Sports/Gaming

5TH
EDITION

Business Analytics:
Data Analysis and Decision Making

S. Christian Albright
Kelly School of Business, Indiana University, Emeritus

Wayne L. Winston
Kelly School of Business, Indiana University

With cases by

Mark Broadie
Graduate School of Business, Columbia University

Peter Kolesar
Graduate School of Business, Columbia University

Lawrence L. Lapin
San Jose State University

William D. Whisler
Emeritus, California State University, Hayward

CENGAGE
Learning·

Australia • Brazil • Japan • Korea • Mexico • Singapore • Spain • United Kingdom • United States

CENGAGE
Learning·

Business Analytics: Data Analysis and Decision Making, Fifth Edition
S. Christian Albright and Wayne L. Winston

Product Director: Joe Sabatino

Product Manager: Aaron Arnsparger

Content Developer: Krista Kellman

Product Assistant: Brad Sullender

Marketing Director: Natalie King

Assoc. Market Development Manager:
    Roy Rosa

Sr. Content Project Manager: Holly Henjum

Media Developer: Chris Valentine

Manufacturing Planner: Ron Montgomery

Marketing Coordinator: Eileen Corcoran

Composition and Production Service:
    diacriTech

Sr. Art Director: Stacy Jenkins Shirley

Sr. Rights Acquisitions Specialist: John Hill

Cover Designer: Joe Devine/
    Red Hangar Design

Cover Image: © nadla/iStockphoto

Screenshots are used with permission from Microsoft Corporation, Microsoft Excel® is a registered trademark of Microsoft Corporation. © 2013 Microsoft.

@RISK, StatTools, PrecisionTree, TopRank, RISKOptimizer, NeuralTools®, and Evolver™, are © 2013 Palisade.com.

Except where otherwise noted, all content is © Cengage Learning 2015.

Library of Congress Control Number: 2013946375

ISBN-13: 978-1-133-58826-9

ISBN-10: 1-133-58826-3

Cengage Learning
200 First Stamford Place, 4th Floor
Stamford CT 06902
USA

Cengage Learning is a leading provider of customized learning solutions with office locations around the globe, including Singapore, the United Kingdom, Australia, Mexico, Brazil, and Japan. Locate your local office at: **www.cengage.com/global**

Cengage Learning products are represented in Canada by Nelson Education, Ltd.

To learn more about Cengage Learning Solutions, visit **www.cengage.com**

Purchase any of our products at your local college store or at our preferred online store **www.cengagebrain.com**

Printed in the United States of America
1 2 3 4 5 6 7 17 16 15 14 13

To my wonderful wife Mary—my best friend and travel mate; to Sam, Lindsay, Teddy, and Archer, our second adorable grandson; and to Bryn, our ball-playing Welsh corgi!   *S.C.A*

To my wonderful family   *W.L.W.*

About the Authors

© Cengage Learning

S. Christian Albright got his B.S. degree in Mathematics from Stanford in 1968 and his PhD in Operations Research from Stanford in 1972. He taught in the Operations & Decision Technologies Department in the Kelley School of Business at Indiana University (IU) for close to 40 years, before retiring from teaching in 2011. While at IU, he taught courses in management science, computer simulation, statistics, and computer programming to all levels of business students, including undergraduates, MBAs, and doctoral students. In addition, he taught simulation modeling at General Motors and Whirlpool, and he taught database analysis for the Army. He published over 20 articles in leading operations research journals in the area of applied probability, and he has authored the books *Statistics for Business and Economics, Practical Management Science, Spreadsheet Modeling and Applications, Data Analysis for Managers*, and *VBA for Modelers*. He currently works with the Palisade Corporation developing training materials for its software products, he has developed a commercial version of his Excel® tutorial, called ExcelNow!, and he continues to revise his textbooks.

On the personal side, Chris has been married for 42 years to his wonderful wife, Mary, who retired several years ago after teaching 7th grade English for 30 years. They have one son, Sam, who lives in Philadelphia with his wife Lindsay and their two sons, Teddy and Archer. Chris has many interests outside the academic area. They include activities with his family (especially traveling with Mary), going to cultural events at IU, power walking while listening to books on his iPod, and reading. And although he earns his livelihood from statistics and management science, his *real* passion is for playing classical piano music.

© Cengage Learning

Wayne L. Winston is Professor of Operations & Decision Technologies in the Kelley School of Business at Indiana University, where he has taught since 1975. Wayne received his B.S. degree in Mathematics from MIT and his PhD in Operations Research from Yale. He has written the successful textbooks *Operations Research: Applications and Algorithms, Mathematical Programming: Applications and Algorithms, Simulation Modeling Using @RISK, Practical Management Science, Data Analysis and Decision Making, Financial Models Using Simulation and Optimization*, and *Mathletics*. Wayne has published more than 20 articles in leading journals and has won many teaching awards, including the school-wide MBA award four times. He has taught classes at Microsoft, GM, Ford, Eli Lilly, Bristol-Myers Squibb, Arthur Andersen, Roche, PricewaterhouseCoopers, and NCR. His current interest is showing how spreadsheet models can be used to solve business problems in all disciplines, particularly in finance and marketing.

Wayne enjoys swimming and basketball, and his passion for trivia won him an appearance several years ago on the television game show *Jeopardy!*, where he won two games. He is married to the lovely and talented Vivian. They have two children, Gregory and Jennifer.

Brief Contents

Contents

Preface

With today's technology, companies are able to collect tremendous amounts of data with relative ease. Indeed, many companies now have more data than they can handle. However, the data are usually meaningless until they are analyzed for trends, patterns, relationships, and other useful information. This book illustrates in a practical way a variety of methods, from simple to complex, to help you analyze data sets and uncover important information. In many business contexts, data analysis is only the first step in the solution of a problem. Acting on the solution and the information it provides to make good decisions is a critical next step. Therefore, there is a heavy emphasis throughout this book on analytical methods that are useful in decision making. Again, the methods vary considerably, but the objective is always the same—to equip you with decision-making tools that you can apply in your business careers.

We recognize that the majority of students in this type of course are *not* majoring in a quantitative area. They are typically business majors in finance, marketing, operations management, or some other business discipline who will need to analyze data and make quantitative-based decisions in their jobs. We offer a hands-on, example-based approach and introduce fundamental concepts as they are needed. Our vehicle is spreadsheet software—specifically, Microsoft Excel®. This is a package that most students already know and will almost surely use in their careers. Our MBA students at Indiana University are so turned on by the required course that is based on this book that *almost all* of them (mostly finance and marketing majors) take at least one of our follow-up elective courses in spreadsheet modeling. We are convinced that students see value in quantitative analysis when the course is taught in a practical and example-based approach.

Rationale for Writing This Book

Business Analytics: Data Analysis and Decision Making is different from the many fine textbooks written for statistics and management science. Our rationale for writing this book is based on three fundamental objectives.

- **Integrated coverage and applications.** The book provides a unified approach to business-related problems by integrating methods and applications that have been traditionally taught in separate courses, specifically statistics and management science.

- **Practical in approach.** The book emphasizes realistic business examples and the processes managers actually use to analyze business problems. The emphasis is *not* on abstract theory or computational methods.

- **Spreadsheet-based teaching.** The book provides students with the skills to analyze business problems with tools they have access to and will use in their careers. To this end, we have adopted Excel and commercial spreadsheet add-ins.

Integrated Coverage and Applications

In the past, many business schools, including ours at Indiana University, have offered a required statistics course, a required decision-making course, and a required management science course—or some subset of these. A current trend, however, is to have only one required course that covers the basics of statistics, some regression analysis, some decision making under uncertainty, some linear programming, some simulation, and possibly others. Essentially, faculty in the quantitative area get one opportunity to teach all business students, so we attempt to cover a variety of useful quantitative methods. We are not necessarily arguing that this trend is ideal, but rather that it is a reflection of the reality at our university and, we suspect, at many others. After several years of teaching this course, we have found it to be a great opportunity to attract students to the subject and to more advanced study.

The book is also integrative in another important aspect. It not only integrates a number of analytical methods, but it also applies them to a wide variety of business problems—that is, it analyzes realistic examples from many business disciplines. We include examples, problems, and cases that deal with portfolio optimization, workforce scheduling, market share analysis, capital budgeting, new product analysis, and many others.

Practical in Approach

This book has been designed to be very example-based and practical. We strongly believe that students learn best by working through examples, and they appreciate the material most when the examples are realistic and interesting. Therefore, our approach in the book differs in two important ways from many competitors. First, there is just enough conceptual development to give students an understanding and appreciation for the issues raised in the examples. We often introduce important concepts, such as standard deviation as a measure of variability, in the context of examples rather than discussing them in the abstract. Our experience is that students gain greater intuition and understanding of the concepts and applications through this approach.

Second, we place virtually no emphasis on hand calculations. We believe it is more important for students to understand why they are conducting an analysis and what it means than to emphasize the tedious calculations associated with many analytical techniques. Therefore, we illustrate how powerful software can be used to create graphical and numerical outputs in a matter of seconds, freeing the rest of the time for in-depth interpretation of the results, sensitivity analysis, and alternative modeling approaches. In our own courses, we move directly into a discussion of examples, where we focus almost exclusively on interpretation and modeling issues, and we let the software perform the number crunching.

Spreadsheet-based Teaching

We are strongly committed to teaching spreadsheet-based, example-driven courses, regardless of whether the basic area is data analysis or management science. We have found tremendous enthusiasm for this approach, both from students and from faculty around the world who have used our books. Students learn and remember more, and they appreciate the material more. In addition, instructors typically enjoy teaching more, and they usually receive immediate reinforcement through better teaching evaluations. We were among the first to move to spreadsheet-based teaching about two decades ago, and we have never regretted the move.

What We Hope to Accomplish in This Book

Condensing the ideas in the previous paragraphs, we hope to:

- reverse negative student attitudes about statistics and quantitative methods by making these topics real, accessible, and interesting;

- give students plenty of hands-on experience with real problems and challenge them to develop their intuition, logic, and problem-solving skills;

- expose students to real problems in many business disciplines and show them how these problems can be analyzed with quantitative methods; and

- develop spreadsheet skills, including experience with powerful spreadsheet add-ins, that add immediate value to students' other courses and for their future careers.

New in the Fifth Edition

There are several important changes in this edition.

- *Business Analytics Focus:* The term *business analytics* is now in the title of the book. This term is now ubiquitous in our area, being extremely popular with both academics and business people, and we are pleased that our methods are now so highly regarded. However, an argument can certainly be made that the methods in this book, methods we have taught for years, are essentially what the field of Business Analytics is all about. Granted, a major focus of Business Analytics is on using *large* data sets to help make good decisions. Therefore, we have added the chapter discussed in the next bullet.

- *Data Mining Coverage:* Chapter 17 on Data Mining is completely new. This topic, which we were hardly aware of just 15 years ago, is now an extremely important part of Business Analytics. Part of the reason for this is that virtually all companies have access to large data sets that they need to make sense of. Another part of the reason is that there are now powerful algorithms and accompanying software packages to perform the analyses. The topic itself is huge, with many books of various mathematical levels devoted entirely to it, and it is impossible to cover it adequately in a single chapter. However, we believe this new chapter provides an exciting, hands-on introduction to data mining.

- *Content Reductions:* Because of the combination of statistical and management science topics, the book has always been long. With the addition of the data mining chapter, it got even longer, and something had to be cut. Therefore, parts of various chapters, particularly Chapter 4 (Probability and Probability Distributions), have been deleted. Based on user surveys, we tried to cut only the material that was used least often, but if any of your favorite sections are missing, you can contact Cengage or the authors, and we will provide you with PDF versions from the fourth edition. A complete list of deleted sections follows:[1]

- Section 3.6: An Extended Example
- Section 4.5: Probability Distributions of Two Random Variables: Scenario Approach
- Section 4.6: Probability Distribution of Two Random Variables: Joint Probability Approach
- Section 4.7: Independent Random Variables (this is now discussed briefly in Section 4.2.4)
- Section 4.8: Weighted Sums of Random Variables
- Section 5.7: Fitting a Probability Distribution to Data with @RISK
- Section 9.7: One-Way ANOVA (this is now discussed extensively in the online Chapter 19: ANOVA and Experimental Design)
- Section 11.7: The Partial F Test
- Section 12.6: Autoregression Models

- **Advanced Statistical Coverage:** Three online chapters are available: Chapter 18 (Importing Data into Excel), Chapter 19 (Analysis of Variance and Experimental Design), and Chapter 20 (Statistical Process Control). The latter two of these are new online chapters, updated versions of "advanced statistical" chapters that appeared in our old *Data Analysis for Managers* book.
- **Tutorial Videos:** To help students learn, we created more than 50 videos that explain concepts and work through examples. Students can access the videos for free on the textbook companion website. A complete list of videos is available on the website and video icons appear in the margins of the textbook next to relevant topics.
- **Updated to Office 2013:** As we were creating this edition of the book, Microsoft released Office 2013. Therefore, all of the screenshots in the book are from this newer version. However, the changes from 2010 to 2013 (or even from 2007 to 2013) are not that extensive, at least for our

purposes. Therefore, if you are still using Office 2007 or 2010, this book should work fine for you.

- **Updated Problems:** As in the previous edition, we modified a number of problems, usually to update their data, and we added several brand-new problems. We also created a file, essentially a database of problems, which is available to instructors. This file, **DADM 5e Problem Database.xlsx,** indicates the context of each of the problems, and it also shows the correspondence between problems in this edition and problems in the previous edition.
- **Suggested Solutions for Conceptual Questions:** In addition to Problems, each chapter also includes Conceptual Questions to assess student comprehension of concepts on a broad level. New for this edition, suggested solutions for these Conceptual Questions have been provided.

Software

This book is based entirely on Microsoft Excel, the spreadsheet package that has become the standard analytical tool in business. Excel is an extremely powerful package, and one of our goals is to convert *casual* users into *power* users who can take full advantage of its features. If you learn no more than this, you will be acquiring a valuable skill for the business world. However, Excel has some limitations. Therefore, this book includes several Excel add-ins that greatly enhance Excel's capabilities. As a group, these add-ins comprise what is arguably the most impressive assortment of spreadsheet-based software accompanying any book on the market.

DecisionTools® Suite Add-in

The textbook website for *Business Analytics: Data Analysis and Decision Making* provides a link to the powerful DecisionTools® Suite by Palisade Corporation. (The version available is compatible with Excel 2013 and previous versions of Excel.) This suite includes six separate add-ins:

- **@RISK**, an add-in for simulation
- **StatTools**, an add-in for statistical data analysis
- **PrecisionTree**, a graphical-based add-in for creating and analyzing decision trees
- **TopRank**, an add-in for performing what-if analyses

---

[1] These section numbers refer to the numbering in the previous (fourth) edition.

- **NeuralTools®**, an add-in for estimating complex, nonlinear relationships
- **Evolver™**, an add-in for performing optimization (an alternative to Excel's Solver)

We use @RISK and PrecisionTree extensively in the chapters on simulation and decision making under uncertainty, and we use StatTools extensively in the data analysis chapters.

Online access to the DecisionTools Suite, available with new copies of the book, is an academic version, slightly scaled down from the professional version that sells for hundreds of dollars and is used by many leading companies. It functions for two years when properly installed, and it puts only modest limitations on the size of data sets or models that can be analyzed.[2]

SolverTable Add-in

We also include SolverTable, a supplement to Excel's built-in Solver for optimization.[3] If you have ever had difficulty understanding Solver's sensitivity reports, you will appreciate SolverTable. It works like Excel's data tables, except that for each input (or pair of inputs), the add-in runs Solver and reports the *optimal* output values. SolverTable is used extensively in the optimization chapters.

Windows versus Mac

In our own courses, we have seen an increasing number of students using Macintosh laptops rather than Windows laptops. Fortunately, this is *not* a problem, and our students have followed along fine with their Macs. However, these students should be advised to use a Windows emulation program (Bootcamp or Parallels are good candidates), along with Office for *Windows*. If they use Office for the Mac, they are bound to be confused, and there is no guarantee that the add-ins used throughout the book will work. In fact, the Palisade add-ins are guaranteed *not* to work.

Potential Course Structures

Although we have used the book for our own required one-semester course, there is admittedly much more material than can be covered adequately in one semester. We have tried to make the book as modular as possible, allowing an instructor to cover, say, simulation before optimization or vice-versa, or to omit either of these topics. The one exception is statistics. Due to the natural progression of statistical topics, the basic topics in the early chapters should be covered before the more advanced topics (regression and time series analysis) in the later chapters. With this in mind, there are several possible ways to cover the topics.

- **One-semester Required Course, with No Statistics Prerequisite** (or where MBA students need a refresher for whatever statistics they learned previously): If data analysis is the primary focus of the course, then Chapters 2–5, 7–11, and possibly Chapter 17 should be covered. Depending on the time remaining, any of the topics in Chapters 6 (decision making under uncertainty), 12 (time series analysis), 13–14 (optimization), or 15–16 (simulation) can be covered in practically any order.

- **One-semester Required Course, with a Statistics Prerequisite**: Assuming that students know the basic elements of statistics (up through hypothesis testing), the material in Chapters 2–5 and 7–9 can be reviewed quickly, primarily to illustrate how Excel and add-ins can be used to do the number crunching. The instructor can then choose among any of the topics in Chapters 6, 10–11, 12, 13–14, or 15–16 (in practically any order), or to fill the remainder of the course.

- **Two-semester Required Sequence**: Given the luxury of spreading the topics over two semesters, the entire book, or at least most of it, can be covered. The statistics topics in Chapters 2–5 and 7–9 should be covered in chronological order before other statistical topics (regression and time series analysis), but the remaining chapters can be covered in practically any order.

Custom Publishing

Cengage Learning is dedicated to making the educational experience unique for all learners by creating custom materials that best suit your course needs. With Cengage Learning you can create a custom solution where you have the ability to choose your book's content, length, sequence, even the cover design. You may combine content from multiple Cengage Learning titles and add other materials, including your own original work, to create your ideal customized

---

[2] Visit www.kelley.iu.edu/albrightbooks for specific details on these limitations.

[3] Although SolverTable is available on this textbook's website, it is also available for free from Albright's website, www.kelley.iu.edu /albrightbooks.

text. If you would like to learn more about our custom publishing services, please contact your Cengage Learning representative[4] or visit us at www.cengage.com/custom.

Instructor Supplements

Textbook Website: cengage.com/login

The companion website provides immediate access to an array of teaching resources—including data and solutions files for all of the Examples, Problems, and Cases in the book, Chapters 18–20 and Appendix A, Test Bank files, PowerPoint slides, and access to the DecisionTools® Suite by Palisade Corporation and the SolverTable add-in. Also, new for this edition, the website features more than 50 videos that explain concepts and work through examples. You can easily download the instructor resources you need from the password-protected, instructor-only section of the site.

Test Bank

Cengage Learning Testing Powered by Cognero is a flexible, online system that allows you to:

- author, edit, and manage test bank content from multiple Cengage Learning solutions

- create multiple test versions in an instant

- deliver tests from your LMS, your classroom, or wherever you want

Student Supplements

Textbook Website: www.cengagebrain.com

Every new student edition of this book comes with access to the *Business Analytics: Data Analysis and Decision Making, 5e* textbook website that links to the following files and tools:

- Excel files for the examples in the chapters (usually two versions of each—a template, or data-only version, and a finished version)

- Data files required for the Problems and Cases

- **excel_tutorial.xlsm**, which contains a useful tutorial for getting up to speed in Excel

- Chapters 18–20 and Appendix A

- DecisionTools® Suite software by Palisade Corporation (described earlier)

- SolverTable add-in

- More than 50 tutorial videos that explain concepts and work through examples

To access resources, go to www.cengagebrain.com, search by ISBN 9781133629603, click on the "Free Materials" tab, and select "Access Now." The resources you need will be listed both per chapter (by selecting a chapter from the drop-down list) and for the entire book (under Book Resources).

Student Solutions

Student Solutions to many of the problems (indicated in the text with a colored box around the problem number) are available in Excel format. You can purchase access to Student Solutions files by going to www.cengagebrain.com, searching by ISBN 9781285871332, and adding the product to your cart.

Acknowledgements

The authors would like to thank several people who helped make this book a reality. First, the authors are indebted to Peter Kolesar, Mark Broadie, Lawrence Lapin, and William Whisler for contributing some of the excellent case studies that appear throughout the book.

We are also grateful to many of the professionals who worked behind the scenes to make this book a success: Joe Sabatino, Product Director; Krista Kellman, Content Developer; Holly Henjum, Senior Content Project Manager; Roy Rosa, Associate Market Development Manager; and Product Assistant, Brad Sullender.

We also extend our sincere appreciation to the reviewers who provided feedback on the authors' proposed changes that resulted in this fifth edition:

John Aloysius, *Walton College of Business, University of Arkansas*

Henry F. Ander, *Arizona State University*

Dr. Baabak Ashuri, *School of Building Construction, Georgia Institute of Technology*

James Behel, *Harding University*

Robert H. Burgess, *Scheller College of Business, Georgia Institute of Technology*

Paul Damien, *McCombs School of Business, University of Texas in Austin*

Parviz Ghandforoush, *Virginia Tech*

---

[4] Find your Learning Consultant at sites.cengage.com/repfinder.

Betsy Greenberg, *University of Texas*

Anissa Harris, *Harding University*

Tim James, *Arizona State University*

Norman Johnson, *C.T. Bauer College of Business, University of Houston*

Shivraj Kanungo, *The George Washington University*

Miguel Lejeune, *The George Washington University*

José Lobo, *Arizona State University*

Stuart Low, *Arizona State University*

Lance Matheson, *Virginia Tech*

Patrick R. McMullen, *Wake Forest University*

Barbara A. Price, PhD, *Georgia Southern University*

Laura Wilson-Gentry, *University of Baltimore*

Toshiyuki Yuasa, *University of Houston*

S. Christian Albright

Wayne L. Winston

August 2013

Introduction to Data Analysis and Decision Making

Konstantin Chagin/Shutterstock.com

HOTTEST NEW JOBS: STATISTICS AND MATHEMATICS

Much of this book, as the title implies, is about data analysis. The term *data analysis* has long been synonymous with the term *statistics*, but in today's world, with massive amounts of data available in business and many other fields such as health and science, data analysis goes beyond the more narrowly focused area of traditional statistics. But regardless of what it is called, data analysis is currently a hot topic and promises to get even hotter in the future. The data analysis skills you learn here, and possibly in follow-up quantitative courses, might just land you a very interesting and lucrative job.

This is exactly the message in a recent *New York Times* article, "For Today's Graduate, Just One Word: Statistics," by Steve Lohr. (A similar article, "Math Will Rock Your World," by Stephen Baker, was the cover story for *BusinessWeek*. Both articles are available online by searching for their titles.) The statistics article begins by chronicling a Harvard anthropology and archaeology graduate, Carrie Grimes, who began her career by mapping the locations of Mayan artifacts in places like Honduras. As she states, "People think of field archaeology as Indiana Jones, but much of what you really do is data analysis." Since then, Grimes has leveraged her data analysis skills to get a job with Google, where she and many other people with a quantitative background are analyzing huge amounts of data to improve the company's search engine. As the chief economist at Google, Hal Varian, states, "I keep saying that the sexy job in the next 10 years will be statisticians. And I'm not kidding." The salaries for statisticians with doctoral degrees currently *start* at $125,000, and they will probably continue to increase. (The math article indicates that mathematicians are also in great demand.)

Why is this trend occurring? The reason is the explosion of digital data—data from sensor signals, surveillance tapes, Web clicks, bar scans, public records, financial transactions, and more. In years past, statisticians typically analyzed relatively small data sets, such as opinion polls with about 1000 responses. Today's massive data sets require new statistical methods, new computer software, and most importantly for you, more young people trained in these methods and the corresponding software. Several particular areas mentioned in the articles include (1) improving Internet search and online advertising, (2) unraveling gene sequencing information for cancer research, (3) analyzing sensor and location data for optimal handling of food shipments, and (4) the recent Netflix contest for improving the company's recommendation system.

The statistics article mentions three specific organizations in need of data analysts. The first is government, where there is an increasing need to sift through mounds of data as a first step toward dealing with long-term economic needs and key policy priorities. The second is IBM, which created a Business Analytics and Optimization Services group in April 2009. This group will use the more than 200 mathematicians, statisticians, and data analysts already employed by the company, but IBM intends to retrain or hire 4000 more analysts to meet its needs. The third is Google, which needs more data analysts to improve its search engine. You may think that today's search engines are unbelievably efficient, but Google knows they can be improved. As Ms. Grimes states, "Even an improvement of a percent or two can be huge, when you do things over the millions and billions of times we do things at Google."

Of course, these three organizations are not the only organizations that need to hire more skilled people to perform data analysis and other analytical procedures. It is a need faced by *all* large organizations. Various recent technologies, the most prominent by far being the Web, have given organizations the ability to gather massive amounts of data easily. Now they need people to make sense of it all and use it to their competitive advantage. ■

1-1 INTRODUCTION

We are living in the age of technology. This has two important implications for everyone entering the business world. First, technology has made it possible to collect huge amounts of data. Retailers collect point-of-sale data on products and customers every time a transaction occurs; credit agencies have all sorts of data on people who have or would like to obtain credit; investment companies have a limitless supply of data on the historical patterns of stocks, bonds, and other securities; and government agencies have data on economic trends, the environment, social welfare, consumer product safety, and virtually everything else imaginable. It has become relatively *easy* to collect the data. As a result, data are plentiful. However, as many organizations are now beginning to discover, it is quite a challenge to make sense of all the data they have collected.

A second important implication of technology is that it has given many more people the power and responsibility to analyze data and make decisions on the basis of quantitative analysis. People entering the business world can no longer pass all of the quantitative analysis to the "quant jocks," the technical specialists who have traditionally done the number crunching. The vast majority of employees now have a desktop or laptop computer at their disposal, access to relevant data, and training in easy-to-use software, particularly spreadsheet and database software. For these employees, statistics and other quantitative methods are no longer forgotten topics they once learned in college. Quantitative analysis is now an integral part of their daily jobs.

A large amount of data already exists, and it will only increase in the future. Many companies already complain of swimming in a sea of data. However, enlightened companies are seeing this expansion as a source of competitive advantage. In fact, one of the hottest topics in today's business world is **business analytics**. This term has been created to encompass all of the types of analysis discussed in this book, so it isn't really new; we have been teaching it for years. The new aspect of business analytics is that it typically implies the analysis of very *large* data sets, the kind that companies currently encounter. By using quantitative methods to uncover the *information* in these data sets and then acting on this information—again guided by quantitative analysis—companies are able to gain advantages that their less enlightened competitors are not able to gain. Here are several pertinent examples.

- Direct marketers analyze enormous customer databases to see which customers are likely to respond to various products and types of promotions. Marketers can then target different classes of customers in different ways to maximize profits—and give their customers what they want.

- Hotels and airlines also analyze enormous customer databases to see what their customers want and are willing to pay for. By doing this, they have been able to devise very clever pricing strategies, where different customers pay different prices for the same accommodations. For example, a business traveler typically makes a plane reservation closer to the time of travel than a vacationer. The airlines know this. Therefore, they reserve seats for these business travelers and charge them a higher price for the same seats. The airlines profit from clever pricing strategies, and the customers are happy.

- Financial planning services have a virtually unlimited supply of data about security prices, and they have customers with widely differing preferences for various types of investments. Trying to find a match of investments to customers is a very challenging problem. However, customers can easily take their business elsewhere if good decisions are not made on their behalf. Therefore, financial planners are under extreme competitive pressure to analyze masses of data so that they can make informed decisions for their customers.[1]

- We all know about the pressures U.S. manufacturing companies have faced from foreign competition in the past couple of decades. The automobile companies, for example, have had to change the way they produce and market automobiles to stay in business. They have had to improve quality and cut costs by orders of magnitude. Although the struggle continues, much of the success they have had can be attributed to data analysis and wise decision making. Starting on the shop floor and moving up through the organization, these companies now measure almost everything, analyze these measurements, and then act on the results of their analysis.

We talk about companies analyzing data and making decisions. However, *companies* don't really do this; *people* do it. And who will these people be in the future? They will be *you*! We know from experience that students in all areas of business, at both the undergraduate and graduate level, will be *required* to describe large complex data sets, run regression analyses, make quantitative forecasts, create optimization models, and run simulations. You are the person who will be analyzing data and making important decisions to help

---

[1]For a great overview of how quantitative techniques have been used in the financial world, read the book *The Quants*, by Scott Patterson (Random House, 2010). It describes how quantitative models made millions for a lot of bright young analysts, but it also describes the dangers of relying totally on quantitative models, at least in the complex world of global finance.

your company gain a competitive advantage. And if you are *not* willing or able to do so, there will be plenty of other technically trained people who will be more than happy to replace you.

The goal of this book is to teach you how to use a variety of quantitative methods to analyze data and make decisions in a very hands-on way. We discuss a number of quantitative methods and illustrate their use in a large variety of realistic business situations. As you will see, this book includes many examples from finance, marketing, operations, accounting, and other areas of business. To analyze these examples, we take advantage of the Microsoft Excel® spreadsheet software, together with a number of powerful Excel add-ins. In each example we provide step-by-step details of the method and its implementation in Excel.

This is *not* a "theory" book. It is also not a book where you can lean comfortably back in your chair and read about how *other* people use quantitative methods. It is a "get your hands dirty" book, where you will learn best by actively following the examples throughout the book on your own PC. By the time you have finished, you will have acquired some very useful skills for today's business world.

1-2 OVERVIEW OF THE BOOK

This book is packed with quantitative methods and examples, probably more than can be covered in any single course. Therefore, we purposely intend to keep this introductory chapter brief so that you can get on with the analysis. Nevertheless, it is useful to introduce the methods you will be learning and the tools you will be using. This section provides an overview of the methods covered in this book and the software that is used to implement them. Then the next section presents a brief discussion of models and the modeling process. The primary goal at this point is to stimulate your interest in what follows.

1-2a The Methods

This book is rather unique in that it combines topics from two separate fields: statistics and management science. Statistics is the study of data analysis, whereas management science is the study of model building, optimization, and decision making. In the academic arena these two fields have traditionally been separated, sometimes widely. Indeed, they are often housed in separate academic departments. However, from a user's standpoint it makes little sense to separate them. Both are useful in accomplishing what the title of this book promises: data analysis and decision making.

Therefore, we do not distinguish between the statistics and the management science parts of this book. Instead, we view the entire book as a collection of useful quantitative methods that can be used to analyze data and help make business decisions. In addition, our choice of software helps to integrate the various topics. By using a single package, Excel, together with a number of add-ins, you will see that the methods of statistics and management science are similar in many important respects. Most importantly, their combination gives you the power and flexibility to solve a wide range of business problems.

Three important themes run through this book. Two of them are in the title: data analysis and decision making. The third is *dealing with uncertainty*.[2] Each of these themes has subthemes. Data analysis includes data description, data inference, and the search for relationships in data. Decision making includes *optimization* techniques for problems with no uncertainty, *decision analysis* for problems with uncertainty, and structured *sensitivity*

---

[2]The fact that the uncertainty theme did not find its way into the title of this book does not detract from its importance. We just wanted to keep the title reasonably short!

analysis. Dealing with uncertainty includes measuring uncertainty and modeling uncertainty explicitly. There are obvious overlaps between these themes and subthemes. When you make inferences from data and search for relationships in data, you must deal with uncertainty. When you use *decision trees* to help make decisions, you must deal with uncertainty. When you use *simulation models* to help make decisions, you must deal with uncertainty, and then you often make inferences from the simulated data.

Figure 1.1 shows where these themes and subthemes are discussed in the book. The next few paragraphs discuss the book's contents in more detail.

Figure 1.1
Themes and
Subthemes

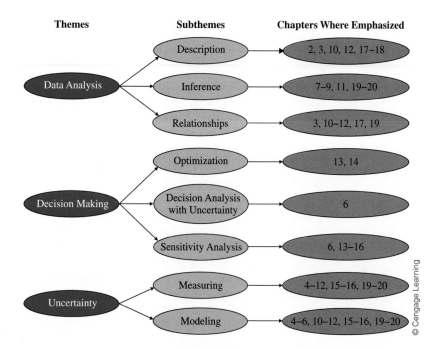

We begin in Chapters 2 and 3 by illustrating a number of ways to summarize the information in data sets. These include graphical and tabular summaries, as well as numerical summary measures such as means, medians, and standard deviations. The material in these two chapters is elementary from a mathematical point of view, but it is extremely important. As stated earlier, organizations are now able to collect huge amounts of raw data, but what does it all mean? Although there are very sophisticated methods for analyzing data, some of which are covered in later chapters, the "simple" methods in Chapters 2 and 3 are crucial for obtaining an initial understanding of the data. Fortunately, Excel and available add-ins now make this quite easy. For example, Excel's pivot table tool for "slicing and dicing" data is an analyst's dream come true. You will be amazed by the insights you can gain from pivot tables—with very little effort.

Uncertainty is a key aspect of most business problems. To deal with uncertainty, you need a basic understanding of probability. We discuss the key concepts in Chapters 4 and 5. Chapter 4 covers basic rules of probability and then discusses the extremely important concept of probability distributions. Chapter 5 follows up this discussion by focusing on two of the most important probability distributions, the normal and binomial distributions.

One of the best ways to make probabilistic concepts easier to understand is by using computer simulation. Therefore, simulation is a common theme that runs through this book, beginning in Chapter 4. Although the final Chapters 15 and 16 are devoted entirely to simulation, we do not hesitate to use simulation early and often to illustrate statistical concepts.

In Chapter 6 we apply probability to decision making under uncertainty. These types of problems—faced by all companies on a continual basis—are characterized by the need to make a decision *now,* even though important information, such as demand for a product or returns from investments, will not be known until later. The methods in Chapter 6 provide a rational basis for making such decisions. These methods do not guarantee perfect outcomes—the future could unluckily turn out differently than expected—but they do enable decision makers to proceed rationally and make the best of the given circumstances. Additionally, the software used to implement these methods allows decision makers, with very little extra work, to see how sensitive the optimal decisions are to inputs. This is crucial, because the inputs to many business problems are, at best, educated guesses. Finally, we examine the role of risk aversion in these types of decision problems.

In Chapters 7, 8, and 9 we discuss sampling and statistical inference. Here the basic problem is to estimate one or more characteristics of a population. If it is too expensive or time-consuming to learn about the *entire* population—and it usually is—it is instead common to select a random sample from the population and then use the information in the sample to *infer* the characteristics of the population. You see this continually on news shows that describe the results of various polls. You also see it in many business contexts. For example, auditors typically sample only a fraction of a company's records. Then they infer the characteristics of the entire population of records from the results of the sample to conclude whether the company has been following acceptable accounting standards.

In Chapters 10 and 11 we discuss the extremely important topic of regression analysis, which is used to study relationships between variables. The power of regression analysis is its generality. Every part of a business has variables that are related to one another, and regression can often be used to estimate relationships between these variables. In managerial accounting, regression is used to estimate how overhead costs depend on direct labor hours and production volume. In marketing, regression is used to estimate how sales volume depends on advertising and other marketing variables. In finance, regression is used to estimate how the return of a stock depends on the "market" return. In real estate studies, regression is used to estimate how the selling price of a house depends on the assessed valuation of the house and characteristics such as the number of bedrooms and square footage.

From regression, we move to time series analysis and forecasting in Chapter 12. This topic is particularly important for providing inputs into business decision problems. For example, manufacturing companies must forecast demand for their products to make sensible decisions about order quantities from their suppliers. Similarly, fast-food restaurants must forecast customer arrivals, sometimes down to the level of 15-minute intervals, so that they can staff their restaurants appropriately. There are many approaches to forecasting, ranging from simple to complex. Some involve regression-based methods, whereas other methods are based on extrapolation. In an extrapolation method the historical patterns of a time series variable, such as product demand or customer arrivals, are studied carefully and are then *extrapolated* into the future to obtain forecasts. In Chapter 12 we discuss both regression and extrapolation methods for forecasting.

Chapters 13 and 14 are devoted to spreadsheet optimization, with emphasis on linear programming. We assume a company must make several decisions, and there are constraints that limit the possible decisions. The job of the decision maker is to choose the decisions such that all of the constraints are satisfied and an objective, such as total profit or total cost, is optimized. The solution process consists of two steps. The first step is to build a spreadsheet model that relates the decision variables to other relevant quantities by means of logical formulas. In this first step there is no attempt to find the *optimal* solution; its only purpose is to relate all relevant quantities in a logical way. The second step is then to find the optimal solution. Fortunately, Excel contains a Solver add-in that performs the optimization. All you need to do is specify the objective, the decision variables, and the constraints; Solver then uses powerful algorithms to find the optimal solution. As with regression, the power of this approach is its generality. An enormous variety of problems can be solved with spreadsheet optimization.

Chapters 15 and 16 illustrate a number of computer simulation models. This is not your first exposure to simulation—it is used in a number of previous chapters to illustrate statistical concepts—but here it is studied in its own right. As mentioned earlier, most business problems have some degree of uncertainty. The demand for a product is unknown, future interest rates are unknown, the delivery lead time from a supplier is unknown, and so on. Simulation allows you to build this uncertainty *explicitly* into spreadsheet models. Essentially, some cells in the model contain random values with given probability distributions. Every time the spreadsheet recalculates, these random values change, which causes "bottom-line" output cells to change as well. The trick then is to force the spreadsheet to recalculate many times and keep track of interesting outputs. In this way you can see which output values are most likely, and you can see best-case and worst-case results.

Spreadsheet simulations can be performed entirely with Excel's built-in tools, but this is quite tedious. Therefore, we use a spreadsheet add-in to streamline the process. In particular, you will learn how the @RISK add-in from Palisade Corporation can be used to run replications of a simulation, keep track of outputs, create useful charts, and perform sensitivity analyses. With the inherent power of spreadsheets and the ease of using add-ins such as @RISK, spreadsheet simulation is becoming one of the most popular quantitative tools in the business world.

Chapter 17 is new to this edition. It provides a brief introduction to data mining, a topic of increasing importance in today's data-driven world. Data mining is all about exploring data sets, especially large data sets, for relationships and patterns that can help companies gain a competitive advantage. It employs a number of relatively new technologies to implement various algorithms, several of which are discussed in this chapter.

Finally, there are three online chapters, 18–20, that complement topics included in the book itself. Chapter 18 discusses methods for importing the right data into Excel in the first place. Chapter 19 discusses analysis of variance (ANOVA) and experimental design. Chapter 20 discusses quality control and statistical process control. These three online chapters follow the same structure as the chapters in the book, complete with many examples and problems.

1-2b The Software

The quantitative methods in this book can be used to analyze a wide variety of business problems. However, they are not of much practical use unless you have the software to do the number crunching. Very few business problems are small enough to be solved with pencil and paper. They require powerful software.

The software included in new copies of this book, together with Microsoft Excel, provides you with a powerful combination. This software is being used—and will continue to be used—by leading companies all over the world to analyze large, complex problems. We firmly believe that the experience you obtain with this software, through working the examples and problems in this book, will give you a key competitive advantage in the marketplace.

It all begins with Excel. All of the quantitative methods that we discuss are implemented in Excel. Specifically, in this edition, we use Excel 2013.[3] We cannot forecast the

---

[3] As you probably know, Microsoft made sweeping changes to Excel when it went from version 2003 to version 2007. The subsequent move to version 2010 introduced a few new changes, but nothing too dramatic, and the same is true of the most recent version, Excel 2013. If you are using version 2007 or 2010, you will see a few differences in the screenshots (which are from version 2013), but you should be able to follow along without trouble.

state of computer software in the long-term future, but Excel is currently *the* most heavily used spreadsheet package on the market, and there is every reason to believe that this state will persist for many years. Most companies use Excel, most employees and most students have been trained in Excel, and Excel is a *very* powerful, flexible, and easy-to-use package.

Built-in Excel Features

Virtually everyone in the business world knows the basic features of Excel, but relatively few know some of its more powerful features. In short, relatively few people are the "power users" we expect you to become by working through this book. To get you started, the file **excel_tutorial.xlsm** explains some of the "intermediate" features of Excel—features that we expect you to be able to use (see the Preface for instructions on how to access the resources that accompany this textbook). These include the **SUMPRODUCT**, **VLOOKUP**, **IF**, **NPV**, and **COUNTIF**, functions. They also include range names, data tables, Paste Special, Goal Seek, and many others. Finally, although we assume you can perform routine spreadsheet tasks such as copying and pasting, the tutorial provides many tips to help you perform these tasks more efficiently.[4]

In the body of the book, we describe several of Excel's advanced features in more detail. For example, we introduce pivot tables in Chapter 3. This Excel tool enables you to summarize data sets in an almost endless variety of ways. As another example, we introduce Excel's **RAND** and **RANDBETWEEN** functions for generating random numbers in Chapter 4. These functions are used in all spreadsheet simulations (at least those that do not take advantage of an add-in). In short, when an Excel tool is useful for a particular type of analysis, we usually provide step-by-step instructions on how to use it.

Solver Add-in

Chapters 13 and 14 make heavy use of Excel's Solver add-in. This add-in, developed by Frontline Systems®, not Microsoft, uses powerful algorithms—all behind the scenes—to perform spreadsheet optimization. Before this type of spreadsheet optimization add-in was available, specialized (nonspreadsheet) software was required to solve optimization problems. Now you can do it all within the familiar Excel environment.

SolverTable Add-in

An important theme throughout this book is sensitivity analysis: How do outputs change when inputs change? Typically these changes are made in spreadsheets with a data table, a built-in Excel tool. However, data tables don't work in optimization models, where we want to see how the *optimal* solution changes when certain inputs change. Therefore, we include an Excel add-in called SolverTable, which works almost exactly like Excel's data tables. (This add-in was developed by Albright.) Chapters 13 and 14 illustrate the use of SolverTable.

DecisionTools Suite

In addition to SolverTable and built-in Excel add-ins, an educational version of Palisade Corporation's powerful DecisionTools® Suite is available (see the Preface for instructions on how to access it). All of the programs in this suite are Excel add-ins, so the learning curve isn't very steep. There are six separate add-ins in this suite: @RISK, StatTools,

---

[4]Albright and a couple of colleagues have created a more robust commercial version of this tutorial called **ExcelNow!**. The **excel_tutorial.xlsm** file explains how you can upgrade to this commercial version at a very reasonable price.

PrecisionTree, NeuralTools, TopRank, and Evolver.[5] We use only the first four in this book, but all are useful for certain tasks and are described briefly below.

@RISK

The simulation add-in @RISK enables you to run as many replications of a spreadsheet simulation as you like. As the simulation runs, @RISK automatically keeps track of the outputs you select, and it then displays the results in a number of tabular and graphical forms. @RISK also enables you to perform a sensitivity analysis, so that you can see which inputs have the most effect on the outputs. Finally, @RISK provides a number of spreadsheet functions that enable you to generate random numbers from a variety of probability distributions.

RISKOptimizer, part of @RISK, combines optimization with simulation. There are often times when you want to use simulation to model some business problem, but you also want to optimize a summary measure, such as a mean, of an output distribution. This optimization can be performed in a trial-and-error fashion, where you try a few values of the decision variable(s) and see which provides the best solution. However, RISKOptimizer provides a more automatic optimization procedure.

StatTools

Much of this book discusses basic statistical analysis. Fortunately, the Palisade suite includes a statistical add-in called StatTools. StatTools is powerful, easy to use, and capable of generating output quickly in an easily interpretable form.

PrecisionTree

The PrecisionTree add-in is used in Chapter 6 to analyze decision problems with uncertainty. The primary method for performing this type of analysis is to draw a decision tree. Decision trees are inherently graphical, and they have always been difficult to implement in spreadsheets, which are based on rows and columns. However, PrecisionTree does this in a very clever and intuitive way. Equally important, once the basic decision tree is built, you can use PrecisionTree to perform a sensitivity analysis on the model's inputs.

NeuralTools

Chapters 10 and 11 discuss how regression can be used to find a linear equation that quantifies the relationship between a dependent variable and one or more explanatory variables. Although linear regression is a powerful tool, it is not capable of quantifying all possible relationships. The NeuralTools add-in mimics the working of the human brain to find "neural networks" that quantify complex nonlinear relationships. It is used in Chapter 17 as one of several possible classification methods.

Evolver

Chapters 13 and 14 discuss how the built-in Solver add-in can optimize linear models and even some nonlinear models. But there are some "non-smooth" nonlinear models that Solver cannot handle. Fortunately, there are other optimization algorithms for such models, including "genetic" algorithms. The Evolver add-in implements these genetic algorithms. As of version 6.0, it also implements a very powerful optimization engine called OptQuest. Evolver can now solve practically any problem that Solver can solve, and it can even solve problems that are too large for Solver. (We continue to use Solver in the optimization chapters, however, because it is built into Excel.)

---

[5]The Palisade suite used to have another separate add-in, RISKOptimizer. Now RISKOptimizer is contained entirely in @RISK.

TopRank

TopRank is a "what-if" add-in used for sensitivity analysis. It starts with any spreadsheet model, where a set of inputs, along with a number of spreadsheet formulas, leads to one or more outputs. TopRank then performs a sensitivity analysis to see which inputs have the largest effect on a given output. For example, it might indicate which input affects after-tax profit the most: the tax rate, the risk-free rate for investing, the inflation rate, or the price charged by a competitor. Unlike @RISK, TopRank does not explicitly model uncertainty.

Software Guide

Figure 1.2 illustrates how these add-ins are used throughout the book. Excel doesn't appear explicitly in this figure because it is used extensively in *all* of the chapters.

Figure 1.2

Software Guide

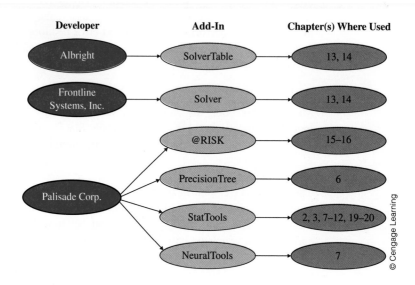

© Cengage Learning

With Excel and the add-ins available with the book, you have a wealth of software at your disposal. The examples and step-by-step instructions throughout the book will help you become a power user of this software. Admittedly, this takes plenty of practice and a willingness to experiment, but it is certainly within your grasp. When you are finished, it is very likely that you will rate "improved software skills" as the most valuable thing you have learned from the book.

1-3 MODELING AND MODELS

The term *model* has already appeared several times in this chapter. Models and the modeling process are key elements throughout the book, so we explain them here in more detail.[6]

A model is an abstraction of a real problem. A model tries to capture the essence and key features of the problem without getting bogged down in relatively unimportant details. There are different types of models, and depending on an analyst's preferences and skills, each can be a valuable aid in solving a real problem. We briefly describe three types of models here: graphical models, algebraic models, and spreadsheet models.

---

[6]Management scientists tend to use the terms *model* and *modeling* more than statisticians. However, many traditional statistics topics such as regression analysis and forecasting are definitely applications of modeling.

1-3a Graphical Models

Graphical models are probably the most intuitive and least quantitative type of model. They attempt to portray graphically how different elements of a problem are related—what affects what. A very simple graphical model appears in Figure 1.3. It is called an **influence diagram**.

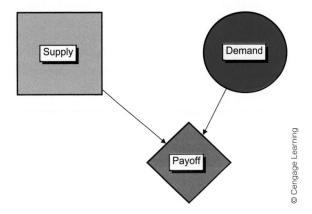

© Cengage Learning

Figure 1.3

Influence Diagram

This particular influence diagram is for a company that is trying to decide how many souvenirs to order for the upcoming Olympics. The essence of the problem is that the company will order a certain supply, customers will request a certain demand, and the combination of supply and demand will yield a certain payoff for the company. The diagram indicates fairly intuitively what affects what. As it stands, the diagram does not provide enough quantitative details to "solve" the company's problem, but this is usually not the purpose of a graphical model. Instead, its purpose is usually to show the important elements of a problem and how they are related. For complex problems, this can be very enlightening information for management.

1-3b Algebraic Models

Algebraic models are at the opposite end of the spectrum. Using algebraic equations and inequalities, they specify a set of relationships in a very precise way. Their preciseness and lack of ambiguity are very appealing to people with a mathematical background. In addition, algebraic models can usually be stated concisely and with great generality.

A typical example is the "product mix" problem in Chapter 13. A company can make several products, each of which contributes a certain amount to profit and consumes certain amounts of several scarce resources. The problem is to select the product mix that maximizes profit subject to the limited availability of the resources. *All* product mix problems can be stated algebraically as follows:

Algebraic Product Mix Model

$$\max \sum_{j=1}^{n} p_j x_j \qquad\qquad (1.1)$$

$$\text{subject to } \sum_{j=1}^{n} a_{ij} x_j \leq b_i, \;\; 1 \leq i \leq m \qquad\qquad (1.2)$$

$$0 \leq x_j \leq u_j, \;\; 1 \leq j \leq n \qquad\qquad (1.3)$$

Here x_j is the amount of product j produced, u_j is an upper limit on the amount of product j that can be produced, p_j is the unit profit margin for product j, a_{ij} is the amount of resource i consumed by each unit of product j, b_i is the amount of resource i available, n is the number of products, and m is the number of scarce resources. This algebraic model states very concisely that we should maximize total profit [expression (1.1)], subject to consuming no more of each resource than is available [inequality (1.2)], and all production quantities should be between 0 and their upper limits [inequality (1.3)].

Algebraic models appeal to mathematically trained analysts. They are concise, they spell out exactly which data are required (the values of the u_js, the p_js, the a_{ij}s, and the b_is would need to be estimated from company data), they scale well (a problem with 500 products and 100 resource constraints is just as easy to state as one with only five products and three resource constraints), and many software packages accept algebraic models in essentially the same form as shown here, so that no "translation" is required. Indeed, algebraic models were the preferred type of model for years—and still are by many analysts. Their main drawback is that they require an ability to work with abstract mathematical symbols. Some people have this ability, but many perfectly intelligent people do not.

1-3c Spreadsheet Models

An alternative to algebraic modeling is spreadsheet modeling. Instead of relating various quantities with algebraic equations and inequalities, they are related in a spreadsheet with cell formulas. In our experience, this process is much more intuitive to most people. One of the primary reasons for this is the instant feedback available from spreadsheets. If you enter a formula incorrectly, it is often immediately obvious (from error messages or unrealistic numbers) that you have made an error, which you can then go back and fix. Algebraic models provide no such immediate feedback.

A specific comparison might help at this point. You already saw a general algebraic model of the product mix problem. Figure 1.4, taken from Chapter 13, illustrates a spreadsheet model for a specific example of this problem. The spreadsheet model should be fairly self-explanatory. All quantities in shaded cells (other than in rows 16 and 25) are inputs to the model, the quantities in row 16 are the decision variables (they correspond to the x_js in the algebraic model), and all other quantities are created through appropriate Excel formulas. To indicate constraints, inequality signs have been entered as labels in appropriate cells.

Although a well-designed and well-documented spreadsheet model such as the one in Figure 1.4 is undoubtedly more intuitive for most people than its algebraic counterpart, the art of developing good spreadsheet models is not easy. Obviously, they must be *correct*. The formulas relating the various quantities must have the correct syntax, the correct cell references, and the correct logic. In complex models this can be quite a challenge.

However, correctness is not enough. If spreadsheet models are to be used in the business world, they must also be well designed and well documented. Otherwise, no one other than you (and maybe not even you after a few weeks have passed) will be able to understand what your models do or how they work. The strength of spreadsheets is their flexibility—you are limited only by your imagination. However, this flexibility can be a liability in spreadsheet modeling unless you design your models carefully.

Note the clear design in Figure 1.4. Most of the inputs are grouped at the top of the spreadsheet. All of the financial calculations are done at the bottom. When there are constraints, the two sides of the constraints are placed next to each other (as in the range B21:D22). Colored backgrounds (which appear on the screen but not in the book) are used for added clarity, and descriptive labels are used liberally. Excel itself imposes none of these "rules," but you should impose them on yourself.

Figure 1.4 Optimal Solution for Product Mix Model

	A	B	C	D	E	F	G
1	**Assembling and testing computers**				Range names used:		
2					Hours_available	=Model!$D$21:$D$22	
3	Cost per labor hour assembling	$11			Hours_used	=Model!$B$21:$B$22	
4	Cost per labor hour testing	$15			Maximum_sales	=Model!$B$18:$C$18	
5					Number_to_produce	=Model!$B$16:$C$16	
6	Inputs for assembling and testing a computer				Total_profit	=Model!$D$25	
7		Basic	XP				
8	Labor hours for assembly	5	6				
9	Labor hours for testing	1	2				
10	Cost of component parts	$150	$225				
11	Selling price	$300	$450				
12	Unit margin	$80	$129				
13							
14	Assembling, testing plan (# of computers)						
15		Basic	XP				
16	Number to produce	560	1200				
17		<=	<=				
18	Maximum sales	600	1200				
19							
20	Constraints (hours per month)	Hours used		Hours available			
21	Labor availability for assembling	10000	<=	10000			
22	Labor availability for testing	2960	<=	3000			
23							
24	Net profit ($ this month)	Basic	XP	Total			
25		$44,800	$154,800	$199,600			

© Cengage Learning

We have made a conscious effort to establish good habits for you to follow throughout the book. We have designed our spreadsheet models so that they are as clear as possible. This does not mean that you have to copy everything we do—everyone tends to develop their own spreadsheet style—but our models should give you something to emulate. Just remember that in the business world, you typically start with a *blank* spreadsheet. It is then up to you to develop a model that is not only correct but is also intelligible to you and others. This takes a lot of practice and a lot of editing, but it is a skill well worth developing.

1-3d A Seven-Step Modeling Process

Most of the modeling you will do in this book is only part of an overall modeling process typically done in the business world. We portray it as a seven-step process, as discussed here. Admittedly, not all problems require all seven steps. For example, the analysis of survey data might entail primarily steps 2 (data analysis) and 5 (decision making) of the process, without the formal model building discussed in steps 3 and 4.

The Modeling Process

1. **Define the problem.** Typically, a company does not develop a model unless it believes it has a problem. Therefore, the modeling process really begins by identifying an underlying problem. Perhaps the company is losing money, perhaps its market share is declining, or perhaps its customers are waiting too long for service. Any number

of problems might be evident. However, as several people have warned [see Miser (1993) and Volkema (1995) for examples], this step is not always as straightforward as it might appear. The company must be sure that it has identified the *correct* problem before it spends time, effort, and money trying to solve it.

For example, Miser cites the experience of an analyst who was hired by the military to investigate overly long turnaround times between fighter planes landing and taking off again to rejoin the battle. The military was convinced that the problem was caused by inefficient ground crews; if they were faster, turnaround times would decrease. The analyst nearly accepted this statement of the problem and was about to do classical time-and-motion studies on the ground crew to pinpoint the sources of their inefficiency. However, by snooping around, he found that the problem obviously lay elsewhere. The trucks that refueled the planes were frequently late, which in turn was due to the inefficient way they were refilled from storage tanks at another location. Once this latter problem was solved—and its solution was embarrassingly simple—the turnaround times decreased to an acceptable level without any changes on the part of the ground crews. If the analyst had accepted the military's statement of the problem, the *real* problem might never have been located or solved.

2. **Collect and summarize data.** This crucial step in the process is often the most tedious. All organizations keep track of various data on their operations, but these data are often not in the form an analyst requires. They are also typically scattered in different places throughout the organization, in all kinds of different formats. Therefore, one of the first jobs of an analyst is to gather exactly the right data and summarize the data appropriately—as discussed in detail in Chapters 2 and 3—for use in the model. Collecting the data typically requires asking questions of key people (such as the accountants) throughout the organization, studying existing databases, and performing time-consuming observational studies of the organization's processes. In short, it entails a lot of legwork. Fortunately, many companies have understood the need for good clean data and have spent large amounts of time and money to build *data warehouses* for quantitative analysis.

3. **Develop a model.** This is the step we emphasize, especially in the latter chapters of the book. The form of the model varies from one situation to another. It could be a graphical model, an algebraic model, or a spreadsheet model. The key is that the model must capture the important elements of the business problem in such a way that it is understandable by all parties involved. This latter requirement is why we favor spreadsheet models, especially when they are well designed and well documented.

4. **Verify the model.** Here the analyst tries to determine whether the model developed in the previous step is an accurate representation of reality. A first step in determining how well the model fits reality is to check whether the model is valid for the current situation. This verification can take several forms. For example, the analyst could use the model with the company's current values of the input parameters. If the model's outputs are then in line with the outputs currently observed by the company, the analyst has at least shown that the model can duplicate the current situation.

A second way to verify a model is to enter a number of input parameters (even if they are not the company's current inputs) and see whether the outputs from the model are *reasonable*. One common approach is to use extreme values of the inputs to see whether the outputs behave as they should. If they do, this is another piece of evidence that the model is reasonable.

If certain inputs are entered in the model and the model's outputs are *not* as expected, there could be two causes. First, the model could be a poor representation of reality. In this case it is up to the analyst to refine the model so that it is more realistic. The second possible cause is that the model is fine but our intuition is not very good. In this case the fault lies with us, not the model. The fact that outcomes sometimes defy intuition is an important reason why models are important. These models prove that our ability to predict outcomes in complex environments is often not very good.

5. **Select one or more suitable decisions.** Many, but not all, models are decision models. For any specific decisions, the model indicates the amount of profit obtained, the amount of cost incurred, the level of risk, and so on. If the model is working correctly, as discussed in step 4, then it can be used to see which decisions produce the *best* outputs.

6. **Present the results to the organization.** In a classroom setting you are typically finished when you have developed a model that correctly solves a particular problem. In the business world a correct model, even a useful one, does not always suffice. An analyst typically has to "sell" the model to management. Unfortunately, the people in management are sometimes not as well trained in quantitative methods as the analyst, so they are not always inclined to trust complex models.

   There are two ways to mitigate this problem. First, it is helpful to include relevant people throughout the company in the modeling process—from beginning to end—so that everyone has an understanding of the model and feels an ownership of it. Second, it helps to use a *spreadsheet* model whenever possible, especially if it is designed and documented properly. Almost everyone in today's business world is comfortable with spreadsheets, so spreadsheet models are more likely to be accepted.

7. **Implement the model and update it over time.** Again, there is a big difference between a classroom situation and a business situation. When you turn in a classroom assignment, you are typically finished with that assignment and can await the next one. In contrast, an analyst who develops a model for a company usually cannot pack up his bags and leave. If the model is accepted by management, the company will then need to implement it company-wide. This can be very time consuming and politically difficult, especially if the model's suggestions represent a significant change from the past. At the very least, employees must be trained how to use the model on a day-to-day basis.

   In addition, the model will probably have to be updated over time, either because of changing conditions or because the company sees more potential uses for the model as it gains experience using it. This presents one of the greatest challenges for a model developer, namely, the ability to develop a model that *can* be modified as the need arises.

1-4 CONCLUSION

In this chapter we have tried to convince you that the skills in this book are important for *you* to know as you enter the business world. The methods we discuss are no longer the sole province of the "quant jocks." By having a PC on your desk that is loaded with powerful software, you incur a responsibility to use this software to analyze business problems effectively. We have described the types of problems you will learn to analyze in this book, along with the software you will use to analyze them. We also discussed the modeling process, a theme that runs throughout this book. Now it is time for you to get started!

Cruise ship traveling has become big business. Many cruise lines are now competing for customers of all age groups and socioeconomic levels. They offer all types of cruises, from relatively inexpensive 3- to 4-day cruises in the Caribbean, to 12- to 15-day cruises in the Mediterranean, to several-month around-the-world cruises. Cruises have several features that attract customers, many of whom book six months or more in advance: (1) they offer a relaxing, everything-done-for-you way to travel; (2) they serve food that is plentiful, usually excellent, and included in the price of the cruise; (3) they stop at a number of interesting ports and offer travelers a way to see the world; and (4) they provide a wide variety of entertainment, particularly in the evening.

This last feature, the entertainment, presents a difficult problem for a ship's staff. A typical cruise might have well over 1000 passengers, including elderly singles and couples, middle-aged people with or without children, and young people, often honeymooners. These various types of passengers have varied tastes in terms of their after-dinner preferences in entertainment. Some want traditional dance music, some want comedians, some want rock music, some want movies, some want to go back to their cabins and read, and so on. Obviously, cruise entertainment directors want to provide the variety of entertainment their customers desire—within a reasonable budget—because satisfied customers tend to be repeat customers. The question is how to provide the right mix of entertainment.

On a cruise one of the authors and his wife took a few years ago, the entertainment was of high quality and there was plenty of variety. A seven-piece show band played dance music nightly in the largest lounge, two other small musical combos played nightly at two smaller lounges, a pianist played nightly at a piano bar in an intimate lounge, a group of professional singers and dancers played Broadway-type shows about twice weekly, and various professional singers and comedians played occasional single-night performances.[7] Although this entertainment was free to all of the passengers, much of it had embarrassingly low attendance. The nightly show band and musical combos, who were contracted to play nightly until midnight, often had less than a half-dozen people in the audience—sometimes literally none. The professional singers, dancers, and comedians attracted larger audiences, but there were still plenty of empty seats. In spite of this, the cruise staff posted a weekly schedule, and they stuck to it regardless of attendance. In a short-term financial sense, it didn't make much difference. The performers got paid the same whether anyone was in the audience or not, the passengers had already paid (indirectly) for the entertainment as part of the cost of the cruise, and the only possible opportunity cost to the cruise line (in the short run) was the loss of liquor sales from the lack of passengers in the entertainment lounges. The morale of the entertainers was not great—entertainers love packed houses—but they usually argued, philosophically, that their hours were relatively short and they were still getting paid to see the world.

If you were in charge of entertainment on this ship, how would you describe the problem with entertainment: Is it a problem with deadbeat passengers, low-quality entertainment, or a mismatch between the entertainment offered and the entertainment desired? How might you try to solve the problem? What constraints might you have to work within? Would you keep a strict schedule such as the one followed by this cruise director, or would you play it more by ear? Would you gather data to help solve the problem? What data would you gather? How much would financial considerations dictate your decisions? Would they be long-term or short-term considerations?

---

[7]There was also a moderately large onboard casino, but it tended to attract the same people every night, and it was always closed when the ship was in port.

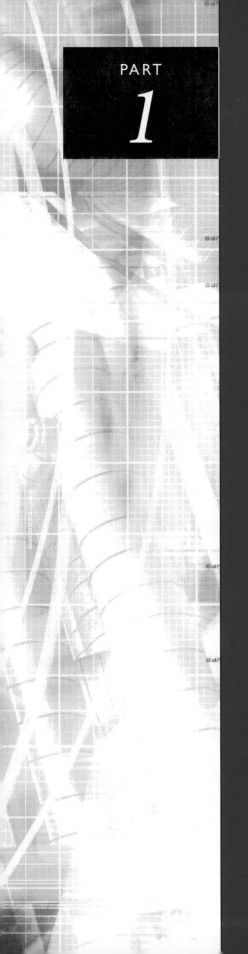

PART

1

Exploring Data

Describing the Distribution of a Single Variable

ZUMA Press, Inc./Alamy

RECENT PRESIDENTIAL ELECTIONS

Presidential elections in the United States are scrutinized more than ever. It hardly seems that one is over before we start hearing plans and polls for the next. There is thorough coverage of the races leading up to the elections, but it is also interesting to analyze the results after the elections have been held. This is not difficult, given the many informative Web sites that appear immediately with election results. For example, a Web search for "2012 presidential election results" finds many sites with in-depth results, interactive maps, and more. In addition, the resulting data can often be imported into Excel® rather easily for further analysis.

The file **Presidential Elections 2000–2012.xlsx** contains such downloaded data for the 2000 (Bush versus Gore), 2004 (Bush versus Kerry), 2008 (Obama versus McCain), and 2012 (Obama versus Romney) elections. The results of the 2000 election are particularly interesting. As you might remember, this was one of the closest elections of all time, with Bush defeating Gore by a very narrow margin in the electoral vote, 271 to 266, following a disputed recount in Florida. In fact, Gore actually beat Bush in the total count of U.S. votes, 50,999,897 to 50,456,002. However, because of the all-or-nothing nature of electoral votes in each state, Bush's narrow margin of victory in many closely contested states won him a lot of electoral votes. In contrast, Gore outdistanced Bush by a wide margin in several large states, winning him the same electoral votes he would have won even if these races had been much closer.

A closer analysis of the state-by-state results shows how this actually happened. In the Excel file, we created two new columns: **Bush Votes**

minus Gore Votes and **Pct for Bush minus Pct for Gore**, with a value for each state (including the District of Columbia). We then created column charts of these two variables, as shown in Figures 2.1 and 2.2.

Figure 2.1   Chart of Vote Differences

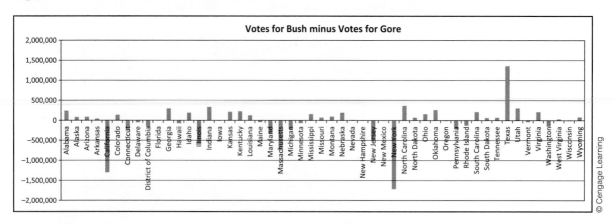

Figure 2.2   Chart of Percent Differences

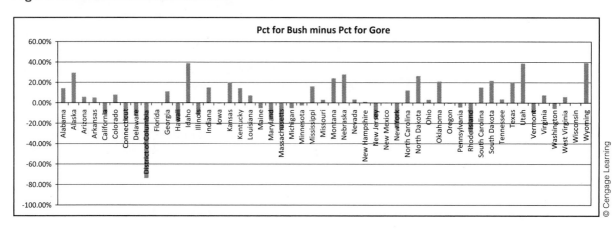

Each of these charts tells the same story, but in slightly different ways. From Figure 2.1, you can see how Gore won big (large vote difference) in several large states, most notably California, Massachusetts, and New York. Bush's only comparable margin of victory was in his home state of Texas. However, Bush won a lot of close races in states with relatively few electoral votes—but enough to add up to an overall win. As Figure 2.2 indicates, many of these "close" races, such as Alaska and Idaho for Bush and District of Columbia for Gore, were not that close after all, at least not from a percentage standpoint. This is one case of many where multiple charts can be created to "tell a story." Perhaps an argument can be made that Figure 2.1 tells the story best, but Figure 2.2 is also interesting.

The bottom line is that the election could easily have gone the other way. With one more swing state, particularly Florida, Al Gore would have been president. On the other hand, Gore won some very close races as well, particularly in Iowa, Minnesota,

New Mexico, and Oregon. If these had gone the other way, the popular vote would still have been very close, but Bush's victory in the electoral vote would have been more impressive. ■

2-1 INTRODUCTION

The goal of this chapter and the next chapter is very simple: to make sense of data by constructing appropriate summary measures, tables, and graphs. Our purpose here is to present the data in a form that makes sense to people. There are numerous ways to do this, limited only by your imagination, but there are several tools used most often: (1) a variety of graphs, including bar charts, pie charts, histograms, scatterplots, and time series graphs; (2) numerical summary measures such as counts, percentages, averages, and measures of variability; and (3) tables of summary measures such as totals, averages, and counts, grouped by categories. These terms might not all be familiar to you at this point, but you have undoubtedly seen examples of them in newspapers, magazine articles, and books.

The material in these two chapters is *simple, complex*, and *important*. It is simple because there are no difficult mathematical concepts. With the possible exception of variance, standard deviation, and correlation, all of the numerical measures, graphs, and tables are natural and easy to understand.

It is customary to refer to the raw numbers as data and the output of data analysis as information. You start with the data, and you hope to end with information that an organization can use for competitive advantage.

If it is so easy, why do we also claim that the material in this chapter is complex? The data sets available to companies in today's digital world tend to be extremely large and filled with "unstructured" data. As you will see, even in data sets that are quite small in comparison with those that real companies face, it is a challenge to summarize the data so that the important *information* stands out clearly. It is easy to produce summary measures, graphs, and tables, but the real goal is to produce the most *appropriate* ones.

The typical employees of today—not just the managers and technical specialists—have a wealth of easy-to-use tools at their disposal, and it is frequently up to them to summarize data in a way that is both meaningful and useful to their constituents: people within their company, their company's suppliers, and their company's customers. It takes some training and practice to do this effectively.

Because today's companies are inundated with data, and because virtually every employee in the company must summarize data to some extent, the material in this chapter and the next one is arguably the most important material in the book. There is sometimes a tendency to race through the "descriptive statistics" chapters to get to the more "interesting" material in later chapters as quickly as possible. We resist this tendency. The material covered in these two chapters deserves close examination, and this takes some time.

Data analysis in the real world is never done in a vacuum. It is done to solve a problem. Typically, there are four steps that are followed, whether the context is business, medical science, or any other field. The first step is to recognize a problem that needs to be solved. Perhaps a retail company is experiencing decreased sales in a particular region or for a particular product. Why is this happening? The second step is to gather data to help understand and then solve the problem. This might be done through a survey of customers, by assembling data from already-existing company systems, by finding relevant data on the Web, or from other sources. Once the data is gathered, the third step is to analyze the data using the tools you will learn in the book. The fourth step is to act on this analysis by changing policies, undertaking initiatives, publishing reports, and so on. Of course, the analysis can sometimes repeat steps. For example, once a given set of data is analyzed, it might be apparent that even more data needs to be collected.

Use your imagination to ask interesting questions about the many data sets available to you. We will supply you with the tools to answer these questions.

As we discuss the tools for analyzing data, we will often jump into the third step directly, providing you with a data set to analyze. Although this data set may not be directly connected to the goal of solving some company's problem, you should still strive to ask interesting questions of the data. (We have tried to include interesting data sets, often containing real data, that make this possible.) If the data set contains salaries, you might ask what drives these salaries. Does it depend on the industry a person is in? Does it depend on gender? Does it depend on educational background? Is the salary structure, whatever it is, changing over time? If the data set contains cost-of-living indexes, there are also a lot of interesting questions you can ask. How are the indexes changing over time? Does this behavior vary in different geographical regions? Does this behavior vary across different items such as housing, food, and automobiles? These early chapters provide you with many tools to answer such questions, but it is up to you to ask good questions—and then take advantage of the most appropriate tools to answer them.

The material in these chapters is organized as follows. This chapter discusses a number of ways to analyze one variable at a time. The next chapter discusses ways to discover relationships between variables. In addition, there is a bonus Chapter 18 on importing data from external sources into Excel, a natural companion to Chapters 2 and 3. This bonus chapter is available on this textbook's Web site (see Preface for instructors on accessing the resources that accompany this book).

2-2 BASIC CONCEPTS

We begin with a short discussion of several important concepts: populations and samples, data sets, variables and observations, and types of data.

2-2a Populations and Samples

First, we distinguish between a population and a sample. A **population** includes all of the entities of interest: people, households, machines, or whatever. The following are three typical populations:

- All potential voters in a presidential election
- All subscribers to cable television
- All invoices submitted for Medicare reimbursement by nursing homes

In these situations and many others, it is virtually impossible to obtain information about all members of the population. For example, it is far too costly to ask all potential voters which presidential candidates they prefer. Therefore, we often try to gain insights into the characteristics of a population by examining a **sample**, or subset, of the population. In later chapters, we examine populations and samples in some depth, but for now it is enough to know that samples should be *representative* of the population so that observed characteristics of the sample can be generalized to the population as a whole.

> A **population** includes all of the entities of interest in a study. A **sample** is a subset of the population, often randomly chosen and preferably representative of the population as a whole.

A famous example where a sample was *not* representative is the case of the *Literary Digest* fiasco of 1936. In the 1936 presidential election, subscribers to the *Literary Digest*, a highbrow literary magazine, were asked to mail in a ballot with their preference for president. Overwhelmingly, these ballots favored the Republican candidate, Alf Landon, over the Democratic candidate, Franklin D. Roosevelt. Despite this, FDR was a landslide winner. The discrepancy arose because the readers of the *Literary Digest* were not at all representative of most voters in 1936. Most voters in 1936 could barely make ends meet, let alone subscribe to a literary magazine. Thus, the typical lower-to-middle-income voter had almost no chance of being chosen in this sample.

Today, Gallup, Harris, and other pollsters make a conscious effort to ensure that their samples—which usually include about 1000 to 1500 people—are representative of the population. (It is truly remarkable, for example, that a sample of 1500 voters can almost surely predict a candidate's actual percentage of votes correctly to within 3 percent. We explain why this is possible in Chapters 7 and 8.) The important point is that a representative sample of reasonable size can provide a lot of important information about the population of interest.

We use the terms *population* and *sample* a few times in this chapter, which is why we have defined them here. However, the distinction is not really important until later chapters. Our intent in this chapter is to focus entirely on the data in a given data set, not to generalize beyond it. Therefore, the given data set could be a population or a sample from a population. For now, the distinction is irrelevant.

2-2b Data Sets, Variables, and Observations

We now discuss the types of data sets we will examine. Although the focus of this book is Excel, virtually all statistical software packages use the same concept of a data set: A **data set** is generally a rectangular array of data where the columns contain **variables**, such as height, gender, and income, and each row contains an **observation**. Each observation includes the attributes of a particular member of the population: a person, a company, a city, a machine, or whatever. This terminology is common, but other terms are often used. A variable (column) is often called a **field** or an **attribute**, and an observation (row) is often called a **case** or a **record**. Also, data sets are occasionally rearranged, so that the variables are in rows and the observations are in columns. However, the most common arrangement by far is to have variables in columns, with variable names in the top row, and observations in the remaining rows.

> A **data set** is usually a rectangular array of data, with variables in columns and observations in rows. A **variable** (or **field** or **attribute**) is a characteristic of members of a population, such as height, gender, or salary. An **observation** (or **case** or **record**) is a list of all variable values for a single member of a population.

| EXAMPLE | 2.1 Data from an Environmental Survey |

The data set shown in Figure 2.3 represents 30 responses from a questionnaire concerning the president's environmental policies, where 20 of the observations have been hidden. (See the file **Questionnaire Data.xlsx**.) Identify the variables and observations.

Figure 2.3
Environmental
Survey Data

	A	B	C	D	E	F	G
1	**Person**	**Age**	**Gender**	**State**	**Children**	**Salary**	**Opinion**
2	1	35	Male	Minnesota	1	$65,400	5
3	2	61	Female	Texas	2	$62,000	1
4	3	35	Male	Ohio	0	$63,200	3
5	4	37	Male	Florida	2	$52,000	5
6	5	32	Female	California	3	$81,400	1
7	6	33	Female	New York	3	$46,300	5
28	27	27	Male	Illinois	3	$45,400	2
29	28	63	Male	Michigan	2	$53,900	1
30	29	52	Male	California	1	$44,100	3
31	30	48	Female	New York	2	$31,000	4

© Cengage Learning

Objective   To illustrate variables and observations in a typical data set.

Solution

Each observation lists the person's age, gender, state of residence, number of children, annual salary, and opinion of the president's environmental policies. These six pieces of information represent the variables. It is customary to include a row (row 1 in this case) that lists variable names. These variable names should be concise but meaningful. Note that an index of the observation is often included in column A. If you sort on other variables, you can always sort on the index to get back to the original sort order.

As you will see shortly when you use the powerful statistical add-in for Excel called StatTools, the concept of a data set is crucial. Before you can perform any statistical analysis on a data set with StatTools, you must designate a rectangular range as a StatTools data set. This is easy, but it must be done. As you will also see, StatTools allows several layouts for data sets, including one where the variables are in rows and the observations are in columns. However, the default layout, the one you will see over 99% of the time, is the one shown in Figure 2.3, where variables are in columns, observations are in rows, and the top row contains variable names. ■

2-2c Types of Data

There are several ways to categorize data, as we explain in the context of Example 2.1. A basic distinction is between **numerical** and **categorical** data. The distinction is whether you intend to do any arithmetic on the data. It makes sense to do arithmetic on numerical data, but not on categorical data. (Actually, there is a third **data type**, a **date** variable. As you may know, Excel stores dates as numbers, but for obvious reasons, dates are treated differently from typical numbers.)

Three types of variables that appear to be numerical but are usually treated as categorical are phone numbers, zip codes, and Social Security numbers. Do you see why? Can you think of others?

> A variable is **numerical** if meaningful arithmetic can be performed on it. Otherwise, the variable is **categorical**.

In the questionnaire data, Age, Children, and Salary are clearly numerical. For example, it makes perfect sense to sum or average any of these. In contrast, Gender and State are clearly categorical because they are expressed as text, not numbers.

The Opinion variable is less obvious. It is expressed numerically, on a 1-to-5 scale. However, these numbers are really only *codes* for the categories "strongly disagree," "disagree," "neutral," "agree," and "strongly agree." There is never any intent to perform arithmetic on these numbers; in fact, it is not really appropriate to do so. Therefore, it is most appropriate to treat the Opinion variable as categorical. Note, too, that there is a definite ordering of its categories, whereas there is no natural ordering of the categories for the Gender or State variables. When there is a natural ordering of categories, the variable is classified as **ordinal**. If there is no natural ordering, as with the Gender variable or the State variable, the variable is classified as **nominal**. Remember, though, that both ordinal and nominal variables are categorical.

> A categorical variable is **ordinal** if there is a natural ordering of its possible categories. If there is no natural ordering, it is **nominal**.

Excel Tip: Horizontal Alignment Conventions
Excel automatically right-aligns numbers and left-aligns text. We will use this automatic formatting, but starting in this edition, we will add our own. Specifically, we will right-align all numbers that are available for arithmetic; we will left-align all text such as Male, Female, Yes, *and* No; *and we will center-align everything else, including dates, indexes such as the Person*

column, numbers that are indicators of categories such as in the Opinion column, and numbers such as phone numbers that aren't available for arithmetic. You don't need to follow this convention, but it helps to identify variable types.

Excel Tip: Documenting with Cell Comments
How do you remember, for example, that "1" stands for "strongly disagree" in the Opinion variable? You can enter a comment—a reminder to yourself and others—in any cell. To do so, right-click a cell and select Insert Comment. A small red tag appears in any cell with a comment. Moving the cursor over that cell causes the comment to appear. You will see numerous comments in the files that accompany the book.

Categorical variables can be coded numerically. In Figure 2.3, Gender has not been coded, whereas Opinion has been coded. This is largely a matter of taste—so long as you realize that coding a categorical variable does not make it numerical and available for arithmetic operations. An alternative way of displaying the data appears in Figure 2.4. Now Opinion has been replaced by text, and Gender has been coded as 1 for males and 0 for females. This 0–1 coding for a categorical variable is very common. Such a variable is called a **dummy variable**, and it often simplifies the analysis. You will see dummy variables often throughout the book.

> A **dummy variable** is a 0–1 coded variable for a specific category. It is coded as 1 for all observations in that category and 0 for all observations not in that category.

Figure 2.4   Environmental Data Using a Different Coding

	A	B	C	D	E	F	G	H	I	J	K	L
1	Person	Age	Gender	State	Children	Salary	Opinion					
2	1	Middle-aged	1	Minnesota	1	$65,400	Strongly agree					
3	2	Elderly	0	Texas	2	$62,000	Strongly disagree		Note the formulas in columns B, C, and			
4	3	Middle-aged	1	Ohio	0	$63,200	Neutral		G that generate this recorded data. The			
5	4	Middle-aged	1	Florida	2	$52,000	Strongly agree		formulas in columns B and G are based			
6	5	Young	0	California	3	$81,400	Strongly disagree		on the lookup tables below.			
7	6	Young	0	New York	3	$46,300	Strongly agree					
8	7	Elderly	0	Minnesota	2	$49,600	Strongly disagree					
9	8	Middle-aged	1	New York	1	$45,900	Strongly disagree		Age lookup table (range name AgeLookup)			
10	9	Middle-aged	1	Texas	3	$47,700	Agree		0	Young		
11	10	Young	0	Texas	1	$59,900	Agree		35	Middle-aged		
12	11	Middle-aged	1	New York	1	$48,100	Agree		60	Elderly		
13	12	Middle-aged	0	Virginia	0	$58,100	Neutral					
14	13	Middle-aged	0	Illinois	2	$56,000	Strongly disagree		Opinion lookup table (range name OpinionLookup)			
15	14	Middle-aged	0	Virginia	2	$53,400	Strongly disagree		1	Strongly disagree		
16	15	Middle-aged	0	New York	2	$39,000	Disagree		2	Disagree		
17	16	Middle-aged	1	Michigan	1	$61,500	Disagree		3	Neutral		
18	17	Middle-aged	1	Ohio	0	$37,700	Strongly disagree		4	Agree		
19	18	Middle-aged	0	Michigan	2	$36,700	Agree		5	Strongly agree		
28	27	Young	1	Illinois	3	$45,400	Disagree					
29	28	Elderly	1	Michigan	2	$53,900	Strongly disagree					
30	29	Middle-aged	1	California	1	$44,100	Neutral					
31	30	Middle-aged	0	New York	2	$31,000	Agree					

© Cengage Learning

In addition, the Age variable has been categorized as "young" (34 years or younger), "middle-aged" (from 35 to 59 years), and "elderly" (60 years or older). This method of categorizing a numerical variable is called **binning** (putting the data into discrete bins), and it is also very common. (It is also called **discretizing**.) The purpose of the study dictates whether age should be treated numerically or categorically; there is no absolute right or wrong way.

> A **binned** (or **discretized**) **variable** corresponds to a numerical variable that has been categorized into discrete categories. These categories are usually called **bins**.

Excel Tip: VLOOKUP Function

As Figure 2.4 indicates, we used lookup tables, along with the very important VLOOKUP function, to transform the data set from Figure 2.3 to Figure 2.4. Take a look at these functions in the questionnaire file. There is arguably no more important Excel function than VLOOKUP, so you should definitely learn how to use it.

Numerical variables can be classified as **discrete** or **continuous**. The basic distinction is whether the data arise from counts or continuous measurements. The variable Children is clearly a count (discrete), whereas the variable Salary is best treated as continuous. This distinction between discrete and continuous variables is sometimes important because it dictates the most natural type of analysis.

A numerical variable is **discrete** if it results from a count, such as the number of children. A **continuous** variable is the result of an essentially continuous measurement, such as weight or height.

Data sets can also be categorized as cross-sectional or time series. The opinion data set in Example 2.1 is **cross-sectional**. A pollster evidently sampled a cross section of people at one particular point in time. In contrast, **time series** data occur when one or more variables are tracked through time. A typical time series variable is the series of daily closing values of the Dow Jones Industrial Average (DJIA). Very different types of analyses are appropriate for cross-sectional and time series data, as will become apparent in this and later chapters.

Cross-sectional data are data on a cross section of a population at a distinct point in time. **Time series** data are data collected over time.

A time series data set generally has the same layout—variables in columns and observations in rows—but now each variable is a time series. Also, one of the columns usually indicates the time period. A typical example appears in Figure 2.5. (See the file **Toy Revenues.xlsx**.) It has quarterly observations on revenues from toy sales over a four-year period in column B, with the time periods listed chronologically in column A.

Figure 2.5

Typical Time Series Data Set

	A	B	C	D	E	F
1	Quarter	Revenue				
2	Q1-2010	1026				
3	Q2-2010	1056		All monetary values are in		
4	Q3-2010	1182		thousands of dollars.		
5	Q4-2010	2861				
6	Q1-2011	1172				
7	Q2-2011	1249				
8	Q3-2011	1346				
9	Q4-2011	3402				
10	Q1-2012	1286				
11	Q2-2012	1317				
12	Q3-2012	1449				
13	Q4-2012	3893				
14	Q1-2013	1462				
15	Q2-2013	1452				
16	Q3-2013	1631				
17	Q4-2013	4200				

© Cengage Learning

2-3 DESCRIPTIVE MEASURES FOR CATEGORICAL VARIABLES

This section discusses methods for describing a categorical variable. Because it is not appropriate to perform arithmetic on the values of the variable, there are only a few possibilities for describing the variable, and these are all based on *counting*. First, you can count the *number* of categories. Many categorical variables such as Gender have only two categories. Others such as Region can have more than two categories. As you count the categories, you can also give the categories *names*, such as Male and Female. Keep in mind that categorical variables, such as Opinion in Example 2.1, can be coded numerically. In these cases, it is still a good idea to supply text descriptions of these categories, such as "strongly agree," and it is often useful to substitute these meaningful descriptions for the numerical codes, as in Figure 2.4. This is especially useful for statistical reports.

The only meaningful way to summarize categorical data is with counts of observations in the categories.

Once you know the number of categories and their names, you can count the number of observations in each category (this is referred to as the **count of categories**). The resulting counts can be reported as "raw counts" or they can be transformed into percentages of totals. For example, if there are 1000 observations, you can report that there are 560 males and 440 females, or you can report that 56% of the observations are males and 44% are females. In fact, it is often useful to report the counts in both of these ways. Finally, once you have the counts, you can display them graphically, usually in a column chart or possibly a pie chart. Example 2.2 illustrates how to do this in Excel.

EXAMPLE | **2.2 SUPERMARKET SALES**

The file **Supermarket Transactions.xlsx** contains over 14,000 transactions made by supermarket customers over a period of approximately two years. (The data are not real, but real supermarket chains have huge data sets just like this one.) A small sample of the data appears in Figure 2.6. Column B contains the date of the purchase, column C is a unique identifier for each customer, columns D–H contain information about the customer, columns I–K contain the location of the store, columns L–N contain information about the product purchased (these columns have been hidden to conserve space), and the last two columns indicate the number of items purchased and the amount paid. Which of the variables are categorical, and how can these categorical variables be summarized?

Figure 2.6   Supermarket Data Set

	A	B	C	D	E	F	G	H	I	J	K	O	P
1	Transaction	Purchase Date	Customer ID	Gender	Marital Status	Home Owner	Children	Annual Income	City	State or Province	Country	Units Sold	Revenue
2	1	12/18/2011	7223	F	S	Y	2	$30K - $50K	Los Angeles	CA	USA	5	$27.38
3	2	12/20/2011	7841	M	M	Y	5	$70K - $90K	Los Angeles	CA	USA	5	$14.90
4	3	12/21/2011	8374	F	M	N	2	$50K - $70K	Bremerton	WA	USA	3	$5.52
5	4	12/21/2011	9619	M	M	Y	3	$30K - $50K	Portland	OR	USA	4	$4.44
6	5	12/22/2011	1900	F	S	Y	3	$130K - $150K	Beverly Hills	CA	USA	4	$14.00
7	6	12/22/2011	6696	F	M	Y	3	$10K - $30K	Beverly Hills	CA	USA	3	$4.37
8	7	12/23/2011	9673	M	S	Y	2	$30K - $50K	Salem	OR	USA	4	$13.78
9	8	12/25/2011	354	F	M	Y	2	$150K +	Yakima	WA	USA	6	$7.34
10	9	12/25/2011	1293	M	M	Y	3	$10K - $30K	Bellingham	WA	USA	1	$2.41
11	10	12/25/2011	7938	M	S	N	1	$50K - $70K	San Diego	CA	USA	2	$8.96

Objective   To summarize categorical variables in a large data set.

Solution

Most of the variables in this data set are categorical. Only Children, Units Sold, and Revenue are numerical. Purchase Date is a date variable, and Transaction and Customer ID are used only to identify transactions and customers. All of the others are categorical. This includes Annual Income, which has been binned into categories. Three of these categorical variables—Gender, Marital Status, and Homeowner—have only two categories. The others have more than two categories.

The first question is how you can discover all of the categories for a variable such as State or Province. Without good tools, this is not a trivial problem. One option is to sort on this variable and then manually go through the list, looking for the different categories. Fortunately, there are much easier ways, using Excel's built-in table and pivot table tools. We will postpone these for later and deal for now only with the "easy" categorical variables.

Figure 2.7 displays summaries of Gender, Marital Status, Homeowner, and Annual Income, along with several corresponding charts for Gender. Each of the counts in column S can be obtained with Excel's COUNTIF function. For example, the formula in cell S3 is **=COUNTIF($D$2:$D$14060,R3)**. This function takes two arguments, the data range and a criterion, so it is perfect for counting observations in a category. Then, to get the percentages in column T, each count is divided by the total number of observations. (As a check, it is a good idea to sum these percentages. They should sum to 100% for each variable, as they do here.)

Figure 2.7 Summaries of Categorical Variables

	R	S	T	U	V	W	X	Y	Z	AA	AB	AC	AD	AE
1	Categorical summaries													
2	Gender	Count	Percent											
3	M	6889	49.0%											
4	F	7170	51.0%											
5			100.0%											
6														
7	Marital Status	Count	Percent											
8	S	7193	51.2%											
9	M	6866	48.8%											
10			100.0%											
11														
12	Homeowner	Count	Percent											
13	Y	8444	60.1%											
14	N	5615	39.9%											
15			100.0%											
16														
17	Annual Income	Count	Percent											
18	$10K - $30K	3090	22.0%											
19	$30K - $50K	4601	32.7%											
20	$50K - $70K	2370	16.9%											
21	$70K - $90K	1709	12.2%											
22	$90K - $110K	613	4.4%											
23	$110K - $130K	643	4.6%											
24	$130K - $150K	760	5.4%											
25	$150K +	273	1.9%											
26			100.0%											
27														
28														
29														
30														

When you have a choice between a "simple" chart and a "fancier" chart, keep it simple. Simple charts tend to reveal the information in the data more clearly.

As the charts indicate, you get essentially the same chart whether you graph the counts or the percentages. However, be careful with misleading scales. If you select the range R2:S4 and then insert a column chart, you get the top left chart by default. Its vertical scale starts well above 6000, which makes it appear that there are *many* more females than males. By resetting the vertical scale to start at 0, as in the two middle charts, you see more accurately that there are almost as many males as females. Finally, you can decide whether you prefer a column chart or a pie chart. We tend to prefer column charts, but this is entirely a matter of taste. (We also tend to prefer column charts to horizontal bar charts, but this is again a matter of taste.) Our only recommendation in general is to keep charts *simple* so that the information they contain emerges as clearly as possible.

Excel Tip: *Creating an Excel Chart Efficiently*
If you are new to Excel charts, particularly in post-2003 versions of Excel, you should try creating the charts in Figure 2.7 on your own. One way is to select a blank cell, select a desired chart type from the Insert ribbon, and then designate the data to be included in the chart. However, it is usually more efficient to select the data to be charted and then insert the chart. For example, try highlighting the range R2:S4 and then inserting a column chart. Except for a little cleanup (deleting the legend, changing the chart title, and possibly changing the vertical scale), you get almost exactly what you want with very little work.

If this example of summarizing categorical variables appears to be overly tedious, be patient. As indicated earlier, Excel has some powerful tools, especially pivot tables, that make this summarization much easier. We discuss pivot tables in depth in the next chapter. For now, just remember that the only meaningful way to summarize a categorical variable is to count observations in each of its categories.

Before leaving this section, we mention one other efficient way to find counts for a categorical variable. This method uses dummy (0–1) variables. To see how it works, focus on any category of some categorical variable, such as M for Gender. Recode the variable so that each M is replaced by a 1 and all other values are replaced by 0. (This can be done in Excel in a new column, using a simple IF formula. See column E of Figure 2.8) Now you can find the count of males by *summing* the 0s and 1s, and you can find the percentage of males by *averaging* the 0s and 1s. That is, the formulas in cells E14061 and E14062 use

Figure 2.8

Summarizing a Category with a Dummy Variable

⬛	A	B	C	D	E
1	Transaction	Purchase Date	Customer ID	Gender	Gender Dummy for M
2	1	12/18/2011	7223	F	0
3	2	12/20/2011	7841	M	1
4	3	12/21/2011	8374	F	0
5	4	12/21/2011	9619	M	1
6	5	12/22/2011	1900	F	0
7	6	12/22/2011	6696	F	0
8	7	12/23/2011	9673	M	1
9	8	12/25/2011	354	F	0
10	9	12/25/2011	1293	M	1
11	10	12/25/2011	7938	M	1
14055	14054	12/29/2013	2032	F	0
14056	14055	12/29/2013	9102	F	0
14057	14056	12/29/2013	4822	F	0
14058	14057	12/31/2013	250	M	1
14059	14058	12/31/2013	6153	F	0
14060	14059	12/31/2013	3656	M	1
14061				Count	6889
14062				Percent	49.0%

© Cengage Learning

the SUM and AVERAGE functions on the data in column E. You should convince yourself why this works (for example, what arithmetic are you really doing when you average 0s and 1s?), and you should remember this method. It is one reason why dummy variables are used so frequently in data analysis. ■

PROBLEMS

Note: Student solutions for problems whose numbers appear within a color box are available for purchase at www.cengagebrain.com.

Level A

1. The file **P02_01.xlsx** indicates the gender and nationality of the MBA incoming class in two successive years at the Kelley School of Business at Indiana University.
   a. For each year, create tables of counts of gender and of nationality. Then create column charts of these counts. Do they indicate any noticeable change in the composition of the two classes?
   b. Repeat part **a** for nationality, but recode this variable so that all nationalities that have counts of 1 or 2 are classified as Other.

2. The file **P02_02.xlsx** contains information on over 200 movies that were released in 2006 and 2007.
   a. Create two column charts of counts, one of the different genres and one of the different distributors.
   b. Recode the Genre column so that all genres with a count of 10 or less are lumped into a category called Other. Then create a column chart of counts for this recoded variable. Repeat similarly for the Distributor variable.

3. The file **P02_03.xlsx** contains data from a survey of 399 people regarding a government environmental policy.
   a. Which of the variables in this data set are categorical? Which of these are nominal; which are ordinal?
   b. For each categorical variable, create a column chart of counts.
   c. Recode the data into a new data set, making four transformations: (1) change Gender to list "Male"

or "Female"; (2) change Children to list "No children" or "At least one child"; (3) change Salary to be categorical with categories "Less than $40K," "Between $40K and $70K," "Between $70K and $100K," and "Greater than $100K " (where you can treat the breakpoints however you like); and (4) change Opinion to be a numerical code from 1 to 5 for Strongly Disagree to Strongly Agree. Then create a column chart of counts for the new Salary variable.

4. The file **P02_04.xlsx** contains salary data on all Major League Baseball players for each year from 2002 to 2011. (The 2011 sheet is used for examples later in this chapter.) For any three selected years, create a table of counts of the various positions, expressed as percentages of all players for the year. Then create a column chart of these percentages for these years. Do they remain fairly constant from year to year?

Level B

5. The file **DJIA Monthly Close.xlsx** contains monthly values of the Dow Jones Industrial Average from 1950 through 2011. It also contains the percentage changes from month to month. (This file will be used for an example later in this chapter.) Create a new column for recoding the percentage changes into six categories: Large negative ($<-3\%$), Medium negative ($<-1\%$, $\geqslant -3\%$), Small negative ($<0\%$, $\geqslant -1\%$), Small positive ($<1\%$, $\geqslant 0\%$), Medium positive ($<3\%$, $\geqslant 1\%$), and Large positive ($\geqslant 3\%$). Then create a column chart of the counts of this categorical variable. Comment on its shape.

2-4 DESCRIPTIVE MEASURES FOR NUMERICAL VARIABLES

There are many ways to summarize numerical variables, both with numerical summary measures and with charts, and we discuss the most common ways in this section. But before we get into details, it is important to understand the basic goal of this section. We begin with a numerical variable such as Salary, where there is one observation for each person. Our basic goal is to learn how these salaries are distributed across people. To do this, we can ask a number of questions, including the following. (1) What are the most "typical" salaries? (2) How spread out are the salaries? (3) What are the "extreme" salaries on either end? (4) Is a chart of the salaries symmetric about some middle value, or is it skewed in some direction? (5) Does the chart of salaries have any other peculiar features besides possible skewness? In the next chapter, we explore methods for checking whether a variable such as Salary is related to *other* variables, but for now we simply want to explore the distribution of values in the Salary column.

Excel has a number of built-in tools for summarizing numerical variables, and we will discuss these. However, even better tools are available in Excel add-ins, and in this section we will introduce a very powerful add-in from Palisade Corporation called StatTools. There are two important advantages of StatTools over other statistical software. First, it works inside Excel, which is an obvious advantage for the many users who prefer to work in Excel. Second, it is extremely easy to learn, with virtually no learning curve. Just keep in mind that StatTools is not part of Microsoft Office. You get the academic version of StatTools free with this book, but if you eventually want to use StatTools in your job, you will have to persuade your company to purchase it. (Many of our graduates have done exactly that.)

2-4a Numerical Summary Measures

Throughout this section, we focus on a Salary variable. Specifically, we examine the 2011 salaries for Major League Baseball players, as described in Example 2.3.

CHANGES IN EXCEL 2010

Microsoft modified many of the statistical functions and added a few new ones in Excel 2010. Although Microsoft advertises the superiority of the new functions, all of the old functions can still be used. When a modified or new function is relevant, we indicate this in the text.

EXAMPLE | **2.3 BASEBALL SALARIES**

The file **Baseball Salaries 2011.xlsx** contains data on 843 Major League Baseball (MLB) players in the 2011 season. There are four variables, as shown in Figure 2.9: the player's name, team, position, and salary. How can these 843 salaries be summarized?

Figure 2.9
Baseball Salaries

	A	B	C	D
1	Player	Team	Position	Salary
2	A.J. Burnett	New York Yankees	Pitcher	$16,500,000
3	A.J. Ellis	Los Angeles Dodgers	Catcher	$421,000
4	A.J. Pierzynski	Chicago White Sox	Catcher	$2,000,000
5	Aaron Cook	Colorado Rockies	Pitcher	$9,875,000
6	Aaron Crow	Kansas City Royals	Pitcher	$1,400,000
7	Aaron Harang	San Diego Padres	Pitcher	$3,500,000
8	Aaron Heilman	Arizona Diamondbacks	Pitcher	$2,000,000
9	Aaron Hill	Toronto Blue Jays	Second Baseman	$5,000,000
10	Aaron Laffey	Seattle Mariners	Pitcher	$431,600
11	Aaron Miles	Los Angeles Dodgers	Second Baseman	$500,000
12	Aaron Rowand	San Francisco Giants	Outfielder	$13,600,000
13	Adam Dunn	Chicago White Sox	Designated Hitter	$12,000,000
14	Adam Everett	Cleveland Indians	Shortstop	$700,000

© Cengage Learning

Objective   To learn how salaries are distributed across all 2011 MLB players.

Solution

The various numerical summary measures can be categorized into several groups: measures of central tendency; minimum, maximum, percentiles, and quartiles; measures of variability; and measures of shape. We explain each of these in this extended example. ∎

Measures of Central Tendency

There are three common measures of central tendency, all of which try to answer the basic question of which value is most "typical." These are the mean, the median, and the mode.

The **mean** is the average of all values. If the data set represents a sample from some larger population, this measure is called the **sample mean** and is denoted by $\bar{X}$ (pronounced "X-bar"). If the data set represents the entire population, it is called the **population mean** and is denoted by μ (the Greek letter *mu*). This distinction is not important in this chapter, but it will become relevant in later chapters when we discuss statistical inference. In either case, the formula for the mean is given by Equation (2.1).

Formula for the Mean

$$\text{Mean} = \frac{\sum_{i=1}^{n} X_i}{n}$$

(2.1)

Here, n is the number of observations and X_i is the value of observation i. Equation (2.1) says to add all the observations and divide by n, the number of observations. The Σ (Greek capital *sigma*) symbol means to sum from $i = 1$ to $i = n$, that is, to sum over all observations.

For Excel data sets, you can calculate the mean with the AVERAGE function. This is shown for the baseball data (along with a lot of other summary measures we will discuss shortly) in Figure 2.10. Specifically, the average salary for all players is a whopping $3,305,055. Is this a "typical" salary? Keep reading.

The **median** is the middle observation when the data are sorted from smallest to largest. If the number of observations is odd, the median is literally the middle observation. For example, if there are nine observations, the median is the fifth smallest (or fifth largest). If the number of observations is even, the median is usually defined as the average of the two middle observations (although there are some slight variations of this definition). For example, if there are 10 observations, the median is usually defined as the average of the fifth and sixth smallest values.

For highly skewed data, the median is typically a better measure of central tendency. The median is unaffected by the extreme values, whereas the mean can be very sensitive to extreme values.

The median can be calculated in Excel with the MEDIAN function. Figure 2.10 shows that the median salary is $1,175,000. In words, half of the players make less than this, and half make more. Why is the median in this example so much smaller than the mean, and which is more appropriate? These are important questions, and they are relevant questions for many real-world data sets. As you might expect, the vast majority of baseball players have relatively modest salaries that are dwarfed by the astronomical salaries of a few stars. Because it is an average, the mean is strongly influenced by these really large values, so it is quite high. In contrast, the median is completely unaffected by the magnitude of the really large salaries, so it is much smaller. (For example, the median would not change by a single cent if Alex Rodriguez made $32 *trillion* instead of his $32 million, but the mean would increase to almost $38 million.)

Figure 2.10 Summary Measures of Baseball Salaries Using Excel Functions

◢	A	B	C	D	E	F
1	**Measures of central tendency**				**Measures of variability**	
2	Mean	$3,305,055			Range	$31,586,000
3	Median	$1,175,000			Interquartile range	$3,875,925
4	Mode	$414,000	57		Variance	20,563,887,478,833
5					Standard deviation	$4,534,742
6	**Min, max, percentiles, quartiles**				Mean absolute deviation	$3,249,917
7	Min	$414,000				
8	Max	$32,000,000			**Measures of shape**	
9	P01	$414,000	0.01		Skewness	2.2568
10	P05	$414,000	0.05		Kurtosis	5.7233
11	P10	$416,520	0.10			
12	P20	$424,460	0.20		**Percentages of values less than given values**	
13	P50	$1,175,000	0.50		Value	Percentage less than
14	P80	$5,500,000	0.80		$1,000,000	46.38%
15	P90	$9,800,000	0.90		$1,500,000	54.69%
16	P95	$13,590,000	0.95		$2,000,000	58.36%
17	P99	$20,000,000	0.99		$2,500,000	63.23%
18	Q1	$430,325	1		$3,000,000	66.55%
19	Q2	$1,175,000	2			
20	Q3	$4,306,250	3			

© Cengage Learning

In many situations like this, where the data are skewed to the right (a few extremely large salaries not balanced by any extremely small salaries), most people would argue that the median is a more representative measure of central tendency than the mean. However, both are often quoted. And for variables that are *not* skewed in one direction or the other, the mean and median are often quite close to one another.

The **mode** is the value that appears most often, and it can be calculated in Excel with the MODE function. In most cases where a variable is essentially continuous, the mode is not very interesting because it is often the result of a few lucky ties. However, the mode for the salary data in Figure 2.10 is not a result of luck. Its value, $414,000, is the minimum possible salary set by the league. As shown in cell C4 (with a COUNTIF formula), this value occurred 57 times. In other words, close to 7% of the players earn the minimum possible salary. This is a good example of learning something you probably didn't know simply by exploring the data.

CHANGES IN EXCEL 2010

Two new versions of the MODE function were introduced in Excel 2010: MODE.MULT and MODE.SNGL. The latter is the same as the older MODE function. The MULT version returns multiple modes if there are multiple modes.

Minimum, Maximum, Percentiles, and Quartiles

Given a certain percentage such as 25%, what is the salary value such that this percentage of salaries is below it? This type of question leads to **percentiles** and **quartiles**. Specifically, for any percentage p, the pth percentile is the value such that a percentage p of all values are less than it. Similarly, the first, second, and third quartiles are the percentiles corresponding to $p = 25\%$, $p = 50\%$, and $p = 75\%$. These three values divide the data into four groups, each with (approximately) a quarter of all observations. Note that the second quartile is equal to the median by definition. To complete this group of descriptive measures, we add the **minimum** and **maximum** values, with the obvious meanings.

You are probably aware of percentiles from standardized tests. For example, if you learn that your score in the verbal SAT test is at the 93rd percentile, this means that you scored better than 93% of those taking the test.

The minimum and maximum can be calculated with Excel's MIN and MAX functions. For the percentiles and quartiles, you can use Excel's PERCENTILE and QUARTILE functions. The PERCENTILE function takes two arguments: the data range and a value of p between 0 and 1. (It has to be between 0 and 1. For example, if you want the 95th percentile, you must enter the second argument as 0.95, not as 95.) The QUARTILE function also takes two arguments: the data range and 1, 2, or 3, depending on which quartile you want. Figure 2.10 shows the minimum, maximum, the three quartiles, and several commonly requested percentiles for the baseball data. Note that at least 25% of the players make within $16,325 of the league minimum, and more than a quarter of all players make more than $4.3 million. In fact, more than 1% of the players make more than $20 million, with Alex Rodriguez topping the list at $32 million. And they say it's just a game!

Excel Tip: Entering Arguments for Copying
Note the values in column C of Figure 2.10 for percentiles and quartiles. These allow you to enter one formula for the percentiles and one for quartiles that can then be copied down. Specifically, the formulas in cells B9 and B18 are

= PERCENTILE(Data!$D$2:$D$844,C9)

and

= QUARTILE(Data!$D$2:$D$844,C18).

(Here, Data! is a reference to the worksheet that contains the data.) Always look for ways to make your Excel formulas copyable. It saves time and it avoids errors. And if you don't want the values in column C to be visible, just color them white.

CHANGES IN EXCEL 2010

Excel's PERCENTILE and QUARTILE functions can give strange results when there are only a few observations. For this reason, Microsoft added new functions in Excel 2010: PERCENTILE.EXC, PERCENTILE.INC, QUARTILE.EXC, and QUARTILE.INC, where EXC and INC stand for exclusive and inclusive. The INC functions work just like the older PERCENTILE and QUARTILE functions. The EXC versions are recommended especially for a small number of observations.

If you are given a certain salary figure such as $1 million, you might want to find the percentage of all salaries less than this. This is essentially the opposite of a percentile question. In a percentile question, you are given a percentage and you want to find a value. Now you are given a value and you want to find a percentage. You can find this percentage in Excel by dividing a COUNTIF function by the total number of observations. A few such values are shown in the bottom right of Figure 2.10. The typical formula in cell F14, which is then copied down, is

=COUNTIF(Data!$D$2:$D$844,"<"&E14)/COUNT(Data!$D$2:$D$844).

The following Excel tip explains this formula in more detail.

Excel Tip: **Creating a Condition with Concatenation**
The condition in this COUNTIF formula is a bit tricky. You literally want it to be "< 1000000", but you want the formula to refer to the values in column E to enable copying. Therefore, you can **concatenate** *(or string together) the literal part, "<", and the variable part, the reference to cell E14. The ampersand symbol (&) in the middle is the symbol used to concatenate in Excel. This use of concatenation to join literal and variable parts is especially useful in functions like COUNTIF that require a condition, so you should learn how to use it.*

Measures of Variability

If you learn that the mean (or median) salary in some company is $100,000, this tells you something about the "typical" salary, but it tells you nothing about the variability of the salaries. Percentiles and quartiles certainly tell you something about variability. In fact, by seeing a lot of percentiles, you know almost exactly how the data are spread out. (Just look at the list of percentiles in Figure 2.10 and add a few more if you want to fill in the gaps.) In this subsection, we list a few other measures that summarize variability. These include the range, the interquartile range, the variance and standard deviation, and the mean absolute deviation. None of these says as much about variability as a complete list of percentiles, but they are all useful.

The **range** is a fairly crude measure of variability. It is defined as the maximum value minus the minimum value. For the baseball salaries, this range is $31.586 million. This value certainly indicates how spread out the salaries are, but it is too sensitive to the extremes. For example, if Alex Rodriguez's salary increased to $42 million, the range would increase by $10 million—just because of one player. A less sensitive measure is the **interquartile range** (abbreviated **IQR**). It is defined as the third quartile minus the first quartile, so it is really the range of the middle 50% of the data. For the baseball data, the IQR is $3,875,925. If you excluded the 25% of players with the lowest salaries and the 25% with the highest salaries, this IQR would be the range of the remaining salaries.

The range or a modified range such as the IQR probably seems like a natural measure of variability, but there is another measure that is quoted much more frequently: standard deviation. Actually, there are two related measures, variance and standard deviation, and we begin with a definition of variance. The **variance** is essentially the average of the squared deviations from the mean, where if X_i is a typical observation, its squared deviation from the mean is $(X_i - \text{mean})^2$. As in the discussion of the mean, there is a **sample variance**, denoted by s^2, and a **population variance**, denoted by σ^2 (where σ is the Greek letter *sigma*). They are defined as follows:

Formula for Sample Variance

$$s^2 = \frac{\sum_{i=1}^{n}(X_i - \text{mean})^2}{n - 1}$$

(2.2)

Formula for Population Variance

$$\sigma^2 = \frac{\sum_{i=1}^{n}(X_i - \text{mean})^2}{n} \qquad (2.3)$$

Technical Note: Denominators of Variance Formulas

It is traditional to use the capital letter N for the population size and lowercase n for the sample size, but we won't worry about this distinction in this chapter. Furthermore, there is a technical reason why the sample variance uses n−1 in the denominator, not n, and this is explained in a later chapter. However, the difference is negligible when n is large. Excel implements both of these formulas. You can use the VAR function to obtain the sample variance (denominator n−1), and you can use the VARP function to obtain the population variance (denominator n).

To understand why the variance is indeed a measure of variability, look closely at either formula. If all observations are close to the mean, their squared deviations from the mean will be relatively small, and the variance will be relatively small. On the other hand, if at least a few of the observations are far from the mean, their squared deviations from the mean will be large, and this will cause the variance to be large. Note that because deviations from the mean are *squared*, an observation a certain amount *below* the mean contributes the same to variance as an observation that same amount *above* the mean.

There is a fundamental problem with variance as a measure of variability: It is in *squared* units. For example, if the observations are measured in dollars, the variance is in squared dollars. A more natural measure is the square root of variance. This is called the **standard deviation**. Again, there are two versions of standard deviation. The **sample standard deviation**, denoted by *s*, is the square root of the quantity in Equation (2.2). The **population standard deviation**, denoted by σ, is the square root of the quantity in Equation (2.3).

To calculate either standard deviation in Excel, you can first find the variance with the VAR or VARP function and then take its square root. Alternatively, you can find it directly with the STDEV (sample) or STDEVP (population) function.

CHANGES IN EXCEL 2010

The functions for variance and standard deviation were renamed in Excel 2010 to VAR.S, VAR.P, STDEV.S, and STDEV.P. However, the older versions still work fine.

The data in Figure 2.11 help clarify these concepts. It is in the file **Variability.xlsx**. (It will help if you open this file and look at its formulas as you read this.) The variable Diameter1 on the left has relatively low variability; its 10 values vary closely around its mean of approximately 100 (found in cell A16 with the AVERAGE function). To show how variance is calculated, we explicitly calculated the 10 squared deviations from the mean in column B. Then either variance, sample or population, can be calculated (in cells A19 and A22) as the sum of squared deviations divided by 9 or 10. Alternatively, they can be calculated more directly (in cells B19 and B22) with Excel's VAR and VARP functions. Next, either standard deviation, sample or population, can be calculated as the square root of the corresponding variance or with Excel's STDEV or STDEVP functions.

The calculations are exactly the same for Diameter2 on the right. This variable also has mean approximately equal to 100, but its observations vary much more around 100 than the observations for Diameter1. As expected, this increased variability is obvious in a comparison of the variances and standard deviations for the two suppliers.

Figure 2.11   Calculating Variance and Standard Deviation

	A	B	C	D	E	F
1	Low variability supplier				High variability supplier	
2						
3	Diameter1	Sq dev from mean			Diameter2	Sq dev from mean
4	102.61	6.610041			103.21	9.834496
5	103.25	10.310521			93.66	41.139396
6	96.34	13.682601			120.87	432.473616
7	96.27	14.205361			110.26	103.754596
8	103.77	13.920361			117.31	297.079696
9	97.45	6.702921			110.23	103.144336
10	98.22	3.308761			70.54	872.257156
11	102.76	7.403841			39.53	3665.575936
12	101.56	2.313441			133.22	1098.657316
13	98.16	3.530641			101.91	3.370896
14						
15	Mean				Mean	
16	100.039				100.074	
17						
18	Sample variance				Sample variance	
19	9.1098	9.1098			736.3653	736.3653
20						
21	Population variance				Population variance	
22	8.1988	8.1988			662.7287	662.7287
23						
24	Sample standard deviation				Sample standard deviation	
25	3.0182	3.0182			27.1361	27.1361
26						
27	Population standard deviation				Population standard deviation	
28	2.8634	2.8634			25.7435	25.7435

Variability is usually the enemy. Being close to a target value on average is not good enough if there is a lot of variability around the target.

This example also indicates why variability is important. Imagine that you are about to buy 10 parts from one of two suppliers, and you want each part's diameter to be close to 100 centimeters. Furthermore, suppose that Diameter1 in the example represents 10 randomly selected parts from supplier 1, whereas Diameter2 represents 10 randomly selected parts from Supplier 2. You can see that both suppliers are very close to the target of 100 *on average*, but the increased variability for Supplier 2 makes this supplier much less attractive. There is a famous saying in operations management: **Variability is the enemy**. This example illustrates exactly what this saying means.

Empirical Rules for Interpreting Standard Deviation

Now you know how to *calculate* the standard deviation, but there is a more important question: How do you interpret its value? Fortunately, the standard deviation often has a very natural interpretation, which is why it is quoted so frequently. This interpretation can be stated as three **empirical rules**. Specifically, if the values of this variable are approximately *normally* distributed (symmetric and bell-shaped), then the following rules hold:

- Approximately 68% of the observations are within one standard deviation of the mean, that is, within the interval $\overline{X} \pm s$.

- Approximately 95% of the observations are within two standard deviations of the mean, that is, within the interval $\overline{X} \pm 2s$.

- Approximately 99.7% of the observations—almost all of them—are within three standard deviations of the mean, that is, within the interval $\overline{X} \pm 3s$.

Fortunately, many variables in real-world data are approximately normally distributed, so these empirical rules correctly apply. (The normal distribution is discussed in much more depth in Chapter 5.)

FUNDAMENTAL INSIGHT

Usefulness of Standard Deviation

Variability is an important property of any numerical variable, and there are several measures for quantifying the amount of variability. Of these, standard deviation is by far the most frequently quoted measure. It is measured in the same units as the variable, it has a long tradition, and, at least for many data sets, it obeys the empirical rules discussed here. These empirical rules give a very specific meaning to standard deviation.

As an example, if the parts supplied by the suppliers in Figure 2.11 have diameters that are approximately normally distributed, then the intervals in the empirical rules for supplier 1 are about 100 ± 3, 100 ± 6, and 100 ± 9. Therefore, about 68% of this supplier's parts will have diameters from 97 to 103, 95% will have diameters from 94 to 106, and almost none will have diameters below 91 or above 109. Obviously, the situation for supplier 2 is much worse. With a standard deviation slightly larger than 25, the second empirical rule implies that about 1 out of every 20 of this supplier's parts will be below 50 or above 150. It is clear that supplier 2 has to do something to reduce its variability. In fact, this is exactly what almost all suppliers are continuously trying to do: reduce variability.

Returning to the baseball data, Figure 2.10 indicates that the standard deviation of salaries is about $4.535 million. (The variance is shown, but because it is in squared dollars, it is a huge value with no meaningful interpretation.) Can the empirical rules be applied to these baseball salaries? The answer is that you can always try, but if the salaries are not at least approximately normally distributed, the rules won't be very accurate. And because of obvious skewness in the salary data (due to the stars with astronomical salaries), the assumption of a normal distribution is not a good one.

Nevertheless, the rules are checked in Figure 2.12. For each of the three rules, the lower and upper endpoints of the corresponding interval are found in columns I and J. Right away there are problems. Because the standard deviation is *larger* than the mean, all three lower endpoints are *negative*, which automatically means that there can be no salaries below them. But

Figure 2.12   Empirical Rules for Baseball Salaries

	H	I	J	K	L	M	N	O
1	Do empirical rules apply?							
2		Lower endpoint	Upper endpoint	# below lower	# above upper	% below lower	% above upper	% between
3	Rule 1	−$1,229,688	$7,839,797	0	108	0%	13.20%	86.80%
4	Rule 2	−$5,764,430	$12,374,539	0	54	0%	6.60%	93.40%
5	Rule 3	−$10,299,172	$16,909,281	0	19	0%	2.32%	97.68%

© Cengage Learning

continuing anyway, the COUNTIF was used (again with concatenation) to find the number of salaries above the upper endpoints in column L, and the corresponding percentages appear in column N. Finally, subtracting columns M and N from 100% in column O gives the percentages between the endpoints. These three percentages, according to the empirical rules, should be about 68%, 95%, and 99.7%. Rules 2 and 3 are not way off, but rule 1 isn't even close.

The point of these calculations is that even though the empirical rules give substantive meaning to the standard deviation for many variables, they should be applied with caution, especially when the data are clearly skewed.

Before leaving variance and standard deviation, you might ask why the deviations from the mean are *squared* in the definition of variance. Why not simply take the *absolute* deviation from the mean? For example, if the mean is 100 and two observations have values 95 and 105, then each has a *squared* deviation of 25, but each has an *absolute* deviation of only 5. Wouldn't this latter value be a more natural measure of variability? Intuitively, it would, but there is a long history of using squared deviations. They have many attractive theoretical properties that are not shared by absolute deviations. Still, some analysts quote the **mean absolute deviation** (abbreviated as **MAD**) as another measure of variability, particularly in time series analysis. It is defined as the average of the absolute deviations.

Formula for Mean Absolute Deviation

$$\text{MAD} = \frac{\sum_{i=1}^{n} |X_i - \text{mean}|}{n}$$

(2.4)

There is another empirical rule for MAD: For many (but not all) variables, the standard deviation is approximately 25% larger than MAD, that is, $s \approx 1.25\text{MAD}$. Fortunately, Excel has a function, AVEDEV, that performs the calculation in Equation (2.4). Using it for the baseball salaries in Figure 2.10, you can see that MAD is about $3.25 million. If this is multiplied by 1.25, the result is slightly over $4 million, which is not too far from the standard deviation.

Measures of Shape

There are two final measures of a distribution you will hear occasionally: **skewness** and **kurtosis**. Each of these has not only an intuitive meaning but also a specific numeric measure. We have already mentioned skewness in terms of the baseball salaries. It occurs when there is a lack of symmetry. A few stars have really large salaries, and no players have really small salaries. Alternatively, the largest salaries are much farther to the right of the mean than the smallest salaries are to the left of the mean. This lack of symmetry is usually apparent from a histogram of the salaries, discussed in the next section. We say that these salaries are **skewed to the right** (or **positively skewed**) because the skewness is due to the really *large* salaries. If the skewness were due to really small values (as might occur with temperature lows in Antarctica), then we would call it **skewness to the left** (or **negatively skewed**).

In either case, a measure of skewness can be calculated with Excel's SKEW function. For the baseball data, it is approximately 2.3, as shown in Figure 2.10. You don't need to know exactly what this value means. Simply remember that (1) it is positive when there is skewness to the right, (2) it is negative when there is skewness to the left, (3) it is approximately zero when there is no skewness (the symmetric case), and (4) its magnitude increases as the degree of skewness increases.

Kurtosis is all about extreme events—the kind that occurred in late 2008 and sent Wall Street into a panic.

The other measure, kurtosis, has to do with the "fatness" of the tails of the distribution relative to the tails of a normal distribution. Remember from the third empirical rule that a normal distribution has almost all of its observations within three standard deviations of the mean. In contrast, a distribution with high kurtosis has many more extreme observations. Is this important in reality? It certainly is. For example, many researchers believe the Wall Street meltdown in late 2008 was at least partly due to financial analysts relying on the normal distribution, whereas in reality the actual distribution had much fatter tails. More specifically, financial analysts followed complex mathematical models that indicated really extreme events would virtually never occur. Unfortunately, a number of extreme events *did* occur, and they sent the economy into a deep recession.[1]

Although kurtosis can be calculated in Excel with the KURT function (it is about 5.7 for the baseball salaries), we won't have any use for this measure in the book. Nevertheless, when you hear the word kurtosis, think of fat tails and extreme events. And if you plan to work on Wall Street, you should definitely learn more about kurtosis.

Numerical Summary Measures in the Status Bar

You might have noticed that summary measures sometimes appear automatically in the status bar at the bottom of your Excel window. The rule is that if you select multiple cells (in a single column or even in multiple columns), selected summary measures appear for the selected cells. (Nothing appears if only a single cell is selected.) These can be very handy for quick lookups. Also, you can choose the summary measures that appear by right-clicking the status bar and selecting your favorites.

2-4b Numerical Summary Measures with StatTools

Introduction to StatTools

In the previous subsection, Excel's built-in functions (AVERAGE, STDEV, and others) were used to calculate a number of summary measures. A much quicker way is to use Palisade's StatTools add-in. As we promised earlier, StatTools requires almost no learning curve. After you go through this section, you will know everything you need to know to use StatTools like a professional.

EXAMPLE | **2.3 BASEBALL SALARIES (CONTINUED)**

Use the StatTools add-in to generate the same summary measures of baseball salaries that were calculated in the previous subsection.

Objective   To learn the fundamentals of StatTools and to use this add-in to generate summary measures of baseball salaries.

Solution

Because this is your first exposure to StatTools, we first explain how to get started. StatTools is part of the Palisade DecisionTools Suite®, and you have the free academic version of this suite as a result of purchasing the book. The explanations and screenshots in the book are based on version 6.0 of the suite. (It is possible that by the time you are reading this, you might have a later version.) In any case, you must install the suite before you can use StatTools.

Once the suite is installed, you can load StatTools by double-clicking the StatTools item in the list of programs on the Windows Start menu. (It is in the Palisade group.) If Excel is already running, this will load StatTools on top of Excel. If Excel isn't running, this will launch Excel and load StatTools as well. You will know that StatTools is loaded when you see the StatTools tab and ribbon, as shown in Figure 2.13.

---

[1]The popular book *The Black Swan*, by Nassim Nicholas Taleb (Random House, 2007), is all about extreme events and the trouble they can cause.

Figure 2.13 StatTools Ribbon

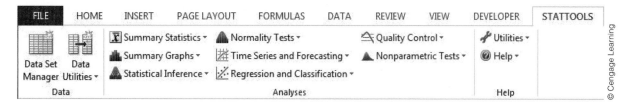

© Cengage Learning

The buttons in the Analyses group on this ribbon are for performing the various statistical analyses, many of which are explained in the book. But before you can use these, you need to know a few basic features of StatTools. ∎

Basic StatTools Features

1. There is an Application Settings item on the Utilities dropdown list. When you click it, you get the dialog box in Figure 2.14. (All of the other add-ins in the Palisade

Figure 2.14

Application Settings Dialog Box

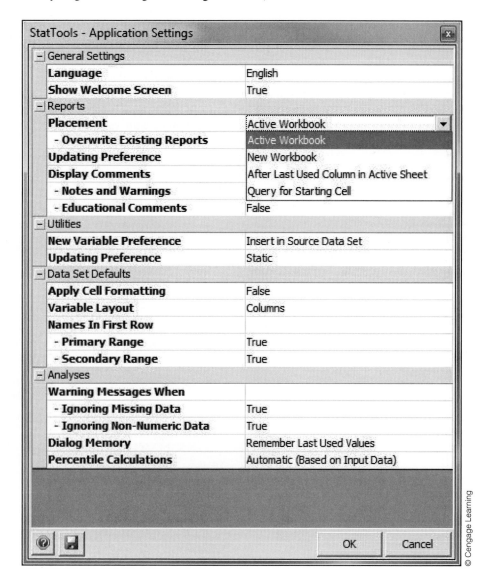

© Cengage Learning

suite have a similar Application Settings item.) This is where you can change overall settings of StatTools. You can experiment with these settings, but the only one you will probably ever need to change is the Reports Placement setting—where your results are placed. The dropdown list in Figure 2.14 shows the four possibilities. We tend to prefer the Active Workbook option (this places the results on a new worksheet) or the Query for Starting Cell option (this lets you choose the cell where your results will start).

2. If you want to unload StatTools without closing Excel, you can select Unload StatTools Add-In from the Utilities dropdown list.

3. Although you probably won't need it, there is plenty of online help, including example spreadsheets, on the Help dropdown list. (These example files were created by the first author of this book.)

4. This is the important one. Before you can perform any statistical analysis, you must define a StatTools data set. You do this by clicking the Data Set Manager button. Try it now. With the **Baseball Salaries 2011.xlsx** file open, make sure any cell in the data set is selected, and click the Data Set Manager button. You will first be asked whether you want to add the range $A$1:$D$844 as a new StatTools data set. Click Yes. Then you will see the dialog box in Figure 2.15. StatTools makes several guesses about your data set. They are generally correct, but you can always override them. First, it gives your data set a generic name, such as Data Set #1. You can accept this or supply a more meaningful name. The latter is especially useful if your file contains more than one data set. Second, you can override the data range. (Note that this range *should* include the variable names in row 1.) Third, the default layout is that variables are in columns, with variable names in the top row. You should override these settings only in rare cases where your data set has the roles of rows and columns reversed. (The Multiple button is for very unusual cases. We will not discuss it here.) Finally, if you want to apply some color to your data set, you can check the Apply Cell Formatting option. (We generally don't.)

Figure 2.15

Data Set Manager
Dialog Box

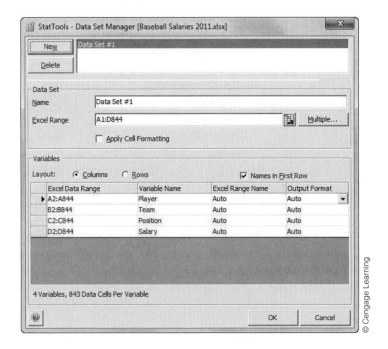

For now, simply click OK. You now have a StatTools data set, and you can begin the analysis. Fortunately, this step has to be done only once. If you save the file and reopen it at a later date, StatTools remembers this data set. So when we said that StatTools has a short learning curve, this is it—simply remember to designate a StatTools data set before you begin any analysis.

Now that the preliminaries are over, you can quickly generate the summary measures for the Salary variable. To do so, select One-Variable Summary from the Summary Statistics dropdown list. You will see the dialog box in Figure 2.16. (If you see two columns of variables in the top pane, click the Format button and select Unstacked.) This is a typical StatTools dialog box. In the top section, you can select a StatTools data set and one or more variables. In the bottom section, you can select the measures you want. For this example, we have chosen all of the measures. (In addition, you can add other percentiles if you like.) Before you click OK, click the "double-check" button to the left of the OK button. This brings up the Application Settings dialog box already shown in Figure 2.14. This is your last chance to designate where you want to place the results. (We chose Active Workbook, which means that the results are placed in a new worksheet automatically named One Var Summary.)

StatTools Tip: *Saving Favorite StatTools Choices*
In general, you might want to choose only your favorite summary measures, such as mean, median, standard deviation, minimum, and maximum. This requires you to uncheck all of the others. To avoid all of this unchecking in future analyses, you can click the Save button in the middle of the bottom left group. This saves your choices as the defaults from then on.

Figure 2.16

One Variable Summary Dialog Box

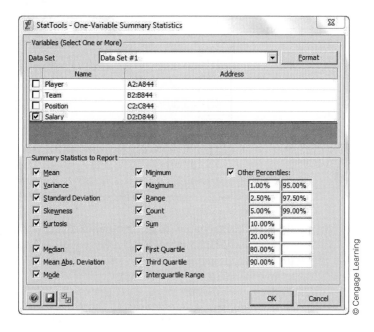

The results appear in Figure 2.17. If you compare these to the measures from Excel functions in Figure 2.10, you will see some slight discrepancies in the percentiles and quartiles. (The kurtosis is also quite different.) When Palisade developed StatTools, it did not fully trust Excel's statistical functions, so it developed its own based on best practices from

Figure 2.17

Summary Measures for Salaries

◢	A	B
7		**Salary**
8	*One Variable Summary*	Data Set #1
9	Mean	$3305054.67
10	Variance	20563887478832.70
11	Std. Dev.	$4534742.27
12	Skewness	2.2568
13	Kurtosis	8.7233
14	Median	$1175000.00
15	Mean Abs. Dev.	$3249917.17
16	Mode	$414000.00
17	Minimum	$414000.00
18	Maximum	$32000000.00
19	Range	$31586000.00
20	Count	$843
21	Sum	$2786161091.00
22	1st Quartile	$430150.00
23	3rd Quartile	$4312500.00
24	Interquartile Range	$3882350.00
25	1.00%	$414000.00
26	2.50%	$414000.00
27	5.00%	$414000.00
28	10.00%	$416500.00
29	20.00%	$424300.00
30	80.00%	$5500000.00
31	90.00%	$9875000.00
32	95.00%	$13600000.00
33	97.50%	$16174974.00
34	99.00%	$20000000.00

© Cengage Learning

the statistical literature. In fact, if you select any of the result cells, you will see functions such as StatMean, StatStdDev, StatPercentile, and so on. Don't be overly concerned that the percentiles and quartiles don't exactly match. Both sets provide the same basic picture of how the salaries are distributed.

Technical Note: Discrepancies in Percentiles and Quartiles

Why is there a discrepancy at all in the percentiles and quartiles? Suppose, for example, that you want the 95th percentile and there are 843 observations. By definition, the 95th percentile is the value such that 95% of the values are below it and 5% are above it. Now, 95% of 843 is 801.80. This suggests that you should sort the 843 observations in increasing order and locate the 801st and 802nd smallest. For the baseball data, these salaries are $13,600,000 and $14,000,000. Excel reports the 95th percentile as $13,590,000, whereas StatTools reports it as $13,600,000. In words, Excel interpolates and StatTools *doesn't, but either is reasonable. As for kurtosis, Excel provides an index that is 0 for a normal distribution, whereas StatTools returns a value 3 for a normal distribution. So the two indexes differ by 3. (For what it's worth, Wikipedia indicates that either definition of kurtosis is acceptable.)*

If you open a file and it has errors in StatTools outputs, load StatTools. It is possible that you might have to close the file and reopen it.

There are several other things to note about the StatTools output. First, it formats the results according to its own rules. If you would like fewer or more decimals or any other formatting changes, you can certainly reformat in the usual way. Second, the fact that there are *formulas* in these result cells indicates that they are "live." If you go back to the data and change any of the salaries, the summary measures will update automatically. This is true for most, but not quite all, StatTools outputs. (Regression analysis, discussed in Chapters 10 and 11, is the most important situation where the StatTools results are not live.) Finally, if you open a file with StatTools outputs but StatTools is not loaded, you might see #VALUE! errors in the cells. These can be fixed by loading StatTools. (You might have to close the file, load StatTools, and open the file again.)

2-4c Charts for Numerical Variables

There are many graphical ways to indicate the distribution of a numerical variable, but the two we prefer and discuss in this subsection are **histograms** and **box plots** (also called **box-whisker plots**). Each of these is useful primarily for cross-sectional variables. If they are used for time series variables, the time dimension is lost. Therefore, we discuss **time series graphs** for time series variables separately in the next section.

FUNDAMENTAL INSIGHT

Histograms Versus Summary Measures

It is important to remember that each of the summary measures we have discussed for a numerical variable—mean, median, standard deviation, and others—describes only one aspect of a numerical variable. In contrast, a histogram provides the complete picture. It indicates the "center" of the distribution, the variability, the skewness, and other aspects, all in one convenient chart.

Histograms

A histogram is the most common type of chart for showing the distribution of a numerical variable. It is based on binning the variable—that is, dividing it up into discrete categories. The histogram is then a column chart of the counts in the various categories (with no gaps between the vertical bars). In general, a histogram is great for showing the shape of a distribution. We are particularly interested in whether the distribution is symmetric or is skewed in one direction. The concept is a simple one, as illustrated in the following continuation of the baseball salary example.

EXAMPLE **2.3 BASEBALL SALARIES (CONTINUED)**

We have already mentioned that the baseball salaries are skewed to the right. How does this show up in a histogram of salaries?

Objective To see the shape of the salary distribution through a histogram.

Solution

It is possible to create a histogram with Excel tools only—no add-ins—but it is a tedious process. First, the bins must be defined. If you do it yourself, you will probably choose "nice" bins, such as $400,000 to $800,000; $800,000 to $1,200,000; and so on. But there is also the question of *how many* bins to use and what their endpoints should be, and these are not always easy choices. In any case, once the bins have been selected, the number of observations in each bin must be counted. This can be done in Excel with the COUNTIF function. (You can also do this with the COUNTIFS and FREQUENCY functions, but we won't discuss them here.) The resulting table of counts is usually called a **frequency table**. Finally, a column chart of the counts must be created. If you are interested, we have indicated the steps in the Excel Histogram sheet of the finished version of the baseball file.

A histogram can be created with Excel tools only, but the process is quite tedious. It is much easier to use StatTools.

It is much easier to create a histogram with StatTools. As with all StatTools analyses, the first step is to designate a StatTools data set, which has already been done for the baseball salary data. To create a histogram, select Histogram from the Summary Graphs dropdown list to obtain the dialog box in Figure 2.18. At this point, all you really need to do is select the Salary variable and click OK. This gives you the default bins, indicated by "auto" values. Essentially, StatTools checks your data and chooses "good" bins. The resulting histogram, along with the bin data it is based on, appears in Figure 2.19. StatTools has used 11 bins, with the endpoints indicated in columns B and C. The histogram is then a column chart (with no gaps between the vertical bars) of the counts in column E. (These counts are also called **frequencies**.)

Figure 2.18

StatTools Histogram Dialog Box

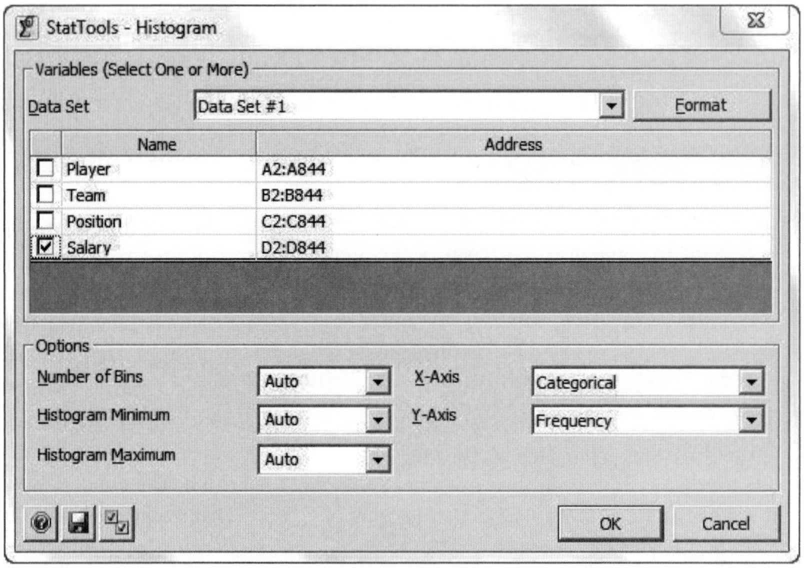

In many situations, you can accept the StatTools defaults for histogram bins. They generally show the big picture quite well, which is the main goal.

You could argue that the bins chosen by StatTools aren't very "nice." For example, the upper limit of the first bin is $3,285,454.55. If you want to fine-tune these, you can enter your own bins instead of the "auto" values in Figure 2.18. We illustrate this in the next example, but it is largely beside the point for answering the main question about baseball salaries. The StatTools default histogram shows very clearly that the salaries are skewed to the right, and fine-tuning bins won't change this primary finding. The vast majority of the players are in the lowest two categories, and the salaries of the stars account for the long tail to the right. This big picture finding is typically all you want from a histogram. ∎

When is it useful to fine-tune the StatTools histogram bins? One good example is when the values of the variable are integers, as illustrated next.

Figure 2.19 Histogram of Salaries

	A	B	C	D	E	F	G
7				Salary/Baseball 2011 data			
8	*Histogram*	**Bin Min**	**Bin Max**	**Bin Midpoint**	**Freq.**	**Rel. Freq.**	**Prb. Density**
9	Bin #1	$414000.00	$3285454.55	$1849727.27	587	0.6963	0.000000242
10	Bin #2	$3285454.55	$6156909.09	$4721181.82	111	0.1317	0.000000046
11	Bin #3	$6156909.09	$9028363.64	$7592636.36	54	0.0641	0.000000022
12	Bin #4	$9028363.64	$11899818.18	$10464090.91	26	0.0308	0.000000011
13	Bin #5	$11899818.18	$14771272.73	$13335545.45	34	0.0403	0.000000014
14	Bin #6	$14771272.73	$17642727.27	$16207000.00	13	0.0154	0.000000005
15	Bin #7	$17642727.27	$20514181.82	$19078454.55	12	0.0142	0.000000005
16	Bin #8	$20514181.82	$23385636.36	$21949909.09	3	0.0036	0.000000001
17	Bin #9	$23385636.36	$26257090.91	$24821363.64	2	0.0024	0.000000001
18	Bin #10	$26257090.91	$29128545.45	$27692818.18	0	0.0000	0.000000000
19	Bin #11	$29128545.45	$32000000.00	$30564272.73	1	0.0012	0.000000000

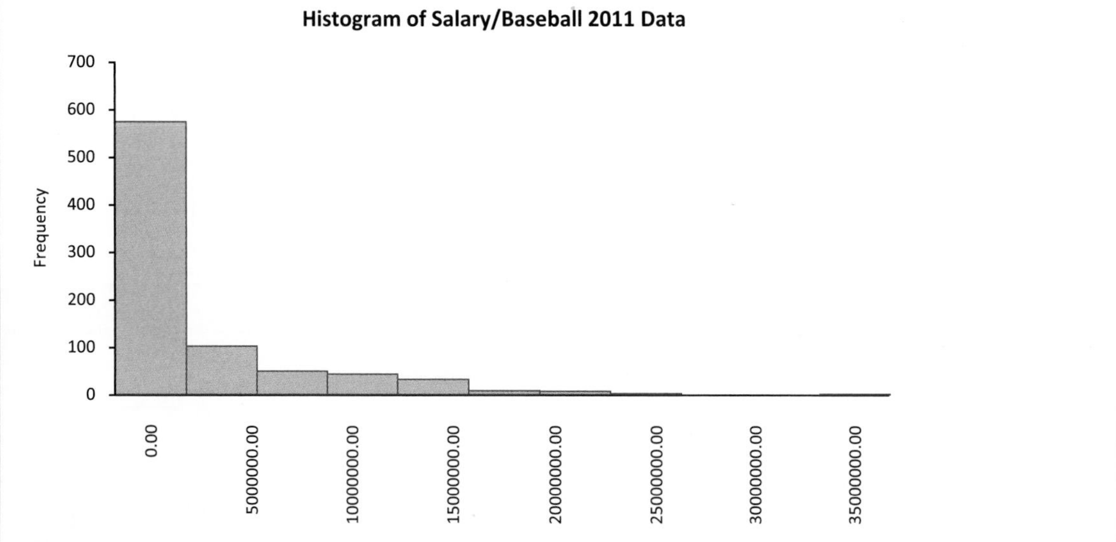

© Cengage Learning

EXAMPLE

2.4 LOST OR LATE BAGGAGE AT AIRPORTS

For a quick analysis, feel free to accept StatTools's automatic histogram options. However, don't be afraid to experiment with these options in defining your own bins. The goal is to make the histogram as meaningful and easy to read as possible.

The file **Late or Lost Baggage.xlsx** contains information on 456 flights into an airport. (This is not real data.) For each flight, it lists the number of bags that were either late or lost. Some of the data are shown in Figure 2.20. What is the most natural histogram for this data set?

Objective To fine-tune a histogram for a variable with integer counts.

Solution

From a scan of the data (sort from lowest to highest), it is apparent that all flights had from 0 to 8 late or lost bags. Therefore, the most natural histogram is one that shows the count of each possible value. If you use the default settings in StatTools, this is *not* what you will get. However, if you fill in the Histogram dialog box as shown in Figure 2.21,

Figure 2.20

Data on Late or Lost Baggage

◢	A	B
1	**Flight**	**Bags late or lost**
2	1	0
3	2	3
4	3	5
5	4	0
6	5	2
7	6	2
8	7	1
9	8	5
10	9	1
11	10	3
12	11	3
13	12	4
14	13	5
15	14	4
16	15	3

© Cengage Learning

Figure 2.21

Histogram Dialog Box with Desired Bins

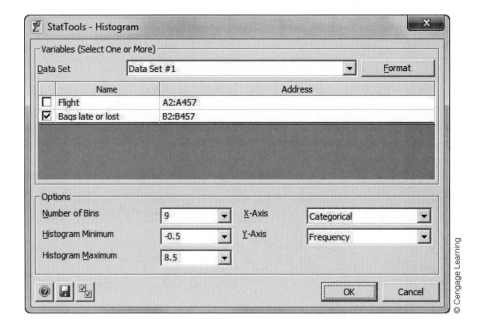

© Cengage Learning

you will get exactly what you want. The resulting histogram appears in Figure 2.22. Do you see the trick? When you request 9 bins and set the minimum and maximum to −0.5 and 8.5, StatTools divides the range from −0.5 to 8.5 into 9 equal-length bins: −0.5 to 0.5, 0.5 to 1.5, and on up to 7.5 to 8.5. Of course, each bin contains only one possible value, the integer in the middle. So you get the count of 0s, the count of 1s, and so on. As an extra benefit, StatTools always labels the horizontal axis with the midpoints of the bins, which

Figure 2.22   Histogram of Counts

	A	B	C	D	E	F	G
7				Bags late or lost/Baggage Data			
8	*Histogram*	**Bin Min**	**Bin Max**	**Bin Midpoint**	**Freq.**	**Rel. Freq.**	**Prb. Density**
9	Bin #1	−0.500	0.500	0.000	16	0.0351	0.04
10	Bin #2	0.500	1.500	1.000	67	0.1469	0.15
11	Bin #3	1.500	2.500	2.000	113	0.2478	0.25
12	Bin #4	2.500	3.500	3.000	101	0.2215	0.22
13	Bin #5	3.500	4.500	4.000	77	0.1689	0.17
14	Bin #6	4.500	5.500	5.000	44	0.0965	0.10
15	Bin #7	5.500	6.500	6.000	23	0.0504	0.05
16	Bin #8	6.500	7.500	7.000	13	0.0285	0.03
17	Bin #9	7.500	8.500	8.000	2	0.0044	0.00

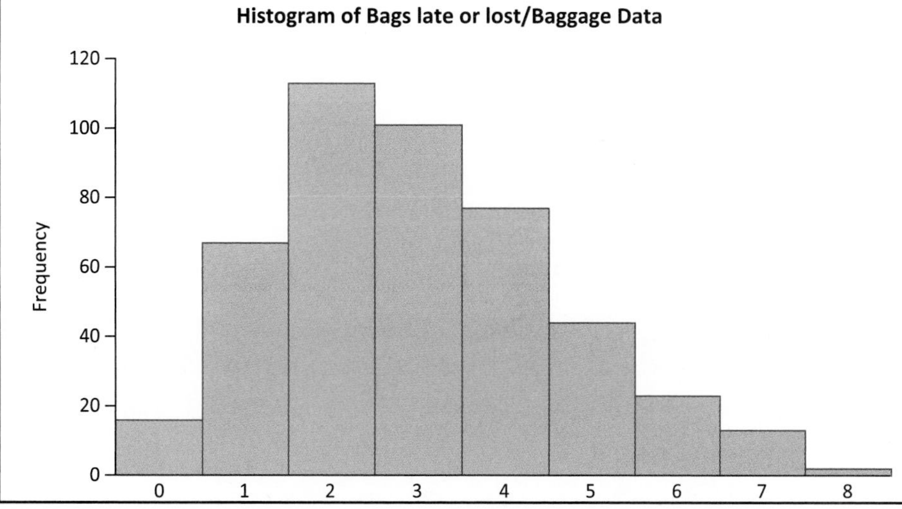

Histogram of Bags late or lost/Baggage Data

© Cengage Learning

are exactly the integers you want. (For an even nicer look, you can format these horizontal axis values with no decimals.)

The point of this example is that you *do* have control over the histogram bins if you are not satisfied with the StatTools defaults. Just keep one technical detail in mind. If a bin extends, say, from 2.7 to 3.4, its count is the number of observations greater than 2.7 and less than *or equal to* 3.4. In other words, observations equal to the right endpoint are counted, but observations equal to the left endpoint are not. (They are counted in the *previous* bin.) So in this example, if you designate the minimum and maximum as −1 and 8 in Figure 2.21, you will get the same histogram, but with different midpoints on the horizontal axis. ∎

Box Plots

A **box plot** (also called a box-whisker plot) is an alternative type of chart for showing the distribution of a variable. For the distribution of a single variable, a box plot is not nearly as popular as a histogram, but as you will see in the next chapter, side-by-side box plots are very useful for *comparing* distributions, such as salaries for men versus salaries for women. As with histograms, box plots are "big picture" charts. They show you at a glance some of the key features of a distribution. We explain how they do this in the following continuation of the baseball salary example.

EXAMPLE | **2.3 BASEBALL SALARIES (CONTINUED)**

A histogram of the salaries clearly indicated the skewness to the right. Does a box plot of salaries indicate the same behavior?

Objective   To illustrate the features of a box plot, particularly how it indicates skewness.

Solution

Excel has no built-in box plot chart type. In this case, you must rely on StatTools.

This time you *must* rely on StatTools. There is no easy way to create a box plot with Excel tools only. Fortunately, it is easy with StatTools. Select Box-Whisker Plot from the Summary Graphs dropdown list and fill in the resulting dialog box as in Figure 2.23— there are no other choices to make. The box plot appears in Figure 2.24. (StatTools also

Figure 2.23

StatTools
Box-Whisker Plot
Dialog Box

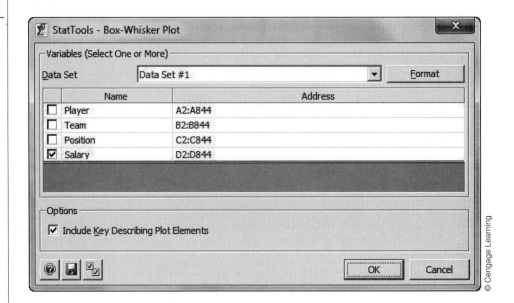

Figure 2.24

Box Plot of Salaries

Box-Whisker Plot of Salary/Baseball 2011 Data

lists some mysterious values, including errors, below the box plot. You can ignore these, but don't delete them. They are the basis for the box plot itself.)

To help you understand the elements of a box plot, StatTools provides the generic box plot shown in Figure 2.25. (It is not drawn to scale.) You can get this by checking the Include Key Describing Plot Elements option in Figure 2.23, although you will probably want to do this only once or twice. As this generic diagram indicates, the box itself extends, left to right, from the 1st quartile to the 3rd quartile. This means that it contains the middle half of the data. The line inside the box is positioned at the median, and the x inside the box is positioned at the mean. The lines (whiskers) coming out either side of the box extend to 1.5 IQRs (interquartile ranges) from the quartiles. These generally include most of the data outside the box. More distant values, called outliers, are denoted separately with small squares. They are hollow for "mild" outliers, and solid for "extreme" outliers, as indicated in the explanation.

Figure 2.25

Elements of a Generic Box Plot

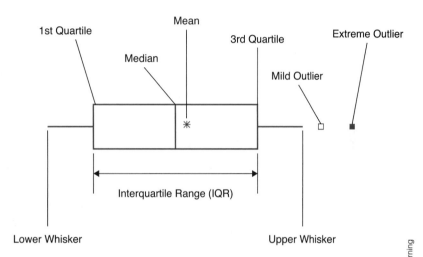

Whiskers extend to the furthest observations that are no more than 1.5 IQR from the edges of the box. Mild outliers are observations between 1.5 IQR and 3 IQR from the edges of the box. Extreme outliers are greater than 3 IQR from the edges of the box.

© Cengage Learning

The box plot of salaries in Figure 2.24 should now make more sense. It is typical of an extremely right-skewed distribution. The mean is much larger than the median, there is virtually no whisker out of the left side of the box (because the first quartile is barely above the minimum value—remember all the players earning $414,000?), and there are many outliers to the right (the stars). In fact, many of these outliers overlap one another. You can decide whether you prefer the histogram of salaries to the box plot or vice versa, but both are clearly telling the same story.

Box plots have existed for several decades, and they are probably more popular now than ever. The implementation of box plots in StatTools is just one version of what you might see. Some software packages draw box plots vertically, not horizontally. Also, some vary the height of the box to indicate some other feature of the distribution. (The height of the box is irrelevant in StatTools's box plots.) Nevertheless, they all follow the same basic rules and provide the same basic information. ■

Box Plots Versus Histograms

Box plots and histograms are complementary ways of displaying the distribution of a numerical variable. Although histograms are much more popular and are arguably more intuitive, box plots are still informative. Besides, side-by-side box plots are very useful for comparing two or more populations.

PROBLEMS

Level A

6. The file **P02_06.xlsx** lists the average time (in minutes) it takes citizens of 379 metropolitan areas to travel to work and back home each day.
   a. Create a histogram of the daily commute times.
   b. Find the most representative average daily commute time across this distribution.
   c. Find a useful measure of the variability of these average commute times around the mean.
   d. The empirical rule for standard deviations indicates that approximately 95% of these average travel times will fall between which two values? For this particular data set, is this empirical rule at least approximately correct?

7. The file **P02_07.xlsx** includes data on 204 employees at the (fictional) company Beta Technologies.
   a. Indicate the data type for each of the six variables included in this data set.
   b. Create a histogram of the Age variable. How would you characterize the age distribution for these employees?
   c. What proportion of these full-time Beta employees are female?
   d. Find appropriate summary measures for each of the numerical variables in this data set.
   e. For the Salary variable, explain why the empirical rules for standard deviations do or do not apply.

8. The file **P02_08.xlsx** contains data on 500 shipments of one of the computer components that a company manufactures. Specifically, the proportion of items that are defective is listed for each shipment.
   a. Create a histogram that will help a production manager understand the variation of the proportion of defective components in the company's shipments.
   b. Is the mean or median the most appropriate measure of central location for this data set? Explain your reasoning.
   c. Discuss whether the empirical rules for standard deviations apply. Can you tell, or at least make an educated guess, by looking at the shape of the histogram? Why?

9. The file **P02_09.xlsx** lists the times required to service 200 consecutive customers at a (fictional) fast-food restaurant.
   a. Create a histogram of the customer service times. How would you characterize the distribution of service times?
   b. Calculate the mean, median, and first and third quartiles of this distribution.
   c. Which measure of central tendency, the mean or the median, is more appropriate in describing this distribution? Explain your reasoning.
   d. Find and interpret the variance and standard deviation of these service times.
   e. Are the empirical rules for standard deviations applicable for these service times? If not, explain why. Can you tell whether they apply, or at least make an educated guess, by looking at the shape of the histogram? Why?

10. The file **P02_10.xlsx** contains midterm and final exam scores for 96 students in a corporate finance course.
    a. Create a histogram for each of the two sets of exam scores.
    b. What are the mean and median scores on each of these exams?
    c. Explain why the mean and median values are different for these data.
    d. Based on your previous answers, how would you characterize this group's performance on the midterm and on the final exam?
    e. Create a new column of differences (final exam score minus midterm score). A positive value means the student improved, and a negative value means the student did the opposite. What are the mean and median of the differences? What does a histogram of the differences indicate?

11. The file **P02_11.xlsx** contains data on 148 houses that were recently sold in a (fictional) suburban community. The data set includes the selling price of each house,

along with its appraised value, square footage, number of bedrooms, and number of bathrooms.

   a. Which of these variables are continuous? Which are discrete?

   b. Create histograms for the appraised values and selling prices of the houses. How are these two distributions similar? How are they different?

   c. Find the maximum and minimum sizes (measured in square footage) of all sample houses.

   d. Find the house(s) at the 80th percentile of all sample houses with respect to appraised value. Find the house(s) at the 80th percentile of all sample houses with respect to selling price.

   e. What are the typical number of bedrooms and the typical number of bathrooms in this set of houses? How do you interpret the word "typical?"

12. The file **P02_12.xlsx** includes data on the 50 top graduate programs in the United States, according to a recent *U.S. News & World Report* survey.

   a. Indicate the type of data for each of the 10 variables considered in the formulation of the overall ranking.

   b. Create a histogram for each of the numerical variables in this data set. Indicate whether each of these distributions is approximately symmetric or skewed. Which, if any, of these distributions are skewed to the right? Which, if any, are skewed to the left?

   c. Identify the schools with the largest and smallest annual out-of-state tuition and fee levels.

   d. Find the annual out-of-state tuition and fee levels at each of the 25th, 50th, and 75th percentiles for these schools. For post-2007 Excel users only, find these percentiles using both the PERCENTILE. INC and PERCENTILE.EXE functions. Can you explain how and why they are different (if they are indeed different)?

   e. Create a box plot to characterize this distribution of these MBA salaries. Is this distribution essentially symmetric or skewed? If there are any outliers on either end, which schools do they correspond to? Are these same schools outliers in box plots of any of the other numerical variables (from columns E to L)?

13. The file **P02_13.xlsx** contains the thickness (in centimeters) of 252 mica pieces. A piece meets specifications if its thickness is between 7 and 15 centimeters.

   a. What fraction of mica pieces meets specifications?

   b. Are the empirical rules for standard deviations at least approximately valid for these data? Can you tell, or at least make an educated guess, by looking at a histogram of the data?

   c. If the histogram of the data is approximately bell-shaped and you want about 95% of the observations to meet specifications, is it sufficient for the average and standard deviation to be, at least approximately, 11 and 2 centimeters, respectively?

14. Recall that the file **Supermarket Transactions.xlsx** contains over 14,000 transactions made by supermarket customers over a period of approximately two years. Using these data, create side-by-side box plots for revenues broken down by state or province. Are these distributions essentially symmetric or skewed? Note that these box plots include revenues from countries besides the U.S. Do whatever it takes to create side-by-side box plots of revenue for only states within the U.S.

(Hint: StatTools will not let you define a second data set that is a subset of an existing data set. But you can copy data for the second question to a new worksheet or some other range of the data sheet.)

15. Recall that the file **Baseball Salaries 2011.xlsx** contains data on 843 MLB players in the 2011 season. Using these data, create a box plot to characterize the distribution of salaries of all pitchers. Do the same for non-pitchers. Summarize your findings. (See the hint in the previous problem.)

16. The file **P02_16.xlsx** contains traffic data from 256 weekdays on four variables. Each variable lists the number of vehicle arrivals to a tollbooth during a specific five-minute period of the day.

   a. Create a histogram of each variable. How would you characterize and compare these distributions?

   b. Find a table of summary measures for these variables that includes (at least) the means, medians, standard deviations, first and third quartiles, and 5th and 95th percentiles. Use these to compare the arrival process at the different times of day.

Level B

17. The file **P02_17.xlsx** contains salaries of 200 recent graduates from a (fictional) MBA program.

   a. What salary level is most indicative of those earned by students graduating from this MBA program this year?

   b. Do the empirical rules for standard deviations apply to these data? Can you tell, or at least make an educated guess, by looking at the shape of the histogram? Why?

   c. If the empirical rules apply here, between which two numbers can you be about 68% sure that the salary of any one of these 200 students will fall?

   d. If the MBA program wants to make a statement such as "Some of our recent graduates started out making X dollars or more, and almost all of them started out making at least Y dollars" for their promotional materials, what values of X and Y would you suggest they use? Defend your choice.

   e. As an admissions officer of this MBA program, how would you proceed to use these findings to market the program to prospective students?

18. The file **P02_18.xlsx** contains daily values of the Standard & Poor's 500 Index from 1970 to early 2012. It also contains percentage changes in the index from each day to the next.
    a. Create a histogram of the percentage changes and describe its shape.
    b. Check the percentage of these percentage changes that are more than k standard deviations from the mean for $k = 1, 2, 3, 4,$ and 5. Are these approximately what the empirical rules indicate or are there "fat" tails? Do you think this has any real implications for the financial markets? (Note that we have discussed the empirical rules only for $k = 1, 2,$ and 3. For $k = 4$ and 5, they indicate that only 0.006% and 0.0001% of the observations should be this distant from the mean.)

2-5 TIME SERIES DATA

When we analyze time series variables, summary measures such as means and standard deviations and charts such as histograms and box plots often don't make much sense. Our main interest in time series variables is how they change over time, and this information is lost in traditional summary measures and in histograms or box plots. Imagine, for example, that you are interested in daily closing prices of a stock that has historically been between 20 and 60. If you create a histogram with a bin such as 45 to 50, you will get a count of all daily closing prices in this interval—but you won't know when they occurred. The histogram is missing a key feature: time. Similarly, if you report the *mean* of a time series such as the monthly Dow Jones average over the past 40 years, you will get a measure that isn't very relevant for the current and future values of the Dow.

Therefore, we turn to a different but very intuitive type of graph called a **time series graph**. This is a graph of the values of one or more time series, using time on the horizontal axis, and it is always the place to start a time series analysis. We illustrate some possibilities in Example 2.5.

EXAMPLE | **2.5 CRIME IN THE U.S.**

The file **Crime in US.xlsx** contains annual data on violent and property crimes for the years 1960 to 2010. Part of the data is listed in Figure 2.26. This shows the number of crimes. The rates per 100,000 population are not shown, but they can be calculated easily.

Figure 2.26 Crime Data

	A	B	C	D	E	F	G	H	I	J	K
1	Year	Population	Violent crime total	Murder and nonnegligent manslaughter	Rape	Robbery	Aggravated assault	Property crime total	Burglary	Larceny-theft	Motor vehicle theft
2	1960	179,323,175	288,460	9,110	17,190	107,840	154,320	3,095,700	912,100	1,855,400	328,200
3	1961	182,992,000	289,390	8,740	17,220	106,670	156,760	3,198,600	949,600	1,913,000	336,000
4	1962	185,771,000	301,510	8,530	17,550	110,860	164,570	3,450,700	994,300	2,089,600	366,800
5	1963	188,483,000	316,970	8,640	17,650	116,470	174,210	3,792,500	1,086,400	2,297,800	408,300
6	1964	191,141,000	364,220	9,360	21,420	130,390	203,050	4,200,400	1,213,200	2,514,400	472,800
7	1965	193,526,000	387,390	9,960	23,410	138,690	215,330	4,352,000	1,282,500	2,572,600	496,900
8	1966	195,576,000	430,180	11,040	25,820	157,990	235,330	4,793,300	1,410,100	2,822,000	561,200
9	1967	197,457,000	499,930	12,240	27,620	202,910	257,160	5,403,500	1,632,100	3,111,600	659,800
10	1968	199,399,000	595,010	13,800	31,670	262,840	286,700	6,125,200	1,858,900	3,482,700	783,600

Are there any apparent trends in this data? If so, are the trends the same for the different types of crime?

Excel Tip: Formatting Long Variable Names
Note the format of the variable names in row 1. If you have long variable names, one pos-sibility is to align them vertically and check the Wrap Text option. (These are both available through the Format Cells command, which can be accessed by right-clicking any cell.) With these changes, the row 1 labels are neither too tall nor too wide.

Objective   To see how time series graphs help to detect trends in crime data.

Solution

It is actually quite easy to create a time series graph with Excel tools only—no add-ins. We illustrate the process to the right of the data in the finished version of the crime file. But StatTools is a bit quicker and easier. We illustrate a few of the many time series graphs you could create from this data set. As usual, start by designating a StatTools data set. Then select Time Series Graph from the Time Series and Forecasting dropdown list. (Note that this item is *not* in the Summary Graphs group.) The resulting dialog box appears in Figure 2.27. At the top, you can choose between a graph with a label and one without a label. The label is for time, so if you have a time variable (in this case, Year), choose the "with label" option. This leads to two columns of variables, one for the label (Lbl) and one for values (Val). Check Year in the Lbl column and select one or more variables in the Val column. For this first graph, we selected the Violent crime total and Property crime total variables to get started.

Figure 2.27
StatTools Time
Series Graph
Dialog Box

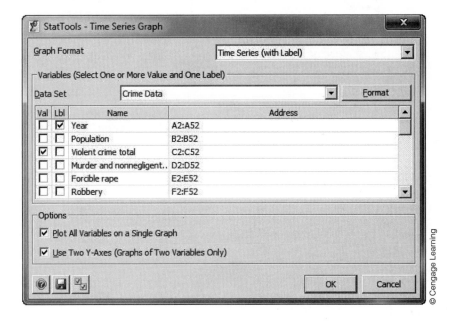

© Cengage Learning

When you select multiple Val variables, the first option at the bottom lets you plot all variables in a single graph or create a separate graph for each. We chose a single graph. Furthermore, when you select *exactly two* Val variables, you can use two different Y-axis scales for the two variables. This is useful when they are of very different magnitudes, as is the case for violent and property crimes, so we checked this option. (This option isn't available if you select *more* than two Val variables. In that case, all are forced to share

The whole purpose of time series graphs is to detect historical patterns in the data. In this crime example, you are looking for broad trends.

the same Y-axis scale.) The resulting time series graph appears in Figure 2.28. The graph shows that both types of crimes increased sharply until the early 1990s and have gradually decreased since then.

However, the time series population in Figure 2.29 indicates that the U.S. population has increased steadily since 1960, so it is possible that the trend in crime *rates* is different than the trends in Figure 2.28. This is indeed true, as seen in Figure 2.30. It shows the good news that the crime rate has been falling since its peak in the early 1990s.[2]

Figure 2.28 Total Violent and Property Crimes

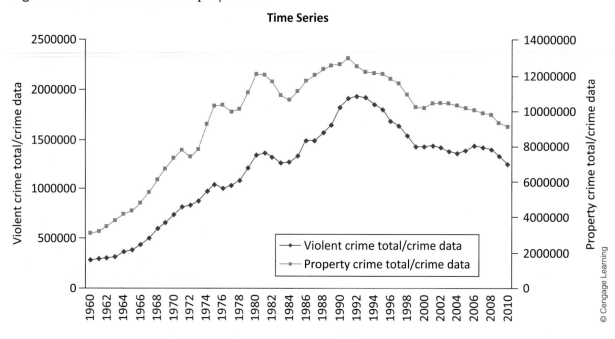

Figure 2.29 Population Totals

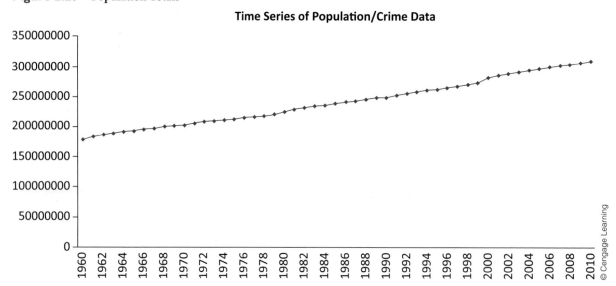

[2]Why did this occur? One compelling reason was suggested by Levitt and Dubner in their popular book *Freakonomics*. You can read their somewhat controversial analysis to see if you agree.

Figure 2.30 Violent and Property Crime Rates

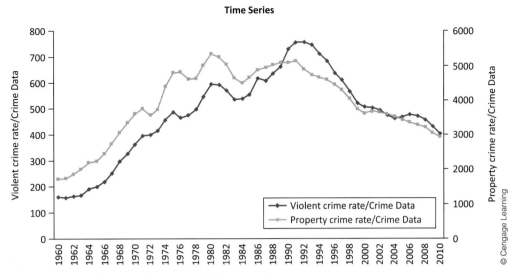

StatTools Tip: StatTools Remembers Previous Choices
StatTools remembers your previous choices for any particular type of analysis such as time series graphs. Therefore, if you run another analysis of the same type, make sure you uncheck variables you don't want in the current analysis.

Because it is so easy, we also created two more time series graphs that appear in Figures 2.31 and 2.32. The first shows the crime rates for the various types of violent crimes, and the second does the same for property crimes. The patterns (up, then down) are similar for each type of crime, but they are certainly not identical. For example, the larceny-theft and motor vehicle theft rates both peaked in the early 1990s, but the burglary rate was well in decline by this time. Finally, Figure 2.31 indicates one problem with having multiple time series variables on a single graph—any variable with small values can become dominated by variables with much larger values. It might be a good idea to create two separate graphs for these four variables, with murder and rape on one and robbery and aggravated assault on the other. Then you could see the murder and rape patterns more clearly. ■

Figure 2.31 Rates of Violent Crime Types

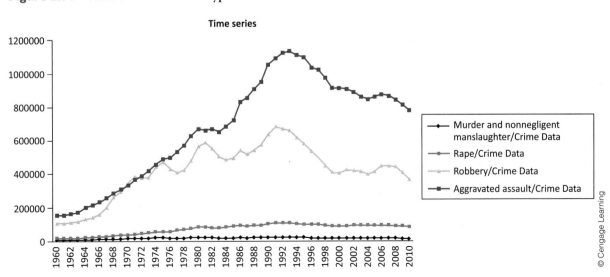

Figure 2.32   Rates of Property Crime Types

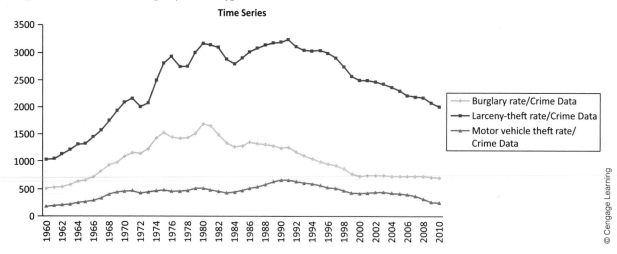

CHANGES IN EXCEL 2010

One feature introduced in Excel 2010 is the *sparkline*. This is a mini-chart embedded in a cell. Although it applies to any kind of data, it is especially useful for time series data. Try the following. Open a file, such as the problem file **P03_30.xlsx**, that has multiple time series—one per column. Highlight the cell below the last time series value of the first time series and click the Line button in the Sparklines group on the Insert ribbon. In the resulting dialog box, select the data in the first time series. You will get a mini-time-series graph in the cell. Now copy this cell across for the other time series, and increase the row height to expand the graphs. Change any of the time series values to see how the sparklines change automatically. We suspect that these instant sparkline graphs are becoming quite popular.

As mentioned earlier, traditional summary measures such as means, medians, and standard deviations are often not very meaningful for time series data, at least not for the original data. However, it is often useful to find differences or percentage changes in the data from period to period and then report traditional summary measures of these. Example 2.6 illustrates these ideas.

EXAMPLE | 2.6 THE DJIA INDEX

The Dow Jones Industrial Average (DJIA or simply "the Dow") is an index of 30 large publicly traded U.S. stocks and is one of the most quoted stock indexes. The file **DJIA Monthly Close.xlsx** contains monthly values of the Dow from 1950 through 2011. What is a useful way to summarize the data in this file?

Objective   To find useful ways to summarize the monthly Dow data.

Solution

A time series graph and a few summary measures of the Dow appear in Figure 2.33. The graph clearly shows a gradual increase through the early 1990s (except for Black Monday in 1987), then a sharp increase through the rest of the 1990s, and finally huge swings since 2000. The mean (3484), the median (969), and any of the other traditional summary measures are of historical interest at best.

Figure 2.33 Summary Measures and Graph of the Dow

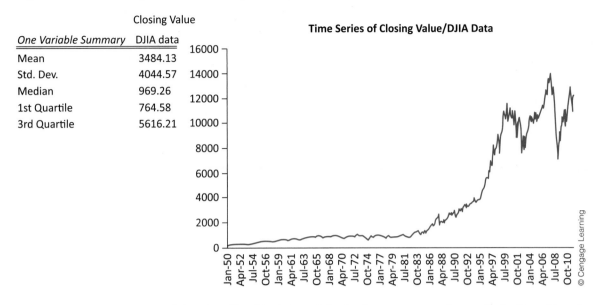

One Variable Summary	Closing Value DJIA data
Mean	3484.13
Std. Dev.	4044.57
Median	969.26
1st Quartile	764.58
3rd Quartile	5616.21

Time Series of Closing Value/DJIA Data

© Cengage Learning

In situations like this, it is useful to look at percentage changes in the Dow. These have been calculated in the file and have been used to create the summary measures and time series graph in Figure 2.34. The graph shows that these percentage changes have fluctuated around zero, sometimes with wild swings (like Black Monday). Actually, the mean and median of the percentage changes are slightly positive, about 0.64% and 0.85%, respectively. In addition, the quartiles show that 25% of the changes have been less than −1.72% and 25% have been greater than 3.29%. Finally, the empirical rules indicate, for example, that about 95% of the percentage changes over this period have been no more than two standard deviations (8.36%) from the mean. (You can check that the actual percentage within two standard deviations of the mean is close to 95%, so this empirical rule applies very well.)[3] ■

Figure 2.34 Summary Measures and Graph of Percentage Changes of the Dow

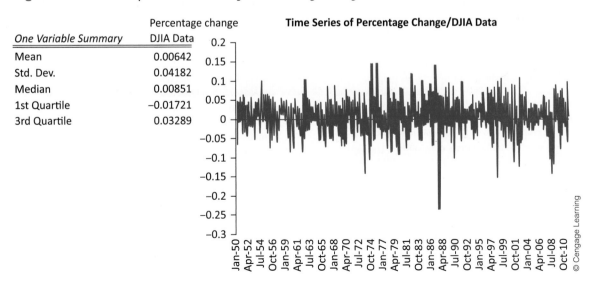

One Variable Summary	Percentage change DJIA Data
Mean	0.00642
Std. Dev.	0.04182
Median	0.00851
1st Quartile	−0.01721
3rd Quartile	0.03289

Time Series of Percentage Change/DJIA Data

© Cengage Learning

[3]One of the problems asks you to check whether all three of the empirical rules apply to similar stock price data. The extreme tails are where there are some surprises.

PROBLEMS

Level A

19. The file **P02_19.xlsx** lists annual percentage changes in the Consumer Price Index (CPI) from 1914 through 2010. Find and interpret the first and third quartiles and the interquartile range for these annual percentage changes. Discuss whether these are meaningful summary measures for this time series data set. Suppose that the data set listed the actual CPI values, not percentage changes, for each year. Would the quartiles and interquartile range be meaningful in this case? Why or why not?

20. The Consumer Confidence Index (CCI) attempts to measure people's feelings about general business conditions, employment opportunities, and their own income prospects. Monthly average values of the CCI are listed in the file **P02_20.xlsx**.
   a. Create a time series graph of the CCI values.
   b. Have U.S. consumers become more or less confident through time?
   c. How would you explain recent variations in the overall trend of the CCI?

21. The file **P02_21.xlsx** contains monthly interest rates on 30-year fixed-rate mortgages in the U.S. from 1977 to 2009. The file also contains rates on 15-year fixed-rate mortgages from late 1991 to 2009. What conclusion(s) can you draw from a time series graph of these mortgage rates? Specifically, what has been happening to mortgage rates in general, and how does the behavior of the 30-year rates compare to the behavior of the 15-year rates?

22. The file **P02_22.xlsx** contains annual trade balances (exports minus imports) from 1980 to 2010.
   a. Create a times series graph for each of the three time series in this file.
   b. Characterize recent trends in the U.S. balance of trade figures using your time series graphs.

23. What has happened to the total number and average size of farms in the U.S. since the middle of the 20th century? Answer this question by creating a time series graph of the data from the U.S. Department of Agriculture in the file **P02_23. xlsx**. Is the observed result consistent with your knowledge of the structural changes within the U.S. farming economy?

24. Is educational attainment in the U.S. on the rise? Explore this question by creating time series graphs for each of the variables in the file **P02_24.xlsx**. Comment on any observed trends in the annual educational attainment of the general U.S. population over the given period.

25. The monthly averages of the federal funds rate and the bank prime loan rate are listed in the file **P02_25.xlsx**.
   a. Describe the time series behavior of these two variables. Can you discern any cyclical or other patterns in the times series graphs of these key interest rates?
   b. Discuss whether it would make much sense, especially to a person at the present time, to quote traditional summary measures such as means or percentiles of these series.

Level B

26. In which months of the calendar year do U.S. gasoline service stations typically have their *lowest* retail sales levels? In which months of the calendar year do the service stations typically have their *highest* retail sales levels? Create time series graphs for the monthly data in the file **P02_26.xlsx** to respond to these two questions. There are really two series, one of actual values and one of seasonally adjusted values. The latter adjusts for any possible seasonality, such as higher values in June and lower values in January, so that any trends are more apparent.

27. The file **P02_27.xlsx** contains monthly data for total U.S. retail sales of building materials, garden materials, and supplies dealers. There are really two series, one of actual values and one of seasonally adjusted values. The latter adjusts for any possible seasonality, such as higher values in June and lower values in January, so that any trends are more apparent.
   a. Is there an observable trend in these data? That is, do the values of the series tend to increase or decrease over time?
   b. Is there a seasonal pattern in these data? If so, what is the seasonal pattern?

28. The file **P02_28.xlsx** contains total monthly U.S. retail sales data for a number of years. There are really two series, one of actual sales and one of seasonally adjusted sales. The latter adjusts for any possible seasonality, such as higher sales in December and lower sales in February, so that any trends are more apparent.
   a. Create a graph of both time series and comment on any observable trends, including a possible seasonal pattern, in the data. Does seasonal adjustment make a difference? How?
   b. Based on your time series graph of actual sales, make a qualitative projection about the total retail sales levels for the next 12 months. Specifically, in which months of the subsequent year do you expect retail sales levels to be *highest?* In which months of the subsequent year do you expect retail sales levels to be *lowest?*

2-6 OUTLIERS AND MISSING VALUES

Most textbooks on data analysis, including this one, tend to use example data sets that are "cleaned up." Unfortunately, the data sets you are likely to encounter in your job are often not so clean. Two particular problems you will encounter are outliers and missing data, the topics of this section. There are no easy answers for dealing with these problems, but you should at least be aware of the issues.

2-6a Outliers

An **outlier** is literally a value or an entire observation (row) that lies well outside of the norm. For the baseball data, Alex Rodriguez's salary of $32 million is definitely an outlier. This is indeed his correct salary—the number wasn't entered incorrectly—but it is way beyond what most players make. Actually, statisticians disagree on an exact definition of an outlier. Going by the third empirical rule, you might define an outlier as any value more than three standard deviations from the mean, but this is only a rule of thumb. Let's just agree to define outliers as *extreme* values, and then for any particular data set, you can decide how extreme a value needs to be to qualify as an outlier.

Sometimes an outlier is easy to detect and deal with. For example, this is often the case with data entry errors. Suppose a data set includes a Height variable, a person's height measured in inches, and you see a value of 720. This is certainly an outlier—and it is certainly an error. Once you spot it, you can go back and check this observation to see what the person's height should be. Maybe an extra 0 was accidentally appended and the true value is 72. In any case, this type of outlier is usually easy to discover and fix.

Sometimes a careful check of the variable values, one variable at a time, will not reveal any outliers, but there still might be unusual *combinations* of values. For example, it would be strange to find a person with Age equal to 10 and Height equal to 72. Neither of these values is unusual by itself, but the combination is certainly unusual. Again, this would probably be a result of a data entry error, but it would be harder to spot. (The scatterplots discussed in the next chapter are useful for spotting unusual combinations.)

It isn't always easy to detect outliers, but an even more important issue is what to do about them when they are detected. Of course, if they are due to data entry errors, they can be fixed, but what if they are legitimate values like Alex Rodriguez's salary? One or a few wild outliers like this one can dominate a statistical analysis. For example, they can make a mean or standard deviation much different than if the outliers were not present.

For this reason, some people argue, possibly naïvely, that outliers should be eliminated before running statistical analyses. However, it is *not* appropriate to eliminate outliers simply to produce "nicer" results. There has to be a legitimate reason for eliminating outliers, and such a reason sometimes exists. For example, suppose you want to analyze salaries of "typical" managers at your company. Then it is probably appropriate to eliminate the CEO and possibly other high-ranking executives from the analysis, arguing that they aren't really part of the population of interest and would just skew the results. Or if you are interested in the selling prices of "typical" homes in your community, it is probably appropriate to eliminate the few homes that sell for over $2 million, again arguing that these are not the types of homes you are interested in.

One good way of dealing with outliers is to report results with the outliers and without them.

Probably the best advice for dealing with outliers is to run the analyses two ways: with the outliers and without them. This way, you can report the results both ways—and you are being honest.

2-6b Missing Values

There are no missing data in the baseball salary data set. All 843 observations have a value for each of the four variables. For real data sets, however, this is probably the exception rather than the rule. Unfortunately, most real data sets have gaps in the data. This could be because a person didn't want to provide all the requested personal information (what business is it of yours how old I am or whether I drink alcohol?), it could be because data doesn't exist (stock prices in the 1990s for companies that went public after 2000), or it could be because some values are simply unknown. Whatever the reason, you will undoubtedly encounter data sets with varying degrees of **missing values**.

As with outliers, there are two issues: how to detect missing values and what to do about them. The first issue isn't as simple as you might imagine. For an Excel data set, you might expect missing data to be obvious from blank cells. This is certainly one possibility, but there are others. Missing data are coded in a variety of strange ways. One common method is to code missing values with an unusual number such as −9999 or 9999. Another method is to code missing values with a symbol such as − or *. If you know the code (and it is often supplied in a footnote), then it is usually a good idea, at least in Excel, to perform a global search and replace, replacing all of the missing value codes with blanks.

The more important issue is what to do about missing values. One option is to ignore them. Then you will have to be aware of how the software deals with missing values. For example, if you use Excel's AVERAGE function on a column of data with missing values, it reacts the way you would hope and expect—it adds all the nonmissing values and divides by the number of nonmissing values. StatTools reacts in the same way for all of the measures discussed in this chapter (after alerting you that there are indeed missing values). We will say more about how StatTools deals with missing data for other analyses in later chapters. If you are using other statistical software such as SPSS or SAS, you should read its online help to learn how its various statistical analyses deal with missing data.

Because this is such an important topic in real-world data analysis, researchers have studied many ways of filling in the gaps so that the missing data problem goes away (or is at least disguised). One possibility is to fill in all of the missing values in a column with the average of the nonmissing values in that column. Indeed, this is an option in some software packages, but we don't believe it is usually a very good option. (Is there any reason to believe that missing values would be *average* values if they were known? Probably not.) Another possibility is to examine the nonmissing values in the *row* of any missing value. It is possible that they provide some clues on what the missing value should be. For example, if a person is male, is 55 years old, has an MBA degree from Harvard, and has been a manager at an oil company for 25 years, this should probably help to predict his missing salary. (It probably isn't below $100,000.) We will not discuss this issue any-further here because it is quite complex, and there are no easy answers. But be aware that you will undoubtedly have to deal with missing data at some point in your job, either by ignoring the missing values or by filling in the gaps in some way.

PROBLEMS

Level A

29. The file **P02_29.xlsx** contains monthly percentages of on-time arrivals at several of the largest U.S. airports and all of the major airlines from 1988 to 2008. The "By Airline" sheet contains a lot of missing data, presumably because some of the airlines were not in existence in 1988 and some went out of business before 2008. The "By Airport" sheet contains missing data only for Atlantic City International Airport (and we're not sure why).

a. Use StatTools to calculate summary measures (means, medians, standard deviations, and any other measures you would like to report) for each airline and each airport. How does it deal with missing data?

b. Use StatTools to create histograms for a few of the airports and a few of the airlines, including Atlantic City International. How does it deal with missing data?

c. Use StatTools to create time series graphs for a few of the airports and a few of the airlines, including Atlantic City International. How does it deal with missing data?

d. Which airports and which airlines have done a good job? Which would you like to avoid?

30. *The Wall Street Journal CEO Compensation Study* analyzed CEO pay for many U.S. companies with fiscal year 2008 revenue of at least $5 billion that filed their proxy statements between October 2008 and March 2009. The data are in the file **P02_30.xlsx**.

a. Create a new variable that is the sum of salary and bonus, and create a box plot of this new variable.

b. As the box plot key indicates, mild outliers are observations between 1.5 IQR (interquartile range) and 3.0 IQR from the edge of the box, whereas extreme outliers are greater than 3 IQR from the edge of the box. Use these definitions to identify the names of all CEOs who are mild outliers and all those who are extreme outliers.

Level B

31. There is no consistent way of defining an outlier that everyone agrees upon. For example, some people refer to an outlier that is any observation more than three standard deviations from the mean. Other people use the box plot definition, where an outlier (moderate or extreme) is any observation more than 1.5 IQR from the edges of the box, and some people care only about

the *extreme* box plot-type outliers, those that are 3.0 IQR from the edges of the box. The file **P02_18.xlsx** contains daily percentage changes in the S&P 500 index over many years. Identify outliers—days when the percentage change was unusually large in either a negative or positive direction—according to each of these three definitions. Which definition produces the most outliers?

32. Sometimes it is possible that missing data are predictive in the sense that rows with missing data are somehow different from rows without missing data. Check this with the file **P02_32.xlsx**, which contains blood pressures for 1000 (fictional) people, along with variables that can be related to blood pressure. These other variables have a number of missing values, presumably because the people didn't want to report certain information.

a. For each of these other variables, find the mean and standard deviation of blood pressure for all people without missing values and for all people with missing values. Can you conclude that the presence or absence of data for any of these other variables has anything to do with blood pressure?

b. Some analysts suggest filling in missing data for a variable with the *mean* of the nonmissing values for that variable. Do this for the missing data in the blood pressure data. In general, do you think this is a valid way of filling in missing data? Why or why not?

2-7 EXCEL TABLES FOR FILTERING, SORTING, AND SUMMARIZING

This section discusses a great tool that was introduced in Excel 2007: tables. Tables were somewhat available in previous versions of Excel, but they were never called tables before, and some of the really useful features of Excel 2007 tables were new at the time.

It is useful to begin with some terminology and history. Earlier in this chapter, we discussed data arranged in a rectangular range of rows and columns, where each row is an observation and each column is a variable, with variable names at the top of each column. Informally, we refer to such a range as a data set. In fact, this is the technical term used by StatTools. In previous versions of Excel, data sets of this form were called *lists*, and Excel provided several tools for dealing with lists. In Excel 2007, recognizing the importance of data sets, Microsoft made them much more prominent and provided even better tools for analyzing them. Specifically, you now have the ability to designate a rectangular data set as a table and then employ a number of powerful tools for analyzing tables. These tools include filtering, sorting, and summarizing.

We illustrate Excel tables in Example 2.7. Before proceeding, however, we mention one important caveat. Some of the tools discussed in this section do not work on an Excel file in the old .xls format. Therefore, you should apply them only to files saved in the new .xlsx format (new to Excel 2007).

EXAMPLE | **2.7 HyTex's Customer Data**

The file **Catalog Marketing.xlsx** contains data on 1000 customers of HyTex, a (fictional) direct marketing company, for the current year. A sample of the data appears in Figure 2.35. The definitions of the variables are fairly straightforward, but details about several of them are listed in cell comments in row 1. HyTex wants to find some useful and quick information about its customers by using an Excel table. How can it proceed?

Figure 2.35 HyTex Customer Data

	A	B	C	D	E	F	G	H	I	J	K	L	M	N	O
1	Person	Age	Gender	Own Home	Married	Close	Salary	Children	History	Catalogs	Region	State	City	First Purchase	Amount Spent
2	1	1	0	0	0	1	$16,400	1	1	12	South	Florida	Orlando	10/23/2008	$218
3	2	2	0	1	1	0	$108,100	3	3	18	Midwest	Illinois	Chicago	5/25/2006	$2,632
4	3	2	1	1	1	1	$97,300	1	NA	12	South	Florida	Orlando	8/18/2012	$3,048
5	4	3	1	1	1	1	$26,800	0	1	12	East	Ohio	Cleveland	12/26/2009	$435
6	5	1	1	0	0	1	$11,200	0	NA	6	Midwest	Illinois	Chicago	8/4/2012	$106
7	6	2	0	0	0	1	$42,800	0	2	12	West	Arizona	Phoenix	3/4/2010	$759
8	7	2	0	0	0	1	$34,700	0	NA	18	Midwest	Kansas	Kansas City	6/11/2012	$1,615
9	8	3	0	1	1	0	$80,000	0	3	6	West	California	San Francisco	8/17/2006	$1,985
10	9	2	1	1	0	1	$60,300	0	NA	24	Midwest	Illinois	Chicago	5/29/2012	$2,091
11	10	3	1	1	1	0	$62,300	0	3	24	South	Florida	Orlando	6/9/2008	$2,644

© Cengage Learning

Objective To illustrate Excel tables for analyzing the HyTex data.

Solution

*You can also designate a table by selecting any option on the Format as Table dropdown on the Home ribbon. A third alternative is even easier: select any cell in the data set and press **Ctrl+t**.*

The range A1:O1001 is in the form of a data set—it is a rectangular range bounded by blank rows and columns, where each row is an observation, each column is a variable, and variable names appear in the top row. Therefore, it is a candidate for an Excel table. However, it doesn't benefit from the new table tools until you actually *designate* it as a table. To do so, select *any* cell in the data set, click the Table button in the left part of the Insert ribbon (see Figure 2.36), and accept the default options. Two things happen. First, the data set is designated as a table, it is formatted nicely, and a dropdown arrow appears next to each variable name, as shown in Figure 2.37. Second, a new Table Tools Design ribbon becomes available (see Figure 2.38). This ribbon is available any time the active cell is inside a table. Note that the table is named Table1 by default (if this is the first table). However, you can change this to a more descriptive name if you like.

Figure 2.36 Insert Ribbon with Table Button

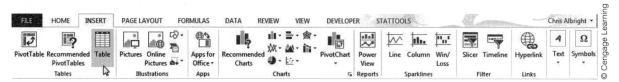

© Cengage Learning

One handy feature of Excel tables is that the variable names remain visible even when you scroll down the screen. Try it to see how it works. When you scroll down far enough that the variable names would disappear, the column headers, A, B, C, and so on, change to the variable names. Therefore, you no longer need to freeze panes or split the screen to see the variable names. However, this works only when the active cell is within the table. If you click outside the table, the column headers revert back to A, B, C, and so on.

Figure 2.37 Table with Dropdown Arrows Next to Variable Names

	A	B	C	D	E	F	G	H	I	J	K	L	M	N	O
1	Person	Age	Gender	Own Home	Married	Close	Salary	Children	History	Catalogs	Region	State	City	First Purchase	Amount Spent
2	1	1	0	0	0	1	$16,400	1	1	12	South	Florida	Orlando	10/23/2008	$218
3	2	2	0	1	1	0	$108,100	3	3	18	Midwest	Illinois	Chicago	5/25/2006	$2,632
4	3	2	1	1	1	1	$97,300	1	NA	12	South	Florida	Orlando	8/18/2012	$3,048
5	4	3	1	1	1	1	$26,800	0	1	12	East	Ohio	Cleveland	12/26/2009	$435
6	5	1	1	0	0	1	$11,200	0	NA	6	Midwest	Illinois	Chicago	8/4/2012	$106
7	6	2	0	0	0	1	$42,800	0	2	12	West	Arizona	Phoenix	3/4/2010	$759
8	7	2	0	0	0	1	$34,700	0	NA	18	Midwest	Kansas	Kansas City	6/11/2012	$1,615
9	8	3	0	1	1	0	$80,000	0	3	6	West	California	San Francisco	8/17/2006	$1,985
10	9	2	1	1	0	1	$60,300	0	NA	24	Midwest	Illinois	Chicago	5/29/2012	$2,091

© Cengage Learning

Figure 2.38 Table Tools Design Ribbon

© Cengage Learning

The dropdown arrows next to the variable names allow you to filter in many different ways. For example, click the Own Home dropdown list, uncheck Select All, and check 1. This filters out all customers except those who own their own home. Filtering is discussed in much more detail later on, but at this point, just be aware that filtering does not *delete* any observations; it only hides them. There are three indications that the table has been filtered: (1) the row numbers are colored blue and some are missing; (2) a message appears at the bottom of the screen indicating that only 516 out of 1000 records are visible; and (3) there is a filter icon next to the Own Home dropdown arrow. It is easy to remove this filter by opening the Own Home dropdown list and selecting Clear Filter (but don't do so yet).

As illustrated in Figure 2.38, there are various options you can apply to tables, including the following:

- A number of table styles are available for making the table attractive. You can experiment with these, including the various table styles and table style options. Note the dropdown list in the Table Styles group. It gives you many more styles than the ones originally visible. In particular, at the top left of options, there is a "no color" style you might prefer.

- In the Tools group, you can click Convert to Range. This undesignates the range as a table (and the dropdown arrows disappear).

- In the Properties group, you can change the name of the table. You can also click the Resize Table button to expand or contract the table range.

The Total row in an Excel table summarizes only the visible data. The data that has been filtered out is ignored.

- A particularly useful option is the Total Row in the Table Style Options group. If you check this, a new row is appended to the bottom of the table (see Figure 2.39). It creates a sum formula in the rightmost column.[4] This sum includes *only* the nonhidden rows. To prove this to youself, clear the Own Home filter and check the sum. It increases to $1,216,768. This total row is quite flexible. First, you can summarize the last column by a number of summary measures, such as Average, Max, Min, Count, and others. To do so, select cell O1002 and click the dropdown list that appears. Second, you can summarize any other column in the table in the same way. For example, if you select cell G1002, a dropdown list appears for Salary, and you can then summarize Salary with the same summarizing options.

---

[4]The actual formula is **=SUBTOTAL(109,[AmountSpent])**, where 109 is a code for summing. However, you never need to type any such formula; you can choose the summary function you want from the dropdown list.

Figure 2.39   Total Row

	Children	History	Catalogs	Region	State	City	First Purchase	Amount Spent
994	0	3	18	Midwest	Ohio	Cincinnati	10/23/2009	$1,857
996	0	2	6	South	Florida	Miami	7/7/2010	$654
997	0	2	12	West	Washington	Seattle	8/14/2012	$843
999	0	3	18	East	Pennsylvania	Philadelphia	8/9/2010	$2,546
1001	1	3	24	West	Utah	Salt Lake City	3/9/2009	$2,464
1002								$796,260

Excel tables have a lot of built-in intelligence. Although there is not enough space here to give a full account, try the following to see what we mean:

- In cell R2, enter a formula by typing an equals sign, pointing to cell O2, typing a divide sign (/), and pointing to cell G2. You do *not* get the usual formula **=O2/G2**. Instead you get **=Table1[[#This Row],[AmountSpent]]/Table1[[#This Row],[Salary]]**. This is certainly not the Excel syntax you are used to, but it makes perfect sense.[5]

- Similarly, you can expand the table with a new variable, such as the ratio of Amount Spent to Salary. Start by typing the variable name Ratio in cell P1. Then in cell P2, enter a formula exactly as you did in the previous bullet. You will notice two things. First, as soon as you enter the Ratio label, column P becomes part of the table. Second, as soon as you enter the new formula in one cell, it is copied to all of column P. This is what we mean by table intelligence.

- Excel tables expand automatically as new rows are added to the bottom or new columns are added to the right. (You saw this latter behavior in the previous bullet.) To appreciate the benefit of this, suppose you have a monthly time series data set. You designate it as a table and then build a line chart from it to show the time series behavior. Later on, if you add new data to the bottom of the table, the chart will *automatically* update to include the new data. This is a great feature. In fact, when we discuss pivot tables in the next chapter, we will recommend basing them on tables, not ranges, whenever possible. Then they too will update automatically when new data are added to the table. ■

Filtering

We now discuss ways of filtering data sets—that is, finding records that match particular criteria. Before getting into details, there are two aspects of filtering you should be aware of. First, this section is concerned with the types of filters called AutoFilter in pre-2007 versions of Excel. The term AutoFilter implied that these were very simple filters, easy to learn and apply. If you wanted to do any complex filtering, you had to move beyond AutoFilter to Excel's Advanced Filter tool. Starting in version 2007, Excel still has Advanced Filter. However, the term AutoFilter has been changed to Filter to indicate that these "easy" filters are now more powerful than the old AutoFilter. Fortunately, they are just as easy as AutoFilter.

Filtering is possible without using Excel tables, but there are definitely advantages to filtering with Excel tables.

Second, one way to filter is to create an Excel table, as indicated in the previous sub-section. This automatically provides the dropdown arrows next to the field names that allow you to filter. Indeed, this is the way we will filter in this section: on an existing table. However, a designated table is not required for filtering. You can filter on any rectangular

---

[5]If you don't like this type of formula, you can go to Excel Options and uncheck the "Use table names in formulas" option in the Formulas group.

data set with variable names. There are actually three ways to do so. For each method, the active cell should be a cell inside the data set.

- Use the Filter button from the Sort & Filter dropdown list on the Home ribbon.

- Use the Filter button from the Sort & Filter group on the Data ribbon.

- Right-click any cell in the data set and select Filter. You get several options, the most popular of which is Filter by Selected Cell's Value. For example, if the selected cell has value 1 and is in the Children column, then only customers with a single child will remain visible. (This behavior should be familiar to Access users.)

The point is that Microsoft realizes how important filtering is to Excel users. Therefore, they have made filtering a very prominent and powerful tool in all versions of Excel since 2007.

As far as we can tell, the two main advantages of filtering on a table, as opposed to the three options just listed, are the nice formatting (banded rows, for example) provided by tables, and, more importantly, the total row. If this total row is showing, it summarizes *only* the visible records; the hidden rows are ignored.

We now continue Example 2.7 to illustrate a number of filtering possibilities. We won't lead you through a lot of descriptions and screenshots. Once you know the possibilities that are available, you should find them quite easy to use.

EXAMPLE | **2.7 HyTex's Customer Data (Continued)**

HyTex wants to analyze its customer data by applying one or more filters to the data. It has already designated the data set as an Excel table. What types of filters might be useful?

Objective   To investigate the types of filters that can be applied to the HyTex data.

Solution

There is almost no limit to the filters you can apply, but here are a few possibilities.

- **Filter on one or more values in a field.** Click the Catalogs dropdown arrow. You will see five checkboxes, all checked: Select All, 6, 12, 18, and 24. To select one or more values, uncheck Select All and then check any values you want to filter on, such as 6 and 24. In this case, only customers who received 6 or 24 catalogs will remain visible. (In pre-2007 versions of Excel, it wasn't possible to select more than one value this way. Now it's easy.)

- **Filter on more than one field.** With the Catalogs filter still in place, create a filter on some other field, such as customers with one child. When there are filters on multiple fields, only records that meet *all* of the criteria are visible, in this case customers with one child who received 6 or 24 catalogs.

- **Filter on a continuous numerical field.** The Salary and Amount Spent fields are basically continuous fields, so it would not make much sense to filter on one or a few particular values. However, it does make sense to filter on *ranges* of values, such as all salaries greater than $75,000. This is easy. Click the dropdown arrow next to Salary and select Number Filters. You will see a number of obvious possibilities, including Greater Than.

- **Top 10 and Above/Below Average filters.** Continuing the previous bullet, the Number Filters include Top 10, Above Average, and Below Average options. These are particularly useful if you like to see the highs and the lows. The Above Average and Below Average filters do exactly what their names imply. The Top 10 filter is

The number of ways you can filter with Excel's newest tools is virtually unlimited. Don't be afraid to experiment. You can always clear filters to get back to where you started.

actually more flexible than its name implies. It can be used to select the top *n* items (where you can choose *n*), the bottom *n* items, the top *n* percent of items, or the bottom *n* percent of items. Note that if a Top 10 filter is used on a text field, the ordering is alphabetical. If it is used on a date field, the ordering is chronological.

- **Filter on a text field.** If you click the dropdown arrow for a text field such as Region, you can choose one or more of its values, such as East and South, to filter on. You can also select the Text Filters item, which provides a number of choices, including Begins With, Ends With, Contains, and others. For example, if there were an Address field, you could use the Begins With option to find all addresses that begin with P.O. Box.

- **Filter on a date field.** Starting in version 2007, Excel has great built-in intelligence for filtering on dates. If you click the First Purchase dropdown arrow, you will see an item for each year in the data set with plus signs next to them. By clicking on the plus signs, you can drill down to months and then days for as much control as you need. Figure 2.40 shows one possibility, where we have filtered out all dates except the first part of July 2012. In addition, if you select the Date Filters item, you get a number of possibilities, such as Yesterday, Next Week, Last Month, and many others.

Figure 2.40

Filtering on a Date Variable

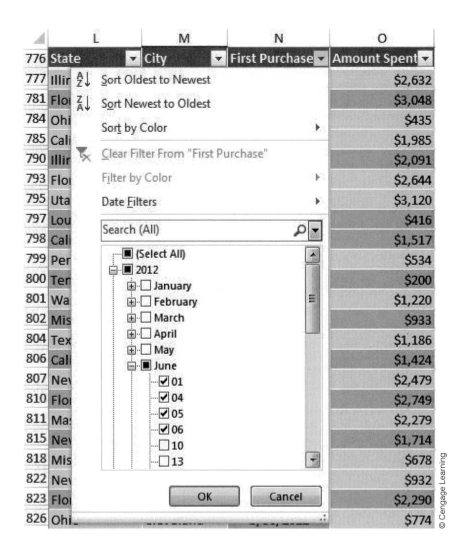

© Cengage Learning

- **Filter on color or icon.** Starting in version 2007, Excel has many ways to color cells or enter icons in cells. Often the purpose is to denote the sizes of the numbers in the cells, such as red for small numbers and green for large numbers. We won't cover the possibilities in this book, but you can experiment with Conditional Formatting on the Home ribbon. The point is that cells are often colored in certain ways or contain certain icons. Therefore, Excel allows you to filter on background color, font color, or icon. For example, if certain salaries are colored yellow, you can isolate them by filtering on yellow.

- **Use a custom filter.** If nothing else works, you can try a custom filter, available at the bottom of the Number Filters, Text Filters, and Date Filters lists. Figures 2.41 and 2.42 illustrate two possibilities. The first of these filters out all salaries between $25,000 and $75,000. Without a custom filter, this wouldn't be possible. The second filter uses the * wildcard to find regions ending in *est* (West and Midwest). Admittedly, this is an awkward way to perform this filter, but it indicates how flexible custom filters can be.

Figure 2.41

Custom Filter for Salary

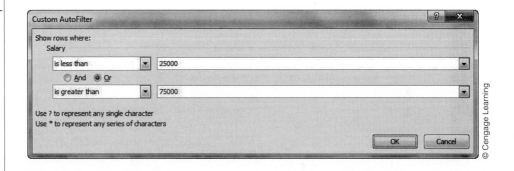

Figure 2.42

Custom Filter for Region

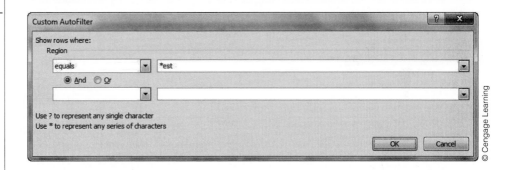

We remind you once again that if you filter on an Excel table and you have summary measures in a total row at the bottom of the table, these summary measures are based *only* on the filtered data; they ignore the hidden rows.

One final comment about filters is that when you click the dropdown arrow for any variable, you always get three items at the top for *sorting*, not filtering (see Figure 2.40, for example). These allow you to perform the obvious sorts, from high to low or vice versa, and they even allow you to sort on color. As with filtering, you do not need to designate an Excel table to perform sorting (the popular A-Z and Z-A buttons work just fine without tables), but sorting is made even easier with tables.

Excel Tip: Other Useful Ways to Filter

The Advanced Filter tool is useful for implementing an OR filter, such as all customers who are either male with salary above $40,000 OR female with at least two children. In fact, it is probably the most natural way to implement such a filter. However, there is another way that is used in the solutions of a few problems in Chapter 2. Suppose you want a filter of the type A OR B, where A and B are any conditions, maybe even AND conditions. Create two columns, Condition A and Condition B. Fill each with an IF formula that returns Yes or No, depending on whether the condition holds in that row. Then create a third new column, Condition A or B, and fill it with a formula like =IF(OR(conditionA, conditionB), "Yes", "No"), where conditionA and conditionB are references to the Yes/No values in the Condition A and Condition B columns. Then you can filter on Yes in this last column to obtain the desired results.

Now that you know the possibilities, here is one particular filter you can try. Suppose HyTex wants information about all middle-aged married customers with at least two children who have above average salaries, own their own home, and live in Indiana or Kentucky. You should be able to create this filter in a few seconds. The result, sorted in decreasing order of Amount Spent and shown in Figure 2.43, indicates that the average salary for these 10 customers is $84,750, and their total amount spent at HyTex is $14,709. (We summarized Salary by average and Amount Spent by sum in the total row.) ∎

Figure 2.43   Results from a Typical Filter

	A	B	C	D	E	F	G	H	I	J	K	L	M	N	O
1	Person	Age	Gender	Own Home	Married	Close	Salary	Children	History	Catalogs	Region	State	City	First Purchase	Amount Spent
155	154	2	0	1	1	0	$96,800	3	NA	24	Midwest	Kentucky	Louisville	4/28/2012	$3,082
163	162	2	0	1	1	1	$62,200	3	NA	24	Midwest	Indiana	Indianapolis	6/7/2008	$2,119
245	244	2	1	1	1	0	$82,400	2	3	24	Midwest	Indiana	Indianapolis	3/25/2011	$2,035
370	369	2	1	1	1	0	$113,400	3	3	18	Midwest	Kentucky	Louisville	11/25/2011	$1,790
430	429	2	1	1	1	1	$113,000	2	2	18	Midwest	Kentucky	Louisville	6/15/2011	$1,554
570	569	2	1	1	1	1	$70,400	2	NA	12	Midwest	Indiana	Indianapolis	4/12/2007	$1,127
764	763	2	0	1	1	1	$85,500	2	2	18	Midwest	Kentucky	Louisville	7/3/2012	$895
790	789	2	1	1	1	1	$74,500	2	2	12	Midwest	Indiana	Indianapolis	3/7/2012	$824
804	803	2	0	1	1	1	$72,200	2	2	18	Midwest	Kentucky	Louisville	5/29/2011	$715
851	850	2	1	1	1	1	$77,100	2	2	6	Midwest	Indiana	Indianapolis	6/17/2012	$568
1002	Total						$84,750								$14,709

© Cengage Learning

PROBLEMS

Level A

33. The file **P02_03.xlsx** contains data from a survey of 399 people regarding an environmental policy. Use filters for each of the following.

a. Identify all respondents who are female, middle-aged, and have two children. What is the average salary of these respondents?

b. Identify all respondents who are elderly and strongly disagree with the environmental policy. What is the average salary of these respondents?

c. Identify all respondents who strongly agree with the environmental policy. What proportion of these individuals are young?

d. Identify all respondents who are either (1) middle-aged men with at least one child and an annual salary of at least $50,000, or (2) middle-aged women with two or fewer children and an annual salary of at least $30,000.

What are the mean and median salaries of the respondents who meet these conditions? What proportion of the respondents who satisfy these conditions agree or strongly agree with the environmental policy?

34. The file **P02_07.xlsx** includes data on 204 employees at the (fictional) company Beta Technologies. Use filters for each of the following.

a. Identify all employees who are male and have exactly 4 years of post-secondary education. What is the average salary of these employees?

b. Find the average salary of all female employees who have exactly 4 years of post-secondary education. How does this mean salary compare to the one obtained in part **a**?

c. Identify all employees who have more than 4 years of post-secondary education. What proportion of these employees are male?

d. Identify all full-time employees who are either (1) females between the ages of 30 and 50 (inclusive) with at least 5 years of prior work experience, at least 10 years of prior work experience at Beta, and at least 4 years of postsecondary education; or (2) males between the ages of 40 and 60 (inclusive) with at least 6 years of prior work experience, at least 12 years of prior work experience at Beta, and at least 4 years of postsecondary education.

e. For those employees who meet the conditions specified in part **d**, compare the mean salary of the females with that of the males. Also, compare the median salary of the female employees with that of the male employees.

f. What proportion of the full-time employees identified in part **d** earns less than $50,000 per year?

35. The file **P02_35.xlsx** contains (fictional) data from a survey of 500 randomly selected households. Use Excel filters to answer the following questions.

a. What are the average monthly home mortgage payment, average monthly utility bill, and average total debt (excluding the home mortgage) of all homeowners residing in the southeast part of the city?

b. What are the average monthly home mortgage payment, average monthly utility bill, and average total debt (excluding the home mortgage) of all homeowners residing in the northwest part of the city? How do these results compare to those found in part **a**?

c. What is the average annual income of the first household wage earners who rent their home (house or apartment)? How does this compare to the average annual income of the first household wage earners who own their home?

d. What proportion of the surveyed households contains a single person who owns his or her home?

36. Recall that the file **Supermarket Transactions.xlsx** contains over 14,000 transactions made by supermarket customers over a period of approximately two years. Use Excel filters to answer the following questions.

a. What proportion of these transactions are made by customers who are married?

b. What proportion of these transactions are made by customers who do not own a home?

c. What proportion of these transactions are made by customers who have at least one child?

d. What proportion of these supermarket customers are single and own a home?

Level B

37. The file **P02_35.xlsx** contains (fictional) data from a survey of 500 randomly selected households. Use Excel filters to answer the following questions.

a. Identify households that own their home and have a monthly home mortgage payment in the top quartile of the monthly payments for all households.

b. Identify households with monthly expenditures on utilities that are within two standard deviations of the mean monthly expenditure on utilities for all households.

c. Identify households with total indebtedness (excluding home mortgage) less than 10% of the household's primary annual income level.

2-8 CONCLUSION

The summary measures, charts, and tables discussed in this chapter are extremely useful for describing variables in data sets. The methods in this chapter (and the next chapter) are often called *exploratory* methods because they allow you to explore the characteristics of the data and at least tentatively answer interesting questions. Most of these tools have been available for many years, but with the powerful software now accessible to virtually everyone, the tools can be applied quickly and easily to gain insights. We can promise that you will be using many if not all of these tools in your job. Indeed, the knowledge you gain from these early chapters is arguably the most valuable knowledge you will gain from the book.

To help you remember which analyses are appropriate for different questions and different data types, and which tools are useful for performing the various analyses, we have created a taxonomy in the file **Data Analysis Taxonomy.xlsx**. (It doesn't fit nicely on the printed page.) Feel free to refer back to the diagram in this file as you apply the tools in this chapter and the next chapter.

Summary of Key Terms

Term	Explanation	Excel	Pages	Equation
Population	Includes all objects of interest in a study—people, households, machines, etc.		22	
Sample	Representative subset of population, usually chosen randomly		22	
Variable (or field or attribute)	Attribute or measurement of members of a population, such as height, gender, or salary		23	
Observation (or case or record)	List of all variable values for a single member of a population		23	
Data set	(Usually) a rectangular array of data, with variables in columns, observations in rows, and variable names in the top row		23	
Data type	Several categorizations are possible: numerical versus categorical, discrete versus continuous, cross-sectional versus time series; categorical can be nominal or ordinal		24	
Dummy variable	A variable coded 1 or 0: 1 for observations in a category, 0 for observations not in the category		25	
Binned (or discretized) variable	Numerical variable that has been categorized into discrete categories called bins		25	
StatTools	Palisade add-in for data analysis in Excel	StatTools ribbon	31	
Mean	Average of observations	AVERAGE or StatTools	32	2.1
Median	Middle observation after sorting	MEDIAN or StatTools	32	
Mode	Most frequent observation	MODE	33	
Percentiles	Values that have specified percentages of observations below them	PERCENTILE or StatTools	34	
Quartiles	Values that have 25%, 50%, or 75% of observations below them	QUARTILE or StatTools	34	
Minimum	Smallest observation	MIN or StatTools	34	
Maximum	Largest observation	MAX or StatTools	34	
Concatenate	String together two or more pieces of text	& character (or CONCATENATE)	35	
Range	Difference between largest and smallest observations	MAX, MIN, or StatTools	35	
Interquartile range (IQR)	Difference between first and third quartiles	QUARTILE or StatTools	35	
Variance	Measure of variability; essentially the average of squared deviations from the mean	VAR (or VARP) or StatTools	35	2.2, 2.3
Standard deviation	Measure of variability in same units as observations; square root of variance	STDEV (or STDEVP) or StatTools	36	
Empirical rules	Rules that specify approximate percentage observations within one, two, or three standard deviations of mean for bell-shaped distributions		38	
Mean absolute Deviation (MAD)	Another measure of variability; average of absolute deviations from the mean	AVEDEV or StatTools	39	2.4

Term	Explanation	Excel	Pages	Equation
Skewness	When one tail of a distribution is longer than the other	SKEW or StatTools	39	
Kurtosis	Measure of "fatness" of tails of a distribution	KURT or StatTools	39	
Histogram	Chart of bin counts for a numerical variable; shows shape of the distribution	StatTools	45	
Frequency table	Contains counts of observations in specified categories	COUNTIF or FREQUENCY	46	
Box plots	Alternative chart that shows the distribution of a numerical variable	StatTools	45	
Time series graph	Graph showing behavior through time of one or more time series variables	StatTools	54	
Outlier	Observation that lies outside of the general range of observations in a data set		61	
Missing values	Values that are not reported in a data set		62	
Excel tables	Rectangular ranges specified as *tables*; especially useful for sorting and filtering	Table from Insert ribbon	63	

PROBLEMS

Conceptual Questions

C.1. An airline analyst wishes to estimate the proportion of all American adults who are afraid to fly because of potential terrorist attacks. To estimate this percentage, the analyst decides to survey 1500 Americans from across the nation. Identify the relevant sample and population in this situation.

C.2. The number of children living in each of a large number of randomly selected households is an example of which data type? Be specific.

C.3. Does it make sense to construct a histogram for the state of residence of randomly selected individuals in a sample? Explain why or why not.

C.4. Characterize the likely shape of a histogram of the distribution of scores on a midterm exam in a graduate statistics course.

C.5. A researcher is interested in determining whether there is a relationship between the number of room air-conditioning units sold each week and the time of year. What type of descriptive chart would be most useful in performing this analysis? Explain your choice.

C.6. Suppose that the histogram of a given income distribution is positively skewed. What does this fact imply about the relationship between the mean and median of this distribution?

C.7. "The midpoint of the line segment joining the first quartile and third quartile of any distribution is the median." Is this statement true or false? Explain your answer.

C.8. Explain why the standard deviation would likely *not* be a reliable measure of variability for a distribution of data that includes at least one extreme outlier.

C.9. Explain how a box plot can be used to determine whether the associated distribution of values is essentially symmetric.

C.10. Suppose that you collect a random sample of 250 salaries for the salespersons employed by a large PC manufacturer. Furthermore, assume that you find that two of these salaries are considerably higher than the others in the sample. Before analyzing this data set, should you delete the unusual observations? Explain why or why not.

Level A

38. The file **P02_35.xlsx** contains (fictional) data from a survey of 500 randomly selected households.
   a. Indicate the type of data for each of the variables included in the survey.
   b. For each of the categorical variables in the survey, indicate whether the variable is nominal or ordinal, and why.
   c. Create a histogram for each of the numerical variables in this data set. Indicate whether each of these distributions is approximately symmetric or skewed. Which, if any, of these distributions are skewed to the right? Which, if any, are skewed to the left?

d. Find the maximum and minimum debt levels for the households in this sample.

e. Find the indebtedness levels at each of the 25th, 50th, and 75th percentiles.

f. Find and interpret the interquartile range for the indebtedness levels of these households.

39. The file **P02_39.xlsx** contains SAT test scores (two verbal components, a mathematical component, and the sum of these three) for each state and Washington DC in 2009. It also lists the percentage of high school graduates taking the test in each of the states.

a. Create a histogram for each of the numerical variables. Are these distributions essentially symmetric or are they skewed?

b. Compare the distributions of the average verbal scores and average mathematical scores. In what ways are these distributions similar? In what ways are they different?

c. Find the mean, median, and mode of the set of percentages taking the test.

d. For each of the numerical variables, which is the most appropriate measure of central tendency? Why?

e. How does the mean of the Combined variable relate to the means of the Critical Reading, Math, and Writing variables? Is the same true for medians?

40. *The Wall Street Journal CEO Compensation Study* analyzed CEO pay from many U.S. companies with fiscal year 2008 revenue of at least $5 billion that filed their proxy statements between October 2008 and March 2009. The data are in the file **P02_30.xlsx**.

a. Create histograms to gain a clearer understanding of the distributions of annual base salaries and bonuses earned by the surveyed CEOs in fiscal 2008. How would you characterize these histograms?

b. Find the annual salary below which 75% of all given CEO salaries fall.

c. Find the annual bonus above which 55% of all given CEO bonuses fall.

d. Determine the range of the middle 50% of all given total direct compensation figures. For the 50% of the executives that do not fall into this middle 50% range, is there more variability in total direct compensation to the right than to the left? Explain.

41. The file **P02_41.xlsx** contains monthly returns on American Express stock for several years. As the formulas in the file indicate, each return is the percentage change in the adjusted closing price from one month to the next. Do monthly stock returns appear to be skewed or symmetric?

On average, do they tend to be positive, negative, or zero?

42. The file **P02_42.xlsx** contains monthly returns on Mattel stock for several years. As the formulas in the file indicate, each return is the percentage change in the adjusted closing price from one month to the next. Create a histogram of these returns and summarize what you learn from it. On average, do the returns tend to be positive, negative, or zero?

43. The file **P02_43.xlsx** contains U.S. Bureau of Labor Statistics data on the year-to-year percentage changes in the wages and salaries of workers in private industries, including both white-collar and blue-collar occupations.

a. Create box plots to summarize these distributions of annual percentage changes. Comparing the box plots for white-collar and blue-collar workers, discuss the similarities or differences you see.

b. Given that these are time series variables, what information is omitted from the box plots? Are box plots even relevant?

44. The file **P02_44.xlsx** contains annual data on the percentage of Americans under the age of 18 living below the poverty level.

a. In which years of the sample has the poverty rate for American children exceeded the rate that defines the third quartile of these data?

b. In which years of the sample has the poverty rate for American children fallen below the rate that defines the first quartile of these data?

c. What is the typical poverty rate for American children during this period?

d. Create and interpret a time series graph for these data. How successful have Americans been recently in their efforts to win "the war against poverty" for the nation's children?

e. Given that this data set is a time series, discuss whether the measures requested in parts **a-c** are very meaningful at the current time.

Level B

45. The file **P02_45.xlsx** contains the salaries of 135 business school professors at a (fictional) large state university.

a. If you increased every professor's salary by $1000, what would happen to the mean and median salary?

b. If you increased every professor's salary by $1000, what would happen to the standard deviation of the salaries?

c. If you increased every professor's salary by 5%, what would happen to the standard deviation of the salaries?

46. The file **P02_46.xlsx** lists the fraction of U.S. men and women of various heights and weights. Use these data to estimate the mean and standard deviation of the height of American men and women. (*Hint*: Assume all heights in a group are concentrated at the group's midpoint.) Do the same for weights.

47. Recall that HyTex Company is a direct marketer of technical products and that the file **Catalog Marketing.xlsx** contains recent data on 1000 HyTex customers.
   a. Identify all customers in the data set who are 55 years of age or younger, female, single, and who have had at least some dealings with HyTex before this year. Find the average number of catalogs sent to these customers and the average amount spent by these customers this year.
   b. Do any of the customers who satisfy the conditions stated in part **a** have salaries that fall in the bottom 10% of all 1000 combined salaries in the data set? If so, how many?
   c. Identify all customers in the sample who are more than 30 years of age, male, homeowners, married, and who have had little if any dealings with HyTex before this year. Find the average combined household salary and the average amount spent by these customers this year.
   d. Do any of the customers who satisfy the conditions stated in part **c** have salaries that fall in the top 10% of all 1000 combined salaries in the data set? If so, how many?

48. Recall that the file **Baseball Salaries 2011.xlsx** contains data on 843 MLB players in the 2011 season. Using this data set, answer the following questions:
   a. Find the mean and median of the salaries of all shortstops. Are any of these measures influenced significantly by one or more unusual observations?
   b. Find the standard deviation, first and third quartiles, and 5th and 95th percentiles for the salaries of all shortstops. Are any of these measures influenced significantly by one or more unusual observations?
   c. Create a histogram of the salaries of all shortstops. Are any of these measures influenced significantly by one or more unusual observations?

49. In 1969 and again in 1970, a lottery was held to determine who would be drafted and sent to Vietnam in the following year. For each date of the year, a ball was put into an urn. For example, in the first lottery, January 1 was number 305 and February 14 was number 4. This means that a person born on February 14 would be drafted before a person born on January 1. The file **P02_49.xlsx** contains the "draft

number" for each date for the two lotteries. Do you notice anything unusual about the results of either lottery? What do you think might have caused this result? (*Hint*: Create a box plot for each month's numbers.)

50. The file **P02_50.xlsx** contains the average price of gasoline in each of the 50 states. (*Note*: You will need to manipulate the data to some extent before performing the analyses requested below.)
   a. Compare the distributions of gasoline price data (one for each year) across states. Specifically, are the mean and standard deviation of these distributions changing over time? If so, how do you explain the trends?
   b. In which regions of the country have gasoline prices changed the most?
   c. In which regions of the country have gasoline prices remained relatively stable?

51. The file **P02_51.xlsx** contains data on U.S. home-ownership rates.
   a. Employ numerical summary measures to characterize the changes in homeownership rates across the country during this period.
   b. Do the trends appear to be uniform across the U.S. or are they unique to certain regions of the country? Explain.

52. Recall that HyTex Company is a direct marketer of technical products and that the file **Catalog Marketing.xlsx** contains recent data on 1000 HyTex customers.
   a. Identify all customers who are either (1) home-owners between the ages of 31 and 55 who live reasonably close to a shopping area that sells similar merchandise, and have a combined salary between $40,000 and $90,000 (inclusive) and a history of being a medium or high spender at HyTex; or (2) homeowners greater than the age of 55 who live reasonably close to a shopping area that sells similar merchandise and have a combined salary between $40,000 and $90,000 (inclusive) and a history of being a medium or high spender at HyTex.
   b. Characterize the subset of customers who satisfy the conditions specified in part **a**. In particular, what proportion of these customers are women? What proportion of these customers are married? On average, how many children do these customers have? Finally, how many catalogs do these customers typically receive, and how much do they typically spend each year at HyTex?
   c. In what ways are the customers who satisfy condition 1 in part **a** different from those who satisfy condition 2 in part **a**? Be specific.

53. Recall that the file **Supermarket Transactions.xlsx** contains data on over 14,000 transactions. There are two numerical variables, Units Sold and Revenue. The first of these is discrete and the second is continuous. For each of the following, do whatever it takes to create a bar chart of counts for Units Sold and a histogram of Revenue for the given subpopulation of purchases.

    a. All purchases made during January and February of 2012.

    b. All purchase made by married female homeowners.

    c. All purchases made in the state of California.

    d. All purchases made in the Produce product department.

54. The file **P02_54.xlsx** contains daily values of an EPA air quality index in Washington DC and Los Angeles from January 1980 through April 2009. For some unknown reason, the source provides slightly different dates for the two cities.

    a. Starting in column G, create three new columns: Date, Wash DC Index, and LA Index. Fill the new date column with *all* dates from 1/1/1980 to 4/30/2009. Then use lookup functions to fill in the two new index columns, entering the observed index if available or a blank otherwise. (*Hint*: Use a combination of the VLOOKUP function with False as the last argument and the IFERROR function. Look up the latter in online help if you have never seen it before.)

    b. Create a separate time series graph of each new index column. Because there are so many dates, it is difficult to see how the graph deals with missing data, but see if you can determine this (maybe by expanding the size of the graph or trying a smaller example). In spite of the few missing points, explain the patterns in the graphs and how Washington DC compares to Los Angeles. (*Note*: StatTools will not let you create a time series graph with missing data in the *middle* of the series, but you can create a line chart manually in Excel, without StatTools.)

55. The file **P02_55.xlsx** contains monthly sales (in millions of dollars) of beer, wine, and liquor. The data have not been seasonally adjusted, so there might be seasonal patterns that can be discovered. For any month in any year, define that month's seasonal index as the ratio of its sales value to the average sales value over all months of that year.

    a. Calculate these seasonal indexes, one for each month in the series. Do you see a consistent pattern from year to year? If so, what is it?

    b. To "deseasonalize" the data and get the seasonally adjusted series often reported, divide each monthly sales value by the corresponding seasonal index from part **a**. Then create a time series graph of both series, the actual sales and the seasonally adjusted sales. Explain how they are different and why the seasonally adjusted series might be of interest.

56. The file **P02_56.xlsx** contains monthly values of indexes that measure the amount of energy necessary to heat or cool buildings due to outside temperatures. (See the explanation in the Source sheet of the file.) These are reported for each state in the U.S. and also for several regions, as listed in the Locations sheet, from 1931 to 2000. Create summary measures and/or charts to see whether there is any indication of temperature changes (global warming?) through time, and report your findings.

57. The file **P02_57.xlsx** contains data on mortgage loans in 2008 for each state in the U.S. The file is different from similar ones in this chapter in that each state has its own sheet with the same data laid out in the same format. Each state sheet breaks down all mortgage applications by loan purpose, applicant race, loan type, outcome, and denial reason (for those that were denied). The question is how a *single* data set for all states can be created for analysis. The Typical Data Set sheet indicates a simple way of doing this, using the powerful but little-known INDIRECT function. This sheet is basically a template for bringing in any pieces of data from the state sheet you would like to examine.

    a. Create histograms and summary measures for the example data given in the Typical Data Set sheet and write a short report on your findings.

    b. Create a copy of the Typical Data Set sheet and repeat part **a** on this copy for at least one other set of variables (of your choice) from the state sheets.

CASE 2.1 CORRECT INTERPRETATION OF MEANS

A mean, as defined in this chapter, is a simple concept—it is the average of a set of numbers. But even this simple concept can cause confusion if you aren't careful. The data in Figure 2.44 are typical of data presented by marketing researchers for a type of product, in this case beer. (See the file **C02_01.xlsx**.)

Each value is an average of the number of six- packs of beer purchased per customer during a month. For the individual brands, the value is the average only for the customers who purchased at least one six-pack of that brand. For example, the value for Miller is the average number of six-packs purchased of *all* of these brands for customers who purchased at least one six-pack of Miller. In contrast, the "Any" average is the average number of six-packs

purchased of these brands for all customers in the population.

Is there a paradox in these averages? On first glance, it might appear unusual, or even impossible, that the "Any" average is less than each brand average. Make up your own (small) data set, where you list a number of customers, along with the number of six-packs of each brand of beer each customer purchased, and calculate the averages for your data that correspond to those in Figure 2.44. Do you get the same result (that the "Any" average is lower than all of the others)? Are you *guaranteed* to get this result? Does it depend on the amount of brand loyalty in your population, where brand loyalty is greater when customers tend to stick to the same brand, rather than buying multiple brands? Write up your results in a concise report.

Figure 2.44 Average Beer Purchases

⬜	A	B	C	D	E	F	G	H
1	Miller	Budweiser	Coors	Michelob	Heineken	Old Milwaukee	Rolling Rock	Any
2	6.77	6.66	6.64	7.11	7.29	7.3	7.17	4.71

© Cengage Learning

CASE 2.2 THE DOW JONES INDUSTRIAL AVERAGE

The monthly closing values of the Dow Jones Industrial Average (DJIA) for the period beginning in January 1950 are given in the file **C02_02.xlsx**. According to Wikipedia, the Dow Jones Industrial Average, also referred to as the Industrial Average, the Dow Jones, the Dow 30, or simply the Dow, is one of several stock market indices created by Charles Dow. The average is named after Dow and one of his business associates, statistician Edward Jones. It is an index that shows how 30 large, publicly owned companies based in the U.S. have traded during a standard trading session in the stock market. It is the second oldest U.S. market index after the Dow Jones Transportation Average, which Dow also created.

The *Industrial* portion of the name is largely historical, as many of the modern 30 components have little or nothing to do with traditional heavy industry. The average is price-weighted, and to compensate for the effects of stock splits and other adjustments, it is currently a scaled average. The value of the Dow is not the actual average of the prices of its component stocks, but rather the sum of the component prices divided by a *divisor*, which changes whenever one of the component stocks has a stock split or stock dividend, so as to generate a consistent value for the index.

Along with the NASDAQ Composite, the S&P 500 Index, and the Russell 2000 Index, the Dow is among the most closely watched benchmark indices for tracking stock market activity. Although Dow compiled the index to gauge the performance of the industrial sector within the U.S. economy, the index's performance continues to be influenced not only by corporate and economic reports, but also by domestic and foreign political events such as war and terrorism, as well as by natural disasters that could potentially lead to economic harm.

Using the summary measures and graphical tools from this chapter, analyze this important time series over the given period. Summarize in detail the behavior of the monthly closing values of the Dow and the associated monthly percentage changes in the closing values of the Dow.

CASE | 2.3 HOME AND CONDO PRICES

The file **C02_03.xlsx** contains an index of home prices and a seasonally adjusted (SA) version of this index for several large U.S. cities. It also contains a condo price index for several large cities and a national index. (The data are explained in the Source sheet.) Use the tools in this chapter to explore these data, and write a report of your findings. Some important questions you can answer are the following: Are there trends over time? Are there differences across cities? Are there differences across months? Do condo prices mirror home prices? Why are *seasonally adjusted* indexes published?

Finding Relationships among Variables

Monkey Business Images/Shutterstock.com

PREDICTORS OF SUCCESSFUL MOVIES

The movie industry is a high-profile industry with a highly variable revenue stream. In 1998, U.S. moviegoers spent close to $7 billion at the box office alone. Ten years later, the figure was slightly higher, despite the number of people watching DVDs and other media at home. With this much money at stake, it is not surprising that movie studios are interested in knowing what variables are useful for predicting a movie's financial success. The article by Simonoff and Sparrow (2000) examines this issue for 311 movies released in 1998 and late 1997. (They obtained their data from a public Web site, www.imdb.com.) Although it is preferable to examine movie *profits*, the costs of making movies are virtually impossible to obtain. Therefore, the authors focused instead on revenues—specifically, the total U.S. domestic gross revenue for each film.

Simonoff and Sparrow obtained prerelease information on a number of variables that were thought to be possible predictors of gross revenue. (Prerelease means that this information is known about a film *before* the film is actually released.) These variables include: (1) the genre of the film, categorized as action, children's, comedy, documentary, drama, horror, science fiction, or thriller; (2) the Motion Picture Association of America (MPAA) rating of the film, categorized as G (general audiences), PG (parental guidance suggested), PG-13 (possibly unsuitable for children under 13), R (children not admitted unless accompanied by an adult), NC-17 (no one under 17 admitted), or U (unrated); (3) the country of origin of the movie, categorized as United States, English-speaking but non–United States, or non–English-speaking; (4) number of actors and actresses in the movie who were listed in *Entertainment Weekly*'s lists of the 25 Best Actors and 25 Best Actresses, as of 1998; (5) number of actors and actresses in the movie who were among the top 20 actors and top 20 actresses in average box office gross per movie in their careers; (6) whether the movie was a sequel; (7) whether the movie was released before a holiday weekend; (8) whether the movie was released during the Christmas season; and (9) whether the movie was released during the summer season.

To get a sense of whether these variables are related to gross revenue, we could calculate a lot of summary measures and create numerous tables. However, we agree with Simonoff and Sparrow that the information is best presented in a series of *side-by-side box plots*. (See Figure 3.1.) These box plots are slightly different from the versions introduced in the previous chapter, but they accomplish exactly the same thing. (There are two differences: First, their box plots are vertical; ours are horizontal. Second, their box plots capture an extra piece of information—the *widths* of their boxes are proportional to the square roots of the sample sizes, so that wide boxes correspond to categories with more movies. In contrast, the *heights* of our boxes carry no information about sample size.) Basically, each box and the lines and points extending above and below it indicate the distribution of gross revenues for any category. Remember that the box itself, from bottom to top, captures the middle 50% of the revenues in the category, the line in the middle of the box represents the median revenue, and the lines and dots indicate possible skewness and outliers.

These particular box plots indicate some interesting and possibly surprising information about the movie business. First, almost all of the box plots indicate a high degree of variability and skewness to the right, where there are a few movies that gross extremely large amounts compared to the "typical" movies in the category. Second, genre certainly makes a difference. There are more comedies and dramas (wider boxes), but they typically gross considerably less than action, children's, and science fiction films. Third, the same is true of R-rated movies compared to movies rated G, PG, or PG-13—there are more of them, but they typically gross much less. Fourth, U.S. movies do considerably better than foreign movies. Fifth, it helps to have stars, although there are quite a few "sleepers" that succeed without having big-name stars. Sixth, sequels do better, presumably reflecting the success of the earlier films. Finally, the release date makes a big difference. Movies released before holidays, during the Christmas season, or during the summer season tend to have larger gross revenues. Indeed, as Simonoff and Sparrow discuss, movie studios compete fiercely for the best release dates.

Are these prerelease variables sufficient to predict gross revenues accurately? As you might expect from the amount of variability in most of the box plots in Figure 3.1, the answer is "no." Many intangible factors evidently determine the ultimate success of a movie, so that some, such as *There's Something About Mary,* do much better than expected, and others, such as *Godzilla,* do worse than expected. We will revisit this movie data set in the chapter opener to Chapter 11. There, you will see how Simonoff and Sparrow use *multiple regression* to predict gross revenue—with limited success. ■

3-1 INTRODUCTION

The previous chapter introduced a number of summary measures, graphs, and tables to describe the distribution of a single variable. For a variable such as baseball salary, the entire focus was on how salaries were distributed over some range. This is an important first step in any exploratory data analysis—to look closely at variables one at a time—but it is almost never the *last* step. The primary interest is usually in *relationships* between variables. For example, it is natural to ask what drives baseball salaries. Does it depend on qualitative factors, such as the player's team or position? Does it depend on quantitative factors, such as the number of hits the player gets or the number of strikeouts? To answer these questions, you have to examine relationships between various variables and salary.

Figure 3.1 Box Plots of Domestic Gross Revenues for 1998 Movies

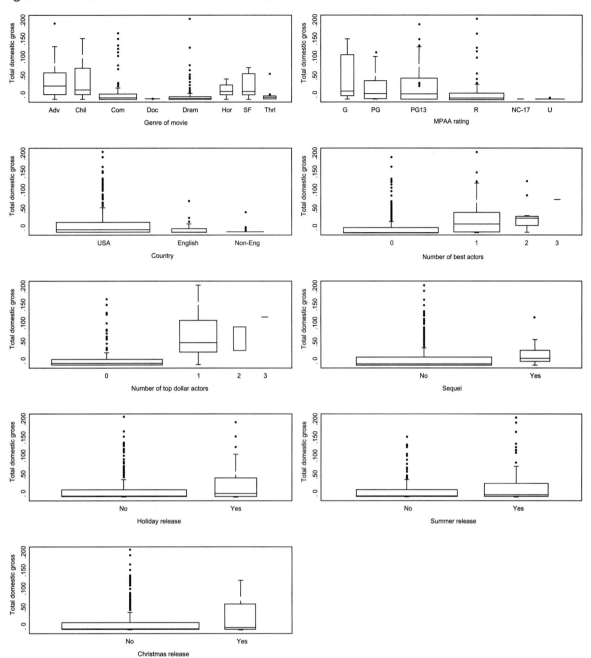

Source: From "Predicting Movie Grosses, Winners and Losers, Blockbusters and Sleepers" by J.S. Simonoff & I.R. Sparrow, CHANCE, pp. 15–22, Vol. 13, No. 3, Summer 2000. Used by permission of American Statistical Association.

A key issue in this chapter is that different tools should be used to examine relationships, depending on whether the variables involved are numeric or categorical.

This chapter again discusses numerical summary measures, graphs, and tables, but they now involve at least two variables at a time. The most useful numerical summary measure is correlation, a measure that applies primarily to numerical variables. The most useful graph is a scatterplot, which again applies primarily to numerical variables. Other tools are used for relationships involving categorical variables. For example, to break down a numerical variable by a categorical variable, as in the chapter opener with movie gross revenues, it is often useful to create side-by-side box plots as in Figure 3.1. Finally, we discuss Excel®'s arguably most powerful tool, the pivot table. A pivot table enables you to break down one variable by others so that all sorts of relationships can be uncovered very quickly.

As you read this chapter, remember that the diagram in the file **Data Analysis Taxonomy.xlsx** is available. This diagram gives you the big picture of which analyses are appropriate for which data types and which tools are best for performing the various analyses.

3-2 RELATIONSHIPS AMONG CATEGORICAL VARIABLES

Consider a data set with at least two categorical variables, Smoking and Drinking. Each person is categorized into one of three smoking categories: nonsmoker (NS), occasional smoker (OS), and heavy smoker (HS). Similarly, each person is categorized into one of three drinking categories: nondrinker (ND), occasional drinker (OD), and heavy drinker (HD). Do the data indicate that smoking and drinking habits are related? For example, do nondrinkers tend to be nonsmokers? Do heavy smokers tend to be heavy drinkers?

Use a crosstabs, a table of counts of joint categories, to discover relationships between two categorical variables.

As discussed in the previous chapter, the most meaningful way to describe a categorical variable is with counts, possibly expressed as percentages of totals, and corresponding charts of the counts. The same is true of examining relationships between two categorical variables. We can find the counts of the categories of either variable separately, and more importantly, we can find counts of the *joint* categories of the two variables, such as the count of all nondrinkers who are also nonsmokers. Again, corresponding percentages of totals and charts help tell the story.

It is customary to display all such counts in a table called a **crosstabs** (for crosstabulations). This is also sometimes called a **contingency table**. Example 3.1 illustrates these tables.

EXAMPLE	**3.1 RELATIONSHIP BETWEEN SMOKING AND DRINKING**

The file **Smoking Drinking.xlsx** lists the smoking and drinking habits of 8761 adults. (This is fictional data.) The categories have been coded so that "N," "O," and "H" stand for "Non," "Occasional," and "Heavy," and "S" and "D" stand for "Smoker" and "Drinker." Is there any indication that smoking and drinking habits are related? If so, how are they related?

Objective   To use a crosstabs to explore the relationship between smoking and drinking.

Solution

The first question is the data format. If you are lucky, you will be given a table of counts. However, it is also possible that you will have to create these counts. In the file for this example, the data are in long columns, a small part of which is shown in Figure 3.2. (Presumably, there could be other variables describing these people, but only the Smoking and Drinking variables are relevant here.)

To create the crosstabs, start by entering the category headings in Figure 3.3. The goal is to fill the table with counts of joint categories, along with row and column sums. If you

Figure 3.2

Smoking and Drinking Data

◢	A	B	C
1	Person	Smoking	Drinking
2	1	NS	OD
3	2	NS	HD
4	3	OS	HD
5	4	HS	ND
6	5	NS	OD
7	6	NS	ND
8	7	NS	OD
9	8	NS	ND
10	9	OS	HD
11	10	HS	HD

© Cengage Learning

Figure 3.3

Headings for Crosstabs

◢	E	F	G	H	I
1	Crosstabs from COUNTIFS formulas				
2					
3		NS	OS	HS	Total
4	ND				
5	OD				
6	HD				
7	Total				

© Cengage Learning

are thinking about using the COUNTIF function to obtain the joint counts, you are close. Unfortunately, the COUNTIF function lets you specify only a single criterion, but there are now *two* criteria, one for smoking and one for drinking. Fortunately, Excel has a function (introduced in Excel 2007) designed exactly for this: COUNTIFS. It enables you to specify any number of range-criterion pairs. In fact, you can fill in the entire table with a single formula entered in cell F4 and copied to the range F4:H6:

=COUNTIFS($B$2:$B$8762,F$3,$C$2:$C$8762,$E4)

The first two arguments are for the condition on smoking; the last two are for the condition on drinking. You can then sum across rows and down columns to get the totals.

The resulting counts appear in the top table in Figure 3.4. For example, among the 8761 people, 4912 are nonsmokers, 2365 are heavy drinkers, and 733 are nonsmokers *and* heavy drinkers. Because the totals are far from equal (there are many more nonsmokers than heavy smokers, for example), any relationship between smoking and drinking is difficult to detect in these raw counts. Therefore, it is useful to express the counts as percentages of row in the middle table and as percentages of column in the bottom table.

The latter two tables indicate, in complementary ways, that there is definitely a relationship between smoking and drinking. If there were no relationship, the rows in the middle table would be practically identical, as would the columns in the bottom table. (Make sure you understand why this is true.) But they are far from identical. For example,

Relationships between the two variables are usually more evident when the counts are expressed as percentages of row totals or percentages of column totals.

Figure 3.4

Crosstabs of
Smoking and
Drinking

	E	F	G	H	I
1	Crosstabs from COUNTIFS formulas				
2					
3		NS	OS	HS	Total
4	ND	2118	435	163	2716
5	OD	2061	1067	552	3680
6	HD	733	899	733	2365
7	Total	4912	2401	1448	8761
8					
9	Shown as percentages of row				
10		NS	OS	HS	Total
11	ND	78.0%	16.0%	6.0%	100.0%
12	OD	56.0%	29.0%	15.0%	100.0%
13	HD	31.0%	38.0%	31.0%	100.0%
14					
15	Shown as percentages of column				
16		NS	OS	HS	
17	ND	43.1%	18.1%	11.3%	
18	OD	42.0%	44.4%	38.1%	
19	HD	14 9%	37 4%	50 6%	
20	Total	100.0%	100.0%	100.0%	

© Cengage Learning

the middle table indicates that only 6% of the nondrinkers are heavy smokers, whereas 31% of the heavy drinkers are heavy smokers. Similarly, the bottom table indicates that 43.1% of the nonsmokers are nondrinkers, whereas only 11.3% of the heavy smokers are nondrinkers. In short, these tables indicate that smoking and drinking habits tend to go with one another. These tendencies are reinforced by the column charts of the two percentage tables in Figure 3.5. ■

Figure 3.5   Column Charts of Smoking and Drinking Percentages

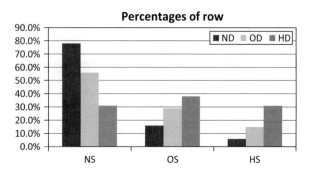

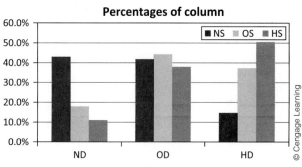

© Cengage Learning

Counts Versus Percentages

There is no single correct way to display the data in a crosstabs. Ultimately, the data are always counts, but they can be shown as raw counts, percentages of row totals, percentages of column totals, or even percentages of the overall total. Nevertheless, when you are looking for relationships between two categorical variables, showing the counts as percentages of row totals or percentages of column totals usually makes any relationships stand out more clearly. Corresponding charts are also very useful.

Excel Tip: Creating Charts from Crosstabs

It takes almost no work to create these charts. To get the one on the left, highlight the range E10:H13 and insert a column chart from the Insert ribbon. Do the same with the range E16:H19 to get the chart on the right, except that it will have smoking on the horizontal axis and drinking in the legend. To reverse their roles, simply click the Switch Row/Column button on the Chart Tools Design ribbon.

Although this example illustrates that it doesn't take too much work to create crosstabs and corresponding charts, you will see a much quicker and easier way when pivot tables are discussed later in this chapter.

PROBLEMS

Note: Student solutions for problems whose numbers appear within a colored box are available for purchase at www.cengagebrain.com.

Level A

1. The file **P02_01.xlsx** indicates the gender and nationality of the MBA incoming class in two successive years at the Kelley School of Business at Indiana University.

  a. For each year separately, recode Nationality so that all nationalities with a count of 1 or 2 are listed as Other.

  b. For each year, create a crosstabs of Gender versus the recoded Nationality and an associated column chart. Does there seem to be any relationship between Gender and the recoded Nationality? Is the pattern about the same in the two years?

2. The file **P02_03.xlsx** contains data from a survey of 399 people regarding a government environmental policy.

  a. Create a crosstabs and an associated column chart for Gender versus Opinion. Express the counts as percentages so that for either gender, the percentages add to 100%. Discuss your findings. Specifically, do the two genders tend to differ in their opinions about the environmental policy?

  b. Repeat part **a** with Age versus Opinion.

  c. Recode Salary to be categorical with categories "Less than $40K," "Between $40K and $70K," "Between $70K and $100K," and "Greater than $100K" (where you can treat the breakpoints

however you like). Then repeat part **a** with this new Salary variable versus Opinion.

3. The file **P02_02.xlsx** contains data about 211 movies released in 2006 and 2007.

  a. Recode Distributor so that all distributors except for Paramount Pictures, Buena Vista, Fox Searchlight, Universal, Warner Bros., 20th Century Fox, and Sony Pictures are listed as Other. (Those in Other released fewer than 16 movies.) Similarly, recode Genre so that all genres except for Action, Adventure, Thriller/Suspense, Drama, and Comedy are listed as Other. (Again, those in Other are genres with fewer than 16 movies.)

  b. Create a crosstabs and an associated column chart for these two recoded variables. Express the counts as percentages so that for any distributor, the percentages add to 100%. Discuss your findings.

4. Recall from Chapter 2 that the file **Supermarket Transactions.xlsx** contains over 14,000 transactions made by supermarket customers over a period of approximately two years. To understand which customers purchase which products, create a crosstabs and an associated column chart for each of the following. For each, express the counts as percentages so that for any value of the first variable listed, the percentages add to 100%. Do any patterns stand out?

  a. Gender versus Product Department

  b. Marital Status versus Product Department

  c. Annual Income versus Product Department

Level B

5. Recall from Chapter 2 that HyTex Company is a direct marketer of technical products and that the file **Catalog Marketing.xlsx** contains recent data on 1000 HyTex customers. To understand these customers, first recode Salary and Amount Spent as indicated in part **a**, and then create each of the requested crosstabs and an associated column chart in parts **b** to **e**. Express each count as a percentage, so that for any value of the first variable listed, the percentages add up to 100%. Do any patterns stand out?

    a. Find the first, second, and third quartiles of Salary, and then recode Salary as 1 to 4, depending on which quarter of the data each value falls into. For example, the first salary, $16,400, is recoded as 1 because $16,400 is less than the first quartile, $29,975. Recode Amount Spent similarly, based on its quartiles. (*Hint*: The recoding can be done most easily with lookup tables.)

    b. Age versus the recoded Amount Spent

    c. Own Home versus the recoded Amount Spent

    d. History versus the recoded Amount Spent

    e. The recoded Salary versus the recoded Amount Spent

6. The smoking/drinking example in this section used the function COUNTIFS function (introduced in Excel 2007) to find the counts of the joint categories. Without using this function (or pivot tables), devise another way to get the counts. The raw data are in the file **Smoking Drinking.xlsx**. (*Hint*: One possibility is to concatenate the values in columns B and C into a new column D. But feel free to find the counts in any way you like.)

3-3 RELATIONSHIPS AMONG CATEGORICAL VARIABLES AND A NUMERICAL VARIABLE

The comparison problem, where a numerical variable is compared across two or more subpopulations, is one of the most important problems faced by data analysts in all fields of study.

This section describes a very common situation where you want to break down a numerical variable such as salary by a categorical variable such as gender. This is precisely what pivot tables were built for, as you will see later in the chapter. For now, however, numerical and graphical tools in StatTools will be used. This general problem, typically referred to as the **comparison problem**, is one of the most important problems in data analysis. It occurs whenever you want to compare a numerical measure across two or more subpopulations. Here are some examples:

- The subpopulations are males and females, and the numerical measure is salary.

- The subpopulations are different regions of the country, and the numerical measure is the cost of living.

- The subpopulations are different days of the week, and the numerical measure is the number of customers going to a particular fast-food chain.

- The subpopulations are different machines in a manufacturing plant, and the numerical measure is the number of defective parts produced per day.

- The subpopulations are patients who have taken a new drug and those who have taken a placebo, and the numerical measure is the recovery rate from a particular disease.

- The subpopulations are undergraduates with various majors (business, English, history, and so on), and the numerical measure is the starting salary after graduating.

    The list could go on and on. The discussion of the comparison problem begins in this chapter, where exploratory methods are used to investigate whether there appear to be differences across the subpopulations on the numerical variable of interest. In later chapters, inferential methods—confidence intervals and hypothesis tests—are used to see whether the differences in *samples* from the subpopulations can be generalized to the subpopulations as a whole.

Breaking Down By Category

There is arguably no more powerful data analysis technique than breaking down a numerical variable by a categorical variable. The methods in this chapter, especially side-by-side box plots and pivot tables, get you started with this general comparison problem. They allow you to see quickly, with charts and/or numerical summary measures, how two or more categories compare. More sophisticated techniques for comparing across categories are discussed in later chapters.

3-3a Stacked and Unstacked Formats

The stacked format is by far the most common. There are one or more long numerical variables and another long variable that specifies which category each observation is in.

There are two possible **data formats** you will see, stacked and unstacked. This concept is crucial for understanding how StatTools deals with comparison problems. Consider salary data on males and females. (There could be other variables in the data set, but they aren't relevant here.) The data are **stacked** if there are two "long" variables, Gender and Salary, as indicated in Figure 3.6. The idea is that the male salaries are stacked in with the female salaries. This is the format you will see in the majority of situations. However, you will occasionally see data in **unstacked** format, as shown in Figure 3.7. (Note that both tables list exactly the same data. See the file **Stacked Unstacked Data.xlsx**.) Now there are two "short" variables, Female Salary and Male Salary. In addition, it is very possible that the two variables have different lengths. This is the case here because there are more females than males.

Figure 3.6

Stacked Data

	A	B
1	**Gender**	**Salary**
2	Male	81600
3	Female	61600
4	Female	64300
5	Female	71900
6	Male	76300
7	Female	68200
8	Male	60900
9	Female	78600
10	Female	81700
11	Male	60200
12	Female	69200
13	Male	59000
14	Male	68600
15	Male	51900
16	Female	64100
17	Male	67600
18	Female	81100
19	Female	77000
20	Female	58800
21	Female	87800
22	Male	78900

© Cengage Learning

Figure 3.7

Unstacked Data

◢	A	B
1	Female Salary	Male Salary
2	61600	81600
3	64300	76300
4	71900	60900
5	68200	60200
6	78600	59000
7	81700	68600
8	69200	51900
9	64100	67600
10	81100	78900
11	77000	
12	58800	
13	87800	

© Cengage Learning

StatTools is capable of dealing with either stacked or unstacked format. (Not all statistical software can make this claim. Some packages require stacked format.) Nevertheless, there are a few times when you might want to convert from stacked to unstacked format or vice versa. StatTools has utilities for doing this. These utilities are found on the Data Utilities (*not* the Utilities) dropdown list on the StatTools ribbon. They are very simple to use, and you can try them on the data in Figures 3.6 and 3.7. (If you need help, open the finished version of the **Stacked Unstacked Data.xlsx** file, which includes instructions for using these data utilities.)

We now return to the baseball data to see which, if any, of the categorical variables makes a difference in player salaries.

EXAMPLE | **3.2 BASEBALL SALARIES**

The file **Baseball Salaries 2011 Extra.xlsx** contains the same 2011 baseball data examined in the previous chapter. In addition, several extra categorical variables are included:

- Pitcher (Yes for all pitchers, No for the others)
- League (American or National)
- Division (National West, American East, and so on)
- Yankees (Yes if team is New York Yankees, No otherwise)
- Playoff Team 2011 (Yes for the eight teams that made it to the playoffs, No for the others)
- World Series Team 2011 (Yes for St. Louis Cardinals and Texas Rangers, No for others)

Do pitchers (or any other positions) earn more than others? Does one league pay more than the other, or do any divisions pay more than others? How does the notoriously high Yankees payroll compare to the others? Do the successful teams from 2011 tend to have larger 2011 payrolls?

Objective To learn methods in StatTools for breaking down baseball salaries by various categorical variables.

Solution

It is useful to look first at some numerical summary measures for salary. These are the same summary measures from the previous chapter, but now we want to break them down by position. Fortunately, StatTools makes this easy. To get started, designate the range as a StatTools data set in the usual way and then select One-Variable Summary from the Summary Statistics dropdown list. Then the key is to click the Format button (see Figure 3.8) and choose Stacked (if it isn't already selected). When you choose Stacked, you get two lists of variables to choose from. In the Cat (categorical) list, choose the variable that you want to categorize by, in this case Position. In the Val (value) list, choose the variable that you want to summarize, in this case Salary. Then select any of the summary measures you would like to see, such as those checked in Figure 3.8.

Figure 3.8

One-Variable Summary Dialog Box with Stacked Format

The results appear in Figure 3.9. This table lists each of the requested summary measures for each of the nine positions in the data set. If you want to see salaries broken down by team or any other categorical variable, you can easily run this analysis again and choose a different Cat variable.[1]

Figure 3.9   Summary Measures of Salary for Various Positions

	A	B	C	D	E	F	G	H	I	J
7		Salary (Catcher)	Salary (Designated Hitter)	Salary (First Baseman)	Salary (Infielder)	Salary (Outfielder)	Salary (Pitcher)	Salary (Second Baseman)	Salary (Shortstop)	Salary (Third Baseman)
8	*One Variable Summary*	Baseball 2011 Data	Baseball 2011 Data	Baseball 2011 Data	Baseball 2011 Data	Baseball 2011 Data	Baseball 2011 Data	Baseball 2011 Data	Baseball 2011 Data	Baseball 2011 Data
9	Mean	$2252780.70	$7110181.88	$5452236.81	$3162678.71	$4018200.30	$2943853.37	$2776197.15	$2852726.28	$4309856.85
10	Std. Dev.	$3539587.29	$4783000.51	$6692183.63	$5795695.23	$5210328.15	$4043494.94	$3387236.65	$3564560.06	$5943914.21
11	Median	$850000.00	$4250000.00	$2000000.00	$428600.00	$1250000.00	$1095000.00	$1000000.00	$1350000.00	$2050000.00
12	Minimum	$414000.00	$2020000.00	$414000.00	$414000.00	$414000.00	$414000.00	$414000.00	$414000.00	$414000.00
13	Maximum	$23000000.00	$1300000.00	$23125000.00	$16174974.00	$26187500.00	$24285714.00	$15285714.00	$14729364.00	$32000000.00
14	Count	69	8	42	7	152	413	59	47	46
15	1st Quartile	$424000.00	$2500000.00	$427500.00	$414000.00	$443000.00	$431500.00	$425000.00	$425400.00	$478000.00
16	3rd Quartile	$3000000.00	$12000000.00	$7410655.00	$2285677.00	$6000000.00	$3750000.00	$4500000.00	$4300000.00	$5500000.00

There are a lot of numbers to digest in Figure 3.9, so it is difficult to get a clear picture of differences across positions. It is more enlightening to see a graphical summary of this information. There are several types of graphs you can use. Our favorite way, which will be discussed shortly, is to create side-by-side box plots (the same type of chart illustrated

---

[1]For baseball fans, don't be fooled by the low mean for the Infielder position. There are only seven players in this category, evidently the "utility" infielders who can play several positions—and don't command high salaries.

in the chapter opener). Another possibility is to create side-by-side histograms, with one histogram for each category. This is easy with StatTools, using the Stacked format option exactly as was used for summary measures. However, you should *not* accept the default bins because they will differ across categories and prevent a fair comparison. So make sure you enter your own bins. (See the finished version of the baseball file for an illustration of side-by-side histograms done with default bins and with specified bins.) A third possibility is to use pivot tables and corresponding pivot charts, as discussed later in this chapter.

For now, we illustrate side-by-side box plots. These are very easy to obtain. You select Box-Whisker Plot from the Summary Graphs dropdown list and fill in the resulting dialog box as shown in Figure 3.10. Again, the key is to select the Stacked format so that you can choose a Cat variable and a Val variable.

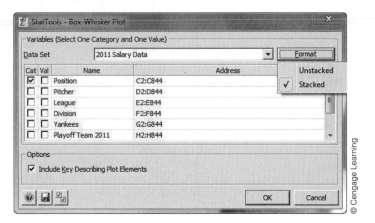

The results appear in Figure 3.11. There is a separate box plot for each category of the Position variable, and each has exactly the same interpretation as in the previous chapter. Now the differences between positions emerge fairly clearly. A few of the conclusions that can be made follow.

- The salaries for all positions are skewed to the right (mean greater than median, long lines and outliers to the right).
- As a whole, first basemen tend to be the highest paid players, followed by outfielders and third basemen. The designated hitters also make a lot, but there are only eight of them in the data set.
- As a whole, pitchers don't make as much as first basemen, outfielders, and third basemen, but there are a lot of pitchers who are high-earning outliers.
- Except for a few notable exceptions, catchers, shortstops, and second basemen tend to be paid somewhat less than the other positions.

Because these side-by-side box plots are so easy to obtain, you can generate a lot of them to provide insights into the salary data. Several interesting examples appear in Figures 3.12–3.14. From these box plots, we can conclude the following:

- Pitchers make somewhat less than other players, although there are many outliers in each group.
- The Yankees payroll is indeed *much* larger than the payrolls for the rest of the teams. In fact, it is so large that Alex Rodriguez's $32 million is considered only a *mild* outlier relative to the rest of the team.
- Aside from the many outliers, the playoff teams from 2011 tend to have slightly larger payrolls than the non-playoff teams. The one question we cannot answer, however, at least not without additional data, is whether these larger payrolls are a cause or an effect of being successful.

Figure 3.11

Box Plots of Salary
by Position

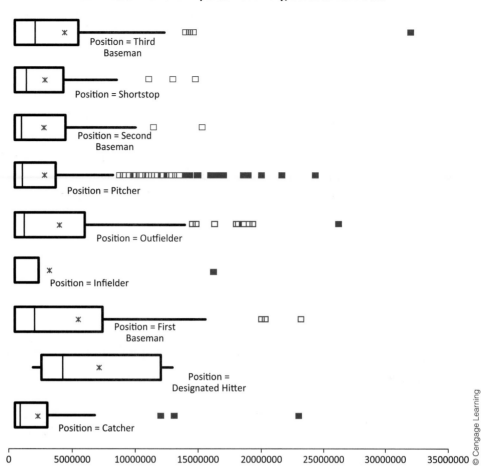

Box-Whisker Plot of Comparison of Salary/Baseball 2011 Data

Figure 3.12

Box Plots of Salary
by Pitcher

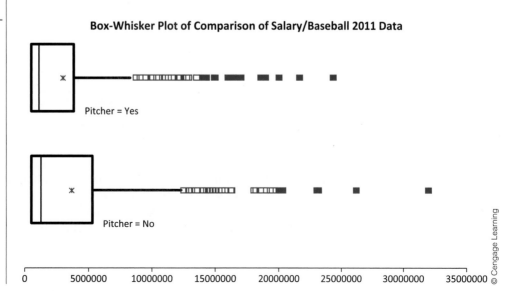

Box-Whisker Plot of Comparison of Salary/Baseball 2011 Data

Figure 3.13

Box Plots of Salary by Yankees

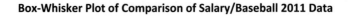

Box-Whisker Plot of Comparison of Salary/Baseball 2011 Data

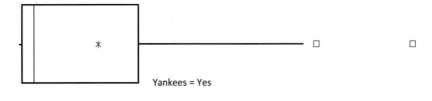

Yankees = Yes

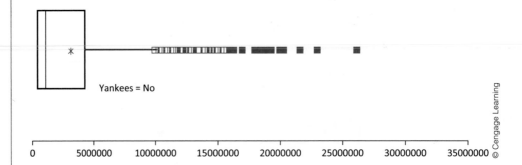

Yankees = No

| 0 | 5000000 | 10000000 | 15000000 | 20000000 | 25000000 | 30000000 | 35000000 |

Figure 3.14

Box Plots of Salary by Playoff Team

Box-Whisker Plot of Comparison of Salary/Baseball 2011 Data

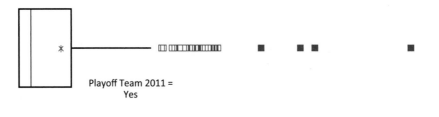

Playoff Team 2011 = Yes

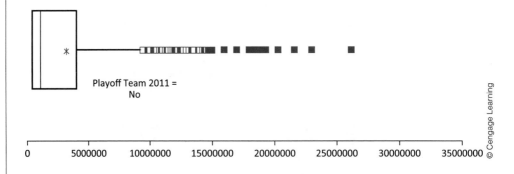

Playoff Team 2011 = No

| 0 | 5000000 | 10000000 | 15000000 | 20000000 | 25000000 | 30000000 | 35000000 |

You can often create a categorical variable on the fly with an IF formula and then use it for side-by-side box plots. We did this with the Yankees.

There is one StatTools limitation you should be aware of. The academic version allows only 12 categories for box plots. Therefore, you can't choose Team as the Cat variable because there are 30 teams. However, it is possible to isolate one or more teams in a column and then base the box plots on this column, as we did for the Yankees. As another example, if you were interested in comparing the Yankees, the Red Sox, and all the others, you could create another column with three values: Yankees, Red Sox, and Other. ∎

PROBLEMS

Level A

7. Recall that the file **Baseball Salaries 2011 Extra.xlsx** contains data on 843 Major League Baseball (MLB) players during the 2011 season. Use StatTools to find the mean, median, standard deviation, and first and third quartiles of Salary, broken down by each of the following categories. Comment on your findings.
 a. Team
 b. Division
 c. Whether they played for the Yankees
 d. Whether they were in the playoffs

8. The file **P02_07.xlsx** includes data on 204 employees at the (fictional) company Beta Technologies. Use StatTools to find the mean, median, and standard deviation of Annual Salary, broken down by each of the following categories. Comment on your findings.
 a. Gender
 b. A recoded version of Education, with new values 1 for Education less than 4, 2 for Education equal to 4, and 3 for Education greater than 4
 c. A recoded version of Age, with people aged less than 34 listed as Young, those aged at least 34 and less than 50 listed as Middle-aged, and those aged at least 50 listed as Older

9. The file **Golf Stats.xlsx** contains data on the 200 top golfers each year from 2003 to 2011. (This data set is used in an example in the next section.) Create a recoded Age variable, with values "Twenties," "Thirties," and "Forties," based on their ages in the 2011 sheet. Then use StatTools to calculate the mean, median, and standard deviation of the following 2011 variables, broken down by the recoded Age. Comment on whether it appears that golfers peak in their thirties.
 a. Earnings
 b. Yards/Drive and Driving Accuracy
 c. Greens in Regulation
 d. Putting Average (Golfers want this to be small.)

10. Recall from Chapter 2 that HyTex Company is a direct marketer of technical products and that the file **Catalog Marketing.xlsx** contains recent data on 1000 HyTex customers. Use StatTools to find the mean, median, and standard deviation of Amount Spent, broken down by the following variables. Then create side-by-side box plots of Amount Spent, broken down by the same variables. Comment on how the box plots complement the summary measures.
 a. Age
 b. Gender
 c. Close
 d. Region
 e. Year of first purchase. (*Hint*: For this one, use Excel's YEAR function to create a Year column.)

 f. The combination of Married and Own Home. (For this one, create a code variable, with values from 1 to 4, for the four combinations of Married and Own Home. Alternatively, create a text variable with values such as "Not married, Owns home.")

11. The file **P02_35.xlsx** contains data from a survey of 500 randomly selected households.
 a. Create a new column Has Second Income with values "Yes" and "No" depending on whether the household has a reported second income.
 b. Use StatTools to find the mean, median, and standard deviation of First Income, broken down by the variable you created in part **a**. Is there any indication that first income tends to be any larger or smaller, or has more or less variation, depending on whether there is a second income?
 c. Repeat part **b** for each of the Monthly Payment and Debt variables.

12. The file **P02_02.xlsx** contains data about 211 movies released in 2006 and 2007.
 a. Recode Genre so that all genres except for Action, Adventure, Thriller/Suspense, Drama, and Comedy are listed as Other. (Those in Other are genres with fewer than 16 movies.)
 b. Use StatTools to find the mean, median, and standard deviation of Total US Gross, broken down by the recoded Genre variable. Also, create side-by-side box plots of Total US Gross, again broken down by the recoded Genre variable. Comment on what the results say about the popularity of different genres.

13. *The Wall Street Journal CEO Compensation Study* analyzed chief executive officer (CEO) pay from many U.S. companies with fiscal year 2008 revenue of at least $5 billion that filed their proxy statements between October 2008 and March 2009. The data are in the file **P02_30.xlsx**.
 a. Create a new variable Total 2008, the sum of Salary 2008 and Bonus 2008. (Actually, this is not "total" compensation because it omits the very lucrative compensation from stock options.) Also, recode Company Type so that the Technology and Telecommunications are collapsed into a Tech/Telecomm category.
 b. Use StatTools to find the mean, median, and standard deviation of Total 2008, broken down by the recoded Company Type. Also, create side-by-side box plots of Total 2008, again broken down by the recoded Company Type. What do the results tell you about differences in level or variability across company types?

14. The file **P02_55.xlsx** contains monthly sales (in millions of dollars) of beer, wine, and liquor. The data have not been seasonally adjusted, so there might be seasonal patterns that can be discovered.
    a. Create a new Month Name variable with values Jan, Feb, and so on. (Use Excel's MONTH function and then a lookup table.)
    b. Use StatTools to create side-by-side box plots of Total Sales, broken down by Month Name. Is there any evidence of differences across months for either the level of sales or the variability of sales?

15. The file **P03_15.xlsx** contains monthly data on the various components of the Consumer Price Index (CPI). The source claims that these data have been seasonally adjusted. The following parts ask you to check this claim.
    a. Create a new Month Name variable with values Jan, Feb, and so on. (Use Excel's MONTH function and then a lookup table.)
    b. Create side-by-side box plots of each component of the CPI (including the All Items variable), broken down by the Month Name variable from part **a**. What results would you expect for "seasonally adjusted" data? Are your results in line with this?

16. The file **P02_11.xlsx** contains data on 148 houses that were recently sold in a (fictional) suburban community. The data set includes the selling price of each house, along with its appraised value, square footage, number of bedrooms, and number of bathrooms.
    a. Create two new variables, Ratio 1 and Ratio 2. Ratio 1 is the ratio of Appraised Value to Selling Price, and Ratio 2 is the ratio of Selling Price to Square Feet. Identify any obvious outliers in these two Ratio variables.
    b. Use StatTools to find the mean, median, and standard deviation of each Ratio variable, broken down by Bedrooms. Also, create side-by-side box plots of each Ratio variable, again broken down by Bedrooms. Comment on the results.
    c. Repeat part **b** with Bedrooms replaced by Bathrooms.
    d. If you repeat parts **b** and **c** with any obvious outlier(s) from part **a** removed, do the conclusions change in any substantial way?

Level B

17. The file **P02_32.xlsx** contains blood pressures for 1000 people, along with variables that can be related to blood pressure. These other variables have a number of missing values, probably because some people didn't want to report certain information. For each of the Alcohol, Exercise, and Smoke variables, use StatTools to find the mean, median, and standard deviation of Blood Pressure, broken down by whether the data for that variable are missing. For example,

there should be one set of statistics for people who reported their alcohol consumption and another for those who didn't report it. Based on your results, does it appear that there is any difference in blood pressure between those who reported and those who didn't?

18. The file **P03_18.xlsx** contains the times in the Chicago marathon for the top runners each year (the top 10,000 in 2006 and the top 20,000 in 2007 and 2008).
    a. Merge the data in these three sheets into a single sheet named 2006–2008, and in the new sheet, create a variable Year that lists the year.
    b. The Time variable, shown as something like 2:16:12, is really stored as a time, the fraction of day starting from midnight. So 2:16:12, for example, which means 2 hours, 16 minutes, and 12 seconds, is stored as 0.0946, meaning that 2:16:12 AM is really 9.46% of the way from midnight to the next midnight. This isn't very useful. Do whatever it takes to recode the times into a new Minutes variable with two decimals, so that 2:16:12 becomes 136.20 minutes. (*Hint*: Look up Time functions in Excel's online help.)
    c. Create a new variable Nationality to recode Country as "KEN, ETH," "USA," or "Other," depending on whether the runner is from Kenya/Ethiopia (the usual winners), the USA, or some other country.
    d. Use StatTools to find the mean, median, standard deviation, and first and third quartiles of Minutes, broken down by Nationality. Also, create side-by-side box plots of Minutes, again broken down by Nationality. Comment on the results.
    e. Repeat part **d**, replacing Nationality by Gender.

19. The file **P02_18.xlsx** contains daily values of the S&P Index from 1970 to early 2012. It also contains percentage changes in the index from each day to the next.
    a. Create a new variable President that lists the U.S. presidents Nixon through Obama on each date. You can look up the presidents and dates online.
    b. Use StatTools to find the mean, median, standard deviation, and first and third quartiles of % Change, broken down by President. Also, create side-by-side box plots of % Change, again broken down by President. Comment on the results.

20. The file **P02_56.xlsx** contains monthly values of indexes that measure the amount of energy necessary to heat or cool buildings due to outside temperatures. (See the explanation in the Source sheet of the file.) These are reported for each state in the U.S. and also for several regions, as listed in the Locations sheet, from 1931 to 2000.
    a. For each of the Heating Degree Days and Cooling Degree Days sheets, create a new Season variable with values "Winter," "Spring," "Summer," and

"Fall." Winter consists of December, January, and February; Spring consists of March, April, and May; Summer consists of June, July, and August; and Fall consists of September, October, and November.

b. Use StatTools to find the mean, median, and standard deviation of Heating Degree Days (HDD), broken down by Season, for the 48 contiguous states location (code 5999). (Ignore the first and last rows for the given location, the ones that contain -9999, the code for missing values.) Also, create side-by-side box plots of HDD, broken down by season. Comment on the results. Do they go in the direction you would expect? Do the same for Cooling Degree Days (which has no missing data).

c. Repeat part b for California (code 0499).

d. Repeat part b for the New England group of states (code 5801).

3-4 RELATIONSHIPS AMONG NUMERICAL VARIABLES

This section discusses methods for finding relationships among numerical variables. For example, we might want to examine the relationship between heights and weights of people, or between salary and years of experience of employees. To study such relationships, we introduce two new summary measures, correlation and covariance, and a new type of chart called a scatterplot.

In general, don't use correlations that involve coded categorical variables such as 0–1 dummies. The methods from the previous two sections are more appropriate.

Note that these measures can be applied to *any* variables that are displayed numerically. However, they are appropriate only for truly numerical variables, not for categorical variables that have been coded numerically. In particular, many people create dummy (0–1) variables for categorical variables such as Gender and then include these dummies in a table of correlations. This is certainly possible, and we do not claim that it is wrong. However, if you want to investigate relationships involving categorical variables, it is better to employ the tools in the previous two sections.

3-4a Scatterplots

We first discuss scatterplots, a graphical method for detecting relationships between two numerical variables.[2] Then we will discuss the numerical summary measures, correlation and covariance, in the next subsection. (We do it in this order because correlation and covariance make more sense once you understand scatterplots.) A **scatterplot** is a scatter of points, where each point denotes the values of an observation for two selected variables. The two variables are often labeled generically as *X* and *Y*, so a scatterplot is sometimes called an **X-Y chart**. The whole purpose of a scatterplot is to make a relationship (or the lack of it) apparent. Do the points tend to rise upward from left to right? Do they tend to fall downward from left to right? Does the pattern tend to be linear, nonlinear, or no particular shape? Do any points fall outside the general pattern? The answers to these questions provide information about the possible relationship between the two variables. The process is illustrated in Example 3.3.

EXAMPLE	3.3 GOLF STATS ON THE PGA TOUR

For the past decade or so, the Professional Golf Association (PGA) has kept statistics on all PGA Tour players, and these stats are published on the Web. We imported yearly data from 2003–2011 into the file **Golf Stats.xlsx**. The file includes an observation for each of the top 200 earners for each year, including age, earnings, events played, rounds played, 36-hole cuts made (only the top scorers on Thursday and Friday get to play on the weekend; the others don't make the cut), top 10s, and wins. It also includes stats about

[2]Some people spell these plots as *scatterplots*, others *scatter plots*. We (and StatTools) prefer the one-word spelling.

efficiency in the various parts of the game (driving, putting, greens in regulation, and sand saves), as well as good holes (eagles and birdies) and bad holes (bogies). A sample of the data for 2011 appears in Figure 3.15, with the data sorted in decreasing order of earnings and a few variables not shown. What relationships can be uncovered in these data for any particular year?

Figure 3.15   Golf Stats

	A	B	C	D	E	F	G	H	I	J	K	L	M	N
1	Rank	Player	Age	Events	Rounds	Cuts Made	Top 10s	Wins	Earnings	Yards/Drive	Driving Accuracy	Greens in Regulation	Putting Average	Sand Save Pct
2	1	Luke Donald	34	19	67	17	14	2	6,683,215	284.1	64.3	67.3	1.7	59.1
3	2	Webb Simpson	26	26	98	23	12	2	6,347,354	296.2	61.9	69.8	1.731	52
4	3	Nick Watney	30	22	77	19	10	2	5,290,674	301.9	58.2	66.9	1.738	48.1
5	4	K.J. Choi	41	22	75	18	8	1	4,434,691	285.6	62	65.9	1.787	55.6
6	5	Dustin Johnson	27	21	71	17	6	1	4,309,962	314.2	57.2	68.4	1.759	41.5
7	6	Matt Kuchar	33	24	88	22	9	0	4,233,920	286.2	64.7	67	1.735	58.9
8	7	Bill Haas	29	26	92	22	7	1	4,088,637	296.6	63.6	69.4	1.775	43.9
9	8	Steve Striker	44	19	69	18	5	2	3,992,785	288.8	62.5	66	1.71	52.1
10	9	Jason Day	24	21	73	18	10	0	3,962,647	302.6	54.7	64.9	1.737	61
11	10	David Toms	45	23	79	16	7	1	3,858,090	279.1	71.8	66.6	1.749	55.9

© Cengage Learning

Objective   To use scatterplots to search for relationships in the golf data.

Solution

Scatterplots are great for initial exploration of the data. If a scatterplot suggests a relationship between two variables, other methods can then be used to examine this relationship in more depth.

This example is typical in that there are many numerical variables, and it is up to you to search for possible relationships. A good first step is to ask some interesting questions and then try to answer them with scatterplots. For example, do younger players play more events? Are earnings related to age? Which is related most strongly to earnings: driving, putting, or greens in regulation? Do the answers to these questions remain the same from year to year? This example is all about *exploring* the data, and we will answer only a few of the questions that could be asked. Fortunately, scatterplots are easy to create, especially with StatTools, so you can do a lot of exploring very quickly.

It is possible to create a scatterplot with Excel tools only—that is, without StatTools. To do so, you highlight any two variables of interest and select a scatter chart of the top left type from the Insert ribbon. At this point, you will probably want to modify the chart by deleting the legend, inserting some titles, and possibly changing some formatting. Also, you might want to swap the roles of the X and Y variables. The point is that you can do it, but the process is somewhat tedious, especially if you want to create a *lot* of scatterplots.

Excel Tip: Selecting Multiple Ranges Efficiently
How do you select two long variables such as Age and Earnings? Here are the steps that make it easy. (1) Select the Age label in cell B1. (2) Hold down the Shift and Ctrl keys and press the down arrow key. This selects the Age column. (3) Hold down the Ctrl key and select the Earnings label in cell H1. (4) Hold down the Shift and Ctrl keys and press the down arrow key. Now both columns are selected.

StatTools allows you to create many scatterplots at once. Just select multiple X variables and/or multiple Y variables.

It is much easier to use StatTools. Begin by designating a StatTools data set called 2011 Data (to distinguish it from data sets you might want to create for the other years). Then select Scatterplot from the Summary Graphs dropdown list. In the resulting dialog box shown in Figure 3.16, you *must* select at least one X variable and at least one Y variable. However, you are allowed to select multiple X variables and/or multiple Y variables. Then a scatterplot will be created for *each* X-Y pair selected. For example, if you want to see how a number of variables are related to Earnings, you can select Earnings as the Y variable and the others as X variables, as shown in the figure. Note that StatTools shows the associated correlation below each scatterplot if you check the Display Correlation Coefficient option. Correlations will be discussed shortly.

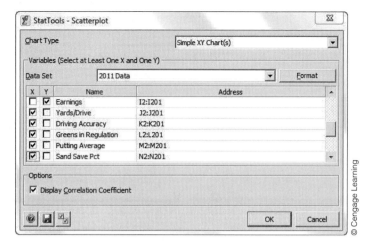

Figure 3.16
StatTools Scatterplot
Dialog Box

Several scatterplots appear in Figures 3.17 through 3.20. (In a few of these, we modified the scale on the horizontal axis so that the scatter fills the chart.) The scatterplots in Figure 3.17 indicate the possibly surprising results that age is practically unrelated to the number of events played and earnings. Each scatter is basically a shapeless swarm of points, and a shapeless swarm always indicates "no relationship." The scatterplots in Figure 3.18 confirm what you would expect. Specifically, players who play in more events

Figure 3.17   Scatterplots of Age Versus Events and Earnings

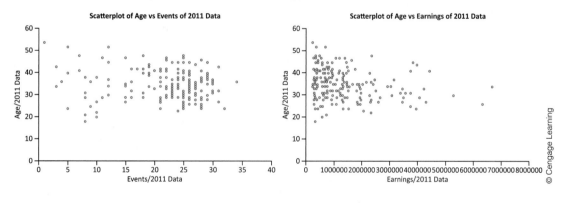

Figure 3.18   Scatterplots of Earnings Versus Events and Cuts Made

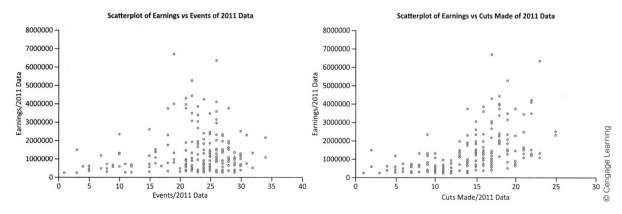

tend to earn more, although there are a number of exceptions to this pattern. Also, players who make more 36-hole cuts tend to earn more.

Remember that all StatTools charts are really Excel charts, so you can modify them as you like with the usual Excel chart tools.

Excel Tip: Data Labels in Scatterplots

Unfortunately, there is no automatic way to enter a label such as "Luke Donald" next to a point in a scatterplot. We had to insert the text boxes manually in Figure 3.18. If you click twice on a point (don't double-click, but slowly click twice), you can select this point. Then if you right-click, you have the option of adding a data label. However, this data label is always the value of the Y variable. In this case, it would be Luke's earnings, not his name.

StatTools Tip: Selecting Multiple Variables in StatTools

If you right-click the X or Y label in the StatTools Scatterplot dialog box, you can select or deselect all variables in the list. This is a handy shortcut if there are many variables. This same shortcut is available elsewhere in StatTools, such as in the Correlations and Covariances dialog box discussed next.

StatTools Tip: New Scatterplot Options in StatTools 6.0

*There are two new features in StatTools 6.0 scatterplots. First, you are allowed to check both the X and Y boxes for any variable. By doing this for several variables, you can easily get a matrix of scatterplots, where each variable is plotted against each other variable. For example, the finished version of the golf stats file has a matrix of scatterplots for 2010 and another for 2011. If you want to see how variables are related to Earnings, look at the Earnings "row" of scatterplots. Second, in the Chart Type dropdown list, you can select **Break Down by Categorical Variable**. This allows you to select a categorical variable such as Gender. Then all resulting scatterplots will color all Male points one color and all Female points another color.*

Golfers will be particularly interested in the scatterplots in Figures 3.19 and 3.20. First, the scatterplots in Figure 3.19 indicate almost no relationships between earnings and the two components of driving, length (yards per drive) and accuracy (percentage of fairways hit). At least in 2011, neither driving length nor driving accuracy seems to have much effect on earnings. In contrast, there is a reasonably strong upward relationship between greens hit in regulation and earnings. You would probably expect players who hit a lot of greens in regulation to earn more, and this appears to be the case. Finally, there is a definite *downward* relationship between putting average and earnings. Does this mean that better putters earn *less*? Absolutely not! The putting stat is the average number of putts per hole,

Figure 3.19 Scatterplots of Earnings Versus Driving Length and Driving Accuracy

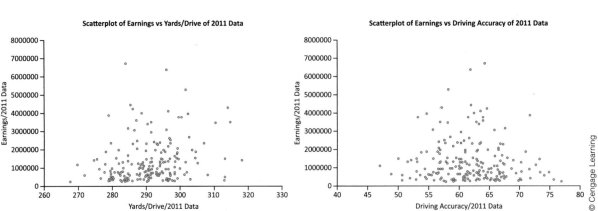

Figure 3.20 Scatterplots of Earnings Versus Greens in Regulation and Putting Average

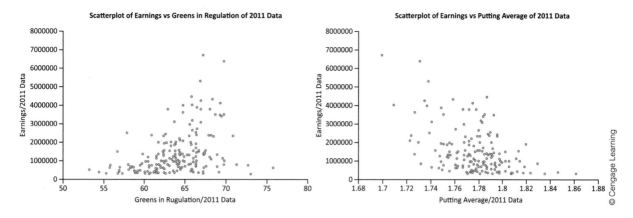

so that a *lower* value is better. Therefore, the downward relationship indicated in the chart is expected. In fact, the driving and putting scatterplots tend to confirm the old saying in golf: Drive for show, putt for dough.

You could obviously ask many more questions about the relationships in this golf data set and then attempt to answer them with scatterplots. For example, are the relationships (or lack of them) in the above scatterplots consistent through the years? Or should Earnings per Round be used instead of Earnings as the Y variable? Or are there other variables not shown here, such as the percentage of putts of less than 10 feet made, that are more highly related to Earnings? You now have a powerful tool, scatterplots, for examining relationships, and the tool is easy to implement. We urge you to use it—a lot. ■

Trend Lines in Scatterplots

Excel allows you to superimpose a trend line, linear or curved, on a scatterplot. It is an easy way to quantify the relationship apparent in the scatterplot.

Chapters 10 and 11 discuss regression, a method for quantifying relationships between variables. We can provide a gentle introduction to regression at this point by discussing the very useful Trendline tool in Excel. Once you have a scatterplot, Excel enables you to superimpose one of several trend lines on the scatterplot. Essentially, a **trend line** is a line or curve that "fits" the scatter as well as possible. This could indeed be a straight line, or it could be one of several types of curves. (By the way, you can also superimpose a trend line on a time series graph, exactly as described here for scatterplots.)

To illustrate the Trendline option, we created the scatterplot of driving length versus driving accuracy in Figure 3.21. If you are a golfer, you are probably not surprised to see that the longest hitters tend to be less accurate. This scatterplot is definitely downward sloping, and it appears to follow a straight line reasonably well.

Therefore, it is reasonable to fit a linear trend line to this scatterplot. To do this, right-click on any point on the chart, select Add Trendline, and fill out the resulting dialog box as shown in Figure 3.22. Note that we have checked the Display Equation on Chart option. The result (after moving the equation to a blank part of the chart) appears in Figure 3.23. The equation you see is a regression equation. It states that driving length (y) is 356.81 minus 1.0623 times driving accuracy (x). This line is certainly not a perfect fit because there are many points well above the line and others below the line. Still, it quantifies the downward relationship reasonably well.

Figure 3.21

Scatterplots of
Driving Length
Versus Driving
Accuracy

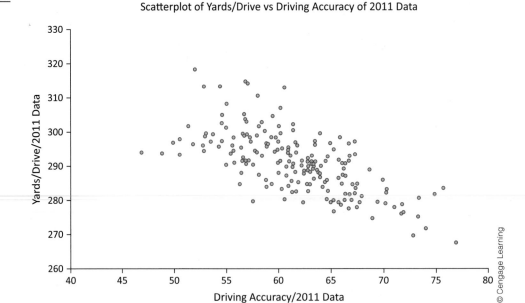

Figure 3.22

More Trendline
Options Dialog Box

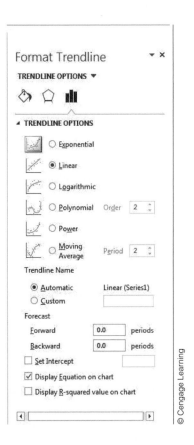

The tools in this subsection, scatterplots and trend lines superimposed on scatterplots, are among the most valuable tools you will learn in the book. When you are interested in a possible relationship between two numerical variables, these are the tools you should use first.

Figure 3.23

Scatterplot with
Trend Line
and Equation
Superimposed

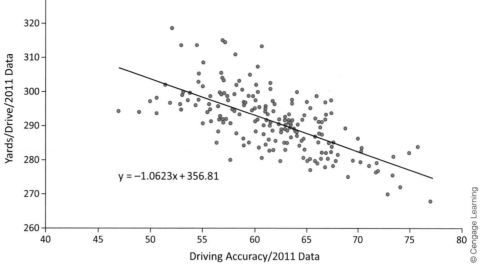

Scatterplot of Yards/Drive vs Driving Accuracy of 2011 Data

$y = -1.0623x + 356.81$

© Cengage Learning

3-4b Correlation and Covariance

Many numerical summary measures were discussed in Chapter 2, all of which involve a *single* variable. The two measures discussed in this section, correlation and covariance, involve *two* variables. Specifically, each measures the strength and direction of a *linear* relationship between two numerical variables. Intuitively, the relationship is "strong" if the points in a scatterplot cluster tightly around some straight line. If this straight line rises from left to right, the relationship is *positive* and the measures will be positive numbers. If it falls from left to right, the relationship is *negative* and the measures will be negative numbers.

To measure the covariance or correlation between two numerical variables X and Y—indeed, to form a scatterplot of X versus Y—X and Y must be "paired" variables. That is, they must have the same number of observations, and the X and Y values for any observation should be naturally paired. For example, each observation could be the height and weight for a particular person, the time in a store and the amount purchased for a particular customer, and so on.

With this in mind, let X_i and Y_i be the paired values for observation i, and let n be the number of observations. Then the **covariance** between X and Y, denoted by Covar(X, Y), is given by the following formula.

Formula for Covariance

$$\text{Covar}(X, Y) = \frac{\sum_{i=1}^{n}(X_i - \overline{X})(Y_i - \overline{Y})}{n - 1} \tag{3.1}$$

You will probably never have to use Equation (3.1) directly—Excel has a built-in COVAR function that does it for you, and StatTools also calculates covariances automatically—but the formula does indicate what covariance is all about. It is essentially an average of products of deviations from means. If X and Y vary in the *same* direction, then when X is above its mean, Y will tend to be above its mean, and when X is below its mean,

Y will tend to be below its mean. In either case, the product of deviations will be positive—a positive times a positive or a negative times a negative—so the covariance will be positive. The opposite is true when *X* and *Y* vary in *opposite* directions. Then the covariance will be negative.

CHANGES IN EXCEL 2010

Excel's old COVAR function actually uses denominator *n*, so it gives the population covariance, not the sample covariance (denominator *n*–1) in Equation (3.1). Starting in Excel 2010, both versions are available, named COVARIANCE.P (population) and COVARIANCE.S (sample).

Covariance is too sensitive to the measurement scales of X and Y to make it interpretable, so it is better to rely on correlation, which is unaffected by measurement scales.

Covariance has a serious limitation as a descriptive measure because it is very sensitive to the *units* in which *X* and *Y* are measured. For example, the covariance can be inflated by a factor of 1000 simply by measuring *X* in dollars rather than thousands of dollars. This limits the usefulness of covariance as a descriptive measure, and we will use it very little in the book.[3]

In contrast, the **correlation**, denoted by Correl(*X*, *Y*), remedies this problem. It is a *unitless* quantity that is unaffected by the measurement scale. For example, the correlation is the same regardless of whether the variables are measured in dollars, thousands of dollars, or millions of dollars. The correlation is defined by Equation (3.2), where Stdev(*X*) and Stdev(*Y*) denote the standard deviations of *X* and *Y*. Again, you will probably never have to use this formula for calculations—Excel does it for you with the built-in CORREL function, and StatTools also calculates correlations automatically—but it does show how correlation and covariance are related to one another.

Formula for Correlation

$$\text{Correl}(X, \ Y) = \frac{\text{Covar}(X, \ Y)}{\text{Stdev}(X) \ \times \ \text{Stdev}(Y)} \tag{3.2}$$

Correlation is useful only for measuring the strength of a linear relationship. Strongly related variables can have correlation close to 0 if the relationship is nonlinear.

The correlation is not only unaffected by the units of measurement of the two variables, but it is *always* between −1 and +1. The closer it is to either of these two extremes, the closer the points in a scatterplot are to a straight line, either in the negative or positive direction. On the other hand, if the correlation is close to 0, the scatterplot is typically a "cloud" of points with no apparent relationship. However, although it is not common, it is also *possible* that the points are close to a curve and have a correlation close to 0. This is because correlation is relevant only for measuring *linear* relationships.

When there are several numerical variables in a data set, it is useful to create a table of covariances and/or correlations. Each value in the table then corresponds to a particular pair of variables. StatTools allows you to do this easily, as illustrated in the following continuation of the golf example. However, we first make three important points about the roles of scatterplots, correlations, and covariances.

- **A correlation is a single-number summary of a scatterplot.** It never conveys as much information as the full scatterplot; it only summarizes the information in the scatterplot. Still, it is often more convenient to report a table of correlations for many variables than to report an unwieldy number of scatterplots.

- **You are usually on the lookout for large correlations, those near −1 or +1.** But how large is "large"? There is no generally agreed-upon cutoff, but by looking at a

---

[3]Don't write off covariance too quickly, however. If you plan to take a finance course in investments, you will see plenty of covariances.

number of scatterplots and their corresponding correlations, you will start to get a sense of what a correlation such as −0.5 or +0.7 really means in terms of the strength of the linear relationship between the variables. (In addition, a concrete meaning will be given to the *square* of a correlation in Chapters 10 and 11.)

■ **Do not even try to interpret covariances numerically except possibly to check whether they are positive or negative.** For interpretive purposes, concentrate on correlations.

EXAMPLE | 3.3 GOLF STATS (CONTINUED)

In the previous subsection, you saw how relationships between several of the golf variables can be detected with scatterplots. What further insights are possible by looking at correlations between these variables?

Objective To use correlations to understand relationships in the golf data.

Solution

With the many numerical variables in the golf data set, it is indeed unwieldy to create scatterplots for all pairs of variables, but it is easy to create a table of correlations with StatTools.[4] (If you want only one correlation, you can instead use Excel's CORREL function.) As an example, we will create a table of correlations for the golf data in 2011. To do so, select Correlation and Covariance from the Summary Statistics dropdown list, and fill in the resulting dialog box as shown in Figure 3.24. There are several options. First, you can check as many numerical variables as you like. We checked a few but not all. Second, you can ask for a table of correlations and/or a table of covariances. (There is a third option, new to StatTools 6.0, where you can ask for Spearman rank-order correlations, but this option is not discussed here.) We asked for correlations only. Finally, correlations (and covariances) are symmetric in that the correlation between any two variables X and Y is the same as the correlation between Y and X. Therefore, you can choose any of the three table structure options and receive exactly the same information. We tend to favor the Entries Below the Diagonal Only option.

You typically scan a table of correlations for the large correlations, either positive or negative. Conditional formatting is useful, especially if the table is a large one.

The resulting table of correlations appears in Figure 3.25. You can ignore the 1.000 values along the diagonal because a variable is always perfectly correlated with itself. Besides these, you are typically looking for relatively large values, either positive or negative. When the table is fairly large, conditional formatting is useful. Although it doesn't show up on the printed page, we formatted all correlations between 0.6 and 0.999 as red and all correlations between −1.0 and −0.6 as green. (See the finished version of the golf file for instructions on how to create the conditional formatting.) There are three large positive values involving events, rounds, and cuts made. None of these should come as a

---

[4]Remember that version 6.0 of StatTools can easily create a *matrix* of scatterplots, but this can be a lot of information to digest if it involves many variables.

Figure 3.24
StatTools
Correlation and
Covariance Dialog
Box

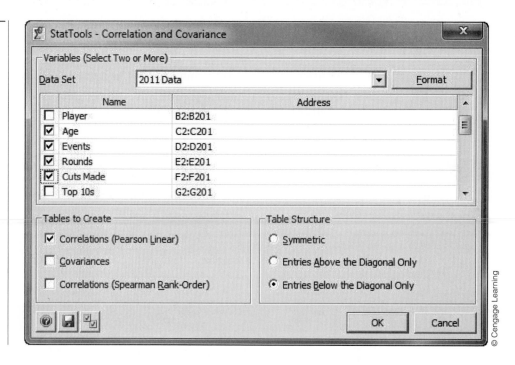

Figure 3.25 Correlations for Golf Data

	A	B	C	D	E	F	G	H	I	J	K
7		Age	Events	Rounds	Cuts Made	Earnings	Yards/Drive	Driving Accuracy	Greens in Regulation	Putting Average	Sand Save Pct
8	*Correlation Table*	2011 Data	2011 Data	2011 Data	2011 Data	2011 Data	2011 Data	2011 Data	2011 Data	2011 Data	2011 Data
9	Age	1.000									
10	Events	−0.094	1.000								
11	Rounds	−0.117	0.965	1.000							
12	Cuts Made	−0.175	0.748	0.884	1.000						
13	Earnings	−0.209	0.139	0.282	0.533	1.000					
14	Yards/Drive	−0.396	−0.008	0.040	0.140	0.238	1.000				
15	Driving Accuracy	0.294	0.050	0.071	0.046	−0.056	−0.666	1.000			
16	Greens in Reg.	−0.031	−0.114	−0.002	0.214	0.400	0.090	0.241	1.000		
17	Putting Average	0.170	0.118	−0.082	−0.316	−0.461	0.000	0.115	0.045	1.000	
18	Sand Save Pct	0.220	−0.143	−0.090	0.027	0.161	−0.358	0.156	0.050	−0.306	1.000

surprise. There is only one large negative correlation, the one between driving length and driving accuracy, and you already saw the corresponding scatterplot in Figure 3.21. So if you want to know what a correlation of approximately −0.6 actually means, look at the scatterplot in this figure. It indicates a definite downward trend, but there is still quite a lot of variability around the best-fitting straight line.

Again, a correlation is only a summary of a scatterplot. Therefore, you can learn more about any interesting-looking correlations by creating the corresponding scatterplot. For example, the scatterplot corresponding to the 0.884 correlation between Cuts Made and Rounds appears in Figure 3.26. (We also superimposed a trend line.) This chart shows the strong linear relationship between cuts made and rounds played, but it also shows that there is still considerable variability around the best-fitting straight line, even with a correlation as large as 0.884. ∎

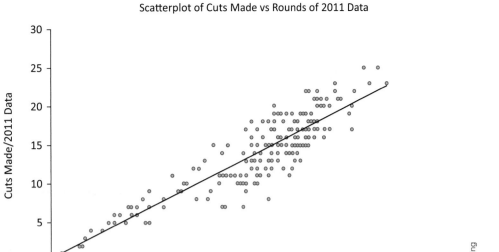

Figure 3.26
Scatterplot of Cuts Made Versus Rounds

Scatterplot of Cuts Made vs Rounds of 2011 Data

Correlation   0.884

PROBLEMS

Level A

21. The file **P02_07.xlsx** includes data on 204 employees at the (fictional) company Beta Technologies.

   a. Create a table of correlations between the variables Age, Prior Experience, Beta Experience, Education, and Annual Salary. Which of the first four of these variables is most highly correlated (in a positive direction) with Annual Salary?

   b. Create scatterplots of Annual Salary (Y axis) versus each of Age, Prior Experience, Beta Experience, and Education.

   c. For the variable from part **a** most highly correlated with Annual Salary, create a (linear) trend line in its scatterplot with the corresponding equation shown in the chart. What does this equation imply about the relationship between the two variables? Be specific.

22. The file **P03_22.xlsx** lists financial data on movies released since 1980 with budgets of at least $20 million.

   a. Reduce the size of this data set by deleting all movies with a budget of more than $100 million. Also, delete all movies where US Gross and/or Worldwide Gross is listed as Unknown.

   b. For the remaining movies, create a table of correlations between the variables Budget, US Gross, and Worldwide Gross. Comment on the results. Are there any surprises?

   c. For the movies remaining after part **a**, create a scatterplot of Worldwide Gross (Y axis) versus US Gross and another scatterplot of US Gross (Y axis) versus Budget. Briefly explain any patterns you see in these scatterplots. Do they seem to be consistent with the corresponding correlations?

23. The file **P02_10.xlsx** contains midterm and final exam scores for 96 students in a corporate finance course.

   a. Do the students' scores for the two exams tend to go together, so that those who do poorly on the midterm tend to do poorly on the final, and those who do well on the midterm tend to do well on the final? Create a scatterplot, along with a correlation, to answer this question.

   b. Superimpose a (linear) trend line on the scatterplot, along with the equation of the line. Based on this equation, what would you expect a student with a 75 on the midterm to score on the final exam?

24. Recall that the file **Golf Stats.xlsx** contains data on the 200 top golfers each year from 2003 to 2011. The question to be explored in this problem is what drives earnings, and whether this is consistent from year to year.

a. For at least three of the years, create two new variables, Birdies/Round and Earnings/Event. The latter is potentially a better measure of earnings because some players enter more events than others.

b. Create a separate table of correlations for each of the selected years that includes Earnings/Event, Yards/Drive, Driving Accuracy, Greens in Regulation, Putting Average, Sand Save Pct, and Birdies/Round. (StatTools will warn you about missing data, but don't worry about it.) Explain whether these correlations help answer the questions posed above.

c. There is a saying in golf: "Drive for show, putt for dough." Create a separate set of scatterplots for each of the selected years of Earnings/Event (Y axis) versus each of Yards/Drive, Driving Accuracy, and Putting Average. Discuss whether these scatterplots tend to support the saying.

25. The file **P02_02.xlsx** contains data about 211 movies released in 2006 and 2007. The question to be explored in this problem is whether the total gross for a movie can be predicted from how it does in its first week or two.

a. Create a table of correlations between the five variables 7-day Gross, 14-day Gross, Total US Gross, International Gross, and US DVD Sales. (StatTools will warn you about missing data, but don't worry about it.) Does it appear that the last three variables are related to either of the first two?

b. Explore the basic question further by creating a scatterplot of each of Total US Gross, International Gross, and US DVD Sales (Y axis) versus each of 7-day Gross and 14-day Gross (X axis)—six scatterplots in all. Do these support the claim that you can tell how well a movie will do by seeing how it does in its first week or two?

26. The file **P02_39.xlsx** lists the average high school student scores on the SAT exam by state. There are three components of the SAT: critical reading, math, and writing. These components are listed, along with their sum. The percentage of all potential students who took the SAT is also listed by state. Create correlations and scatterplots to explore the following relationships and comment on the results.

a. The relationship between the combined score and the percentage taking the exam.

b. The relationship between the critical reading and writing components.

c. The relationship between a combined verbal component (the average of critical reading and writing) and the math component.

d. The relationship between each of critical reading, math, and writing with the combined score. Are these bound to be highly correlated because the

sum of the three components *equals* the combined score?

27. The file **P02_16.xlsx** contains traffic data from 256 weekdays on four variables. Each variable lists the number of arrivals during a specific 5-minute period of the day.

a. What would it mean, in the context of traffic, for the data in the four columns to be positively correlated? Based on your observations of traffic, would you expect positive correlations?

b. Create a table of correlations and check whether these data behave as you would expect.

28. The file **P02_11.xlsx** contains data on 148 houses that were recently sold in a (fictional) suburban community. The data set includes the selling price of each house, along with its appraised value, square footage, number of bedrooms, and number of bathrooms.

a. Create a table of correlations between all of the variables. Comment on the magnitudes of the correlations. Specifically, which of the last three variables, Square Feet, Bedrooms, and Bathrooms, are highly correlated with Selling Price?

b. Create four scatterplots to show how the other four variables are related to Selling Price. In each, Selling Price should be on the Y axis. Are these in line with the correlations in part **a**?

c. You might think of the difference, Selling Price minus Appraised Value, as the "error" in the appraised value, in the sense that this difference is how much more or less the house sold for than the appraiser expected. Find the correlation between this difference and Selling Price, and find the correlation between the *absolute value* of this difference and Selling Price. If either of these correlations is reasonably large, what is it telling us?

Level B

29. The file **P03_29.xlsx** contains monthly prices of four precious metals: gold, silver, platinum, and palladium. The question to be explored here is whether changes in these commodities move together through time.

a. Create time series graphs of the four series. Do the series appear to move together?

b. Create four new difference variables, one for each metal. Each should list this month's price minus the previous month's price. Then create time series graphs of the differences. Note that there will be missing data for Jan-97 because the Dec-96 prices are not listed. Also, because the source for this data set listed prices for platinum and palladium through Nov-08 only, there will be missing data at the end of these series.

c. Create a table of correlations between the differences created in part **b**. Based on this table, comment on whether the changes in the prices of these metals tend to move together over time.

d. For all correlations in part **c** above 0.6, create the corresponding scatterplots of the differences (for example, gold differences versus silver differences). Do these, along with the time series graphs from parts **a** and **b**, provide a clearer picture of how these series move together over time? Discuss in some detail.

e. Check with your own formulas using Excel's CORREL function that StatTools uses data through Dec-09 for the correlation between gold and silver, but it uses data through Nov-08 for correlations between gold and platinum. That is, check that StatTools uses all of the available data for either correlation.

30. The file **P03_30.xlsx** contains monthly data on exchange rates of various currencies versus the U.S. dollar. It is of interest to financial analysts and economists to see whether exchange rates move together through time. You could find the correlations between the exchange rates themselves, but it is often more useful with time series data to check for correlations between *differences* from month to month.

a. Create a column of differences for each currency. For example, the difference corresponding to Jan-06 will be blank for each currency because the Dec-05 value isn't listed, but the difference for euros in Feb-06 will be 0.8375 − 0.8247.

b. Create a table of correlations between all of the *original* variables. Then on the same sheet, create a second table of correlations between the difference variables. On this same sheet, enter two cutoff values, one positive such as 0.6 and one negative such as −0.5, and use conditional formatting to color all correlations (in both tables) above the positive cutoff green and all correlations below the negative cutoff red. Do it so that the 1s on the diagonal are not colored.

c. Based on the second table and your coloring, can you conclude that these currencies tend to move together in the same direction? If not, what can you conclude?

d. Can you explain how the correlation between two currencies like the Chinese yuan and British pound can be fairly highly negatively correlated, whereas the correlation between their differences is essentially zero? Would you conclude that these two currencies "move together?" (*Hint*: There is no easy answer, but scatterplots and time series graphs for these two currencies and their differences are revealing.)

31. The file **P02_35.xlsx** contains data from a survey of 500 randomly selected (fictional) households.

a. Create a table of correlations between the last five variables (First Income to Debt). On the sheet with these correlations, enter a "cutoff" correlation such as 0.5 in a blank cell. Then use conditional

formatting to color green all correlations in the table at least as large as this cutoff, but don't color the 1s on the diagonal. The coloring should change automatically as you change the cutoff. This is always a good idea for highlighting the "large" correlations in a correlations table.

b. When you create the table of correlations, you are warned about the missing values for Second Income. Do some investigation to see how StatTools deals with missing values and correlations. There are two basic possibilities (and both of these are options in some software packages). First, it could delete all rows that have missing values for *any* variables and then calculate all of the correlations based on the remaining data. Second, when it creates the correlation for any *pair* of variables, it could (temporarily) delete only the rows that have missing data for these two variables and then calculate the correlation on what remains for these two variables. Why would you prefer the second option? How does StatTools do it?

32. We have indicated that if you have two categorical variables and you want to check whether they are related, the best method is to create a crosstabs, possibly with the counts expressed as percentages. But suppose both categorical variables have only two categories and these variables are coded as dummy 0–1 variables. Then there is nothing to prevent you from finding the correlation between them with the same Equation (3.2) from this section, that is, with Excel's CORREL function. However, if we let $C(i, j)$ be the count of observations where the first variable has value i and the second variable has value j, there are only four joint counts that can have any bearing on the relationship between the two variables: $C(0,0)$, $C(0,1)$, $C(1,0)$, and $C(1,1)$. Let $C_1(1)$ be the count of 1s for the first variable and let $C_2(1)$ be the count of 1s for the second variable. Then it is clear that $C_1(1) = C(1,0) + C(1,1)$ and $C_2(1) = C(0,1) + C(1,1)$, so $C_1(1)$ and $C_2(1)$ are determined by the joint counts. It can be shown algebraically that the correlation between the two 0–1 variables is

$$\frac{nC(1,1) - C_1(1)C_2(1)}{\sqrt{C_1(1)(n - C_1(1))}\sqrt{C_2(1)(n - C_2(1))}}$$

To illustrate this, the file **P03_32.xlsx** contains two 0–1 variables. (The values were generated randomly.) Create a crosstabs to find the required counts, and use the above formula to calculate the correlation. Then use StatTools (or Excel's CORREL function) to find the correlation in the usual way. Do your two results match? (Again, we do not necessarily recommend finding correlations between 0–1 variables. A crosstabs is more meaningful and easier to interpret.)

3-5 PIVOT TABLES

We now discuss one of Excel's most powerful—and easy-to-use—tools, the **pivot table**. Pivot tables allow you to break the data down by categories so that you can see, for example, average sales by gender, by region of country, by time of day, or any combination of these. Sometimes pivot tables are used to display counts, such as the number of customers broken down by gender and region of country. These tables of counts, often called crosstabs or contingency tables, have been used by statisticians for years. However, crosstabs typically list only counts, whereas pivot tables can list counts, sums, averages, and other summary measures.[5]

It is easiest to understand pivot tables by means of examples, so we illustrate several possibilities in Example 3.4.

EXAMPLE | **3.4 CUSTOMER ORDERS AT ELECMART**

The file **Elecmart Sales.xlsx** (see Figure 3.27) contains data on 400 customer orders during a period of several months for the fictional Elecmart company.[6] There are several categorical variables and several numerical variables. The categorical variables include the day of week, time of day, region of country, type of credit card used, gender of customer, and buy category of the customer (high, medium, or low) based on previous behavior. Even the date variable can be treated as a categorical variable. The numerical variables include the number of items ordered, the total cost of the order, and the price of the highest-priced item purchased. How can the manager of Elecmart use pivot tables to summarize the data so that she can understand the buying patterns of her customers?

Objective To use pivot tables to break down the customer order data by a number of categorical variables.

Figure 3.27 Elecmart Data

	A	B	C	D	E	F	G	H	I	J
1	Date	Day	Time	Region	Card Type	Gender	Buy Category	Items Ordered	Total Cost	High Item
2	6-Mar	Tue	Morning	West	ElecMart	Female	High	4	$136.97	$79.97
3	6-Mar	Tue	Morning	West	Other	Female	Medium	1	$25.55	$25.55
4	6-Mar	Tue	Afternoon	West	ElecMart	Female	Medium	5	$113.95	$90.47
5	6-Mar	Tue	Afternoon	NorthEast	Other	Female	Low	1	$6.82	$6.82
6	6-Mar	Tue	Afternoon	West	ElecMart	Male	Medium	4	$147.32	$83.21
7	6-Mar	Tue	Afternoon	NorthEast	Other	Female	Medium	5	$142.15	$50.90
8	7-Mar	Wed	Evening	West	Other	Male	Low	1	$18.65	$18.65
9	7-Mar	Wed	Evening	South	Other	Male	High	4	$178.34	$161.93
10	7-Mar	Wed	Evening	West	Other	Male	Low	2	$25.83	$15.91
11	8-Mar	Thu	Morning	MidWest	Other	Female	Low	1	$18.13	$18.13
12	8-Mar	Thu	Morning	NorthEast	ElecMart	Female	Medium	2	$54.52	$54.38
13	8-Mar	Thu	Afternoon	South	Other	Male	Medium	2	$61.93	$56.32
14	9-Mar	Fri	Morning	NorthEast	ElecMart	Male	High	3	$147.68	$96.64
15	9-Mar	Fri	Afternoon	NorthEast	Other	Male	Low	1	$27.24	$27.24

© Cengage Learning

---

[5]To be fair, many other statistical software packages, such as SPSS and SAS, now emulate Excel pivot tables.

[6]Users of previous editions of the book will notice that the year in this data set has been changed from 2006 to 2012. This changes the days of the week in column B, so any pivot tables that use the Day field, such as the pivot table in Figure 3.41, will be different from before.

Solution

Pivot tables are perfect for breaking down data by categories. Many people refer to this as "slicing and dicing" the data.

First, we preview the results you can obtain. Pivot tables are useful for breaking down numerical variables by categories, or for counting observations in categories and possibly expressing the counts as percentages. So, for example, you might want to see how the average total cost for females differs from the similar average for males. Or you might simply want to see the percentage of the 400 sales made by females. Pivot tables allow you to find such averages and percentages easily.

Actually, you could find such averages or percentages without using pivot tables. For example, you could sort on gender and then find the average of the Female rows and the average of the Male rows. However, this takes time, and more complex breakdowns are even more difficult and time-consuming. They are all easy and quick with pivot tables. Besides that, the resulting tables can be accompanied with corresponding charts that require virtually no extra effort to create. Pivot tables are a manager's dream. Fortunately, Excel makes them a manager's *reality*.

As you can see, there is a new Recommended Pivot Tables option in Excel 2013. It guesses which pivot tables you might want.

We begin by building a pivot table to find the sum of Total Cost broken down by time of day and region of country. Although we show this in a number of screen shots, just to help you get the knack of it, the process takes only a few seconds after you gain some experience with pivot tables.

To start, click the PivotTable button at the far left on the Insert ribbon (see Figure 3.28). This produces the dialog box in Figure 3.29. The top section allows you to specify the

---

Figure 3.28 PivotTable Button on the Insert Ribbon

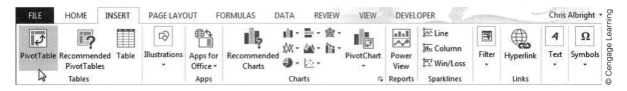

Figure 3.29

Create PivotTable Dialog Box

table or range that contains the data. (You can also specify an external data source, but we will not cover this option here.) The bottom section allows you to select the location where you want the results to be placed. If you start by selecting any cell inside the data set, Excel's guess for the table or range is usually correct, although you can override it if necessary. Make sure the range selected for this example is A1:J401. This selected range should include the variable names at the top of each column. Then click OK. Note that with these settings, the pivot table will be placed in a new worksheet with a generic name such as Sheet1. We recommend that you rename it something like PivotTable1.

This produces a blank pivot table, as shown in Figure 3.30. Also, assuming any cell inside this blank pivot table is selected, the PivotTable Tools "super tab" is visible. This super tab has two ribbons, Analzye and Design. (The Analyze ribbon was named Options in Excel 2007 and 2010. To avoid confusing users of those versions, we will refer to it as the Analyze/Options ribbon from here on.) The Analyze/Options ribbon appears in Figure 3.31, and the Design ribbon appears in Figure 3.32. Each of these has a variety of buttons for manipulating pivot tables, some of which we will explore shortly. Finally, the PivotTable Fields pane in Figure 3.33 is visible. By default, it is docked at the right of the screen, but you can move it if you like.

Note that the two pivot table ribbons and the PivotTable Fields pane are visible only when the active cell is inside a pivot table. If you click outside the pivot table, say, in cell D1, all three of these will disappear. Don't worry. You can get them back by selecting any cell inside the pivot table.

We refer to the PivotTable Tools Analyze/Options ribbon, but you will see it as either the Options ribbon (Excel 2010 and earlier) or the Analyze ribbon (Excel 2013).

Figure 3.30
Blank Pivot Table

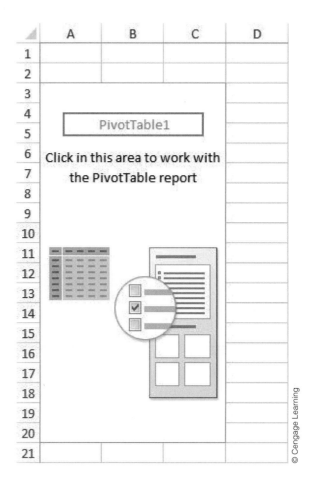

© Cengage Learning

Figure 3.31 PivotTable Analyze/Options Ribbon

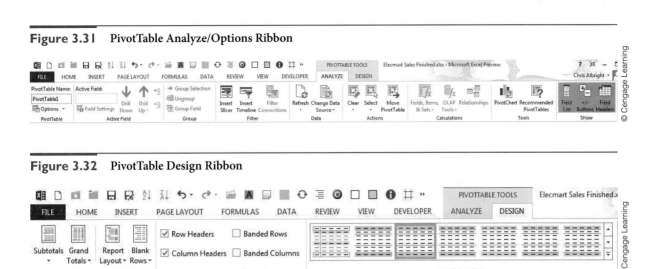

Figure 3.32 PivotTable Design Ribbon

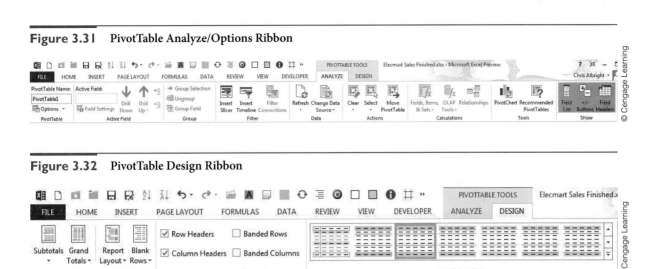

Figure 3.33
PivotTable Field List

The pivot table "look" changed considerably in Excel 2007, but the functionality is very similar.

If you have used pivot tables in a pre-2007 version of Excel, the blank pivot table in Figure 3.30 will look different. Here are two things to be aware of. First, if you open a file in the old .xls format (Excel 2003 or earlier) and go through the same steps as above, you will get an "old style" pivot table, as shown in Figure 3.34. Second, if you prefer the old style, Excel 2007 or later lets you revert back to it. To do so, right-click the pivot table, select PivotTable Options, select the Display tab, and check the Classic PivotTable layout option (see Figure 3.35).

Figure 3.34
Old-Style Blank
Pivot Table

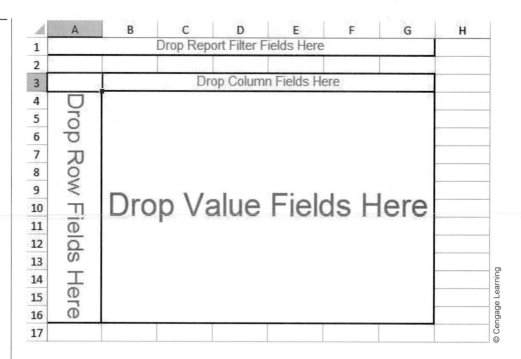

Figure 3.35
Switching to Classic
PivotTable Layout

The PivotTable Fields pane indicates that a pivot table has four areas. These are for Filters, Rows, Columns, and Values. They correspond to the four areas in Figure 3.34 where you can put fields.[7] Note that the terminology has changed slightly through different versions of Excel. The terminology used here is for Excel 2013.

Essentially, a Rows field has categories that go down the left side of a pivot table, a Columns field has categories that go across the top of a pivot table, a Filters field lets you filter the whole pivot table by its categories, and a Values field contains the data you want to summarize. Typically (but not always), you will place categorical variables in the Filters, Rows, and/or Columns areas, and you will place numeric variables in the Values area.

In the present example, check the Time, Region, and Total Cost boxes in the upper half of the PivotTable Fields pane. With no extra work whatsoever, you get the pivot table in Figure 3.36. It shows the sum of Total Cost, broken down by time of day and region of country. For example, the total cost of orders in the morning in the South was $3835.86, and the total cost of orders in the morning (over all regions) was $18,427.31.

Figure 3.36

Sum of Total Cost by Time and Region (Compact Layout)

	A	B
1		
2		
3	Row Labels ▼	Sum of Total Cost
4	⊟Afternoon	24265.6
5	MidWest	3187.16
6	NorthEast	8159.78
7	South	5729.72
8	West	7188.94
9	⊟Evening	18834.3
10	MidWest	2552.89
11	NorthEast	5941.49
12	South	3864.12
13	West	6475.8
14	⊟Morning	18427.31
15	MidWest	3878.22
16	NorthEast	5084.57
17	South	3835.86
18	West	5628.66
19	Grand Total	61527.21

© Cengage Learning

Excel applies two rules to variables checked at the top of the PivotTable Fields pane:

- When you check a text variable or a date variable in the field list, it is added to the Rows area.

- When you check a numeric variable in the field list, it is added to the Values area and summarized with the Sum function.

This is exactly what happens when you check Time, Region, and Total Cost. However, this is just the beginning. With very little work, you can do a lot more. Some of the many possibilities are explained in the remainder of this example.

First, however, we mention the new look of pivot tables in Excel 2007 and later. Notice that the pivot table in Figure 3.36 has *both* Rows fields, Time and Region, in column A. This wasn't possible in pre-2007 pivot tables, where the two Rows fields would have been in separate columns. Microsoft decided to offer this new layout because of its clean,

Starting with Excel 2007, there are three different layouts for pivot tables, but the differences are relatively minor. Ultimately, it is a matter of taste.

[7]In discussing pivot tables, Microsoft uses the term *field* rather than *variable*, so we will do so as well.

streamlined look. In fact, you can now choose from three layouts: Compact, Outline, or Tabular. These are available from the Report Layout dropdown list on the Design ribbon. When you create a pivot table (in an .xlsx file), you get the compact layout by default. If you would rather have the tabular or outline layout, it is easy to switch to them. In particular, the tabular layout, shown in Figure 3.37, is closer to what was used in pre-2007 versions of Excel. (Outline layout, not shown here, is very similar to tabular layout except for the placement of its subtotals.)

Figure 3.37

Sum of Total Cost by Time and Region (Tabular Layout)

	A	B	C
1			
2			
3	**Time** ▼	**Region** ▼	**Sum of Total Cost**
4	⊟**Afternoon**	MidWest	3187.16
5		NorthEast	8159.78
6		South	5729.72
7		West	7188.94
8	**Afternoon Total**		**24265.6**
9	⊟**Evening**	MidWest	2552.89
10		NorthEast	5941.49
11		South	3864.12
12		West	6475.8
13	**Evening Total**		**18834.3**
14	⊟**Morning**	MidWest	3878.22
15		NorthEast	5084.57
16		South	3835.86
17		West	5628.66
18	**Morning Total**		**18427.31**
19	**Grand Total**		**61527.21**

© Cengage Learning

One significant advantage to using tabular (or outline) layout instead of compact layout is that you can see which fields are in the Rows and Columns areas. Take another look at the pivot table in Figure 3.36. It is fairly obvious that categories such as Afternoon and Morning have to do with time of day and that categories such as Midwest and South have to do with region of country. However, there are no labels that explicitly name the Rows fields. In contrast, the tabular layout in Figure 3.37 names them explicitly. You can choose the layout you prefer.

Hiding Categories (Filtering)

The pivot table in Figure 3.36 shows all times of day for all regions, but this is not necessary. You can filter out any of the times or regions you don't want to see. To understand how this works, make sure the Analyze/Options ribbon is visible. In the Active Field group, you will notice that one of the fields is designated as the active field. The active field corresponds to the active cell. If the active cell contains a Time category, such as Evening, then Time is the active field. If the active cell contains a Region category such as NorthEast, then Region is the active field. If the active cell contains any of the numbers, then Sum of Total Cost is the active field.

Once you understand the active field concept, then the way Excel implements filtering makes sense. If Time is the active field and you click the Row Labels dropdown arrow, you see the dialog box in Figure 3.38. To see data only for Afternoon and Morning, for example, uncheck the Select All item and then check the Afternoon and Morning items. Similarly, if Region is the active field and you click the Row Labels dropdown arrow, you

Figure 3.38
Filtering on Time

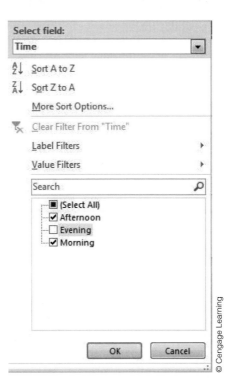

© Cengage Learning

can check the regions you want to filter on. (If you are in tabular layout, it is more straightforward, because each Rows field then has its own dropdown list.) For example, the pivot table in Figure 3.39 is obtained by filtering out the Evening and NorthEast categories. Note how the filter symbols replace the arrows in row 3 to indicate that some categories have been filtered out. Also, note that the updated subtotals for Morning and Afternoon and the updated grand total for all categories do *not* include the hidden categories.[8]

Figure 3.39
Pivot Table with
Hidden Categories

	A	B	C
1			
2			
3	**Time** ⬛	**Region** ⬛	**Sum of Total Cost**
4	⊟Afternoon	MidWest	3187.16
5		South	5729.72
6		West	7188.94
7	**Afternoon Total**		**16105.82**
8	⊟Morning	MidWest	3878.22
9		South	3835.86
10		West	5628.66
11	**Morning Total**		**13342.74**
12	**Grand Total**		**29448.56**

© Cengage Learning

Sorting on Values or Categories

It is easy to sort in a pivot table, either by the numbers in the Values area of the table or by the labels in a Rows or Columns field. To sort by the numbers in the Values area, right-click any number and select Sort. If a simple A–Z or Z–A sort isn't enough, you can select More Sort Options. For example, this allows you to sort on the *column* of numbers that contains the selected cell or on the *row* of numbers that contains this cell.

---

[8]You have probably noticed that the dialog box in Figure 3.38 is exactly like the one for Excel tables discussed in the previous chapter. This is no accident. You already learned how to filter tables, so there is nothing new to learn for filtering pivot tables.

To sort on the labels of a Rows or Columns field, you can again right-click any of the categories such as Morning and select Sort. Alternatively, you can click the drop-down arrow for the field, such as Time in Figure 3.39, and you will get the dialog box in Figure 3.38 that allows both sorting and filtering.

However, be aware that sorting on labels is always in alphabetical or reverse alphabetical order. This is not always what you want. For example, suppose you want the natural sort order: Morning, Afternoon, Evening. This isn't the A–Z or Z–A order, but it is still possible to sort *manually*. The trick is to select the cell of some label such as Morning and place the cursor on the border of the cell so that it becomes a four-sided arrow. Then you can drag the label up or down, or to the left or right. It takes a little practice, but it isn't difficult. The times of day in the remaining screenshots will be shown in the natural order: Morning, Afternoon, Evening. ∎

Changing Locations of Fields (Pivoting)

Starting with the pivot table in Figure 3.39, you can choose where to place either Time or Region; it does *not* have to be in the Rows area. To place the Region variable in the Columns area, for example, drag the Region button from the Rows area of the PivotTable Fields pane to the Columns area. The pivot table changes automatically, as shown in Figure 3.40. (We removed the filters on Time and Region.)

Figure 3.40

Placing Region in the Columns Area

	A	B	C	D	E	F
1						
2						
3	Sum of Total Cost	Column Labels ▼				
4	Row Labels ▼	MidWest	NorthEast	South	West	Grand Total
5	Morning	3878.22	5084.57	3835.86	5628.66	18427.31
6	Afternoon	3187.16	8159.78	5729.72	7188.94	24265.6
7	Evening	2552.89	5941.49	3864.12	6475.8	18834.3
8	Grand Total	9618.27	19185.84	13429.7	19293.4	61527.21

© Cengage Learning

Changing the locations of fields in pivot tables has always been easy, but the user interface introduced in Excel 2007 makes it even easier. We favor dragging the fields to the various areas, but you can experiment with the various options.

Alternatively, you can categorize by a third field such as Day and locate it in a different area. As before, if you check Day in the PivotTable Fields pane, it goes to the Rows area by default, but you can then drag it to another area. The pivot table in Figure 3.41 shows the result of placing Day in the Filters area. By clicking the dropdown arrow in row 1, you can then show the pivot table for all days or any particular day. In fact, you can check the Show Multiple Items option. (This option wasn't available before Excel 2007.) We checked this option and then selected Friday and Saturday to obtain the pivot table in Figure 3.41. It reports data only for Fridays and Saturdays.

Figure 3.41

Filtering on Day in the Filters Area

	A	B	C	D	E	F
1	Day	(Multiple Items) ▼				
2						
3	Sum of Total Cost	Column Labels ▼				
4	Row Labels ▼	MidWest	NorthEast	South	West	Grand Total
5	Morning	785.53	695.26	1382.32	2219.14	5082.25
6	Afternoon	147.93	1600.23	2009.2	1599.69	5357.05
7	Evening	247.35	2117.08	1632.31	2326.94	6323.68
8	Grand Total	1180.81	4412.57	5023.83	6145.77	16762.98

© Cengage Learning

This ability to categorize by multiple fields and rearrange the fields as you like is a big reason why pivot tables are so powerful and useful—and easy to use.

Changing Field Settings

Depending on which field is the active field, you can change various settings in the Field Settings dialog box. You can get to this dialog box in at least two ways. First, there is a Field Setting button on the Analyze/Options ribbon. Second, you can right-click any of the pivot table cells and select the Field Settings item. The field settings are particularly useful for fields in the Values area.

The key to summarizing the data the way you want it summarized is the Value Field Settings dialog box. Get used to it because you will use it often.

For now, right-click any number in the pivot table in Figure 3.41 and select Value Field Settings to obtain the dialog box in Figure 3.42. This allows you to choose how you want to summarize the Total Cost variable—by Sum, Average, Count, or several others. You can also click the Number Format button to choose from the usual number formatting options, and you can click the Show Values As tab to display the data in various ways (more on this later). If you choose Average and format as currency with two decimals, the resulting pivot table appears as in Figure 3.43. Now each number is the average of Total Cost for all orders in its combination of categories. For example, the average of Total Cost for all Friday and Saturday morning orders in the South is $107.69, and the average of *all* Friday and Saturday orders in the South is $109.10.

Figure 3.42
Value Field Settings Dialog Box

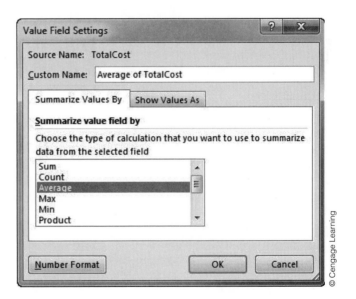

Figure 3.43
Pivot Table with Average of Total Cost

	A	B	C	D	E	F
1	Day	(Multiple Items) 🔽				
2						
3	Average of Total Cost	Column Labels 🔽				
4	Row Labels 🔽	MidWest	NorthEast	South	West	Grand Total
5	Morning	$157.11	$139.05	$153.59	$158.51	$154.01
6	Afternoon	$73.97	$145.48	$143.51	$159.97	$144.79
7	Evening	$82.45	$192.46	$163.23	$193.91	$175.66
8	Grand Total	$118.08	$163.43	$152.24	$170.72	$158.14

Pivot Charts

It is easy to accompany pivot tables with **pivot charts**. These charts are not just typical Excel charts; they adapt automatically to the underlying pivot table. If you make a change to the pivot table, such as pivoting the Rows and Columns fields, the pivot chart makes the same change automatically. To create a pivot chart, click anywhere inside the pivot table, select the PivotChart button on the Analyze/Options ribbon, and select a chart type. That's all there is to it. The resulting pivot chart (using the default column chart option) for the pivot table in Figure 3.43 appears in Figure 3.44. If you decide to pivot the Rows and Columns fields, the pivot chart changes automatically, as shown in Figure 3.45. Note that the categories on the horizontal axis are always based on the Rows field, and the categories in the legend are always based on the Columns field.

Figure 3.44

Pivot Chart Based on Pivot Table

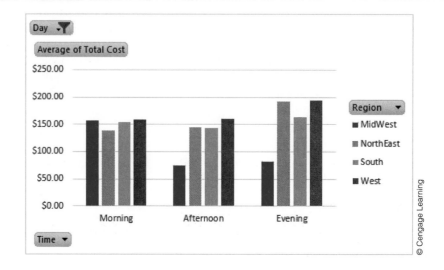

Figure 3.45

Pivot Chart after Pivoting Rows and Columns Fields

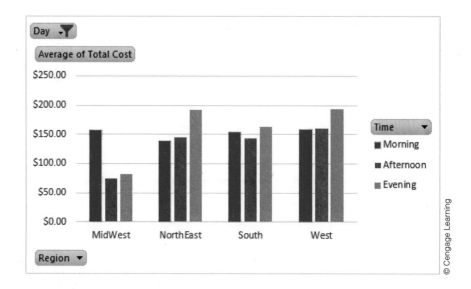

Note that when you activate a pivot chart, the PivotTable Tools "super tab" changes to PivotChart Tools. This super tab includes three ribbons for manipulating pivot charts: Analyze, Design, and Format (see Figure 3.46, where slight ribbon changes from Excel 2010 to Excel 2013 are again apparent). There is not enough space here to discuss the many options on these ribbons, but they are intuitive and easy to use. As usual, don't be afraid to experiment.

Figure 3.46   PivotChart Tools Tabs

Multiple Variables in the Values Area

More than a single variable can be placed in the Values area. In addition, a given variable in the Values area can be summarized by more than one summarizing function. This can create a rather busy pivot table, so we indicate our favorite way of doing it. Starting with the pivot table in Figure 3.43, drag Total Cost in the top of the PivotTable Fields pane (the item that is already checked) to the Values area. The bottom part of the Field List should now appear as in Figure 3.47, and the pivot table should now appear as in Figure 3.48. (The South and West regions have been filtered out to conserve space.) Note in particular the Values button in the Columns area. This button controls the placement of the data in the pivot table. You have a number of options for this button: (1) leave it where it is, (2) drag it above the Time button, (3) drag it to the Rows area, below the Region button, or (4) drag it to the Rows area, above the Region button. You can experiment with these options, but we tend to prefer option (2), which leads to the pivot table in Figure 3.49.

Figure 3.47

Choosing Two Values Fields

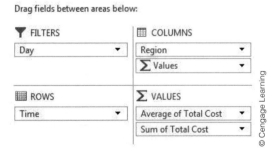

Figure 3.48   Pivot Table with Two Values Fields

	A	B	C	D	E	F	G
1	Day	(Multiple Items)					
2							
3		Column Labels					
4		MidWest		NorthEast		Total Average of Total Cost	Total Sum of Total Cost
5	Row Labels	Average of Total Cost	Sum of Total Cost	Average of Total Cost	Sum of Total Cost		
6	Morning	$157.11	785.53	$139.05	695.26	$148.08	1480.79
7	Afternoon	$73.97	147.93	$145.48	1600.23	$134.47	1748.16
8	Evening	$82.45	247.35	$192.46	2117.08	$168.89	2364.43
9	Grand Total	$118.08	1180.81	$163.43	4412.57	$151.17	5593.38

Figure 3.49

Rearranged Pivot
Table with Two
Values Fields

	A	B	C	D
1	Day	(Multiple Items) ⫪		
2				
3		Column Labels ⫪		
4	Row Labels ▾	MidWest	NorthEast	Grand Total
5	**Average of Total Cost**			
6	Morning	$157.11	$139.05	$148.08
7	Afternoon	$73.97	$145.48	$134.47
8	Evening	$82.45	$192.46	$168.89
9	**Sum of Total Cost**			
10	Morning	785.53	695.26	1480.79
11	Afternoon	147.93	1600.23	1748.16
12	Evening	247.35	2117.08	2364.43
13	**Total Average of Total Cost**	**$118.08**	**$163.43**	**$151.17**
14	**Total Sum of Total Cost**	**1180.81**	**4412.57**	**5593.38**

© Cengage Learning

In a similar manner, you can experiment with the buttons in the Values area. However, the effect here is less striking. If you drag the Sum of Total Cost button *above* the Average of Total Cost button in the field list, the effect is simply to switch the ordering of these summaries in the pivot table, as shown in Figure 3.50.

	A	B	C	D
1	Day	(Multiple Items) ⫪		
2				
3		Column Labels ⫪		
4	Row Labels ▾	MidWest	NorthEast	Grand Total
5	**Sum of Total Cost**			
6	Morning	785.53	695.26	1480.79
7	Afternoon	147.93	1600.23	1748.16
8	Evening	247.35	2117.08	2364.43
9	**Average of Total Cost**			
10	Morning	$157.11	$139.05	$148.08
11	Afternoon	$73.97	$145.48	$134.47
12	Evening	$82.45	$192.46	$168.89
13	**Total Sum of Total Cost**	**1180.81**	**4412.57**	**5593.38**
14	**Total Average of Total Cost**	**$118.08**	**$163.43**	**$151.17**

© Cengage Learning

Summarizing by Count

The variable in the Values area, whatever it is, can be summarized by the Count function. This is useful when you want to know, for example, how *many* of the orders were placed by females in the South. When summarizing by Count, the key is to understand that the actual variable placed in the Values area is *irrelevant*, so long as you summarize it by the Count function. To illustrate, start with the pivot table in Figure 3.43, where Total Cost is summarized with the Average function, and delete the Day filter. Next, right-click any number in the pivot table, select Value Field Settings, and select the Count function (see Figure 3.51). The default Custom Name you will see in this dialog box, Count of Total Cost, is misleading, because Total Cost has nothing to do with the counts obtained. Therefore, we like to change this Custom Name label to Count, as shown in the figure. The resulting pivot table,

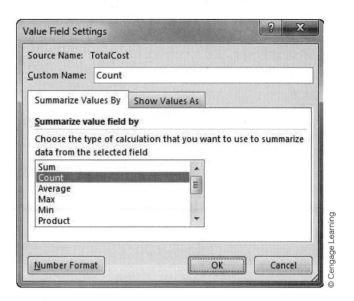

Figure 3.51

Field Settings Dialog Box with Count Selected

© Cengage Learning

with values formatted as numbers with zero decimals (and the filter on Day removed), appears in Figure 3.52. For example, 27 of the 400 orders were placed in the morning in the South, and 115 of the 400 orders were placed in the NorthEast. (Do you now see why the counts have nothing to do with Total Cost?) This type of pivot table, with counts for various categories, is the same as the *crosstabs* discussed in Section 3-2. However, it has now been created much more easily with a pivot table.

Counts can be displayed in a number of ways. You should choose the way that best answers the question you are asking.

When data are summarized by counts, there are a number of ways they can be displayed. The pivot table in Figure 3.52 shows "raw counts." Depending on the type of information you want, it might be more useful to display the counts as percentages. Three particular options are typically chosen: as percentages of total, as percentages of row totals, and as percentages of column totals. When shown as percentages of total, the percentages in the table sum to 100%; when shown as percentages of row totals, the percentages in *each* row sum to 100%; when shown as percentages of column totals, the percentages in *each* column sum to 100%. Each of these options can be useful, depending on the question you are trying to answer. For example, if you want to know whether the daily pattern of orders varies from region to region, showing the counts as percentages of column totals is useful so that you can compare columns. But if you want to see whether the regional ordering pattern varies by time of day, showing the counts as percentages of row totals is useful so that you can compare rows.

As an example, to display the counts as percentages of column totals, right-click any number in the pivot table, select **Show Values As**, and select the option you want.

Figure 3.52

Pivot Table with Counts

	A	B	C	D	E	F
1						
2						
3	Count	Column Labels ▼				
4	Row Labels ▼	MidWest	NorthEast	South	West	Grand Total
5	Morning	26	33	27	38	124
6	Afternoon	26	48	39	41	154
7	Evening	19	34	27	42	122
8	Grand Total	71	115	93	121	400

© Cengage Learning

(You can also get to these options from the **Show Values As** tab in the Value Field Settings dialog box in Figure 3.53.) The resulting pivot table and corresponding pivot chart appear in Figure 3.54. As you can see by comparing columns, the pattern of regional orders varies somewhat by time of day.

Figure 3.53
Value Field Settings Dialog Box with "Show Values As" Options

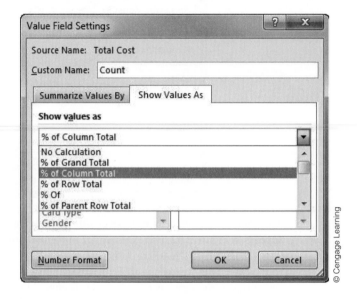

Figure 3.54
Pivot Table and Pivot Chart with Counts As Percentages of Column Totals

	A	B	C	D	E	F
1						
2						
3	Count	Column Labels ▾				
4	Row Labels ▾	MidWest	NorthEast	South	West	Grand Total
5	Morning	36.62%	28.70%	29.03%	31.40%	31.00%
6	Afternoon	36.62%	41.74%	41.94%	33.88%	38.50%
7	Evening	26.76%	29.57%	29.03%	34.71%	30.50%
8	Grand Total	100.00%	100.00%	100.00%	100.00%	100.00%

Sometimes it is useful to see the raw counts *and* the percentages. This can be done easily by dragging any variable to the Values area, summarizing it by Count, and displaying it as "Normal." Figure 3.55 shows one possibility, where we have changed the custom names of the two Count variables to make them more meaningful. Alternatively, the counts and percentages could be shown in two separate pivot tables.

Pivot Table Tip: Right-Clicking to Choose Options
We keep saying to make changes in the Value Field Settings dialog box. However, you can also make changes directly by right-clicking a value in the pivot table. For example, when you right-click a number in the Values area, you see Number Format, Summarize Values By, and Show Values As menu items, among others.

Grouping

Finally, categories in a Rows or Columns variable can be grouped. This is especially useful when a Rows or Columns variable has many distinct values. Because a pivot table creates a row or column for each distinct value, the results can be unwieldy. We present two possibilities. First, suppose you want to summarize Sum of Total Cost by Date. Starting with

Figure 3.55

Pivot Table with Percentages of Row Totals and Raw Counts

Row Labels	Column Labels ▼ MidWest	NorthEast	South	West	Grand Total
Raw Count					
Morning	26	33	27	38	124
Afternoon	26	48	39	41	154
Evening	19	34	27	42	122
Count of Column					
Morning	36.62%	28.70%	29.03%	31.40%	31.00%
Afternoon	36.62%	41.74%	41.94%	33.88%	38.50%
Evening	26.76%	29.57%	29.03%	34.71%	30.50%
Total Raw Count	71	115	93	121	400
Total Count of Column	100.00%	100.00%	100.00%	100.00%	100.00%

© Cengage Learning

a blank pivot table, check both Date and Total Cost in the PivotTable Fields pane. This creates a separate row for each distinct date in the data set—more than 100 separate dates. This is too much detail, so it is useful to group on the Date variable. To do so, right-click any date in column A and select Group. (Group options are also available on the Analyze/Options ribbon.) Accept the default selections in the Grouping dialog box (see Figure 3.56) to obtain the pivot table in Figure 3.57.

*Pivot Table Tip: **Grouping on Dates***

Suppose you have multiple years of data and you would like a monthly grouping such as January 2007 through December 2009. If you simply select Months as in Figure 3.56, all of the Januaries, for example, will be lumped together. The trick is to select both Months and Years in the dialog box.

Figure 3.56

Grouping Dialog Box

© Cengage Learning

Figure 3.57

Pivot Table after Grouping by Month

Row Labels ▼	Sum of Total Cost
Mar	$9,383.26
Apr	$14,589.91
May	$19,468.11
Jun	$18,085.93
Grand Total	**$61,527.21**

© Cengage Learning

As a second possibility for grouping, suppose you want to see how the average of Total Cost varies by the amount of the highest priced item in the order. You can drag Total Cost to the Values area, summarized by Average, and drag High Item to the Rows area. Because High Item has nearly 400 distinct values, the resulting pivot table is virtually worthless. Again, however, the trick is to group on the Rows variable. This time there are no natural groupings as there are for a date variable, so it is up to you to create the groupings. Excel provides a suggestion, as shown in Figure 3.58, but you can override it. For example, changing the bottom entry to 50 leads to the pivot table in Figure 3.59. Some experimentation is typically required to obtain the grouping that presents the results in the most appropriate way.

Figure 3.58

Grouping Dialog Box for a Non-Date Variable

Figure 3.59

Pivot Table after Grouping by 50 on High Item

	A	B
1		
2		
3	Row Labels ▾	Average of Total Cost
4	6.82-56.82	$72.78
5	56.82-106.82	$139.66
6	106.82-156.82	$172.71
7	156.82-206.82	$253.55
8	206.82-256.82	$324.26
9	256.82-306.82	$328.92
10	306.82-356.82	$361.53
11	356.82-406.82	$415.17
12	Grand Total	$153.82

By now, we have illustrated the pivot table features that are most commonly used. Be aware, however, that there are *many* more features available. These include (but are not limited to) the following:

- Showing/hiding subtotals and grand totals (check the Layout options on the Design ribbon)
- Dealing with blank rows, that is, categories with no data (right-click any number, choose PivotTable Options, and check the options on the Layout & Format tab)
- Displaying the data behind a given number in a pivot table (double-click any number in the Values area to get a new worksheet)
- Formatting a pivot table with various styles (check the style options on the Design ribbon)
- Moving or renaming pivot tables (check the PivotTable and Action groups on the Analyze/Options ribbon)
- Refreshing pivot tables as the underlying data changes (check the Refresh dropdown list on the Analyze/Options ribbon)
- Creating pivot table formulas for calculated fields or calculated items (check the Formulas dropdown list on the Analyze/Options ribbon)
- Basing pivot tables on external databases (not covered here)

Not only are these (and other) features available, but Excel usually provides more than one way to implement them. The suggestions above are just some of the ways they can be implemented. The key to learning pivot table features is to *experiment*. There are entire books written about pivot tables, but we don't recommend them. You can learn a lot more, and a lot more quickly, by experimenting with data such as the Elecmart data. Don't be afraid to mess up. Pivot tables are very forgiving, and you can always start over.

Excel Tip: **How Excel Stores Pivot Table Data**
When you create a pivot table, Excel stores a snapshot of your source data in memory in a pivot cache. The amount of memory depends on the size of the data source, but it can be large. Then if you create a second pivot table, even if it is based on the same data source, a second pivot cache is created. This is obviously a waste of memory if the same data source is cached for each extra pivot table. Fortunately, there is a workaround. If you copy the first pivot table and paste it to another location, you get a second pivot table, which can be manipulated independently of the first, but it is not accompanied by an extra pivot cache. So if you want to create multiple pivot tables from the same data source, this copy/paste approach is the way to go.

We complete this section by providing one last example to illustrate how pivot tables can answer business questions very quickly.

EXAMPLE | **3.5 FROZEN LASAGNA DINNERS**

The file **Lasagna Triers.xlsx** contains data on over 800 potential customers being tracked by a (fictional) company that has been marketing a frozen lasagna dinner. The file contains a number of demographics on these customers, as indicated in Figure 3.60: their age, weight, income, pay type, car value, credit card debt, gender, whether they live alone, dwelling type, monthly number of trips to the mall, and neighborhood. It also indicates whether they have tried the company's frozen lasagna. The company wants to understand why some potential customers are triers and others are not. Does gender make a difference? Does income make a difference? In general, what distinguishes triers from nontriers? How can the company use pivot tables to explore these questions?

Figure 3.60 Lasagna Trier Data

	A	B	C	D	E	F	G	H	I	J	K	L	M
1	Person	Age	Weight	Income	Pay Type	Car Value	CC Debt	Gender	Live Alone	Dwell Type	Mall Trips	Nbhd	Have Tried
2	1	48	175	65500	Hourly	2190	3510	Male	No	Home	7	East	No
3	2	33	202	29100	Hourly	2110	740	Female	No	Condo	4	East	Yes
4	3	51	188	32200	Salaried	5140	910	Male	No	Condo	1	East	No
5	4	56	244	19000	Hourly	700	1620	Female	No	Home	3	West	No
6	5	28	218	81400	Salaried	26620	600	Male	No	Apt	3	West	Yes
7	6	51	173	73000	Salaried	24520	950	Female	No	Condo	2	East	No
8	7	44	182	66400	Salaried	10130	3500	Female	Yes	Condo	6	West	Yes
9	8	29	189	46200	Salaried	10250	2860	Male	No	Condo	5	West	Yes
10	9	28	200	61100	Salaried	17210	3180	Male	No	Condo	10	West	Yes
11	10	29	209	9800	Salaried	2090	1270	Female	Yes	Apt	7	East	Yes

© Cengage Learning

Pivot tables, with counts in the Values area, are a great way to discover which variables have the largest effect on a Yes/No variable.

Objective To use pivot tables to explore which demographic variables help to distinguish lasagna triers from nontriers.

Solution

The key is to set up a pivot table that shows counts of triers and nontriers for different categories of any of the potential explanatory variables. For example, one such pivot table shows the percentages of triers and nontriers for males and females separately. If the percentages are different for males than for females, the company will know that gender has an effect. On the other hand, if the percentages for males and females are about the same, the company will know that gender does not make much of a difference.

The typical pivot table should be set up as shown in Figure 3.61. The Rows variable is any demographic variable you want to investigate—in this case, Gender. The Columns variable is Have Tried (Yes or No). The Values variable can be *any* variable, as long as it is expressed as a count. Finally, it is useful to show these counts as percentage of row totals. This way you can easily look down column C to see whether the percentage in one category (Female) who have tried the product is any different from the percentage in another category (Male) who have tried the product. As you can see, males are somewhat more likely to try the product than females: 60.92% versus 54.27%. This is also apparent from the associated pivot chart.

Figure 3.61   Pivot Table and Pivot Chart for Examining the Effect of Gender

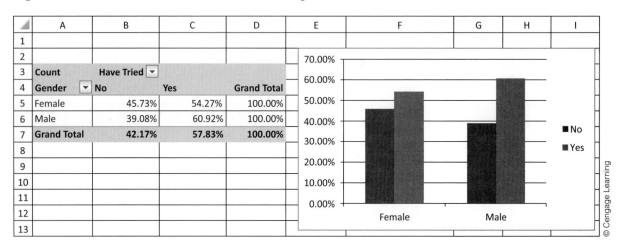

Once this generic pivot table and associated pivot chart are set up, you can easily explore other demographic variables by swapping them for Gender. For example, Figure 3.62 indicates that people who live alone are (not surprisingly) *much* more likely to try this frozen microwave product than people who don't live alone.

Figure 3.62   Pivot Table and Pivot Chart for Examining the Effect of Live Alone

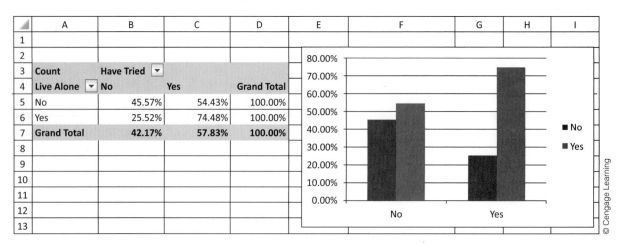

As another example, Figure 3.63 indicates that people with larger incomes are slightly more likely to try the product. There are two things to note about this income pivot table. First, because there are so many individual income values, grouping is useful. You can experiment with the grouping to get the most meaningful results. Second, you should be a bit skeptical about the last group, which has 100% triers. It is possible that there are only one or two people in this group. (It turns out that there are four.) For this reason, it is a good idea to create two pivot tables of the counts, one showing percentage of row totals and one showing the raw counts. This second pivot table is shown at the bottom of Figure 3.63.

Figure 3.63 Pivot Table and Pivot Chart for Examining the Effect of Income

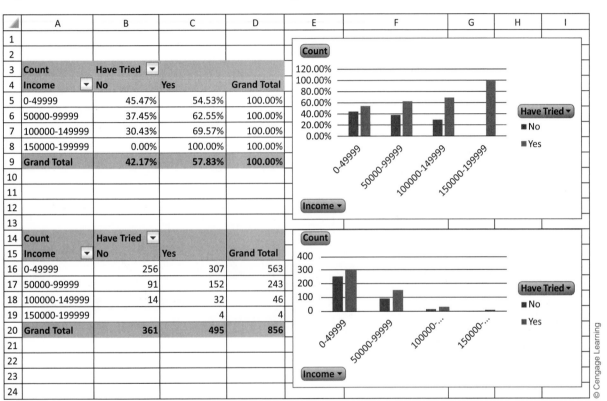

The problem posed in this example is a common one in real business situations. One variable indicates whether people are in one group or another (triers or nontriers), and there are a lot of other variables that could potentially explain why some people are in one group and others are in the other group. There are a number of sophisticated techniques for attacking this *classification* problem, and some of these are discussed in Chapter 17. However, you can go a long way toward understanding which variables are important by the simple pivot table method illustrated here. ∎

CHANGES IN EXCEL 2010 AND 2013

Microsoft made the already user-friendly pivot tables even friendlier in Excel 2010 with the addition of **slicers**. These are essentially lists of the distinct values of any variable, which you can then filter on. You add a slicer from the Analyze/Options ribbon under PivotTable Tools. For example, in the

Elecmart sales data, you can choose Region as a slicer. You then see a list on the screen with a button for each possible value: Midwest, Northeast, South, and West. You can then click any combination of these buttons to filter on the chosen regions. Note that a slicer variable does *not* have to be part of the pivot table. For example, if you are showing sum of Total Cost, and Region is not part of the pivot table, a Region slicer will still filter sum of Total Cost for the regions selected. On the other hand, if Region is already in the Rows area, say, you can filter on it through the slicer. In this case, selecting regions from the slicer is equivalent to filtering on the same regions in the Rows area. Basically, the slicers have been added as a convenience to users. They make filtering easier and more transparent.

A similar Timeline feature was added in Excel 2013. A timeline is like a slicer, but it is specifically for filtering on a date variable. (In the Preview version of Excel 2013 used to develop this book, the Timeline feature seems to have a bug. It doesn't work properly for a field named Date, but it works fine if the field name is changed to something like Purchase Date. Possibly, Date is a reserved key word.)

As an example, Figure 3.64 shows a pivot table accompanied by two slicers and a timeline. The Rows field is Time, which has been filtered in the usual way (through the dropdown list in the Rows area) to show only Afternoon and Evening. The two slicers appear next to the pivot table. The Region slicer has been filtered on Midwest and South, and the Gender slicer has been filtered on Male. Note that the Date field for the timeline has been renamed to Purchase Date so that the timeline works properly. Here you can see that the sum of Total Cost for all sales in the evening by males in the Midwest and South during the months of April and May is $2442.05.

Figure 3.64   Pivot Table with Slicers and a Timeline

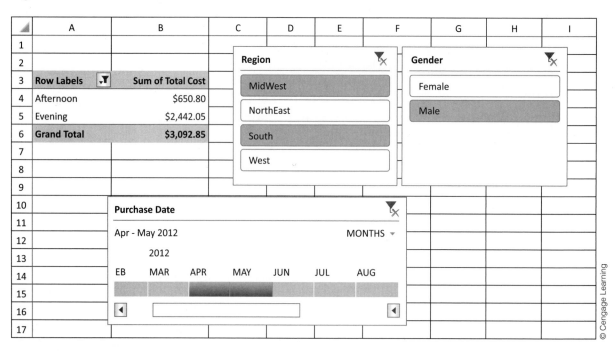

© Cengage Learning

PROBLEMS

Level A

33. Solve problem 1 with pivot tables and create corresponding pivot charts. Express the counts as percentages of row totals. What do these percentages indicate

about this particular data set? Then repeat, expressing the counts as percentages of column totals.

34. Solve problem 2 with pivot tables and create corresponding pivot charts. Express the counts as percentages of row totals. What do these percentages indicate about this particular data set? Then repeat, expressing the counts as percentages of column totals.

35. Solve problem 3 with pivot tables and create corresponding pivot charts. Express the counts as percentages of row totals. What do these percentages indicate about this particular data set? Then repeat, expressing the counts as percentages of columns totals.

36. Solve problem 4 with pivot tables and create corresponding pivot charts. Express the counts as percentage of row totals. What do these percentages indicate about this particular data set? Then repeat, expressing the counts as percentages of column totals.

37. Solve problem 7 with pivot tables and create corresponding pivot charts. However, find only means and standard deviations, not medians or quartiles. (This is one drawback of pivot tables. Medians, quartiles, and percentiles are not in the list of summary measures.)

38. Solve problem 8 with pivot tables and create corresponding pivot charts. However, find only means and standard deviations, not medians. (This is one drawback of pivot tables. Medians are not among their summary measures.)

39. Solve problem 9 with pivot tables and create corresponding pivot charts. However, find only means and standard deviations, not medians. (This is one drawback of pivot tables. Medians are not among their summary measures.)

40. The file **P03_40.xlsx** contains monthly data on the number of border crossings from Mexico into four southwestern states.
   a. Restructure this data set on a new sheet so that there are three long columns: Month, State, and Crossings. Essentially, you should stack the original columns B through E on top of one another to get the Crossings column, and you should also indicate which state each row corresponds to in the State column. The Month column should have four replicas of the original Month column.
   b. Create a pivot table and corresponding pivot table chart based on the restructured data. It should break down the average of Crossings by Year and State. Comment on any patterns you see in the chart.

41. *The Wall Street Journal CEO Compensation Study* analyzed CEO pay from many U.S. companies with fiscal year 2008 revenue of at least $5 billion that filed their proxy statements between October 2008 and March 2009. The data are in the file **P02_30.xlsx**.
   a. Create a pivot table and a corresponding pivot chart that simultaneously shows average of Salary 2008 and average of Bonus 2008, broken down by Company Type. Comment on any striking results in the chart.
   b. In the Data sheet, create a new column, Total 2008, which is the sum of Salary 2008 and Bonus 2008.

Then create two pivot tables and corresponding pivot charts on a single sheet. The first should show the counts of CEOs broken down by Company Type, and the second should simultaneously show the average of Total 2008, the minimum of Total 2008, and the maximum of Total 2008, all broken down by Company Type. Comment on any striking results in these charts.

42. One pivot table element we didn't explain is a **calculated item**. This is usually a new category for some categorical variable that is created from existing categories. It is easiest to learn from an example. Open the file **Elecmart Sales.xlsx** from this section, create a pivot table, and put Day in the Rows area. Proceed as follows to create two new categories, Weekday and Weekend.
   a. Select any day and select Calculated Item from the Formulas dropdown list on the PivotTable Tools Options ribbon. This will open a dialog box. Enter Weekend in the Name box and enter the formula **=Sat+Sun** in the formula box. (You can double-click the items in the Items list to help build this formula.) When you click OK, you will see Weekend in the pivot table.
   b. Do it yourself. Create another calculated item, Weekday, for Mon through Fri.
   c. Filter out all of the individual days from the row area, so that only Weekday and Weekend remain, and then find the sum of Total Cost for these two new categories. How can you check whether these sums are what you think they should be? (Notes about calculated items: First, if you have Weekend, Weekday, and some individual days showing in the Rows area, the sum of Total Cost will double-count these individual days, so be careful about this. Second, be aware that if you create a calculated item from some variable such as Day, you are no longer allowed to drag that variable to the Filters area.)

43. Building on the previous problem, another pivot table element we didn't explain is a **calculated field**. This is usually a new numerical variable built from numerical variables that can be summarized in the Values area. It acts somewhat like a new column in the spreadsheet data, but there is an important difference. Again, it is easiest to learn from an example. Open the file **Elecmart Sales.xlsx** and follow the instructions below.
   a. Create a new column in the data, CostPerItem, which is Total Cost divided by Items Ordered. Then create a pivot table and find the average of CostPerItem, broken down by Region. You should find averages such as $50.41 for the MidWest. Explain exactly how this value was calculated. Would such an average be of much interest to a manager at Elecmart? Why or why not?

b. Select any average in the pivot table and then select Calculated Field from the Formulas dropdown list on the Analyze/Options ribbon. This will open a dialog box. Enter CF_CostPerItem in the name box (we added CF, for calculated field, because we are not allowed to use the CostPerItem name that already exists), enter the formula **=TotalCost/ItemsOrdered**, and click OK. You should now see a new column in the pivot table, Sum of CF_CostPerItem, with *different* values than in the Average of CostPerItem column. For example, the new value for the MidWest should be $46.47. Do some investigation to understand how this "sum" was calculated. From a manager's point of view, does it make any sense? (Note on calculated fields: When you summarize a calculated field, it doesn't matter whether you express it as sum, average, max, or any other summary measure. It is calculated in exactly the same way in each case.)

44. The file **P02_18.xlsx** contains daily values of the S&P Index from 1970 to early 2012. It also contains percentage changes in the index from each day to the next. Create a pivot table with average of % Change in the Values area and Date in the Rows area. You will see every single date, with no real averaging taking place. This problem lets you explore how you can group naturally on a date variable. For each part below, explain the result briefly.
  a. Group by Month.
  b. Group by Year.
  c. Group by Month and Year (select both in the Group dialog box). Can you make it show the year averages from part **b**?
  d. Group by Quarter.
  e. Group by Month and Quarter. Can you make it show the averages from part **c**?
  f. Group by Quarter and Year.
  g. Group by Month, Quarter, and Year.

45. (*For Excel 2010 or later users only*) Using the **Elecmart Sales.xlsx** file from this section, experiment with slicers as follows.
  a. Create a pivot table that shows the average of Total Cost, broken down by Region in the Rows area and Time in the Columns area. Then insert two slicers, one for Region and one for Time. Select the West and NorthEast buttons on the Region slicer and the Morning and Afternoon buttons on the Time slicer. Explain what happens in the pivot table.
  b. Create a pivot table that shows the average of Total Cost, broken down by Region in the Rows area and Time in the Columns area. Insert a Day slicer and select the Sat and Sun buttons. Explain what averages are now showing in the pivot table. Verify this by deleting the slicer and placing Days in the Filters area, with Sat and Sun selected.

46. (*For Excel 2010 or later users only*) We used the **Lasagna Triers.xlsx** file in this section to show how pivot tables can help explain which variables are related to the buying behavior of customers. Illustrate how the same information could be obtained with slicers. Specifically, set up the pivot table as in the example, but use a slicer instead of a Rows variable. Then set it up exactly as in the example, *with* a Rows variable, but include a slicer for some other variable. Comment on the type of results you obtain with these two versions. Do slicers appear to provide any advantage in this type of problem?

Level B

47. Solve problem 5 with pivot tables and create corresponding pivot charts. If you first find the quartiles of Salary and Amount Spent (by any method), is it possible to create the desired crosstabs by grouping, *without* recoding these variables?

48. Solve problem 17 with pivot tables. However, find only means and standard deviations, not medians. (This is one drawback of pivot tables. Medians are not among their summary measures.)

49. The file **P03_22.xlsx** lists financial data on movies released since 1980 with budgets of at least $20 million.
  a. Create three new variables, Ratio1, Ratio2, and Decade. Ratio1 should be US Gross divided by Budget, Ratio2 should be Worldwide Gross divided by Budget, and Decade should list 1980s, 1990s, or 2000s, depending on the year of the release date. If either US Gross or Worldwide Gross is listed as "Unknown," the corresponding ratio should be blank. (*Hint*: For Decade, use the YEAR function to fill in a new Year column. Then use a lookup table to populate the Decade column.)
  b. Use a pivot table to find counts of movies by various distributors. Then go back to the data and create one more column, Distributor New, which lists the distributor for distributors with at least 30 movies and lists Other for the rest. (*Hint*: Use a lookup table to populate Distributor New, but also use an IF to fill in Other where the distributor is missing.)
  c. Create a pivot table and corresponding pivot chart that shows average and standard deviation of Ratio1, broken down by Distributor New, with Decade in the Filters area. Comment on any striking results.
  d. Repeat part **c** for Ratio2.

50. The file **P03_50.xlsx** lists NBA salaries for five seasons. (Each NBA season straddles two calendar years.)
  a. Merge all of the data into a single new sheet called All Data. In this new sheet, add a new column Season that lists the season, such as 2006–2007.

b. Note that many of the players list a position such as C-F or F-C. Presumably, the first means the player is primarily a center but sometimes plays forward, whereas the second means the opposite. Recode these so that only the primary position remains (C in the first case, F in the second). To complicate matters further, the source lists positions differently in 2007–2008 than in other years. It lists PG and SG (point guard and shooting guard) instead of just G, and it lists SF and PF (small forward and power forward) instead of just F. Recode the positions for this season to be consistent with the other seasons (so that there are only three positions: G, F, and C).

c. Note that many players have (p) or (t) in their Contract Thru value. The Source sheet explains this. Create two new columns in the All Data sheet, Years Remaining and Option. The Years Remaining column should list the years remaining in the contract. For example, if the season is 2004–2005 and the contract is through 2006–2007, years remaining should be 2. The Option column should list Player if there is a (p), Team if there is a (t), and blank if neither.

d. Use a pivot table to find the average Salary by Season. Change it to show average Salary by Team. Change it to show average Salary by Season and Team. Change it to show average Salary by Primary Position. Change it to show average Salary by Team and Primary Position, with filters for Season, Contract Years, Years Remaining, and Option. Comment on any striking findings.

51. The file **P02_29.xlsx** contain monthly percentages of on-time arrivals at several of the largest U.S. airports.

a. Explain why the current format of either data set limits the kind of information you can obtain with a pivot table. For example, does it allow you find the average on-time arrival percentage by year for any selected subset of airports, such as the average for O'Hare, Los Angeles International, and La Guardia?

b. Restructure the data appropriately and then use a pivot table to answer the specific question in part **a**.

3-6 CONCLUSION

Finding relationships among variables is arguably the most important task in data analysis. This chapter has equipped you with some very powerful tools for detecting relationships. As we have discussed, the tools vary depending on whether the variables are categorical or numerical. (Again, refer to the diagram in the **Data Analysis Taxonomy.xlsx** file.) Tables and charts of counts are useful for relationships among categorical variables. Summary measures broken down by categories and side-by-side box plots are useful for finding relationships between a categorical and a numerical variable. Scatterplots and correlations are useful for finding relationships among numerical variables. Finally, pivot tables are useful for all types of variables.

Summary of Key Terms

Term	Explanation	Excel	Pages	Equation
Crosstabs (or contingency table)	Table of counts of joint categories of two categorical variables	COUNTIFS function or pivot table	82	
Comparison problem	Comparing a numerical variable across two or more subpopulations		86	
Stacked or unstacked data formats	Stacked means long columns, one for categories and another for values; unstacked means a separate values column for each category		87	
Scatterplot (or X-Y chart)	Chart for detecting a relationship between two numerical variables; one point for each observation	Scatter from Insert ribbon or StatTools	95	
Trend line	Line or curve fit to scatterplot (or time series graph)	Right-click on chart point, select Add Trendline	99	

(continued)

Summary of Key Terms   (*Continued*)

Term	Explanation	Excel	Pages	Equation
Covariance	Measure of linear relationship between two numerical variables, but affected by units of measurement	COVAR function or StatTools	101	3.1
Correlation	Measure of linear relationship between two numerical variables, always from −1 to +1	CORREL function or StatTools	102	3.2
Pivot table	Table for breaking down data by category; can show counts, averages, or other summary measures	PivotTable from Insert ribbon	108	
Pivot chart	Chart corresponding to a pivot table	PivotChart from PivotTable Tools Analyze/Options ribbon	118	
Slicers	Graphical elements for filtering in pivot tables	New to Excel 2010	127	

PROBLEMS

Conceptual Questions

C.1. When you are trying to discover whether there is a relationship between two categorical variables, why is it useful to transform the counts in a crosstabs to percentages of row or column totals? Once you do this, how can you tell if the variables are related?

C.2. Suppose you have a crosstabs of two "Yes/No" categorical variables, with the counts shown as percentages of row totals. What will these percentages look like if there is absolutely no relationship between the variables? Besides this case, list all possible *types* of relationships that could occur. (There aren't many.)

C.3. If you suspect that a company's advertising expenditures in a given month affect its sales in *future* months, what correlations would you look at to confirm your suspicions? How would you find them?

C.4. Suppose you have customer data on whether they have bought your product in a given time period, along with various demographics on the customers. Explain how you could use pivot tables to see which demographics are the primary drivers of their "yes/no" buying behavior.

C.5. Suppose you have data on student achievement in high school for each of many school districts. In spreadsheet format, the school district is in column A, and various student achievement measures are in columns B, C, and so on. If you find fairly low correlations (magnitudes from 0 to 0.4, say) between the variables in these achievement columns, what exactly does this mean?

C.6. A supermarket transactions data set is likely to have "hierarchical" columns of data. For example, for the product sold, there might be columns like Product Family, Product Department, Product Category, and maybe even more. (See the file **Supermarket Transactions.xlsx** from Chapter 2 as an example.) Another hierarchy is for store location, where there might be columns for Country, State or Province, City, and possibly more. One more hierarchy is time, with the hierarchy Year, Quarter, Month, and so on. How could a supermarket manager use pivot tables to "drill down" through a hierarchy to examine revenues? For example, you might start at the Drink level, then drill down to Alcoholic Beverages, and then to Beer and Wine? Illustrate with the file mentioned.

C.7. Suppose you have a large data set for some sport. Each row might correspond to a particular team (as in the file **P03_57.xlsx** on football outcomes, for example) or it might even correspond to a given play. Each row contains one or more measures of success as well as many pieces of data that could be drivers of success. How might you find the most important drivers of success if the success measure is categorical (such as Win or Lose)? How might you find the most important drivers of success if the success measure is numerical and basically continuous (such as Points Scored in basketball)?

C.8. If two variables are highly correlated, does this imply that changes in one *cause* changes in the other? If not, give at least one example from the real world that illustrates what else could cause a high correlation.

C.9. Suppose there are two commodities A and B with strongly negatively correlated daily returns, such as a stock and gold. Is it possible to find another commodity with daily returns that are strongly negatively correlated with *both* A and B?

C.10. In checking whether several times series, such as monthly exchange rates of various currencies, move together, why do most analysts look at correlations between their *differences* rather than correlations between the original series?

Level A

52. Unfortunately, StatTools doesn't have a stacked option for its correlation procedure, which would allow you to get a separate table of correlations for each category of a categorical variable. The only alternative is to sort on the categorical variable, insert some blank rows between values of different categories, copy the headings to each section, create separate StatTools data sets for each, and then ask for correlations from each. Do this with the movie data in the file **P02_02.xlsx**. Specifically, separate the data into three data sets based on Genre: one for Comedy, one for Drama, and one for all the rest. For this problem, you can ignore the third group. For each of Comedy and Drama, create a table of correlations between 7-day Gross, 14-day Gross, Total US Gross, International Gross, and US DVD Sales. Comment on whether the correlation structure is much different for these two popular genres.

53. The file **P03_53.xlsx** lists campaign contributions, by number of contributors and contribution amount, by state (including Washington DC) for the four leading contenders in the 2008 presidential race. Create a scatterplot and corresponding correlation between Dollar Amount (Y axis) and Contributors for each of the four contenders. For each scatterplot, superimpose a linear trend line and show the corresponding equation. Interpret each equation and compare them across candidates. Finally, identify the state for any points that aren't on or very close to the corresponding trend line.

54. The file **P03_54.xlsx** lists data for 593 movies released in 2011. Obviously, some movies are simply more popular than others, but success in 2011, measured by 2011 gross or 2011 tickets sold, could also be influenced by the release date. To check this, create a new variable, Days Out, which is the number of days the movie was out during 2011. For example, a movie released on 12/15 would have Days Out equal to 17 (which includes the release day). Create two scatterplots and corresponding correlations, one of 2011 Gross (Y axis) versus Days Out and one of 2011 Tickets Sold (Y axis) versus Days Out. Describe the behavior you see. Do you think a movie's success can be predicted very well just by knowing how many days it has been out?

55. The file **P03_55.xlsx** lists the average salary for each MLB team from 2004 to 2011, along with the number of team wins in each of these years.
   a. Create a table of correlations between the Wins columns. What do these correlations indicate? Are they higher or lower than you expected?
   b. Create a table of correlations between the Salary columns. What do these correlations indicate? Are they higher or lower than you expected?
   c. For each year, create a scatterplot and the associated correlations between Wins for that year (Y axis) and Salary for that year. Does it appear that teams are buying their way to success?
   d. The coloring in the Wins columns indicates the playoff teams. Create a new Yes/No column for each year, indicating whether the team made it to the playoffs that year. Then create a pivot table for each year showing average of Salary for that year, broken down by the Yes/No column for that year. Do these pivot tables indicate that teams are buying their way into the playoffs?

56. The file **P03_56.xlsx** lists the average salary for each NBA team from the 2004–2005 season to the 2009–2010 season, along with the number of team wins each of these years. Answer the same questions as in the previous problem for this basketball data.

57. The file **P03_57.xlsx** lists the average salary for each NFL team from 2002 to 2009, along with the number of team wins each of these years. Answer the same questions as in problem 55 for this football data.

58. The file **P03_58.xlsx** lists salaries of MLB players in the years 2007 to 2009. Each row corresponds to a particular player. As indicated by blank salaries, some players played in one of these years, some played in two of these years, and the rest played in all three years.
   a. Create a new Yes/No variable, All 3 Years, that indicates which players played all three years.
   b. Create two pivot tables and corresponding pivot charts. The first should show the count of players by position who played all three years. The second should show the average salary each year, by position, for all players who played all three years. (For each of these, put the All 3 Years variable in the Filters area.) Explain briefly what these two pivot tables indicate.
   c. Define a StatTools data set on only the players who played all three years. Using this data set, create a table of correlations of the three salary variables. What do these correlations indicate about player salaries?

59. The file **P03_59.xlsx** lists the results of about 20,000 runners in the 2008 New York Marathon.
   a. For all runners who finished in 3.5 hours or less, create a pivot table and corresponding pivot chart

of average of Time by Gender. (To get a fairer comparison in the chart, change it so that the vertical axis starts at zero.) For the same runners, and on the same sheet, create another pivot table and pivot chart of counts by Gender. Comment on the results.

b. For all runners who finished in 3.5 hours or less, create a pivot table and corresponding pivot chart of average of Time by Age. Group by Age so that the teens are in one category, those in their twenties are in another category, and so on. For the same runners, and on the same sheet, create another pivot table and pivot chart of counts of these age groups. Comment on the results.

c. For all runners who finished in 3.5 hours or less, create a single pivot table of average of Time and of counts, broken down by Country. Then filter so that only the 10 countries with the 10 lowest average times appear. Finally, sort on average times so that the fastest countries rise to the top. Guess who the top two are! (*Hint*: Try the Value Filters for the Country variable.) Comment on the results.

60. The file **P02_12.xlsx** includes data on the 50 top graduate programs in the U.S., according to a recent *U.S. News & World Report* survey.

a. Create a table of correlations between all of the numerical variables. Discuss which variables are highly correlated with which others.

b. The Overall score is the score schools agonize about. Create a scatterplot and corresponding correlation of each of the other variables versus Overall, with Overall always on the Y axis. What do you learn from these scatterplots?

61. Recall from an example in the previous chapter that the file **Supermarket Transactions.xlsx** contains over 14,000 transactions made by supermarket customers over a period of approximately two years. Set up a single pivot table and corresponding pivot chart, with some instructions to a user (like the supermarket manager) in a text box, on how the user can get answers to any typical question about the data. For example, one possibility (of many) could be total revenue by product department and month, for any combination of gender, marital status, and homeowner. (The point is to get you to explain pivot table basics to a nontechnical user.)

62. The file **P03_15.xlsx** contains monthly data on the various components of the Consumer Price Index.

a. Create differences for each of the variables. You can do this quickly with StatTools, using the Difference item in the Data Utilities dropdown list, or you can create the differences with Excel formulas.

b. Create a times series graph for each CPI component, including the All Items component. Then create a time series graph for each difference variable. Comment on any patterns or trends you see.

c. Create a table of correlations between the differences. Comment on any large correlations (or the lack of them).

d. Create a scatterplot for each difference variable versus the difference for All Items (Y axis). Comment on any patterns or outliers you see.

Level B

63. The file **P03_63.xlsx** contains financial data on 85 U.S. companies in the Computer and Electronic Product Manufacturing sector (NAICS code 334) with 2009 earnings before taxes of at least $10,000. Each of these companies listed R&D (research and development) expenses on its income statement. Create a table of correlations between all of the variables and use conditional formatting to color green all correlations involving R&D that are strongly positive or negative. (Use cutoff values of your choice to define "strongly.") Then create scatterplots of R&D (Y axis) versus each of the other most highly correlated variables. Comment on any patterns you see in these scatterplots, including any obvious outliers, and explain why (or if) it makes sense that these variables are highly correlated with R&D. If there are highly correlated variables with R&D, can you tell which way the causality goes?

64. The file **P03_64.xlsx** lists monthly data since 1950 on the well-known Dow Jones Industrial Average (DJIA), as well as the less well-known Dow Jones Transportation Average (DJTA) and Dow Jones Utilities Average (DJUA). Each of these is an index based on 20 to 30 leading companies (which change over time).

a. Create monthly differences in three new columns. The Jan-50 values will be blank because there are no Dec-49 values. Then, for example, the Feb-50 difference is the Feb-50 value minus the Jan-50 value. (You can easily calculate these with Excel formulas, but you might want to try the StatTools Difference procedure from its Data Utilities dropdown list.)

b. Create a table of correlations of the three difference columns. Does it appear that the three Dow indexes tend to move together through time?

c. It is possible (and has been claimed) that one of the indexes is a "leading indicator" of another. For example, a change in the DJUA in September might predict a similar change in the DJIA in the following December. To check for such behavior, create "lags" of the difference variables. To do so, select Lag from the StatTools Data Utilities dropdown list, select one of the difference variables, and enter the number of lags you want.

For this problem, try four lags. Then press OK and accept the StatTools warnings. Do this for each of the three difference variables. You should end up with 12 lag variables. Explain in words what these lag variables contain. For example, what is the Dec-50 lag3 of the DJIA difference?

d. Create a table of correlations of the three differences and the 12 lags. Use conditional formatting to color green all correlations greater than 0.5 (or any other cutoff you choose). Does it appear that any index is indeed a leading indicator of any other? Explain.

65. The file **P03_65.xlsx** lists a lot of data for each NBA team for the seasons 2004–2005 to 2008–2009. The variables are divided into groups: (1) Overall success, (2) Offensive, and (3) Defensive. The basic question all basketball fans (and coaches) ponder is what causes success or failure.

a. Explore this question by creating a correlation matrix with the variable Wins (the measure of success) and all of the variables in groups (2) and (3). Based on these correlations, which five variables appear to be the best predictors of success? (Keep in mind that negative correlations can also be important.)

b. Explore this question in a different way, using the Playoff Team column as a measure of success. Here, it makes sense to proceed as in the Lasagna Triers example in Section 3-5, using the variables in groups (2) and (3) as the predictors. However, these predictors are all basically continuous, so grouping would be required for all of them in the pivot table, and grouping is always somewhat arbitrary. Instead, create a copy of the Data sheet. Then for each variable in groups (2) to (13), create a formula that returns 1, 2, 3, or 4, depending on which quarter of that variable the value falls in (1 if it is less than or equal to the first quartile, and so on). (This sounds like a lot of work, but a *single* copyable formula will work for the entire range.) Now use these discrete variables as predictors and proceed as in the Lasagna Triers example. List the five variables that appear to be the best (or at least good) predictors of making the playoffs.

66. The file **P03_66.xlsx** lists a lot of data for each NFL team for the years 2004 to 2009. The variables are divided into groups: (1) Overall success, (2) Team Offense, (3) Passing Offense, (4) Rushing Offense, (5) Turnovers Against, (6) Punt Returns, (7) Kick Returns, (8) Field Goals, (9) Punts, (10) Team Defense, (11) Passing Defense, (12) Rushing Defense, and (13) Turnovers Caused. The basic question all football fans (and coaches) ponder is what causes success or failure. Answer the same questions as in the previous problem for this football data, but use all of the variables in groups (2) to (13) as possible predictors.

67. The file **P02_57.xlsx** contains data on mortgage loans in 2008 for each state in the U.S. The file is different from others in this chapter in that each state has its own sheet with the same data in the same format. Each state sheet breaks down all mortgage applications by loan purpose, applicant race, loan type, outcome, and denial reason (for those that were denied). The question is how a *single* data set for all states can be created for analysis. The Typical Data Set sheet indicates a simple way of doing this, using the powerful but little-known INDIRECT function. This sheet is basically a template for bringing in any pieces of data from the state sheets you would like to examine.

a. Do whatever it takes to populate the Typical Data Set sheet with information in the range B7:D11 and B14:D14 (18 variables in all) of each state sheet. Add appropriate labels in row 3, such as Asian Dollar Amount Applied For.

b. Create a table of correlations between these variables. Color yellow all correlations between a given applicant race, such as those between Asian Mortgage Application, Asian Dollar Amount Applied For, and Asian Average Income. Comment on the magnitudes of these. Are there any surprises?

c. Create scatterplots of White Dollar Amount Applied For (X axis) versus the similar variable for each of the other five applicant races. Comment on any patterns in these scatterplots, and identify any obvious outliers.

CASE 3.1 CUSTOMER ARRIVALS AT BANK98

Bank98 operates a main location and three branch locations in a medium-size city. All four locations perform similar services, and customers typically do business at the location nearest them. The bank has recently had more congestion—longer waiting lines—than it (or its customers) would like. As part of a study to learn the causes of these long lines and to suggest possible solutions, all locations have kept track of customer arrivals during one-hour intervals for the past 10 weeks. All branches are open Monday through Friday from 9 A.M. until 5 P.M. and on Saturday from 9 A.M. until noon. For each location, the file **C03_01.xlsx** contains the number of customer arrivals during each hour of a 10-week period. The manager of Bank98 has hired you to make some sense of these data. Specifically, your task is to present charts and/or tables that indicate how customer traffic into the bank locations varies by day of week and hour of day. There is also interest in whether any daily or hourly patterns you observe are stable across weeks. Although you don't have full information about the way the bank currently runs its operations—you know only its customer arrival pattern and the fact that it is currently experiencing long lines—you are encouraged to append any suggestions for improving operations, based on your analysis of the data.

CASE 3.2 SAVING, SPENDING, AND SOCIAL CLIMBING

The best-selling book *The Millionaire Next Door* by Thomas J. Stanley and William D. Danko (Longstreet Press, 1996) presents some very interesting data on the characteristics of millionaires. We tend to believe that people with expensive houses, expensive cars, expensive clothes, country club memberships, and other outward indications of wealth are the millionaires. The authors define wealth, however, in terms of savings and investments, not consumer items. In this sense, they argue that people with a lot of expensive *things* and even large incomes often have surprisingly little wealth. These people tend to spend much of what they make on consumer items, often trying to keep up with, or impress, their peers.

In contrast, the real millionaires, in terms of savings and investments, frequently come from "unglamorous" professions (particularly teaching), own unpretentious homes and cars, dress in inexpensive clothes, and otherwise lead rather ordinary lives.

Consider the (fictional) data in the file **C03_02.xlsx**. For several hundred couples, it lists their education level, their annual combined salary, the market value of their home and cars, the amount of savings they have accumulated (in savings accounts, stocks, retirement accounts, and so on), and a self-reported "social climber index" on a scale of 1 to 10 (with 1 being very unconcerned about social status and material items and 10 being very concerned about these). Prepare a report based on these data, supported by relevant charts and/or tables, that could be used in a book such as *The Millionaire Next Door*. Your conclusions can either support or contradict those of Stanley and Danko.

CASE 3.3 CHURN IN THE CELLULAR PHONE MARKET

The term **churn** is very important to managers in the cellular phone business. Churning occurs when a customer stops using one company's service and switches to another company's service. Obviously, managers try to keep churning to a minimum, not only by offering the best possible service, but by trying to identify conditions that lead to churning and taking steps to stop churning before it occurs. For example, if a company learns that customers tend to churn at the end of their two-year contract, they could offer customers an incentive to stay a month or two before the end of their two-year contract. The file **C03_03.xlsx** contains data on over 2000 customers of a particular cellular phone company. Each row contains the activity of a particular customer for a given time period, and the last column indicates whether the customer churned during this time period. Use the tools in this chapter (and possibly the previous chapter) to learn (1) how these variables are distributed, (2) how the variables in columns B–R are related to each other, and (3) how the variables in columns B–R are related to the Churn variable in column S. Write a short report of your findings, including any recommendations you would make to the company to reduce churn.

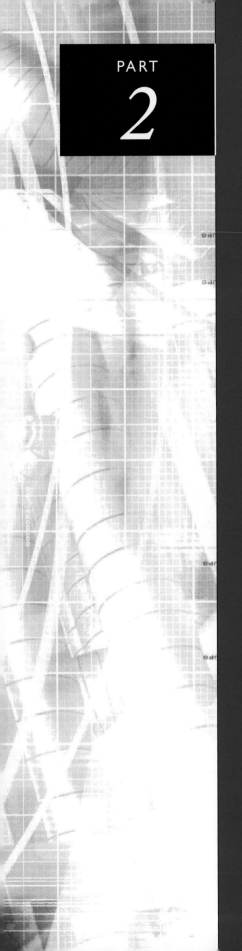

PART 2

Probability and Decision Making under Uncertainty

Rob Walls/Alamy

CHAPTER 4

Probability and Probability Distributions

GAME AT MCDONALD'S

Several years ago, McDonald's ran a campaign in which it gave game cards to its customers. These game cards made it possible for customers to win hamburgers, french fries, soft drinks, and other fast-food items, as well as cash prizes. Each card had 10 covered spots that could be uncovered by rubbing them with a coin. Beneath three of these spots were "zaps." Beneath the other seven spots were names of prizes, two of which were identical. For example, one card might have two pictures of a hamburger, one picture of a Coke, one of french fries, one of a milk shake, one of $5, one of $1000, and three zaps. For this card the customer could win a hamburger. To win on any card, the customer had to uncover the two matching spots (which showed the potential prize for that card) before uncovering a zap; any card with a zap uncovered was automatically void. Assuming that the two matches and the three zaps were arranged randomly on the cards, what is the probability of a customer winning?

We label the two matching spots M_1 and M_2, and the three zaps Z_1, Z_2, and Z_3. Then the probability of winning is the probability of uncovering M_1 *and* M_2 before uncovering Z_1, Z_2, *or* Z_3. In this case the relevant set of outcomes is the set of all orderings of M_1, M_2, Z_1, Z_2, and Z_3, shown in the order they are uncovered. As far as the outcome of the game is concerned, the other five spots on the card are irrelevant. Thus, an outcome such as M_2, M_1, Z_3, Z_1, Z_2 is a winner, whereas M_2, Z_2, Z_1, M_1, Z_3 is a loser. Actually, the first of these would be declared a winner as soon as M_1 was uncovered, and the second would be declared a loser as soon as Z_2 was uncovered. However, we show the whole sequence of Ms and Zs so that we can count outcomes correctly. We then find the probability of winning using an equally likely argument. Specifically, we divide the number of outcomes that are winners by the total number of outcomes. It can be shown that the number of outcomes that are winners is 12, whereas the total number of outcomes is 120. Therefore, the probability of a winner is $12/120 = 0.1$.

This calculation, which shows that on average, 1 out of 10 cards could be winners, was obviously important for McDonald's. Actually, this provides only an upper bound on the fraction of cards where a prize was awarded. Many customers threw their cards away without playing the game, and even some of the winners neglected to claim their prizes. So, for example, McDonald's knew that if they made 50,000 cards where a milk shake was the winning prize, somewhat less than 5000 milk shakes would be given away. Knowing approximately what their expected "losses" would be from winning cards, McDonald's was able to design the game (how many cards of each type to print) so that the expected extra revenue (from customers attracted to the game) would cover the expected losses. ■

4-1 INTRODUCTION

A key aspect of solving real business problems is dealing appropriately with uncertainty. This involves recognizing explicitly that uncertainty exists and using quantitative methods to model uncertainty. If you want to develop realistic business models, you cannot simply act as if uncertainty doesn't exist. For example, if you don't know next month's demand, you shouldn't build a model that assumes next month's demand is a sure 1500 units. This is only wishful thinking. You should instead incorporate demand uncertainty explicitly into your model. To do this, you need to know how to deal quantitatively with uncertainty. This involves probability and probability distributions. We introduce these topics in this chapter and then use them in a number of later chapters.

There are many sources of uncertainty. Demands for products are uncertain, times between arrivals to a supermarket are uncertain, stock price returns are uncertain, changes in interest rates are uncertain, and so on. In many situations, the uncertain quantity—demand, time between arrivals, stock price return, change in interest rate—is a numerical quantity. In the language of probability, it is called a **random variable**. More formally, a random variable associates a numerical value with each possible random outcome.

Associated with each random variable is a **probability distribution** that lists all of the possible values of the random variable and their corresponding probabilities. A probability distribution provides very useful information. It not only indicates the possible values of the random variable, but it also indicates how likely they are. For example, it is useful to know that the possible demands for a product are, say, 100, 200, 300, and 400, but it is even more useful to know that the probabilities of these four values are, say, 0.1, 0.2, 0.4, and 0.3. This implies, for example, that there is a 70% chance that demand will be at least 300.

It is often useful to summarize the information from a probability distribution with numerical summary measures. These include the mean, variance, and standard deviation. As their names imply, these summary measures are much like the corresponding summary measures in Chapters 2 and 3. However, they are *not* identical. The summary measures in this chapter are based on probability distributions, not an observed data set. We will use numerical examples to explain the difference between the two—and how they are related.

The purpose of this chapter is to explain the basic concepts and tools necessary to work with probability distributions and their summary measures. We begin by briefly discussing the basic rules of probability. We also introduce *computer simulation,* an extremely useful tool for illustrating important concepts in probability and statistics.

Modeling uncertainty, as we will be doing in the next few chapters and later in Chapters 15 and 16, is sometimes difficult, depending on the complexity of the model, and it is easy to get so caught up in the details that you lose sight of the big picture. For this reason, the flow chart in Figure 4.1 is useful. (A colored version of this chart is available in the file **Modeling Uncertainty Flow Chart.xlsx.**) Take a close look at the middle row of this chart. We begin with inputs, some of which are uncertain quantities, we use Excel®

Figure 4.1   Flow Chart for Modeling Uncertainty

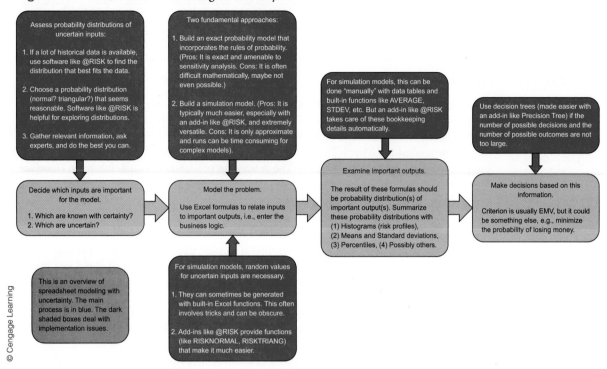

© Cengage Learning

formulas to incorporate the logic of the model, and we end with probability distributions of important outputs. Finally, we use this information to make decisions. (The abbreviation EMV stands for expected monetary value. It is discussed extensively in Chapter 6.) The other boxes in the chart deal with implementation issues, particularly with the software you can use to perform the analysis. Study this chart carefully and return to it as you proceed through the next few chapters and Chapters 15 and 16.

Before proceeding, we discuss two terms you often hear in the business world: *uncertainty* and *risk*. They are sometimes used interchangeably, but they are not really the same. You typically have no control over uncertainty; it is something that simply exists. A good example is the uncertainty in exchange rates. You cannot be sure what the exchange rate between the U.S. dollar and the euro will be a year from now. All you can try to do is *measure* this uncertainty with a probability distribution.

In contrast, risk depends on your position. Even though you don't know what the exchange rate will be, it makes no difference to you—there is no risk—if you have no European investments, you aren't planning a trip to Europe, and you don't have to buy or sell anything in Europe. You have risk only when you stand to gain or lose money depending on the eventual exchange rate. Of course, the form of your risk depends on your position. If you are holding euros in a money market account, you are hoping that euros gain value relative to the dollar. But if you are planning a European vacation, you are hoping that euros lose value relative to the dollar.

Uncertainty and risk are inherent in many of the examples in this book. By learning about probability, you will learn how to measure uncertainty, and you will also learn how to measure the risks involved in various decisions. One important topic you will *not* learn much about is risk *mitigation* by various types of hedging. For example, if you know you have to purchase a large quantity of some product from Europe a year from now, you face the risk that the value of the euro could increase dramatically, thus costing you a lot of money. Fortunately, there are ways to hedge this risk, so that if the euro does increase relative to the dollar, your hedge minimizes your losses. Hedging risk is an extremely important topic, and it is practiced daily in the real world, but it is beyond the scope of this book.

4-2 PROBABILITY ESSENTIALS

We begin with a brief discussion of probability. The concept of probability is one that we all encounter in everyday life. When a weather forecaster states that the chance of rain is 70%, he or she is making a probability statement. When a sports commentator states that the odds against the Miami Heat winning the NBA Championship are 3 to 1, he or she is also making a probability statement. The *concept* of probability is quite intuitive. However, the *rules* of probability are not always as intuitive or easy to master. We examine the most important of these rules in this section.

> A **probability** is a number between 0 and 1 that measures the likelihood that some event will occur. An event with probability 0 cannot occur, whereas an event with probability 1 is certain to occur. An event with probability greater than 0 and less than 1 involves uncertainty. The closer its probability is to 1, the more likely it is to occur.

As the examples in the preceding paragraph illustrate, probabilities are sometimes expressed as percentages or odds. However, these can easily be converted to probabilities on a 0-to-1 scale. If the chance of rain is 70%, then the probability of rain is 0.7. Similarly, if the odds against the Heat winning are 3 to 1, then the probability of the Heat winning is 1/4 (or 0.25).

There are only a few probability rules you need to know, and they are discussed in the next few subsections. Surprisingly, these are the *only* rules you need to know. Probability is not an easy topic, and a more thorough discussion of it would lead to considerable mathematical complexity, well beyond the level of this book. However, it is all based on the few relatively simple rules discussed next.

4-2a Rule of Complements

The simplest probability rule involves the *complement* of an event. If A is any event, then the **complement of A**, denoted by $\overline{A}$ (or in some books by A^c), is the event that A does *not* occur. For example, if A is the event that the Dow Jones Industrial Average will finish the year at or above the 14,000 mark, then the complement of A is that the Dow will finish the year below 14,000.

If the probability of A is $P(A)$, then the probability of its complement, $P(\overline{A})$, is given by Equation (4.1). Equivalently, the probability of an event and the probability of its complement sum to 1. For example, if you believe that the probability of the Dow finishing at or above 14,000 is 0.25, then the probability that it will finish the year below 14,000 is $1 - 0.25 = 0.75$.

> *Rule of Complements*
> $$P(\overline{A}) = 1 - P(A) \tag{4.1}$$

4-2b Addition Rule

Events are **mutually exclusive** if at most one of them can occur. That is, if one of them occurs, then none of the others can occur. For example, consider the following three events involving a company's annual revenue for the coming year: (1) revenue is less than $1 million, (2) revenue is at least $1 million but less than $2 million, and (3) revenue is at least

$2 million. Clearly, only one of these events can occur. Therefore, they are mutually exclusive. They are also **exhaustive events**, which means that they exhaust all possibilities—one of these three events *must* occur. Let A_1 through A_n be any n events. Then the *addition rule* of probability involves the probability that at least one of these events will occur. In general, this probability is quite complex, but it simplifies considerably when the events are mutually exclusive. In this case the probability that at least one of the events will occur is the sum of their individual probabilities, as shown in Equation (4.2). Of course, when the events are mutually exclusive, "at least one" is equivalent to "exactly one." In addition, if the events A_1 through A_n are exhaustive, then the probability is one because one of the events is certain to occur.

Addition Rule for Mutually Exclusive Events

$$P(\text{at least one of } A_1 \text{ through } A_n) = P(A_1) + P(A_2) + \cdots + P(A_n) \qquad \textbf{(4.2)}$$

In a typical application, the events A_1 through A_n are chosen to partition the set of all possible outcomes into a number of mutually exclusive events. For example, in terms of a company's annual revenue, define A_1 as "revenue is less than $1 million," A_2 as "revenue is at least $1 million but less than $2 million," and A_3 as "revenue is at least $2 million." Then these three events are mutually exclusive and exhaustive. Therefore, their probabilities must sum to 1. Suppose these probabilities are $P(A_1) = 0.5$, $P(A_2) = 0.3$, and $P(A_3) = 0.2$. (Note that these probabilities *do* sum to 1.) Then the additive rule enables you to calculate other probabilities. For example, the event that revenue is at least $1 million is the event that either A_2 or A_3 occurs. From the addition rule, its probability is

$$P(\text{revenue is at least \$1 million}) = P(A_2) + P(A_3) = 0.5$$

Similarly,

$$P(\text{revenue is less than \$2 million}) = P(A_1) + P(A_2) = 0.8$$

and

$$P(\text{revenue is less than \$1 million } or \text{ at least \$2 million}) = P(A_1) + P(A_3) = 0.7$$

Again, the addition rule works only for mutually exclusive events. If the events overlap, the situation is more complex. For example, suppose you are dealt a bridge hand (13 cards from a 52-card deck). Let H, D, C, and S, respectively, be the events that you get at least 5 hearts, at least 5 diamonds, at least 5 clubs, and at least 5 spades. What is the probability that at least one of these four events occurs? It is not the sum of their individual probabilities because they are not mutually exclusive. For example, you could get 5 hearts *and* 5 spades. Probabilities such as this one are actually quite difficult to calculate, and we will not pursue them here. Just be aware that the addition rule does not apply unless the events are mutually exclusive.

4-2c Conditional Probability and the Multiplication Rule

Probabilities are always assessed relative to the information currently available. As new information becomes available, probabilities can change. For example, if you read that LeBron James suffered a season-ending injury, your assessment of the probability that the Heat will win the NBA Championship would obviously change. A formal way to revise probabilities on the basis of new information is to use *conditional probabilities.*

Let A and B be any events with probabilities $P(A)$ and $P(B)$. Typically, the probability $P(A)$ is assessed without knowledge of whether B occurs. However, if you are *told* that B has occurred, then the probability of A might change. The new probability of A is called the **conditional probability** of *A* given *B*, and it is denoted by $P(A|B)$. Note that there is still uncertainty involving the event to the left of the vertical bar in this notation; you do not know whether it will occur. However, there is no uncertainty involving the event to the right of the vertical bar; you *know* that it has occurred. The conditional probability can be calculated with the following formula.

Conditional Probability

$$P(A|B) = \frac{P(A \text{ and } B)}{P(B)} \tag{4.3}$$

The numerator in this formula is the probability that *both A* and *B* occur. This probability must be known to find $P(A|B)$. However, in some applications $P(A|B)$ and $P(B)$ are known. Then you can multiply both sides of Equation (4.3) by $P(B)$ to obtain the following **multiplication rule** for $P(A \text{ and } B)$.

Multiplication Rule

$$P(A \text{ and } B) = P(A|B)\,P(B) \tag{4.4}$$

The conditional probability formula and the multiplication rule are both valid; in fact, they are equivalent. The one you use depends on which probabilities you know and which you want to calculate, as illustrated in Example 4.1.

EXAMPLE | **4.1 ASSESSING UNCERTAINTY AT BENDER COMPANY**

Bender Company supplies contractors with materials for the construction of houses. The company currently has a contract with one of its customers to fill an order by the end of July. However, there is some uncertainty about whether this deadline can be met, due to uncertainty about whether Bender will receive the materials it needs from one of its suppliers by the middle of July. Right now it is July 1. How can the uncertainty in this situation be assessed?

Objective   To apply probability rules to calculate the probability that Bender will meet its end-of-July deadline, given the information the company has at the beginning of July.

Solution

Let *A* be the event that Bender meets its end-of-July deadline, and let *B* be the event that Bender receives the materials from its supplier by the middle of July. The probabilities Bender is best able to assess on July 1 are probably $P(B)$ and $P(A|B)$. At the beginning of July, Bender might estimate that the chances of getting the materials on time from its supplier are 2 out of 3, so that $P(B) = 2/3$. Also, thinking ahead, Bender estimates that *if* it receives the required materials on time, the chances of meeting the end-of-July deadline are 3 out of 4. This is a conditional probability statement, namely, that $P(A|B) = 3/4$. Then the multiplication rule implies that

$$P(A \text{ and } B) = P(A|B)P(B) = (3/4)(2/3) = 0.5$$

That is, there is a fifty-fifty chance that Bender will get its materials on time *and* meet its end-of-July deadline.

This uncertain situation is depicted graphically in the form of a **probability tree** in Figure 4.2. Note that Bender initially faces (at the leftmost branch of the tree) the uncertainty of whether event B or its complement will occur. Regardless of whether event B occurs, Bender must next confront the uncertainty regarding event A. This uncertainty is reflected in the set of two parallel pairs of branches in the right half of the tree. Hence, there are four mutually exclusive outcomes regarding the two uncertain events, as listed to the right of the tree. Initially, Bender is interested in the first possible outcome, the joint occurrence of events A and B, the top probability in the figure. Another way to compute this probability is to multiply the probabilities associated with the branches leading to this outcome, that is, the probability of B times the probability of A given B. As the figure indicates, this is $(3/4)(2/3)$, or 0.5.

Figure 4.2

Probability Tree for Bender Example

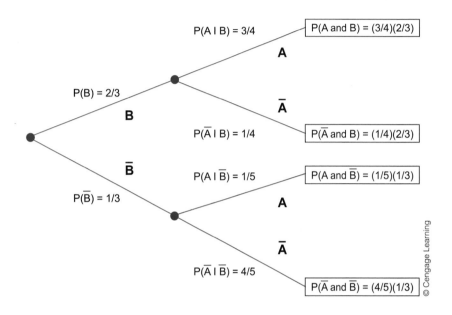

There are several other probabilities of interest in this example. First, let $\bar{B}$ be the complement of B; it is the event that the materials from the supplier do *not* arrive on time. We know that $P(\bar{B}) = 1 - P(B) = 1/3$ from the rule of complements. However, we do not yet know the conditional probability $P(A|\bar{B})$, the probability that Bender will meet its end-of-July deadline, given that it does not receive the materials from the supplier on time. In particular, $P(A|\bar{B})$ is *not* equal to $1 - P(A|B)$. (Can you see why?) Suppose Bender estimates that the chances of meeting the end-of-July deadline are 1 out of 5 if the materials do not arrive on time, so that $P(A|\bar{B}) = 1/5$. Then a second use of the multiplication rule gives

$$P(A \text{ and } \bar{B}) = P(A|\bar{B})P(\bar{B}) = (1/5)(1/3) = 0.0667$$

In words, there is only 1 chance out of 15 that the materials will not arrive on time *and* Bender will meet its end-of-July deadline. This is the third (from the top) probability listed at the right of the tree.

The bottom line for Bender is whether it will meet its end-of-July deadline. After mid-July, this probability is either $P(A|B) = 3/4$ or $P(A|\bar{B}) = 1/5$ because by this time, Bender will *know* whether the materials arrived on time. But on July 1, the relevant probability is $P(A)$—there is still uncertainty about whether B or $\bar{B}$ will occur. Fortunately, you can calculate $P(A)$ from the probabilities you already know. The logic is that A consists of the two mutually exclusive events $(A$ and $B)$ and $(A$ and $\overline{B})$. That is, if A is to occur, it must occur with B or with $\overline{B}$. Therefore, the *addition* rule for mutually exclusive events implies that

$$P(A) = P(A \text{ and } B) + P(A \text{ and } \overline{B}) = 1/2 + 1/15 = 17/30 = 0.5667$$

The chances are 17 out of 30 that Bender will meet its end-of-July deadline, given the information it has at the beginning of July. ∎

4-2d Probabilistic Independence

A concept that is closely tied to conditional probability is probabilistic independence. You just saw that the probability of an event A can depend on whether another event B has occurred. Typically, the probabilities $P(A)$, $P(A|B)$, and $P(A|\overline{B})$ are all different, as in Example 4.1. However, there are situations where all of these probabilities are equal. In this case, A and B are **probabilistically independent events**. This does *not* mean they are mutually exclusive. Rather, probabilistic independence means that knowledge of one event is of no value when assessing the probability of the other.

When two events are probabilistically independent, the multiplication rule simplifies to Equation (4.5). This follows by substituting $P(A)$ for $P(A|B)$ in the multiplication rule, which is allowed because of independence. In words, the probability that both events occur is the product of their individual probabilities.

Multiplication Rule for Independent Events
$$P(A \text{ and } B) = P(A)P(B) \tag{4.5}$$

How can you tell whether events *are* probabilistically independent? Unfortunately, this issue usually cannot be settled with mathematical arguments. Typically, you need empirical data to decide whether independence is reasonable. As a simple example, let A be the event that a family's first child is male, and let B be the event that its second child is male. Are A and B independent? You could argue that they aren't independent if you believe, say, that a boy is more likely to be followed by another boy than by a girl. You could argue that they are independent if you believe the chances of the second child being a boy are the same, regardless of the gender of the first child. (Note that neither argument implies that boys and girls are equally likely.)

In any case, the only way to settle the argument is to observe many families with at least two children. If you observe, say, that 55% of all families with first child male also have the second child male, and only 45% of all families with first child female have the second child male, then you can make a good case that A and B are *not* independent.

The concept of independence carries over to random variables. Two random variables, X and Y, are independent if any two events, one involving only X and the other involving only Y, are independent. The idea is that knowledge of X is of no help in predicting Y, and vice versa. For example, if X is the amount of rain in Seattle in March and Y is the amount of rain in Seattle in June, it might be realistic to assume that X and Y are independent random variables. March weather probably doesn't have much effect on June weather. On the other hand, if X and Y are the changes in stock prices of two companies in the same industry from one day to the next, it might not be realistic to assume that X and Y are independent. The reason is that they might both be subject to the same economic influences.

Note that the multiplication rule applies to events involving independent random variables. For example, if X and Y are independent, then $P(X = 10 \text{ and } Y = 15) = P(X = 10)P(Y = 15)$.

It is probably fair to say that most events in the real world are not truly independent. However, because of the simplified multiplication rule for independent events, many mathematical models assume that events are independent; the math is much easier with this assumption. The question then is whether the results from such a model are believable. This depends on how unrealistic the independence assumption really is.

4-2e Equally Likely Events

Much of what you know about probability is probably based on situations where outcomes are equally likely. These include flipping coins, throwing dice, drawing balls from urns, and other random mechanisms that are often discussed in introductory probability books. For example, suppose an urn contains 20 red marbles and 10 blue marbles. You plan to randomly select five marbles from the urn, and you are interested, say, in the probability of selecting at least three red marbles. To find this probability, you argue that every possible set of five marbles is equally likely to be chosen. Then you *count* the number of sets of five marbles that contain at least three red marbles, you count the total number of sets of five marbles that could be selected, and you set the desired probability equal to the ratio of these two counts.

It is true that many probabilities, particularly in games of chance, *can* be calculated by using an equally likely argument. It is also true that probabilities calculated in this way satisfy all of the rules of probability, including the rules we have already discussed. However, many probabilities, especially those in business situations, *cannot* be calculated by equally likely arguments for the simple reason that the possible outcomes are not equally likely. For example, just because you are able to identify five possible scenarios for a company's future, there is probably no reason whatsoever to conclude that each scenario has probability 1/5.

The bottom line is that there is no need in this book to discuss complex counting rules for equally likely outcomes. If you dreaded learning about probability in terms of balls and urns, rest assured that you will *not* have to do so here.

4-2f Subjective Versus Objective Probabilities

We now ask a very basic question: Where do the probabilities in a probability distribution come from? A complete answer to this question could lead to a chapter by itself, so we only briefly discuss the issues involved. There are essentially two distinct ways to assess probabilities, objectively and subjectively. **Objective probabilities** are those that can be estimated from long-run proportions, whereas **subjective probabilities** cannot be estimated from long-run proportions. Some examples will clarify this distinction.

Consider throwing two dice and observing the sum of the two sides that face up. What is the probability that the sum of these two sides is 7? You might argue as follows. Because there are $6 \times 6 = 36$ ways the two dice can fall, and because exactly 6 of these result in a sum of 7, the probability of a 7 is $6/36 = 1/6$. This is the equally likely argument discussed previously. It reduces probability to counting.

What if the dice are weighted in some way? Then the equally likely argument is no longer valid. You can, however, toss the dice many times and record the proportion of tosses that result in a sum of 7. This proportion is called a *relative frequency*.

> The **relative frequency** of an event is the proportion of times the event occurs out of the number of times the random experiment is run.

A famous result called the *law of large numbers* states that this relative frequency, in the long run, will get closer and closer to the "true" probability of a 7. This is exactly what we mean by an objective probability. It is a probability that can be estimated as the long-run proportion of times an event occurs in a sequence of many identical experiments.

If you are flipping coins, throwing dice, or spinning roulette wheels, objective probabilities are certainly relevant. You don't need a person's *opinion* of the probability that a roulette wheel, say, will end up pointing to a red number; you can simply spin it many times and keep track of the proportion of times it points to a red number. However, there are many situations, particularly in business, that cannot be repeated many times—or even more than once—under identical conditions. In these situations objective probabilities make no sense (and equally likely arguments usually make no sense either), so you must use subjective probabilities. A subjective probability is one person's assessment of the likelihood that a certain event will occur. We assume that the person making the assessment uses all of the information available to make the most rational assessment possible.

This definition of subjective probability implies that one person's assessment of a probability can differ from another person's assessment of the *same* probability. For example, consider the probability that the San Francisco 49ers will win the next Super Bowl. If you ask a casual football observer to assess this probability, you will get one answer, but if you ask a person with a lot of inside information about injuries, team cohesiveness, and so on, you might get a very different answer. Because these probabilities are *subjective,* people with different information typically assess probabilities in different ways.

Subjective probabilities are usually relevant for unique, one-time situations. However, most situations are not completely unique; you often have some history to guide you. That is, historical relative frequencies can be factored into subjective probabilities. For example, suppose a company is about to market a new product. This product might be different in some ways from any products the company has marketed before, but it might also share some features with the company's previous products. If the company wants to assess the probability that the new product will be a success, it will certainly analyze the unique features of this product and the current state of the market to obtain a subjective assessment. However, the company will also look at its past successes and failures with reasonably similar products. If the proportion of successes with past products was 20%, say, then this value might be a starting point in the assessment of *this* product's probability of success.

All of the "given" probabilities in this chapter and later chapters can be placed somewhere on the objective-to-subjective continuum, usually closer to the subjective end. An important implication of this is that these probabilities are not cast in stone; they are only educated guesses. Therefore, it is always a good idea to run a *sensitivity analysis* (especially in Excel, where this is easy to do) to see how "bottom-line" results depend on the given probabilities. Sensitivity analysis is especially important in Chapter 6, when we study decision making under uncertainty.

PROBLEMS

Note: Student solutions for problems whose numbers appear within a colored box are available for purchase at www .cengagebrain.com.

Level A

1. In a particular suburb, 30% of the households have installed electronic security systems.
  a. If a household is chosen at random from this suburb, what is the probability that this household has *not* installed an electronic security system?
  b. If two households are chosen at random from this suburb, what is the probability that *neither* has installed an electronic security system?

2. Several major automobile producers are competing to have the largest market share for sport utility vehicles (SUVs) in the coming quarter. A professional automobile market analyst assesses that the odds of General Motors *not* being the market leader are 6 to 1. The odds against Toyota and Ford having the largest market share in the coming quarter are similarly assessed to be 12 to 5 and 8 to 3, respectively.
  a. Find the probability that General Motors will have the largest market share for SUVs in the coming quarter.
  b. Find the probability that Toyota will have the largest market share for SUVs in the coming quarter.

c. Find the probability that Ford will have the largest market share for SUVs in the coming quarter.

d. Find the probability that some other automobile manufacturer will have the largest market share for SUVs in the coming quarter.

3. The publisher of a popular financial periodical has decided to undertake a campaign in an effort to attract new subscribers. Market research analysts in this company believe that there is a 1 in 4 chance that the increase in the number of new subscriptions resulting from this campaign will be less than 3000, and there is a 1 in 3 chance that the increase in the number of new subscriptions resulting from this campaign will be between 3000 and 5000. What is the probability that the increase in the number of new subscriptions resulting from this campaign will be less than 3000 *or* more than 5000?

4. Suppose that 18% of the employees of a given corporation engage in physical exercise activities during the lunch hour. Moreover, assume that 57% of all employees are male, and 12% of all employees are males who engage in physical exercise activities during the lunch hour.

a. If you choose an employee at random from this corporation, what is the probability that this person is a female who engages in physical exercise activities during the lunch hour?

b. If you choose an employee at random from this corporation, what is the probability that this person is a female who does not engage in physical exercise activities during the lunch hour?

5. In a study designed to gauge married women's participation in the workplace today, the data provided in the file **P04_05.xlsx** were obtained from a sample of 750 randomly selected married women. Consider a woman selected at random from this sample in answering the following questions.

a. What is the probability that this woman has a job outside the home?

b. What is the probability that this woman has at least one child?

c. What is the probability that this woman has a full-time job and no more than one child?

d. What is the probability that this woman has a part-time job or at least one child, but not both?

6. Suppose that you draw a single card from a standard deck of 52 playing cards.

a. What is the probability that this card is a diamond *or* club?

b. What is the probability that this card is not a 4?

c. Given that this card is a black card, what is the probability that it is a spade?

d. Let E_1 be the event that this card is a black card. Let E_2 be the event that this card is a spade. Are E_1 and E_2 independent events? Why or why not?

e. Let E_3 be the event that this card is a heart. Let E_4 be the event that this card is a 3. Are E_3 and E_4 independent events? Why or why not?

Level B

7. In a large accounting firm, the proportion of accountants with MBA degrees and at least five years of professional experience is 75% as large as the proportion of accountants with no MBA degree and less than five years of professional experience. Furthermore, 35% of the accountants in this firm have MBA degrees, and 45% have fewer than five years of professional experience. If one of the firm's accountants is selected at random, what is the probability that this accountant has an MBA degree or at least five years of professional experience, but not both?

8. A local beer producer sells two types of beer, a regular brand and a light brand with 30% fewer calories. The company's marketing department wants to verify that its traditional approach of appealing to local white-collar workers with light beer commercials and appealing to local blue-collar workers with regular beer commercials is indeed a good strategy. A randomly selected group of 400 local workers are questioned about their beer-drinking preferences, and the data in the file **P04_08.xlsx** are obtained.

a. If a blue-collar worker is chosen at random from this group, what is the probability that he/she prefers light beer (to regular beer or no beer at all)?

b. If a white-collar worker is chosen at random from this group, what is the probability that he/she prefers light beer (to regular beer or no beer at all)?

c. If you restrict your attention to workers who like to drink beer, what is the probability that a randomly selected blue-collar worker prefers to drink light beer?

d. If you restrict your attention to workers who like to drink beer, what is the probability that a randomly selected white-collar worker prefers to drink light beer?

e. Does the company's marketing strategy appear to be appropriate? Explain why or why not.

9. Suppose that two dice are tossed. For each die, it is equally likely that 1, 2, 3, 4, 5, or 6 dots will turn up. Let S be the sum of the two dice.

a. What is the probability that S will be 5 or 7?

b. What is the probability that S will be some number other than 4 or 8?

c. Let E_1 be the event that the first die shows a 3. Let E_2 be the event that S is 6. Are E_1 and E_2 independent events?

d. Again, let E_1 be the event that the first die shows a 3. Let E_3 be the event that S is 7. Are E_1 and E_3 independent events?

e. Given that S is 7, what is the probability that the first die showed 4 dots?

f. Given that the first die shows a 3, what is the probability that S is an even number?

4-3 PROBABILITY DISTRIBUTION OF A SINGLE RANDOM VARIABLE

We now discuss the topic of most interest in this chapter, *probability distributions*. In this section we examine the probability distribution of a single random variable.

There are really two types of random variables: discrete and continuous. A **discrete** random variable has only a finite number of possible values, whereas a **continuous** random variable has a continuum of possible values.[1] Usually a discrete distribution results from a count, whereas a continuous distribution results from a measurement. For example, the number of children in a family is clearly discrete, whereas the amount of rain this year in San Francisco is clearly continuous.

This distinction between counts and measurements is not always clear-cut. For example, what about the demand for televisions at a particular store next month? The number of televisions demanded is clearly an integer (a count), but it probably has many possible values, such as all integers from 0 to 100. In some cases like this, we often approximate in one of two ways. First, we might use a discrete distribution with only a few possible values, such as all multiples of 20 from 0 to 100. Second, we might approximate the possible demand as a continuum from 0 to 100. The reason for such approximations is to simplify the mathematics, and they are frequently used.

Mathematically, there is an important difference between discrete and continuous probability distributions. Specifically, a proper treatment of continuous distributions, analogous to the treatment we provide in this chapter, requires calculus—which we do not presume for this book. Therefore, we discuss only discrete distributions in this chapter. In later chapters we often *use* continuous distributions, particularly the bell-shaped normal distribution, but we simply state their properties without deriving them mathematically.

The essential properties of a discrete random variable and its associated probability distribution are quite simple. We discuss them in general and then analyze a numerical example.

Usually, capital letters toward the end of the alphabet, such as X, Y, and Z, are used to denote random variables.

Let X be a random variable. To specify the probability distribution of X, we need to specify its possible values and their probabilities. We assume that there are k possible values, denoted $v_1, v_2, \ldots, v_k$. The probability of a typical value v_i is denoted in one of two ways, either $P(X = v_i)$ or $p(v_i)$. The first is a reminder that this is a probability involving the random variable X, whereas the second is a shorthand notation. Probability distributions must satisfy two criteria: (1) the probabilities must be nonnegative, and (2) they must sum to 1. In symbols, we must have

$$\sum_{i=1}^{k} p(v_i) = 1, \quad p(v_i) \geq 0$$

A discrete probability distribution is a set of possible values and a corresponding set of probabilities that sum to 1.

This is basically all there is to it: a list of possible values and a list of associated probabilities that sum to 1. It is also sometimes useful to calculate *cumulative* probabilities. A **cumulative probability** is the probability that the random variable is *less than or equal to* some particular value. For example, assume that 10, 20, 30, and 40 are the possible values of a random variable X, with corresponding probabilities 0.15, 0.25, 0.35, and 0.25. Then a typical cumulative probability is $P(X \leq 30)$. From the addition rule it can be calculated as

$$P(X \leq 30) = P(X = 10) + P(X = 20) + P(X = 30) = 0.75$$

---

[1]Actually, a more rigorous discussion allows a discrete random variable to have an infinite number of possible values, such as all positive integers.

The point is that the cumulative probabilities are completely determined by the individual probabilities.

4-3a Summary Measures of a Probability Distribution

It is often convenient to summarize a probability distribution with two or three well-chosen numbers. The first of these is the **mean**, often denoted μ. It is also called the **expected value** of X and denoted $E(X)$ (for *expected* X). The mean is a weighted sum of the possible values, weighted by their probabilities, as shown in Equation (4.6). In much the same way that an average of a set of numbers indicates "central location," the mean indicates the "center" of the probability distribution.

Mean of a Probability Distribution, μ

$$\mu = E(X) = \sum_{i=1}^{k} v_i p(v_i) \qquad \textbf{(4.6)}$$

To measure the variability in a distribution, we calculate its variance or standard deviation. The **variance**, denoted by σ^2 or $\text{Var}(X)$, is a weighted sum of the squared deviations of the possible values from the mean, where the weights are again the probabilities. This is shown in Equation (4.7). As in Chapter 2, the variance is expressed in the *square* of the units of X, such as dollars squared. Therefore, a more natural measure of variability is the **standard deviation**, denoted by σ or $\text{Stdev}(X)$. It is the square root of the variance, as indicated by Equation (4.8).

Variance of a Probability Distribution, σ^2

$$\sigma^2 = Var(X) = \sum_{i=1}^{k} (v_i - E(X))^2 p(v_i) \qquad \textbf{(4.7)}$$

Standard Deviation of a Probability Distribution, σ

$$\sigma = \text{Stdev}(X) = \sqrt{\text{Var}(X)} \qquad \textbf{(4.8)}$$

Equation (4.7) is useful for understanding variance as a weighted average of squared deviations from the mean. However, the following is an equivalent formula for variance and is somewhat easier to implement in Excel. (It can be derived with straightforward algebra.) In words, you find the weighted average of the squared values, weighted by their probabilities, and then subtract the square of the mean.

Variance (computing formula)

$$\sigma^2 = \sum_{i=1}^{k} v_i^2 p(v_i) - \mu^2 \qquad \textbf{(4.9)}$$

We now consider a typical example.

4.2 MARKET RETURN SCENARIOS FOR THE NATIONAL ECONOMY

In reality, there is a continuum of possible returns. The assumption of only five possible returns is clearly an approximation to reality, but such an assumption is often useful.

An investor is concerned with the market return for the coming year, where the market return is defined as the percentage gain (or loss, if negative) over the year. The investor believes there are five possible scenarios for the national economy in the coming year: rapid expansion, moderate expansion, no growth, moderate contraction, and serious contraction. Furthermore, she has used all of the information available to her to estimate that the market returns for these scenarios are, respectively, 23%, 18%, 15%, 9%, and 3%. That is, the possible returns vary from a high of 23% to a low of 3%. Also, she has assessed that the probabilities of these outcomes are 0.12, 0.40, 0.25, 0.15, and 0.08. Use this information to describe the probability distribution of the market return.

Objective To compute the mean, variance, and standard deviation of the probability distribution of the market return for the coming year.

Solution

To make the connection between the general notation and this particular example, let X denote the market return for the coming year. Then each possible economic scenario leads to a possible value of X. For example, the first possible value is $v_1 = 23\%$, and its probability is $p(v_1) = 0.12$. These values and probabilities appear in columns B and C of Figure 4.3. (See the file **Market Return.xlsx**.) Note that the five probabilities sum to 1, as they should. This probability distribution implies, for example, that the probability of a market return at least as large as 18% is $0.12 + 0.40 = 0.52$ because it could occur as a result of rapid or moderate expansion of the economy. Similarly, the probability that the market return is 9% or less is $0.15 + 0.08 = 0.23$ because this could occur as a result of moderate or serious contraction of the economy.

Figure 4.3 Probability Distribution of Market Returns

	A	B	C	D	E	F	G	H
1	Mean, variance, and standard deviation of the market return					Range names used		
2						Market_return	=Market!$C$4:$C$8	
3	Economic outcome	Probability	Market return	Sq dev from mean		Mean	=Market!$B$11	
4	Rapid Expansion	0.12	0.23	0.005929		Probability	=Market!$B$4:$B$8	
5	Moderate Expansion	0.40	0.18	0.000729		Sq_dev_from_mean	=Market!$D$4:$D$8	
6	No Growth	0.25	0.15	0.000009		Stdev	=Market!$B$13	
7	Moderate Contraction	0.15	0.09	0.003969		Variance	=Market!$B$12	
8	Serious Contraction	0.08	0.03	0.015129				
9								
10	Summary measures of return							
11	Mean	15.3%						
12	Variance	0.002811	0.002811	←———		Quick alternative formula		
13	Stdev	5.3%	5.3%					

© Cengage Learning

The summary measures of this probability distribution appear in the range B11:B13. They can be calculated with the following steps. (Note that the formulas make use of the range names listed in the figure.)

Procedure for Calculating Summary Measures

1. **Mean return.** Calculate the mean return in cell B11 with the formula

   =SUMPRODUCT(Market_return,Probability)

Excel Tip: Excel's SUMPRODUCT Function

Excel's SUMPRODUCT function is a gem, and you should use it whenever possible. It takes (at least) two arguments, which must be ranges of exactly the same size and shape. It sums the products of the values in these ranges. For example, =SUMPRODUCT (A1:A3,B1:B3) is equivalent to the formula =A1*B1 + A2*B2 + A3*B3. If the ranges contain only a few cells, there isn't much advantage to using SUMPRODUCT, but when the ranges are large, such as A1:A100 and B1:B100, SUMPRODUCT is the only viable choice.

This formula illustrates the general rule in Equation (4.6): The mean is the sum of products of possible values and probabilities.

2. **Squared deviations.** To get ready to compute the variance from Equation (4.7), calculate the squared deviations from the mean by entering the formula

=(C4-Mean)^2

in cell D4 and copying it down through cell D8.

3. **Variance.** Calculate the variance of the market return in cell B12 with the formula

=SUMPRODUCT(Sq_dev_from_mean,Probability)

As always, range names are not required, but they make the Excel formulas easier to read. You can use them or omit them, as you wish.

This illustrates the general formula for variance in Equation (4.7). The variance is always a sum of products of squared deviations from the mean and probabilities. Alternatively, you can skip the calculation of the squared deviations from the mean and use Equation (4.9) directly. This is done in cell C12 with the formula

=SUMPRODUCT(Market_return,Market_return,Probability)-Mean^2

By entering the Market_return range twice in this SUMPRODUCT formula, you get the squares. From now on, we will use this simplified formula for variance and dispense with squared deviations from the mean. But regardless of how it is calculated, you should remember the essence of variance: It is a weighted average of squared deviations from the mean.

4. **Standard deviation.** Calculate the standard deviation of the market return in cell B13 with the formula

=SQRT(Variance)

You can see that the mean return is 15.3% and the standard deviation is 5.3%. What do these measures really mean? First, the mean, or *expected,* return does not imply that the most likely return is 15.3%, nor is this the value that the investor "expects" to occur. In fact, the value 15.3% is not even a possible market return (at least not according to the model). You can understand these measures better in terms of long-run averages. Specifically, if you could imagine the coming year being repeated many times, each time using the probability distribution in columns B and C to generate a market return, then the average of these market returns would be close to 15.3%, and their standard deviation—calculated as in Chapter 2—would be close to 5.3%.

Before leaving this section, we emphasize a key point, a point that is easy to forget with all the details. The whole point of discussing probability and probability distributions, especially in the context of business problems, is that uncertainty is often a key factor, and you cannot simply ignore it. For instance, the mean return in this example is 15.3%. However, it would be far from realistic to treat the actual return as a sure 15.3%, with no uncertainty. If you did this, you would be ignoring the uncertainty completely, and it is often the uncertainty that makes business problems interesting—and adds risk. Therefore, to model such problems in a realistic way, you must deal with probability and probability distributions. ∎

4-3b Conditional Mean and Variance

There are many situations where the mean and variance of a random variable depend on some external event. In this case, you can *condition* on the outcome of the external event to find the overall mean and variance (or standard deviation) of the random variable.

It is best to motivate this with an example. Consider the random variable X, representing the percentage change in the price of stock A from now to a year from now. This change is driven partly by circumstances specific to company A, but it is also driven partly by the economy as a whole. In this case, the outcome of the economy is the external event. Let's assume that the economy in the coming year will be awful, stable, or great with probabilities 0.20, 0.50, and 0.30, respectively. In addition, we make the following assumptions.

- Given that the economy is awful, the mean and standard deviation of X are −20% and 30%.
- Given that the economy is stable, the mean and standard deviation of X are 5% and 20%.
- Given that the economy is great, the mean and standard deviation of X are 25% and 15%.

Each of these statements is a statement about X, conditional upon the economy. What can you say about the *unconditional* mean and standard deviation of X? That is, what are the mean and standard deviation of X *before* you learn the state of the economy? The answers come from Equations (4.10) and (4.11). In the context of the example, p_i is the probability of economy state i, and $E_i(X)$ and $Var_i(X)$ are the mean and variance of X, given that economy state i occurs.

Conditional Mean Formula

$$E(X) = \sum_{i=1}^{k} E_i(X)p_i \qquad \text{(4.10)}$$

Conditional Variance Formula

$$Var(X) = \sum_{i=1}^{k} \left[Var_i(X) + [E_i(X)]^2 \right] p_i - [E(X)]^2 \qquad \text{(4.11)}$$

In the example, the mean percentage change in the price of stock A, from Equation (4.10), is

$$E(X) = 0.2(-20\%) + 0.5(5\%) + 0.3(25\%) = 6\%$$

To calculate the standard deviation of X, first use Equation (4.11) to calculate the variance, and then take its square root. The variance is

$$Var(X) = \{0.2[(30\%)^2 + (-20\%)^2] + 0.5[(20\%)^2 + (5\%)^2]$$
$$+ 0.2[(15\%)^2 + (25\%)^2]\} - (6\%)^2 = 0.06915$$

Taking the square root gives

$$Stdev(X) = \sqrt{0.06915} = 26.30\%$$

Of course, these calculations can be done easily in Excel. See the file **Stock Price and Economy.xlsx** for details.

The point of this example is that it is often easier to assess the uncertainty of some random variable X by conditioning on every possible outcome of some external event like the economy. However, *before* that outcome is known, the relevant mean and standard deviation of X are those calculated from Equations (4.10) and (4.11). In this particular example, *before* you know the state of the economy, the relevant mean and standard deviation of the change in the price of stock A are 6% and 26.3%, respectively.

PROBLEMS

Level A

10. A fair coin (i.e., heads and tails are equally likely) is tossed three times. Let X be the number of heads observed in three tosses of this fair coin.
  a. Find the probability distribution of X.
  b. Find the probability that two or fewer heads are observed in three tosses.
  c. Find the probability that at least one head is observed in three tosses.
  d. Find the expected value of X.
  e. Find the standard deviation of X.

11. Consider a random variable with the following probability distribution: $P(X = 0) = 0.1$, $P(X = 1) = 0.2$, $P(X = 2) = 0.3$, $P(X = 3) = 0.3$, and $P(X = 4) = 0.1$.
  a. Find $P(X \leq 2)$.
  b. Find $P(1 < X \leq 3)$.
  c. Find $P(X > 0)$.
  d. Find $P(X > 3 | X > 2)$.
  e. Find the expected value of X.
  f. Find the standard deviation of X.

12. A study has shown that the probability distribution of X, the number of customers in line (including the one being served, if any) at a checkout counter in a department store, is given by $P(X = 0) = 0.25$, $P(X = 1) = 0.25$, $P(X = 2) = 0.20$, $P(X = 3) = 0.20$, and $P(\geq 4) = 0.10$. Consider a newly arriving customer to the checkout line.
  a. What is the probability that this customer will not have to wait behind anyone?
  b. What is the probability that this customer will have to wait behind at least one customer?
  c. On average, the newly arriving customer will have to wait behind how many other customers?

13. A construction company has to complete a project no later than three months from now or there will be significant cost overruns. The manager of the construction company believes that there are four possible values for the random variable X, the number of months from now it will take to complete this project: 2, 2.5, 3, and 3.5. The manager currently thinks that the probabilities of these four possibilities are in the ratio 1 to 2 to 4 to 2. That is, $X = 2.5$ is twice as likely as $X = 2$, $X = 3$ is twice as likely as $X = 2.5$, and $X = 3.5$ is half as likely as $X = 3$.
  a. Find the probability distribution of X.
  b. What is the probability that this project will be completed in less than three months from now?

  c. What is the probability that this project will *not* be completed on time?
  d. What is the expected completion time (in months) of this project from now?
  e. How much variability (in months) exists around the expected value you found in part **d**?

14. Three areas of southern California are prime candidates for forest fires each dry season. You believe (based on historical evidence) that each of these areas, independently of the others, has a 30% chance of having a major forest fire in the next dry season.
  a. Find the probability distribution of X, the number of the three regions that have major forest fires in the next dry season.
  b. What is the probability that none of the areas will have a major forest fire?
  c. What is the probability that all of them will have a major forest fire?
  d. What is expected number of regions with major forest fires?
  e. Each major forest fire is expected to cause $20 million in damage and other expenses. What is the expected amount of damage and other expenses in these three regions in the next dry season?

Level B

15. The National Football League playoffs are just about to begin. Because of their great record in the regular season, the Steelers get a bye in the first week of the playoffs. In the second week, they will play the winner of the game between the Ravens and the Patriots. A football expert estimates that the Ravens will beat the Patriots with probability 0.45. This same expert estimates that if the Steelers play the Ravens, the mean and standard deviation of the point spread (Steelers points minus Ravens points) will be 6.5 and 10.5, whereas if the Steelers play the Patriots, the mean and standard deviation of the point spread (Steelers points minus Patriots points) will be 3.5 and 12.5. Find the mean and standard deviation of the point spread (Steelers points minus their opponent's points) in the Steelers game.

16. Because of tough economic times, the Indiana legislature is debating a bill that could have significant negative implications for public school funding. There are three possibilities for this bill: (1) it could be passed in essentially its current version; (2) it could be passed but with amendments that make it less harsh on public school funding; or (3) it could be defeated. The probabilities of these three events are estimated to be 0.4, 0.25, and 0.35, respectively. The estimated effect on percentage changes in salaries next year at Indiana University are estimated as follows. If the bill is passed in its current version, the mean and standard deviation of salary percentage change will be 0% and 1%. If the bill is passed with amendments, the mean and standard deviation will be 1.5% and 3.5%. Finally, if the bill is defeated, the mean and standard deviation will be 3.5% and 6%. Find the mean and standard deviation of the percentage change in salaries next year at Indiana University.

17. The "house edge" in any game of chance is defined as

$$\frac{E(\text{player's loss on a bet})}{\text{Size of player's loss on a bet}}$$

For example, if a player wins \$10 with probability 0.48 and loses \$10 with probability 0.52 on any bet, the house edge is

$$\frac{-[10(0.48) - 10(0.52)]}{10} = 0.04$$

Give an interpretation to the house edge that relates to how much money the house is likely to win on average. Which do you think has a larger house edge: roulette or sports gambling? Why?

4-4 INTRODUCTION TO SIMULATION

In the previous section, we asked you to imagine many repetitions of an event, with each repetition resulting in a different random outcome. Fortunately, you can do more than *imagine;* you can make it happen with computer simulation. **Simulation** is an extremely useful tool that can be used to incorporate uncertainty explicitly into spreadsheet models. A simulation model is the same as a regular spreadsheet model except that some cells contain random quantities. Each time the spreadsheet recalculates, new values of the random quantities are generated, and these typically lead to different bottom-line results. By forcing the spreadsheet to recalculate many times, a business manager is able to discover the results that are most likely to occur, those that are least likely to occur, and best-case and worst-case results. We use simulation several places in this book to help explain concepts in probability and statistics. We begin in this section by using simulation to explain the connection between summary measures of probability distributions and the corresponding summary measures from Chapter 2.

We continue to use the market return distribution in Figure 4.3. Because this is your first discussion of computer simulation in Excel, we proceed in some detail. Our goal is to simulate many returns (we arbitrarily choose 400) from this distribution and analyze the resulting returns. We want each simulated return to have probability 0.12 of being 23%, probability 0.40 of being 18%, and so on. Then, using the methods for summarizing data from Chapter 2, we calculate the average and standard deviation of the 400 simulated returns.

The method for simulating many market returns is straightforward once you know how to simulate a *single* market return. The key to this is Excel's RAND function, which generates a random number between 0 and 1. The RAND function has no arguments, so every time you use it, you must enter =RAND(). (Although there is nothing inside the parentheses next to RAND, the parentheses cannot be omitted.) That is, to generate a random number between 0 and 1 in any cell, you enter the formula

=RAND()

in that cell. The RAND function can also be used as part of another function. For example, you can simulate the result of a single flip of a fair coin with the formula

=IF(RAND()<=0.5,"Heads","Tails")

Random numbers generated with Excel's RAND function are said to be **uniformly distributed** between 0 and 1 because all decimal values between 0 and 1 are equally likely. These uniformly distributed random numbers can then be used to generate numbers from any discrete distribution such as the market return distribution in Figure 4.3. To see how this is done, note first that there are five possible values in this distribution. Therefore, we divide the interval from 0 to 1 into five parts with lengths equal to the probabilities in the probability distribution. Then we see which of these parts the random number from RAND falls into and generate the associated market return. If the random number is between 0 and 0.12 (of length 0.12), we generate 23% as the market return; if the random number is between 0.12 and 0.52 (of length 0.40), we generate 18% as the market return; and so on. See Figure 4.4.

Figure 4.4

Associating RAND Values with Market Returns

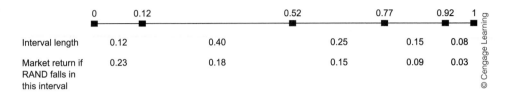

	0	0.12	0.52	0.77	0.92 1
Interval length	0.12	0.40	0.25	0.15	0.08
Market return if RAND falls in this interval	0.23	0.18	0.15	0.09	0.03

This procedure is accomplished most easily in Excel through the use of a lookup table. A lookup table is useful when you want to compare a particular value to a set of values and, depending on where the particular value falls, assign the appropriate value from an associated list of values. In this case we want to compare a generated random number to values falling in each of the five intervals shown in Figure 4.4, and then report the corresponding market return. This process is made relatively simple in Excel by applying the VLOOKUP function, as explained in the following steps.[2] (Refer to Figure 4.5 and the **Market Return.xlsx** file.)

Figure 4.5 **Simulation of Market Returns**

	A	B	C	D	E	F	G	H	I
1	Simulating market returns					Range names used			
2						LTable	=Simulation!$D$13:$E$17		
3	Summary statistics from simulation below					Simulated_market_return	=Simulation!$B$13:$B$412		
4	Average return	0.151							
5	Stdev of returns	0.051							
6									
7	Exact values from previous sheet (for comparison)								
8	Average return	0.153							
9	Stdev of returns	0.053							
10									
11	Simulation			Lookup table					
12	Random #	Simulated market return		Cum Prob	Return				
13	0.798539	0.09		0	0.23				
14	0.667815	0.15		0.12	0.18				
15	0.583578	0.15		0.52	0.15				
16	0.049406	0.23		0.77	0.09				
17	0.916760	0.09		0.92	0.03				
18	0.639143	0.15							
19	0.450413	0.18							
411	0.751662	0.15							
412	0.524991	0.15							

[2]This could also be accomplished with nested IF functions, but the resulting formula would be much more complex.

Procedure for Generating Random Market Returns in Excel

1. **Lookup table.** Copy the possible returns to the range E13:E17. Then enter the *cumulative* probabilities next to them in the range D13:D17. To do this, enter the value 0 in cell D13. Then enter the formula

   =D13+Market!B4

   in cell D14 and copy it down through cell D17. (Note that the Market!B4 in this formula refers to cell B4 in the Market sheet, that is, cell B4 in Figure 4.3.) Each value in column D is the current probability plus the previous value. The table in this range, D13:E17, becomes the lookup range. For convenience, we have named this range LTable.

2. **Random numbers.** Enter random numbers in the range A13:A412. An easy way to do this is to select the range, then type the formula

   =RAND()

   and finally press Ctrl+Enter. Note that these random numbers are "live." That is, each time you do any calculation in Excel or press the recalculation F9 key, these random numbers change.

   Excel Tip: Copying a Formula with Ctrl+Enter
   A quick way to enter a formula (or value) into a range of cells is to select the range, type the formula (or value), and press Ctrl+Enter (both keys at once). This is equivalent to entering the formula in the first cell of the range and then copying it to the rest of the range.

3. **Market returns.** Generate the random market returns by referring the random numbers in column A to the lookup table. Specifically, enter the formula

   =VLOOKUP(A13,LTable,2)

   in cell B13 and copy it down through cell B412. This formula compares the random number in cell A13 to the cumulative probabilities in the first column of the lookup table and sees where it "fits," as illustrated in Figure 4.4. Then it returns the corresponding market return in the second column of the lookup table. (It uses the *second* column because the third argument of the VLOOKUP function is 2.)

   Excel Tip: Excel's VLOOKUP Function
   In general, the VLOOKUP function takes four arguments: (1) the value to be compared, (2) a table of lookup values, with the values to be compared against always in the leftmost column, and (3) the column number of the lookup table that contains the "answer," and (4) whether you are looking for an approximate match or an exact match for the lookup value. When you are looking for an approximate match, as in this example, the fourth argument can be omitted.

4. **Summary statistics.** Summarize the 400 market returns by entering the formulas

   =AVERAGE(Simulated_market_return)

   and

   =STDEV(Simulated_market_return)

   in cells B4 and B5. For comparison, copy the average and standard deviation from the Market sheet in Figure 4.3 to cells B8 and B9.

Now let's step back and see what has been accomplished. The following points are relevant.

- Simulations like this are very common, and we will continue to use them to illustrate concepts in probability and statistics.

- The numbers you obtain will be different from the ones in Figure 4.5 because of the nature of simulation. The results depend on the particular random numbers that happen to be generated.

- The way we entered cumulative probabilities and then used a lookup table is generally the best way to generate random numbers from a discrete probability distribution. However, there is an easier way if a simulation add-in is available, as will be discussed in Chapter 15.

- Each generated market return in the Simulated_market_return range is one of the five possible market returns. If you count the number of times each return appears and then divide by 400, the number of simulated values, you will see that the resulting fractions are approximately equal to the original probabilities. For example, the fraction of times the highest return 23% appears is about 0.12. This is the essence of what it means to simulate from a given probability distribution.

- The average and standard deviation in cells B4 and B5, calculated from the formulas in Chapter 2, are very close to the mean and standard deviation of the probability distribution in cells B8 and B9. However, these measures are calculated in entirely different ways. Specifically, the average in cell B4 is a simple average of 400 numbers, whereas the mean in cell B8 is a weighted sum of the possible market returns, weighted by their probabilities.

This last point allows you to interpret the summary measures of a probability distribution. Specifically, the mean and standard deviation of a probability distribution are approximately what you would obtain if you calculated the average and standard deviation, using the formulas from Chapter 2, of many simulated values from this distribution. In other words, the mean is the long-run average of the simulated values. Similarly, the standard deviation measures their variability.

You might ask whether this long-run average interpretation of the mean is relevant if the situation is going to occur only once. For example, the market return in the example is for "the coming year," and the coming year will occur only once. So what is the use of a long-run average? In this type of situation, the long-run average interpretation is not very relevant, but fortunately, there is another use of the expected value that we exploit in Chapter 6. Specifically, when a decision maker must choose among several actions that have uncertain outcomes, the preferred decision is often the one with the largest expected (monetary) value. This makes the expected value of a probability distribution extremely important in decision-making contexts.

FUNDAMENTAL INSIGHT

Role of Simulation

Spreadsheet simulation is one of the most important tools in an analyst's arsenal. For this reason, it will be discussed in much more depth in later chapters, particularly Chapters 15 and 16. Simulation doesn't show you what *will* occur; instead, it shows you many of the possible scenarios that *might* occur. By seeing a variety of scenarios, including those that are "typical" and those that are "extreme," you understand the situation much better and can make more informed decisions relative to reward and risk.

PROBLEMS

Level A

18. A quality inspector picks a sample of 15 items at random from a manufacturing process known to produce 10% defective items. Let X be the number of defective items found in the random sample of 15 items. Assume that the condition of each item is independent of that of each of the other items in the sample. The probability distribution of X is provided in the file **P04_18.xlsx**.

    a. Use simulation to generate 500 values of this random variable X.

    b. Calculate the mean and standard deviation of the simulated values. How do they compare to the mean and standard deviation of the given probability distribution?

19. A personnel manager of a large manufacturing plant is investigating the number of reported on-the-job accidents at the facility over the past several years. Let X be the number of such accidents reported during a one-month period. Based on past records, the manager has established the probability distribution for X as shown in the file **P04_19.xlsx**.
   a. Use simulation to generate 1000 values of this random variable X.
   b. Is the simulated distribution indicative of the given probability distribution? Explain why or why not.

20. Let X be the number of heads when a fair coin is flipped four times.
   a. Find the distribution of X and then use simulation to generate 1000 values of X.
   b. Is the simulated distribution indicative of the given probability distribution? Explain why or why not.
   c. Calculate the mean and standard deviation of the simulated values. How do they compare to the mean and standard deviation of the given probability distribution?

21. The probability distribution of X, the number of customers in line (including the one being served, if any) at a checkout counter in a department store, is given by $P(X = 0) = 0.25$, $P(X = 1) = 0.25$, $P(X = 2) = 0.20$, $P(X = 3) = 0.20$, and $P(X = 4) = 0.10$.

   a. Use simulation to generate 500 values of this random variable X.
   b. Is the simulated distribution indicative of the given probability distribution? Explain why or why not.
   c. Calculate the mean and standard deviation of the simulated values. How do they compare to the mean and standard deviation of the given probability distribution?
   d. Repeat parts **a** through **c** with 5000 simulated values rather than 500. Explain any differences you observe.

Level B

22. Suppose Michigan is favored by 17.5 points over Indiana. If you bet a "unit" on Indiana and Indiana loses by 17 or less, you win $10. If Indiana loses by 18 or more points, you lose $11. Find the mean and standard deviation of your winnings on a single bet. Assume that there is a 0.5 probability that you will win your bet and a 0.5 probability that you will lose your bet. Also simulate 1600 "bets" to estimate the average loss per bet. (*Note:* Do not be too disappointed if you are off by up to 50 cents. It takes many, say 10,000, simulated bets to get a really good estimate of the mean loss per bet. This is because there is a lot of variability on each bet.)

4-5 CONCLUSION

This chapter has introduced some very important concepts, including the basic rules of probability, random variables, probability distributions, and summary measures of probability distributions. We have also shown how computer simulation can be used to help explain some of these concepts. Many of the concepts presented in this chapter are used in later chapters, so it is important to learn them now. In particular, we rely heavily on probability distributions in Chapter 6 when we discuss decision making under uncertainty. There you will learn how the expected value of a probability distribution is the primary criterion for making decisions. We will also continue to use computer simulation in later chapters to help explain statistical concepts.

Summary of Key Terms

Term	Explanation	Excel	Page	Equation
Random variable	Associates a numerical value with each possible outcome in a situation involving uncertainty		140	
Probability	A number between 0 and 1 that measures the likelihood that some event will occur		142	
Rule of complements	The probability of any event and the probability of its complement sum to 1	Basic formulas	142	4.1
Mutually exclusive events	Events where only one of them can occur		142	
Exhaustive events	Events where at least one of them must occur		143	

Term	Explanation	Excel	Page	Equation
Addition rule for mutually exclusive events	The probability that at least one of a set of mutually exclusive events will occur is the sum of their probabilities	Basic formulas	143	4.2
Conditional probability formula	Updates the probability of an event, given the knowledge that another event has occurred	Basic formulas	144	4.3
Multiplication rule	Formula for the probability that two events both occur	Basic formulas	144	4.4
Probability tree	A graphical representation of how events occur through time, useful for calculating probabilities		145	
Probabilistically independent events	Events where knowledge that one of them has occurred is of no value in assessing the probability that the other will occur		146	4.5
Relative frequency	The proportion of times the event occurs out of the number of times a random experiment is performed		147	
Cumulative probability	"Less than or equal to" probabilities associated with a random variable		150	
Mean (or expected value) of a probability distribution	A measure of central tendency—the weighted sum of the possible values, weighted by their probabilities	Basic formulas	151	4.6
Variance of a probability distribution	A measure of variability: the weighted sum of the squared deviations of the possible values from the mean, weighted by the probabilities	Basic formulas	151	4.7, 4.9
Standard deviation of a probability distribution	A measure of variability: the square root of the variance	Basic formulas	151	4.8
Simulation	An extremely useful tool that can be used to incorporate uncertainty explicitly into spreadsheet models		156	
Uniformly distributed random numbers	Random numbers such that all decimal values between 0 and 1 are equally likely	=RAND()	156	

PROBLEMS

Conceptual Questions

C.1. Suppose that you want to find the probability that event *A* or event *B* will occur. If these two events are *not* mutually exclusive, explain how you would proceed.

C.2. "If two events are mutually exclusive, they must *not* be independent events." Is this statement true or false? Explain your choice.

C.3. Is the number of passengers who show up for a particular commercial airline flight a discrete or a continuous random variable? Is the time between flight arrivals at a major airport a discrete or a continuous random variable? Explain your answers.

C.4. Suppose that officials in the federal government are trying to determine the likelihood of a major small-pox epidemic in the United States within the next 12 months. Is this an example of an objective probability or a subjective probability? How might the officials assess this probability?

C.5. Consider the statement, "When there are a finite number of outcomes, then all probability is just a matter of counting. Specifically, if *n* of the outcomes are favorable to some event *E*, and there are *N* outcomes total, then the probability of *E* is *n/N*." Is this statement always true? Is it always false?

C.6. If there is uncertainty about some monetary outcome and you are concerned about return and risk, then all you need to see are the mean and standard deviation. The entire distribution provides no extra useful information. Do you agree or disagree? Provide an example to back up your argument.

C.7. Choose at least one uncertain quantity of interest to you. For example, you might choose the highest price of gas between now and the end of the year, the highest point the Dow Jones Industrial Average will reach between now and the end of the year, the number of majors Tiger Woods will win in his career, and so on. Using all of the information and insight you have, assess the probability distribution of this uncertain quantity. Is there one "right answer?"

C.8. Historically, the most popular measure of variability has been the standard deviation, the square root of the weighted sum of *squared* deviations from the mean, weighted by their probabilities. Suppose analysts had always used an alternative measure of variability, the weighted sum of the *absolute* deviations from the mean, again weighted by their probabilities. Do you think this would have made a big difference in the theory and practice of probability and statistics?

C.9. Suppose a person flips a coin, but before you can see the result, the person puts her hand over the coin. At this point, does it make sense to talk about the *probability* that the result is heads? Is this any different from the probability of heads *before* the coin was flipped?

C.10. Consider an event that will either occur or not. For example, the event might be that California will experience a major earthquake in the next five years. You let p be the probability that the event will occur. Does it make any sense to have a probability distribution of p? Why or why not? If so, what might this distribution look like? How would you interpret it?

C.11. Suppose a couple is planning to have two children. Let B1 be the event that the first child is a boy, and let B2 be the event that the second child is a boy. You and your friend get into an argument about whether B1 and B2 are *independent* events. You think they are independent and your friend thinks they aren't. Which of you is correct? How could you settle the argument?

Level A

23. A business manager who needs to make many phone calls has estimated that when she calls a client, the probability that she will reach the client right away is 60%. If she does not reach the client on the first call, the probability that she will reach the client with a subsequent call in the next hour is 20%.
   a. Find the probability that the manager reaches her client in two or fewer calls.
   b. Find the probability that the manager reaches her client on the second call but not on the first call.
   c. Find the probability that the manager is unsuccessful on two consecutive calls.

24. Suppose that a marketing research firm sends questionnaires to two different companies. Based on historical evidence, the marketing research firm believes that each company, independently of the other, will return the questionnaire with probability 0.40.
   a. What is the probability that *both* questionnaires are returned?
   b. What is the probability that *neither* of the questionnaires is returned?
   c. Now, suppose that this marketing research firm sends questionnaires to *ten* different companies. Assuming that each company, independently of the others, returns its completed questionnaire with probability 0.40, how do your answers to parts **a** and **b** change?

25. Based on past sales experience, an appliance store stocks five window air conditioner units for the coming week. No orders for additional air conditioners will be made until next week. The weekly consumer demand for this type of appliance has the probability distribution given in the file **P04_25.xlsx**.
   a. Let X be the number of window air conditioner units left at the end of the week (if any), and let Y be the number of special stockout orders required (if any), assuming that a special stockout order is required each time there is a demand and no unit is available in stock. Find the probability distributions of X and Y.
   b. Find the expected value of X and the expected value of Y.
   c. Assume that this appliance store makes a $60 profit on each air conditioner sold from the weekly available stock, but the store loses $20 for each unit sold on a special stockout order basis. Let Z be the profit that the store earns in the coming week from the sale of window air conditioners. Find the probability distribution of Z.
   d. Find the expected value of Z.

26. Simulate 1000 weekly consumer demands for window air conditioner units with the probability distribution given in the file **P04_25.xlsx**. How does your simulated distribution compare to the given probability distribution? Explain any differences between these two distributions.

27. The probability distribution of the weekly demand for copier paper (in hundreds of reams) used in the duplicating center of a corporation is provided in the file **P04_27.xlsx**.
   a. Find the mean and standard deviation of this distribution.
   b. Find the probability that weekly copier paper demand is at least one standard deviation above the mean.
   c. Find the probability that weekly copier paper demand is within one standard deviation of the mean.

28. Consider the probability distribution of the weekly demand for copier paper (in hundreds of reams) used in a corporation's duplicating center, as shown in the file **P04_27.xlsx**.

a. Use simulation to generate 500 values of this random variable.

b. Find the mean and standard deviation of the simulated values.

c. Use your simulated values to estimate the probability that weekly copier paper demand is within one standard deviation of the mean. Why is this only an estimate, not an exact value?

29. The probability distribution of the weekly demand for copier paper (in hundreds of reams) used in the duplicating center of a corporation is provided in the file **P04_27.xlsx**. Assuming that it costs the duplicating center $5 to purchase a ream of paper, find the mean and standard deviation of the weekly copier paper cost for this corporation.

30. A roulette wheel contains the numbers 0, 00, and 1 to 36. If you bet $1 on a single number coming up, you earn $35 if the number comes up and lose $1 otherwise. Find the mean and standard deviation of your winnings on a single bet. Then find the mean and standard deviation of your net winnings if you make 100 bets. You can assume (realistically) that the results of the 100 spins are independent. Finally, provide an interval such that you are 95% sure your net winnings from 100 bets will be inside this interval.

31. You are involved in a risky business venture where three outcomes are possible: (1) you will lose not only your initial investment ($5000) but an additional $3000; (2) you will just make back your initial investment (for a net gain of $0); or (3) you will make back your initial investment plus an extra $10,000. The probability of (1) is half as large as the probability of (2), and the probability of (3) is one-third as large as the probability of (2).

a. Find the individual probabilities of (1), (2), and (3). (They should sum to 1.)

b. Find the expected value and standard deviation of your net gain (or loss) from this venture.

Level B

32. Equation (4.7) for variance indicates exactly what variance is: the weighted average of squared deviations from the mean, weighted by the probabilities. However, the computing formula for variance, Equation (4.9), is more convenient for spreadsheet calculations. Show algebraically that the two formulas are equivalent.

33. The basic game of craps works as follows. You throw two dice. If the sum of the two faces showing up is 7 or 11, you win and the game is over. If the sum is 2, 3, or 12, you lose and the game is over. If the sum is anything else (4, 5, 6, 8, 9, or 10), that value becomes your "point." You then keep throwing the dice until the sum matches your point or equals 7. If your point occurs first, you win and the game is over. If 7 occurs

first, you lose and the game is over. What is the probability that you win the game?

34. Consider an individual selected at random from a sample of 750 married women (see the data in the file **P04_05.xlsx**) in answering each of the following questions.

a. What is the probability that this woman does not work outside the home, given that she has at least one child?

b. What is the probability that this woman has no children, given that she works part time?

c. What is the probability that this woman has at least two children, given that she does not work full time?

35. Suppose that 8% of all managers in a given company are African American, 13% are women, and 17% have earned an MBA degree from a top-10 graduate business school. Let A, B, and C be, respectively, the events that a randomly selected individual from this population is African American, is a woman, and has earned an MBA from a top-10 graduate business school.

a. Do you believe that A, B, and C are independent events? Explain why or why not.

b. Assuming that A, B, and C *are* independent events, find the probability that a randomly selected manager from this company is a white male and has earned an MBA degree from a top-10 graduate business school.

c. If A, B, and C are *not* independent events, can you calculate the probability requested in part **b** from the information given? What further information would you need?

36. Two gamblers play a version of roulette with a wheel as shown in the file **P04_36.xlsx**. Each gambler places four bets, but their strategies are different, as explained below. For each gambler, use the rules of probability to find the distribution of their net winnings after four bets. Then find the mean and standard deviation of their net winnings. The file gets you started.

a. Player 1 always bets on red. On each bet, he either wins or loses what he bets. His first bet is for $10. From then on, he bets $10 following a win, and he doubles his bet after a loss. (This is called a martingale strategy and is used frequently at casinos.) For example, if he spins red, red, not red, and not red, his bets are for $10, $10, $10, and $20, and he has a net loss of $10. Or if he spins not red, not red, not red, and red, then his bets are for $10, $20, $40, and $80, and he has a net gain of $10.

b. Player 2 always bets on black and green. On each bet, he places $10 on black and $2 on green. If red occurs, he loses all $12. If black occurs, he wins a net $8 ($10 gain on black, $2 loss on green). If green occurs, he wins a net $50 ($10 loss on black, $60 gain on green).

37. Suppose the New York Yankees and Philadelphia Phillies (two Major League Baseball teams) are playing a best-of-three series. The first team to win two games is the winner of the series, and the series ends as soon as one team has won two games. The first game is played in New York, the second game is in Philadelphia, and if necessary the third game is in New York. The probability that the Yankees win a game in their home park is 0.55. The probability that the Phillies win a game in their home park is 0.53. You can assume that the outcomes of the games are probabilistically independent.

   a. Find the probability that the Yankees win the series.

   b. Suppose you are a Yankees fan, so you place a bet on each game played where you win $100 if the Yankees win the game and you lose $105 if the Yankees lose the game. Find the distribution of your net winnings. Then find the mean and standard deviation of this distribution. Is this betting strategy favorable to you?

   c. Repeat part **a**, but assume that the games are played in Philadelphia, then New York, then Philadelphia. How much does this "home field advantage" help the Phillies?

   d. Repeat part **a**, but now assume that the series is a best-of-five series, where the first team that wins three games wins the series. Assume that games alternate between New York and Philadelphia, with the first game in New York.

38. The application at the beginning of this chapter describes the campaign McDonald's used several years ago, where customers could win various prizes.

   a. Verify the figures that are given in the description. That is, argue why there are 10 winning outcomes and 120 total outcomes.

   b. Suppose McDonald's had designed the cards so that each card had two zaps and three pictures of the winning prize (and again five pictures of other irrelevant prizes). The rules are the same as before: To win, the customer must uncover all three pictures of the winning prize before uncovering a zap. Would there be more or fewer winners with this design? Argue by calculating the probability that a card is a winner.

   c. Going back to the original game (as in part **a**), suppose McDonald's printed one million cards, each of which was eventually given to a customer. Assume that the (potential) winning prizes on these were: 500,000 Cokes worth $0.40 each, 250,000 french fries worth $0.50 each, 150,000 milk shakes worth $0.75 each, 75,000

hamburgers worth $1.50 each, 20,000 cards with $1 cash as the winning prize, 4000 cards with $10 cash as the winning prize, 800 cards with $100 cash as the winning prize, and 200 cards with $1000 cash as the winning prize. Find the expected amount (the dollar equivalent) that McDonald's gave away in winning prizes, assuming everyone played the game and claimed the prize if they won. Also find the standard deviation of this amount.

39. A manufacturing company is trying to decide whether to sign a contract with the government to deliver an instrument to the government no later than eight weeks from now. Due to various uncertainties, the company isn't sure when it will be able to deliver the instrument. Also, when the instrument is delivered, there is a chance that the government will judge it as being of inferior quality. The company estimates that the probability distribution of the time it takes to deliver the instrument is as given in the file **P04_39.xlsx**. Independently of this, it estimates that the probability of rejection due to inferior quality is 0.15. If the instrument is delivered at least a week ahead of time and the government judges the quality to be inferior, the company will have time to fix the problem (with certainty) and still meet the deadline. However, if the delivery is late, or if it is exactly on time but of inferior quality, the government won't pay up. The company expects its cost of manufacturing the instrument to be $45,000. This is a sunk cost that will be incurred regardless of timing or the quality of the instrument. The company also estimates that the cost to fix an inferior instrument depends on the number of weeks left to fix it: $7500 if there are three weeks left, $10,000 if there are two weeks left, and $15,000 if there is one week left. The government will pay $70,000 for an instrument of sufficient quality delivered on time, but it will pay nothing otherwise. Find the distribution of profit or loss to the company. Then find the mean and standard deviation of this distribution. Do you think the company should sign the contract?

40. Have you ever watched the odds at a horse race? You might hear that the odds against a given horse winning are 9 to 1, meaning that the horse has a probability $1/(1 + 9) = 1/10$ of winning. However, these odds, after being converted to probabilities, typically add to something greater than one. Why is this? Suppose you place a bet of $10 on this horse. It seems that it is a fair bet if you lose your $10 if the horse loses, but you win $90 if the horse wins. However, argue why this isn't really fair to you, that is, argue why your expected winnings are negative.

4.1 SIMPSON'S PARADOX

The results we obtain with conditional probabilities can be quite counterintuitive, even paradoxical. This case is similar to one described in an article by Blyth (1972), and is usually referred to as Simpson's paradox. [Two other examples of Simpson's paradox are described in articles by Westbrooke (1998) and Appleton et al. (1996).] Essentially, Simpson's paradox says that even if one treatment has a better effect than another on *each* of two separate subpopulations, it can have a *worse* effect on the population as a whole.

Suppose that the population is the set of managers in a large company. We categorize the managers as those with an MBA degree (the Bs) and those without an MBA degree (the $\bar{B}$s). These categories are the two "treatment" groups. We also categorize the managers as those who were hired directly out of school by this company (the Cs) and those who worked with another company first (the $\bar{C}$s). These two categories form the two "subpopulations." Finally, we use as a measure of effectiveness those managers who have been promoted within the past year (the As).

Assume the following conditional probabilities are given:

$$P(A|B \text{ and } C) = 0.10, P(A|\bar{B} \text{ and } C) = 0.05 \qquad (4.12)$$

$$P(A|B \text{ and } \bar{C}) = 0.35, P(A|\bar{B} \text{ and } \bar{C}) = 0.20 \qquad (4.13)$$

$$P(C|B) = 0.90, P(C|\bar{B}) = 0.30 \qquad (4.14)$$

Each of these can be interpreted as a proportion. For example, the probability $P(A|B \text{ and } C)$ implies that 10% of all managers who have an MBA degree and were hired by the company directly out of school were promoted last year. Similar explanations hold for the other probabilities.

Joan Seymour, the head of personnel at this company, is trying to understand these figures. From the probabilities in Equation (4.12), she sees that among the subpopulation of workers hired directly out of school, those with an MBA degree are twice as likely to be promoted as those without an MBA degree. Similarly, from the probabilities in Equation (4.13), she sees that among the subpopulation of workers hired after working with another company, those with an MBA degree are *almost* twice as likely to be promoted as those without an MBA degree. The information provided by the probabilities in Equation (4.14) is somewhat different. From these, she sees that employees with MBA degrees are three times as likely as those without MBA degrees to have been hired directly out of school.

Joan can hardly believe it when a whiz-kid analyst uses these probabilities to show—correctly—that

$$P(A|B) = 0.125, P(A|\bar{B}) = 0.155 \qquad (4.15)$$

In words, those employees *without* MBA degrees are more likely to be promoted than those with MBA degrees. This appears to go directly against the evidence in Equations (4.12) and (4.13), both of which imply that MBAs have an advantage in being promoted. Can you derive the probabilities in Equation (4.15)? Can you shed any light on this "paradox"?

Normal, Binomial, Poisson, and Exponential Distributions

CHALLENGING CLAIMS OF *THE BELL CURVE*

One of the most controversial books in recent years is *The Bell Curve* (The Free Press, 1994). The authors are the late Richard Herrnstein, a psychologist, and Charles Murray, an economist, both of whom had extensive training in statistics. The book is a scholarly treatment of differences in intelligence, measured by IQ, and their effect on socioeconomic status (SES). The authors argue, by appealing to many past studies and presenting many statistics and graphs, that there are significant differences in IQ among different groups of people, and that these differences are at least partially responsible for differences in SES. Specifically, their basic claims are that (1) there is a quantity, intelligence, that can be measured by an IQ test; (2) the distribution of IQ scores is essentially a symmetric bell-shaped curve; (3) IQ scores are highly correlated with various indicators of success; (4) IQ is determined predominantly by genetic factors and less so by environmental factors; and (5) African Americans score significantly lower—about 15 points lower—on IQ than whites.

Although the discussion of this latter point takes up a relatively small part of the book, it has generated by far the most controversy. Many criticisms of the authors' racial thesis have been based on emotional arguments. However, it can also be criticized on entirely statistical grounds, as Barnett (1995) has done.[1] Barnett never states that the analysis by Herrnstein and Murray is *wrong*. He merely states that (1) the assumptions behind some of the analysis are at best questionable, and (2) some of the crucial details are not made as explicit as they should have been. As he states, "The issue is not that *The Bell Curve* is demonstrably wrong, but that it falls so far short

---

[1]Arnold Barnett is a professor in operations research at MIT's Sloan School of Management. He specializes in data analysis of health and safety issues.

of being demonstrably right. The book does not meet the burden of proof we might reasonably expect of it."

For example, Barnett takes issue with the claim that the genetic component of IQ is, in the words of Herrnstein and Murray, "unlikely to be smaller than 40 percent or higher than 80 percent." Barnett asks what it would mean if genetics made up, say, 60% of IQ. His only clue from the book is in an endnote, which implies this definition: If a large population of genetically identical newborns grew up in randomly chosen environments, and their IQs were measured once they reached adulthood, then the variance of these IQs would be 60% less than the variance for the entire population. The key word is *variance*. As Barnett notes, however, this statement implies that the corresponding drop in *standard deviation* is only 37%. That is, even if all members of the population were exactly the same genetically, differing environments would create a standard deviation of IQs 63% as large as the standard deviation that exists today. If this is true, it is hard to argue, as Herrnstein and Murray have done, that environment plays a minor role in determining IQ.

Because the effects of different racial environments are so difficult to disentangle from genetic effects, Herrnstein and Murray try at one point to bypass environmental influences on IQ by matching blacks and whites from similar environments. They report that blacks in the top decile of SES have an average IQ of 104, but that whites within that decile have an IQ one standard deviation higher. Even assuming that they have their facts straight, Barnett criticizes the vagueness of their claim. What standard deviation are they referring to: the standard deviation of the entire population or the standard deviation of only the people in the upper decile of SES? The latter is certainly much smaller than the former. Should we assume that the "top-decile blacks" are in the top decile of the black population or of the overall population? If the latter, then the matched comparison between blacks and whites is flawed because the wealthiest 10% of whites have far more wealth than the wealthiest 10% of blacks. Moreover, even if the reference is to the pooled national population, the matching is imperfect. It is possible that the blacks in this pool could average around the ninth percentile, whereas the whites could average around the fourth percentile, with a significant difference in income between the two groups.

The problem is that Herrnstein and Murray never state these details explicitly. Therefore, we have no way of knowing—without collecting and analyzing all of the data ourselves—whether their results are essentially correct. As Barnett concludes his article, "I believe that *The Bell Curve*'s statements about race would have been better left unsaid even if they were definitely true. And they are surely better left unsaid when, as we have seen, their meaning and accuracy [are] in doubt." ∎

5-1 INTRODUCTION

The previous chapter discussed probability distributions in general. This chapter investigates several specific distributions that commonly occur in a variety of business applications. The first of these is a continuous distribution called the *normal* distribution. It is characterized by a symmetric bell-shaped curve and is the cornerstone of statistical theory. The second distribution is a discrete distribution called the *binomial* distribution. It is relevant when we sample from a population with only two types of members or when we perform a series of independent, identical *experiments* with only two possible outcomes. The other two distributions we will discuss briefly are the *Poisson* and *exponential* distributions. These are often used when we are counting events of some type through time, such as arrivals to a bank. In this case, the Poisson distribution, which is discrete, describes the *number* of arrivals in any period of time, and the exponential distribution, which is continuous, describes the *times* between arrivals.

The main goals in this chapter are to present the properties of these distributions, give some examples of when they apply, and show how to perform calculations involving them. Regarding this last objective, analysts have traditionally used special tables to find probabilities or values for the distributions in this chapter. However, these tasks have been simplified with the statistical functions available in Excel®. Given the availability of these Excel functions, the traditional tables are no longer necessary.

We cannot overemphasize the importance of these distributions. Almost all of the statistical results discussed in later chapters are based on either the normal distribution or the binomial distribution. The Poisson and exponential distributions play a less important role in this book, but they are nevertheless extremely important in many management science applications. Therefore, it is important for you to become familiar with these distributions before proceeding.

5-2 THE NORMAL DISTRIBUTION

The single most important distribution in statistics is the normal distribution. It is a continuous distribution and is the basis of the familiar symmetric bell-shaped curve. Any particular normal distribution is specified by its mean and standard deviation. By changing the mean, the normal curve shifts to the right or left. By changing the standard deviation, the curve becomes more or less spread out. Therefore, there are really many normal distributions, not just a single one. We say that the normal distribution is a *two-parameter family*, where the two parameters are the mean and the standard deviation.

5-2a Continuous Distributions and Density Functions

We first take a moment to discuss continuous probability distributions in general. In the previous chapter we discussed discrete distributions, characterized by a list of possible values and their probabilities. The same basic idea holds for continuous distributions such as the normal distribution, but the mathematics is more complex. Now instead of a list of possible values, there is a *continuum* of possible values, such as all values between 0 and 100 or all values greater than 0. Instead of assigning probabilities to each individual value in the continuum, the total probability of 1 is spread over this continuum. The key to this spreading is called a *density function,* which acts like a histogram. The higher the value of the density function, the more likely this region of the continuum is.

> A **density function**, usually denoted by $f(x)$, specifies the probability distribution of a continuous random variable X. The higher $f(x)$ is, the more likely x is. Also, the total area between the graph of $f(x)$ and the horizontal axis, which represents the total probability, is equal to 1. Finally, $f(x)$ is nonnegative for all possible values of X.

As an example, consider the density function shown in Figure 5.1. (This is *not* a normal density function.) It indicates that all values in the continuum from 25 to 100 are possible, but that the values near 70 are most likely. (This density function might correspond to scores on an exam.) More specifically, because the height of the density at 70 is approximately twice the height of the curve at 84 or 53, a value near 70 is approximately twice as likely as a value near 84 or a value near 53. In this sense, the height of the density function indicates *relative* likelihoods.

Figure 5.1

A Skewed Density
Function

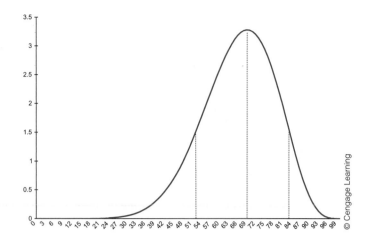

*For continuous distribu-
tions, probabilities are
areas under the density
function. These prob-
abilities can often be
calculated with Excel
functions.*

Probabilities are found from a density function as areas under the curve. For example, the area of the designated region in Figure 5.2 represents the probability of a score between 65 and 75. Also, the area under the *entire* curve is 1 because the total probability of all possible values is always 1. Unfortunately, this is about as much as we can say without calculus. Integral calculus is required to find areas under curves. Fortunately, statistical tables have been constructed to find such areas for a number of well-known density functions, including the normal. Even better, Excel functions have been developed to find these areas—without the need for bulky tables. We take advantage of these Excel functions in the rest of this chapter.

Figure 5.2

Probability as the
Area Under the
Density

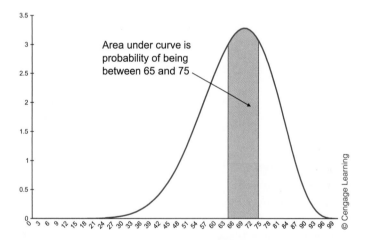

As in the previous chapter, the mean is a measure of central tendency of the distribution, and the standard deviation (or variance) measures the variability of the distribution. Again, however, calculus is generally required to calculate these quantities. We will simply list their values (which *were* obtained through calculus) for the normal distribution and any other continuous distributions where we need them. By the way, the mean for the (nonnormal) density in Figure 5.1 is slightly *less* than 70—it is always to the left of the peak for a left-skewed distribution and to the right of the peak for a right-skewed distribution— and the standard deviation is approximately 15.

5-2b The Normal Density

The **normal distribution** is a continuous distribution with possible values ranging over the *entire* number line—from "minus infinity" to "plus infinity." However, only a relatively small range has much chance of occurring. The normal density function is actually quite complex, in spite of its "nice" bell-shaped appearance. For the sake of completeness, we list the formula for the normal density function in Equation (5.1). Here, μ and σ are the mean and standard deviation of the distribution.

Normal Density Function

$$f(x) = \frac{1}{\sqrt{2\pi}\sigma} e^{-(x-\mu)^2/(2\sigma^2)} \quad \text{for} \quad -\infty < x < +\infty \quad\quad \textbf{(5.1)}$$

The curves in Figure 5.3 illustrate several normal density functions for different values of μ and σ. The mean μ can be any number: negative, positive, or zero. As you can see, the effect of increasing or decreasing the mean μ is to shift the curve to the right or the left. On the other hand, the standard deviation σ must be a *positive* number. It controls the spread of the normal curve. When σ is small, the curve is more peaked; when σ is large, the curve is more spread out. For shorthand, we use the notation $N(\mu, \sigma)$ to refer to the normal distribution with mean μ and standard deviation σ. For example, $N(-2, 1)$ refers to the normal distribution with mean -2 and standard deviation 1.

Figure 5.3

Several Normal Density Functions

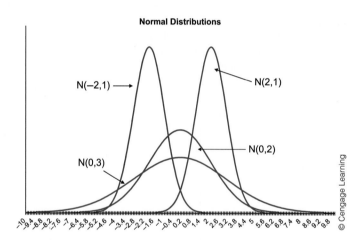

FUNDAMENTAL INSIGHT

Why the Normal Distribution?

The normal density in Equation (5.1) is certainly not very intuitive, so why is the normal distribution the basis for so much of statistical theory? One reason is practical. Many histograms based on real data resemble the bell-shaped normal curve to a remarkable extent. Granted, not all histograms are symmetric and bell-shaped, but a surprising number are. Another reason is theoretical. In spite of the complexity of Equation (5.1), the normal distribution has many appealing properties that have enabled researchers to build the rich statistical theory that finds widespread use in business, the sciences, and other fields.

5-2c Standardizing: *Z*-Values

There are infinitely many normal distributions, one for each pair μ and σ. We single out one of these for special attention, the *standard* normal distribution. The **standard normal** distribution has mean 0 and standard deviation 1, so we denote it by $N(0, 1)$. It is also referred to as the *Z* distribution. Suppose the random variable *X* is normally distributed with mean μ and standard deviation σ. We define the random variable *Z* by Equation (5.2).

This operation is called *standardizing*. That is, to **standardize** a variable, you subtract its mean and then divide the difference by the standard deviation. When X is normally distributed, the standardized variable is $N(0, 1)$.

> *Standardizing a Normal Random Variable*
> $$Z = \frac{X - \mu}{\sigma} \tag{5.2}$$

One reason for standardizing is to measure variables with different means and/or standard deviations on a single scale. For example, suppose several sections of a college course are taught by different instructors. Because of differences in teaching methods and grading procedures, the distributions of scores in these sections might differ, possibly by a wide margin. However, if each instructor calculates his or her mean and standard deviation and then calculates a Z-value for each student, the distributions of the Z-values should be approximately the same in each section.

It is easy to interpret a Z-value. It is the number of standard deviations to the right or the left of the mean. If Z is positive, the original value (in this case, the original score) is to the *right* of the mean; if Z is negative, the original score is to the *left* of the mean. For example, if the Z-value for some student is 2, then this student's score is two standard deviations above the mean. If the Z-value for another student is −0.5, then this student's score is half a standard deviation below the mean. We illustrate Z-values in Example 5.1.

EXAMPLE | **5.1 STANDARDIZING RETURNS FROM MUTUAL FUNDS**

The annual returns for 30 mutual funds appear in Figure 5.4. (See the file **Standardizing.xlsx**.) Find and interpret the Z-values of these returns.

Objective   To use Excel to standardize annual returns of various mutual funds.

Figure 5.4   Mutual Fund Returns and Z-Values

	A	B	C	D	E	F	G	H
1	**Standardizing mutual fund returns**							
2								
3	Summary statistics from returns below				Calculated two different ways — the second with the Standardize function			
4	Mean	0.091						
5	Stdev	0.047						
6								
7	Fund	Annual return	Z value	Z value		**Range names used**		
8	1	0.007	−1.8047	−1.8047		Annual_return	=Data!$B$8:$B$37	
9	2	0.080	−0.2363	−0.2363		Mean	=Data!$B$4	
10	3	0.082	−0.1934	−0.1934		Stdev	=Data!$B$5	
11	4	0.123	0.6875	0.6875				
12	5	0.022	−1.4824	−1.4824				
13	6	0.054	−0.7949	−0.7949				
36	29	0.078	−0.2793	−0.2793				
37	30	0.066	−0.5371	−0.5371				

Solution

The 30 annual returns appear in column B of Figure 5.4. Their mean and standard deviation are calculated in cells B4 and B5 with the AVERAGE and STDEV functions. The corresponding Z-values are calculated in column C by entering the formula

=(B8-Mean)/Stdev

in cell C8 and copying it down column C.

There is an equivalent way to calculate these Z-values in Excel. This is done in column D by using Excel's STANDARDIZE function directly. To use this function, enter the formula

=STANDARDIZE(B8,Mean,Stdev)

in cell D8 and copy it down column D.

The Z-values in Figure 5.4 range from a low of -1.80 to a high of 2.19. Specifically, the return for stock 1 is about 1.80 standard deviations below the mean, whereas the return for fund 17 is about 2.19 standard deviations above the mean. As you will see shortly, these values are typical: Z-values are usually in the range from -2 to $+2$ and values beyond -3 or $+3$ are very uncommon. (Recall the *empirical rules* for interpreting standard deviation first discussed in Chapter 2.) Also, the Z-values automatically have mean 0 and standard deviation 1, as you can see in cells C5 and C6 by using the AVERAGE and STDEV functions on the Z-values in column C (or D). ∎

5-2d Normal Tables and Z-Values[2]

A common use for Z-values and the standard normal distribution is in calculating probabilities and percentiles by the traditional method. This method is based on a table of the standard normal distribution found in many statistics textbooks. Such a table is given in Figure 5.5. The body of the table contains probabilities. The left and top margins contain possible values. Specifically, suppose you want to find the probability that a standard normal random variable is less than 1.35. You locate 1.3 along the left and 0.05—the second decimal in 1.35—along the top, and then read into the table to find the probability 0.9115. In words, the probability is about 0.91 that a standard normal random variable is less than 1.35.

Alternatively, if you are given a probability, you can use the table to find the value with this much probability to the left of it under the standard normal curve. This is called a *percentile* calculation. For example, if the probability is 0.75, you can find the 75th percentile by locating the probability in the table closest to 0.75 and then reading to the left and up. With interpolation, the required value is approximately 0.675. In words, the probability of being to the left of 0.675 under the standard normal curve is approximately 0.75.

You can perform the same kind of calculations for *any* normal distribution if you first standardize. As an example, suppose that X is normally distributed with mean 100 and standard deviation 10. We will find the probability that X is less than 115 and the 85th percentile of this normal distribution. To find the probability that X is less than 115, first standardize the value 115. The corresponding Z-value is

$$Z = (115 - 100)/10 = 1.5$$

Now look up 1.5 in the table (1.5 row, 0.00 column) to obtain the probability 0.9332. For the percentile question, first find the 85th percentile of the standard normal distribution. Interpolating, a value of approximately 1.037 is obtained. Then set this value equal to a standardized value:

$$Z = 1.037 = (X - 100)/10$$

---

[2]If you intend to rely on Excel functions for normal calculations, you can skip this subsection.

Figure 5.5 Normal Probabilities

z	0.00	0.01	0.02	0.03	0.04	0.05	0.06	0.07	0.08	0.09
0.0	0.5000	0.5040	0.5080	0.5120	0.5160	0.5199	0.5239	0.5279	0.5319	0.5359
0.1	0.5398	0.5438	0.5478	0.5517	0.5557	0.5596	0.5636	0.5675	0.5714	0.5753
0.2	0.5793	0.5832	0.5871	0.5910	0.5948	0.5987	0.6026	0.6064	0.6103	0.6141
0.3	0.6179	0.6217	0.6255	0.6293	0.6331	0.6368	0.6406	0.6443	0.6480	0.6517
0.4	0.6554	0.6591	0.6628	0.6664	0.6700	0.6736	0.6772	0.6808	0.6844	0.6879
0.5	0.6915	0.6950	0.6985	0.7019	0.7054	0.7088	0.7123	0.7157	0.7190	0.7224
0.6	0.7257	0.7291	0.7324	0.7357	0.7389	0.7422	0.7454	0.7486	0.7517	0.7549
0.7	0.7580	0.7611	0.7642	0.7673	0.7704	0.7734	0.7764	0.7794	0.7823	0.7852
0.8	0.7881	0.7910	0.7939	0.7967	0.7995	0.8023	0.8051	0.8078	0.8106	0.8133
0.9	0.8159	0.8186	0.8212	0.8238	0.8264	0.8289	0.8315	0.8340	0.8365	0.8389
1.0	0.8413	0.8438	0.8461	0.8485	0.8508	0.8531	0.8554	0.8577	0.8599	0.8621
1.1	0.8643	0.8665	0.8686	0.8708	0.8729	0.8749	0.8770	0.8790	0.8810	0.8830
1.2	0.8849	0.8869	0.8888	0.8907	0.8925	0.8944	0.8962	0.8980	0.8997	0.9015
1.3	0.9032	0.9049	0.9066	0.9082	0.9099	0.9115	0.9131	0.9147	0.9162	0.9177
1.4	0.9192	0.9207	0.9222	0.9236	0.9251	0.9265	0.9279	0.9292	0.9306	0.9319
1.5	0.9332	0.9345	0.9357	0.9370	0.9382	0.9394	0.9406	0.9418	0.9429	0.9441
1.6	0.9452	0.9463	0.9474	0.9484	0.9495	0.9505	0.9515	0.9525	0.9535	0.9545
1.7	0.9554	0.9564	0.9573	0.9582	0.9591	0.9599	0.9608	0.9616	0.9625	0.9633
1.8	0.9641	0.9649	0.9656	0.9664	0.9671	0.9678	0.9686	0.9693	0.9699	0.9706
1.9	0.9713	0.9719	0.9726	0.9732	0.9738	0.9744	0.9750	0.9756	0.9761	0.9767
2.0	0.9772	0.9778	0.9783	0.9788	0.9793	0.9798	0.9803	0.9808	0.9812	0.9817
2.1	0.9821	0.9826	0.9830	0.9834	0.9838	0.9842	0.9846	0.9850	0.9854	0.9857
2.2	0.9861	0.9864	0.9868	0.9871	0.9875	0.9878	0.9881	0.9884	0.9887	0.9890
2.3	0.9893	0.9896	0.9898	0.9901	0.9904	0.9906	0.9909	0.9911	0.9913	0.9916
2.4	0.9918	0.9920	0.9922	0.9925	0.9927	0.9929	0.9931	0.9932	0.9934	0.9936
2.5	0.9938	0.9940	0.9941	0.9943	0.9945	0.9946	0.9948	0.9949	0.9951	0.9952
2.6	0.9953	0.9955	0.9956	0.9957	0.9959	0.9960	0.9961	0.9962	0.9963	0.9964
2.7	0.9965	0.9966	0.9967	0.9968	0.9969	0.9970	0.9971	0.9972	0.9973	0.9974
2.8	0.9974	0.9975	0.9976	0.9977	0.9977	0.9978	0.9979	0.9979	0.9980	0.9981
2.9	0.9981	0.9982	0.9982	0.9983	0.9984	0.9984	0.9985	0.9985	0.9986	0.9986
3.0	0.9987	0.9987	0.9987	0.9988	0.9988	0.9989	0.9989	0.9989	0.9990	0.9990
3.1	0.9990	0.9991	0.9991	0.9991	0.9992	0.9992	0.9992	0.9992	0.9993	0.9993
3.2	0.9993	0.9993	0.9994	0.9994	0.9994	0.9994	0.9994	0.9995	0.9995	0.9995
3.3	0.9995	0.9995	0.9995	0.9996	0.9996	0.9996	0.9996	0.9996	0.9996	0.9997
3.4	0.9997	0.9997	0.9997	0.9997	0.9997	0.9997	0.9997	0.9997	0.9997	0.9998

Finally, solve for X to obtain 110.37. In words, the probability of being to the left of 110.37 in the $N(100,10)$ distribution is about 0.85.

There are some obvious drawbacks to using the standard normal table for probability calculations. The first is that there are holes in the table—interpolation is often necessary. A second drawback is that the standard normal table takes different forms in different textbooks. These differences are rather minor, but they can easily cause confusion. Finally, the table requires you to perform calculations. For example, you often need to standardize. More importantly, you often have to use the symmetry of the normal distribution to find probabilities that are not in the table. As an example, to find the probability that Z is less than -1.5, you must go through some mental gymnastics. First, by symmetry this is the same as the probability that Z is greater than 1.5. Then, because only left-tail ("less than") probabilities are tabulated, you must find the probability that Z is less than 1.5 and subtract this probability from 1. The chain of reasoning is

$$P(Z < -1.5) = P(Z > 1.5) = 1 - P(Z < 1.5) = 1 - 0.9332 = 0.0668$$

This is not too difficult, given a bit of practice, but it is easy to make a mistake. Excel functions make the whole procedure much easier and less error-prone.

5-2e Normal Calculations in Excel

Two types of calculations are typically made with normal distributions: finding probabilities and finding percentiles. Excel makes each of these fairly simple. The functions used for normal probability calculations are NORMDIST and NORMSDIST. The main difference between these is that the one with the "S" (for standardized) applies only to $N(0, 1)$ calculations, whereas NORMDIST applies to *any* normal distribution. On the other hand, percentile calculations that take a probability and return a value are often called *inverse* calculations. Therefore, the Excel functions for these are named NORMINV and NORMSINV. Again, the "S" in the second of these indicates that it applies to the standard normal distribution.

The NORMDIST and NORMSDIST functions return left-tail probabilities, such as the probability that a normally distributed variable is *less than* 35. The syntax for these functions is

=NORMDIST(x,μ,σ,1)

and

=NORMSDIST (x)

Here, x is a number you supply, and μ and σ are the mean and standard deviation of the normal distribution. The last argument in the NORMDIST function, 1, is used to obtain the *cumulative* normal probability, the type usually required. (This 1 is a nuisance to remember, but it is necessary.) Note that NORMSDIST takes only one argument (because μ and σ are known to be 0 and 1), so it is easier to use—when it applies.

The NORMINV and NORMSINV functions return values for user-supplied probabilities. For example, if you supply the probability 0.95, these functions return the 95th percentile. Their syntax is

=NORMINV(p,μ,σ)

and

=NORMSINV(p)

where p is a probability you supply. These are analogous to the NORMDIST and NORMSDIST functions (except there is no fourth argument in the NORMINV function).

CHANGES IN EXCEL 2010

Many of the statistical functions were revamped in Excel 2010, as we will point out throughout the next few chapters. Microsoft wanted a more consistent naming convention that would make functions better match the ways they are used in statistical inference. All of the old functions, including the normal functions discussed here, are still available for compatibility, but Microsoft is hoping that users will switch to the new functions. The new normal functions are NORM.DIST, NORM.S.DIST, NORM.INV, and NORM.S.INV. These work exactly like the old normal functions except that NORM.S.DIST takes the same last "cumulative" argument, as was explained above for NORMDIST. The new and old functions are both shown in the file for the next example.

Probability and Percentile Calculations

There are two basic types of calculations involving probability distributions, normal or otherwise. In a probability calculation, you provide a possible value, and you ask for the probability of being less than or equal to this value. In a percentile calculation, you provide a probability, and you ask for the value that has this probability to the left of it. Excel's statistical functions, especially with the new names introduced in Excel 2010, use DIST in functions that perform probability calculations and INV (for inverse) in functions that perform percentile calculations.

We illustrate these Excel functions in Example 5.2.[3]

EXAMPLE | **5.2 NORMAL CALCULATIONS IN EXCEL**

Use Excel to calculate the following probabilities and percentiles for the standard normal distribution: (a) $P(Z < -2)$, (b) $P(Z > 1)$, (c) $P(-0.4 < Z < 1.6)$, (d) the 5th percentile, (e) the 75th percentile, and (f) the 99th percentile. Then for the $N(75, 8)$ distribution, find the following probabilities and percentiles: (a) $P(X < 70)$, (b) $P(X > 73)$, (c) $P(75 < X < 85)$, (d) the 5th percentile, (e) the 60th percentile, and (f) the 97th percentile.

Objective   To calculate probabilities and percentiles for standard normal and general normal distributions in Excel.

Solution

The solution appears in Figure 5.6. (See the file **Normal Calculations.xlsx**.) The $N(0, 1)$ calculations are in rows 7 through 14; the $N(75, 8)$ calculations are in rows 23 through 30. For your convenience, the formulas used in column B are spelled out in column D (as labels). Note that the standard normal calculations use the normal functions with the "S" in the middle; the rest use the normal functions without the "S"—and require more arguments. (The new Excel 2010 functions don't appear in this figure, but they are included in the file.)

Note the following for normal *probability* calculations:

- For "less than" probabilities, use NORMDIST or NORMSDIST directly. (See rows 7 and 23.)
- For "greater than" probabilities, subtract the NORMDIST or NORMSDIST function from 1. (See rows 8 and 24.)
- For "between" probabilities, subtract the two NORMDIST or NORMSDIST functions. For example, in row 9 the probability of being between −0.4 and 1.6 is the probability of being less than 1.6 minus the probability of being less than −0.4.

The percentile calculations are even more straightforward. In most percentile problems you want to find the value with a certain probability to the *left* of it. In this case you use the NORMINV or NORMSINV function with the specified probability as the first argument. See rows 12 through 14 and 28 through 30.

---

[3]Actually, we already illustrated the NORMSDIST function; it was used to create the body of Figure 5.5. In other words, you can use it to build your own normal probability table.

Figure 5.6 Normal Calculations with Excel Functions

	A	B	C	D	E	F	G	H	I
1	**Normal probability calculations**								
2									
3	**Examples with standard normal**								
4									
5	**Probability calculations**								
6	Range	Probability		Formula					
7	Less than −2	0.0228		=NORMSDIST(−2)					
8	Greater than 1	0.1587		=1-NORMSDIST(1)					
9	Between −0.4 and 1.6	0.6006		=NORMSDIST(1.6)-NORMSDIST(−0.4)					
10									
11	**Percentiles**								
12	5th	−1.645		=NORMSINV(0.05)					
13	75th	0.674		=NORMSINV(0.75)					
14	99th	2.326		=NORMSINV(0.99)					
15									
16	**Examples with nonstandard normal**								
17				Range names used:					
18	Mean	75		Mean	=Normal!$B$18				
19	Stdev	8		Stdev	=Normal!$B$19				
20									
21	**Probability calculations**								
22	Range	Probability		Formula					
23	Less than 70	0.2660		=NORMDIST(70,Mean,Stdev,1)					
24	Greater than 73	0.5987		=1-NORMDIST(73,Mean,Stdev,1)					
25	Between 75 and 85	0.3944		=NORMDIST(85,Mean,Stdev,1)-NORMDIST(75,Mean,Stdev,1)					
26									
27	**Percentiles**								
28	5th	61.841		=NORMINV(0.05,Mean,Stdev)					
29	60th	77.027		=NORMINV(0.6,Mean,Stdev)					
30	97th	90.046		=NORMINV(0.97,Mean,Stdev)					

Note that when you are doing probability calculations on *any* continuous distribution, including the normal distribution, there is no need to distinguish between "less than" and "less than or equal to" events, or between "greater than" and "greater than or equal to" events. The reason is that there is no *positive* probability of being equal to any particular value. However, as you will see when we discuss the binomial distribution, this is not true of discrete distributions. ■

There are a couple of variations of percentile calculations. First, suppose you want the value with probability 0.05 to the *right* of it. This is the same as the value with probability 0.95 to the left of it, so you use NORMINV or NORMSINV with probability argument 0.95. For example, the value with probability 0.4 to the right of it in the N(75, 8) distribution is 77.027. (See cell B29 in Figure 5.6.)

As a second variation, suppose you want to find an interval of the form −x to x, for some positive number x, with (1) probability 0.025 to the left of −x, (2) probability 0.025 to the right of x, and (3) probability 0.95 between −x and x. This is a very common problem in statistical inference. In general, you want a probability (such as 0.95) to be in the middle of the interval so that half of the remaining probability (0.025) is in each of the tails. (See Figure 5.7.) Then the required x can be found with NORMINV or NORMSINV, using probability argument 0.975, because there must be a total probability of 0.975 to the left of x.

For example, if the relevant distribution is the standard normal, the required value of x is 1.96, found with the function NORMSINV (0.975). Similarly, if you want probability 0.90 in the middle and probability 0.05 in each tail, the required x is 1.645, found with the function NORMSINV (0.95). Remember these two numbers, 1.96 and 1.645. They occur frequently in statistical applications.

Figure 5.7

Typical Normal Probabilities

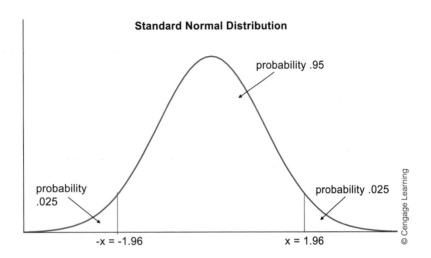

By substituting the values 1, 2, and 3 for k, we find the following probabilities:

5-2f Empirical Rules Revisited

We introduced three empirical rules in Chapter 2 that apply to many data sets. Namely, about 68% of the data fall within one standard deviation of the mean, about 95% fall within two standard deviations of the mean, and almost all fall within three standard deviations of the mean. For these rules to hold with real data, the distribution of the data must be at least approximately symmetric and bell-shaped. Let's look at these rules more closely.

Let X be normally distributed with mean μ and standard deviation σ. To perform a probability calculation on X, we can first standardize X and then perform the calculation on the standardized variable Z. Specifically, we will find the probability that X is within k standard deviations of its mean for $k = 1$, $k = 2$, and $k = 3$. In general, this probability is $P(\mu - k\sigma < X < \mu + k\sigma)$. But by standardizing the values $\mu - k\sigma$ and $\mu + k\sigma$, we obtain the equivalent probability $P(-k < Z < k)$, where Z has a $N(0, 1)$ distribution. This latter probability can be calculated in Excel with the formula

The normal distribution is the basis for the empirical rules introduced in Chapter 2.

= NORMSDIST(k)−NORMSDIST($-k$)

By substituting the values 1, 2, and 3 for k, we find the following probabilities:

$P(-1 < Z < 1) = 0.6827$

$P(-2 < Z < 2) = 0.9545$

$P(-3 < Z < 3) = 0.9973$

As you can see, there is virtually no chance of being beyond three standard deviations from the mean, the chances are about 19 out of 20 of being within two standard deviations of the mean, and the chances are about 2 out of 3 of being within one standard deviation of the mean. These probabilities are the basis for the empirical rules in Chapter 2. These rules more closely approximate reality as the histograms of observed data become more bell-shaped.

5-2g Weighted Sums of Normal Random Variables

One very attractive property of the normal distribution is that if you create a weighted sum of normally distributed random variables, the weighted sum is also normally distributed. In fact, this is true even if the random variables are *not* independent.

Specifically, if X_1 through X_n are n independent and normally distributed random variables with common mean μ and common standard deviation σ, then the sum $X_1 + \cdots + X_n$ is normally distributed with mean $n\mu$ (sum of the means), variance $n\sigma^2$ (sum of the variances), and standard deviation $\sqrt{n}\sigma$ (square root of the variance). More generally, if a_1 through a_n are any constants, then the weighted sum $a_1X_1 + \cdots + a_nX_n$ is normally distributed with mean $a_1\mu_1 + \cdots + a_n\mu_n$ and variance $a_1^2\sigma_1^2 + \cdots + a_n^2\sigma_n^2$. You will need this fact to solve a few of the problems in this chapter.

5-3 APPLICATIONS OF THE NORMAL DISTRIBUTION

In this section we apply the normal distribution to a variety of business problems.

EXAMPLE	5.3 Personnel Testing at ZTel

The personnel department of ZTel, a large communications company, is reconsidering its hiring policy. Each applicant for a job must take a standard exam, and the hire or no-hire decision depends at least in part on the result of the exam. The scores of all applicants have been examined closely. They are approximately normally distributed with mean 525 and standard deviation 55.

The current hiring policy occurs in two phases. The first phase separates all applicants into three categories: automatic accepts, automatic rejects, and maybes. The automatic accepts are those whose test scores are 600 or above. The automatic rejects are those whose test scores are 425 or below. All other applicants (the maybes) are passed on to a second phase where their previous job experience, special talents, and other factors are used as hiring criteria. The personnel manager at ZTel wants to calculate the percentage of applicants who are automatic accepts or rejects, given the current standards. She also wants to know how to change the standards to automatically reject 10% of all applicants and automatically accept 15% of all applicants.

Objective To determine test scores that can be used to accept or reject job applicants at ZTel.

Solution

Let X be the test score of a typical applicant. Then historical data suggest that the distribution of X is $N(525, 55)$. A probability such as $P(X \leq 425)$ can be interpreted as the probability that a typical applicant is an automatic reject, or it can be interpreted as the percentage of *all* applicants who are automatic rejects. Given this observation, the solution to ZTel's problem appears in Figure 5.8. (See the file **Personnel Decisions.xlsx**.) The probability that a typical applicant is automatically accepted is 0.0863, found in cell B10 with the formula

=1–NORMDIST(B7,Mean,Stdev,1)

Figure 5.8 Calculations for Personnel Example

	A	B	C	D	E	F
1	**Personnel Decisions**					
2				**Range names used:**		
3	Mean of test scores	525		Mean	=Model!$B$3	
4	Stdev of test scores	55		Stdev	=Model!$B$4	
5						
6	**Current Policy**					
7	Automatic accept point	600				
8	Automatic reject point	425				
9						
10	Percent accepted	8.63%		=1-NORMDIST(B7,Mean,Stdev,1)		
11	Percent rejected	3.45%		=NORMDIST(B8,Mean,Stdev,1)		
12						
13	**New Policy**					
14	Percent accepted	15%				
15	Percent rejected	10%				
16						
17	Automatic accept point	582		=NORMINV(1-B14,Mean,Stdev)		
18	Automatic reject point	455		=NORMINV(B15,Mean,Stdev)		

© Cengage Learning

Similarly, the probability that a typical applicant is automatically rejected is 0.0345, found in cell B11 with the formula

=NORMDIST(B8,Mean,Stdev,1)

Therefore, ZTel automatically accepts about 8.6% and rejects about 3.5% of all applicants under the current policy.

To find new cutoff values that reject 10% and accept 15% of the applicants, we need the 10th and 85th percentiles of the $N(525, 55)$ distribution. These are 455 and 582 (rounded to the nearest integer), respectively, found in cells B17 and B18 with the formulas

=NORMINV(1–B14,Mean,Stdev)

and

=NORMINV(B15,Mean,Stdev)

To accomplish its objective, ZTel needs to raise the automatic rejection point from 425 to 455 and lower the automatic acceptance point from 600 to 582. ∎

EXAMPLE | **5.4 QUALITY CONTROL AT PAPERSTOCK**

PaperStock Company runs a manufacturing facility that produces a paper product. The fiber content of this product is supposed to be 20 pounds per 1000 square feet. (This is typical for the type of paper used in grocery bags, for example.) Because of random variations in the inputs to the process, however, the fiber content of a typical 1000-square-foot roll varies according to a $N(\mu, \sigma)$ distribution. The mean fiber content (μ) can be controlled—that is, it can be set to any desired level by adjusting an instrument on the machine. The variability in fiber content, as measured by the standard deviation σ, is 0.10 pound when the process is "good," but it sometimes increases to 0.15 pound when the machine goes "bad." A given roll of this product must be rejected if its actual fiber content is less than 19.8 pounds or greater than 20.3 pounds. Calculate the probability that a given roll is rejected, for a setting of $\mu = 20$, when the machine is "good" and when it is "bad."

Objective   To determine the machine settings that result in paper of acceptable quality at PaperStock Company.

Solution

Let X be the fiber content of a typical roll. The distribution of X will be either $N(20, 0.10)$ or $N(20, 0.15)$, depending on the status of the machine. In either case, the probability that the roll must be rejected can be calculated as shown in Figure 5.9. (See the file **Paper Machine Settings.xlsx**.) The formula for rejection in the "good" case appears in cell B12:

=NORMDIST(B8,Mean,Stdev_good,1)+(1-NORMDIST(B9,Mean,Stdev_good,1))

Figure 5.9   Calculations for Paper Quality Example

	A	B	C	D	E	F	G	H	I	J
1	Paper Machine Settings			Range names used:						
2				Mean	=Model!$B$3					
3	Mean	20		Stdev_bad	=Model!$B$5					
4	Stdev in good case	0.1		Stdev_good	=Model!$B$4					
5	Stdev in bad case	0.15								
6										
7	Reject region									
8	Lower limit	19.8								
9	Upper limit	20.3								
10										
11	Probability of reject									
12	in good case	0.024		=NORMDIST(B8,Mean,Stdev_good,1)+(1-NORMDIST(B9,Mean,Stdev_good,1))						
13	in bad case	0.114		=NORMDIST(B8,Mean,Stdev_bad,1)+(1-NORMDIST(B9,Mean,Stdev_bad,1))						
14										
15	Data table of rejection probability as a function of the mean and good standard deviation									
16				Standard deviation						
17		0.024	0.1	0.11	0.12	0.13	0.14	0.15		
18		19.7	0.841	0.818	0.798	0.779	0.762	0.748		
19		19.8	0.500	0.500	0.500	0.500	0.500	0.500		
20		19.9	0.159	0.182	0.203	0.222	0.240	0.256		
21	Mean	20.0	0.024	0.038	0.054	0.072	0.093	0.114		
22		20.1	0.024	0.038	0.054	0.072	0.093	0.114		
23		20.2	0.159	0.182	0.203	0.222	0.240	0.256		
24		20.3	0.500	0.500	0.500	0.500	0.500	0.500		
25		20.4	0.841	0.818	0.798	0.779	0.762	0.748		

To form this data table, enter the formula = B12 in cell B17, highlight the range B17:H25, and create a data table with row input cell B4 and column input cell B3.

This is the sum of two probabilities: the probability of being to the left of the lower limit and the probability of being to the right of the upper limit. These probabilities of rejection are represented graphically in Figure 5.10. A similar formula for the "bad" case appears in cell B13, using Stdev_bad in place of Stdev_good.

You can see that the probability of a rejected roll in the "good" case is 0.024; in the "bad" case it is 0.114. That is, when the standard deviation increases by 50% from 0.10 to 0.15, the percentage of rolls rejected more than quadruples, from 2.4% to 11.4%.

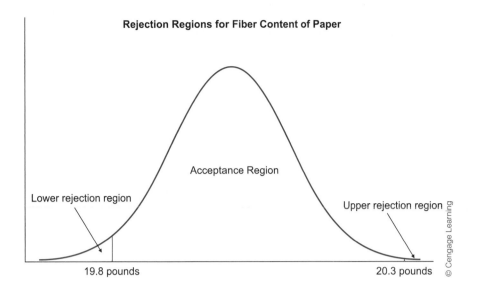

Figure 5.10

Rejection Regions for Paper Quality Example

Rejection Regions for Fiber Content of Paper

Acceptance Region

Lower rejection region

Upper rejection region

19.8 pounds

20.3 pounds

© Cengage Learning

It is certainly possible that the true process mean and "good" standard deviation will not always be equal to the values in cells B3 and B4. Therefore, it is useful to see how sensitive the rejection probability is to these two parameters. You can do this with a two-way data table, as shown in Figure 5.9. The tabulated values show that the probability of rejection varies greatly even for small changes in the key inputs. In particular, a combination of a badly centered mean and a large standard deviation can make the probability of rejection quite large. ∎

EXAMPLE **5.5 ANALYZING AN INVESTOR'S AFTER-TAX PROFIT**

Howard Davis invests \$10,000 in a certain stock on January 1. By examining past movements of this stock and consulting with his broker, Howard estimates that the annual return from this stock, X, is normally distributed with mean 5% and standard deviation 14%. Here X (when expressed as a decimal) is the profit Howard receives per dollar invested. It means that on December 31, his \$10,000 will have grown to $10,000(1 + X)$ dollars. Because Howard is in the 33% tax bracket, he will then have to pay the Internal Revenue Service 33% of his profit, if he makes a profit. However, he doesn't have to pay any tax if he loses money. Calculate the probability that Howard will have to pay the IRS at least \$400, and calculate the probability that he won't have to pay any tax. Also, calculate the dollar amount such that Howard's after-tax profit is 90% certain to be less than this amount; that is, calculate the 90th percentile of his after-tax profit.

Objective To determine the after-tax profit Howard Davis can be 90% certain of earning.

Solution

Howard's before-tax profit is $10,000X$ dollars, so the amount he pays the IRS is $0.33(10,000X)$, or $3300X$ dollars. We want the probability that this is at least \$400. Because $3300X > 400$ is the same as $X > 4/33$, the probability of this outcome can be found as in Figure 5.11. (See the file **Tax on Stock Return.xlsx**.) It is calculated with the formula

=1-NORMDIST(400/(Amount_invested*Tax_rate),Mean,Stdev,1)

in cell B8. As you can see, Howard has about a 30% chance of paying at least \$400 in taxes.

The probability that he doesn't have to pay any tax is easier. It is the probability the return on the stock is negative. This is 0.36, found in cell B9 with the formula shown to its right.

Figure 5.11 Calculations for Taxable Returns Example

▲	A	B	C	D	E	F	G	H	I
1	Tax on Stock Return								
2				Range names used:					
3	Amount invested	$10,000		Amount_invested	=Model!$B$3				
4	Mean	5%		Mean	=Model!$B$4				
5	Stdev	14%		Stdev	=Model!$B$5				
6	Tax rate	33%		Tax_rate	=Model!$B$6				
7									
8	Probability he pays at least $400 in taxes	0.305		=1-NORMDIST(400/(Amount_invested*Tax_rate),Mean,Stdev,1)					
9	Probability of no tax	0.360		=NORMDIST(0,Mean,Stdev,1)					
10									
11	90th percentile of stock return	22.94%		=NORMINV(0.9,Mean,Stdev)					
12	90th percentile of after-tax return	$1,537		=(1-Tax_rate)*Amount_invested*B10					

To answer the last question, note that the after-tax profit (when X is positive) is 67% of the before-tax profit, or $6700X$ dollars, and we want its 90th percentile. If this percentile is x, then we know that $P(6700X < x) = 0.90$, which is the same as $P(X < x/6700) = 0.90$. In words, we want the 90th percentile of the X distribution to be $x/6700$. From cell B11 of Figure 5.11, the 90th percentile is 22.94%, so the required value of x is $1,537. ■

It is sometimes tempting to model every continuous random variable with a normal distribution. This can be dangerous for at least two reasons. First, not all random variables have a *symmetric* distribution. Some are skewed to the left or the right, and for these the normal distribution can be a poor approximation to reality. The second problem is that many random variables in real applications must be *nonnegative*, and the normal distribution allows the possibility of negative values. The following example shows how a normal assumption can get you into trouble if you aren't careful.

EXAMPLE **5.6 PREDICTING DEMAND FOR MICROWAVE OVENS**

Highland Company is a retailer that sells microwave ovens. The company wants to model its demand for microwaves over the next 12 years. Using historical data as a guide, it assumes that demand in year 1 is normally distributed with mean 5000 and standard deviation 1500. It assumes that demand in each subsequent year is normally distributed with mean equal to the *actual* demand from the previous year and standard deviation 1500. For example, if demand in year 1 is 4500, then the *mean* demand in year 2 is 4500. This assumption is plausible because it leads to correlated demands. For example, if demand is high one year, it will tend to be high the next year. Investigate the ramifications of this model, and suggest models that might be more realistic.

Objective To construct and analyze a spreadsheet model for microwave oven demand over the next 12 years using Excel's NORMINV function, and to show how models using the normal distribution can lead to nonsensical outcomes unless they are modified appropriately.

Solution

To generate a random number from a normal distribution, use NORMINV with three arguments: RAND(), the mean, and the standard deviation.

The best way to analyze this model is with simulation, much as in Chapter 4. To do this, you must be able to simulate normally distributed random numbers in Excel. You can do this with the NORMINV function. Specifically, to generate a normally distributed number with mean μ and standard deviation σ, use the formula

=NORMINV(RAND(),μ,σ)

Because this formula uses the RAND function, it generates a *different* random number each time it is used—and each time the spreadsheet recalculates.[4]

The spreadsheet in Figure 5.12 shows a simulation of yearly demands over a 12-year period. (See the file **Oven Demand Simulation.xlsx**.) To simulate the demands in row 15, enter the formula

=NORMINV(RAND(),B6,B7)

in cell B15. Then enter the formula

=NORMINV(RAND(),B15,$B$11)

in cell C15 and copy it across row 15. (Note how the mean demand in any year is the *simulated* demand from the previous year.) As the accompanying time series graph of these demands indicates, the model seems to be performing well.

Figure 5.12   One Set of Demands for Model 1 in the Microwave Example

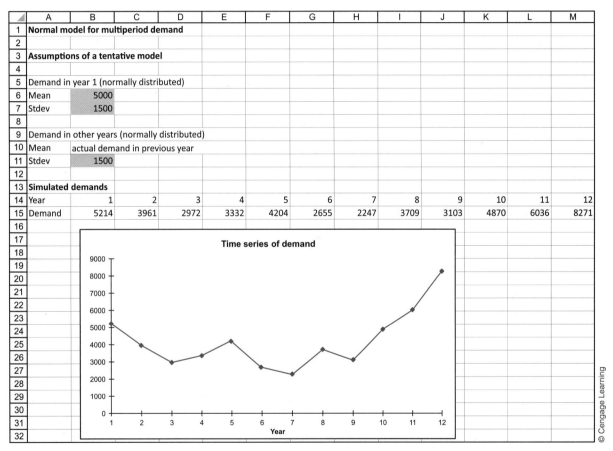

However, the simulated demands in Figure 5.12 are only one set of possible demands. Remember that each time the spreadsheet recalculates, all of the random numbers change. Figure 5.13 shows a different set of random numbers generated by the *same* formulas. Clearly, the model is not working well in this case—some demands are negative, which

[4]To see why this formula makes sense, note that the RAND function in the first argument generates a uniformly distributed random value between 0 and 1. Therefore, the effect of the formula is to generate a random *percentile* from the normal distribution.

makes no sense. The problem is that if the actual demand is low in one year, there is a fairly good chance that the next normally distributed demand will be negative. You can check (by recalculating many times) that the demand sequence is *usually* all positive, but every now and then a nonsense sequence as in Figure 5.13 appears. We need a new model!

Figure 5.13 Another Set of Demands for Model 1 in the Microwave Example

	A	B	C	D	E	F	G	H	I	J	K	L	M
1	Normal model for multiperiod demand												
2													
3	Assumptions of a tentative model												
4													
5	Demand in year 1 (normally distributed)												
6	Mean	5000											
7	Stdev	1500											
8													
9	Demand in other years (normally distributed)												
10	Mean	actual demand in previous year											
11	Stdev	1500											
12													
13	Simulated demands												
14	Year	1	2	3	4	5	6	7	8	9	10	11	12
15	Demand	3362	2665	2323	147	−1012	−2048	−1269	618	197	483	18	2641
16													
17													
18				Time series of demand									
19		4000											
20		3000											
21													
22		2000											
23													
24		1000											
25		0											
26			1 2 3 4 5 6 7 8 9 10 11 12										
27		−1000											
28													
29		−2000											
30		−3000											
31				Year									
32													

One way to modify the model is to let the standard deviation and mean move together. That is, if the mean is low, then the standard deviation will also be low. This minimizes the chance that the *next* random demand will be negative. Besides, this type of model is probably more realistic. If demand in one year is low, there could be less variability in next year's demand. Figure 5.14 illustrates one way (but not the only way) to model this changing standard deviation.

We let the standard deviation of demand in any year (after year 1) be the original standard deviation, 1500, multiplied by the ratio of the expected demand for this year to the expected demand in year 1. For example, if demand in some year is 500, the expected demand next year is 500, and the standard deviation of next year's demand is reduced to 1500(500/5000) = 150. The only change to the spreadsheet model is in row 15, where cell C15 contains the formula

=NORMINV(RAND(),B15,$B$7*B15/$B$6)

and is copied across row 15. Now the chance of a negative demand is practically negligible because this would require a value more than three standard deviations below the mean.

Figure 5.14 Generated Demands for Model 2 in Microwave Example

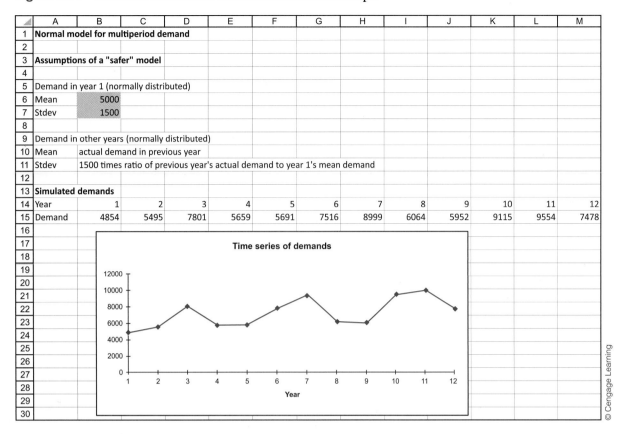

	A	B	C	D	E	F	G	H	I	J	K	L	M
1	Normal model for multiperiod demand												
2													
3	Assumptions of a "safer" model												
4													
5	Demand in year 1 (normally distributed)												
6	Mean	5000											
7	Stdev	1500											
8													
9	Demand in other years (normally distributed)												
10	Mean	actual demand in previous year											
11	Stdev	1500 times ratio of previous year's actual demand to year 1's mean demand											
12													
13	Simulated demands												
14	Year	1	2	3	4	5	6	7	8	9	10	11	12
15	Demand	4854	5495	7801	5659	5691	7516	8999	6064	5952	9115	9554	7478
16													
17													
...													

Unfortunately, the model in Figure 5.14 is still not foolproof. By recalculating many times, negative demands still appear occasionally. To be even safer, it is possible to *truncate* the demand distribution at some nonnegative value such as 250, as shown in Figure 5.15. Now a random demand is generated as in the previous model, but if this randomly generated value is below 250, it is replaced by 250. This is done with the formulas

=MAX(NORMINV(RAND(),B8,B9),D5)

and

=MAX(NORMINV(RAND(),B17,$B$9*B17/$B$8),$D$5)

in cells B17 and C17 and copying this latter formula across row 17. Whether this is the way the demand process works for Highland's microwaves is an open question, but at least it prevents demands from becoming negative—or even falling below 250. Moreover, this type of truncation is a common way of modeling when you want to use a normal distribution but for physical reasons cannot allow the random quantities to become negative.

Before leaving this example, we challenge your intuition. In the final model in Figure 5.15, the demand in any year (say, year 6) is, aside from the truncation, normally distributed with a mean and standard deviation that depend on the previous year's demand. Does this mean that if you recalculate many times and keep track of the year 6 demand each time, the resulting histogram of these year 6 demands will be normally distributed? Perhaps surprisingly, the answer is a clear no. Evidence of this appears in

Figure 5.15   Generated Demands for a Truncated Model in Microwave Example

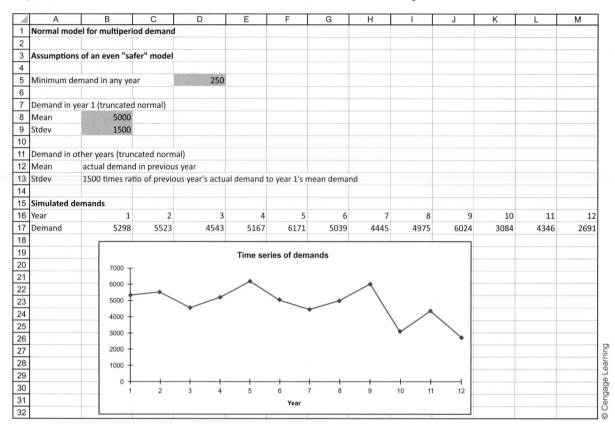

Figure 5.16

Replication of Demand in Year 6

	A	B	C	D	E
36	Replication	Demand			
37		1312		Average	5196
38	1	2026		Stdev	4132
39	2	2232			
40	3	15344			
41	4	2364			
42	5	3709			
434	397	8802			
435	398	5786			
436	399	5836			
437	400	3307			

Figures 5.16 and 5.17. In Figure 5.16 we use a data table to obtain 400 replications of demand in year 6 (in column B). Then we use StatTools's histogram procedure to create a histogram of these simulated demands in Figure 5.17. It is clearly skewed to the right and *nonnormal*.

What causes this distribution to be nonnormal? It is *not* the truncation. Truncation has a relatively minor effect because most of the demands don't need to be truncated. The real reason is that the distribution of year 6 demand is only normal *conditional* on the demand in year 5. That is, if we fix the demand in year 5 at any level and then replicate year 6

Figure 5.17 Histogram of Year 6 Demands

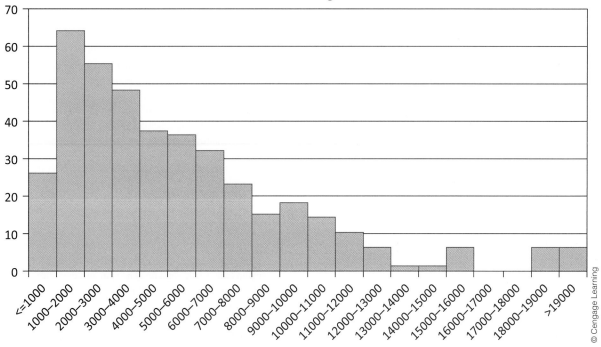

demand many times, the resulting histogram *is* normally shaped. But the year 5 demand is *not* fixed. It varies from replication to replication, and this variation causes the skewness in Figure 5.17. Admittedly, the reason for this skewness is not intuitively obvious, but simulation makes it easy to demonstrate. ∎

PROBLEMS

Note: Student solutions for problems whose numbers appear within a colored box are available for purchase at www .cengagebrain.com.

Level A

1. The grades on the midterm examination given in a large managerial statistics class are normally distributed with mean 75 and standard deviation 9. The instructor of this class wants to assign an A grade to the top 10% of the scores, a B grade to the next 10% of the scores, a C grade to the next 10% of the scores, a D grade to the next 10% of the scores, and an F grade to all scores below the 60th percentile of this distribution. For each possible letter grade, find the lowest acceptable score within the established range. For example, the lowest acceptable score for an A is the score at the 90th percentile of this normal distribution.

2. Suppose it is known that the distribution of purchase amounts by customers entering a popular retail store is approximately normal with mean $75 and standard deviation $20.
   a. What is the probability that a randomly selected customer spends less than $85 at this store?
   b. What is the probability that a randomly selected customer spends between $65 and $85 at this store?
   c. What is the probability that a randomly selected customer spends more than $45 at this store?
   d. Find the dollar amount such that 75% of all customers spend no more than this amount.
   e. Find the dollar amount such that 80% of all customers spend at least this amount.
   f. Find two dollar amounts, equidistant from the mean, such that 90% of all customer purchases are between these values.

3. A machine used to regulate the amount of a certain chemical dispensed in the production of a particular type of cough syrup can be set so that it discharges an average of μ milliliters (ml) of the chemical in each bottle of cough syrup. The amount of chemical placed into each bottle of cough syrup is known to have a normal distribution with a standard deviation of 0.250 ml. If this machine discharges more than 2 ml of the chemical when preparing a given bottle of this cough syrup, the bottle is considered to be unacceptable by industry standards. Determine the setting for μ so that no more than 1% of the bottles of cough syrup prepared by this machine will be rejected.

4. Assume that the monthly sales for Toyota passenger cars follow a normal distribution with mean 5000 cars and standard deviation 1400 cars.
  a. There is a 1% chance that Toyota will sell more than what number of passenger cars during the next year? (You can assume that sales in different months are probabilistically independent.)
  b. What is the probability that Toyota will sell between 55,000 and 65,000 passenger cars during the next year?

5. An investor has invested in nine different investments. The dollar returns on the different investments are probabilistically independent, and each return follows a normal distribution with mean $50,000 and standard deviation $10,000.
  a. There is a 1% chance that the total return on the nine investments is less than what value?
  b. What is the probability that the investor's total return is between $400,000 and $520,000?

6. Scores on an exam appear to follow a normal distribution with $\mu = 60$ and $\sigma = 20$. The instructor wishes to give a grade of D to students scoring between the 10th and 30th percentiles on the exam. For what range of scores should a D be given? What percentage of the students will get a D?

7. Suppose that the weight of a typical American male follows a normal distribution with $\mu = 180$ lb and $\sigma = 30$ lb. Also, suppose 91.92% of all American males weigh more than I weigh.
  a. What fraction of American males weigh more than 225 pounds?
  b. How much do I weigh?
  c. If I weighed 20 pounds more than I do, what percentile would I be in?

8. Assume that the length of a typical televised baseball game, including all the commercial time-outs, is normally distributed with mean 2.45 hours and standard deviation 0.37 hour. Consider a televised baseball game that begins at 2:00 in the afternoon. The next regularly scheduled broadcast is at 5:00.
  a. What is the probability that the game will cut into the next show, that is, go past 5:00?
  b. If the game is over before 4:30, another half-hour show can be inserted into the 4:30–5:00 slot. What is the probability of this occurring?

9. The amount of a soft drink that goes into a typical 12-ounce can varies from can to can. It is normally distributed with an adjustable mean μ and a fixed standard deviation of 0.05 ounce. (The adjustment is made to the filling machine.)
  a. If regulations require that cans have at least 11.9 ounces, what is the smallest mean μ that can be used so that at least 99.5% of all cans meet the regulation?
  b. If the mean setting from part **a** is used, what is the probability that a typical can has at least 12 ounces?

10. Suppose that the demands for a company's product in weeks 1, 2, and 3 are each normally distributed. The means are 50, 45, and 65. The standard deviations are 10, 5, and 15. Assume that these three demands are probabilistically independent.
  a. Suppose that the company currently has 180 units in stock, and it will not be receiving any more shipments from its supplier for at least three weeks. What is the probability that stock will run out during this three-week period?
  b. How many units should the company currently have in stock so that it can be 98% certain of not running out during this three-week period? Again, assume that it won't receive any more shipments during this period.

Level B

11. Matthew's Bakery prepares peanut butter cookies for sale every morning. It costs the bakery $0.50 to bake each peanut butter cookie, and each cookie is sold for $1.25. At the end of the day, leftover cookies are discounted and sold the following day at $0.40 per cookie. The daily demand (in dozens) for peanut butter cookies at this bakery is known to be normally distributed with mean 200 and standard deviation 60. The manager of Matthew's Bakery is trying to determine how many dozen peanut butter cookies to make each morning to maximize the product's contribution to bakery profits. Use simulation to find a very good, if not optimal, production plan.

12. The manufacturer of a particular bicycle model has the following costs associated with the management of this product's inventory. In particular, the company currently maintains an inventory of 1000 units of this bicycle model at the beginning of each year. If X units are demanded each year and X is less than 1000, the excess supply, $1000 - X$ units, must be stored until next year at a cost of $50 per unit. If X is greater than 1000 units, the excess demand, $X - 1000$ units, must be produced separately at an extra cost of $80 per unit. Assume that the annual demand (X) for this bicycle model is normally distributed with mean 1000 and standard deviation 75.

   a. Find the expected annual cost associated with managing potential shortages or surpluses of this product. (*Hint:* Use simulation to approximate the answer. An exact solution using probability arguments is beyond the level of this book.)

   b. Find two annual total cost levels, equidistant from the expected value found in part **a**, such that 95% of all costs associated with managing potential shortages or surpluses of this product are between these values. (Continue to use simulation.)

   c. Comment on this manufacturer's annual production policy for this bicycle model in light of your findings in part **b**.

13. Suppose that a particular production process fills detergent in boxes of a given size. Specifically, this process fills the boxes with an amount of detergent (in ounces) that is normally distributed with mean 50 and standard deviation 0.5.

   a. Simulate this production process for the filling of 500 boxes of detergent. Find the mean and standard deviation of your simulated sample weights. How do your sample statistics compare to the theoretical population parameters in this case? How well do the empirical rules apply in describing the variation in the weights in your simulated detergent boxes?

   b. A box of detergent is rejected by quality control personnel if it is found to contain less than 49 ounces or more than 51 ounces of detergent. Given these quality standards, what proportion of all boxes are rejected? What step(s) could the supervisor of this production process take to reduce this proportion to 1%?

14. It is widely known that many drivers on interstate highways in the United States do not observe the posted speed limit. Assume that the actual rates of speed driven by U.S. motorists are normally distributed with mean μ mph and standard deviation 5 mph. Given this information, answer each of the following independent questions. (*Hint:* Use Goal Seek in parts **a** and **b**, and use the Solver add-in with no objective in part **c**. Solver is usually used to optimize, but it can also be used to solve equations with multiple unknowns.)

   a. If 40% of all U.S. drivers are observed traveling at 65 mph or more, what is the mean μ?

   b. If 25% of all U.S. drivers are observed traveling at 50 mph or less, what is the mean μ?

   c. Suppose now that the mean μ and standard deviation σ of this distribution are both unknown. Furthermore, it is observed that 40% of all U.S. drivers travel at less than 55 mph and 10% of all U.S. drivers travel at more than 70 mph. What must μ and σ be?

15. The lifetime of a certain manufacturer's washing machine is normally distributed with mean 4 years. Only 15% of all these washing machines last at least 5 years. What is the standard deviation of the lifetime of a washing machine made by this manufacturer?

16. You have been told that the distribution of regular unleaded gasoline prices over all gas stations in Indiana is normally distributed with mean $3.25 and standard deviation $0.075, and you have been asked to find two dollar values such that 95% of all gas stations charge somewhere between these two values. Why is each of the following an acceptable answer: between $3.076 and $3.381, or between $3.103 and $3.397? Can you find any other acceptable answers? Which of the many possible answers would you give if you are asked to obtain the *shortest* interval?

17. A fast-food restaurant sells hamburgers and chicken sandwiches. On a typical weekday the demand for hamburgers is normally distributed with mean 313 and standard deviation 57; the demand for chicken sandwiches is normally distributed with mean 93 and standard deviation 22.

   a. How many hamburgers must the restaurant stock to be 98% sure of not running out on a given day?

   b. Answer part **a** for chicken sandwiches.

   c. If the restaurant stocks 400 hamburgers and 150 chicken sandwiches for a given day, what is the probability that it will run out of hamburgers or chicken sandwiches (or both) that day? Assume that the demand for hamburgers and the demand for chicken sandwiches are probabilistically independent.

   d. Why is the independence assumption in part **c** probably not realistic? Using a more realistic assumption, do you think the probability requested in part **c** would increase or decrease?

18. Referring to the box plots introduced in Chapter 2, the sides of the "box" are at the first and third quartiles, and the difference between these (the length of the box) is called the interquartile range (IQR). A *mild* outlier is an observation that is between 1.5 and 3 IQRs from the box, and an

extreme outlier is an observation that is more than 3 IQRs from the box.

a. If the data are normally distributed, what percentage of values will be mild outliers? What percentage will be extreme outliers? Why don't the answers depend on the mean and/or standard deviation of the distribution?

b. Check your answers in part **a** with simulation. Simulate a large number of normal random numbers (you can choose any mean and standard deviation), and count the number of mild and extreme outliers with appropriate formulas. Do these match, at least approximately, your answers to part **a**?

5-4 THE BINOMIAL DISTRIBUTION

The normal distribution is undoubtedly the most important probability distribution in statistics. Not far behind, however, is the *binomial* distribution. The **binomial distribution** is a discrete distribution that can occur in two situations: (1) when sampling from a population with only two types of members (males and females, for example), and (2) when performing a sequence of identical experiments, each of which has only two possible outcomes.

Imagine any experiment that can be repeated many times under identical conditions. It is common to refer to each repetition of the experiment as a *trial*. We assume that the outcomes of successive trials are probabilistically independent of one another and that each trial has only two possible outcomes. We label these two possibilities generically as *success* and *failure*. In any particular application the outcomes might be Democrat/Republican, defective/nondefective, went bankrupt/remained solvent, and so on. We label the probability of a success on each trial as p, and the probability of a failure as $1 - p$. We let n be the number of trials.

> **FUNDAMENTAL INSIGHT**
>
> **What the Binomial Distribution Describes**
> Unlike the normal distribution, which can describe many types of random phenomena, the binomial distribution is relevant for a very common and specific situation: the number of *successes* in a fixed number of *trials*, where the trials are probabilistically independent and the probability of success remains constant across trials. Whenever this situation occurs, the binomial distribution is the relevant distribution.

> Consider a situation where there are n independent, identical trials, where the probability of a success on each trial is p and the probability of a failure is $1 - p$. Define X to be the random number of successes in the n trials. Then X has a **binomial distribution** with parameters n and p.

For example, the binomial distribution with parameters 100 and 0.3 is the distribution of the number of successes in 100 trials when the probability of success is 0.3 on each trial. A simple example that you can keep in mind throughout this section is the number of heads you would see if you flipped a coin n times. Assuming the coin is well balanced, the relevant distribution is binomial with parameters n and $p = 0.5$. This coin-flipping example is often used to illustrate the binomial distribution because of its simplicity, but you will see that the binomial distribution also applies to many important business situations.

To understand how the binomial distribution works, consider the coin-flipping example with $n = 3$. If X represents the number of heads in three flips of the coin, then the possible values of X are 0, 1, 2, and 3. You can find the probabilities of these values by considering the eight possible outcomes of the three flips: (T,T,T), (T,T,H), (T,H,T), (H,T,T), (T,H,H), (H,T,H), (H,H,T), and (H,H,H). Because of symmetry (the well-balanced property of the coin), each of these eight possible outcomes must have the same probability, so each must have probability 1/8. Next, note that one of the outcomes has $X = 0$, three outcomes have $X = 1$, three outcomes have $X = 2$, and one outcome has $X = 3$. Therefore, the probability distribution of X is

$$P(X = 0) = 1/8, \quad P(X = 1) = 3/8, \quad P(X = 2) = 3/8, \quad P(X = 3) = 1/8$$

This is a special case of the binomial distribution, with $n = 3$ and $p = 0.5$. In general, where n can be any positive integer and p can be any probability between 0 and 1, there is a rather complex formula for calculating $P(X = k)$ for any integer k from 0 to n. Instead of presenting this formula, we will discuss how to calculate binomial probabilities in Excel. You do this with the BINOMDIST function. The general form of this function is

= BINOMDIST($k, n, p,$ cum)

The middle two arguments are the number of trials n and the probability of success p on each trial. The first parameter k is an integer number of successes that you specify. The last parameter, *cum*, is either 0 or 1. It is 1 if you want the probability of *less than or equal to k* successes, and it is 0 if you want the probability of *exactly k* successes. We illustrate typical binomial calculations in Example 5.7.

CHANGES IN EXCEL 2010

As with the new normal functions, there are new binomial functions in Excel 2010. The BINOMDIST and CRITBINOM functions in the following example have been replaced by BINOM.DIST and BINOM.INV, but the old functions still work fine. Both versions are indicated in the file for the following example.

EXAMPLE | **5.7 BINOMIAL CALCULATIONS IN EXCEL**

Suppose that 100 identical batteries are inserted in identical flashlights. Each flashlight takes a single battery. After eight hours of continuous use, a given battery is still operating with probability 0.6 or has failed with probability 0.4. Let X be the number of successes in these 100 trials, where a success means that the battery is still functioning. Find the probabilities of the following events: (a) exactly 58 successes, (b) no more than 65 successes, (c) less than 70 successes, (d) at least 59 successes, (e) greater than 65 successes, (f) between 55 and 65 successes (inclusive), (g) exactly 40 failures, (h) at least 35 failures, and (i) less than 42 failures. Then find the 95th percentile of the distribution of X.

Objective To use Excel's BINOMDIST and CRITBINOM functions for calculating binomial probabilities and percentiles in the context of flashlight batteries.

Solution

Figure 5.18 shows the solution to all of these problems. (See the file **Binomial Calculations. xlsx**.) The probabilities requested in parts (a) through (f) all involve the number of successes X. The key to these is the wording of phrases such as "no more than," "greater than," and so on. In particular, you have to be careful to distinguish between probabilities such as $P(X < k)$ and $P(X \leq k)$. The latter includes the possibility of having $X = k$ and the former does not.

Figure 5.18 Typical Binomial Calculations

	A	B	C	D	E	F	G	H	I	J
1	**Binomial Probability Calculations**									
2				**Range names used:**						
3	Number of trials	100		NTrials	=BinomCalcs!$B$3					
4	Probability of success on each trial	0.6		PSuccess	=BinomCalcs!$B$4					
5										
6	**Event**	**Probability**		**Formula**						
7	Exactly 58 successes	0.0742		=BINOMDIST(58,NTrials,PSuccess,0)						
8	No more than 65 successes	0.8697		=BINOMDIST(65,NTrials,PSuccess,1)						
9	Less than 70 successes	0.9752		=BINOMDIST(69,NTrials,PSuccess,1)						
10	At least 59 successes	0.6225		=1-BINOMDIST(58,NTrials,PSuccess,1)						
11	Greater than 65 successes	0.1303		=1-BINOMDIST(65,NTrials,PSuccess,1)						
12	Between 55 and 65 successes (inclusive)	0.7386		=BINOMDIST(65,NTrials,PSuccess,1)-BINOMDIST(54,NTrials,PSuccess,1)						
13										
14	Exactly 40 failures	0.0812		=BINOMDIST(40,NTrials,1-PSuccess,0)						
15	At least 35 failures	0.8697		=1-BINOMDIST(34,NTrials,1-PSuccess,1)						
16	Less than 42 failures	0.6225		=BINOMDIST(41,NTrials,1-PSuccess,1)						
17										
18	**Finding the 95th percentile (trial and error)**									
19	Trial values	CumProb								
20	65	0.8697		=BINOMDIST(A20,NTrials,PSuccess,1)						
21	66	0.9087		(Copy down)						
22	67	0.9385								
23	68	0.9602								
24	69	0.9752								
25	70	0.9852								
26				Formula in cell A27:						
27	68	0.95		=CRITBINOM(NTrials,PSuccess,B27)						

With this in mind, the probabilities requested in (a) through (f) become:

a. $P(X = 58)$

b. $P(X \le 65)$

c. $P(X < 70) = P(X \le 69)$

d. $P(X \ge 59) = 1 - P(X < 59) = 1 - P(X \le 58)$

e. $P(X > 65) = 1 - P(X \le 65)$

f. $P(55 \le X \le 65) = P(X \le 65) - P(X < 55) = P(X \le 65) - P(X \le 54)$

Note how we have manipulated each of these so that it includes only terms of the form $P(X = k)$ or $P(X \le k)$ for suitable values of k. These are the types of probabilities that can be handled directly by the BINOMDIST function. The answers appear in the range B7:B12, and the corresponding formulas are shown (as labels) in column D. (The Excel 2010 functions do not appear in this figure, but they are included in the file.)

The probabilities requested in (g) through (i) involve *failures* rather than successes. But because each trial results in either a success or a failure, the number of failures is also binomially distributed, with parameters n and $1 - p = 0.4$. So in rows 14 through 16 the requested probabilities are calculated in exactly the same way, except that 1-PSuccess is substituted for PSuccess in the third argument of the BINOMDIST function.

Finally, to calculate the 95th percentile of the distribution of X, you can proceed by trial and error. For each value k from 65 to 70, the probability $P(X \le k)$ is calculated in column B with the BINOMDIST function. Note that there is no value k such that $P(X \leq k) = 0.95$ exactly. Specifically, $P(X \leq 67)$ is slightly less than 0.95 and $P(X \leq 68)$ is slightly greater than 0.95. Therefore, the meaning of the "95th percentile" is somewhat ambiguous. If you want the largest value k such that $P(X \leq k) \leq 0.95$, then this k is 67. If instead you want the smallest value k such that $P(X \leq k) \geq 0.95$, then this value is 68. The latter interpretation is the one usually accepted for binomial percentiles.

In fact, Excel has another built-in function, CRITBINOM (or BINOM.INV beginning in Excel 2010), for finding this value of k. This function is illustrated in row 27 of Figure 5.18. Now you enter the requested probability, 0.95, in cell B27 and the formula

=CRITBINOM(NTrials,PSuccess,B27)

in cell A27. It returns 68, the smallest value k such that $P(X \leq k) \geq 0.95$ for this binomial distribution. ∎

5-4a Mean and Standard Deviation of the Binomial Distribution

It can be shown that the mean and standard deviation of a binomial distribution with parameters n and p are given by the following equations.

Mean and Standard Deviation of the Binomial Distribution

$$E(X) = np \tag{5.3}$$

$$\text{Stdev}(X) = \sqrt{np(1 - p)} \tag{5.4}$$

The formula for the mean is quite intuitive. For example, if you observe 100 trials, each with probability of success 0.6, your best guess for the number of successes is $100(0.6) = 60$. The standard deviation is less obvious but still very useful. It indicates how far the actual number of successes is likely to deviate from the mean. In this case the standard deviation is $\sqrt{100(0.6)(0.4)} = 4.90$.

Fortunately, the empirical rules discussed in Chapter 2 also apply, at least approximately, to the binomial distribution. That is, there is about a 95% chance that the actual number of successes will be within two standard deviations of the mean, and there is almost no chance that the number of successes will be more than three standard deviations from the mean. So for this example, it is very likely that the number of successes will be in the range of approximately 50 to 70, and it is very unlikely that there will be fewer than 45 or more than 75 successes.

This reasoning is extremely useful. It provides a rough estimate of the number of successes you are likely to observe. Suppose 1000 parts are sampled randomly from an assembly line and, based on historical performance, the percentage of parts with some type of defect is about 5%. Translated into a binomial model, each of the 1000 parts, independently of the others, has some type of defect with probability 0.05. Would it be surprising to see, say, 75 parts with a defect? The mean is $1000(0.05) = 50$ and the standard deviation is $\sqrt{1000(0.05)(0.95)} = 6.89$. Therefore, the number of parts with defects is 95% certain to be within $50 \pm 2(6.89)$, or approximately from 36 to 64. Because 75 is slightly beyond three standard deviations from the mean, it is highly unlikely that there would be 75 (or more) defective parts.

5-4b The Binomial Distribution in the Context of Sampling

We now discuss how the binomial distribution applies to sampling from a population with two types of members. Let's say these two types are men and women, although in applications they might be Democrats and Republicans, users of our product and nonusers, and so on. We assume that the population has N members, of whom N_M are men and N_W are women (where $N_M + N_W = N$). If you sample n of these randomly, you are typically interested in the composition of the sample. You might expect the number of men in the sample to be binomially distributed with parameters n and $p = N_M/N$, the fraction of men in the population. However, this depends on how the sampling is performed.

If sampling is done **without replacement**, each member of the population can be sampled only once. That is, once a person is sampled, his or her name is struck from the list and cannot be sampled again. If sampling is done **with replacement**, then it is possible, although maybe not likely, to select a given member of the population more than once. Most real-world sampling is performed *without* replacement. There is no point in obtaining information from the same person more than once. However, *the binomial model applies only to sampling with replacement*. Because the composition of the remaining population keeps changing as the sampling progresses, the binomial model provides only an approximation if sampling is done without replacement. If there is no replacement, the value of p, the proportion of men in this case, does *not* stay constant, a requirement of the binomial model. The appropriate distribution for sampling without replacement is called the *hypergeometric* distribution, a distribution we will not discuss here.[5]

If n is small relative to N, however, the binomial distribution is a very good approximation to the hypergeometric distribution and can be used even if sampling is performed without replacement. A rule of thumb is that if n is no greater than 10% of N, that is, no more than 10% of the population is sampled, then the binomial model can be used safely. Of course, most national polls sample considerably less than 10% of the population. In fact, they often sample only about a thousand people from the hundreds of millions in the entire population. The bottom line is that in most real-world sampling contexts, the binomial model is perfectly adequate.

5-4c The Normal Approximation to the Binomial

If n is large and p is not too close to 0 or 1, the binomial distribution is bell-shaped and can be approximated well by the normal distribution.

If you graph the binomial probabilities, you will see an interesting phenomenon—namely, the graph begins to look symmetric and bell-shaped when n is fairly large and p is not too close to 0 or 1. An example is illustrated in Figure 5.19 with the parameters $n = 30$ and $p = 0.4$. Generally, if $np > 5$ and $n(1-p) > 5$, the binomial distribution can be approximated well by a normal distribution with mean np and standard deviation $\sqrt{np(1-p)}$.

One practical consequence of the normal approximation to the binomial is that the empirical rules can be applied. That is, when the binomial distribution is approximately symmetric and bell-shaped, there is about a 68% chance that the number of successes will be within one standard deviation of the mean. Similarly, there is about a 95% chance that the number of successes will be within two standard deviations of the mean, and the number of successes will almost surely be within three standard deviations of the mean. Here, the mean is np and the standard deviation is $\sqrt{np(1-p)}$.

[5]Excel has a function **HYPGEOMDIST** for sampling without replacement that works much like the BINOMDIST function. You can look it up under the Statistical category of Excel functions.

Figure 5.19
Bell-shaped Binomial Distribution

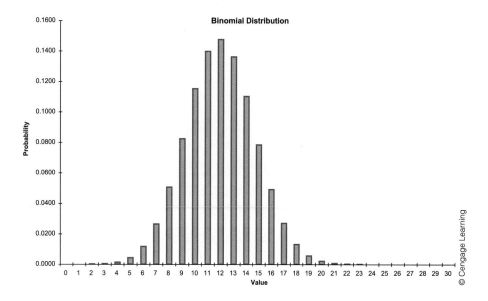

© Cengage Learning

Excel Tip: **Continuity Correction**

Because the normal distribution is continuous and the binomial distribution is discrete, the normal approximation to the binomial can be improved slightly with a continuity correction. If you want to approximate a binomial probability such as $P(36 \leq X \leq 45)$, expand the interval by 0.5 on each end in the normal approximation. That is, approximate with the normal probability $P(35.5 \leq X \leq 45.5)$. Similarly, approximate binomial $P(X \leq 45)$ with normal $P(X \leq 45.5)$, or binomial $P(X \geq 36)$ with normal $P(X \geq 35.5)$.

5-5 APPLICATIONS OF THE BINOMIAL DISTRIBUTION

The binomial distribution finds many applications in the business world and elsewhere. We discuss a few typical applications in this section.

EXAMPLE | 5.8 IS THIS MUTUAL FUND REALLY A WINNER?

An investment broker at the Michaels & Dodson Company claims that he has found a real winner. He has tracked a mutual fund that has beaten a standard market index in 37 of the past 52 weeks. Could this be due to chance, or has he *really* found a winner?

Objective To determine the probability of a mutual fund outperforming a standard market index at least 37 out of 52 weeks.

Solution

The broker is no doubt tracking a lot of mutual funds, and he is probably reporting only the best of these. Therefore, we will check whether the best of *many* mutual funds could do at least this well purely by chance. To do this, we first specify what we mean by "purely by chance." This means that each week, a given fund has a fifty-fifty chance of beating the market index, independently of performance in other weeks. In other words, the number of weeks where a given fund outperforms the market index is binomially distributed with $n = 52$ and $p = 0.5$. With this in mind, cell B6 of Figure 5.20 shows the probability that a given fund does at least as well—beats the market index at least 37 out of 52 weeks—as the reported fund. (See the **Beating the Market.xlsx** file.) Because $P(X \geq 37) = 1 - P(X \leq 36)$, the relevant formula is

=1–BINOMDIST(B3–1,B4,0.5,1)

Obviously, this probability, 0.00159, is quite small. A single fund isn't likely to beat the market this often purely by chance.

Figure 5.20   Binomial Calculations for Investment Example

	A	B	C	D	E	F	G
1	Beating the market						
2							
3	Weeks beating market index	37					
4	Total number of weeks	52					
5							
6	Probability of doing at least this well by chance	0.00159		=1-BINOMDIST(B3-1,B4,0.5,1)			
7							
8	Number of mutual funds	400					
9	Probability of at least one doing at least this well	0.471		=1-BINOMDIST(0,B8,B6,1)			
10							
11	Two-way data table of the probability in B9 as a function of values in B3 and B8						
12			Number of weeks beating the market index				
13		0.471	36	37	38	39	40
14	Number of mutual funds	200	0.542	0.273	0.113	0.040	0.013
15		300	0.690	0.380	0.164	0.060	0.019
16		400	0.790	0.471	0.213	0.079	0.025
17		500	0.858	0.549	0.258	0.097	0.031
18		600	0.904	0.616	0.301	0.116	0.038

© Cengage Learning

However, the probability that the *best* of many mutual funds does at least this well is much larger. To calculate this probability, assume that 400 funds are being tracked, and let *Y* be the number of these that beat the market at least 37 of 52 weeks. Then *Y* is also binomially distributed, with parameters $n = 400$ and $p = 0.00159$, the probability calculated previously. To see whether *any* of the 400 funds beats the market at least 37 of 52 weeks, calculate $P(Y \geq 1) = 1 - P(Y = 0)$ in cell B9 with the formula

=1–BINOMDIST(0,B8,B7,1)

(Can you see why the fourth argument could be 0 *or* 1?) The resulting probability is nearly 0.5—that is, there is nearly a fifty-fifty chance that at least one of 400 funds will do as well as the reported fund. This certainly casts doubt on the broker's claim that he has found a real winner. It is more likely that his star fund just got lucky and will perform no better than average in succeeding weeks.

To see how the probability in cell B9 depends on the level of success of the reported fund (the value in cell B3) and the number of mutual funds being tracked (in cell B8), you can create a two-way data table in the range B13:G18. (The formula in cell B13 is = **B9**, the row input cell is B3, and the column input cell is B8.) As you saw, beating the market 37 times out of 52 is no big deal with 400 funds, but beating it 40 times out of 52, even with 600 funds, is something worth reporting. The probability of this happening purely by chance is only 0.038, or less than 1 out of 25. ∎

Example 5.9 requires a normal calculation to find a probability p, which is then used in a binomial calculation.

| EXAMPLE | **5.9 DAILY SALES AT A SUPERMARKET** |

Customers at a supermarket spend varying amounts. Historical data indicate that the amount spent per customer is normally distributed with mean $85 and standard deviation $30. If 500 customers shop in a given day, calculate the mean and standard deviation of the number who spend at least $100. Then calculate the probability that at least 30% of all customers spend at least $100.

Objective   To use the normal *and* binomial distributions to calculate the typical number of customers who spend at least $100 per day and the probability that at least 30% of all 500 daily customers spend at least $100.

Solution

Both questions involve the number of customers who spend at least $100. Because the amounts spent are normally distributed, the probability that a typical customer spends at least $100 is found with the NORMDIST function. This probability, 0.309, appears in cell B7 of Figure 5.21. (See the file **Supermarket Spending.xlsx**.) It is calculated with the formula

=1-NORMDIST(100,B4,B5,1)

This probability is then used as the parameter p in a binomial model. The mean and standard deviation of the number who spend at least $100 are calculated in cells B13 and B14 as np and $\sqrt{np(1-p)}$ using $n = 500$, the number of shoppers, and $p = 0.309$. The expected number who spend at least $100 is slightly greater than 154, and the standard deviation of this number is slightly greater than 10.

To answer the second question, note that 30% of 500 customers is 150 customers. Then the probability that at least 30% of the customers spend at least $100 is the probability that a binomially distributed random variable, with $n = 500$ and $p = 0.309$, is at least 150. This binomial probability, which turns out to be about 2/3, is calculated in cell B16 with the formula

=1-BINOMDIST(0.3*B10-1,B10,B7,1)

Note that the first argument evaluates to 149. This is because the probability of *at least* 150 customers is one minus the probability of less than or equal to 149 customers. ∎

Figure 5.21 Calculations for Supermarket Example

	A	B	C	D	E	F
1	**Supermarket spending**					
2						
3	Amount spent per customer (normally distributed)					
4	Mean	$85				
5	StDev	$30				
6						
7	Probability that a customer spends at least $100	0.309		=1-NORMDIST(100,B4,B5,1)		
8						
9						
10	Number of customers	500				
11						
12	Mean and stdev of number who spend at least $100					
13	Mean	154.27		=B10*B7		
14	StDev	10.33		=SQRT(B10*B7*(1-B7))		
15						
16	Probability at least 30% spend at least $100	0.676		=1-BINOMDIST(0.3*B10-1,B10,B7,1)		

© Cengage Learning

EXAMPLE | **5.10 OVERBOOKING BY AIRLINES**

This example presents a simplified version of calculations used by airlines when they overbook flights. They realize that a certain percentage of ticketed passengers will cancel at the last minute. Therefore, to avoid empty seats, they sell more tickets than there are seats, hoping that just about the right number of passengers show up. We assume that the no-show rate is 10%. In binomial terms, we assume that each ticketed passenger, independently of the others, shows up with probability 0.90 and cancels with probability 0.10.

For a flight with 200 seats, the airline wants to see how sensitive various probabilities are to the number of tickets it issues. In particular, it wants to calculate (a) the probability that more than 205 passengers show up, (b) the probability that more than 200 passengers show up, (c) the probability that at least 195 seats are filled, and (d) the probability that at least 190 seats are filled. The first two of these are "bad" events from the airline's perspective; they mean that some customers will be bumped from the flight. The last two events are "good" in the sense that the airline wants most of the seats to be occupied.

Objective   To assess the benefits and drawbacks of airline overbooking.

Solution

To solve the airline's problem, we use the BINOMDIST function and a data table. The solution appears in Figure 5.22. (See the file **Airline Overbooking.xlsx**.) For any number of tickets issued in cell B6, the required probabilities are calculated in row 10. For example, the formulas in cells B10 and D10 are

=1-BINOMDIST(205,NTickets,1-PNoShow,1)

and

=1-BINOMDIST(194,NTickets,1-PNoShow,1)

Figure 5.22 Binomial Calculations for Overbooking Example

	A	B	C	D	E	F
1	**Airline overbooking**			**Range names used:**		
2				NTickets	=Overbooking!$B$6	
3	Number of seats	200		PNoShow	=Overbooking!$B$4	
4	Probability of no-show	0.1				
5						
6	Number of tickets issued	215				
7						
8	**Required probabilities**					
9		More than 205 show up	More than 200 show up	At least 195 seats filled	At least 190 seats filled	
10		0.001	0.050	0.421	0.820	
11						
12	Data table showing sensitivity of probabilities to number of tickets issued					
13	Number of tickets issued	More than 205 show up	More than 200 show up	At least 195 seats filled	At least 190 seats filled	
14		0.001	0.050	0.421	0.820	
15	206	0.000	0.000	0.012	0.171	
16	209	0.000	0.001	0.064	0.384	
17	212	0.000	0.009	0.201	0.628	
18	215	0.001	0.050	0.421	0.820	
19	218	0.013	0.166	0.659	0.931	
20	221	0.064	0.370	0.839	0.978	
21	224	0.194	0.607	0.939	0.995	
22	227	0.406	0.802	0.981	0.999	
23	230	0.639	0.920	0.995	1.000	
24	233	0.822	0.974	0.999	1.000	

© Cengage Learning

Note that the condition "more than" requires a slightly different calculation from "at least." The probability of more than 205 is one minus the probability of less than or equal to 205, whereas the probability of at least 195 is one minus the probability of less than or equal to 194. Also, note that a passenger who shows up is called a success. Therefore, the third argument of each BINOMDIST function is one minus the no-show probability.

To see how sensitive these probabilities are to the number of tickets issued, we create a one-way data table at the bottom of the spreadsheet. It is *one-way* because there is only one *input,* the number of tickets issued, even though four output probabilities are tabulated. (To create the data table, list several possible numbers of tickets issued along the side in column A and create links to the probabilities in row 10 and in row 14. That is, enter the formula =B10 in cell B14 and copy it across row 14. Then form a data table using the range A14:E24, no row input cell, and column input cell B6.)

The results are as expected. As the airline issues more tickets, there is a larger chance of having to bump passengers from the flight, but there is also a larger chance of filling most seats. In reality, the airline has to make a trade-off between these two, taking its various costs and revenues into account. ■

The following is another simplified example of a real problem that occurs every time you watch election returns on TV. This problem is of particular interest in light of the highly unusual events that took place during election night television coverage of the U.S. presidential election in 2000, where the networks declared Al Gore an early winner in at least one state that he eventually lost. The basic question is how soon the networks can declare one of the candidates the winner, based on early voting returns. Our example is somewhat unrealistic because it ignores the possibility that early tabulations can be biased one way or the other. For example, the earliest reporting precincts might be known to be more heavily in favor of the Democrat than the population in general. Nevertheless, the example indicates why the networks are able to make early conclusions based on such seemingly small amounts of data.

EXAMPLE | 5.11 PROJECTING ELECTION WINNERS FROM EARLY RETURNS

We assume that there are N voters in the population, of whom N_R will vote for the Republican and N_D will vote for the Democrat. The eventual winner will be the Republican if $N_R > N_D$ and will be the Democrat otherwise, but we won't know which until all of the votes are tabulated. (To simplify the example, we assume there are only two candidates and that the election will *not* end in a tie.) Let's suppose that a small percentage of the votes have been counted and the Republican is currently ahead 540 to 460. On what basis can the networks declare the Republican the winner, especially if there are millions of voters in the population?

Objective To use a binomial model to determine whether early returns reflect the eventual winner of an election between two candidates.

Solution

Let $n = 1000$ be the total number of votes that have been tabulated. If X is the number of Republican votes so far, we are given that $X = 540$. Now we pose the following question. If the Democrat were going to be the eventual winner, that is, $N_D > N_R$, and we randomly sampled 1000 voters from the population, how likely is it that at least 540 of these voters would be in favor of the Republican? If this is very *unlikely*, then the only reasonable conclusion is that the Democrat will *not* be the eventual winner. This is the reasoning the networks might use to declare the Republican the winner so early in the tabulation.

We use a binomial model to see how unlikely the event "at least 540 out of 1000 " is, assuming that the Democrat will be the eventual winner. We need a value for p, the probability that a typical vote is for the Republican. This probability should be the proportion of voters in the entire population who favor the Republican. All we know is that this probability is less than 0.5, because we have *assumed* that the Democrat will eventually win. In Figure 5.23, we show how the probability of at least 540 out of 1000 varies with values of p less than, but close to, 0.5. (See the file **Election Returns.xlsx**.)

We enter a trial value of 0.49 for p in cell B3 and then calculate the required probability in cell B9 with the formula

=1-BINOMDIST(B6-1,B5,B3,1)

Then we use this to create the data table at the bottom of the spreadsheet. This data table tabulates the probability of the given lead (at least 540 out of 1000) for various values of p less than 0.5. As shown in the last few rows, even if the eventual outcome were going to be a virtual tie—with the Democrat slightly ahead—there would still be *very* little chance of the Republican being at least 80 votes ahead so far. But because the Republican *is* currently ahead by 80 votes, the networks feel safe in declaring the Republican the winner. Admittedly, the probability model they use is more complex than our simple binomial model, but the idea is the same. ∎

Figure 5.23 Binomial Calculations for Voting Example

	A	B	C	D	E	F
1	**Election returns**					
2						
3	Population proportion for Republican	0.49				
4						
5	Votes tabulated so far	1000				
6	Votes for Republican so far	540				
7						
8	P(at least this many R votes)-binomial	0.0009		=1-BINOMDIST(B6-1,B5,B3,1)		
9						
10	Data table showing sensitivity of this probability to population proportion for Republican					
11	Population proportion for Republican	Probability				
12		0.0009				
13	0.490	0.0009				
14	0.492	0.0013				
15	0.494	0.0020				
16	0.496	0.0030				
17	0.498	0.0043				
18	0.499	0.0052				

The final example in this section challenges the two assumptions of the binomial model. So far, we have assumed that the outcomes of successive trials have the same probability p of success and are probabilistically independent. There are many situations where either or both of these assumptions are questionable. For example, consider successive items from a production line, where each item either meets specifications (a success) or doesn't (a failure). If the process deteriorates over time, at least until it receives maintenance, the probability p of success will slowly decrease. But even if p remains constant, defective items could come in bunches (because of momentary inattentiveness on the part of a worker, say), which would invalidate the independence assumption.

If you believe that the binomial assumptions are invalid, then you must specify an alternative model that reflects reality more closely. This is not easy—all kinds of *nonbinomial* assumptions can be imagined. Furthermore, when you make such assumptions, there are probably no simple formulas to use, such as the BINOMDIST formulas we have been using. Simulation might be the only (simple) alternative, as illustrated in Example 5.12.

EXAMPLE **5.12 Shooting Streaks in Basketball**

Do basketball players shoot in streaks? This question has been debated by thousands of basketball fans, and it has been studied statistically by academic researchers. Most fans believe the answer is yes, arguing that players clearly alternate between hot streaks where they can't miss and cold streaks where they can't hit the broad side of a barn. This situation does not fit a binomial model where, say, a "450 shooter" has a 0.450 probability of making each shot and a 0.550 probability of missing, independently of other shots. If the binomial model does not apply, what model is appropriate, and how could it be used

5-5 Applications of the Binomial Distribution **201**

to calculate a typical probability such as the probability of making at least 13 shots out of 25 attempts?[6]

Objective   To formulate a nonbinomial model of basketball shooting, and to use it to find the probability of a "450 shooter" making at least 13 out of 25 shots.

Solution

This example is quite open-ended. There are numerous alternatives to the binomial model that could capture the "streakiness" most fans believe in, and the one we suggest here is by no means the only possibility. We challenge you to develop others.

The model we propose assumes that this shooter makes 45% of his shots in the long run. The probability that he makes his first shot in a game is 0.45. In general, consider his nth shot. If he has made his last k shots, we assume the probability of making shot n is $0.45 + kd_1$. On the other hand, if he has missed his last k shots, we assume the probability of making shot n is $0.45 - kd_2$. Here, d_1 and d_2 are small values (0.01 and 0.02, for example) that indicate how much the shooter's probability of success increases or decreases depending on his current streak. The model implies that the shooter gets better the more shots he makes and worse the more he misses.

To implement this model, we use simulation as shown in Figure 5.24 (with many hidden rows). (See the file **Basketball Simulation.xlsx**.) Actually, we first do a baseline binomial calculation in cell B9, using the parameters $n = 25$ and $p = 0.450$. The formula in cell B9 is

=1-BINOMDIST(12,B7,B3,1)

If the player makes each shot with probability 0.45, independently of the other shots, then the probability that he will make over half of his 25 shots is 0.306—about a 30% chance. (Remember that this is a binomial calculation for a situation where the binomial distribution probably does not apply.) The simulation in the range A17:D41 shows the results of 25 random shots according to the *nonbinomial* model we have assumed. Column B indicates the length of the current streak, where a negative value indicates a streak of misses and a positive value indicates a streak of makes. Column C indicates the probability of a make on the current shot, and column D contains 1s for makes and 0s for misses. Here are step-by-step instructions for developing this model.

1. **First shot.** Enter the formulas

    =B3

    and

    =IF(RAND()<C17,1,0)

    in cells C17 and D17 to determine the outcome of the first shot.

2. **Second shot.** Enter the formulas

    =IF(D17=0,-1,1)

    =IF(B18<0,$B$3+B18*$B$5,$B$4+B18*$B$5)

    and

    =IF(RAND()C18,1,0)

---

[6]There are obviously a lot of extenuating circumstances surrounding any shot: the type of shot (layup versus jump shot), the type of defense, the score, the time left in the game, and so on. For this example, we focus on a pure jump shooter who is unaffected by the various circumstances in the game.

Figure 5.24 Simulation of Basketball Shooting Model

	A	B	C	D	E	F	G	H	I
1	**Basketball shooting simulation**								
2									
3	Long-run average	0.45							
4	Increment d1 after a make	0.015							
5	Increment d2 after a miss	0.015							
6									
7	Number of shots	25							
8									
9	P (at least 13 out of 25)-binomial	0.306							
10									
11	Summary statistics from simulation below				Compare these	Fraction of reps with at least 13 from table below			
12	Number of makes	11				0.288			
13	At least 13 makes ?	0							
14									
15	Simulation of makes and misses using nonbinomial model					Data table to replicate 25 shots many times			
16		Shot	Streak	P(make)	Make?		Rep	At least 13?		
17		1	NA	0.45	0			0		
18		2	−1	0.435	1		1	0		
19		3	1	0.465	0		2	0		
20		4	−1	0.435	0		3	0		
21		5	−2	0.42	0		4	1		
37		21	4	0.51	1		20	1		
38		22	5	0.525	1		21	1		
39		23	6	0.54	0		22	0		
40		24	−1	0.435	0		23	0		
41		25	−2	0.42	0		24	0		
42							25	0		
43							26	1		
265							248	0		
266							249	1		
267							250	1		

© Cengage Learning

in cells B18, C18, and D18. The first of these indicates that by the second shot, the shooter will have a streak of one make or one miss. The second formula is the important one. It indicates how the probability of a make changes depending on the current streak. The third formula simulates a make or a miss, using the probability in cell C18.

3. **Length of streak on third shot.** Enter the formula

=IF(AND(B18<0,D18=0),B18-1,IF(AND(B18<0,D18=1),1,

IF(ANDB18>0,D18=0),−1,B18+1)))

in cell B19 and copy it down column B. This nested IF formula checks for all four combinations of the previous streak (negative or positive, indicated in cell B18) and the most recent shot (make or miss, indicated in cell D18) to see whether the current streak continues by 1 or a new streak starts.

4. **Results of remaining shots.** The logic for the formulas in columns C and D is the same for the remaining shots as for shot 2, so copy the formulas in cells C18 and D18 down their respective columns.

5. **Summary of 25 shots.** Enter the formulas

=SUM(D17:D41)

and

=IF(B12>=13,1,0)

in cells B12 and B13 to summarize the results of the 25 simulated shots. In particular, the value in cell B13 is 1 only if at least 13 of the shots are successes.

What about the *probability* of making at least 13 shots with this nonbinomial model? So far, we have simulated one set of 25 shots and have reported whether at least 13 of the shots are successes. We need to replicate this simulation many times and report the fraction of the replications where at least 13 of the shots are successes. We do this with a data table in columns F and G.

To create this table, enter the replication numbers 1 through 250 (you could use any number of replications) in column F. Then put a link to B13 in cell G17 by entering the formula = **B13** in this cell. Essentially, we are recalculating this value 250 times, each with different random numbers. To do this, highlight the range F17:G267, and create a data table with no row input cell and *any blank cell* (such as F17) as the column input cell. This causes Excel to recalculate the basic simulation 250 times, each time with different random numbers. (This trick of using a blank column input cell will be discussed in more detail in Chapter 15.) Finally, enter the formula

=AVERAGE(G18:G267)

in cell F12 to calculate the fraction of the replications with at least 13 makes out of 25 shots.

After finishing all of this, note that the spreadsheet is "live" in the sense that if you press the F9 recalculation key, all of the simulated quantities change with new random numbers. In particular, the estimate in cell F12 of the probability of at least 13 makes out of 25 shots changes. It is sometimes less than the binomial probability in cell B9 and sometimes greater. In general, the two probabilities are roughly the same. The bottom line? Even if the world doesn't behave exactly as the binomial model indicates, probabilities of various events can often be approximated fairly well by binomial probabilities—which saves you the trouble of developing and working with more complex models. ∎

PROBLEMS

Level A

19. In a typical month, an insurance agent presents life insurance plans to 40 potential customers. Historically, one in four such customers chooses to buy life insurance from this agent. Based on the relevant binomial distribution, answer the following questions about X, the number of customers who will buy life insurance from this agent in the coming month:
   a. What is the probability X is exactly 5?
   b. What is the probability that X is no more than 10?
   c. What is the probability that X is at least 20?
   d. Determine the mean and standard deviation of X.
   e. What is the probability that X will be within two standard deviations of the mean?
   f. What is the probability that X will be within three standard deviations of the mean?

20. Continuing the previous exercise, use the normal approximation to the binomial to answer each of the questions posed in parts **a** through **f**. How well does the normal approximation perform in this case? Explain.

21. Many vehicles used in space travel are constructed with redundant systems to protect flight crews and their valuable equipment. In other words, backup systems are included within many vehicle components so that if one or more systems fail, backup systems will assure the safe operation of the given component and thus the entire vehicle. For example, consider one particular component of the U.S. space shuttle that has n duplicated systems (i.e., one original system and $n - 1$ backup systems). Each of these systems functions, independently of the others, with probability 0.98. This shuttle component functions successfully provided that *at least* one of the *n* systems functions properly.

a. Find the probability that this shuttle component functions successfully if $n = 2$.

b. Find the probability that this shuttle component functions successfully if $n = 4$.

c. What is the minimum number *n* of duplicated systems that must be incorporated into this shuttle component to ensure at least a 0.9999 probability of successful operation?

22. Suppose that a popular hotel for vacationers in Orlando, Florida, has a total of 300 identical rooms. As many major airline companies do, this hotel has adopted an overbooking policy in an effort to maximize the usage of its available lodging capacity. Assume that each potential hotel customer holding a room reservation, independently of other customers, cancels the reservation or simply does not show up at the hotel on a given night with probability 0.15.

a. Find the largest number of room reservations that this hotel can book and still be at least 95% sure that everyone who shows up at the hotel will have a room on a given night.

b. Given that the hotel books the number of reservations found in part **a**, find the probability that at least 90% of the available rooms will be occupied on a given night.

c. Given that the hotel books the number of reservations found in part **a**, find the probability that at most 80% of the available rooms will be occupied on a given night.

d. How does your answer to part **a** change as the required assurance rate increases from 95% to 97%? How does your answer to part **a** change as the required assurance rate increases from 95% to 99%?

e. How does your answer to part **a** change as the cancellation rate varies between 5% and 25% (in increments of 5%)? Assume now that the required assurance rate remains at 95%.

23. A production process manufactures items with weights that are normally distributed with mean 15 pounds and standard deviation 0.1 pound. An item is considered to be defective if its weight is less than 14.8 pounds or greater than 15.2 pounds. Suppose that these items are currently produced in batches of 1000 units.

a. Find the probability that at most 5% of the items in a given batch will be defective.

b. Find the probability that at least 90% of the items in a given batch will be acceptable.

c. How many items would have to be produced in a batch to guarantee that a batch consists of no more than 1% defective items?

24. Past experience indicates that 30% of all individuals entering a certain store decide to make a purchase. Using (a) the binomial distribution and (b) the normal approximation to the binomial, find that probability that 10 or more of the 30 individuals entering the store in a given hour will decide to make a purchase. Compare the results obtained using the two different approaches. Under what conditions will the normal approximation to this binomial probability become even more accurate?

25. Suppose that the number of ounces of soda put into a soft-drink can is normally distributed with $\mu = 12.05$ ounces and $\sigma = 0.03$ ounce.

a. Legally, a can must contain at least 12 ounces of soda. What fraction of cans will contain at least 12 ounces of soda?

b. What fraction of cans will contain less than 11.9 ounces of soda?

c. What fraction of cans will contain between 12 and 12.08 ounces of soda?

d. One percent of all cans will weigh more than what value?

e. Ten percent of all cans will weigh less than what value?

f. The soft-drink company controls the mean weight in a can by setting a timer. For what mean should the timer be set so that only 1 in 1000 cans will be underweight?

g. Every day the company produces 10,000 cans. The government inspects 10 randomly chosen cans each day. If at least two are underweight, the company is fined $10,000. Given that $\mu = 12.05$ ounces and $\sigma = 0.03$ ounce, what is the probability that the company will be fined on a given day?

26. Suppose that 53% of all registered voters prefer presidential candidate Smith to presidential candidate Jones. (You can substitute the names of the most recent presidential candidates.)

a. In a random sample of 100 voters, what is the probability that the sample will indicate that Smith will win the election (that is, there will be more votes in the sample for Smith)?

b. In a random sample of 100 voters, what is the probability that the sample will indicate that Jones will win the election?

c. In a random sample of 100 voters, what is the probability that the sample will indicate a dead heat (fifty-fifty)?

d. In a random sample of 100 voters, what is the probability that between 40 and 60 (inclusive) voters will prefer Smith?

27. Assume that, on average, 95% of all ticket holders show up for a flight. If a plane seats 200 people, how many tickets should be sold to make the chance of an overbooked flight as close as possible to 5%?

28. Suppose that 55% of all people prefer Coke to Pepsi. We randomly choose 500 people and ask them if they prefer Coke to Pepsi. What is the probability that our

survey will (erroneously) indicate that Pepsi is preferred by more people than Coke? Does this probability increase or decrease as we take larger and larger samples? Why?

29. A firm's office contains 150 PCs. The probability that a given PC will not work on a given day is 0.05.

   a. On a given day what is the probability that exactly one computer will not be working?

   b. On a given day what is the probability that at least two computers will not be working?

   c. What assumptions do your answers in parts **a** and **b** require? Do you think they are reasonable? Explain.

30. Suppose that 4% of all tax returns are audited. In a group of n tax returns, consider the probability that at most two returns are audited. How large must n be before this probability is less than 0.01?

31. Suppose that the height of a typical American female is normally distributed with $\mu = 64$ inches and $\sigma = 4$ inches. We observe the height of 500 American females.

   a. What is the probability that fewer than 35 of the 500 women will be less than 58 inches tall?

   b. Let X be the number of the 500 women who are less than 58 inches tall. Find the mean and standard deviation of X.

32. In basketball, a player who is fouled in the act of shooting gets to shoot two free throws. Suppose we hear that one player is an "85% free throw shooter." If this player is fouled 25 times in the act of shooting (maybe over a period of several games), find the distribution of occasions where he makes both free throws. That is, if X is the number of times he makes both free throws, find $P(X = k)$ for each k from 0 to 25. How likely is it that he will make both free throws on at least 20 of the 25 occasions?

Level B

33. Many firms utilize sampling plans to control the quality of manufactured items ready for shipment. To illustrate the use of a sampling plan, suppose that a particular company produces and ships electronic computer chips in lots, each lot consisting of 1000 chips. This company's sampling plan specifies that quality control personnel should randomly sample 50 chips from each lot and accept the lot for shipping if the number of defective chips is four or fewer. The lot will be rejected if the number of defective chips is five or more.

   a. Find the probability of accepting a lot as a function of the actual fraction of defective chips. In particular, let the actual fraction of defective chips in a given lot equal any of 0.02, 0.04, 0.06, 0.08, 0.10, 0.12, 0.14, 0.16, 0.18. Then compute the lot acceptance probability for each of these lot defective fractions.

   b. Construct a graph showing the probability of lot acceptance for each of the lot defective fractions, and interpret your graph.

   c. Repeat parts **a** and **b** under a revised sampling plan that calls for accepting a given lot if the number of defective chips found in the random sample of 50 chips is *five* or fewer. Summarize any notable differences between the two graphs.

34. Suppose you play a game at a casino where your probability of winning each game is 0.49. On each game, you bet $10, which you either win or lose. Let $P(n)$ be the probability that you are ahead by at least $50 after n games. Graph this probability versus n for n equal to multiples of 50 up to 1000. Discuss the behavior of this function and why it behaves as it does.

35. Comdell Computer receives computer chips from Chipco. Each batch sent by Chipco is inspected as follows: 35 chips are tested and the batch passes inspection if at most one defective chip is found in the set of 35 tested chips. Past history indicates an average of 1% of all chips produced by Chipco are defective. Comdell has received 10 batches this week. What is the probability that at least nine of the batches will pass inspection?

36. A standardized test consists entirely of multiple-choice questions, each with five possible choices. You want to ensure that a student who randomly guesses on each question will obtain an expected score of zero. How can you accomplish this?

37. In the current tax year, suppose that 5% of the millions of individual tax returns are fraudulent. That is, they contain errors that were purposely made to cheat the government.

   a. Although these errors are often well concealed, let's suppose that a thorough IRS audit will uncover them. If a random 250 tax returns are audited, what is the probability that the IRS will uncover at least 15 fraudulent returns?

   b. Answer the same question as in part **a**, but this time assume there is only a 90% chance that a given fraudulent return will be spotted as such if it is audited.

38. Suppose you work for a survey research company. In a typical survey, you mail questionnaires to 150 companies. Of course, some of these companies might decide not to respond. Assume that the nonresponse rate is 45%; that is, each company's probability of not responding, independently of the others, is 0.45.

   a. If your company requires at least 90 responses for a valid survey, find the probability that it will get this many. Use a data table to see how your answer varies as a function of the nonresponse rate (for a reasonable range of response rates surrounding 45%).

b. Suppose your company does this survey in two "waves." It mails the 150 questionnaires and waits a certain period for the responses. As before, assume that the nonresponse rate is 45%. However, after this initial period, your company follows up (by telephone, say) on the nonrespondents, asking them to please respond. Suppose that the nonresponse rate on this second wave is 70%; that is, each original nonrespondent now responds with probability 0.3, independently of the others. Your company now wants to find the probability of obtaining at least 110 responses total. It turns out that this is a difficult probability to calculate directly. So instead, approximate it with simulation.

39. Suppose you are sampling from a large population, and you ask the respondents whether they believe men should be allowed to take paid paternity leave from their jobs when they have a new child. Each person you sample is equally likely to be male or female. The population proportion of females who believe males should be granted paid paternity leave is 56%, and the population proportion of males who favor it is 48%. If you sample 200 people and count the number who believe males should be granted paternity leave, is this number binomially distributed? Explain why or why not. Would your answer change if you knew your sample was going to consist of exactly 100 males and 100 females?

40. A woman claims that she is a fortune-teller. Specifically, she claims that she can predict the direction of the change (up or down) in the Dow Jones Industrial Average for the next 10 days. For example, one possible prediction might be U, U, D, U, D, U, U, D, D, D. (You can assume that she makes all 10 predictions right now, although that does not affect your answer to the question.) Obviously, you are skeptical, thinking that she is just guessing, so you would be surprised if her predictions are accurate. Which would surprise you more: (1) she predicts at least 8 out of 10 correctly, or (2) she predicts at least 6 out of 10 correctly on each of four separate occasions? Answer by assuming that (1) she is really guessing and (2) each day the Dow is equally likely to go up or down.

5-6 THE POISSON AND EXPONENTIAL DISTRIBUTIONS

The final two distributions in this chapter are called the *Poisson* and *exponential distributions*. In most statistical applications, including those in the rest of this book, these distributions play a much less important role than the normal and binomial distributions. For this reason, we will not analyze them in much detail. However, in many applied management science models, the Poisson and exponential distributions are key distributions. For example, much of the study of probabilistic inventory models, queuing models, and reliability models relies heavily on these two distributions.

5-6a The Poisson Distribution

The **Poisson distribution** is a discrete distribution. It usually applies to the *number* of events occurring within a specified period of time or space. Its possible values are all of the nonnegative integers: 0, 1, 2, and so on—there is no upper limit. Even though there is an infinite number of possible values, this causes no real problems because the probabilities of all sufficiently large values are essentially 0.

The Poisson distribution is characterized by a single parameter, usually labeled λ (Greek lambda), which must be positive. By adjusting the value of λ, we are able to produce different Poisson distributions, all of which have the same basic shape as in Figure 5.25. That is, they first increase and then decrease. It turns out that λ is easy to interpret. It is both the mean and the variance of the Poisson distribution. Therefore, the standard deviation is $\sqrt{\lambda}$.

Typical Examples of the Poisson Distribution

- A bank manager is studying the arrival pattern to the bank. The events are customer arrivals, the number of arrivals in an hour is Poisson distributed, and λ represents the expected number of arrivals per hour.

- An engineer is interested in the lifetime of a type of battery. A device that uses this type of battery is operated continuously. When the first battery fails, it is replaced by a second; when the second fails, it is replaced by a third, and so on. The events are battery failures, the number of failures that occur in a month is Poisson distributed, and λ represents the expected number of failures per month.

- A retailer is interested in the number of customers who order a particular product in a week. Then the events are customer orders for the product, the number of customer orders in a week is Poisson distributed, and λ is the expected number of orders per week.

- In a quality control setting, the Poisson distribution is often relevant for describing the number of defects in some unit of space. For example, when paint is applied to the body of a new car, any minor blemish is considered a defect. Then the number of defects on the hood, say, might be Poisson distributed. In this case, λ is the expected number of defects per hood.

These examples are representative of the many situations where the Poisson distribution has been applied. The parameter λ is often called a *rate*—arrivals per hour, failures per month, and so on. If the unit of time is changed, the rate must be modified accordingly. For example, if the number of arrivals to a bank in a single hour is Poisson distributed with rate $\lambda = 30$, then the number of arrivals in a half-hour period is Poisson distributed with rate $\lambda = 15$.

We can use Excel to calculate Poisson probabilities much as we did with binomial probabilities. The relevant function is the POISSON function. It takes the form

=POISSON(k,λ,cum)

The third argument *cum* works exactly as in the binomial case. If it is 0, the function returns $P(X = k)$; if it is 1, the function returns $P(X \leq k)$. As examples, if $\lambda = 5$ **=POISSON(7,5,0)** returns the probability of exactly 7, **=POISSON(7,5,1)** returns the probability of less than or equal to 7, and **=1-POISSON(3,5,1)** returns the probability of greater than 3.

CHANGES IN EXCEL 2010

The POISSON function has been replaced in Excel 2010 by POISSON.DIST. Either version can be used, and they work exactly the same way. Both versions are shown in the file for the following example. (Curiously, there is still no POISSON.INV function.)

Example 5.13 shows how a manager or consultant could use the Poisson distribution.

EXAMPLE 5.13 MANAGING TV INVENTORY AT KRIEGLAND

Kriegland is a department store that sells various brands of plasma screen TVs. One of the manager's biggest problems is to decide on an appropriate inventory policy for stocking TVs. He wants to have enough in stock so that customers receive their requests right away, but he does not want to tie up too much money in inventory that sits on the storeroom floor.

Most of the difficulty results from the unpredictability of customer demand. If this demand were constant and known, the manager could decide on an appropriate inventory policy fairly easily. But the demand varies widely from month to month in a random manner. All the manager knows is that the historical average demand per month is approximately 17. Therefore, he decides to call in a consultant. The consultant immediately suggests using a probability model. Specifically, she attempts to find the probability distribution of demand in a typical month. How might she proceed?

Objective   To model the probability distribution of monthly demand for plasma screen TVs with a particular Poisson distribution.

Solution

Let X be the demand in a typical month. The consultant knows that there are many possible values of X. For example, if historical records show that monthly demands have always been between 0 and 40, the consultant knows that almost all of the probability should be assigned to the values 0 through 40. However, she does not relish the thought of finding 41 probabilities, $P(X = 0)$ through $P(X = 40)$, that sum to 1 and reflect historical frequencies. Instead, she discovers from the manager that the histogram of demands from previous months is shaped much like the graph in Figure 5.25. That is, it rises to some peak and then falls.

Figure 5.25

Typical Poisson Distribution

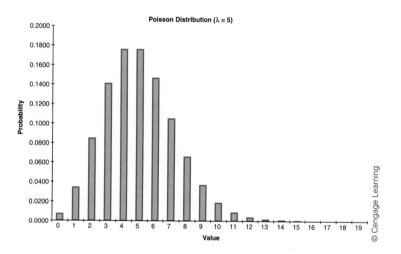

Knowing that a Poisson distribution has this same basic shape, the consultant decides to model the monthly demand with a Poisson distribution. To choose a particular Poisson distribution, all she has to do is choose a value of λ, the mean demand per month. Because the historical average is approximately 17, she chooses $\lambda = 17$. Now she can test the Poisson model by calculating probabilities of various events and asking the manager whether these probabilities are reasonable approximations to reality.

For example, the Poisson probability that monthly demand is less than or equal to 20, $P(X \leq 20)$, is 0.805 [using the Excel function **POISSON(20,17,1)**], and the probability that demand is between 10 and 15 inclusive, $P(10 \leq X \leq 15)$, is 0.345 [using **POISSON(15,17,1)-POISSON(9,17,1)**]. Figure 5.26 illustrates various probability calculations and shows the graph of the individual Poisson probabilities. (See the file **Poisson Demand Distribution.xlsx**.)

If the manager believes that these probabilities and other similar probabilities are reasonable, then the *statistical* part of the consultant's job is finished. Otherwise, she must try a different Poisson distribution—a different value of λ—or perhaps a different type of distribution altogether. ∎

Figure 5.26 Poisson Calculations for TV Example

	A	B	C	D	E	F	G	H	I	J	K
1	Poisson distribution for monthly demand										
2				Range name used:							
3	Mean monthly demand (λ)	17		Mean	=Sheet1!$B$3						
4											
5	Representative probability calculations										
6	Less than or equal to 20	0.805		=POISSON(20,Mean,1)							
7	Between 10 and 15 (inclusive)	0.345		=POISSON(15,Mean,1)-POISSON(9,Mean,1)							
8											
9	Individual probabilities										
10	Value	Prob									
11	0	0.000		=POISSON(A11,MeanDem,0)							
12	1	0.000									
13	2	0.000									
14	3	0.000									
15	4	0.000									
16	5	0.000									
17	6	0.001									
18	7	0.003									
19	8	0.007									
20	9	0.014									
21	10	0.023									
22	11	0.036									
23	12	0.050									
24	13	0.066									
25	14	0.080									
26	15	0.091									
27	16	0.096									
28	17	0.096									
29	18	0.091									
30	19	0.081									
31	20	0.069									
32	21	0.056									
33	22	0.043									
34	23	0.032									
35	24	0.023									
36	25	0.015									
37	26	0.010									
38	27	0.006									
39	28	0.004									
40	29	0.002									
41	30	0.001									
42	31	0.001									
43	32	0.000									
44	33	0.000									
45	34	0.000									
46	35	0.000									
47	36	0.000									
48	37	0.000									
49	38	0.000									
50	39	0.000									
51	40	0.000									

Poisson Distribution with λ = 17

5-6b The Exponential Distribution

Suppose that a bank manager is studying the pattern of customer arrivals at her branch location. As indicated previously in this section, the number of arrivals in an hour at a facility such as a bank is often well described by a Poisson distribution with parameter λ, where λ represents the expected number of arrivals per hour. An alternative way to view the uncertainty in the arrival process is to consider the *times* between customer arrivals. The most common probability distribution used to model these times, often called *interarrival times,* is the *exponential* distribution.

In general, the *continuous* random variable X has an **exponential distribution** with parameter λ (with $\lambda > 0$) if the density function of X has the form $f(x) = \lambda e^{-\lambda x}$ for $x > 0$. This density function has the shape shown in Figure 5.27. Because this density function decreases continuously from left to right, its most likely value is $x = 0$. Alternatively, if you collect many observations from an exponential distribution and draw a histogram of the observed values, you should expect it to resemble the smooth curve shown in Figure 5.27, with the tallest bars to the left. The mean and standard deviation of this distribution are easy to remember. They are both equal to the *reciprocal* of the parameter λ. For example, an exponential distribution with parameter $\lambda = 0.1$ has mean and standard deviation both equal to 10.

Figure 5.27

Exponential Density Function

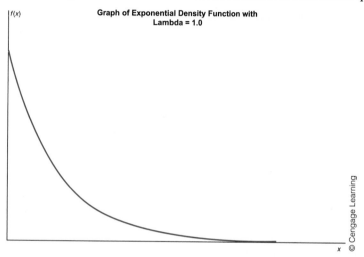

As with the normal distribution, you usually want probabilities to the left or right of a given value. For any exponential distribution, the probability to the left of a given value $x > 0$ can be calculated with Excel's EXPONDIST function. This function takes the form

=EXPONDIST($x,\lambda,1$)

For example, if $x = 0.5$ and $\lambda = 5$ (so that the mean equals $1/5 = 0.2$), the probability of being less than 0.5 can be found with the formula

=EXPONDIST(0.5,5,1)

This returns the probability 0.918. Of course, the probability of being greater than 0.5 is then $1 - 0.918 = 0.082$.

CHANGES IN EXCEL 2010

The EXPONDIST function has been replaced in Excel 2010 by EXPON.DIST. Either version can be used, and they work exactly the same way. (As with the Poisson distribution, there is no EXPON.INV function.)

Returning to the bank manager's analysis of customer arrival data, when the times between arrivals are exponentially distributed, you sometimes hear that "arrivals occur according to a Poisson process." This is because there is a close relationship between the exponential distribution, which measures *times* between events such as arrivals, and the **Poisson distribution**, which counts the *number* of events in a certain length of time. The details of this relationship are beyond the level of this book, so we will not explore the topic further. But if you hear, for example, that customers arrive at a facility according to a Poisson process at the rate of six per hour, then the corresponding times between arrivals are exponentially distributed with mean 1/6 hour.

PROBLEMS

Level A

41. The annual number of industrial accidents occurring in a particular manufacturing plant is known to follow a Poisson distribution with mean 12.
   a. What is the probability of observing exactly 12 accidents during the coming year?
   b. What is the probability of observing no more than 12 accidents during the coming year?
   c. What is the probability of observing at least 15 accidents during the coming year?
   d. What is the probability of observing between 10 and 15 accidents (inclusive) during the coming year?
   e. Find the smallest integer k such that we can be at least 99% sure that the annual number of accidents occurring will be less than k.

42. Suppose that X, the number of customers arriving each hour at the only checkout counter in a local pharmacy, is approximately Poisson distributed with an expected arrival rate of 20 customers per hour.
   a. Find the probability that X is exactly 10.
   b. Find the probability that X is at least 5.
   c. Find the probability that X is no more than 25.
   d. Find the probability that X is between 10 and 30 (inclusive).
   e. Find the largest integer k such that we can be at least 95% sure that X will be greater than k.
   f. Recalling the relationship between the Poisson and exponential distributions, find the probability that the time between two successive customer arrivals is more than four minutes. Find the probability that it is less than two minutes.

43. Suppose the number of baskets scored by the Indiana University basketball team in one minute follows a Poisson distribution with $\lambda = 1.5$. In a 10-minute span of time, what is the probability that Indiana University scores exactly 20 baskets; at most 20 baskets?

(Use the fact that if the rate per minute is λ, then the rate in t minutes is λt.)

44. Suppose that the times between arrivals at a bank during the peak period of the day are exponentially distributed with a mean of 45 seconds. If you just observed an arrival, what is the probability that you will need to wait for more than a minute before observing the next arrival? What is the probability you will need to wait at least two minutes?

Level B

45. Consider a Poisson random variable X with parameter $\lambda = 2$.
   a. Find the probability that X is within one standard deviation of its mean.
   b. Find the probability that X is within two standard deviations of its mean.
   c. Find the probability that X is within three standard deviations of its mean.
   d. Do the empirical rules we learned previously seem to be applicable in working with the Poisson distribution where $\lambda = 2$? Explain why or why not.
   e. Repeat parts **a** through **d** for the case of a Poisson random variable where $\lambda = 20$.

46. Based on historical data, the probability that a major league pitcher pitches a no-hitter in a game is about 1/1300.
   a. Use the binomial distribution to determine the probability that in 650 games 0, 1, 2, or 3 no-hitters will be pitched. (Find the separate probabilities of these four events.)
   b. Repeat part **a** using the Poisson approximation to the binomial. This approximation says that if n is large and p is small, a binomial distribution with parameters n and p is approximately the same as a Poisson distribution with $\lambda = np$.

5-7 CONCLUSION

We have covered a lot of ground in this chapter, and much of the material, especially that on the normal distribution, will be used in later chapters. The normal distribution is the cornerstone for much of statistical theory. As you will see in later chapters on statistical inference and regression, an assumption of normality is behind most of the procedures we use. Therefore, it is important for you to understand the properties of the normal distribution and how to work with it in Excel. The binomial, Poisson, and exponential distributions, although not used as frequently as the normal distribution in this book, are also extremely important. The examples we have discussed indicate how these distributions can be used in a variety of business situations.

Although we have attempted to stress *concepts* in this chapter, we have also described the details necessary to work with these distributions in Excel. Fortunately, these details are not too difficult to master once you understand Excel's built-in functions, especially NORMDIST, NORMINV, and BINOMDIST. Figures 5.6 and 5.18 provide typical examples of these functions. We suggest that you keep a copy of these figures handy.

Summary of Key Terms

Term	Explanation	Excel	Page	Equation
Density function	Specifies the probability distribution of a continuous random variable		168	
Normal distribution	A continuous distribution with possible values ranging over the *entire* number line; its density function is a symmetric bell-shaped curve		169	5.1
Standardizing a normal random variable	Transforms any normal distribution with mean μ and standard deviation σ to the *standard* normal distribution with mean 0 and standard deviation 1	STANDARDIZE	170	5.2
Normal calculations in Excel	Useful for finding probabilities and percentiles for nonstandard and standard normal distributions	NORMDIST, NORMSDIST, NORMINV, NORMSINV	175	
Empirical rules for normal distribution	About 68% of the data fall within one standard deviation of the mean, about 95% of the data fall within two standard deviations of the mean, and almost all fall within three standard deviations of the mean		177	
Binomial distribution	The distribution of the number of successes in n independent, identical trials, where each trial has probability p of success	BINOMDIST CRITBINOM	190	
Mean and standard deviation of a binomial distribution	The mean and standard deviation of a binomial distribution with parameters n and p are np and $\sqrt{np(1-p)}$, respectively		193	5.3, 5.4
Sampling without replacement	Sampling where no member of the population can be sampled more than once		194	
Sampling with replacement	Sampling where any member of the population can be sampled more than once		194	
Normal approximation to the binomial distribution	If $np > 5$ and $n(1-p) > 5$, the binomial distribution can be approximated well by a normal distribution with mean np and standard deviation $\sqrt{np(1-p)}$		194	
Poisson distribution	A discrete probability distribution that often describes the number of events occurring within a specified period of time or space; mean and variance both equal the parameter λ	POISSON	207	
Exponential distribution	A continuous probability distribution useful for measuring *times* between events, such as customer arrivals to a service facility; mean and standard deviation both equal $1/\lambda$	EXPONDIST	210	

PROBLEMS

Conceptual Questions

C.1. For each of the following uncertain quantities, discuss whether it is reasonable to assume that the probability distribution of the quantity is normal. If the answer isn't obvious, discuss how you could discover whether a normal distribution is reasonable.

   a. The change in the Dow Jones Industrial Average between now and a year from now

   b. The length of time (in hours) a battery that is in continuous use lasts

   c. The time between two successive arrivals to a bank

   d. The time it takes a bank teller to service a random customer

   e. The length (in yards) of a typical drive on a par 5 by Phil Michelson

   f. The amount of snowfall (in inches) in a typical winter in Minneapolis

   g. The average height (in inches) of all boys in a randomly selected seventh-grade middle school class

   h. Your bonus from finishing a project, where your bonus is $1000 per day under the deadline if the project is completed before the deadline, your bonus is $500 if the project is completed right on the deadline, and your bonus is $0 if the project is completed after the deadline

   i. Your gain on a call option on a stock, where you gain nothing if the price of the stock a month from now is less than or equal to $50 and you gain $(P-50)$ dollars if the price P a month from now is greater than $50

C.2. For each of the following uncertain quantities, discuss whether it is reasonable to assume that the probability distribution of the quantity is binomial. If you think it is, what are the parameters n and p? If you think it isn't, explain your reasoning.

   a. The number of wins the Boston Red Sox baseball team has next year in its 81 home games

   b. The number of free throws Kobe Bryant misses in his next 250 attempts

   c. The number of free throws it takes Kobe Bryant to achieve 100 successes

   d. The number out of 1000 randomly selected customers in a supermarket who have a bill of at least $150

   e. The number of trading days in a typical year where Microsoft's stock price increases

   f. The number of spades you get in a 13-card hand from a well-shuffled 52-card deck

   g. The number of adjacent 15-minute segments during a typical Friday where at least 10 customers enter a McDonald's restaurant

   h. The number of pages in a 500-page book with at least one misprint on the page

C.3. The Poisson distribution is often appropriate in the "binomial" situation of n independent and identical trials, where each trial has probability p of success, but n is very large and p is very small. In this case, the Poisson distribution is relevant for the number of successes, and its parameter (its mean) is np. Discuss some situations where such a Poisson model might be appropriate. How would you measure n and p, or would you measure only their product np? Here is one to get you started: the number of traffic accidents at a particular intersection in a given year.

C.4. One disadvantage of a normal distribution is that there is always some probability that a quantity is negative, even when this makes no sense for the uncertain quantity. For example, the time a light bulb lasts cannot be negative. In any particular situation, how would you decide whether you could ignore this disadvantage for all practical purposes?

C.5. Explain why probabilities such as $P(X < x)$ and $P(X \le x)$ are equal for a continuous random variable.

C.6. State the major similarities and differences between the *binomial* distribution and the *Poisson* distribution.

C.7. You have a bowl with 100 pieces of paper inside, each with a person's name written on it. It turns out that 50 of the names correspond to males and the other 50 to females. You reach inside and grab five pieces of paper. If X is the random number of male names you choose, is X binomially distributed? Why or why not?

C.8. A distribution we didn't discuss is the Bernoulli distribution. It is a binomial distribution with $n = 1$. In other words, it is the number of successes (0 or 1) in a single trial when the probability of success is p. What are the mean and standard deviation of a Bernoulli distribution? Discuss how a binomial random variable can be expressed in terms of n independent Bernoulli random variables, each with the same parameter p.

C.9. For real applications, the normal distribution has two potential drawbacks: (1) it can be negative, and (2) it isn't symmetric. Choose some continuous random numeric outcomes of interest to you. Are either potential drawbacks really drawbacks for your random outcomes? If so, which is the more serious drawback?

C.10. Many basketball players and fans believe strongly in the "hot hand." That is, they believe that players tend to shoot in streaks, either makes or misses. If this is the case, why does the binomial distribution not apply, at least not exactly, to the number of makes in a given number of shots? Which assumption of the binomial model is violated, the independence of successive shots or the constant probability of success on each shot? Or can you tell?

C.11. Suppose the demands in successive weeks for your product are normally distributed with mean 100 and standard deviation 20, and suppose your lead time for receiving a placed order is three weeks. A quantity of interest to managers is the lead-time demand, the total demanded over three weeks. Why does the formula for the standard deviation of lead-time demand include a square root of 3? What assumptions are behind this?

Level A

47. Suppose the annual return on XYZ stock follows a normal distribution with mean 12% and standard deviation 30%.
   a. What is the probability that XYZ's value will decrease during a year?
   b. What is the probability that the return on XYZ during a year will be at least 20%?
   c. What is the probability that the return on XYZ during a year will be between −6% and 9%?
   d. There is a 5% chance that the return on XYZ during a year will be greater than what value?
   e. There is a 1% chance that the return on XYZ during a year will be less than what value?
   f. There is a 95% chance that the return on XYZ during a year will be between which two values (equidistant from the mean)?

48. Assume the annual mean return on ABC stock is around 15% and the annual standard deviation is around 25%. Assume the annual and daily returns on ABC stock are normally distributed.
   a. What is the probability that ABC will lose money during a year?
   b. There is a 5% chance that ABC will earn a return of at least what value during a year?
   c. There is a 10% chance that ABC will earn a return of less than or equal to what value during a year?
   d. What is the probability that ABC will earn at least 35% during a year?
   e. Assume there are 252 trading days in a year. What is the probability that ABC will lose money on a given day? (*Hint*: Let Y be the annual return on ABC and X_i be the return on ABC on day i. Then [approximately] $Y = X_1 + X_2 + \ldots + X_{252}$.)

49. Suppose Comdell Computer receives its hard drives from Diskco. On average, 4% of all hard disk drives received by Comdell are defective.
   a. Comdell has adopted the following policy. It samples 50 hard drives in each shipment and accepts the shipment if all hard drives in the sample are nondefective. What fraction of shipments will Comdell accept?
   b. Suppose instead that the shipment is accepted if at most one hard drive in the sample is defective. What fraction of shipments will Comdell accept?

   c. What is the probability that a sample of size 50 will contain at least 10 defectives?

50. A family is considering a move from a midwestern city to a city in California. The distribution of housing costs where the family currently lives is normal, with mean $105,000 and standard deviation $18,200. The distribution of housing costs in the California city is normal with mean $235,000 and standard deviation $30,400. The family's current house is valued at $110,000.
   a. What percentage of houses in the family's current city cost less than theirs?
   b. If the family buys a $200,000 house in the new city, what percentage of houses there will cost less than theirs?
   c. What price house will the family need to buy to be in the same percentile (of housing costs) in the new city as they are in the current city?

51. The number of traffic fatalities in a typical month in a given state has a normal distribution with mean 125 and standard deviation 31.
   a. If a person in the highway department claims that there will be at least m fatalities in the next month with probability 0.95, what value of m makes this claim true?
   b. If the claim is that there will be no more than n fatalities in the next month with probability 0.98, what value of n makes this claim true?

52. It can be shown that a sum of normally distributed random variables is also normally distributed. Do *all* functions of normal random variables lead to normal random variables? Consider the following. SuperDrugs is a chain of drugstores with three similar-size stores in a given city. The sales in a given week for any of these stores is normally distributed with mean $15,000 and standard deviation $3000. At the end of each week, the sales figure for the store with the largest sales among the three stores is recorded. Is this maximum value normally distributed? To answer this question, simulate a weekly sales figure at each of the three stores and calculate the maximum. Then replicate this maximum 500 times and create a histogram of the 500 maximum values. Does it appear to be normally shaped? Whatever this distribution looks like, use your simulated values to estimate the mean and standard deviation of the maximum.

53. In the game of baseball, every time a player bats, he is either successful (gets on base) or he fails (doesn't get on base). (This is all you need to know about baseball for this problem!) His on-base percentage, usually expressed as a decimal, is the percentage of times he is successful. Let's consider a player who is theoretically a 0.375 on-base batter. Specifically, assume that each time he bats, he is successful with probability 0.375 and unsuccessful with probability 0.625. Also, assume that he bats 600 times in a season. What can you say about his on-base percentage, (# of successes)/600, for the season? (*Hint*: Each on-base percentage is equivalent to a number of successes. For example, 0.380 is equivalent to 228 successes because 0.380*600 = 228.)

   a. What is the probability that his on-base percentage will be *less than* 0.360?

   b. What is the probability that his on-base percentage will be *greater than* 0.370?

   c. What is the probability that his on-base percentage will be *less than or equal to* 0.400?

54. In the financial world, there are many types of complex instruments called derivatives that *derive* their value from the value of an underlying asset. Consider the following simple derivative. A stock's current price is $80 per share. You purchase a derivative whose value to you becomes known a month from now. Specifically, let P be the price of the stock in a month. If P is between $75 and $85, the derivative is worth nothing to you. If P is less than $75, the derivative results in a loss of 100*(75–P) dollars to you. (The factor of 100 is because many derivatives involve 100 shares.) If P is greater than $85, the derivative results in a gain of 100*(P–85) dollars to you. Assume that the distribution of the *change* in the stock price from now to a month from now is normally distributed with mean $1 and standard deviation $8. Let P (big loss) be the probability that you lose at least $1000 (that is, the price falls below $65), and let P (big gain) be the probability that you gain at least $1000 (that is, the price rises above $95). Find these two probabilities. How do they compare to one another?

Level B

55. When you sum 30 or more independent random variables, the sum of the random variables will usually be approximately normally distributed, even if each individual random variable is not normally distributed. Use this fact to estimate the probability that a casino will be behind after 90,000 roulette bets, given that it wins $1 or loses $35 on each bet with probabilities 37/38 and 1/38.

56. The daily demand for six-packs of Coke at Mr. D's supermarket follows a normal distribution with mean 120 and standard deviation 30. Every Monday the Coke delivery driver delivers Coke to Mr. D's. If Mr. D's wants to have only a 1% chance of running out of Coke by the end of the week, how many should Mr. D's order for the week? Assume orders are placed on Sunday at midnight. Also assume that demands on different days are probabilistically independent.

57. Many companies use sampling to determine whether a batch should be accepted. An (n, c) sampling plan consists of inspecting n randomly chosen items from a batch and accepting the batch if c or fewer sampled items are defective. Suppose a company uses a $(100, 5)$ sampling plan to determine whether a batch of 10,000 computer chips is acceptable.

   a. The "producer's risk" of a sampling plan is the probability that an acceptable batch will be rejected by the sampling plan. Suppose the customer considers a batch with 3% defectives acceptable. What is the producer's risk for this sampling plan?

   b. The "consumer's risk" of a sampling plan is the probability that an unacceptable batch will be accepted by the sampling plan. Our customer says that a batch with 9% defectives is unacceptable. What is the consumer's risk for this sampling plan?

58. Suppose that if a presidential election were held today, 53% of all voters would vote for candidate Smith over candidate Jones. (You can substitute the names of the most recent presidential candidates.) This problem shows that even if there are 100 million voters, a sample of several thousand is enough to determine the outcome, even in a fairly close election.

   a. If 1500 voters are sampled randomly, what is the probability that the sample will indicate (correctly) that Smith is preferred to Jones?

   b. If 6000 voters are sampled randomly, what is the probability that the sample will indicate (correctly) that Smith is preferred to Jones?

59. A soft-drink factory fills bottles of soda by setting a timer on a filling machine. It has generally been observed that the distribution of the number of ounces the machine puts into a bottle is normal, with standard deviation 0.05 ounce. The company wants 99.9% of all its bottles to have at least 16 ounces of soda. To what value should the mean amount put in each bottle be set? (Of course, the company does not want to fill any more than is necessary.)

60. The time it takes you to swim 100 yards in a race is normally distributed with mean 62 seconds and standard deviation 2 seconds. In your next five races, what is the probability that you will swim under a minute exactly twice?

61. A company assembles a large part by joining two smaller parts together. Assume that the smaller parts are normally distributed with a mean length of 1 inch and a standard deviation of 0.01 inch.

   a. What fraction of the larger parts are longer than 2.05 inches?

   b. What fraction of the larger parts are between 1.96 inches and 2.02 inches long?

62. (*Suggested by Sam Kaufmann, Indiana University MBA, who has run Harrah's Lake Tahoe Casino.*) A high roller has come to the casino to play 300 games of craps. For each game of craps played there is a 0.493 probability that the high roller will win $1 and a 0.507 probability that the high roller will lose $1.

After 300 games of craps, what is the probability that the casino will be behind more than $10?

63. *(Suggested by Sam Kaufmann, Indiana University MBA, who has run Harrah's Lake Tahoe Casino.)* A high roller comes to the casino intending to play 500 hands of blackjack for $1 a hand. On each hand, the high roller will win $1 with probability 0.48 and lose $1 with probability 0.52. After the 500 hands, what is the probability that the casino has lost more than $40?

64. A soft-drink company produces 100,000 12-ounce bottles of soda per year. By adjusting a dial, the company can set the mean number of ounces placed in a bottle. Regardless of the mean, the standard deviation of the number of ounces in a bottle is 0.05 ounce. The soda costs 5 cents per ounce. Any bottle weighing less than 12 ounces will incur a $10 fine for being underweight. Determine a setting for the mean number of ounces per bottle of soda that minimizes the expected cost per year of producing soda. Your answer should be accurate within 0.001 ounce. Does the number of bottles produced per year influence your answer?

65. The weekly demand for TVs at Lowland Appliance is normally distributed with mean 400 and standard deviation 100. Each time an order for TVs is placed, it arrives exactly four weeks later. That is, TV orders have a four-week lead time. Lowland doesn't want to run out of TVs during any more than 1% of all lead times. How low should Lowland let its TV inventory drop before it places an order for more TVs? (*Hint*: How many standard deviations above the mean lead-time demand must the reorder point be for there to be a 1% chance of a stockout during the lead time?)

66. An elevator rail is assumed to meet specifications if its diameter is between 0.98 and 1.01 inches. Each year a company produces 100,000 elevator rails. For a cost of $10/\sigma^2$ per year the company can rent a machine that produces elevator rails whose diameters have a standard deviation of σ. (The idea is that the company must pay more for a smaller variance.) Each such machine will produce rails having a mean diameter of one inch. Any rail that does not meet specifications must be reworked at a cost of $12. Assume that the diameter of an elevator rail follows a normal distribution.
   a. What standard deviation (within 0.001 inch) minimizes the annual cost of producing elevator rails? You do not need to try standard deviations in excess of 0.02 inch.
   b. For your answer in part **a**, one elevator rail in 1000 will be at least how many inches in diameter?

67. A 50-question true–false examination is given. Each correct answer is worth 10 points. Consider an unprepared student who randomly guesses on each question.
   a. If no points are deducted for incorrect answers, what is the probability that the student will score at least 350 points?

   b. If 5 points are deducted for each incorrect answer, what is the probability that the student will score at least 200 points?
   c. If 10 points are deducted for each incorrect answer, what is the probability that the student will receive a negative score?

68. What caused the crash of TWA Flight 800 in 1996? Physics professors Hailey and Helfand of Columbia University believe there is a reasonable possibility that a meteor hit Flight 800. They reason as follows. On a given day, 3000 meteors of a size large enough to destroy an airplane hit the earth's atmosphere. Approximately 50,000 flights per day, averaging two hours in length, have been flown from 1950 to 1996. This means that at any given point in time, planes in flight cover approximately two-billionths of the world's atmosphere. Determine the probability that at least one plane in the last 47 years has been downed by a meteor. (*Hint*: Use the Poisson approximation to the binomial. This approximation says that if n is large and p is small, a binomial distribution with parameters n and p is approximately Poisson distributed with $\lambda = np$.)

69. In the decade 1982 through 1991, 10 employees working at the Amoco Company chemical research center were stricken with brain tumors. The average employment at the center was 2000 employees. Nationwide, the average incidence of brain tumors in a single year is 20 per 100,000 people. If the incidence of brain tumors at the Amoco chemical research center were the same as the nationwide incidence, what is the probability that at least 10 brain tumors would have been observed among Amoco workers during the decade 1982 through 1991? What do you conclude from your analysis? (Source: AP wire service report, March 12, 1994)

70. Claims arrive at random times to an insurance company. The daily amount of claims is normally distributed with mean $1570 and standard deviation $450. Total claims on different days each have this distribution, and they are probabilistically independent of one another.
   a. Find the probability that the amount of total claims over a period of 100 days is at least $150,000.
   b. If the company receives premiums totaling $165,000, find the probability that the company will net at least $10,000 for the 100-day period.

71. A popular model for stock prices is the following. If p_0 is the current stock price, then the price k periods from now, p_k, (where a period could be a day, week, or any other convenient unit of time, and k is any positive integer) is given by

$$p_k = p_0 \exp((\mu - 0.5\sigma^2)k + sZ\sqrt{k})$$

Here, exp is the exponential function (EXP in Excel), μ is the mean percentage growth rate per period of the stock, σ is the standard deviation of the growth rate per period, and Z is a standard normal random variable. Both μ and σ are typically estimated from actual stock price data, and they are typically expressed in decimal form, such as $\mu = 0.01$ for a 1% mean growth rate.

a. Suppose a period is defined as a month, the current price of the stock (as of the end of December 2012) is $75, $\mu = 0.006$, and $\sigma = 0.028$. Use simulation to obtain 500 possible stock price changes from the end of December 2012 to the end of December 2015. Each simulated change will be the price at the end of 2015 minus the price at the end of 2012. (Note that you can simulate a given change in one line and then copy it down.) Create a histogram of these changes to see whether the stock price change is at least approximately normally distributed. Also, use the simulated data to estimate the mean price change and the standard deviation of the change.

b. Use simulation to generate the ending stock prices for each month in 2013. (Use $k = 1$ to get January's price from December's, use $k = 1$ again to get February's price from January's, and so on.) Then use a data table to replicate the ending December 2013 stock price 500 times. Create a histogram of these 500 values. Do they appear to resemble a normal distribution?

72. Your company is running an audit on Sleaze Company. Because Sleaze has a bad habit of overcharging its customers, the focus of your audit is on checking whether the billing amounts on its invoices are correct. Assume that each invoice is for too high an amount with probability 0.06 and for too low an amount with probability 0.01 (so that the probability of a correct billing is 0.93). Also, assume that the outcome for any invoice is probabilistically independent of the outcomes for other invoices.

a. If you randomly sample 200 of Sleaze's invoices, what is the probability that you will find at least 15 invoices that overcharge the customer? What is the probability you won't find any that undercharge the customer?

b. Find an integer k such that the probability is at least 0.99 that you will find at least k invoices that overcharge the customer. (*Hint*: Use trial and error with the BINOMDIST function to find k.)

73. Continuing the previous problem, suppose that when Sleaze overcharges a customer, the distribution of the amount overcharged (expressed as a percentage of the correct billing amount) is normally distributed with mean 15% and standard deviation 4%.

a. What percentage of overbilled customers are charged at least 10% more than they should pay?

b. What percentage of *all* customers are charged at least 10% more than they should pay?

c. If your auditing company samples 200 randomly chosen invoices, what is the probability that it

will find at least five where the customer was overcharged by at least 10%?

74. Your manufacturing process makes parts such that each part meets specifications with probability 0.98. You need a batch of 250 parts that meet specifications. How many parts must you produce to be at least 99% certain of producing at least 250 parts that meet specifications?

75. Let X be normally distributed with a given mean and standard deviation. Sometimes you want to find two values a and b such that $P(a < X < b)$ is equal to some specific probability such as 0.90 or 0.95. There are many answers to this problem, depending on how much probability you put in each of the two tails. For this question, assume the mean and standard deviation are $\mu = 100$ and $\sigma = 10$, and that you want to find a and b such that $P(a < X < b) = 0.90$.

a. Find a and b so that there is probability 0.05 in each tail.

b. Find a and b so that there is probability 0.025 in the left tail and 0.075 in the right tail.

c. The usual answer to the general problem is the answer from part a, that is, where you put equal probability in the two tails. It turns out that this is the answer that minimizes the length of the interval from a to b. That is, if you solve the following problem: minimize $(b - a)$, subject to $P(a < X < b) = 0.90$, you will get the same answer as in part **a**. Verify this by using Excel's Solver add-in.

76. As any credit-granting agency knows, there are always some customers who default on credit charges. Typically, customers are grouped into relatively homogeneous categories, so that customers within any category have approximately the same chance of defaulting on their credit charges. Here we will look at one particular group of customers. We assume each of these customers has (1) probability 0.07 of defaulting on his or her current credit charges, and (2) total credit charges that are normally distributed with mean $350 and standard deviation $100. We also assume that if a customer defaults, 20% of his or her charges can be recovered. The other 80% are written off as bad debt.

a. What is the probability that a typical customer in this group will default and produce a write-off of more than $250 in bad debt?

b. If there are 500 customers in this group, what are the mean and standard deviation of the number of customers who will meet the description in part **a**?

c. Again assuming there are 500 customers in this group, what is the probability that at least 25 of them will meet the description in part **a**?

d. Suppose now that nothing is recovered from a default—the whole amount is written off as bad debt. Show how to simulate the total amount of bad debt from 500 customers in just two cells, one with a binomial calculation, the other with a normal calculation.

77. The Excel functions discussed in this chapter are useful for solving a lot of probability problems, but there are other problems that, even though they are similar to normal or binomial problems, cannot be solved with these functions. In cases like this, simulation can often be used. Here are a couple of such problems for you to simulate. For each example, simulate 500 replications of the experiment.

  a. You observe a sequence of parts from a manufacturing line. These parts use a component that is supplied by one of two suppliers. Each part made with a component from supplier 1 works properly with probability 0.95, and each part made with a component from supplier 2 works properly with probability 0.98. Assuming that 100 of these parts are made, 60 from supplier 1 and 40 from supplier 2, you want the probability that at least 97 of them work properly.

  b. Here we look at a more generic example such as coin flipping. There is a sequence of trials where each trial is a success with probability p and a failure with probability $1 - p$. A run is a sequence of consecutive successes or failures. For most of us, intuition says that there should not be long runs. Test this by finding the probability that there is at least one run of length at least six in a sequence of 15 trials. (The run could be of 0s or 1s.) You can use any value of p you like—or try different values of p.

78. You have a device that uses a single battery, and you operate this device continuously, never turning it off. Whenever a battery fails, you replace it with a brand new one immediately. Suppose the lifetime of a typical battery has an exponential distribution with mean 205 minutes. Suppose you operate the device continuously for three days, making battery changes when necessary. Find the probability that you will observe at least 25 failures. (*Hint*: The number of failures is Poisson distributed.)

79. In the previous problem, we ran the experiment for a certain number of days and then asked about the number of failures. In this problem, we take a different point of view. Suppose you operate the device, starting with a new battery, until you have observed 25 battery failures. What is the probability that at least 15 of these 25 batteries lived at least 3.5 hours? (*Hint*: Each lifetime is exponentially distributed.)

80. In the game of soccer, players are sometimes awarded a penalty kick. The player who kicks places the ball 12 yards from the 24-foot-wide goal and attempts to kick it past the goalie into the net. (The goalie is the only defender.) The question is where the player should aim. Make the following assumptions. (1) The player's kick is off target from where he aims, left or right, by a normally distributed amount with mean 0 and some standard deviation. (2) The goalie typically guesses left or right and dives in that direction at the moment the player kicks. If the goalie guesses wrong, he won't block the kick, but if he guesses correctly, he will be able to block a kick that would have gone into the net as long as the kick is within a distance d from the middle of the goal. The goalie is equally likely to guess left or right. (3) The player never misses high, but he can miss to the right of the goal (if he aims to the right) or to the left (if he aims to the left). For reasonable values of the standard deviation and d, find the probability that the player makes a goal if he aims at a point t feet inside the goal. (By symmetry, you can assume he aims to the right, although the goalie doesn't know this.) What value of t seems to maximize the probability of making a goal?

81. In the 2012 Major League Baseball season, the Baltimore Orioles were ahead after the 7th inning in 74 games, and they won all 74 games. Use an appropriate model to explore how unusual such a streak is. Would you place it in the same category as the famous 56-game hitting streak (at least one hit per game) by Joe DiMaggio in 1941? Discuss the differences, including those that are caused by pressure.

CASE   5.1 EuroWatch Company

EuroWatch Company assembles expensive wristwatches and then sells them to retailers throughout Europe. The watches are assembled at a plant with two assembly lines. These lines are intended to be identical, but line 1 uses somewhat older equipment than line 2 and is typically less reliable. Historical data have shown that each watch coming off line 1, independently of the others, is free of defects with probability 0.98. The similar probability for line 2 is 0.99. Each line produces 500 watches per hour. The production manager has asked you to answer the following questions.

1. She wants to know how many defect-free watches each line is likely to produce in a given hour. Specifically, find the smallest integer k (for each line separately) such that you can be 99% sure that the line will not produce more than k defective watches in a given hour.

2. EuroWatch currently has an order for 500 watches from an important customer. The company plans to fill this order by packing slightly more than 500 watches, all from line 2, and sending this package off to the customer. Obviously, EuroWatch wants to send as few watches as possible, but it wants to be 99% sure that when the customer opens the package, there are at least 500 defect-free watches. How many watches should be packed?

3. EuroWatch has another order for 1000 watches. Now it plans to fill this order by packing slightly more than one hour's production from each line. This package will contain the *same* number of watches from each line. As in the previous question, EuroWatch wants to send as few watches as possible, but it again wants to be 99% sure that when the customer opens the package, there are at least 1000 defect-free watches. The question of how many watches to pack is unfortunately quite difficult because the total number of defect-free watches is *not* binomially distributed. (Why not?) Therefore, the manager asks you to solve the problem with simulation (and some trial and error). (*Hint:* It turns out that it is much faster to simulate small numbers than large numbers, so simulate the number of watches with defects, not the number without defects.)

4. Finally, EuroWatch has a third order for 100 watches. The customer has agreed to pay

$50,000 for the order—that is, $500 per watch. If EuroWatch sends more than 100 watches to the customer, its revenue doesn't increase; it can never exceed $50,000. Its unit cost of producing a watch is $450, regardless of which line it is assembled on. The order will be filled entirely from a single line, and EuroWatch plans to send slightly more than 100 watches to the customer.

If the customer opens the shipment and finds that there are fewer than 100 defect-free watches (which we assume the customer has the ability to do), then he will pay only for the defect-free watches—EuroWatch's revenue will decrease by $500 per watch short of the 100 required—and on top of this, EuroWatch will be required to make up the difference at an expedited cost of $1000 per watch. The customer won't pay a dime for these expedited watches. (If expediting is required, EuroWatch will make sure that the expedited watches are defect-free. It doesn't want to lose this customer entirely.)

You have been asked to develop a spreadsheet model to find EuroWatch's expected profit for any number of watches it sends to the customer. You should develop it so that it responds correctly, regardless of which assembly line is used to fill the order and what the shipment quantity is. (*Hints:* Use the BINOMDIST function, with last argument 0, to fill up a column of probabilities for each possible number of defective watches. Next to each of these, calculate EuroWatch's profit. Then use a SUMPRODUCT to obtain the expected profit. Finally, you can assume that EuroWatch will never send more than 110 watches. It turns out that this large a shipment is not even close to optimal.)

CASE 5.2 CASHING IN ON THE LOTTERY

Many states supplement their tax revenues with state-sponsored lotteries. Most of them do so with a game called lotto. Although there are various versions of this game, they are all basically as follows. People purchase tickets that contain r distinct numbers from 1 to m, where r is generally 5 or 6 and m is generally around 50. For example, in Virginia, the state discussed in this case, $r = 6$ and $m = 44$. Each

ticket costs $1, about 39 cents of which is allocated to the total jackpot.[7] There is eventually a drawing of $r = 6$ distinct numbers from the $m = 44$ possible

[7] Of the remaining 61 cents, the state takes about 50 cents. The other 11 cents is used to pay off lesser prize winners whose tickets match some, but not all, of the winning 6 numbers. To keep this case relatively simple, however, we ignore these lesser prizes and concentrate only on the jackpot.

numbers. Any ticket that matches these 6 numbers wins the jackpot.

There are two interesting aspects of this game. First, the current jackpot includes not only the revenue from this round of ticket purchases but also any jackpots carried over from previous drawings because of no winning tickets. Therefore, the jackpot can build from one drawing to the next, and in celebrated cases it has become huge. Second, if there is more than one winning ticket—a distinct possibility—the winners share the jackpot equally. (This is called *parimutuel* betting.) So, for example, if the current jackpot is $9 million and there are three winning tickets, then each winner receives $3 million.

It can be shown that for Virginia's choice of r and m, there are approximately 7 million possible tickets (7,059,052 to be exact). Therefore, any ticket has about one chance out of 7 million of being a winner. That is, the probability of winning with a single ticket is $p = 1/7,059,052$—not very good odds. If n people purchase tickets, then the number of winners is binomially distributed with parameters n and p. Because n is typically very large and p is small, the number of winners has approximately a Poisson distribution with rate $\lambda = np$. (This makes ensuing calculations somewhat easier.) For example, if 1 million tickets are purchased, then the number of winning tickets is approximately Poisson distributed with $\lambda = 1/7$.

In 1992, an Australian syndicate purchased a huge number of tickets in the Virginia lottery in an attempt to assure itself of purchasing a winner. It worked! Although the syndicate wasn't able to purchase all 7 million possible tickets (it was about 1.5 million shy of this), it did purchase a winning ticket, and there were no other winners. Therefore, the syndicate won a 20-year income stream worth approximately $27 million, with a net present value of approximately $14 million. This made the syndicate a big profit over the cost of the tickets it purchased. Two questions come to mind: (1) Is this hogging of tickets unfair to the rest of the public? (2) Is it a wise strategy on the part of the syndicate (or did it just get lucky)?

To answer the first question, consider how the lottery changes for the general public with the addition of the syndicate. To be specific, suppose the syndicate can invest $7 million and obtain *all* of the possible tickets, making itself a sure winner. Also, suppose n people from the general public

purchase tickets, each of which has 1 chance out of 7 million of being a winner. Finally, let R be the jackpot carried over from any previous lotteries. Then the total jackpot on this round will be $[R + 0.39 (7,000,000 + n)]$ because 39 cents from every ticket goes toward the jackpot. The number of winning tickets for the public will be Poisson distributed with $\lambda = n/7,000,000$. However, any member of the public who wins will *necessarily* have to share the jackpot with the syndicate, which is a sure winner. Use this information to calculate the expected amount the public will win. Then do the same calculation when the syndicate does *not* play. (In this case the jackpot will be smaller, but the public won't have to share any winnings with the syndicate.) For values of n and R that you can select, is the public better off with or without the syndicate? Would you, as a general member of the public, support a move to outlaw syndicates from hogging the tickets?

The second question is whether the syndicate is wise to buy so many tickets. Again assume that the syndicate can spend $7 million and purchase each possible ticket. (Would this be possible in reality?) Also, assume that n members of the general public purchase tickets, and that the carryover from the previous jackpot is R. The syndicate is thus assured of having a winning ticket, but is it assured of covering its costs? Calculate the expected net benefit (in terms of net present value) to the syndicate, using any reasonable values of n and R, to see whether the syndicate can expect to come out ahead.

Actually, the analysis suggested in the previous paragraph is not complete. There are at least two complications to consider. The first is the effect of taxes. Fortunately for the Australian syndicate, it did not have to pay federal or state taxes on its winnings, but a U.S. syndicate wouldn't be so lucky. Second, the jackpot from a $20 million jackpot, say, is actually paid in 20 annual $1 million payments. The Lottery Commission pays the winner $1 million immediately and then purchases 19 "strips" (bonds with the interest not included) maturing at 1-year intervals with face value of $1 million each. Unfortunately, the lottery prize does not offer the liquidity of the Treasury issues that back up the payments. This lack of liquidity could make the lottery less attractive to the syndicate.

CHAPTER

6

Decision Making under Uncertainty

Pressmaster/Shutterstock.com

DECIDING WHETHER TO DEVELOP NEW DRUGS AT BAYER

The formal decision-making process discussed in this chapter is often used to make difficult decisions in the face of much uncertainty, large monetary values, and long-term consequences. Stonebraker (2002) chronicles one such decision-making process he performed for Bayer Pharmaceuticals in 1999. The development of a new drug is a time-consuming and expensive process that is filled with risks along the way. A pharmaceutical company must first get the proposed drug through preclinical trials, where the drug is tested on animals. Assuming this stage is successful (and only about half are), the company can then file an application with the Food and Drug Administration (FDA) to conduct clinical trials on humans. These clinical trials have three phases. Phase 1 is designed to test the safety of the drug on a small sample of healthy patients. Phase 2 is designed to identify the optimal dose of the new drug on patients with the disease. Phase 3 is a statistically designed study to prove the efficacy and safety of the new drug on a larger sample of patients with the disease. Failure at any one of these phases means that further testing stops and the drug is never brought to market. Of course, this means that all costs up to the failure point are lost. If the drug makes it through the clinical tests (and only about 25% of all drugs do so), the company can then apply to the FDA for permission to manufacture and market its drug in the United States. Assuming that the FDA approves, the company is then free to launch the drug in the marketplace.

The study involved the evaluation of a new drug for busting blood clots called BAY 57-9602, and it commenced at a time just prior to the first decision point: whether to conduct preclinical tests. This was the company's first formal use of decision making for evaluating a new drug, so to convince the company of the worth of such a study, Stonebraker did exactly what a successful management science study should do. He formulated the problem and its objectives; he identified risks, costs, and benefits; he involved key people in the organization to help provide the data needed for the decision analysis; and, because much of the resulting data consisted of educated guesses at best, he performed a thorough sensitivity analysis on the inputs. Although we are not told in the article how everything turned out, the analysis did persuade Bayer management to proceed in January 2000 with preclinical testing of the drug.

The article provides a fascinating look at how such a study should proceed. Because there is so much uncertainty, the key is determining probabilities and probability distributions for the various inputs. First, there are uncertainties in the various phases of testing. Each of these can be modeled with a probability of success. For example, the chance of making it through preclinical testing was assessed to be about 65% for BAY 57-9602, although management preferred to use the more conservative benchmark of 50% (based on historical data on other drugs) for the decision analysis. Many of the other uncertain quantities, such as the eventual market share, are continuous random variables. Because the decision tree approach discussed in this chapter requires discrete random variables, usually with only a few possible values, Stonebraker used a popular three-point approximation for all continuous quantities. He asked experts to assess the 10th percentile, the 50th percentile, and the 90th percentile, and he assigned probabilities 0.3, 0.4, and 0.3 to these three values. [The validity of such an approximation is discussed in Keefer and Bodily (1983).]

After getting all such estimates of uncertain quantities from the company experts, the author examined the expected net present value (NPV) of all costs and benefits from developing the new drug. To see which of the various uncertain quantities affected the expected NPV most, he varied each such quantity, one at a time, from its 10th percentile to its 90th percentile, leaving the other inputs at their base 50th percentile values. This identified several quantities that the expected NPV was most sensitive to, including the peak product share, the price per treatment in the United States, and the annual growth rate. The expected NPV was not nearly as sensitive to other uncertain inputs, including the product launch date and the production process yield. Therefore, in the final decision analysis, Stonebraker treated the sensitive inputs as uncertain and the less sensitive inputs as certain at their base values. He also calculated the risk profile from developing the drug. This indicates the probability distribution of NPV, taking all sources of uncertainty into account. Although this risk profile was not exactly optimistic (90% chance of losing money using the conservative probabilities of success, 67% chance of losing money with the more optimistic product-specific probabilities of success), this risk profile compared favorably with Bayer's other potential projects. This evaluation, plus the rigor and defensibility of the study, led Bayer management to give the go-ahead on preclinical testing. ■

6-1 INTRODUCTION

This chapter provides a formal framework for analyzing decision problems that involve uncertainty. Our discussion includes the following:

- criteria for choosing among alternative decisions
- how probabilities are used in the decision-making process
- how early decisions affect decisions made at a later stage

- how a decision maker can quantify the value of information
- how attitudes toward risk can affect the analysis

Throughout, we employ a powerful graphical tool—a decision tree—to guide the analysis. A decision tree enables a decision maker to view all important aspects of the problem at once: the decision alternatives, the uncertain outcomes and their probabilities, the economic consequences, and the chronological order of events. We show how to implement decision trees in Excel® by taking advantage of a very powerful and flexible add-in from Palisade called PrecisionTree.

Many examples of decision making under uncertainty exist in the business world, including the following:

- Companies routinely place bids for contracts to complete a certain project within a fixed time frame. Often these are sealed bids, where each company presents a bid for completing the project in a sealed envelope. Then the envelopes are opened, and the low bidder is awarded the bid amount to complete the project. Any particular company in the bidding competition must deal with the uncertainty of the other companies' bids, as well as possible uncertainty regarding their cost to complete the project if they win the bid. The trade-off is between bidding low to win the bid and bidding high to make a larger profit.

- Whenever a company contemplates introducing a new product into the market, there are a number of uncertainties that affect the decision, probably the most important being the customers' reaction to this product. If the product generates high customer demand, the company will make a large profit. But if demand is low—and, after all, the vast majority of new products do poorly—the company could fail to recoup its development costs. Because the level of customer demand is critical, the company might try to gauge this level by test marketing the product in one region of the country. If this test market is a success, the company can then be more optimistic that a full-scale national marketing of the product will also be successful. But if the test market is a failure, the company can cut its losses by abandoning the product.

- Whenever manufacturing companies make capacity expansion decisions, they face uncertain consequences. First, they must decide whether to build new plants. If they don't expand and demand for their products is higher than expected, they will lose revenue because of insufficient capacity. If they do expand and demand for their products is lower than expected, they will be stuck with expensive underutilized capacity. Of course, in today's global economy, companies also need to decide *where* to build new plants. This decision involves a whole new set of uncertainties, including exchange rates, labor availability, social stability, competition from local businesses, and others.

- Banks must continually make decisions on whether to grant loans to businesses or individuals. As we all know, many banks made many very poor decisions, especially on mortgage loans, during the years leading up to the financial crisis in 2008. They fooled themselves into thinking that housing prices would only increase, never decrease. When the bottom fell out of the housing market, banks were stuck with loans that could never be repaid.

- Utility companies must make many decisions that have significant environmental and economic consequences. For these companies it is not necessarily enough to conform to federal or state environmental regulations. Recent court decisions have found companies liable—for huge settlements—when accidents occurred, even though the companies followed all existing regulations. Therefore, when utility companies decide, say, whether to replace equipment or mitigate the effects of environmental pollution, they must take into account the possible environmental consequences (such as injuries to people) as well as economic consequences (such as lawsuits). An aspect of these situations that makes decision analysis particularly difficult is that the potential "disasters" are often extremely unlikely; hence, their probabilities are difficult to assess accurately.

■ Sports teams continually make decisions under uncertainty. Sometimes these decisions involve long-run consequences, such as whether to trade for a promising but as yet untested pitcher in baseball. Other times these decisions involve short-run consequences, such as whether to go for a fourth down or kick a field goal late in a close football game. You might be surprised at the level of quantitative sophistication in professional sports these days. Management and coaches typically do *not* make important decisions by gut feel. They employ many of the tools in this chapter and in other chapters of this book.

6-2 ELEMENTS OF DECISION ANALYSIS

Although decision making under uncertainty occurs in a wide variety of contexts, all problems have three common elements: (1) the set of decisions (or strategies) available to the decision maker, (2) the set of possible outcomes and the probabilities of these outcomes, and (3) a value model that prescribes monetary values for the various decision–outcome combinations. Once these elements are known, the decision maker can find an optimal decision, depending on the optimality criterion chosen.

Before moving on to realistic business problems, we discuss the basic elements of any decision analysis for a very simple problem. We assume that a decision maker must choose among three decisions, labelled $D1$, $D2$, and $D3$. Each of these decisions has three possible outcomes, labeled $O1$, $O2$, and $O3$.

6-2a Payoff Tables

At the time the decision must be made, the decision maker does *not* know which outcome will occur. However, once the decision is made, the outcome will eventually be revealed, and a corresponding payoff will be received. This payoff might actually be a cost, in which case it is indicated as a negative value. The listing of payoffs for all decision–outcome pairs is called the **payoff table**.[1] For our simple decision problem, this payoff table appears in Table 6.1. For example, if the decision maker chooses decision $D2$ and outcome $O3$ then occurs, a payoff of $30 is received.

> **A payoff table** lists the payoff for each decision–outcome pair. Positive values correspond to *rewards* (or gains) and negative values correspond to *costs* (or losses).

Table 6.1 Payoff Table for Simple Decision Problem

		Outcome		
		O1	*O2*	*O3*
Decision	**D1**	10	10	10
	D2	−10	20	30
	D3	−30	30	80

© Cengage Learning

[1]In situations where all monetary consequences are costs, it is customary to list these costs in a *cost table*. In this case, all monetary values are shown as *positive* costs.

A decision maker gets to decide which row of the payoff table she wants. However, she does not get to choose the column.

This table shows that the decision maker can play it safe by choosing decision $D1$. This provides a sure \$10 payoff. With decision $D2$, rewards of \$20 or \$30 are possible, but a loss of \$10 is also possible. Decision $D3$ is even riskier; the possible loss is greater, and the maximum gain is also greater. Which decision would you choose? Would your choice change if the values in the payoff table were measured in *thousands* of dollars? The answers to these questions are what this chapter is all about. There must be a criterion for making choices, and this criterion must be evaluated so that the *best* decision can be identified. As you will see, it is customary to use one particular criterion for decisions involving moderate amounts of money.

Before proceeding, there is one very important point we need to emphasize: the distinction between good *decisions* and good *outcomes*. In any decision-making problem where there is uncertainty, the "best" decision can have less than great results—in short, you can be unlucky. Regardless of which decision you choose, you might get an outcome that, in hindsight, makes you wish you had made a different decision. For example, if you make decision $D3$, hoping for a large reward, you might get outcome $O1$, in which case you will wish you had chosen decision $D1$ or $D2$. Or if you choose decision $D2$, hoping to limit possible losses, you might get outcome $O3$, in which case you will wish you had chosen decision $D3$. The point is that decision makers must make rational decisions, based on the information they have when the decisions must be made, and then live with the consequences. Second-guessing these decisions, just because of bad luck with the outcomes, is not a fair criticism.

FUNDAMENTAL INSIGHT

What Is a "Good" Decision?

In the context of decision making under uncertainty, a "good" decision is one that is based on the sound decision-making principles discussed in this chapter. Because the decision must usually be made before uncertainty is resolved, a good decision might have unlucky consequences. However, decision makers should not be criticized for unlucky outcomes. They should be criticized only if their analysis *at the time the decision has to be made* is faulty.

6-2b Possible Decision Criteria

What do we mean when we call a decision the "best" decision? We will eventually settle on one particular criterion for making decisions, but we first explore some possibilities. With respect to Table 6.1, one possibility is to choose the decision that maximizes the *worst* payoff. This criterion, called the **maximin criterion**, is appropriate for a very conservative (or pessimistic) decision maker. The worst payoffs for the three decisions are the minimums in the three rows: 10, −10, and −30. The maximin decision maker chooses the decision corresponding to the best of these: decision $D1$ with payoff 10. Such a criterion tends to avoid large losses, but it fails to even consider large rewards. Hence, it is typically *too* conservative and is seldom used.

> The **maximin criterion** finds the worst payoff in each row of the payoff table and chooses the decision corresponding to the best of these.

The maximin and maximax criteria make sense in some situations, but they are generally not used in real decision-making problems.

At the other extreme, the decision maker might choose the decision that maximizes the *best* payoff. This criterion, called the **maximax criterion**, is appropriate for a risk taker (or optimist). The best payoffs for the three decisions are the maximums in the three rows: 10, 30, and 80. The maximax decision maker chooses the decision corresponding to the best of these: decision $D3$ with payoff 80. This criterion looks tempting because it focuses on large gains, but its very serious downside is that it ignores possible losses. Because this type of decision making could eventually bankrupt a company, the maximax criterion is also seldom used.

> The **maximax criterion** finds the best payoff in each row of the payoff table and chooses the decision corresponding to the best of these.

6-2c Expected Monetary Value (EMV)

We have introduced the maximin and maximax criteria because (1) they are occasionally used to make decisions, and (2) they illustrate that there are several "reasonable" criteria for making decisions. In fact, there are other possible criteria that we will not discuss (although a couple are explored in the problems). Instead, we now focus on a criterion that is generally regarded as the preferred criterion in most decision problems. It is called the **expected monetary value criterion**, or **EMV criterion**. To motivate the EMV criterion, we first note that the maximin and maximax criteria make no reference to how *likely* the various outcomes are. However, decision makers typically have at least some idea of these likelihoods, and they ought to use this information in the decision-making process. After all, if outcome O1 in our problem is extremely unlikely, then the pessimist who uses maximin is being overly conservative. Similarly, if outcome O3 is quite unlikely, then the optimist who uses maximax is taking an unnecessary risk.

The EMV approach assesses probabilities for each outcome of each decision and then calculates the *expected* payoff from each decision based on these probabilities. This expected payoff, or EMV, is a weighted average of the payoffs in any given row of the payoff table, weighted by the probabilities of the outcomes. You calculate the EMV for each decision, then choose the decision with the largest EMV. (Note that the terms *expected payoff* and *mean payoff* are equivalent. We will use them interchangeably.)

> The **expected monetary value**, or **EMV**, for any decision is a weighted average of the possible payoffs for this decision, weighted by the probabilities of the outcomes. Using the EMV criterion, you choose the decision with the largest EMV. This is sometimes called "playing the averages."

Where do the probabilities come from? This is a difficult question to answer in general because it depends on each specific situation. In some cases the current decision problem is similar to those a decision maker has faced many times in the past. Then the probabilities can be estimated from the knowledge of previous outcomes. If a certain type of outcome occurred, say, in about 30% of previous situations, an estimate of its current probability might be 0.30.

However, there are many decision problems that have no parallels in the past. In such cases, a decision maker must use whatever information is available, plus some intuition, to assess the probabilities. For example, if the problem involves a new product decision, and one possible outcome is that a competitor will introduce a similar product in the coming year, the decision maker will have to rely on any knowledge of the market and the competitor's situation to assess the probability of this outcome. It is important to note that this assessment can be very subjective. Two decision makers could easily assess the probability of the *same* outcome as 0.30 and 0.45, depending on their information and feelings, and neither could be considered "wrong." This is the nature of assessing probabilities subjectively in real business situations. Still, it is important for the decision maker to consult all relevant sources (historical data, expert opinions, government forecasts, and so on) when assessing these probabilities. As you will see, they are crucial to the decision-making process.

With this general framework in mind, let's assume that a decision maker assesses the probabilities of the three outcomes in Table 6.1 as 0.3, 0.5, and 0.2 if decision $D2$ is made, and as 0.5, 0.2, 0.3 if decision $D3$ is made. Then the EMV for each decision is the sum of products of payoffs and probabilities:

$$\text{EMV for } D1: \ 10 \ (\text{a sure thing})$$
$$\text{EMV for } D2: \ -10(0.3) + 20(0.5) + 30(0.2) = 13$$
$$\text{EMV for } D3: \ -30(0.5) + 30(0.2) + 80(0.3) = 15$$

These calculations lead to the optimal decision: Choose decision $D3$ because it has the largest EMV.

It is important to understand what the EMV of a decision represents—and what it doesn't represent. For example, the EMV of 15 for decision $D3$ does *not* mean that you expect to gain $15 from this decision. The payoff table indicates that the result from $D3$ will be a loss of $30, a gain of $30, or a gain of $80; it will *never* be a gain of $15. The EMV is only a weighted average of the possible payoffs. As such, it can be interpreted in one of two ways. First, imagine that this situation can occur many times, not just once. If decision $D3$ is used each time, then *on average*, you will make a gain of about $15. About 50% of the time you will lose $30, about 20% of the time you will gain $30, and about 30% of the time you will gain $80. These average to $15. For this reason, using the EMV criterion is sometimes referred to as "playing the averages."

But what if the current situation is a one-shot deal that will *not* occur many times in the future? Then the second interpretation of EMV is still relevant. It states that the EMV is a "reasonable" criterion for making decisions under uncertainty. This is actually a point that has been debated in intellectual circles for years—what is the best criterion for making decisions? However, researchers have generally concluded that EMV is reasonable, even for one-shot deals, as long as the monetary values are not too large. For situations where the monetary values are extremely large, we will introduce an alternative criterion in the last section of this chapter. Until then, however, we will use EMV.

This is the gist of decision-making uncertainty. You develop a payoff table, assess probabilities of outcomes, calculate EMVs, and choose the decision with the largest EMV. However, before proceeding to examples, it is useful to introduce a few other concepts: *sensitivity analysis*, *decision trees*, and *risk profiles*.

FUNDAMENTAL INSIGHT

What It Means to Be an EMV Maximizer

An EMV maximizer, by definition, is indifferent when faced with the choice between entering a gamble that has a certain EMV and receiving a sure dollar amount in the amount of the EMV. For example, consider a gamble where you flip a fair coin and win $0 or $1000 depending on whether you get a head or a tail. If you are an EMV maximizer, you are indifferent between entering this gamble, which has EMV $500, and receiving $500 for sure. Similarly, if the gamble is between losing $1000 and winning $500, based on the flip of the coin, and you are an EMV maximizer, you are indifferent between entering this gamble, which has EMV −$250, and *paying* a sure $250 to avoid the gamble. (This latter scenario is the basis of insurance.)

6-2d Sensitivity Analysis

Some of the quantities in a decision analysis, particularly the probabilities, are often intelligent guesses at best. Therefore, it is important, especially in real-world business problems, to accompany any decision analysis with a sensitivity analysis. Here we systematically vary inputs to the problem to see how (or if) the outputs—the EMVs and the best decision—change. For our simple decision problem, this is easy to do in a spreadsheet. The spreadsheet model is shown in Figure 6.1. (See the file **Simple Decision Problem.xlsx**.)

Figure 6.1

Spreadsheet Model of a Simple Decision Problem

◢	A	B	C	D	E	F
1	Simple decision problem under uncertainty					
2						
3			Outcome			
4			O1	O2	O3	EMV
5	Decision	D1	10	10	10	10
6		D2	−10	20	30	13
7		D3	−30	30	80	15
8						
9	Probabilities					
10		D2	0.3	0.5	0.2	
11		D3	0.5	0.2	0.3	

© Cengage Learning

After entering the payoff table and probabilities, we calculate the EMVs in column F as a sum of products, using the formula

=SUMPRODUCT(C6:E6,C10:E10)

in cell F6 and copying it down. (A link to the sure 10 for *D*1 is entered in cell F5.) Then it is easy to change any of the inputs and see whether the optimal decision continues to be *D*3. For example, you can check that if the probabilities for *D*3 change only slightly to 0.6, 0.2, and 0.2, the EMV for *D*3 changes to 4. Now *D*3 is the worst decision and *D*2 is the best, so it appears that the optimal decision is quite sensitive to the assessed probabilities. As another example, if the probabilities remain the same but the last payoff for *D*2 changes from 30 to 45, its EMV changes to 16, and *D*2 becomes the best decision.

Usually, the most important information from a sensitivity analysis is whether the optimal decision continues to be optimal as one or more inputs change.

Given a simple spreadsheet model, it is easy to make a number of ad hoc changes to inputs, as we have done here, to answer specific sensitivity questions. However, it is often useful to conduct a more systematic sensitivity analysis, as we do this later in the chapter. The important thing to realize at this stage is that a sensitivity analysis is not an afterthought to the overall analysis; it is a key component of the analysis.

6-2e Decision Trees

The decision problem we have been analyzing is very basic. You make a decision, you then observe an outcome, you receive a payoff, and that is the end of it. Many decision problems are of this basic form, but many are more complex. In these more complex problems, you make a decision, you observe an outcome, you make a second decision, you observe a second outcome, and so on. A graphical tool called a **decision tree** has been developed to represent decision problems. Decision trees can be used for any decision problems, but they are particularly useful for the more complex types. They clearly show the sequence of events (decisions and outcomes), as well as probabilities and monetary values. The decision tree for the simple problem appears in Figure 6.2. This tree is based on one we drew and calculated by hand. We urge you to try this on your own, at least once. However, later in the chapter we will introduce an Excel add-in that automates the procedure.

Figure 6.2

Decision Tree for Simple Decision Problem

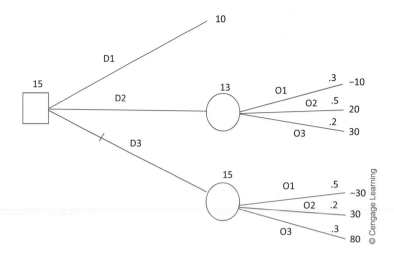

To explain this decision tree, we introduce a number of decision tree conventions that have become standard.

- Decision trees are composed of *nodes* (circles, squares, and triangles) and *branches* (lines).

- The nodes represent points in time. A *decision node* (a square) represents a time when the decision maker makes a decision. A *chance node* (a circle) represents a time when the result of an uncertain outcome becomes known. An *end node* (a triangle) indicates that the problem is completed—all decisions have been made, all uncertainty has been resolved, and all payoffs and costs have been incurred. (When people draw decision trees by hand, they often omit the actual triangles, as we have done in Figure 6.2. However, we still refer to the right-hand tips of the branches as the end nodes.)

- Time proceeds *from left to right*. This means that any branches leading into a node (from the left) have already occurred. Any branches leading out of a node (to the right) have not yet occurred.

- Branches leading out of a decision node represent the possible decisions; the decision maker can choose the preferred branch. Branches leading out of chance nodes represent the possible outcomes of uncertain events; the decision maker has no control over which of these will occur.

- Probabilities are listed on chance branches. These probabilities are *conditional* on the events that have already been observed (those to the left). Also, the probabilities on branches leading out of any chance node must sum to 1.

- Monetary values are shown to the right of the end nodes. (As we discuss shortly, some monetary values are also placed under the branches where they occur in time.)

- EMVs are calculated through a "folding-back" process, discussed next. They are shown above the various nodes. It is then customary to mark the optimal decision branch(es) in some way. We have marked ours with a small notch.

The decision tree in Figure 6.2 follows these conventions. The decision node comes first (to the left) because the decision maker must make a decision *before* observing the uncertain outcome. The chance nodes then follow the decision branches, and the probabilities appear above their branches. (Actually, there is no need for a chance node after the $D1$ branch because its monetary value is a sure 10.) The ultimate payoffs appear next to the end nodes, to the right of the chance branches. The EMVs above the chance nodes are for the various decisions. For example, the EMV for the $D2$ branch is 13. The maximum of the EMVs is for the D2 branch written above the decision node. Because it corresponds to $D3$, we put a notch on the $D3$ branch to indicate that this decision is optimal.

This decision tree is almost a direct translation of the spreadsheet model in Figure 6.1. Indeed, the decision tree is overkill for such a simple problem; the spreadsheet model provides all of the required information. However, decision trees are very useful in business problems. First, they provide a graphical view of the whole problem. This can be useful in its own right for the insights it provides, especially in more complex problems. Second, the decision tree provides a framework for doing all of the EMV calculations. Specifically, it allows you to use the following **folding-back procedure** to find the EMVs and the optimal decision.

Starting from the right of the decision tree and working back to the left:

- At each chance node, calculate an EMV—a sum of products of monetary values and probabilities.
- At each decision node, take a maximum of EMVs to identify the optimal decision.

The folding-back process is a systematic way of calculating EMVs in a decision tree and thereby identifying the optimal decision strategy.

This is exactly what we did in Figure 6.2. At each chance node, we calculated EMVs in the usual way (sums of products) and wrote them above the nodes. Then at the decision node, we took the maximum of the three EMVs and wrote it above this node. Although this procedure entails more work for more complex decision trees, the same two steps—taking EMVs at chance nodes and taking maximums at decision nodes—are the only arithmetic operations required. In addition, the PrecisionTree add-in in the next section does the folding-back calculations for you.

6-2f Risk Profiles

In our small example each decision leads to three possible monetary payoffs with various probabilities. In more complex problems, the number of outcomes could be larger, maybe considerably larger. It is then useful to represent the probability distribution of the monetary values for any decision graphically. Specifically, we show a "spike" chart, where the spikes are located at the possible monetary values, and the heights of the spikes correspond to the probabilities. In decision-making contexts, this type of chart is called a **risk profile**. By looking at the risk profile for a particular decision, you can see the risks and rewards involved. By comparing risk profiles for different decisions, you can gain more insight into their relative strengths and weaknesses.

The **risk profile** for a decision is a "spike" chart that represents the probability distribution of monetary outcomes for this decision.

The risk profile for decision $D3$ appears in Figure 6.3. It shows that a loss of $30 has probability 0.5, a gain of $30 has probability 0.2, and a gain of $80 has probability 0.3. The risk profile for decision $D2$ is similar, except that its spikes are above the values −10, 20,

Figure 6.3

Risk Profile for
Decision *D*3

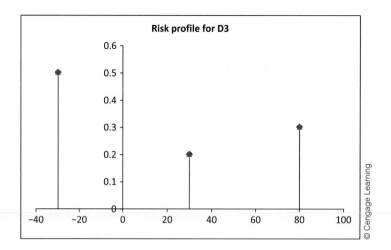

and 30, and the risk profile for decision *D*1 is a single spike of height 1 over the value 10. (The finished version of the **Simple Decision Problem.xlsx** file provides instructions for constructing such a chart with Excel tools.)

A risk profile shows the probability distribution of monetary outcomes, but you typically use only its mean, the EMV, for making decisions.

Note that the EMV for any decision is a summary measure of the risk profile—it is the *mean* of the corresponding probability distribution. Therefore, when you use the EMV criterion for making decisions, you are not using *all* of the information in the risk profiles; you are only comparing their means. Nevertheless, risk profiles can be useful as extra information for making decisions. For example, a manager who sees too much risk in the risk profile of the EMV-maximizing decision might choose to override this decision and instead choose a somewhat less risky alternative.

We now apply all of these concepts to Example 6.1.

EXAMPLE | 6.1 BIDDING FOR A GOVERNMENT CONTRACT AT SCITOOLS

SciTools Incorporated, a company that specializes in scientific instruments, has been invited to make a bid on a government contract. The contract calls for a specific number of these instruments to be delivered during the coming year. The bids must be sealed, so that no company knows what the others are bidding, and the low bid wins the contract. SciTools estimates that it will cost $5000 to prepare a bid and $95,000 to supply the instruments if it wins the contract. On the basis of past contracts of this type, SciTools believes that the possible low bids from the competition, if there is any competition, and the associated probabilities are those shown in Table 6.2. In addition, SciTools believes there is a 30% chance that there will be *no* competing bids. What should SciTools bid to maximize its EMV?

Table 6.2 Data for Bidding Example

Competitors' Low Bid	Probability
Less than $115,000	0.2
Between $115,000 and $120,000	0.4
Between $120,000 and $125,000	0.3
Greater than $125,000	0.1

Objective To develop a decision model that finds the EMV for various bidding strategies and indicates the best bidding strategy.

Where Do the Numbers Come From?

The company has probably done a thorough cost analysis to estimate its cost to prepare a bid and its cost to manufacture the instruments if it wins the contract. (Actually, even if there is uncertainty in the manufacturing cost, the only value required for the decision problem is the *mean* manufacturing cost.) The company's estimates of whether, or how, the competition will bid are probably based on previous bidding experience and some subjectivity. This is discussed in more detail next.

Solution

Let's examine the three elements of SciTools's problem. First, SciTools has two basic strategies: submit a bid or do not submit a bid. If SciTools submits a bid, it must then decide how much to bid. Based on the cost to SciTools to prepare the bid and supply the instruments, there is clearly no point in bidding less than $100,000—SciTools wouldn't make a profit even if it won the bid. (Actually, this isn't totally true. Looking ahead to future contracts, SciTools might make a low bid just to "get in the game" and gain experience. However, we won't consider such a possibility here.) Although any bid amount over $100,000 might be considered, the data in Table 6.2 suggest that SciTools might limit its choices to $115,000, $120,000, and $125,000.[2]

The next element of the problem involves the uncertain outcomes and their probabilities. We have assumed that SciTools knows exactly how much it will cost to prepare a bid and how much it will cost to supply the instruments if it wins the bid. (In reality, these are probably only estimates of the actual costs, and a follow-up study could perform a sensitivity analysis on these quantities.) Therefore, the only source of uncertainty is the behavior of the competitors—will they bid, and if so, how much? From SciTools's stand-point, this is difficult information to obtain. The behavior of the competitors depends on (1) how many competitors are likely to bid and (2) how the competitors assess *their* costs of supplying the instruments. Nevertheless, we assume that SciTools has been involved in similar bidding contests in the past and can reasonably predict competitor behavior from past competitor behavior. The result of such a prediction is the assessed probability distribution in Table 6.2 and the 30% estimate of the probability of no competing bids.

The last element of the problem is the value model that transforms decisions and outcomes into monetary values for SciTools. The value model is straightforward in this example. If SciTools decides not to bid, its monetary value is $0—no gain, no loss. If it makes a bid and is underbid by a competitor, it loses $5000, the cost of preparing the bid. If it bids B dollars and wins the contract, it makes a profit of B minus $100,000—that is, B dollars for winning the bid, minus $5000 for preparing the bid and $95,000 for supplying the instruments. For example, if it bids $115,000 and the lowest competing bid, if any, is greater than $115,000, then SciTools wins the bid and makes a profit of $15,000.

Developing the Payoff Table

The corresponding payoff table, along with probabilities of outcomes, appears in Table 6.3. At the bottom of the table, the probabilities of the various outcomes are listed. For example, the probability that the competitors' low bid is less than $115,000 is 0.7 (the probability

---

[2]The problem with a bid such as $117,000 is that the data in Table 6.2 make it impossible to calculate the probability of SciTools winning the contract if it bids this amount. Other than this, however, there is nothing that rules out such "in-between" bids.

Table 6.3   Payoff Table for SciTools Bidding Example

		No bid	<115	>115, <120	>120, <125	>125
		Competitors' Low Bid ($1000s)				
SciTools' Bid ($1000s)	No bid	0	0	0	0	0
	115	15	−5	15	15	15
	120	20	−5	−5	20	20
	125	25	−5	−5	−5	25
Probability		0.3	0.7(0.2) = 0.14	0.7(0.4) = 0.28	0.7(0.3) = 0.21	0.7(0.1) = 0.07

of at least one competing bid) multiplied by 0.2 (the probability that the lowest competing bid is less than $115,000).

It is sometimes possible to simplify a payoff table to better understand the essence of the problem. In the present example, if SciTools bids, the only necessary information about the competitors' bid(s) is whether SciTools has the lowest bid. That is, SciTools really only cares whether it wins the contract. Therefore, an alternative way of presenting the payoff table is shown in Table 6.4. (See the file **SciTools Bidding Decision 1.xlsx** for these and other calculations. However, we urge you to work this problem on a piece of paper with a calculator, just for practice with the concepts.)

Table 6.4   Alternative Payoff Table for SciTools Bidding Example

		Monetary Value		*Probability That SciTools Wins*
		SciTools Wins	SciTools Loses	
SciTools' Bid ($1000s)	No Bid	NA	0	0.00
	115	15	−5	0.86
	120	20	−5	0.58
	125	25	−5	0.37

© Cengage Learning

The Monetary Value columns of this table indicate the payoffs to SciTools, depending on whether it wins or loses the bid. The rightmost column shows the probability that SciTools wins the bid for each possible decision. For example, if SciTools bids $120,000, then it wins the bid if there are no competing bids (probability 0.3) *or* if there are competing bids and the lowest of these is greater than $120,000 [probability 0.7(0.3 + 0.1) = 0.28]. In this case the total probability that SciTools wins the bid is 0.3 + 0.28 = 0.58.

Developing the Risk Profiles

Table 6.4 contains all the required information to obtain a risk profile for each of SciTools's decisions. Again, each risk profile indicates all possible monetary values and their corresponding probabilities in a spike chart. For example, if SciTools bids $120,000, there are two monetary values possible, a profit of $20,000 and a loss of $5000, and their probabilities are 0.58 and 0.42, respectively. The corresponding risk profile, shown in Figure 6.4, is a spike chart with two spikes, one above −$5000 with height 0.42 and one above $20,000 with height 0.58. On the other hand, if SciTools decides not to bid, there is a sure monetary value of $0—no profit, no loss. Therefore, the risk profile for the "no bid" decision, not shown here, has a single spike above $0 with height 1.

234   Chapter 6   Decision Making under Uncertainty

Figure 6.4

Risk Profile for a
Bid of $120,000

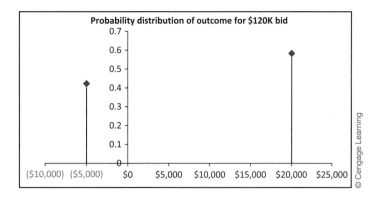

Calculating EMVs

The EMVs for SciTools's problem are listed in Table 6.5. As always, each EMV (other than the EMV of $0 for not bidding) is a sum of products of monetary outcomes and probabilities. These EMVs indicate that if SciTools uses the EMV criterion for making its decision, it should bid $115,000. The EMV from this bid, $12,200, is the largest of the EMVs.

Table 6.5 EMVs for SciTools Bidding Example

Alternative	EMV Calculation	EMV
No bid	0(1)	$0
Bid $115,000	15,000(0.86) + (−5000)(0.14)	$12,200
Bid $120,000	20,000(0.58) + (−5000)(0.42)	$9500
Bid $125,000	25,000(0.37) + (−5000)(0.63)	$6100

As discussed previously, it is important to understand what an EMV implies and what it does not imply. If SciTools bids $115,000, its EMV is $12,200. However, SciTools will definitely *not* earn a profit of $12,200. It will earn $15,000 or it will lose $5000. The EMV of $12,200 represents only a weighted average of these two possible values. Nevertheless, it is the value that is used as the decision criterion. In words, if SciTools is truly an EMV maximizer, it considers this gamble equivalent to a sure return of $12,200.

It is common to place monetary values below the branches where they occur in time.

Developing the Decision Tree

The corresponding decision tree for this problem is shown in Figure 6.5. This is a direct translation of the payoff table and EMV calculations. The company first makes a bidding

Figure 6.5

Decision Tree for
SciTools Bidding
Example

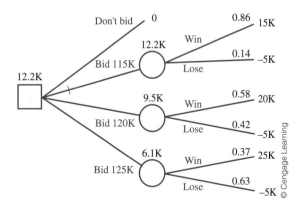

decision, then observes what the competition bids, if anything, and finally receives a payoff. The folding-back process is equivalent to the calculations shown in Table 6.5.

There are often equivalent ways to structure a decision tree. One alternative for this example appears in Figure 6.6. This tree shows exactly how the problem unfolds. The company first decides whether to bid at all. If the company does not make a bid, the profit is a sure $0. Otherwise, the company then decides how much to bid. Note that if the company decides to bid, it incurs a sure cost of $5000, so this cost is placed under the Bid branch. It is a common procedure to place the monetary values on the branches where they occur in time, and we typically do so. Once the company decides how much to bid, it then observes whether there is any competition. If there isn't any, the company wins the bid for sure and makes a corresponding profit. Otherwise, if there is competition, the company eventually discovers whether it wins or loses the bid, with the corresponding probabilities and payoffs. Note that these payoffs are placed below the branches where they occur in time. Also, the *cumulative* payoffs are placed at the ends of the branches. Each cumulative payoff is the sum of all payoffs on branches that lead to that end node.

Figure 6.6

Equivalent Decision Tree for SciTools Bidding Example

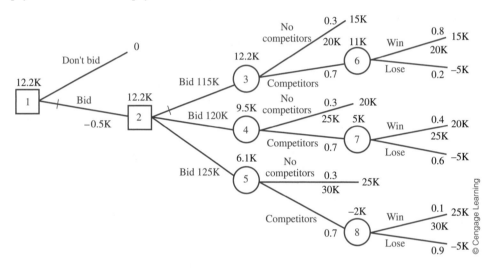

Folding Back the Decision Tree

The folding-back procedure is somewhat more complex than it was for the smaller tree in Figure 6.5. To illustrate, the nodes in Figure 6.6 have been numbered for reference. The EMVs above a selected few of these nodes are calculated as follows:

- Node 7: EMV = 20K(0.40) + (−5K)(0.60) = $5K (uses monetary values from end nodes)
- Node 4: EMV = 20K(0.30) + (5K)(0.70) = $9.5K (uses monetary value from an end node and the EMV from node 7)
- Node 2: EMV = max(12.2K, 9.5K, 6.1K) = $12.2K (uses EMVs from nodes 3, 4, and 5)
- Node 1: EMV = max(0, 12.2K) = $12.2K (uses monetary value from an end node and EMV from node 2)

The results are the same, regardless of whether you use the table of EMVs in Table 6.5, the decision tree in Figure 6.5, or the decision tree in Figure 6.6, because they all calculate the same EMVs in equivalent ways. In each case, the bottom line is that the company should bid $115,000, with a resulting EMV of $12,200. Of course, this decision is not *guaranteed* to produce a good outcome for the company. For example, the competition could bid less than $115,000, in which case SciTools would lose $5000. Alternatively, the competition could bid more than $120,000, in which case SciTools would be kicking itself for not bidding $120,000 and gaining an extra $5000 in profit. Unfortunately, in problems with uncertainty, there is virtually never a guarantee that the optimal decision will produce the best result. The only guarantee is that the EMV-maximizing decision is a rational and defensible decision, given the information known when the decision must be made.

Sensitivity Analysis

The next step in the SciTools decision analysis is to perform a sensitivity analysis. You will eventually see that PrecisionTree, an Excel add-in that helps automate the decision-making process, has some powerful sensitivity analysis tools. However, it is also possible to use Excel data tables. One example is shown in Figure 6.7. (See the finished version of the file **SciTools Bidding Decision 1.xlsx**.) The EMVs are calculated in column G, exactly as described previously. Then you can find the maximum of these in cell B21, and you can use the following formula in cell B22 to find the decision from column B that achieves this maximum:

=INDEX(B16:B19,MATCH(B21,G16:G19,0))

This formula checks which EMV in column G matches the maximum EMV in cell B21 and returns the corresponding decision from column B. (This combination of the INDEX and MATCH functions is often useful for finding the value that corresponds to a maximum or minimum. For an explanation of this combination, see the Preface for instructions on how to access the **excel_tutorial.xlsm** file that is available with this book.)

Figure 6.7 Sensitivity Analysis with a Data Table

▲	A	B	C	D	E	F	G
1	SciTools Bidding Example						
2							
3	Inputs						
4	Cost to prepare a bid	$5,000					
5	Cost to supply instruments	$95,000					
6							
7	Probability of no competing bid	0.3					
8	Comp bid distribution (if they bid)						
9	<$115K	0.2					
10	$115K to $120K	0.4					
11	$120K to $125K	0.3					
12	>$125K	0.1					
13							
14	EMV analysis		Monetary outcomes		Probabilities		
15			SciTools wins	SciTools loses	SciTools wins	SciTools loses	EMV
16		No bid	NA	0	0	1	$0
17	SciTools' Bid	$115,000	$15,000	−$5,000	0.86	0.14	$12,200
18		$120,000	$20,000	−$5,000	0.58	0.42	$9,500
19		$125,000	$25,000	−$5,000	0.37	0.63	$6,100
20							
21	Maximum EMV	$12,200					
22	Best decision	$115,000	$115,000				
23							
24	Data table for sensitivity analysis						
25	Probability of no competing bid	Maximum EMV	Best decision				
26		$12,200	$115,000				
27	0.2	$11,800	$115,000				
28	0.3	$12,200	$115,000				
29	0.4	$12,600	$115,000				
30	0.5	$13,000	$115,000				
31	0.6	$14,200	$125,000				
32	0.7	$16,900	$125,000				

Once the formulas in cells B21 and B22 have been entered, the data table is easy. In Figure 6.7 the probability of no competing bid is allowed to vary from 0.2 to 0.7. The data table shows how the optimal EMV increases over this range. Also, its third column shows that the $115,000 bid is optimal for small values of the input, but that a $125,000 bid becomes optimal for larger values. The main point here is that if you set up a spreadsheet model that links all of the EMV calculations to the inputs, it is easy to use data tables to perform sensitivity analyses on selected inputs. ■

PROBLEMS

Note: Student solutions for problems whose numbers appear within a colored box are available for purchase at www.cengagebrain.com.

Level A

1. For the example in **Simple Decision Problem.xlsx**, are there any probabilities that make the EMV criterion equivalent to the maximin criterion? Are there any probabilities that make the EMV criterion equivalent to the maximax criterion? Explain.

2. Using a data table in Excel, perform a sensitivity analysis on the example in **Simple Decision Problem.xlsx**. Specifically, keep the probabilities in row 10 (for *D*2) as they are, but vary the probability in cell C11 from 0 to 1 in increments of 0.05, and keep the probabilities in cells D11 and E11 in the same ratio as they are currently (2 to 3).

3. In the SciTools example, make two changes: change all references to $115,000 to $110,000, and change all references to $125,000 to $130,000. Rework the EMV calculations and the decision tree. What is the best decision and its corresponding EMV?

4. In the SciTools example, which decision would a maximin decision maker choose? Which decision would a maximax decision maker choose? Would you defend either of these criteria for this particular example? Explain.

5. In the SciTools example, use a two-way data table to see how (or if) the optimal decision changes as the bid cost and the company's production cost change simultaneously. Let the bid cost vary from $2000 to $8000 in increments of $1000, and let the production cost vary from $90,000 to $105,000 in increments of $2500. Explain your results.

6. In the SciTools example, the probabilities for the low bid of competitors, given that there is at least one competing bid, are currently 0.2, 0.4, 0.3, and 0.1. Let the second of these be *p*, and let the others sum to $1 - p$ but keep the same ratios to one another: 2 to 3 to 1. Use a one-way data table to see how (or if) the optimal decision changes as *p* varies from 0.1 to 0.7 in increments of 0.05. Explain your results.

Level B

7. For the example in **Simple Decision Problem.xlsx**, we found that decision *D*3 is the EMV-maximizing decision for the given probabilities. See whether you can find probabilities that make decision *D*1 the best. If the probabilities in row 10 (for *D*2) are the same as the probabilities in row 11 (for *D*3), is it possible for *D*2 to be the best decision? What if these two rows are allowed to be different? Qualitatively, how can you explain the results? That is, which types of probabilities tend to favor the various decisions? (*Hint*: To search for probabilities where *D*2 is better than the other two decisions, given that rows 10 and 11 are the same, you might want to try using Solver.)

8. A decision *d* is said to be *dominated* by another decision *D* if, for every outcome, the payoff from *D* is better than, or no worse than, the payoff from *d*.
   a. Explain why you would never choose a dominated decision using the maximin criterion, the maximax criterion, or the EMV criterion.
   b. Are any of the decisions in the example in **Simple Decision Problem.xlsx** dominated by any others? What about in the SciTools example?

9. Besides the maximin, maximax, and EMV criteria, there are other possible criteria for making decisions. One possibility involves *regret*. The idea behind regret is that if you make any decision and then some outcome occurs, you look at that outcome's column in the payoff table to see how much more you could have made if you had chosen the best payoff in that column. For example, if the decision you make and the outcome you observe lead to a $50 payoff, and if the highest payoff in this outcome's column is $80, then your regret is $30. You regret looking back and seeing how much more you could have made, if only you had made a different decision. Therefore, you calculate the regret for each cell in the payoff table (as the maximum payoff in that column minus the payoff in that cell), calculate the maximum regret in each row, and choose the row with the smallest maximum regret. This is called the *minimax regret criterion*.

a. Apply this criterion to the example in **Simple Decision Problem.xlsx**. Which decision do you choose?

b. Repeat part **a** for the SciTools example.

c. In general, discuss potential strengths and weaknesses of this decision criterion.

10. Referring to the previous problem, another possible criterion is called *expected regret*. Here you calculate the regret for each cell, take a weighted average of these regrets in each row, weighted by the probabilities of the outcomes, and choose the decision with the smallest expected regret.

a. Apply this criterion to the SciTools example. Which decision do you choose?

b. The expected regret criterion is actually *equivalent* to the EMV criterion, in that they always lead to the same decisions. Argue why this is true.

11. In the SciTools example, you might argue that there is a *continuum* of possible low competitor bids (given that there is at least one competing bid), not just four possibilities. In fact, assume the low competitor bid in this case is *normally* distributed with mean $118,000 and standard deviation $4500. Also, assume that SciTools will still either bid or not bid $115,000, $120,000, or $125,000. Use Excel's NORMDIST function to find the EMV for each alternative. Which is the best decision now? Why can't this be represented in a decision tree?

6-3 THE PRECISIONTREE ADD-IN

Decision trees present a challenge for Excel. We must somehow take advantage of Excel's calculating capabilities (to calculate EMVs, for example) and its graphical capabilities (to depict the decision tree). Fortunately, there is a powerful add-in, **PrecisionTree**, developed by Palisade Corporation, that makes the process relatively straightforward. This add-in not only enables you to draw and label a decision tree, but it performs the folding-back procedure automatically and then allows you to perform sensitivity analysis on key input parameters.

The first thing you must do to use PrecisionTree is to "add it in." We assume you have already installed the Palisade DecisionTools® suite. Then to run PrecisionTree, you have two options:

- If Excel is not currently running, you can launch Excel *and* PrecisionTree by clicking the Windows Start button (in Windows 7 and earlier versions) and selecting the PrecisionTree item from the Palisade Decision Tools group in the list of Programs.

- If Excel is currently running, the first procedure will launch PrecisionTree on top of Excel.

You will know that PrecisionTree is ready for use when you see its tab and the associated ribbon (shown in Figure 6.8). If you want to unload PrecisionTree *without* closing Excel, you can do so from its Utilities dropdown list in the Help group.

Figure 6.8 PrecisionTree Ribbon

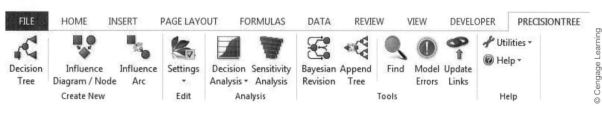

© Cengage Learning

The Decision Tree Model

PrecisionTree is quite easy to use—at least its most basic items are. We will lead you through the steps for the SciTools example. Figure 6.9 shows the results of this procedure, just so that you can see what you are working toward. (See the file **SciTools Bidding Decision 2.xlsx**.) However, we recommend that you work through the steps on your own, starting with a blank spreadsheet.

Figure 6.9 Completed Tree from PrecisionTree

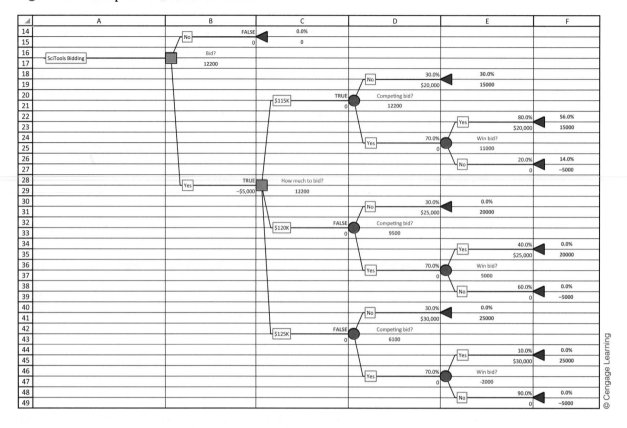

Building the Decision Tree

1. **Inputs.** Enter the inputs shown in Figure 6.10.

Figure 6.10

Inputs for SciTools Bidding Example

	A	B
1	**SciTools Bidding Decision**	
2		
3	**Inputs**	
4	Cost to prepare a bid	$5,000
5	Cost to supply instruments	$95,000
6		
7	Probability of no competing bid	0.3
8	Comp bid distribution (if they bid)	
9	<$115K	0.2
10	$115K to $120K	0.4
11	$120K to $125K	0.3
12	>$125K	0.1

2. **New tree.** Click the Decision Tree button on the PrecisionTree ribbon, and then select cell A14 below the input section to start a new tree. You will immediately see a dialog box where, among other things, you can name the tree. Enter a descriptive name for the tree, such as SciTools Bidding, and click OK. You should now see the beginnings of a tree, as shown in Figure 6.11.

Figure 6.11 Beginnings of a New Tree

⬩	A	B	C
14	SciTools Bidding	100.0%	
15		0	

3. **Decision nodes and branches.** From here on, keep the tree in Figure 6.9 in mind. This is the finished product you eventually want. To obtain decision nodes and branches, click the (only) triangle end node to open the dialog box in Figure 6.12. Click the green square to indicate that you want a decision node, and fill in the dialog box as shown. Then click the Branches (2) tab and supply labels for the branches under Name, as shown in Figure 6.13. By default, you get two branches, which is what you want in this case. However, if you want more than two branches, click Add to get additional branches. Under the "Yes" branch, enter the following link to the bid cost cell, where the minus sign indicates a cost:

=$B$4

Note that it is *usually* a good idea to use absolute cell references in formulas on tree branches, just in case you need to move or copy parts of the tree later on.

Figure 6.12

Dialog Box for Adding a New Decision Node and Branches

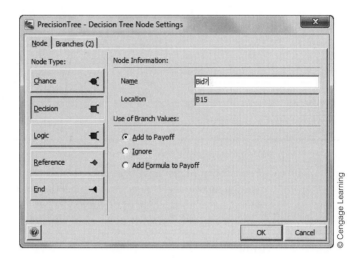

Figure 6.13 Decision Tree with Decision Branches Labeled

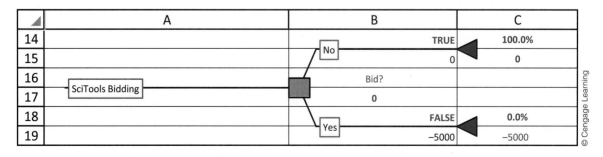

⬩	A	B	C
14		TRUE	100.0%
15		No 0	0
16	SciTools Bidding	Bid?	
17		0	
18		FALSE	0.0%
19		Yes −5000	−5000

PrecisionTree Tip: Allowable Entries

On your computer screen, you will note the color-coding PrecisionTree uses. If you investigate any colored (green, red, or blue) cells, you will see strange formulas that

PrecisionTree uses for its own purposes. You should not modify these formulas. You should enter your own probabilities and monetary values only in the cells with black font.

4. **More decision branches.** The top branch is completed; if SciTools does not bid, there is nothing left to do. So click the bottom end node (the triangle), following SciTools's decision to bid, and proceed as in the previous step to add and label the decision node and three decision branches for the amount to bid. (Again, refer to Figure 6.9.) The tree up to this point should appear as in Figure 6.14. Note that there are no monetary values below these decision branches because no *immediate* payoffs or costs are associated with the bid amount decision.

Figure 6.14 Tree with All Decision Nodes and Branches

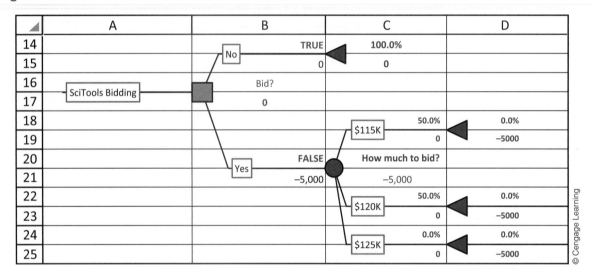

5. **Probability nodes and branches.** Using the same procedure (and using Figure 6.9 as a guide), create chance nodes extending from the "bid $115,000" decision. You should have the skeleton in Figure 6.15.

Figure 6.15 Decision Tree with One Set of Chance Nodes and Branches

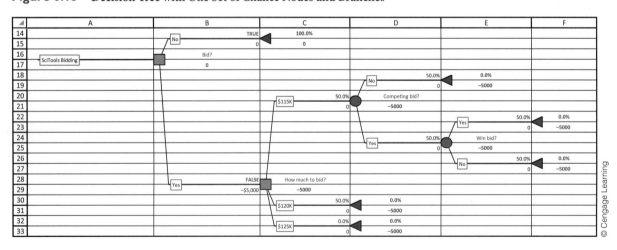

6. **Copying probability nodes and branches.** You could now repeat the same proce-dure from the previous step to build chance nodes and branches following the other bid amount decisions, but because they are structurally equivalent, you can save a lot of time by using PrecisionTree's copy and paste feature. Right-click the leftmost chance node and select Copy SubTree. Then right-click either end node below it and select Paste SubTree. Do this again with the other end node. Decision trees can get very "bushy," but this copy and paste feature can make them much easier to construct.

7. **Enter probabilities on probability branches.** You should now have the decision tree shown in Figure 6.16. It is structurally the same as the completed tree in Figure 6.9, but the probabilities and monetary values on the chance branches are incorrect. Note that each chance branch has a value above and below the branch. The value above is the probability (the default values make the branches equally likely), and the value below is the monetary value (the default values are 0). You can enter any values or formulas in these cells (remember, the cells with black font only), exactly as you do in typical Excel worksheets. As usual, it is a good practice to enter cell references, not numbers, whenever possible.

Figure 6.16   **Structure of Completed Tree**

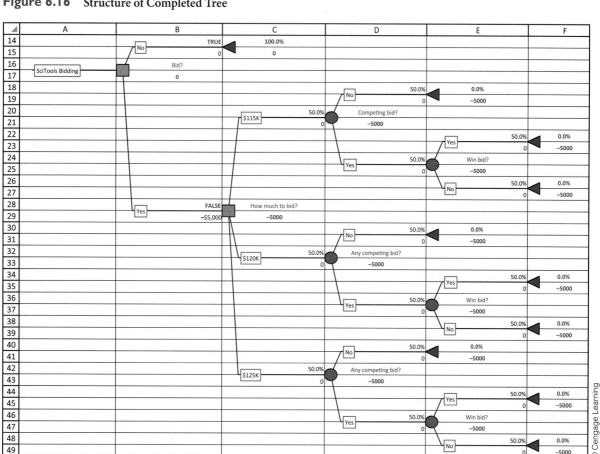

© Cengage Learning

PrecisionTree Tip: **Sum of Probabilities**

PrecisionTree does not enforce the rule that probabilities on branches leading out of a chance node must sum to 1. You must enforce this rule with appropriate formulas. If they do not *sum to 1, you will see #VALUE! errors.*

PrecisionTree Tip: **Entering Monetary Values, Probabilities**

A good practice is to calculate all of the monetary values and probabilities that will be needed in the decision tree in some other area of the spreadsheet. Then the values needed next to the tree branches can be created with simple linking formulas.

We will get you started with the chance branches following the decision to bid $115,000. First, enter the probability of no competing bid in cell D18 with the formula

=$B$7

and enter its complement in cell D24 with the formula

=1-$B$7

Next, enter the probability that SciTools wins the bid in cell E22 with the formula

=SUM($B$10:$B$12)

and enter its complement in cell E26 with the formula

=1-E22

(Remember that SciTools wins the bid only if the competition bids higher, and in this part of the tree, SciTools is bidding $115,000.) For the monetary values, enter the formula

=D9-$B$5

in the two cells, D19 and E23, where SciTools wins the contract. Note that the cost of the bid was already subtracted in cell B29, so it should *not* be subtracted again. This would be double-counting, which you should always avoid in decision trees.

8. **Enter the other formulas on probability branches.** Using the previous step and Figure 6.9 as a guide, enter formulas for the probabilities and monetary values on the other chance branches, those following the decision to bid $120,000 or $125,000.

PrecisionTree Tip: **Copying Subtrees**

Before taking advantage of PrecisionTree's subtree copying capability, it is generally a good idea to fill the subtree as much as possible (with labels, probabilities, and monetary values). In this way, the copies will require less work. Note that formulas on the subtree are copied in the usual Excel way (in terms of relative and absolute addresses), so that the formulas on the copies often have to be adjusted slightly. In this example, you could have sped up the process slightly by completing step 7 before copying. Then step 8 would entail only a few formula adjustments on the copied subtrees.

Interpreting the Decision Tree

To find the optimal decision strategy in any PrecisionTree tree, follow the TRUE labels.

You are finished! The completed tree in Figure 6.9 shows the best strategy and its associated EMV, as discussed previously. In fact, a comparison of the decision tree in Figure 6.6 that was created manually and the tree from PrecisionTree in Figure 6.9 indicates virtually identical results. The best decision strategy is now indicated by the TRUE and FALSE labels above the decision branches (rather than the notches we entered by hand). Each TRUE corresponds to the optimal decision out of a decision node, whereas each FALSE corresponds to a nonoptimal decision. Therefore, you simply follow the TRUE labels. In this case, the company should bid, and its bid amount should be $115,000.

Note that you do *not* have to perform the folding-back procedure manually. PrecisionTree does this for you. Essentially, the tree is completed as soon as you finish entering the relevant inputs. In addition, if you change any of the inputs, the tree reacts automatically. For example, try changing the bid cost in cell B4 from $5000 to some large value such as $20,000. You will see that the tree calculations update automatically, and the best decision is then *not* to bid, with an associated EMV of $0.

PrecisionTree Tip: *Values at End Nodes*

You will notice that there are two values following each triangle end node. The bottom value is the sum of all monetary values on branches leading to this end node. The top value is the probability of getting to this end node when the optimal *strategy is used. This explains why many of these probabilities are 0; the optimal strategy will never lead to these end nodes.*

Policy Suggestion and Risk Profile for Optimal Strategy

The Policy Suggestion shows only the subtree corresponding to the optimal decision strategy.

Once the decision tree is completed, PrecisionTree has several tools you can use to gain more information about the decision analysis. First, you can see a subtree (called a Policy Suggestion) for the *optimal* decision. To do so, choose Policy Suggestion from the Decision Analysis dropdown list and fill in the resulting dialog box as shown in Figure 6.17. (You can experiment with other options.) The Policy Suggestion option shows only the part of the tree that corresponds to the best decision, as shown in Figure 6.18.

Figure 6.17

Dialog Box for Information about Optimal Decision

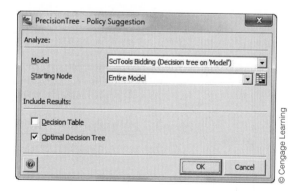

You can also obtain a graphical risk profile of the optimal decision by selecting Risk Profile from the Decision Analysis dropdown list and filling in the resulting dialog box as shown in Figure 6.19. (Again, you can experiment with the other options.) As the risk profile in Figure 6.20 indicates, there are only two possible monetary outcomes if SciTools bids $115,000. It either wins $15,000 or loses $5000, and the former is much more likely. (The associated probabilities are 0.86 and 0.14, respectively.) This graphical information is even more useful when there are a larger number of possible monetary outcomes. You can see what they are and how likely they are.

Figure 6.18 Subtree for Optimal Decision

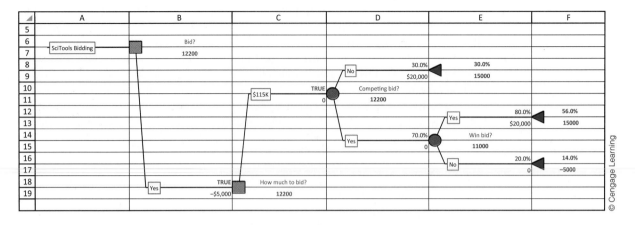

Figure 6.19

Risk Profile Dialog Box

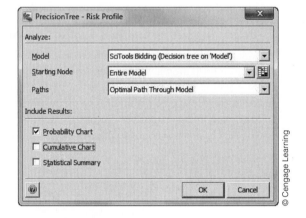

Figure 6.20

Risk Profile of Optimal Decision

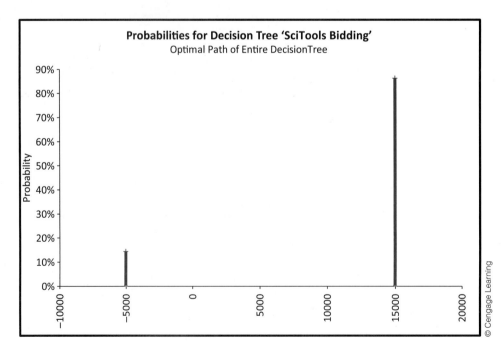

Sensitivity Analysis

We have already stressed the importance of a follow-up sensitivity analysis to any decision problem, and PrecisionTree makes this relatively easy to perform. Of course, you can enter any values in the input cells and watch how the tree changes, but you can obtain more systematic information by clicking PrecisionTree's Sensitivity Analysis button. This brings up the dialog box in Figure 6.21. Although it has a lot of options, it is straightforward once you understand the ideas behind it.

Figure 6.21

Sensitivity Analysis
Dialog Box

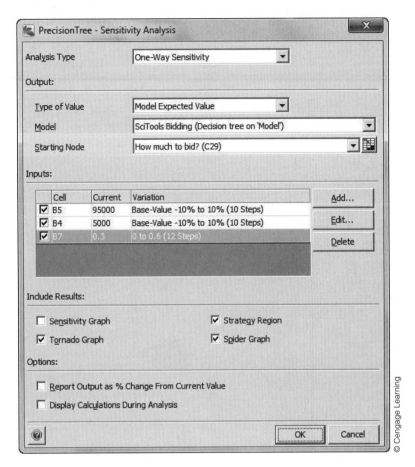

Here are the main options and how to use them.

It takes some practice and experimenting to get used to PrecisionTree's sensitivity analysis tools. However, they are powerful and worth learning.

- The Analysis Type dropdown list allows you to vary one input (One-Way Sensitivity) or two inputs (Two-Way Sensitivity) simultaneously. This is very similar to one-way and two-way data tables in Excel.

- The Starting Node dropdown list lets you choose any node in the tree, and the sensitivity analysis is then performed for the EMV *from that node to the right.* In other words, it assumes you have gotten to that node and are now interested in what will happen from then on. The node selected in the figure, C29, is the leftmost node, so by selecting it, the sensitivity analysis is on the EMV of the entire tree. This is the most common setting.

- You add inputs to vary in the Inputs section. You can add as many as you like, and all of the checked inputs are included in any particular sensitivity analysis. When you add an input to this section, you can specify the range over which you want it to vary. For example, you can vary it by plus or minus 10% in 10 steps from a selected base value, as we did for the production cost in cell B5, or you can vary it from 0 to 0.6 in 12 steps, as we did for the probability of no competing bids in cell B7.

■ The Include Results checkboxes allow you to select up to four types of charts, depending on the type of sensitivity analysis. (The bottom two options are disabled for a two-way sensitivity analysis.) You can experiment with these options, but we will illustrate our favorites shortly.

When you click OK, PrecisionTree varies each of the checked inputs in the middle section, one at a time if you select the One-Way option, and presents the results in new worksheets. By default, these new worksheets are placed in a new workbook. If you would rather have them in the same workbook as the model, select Application Settings from the Utilities dropdown list, and select Active Workbook from the Replace Reports In option. (This is a global setting. It will take effect for all future PrecisionTree analyses.)

Strategy Region Chart

In strategy region charts, the primary interest is in where (or if) lines cross. This is where decisions change.

Figure 6.22 illustrates **a strategy region chart** from a one-way analysis. This chart shows how the EMV varies with the production cost for *both* of the original decisions (bid or don't bid). This type of chart is useful for seeing whether the optimal decision *changes* over the range of the input variable. It does so only if the two lines cross. In this particular graph it is clear that the "Bid" decision dominates the "No bid" decision over the selected production cost range.

Figure 6.22

EMV Versus Production Cost for Each of Two Decisions

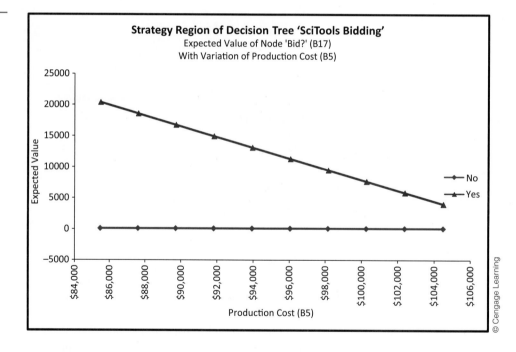

Tornado Chart

Tornado charts and spider charts indicate which inputs the selected EMV is most sensitive to.

A **tornado chart** shows how sensitive the EMV of the *optimal* decision is to each of the selected inputs over the specified ranges. (See Figure 6.23.) The length of each bar shows the change in the EMV in either direction, so inputs with longer bars have a greater effect on the selected EMV. (If you checked the next-to-bottom checkbox in Figure 6.21, the lengths of the bars would indicate *percentage* changes from the base value.) The bars are always arranged from longest on top to shortest on the bottom—hence the name *tornado* chart. Here it is apparent that production cost has the largest effect on EMV, and bid cost has the smallest effect.

Figure 6.23

Tornado Chart for
SciTools Example

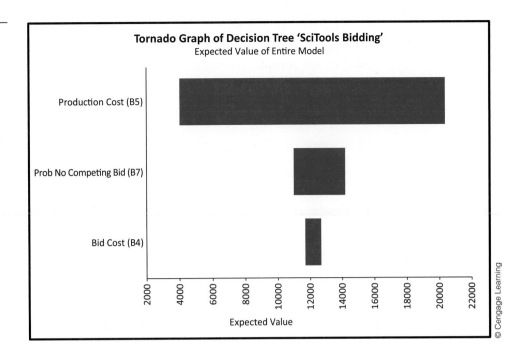

Spider Chart

Finally, a **spider chart** shows how much the optimal EMV varies in magnitude for various percentage changes in the input variables. (See Figure 6.24.) The steeper the slope of the line, the more the EMV is affected by a particular input. It is again apparent that the production cost has a relatively large effect, whereas the other two inputs have relatively small effects.

Figure 6.24

Spider Chart for
SciTools Example

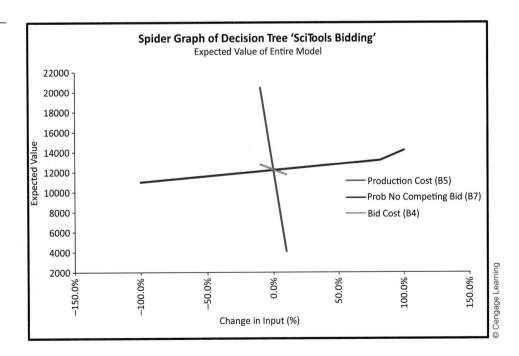

Another Sensitivity Chart

Each time you click the Sensitivity Analysis button, you can run a different sensitivity analysis. For example, you might want to choose cell C29 as the cell to analyze. This is the optimal EMV for the problem, *given* that the company has decided to place a bid. One interesting chart from this analysis is the strategy region chart in Figure 6.25. It indicates how the EMV varies with the probability of no competing bid for *each* of the three bid amount decisions. The $115,000 bid is best for most of the range, but when the probability of no competing bid is sufficiently large (about 0.55), the $120,000 bid becomes best (by a small margin.)

Figure 6.25

Strategy Region Chart for Another EMV Cell

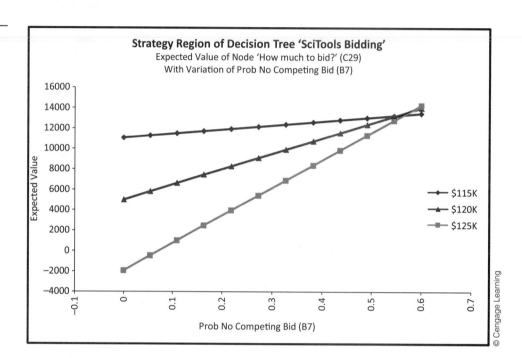

© Cengage Learning

Two-Way Sensitivity Chart

A one-way sensitivity analysis varies only one input at a time. A two-way analysis varies two inputs simultaneously.

Another interesting option is to run a two-way analysis. This shows how the selected EMV varies as each *pair* of inputs varies simultaneously. We analyzed the EMV in cell C29 with this option, using the same inputs as before. A typical result is shown in Figure 6.26. For each of the possible values of production cost and the probability of no competitor bid, this chart indicates which bid amount is optimal. (By choosing cell C29, we are assuming SciTools will bid; the only question is how much.) As you can see, the optimal bid amount remains $115,000 unless the production cost *and* the probability of no competing bid are both large. Then it becomes optimal to bid $120,000 or $125,000. This makes sense intuitively. As the probability of no competing bid increases and a larger production cost must be recovered, it seems reasonable that SciTools should increase its bid.

We reiterate that a sensitivity analysis is always an important component of any real-world decision analysis. If you had to construct decision trees by hand—with paper and pencil—a sensitivity analysis would be tedious, to say the least. You would have to recalculate everything each time through. Therefore, one of the most valuable features of the PrecisionTree add-in is that it enables you to perform sensitivity analyses in a matter of seconds.

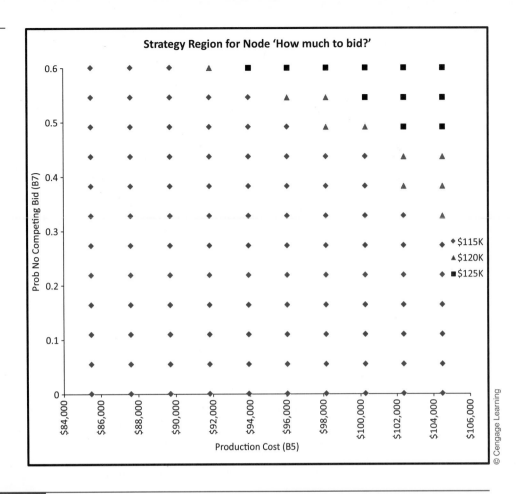

Figure 6.26

Two-Way
Sensitivity Analysis

© Cengage Learning

PROBLEMS

Level A

12. In a tree built with PrecisionTree, there are two blue values at each end node, the top one of which is a probability. Why are so many of these probabilities 0 in the finished tree in Figure 6.9? What do the remaining (positive) probabilities represent?

13. In the SciTools example, we created an Inputs section with the data from the problem statement, and then we cell-referenced these input cells in the tree. Show that you omit the Inputs section and enter the relevant *numbers* (monetary values and probabilities) directly in the tree. Is this any quicker than the method we used? Does it have any drawbacks?

14. For the completed decision tree in Figure 6.9, the monetary values in black are those you enter. The monetary values in color are calculated automatically by PrecisionTree. For this particular example, explain exactly how these latter values are calculated (remember the folding-back process) and what they represent. These include the blue values at the end nodes, the red

values at the chance nodes, and the green values at the decision nodes.

15. For the SciTools example, once you build the tree as in Figure 6.9 and then run a one-way sensitivity analysis with the dialog box filled in as in Figure 6.21, you obtain three strategy charts. (Try it.) Explain exactly what each of these charts represents. (For this problem, you can ignore the tornado and spider charts.)

16. The tornado chart in Figure 6.23 and the spider chart in Figure 6.24 show basically the same information in slightly different forms. Explain in words exactly what information they provide. (If necessary, consult PrecisionTree's online help.)

17. Explain in words what information a two-way sensitivity chart, such as the one in Figure 6.26, provides. Demonstrate how you could provide this same information without PrecisionTree's sensitivity tools, using only data tables. (You can still use the tree built with PrecisionTree.)

6-4 BAYES' RULE

The whole purpose of Bayes' rule is to revise probabilities as new information becomes available.

The examples to this point have required a single decision. We now examine multistage problems, where a decision maker must make at least two decisions that are separated in time, such as when a company must first decide whether to buy information that will help it make a second decision. In multistage decision problems there are typically alternating sets of decision nodes and chance nodes. The decision maker makes a decision, some uncertainty is resolved, the decision maker makes another decision, more uncertainty is resolved, and so on. Before analyzing such problems, we must discuss one important probability issue.

In a multistage decision tree, all chance branches toward the *right* of the tree are conditional on outcomes that have occurred earlier, to their left. Therefore, the probabilities on these branches are of the form $P(A|B)$, read "A given B," where A is an event corresponding to a current chance branch, and B is an event that occurs *before* event A in time. However, when gathering data for the problem, it is sometimes more natural to *assess* conditional probabilities in the opposite order, that is, $P(B|A)$. Whenever this is the case, **Bayes' rule** must be used to obtain the probabilities needed on the tree. Essentially, Bayes' rule is a mechanism for revising probabilities as new information becomes available.

To develop Bayes' rule, let A_1 through A_n be any outcomes. Without any further information, you believe the probabilities of the As are $P(A_1)$ through $P(A_n)$. These are called **prior probabilities**. You then have the possibility of gaining some information. There are several information outcomes you might observe, a typical one of which is labeled B. You assume the probabilities of B, given that any of the As will occur, are known. These probabilities, labeled $P(B|A_1)$ through $P(B|A_n)$, are often called *likelihoods*. Because an information outcome might influence your thinking about the probabilities of the As, you need to find the conditional probability $P(A_i|B)$ for each outcome A_i. This is called the **posterior probability** of A_i. This is where Bayes' rule enters the picture. It states that the posterior probabilities can be calculated from the following formula.

Bayes' rule

$$P(A_i|B) = \frac{P(B|A_i)P(A_i)}{P(B|A_1)P(A_1) + \cdots + P(B|A_n)P(A_n)} \qquad \textbf{(6.1)}$$

In words, Bayes' rule says that the posterior is the likelihood times the prior, divided by a sum of likelihoods times priors. As a side benefit, the denominator in Bayes' rule is also useful in multistage decision trees. It is the probability $P(B)$ of the information outcome.

Denominator of Bayes' rule (Law of Total Probability)

$$P(B) = P(B|A_1)P(A_1) + \cdots + P(B|A_1)P(A_n) \qquad \textbf{(6.2)}$$

This formula is important in its own right. For B to occur, it must occur along with one of the As. Equation (6.2) simply decomposes the probability of B into all of these possibilities. It is sometimes called the **law of total probability**.

In the case where there are only two As, labeled as A and Not A, Bayes' rule takes the following form:

Bayes' rule for two outcomes

$$P(A|B) = \frac{P(B|A)P(A)}{P(B|A)P(A) + P(B|\text{Not } A)P(\text{Not } A)} \qquad \textbf{(6.3)}$$

We illustrate the mechanics of Bayes' rule in Example 6.2. [See Feinstein (1990) for a real application of this example.]

EXAMPLE **6.2 DRUG TESTING COLLEGE ATHLETES**

If an athlete is tested for a certain type of drug use (steroids, say), the test result will be either positive or negative. However, these tests are never perfect. Some drug-free athletes test positive, and some drug users test negative. The former are called *false positives*; the latter are called *false negatives*. Let's assume that 5% of all athletes use drugs, 3% of all tests on drug-free athletes yield false positives, and 7% of all tests on drug users yield false negatives. Suppose a typical athlete is tested. If this athlete tests positive, can you be sure that he is a drug user? If he tests negative, can you be sure he does not use drugs?

Objective   To use Bayes' rule to revise the probability of being a drug user, given the positive or negative results of the test.

Where Do the Numbers Come From?

The estimate that 5% of all athletes are drug users is probably based on a well-known national average. The error rates from the tests are undoubtedly known from extensive experience with the tests. (However, we are not claiming that the numbers used here match reality.)

Solution

Let D and ND denote that a randomly chosen athlete is or is not a drug user, and let $T+$ and $T-$ indicate a positive or negative test result. (The outcomes D and ND correspond to A and Not A in Equation (6.3), and either $T+$ or $T-$ corresponds to B.) The following probabilities are given. First, because 5% of all athletes are drug users, you know that $P(D) = 0.05$ and $P(ND) = 0.95$. These are the prior probabilities. They represent the chance that an athlete is or is not a drug user *prior* to the results of a drug test.

Second, from the information on the accuracy of the drug test, you know the conditional probabilities $P(T+|ND) = 0.03$ and $P(T-|D) = 0.07$. In addition, a drug-free athlete tests either positive or negative, and the same is true for a drug user. Therefore, you also know the probabilities $P(T-|ND) = 0.97$ and $P(T+|D) = 0.93$. These four conditional probabilities of test results given drug user status are the likelihoods of the test results.

Given these priors and likelihoods, you need to calculate posterior probabilities such as $P(D|T+)$, the probability that an athlete who tests positive is a drug user, and $P(ND|T-)$, the probability that an athlete who tests negative is drug free. They are called posterior probabilities because they are assessed *after* the drug test results.

Using Bayes' rule for two outcomes, Equation (6.3), you can calculate

$$P(D|T+) = \frac{P(T+|D)P(D)}{P(T+|D)P(D) + P(T+|ND)P(ND)} = \frac{(0.93)(0.05)}{(0.93)(0.05) + (0.03)(0.95)} = 0.620$$

and

$$P(ND|T-) = \frac{P(T-|ND)P(ND)}{P(T-|D)P(D) + P(T-|ND)P(ND)} = \frac{(0.97)(0.95)}{(0.07)(0.05) + (0.97)(0.95)} = 0.996$$

In words, if the athlete tests positive, there is still a 38% chance that he is *not* a drug user, but if he tests negative, you are virtually sure he is not a drug user. The denominators of these two formulas are the probabilities of the test results. They can be calculated from Equation (6.2):

$$P(T+) = 0.93(0.05) + 0.03(0.95) = 0.075$$

and

$$P(T-) = 0.07(0.05) + 0.97(0.95) = 0.925$$

The first Bayes' rule result might surprise you. After all, the test is reasonably accurate, so if you observe a positive test result, you should be pretty sure that the athlete is a drug user, right? The reason the first posterior probability is "only" 0.620 is that very few athletes in the population are drug users—only 5%. Therefore, you need a lot of evidence to be convinced that a particular athlete is a drug user, and a positive test result from a somewhat inaccurate test is not enough evidence to be totally convincing. On the other hand, a negative test result simply adds confirmation to what you already suspected—that a typical athlete is *not* a drug user. This is why $P(ND|T-)$ is so close to 1.

A More Intuitive Calculation

If you have trouble understanding or implementing Bayes' rule, you are not alone. At least one study has shown that even trained medical specialists have trouble with this type of calculation (in the context of tests for cancer). Most of us do not think intuitively about conditional probabilities. However, there is an equivalent and more intuitive way to obtain the same result.

This alternative procedure, using counts instead of probabilities, is equivalent to Bayes' rule and is probably more intuitive.

Imagine that there are 100,000 athletes. Because 5% of all athletes are drug users, we assume that 5000 of these athletes use drugs and the other 95,000 do not. Now we administer the test to all of them. We expect 3%, or 2850, of the nonusers to test positive (because the false-positive rate is 3%), and we expect 93%, or 4650, of the drug users to test positive (because the false-negative rate is 7%). Therefore, we observe a total of 2850 + 4650 = 7500 positives. If one of these 7500 athletes is chosen at random, what is the probability that a drug user is chosen? It is clearly

$$P(D|T+) = 4650/7500 = 0.620$$

This is the same result we got using Bayes' rule! So if you have trouble with Bayes' rule using probabilities, you can use this alternative method of using *counts*. (By the way, the 100,000 value is irrelevant. We could have used 10,000, 50,000, 1,000,000, or any other convenient value.)

Bayesian Revision with PrecisionTree

Spreadsheet Implementation of Bayes' Rule

It is fairly easy to implement Bayes' rule in a spreadsheet, as illustrated in Figure 6.27 for the drug example. (See the file **Bayes Rule.xlsx**.[3])

The given priors and likelihoods are listed in the ranges B5:C5 and B9:C10. You first use Equation (6.2) to calculate the denominators for Bayes' rule, the unconditional

---

[3]The Bayes2 sheet in this file illustrates how Bayes' rule can be used when there are more than two possible test results and/or drug user categories.

Figure 6.27 Bayes' Rule for Drug-Testing Example

	A	B	C	D	E	F	G	H	I	J	K
1	**Bayes' rule with two outcomes**										
2											
3	Prior probabilities of drug user status				Unconditional probabilities of test results (denominators of Bayes' rule)						
4		User	Non-user		Test positive		0.075				
5		0.05	0.95		Test negative		0.925				
6											
7	Likelihoods of test results, given drug user status				Posterior probabilities of drug user status (Bayes' rule)						
8		User	Non-user				User	Non-user			
9	Test positive	0.93	0.03		Test positive		0.620	0.380			
10	Test negative	0.07	0.97		Test negative		0.004	0.996			

© Cengage Learning

probabilities of the two possible test results, in the range F4:F5. Because each of these is a sum of products of priors and likelihoods, the formula in cell F4 is

=SUMPRODUCT(B$5:C$5,B9:C9)

and this is copied to cell F5. Then you use Equation (6.1) to calculate the posterior probabilities in the range F9:G10. Because each of these is a product of a prior and a likelihood, divided by a denominator, the formula in cell F9 is

=B$5*B9/$F4

and this is copied to the rest of the F9:G10 range.

As we have noted, a positive drug test still leaves a 38% chance that the athlete is *not* a drug user. Is this a valid argument for not requiring drug testing of athletes? We explore this question in a continuation of the drug-testing example in the next section. ■

PROBLEMS

Level A

18. For each of the following, use a one-way data table to see how the posterior probability of being a drug user, given a positive test, varies as the indicated input varies. Write a brief explanation of your results.

   a. Let the input be the prior probability of being a drug user, varied from 0.01 to 0.10 in increments of 0.01.

   b. Let the input be the probability of a false positive from the test, varied from 0 to 0.10 in increments of 0.01.

   c. Let the input be the probability of a false negative from the test, varied from 0 to 0.10 in increments of 0.01.

19. In the drug testing example, assume there are three possible test results: positive, negative, and inconclusive. For a drug user, the probabilities of these outcomes are 0.65, 0.06, and 0.29. For a nonuser, they are 0.03, 0.72, and 0.25. Use Bayes' rule to find a table of all posterior probabilities. (The prior probability of being a drug user is still 0.05.) Then answer the following.

   a. What is the posterior probability that the athlete is a drug user, (1) given that her test results are positive, (2) given that her test results are negative, and (3) given that her drug results are inconclusive?

   b. What is the probability of observing a positive test result, a negative test result, or an inconclusive test result?

20. Referring to the previous problem, find the same probabilities through the counting argument explained in this section. Start with 100,000 athletes and divide them into the various categories. Then find them with the Bayesian Revision tool introduced in PrecisionTree 6.0.

21. Suppose you are a heterosexual white male and are going to be tested to see if you are HIV positive. Assume that if you are HIV positive, your test will always come back positive. Assume that if you are not HIV positive, there is still a 0.001 chance that your test will indicate that you are HIV positive. In reality, 1 of 10,000 heterosexual white males is HIV positive. Your doctor calls and says that you have tested HIV positive. He is sorry but there is a 99.9% (1−0.001) chance that you have HIV. Is he correct? If not, what is the correct probability that you are HIV positive?

Level B

22. The terms *prior* and *posterior* are relative. Assume that the drug test has been performed, and the outcome is positive, which leads to the posterior probabilities in row 20 of Figure 6.27. Now assume there is a *second* test, independent of the first, that can be used as a follow-up. Assume that its false-positive and false-negative rates are 0.02 and 0.06.

    a. Use the posterior probabilities from row 20 as *prior* probabilities in a second Bayes' rule calculation. (Now *prior* means prior to the second test.) If the athlete also tests positive in this second test, what is the posterior probability that he is a drug user?

b. We assumed that the two tests are independent. Why might this not be realistic? If they are not independent, what kind of additional information would you need about the likelihoods of the test results?

23. In the OJ Simpson trial it was accepted that OJ had battered his wife. OJ's lawyer tried to negate the impact of this information by stating that in a one-year period, only 1 out of 2500 battered women are murdered, so the fact that OJ battered his wife does not give much evidence that he was the murderer. The prosecution (foolishly!) let this go unchallenged. Here are the relevant statistics: In a typical year 6.25 million women are battered, 2500 are battered and murdered, and 2250 of the women who were battered and murdered were killed by the batterer. How should the prosecution have refuted the defense's argument?

6-5 MULTISTAGE DECISION PROBLEMS AND THE VALUE OF INFORMATION

In this section we investigate multistage decision problems. In many such problems the first-stage decision is whether to purchase information that will help make a better second-stage decision. In this case the information, if obtained, typically changes the probabilities of later outcomes. To revise the probabilities once the information is obtained, you often need to apply Bayes' rule, as discussed in the previous section. In addition, you typically want to learn how much the information is worth. After all, information usually comes at a price, so you want to know whether the information is worth its price. This leads to an investigation of the value of information, an important theme of this section.

We begin with a continuation of the drug-testing example from the previous section. If drug tests are not completely reliable, should they be used? As you will see, it all depends on the "costs."[4]

EXAMPLE | **6.3 DRUG TESTING COLLEGE ATHLETES**

The administrators at State University are trying to decide whether to institute mandatory drug testing for athletes. They have the same information about priors and likelihoods as in Example 6.2, but they now want to use a decision tree approach to see whether the benefits outweigh the costs.[5]

Objective   To use a multistage decision framework to see whether mandatory drug testing can be justified, given a somewhat unreliable test and a set of "reasonable" monetary values.

---

[4]It might also depend on whether there is a second type of test that could help confirm the findings of the first test. However, we will not consider such a test.
[5]Again, see Feinstein (1990) for an enlightening discussion of this drug-testing problem at a real university.

Where Do the Numbers Come From?

We already discussed the source of the probabilities in Example 6.2. The monetary values we need are discussed in detail here.

Solution

We have already discussed the uncertain outcomes and their probabilities. Now we need to discuss the decision alternatives and the monetary values, the other two elements of a decision analysis. We will assume that there are only two alternatives: perform drug testing on all athletes or don't perform any drug testing. In the former case we will assume that if an athlete tests positive, this athlete is barred from athletics.

Assessing the Monetary Values

The "monetary" values are more difficult to assess. They include

- the benefit B from correctly identifying a drug user and barring this person from athletics
- the cost $C1$ of the test itself for a single athlete (materials and labor)
- the cost $C2$ of falsely accusing a nonuser (and barring this person from athletics)
- the cost $C3$ of not identifying a drug user and allowing this person to participate in athletics
- the cost $C4$ of violating a nonuser's privacy by performing the test.

Real decision problems often involve nonmonetary benefits and costs. These must be assessed, relative to one another, before rational decisions can be made.

It is clear that only $C1$ is a direct monetary cost that is easy to measure. However, the other "costs" and the benefit B are real, and they must be compared on some scale to enable administrators to make a rational decision. We will do so by comparing everything to the cost $C1$, to which we assign value 1. (This does not mean that the cost of testing an athlete is necessarily \$1; it just means that all other monetary values are expressed as multiples of $C1$.) Clearly, there is a lot of subjectivity involved in making these comparisons, so sensitivity analysis on the final decision tree is a must.

Developing a Benefit–Cost Table

Before developing this decision tree, it is useful to form a benefit–cost table for both alternatives and all possible outcomes. Because we will eventually maximize expected net *benefit*, all benefits in this table have a positive sign and all costs have a negative sign. These net benefits are listed in Table 6.6. As before, let D and ND denote that a randomly chosen athlete is or is not a drug user, and let $T+$ and $T-$ indicate a positive or negative test result. The first two columns are relevant if no tests are performed; the last four are relevant when testing is performed. For example, if a positive test is obtained for a nonuser and this athlete is barred from athletics, there are three costs: the cost of the test (C_1), the cost of falsely accusing the athlete (C_2), and the cost of violating the athlete's privacy (C_4). The other entries are obtained similarly.

Table 6.6   Net Benefit for Drug-Testing Example

Ultimate decision	Don't Test		Perform Test			
	D	ND	D and $T+$	ND and $T+$	D and $T-$	ND and $T-$
Bar from athletics	B	$-C_2$	$B-C_1$	$-(C_1+C_2+C_4)$	$B-C_1$	$-(C_1+C_2+C_4)$
Don't bar from athletics	$-C_3$	0	$-(C_1+C_3)$	$-(C_1+C_4)$	$-(C_1+C_3)$	$-(C_1+C_4)$

© Cengage Learning

Developing the Decision Tree Model

The decision model, developed with PrecisionTree and shown in Figures 6.28 and 6.29, is now fairly straightforward. (See the file **Drug Testing Decision.xlsx**.) You first enter all of the benefits and costs in an input section. These, together with the Bayes' rule calculations from Example 6.2, appear at the top of Figure 6.28. Then you use PrecisionTree in the usual way to build the tree in Figure 6.29 and enter the links to the values and probabilities.

Figure 6.28   Inputs and Bayes' Rule Calculations for Drug-Testing Example

	A	B	C	D	E	F	G	H	I	J	K
1	Drug testing decision										
2											
3	Benefits			Given probabilities				Bayesian revision			
4	Identifying user	25		Prior probabilities				Unconditional probabilities of test results			
5					User	Non-user		Positive	0.075		
6	Costs				0.05	0.95		Negative	0.925		
7	Test cost	1									
8	Barring non-user	50		Conditional probabilities of test results				Posterior probabilities			
9	Not identifying user	20			User	Non-user					
10	Violation of privacy	2		Positive	0.93	0.03			User	Non-user	
11				Negative	0.07	0.97		Positive	0.620	0.380	
12	Key probabilities							Negative	0.004	0.996	
13	User	0.05									
14	False Negative	0.07									
15	False Positive	0.03									

It is important to understand the timing (from left to right) in this decision tree. If drug testing is performed, the result of the drug test is observed first (a chance node). Each test result leads to an action (bar from sports or don't), and then the eventual benefit or cost depends on whether the athlete uses drugs (again a chance node). You might argue that the university never knows for certain whether the athlete uses drugs, but you must include this information in the tree to get the correct benefits and costs. On the other hand, if no drug testing is performed, there is no intermediate test result node or branch.

Bayes' rule is required because it yields exactly those probabilities that are needed in the decision tree.

Make sure you understand which probabilities are used in the tree. In the lower part, where no testing takes place, the probabilities are the prior probabilities. There is no test information in this case. In the upper part, where the test is performed, the probabilities for the user and nonuser branches are posterior probabilities, given the results of the test. The reason is that by the time you get to these nodes, the results of the test have already been observed. However, the probabilities for the test results are *unconditional* probabilities, the denominators in Bayes' rule. They are not conditional probabilities such as $P(T+|D)$ because you condition only on information to the *left* of any given branch. In other words, by the time you get to the test result branches, you do not yet know whether the athlete is a user.

New Features in PrecisionTree

Discussion of the Solution

Now we analyze the solution. First, we discuss the benefits and costs shown in Figure 6.28. These were chosen fairly arbitrarily, but with some hope of reflecting reality. The largest cost is falsely accusing (and then barring) a nonuser. This is 50 times as large as the cost of the test. The benefit of identifying a drug user is only half this large, and the cost of not identifying a user is 40% as large as barring a nonuser. The violation of the privacy of a nonuser is twice as large as the cost of the test. Based on these values, the decision tree implies that drug testing should *not* be performed (and no athletes should be barred).

258   Chapter 6   Decision Making under Uncertainty

Figure 6.29   Decision Tree for Drug-Testing Example

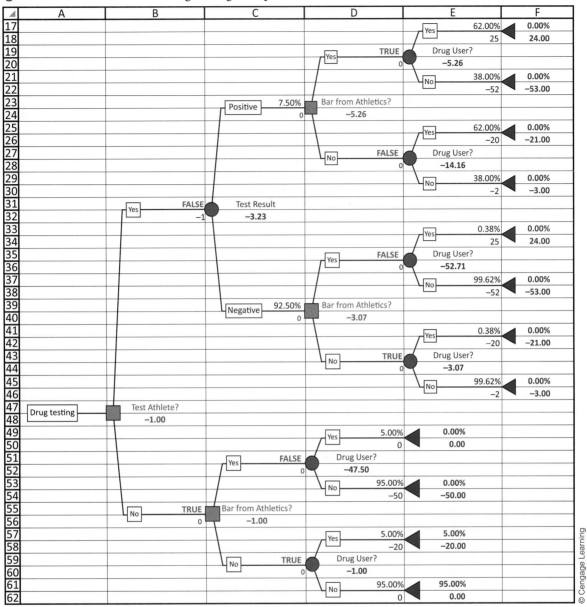

The EMVs for testing and for not testing are both negative, indicating that the costs outweigh the benefits for each, but the EMV for not testing is slightly *less* negative.[6]

Sensitivity Analysis

What would it take to change this decision? We begin with the assumption, probably accepted by most people in our society, that the cost of falsely accusing a nonuser (C_2) is the largest of the benefits and costs in the range B4:B10. In fact, because of possible legal costs, you might argue that C_2 is *more* than 50 times the cost of the test. But if C_2 increases, the scales are tipped even further in the direction of not testing. On the other hand, if the

[6]The university in the Feinstein (1990) study came to the same conclusion.

benefit B from identifying a user and the cost C_3 for not identifying a user increase, testing might become the preferred alternative. We tried this, keeping C_2 constant at 50. When B and C_3 both had value 45, no testing was still optimal, but when they both increased to 50—the same magnitude as C_2—testing won out by a small margin. However, it would be difficult to argue that B and C_3 are of the same magnitude as C_2.

Other than the benefits and costs, the only other input you might vary is the accuracy of the test, measured by the error probabilities in cells B14 and B15. Presumably, if the test makes fewer false positives and false negatives, testing might be a more attractive alternative. We tried this, keeping the benefits and costs the same as those in Figure 6.28 but changing the error probabilities. Even when each error probability was decreased to 0.01, however, the no-testing alternative was still optimal—by a fairly wide margin.

In summary, based on a number of reasonable assumptions and parameter settings, this example has shown that it is difficult to make a case for mandatory drug testing. ∎

6-5a The Value of Information

The drug-testing decision problem represents a typical multistage decision problem. You first decide whether to obtain some information that could be useful—the results of a drug test. If you decide not to obtain the information, you make a decision right away (bar the athlete or don't), based on prior probabilities. If you do decide to obtain the information, you first observe the information and *then* make the final decision, based on posterior probabilities.

The questions we ask now are: How much is the information worth, and if it costs a given amount, should you purchase it? Presumably, information that will help you make your ultimate decision should be worth something, but it might not be clear how much the information is worth. In addition, even if the information is worth something, it might not be worth as much as its actual price. Fortunately, the answers to these questions are embedded in the decision tree itself.

We will find the values of two types of information: sample information and perfect information. **Sample information** is the information from the experiment itself. For example, it is the information from the (less than perfect) drug test. (It has become customary to use the term *sample* information, and we will continue the practice here, but a more precise term would be *imperfect* information.) **Perfect information**, on the other hand, is information from a perfect test—that is, a test that will indicate with certainty which ultimate outcome will occur. In the drug example, this would correspond to a test that never makes mistakes. Admittedly, perfect information is almost never available at any price, but finding its value is still useful because it provides an upper bound on the value of *any* information. For example, if perfect information is valued at $2000, then *no* information can possibly be worth more than $2000.

We will find the **expected value of sample information**, or **EVSI**, and the **expected value of perfect information**, or **EVPI**. They are defined as follows:

The **EVSI** is the most you would be willing to pay for the sample information.

Formula for EVSI
EVSI = EMV with (free) sample information − EMV without information $\qquad$ **(6.4)**

The **EVPI** is the most you would be willing to pay for perfect information.

$$\text{EVPI} = \text{EMV with (free) perfect information} - \text{EMV without information} \qquad \textbf{(6.5)}$$

Information that has no effect on the ultimate decision is worthless.

We first make one important general point about the value of information. Suppose there is an ultimate decision to make. Before making this decision, you can obtain information, supposedly to help you make the ultimate decision. But suppose you make the *same* ultimate decision, regardless of the information you obtain—the same decision you would have made in the absence of information. Can you guess the value of this information? It is zero. The information cannot be worth anything if it never leads to a different decision than you would have made without the information. The moral is that if you plan to pay something for information, you are wasting your money unless this information influences your decision making.

FUNDAMENTAL INSIGHT

The Value of Information

The amount you should be willing to spend for information is the expected increase in EMV you can obtain from having the information. If the actual price of the information is less than or equal to this amount, you should purchase it; otherwise, the information is not worth its price. In addition, information that never affects your decision is worthless, and it should not be purchased at any price. Finally, the value of *any* information can never be greater than the value of perfect information that would eliminate all uncertainty.

We now see how Bayes' rule can be used and the value of information can be evaluated in a typical multistage decision problem.

EXAMPLE 6.4 MARKETING A NEW PRODUCT AT ACME

Acme Company is trying to decide whether to market a new product. As in many new-product situations, there is considerable uncertainty about whether the new product will eventually succeed. Acme believes that it might be wise to introduce the product in a regional test market before introducing it nationally. Therefore, the company's first decision is whether to conduct the test market.

This is clearly an approximation of the real problem. In the real problem, there would be a continuum of possible outcomes, not just three.

Acme estimates that the net cost of the test market is $100,000. We assume this is mostly fixed costs, so that the same cost is incurred regardless of the test-market results. If Acme decides to conduct the test market, it must then wait for the results. Based on the results of the test market, it can then decide whether to market the product nationally, in which case it will incur a fixed cost of $7 million. On the other hand, if the original decision is *not* to run a test market, then the final decision—whether to market the product nationally—can be made without further delay. Acme's unit margin, the difference between its selling price and its unit variable cost, is $18. We assume this is relevant only for the national market.

Acme classifies the results in either the test market or the national market as great, fair, or awful. Each of these results in the national market is accompanied by a forecast of total units sold. These sales volumes (in 1000s of units) are 600 (great), 300 (fair), and 90 (awful). In the absence of any test market information, Acme estimates that probabilities of the three national market outcomes are 0.45, 0.35, and 0.20, respectively.

In addition, Acme has the following historical data from products that were introduced into both test markets and national markets.

■ Of the products that eventually did great in the national market, 64% did great in the test market, 26% did fair in the test market, and 10 did awful in the test market.

- Of the products that eventually did fair in the national market, 18% did great in the test market, 57% did fair in the test market, and 25% did awful in the test market.

- Of the products that eventually did awful in the national market, 9% did great in the test market, 48% did fair in the test market, and 43% did awful in the test market.[7]

The company wants to use a decision tree approach to find the best strategy. It also wants to find the expected value of the information provided by the test market.

Objective To develop a decision tree to find the best strategy for Acme, to perform a sensitivity analysis on the results, and to find EVSI and EVPI.

Where Do the Numbers Come From?

The fixed costs of the test market and the national market are probably accurate estimates, based on planned advertising and overhead expenses. The unit margin is just the difference between the anticipated selling price and the known unit cost of the product. The sales volume estimates are clearly approximations to reality, because the sales from any new product would form a continuum of possible values. Here, the company has "discretized" the problem into three possible outcomes for the national market, and it has estimated the sales for each of these discrete outcomes. The conditional probabilities of national-market results given test-market results are probably based on results from previous products that went through test markets and then national markets.

Solution

We begin by discussing the three basic elements of this decision problem: the possible strategies, the possible outcomes and their probabilities, and the value model. The possible strategies are clear. Acme must first decide whether to run a test market. Then it must decide whether to introduce the product nationally. However, it is important to realize that if Acme decides to run a test market, it can base the national market decision on the results of the test market. In this case its final strategy will be a **contingency plan**, where it conducts the test market, then introduces the product nationally if it receives sufficiently positive test-market results but abandons the product if it receives sufficiently negative test-market results. The optimal strategies from many multistage decision problems involve similar contingency plans.

> In a **contingency plan**, later decisions can depend on earlier decisions and information received.

FUNDAMENTAL INSIGHT

Making Sequential Decisions

Whenever you have a chance to make several sequential decisions and you will learn useful information between decision points, the decision you make initially depends on the decisions you plan to make in the future, and these depend on the information you will learn in the meantime. In other words, when you decide what to do initially, you should look ahead to see what your future options will be, and what your decision will be under each option. Such a contingency plan is typically superior to a *myopic* (short-sighted) plan that doesn't take future options into account when making the initial decision.

---

[7]You can question why the company ever marketed products nationally after awful test-market results, but we will assume that, for whatever reason, the company made a few such decisions—and that a few even turned out to be winners.

Regarding the uncertain outcomes and their probabilities, we note that the given prior probabilities of national-market results in the absence of test-market results will be needed in the part of the tree where Acme decides not to run a test market. However, the historical percentages we quoted are really likelihoods of test-market results, given national-market results. For example, one of these is P(Great test market | Great national market) = 0.64. Such probabilities are the opposite of those needed in the tree. This is because the event to the right of the given sign, "great national market," occurs in time *after* the event to the left of the given sign, "great test market." This is a sure sign that Bayes' rule is required.

The required posterior probabilities of national-market results, given test-market results, are calculated directly from Bayes' rule, Equation (6.1). For example, if NG, NF, and NA represent great, fair, and awful national-market results, respectively, and if TG, TF, and TA represent similar events for the test market, than one typical example of a posterior probability calculation is

$$P(NG|TF) = \frac{P(TF|NG)P(NG)}{P(TF|NG)P(NG) + P(TF|NF)P(NF) + P(TF|NA)P(NA)}$$

$$= \frac{0.26(0.45)}{0.26(0.45) + 0.57(0.35) + 0.48(0.20)} = \frac{0.117}{0.4125} = 0.2836$$

This is a reasonable result. In the absence of test market information, the probability of a great national market is 0.45. However, after a test market with only fair results, the probability of a great national market is revised down to 0.2836. The other posterior probabilities are calculated similarly. In addition, the denominator in this calculation, 0.4125, is the unconditional probability of a fair test market. Such test-market probabilities will be needed in the tree.

Finally, the monetary values in the tree are straightforward. There are fixed costs of test marketing or marketing nationally, which are incurred as soon as these go-ahead decisions are made. From that point, if the company markets nationally, it observes the sales volumes and multiplies them by the unit margin to obtain the profits from sales.

Implementing Bayes' Rule

The inputs and Bayes' rule calculations are shown in Figure 6.30. (See file **Acme Marketing Decisions 1.xlsx**.) You perform the Bayes' rule calculations exactly as in the drug example. To calculate the unconditional probabilities for test-market results, the denominators for Bayes' rule from Equation (6.2), enter the formula

=SUMPRODUCT($D$5:$F$5,I5:K5)

in cell E11 and copy it down to cell E13. To calculate the posterior probabilities from Equation (6.1), enter the formula

=I5*D$5/$E11

in cell I11 and copy it to the range I11:K13.

Figure 6.30 Inputs and Bayes' Rule Calculations for Acme Marketing Example

	A	B	C	D	E	F	G	H	I	J	K	L	M	N	O
1	Acme marketing decisions														
2															
3	Inputs			Prior probabilities of national market results				Likelihoods of test market results (along side), given national market results (along top)							
4	Fixed costs ($1000s)			Great	Fair	Awful			Great	Fair	Awful				
5	Test market	100		0.45	0.35	0.20		Great	0.64	0.18	0.09				
6	National market	7000						Fair	0.26	0.57	0.48				
7								Awful	0.10	0.25	0.43				
8	Unit margin	$18													
9				Bayes' rule calculations				Posterior probabilities of national mkt results (along top), given test mkt results (along side)							
10	Possible quantities sold (1000s of units) in national market			Unconditional probabilities of test market results					Great	Fair	Awful				
11	Great	600		Great	0.3690			Great	0.7805	0.1707	0.0488				
12	Fair	300		Fair	0.4125			Fair	0.2836	0.4836	0.2327				
13	Awful	90		Awful	0.2185			Awful	0.2059	0.4005	0.3936				

© Cengage Learning

Developing the Decision Tree Model

The tree is now straightforward to build and label, as shown in Figure 6.31. Note that the fixed costs of test marketing and marketing nationally appear on the decision branches where they occur in time, so that only the selling profits need to be placed on the probability branches. For example, the formula for the selling profit in cell D22 is

=$B$8*$B$11

Pay particular attention to the probabilities on the branches. The top group are the prior probabilities from the range D5:F5. In the bottom group, the probabilities on the left are

Figure 6.31 Decision Tree for Acme Marketing Example

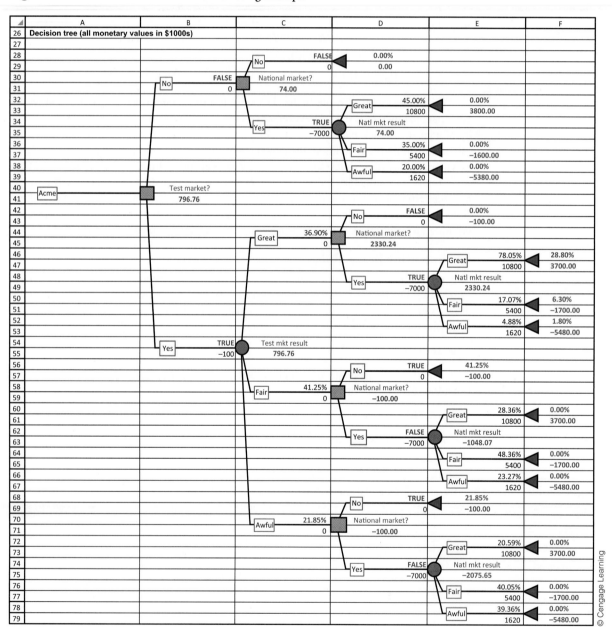

© Cengage Learning

unconditional probabilities of test-market results from the range E11:E13, and those on the right are posterior probabilities of national-market results from the range I11:K13. Again, this corresponds to the standard decision tree convention, where all probabilities on the tree are conditioned on any events that have occurred to the left of them.

Discussion of the Solution

To interpret this tree, note that each value just below each node name is an EMV. (These are colored red or green in Excel.) For example, the 796.76 in cell B30 is the EMV for the entire decision problem. It means that Acme's best EMV from acting optimally is $796,760. As another example, the 74 in cell D24 means that if Acme ever gets to that point—there is no test market and the product is marketed nationally—the EMV is $74,000. Actually, this is the expected selling profit minus the $7 million fixed cost, so the expected selling profit, given that no information from a test market has been obtained, is $7,074,000.

Acme's optimal strategy is apparent by following the TRUE branches from left to right. Acme should first run a test market. If the test-market result is great, the product should be marketed nationally. However, if the test-market result is fair or awful, the product should be abandoned. In these cases the prospects from a national market look bleak, so Acme should cut its losses. (And there *are* losses. In these latter two cases, Acme has already spent $100,000 on the test market and has nothing to show for it.)

Once you have done the work to build the tree, you can reap the benefits of PrecisionTree's tools. For example, its policy suggestion and risk profile outputs are given in Figures 6.32 and 6.33. The policy suggestion shows only the part of the tree corresponding to the optimal strategy. Note that there are two values at each end node. The bottom number is the combined monetary value along this sequence of branches, and the top number is the probability of this sequence of branches. This information leads directly to probability distribution in the risk profile. For this optimal strategy, the only possible monetary outcomes are a gain of $3,700,000 and losses of $100,000, $1,700,000, and $5,480,000. Their respective probabilities are 0.288, 0.631, 0.063, and 0.018. Fortunately, the large possible losses are unlikely enough that the EMV is still positive, $796,760.

Figure 6.32 Policy Suggestion (Optimal Strategy Branches)

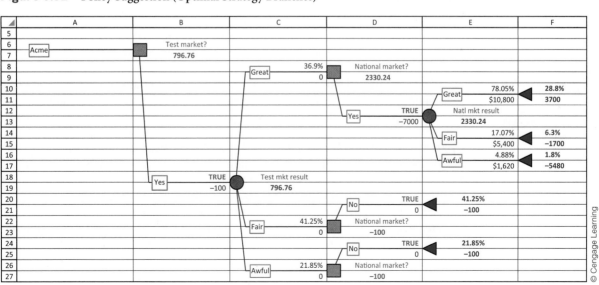

Figure 6.33

Risk Profile of
Optimal Strategy

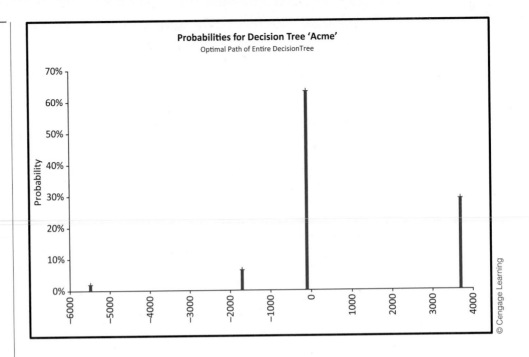

You might argue that the large potential losses and the slightly higher than 70% chance of *some* loss should persuade Acme to abandon the product right away—without a test market. However, this is what "playing the averages" with EMV is all about. Because the EMV of this optimal strategy is greater than 0, the EMV from abandoning the product right away, Acme should go ahead with this optimal strategy if the company is indeed an EMV maximizer. In Section 6-6 we will discuss how this reasoning can change if Acme is a risk-averse decision maker—as it might be with multimillion-dollar losses looming in the future.

Sensitivity Analysis

There are several sensitivity analyses that can be performed on this model. We investigate how things change when the unit margin, currently $18, varies from $8 to $28. This could change the decision about whether to run a test market or to market nationally.

Sensitivity analysis is often important for the insights it provides. It makes you ask, "Why do these results occur?"

We first analyze the overall EMV in cell B30, setting up the sensitivity dialog box as in Figure 6.34. The resulting chart is shown in Figure 6.35. The chart indicates that for small unit margins, it is better *not* to run a test market. The top line, at value 0, corresponds to abandoning the product altogether, whereas the bottom line, at value −100, corresponds to running a test market and then abandoning the product regardless of the results. Similarly, for large unit margins, it is also best not to run a test market. Again, the top line is 100 above the bottom line. However, the reasoning now is different. For large unit margins, the company should market nationally *regardless* of test-market results, so there is no reason to spend money on a test market. Finally, for intermediate unit margins, as in the original model, the chart shows that it is best to run a test market. We hope you agree that this one single chart provides a lot of information and insight.

Figure 6.34

Dialog Box for
Sensitivity Analysis

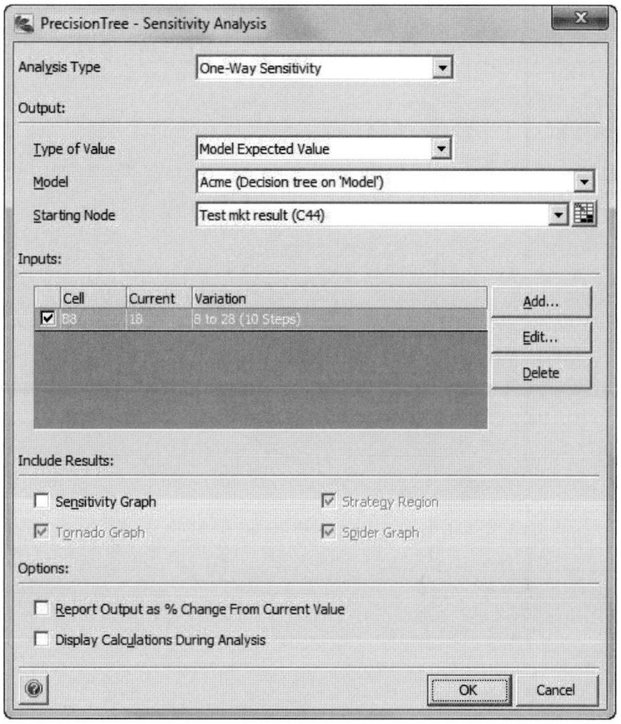

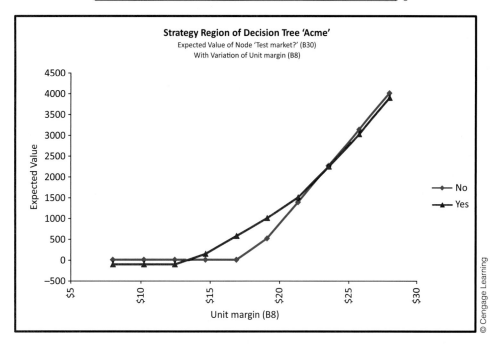

Figure 6.35

Sensitivity Analysis
on Overall Profit

By changing the cell to analyze in Figure 6.34, we can gain additional insight. For example, if no test market is available, the EMV for deciding nationally right away, in cell C20, is relevant. The resulting chart appears in Figure 6.36. Now it is a contest between getting zero profit from abandoning the product and getting a linearly increasing profit from marketing nationally. The breakpoint appears to be slightly below $18. If the unit margin is above this value, Acme should market nationally; otherwise, it should abandon the product.

Figure 6.36

Sensitivity Analysis
for Deciding
Nationally Right
Away

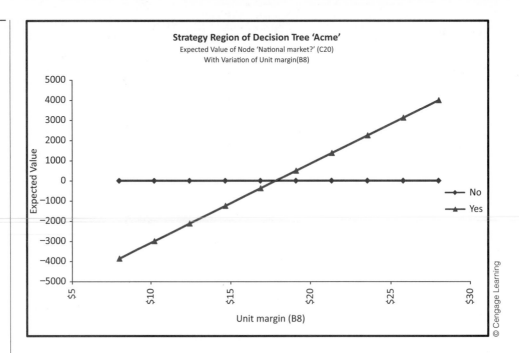

You can also choose to analyze any of the EMVs in cells D34, D48, or D60. Each of these is relevant in the case where the company has run the test market, has observed the test-market results, and is about to decide whether to market nationally. For example, if you choose D60 as the cell to analyze, you obtain the chart in Figure 6.37. It indicates that there are indeed situations—where the unit margin is about $26 or more—when the company should market nationally, even though the test market is awful. In contrast, the chart in Figure 6.38, where we analyze cell D34, indicates the opposite behavior. It shows

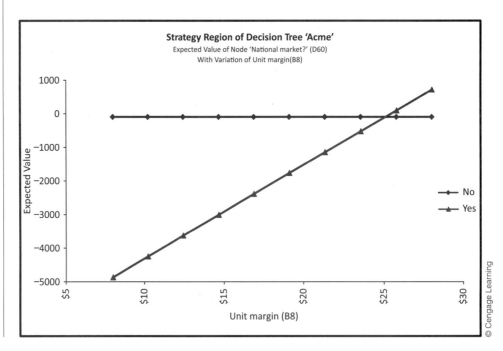

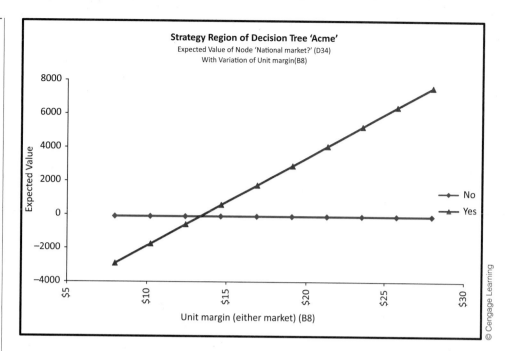

that if the unit margin is low enough—about $13.50 or less—the company should abandon the product nationally, even though the test-market results are great. These are again very useful insights.

Expected Value of Sample Information

The role of the test market in this example is to provide information in the form of more accurate probabilities of national-market results. Information usually costs something, as it does in Acme's problem. Currently, the fixed cost of the test market is $100,000, which is evidently not too much to pay because Acme's best strategy is to run the test market. However, you might ask how much this test market is really worth. This is the expected value of sample information, or EVSI, and it is easy to obtain from the tree. From Figure 6.31, the EMV from test marketing is $796,760, $100,000 of which is the cost of the test market. Therefore, if this test market were free, the expected profit would be $896,760. On the other hand, the EMV from not running a test market is $74,000 (see cell C20 in the tree). From Equation (6.4), the difference is EVSI:

$$\text{EVSI} = \$896,760 - \$74,000 = \$822,760$$

You can check that if you put any value less than 822.76 in the test-market fixed-cost cell (cell B5), the decision to test-market will continue to be best.

Intuitively, running the test market is worth something because it changes the optimal decision. With no test-market information, the best decision is to market nationally. (See the top part of the tree in Figure 6.31.) However, with the test-market information, the ultimate decision depends on the test-market results. Specifically, Acme should market nationally only if the test-market result is great. This is what makes information worth something—its outcome affects the optimal decision.

Expected Value of Perfect Information

It took a lot of work to find EVSI. You had to assess various conditional probabilities, use Bayes' rule, and then build a fairly complex decision tree. In general, Acme might have many sources of information it could obtain that would help it make its national decision; the test market is just one of them. The question, then, is how much such information *could* be worth. This is answered by EVPI, the expected value of perfect information. It provides an upper bound on how much *any* information could be worth, and it is relatively easy to calculate.

Imagine that Acme could purchase an envelope that has the true national-market result—great, fair, or awful—written inside. Once opened, this envelope would remove all uncertainty, and Acme could make an easy decision. (The whole point is that Acme can open the envelope *before* having to make the national decision.) EVPI is what this envelope is worth. To calculate it, you build the tree in Figure 6.39. The key here is that the nodes are reversed in time. You first open the envelope to discover what is inside. This corresponds to the chance node. Then you make the final decision. Given the cost parameters, it is easy to see that Acme should market nationally only if the contents of the envelope reveal that the national market will be great. Otherwise, Acme should abandon the product right away.

This perfect information envelope is obviously a fiction, but it helps to explain how perfect information works.

Figure 6.39

Decision Tree for Evaluating EVPI

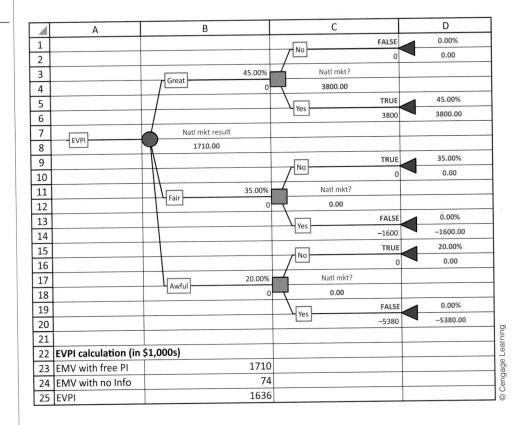

The EVPI calculation is now straightforward. If the envelope (perfect information) is free, the tree in Figure 6.39 indicates that the EMV is $1,710,000. If there is no information, the EMV is $74,000 (cell C31 of Figure 6.31). Therefore, from Equation (6.5),

$$\text{EVPI} = \$1{,}710{,}000 - \$74{,}000 = \$1{,}636{,}000$$

No sample information, test market or otherwise, could possibly be worth more than this. So if some hotshot market analyst offers to provide "extremely reliable" market information to Acme for, say, $1.8 million, Acme knows this information cannot be worth its cost. ∎

PROBLEMS

Level A

24. In deciding whether to perform mandatory drug testing, we claimed that it is difficult to justify such testing under reasonable conditions. Check this yourself in the following questions.

   a. Drug testing ought to be more attractive if the test is more reliable. Keeping the costs the same as in the example, use PrecisionTree's two-way sensitivity tool to see whether the optimal decision (test or not test) changes as the probability of a false positive and the probability of a false negative both change. You can let them vary through some reasonable ranges. Explain the results.

   b. Repeat part **a**, but first double the two monetary values that make the test more attractive: the benefit of identifying a user and the cost of not identifying a user. How do your results differ from those in part **a**?

   c. In this part, keep the probabilities of false positives and false negatives the same, but let the benefits and costs vary. Specifically, let the benefit of identifying a user and the cost of not identifying a user be of the form $25a$ and $20a$, where a is some factor that you can vary. Similarly, let the cost of barring a nonuser and the cost of violating privacy be of the form $50b$ and $2b$. The cost of the test is still 1. (The idea is that large values of a and/or small values of b will make the testing more attractive.) Use PrecisionTree's two-way sensitivity tool to see whether the optimal decision (test or not test) changes for a reasonable range of values of a and b. Discuss your results.

25. In the drug testing decision, find and interpret EVSI and EVPI. Here, "sample" information refers to the information from the imperfect drug test, whereas "perfect" information refers to completely reliable information on whether the athlete uses drugs.

26. Explain in general why EVSI is the same, regardless of the actual cost of the information. For example, in the Acme problem EVSI is the same regardless of whether the actual cost of the test market is $100,000, $200,000, or any other value. Then explain how EVSI, together with the actual cost of the information, leads to the decision about whether to purchase the information.

27. Following up on the previous problem, the *expected net gain from information* is defined as the expected amount gained by having access to the information, at its given cost, as opposed to not having access to the information. Explain how you would calculate this in general. What is its value for the Acme problem?

28. Prior probabilities are often educated guesses at best, so it is worth performing a sensitivity analysis on their values. However, you must make sure that they are varied so that all probabilities are nonnegative and sum to 1. For the Acme problem, perform the following sensitivity analyses on the three prior probabilities and comment on the results.

   a. Vary the probability of a great national market in a one-way sensitivity analysis from 0 to 0.6 in increments of 0.1. Do this in such a way that the probabilities of the two other outcomes, fair and awful, stay in the same ratio as they are currently, 7 to 4.

   b. Vary the probabilities of a great and a fair national market independently in a two-way sensitivity analysis. You can choose the ranges over which these vary, but you must ensure that the three prior probabilities continue to be nonnegative and sum to 1. (For example, you can't choose ranges where the probabilities of great and fair are 0.6 and 0.5.)

29. In the Acme problem, perform a sensitivity analysis on the quantity sold from a great national market (the value in cell B11). Let this value vary over a range of values *greater than* the current value of 600, so that a great national market is even more attractive than before. Does this ever change the optimal strategy? If so, in what way?

30. Using trial and error on the prior probabilities in the Acme problem, find values of them that make EVSI equal to 0. These are values where Acme will make the same decision, regardless of the test-market results it observes. Comment on why the test market is worthless for your particular prior probabilities.

Level B

31. We related EVPI to the value of an envelope that contains the true ultimate outcome. This concept can be extended to "less than perfect" information. For example, in the Acme problem suppose that the company could purchase information that would indicate, with certainty, that one of the following two outcomes will occur: (1) the national market will be great, or (2) the national market will not be great. Note that outcome (2) doesn't say whether the national market will be fair or awful; it just says that it won't be great. How much should Acme be willing to pay for such information?

32. The concept behind EVPI is that you purchase perfect information (the envelope), then open the envelope to see which outcome occurs, and then make an easy decision. You do *not*, however, get to choose what information the envelope contains. In contrast, sometimes a company can pay, not to obtain information, but to influence the outcome. Consider the following version of the Acme problem. There is no possibility of a test market, so Acme must decide right away whether to market nationally. However, suppose Acme can pay to change the probabilities of the national market outcomes from their current values, 0.45, 0.35, and 0.20, to the new values p, $(7/11)(1 - p)$, and $(4/11)(1 - p)$, for some p. (In this way, the probabilities of fair and awful stay in the same ratio as before, 7 to 4, but by making p large, the probability of a great outcome increases.)

a. How much should Acme be willing to pay for the change if $p = 0.6$? If $p = 0.8$? If $p = 0.95$?

b. Are these types of changes realistic? Answer by speculating on the types of actions Acme might be able to take to make the probability of a great national market higher. Do you think such actions would cost more or less than what Acme should be willing to pay for them (from part **a**)?

6-6 RISK AVERSION AND EXPECTED UTILITY

Rational decision makers are sometimes willing to violate the EMV maximization criterion when large amounts of money are at stake. These decision makers are willing to sacrifice some EMV to reduce risk. Are you ever willing to do so personally? Consider the following scenarios.

- You have a chance to enter a lottery where you will win $100,000 with probability 0.1 or win nothing with probability 0.9. Alternatively, you can receive $5000 for certain. How many of you—truthfully—would take the certain $5000, even though the EMV of the lottery is $10,000? Or change the $100,000 to $1,000,000 and the $5000 to $50,000 and ask yourself whether you'd prefer the sure $50,000.

- You can buy collision insurance on your expensive new car or not buy it. The insurance costs a certain premium and carries some deductible provision. If you decide to pay the premium, then you are essentially paying a certain amount to avoid a gamble: the possibility of wrecking your car and not having it insured. You can be sure that the premium is greater than the expected cost of damage; otherwise, the insurance company would not stay in business. Therefore, from an EMV standpoint you should not purchase the insurance. But how many of you drive without this type of insurance?

These examples, the second of which is certainly realistic, illustrate situations where rational people do not behave as EMV maximizers. Then how do they act? This question has been studied extensively by many researchers, both mathematically and behaviorally. Although there is still not perfect agreement, most researchers believe that if certain basic behavioral assumptions hold, people are **expected utility** maximizers—that is, they choose the alternative with the largest expected utility. Although we will not go deeply into the subject of expected utility maximization, the discussion in this section presents the main ideas.

FUNDAMENTAL INSIGHT

Risk Aversion

When large amounts of money are at stake, most of us are risk averse, at least to some extent. We are willing to sacrifice some EMV to avoid risk. The exact way this is done, using utility functions and expected utility, can be difficult to implement in real situations, but the idea is simple. If you are an EMV maximizer, you are indifferent between a gamble with a given EMV and a sure dollar amount equal to the EMV of the gamble. However, if you are risk averse, you prefer the sure dollar amount to the gamble. That is, you are willing to accept a sure dollar amount that is somewhat *less than* the EMV of the gamble, just to avoid risk. The more EMV you are willing to give up, the more risk averse you are.

6-6a Utility Functions

We begin by discussing an individual's **utility function**. This is a mathematical function that transforms monetary values—payoffs and costs—into *utility values*. Essentially, an individual's utility function specifies the individual's preferences for various monetary payoffs and costs and, in doing so, it automatically encodes the individual's attitudes toward risk. Most individuals are *risk averse*, which means intuitively that they are willing to sacrifice some EMV to avoid risky gambles. In terms of the utility function, this means that every extra dollar of payoff is worth slightly less to the individual than the previous dollar, and every extra dollar of cost is considered slightly more costly (in terms of utility) than the previous dollar. The resulting utility functions are shaped as shown in Figure 6.40. Mathematically, these functions are said to be *increasing* and *concave*. The increasing part means that they go uphill—everyone prefers more money to less money. The concave part means that they increase at a decreasing rate. This is the risk-averse behavior.

Figure 6.40

Risk-Averse Utility Function

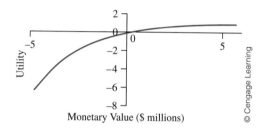

There are two aspects of implementing utility maximization in a real decision analysis. First, an individual's (or company's) utility function must be assessed. This is a time-consuming task that typically involves many trade-offs. It is usually carried out by experts in the field, and we do not discuss the details of the process here. Second, the resulting utility function is used to find the best decision. This second step is relatively straightforward. You substitute utility values for monetary values in the decision tree and then fold back as usual. That is, you calculate expected *utilities* at chance branches and take maximums (of expected *utilities*) at decision branches. We will look at a numerical example later in this section.

6-6b Exponential Utility

As we have indicated, utility assessment is tedious. Even in the best of circumstances, when a trained consultant attempts to assess the utility function of a single person, the process requires the person to make a series of choices between hypothetical alternatives involving uncertain outcomes. Unless the person has some training in probability, these choices will probably be difficult to understand, let alone make, and it is unlikely that the person will answer *consistently* as the questioning proceeds. The process is even more difficult when a *company's* utility function is being assessed. Because different company executives typically have different attitudes toward risk, it can be difficult for these people to reach a consensus on a common utility function.

For these reasons, classes of ready-made utility functions have been developed. One important class is called **exponential utility** and has been used in many financial investment decisions. An exponential utility function has only one adjustable numerical parameter, called the **risk tolerance**, and there are straightforward ways to discover an appropriate value of this parameter for a particular individual or company. So the advantage of using an exponential utility function is that it is relatively easy to assess. The drawback is that exponential utility functions do not capture all types of attitudes toward risk. Nevertheless, their ease of use has made them popular.

An exponential utility function has the following form:

Exponential Utility

$$U(x) = 1 - e^{-x/R} \qquad \text{(6.6)}$$

Here x is a monetary value (a payoff if positive, a cost if negative), $U(x)$ is the utility of this value, and $R > 0$ is the risk tolerance. As the name suggests, the risk tolerance measures how much risk the decision maker will accept. The larger the value of R, the *less* risk averse the decision maker is. That is, a person with a large value of R is more willing to take risks than a person with a small value of R. In the limit, a person with an extremely large value of R is an EMV maximizer.

The **risk tolerance** for an exponential utility function is a single number that specifies an individual's aversion to risk. The higher the risk tolerance, the less risk averse the individual is.

To assess a person's (or company's) exponential utility function, only one number, the value of R, needs to be assessed. There are a couple of tips for doing this. First, it has been shown that the risk tolerance is approximately equal to that dollar amount R such that the decision maker is indifferent between the following two options:

- Option 1: Obtain no payoff at all.
- Option 2: Obtain a payoff of R dollars or a loss of $R/2$ dollars, depending on the flip of a fair coin.

For example, if you are indifferent between a bet where you win \$1000 or lose \$500, with probability 0.5 each, and not betting at all, your R is approximately \$1000. From this criterion it certainly makes intuitive sense that a wealthier person (or company) ought to have a larger value of R. This has been found in practice.

Finding the appropriate risk tolerance value for any company or individual is not necessarily easy, but it is easier than assessing an entire utility function.

A second tip for finding R is based on empirical evidence found by Ronald Howard, a prominent decision analyst. Through his consulting experience with large companies, he discovered tentative relationships between risk tolerance and several financial variables: net sales, net income, and equity. [See Howard (1988).] Specifically, he found that R was approximately 6.4% of net sales, 124% of net income, and 15.7% of equity for the companies he studied. For example, according to this prescription, a company with net sales of \$30 million should have a risk tolerance of approximately \$1.92 million. Howard admits that these percentages are only guidelines. However, they do indicate that larger and more profitable companies tend to have larger values of R, which means that they are more willing to take risks involving large dollar amounts.

We illustrate the use of the expected utility criterion, and exponential utility in particular, in Example 6.5.

6.5 DECIDING WHETHER TO ENTER RISKY VENTURES

$\mathbf{V}$enture Limited is a company with net sales of \$30 million. The company currently must decide whether to enter one of two risky ventures or invest in a sure thing. The gain from the latter is a sure \$125,000. The possible outcomes for the less risky venture are a \$0.5 million loss, a \$0.1 million gain, and a \$1 million gain. The probabilities of these outcomes are 0.25, 0.50, and 0.25, respectively. The possible outcomes of the more risky venture are a \$1 million loss, a \$1 million gain, and a \$3 million gain. The probabilities of these outcomes are 0.35, 0.60, and 0.05, respectively. If Venture Limited must decide on exactly one of these alternatives, what should it do?

Objective To see how the company's risk averseness, determined by its risk tolerance in an exponential utility function, affects its decision.

Where Do the Numbers Come From?

The outcomes for each of the risky alternatives probably form a continuum of possible values. However, as in Example 6.4, the company has classified these into a few possibilities and made intelligent estimates of the monetary consequences and probabilities of these discrete possibilities.

Solution

Don't worry about the actual utility values (for example, whether they are positive or negative). Only the relative magnitudes matter in terms of decision making.

We assume that Venture Limited has an exponential utility function. Also, based on Howard's guidelines, we assume that the company's risk tolerance is 6.4% of its net sales, or \$1.92 million. (A sensitivity analysis on this parameter will be performed later on.) You can substitute into Equation (6.6) to find the utility of any monetary outcome. For example, the gain from the riskless alternative (in \$1000s) is 125, and its utility is

$$U(125) = 1 - e^{-125/1920} = 1 - 0.9370 = 0.0630$$

As another example, the utility of a \$1 million loss is

$$U(-1000) = 1 - e^{-(-1000)/1920} = 1 - 1.6834 = -0.6834$$

These are the values we use (instead of monetary values) in the decision tree.

Developing the Decision Tree Model

Fortunately, PrecisionTree takes care of the details. After building a decision tree and labeling it (with monetary values) in the usual way, select Model Settings from the PrecisionTree Settings dropdown list to open the dialog box shown in Figure 6.41. Then fill in the information under the Utility Function tab as shown in the figure. This says to use an exponential utility function with risk tolerance 1920, the value in cell B5. (As indicated in the spreadsheet, all monetary values are measured in \$1000s.) It also indicates that expected utilities (as opposed to EMVs) should appear in the decision tree.

The tree is built and labeled (with monetary values) exactly as before. PrecisionTree then takes care of calculating the expected utilities.

The completed tree for this example is shown in Figure 6.42. (See the file **Using Exponential Utility.xlsx**.) You build it in exactly the same way as usual and link probabilities and monetary values to its branches in the usual way. For example, there is a link in cell C22 to the monetary value in cell B12. However, the expected values shown in the tree (those shown in color on a computer screen) are expected *utilities*, and the optimal decision is the one with the largest expected utility. In this case the expected utilities for the

Figure 6.41

Dialog Box for Specifying the Exponential Utility Criterion

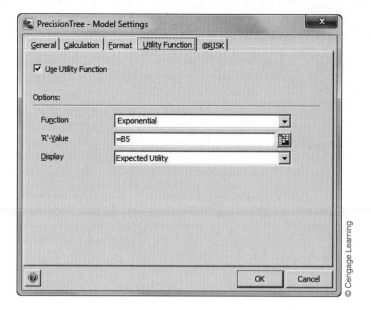

Figure 6.42

Decision Tree for Risky Venture Example

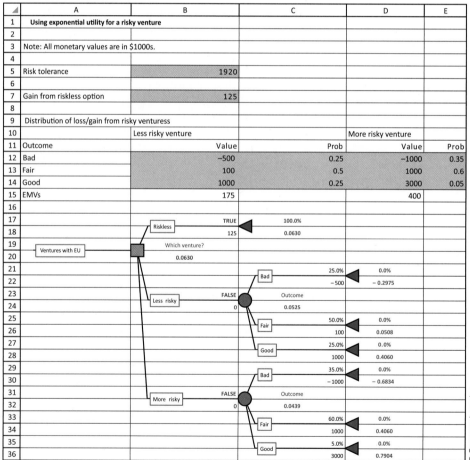

riskless option, investing in the lessrisky venture, and investing in the more risky venture are 0.0630, 0.0525, and 0.0439, respectively. Therefore, the optimal decision is to take the riskless option.

Discussion of the Solution

A risk-averse decision maker typically gives up EMV to avoid risk—when the stakes are large enough.

As indicated in the tree, the riskless option is best in terms of the expected utility criterion; it has the largest expected utility. However, note that the EMVs of the three decisions are $125,000, $175,000, and $400,000. (The latter two of these are calculated in row 15 as the usual SUMPRODUCT of monetary values and probabilities.) So from an EMV point of view, the more risky venture is definitely best. In fact, the ordering of the three alternatives using the EMV criterion is exactly the *opposite* of the ordering using expected utility. But because Venture Limited is sufficiently risk averse and the monetary values are sufficiently large, the company is willing to sacrifice $275,000 of EMV to avoid risk.

Sensitivity Analysis

How sensitive is the optimal decision to the key parameter, the risk tolerance? You can answer this by changing the risk tolerance and watching how the decision tree changes. You can check that when the company becomes *more* risk tolerant, the more risky venture eventually becomes optimal. In fact, this occurs when the risk tolerance increases to approximately $2.210 million. In the other direction, of course, when the company becomes *less* risk tolerant, the riskless decision continues to be optimal. (The "middle" decision, the less risky alternative, is evidently not optimal for *any* value of the risk tolerance.) The bottom line is that the decision considered optimal depends entirely on the attitudes toward risk of Venture Limited's top management. ∎

6-6c Certainty Equivalents

Now let's change the problem slightly so that Venture Limited has only two options. It can either enter the less risky venture or receive a *certain* dollar amount x and avoid the gamble altogether. We want to find the dollar amount x so that the company is indifferent between these two options. If it less enters the less risky venture, its expected utility is 0.0525, calculated earlier. If it receives x dollars for certain, its utility is

$$U(x) = 1 - e^{-x/1920}$$

To find the value x where the company is indifferent between the two options, set $1 - e^{-x/1920}$ equal to 0.0525, or $e^{-x/1920} = 0.9475$, and solve for x. Taking natural logarithms of both sides and multiplying by 1920, the result is

$$x = -1920 \ln(0.9475) = 104$$

(Because of the unit of measure, this is really $104,000.) This value is called the **certainty equivalent** of the risky venture. The company is indifferent between entering the less risky venture and receiving $104,000 for sure to avoid it. Although the EMV of the less risky venture is $175,000, the company acts as if it is equivalent to a sure $104,000. In this sense, the company is willing to give up the difference in EMV, $71,000, to avoid the gamble.

By a similar calculation, the certainty equivalent of the more risky venture is approximately $86,000. That is, the company acts as if this more risky venture is equivalent to a sure $86,000, when in fact its EMV is a hefty $400,000. In this case, the company is willing to give up the difference in EMV, $314,000, to avoid this particular gamble. Again, the reason is that the company wants to avoid risk. You can see these certainty equivalents in PrecisionTree by changing the Display box in Figure 6.41 to show Certainty Equivalent. The resulting tree is shown in Figure 6.43. The certainty equivalents we just discussed appear in cells C24 and C32. (Note that we rounded the values in the text to the nearest $1000. The values in the figure are more exact.)

Figure 6.43   Certainty Equivalents in Tree

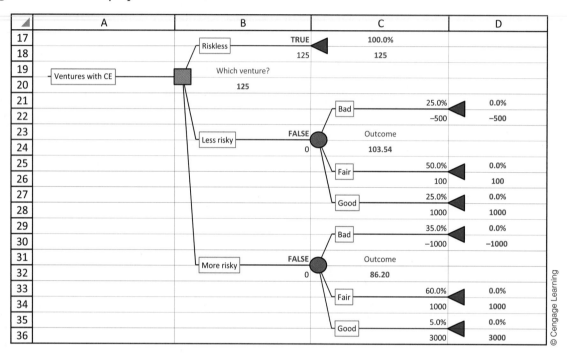

© Cengage Learning

6.4 MARKETING A NEW PRODUCT AT ACME (CONTINUED)

Before concluding this section, we take a last look at the Acme marketing decision from the previous section. Suppose Acme decides to use expected utility as its criterion with an exponential utility function? Is the EMV-maximizing decision still optimal? Remember that this strategy first performed the test market and then marketed nationally only if the test-market results were great.

Objective   To see how risk aversion affects Acme's strategy.

Solution

There is very little work to do. You first enter a risk tolerance value in a blank cell. Then, starting with the tree from Figure 6.31, fill out the dialog box in Figure 6.41, with a link to the risk tolerance cell. (See the finished version of the file **Acme Marketing Decisions 2.xlsx** for the details.) It is then interesting to perform a sensitivity analysis on the risk tolerance. We tried this, letting the risk tolerance vary from 1000 to 10,000 (remember that these are in thousands of dollars) and seeing whether the decision to run a test market changes. The results appear in Figure 6.44.

Figure 6.44   Sensitivity to Risk Tolerance for Acme Decision

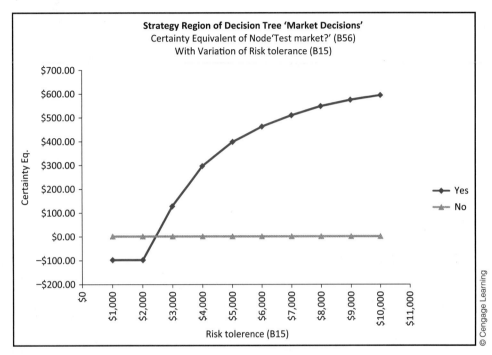

Do you understand why it is better to run the test market only if the risk tolerance is sufficiently large? It is not really because of the cost of the test market. When the risk tolerance is small, the company is so risk averse that it never markets nationally—on *any* of the "National market?" decision nodes. So information from the test market is worthless. However, as *R* increases, the company becomes less risk averse and in some scenarios, its best decision is to market nationally. In these cases, the information from the test market can be worth its price. (If you don't follow this reasoning, open the finished version of the file, try large and small values of the risk tolerance, and see how the TRUE and FALSE values on the decision tree change.) ■

6-6d Is Expected Utility Maximization Used?

The previous discussion indicates that expected utility maximization is a fairly involved task. The question, then, is whether the effort is justified. Theoretically, expected utility maximization might be interesting to researchers, but is it really used in the business world? The answer appears to be: not very often. For example, one article on the practice of decision making [see Kirkwood (1992)] quotes Ronald Howard—the same person we quoted previously—as having found risk aversion to be of practical concern in only 5% to 10% of business decision analyses. This same article quotes the president of a Fortune 500 company as saying, "Most of the decisions we analyze are for a few million dollars. It is adequate to use expected value (EMV) for these."

PROBLEMS

Level A

33. For the risky venture example, create a line chart that includes three series—that is, three lines (or curves). Each line should show the expected utility of a particular decision for a sequence of possible risk tolerance values. This chart should make it clear when the more risky option becomes optimal and whether the less risky option is ever optimal.

34. In the risky venture example, the more risky alternative, in spite of its dominating EMV, is not preferred by a decision maker with a risk tolerance of $1.92 million. Now suppose everything stays the same except for the best monetary outcome of the more risky alternative (the value in cell D14). How much larger must this value be for the decision maker to prefer the more risky alternative? What is the corresponding EMV at that point?

35. In the risky venture example, suppose there is no riskless alternative; the only two possible decisions are the less risky venture and the more risky venture. Explore which of these is the preferred alternative for a range of risk tolerances. Can you find a cutoff point for the risk tolerance such that the less risky venture is preferred for risk tolerances below the cutoff and the more risky venture is preferred otherwise?

Level B

36. Do the absolute magnitudes of the monetary outcomes matter in the risky venture example? Consider the following two possibilities. In each case, multiply all monetary values in the example by a factor of A. (For example, double them if A = 2.) For each part, briefly explain your findings.

a. Currently, an EMV maximizer would choose the most risky venture. Would this continue to be the case for any factor A?

b. Currently, an expected utility maximizer with a risk tolerance of $1.92 million prefers the riskless alternative. Would this continue to be the case for any factor A greater than 1? What about when A is less than 1? You can answer by using trial and error on A.

c. Referring to the dialog box in Figure 6.41, there is a Display dropdown list with three options: expected value (EMV), expected utility, and certainty equivalent. The latter is defined for any gamble as the sure monetary amount a risk-averse person would take as a trade for the risky gamble. For example, you can check that the certainty equivalent for the more risky alternative is 86.2017 (in thousands of dollars). Explain what this really means by calculating the utility of 86.2017 manually and comparing it to the *expected* utility from the more risky venture (as shown on the tree). How does this explain why the decision maker prefers the riskless alternative to the more risky venture?

6-7 CONCLUSION

In this chapter we have discussed methods that can be used in decision-making problems where uncertainty is a key element. Perhaps the most important skill you can gain from this chapter is the ability to approach decision problems with uncertainty in a systematic manner. This systematic approach requires you to list all possible decisions or strategies, list all possible uncertain outcomes, assess the probabilities of these outcomes (possibly with the aid of Bayes' rule), calculate all necessary monetary values, and finally do the necessary calculations to obtain the best decision. If large dollar amounts are at stake, you might also need to perform a utility analysis, where the decision maker's attitudes toward risk are taken into account. Once the basic analysis has been completed, using best guesses for the various parameters of the problem, you should perform a sensitivity analysis to see whether the best decision continues to be best within a range of input parameters.

Summary of Key Terms

Term	Explanation	Excel	Page	Equation
Payoff (or cost) table	A table that lists the payoffs (or costs) for all combinations of decisions and uncertain outcomes		225	
Maximin criterion	The pessimist's criterion; find the worst possible payoff for each decision, and choose the decision with the best of these		226	
Maximax criterion	The optimist's criterion; find the best possible payoff for each decision, and choose the decision with the best of these		227	
Expected monetary value (EMV)	The weighted average of the possible payoffs from a decision, weighted by their probabilities		227	
EMV criterion	Choose the decision with the maximum EMV		227	
Decision tree	A graphical device for illustrating all of the aspects of the decision problem and for finding the optimal decision (or decision strategy)		229	
Folding-back procedure	Calculation method for decision tree; starting at the right, take EMVs at chance nodes, maximums of EMVs at decision nodes		231	
Risk profile	Chart that represents the probability distribution of monetary outcomes for any decision		231	
PrecisionTree	Useful Excel add-in developed by Palisade for building and analyzing decision trees in Excel	Has its own ribbon	239	
PrecisionTree strategy region chart	Useful for seeing how the optimal decision changes as selected inputs vary	Use PrecisionTree Sensitivity Analysis button	248	
PrecisionTree tornado and spider charts	Useful for seeing which inputs affect a selected EMV the most	Use PrecisionTree Sensitivity Analysis button	248–49	
Bayes' rule	Formula for updating probabilities as new information becomes available; *prior probabilities* are transformed into *posterior probabilities*		252	6.1
Law of total probability	The denominator in Bayes' rule, for calculating the (unconditional) probability of an information outcome		252	6.2
Expected value of sample information (EVSI)	The most the (imperfect) *sample information* (such as the results of a test market) would be worth		260	6.4

(continued)

Summary of Key Terms (*Continued*)

Term	Explanation	Excel	Page	Equation
Expected value of perfect information (EVPI)	The most *perfect information* on some uncertain outcome would be worth; represents an upper bound on *any* EVSI		260	6.5
Contingency plan	A decision strategy where later decisions depend on earlier decisions and outcomes observed in the meantime		262	
Utility function	A mathematical function that encodes an individual's (or company's) attitudes toward risk		273	
Exponential utility function, risk tolerance	A popular class of utility functions, where only a single parameter, the risk tolerance, has to be specified		273–74	6.6
Certainty equivalent	The sure dollar value equivalent to the expected utility of a gamble		277	
Expected utility maximization	Choosing the decision that maximizes the expected utility; typically sacrifices EMV to avoid risk when large monetary amounts are at stake		279	

PROBLEMS

Conceptual Questions

C.1. Your company needs to make an important decision that involves large monetary consequences. You have listed all of the possible outcomes and the monetary payoffs and costs from all outcomes and all potential decisions. You want to use the EMV criterion, but you realize that this requires probabilities and you see no way to find the required probabilities. What can you do?

C.2. If your company makes a particular decision in the face of uncertainty, you estimate that it will either gain $10,000, gain $1000, or lose $5000, with probabilities 0.40, 0.30, and 0.30, respectively. You (correctly) calculate the EMV as $2800. However, you distrust the use of this EMV for decision-making purposes. After all, you reason that you will never receive $2800; you will receive $10,000, $1000, or lose $5000. Is this reasoning justified?

C.3. In the previous question, suppose you have the option of receiving a check for $2700 instead of making the risky decision described. Would you make the risky decision, where you *could* lose $5000, or would you take the sure $2700? What would influence your decision?

C.4. In a classic oil-drilling example, you are trying to decide whether to drill for oil on a field that might or might not contain any oil. Before making this decision, you have the option of hiring a geologist to perform some seismic tests and then predict whether there is any oil or not. You assess that if there is actually oil, the geologist will predict there is oil with probability 0.85. You also assess that if there is no oil, the geologist will predict there is no oil with probability 0.90. Why will these two probabilities *not* appear on the decision tree? Which probabilities *will* be on the decision tree?

C.5. Your company has signed a contract with a good customer to ship the customer an order no later than 20 days from now. The contract indicates that the customer will accept the order even if it is late, but instead of paying the full price of $10,000, it will be allowed to pay 10% less, $9000, due to lateness. You estimate that it will take anywhere from 17 to 22 days to ship the order, and each of these is equally likely. You believe you are in good shape, reasoning that the expected days to ship is the average of 17 through 22, or 19.5 days. Because this is less than 20, you will get your full $10,000. What is wrong with your reasoning?

C.6. You must make one of two decisions, each with possible gains and possible losses. One of these decisions is much riskier than the other, having much larger possible gains but also much larger possible losses, and it has a larger EMV than the safer decision. Because you are risk averse and the monetary values are large relative to your wealth, you base your decision on expected utility, and it indicates that you should make the safer decision. It also indicates that the certainty equivalent for the risky decision is $210,000, whereas its EMV is $540,000. What do these two numbers mean? What do you know about the certainty equivalent of the safer decision?

C.7. A potentially huge hurricane is forming in the Caribbean, and there is some chance that it might make a direct hit on Hilton Head Island, South Carolina, where you are in charge of emergency preparedness. You have made plans for evacuating everyone from the island, but such an evacuation is obviously costly and upsetting for all involved, so the decision to evacuate shouldn't be made lightly. Discuss how you would make such a decision. Is EMV a relevant concept in this situation? How would you evaluate the consequences of uncertain outcomes?

C.8. It seems obvious that if you can purchase information before making an ultimate decision, this information should generally be worth something, but explain exactly why (and when) it is sometimes worth nothing.

C.9. Insurance companies wouldn't exist unless customers were willing to pay the price of the insurance and the insurance companies were making a profit. So explain how insurance is a win-win proposition for customers and the company.

C.10. You often hear about the trade-off between risk and reward. Is this trade-off part of decision making under uncertainty when the decision maker uses the EMV criterion? For example, how does this work in investment decisions?

C.11. Can you ever use the material in this chapter to help you make your own real-life decisions? Consider the following. You are about to take an important and difficult exam in one of your MBA courses, and you see an opportunity to cheat. Obviously, from an ethical point of view, you shouldn't cheat, but from a purely monetary point of view, could it also be the wrong decision? To model this, consider the long-term monetary consequences of all possible outcomes.

Level A

37. SweetTooth Candy Company knows it will need 10 tons of sugar six months from now to implement its production plans. Jean Dobson, SweetTooth's purchasing manager, has essentially two options for acquiring the needed sugar. She can either buy the sugar at the going market price when she needs it, six months from now, or she can buy a futures contract now. The contract guarantees delivery of the sugar in six months

but the cost of purchasing it will be based on today's market price. Assume that possible sugar futures contracts available for purchase are for five tons or ten tons only. No futures contracts can be purchased or sold in the intervening months. Thus, SweetTooth's possible decisions are to (1) purchase a futures contract for ten tons of sugar now, (2) purchase a futures contract for five tons of sugar now and purchase five tons of sugar in six months, or (3) purchase all ten tons of needed sugar in six months. The price of sugar bought now for delivery in six months is $0.0851 per pound. The transaction costs for five-ton and ten-ton futures contracts are $65 and $110, respectively. Finally, Ms. Dobson has assessed the probability distribution for the possible prices of sugar six months from now (in dollars per pound). The file **P06_37.xlsx** contains these possible prices and their corresponding probabilities.

  a. Given that SweetTooth wants to acquire the needed sugar in the least costly way, create a cost table that specifies the cost (in dollars) associated with each possible decision and possible sugar price in the future.

  b. Use PrecisionTree to identify the decision that minimizes SweetTooth's expected cost of meeting its sugar demand.

  c. Perform a sensitivity analysis on the optimal decision, letting each of the three currency inputs vary one at a time plus or minus 25% from its base value, and summarize your findings. In response to which of these inputs is the expected cost value most sensitive?

38. Carlisle Tire and Rubber, Inc., is considering expanding production to meet potential increases in the demand for one of its tire products. Carlisle's alternatives are to construct a new plant, expand the existing plant, or do nothing in the short run. The market for this particular tire product may expand, remain stable, or contract. Carlisle's marketing department estimates the probabilities of these market outcomes as 0.25, 0.35, and 0.40, respectively. The file **P06_38.xlsx** contains Carlisle's estimated payoff (in dollars) table.

  a. Use PrecisionTree to identify the strategy that maximizes this tire manufacturer's expected profit.

  b. Perform a sensitivity analysis on the optimal decision, letting each of the monetary inputs vary one at a time plus or minus 10% from its base value, and summarize your findings. In response to which monetary inputs is the expected profit value most sensitive?

39. A local energy provider offers a landowner $180,000 for the exploration rights to natural gas on a certain site and the option for future development. This option, if exercised, is worth an additional $1,800,000 to the landowner, but this will occur only if natural gas is discovered during the exploration phase. The landowner, believing that the energy company's interest in the site is a good indication that gas is present, is tempted to develop the field herself. To do so, she must contract with local experts in natural gas exploration and development. The initial cost for such a contract is $300,000, which is lost forever if no gas is found on the site. If gas is discovered, however, the landowner expects to earn a net profit of $6,000,000. The landowner estimates the probability of finding gas on this site to be 60%.

   a. Create a payoff table that specifies the landowner's payoff (in dollars) associated with each possible decision and each outcome with respect to finding natural gas on the site.

   b. Use PrecisionTree to identify the strategy that maximizes the landowner's expected net earnings from this opportunity.

   c. Perform a sensitivity analysis on the optimal decision, letting each of the inputs vary one at a time plus or minus 25% from its base value, and summarize your findings. In response to which model inputs is the expected profit value most sensitive?

40. Techware Incorporated is considering the introduction of two new software products to the market. In particular, the company has four options regarding these two proposed products: introduce neither product, introduce product 1 only, introduce product 2 only, or introduce both products. Research and development costs for products 1 and 2 are $180,000 and $150,000, respectively. Note that the first option entails no costs because research and development efforts have not yet begun. The success of these software products depends on the trend of the national economy in the coming year and on the consumers' reaction to these products. The company's revenues earned by introducing product 1 only, product 2 only, or both products in various states of the national economy are given in the file **P06_40.xlsx**. The probabilities of observing a strong, fair, or weak trend in the national economy in the coming year are assessed to be 0.30, 0.50, and 0.20, respectively.

   a. Create a payoff table that specifies Techware's net revenue (in dollars) for each possible decision and each outcome with respect to the trend in the national economy.

   b. Use PrecisionTree to identify the strategy that maximizes Techware's expected net revenue from the given marketing opportunities.

   c. Perform a sensitivity analysis on the optimal decision, letting each of the inputs vary one at a time plus or minus 25% from its base value, and summarize your findings. In response to which model inputs is the expected net revenue value most sensitive?

41. Consider an investor with $10,000 available to invest. He has the following options regarding the allocation of his available funds: (1) he can invest in a risk-free savings account with a guaranteed 3% annual rate of return; (2) he can invest in a fairly safe stock, where the possible annual rates of return are 6%, 8%, or 10%; or (3) he can invest in a more risky stock, where the possible annual rates of return are 1%, 9%, or 17%. Note that the investor can place all of his available funds in any one of these options, or he can split his $10,000 into two $5000 investments in any two of these options. The joint probability distribution of the possible return rates for the two stocks is given in the file **P06_41.xlsx**.

   a. Create a payoff table that specifies this investor's return (in dollars) in one year for each possible decision and each outcome with respect to the two stock returns.

   b. Use PrecisionTree to identify the strategy that maximizes the investor's expected earnings in one year from the given investment opportunities.

   c. Perform a sensitivity analysis on the optimal decision, letting the amount available to invest and the risk-free return both vary, one at a time, plus or minus 100% from their base values, and summarize your findings.

42. A buyer for a large department store chain must place orders with an athletic shoe manufacturer six months prior to the time the shoes will be sold in the department stores. In particular, the buyer must decide on November 1 how many pairs of the manufacturer's newest model of tennis shoes to order for sale during the coming summer season. Assume that each pair of this new brand of tennis shoes costs the department store chain $45 per pair. Furthermore, assume that each pair of these shoes can then be sold to the chain's customers for $70 per pair. Any pairs of these shoes remaining unsold at the end of the summer season will be sold in a closeout sale next fall for $35 each. The probability distribution of consumer demand for these tennis shoes during the coming summer season has been assessed by market research specialists and is provided in the file **P06_42.xlsx**. Finally, assume that the department store chain must purchase these tennis shoes from the manufacturer in lots of 100 pairs.

   a. Create a payoff table that specifies the contribution to profit (in dollars) from the sale of the tennis shoes by this department store chain for each possible purchase decision and each outcome with respect to consumer demand.

   b. You could use PrecisionTree to identify the strategy that maximizes the department store chain's expected profit earned by purchasing and subsequently selling pairs of the new tennis shoes. However, show how you can identify the

EMV-maximizing decision directly from the payoff table, without any bushy tree.

c. Perform a sensitivity analysis on the optimal decision, letting the three monetary inputs vary one at a time over reasonable ranges, and summarize your findings. In response to which model inputs is the expected earnings value most sensitive?

43. Each day the manager of a local bookstore must decide how many copies of the community newspaper to order for sale in her shop. She must pay the newspaper's publisher $0.40 for each copy, and she sells the newspapers to local residents for $0.75 each. Newspapers that are unsold at the end of day are considered worthless. The probability distribution of the number of copies of the newspaper purchased daily at her shop is provided in the file **P06_43.xlsx**. Create a payoff table that lists the profit from each order quantity (multiples of 1000 only) and each demand, and use it to find the order quantity that maximizes expected profit. Why is this an easier approach than a decision tree for this particular problem?

44. Two construction companies are bidding against one another for the right to construct a new community center building in Bloomington, Indiana. The first construction company, Fine Line Homes, believes that its competitor, Buffalo Valley Construction, will place a bid for this project according to the distribution shown in the file **P06_44.xlsx**. Furthermore, Fine Line Homes estimates that it will cost $160,000 for its own company to construct this building. Given its fine reputation and long-standing service within the local community, Fine Line Homes believes that it will likely be awarded the project in the event that it and Buffalo Valley Construction submit exactly the same bids. Create a payoff table that lists the profit from each Fine Line bid and each competing bid, and use it to find the bid that maximizes Fine Line's expected profit. Why is this an easier approach than a decision tree for this particular problem?

45. Suppose that you have sued your employer for damages suffered when you recently slipped and fell on an icy surface that should have been treated by your company's physical plant department. Specifically, your injury resulting from this accident was sufficiently serious that you, in consultation with your attorney, decided to sue your company for $500,000. Your company's insurance provider has offered to settle this suit with you out of court. If you decide to reject the settlement and go to court, your attorney is confident that you will win the case but is uncertain about the amount the court will award you in damages. He has provided his assessment of the probability distribution of the court's award to you in the file **P06_45.xlsx**. In addition, there are extra legal fees of $10,000 you will have to pay if you go to court. Let

S be the insurance provider's proposed out-of-court settlement (in dollars). For which values of S will you decide to accept the settlement? For which values of S will you choose to take your chances in court? Assume that you are seeking to maximize the expected net payoff from this litigation.

46. One of your colleagues has $2000 available to invest. Assume that all of this money must be placed in one of three investments: a particular money market fund, a stock, or gold. Each dollar your colleague invests in the money market fund earns a virtually guaranteed 3% annual return. Each dollar he invests in the stock earns an annual return characterized by the probability distribution provided in the file **P06_46.xlsx**. Finally, each dollar he invests in gold earns an annual return characterized by the probability distribution given in the same file.

a. If your colleague must place all of his available funds in a single investment, which investment should he choose to maximize his expected earnings over the next year?

b. Suppose now that your colleague can place all of his available funds in one of these three investments as before, or he can invest $1000 in one alternative and $1000 in another. Assuming that he seeks to maximize his expected total earnings in one year, how should he allocate his $2000?

47. Consider a population of 2000 individuals, 800 of whom are women. Assume that 300 of the women in this population earn at least $60,000 per year, and 200 of the men earn at least $60,000 per year.

a. What is the probability that a randomly selected individual from this population earns less than $60,000 per year?

b. If a randomly selected individual is observed to earn less than $60,000 per year, what is the probability that this person is a man?

c. If a randomly selected individual is observed to earn at least $60,000 per year, what is the probability that this person is a woman?

48. Yearly automobile emissions inspections are required for car owners in the state of Pennsylvania. Suppose that 18% of all inspected cars in Pennsylvania have problems that need to be corrected. Unfortunately, Pennsylvania state inspections fail to detect these problems 12% of the time. On the other hand, assume that an inspection never detects a problem when there is no problem. Consider a car that is inspected and is found to be free of problems. What is the probability that there is indeed something wrong that the inspection has failed to uncover?

49. Consider again the landowner's decision problem described in Problem 39. Suppose now that, at a cost of $90,000, the landowner can request that a soundings test be performed on the site where natural gas is believed to be present. The company that conducts the soundings concedes that 30% of the time the test will indicate that no gas is present when it actually is. When natural gas is not present in a particular site, the soundings test is accurate 90% of the time.

a. Given that the landowner pays for the soundings test and the test indicates that gas is present, what is the landowner's revised estimate of the probability of finding gas on this site?

b. Given that the landowner pays for the soundings test and the test indicates that gas is not present, what is the landowner's revised estimate of the probability of not finding gas on this site?

c. Should the landowner request the given soundings test at a cost of $90,000? Explain why or why not. If not, at what price (if any) would the landowner choose to obtain the soundings test?

50. The CEO of a company in a highly competitive industry believes that one of her key employees is providing confidential information to the competition. She is 90% certain that this informer is the vice president of finance, whose contacts have been extremely valuable in obtaining financing for the company. If she decides to fire this vice president and he is the informer, she estimates that the company will gain $500,000. If she decides to fire this vice president but he is not the informer, the company will lose his expertise and still have an informer within the staff; the CEO estimates that this outcome would cost her company about $2.5 million. If she decides not to fire this vice president, she estimates that the firm will lose $1.5 million regardless of whether he actually is the informer (because in either case the informer is still with the company). Before deciding whether to fire the vice president for finance, the CEO could order lie detector tests. To avoid possible lawsuits, the lie detector tests would have to be administered to all company employees, at a total cost of $150,000. Another problem she must consider is that the available lie detector tests are not perfectly reliable. In particular, if a person is lying, the test will reveal that the person is lying 95% of the time. Furthermore, if a person is not lying, the test will indicate that the person is not lying 85% of the time.

a. To minimize the expected total cost of managing this difficult situation, what strategy should the CEO adopt?

b. Should the CEO order the lie detector tests for all of her employees? Explain why or why not.

c. Determine the maximum amount of money that the CEO should be willing to pay to administer lie detector tests.

d. How sensitive are the results to the accuracy of the lie detector test? Are there any "reasonable" values of the error probabilities that change the optimal strategy?

51. A customer has approached a bank for a $100,000 one-year loan at a 8% interest rate. If the bank does not approve this loan application, the $100,000 will be invested in bonds that earn a 4% annual return. Without additional information, the bank believes that there is a 5% chance that this customer will default on the loan, assuming that the loan is approved. If the customer defaults on the loan, the bank will lose $100,000. At a cost of $1000, the bank can thoroughly investigate the customer's credit record and supply a favorable or unfavorable recommendation. Past experience indicates that in cases where the customer did not default on the approved loan, the probability of receiving a favorable recommendation on the basis of the credit investigation was 0.80. Furthermore, in cases where the customer defaulted on the approved loan, the probability of receiving a favorable recommendation on the basis of the credit investigation was 0.15.

a. What strategy should the bank follow to maximize its expected profit?

b. Calculate and interpret the expected value of sample information (EVSI) for this decision problem.

c. Calculate and interpret the expected value of perfect information (EVPI) for this decision problem.

d. How sensitive are the results to the accuracy of the credit record recommendations? Are there any "reasonable" values of the error probabilities that change the optimal strategy?

52. A company is considering whether to market a new product. Assume, for simplicity, that if this product is marketed, there are only two possible outcomes: success or failure. The company assesses that the probabilities of these two outcomes are p and $1 - p$, respectively. If the product is marketed and it proves to be a failure, the company will have a net loss of $450,000. If the product is marketed and it proves to be a success, the company will have a net gain of $750,000. If the company decides not to market the product, there is no gain or loss. The company is also considering whether to survey prospective buyers of this new product. The results of the consumer survey can be classified as favorable, neutral, or unfavorable. In similar cases where proposed products were eventually market successes, the fractions of cases where the survey results were favorable, neutral, or unfavorable were 0.6, 0.3, and 0.1, respectively. In similar cases where proposed products were eventually market failures, the fractions of cases where the survey results were favorable, neutral, or unfavorable were 0.1, 0.2, and 0.7, respectively. The total cost of administering this survey is C dollars.

a. Let $p = 0.4$. For which values of C, if any, would this company choose to conduct the consumer survey?

b. Let $p = 0.4$. What is the largest amount that this company would be willing to pay for perfect information about the potential success or failure of the new product?

c. Let $p = 0.5$ and $C = \$15,000$. Find the strategy that maximizes the company's expected earnings in this situation. Does the optimal strategy involve conducting the consumer survey? Explain why or why not.

53. The U.S. government is attempting to determine whether immigrants should be tested for a contagious disease. Assume that the decision will be made on a financial basis. Furthermore, assume that each immigrant who is allowed to enter the United States and has the disease costs the country $100,000. Also, each immigrant who is allowed to enter the United States and does not have the disease will contribute $10,000 to the national economy. Finally, assume that x percent of all potential immigrants have the disease. The U.S. government can choose to admit all immigrants, admit no immigrants, or test immigrants for the disease before determining whether they should be admitted. It costs T dollars to test a person for the disease, and the test result is either positive or negative. A person who does not have the disease *always* tests negative. However, 10% of all people who *do* have the disease test negative. The government's goal is to maximize the expected net financial benefits per potential immigrant.

a. If $x = 10$, what is the largest value of T at which the U.S. government will choose to test potential immigrants for the disease?

b. How does your answer to the question in part **a** change if x increases to 15?

c. If $x = 5$ and $T = \$500$, what is the government's optimal strategy?

d. If $x = 5$, calculate and interpret the expected value of perfect information (EVPI) for this decision problem.

54. The senior executives of an oil company are trying to decide whether to drill for oil in a particular field in the Gulf of Mexico. It costs the company $600,000 to drill in the selected field. Company executives believe that if oil is found in this field its estimated value will be $3,400,000. At present, this oil company believes that there is a 45% chance that the selected field actually contains oil. Before drilling, the company can hire a geologist at a cost of $55,000 to prepare a report that contains a recommendation regarding drilling in the selected field. In many similar situations in the past where this geologist has been hired, the geologist has predicted oil on 75% of all fields that have contained oil, and he has predicted no oil on 85% of all fields that have not contained oil.

a. Assuming that this oil company wants to maximize its expected net earnings, use a decision tree to determine its optimal strategy.

b. Calculate and interpret EVSI for this decision problem. Experiment with the accuracy probabilities of the geologist to see how EVSI changes as they change.

c. Calculate and interpret EVPI for this decision problem.

55. FineHair is developing a new product to promote hair growth in cases of male pattern baldness. If FineHair markets the new product and it is successful, the company will earn $1,000,000 in additional profit. If the marketing of this new product proves to be unsuccessful, the company will lose $350,000 in development and marketing costs. In the past, similar products have been successful 30% of the time. At a cost of $50,000, the effectiveness of the new restoration product can be thoroughly tested. In past tests on similar products, the test predicted success on 70% of products that were ultimately successful, and it predicted failure on 75% of products that were ultimately failures.

a. Identify the strategy that maximizes FineHair's expected net earnings in this situation.

b. Calculate and interpret EVSI for this decision problem.

c. Calculate and interpret EVPI for this decision problem.

56. A product manager at Clean & Brite (C&B) wants to determine whether her company should market a new brand of toothpaste. If this new product succeeds in the marketplace, C&B estimates that it could earn $1,800,000 in future profits from the sale of the new toothpaste. If this new product fails, however, the company expects that it could lose approximately $750,000. If C&B chooses not to market this new brand, the product manager believes that there would be little, if any, impact on the profits earned through sales of C&B's other products. The manager has estimated that the new toothpaste brand will succeed with probability 0.50. Before making her decision regarding this toothpaste product, the manager can spend $75,000 on a market research study. Based on similar studies with past products, C&B believes that the study will predict a successful product, given that product would actually be a success, with probability 0.75. It also believes that the study will predict a failure, given that the product would actually be a failure, with probability 0.65.

a. To maximize expected profit, what strategy should the C&B product manager follow?

b. Calculate and interpret EVSI for this decision problem.

c. Calculate and interpret EVPI for this decision problem.

57. An automobile manufacturer is going to produce a new vehicle, the Pioneer, and wants to determine the amount of annual capacity it should build. The company's goal is to maximize the profit from this vehicle over the next 10 years. Each vehicle will sell for $19,000 and incur a variable production cost of $16,000. Building one unit of annual capacity will cost $2000. Each unit of capacity will also cost $2000 per year to maintain, even if the capacity is unused. Demand for the Pioneer is unknown but marketing estimates the distribution of annual demand to be as shown in the file **P06_57.xlsx**. Assume that the number of units sold during a year is the *minimum* of capacity and annual demand.

    a. Explain why a capacity of 130,000 is not a good choice.

    b. Which capacity level should the company choose?

58. Pizza King (PK) and Noble Greek (NG) are competitive pizza chains. PK believes there is a 25% chance that NG will charge $10 per pizza, a 50% chance NG will charge $12 per pizza, and a 25% chance that NG will charge $14 per pizza. If PK charges price p_1 and NG charges price p_2, PK will sell $100 + 25(p_2 - p_1)$ pizzas. It costs PK $4 to make a pizza. PK is considering charging an integer dollar value from $5 to $14 per pizza. To maximize its expected profit, what price should PK charge for a pizza?

59. Many decision problems have the following simple structure. A decision maker has two possible decisions, 1 and 2. If decision 1 is made, a *sure* cost of c is incurred. If decision 2 is made, there are two possible outcomes, with costs c_1 and c_2 and probabilities p and $1 - p$. We assume that $c_1 < c < c_2$. The idea is that decision 1, the riskless decision, has a moderate cost, whereas decision 2, the risky decision, has a low cost c_1 or a high cost c_2.

    a. Find the decision maker's cost table, that is, the cost for each possible decision and each possible outcome.

    b. Calculate the expected cost from the risky decision.

    c. List as many scenarios as you can think of that have this structure. (Here's an example to get you started. Think of insurance, where you pay a sure premium to avoid a large possible loss.)

60. A nuclear power company is deciding whether to build a nuclear power plant at Diablo Canyon or at Roy Rogers City. The cost of building the power plant is $10 million at Diablo and $20 million at Roy Rogers City. If the company builds at Diablo, however, and an earthquake occurs at Diablo during the next five years, construction will be terminated and the company will lose $10 million (and will still have to build a power plant at Roy Rogers City). Without further expert information the company believes there is a 20% chance that an earthquake will occur at Diablo during the next five years. For $1 million, a geologist can be

hired to analyze the fault structure at Diablo Canyon. She will predict either that an earthquake will occur or that an earthquake will not occur. The geologist's past record indicates that she will predict an earthquake on 95% of the occasions for which an earthquake will occur and no earthquake on 90% of the occasions for which an earthquake will not occur. Should the power company hire the geologist? Also, calculate and interpret EVSI and EVPI.

61. Consider again Techware's decision problem described in Problem 40. Suppose now that Techware has an exponential utility function with risk tolerance $350,000.

    a. Find the decision that maximizes Techware's expected utility. How does this optimal decision compare to the optimal decision with an EMV criterion? Explain any difference between the two optimal decisions.

    b. Repeat part **a** when Techware's risk tolerance is $50,000.

62. Consider again the bank's customer loan decision problem in Problem 51. Suppose now that the bank has an exponential utility function with risk tolerance $150,000. Find the strategy that maximizes the bank's expected utility in this case. How does this optimal strategy compare to the optimal decision with an EMV criterion? Explain any difference between the two optimal strategies.

63. The Indiana University basketball team trails by two points with eight seconds to go and has the ball. Should it attempt a two-point shot or a three-point shot? Assume that the Indiana shot will end the game and that no foul will occur on the shot. Assume that a three-point shot has a 30% chance of success, and a two-point shot has a 45% chance of success. Finally, assume that Indiana has a 50% chance of winning in overtime.

Level B

64. George Lindsey (1959) looked at box scores of more than 1000 baseball games and found the expected number of runs scored in an inning for each on-base and out situation to be as listed in the file **P06_64.xlsx**. For example, if a team has a runner on first base with one out, it scores 0.5 run on average until the end of the inning. You can assume throughout this problem that the team batting wants to maximize the expected number of runs scored in the inning.

    a. Use this data to explain why, in most cases, bunting with a man on first base and no outs is a bad decision. In what situation might bunting with a man on first base and no outs be a good decision?

    b. Assume there is a runner on first base with one out. What probability of stealing second makes an attempted steal a good idea?

65. One controversial topic in basketball (college or any other level) is whether to foul a player deliberately with only a few seconds left in the game. Specifically, consider the following scenario. With about 10% seconds left in the game, team A is ahead of team B by three points, and team B is just about to inbound the ball. Assume team A has committed enough fouls so that future fouls result in team B going to the free-throw line. If team A purposely commits a foul as soon as possible, team B will shoot two foul shots (a point apiece). The thinking is that this is better than letting team B shoot a three-point shot, which would be their best way to tie the game and send it into overtime. However, there is a downside to fouling. Team B could make the first free throw, purposely miss the second, get the rebound, and score a two-point shot to tie the game, or even score a three-point shot to win the game. Examine this decision, using reasonable input parameters. This deliberate fouling strategy doesn't seem to be used very often, but do you think it should be used?

66. The following situation actually occurred in a 2009 college football game between Washington and Notre Dame. With about 3.5 minutes left in the game, Washington had fourth down and one yard to go for a touchdown, already leading by two points. Notre Dame had just had two successful goal-line stands from in close, so Washington's coach decided not to go for the touchdown and the virtually sure win. Instead, Washington kicked a field goal, and Notre Dame eventually won in overtime. Use a decision tree, with some reasonable inputs, to see whether Washington made a wise decision or should have gone for the touchdown. Note the only "monetary" values here are 1 and 0. You can think of Washington getting $1 if they win and $0 if they lose. Then the EMV is $1*P(\text{Win}) + 0*P(\text{lose}) = P(\text{Win})$, so maximizing EMV is equivalent to maximizing the probability of winning.

67. Mr. Maloy has just bought a new $30,000 sport utility vehicle. As a reasonably safe driver, he believes that there is only about a 5% chance of being in an accident in the coming year. If he is involved in an accident, the damage to his new vehicle depends on the severity of the accident. The probability distribution for the range of possible accidents and the corresponding damage amounts (in dollars) are given in the file **P06_67.xlsx**. Mr. Maloy is trying to decide whether he is willing to pay $170 each year for collision insurance with a $300 deductible. Note that with this type of insurance, he pays the *first* $300 in damages if he causes an accident and the insurance company pays the remainder.

   a. Create a cost table that specifies the cost (in dollars) associated with each possible decision and type of accident.

   b. Use PrecisionTree to identify the strategy that minimizes Mr. Maloy's annual expected cost.

   c. Perform a sensitivity analysis on the optimal decision with respect to the probability of an accident, the premium, and the deductible amount, and summarize your findings. (You can choose the ranges to test.) In response to which of these three inputs is the expected cost most sensitive?

68. The purchasing agent for a PC manufacturer is currently negotiating a purchase agreement for a particular electronic component with a given supplier. This component is produced in lots of 1000, and the cost of purchasing a lot is $30,000. Unfortunately, past experience indicates that this supplier has occasionally shipped defective components to its customers. Specifically, the proportion of defective components supplied by this supplier has the probability distribution given in the file **P06_68.xlsx**. Although the PC manufacturer can repair a defective component at a cost of $20 each, the purchasing agent learns that this supplier will now assume the cost of replacing defective components in excess of the first 100 faulty items found in a given lot. This guarantee may be purchased by the PC manufacturer prior to the receipt of a given lot at a cost of $1000 per lot. The purchasing agent wants to determine whether it is worthwhile to purchase the supplier's guarantee policy.

   a. Create a cost table that specifies the PC manufacturer's total cost (in dollars) of purchasing and repairing (if necessary) a complete lot of components for each possible decision and each outcome with respect to the proportion of defective items.

   b. Use PrecisionTree to identify the strategy that minimizes the expected total cost of achieving a complete lot of satisfactory microcomputer components.

   c. Perform a sensitivity analysis on the optimal decision with respect to the number of components per lot and the three monetary inputs, and summarize your findings. (You can choose the ranges to test.) In response to which of these inputs is the expected cost most sensitive?

69. A home appliance company is interested in marketing an innovative new product. The company must decide whether to manufacture this product in house or employ a subcontractor to manufacture it. The file **P06_69.xlsx** contains the estimated probability distribution of the cost of manufacturing one unit of this new product (in dollars) if the home appliance company produces the product in house. This file also contains the estimated probability distribution of the cost of purchasing one unit of the product if it comes from the subcontractor. There is also uncertainty about demand for the product in the coming year, as shown in the same file. The company plans to meet all demand, but there is a capacity issue. The subcontractor has unlimited capacity, but the home appliance company has capacity for only 5000 units per year. If it decides to make the product in house and demand is greater than capacity, it will have to purchase the excess demand from an external source at a premium: $225 per unit. Assuming that the company wants to minimize the expected cost of meeting demand in the coming year, should it make the new product in house or buy it from the subcontractor? Do you need a decision tree, or will a cost table with EMV calculations suffice? (You can assume that neither the company nor the subcontractor will ever produce *more* than demand.)

70. A grapefruit farmer in central Florida is trying to decide whether to take protective action to limit damage to his crop in the event that the overnight temperature falls to a level well below freezing. He is concerned that if the temperature falls sufficiently low and he fails to make an effort to protect his grapefruit trees, he runs the risk of losing his entire crop, which is worth approximately $75,000. Based on the latest forecast issued by the National Weather Service, the farmer estimates that there is a 60% chance that he will lose his entire crop if it is left unprotected. Alternatively, the farmer can insulate his fruit by spraying water on all of the trees in his orchards. This action, which would likely cost the farmer *C* dollars, would prevent total devastation but might not completely protect the grapefruit trees from incurring some damage as a result of the unusually cold overnight temperatures. The file **P06_70.xlsx** contains the assessed distribution of possible damages (in dollars) to the insulated fruit in light of the cold weather forecast. The farmer wants to minimize the expected total cost of coping with the threatening weather.
   a. Find the maximum value of *C* below which the farmer should insulate his crop to limit the damage from the unusually cold weather.
   b. Set *C* equal to the value identified in part **a**. Perform sensitivity analysis to determine under what conditions, if any, the farmer would be better off not spraying his grapefruit trees and taking his chances in spite of the threat to his crop.
   c. Suppose that *C* equals $25,000, and in addition to this protection, the farmer can purchase insurance on the crop. Discuss possibilities for reasonable insurance policies and how much they would be worth to the farmer. You can assume that the insurance is relevant only if the farmer purchases the protection, and you can decide on the terms of the insurance policy.

71. A retired partner from a large brokerage firm has $1,000,000 available to invest in particular stocks or bonds. Each investment's annual rate of return depends on the state of the economy in the coming year. The file **P06_71.xlsx** contains the distribution of returns for these stocks and bonds as a function of the economy's state in the coming year. As this file indicates, the returns from stocks and bonds in a fair economy are listed as *X* and *Y*. This investor wants to allocate her $1,000,000 to maximize her expected value of the portfolio one year from now.
   a. If $X = Y = 15\%$, find the optimal investment strategy for this investor. (*Hint*: You could try a decision tree approach, but it would involve a massive tree. It is much easier to find an algebraic expression for the expected final value of the investment when a percentage *p* is put in stocks and the remaining percentage is put in bonds. Given this expression, the best value of *p* should be obvious.)
   b. For which values of *X* (where $10\% < X < 20\%$) and *Y* (where $12.5\% < Y < 17.5\%$), if any, will this investor prefer to place all of her available funds in stocks? Use the same method as in part **a** for each combination of *X* and *Y*.

72. A city in Ohio is considering replacing its fleet of gasoline-powered automobiles with electric cars. The manufacturer of the electric cars claims that this municipality will experience significant cost savings over the life of the fleet if it chooses to pursue the conversion. If the manufacturer is correct, the city will save about $1.5 million dollars. If the new technology employed within the electric cars is faulty, as some critics suggest, the conversion to electric cars will cost the city $675,000. A third possibility is that less serious problems will arise and the city will break even with the conversion. A consultant hired by the city estimates that the probabilities of these three outcomes are 0.30, 0.30, and 0.40, respectively. The city has an opportunity to implement a pilot program that would indicate the potential cost or savings resulting from a switch to electric cars. The pilot program involves renting a small number of electric cars for three months and running them under typical conditions. This program would cost the city $75,000. The city's consultant believes that the results of the pilot program would be significant but not conclusive; she submits the values in the file **P06_72.xlsx**, a compilation of probabilities based on the experience of other cities, to support her contention. For example, the first row of her table indicates that given that a conversion to electric cars actually results in a savings of $1.5 million, the conditional probabilities that the pilot program will indicate that the city saves money, loses money, and breaks even are 0.6, 0.1, and 0.3, respectively. What actions should the city take to maximize its expected savings? When should it run the pilot program, if ever? (Note: If you set up the input section of your spreadsheet in the right way, you will be able

to perform all of the Bayes' rule calculations with a couple of *copyable* formulas.)

73. A manufacturer must decide whether to extend credit to a retailer who would like to open an account with the firm. Past experience with new accounts indicates that 45% are high-risk customers, 35% are moderate-risk customers, and 20% are low-risk customers. If credit is extended, the manufacturer can expect to lose $60,000 with a high-risk customer, make $50,000 with a moderate-risk customer, and make $100,000 with a low-risk customer. If the manufacturer decides not to extend credit to a customer, the manufacturer neither makes nor loses any money. Prior to making a credit extension decision, the manufacturer can obtain a credit rating report on the retailer at a cost of $2000. The credit agency concedes that its rating procedure is not completely reliable. In particular, the credit rating procedure will rate a low-risk customer as a moderate-risk customer with probability 0.10 and as a high-risk customer with probability 0.05. Similarly, the given rating procedure will rate a moderate-risk customer as a low-risk customer with probability 0.06 and as a high-risk customer with probability 0.07. Finally, the rating procedure will rate a high-risk customer as a low-risk customer with probability 0.01 and as a moderate-risk customer with probability 0.05. Find the strategy that maximizes the manufacturer's expected net earnings. (*Note*: If you set up the input section of your spreadsheet in the right way, you will be able to perform all of the Bayes' rule calculations with a couple of *copyable* formulas.)

74. A television network earns an average of $1.6 million each season from a hit program and loses an average of $400,000 each season on a program that turns out to be a flop. Of all programs picked up by this network in recent years, 25% turn out to be hits and 75% turn out to be flops. At a cost of C dollars, a market research firm will analyze a pilot episode of a prospective program and issue a report predicting whether the given program will end up being a hit. If the program is actually going to be a hit, there is a 90% chance that the market researchers will predict the program to be a hit. If the program is actually going to be a flop, there is only a 20% chance that the market researchers will predict the program to be a hit.
   a. Assuming that $C = \$160,000$, find the strategy that maximizes the network's expected profit.
   b. What is the maximum value of C that the network should be willing to pay the market research firm?
   c. Calculate and interpret EVPI for this decision problem.

75. A publishing company is trying to decide whether to publish a new business law textbook. Based on a careful reading of the latest draft of the manuscript, the publisher's senior editor in the business textbook division assesses the distribution of possible payoffs earned by publishing this new book. The file **P06_75.xlsx** contains this probability distribution. Before making a final decision regarding the publication of the book, the editor can learn more about the text's potential for success by thoroughly surveying business law instructors teaching at universities across the country. Historical frequencies based on similar surveys administered in the past are also provided in this file.
   a. Find the strategy that maximizes the publisher's expected payoff if the survey cost is $10,000.
   b. What is the most that the publisher would be willing to pay to conduct a new survey of business law instructors?
   c. Assuming that a survey could be constructed that provides perfect information to the publisher, how much would the company be willing to pay to acquire and implement such a survey?

76. Sharp Outfits is trying to decide whether to ship some customer orders now via UPS or wait until after the threat of another UPS strike is over. If Sharp Outfits decides to ship the requested merchandise now and the UPS strike takes place, the company will incur $60,000 in delay and shipping costs. If Sharp Outfits decides to ship the customer orders via UPS and no strike occurs, the company will incur $4000 in shipping costs. If Sharp Outfits decides to postpone shipping its customer orders via UPS, the company will incur $10,000 in delay costs regardless of whether UPS goes on strike. Let p represent the probability that UPS will go on strike and impact Sharp Outfits's shipments.
   a. For which values of p, if any, does Sharp Outfits minimize its expected total cost by choosing to postpone shipping its customer orders via UPS?
   b. Suppose now that, at a cost of $1000, Sharp Outfits can purchase information regarding the likelihood of a UPS strike in the near future. Based on similar strike threats in the past, the company assesses that if there will be a strike, the information will predict a strike with probability 0.75, and if there will not be a strike, the information will predict no strike with probability 0.85. Provided that $p = 0.15$, what strategy should Sharp Outfits pursue to minimize its expected total cost?
   a. Use the tree from part **b** to find the EVSI when $p = 0.15$. Then use a data table to find EVSI for p from 0.05 to 0.30 in increments of 0.05, and chart EVSI versus p.
   b. Continuing part **b**, compute and interpret the EVPI when $p = 0.15$.

77. A homeowner wants to decide whether he should install an electronic heat pump in his home. Given that the cost of installing a new heat pump is fairly

large, the homeowner wants to do so only if he can count on being able to recover the initial expense over *five* consecutive years of cold winter weather. After reviewing historical data on the operation of heat pumps in various kinds of winter weather, he computes the expected annual costs of heating his home during the winter months with and without a heat pump in operation. These cost figures are shown in the file **P06_77.xlsx**. The probabilities of experiencing a mild, normal, colder than normal, and severe winter are $0.2(1 - x), 0.5(1 - x), 0.3(1 - x)$, and x, respectively. In words, we let the last probability vary, we let the other three be in the ratio 2 to 5 to 3, and we force them to sum to 1.

a. Given that $x = 0.1$, what is the most that the homeowner is willing to pay for the heat pump?

b. If the heat pump costs $500, how large must x be before the homeowner decides it is economically worthwhile to install the heat pump?

c. Given that $x = 0.1$, calculate and interpret EVPI when the heat pump costs $500.

d. Repeat part **c** when $x = 0.15$.

78. Sarah Chang is the owner of a small electronics company. In six months, a proposal is due for an electronic timing system for the next Olympic Games. For several years, Chang's company has been developing a new microprocessor, a critical component in a timing system that would be superior to any product currently on the market. However, progress in research and development has been slow, and Chang is unsure whether her staff can produce the microprocessor in time. If they succeed in developing the microprocessor (probability p_1), there is an excellent chance (probability p_2) that Chang's company will win the $1 million Olympic contract. If they do not, there is a small chance (probability p_3) that she will still be able to win the same contract with an alternative but inferior timing system that has already been developed. If she continues the project, Chang must invest $200,000 in research and development. In addition, making a proposal (which she will decide whether to do after seeing whether the R&D is successful) requires developing a prototype timing system at an additional cost. This additional cost is $50,000 if R&D is successful (so that she can develop the new timing system), and it is $40,000 if R&D is unsuccessful (so that she needs to go with the older timing system). Finally, if Chang wins the contract, the finished product will cost an additional $150,000 to produce.

a. Develop a decision tree that can be used to solve Chang's problem. You can assume in this part of the problem that she is using EMV (of her net profit) as a decision criterion. Build the tree so that she can enter any values for p_1, p_2, and p_3 (in input

cells) and automatically see her optimal EMV and optimal strategy from the tree.

b. If $p_2 = 0.8$ and $p_3 = 0.1$, what value of p_1 makes Chang indifferent between abandoning the project and going ahead with it?

c. How much would Chang benefit if she knew for certain that the Olympic organization would guarantee her the contract? (This guarantee would be in force only if she were successful in developing the product.) Assume $p_1 = 0.4$, $p_2 = 0.8$, and $p_3 = 0.1$.

d. Suppose now that this is a relatively big project for Chang. Therefore, she decides to use expected utility as her criterion, with an exponential utility function. Using some trial and error, see which risk tolerance changes her initial decision from "go ahead" to "abandon" when $p_1 = 0.4$, $p_2 = 0.8$, and $p_3 = 0.1$.

79. Ventron Engineering Company has just been awarded a $2 million development contract by the U.S. Army Aviation Systems Command to develop a blade spar for its Heavy Lift Helicopter program. The blade spar is a metal tube that runs the length of and provides strength to the helicopter blade. Due to the unusual length and size of the Heavy Lift Helicopter blade, Ventron is unable to produce a single-piece blade spar of the required dimensions using existing extrusion equipment and material. The engineering department has prepared two alternatives for developing the blade spar: (1) sectioning or (2) an improved extrusion process. Ventron must decide which process to use. (Backing out of the contract at any point is not an option.) The risk report has been prepared by the engineering department. The information from this report is explained next.

The sectioning option involves joining several shorter lengths of extruded metal into a blade spar of sufficient length. This work will require extensive testing and rework over a 12-month period at a total cost of $1.8 million. Although this process will definitely produce an adequate blade spar, it merely represents an extension of existing technology.

To improve the extrusion process, on the other hand, it will be necessary to perform two steps: (1) improve the material used, at a cost of $300,000, and (2) modify the extrusion press, at a cost of $960,000. The first step will require six months of work, and if this first step is successful, the second step will require another six months of work. If both steps are successful, the blade spar will be available at that time, that is, a year from now. The engineers estimate that the probabilities of succeeding in steps 1 and 2 are 0.9 and 0.75, respectively. However, if either step is unsuccessful (which will be known only in six months for step 1 and in a year for step 2), Ventron will have no alternative but to switch to the sectioning process—and incur the sectioning cost on top of any costs already incurred.

Development of the blade spar must be completed within 18 months to avoid holding up the rest of the contract. If necessary, the sectioning work can be done on an accelerated basis in a six-month period, but the cost of sectioning will then increase from $1.8 million to $2.4 million. The director of engineering, Dr. Smith, wants to try developing the improved extrusion process. He reasons that this is not only cheaper (if successful) for the current project, but its expected side benefits for future projects could be sizable. Although these side benefits are difficult to gauge, Dr. Smith's best guess is an additional $2 million. (These side benefits are obtained only if both steps of the modified extrusion process are completed successfully.)

a. Develop a decision tree to maximize Ventron's EMV. This includes the revenue from this project, the side benefits (if applicable) from an improved extrusion process, and relevant costs. You don't need to worry about the time value of money; that is, no discounting or net present values are required. Summarize your findings in words in the spreadsheet.

b. What value of side benefits would make Ventron indifferent between the two alternatives?

c. How much would Ventron be willing to pay, right now, for perfect information about both steps of the improved extrusion process? (This information would tell Ventron, right now, the ultimate success or failure outcomes of both steps.)

80. Suppose an investor has the opportunity to buy the following contract, a stock call option, on March 1. The contract allows him to buy 100 shares of ABC stock at the end of March, April, or May at a guaranteed price of $50 per share. He can exercise this option at most once. For example, if he purchases the stock at the end of March, he can't purchase more in April or May at the guaranteed price. The current price of the stock is $50. Each month, assume that the stock price either goes up by a dollar (with probability 0.55) or goes down by a dollar (with probability 0.45). If the investor buys the contract, he is hoping that the stock price will go up. The reasoning is that if he buys the contract, the price goes up to $51, and he buys the stock (that is, he exercises his option) for $50, he can then sell the stock for $51 and make a profit of $1 per share. On the other hand, if the stock price goes down, he doesn't have to exercise his option; he can just throw the contract away.

a. Use a decision tree to find the investor's optimal strategy (that is, when he should exercise the option), *assuming* he purchases the contract.

b. How much should he be willing to pay for such a contract?

81. [*Based on Balson et al. (1992).*] An electric utility company is trying to decide whether to replace its PCB transformer in a generating station with a new and safer transformer. To evaluate this decision, the utility needs information about the likelihood of an incident, such as a fire, the cost of such an incident, and the cost of replacing the unit. Suppose that the total cost of replacement as a present value is $75,000. If the transformer is replaced, there is virtually no chance of a fire. However, if the current transformer is retained, the probability of a fire is assessed to be 0.0025. If a fire occurs, the cleanup cost could be high ($80 million) or low ($20 million). The probability of a high cleanup cost, given that a fire occurs, is assessed at 0.2.

a. If the company uses EMV as its decision criterion, should it replace the transformer?

b. Perform a sensitivity analysis on the key parameters of the problem that are difficult to assess, namely, the probability of a fire, the probability of a high cleanup cost, and the high and low cleanup costs. Does the optimal decision from part **a** remain optimal for a wide range of these parameters?

c. Do you believe EMV is the correct criterion to use in this type of problem involving environmental accidents?

82. The ending of the game between the Indianapolis Colts and the New England Patriots (NFL teams) in Fall 2009 was quite controversial. With about two minutes left in the game, the Patriots were ahead 34 to 28 and had the ball on their *own* 28-yard line with fourth down and two yards to go. Their coach, Bill Belichick, decided to go for the first down rather than punt, contrary to conventional wisdom. (See another of his controversial decisions in problem 84.) They didn't make the first down, so that possession went to the Colts, who then scored a touchdown to win by a point. Belichick was harshly criticized by most of the media, but was his unorthodox decision really a bad one?

a. Use a decision tree to analyze the problem. You can make some simplifying decisions: (1) the game would essentially be over if the Patriots made a first down, and (2) at most one score would occur after a punt or a failed first down attempt. (Note that there are no monetary values. However, you can assume the Patriots receive $1 for a win and $0 for a loss, so that maximizing EMV is equivalent to maximizing the probability that the Patriots win.)

b. Show that the Patriots should go for the first down if $p > 1 - q/r$. Here, p is the probability the Patriots make the first down, q is the probability the Colts score a touchdown after a punt, and r is the probability the Colts score a touchdown after the Patriots fail to make a first down. What are your best guesses for these three probabilities? Based on them, was Belichick's decision a good one?

83. Suppose you believe that the price of a particular stock goes up each day with probability p and goes down with probability $1 - p$. You also believe the daily price changes are independent of one another. However, you are not sure of the value of p. Based on your current information, you believe p could be 0.40, 0.45, 0.50, or 0.55, with probabilities 0.15, 0.25, 0.35, and 0.25, respectively. Then you watch the stock price changes for 25 days and observe 12 ups and 13 downs. Use Bayes' rule to find the posterior distribution of p. Based on this posterior distribution, calculate the probability that there will be at least 15 ups in the *next* 30 price changes. (*Hint*: Think in terms of the binomial distribution.)

84. Bill Belichick, coach of the New England Patriots, made another somewhat controversial decision in the 2012 Super Bowl game against the New York Giants. Behind by a score of 17 to 15, the Giants had the ball only a few yards away from scoring a touchdown with about 58 seconds to go, and the Patriots were out of time-outs. At this point, it looked like the Giants were going to run a couple more plays to wind the clock down to a few seconds, and then score an almost sure field goal as time ran out to win 18 to 17. However, Belichick instructed his defense to let the Giants' runner go into the end zone untouched for a touchdown. (The Giants then failed on a two-point conversion, so the score remained 21 to 17.) This gave the ball back to New England with almost a minute to go. They failed to score, and the Giants kept their lead, but should Bellichick be criticized for his decision to "give up" the touchdown? Or should Tom Coughlin, the Giants coach, be criticized for not telling his team *not* to score a touchdown?

CASE 6.1 JOGGER SHOE COMPANY

Jogger Shoe Company is trying to decide whether to make a change in its most popular brand of running shoes. The new style would cost the same to produce and be priced the same, but it would incorporate a new kind of lacing system that (according to its marketing research people) would make it more popular.

There is a fixed cost of $300,000 for changing over to the new style. The unit contribution to before-tax profit for either style is $8. The tax rate is 35%. Also, because the fixed cost can be depreciated and will therefore affect the after-tax cash flow, a depreciation method is needed. You can assume it is straight-line depreciation.

The current demand for these shoes is 190,000 pairs annually. The company assumes this demand will continue for the next three years if the current style is retained. However, there is uncertainty about demand for the new style, if it is introduced. The company models this uncertainty by assuming a normal distribution in year 1, with mean 220,000 and standard deviation 20,000. The company also assumes that this demand, whatever it is, will remain constant for the next three years. However, if demand in year 1 for the new style is sufficiently low, the company can always switch back to the current style and realize an annual demand of 190,000. The company wants a strategy that will maximize the expected net present value (NPV) of total cash flow for the next three years, where a 15% interest rate is used for the purpose of calculating NPV.

CASE 6.2 WESTHOUSER PAPER COMPANY

Westhouser Paper Company in the state of Washington currently has an option to purchase a piece of land with good timber forest on it. It is now May 1, and the current price of the land is $2.2 million. Westhouser does not actually need the timber from this land until the beginning of July, but its top executives fear that another company might buy the land between now and the beginning of July. They assess that there is a 5% chance that a competitor will buy the land during May. If this does not occur, they assess that there is a 10% chance that the competitor will buy the land during June. If Westhouser does not take advantage of its current option, it can attempt to buy the land at the beginning of June or the beginning of July, provided that it is still available.

Westhouser's incentive for delaying the purchase is that its financial experts believe there is a good chance that the price of the land will fall significantly in one or both of the next two months. They assess the possible price decreases and their probabilities in Table 6.7 and Table 6.8. Table 6.7 shows the probabilities of the possible price decreases during May. Table 6.8 lists the *conditional* probabilities of the possible price decreases in June, *given* the price decrease in May. For example, it indicates that if the price decrease in May is $60,000, then the possible

price decreases in June are $0, $30,000, and $60,000 with respective probabilities 0.6, 0.2, and 0.2.

If Westhouser purchases the land, it believes that it can gross $3 million. (This does not count the cost of purchasing the land.) But if it does not purchase the land, Westhouser believes that it can make $650,000 from alternative investments. What should the company do?

Table 6.7 Distribution of Price Decrease in May

Price Decrease	Probability
$0	0.5
$60,000	0.3
$120,000	0.2

© Cengage Learning

Table 6.8 Distribution of Price Decrease in June

Price Decrease in May					
$0		$60,000		$120,000	
June Decrease	Probability	June Decrease	Probability	June Decrease	Probability
$0	0.3	$0	0.6	$0	0.7
$60,000	0.6	$30,000	0.2	$20,000	0.2
$120,000	0.1	$60,000	0.2	$40,000	0.1

© Cengage Learning

CASE | 6.3 BIOTECHNICAL ENGINEERING[8]

Biotechnical Engineering specializes in developing new chemicals for agricultural applications. The company is a pioneer in using the sterile-male procedure to control insect infestations. It operates several laboratories around the world that raise insects and expose them to extra-large doses of radiation, making them sterile. As an alternative to chlorinated hydrocarbon pesticides, such as DDT, the sterile-male procedure has been used frequently with a good track record of success, most notably with the Mediterranean fruit fly (or Medfly).

That pest was controlled in California through the release of treated flies on the premise that the sterile male flies would compete with fertile wild males for mating opportunities. Any female that

has mated with a sterile fly will lay eggs that do not hatch. The California Medfly campaigns required about five successive releases of sterile males—at intervals timed to coincide with the time for newly hatched flies to reach adulthood—before the Medfly was virtually eliminated. (Only sterile flies were subsequently caught in survey traps.) The effectiveness of the sterile-male procedure was enhanced by the release of malathion poisonous bait just a few days before each release, cutting down on the number of viable wild adults.

More recently, Biotechnical Engineering has had particular success in using genetic engineering to

[8]This case was written by Lawrence L. Lapin, San Jose State University.

duplicate various insect hormones and pheromones (scent attractants). Of particular interest is the application of such methods against the Gypsy Moth, a notorious pest that attacks trees. The company has developed synthetic versions of both hormones and pheromones for that moth. It has a synthetic sexual attractant that male moths can detect at great distances. Most promising is the synthetic juvenile hormone.

The juvenile hormone controls moth meta-morphosis, determining the timing for the trans-formation of a caterpillar into a chrysalis and then into an adult. Too much juvenile hormone wreaks havoc with this process, causing caterpillars to turn into freak adults that cannot reproduce.

Biotechnical Engineering has received a government contract to test its new technology in an actual eradication campaign. The company will participate in a small-scale campaign against the Gypsy Moth in the state of Oregon. Because the pest is so damaging, Dr. June Scribner, the administrator in charge, is considering using DDT as an alternative procedure. Of course, that banned substance is only available for government emergency use because of the environmental damage it may cause. In addition to spraying with DDT, two other procedures may be employed: (1) using Biotechnical's scent lure, followed by the release of sterile males, and (2) spraying with the company's juvenile hormone to prevent larvae from developing into adults. Dr. Scribner wants to select the method that yields the best expected payoff, described below.

Although both of the newer procedures are known to work under laboratory conditions, there is some uncertainty about successful propagation of the chemicals in the wild and about the efficacy of the sterile-male procedure with moths.

If the scent-lure program is launched at a cost of $5 million, Biotechnical claims that it will have a fifty-fifty chance of leaving a low number of native males versus a high number. Once the results of that phase are known, a later choice must be made to spray with DDT or to release sterile males; the cost of the sterilization and delivery of the insects to the countryside is an additional $5 million. But if this two-phase program is successful, the net present value of the worth of trees saved is $30 million, including the benefit of avoiding all other forms of environmental damage. The indigenous moth population would be destroyed, and a new infestation could occur only from migrants. Biotechnical's experience with other eradication programs indicates that if the scent lure leaves a small native male population, there is a 90% chance for a successful eradication by using sterile males; otherwise, there is only a 10% chance for success by using sterile males. A failure results in no savings.

The cost of synthesizing enough juvenile hormone is $3 million. Biotechnical maintains that the probability that the hormone can be effectively disseminated is only 0.20. If it works, the worth of the trees saved and environmental damage avoided will be $50 million. This greater level of savings is possible because of the permanent nature of the solution because a successful juvenile hormone can then be applied wherever the moths are known to exist, virtually eliminating the pest from the environment. But if the hormone does not work, the DDT must still be used to save the trees.

DDT constitutes only a temporary solution, and the worth of its savings in trees is far less than the worth of either of the esoteric eradication procedures—if they prove successful. To compare alternatives, Dr. Scribner proposes using the net advantage (crop and environmental savings, minus cost) relative to where she would be were she to decide to use DDT at the outset or were she to be forced to spray with it later. (Regardless of the outcome, Biotechnical will be reimbursed for all expenditures. The decision is hers, not the company's.)

Questions

1. Under Biotechnical's proposal, the selection of DDT without even trying the other procedures would lead to a neutral outcome for the government, having zero payoff. Discuss the benefits of Dr. Scribner's proposed payoff measure.

2. Construct Dr. Scribner's decision tree diagram, using the proposed payoff measure.

3. What action will maximize Dr. Scribner's expected payoff?

4. Dr. Scribner is concerned about the assumed fifty-fifty probability for the two levels of surviving native males following the scent-lure program.

   a. Redo the decision tree analysis to find what action will maximize Dr. Scribner's expected payoff when the probability of low native males is, successively, (1) 0.40 or (2) 0.60 instead.

b. How is the optimal action affected by the probability level assumed for the low native male outcome?

5. Dr. Scribner is concerned about the assumed 0.20 probability for the dissemination success of the juvenile hormone.

   a. Keeping all other probabilities and cash flows at their original levels, redo the decision tree analysis to find what action will maximize Dr. Scribner's expected payoff when the probability of juvenile hormone success is, successively, (1) 0.15 or (2) 0.25 instead.

   b. How is the optimal action affected by the probability level assumed for the juvenile hormone's success?

6. Dr. Scribner is concerned about the assumed probability levels for the success of the sterile-male procedure.

   a. Keeping all other probabilities and cash flows at their original levels, redo the decision tree analysis to find what action will maximize Dr. Scribner's expected payoff when the sterile-male success probabilities are instead as follows:

(1) 80% for a low number of native males and 5% for a high number of native males

(2) 70% for a low number of native males and 15% for a high number of native males

b. How is the optimal action affected by the probability level assumed for the success of the sterile-male procedure?

7. Dr. Scribner is concerned about the assumed levels for the net present value of the worth of trees saved and damage avoided. She believes these amounts are only accurate within a range of ±10%.

   a. Keeping all other probabilities and cash flows at their original levels, redo the decision tree analysis to find what action will maximize Dr. Scribner's expected payoff when the two net present values are instead, successively, (1) 10% lower or (2) 10% higher than originally assumed.

   b. How is the optimal action affected by the level assumed for the NPVs of the savings from using one of the two esoteric Gypsy Moth eradication procedures?

Sampling and Sampling Distributions

mevans/iStockphoto.com

SAMPLE SIZE SELECTION IN A LEGAL CASE

This chapter introduces the important problem of estimating an unknown population quantity by randomly sampling from the population. Sampling is often expensive and/or time-consuming, so a key step in any sampling plan is to determine the sample size that produces a prescribed level of accuracy. Some of the issues in finding an appropriate sample size are discussed in Afshartous (2008). The author was involved as an expert statistical witness for the plaintiff in a court case. Over a period of several years, a service company had collected a flat "special service handling fee" from its client during any month in which a special service request was made. The plaintiff claimed that many of these fees had been charged erroneously and sought to recover all of the money collected from such erroneous fees. The statistical question concerns either the *proportion* of all monthly billing records that were erroneous or the *total number* of all erroneous billing records. Both sides had to agree on a sampling method for sampling through the very large population of billing records. They eventually agreed to *simple* random sampling, as discussed in this chapter. However, there was some contention (and confusion) regarding the appropriate sample size.

Their initial approach was to find a sample size n sufficiently large to accurately estimate p, the unknown proportion of all monthly billing records in error. Specifically, if they wanted to be 95% confident that the error in their estimate of p would be no more than 5%, then a standard sample size formula (provided in Chapter 8) requires n to be 385. (This number is surprisingly independent of the total number of billing records.) Then, for example, if the sample discovered 77 errors, or 20% of the sampled items, they would be 95% confident that between 15% and 25% (20% plus or minus 5%) of *all* billing records were in error.

The author argued that this "plus or minus 5%" does not necessarily provide the desired level of accuracy for the quantity of most interest, the total number of errone-ously charged fees. A couple of numerical examples illustrate his point. Let's suppose that there were 100,000 billing records total and that 20%, or 20,000, were billed erroneously. Then the plus or minus 5% interval translates to an interval from 15,000 to 25,000 bad billings. That is, we are 95% confident that the estimate is not off by more than 5000 billing records on either side. The author defines the *relative error* in this case to be 0.25: the potential error, 5000, divided by the number to be estimated, 20,000. Now change the example slightly so that 60%, or 60,000, were billed erroneously. Then plus or minus 5% translates to the interval from 55,000 to 65,000, and the relative error is 5000/60,000, or 0.083. The point is that the same plus or minus 5% *absolute* error for *p* results in a much smaller *relative* error in the second example.

Using this reasoning, the author suggested that they should choose the sample size to achieve a prescribed *relative* error in the number of bad billings. This can change the magnitude of the sample size considerably. For example, the author shows by means of a rather complicated sample size formula that if a relative error of 0.10 is desired and the value of *p* is somewhere around 0.10, a sample size of about 3600 is required. On the other hand, if a relative error of 0.10 is still desired but the value of *p* is somewhere around 0.5, then the required sample size is only about 400.

Sample size formulas, and statistical arguments that lead to them, are far from intuitive. In this legal case, by keeping the math to a minimum and using simple terminology like *relative error*, the author eventually convinced the others to use his approach, even though it led to a considerably larger sample size than the 385 originally proposed. ∎

7-1 INTRODUCTION

This chapter sets the stage for statistical inference, a topic that is explored in the following few chapters. In a typical statistical inference problem, you want to discover one or more characteristics of a given population. For example, you might want to know the propor-tion of toothpaste customers who have tried, or intend to try, a particular brand. Or you might want to know the average amount owed on credit card accounts for a population of customers at a shopping mall. Generally, the population is large and/or spread out, and it is difficult, maybe even impossible, to contact each member. Therefore, you identify a sample of the population and then obtain information from the members of the sample.

There are two main objectives of this chapter. The first is to discuss the sampling schemes that are generally used in real sampling applications. We focus on several types of *random* samples and see why these are preferable to nonrandom samples. The second objective is to see how the information from a sample of the population—for example, 1% of the population—can be used to infer the properties of the entire population. The key here is the concept of a *sampling distribution*. In this chapter we focus on the sampling distribu-tion of the sample mean, and we discuss the role of a famous mathematical result called the *central limit theorem*. Specifically, we discuss how the central limit theorem is the reason for the importance of the *normal* distribution in statistical inference.

7-2 SAMPLING TERMINOLOGY

We begin by introducing some terminology that is used in sampling. In any sampling problem there is a relevant *population*. A **population** is the set of all members about which a study intends to make inferences, where an *inference* is a statement about a numerical characteristic of the population, such as an average income or the proportion of incomes below \$50,000. It is important to realize that a population is defined in relationship to any particular study. Any analyst planning a survey should first decide which population the conclusions of the study will concern, so that a sample can be chosen from *this* population.

> The relevant **population** contains all members about which a study intends to make inferences.

For example, if a marketing researcher plans to use a questionnaire to infer consumers' reactions to a new product, she must first decide which population of consumers is of interest—all consumers, consumers over 21 years old, consumers who do most of their shopping in shopping malls, or others. Once the relevant consumer population has been designated, a sample from this population can then be surveyed. However, it is important to remember that inferences made from the study pertain only to this *particular* population.

Before you can choose a sample from a given population, you typically need a list of all members of the population. In sampling terminology, this list is called a **frame**, and the potential sample members are called **sampling units**. Depending on the context, sampling units could be individual people, households, companies, cities, or others.

> A **frame** is a list of all members, called **sampling units**, in the population.

It is customary in virtually all statistical literature to let uppercase N be the population size and lowercase n be the sample size. We follow this convention as well.

In this chapter we assume that the population is finite and consists of N sampling units. We also assume that a frame of these N sampling units is available. Unfortunately, there are many situations where a complete frame is practically impossible to obtain. For example, if the purpose of a study is to survey the attitudes of all unemployed teenagers in Chicago, it is practically impossible to obtain a complete frame of them. In this situation the best alternative is to obtain a partial frame from which the sample can be selected. If the partial frame omits any significant segments of the population that a complete frame would include, then the resulting sample could be biased. For instance, if you use the Yellow Pages of a Los Angeles telephone book to choose a sample of restaurants, you automatically omit all restaurants that do not advertise in the Yellow Pages. Depending on the purposes of the study, this could be a serious omission.

There are two basic types of samples: *probability samples* and *judgmental samples*. A **probability sample** is a sample in which the sampling units are chosen from the population according to a random mechanism. In contrast, no formal random mechanism is used to select a **judgmental sample**. In this case the sampling units are chosen according to the sampler's judgment.

> The members of a **probability sample** are chosen according to a random mechanism, whereas the members of a **judgmental sample** are chosen according to the sampler's judgment.

We do not discuss judgmental samples. The reason is very simple—there is no way to measure the accuracy of judgmental samples because the rules of probability do not apply to them. In other words, if a population characteristic is estimated from the observations in a judgmental sample, there is no way to measure the accuracy of this estimate. In addition, it is very difficult to choose a representative sample from a population *without* using some random mechanism. Because our judgment is usually not as good as we think, judgmental samples are likely to contain our own built-in biases. Therefore, we focus exclusively on probability samples from here on.

7-3 METHODS FOR SELECTING RANDOM SAMPLES

In this section we discuss the types of random samples that are used in real sampling applications. Different types of sampling schemes have different properties. There is typically a trade-off between cost and accuracy. Some sampling schemes are cheaper and easier to administer, whereas others are more costly but provide more accurate information. We discuss some of these issues. However, anyone who intends to make a living in survey sampling needs to learn much more about the topic than we can cover here.

7-3a Simple Random Sampling

The simplest type of sampling scheme is appropriately called *simple random sampling*. Consider a population of size N and suppose you want to sample n units from this population. Then a **simple random sample** of size n has the property that every possible sample of size n has the same probability of being chosen. Simple random samples are the easiest to understand, and their statistical properties are the most straightforward. Therefore, we will focus primarily on simple random samples in the rest of this book. However, as we discuss shortly, more complex random samples are often used in real applications.

> A **simple random sample** of size n is one where each possible sample of size n has the same chance of being chosen.

Let's illustrate the concept with a simple random sample for a small population. Suppose the population size is $N = 5$, and the five members of the population are labeled a, b, c, d, and e. Also, suppose the sample size is $n = 2$. Then the possible samples are (a, b), (a, c), (a, d), (a, e), (b, c), (b, d), (b, e), (c, d), (c, e), and (d, e). That is, there are 10 possible samples—the number of ways two members can be chosen from five members. Then a *simple* random sample of size $n = 2$ has the property that each of these 10 possible samples has the same probability, 1/10, of being chosen.

One other property of simple random samples can be seen from this example. If you focus on any member of the population, say, member b, you will see that b is a member of 4 of the 10 samples. Therefore, the probability that b is chosen in a simple random sample is 4/10, or 2/5. In general, any member has the same probability n/N of being chosen in a simple random sample. If you are one of 100,000 members of a population, then the probability that you will be selected in a simple random sample of size 100 is 100/100,000, or 1 out of 1000.

There are several ways simple random samples can be chosen, all of which involve random numbers. One approach that works well for the small example with $N = 5$ and $n = 2$ is to generate a single random number with the RAND function in Excel®. You divide the interval from 0 to 1 into 10 equal subintervals of length 1/10 each and see which of these subintervals the random number falls into. You then choose the corresponding sample. For example, suppose the random number is 0.465. This is in the fifth subinterval, that is, the interval from 0.4 to 0.5, so you choose the fifth sample, (b, c).

For those who have not yet covered the simulation sections of previous chapters: The RAND function in Excel generates numbers that are distributed randomly and uniformly between 0 and 1.

This method is clearly consistent with simple random sampling—each of the samples has the same chance of being chosen—but it is prohibitive when n and N are large. In this case there are too many possible samples to list. Fortunately, there is another method that can be used. The idea is simple. You sort the N members of the population randomly, using Excel's RAND function to generate random numbers for the sort. Then you include the first n members from the sorted sequence in the random sample. This procedure is illustrated in Example 7.1.

EXAMPLE 7.1 SAMPLING FAMILIES TO ANALYZE ANNUAL INCOMES

Consider the frame of 40 families with annual incomes shown in column B of Figure 7.1. (See the file **Random Sampling.xlsm**. The extension is xlsm because this file contains a macro. When you open it, you will need to click the button above the formula bar to enable the macro.) We want to choose a simple random sample of size 10 from this frame. How can this be done? And how do summary statistics of the chosen families compare to the corresponding summary statistics of the population?

Figure 7.1

Population Income Data

	A	B	C	D
1	Simple random sampling			
2				
3	Summary statistics			
4		Mean	Median	Stdev
5	Population	$39,985	$38,500	$7,377
6	Sample			
7				
8	Population			
9	Family	Income		
10	1	$43,300		
11	2	$44,300		
12	3	$34,600		
47	38	$46,900		
48	39	$37,300		
49	40	$41,000		

© Cengage Learning

Objective To illustrate how Excel's random number function, RAND, can be used to generate simple random samples.

Solution

The idea is very simple. You first generate a column of random numbers in column F. Then you sort the rows according to the random numbers and choose the first 10 families in the sorted rows. The following procedure produces the results in Figure 7.2. (See the first sheet in the finished version of the file.)

1. **Random numbers next to a copy.** Copy the original data to columns D and E. Then enter the formula

   =RAND()

   in cell F10 and copy it down column F.

2. **Replace with values.** To enable sorting, you must first "freeze" the random numbers—that is, replace their formulas with values. To do this, copy the range F10:F49 and select Paste Values from the Paste dropdown menu on the Home ribbon.

3. **Sort.** Sort on column F in ascending order. Then the 10 families with the 10 smallest random numbers are the ones in the sample. These are shaded in the figure. (Note that you could instead have chosen the 10 families with the 10 *largest* random numbers. This would be equally valid.)

4. **Means.** Use the AVERAGE, MEDIAN, and STDEV functions in row 6 to calculate summary statistics of the first 10 incomes in column E. Similar summary statistics for the population have already been calculated in row 5. (Cell D5 uses the STDEVP function because this is the *population* standard deviation.)

Figure 7.2

Selecting a Simple
Random Sample

	A	B	C	D	E	F
1	Simple random sampling					
2						
3	Summary statistics					
4		Mean	Median	Stdev		
5	Population	$39,985	$38,500	$7,377		
6	Sample	$41,490	$42,850	$5,323		
7						
8	Population			Random sample		
9	Family	Income		Family	Income	Random #
10	1	$43,300		1	$43,300	0.04545
11	2	$44,300		2	$44,300	0.1496768
12	3	$34,600		12	$51,500	0.23527
13	4	$38,000		7	$42,700	0.2746325
14	5	$44,700		13	$35,900	0.3003506
15	6	$45,600		15	$43,000	0.3197393
16	7	$42,700		6	$45,600	0.3610983
17	8	$36,900		3	$34,600	0.3852641
18	9	$38,400		9	$38,400	0.4427564
19	10	$33,700		14	$35,600	0.4447877
20	11	$44,100		5	$44,700	0.4505899
21	12	$51,500		40	$41,000	0.4597361
47	38	$46,900		39	$37,300	0.8644119
48	39	$37,300		8	$36,900	0.9059098
49	40	$41,000		10	$33,700	0.9637509

© Cengage Learning

To obtain more random samples of size 10 (for comparison), you would need to go through this process repeatedly. To save you the trouble of doing so, we wrote a macro to automate the process. (See the Automated sheet in the finished version of the file.) This sheet looks essentially the same as the sheet in Figure 7.2, except that there is a button to run the macro, and only the required data remain on the spreadsheet. Try clicking this button. Each time you do so, you will get a different random sample—and different summary measures in row 6. By doing this many times and keeping track of the sample summary data, you can see how the summary measures vary from sample to sample. We will have much more to say about this variation later in the chapter. ∎

The procedure described in Example 7.1 can be used in Excel to select a simple random sample of any size from any population. All you need is a frame that lists the population values. Then it is just a matter of inserting random numbers, freezing them, and sorting on the random numbers.

Perhaps surprisingly, simple random samples are used infrequently in real applications. There are several reasons for this.

- Because each sampling unit has the same chance of being sampled, simple random sampling can result in samples that are spread over a large geographical region. This can make sampling extremely expensive, especially if personal interviews are used.

- Simple random sampling requires that all sampling units be identified prior to sampling. Sometimes this is infeasible.

- Simple random sampling can result in underrepresentation or overrepresentation of certain segments of the population. For example, if the primary—but not sole— interest is in the graduate student subpopulation of university students, a simple random sample of *all* university students might not provide enough information about the graduate students.

Despite this, most of the statistical analysis in this book assumes simple random samples. The analysis is considerably more complex for other types of random samples and is best left to more advanced books on sampling.

Using StatTools to Generate Simple Random Samples

The method described in Example 7.1 is simple but somewhat tedious, especially if you want to generate more than one random sample. (Even the macro described at the end of the example works only for that particular file.) Fortunately, a more general method is available in StatTools. This procedure generates any number of simple random samples of any specified sample size from a given data set. It can be found in the Data Utilities (not Utilities) dropdown list on the StatTools ribbon.

EXAMPLE	7.2 SAMPLING ACCOUNTS RECEIVABLE AT SPRING MILLS

The file **Accounts Receivable.xlsx** contains 280 accounts receivable for Spring Mills Company. There are three variables:

- Size: customer size, categorized as small, medium, or large depending on its volume of business with Spring Mills
- Days: number of days since the customer was billed
- Amount: amount of the bill

Generate 25 random samples of size 15 each from the small customers only, calculate the average amount owed in each random sample, and construct a histogram of these 25 averages.

Objective   To illustrate StatTools's method of choosing simple random samples and to demonstrate how sample means are distributed.

Solution

In most real-world applications, you would generate only a *single* random sample from a population, so why do we ask you to generate 25 random samples in this example? The reason is that we want to introduce the concept of a sampling distribution, in this case the sampling distribution of the sample mean. This is the distribution of *all possible* sample means you could generate from all possible samples (of a given size) from a population. By generating a fairly large number of random samples from the population of accounts receivable, you can begin to see what the sampling distribution of the sample mean looks like.

We proceed in several steps. First, because you want random samples of the small customers only and the data are already sorted on Size, you first create a StatTools data set of the small customers only. (It is the range A1:D151.) Then select Random Sample from the StatTools Data Utilities dropdown list to generate 25 samples of size 15 each of the Amount variable.[1] (The Random Sample dialog box should be filled out as shown in Figure 7.3.) These will appear on a new Random Sample sheet, as shown in Figure 7.4 (with many columns hidden). Each of these columns is a random sample of 15 Amount values.

Next, insert a new column A, as shown in Figure 7.4, and calculate the averages in row 17 for each sample with Excel's AVERAGE function. Finally, to obtain a histogram of the averages in row 17, define a second StatTools data set of the data in row 17 of

---

[1]Strictly speaking, the sampling distribution of the sample mean is the distribution of all possible sample means when sampling is done *with replacement*, where any member of the population can be sampled multiple times. However, real-world sampling is almost always done *without replacement*, so this is what we illustrate here.

Figure 7.3

Random Sample Dialog Box

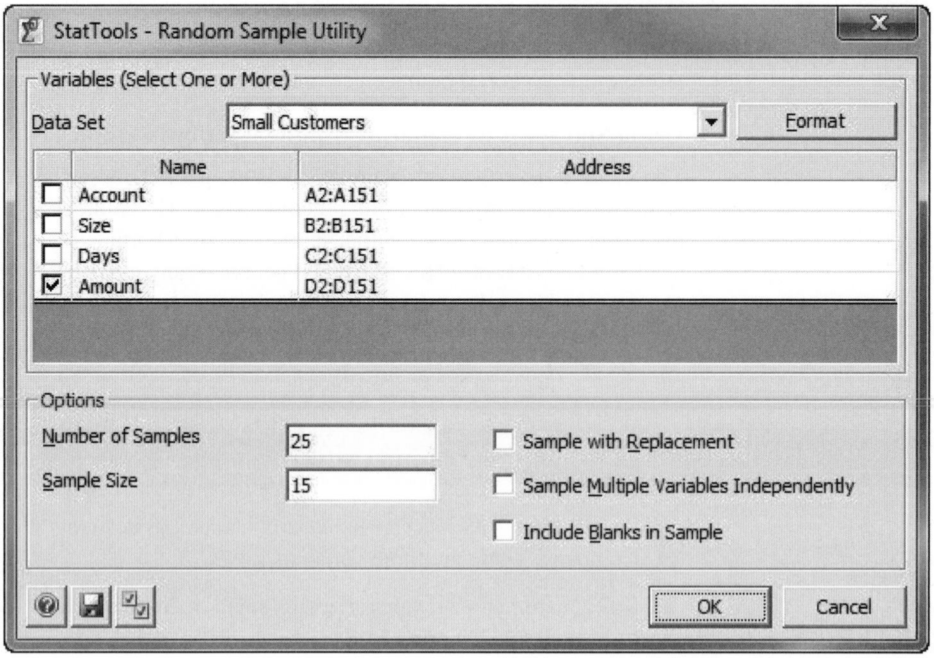

Figure 7.4

Randomly Generated Samples

▲	A	B	C	D	Y	Z
1		Amount(1)	Amount(2)	Amount(3)	Amount(24)	Amount(25)
2		260	200	290	240	260
3		230	240	260	210	290
4		250	310	240	230	300
5		280	250	290	220	240
6		210	210	330	200	250
7		310	270	210	220	270
8		280	270	290	240	270
9		260	190	260	410	250
10		280	240	370	300	230
11		240	190	290	260	240
12		210	240	260	270	250
13		270	240	260	210	150
14		240	240	230	210	180
15		220	300	240	250	310
16		260	320	240	280	200
17	Average	253.333	247.333	270.667	250.000	246.000

Figure 7.4 but, for a change, specify that the only variable for this data set is in a *row,* not a column. (This is an option in the StatTools Data Set Manager.) You can then create a histogram of these 25 averages in the usual way. It appears in Figure 7.5.

The histogram in Figure 7.5 indicates the variability of sample means you might obtain by selecting many *different* random samples of size 15 from this particular population of small customer accounts. This histogram, which is approximately bell-shaped, approximates the sampling distribution of the sample mean. We will come back to this important idea when we discuss sampling distributions in Section 7-4. ∎

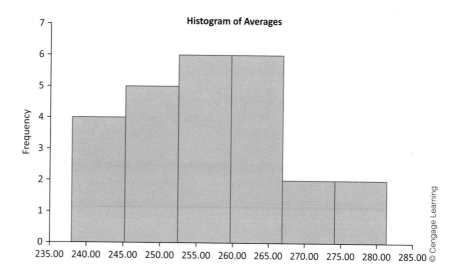

Figure 7.5

Histogram of 25 Sample Averages

In the next several subsections we describe sampling plans that are often used. These plans differ from simple random sampling both in the way the samples are chosen and in the way the data analysis is performed. However, we will barely touch on this latter issue. The details are quite complicated and are better left to a book devoted entirely to sampling.[2]

FUNDAMENTAL INSIGHT

Types of Random Samples

There are actually many methods for choosing random samples, some described only briefly in this book, and they all have their advantages and disadvantages from practical and statistical standpoints. Surprisingly, the simplest of these, where each subset of the population has the same chance of being chosen, is *not* the most frequently used method in real applications. This is basically because other more complex methods can make more efficient use of a given sample size. Nevertheless, the *concepts* you learn here remain essentially the same, regardless of the exact sampling method used.

7-3b Systematic Sampling

Suppose you are asked to select a random sample of 250 names from the white pages of a telephone book. Let's also say that there are 55,000 names listed in the white pages. A **systematic sample** provides a convenient way to choose the sample. First, you divide the population size by the sample size: $55,000/250 = 220$. Conceptually, you can think of dividing the book into 250 "blocks" with 220 names per block. Next, you use a random mechanism to choose a number between 1 and 220. Suppose this number is 131. Then you choose the 131st name and every 220th name thereafter. So you would choose name 131, name 351, name 571, and so on. The result is a systematic sample of size $n = 250$.

In general, one of the first k members is selected randomly, and then every kth member after this one is selected. The value k is called the *sampling interval* and equals the ratio N/n, where N is the population size and n is the desired sample size.

Systematic sampling is quite different from simple random sampling because not every sample of size 250 has a chance of being chosen. In fact, there are only 220 different

[2]See, for example, the excellent book by Levy and Lemeshow (1999).

samples possible (depending on the first number chosen), and each of these is equally likely. Nevertheless, systematic sampling is generally similar to simple random sampling in its statistical properties. The key is the relationship between the ordering of the sampling units in the frame (the white pages of the telephone book in this case) and the purpose of the study.

If the purpose of the study is to analyze personal incomes, then there is probably no relationship between the alphabetical ordering of names in the telephone book and personal income. However, there are situations where the ordering of the sampling units is *not* random, which could make systematic sampling more or less appealing. For example, suppose that a company wants to sample randomly from its customers, and its customer list is in decreasing order of order volumes. That is, the largest customers are at the top of the list and the smallest are at the bottom. Then systematic sampling might be more representative than simple random sampling because it guarantees a wide range of customers in terms of order volumes.

However, some type of cyclical ordering in the list of sampling units can lead to very *unrepresentative* samples. As an extreme, suppose a company has a list of daily transactions (Monday through Saturday) and it decides to draw a systematic sample with the sampling interval equal to 6. Then if the first sampled day is Monday, all other days in the sample will be Mondays. This could clearly bias the sample. Except for obvious examples like this one, however, systematic sampling can be an attractive alternative to simple random sampling and is often used because of its convenience.

7-3c Stratified Sampling

Suppose various subpopulations within the total population can be identified. These subpopulations are called *strata*. Then instead of taking a simple random sample from the entire population, it might make more sense to select a simple random sample from each stratum separately. This sampling method is called **stratified sampling**. It is a particularly useful approach when there is considerable variation *between* the various strata but relatively little variation *within* a given stratum.

> In **stratified sampling**, the population is divided into relatively homogeneous subsets called *strata*, and then random samples are taken from each stratum.

There are several advantages to stratified sampling. One obvious advantage is that separate estimates can be obtained within each stratum—which would not be obtained with a simple random sample from the entire population. Even if the samples from the individual strata are eventually pooled, it cannot hurt to have the total sample broken down into separate samples initially.

A more important advantage of stratified sampling is that the accuracy of the resulting population estimates can be increased by using appropriately defined strata. The trick is to define the strata so that there is less variability *within* the individual strata than in the population as a whole. You want strata such that there is relative homogeneity within the strata, but relative heterogeneity across the strata, with respect to the variable(s) being analyzed. By choosing the strata in this way, you can generally obtain more accuracy for a given sampling cost than you could obtain from a simple random sample at the same cost. Alternatively, you can achieve the same level of accuracy at a lower sampling cost.

The key to using stratified sampling effectively is selecting the appropriate strata. Suppose a company that advertises its product on television wants to estimate the reaction of viewers to the advertising. Here the population consists of all viewers who have seen the advertising. But what are the appropriate strata? The answer depends on the company's objectives and its product. The company could stratify the population by gender, by income, by age, by amount of television watched, by the amount of the product class consumed, and probably others. Without knowing more specific information about the company's objectives, it is impossible to say which of these stratification schemes is most appropriate.

Suppose that you have identified I nonoverlapping strata in a given population. Let N be the total population size, and let N_i be the population size of stratum i, so that

$$N = N_1 + N_2 + \ldots + N_I$$

To obtain a stratified random sample, you must first choose a total sample size n, and then choose a sample size n_i from each stratum i such that

$$n = n_1 + n_2 + \ldots + n_I$$

You can then select a simple random sample of the specified size from *each* stratum exactly as in Example 7.1.

However, how do you choose the individual sample sizes n_1 through n_I, given that the total sample size n has been chosen? For example, if you decide to sample 500 customers in total, how many should come from each stratum? There are many ways to choose sample sizes n_1 through n_I that sum to n, but probably the most popular method is to use **proportional sample sizes**. The idea is very simple. If one stratum has, say, 15% of the total population, then you select 15% of the total sample from this stratum. For example, if the total sample size is $n = 500$, you select $0.15(500) = 75$ members from this stratum.

> With **proportional sample sizes**, the proportion of a stratum in the sample is the same as the proportion of that stratum in the population.

The advantage of proportional sample sizes is that they are very easy to determine. The disadvantage is that they ignore differences in variability among the strata. To illustrate, suppose that you are attempting to estimate the population mean amount paid annually per student for textbooks at a large university. You identify three strata: undergraduates, master's students, and doctoral students. Their population sizes are 20,000, 4000, and 1000, respectively. Therefore, the proportions of students in these strata are $20,000/25,000 = 0.80$, $4000/25,000 = 0.16$, and $1000/25,000 = 0.04$. If the total sample size is $n = 150$, then the sample should include 120 undergraduates, 24 master's students, and 6 doctoral students if proportional sample sizes are used.

However, let σ_i be the standard deviation of annual textbook payments in stratum i, and suppose that $\sigma_1 = \$50$, $\sigma_2 = \$120$, and $\sigma_3 = \$180$. That is, there is considerably more variation in the amounts paid by doctoral students than by undergraduates, with the master's students in the middle. If you are interested in estimating the mean amount spent per student, then despite its small sample size, the doctoral sample is likely to have a large effect on the accuracy of your estimate of the mean. This is because of its relatively large standard deviation. In contrast, you might not need to sample as heavily from the undergraduate population because of its relatively small standard deviation. In general, strata with less variability can afford to be sampled less heavily than proportional sampling calls for, and the opposite is true for strata with larger variability. In fact, there are *optimal* sample size formulas that take the σ_i's into account, but they are not presented here.

Example 7.3 illustrates how stratified sampling can be implemented in Excel.

EXAMPLE 7.3 STRATIFIED SAMPLING FROM CREDIT CARD HOLDERS

The file **Stratified Sampling.xlsx** contains a frame of all 50,000 people in the city of Midtown who have a particular retailer's credit card. The retailer is interested in estimating the average number of *other* credit cards these people own, as well as other information about their use of credit. The company decides to stratify these customers by age, select a stratified sample of size 200 with proportional sample sizes, and then contact these 200 people by phone. How might the company proceed?

Objective   To illustrate how stratified sampling, with proportional sample sizes, can be implemented in Excel.

Solution

First, the company has to decide exactly how to stratify by age. Their reasoning is that different age groups probably have different attitudes and behavior regarding credit. After some preliminary investigation, they decide to use three age categories: 18–30, 31–62, and 63–80. (We assume that no one in the population is younger than 18 or older than 80.)

Figure 7.6 shows how the calculations might then proceed. You begin with the following inputs: (1) the total sample size in cell B3, (2) the definitions of the strata in rows 6 through 8, and (3) the customer data in the range A11:B50010. To see which age category each customer is in, enter the formula

$$= \text{IF}(B11 <= \$D\$6,1,\text{IF}(B11 <= \$D\$7,2,3))$$

in cell C11 and then copy it down column C. Then sort on column C to put all of the customers in the same age groups together.

Figure 7.6

Selecting a Stratified Sample

	A	B	C	D	E	F	G	H
1	**Stratified sampling**							
2								
3	Total sample size	200						
4								
5	Strata based on age					Stratum	Count	Sample size
6	Stratum 1	18	to	30		1	10328	41
7	Stratum 2	31	to	62		2	25402	102
8	Stratum 3	63	to	80		3	14270	57
9								
10	Customer	Age	Stratum	Random #	Stratum index	In sample?		
11	23741	24	1	1.82E-05	1	Yes		
12	49746	21	1	0.0002263	2	Yes		
13	17423	29	1	0.00027	3	Yes		
14	10163	22	1	0.0002908	4	Yes		
15	44672	26	1	0.0005457	5	Yes		
50007	8434	64	3	0.9997092	14267	No		
50008	43033	68	3	0.9998092	14268	No		
50009	35265	79	3	0.9999229	14269	No		
50010	28813	79	3	0.9999873	14270	No		

© Cengage Learning

The next step is to find the proportional sample sizes. First, find the number of customers in stratum 1 with the formula

$$=\text{COUNTIF}(\$C\$11:\$C\$50010,F6)$$

in cell G6 and copy it down to cell G8. Then find the required sample size for stratum 1 in cell H6 with the formula

$$=\text{ROUND}(\$B\$3*G6/50000,0)$$

and copy it down to cell H8. Note that the ROUND function has been used to round to the nearest integer.

Finally, there are a number of ways the sampled members can be chosen. Here is one fairly simple procedure.

1. Enter random numbers with the RAND function in column D and then freeze them.

2. Do a custom sort, first on the strata in column C and then on the random numbers in column D.

3. Enter indexes, starting at 1 for each stratum in column E by entering 1 in cell E11 and then entering the formula

    =IF(C12=C11,E11+1,1)

    in cell E12 and copying down.

4. Create a Yes/No column in column F by entering the formula

    =IF(E11<=VLOOKUP(C11,$F$6:$H$8,3),"Yes","No")

    in cell F11 and copying down.

If you want a different random sample, just repeat these four steps. The setup will appear (with many hidden rows) as in Figure 7.6. You can check that there are as many "Yes" entries for each stratum in column F as required by the proportional sample sizes in column H. ∎

7-3d Cluster Sampling

Suppose that a company is interested in various characteristics of households in a particular city. The sampling units are households. You could select a random sample of households by one of the sampling methods already discussed. However, it might be more convenient to proceed somewhat differently. You could first divide the city into city blocks and consider the city blocks as sampling units. You could then select a simple random sample of city blocks and then sample all of the households in the chosen blocks. In this case the city blocks are called *clusters* and the sampling scheme is called **cluster sampling**.

> In **cluster sampling**, the population is separated into clusters, such as cities or city blocks, and then a random sample of the clusters is selected.

Cluster analysis is typically more convenient and less costly than other random sampling methods.

The primary advantage of cluster sampling is sampling convenience (and possibly lower cost). If an agency is sending interviewers to interview heads of household, it is much easier for them to concentrate on particular city blocks than to contact households throughout the city. The downside, however, is that the inferences drawn from a cluster sample can be less accurate for a given sample size than from other sampling plans.

Consider the following scenario. A nationwide company wants to survey its salespeople with regard to management practices. It decides to randomly select several sales districts (the clusters) and then interview all salespeople in the selected districts. It is likely that in any particular sales district the attitudes toward management are somewhat similar. This overlapping information means that the company is probably not getting the maximum amount of information per sampling dollar spent. Instead of sampling 20 salespeople from a given district, all of whom have similar attitudes, it might be better to sample 20 salespeople from different districts who have a wider variety of attitudes. Nevertheless, the relative convenience of cluster sampling sometimes outweighs these statistical considerations.

Selecting a cluster sample is straightforward. The key is to define the sampling units as the *clusters*—the city blocks, for example. Then a simple random sample of clusters can be chosen exactly as in Example 7.1. Once the clusters are selected, it is typical to sample all of the population members in each selected cluster.

7-3e Multistage Sampling Schemes

The cluster sampling scheme just described, where a sample of clusters is chosen and then all of the sampling units within each chosen cluster are taken, is called a **single-stage** sampling scheme. Real applications are often more complex than this, resulting in **multistage** sampling schemes. For example, the Gallup organization uses multistage sampling in its nationwide surveys. A random sample of approximately 300 locations is chosen in the first stage of the sampling process. City blocks or other geographical areas are then randomly sampled from the first-stage locations in the second stage of the process. This is followed by a systematic sampling of households from each second-stage area. A total of about 1500 households comprise a typical Gallup poll.

We will not pursue the topic of multistage sampling schemes in this book. However, you should realize that real-world sampling procedures can be very complex.

PROBLEMS

Note: Student solutions for problems whose numbers appear within a colored box are available for purchase at www.cengagebrain.com.

Level A

1. The file **P02_07.xlsx** includes data on 204 employees at the (fictional) company Beta Technologies. For this problem, consider this data set as the population frame.

  a. Using the method in this section (not StatTools), generate a simple random sample of size 20 from this population.

  b. Use StatTools to generate 10 simple random samples of size 20 from this population.

  c. Calculate the population mean, median, and standard deviation of Annual Salary. Then calculate the sample mean, median, and standard deviation of Annual Salary for each of the samples in parts **a** and **b**. Comment briefly on how they compare to each other and the population measures.

2. The file **P07_02.xlsx** contains data on the 1995 students who have gone through the MBA program at State University. You can consider this the population of State University's MBA students.

  a. Find the mean and standard deviation for each of the numerical variables in this population. Also, find the following proportions: the proportion of students who are male, the proportion of students who are international (not from the USA), the proportion of students under 30 years of age, and the proportion of students with an engineering undergrad major.

  b. Using the method in this section (not StatTools), generate a simple random sample of 100 students from this population, and find the mean and standard deviation of each numerical variable in the sample. Is there any way to know (without the information in part **a**) whether your summary measures for the sample are lower or higher than the (supposedly unknown) population summary measures?

  c. Use StatTools to generate 10 simple random samples of size 100. For each, find the mean of School Debt and its deviation from the population mean in part **a** (negative if it is below the population mean, positive if it is above the population mean). What is the average of these 10 deviations? What would you expect it to be?

  d. We want random samples to be representative of the population in terms of various demographics. For each of the samples in part **c**, find each of the proportions requested in part **a**. Do these samples appear to be representative of the population in terms of age, gender, nationality, and undergrad major? Why or why not? If they are not representative, is it because there is something wrong with the sampling procedure?

3. The file **P02_35.xlsx** contains data from a survey of 500 randomly selected households.

  a. Suppose you decide to generate a systematic random sample of size 25 from this population of data. How many such samples are there? What is the mean of Debt for each of the first three such samples, using the data in the order given?

b. If you wanted to estimate the (supposedly unknown) population mean of Debt from a systematic random sample as in part **a**, why might it be a good idea to sort first on Debt? If you do so, what is the mean of Debt for each of the first three such samples?

4. Recall from Chapter 2 that the file **Supermarket Transactions.xlsx** contains over 14,000 transactions made by supermarket customers over a period of approximately two years. For this problem, consider this data set the population of transactions.

   a. If you were interested in estimating the mean of Revenue for the population, why *might* it make sense to use a stratified sample, stratified by product family, to estimate this mean?

   b. Suppose you want to generate a stratified random sample, stratified by product family, and have the total sample size be 250. If you use proportional sample sizes, how many transactions should you sample from each of the three product families?

   c. Calculate the population standard deviations for each of the three product families. Given these and the discussion in the book, do you think the *optimal* sample sizes would be much different from the proportional sample sizes?

   d. Using the sample sizes from part **b**, generate a corresponding stratified random sample. What are the individual sample means from the three product families? What are the sample standard deviations?

Level B

5. This problem illustrates an interesting variation of simple random sampling.

   a. Open a blank spreadsheet and use the RAND() function to create a column of 1000 random numbers. Don't freeze them. This is actually a simple random sample from the uniform distribution between 0 and 1. Use the COUNTIF function to count the number of values between 0 and 0.1, between 0.1 and 0.2, and so on. Each such interval should contain about 1/10 of all values. Do they? (Keep pressing the F9 key to see how the results change.)

   b. Repeat part **a**, generating a second column of random numbers, but now generate the first 100 as uniform between 0 and 0.1, the next 100 as uniform between 0.1 and 0.2, and so on, up to 0.9 to 1. (*Hint:* For example, to create a random number uniformly distributed between 0.5 and 0.6, use the formula **=0.5+0.1*RAND()**. Do you see why?) Again, use COUNTIF to find the number of the 1000 values in each of the intervals, although there shouldn't be any surprises this time. Why might this type of random sampling be preferable to the random sampling in part **a**? (Note: The sampling in part **a** is called Monte Carlo sampling, whereas the sampling in part **b** is basically Latin Hypercube sampling, the form of sampling we advocate in Chapters 15 and 16 on simulation.)

6. Another type of random sample is called a *bootstrap sample*. (It comes from the expression "pulling yourself up by your own bootstraps.") Given a data set with n observations, a bootstrap sample, also of size n, is when you randomly sample from the data set *with replacement*. To do so, you keep choosing a random integer from 1 to n and include that item in the sample. The "with replacement" part means that you can sample the same item more than once. For example, if $n = 4$, the sampled items might be 1, 2, 2, and 4. Using the data in the file **Accounts Receivable.xlsx**, illustrate a simple method for choosing bootstrap samples with the RANDBETWEEN and VLOOKUP functions. For each bootstrap sample, find the mean and standard deviation of Days and Amount, and find the counts in the different size categories. How do these compare to the similar measures for the original data set? (For more on bootstrap sampling, do a Web search. Wikipedia has a nice overview.)

7-4 INTRODUCTION TO ESTIMATION

The purpose of any random sample, simple or otherwise, is to estimate properties of a population from the data observed in the sample. The following is a good example to keep in mind. Suppose a government agency wants to know the average household income over the population of all households in Indiana. Then this unknown average is the population parameter of interest, and the government is likely to estimate it by sampling several representative households in Indiana and reporting the average of their incomes.

The mathematical procedures appropriate for performing this estimation depend on which properties of the population are of interest and which type of random sampling scheme is used. Because the details are considerably more complex for more complex sampling schemes such as multistage sampling, we will focus on *simple* random samples, where the mathematical details are relatively straightforward. Details for other sampling schemes such as stratified sampling can be found in Levy and Lemeshow (1999). However, even for more complex sampling schemes, the *concepts* are the same as those we discuss here; only the details change.

Throughout most of this section, we focus on the population mean of some variable such as household income. Our goal is to estimate this population mean by using the data in a randomly selected sample. We first discuss the types of errors that can occur.

7-4a Sources of Estimation Error

There are two basic sources of errors that can occur when you sample randomly from a population: *sampling error* and all other sources, usually lumped together as *nonsampling error*. Sampling error results from "unlucky" samples. As such, the term *error* is somewhat misleading. Suppose, for example, that the mean household income in Indiana is $58,225. (We can only assume that this is the true value. It wouldn't actually be known without taking a census.) A government agency wants to estimate this mean, so it randomly samples 500 Indiana households and finds that their average household income is $60,495. If the agency then infers that the mean of *all* Indiana household incomes is $60,495, the resulting sampling error is the difference between the reported value and the true value: $60,495 − $58,225 = $2270. Note that the agency hasn't done anything wrong. This sampling error is essentially due to bad luck.

> **Sampling error** is the inevitable result of basing an inference on a random sample rather than on the entire population.

We will soon discuss how to measure the *potential* sampling error involved. The point here is that the resulting estimation error is not caused by anything the government agency is doing wrong—it might just get unlucky.

Nonsampling error is quite different and can occur for a variety of reasons. We discuss a few of them.

- Perhaps the most serious type of nonsampling error is **nonresponse bias**. This occurs when a portion of the sample fails to respond to the survey. Anyone who has ever conducted a questionnaire, whether by mail, by phone, or any other method, knows that the percentage of nonrespondents can be quite large. The question is whether this introduces estimation error. If the nonrespondents *would* have responded similarly to the respondents, you don't lose much by not hearing from them. However, because the nonrespondents don't respond, you typically have no way of knowing whether they differ in some important respect from the respondents. Therefore, unless you are able to persuade the nonrespondents to respond—through a follow-up email, for example—you must guess at the amount of nonresponse bias.

- Another source of nonsampling error is **nontruthful responses**. This is particularly a problem when there are sensitive questions in a questionnaire. For example, if the questions "Have you ever had an abortion?" or "Do you regularly use cocaine?" are asked, most people will answer "no," regardless of whether the true answer is "yes" or "no."

  There is a way of getting at such sensitive information, called the *randomized response* technique. Here the investigator presents each respondent with two questions, one of which is the sensitive question. The other is innocuous, such as, "Were you born in the summer?" The respondent is asked to decide randomly which of the two questions to answer—by flipping a coin, say—and then answer the chosen question truthfully. The investigator sees only the answer (yes or no), not the result of the coin flip. That is, the investigator doesn't know which question is being answered.

However, by using probability theory, it is possible for the investigator to infer from many such responses the percentage of the population whose truthful answer to the sensitive question is "yes."

- Another type of nonsampling error is **measurement error**. This occurs when the responses to the questions do not reflect what the investigator had in mind. It might result from poorly worded questions, questions the respondents don't fully understand, questions that require the respondents to supply information they don't have, and so on. Undoubtedly, there have been times when you were filling out a questionnaire and said to yourself, "OK, I'll answer this as well as I can, but I know it's not what they want to know."

- One final type of nonsampling error is **voluntary response bias**. This occurs when the subset of people who respond to a survey differ in some important respect from all potential respondents. For example, suppose a population of students is surveyed to see how many hours they study per night. If the students who respond are predominantly those who get the best grades, the resulting sample mean number of hours could be biased on the high side.

From this discussion and your own experience with questionnaires, you should realize that the potential for nonsampling error is enormous. However, unlike sampling error, it cannot be measured with probability theory. It can be controlled only by using appropriate sampling procedures and designing good survey instruments. We will not pursue this topic any further here. If you are interested, however, you can learn about methods for controlling nonsampling error, such as proper questionnaire design, from books on survey sampling.

7-4b Key Terms in Sampling

We now set the stage for the rest of this chapter, as well as for the next few chapters. Suppose there is some numerical population parameter you would like to know. This parameter could be a population mean, a population proportion, the difference between two population means, the difference between two population proportions, or many others. Unless you measure each member of the population—that is, unless you take a census—you cannot learn the exact value of this population parameter. Therefore, you instead take a random sample of some type and *estimate* the population parameter from the data in the sample.

You typically begin by calculating a **point estimate** (or, simply, an *estimate*) from the sample data. This is a "best guess" of the population parameter. The difference between the point estimate and the true value of the population parameter is called the **sampling error** (or **estimation error**). You then use probability theory to estimate the magnitude of the sampling error. The key to this is the **sampling distribution** of the point estimate, which is defined as the distribution of the point estimates you would see from *all* possible samples (of a given sample size) from the population. Often you report the accuracy of the point estimate with an accompanying *confidence interval*. A **confidence interval** is an interval around the point estimate, calculated from the sample data, that is very likely to contain the true value of the population parameter. (We will say much more about confidence intervals in the next chapter.)

A **point estimate** is a single numeric value, a "best guess" of a population parameter, based on the data in a random sample.

The **sampling error** (or **estimation error**) is the difference between the point estimate and the true value of the population parameter being estimated.

> The **sampling distribution** of any point estimate is the distribution of the point estimates from *all* possible samples (of a given sample size) from the population.

> A **confidence interval** is an interval around the point estimate, calculated from the sample data, that is very likely to contain the true value of the population parameter.

Additionally, there are two other key terms you should know. First, consider the *mean* of the sampling distribution of a point estimate. It is the average value of the point estimates you would see from all possible samples. When this mean is equal to the true value of the population parameter, the point estimate is **unbiased**. Otherwise, it is *biased*. Naturally, unbiased estimates are preferred. Even if they sometimes miss on the low side and sometimes miss on the high side, they tend to be on target on average.

> An **unbiased estimate** is a point estimate such that the mean of its sampling distribution is equal to the true value of the population parameter being estimated.

Unbiased estimates are desirable because they average out to the correct value. However, this isn't enough. Point estimates from different samples should vary as little as possible from sample to sample. If they vary wildly, a point estimate from a *single* random sample isn't very reliable. Therefore, it is common to measure the standard deviation of the sampling distribution of the estimate. This indicates how much point estimates from different samples vary. In the context of sampling, this standard deviation is called the **standard error** of the estimate. Ideally, estimates should have *small* standard errors.

> The **standard error of an estimate** is the standard deviation of the sampling distribution of the estimate. It measures how much estimates vary from sample to sample.

The terms in this subsection are relevant for practically any population parameter you might want to estimate. In the following subsection we discuss them in the context of estimating a population mean.

7-4c Sampling Distribution of the Sample Mean

In this section we discuss the estimation of the population mean from some population. For example, you might be interested in the mean household income for all families in a particular city, the mean diameter of all parts from a manufacturing process, the mean amount of underreported taxes by all U.S. taxpayers, and so on. We label the unknown population mean by μ. (It is common to label population parameters with Greek letters.)

The point estimate of μ typically used, based on a sample from the population, is the sample mean $\overline{X}$, the average of the observations in the sample. There are *other* possible point estimates for a population mean besides the sample mean, such as the sample median, the *trimmed mean* (where all but the few most extreme observations are averaged), and others. However, it turns out that this "natural" estimate, the sample mean, has very good theoretical properties, so it is the point estimate used most often.

How accurate is $\overline{X}$ in estimating μ? That is, how large does the estimation error $\overline{X} - \mu$ tend to be? The sampling distribution of the sample mean $\overline{X}$ provides the key. Before describing this sampling distribution in some generality, we provide some insight into it by revisiting the population of 40 incomes in Example 7.1. There we showed how to generate a single random sample of size 10. For the particular sample we generated (see Figure 7.2), the sample mean was $41,490. Because the population mean of all 40 incomes is $39,985, the estimation error based on this particular sample is the difference $41,490 − $39,985, or $1505 on the high side.

However, this is only one of many possible samples. To see other possibilities, you can use StatTools's procedure for generating random samples to generate 100 random samples of size 10 from the population of 40 incomes. (You must do this by generating four groups of 25 samples each because StatTools limits you to 25 random samples at a time.) You can then calculate the sample mean for each random sample and create a histogram of these sample means. We did this, with the result shown in Figure 7.7. Although this is not *exactly* the sampling distribution of the sample mean (because there are many more than 100 possible samples of size 10 from a population of size 40), it indicates how the possible sample means are distributed. They are most likely to be near the population mean ($39,985), very unlikely to be more than about $3000 from this population mean, and have an approximately bell-shaped distribution.

Figure 7.7

Approximate Sampling Distribution of Sample Mean

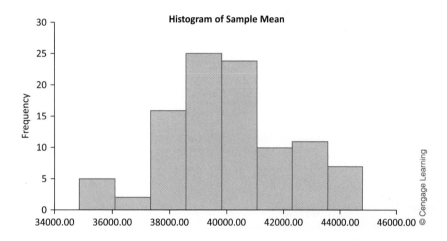

The insights in the previous paragraph can be generalized. It turns out that the sampling distribution of the sample mean has the following properties, regardless of the underlying population. First, it is an unbiased estimate of the population mean, as indicated in Equation (7.1). The sample means from some samples will be too low, and those from other samples will be too high, but on the average, they will be on target.

Unbiased Property of Sample Mean
$$E(\overline{X}) = \mu \qquad\qquad (7.1)$$

The second property involves the variability of the $\overline{X}$ estimate. Recall that the standard deviation of an estimate, called the standard error, indicates how much the estimate varies from sample to sample. The standard error of $\overline{X}$ is given in Equation (7.2). Here, $SE(\overline{X})$ is an abbreviation for the standard error of $\overline{X}$, σ is the standard deviation of the population, and n is the sample size. You can see that the standard error is large when the observations in the population are spread out (large σ), but that the standard error can be reduced by taking a larger sample.[3]

[3]This formula for $SE(\overline{X})$ assumes that the sample size n is small relative to the population size N. As a rule of thumb, we assume that n is no more than 5% of N. Later we provide a "correction" to this formula when n is a larger percentage of N.

> **Standard Error of Sample Mean**
> $$SE(\overline{X}) = \sigma/\sqrt{n} \qquad\qquad (7.2)$$

There is one problem with the standard error in Equation (7.2). Its value depends on another unknown population parameter, σ. Therefore, it is customary to approximate the standard error by substituting the *sample* standard deviation, s, for σ. This leads to Equation (7.3).

> **Approximate Standard Error of Sample Mean**
> $$SE(\overline{X}) = s/\sqrt{n} \qquad\qquad (7.3)$$

As we discuss in the next subsection, the shape of the sampling distribution of $\overline{X}$ is approximately normal. Therefore, you can use the standard error exactly as you have used standard deviations in previous chapters to obtain confidence intervals for the population mean. Specifically, if you go out two standard errors on either side of the sample mean, as shown in Expression (7.4), you are approximately 95% confident of capturing the population mean. Alternatively, you are 95% confident that the estimation error will be no greater than two standard errors in magnitude.

> **(Approximate) Confidence Interval for Population Mean**
> $$\overline{X} \pm 2s/\sqrt{n} \qquad\qquad (7.4)$$

FUNDAMENTAL INSIGHT

Sampling Distributions and Standard Errors

Any point estimate, such as the sample mean, is random because it depends on the random sample that happens to be chosen. The sampling distribution of the point estimate is the probability distribution of point estimates from all possible random samples.

This distribution describes how the sample means would vary from one sample to another. The corresponding standard error is the standard deviation of the sampling distribution. These two concepts, sampling distribution and standard error, are the keys to statistical inference, as discussed here and in the next few chapters.

Example 7.4 illustrates a typical use of sample information.

EXAMPLE | 7.4 ESTIMATING THE MEAN OF ACCOUNTS RECEIVABLE

An internal auditor for a furniture retailer wants to estimate the average of all accounts receivable, where this average is taken over the population of all customer accounts. Because the company has approximately 10,000 accounts, an exhaustive enumeration of all accounts receivable is impractical. Therefore, the auditor randomly samples 100 of the accounts. The data from the sample appear in Figure 7.8. (See the file **Auditing Receivables.xlsx**.) What can the auditor conclude from this sample?

Figure 7.8

Sampling in Auditing Example

	A	B	C	D	E
1	Random sample of accounts receivable				
2					
3	Population size	10000			
4	Sample size	100			
5					
6	Sample of receivables			Summary measures from sample	
7	Account	Amount		Sample mean	$278.92
8	1	$85		Sample stdev	$419.21
9	2	$1,061		Std Error of mean	$41.92
10	3	$0			
11	4	$1,260		With fpc	$41.71
12	5	$924			
13	6	$129			
105	98	$657			
106	99	$86			
107	100	$0			

© Cengage Learning

Objective   To illustrate the meaning of standard error of the mean in a sample of accounts receivable.

Solution

The receivables for the 100 sampled accounts appear in column B. This is the only information available to the auditor, so he must base all conclusions on these sample data. Begin by calculating the sample mean and sample standard deviation in cells E7 and E8 with the formulas

=AVERAGE(B8:B107)

and

=STDEV(B8:B107)

Then use Equation (7.3) to calculate the (approximate) standard error of the mean in cell E9 with the formula

=E8/SQRT(B4)

The auditor should interpret these values as follows. First, the sample mean $279 is a point estimate of the unknown population mean. It provides a best guess for the average of the receivables from all 10,000 accounts. In fact, because the sample mean is an unbiased estimate of the population mean, there is no reason to suspect that $279 either underestimates or overestimates the population mean. Second, the standard error $42 provides a measure of accuracy of the $279 estimate. Specifically, there is about a 95% chance that the estimate differs by no more than two standard errors (about $84) from the true but unknown population mean. Therefore, the auditor can be approximately 95% confident that the mean from all 10,000 accounts is within the interval $279 ± $84, that is, between $195 and $363. ■

It is important to distinguish between the sample standard deviation s and the standard error of the mean, approximated by $s/\sqrt{n}$. The sample standard deviation in the auditing example, $419, measures the variability across *individual* receivables in the sample (or in the population). By scrolling down column B, you can see that there are some very low amounts (many zeros) and some fairly large amounts. This variability is indicated by the rather large sample standard deviation s. However, this value does not measure the accuracy of the sample mean as an estimate of the population mean. To judge *its* accuracy, you need to divide *s* by the square root of the sample size *n*. The resulting standard error, about $42, is much smaller than the sample standard deviation. It indicates that you can be about 95% confident that the sampling error is no greater than $84. In short, sample means vary much less than individual observations from a given population.

The Finite Population Correction

We mentioned that Equation (7.2) [or Equation (7.3)] for the standard error of $\overline{X}$ is appropriate when the sample size *n* is small relative to the population size *N*. Generally, "small" means that *n* is no more than 5% of *N*. In most realistic samples this is certainly true. For example, political polls are typically based on samples of approximately 1000 people from the entire U.S. population.

There are situations, however, when the sample size is greater than 5% of the population. In this case the formula for the standard error of the mean should be modified with a **finite population correction**, or *fpc*, factor. The modified standard error of the mean appears in Equation (7.5), where the *fpc* is given by Equation (7.6). Note that this factor is always less than 1 (when $n > 1$) and it decreases as *n* increases. Therefore, the standard error of the mean decreases—and the accuracy increases—as *n* increases.

Standard Error of Mean with Finite Population Correction Factor

$$\text{SE}(\overline{X}) = fpc \times (s/\sqrt{n})$$
(7.5)

Finite Population Correction Factor

$$fpc = \sqrt{\frac{N - n}{N - 1}}$$
(7.6)

To see how the *fpc* varies with *n* and *N*, consider the values in Table 7.1. Rather than listing *n*, we have listed the percentage of the population sampled, that is, $n/N \times 100\%$. It is clear that when 5% or less of the population is sampled, the *fpc* is very close to 1 and can safely be ignored. In this case you can use $s/\sqrt{n}$ as the standard error of the mean. Otherwise, you should use the modified formula in Equation (7.5).

Table 7.1 Finite Population Correction Factors

N	% Sampled	*fpc*
100	5	0.980
100	10	0.953
10,000	1	0.995
10,000	5	0.975
10,000	10	0.949
1,000,000	1	0.995
1,000,000	5	0.975
1,000,000	10	0.949

© Cengage Learning

If less than 5% of the population is sampled, as is often the case, the fpc can safely be ignored.

In the auditing example, $n/N = 100/100,000 = 0.1\%$. This suggests that the *fpc* can safely be omitted. We illustrate this in cell E11 of Figure 7.8, which uses the formula from Equation (7.5):

=SQRT((B3-B4)/(B3-1))*E9

Clearly, it makes no practical difference in this example whether you use the *fpc* or not. The standard error, rounded to the nearest dollar, is $42 in either case.

Virtually all standard error formulas used in sampling include an *fpc* factor. However, because it is rarely necessary—the sample size is usually very small relative to the population size—we omit it from here on.

7-4d The Central Limit Theorem

Our discussion to this point has concentrated primarily on the mean and standard deviation of the sampling distribution of the sample mean. In this section we discuss this sampling distribution in more detail. Because of an important theoretical result called the **central limit theorem**, this sampling distribution is approximately *normal* with mean μ and standard deviation $\sigma/\sqrt{n}$. This theorem is the reason why the normal distribution appears in so many statistical results. The theorem can be stated as follows.

> For any population distribution with mean μ and standard deviation σ, the sampling distribution of the sample mean $\overline{X}$ is approximately normal with mean μ and standard deviation $\sigma/\sqrt{n}$, and the approximation improves as *n* increases.

The important part of this result is the *normality* of the sampling distribution. We know, without any conditions placed upon the sample size *n*, that the mean and standard deviation are μ and $\sigma/\sqrt{n}$. However, the central limit theorem also implies normality, provided that *n* is reasonably large.

FUNDAMENTAL INSIGHT

The Central Limit Theorem

This important result states that when you sum or average *n* randomly selected values from *any* distribution, normal or otherwise, the distribution of the sum or average is approximately *normal*, provided that *n* is sufficiently large. This is the primary reason why the normal distribution is relevant in so many real applications.

How large must *n* be for the approximation to be valid? Many textbooks suggest $n \geq 30$ as a rule of thumb. However, this depends on the population distribution. If the population distribution is very *nonnormal*—extremely skewed or bimodal, for example—the normal approximation might not be accurate unless *n* is considerably greater than 30. On the other hand, if the population distribution is already approximately symmetric, the normal approximation is quite good for *n* considerably less than 30. In fact, in the special case where the population distribution itself is normal, the sampling distribution of $\overline{X}$ is *exactly* normal for *any* value of *n*.

The central limit theorem is not a simple concept to grasp. To help explain it, we use simulation in Example 7.5.

| EXAMPLE | 7.5 AVERAGE WINNINGS FROM A WHEEL OF FORTUNE |

Suppose you have the opportunity to play a game with a "wheel of fortune" (similar to the one in a popular television game show). When you spin a large wheel, it is equally likely to stop in any position. Depending on where it stops, you win anywhere from $0 to $1000. Let's suppose your winnings are actually based on not one spin, but on the average of n spins of the wheel. For example, if $n = 2$, your winnings are based on the average of two spins. If the first spin results in \$580 and the second spin results in \$320, you win the average, \$450. How does the distribution of your winnings depend on n?

Objective To illustrate the central limit theorem by a simulation of winnings in a game of chance.

Solution

First, what does this experiment have to do with random sampling? Here, the population is the set of all outcomes you could obtain from a *single* spin of the wheel—that is, all dollar values from \$0 to \$1000. Each spin results in one randomly sampled dollar value from this population. Furthermore, because we have assumed that the wheel is equally likely to land in any position, all possible values in the continuum from \$0 to \$1000 have the same chance of occurring. The resulting population distribution is called the *uniform distribution* on the interval from \$0 to \$1000. (See Figure 7.9, where the 1 on the horizontal axis corresponds to \$1000.) It can be shown (with calculus) that the mean and standard deviation of this uniform distribution are $\mu = \$500$ and $\sigma = \$289$.[4]

Figure 7.9

Uniform
Distribution

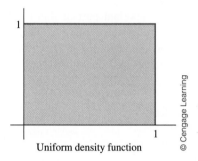

Uniform density function

© Cengage Learning

Before we go any further, take a moment to test your own intuition. If you play this game once and your winnings are based on the average of n spins, how likely is that you will win at least \$600 if $n = 1$? if $n = 3$? if $n = 10$? (The answers are 0.4, 0.27, and 0.14, respectively, where the last two answers are approximate and are based on the central limit theorem or the simulation. So you are much less likely to win big if your winnings are based on the average of many spins.)

Now we analyze the distribution of winnings based on the average of n spins. We do so by means of a sequence of simulations in Excel. (See the file **Wheel of Fortune Simulation.xlsx**, which is set up to work for any number of spins up to 10.) For each simulation, consider 1000 replications of an experiment. Each replication of the experiment simulates n spins of the wheel and calculates the average—that is, the winnings—from these n spins. Based on these 1000 replications, the average and standard deviation of winnings can be calculated, and a histogram of winnings can be formed, for any value of n. These will show clearly how the distribution of winnings depends on n.

The values in Figure 7.10 and the histogram in Figure 7.11 show the results for $n = 1$. Here there is no averaging—you spin the wheel once and win the amount shown. To replicate this experiment 1000 times and collect statistics, proceed as follows.

---

[4]In general, if a distribution is uniform on the interval from a to b, its mean is the midpoint $(a + b)/2$ and its standard deviation is $(b - a)/\sqrt{12}$.

Figure 7.10   Simulation of Winnings from a Single Spin

	A	B	C	D	E	F	G	H	I	J	K	L
1	Wheel of fortune simulation											
2												
3	Minimum winnings	$0									Summary measures of winnings	
4	Maximum winnings	$1,000									Mean	$504
5											Stdev	$294
6	Number of spins	1									P(>600)	0.417
7												
8	Simulation of spins											
9	Spin	1	2	3	4	5	6	7	8	9	10	
10	Replication	Outcome	Outcome	Outcome	Outcome	Outcome	Outcome	Outcome	Outcome	Outcome	Outcome	Winnings
11	1	$443										$443
12	2	$270										$270
13	3	$685										$685
14	4	$786										$786
15	5	$602										$602
16	6	$36										$36
1007	997	$957										$957
1008	998	$192										$192
1009	999	$562										$562
1010	1000	$786										$786

© Cengage Learning

Figure 7.11

Histogram of Simulated Winnings from a Single Spin

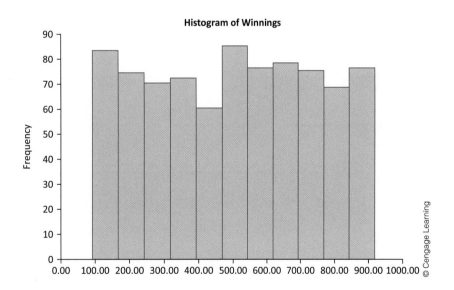

© Cengage Learning

Calculating the Distribution of Winnings by Simulation

1. **Random outcomes.** To generate outcomes uniformly distributed between $0 and $1000, enter the formula

   =IF(B\$9<=\$B\$6,\$B\$3+(\$B\$4−\$B\$3)*RAND(), " ")

   in cell B11 and copy it to the entire range B11:K1010. The effect of this formula, given the values in cells B3 and B4, is to generate a random number between 0 and 1 and multiply it by $1000. The effect of the IF part is to fill as many Outcome columns as there are spins in cell B6 and to leave the rest blank.

2. **Winnings.** Calculate the winnings in each row in column L as the average of the outcomes of the spins in that row. (Note that the AVERAGE function ignores blanks.)

3. **Summary measures.** Calculate the average and standard deviation of the 1000 winnings in column L with the AVERAGE and STDEV functions. These values appear in cells L4 and L5.

4. **Histogram.** Use the StatTools Histogram procedure to create a histogram of the values in column L.

Note the following from Figures 7.10 and 7.11:

▪ The sample mean of the winnings (cell L4) is very close to the population mean, $500.

▪ The standard deviation of the winnings (cell L5) is very close to the population standard deviation, $289.

▪ The histogram is nearly flat.

These properties should come as no surprise. When $n = 1$, the sample mean is a single observation—that is, no averaging takes place. Therefore, the sampling distribution of the sample mean is *equivalent* to the flat population distribution in Figure 7.9.

But what happens when $n > 1$? Figure 7.12 shows the results for $n = 2$. All you need to do is change the number of spins in cell B6, and everything updates automatically. The average winnings are again very close to $500, but the standard deviation of winnings is much lower. In fact, it is close to $\sigma/\sqrt{2} = 289/\sqrt{2} = \$204$, exactly as the theory predicts. In addition, the histogram of winnings is no longer flat. It is triangularly shaped—symmetric, but not yet bell-shaped.

Figure 7.12

Histogram of Simulated Winnings from Two Spins

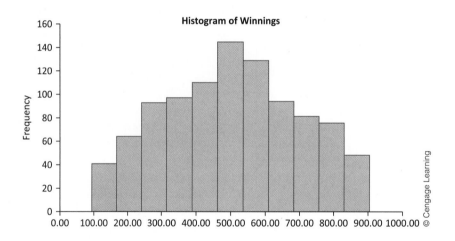

To develop similar simulations for $n = 3$, $n = 6$, $n = 10$, or any other n, simply change the number of spins in cell B6. The resulting histograms appear in Figures 7.13 through 7.15. They clearly show two effects of increasing n: (1) the histogram becomes more bell-shaped, and (2) there is less variability. However, the mean stays right at $500. This behavior is exactly what the central limit theorem predicts. In fact, because the population distribution is symmetric in this example—it is flat—you can see the effect of the central limit theorem for n much less than 30; it is already evident for n as low as 6.

Finally, it is easy to answer the question we posed previously: How does the probability of winning at least $600 depend on n? For any specific value of n, you can find the fraction of the 1000 replications where the average of n spins is greater than $600 with a COUNTIF formula in cell L6. (The value shown in Figure 7.10, 0.417, is only a point estimate of the true probability, which turns out to be very close to 0.4.) ▪

Figure 7.13

Histogram of
Simulated Winnings
from Three Spins

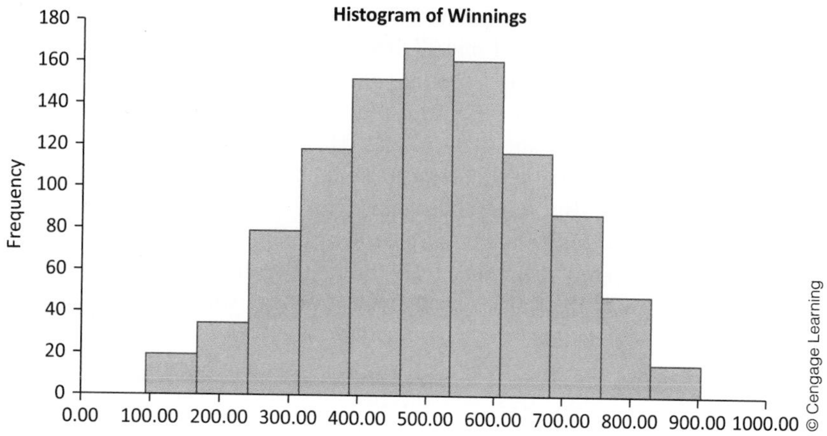

Figure 7.14

Histogram of
Simulated Winnings
from Six Spins

Figure 7.15

Histogram of
Simulated Winnings
from Ten Spins

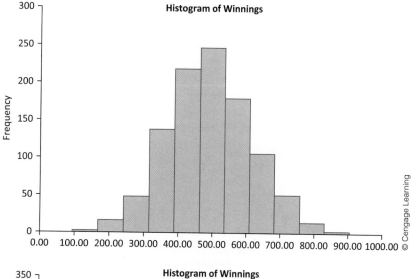

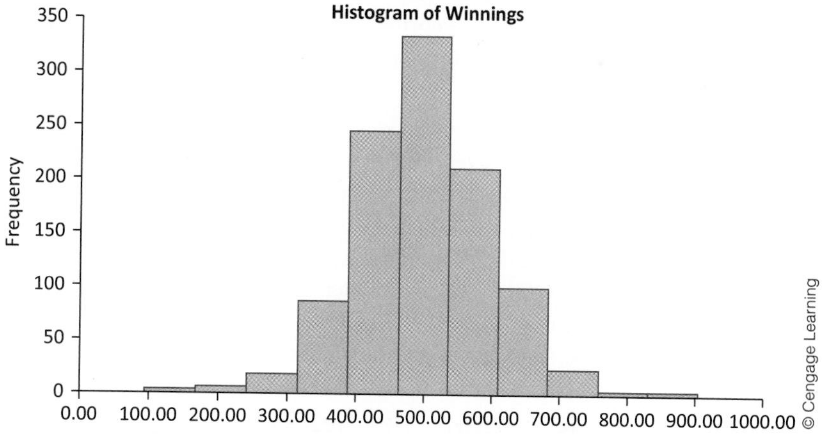

What are the main lessons from this example? For one, you can see that the sampling distribution of the sample mean (winnings) is bell-shaped when *n* is reasonably large. This is in spite of the fact that the population distribution is flat—far from bell-shaped. Actually, the population distribution could have *any* shape, not just uniform, and the bell-shaped property would still hold (although *n* might have to be larger than in the example). This bell-shaped normality property allows you to perform probability calculations with the NORMDIST and NORMINV functions, as discussed in Chapter 5.

Equally important, this example demonstrates the *decreased variability* in the sample means as n increases. Why should an increased sample size lead to decreased variability? This is due to averaging. Think about winning $750 based on the average of two spins. All you need is two lucky spins. In fact, one really lucky spin and an average spin will do. But think about winning $750 based on the average of 10 spins. Now you need a *lot* of really lucky spins—and virtually no unlucky ones. The point is that you are much less likely to obtain a really large (or really small) sample mean when n is large than when n is small. This is exactly what we mean when we say that the variability of the sample means decreases with larger sample sizes.

This decreasing variability is predicted by the formula for the standard error of the mean, $\sigma/\sqrt{n}$. As n increases, the standard error decreases. This is what drives the behaviour in Figures 7.12 through 7.15. In fact, using $\sigma = \$289$, the (theoretical) standard errors for $n = 2$, $n = 3$, $n = 6$, and $n = 10$ are $204, $167, $118, and $91, respectively.

Finally, what does this decreasing variability have to do with estimating a population mean with a sample mean? Very simply, it means that the sample mean tends to be a more *accurate* estimate when the sample size is large. Because of the approximate normality from the central limit theorem, you know from Chapter 5 that there is about a 95% chance that the sample mean will be within two standard errors of the population mean. In other words, there is about a 95% chance that the sampling error will be no greater than two standard errors in magnitude. Therefore, because the standard error decreases as the sample size increases, the sampling error is likely to decrease as well.

FUNDAMENTAL INSIGHT

The Averaging Effect

As you average more and more observations from a given distribution, the variance of the average decreases. This has a very intuitive explanation. For example, suppose you average only two observations. Then it is easy to get an abnormally large (or small) average. All it takes are two abnormally large (or small) observations. But if you average a much larger number of observations, you aren't likely to get an abnormally large (or small) average. The reason is that a few abnormally large observations will typically be cancelled by a few abnormally small observations. This cancellation produces the averaging effect. It also explains why a larger sample size tends to produce a more accurate estimate of a population mean.

To illustrate this, reconsider the auditor in Example 7.4. The standard error based on a sample of size $n = 100$ yielded a sample standard deviation of $419 and a standard error of about $42. Therefore, the sampling error has a 95% chance of being less than two standard errors, or $84, in magnitude. If the auditor believes that this sampling error is too large and therefore randomly samples 300 *more* accounts, the new standard error will be $419/\sqrt{400} \approx \$21$. Now there is about a 95% chance that the sampling error will be no more than $42. Note that because of the square root, small standard errors come at a high price. To decrease the standard error by half, the sample size must be quadrupled.

7-4e Sample Size Selection

The problem of selecting the appropriate sample size in any sampling context is not an easy one (as illustrated in the chapter opener), but it must be faced in the planning stages, *before* any sampling is done. We focus here on the relationship between sampling error and sample size. As we discussed previously, the sampling error tends to decrease as the sample size increases, so the desire to minimize sampling error encourages us to select larger sample sizes. We should note, however, that several other factors encourage us to select *smaller* sample sizes. The ultimate sample size selection must achieve a trade-off between these opposing forces.

What are these other factors? First, there is the obvious cost of sampling. Larger samples cost more. Sometimes, a company or agency might have a budget for a given sampling project. If the sample size required to achieve an acceptable sampling error is 500, but the budget allows for a sample size of only 300, budget considerations will probably prevail.

Another problem caused by large sample sizes is timely collection of the data. Suppose a retailer wants to collect sample data from its customers to decide whether to run an advertising blitz in the coming week. Obviously, the retailer needs to collect the data quickly if they are to be of any use, and a large sample could require too much time to collect.

Finally, a more subtle problem caused by large sample sizes is the increased chance of *nonsampling* error, such as nonresponse bias. As we discussed previously in this chapter, there are many potential sources of nonsampling error, and they are usually very difficult to quantify. However, they are likely to *increase* as the sample size increases. Arguably, the potential increase in *sampling* error from a smaller sample could be more than offset by a decrease in nonsampling error, especially if the cost saved by the smaller sample size is used to reduce the sources of nonsampling error—conducting more follow-up of nonrespondents, for example.

Nevertheless, the determination of sample size is usually driven by sampling error considerations. If you want to estimate a population mean with a sample mean, then the key is the standard error of the mean, given by

$$\text{SE}(\overline{X}) = \sigma/\sqrt{n}$$

The central limit theorem says that if n is reasonably large, there is about a 95% chance that the magnitude of the sampling error will be no more than two standard errors. Because σ is fixed in the formula for $\text{SE}(\overline{X})$, n can be chosen to make $2\text{SE}(\overline{X})$ acceptably small.

FUNDAMENTAL INSIGHT

Effect of Larger Sample Sizes

Accurate estimates of population parameters require small standard errors, and small standard errors require large sample sizes. However, standard errors are typically inversely proportional to the *square root* of the sample size (or sample sizes). The implication is that if you want to decrease the standard error by a given factor, you must increase the sample size by a much larger factor. For example, to decrease the standard error by a factor of 2, you must increase the sample size by a factor of 4. Accurate estimates are not cheap.

We postpone further discussion of sample size selection until the next chapter, where we will discuss in detail how it can be used to control confidence interval length.

7-4f Summary of Key Ideas for Simple Random Sampling

To this point, we have covered some very important concepts. Because we build on these concepts in later chapters, we summarize them here.

Key Concepts of Simple Random Sampling

- To estimate a population mean with a simple random sample, the sample mean is typically used as a "best guess." This estimate is called a *point estimate*. That is, $\overline{X}$ is a point estimate of μ.

- The accuracy of the point estimate is measured by its standard error. It is the standard deviation of the sampling distribution of the point estimate. The standard error of $\overline{X}$ is approximately $s/\sqrt{n}$, where s is the sample standard deviation.

- A *confidence interval* (with 95% confidence) for the population mean extends to approximately two standard errors on either side of the sample mean.
- From the *central limit theorem*, the sampling distribution of $\overline{X}$ is approximately normal when n is reasonably large.
- There is approximately a 95% chance that any particular $\overline{X}$ will be within two standard errors of the population mean μ.
- The sampling error can be reduced by increasing the sample size n. Appropriate sample size formulas for controlling confidence interval length are given in the next chapter.

PROBLEMS

Level A

7. A manufacturing company's quality control personnel have recorded the proportion of defective items for each of 500 monthly shipments of one of the computer components that the company produces. The data are in the file **P07_07.xlsx**. The quality control department manager does not have sufficient time to review all of these data. Rather, she would like to examine the proportions of defective items for a sample of these shipments. For this problem, you can assume that the population is the data from the 500 shipments.
   a. Use Excel to generate a simple random sample of size 25 from the data.
   b. Calculate a point estimate of the population mean from the sample selected in part **a**. What is the sampling error, that is, by how much does the sample mean differ from the population mean?
   c. Calculate a good approximation for the standard error of the mean.
   d. Repeat parts **b** and **c** after generating a simple random sample of size 50 from the population. Is this estimate bound to be more accurate than the one in part **b**? Is its standard error bound to be smaller than the one in part **c**?

8. The manager of a local fast-food restaurant is interested in improving the service provided to customers who use the restaurant's drive-up window. As a first step in this process, the manager asks his assistant to record the time it takes to serve a large number of customers at the final window in the facility's drive-up system. The results are in the file **P07_08.xlsx**, which consists of nearly 1200 service times. For this problem, you can assume that the population is the data in this file.
   a. Use Excel to generate a simple random sample of size 30 from the data.
   b. Calculate a point estimate of the population mean from the sample selected in part **a**. What is the sampling error, that is, by how much does the sample mean differ from the population mean?

   c. Calculate a good approximation for the standard error of the mean.
   d. If you wanted to halve the standard error from part **c**, what approximate sample size would you need? Why is this only approximate?

9. The file **P02_16.xlsx** contains traffic data from 256 weekdays on four variables. Each variable lists the number of arrivals during a specific 5-minute period of the day. For this problem, consider this data set a simple random sample from all possible weekdays.
   a. For each of the four variables, find the sample mean. If each of these is used as an estimate from the corresponding (unknown) population mean, is there any reason to believe that they either underestimate or overestimate the population means? Why or why not?
   b. What are the (approximate) standard errors of the estimates in part **a**? How can you interpret these standard errors? Be as specific as possible.
   c. Is it likely that the estimates in part **a** are accurate to within 0.4 arrival? Why or why not? (Answer for each variable separately.)

10. The file **P02_35.xlsx** contains data from a survey of 500 randomly selected households. For this problem, consider this data set a simple random sample from all possible households, where the number of households in the population is well over 1,000,000.
   a. Create a new variable, Total Income, that is the sum of First Income and Second Income.
   b. For each of the four variables Total Income, Monthly Payment, Utilities, and Debt, find the sample mean. If each of these is used as an estimate from the corresponding (unknown) population mean, is there any reason to believe that they either underestimate or overestimate the corresponding population means? Why or why not?
   c. What are the (approximate) standard errors of the estimates in part **b**? How can you interpret these standard errors? Be as specific as possible. Is the finite population correction required? Why or why not?

d. Is it likely that the estimate of Total Income in part **b** is accurate to within $1500? Why or why not?

11. The file **P02_10.xlsx** contains midterm and final exam scores for 96 students in a corporate finance course. For this problem, assume that these 96 students represent a sample of the 175 students taking the course, and that these 175 students represent the relevant population.

a. Assuming the same instructor is teaching all four sections of this course and that the 96 students are the students in two of these sections, is it fair to say that the 96 students represent a *random* sample from the population? Does it matter?

b. Find the sample mean and the standard error of the sample mean, based on the 96 students in the file. Should the finite population correction be used? What is the standard error without it? What is the standard error with it?

Level B

12. Create a simulation similar to the one in the **Wheel of Fortune Similation.xlsx** file. However, suppose that the outcome of each spin is no longer uniformly distributed between $0 and $1000. Instead, it is the number of 7s you get in 20 rolls of two dice. In other words, each spin results in a binomially distributed random number with parameters $n = 20$ and $p = 1/6$ (because the chance of rolling a 7 is 1 out of 6). The simulation should still allow you to vary the number of "spins" from 1 to 10, and the "winnings" is still the average of the outcomes of the spins. What is

fundamentally different from the simulation in the text? Does the central limit theorem still work? Explain from the results you obtain.

13. Suppose you plan to take a simple random sample from a population with N members. Specifically, you plan to sample a percentage p of the population. If p is 1%, is the finite population correction really necessary? Does the answer depend on N? Explain. Then answer the same questions when p is 5%, 10%, 25%, and 50%, respectively. In general, explain what goes wrong if the finite population correction is really necessary but isn't used.

14. The file **P07_14.xlsx** contains a very small population of only five members. For each member, the height of the person is listed. The purpose of this problem is to let you see exactly what a sampling distribution is. Find the *exact* sampling distribution of the sample mean with sample size 3. Verify that Equation (7.1) holds, that is, the mean of this sampling distribution is equal to the population mean. Also, verify that Equation (7.2) holds, that is, the standard deviation of this sampling distribution is equal to the population standard deviation divided by the square root of 3. (*Hint*: You will have to do this by brute force. There are 125 different samples of size 3 that could be drawn from this population. These include samples with duplicate members, and order counts. For example, they include (1,1,2), (1,2,1), (2,1,1), and (1,1,1). You will need to find the sample mean of each and then find the mean and standard deviation of these sample means.)

7-5 CONCLUSION

This chapter has provided the fundamental concepts behind statistical inference. We discussed ways to obtain random samples from a population; how to calculate a point estimate of a particular population parameter, the population mean; and how to measure the accuracy of this point estimate. The key idea is the sampling distribution of the estimate and specifically its standard deviation, called the standard error of the estimate. Due to the central limit theorem, the sampling distribution of the sample mean is approximately normal, which implies that the sample mean will be within two standard errors of the population mean in approximately 95% of all random samples. In the next two chapters we build on these important concepts.

Summary of Key Terms

Term	Symbol	Explanation	Excel	Page	Equation
Population		Contains all members about which a study intends to make inferences		302	
Frame		A list of all members of the population		303	
Sampling units		Potential members of a sample from a population		303	

(continued)

Summary of Key Terms   (*Continued*)

Term	Symbol	Explanation	Excel	Page	Equation
Probability sample		Any sample that is chosen by using a random mechanism		303	
Judgmental sample		Any sample that is chosen according to a sampler's judgment rather than a random mechanism		303	
Simple random sample		A sample where each member of the population has the same chance of being chosen	StatTools/ Data Utilities	304	
Systematic sample		A sample where one of the first k members is selected randomly, and then every kth member after this one is selected		309	
Stratified sampling		Sampling in which the population is divided into relatively homogeneous subsets called *strata*, and then random samples are taken from each of the strata		310	
Proportional sample sizes (in stratified sampling)		The property of each stratum selected having the same proportion from stratum to stratum		311	
Cluster sampling		A sample where the population is separated into clusters, such as cities or city blocks, and then a random sample of the clusters is selected		313	
Sampling error		The inevitable result of basing an inference on a sample rather than on the entire population		316	
Nonsampling error		Any type of estimation error that is not sampling error, including nonresponse bias, nontruthful responses, measurement error, and voluntary response bias		316	
Point estimate		A single numeric value, a "best guess" of a population parameter, based on the data in a sample		317	
Sampling error (or estimation error)		Difference between the estimate of a population parameter and the true value of the parameter		317	
Sampling distribution		The distribution of the point estimates from *all* possible samples (of a given sample size) from the population		318	
Confidence interval		An interval around the point estimate, calculated from the sample data, where the true value of the population parameter is very likely to be		318	
Unbiased estimate		An estimate where the mean of its sampling distribution equals the value of the parameter being estimated		318	
Standard error of an estimate		The standard deviation of the sampling distribution of the estimate		318	
Mean of sample mean	$E(\bar{X})$	Indicates property of unbiasedness of sample mean		319	7.1
Standard error of sample mean	$SE(\bar{X})$	Indicates how sample means from different samples vary		320	7.2, 7.3
Confidence interval for population mean		An interval that is very likely to contain the population mean mean		320	7.4
Finite population correction	*fpc*	A correction for the standard error when the sample size is fairly large relative to the population size		322	7.5, 7.6
Central limit theorem		States that the distribution of the sample mean is approximately normal for sufficiently large sample sizes		323	

Note: Because the material in this chapter is more conceptual than calculation-based, we have included only conceptual questions here. You will get plenty of practice with calculations in the next two chapters, which build upon the concepts in this chapter.

Conceptual Questions

C.1. Suppose that you want to know the opinions of American secondary school teachers about establishing a national test for high school graduation. You obtain a list of the members of the National Education Association (the largest teachers' union) and mail a questionnaire to 3000 teachers chosen at random from this list. In all, 823 teachers return the questionnaire. Identify the relevant *population*. Do you believe there is a good possibility of nonsampling error? Why or why not?

C.2. A sportswriter wants to know how strongly the residents of Indianapolis, Indiana, support the local minor league baseball team, the Indianapolis Indians. He stands outside the stadium before a game and interviews the first 30 people who enter the stadium. Suppose that the newspaper asks you to comment on the approach taken by this sportswriter in performing the survey. How would you respond?

C.3. A large corporation has 4520 male and 567 female employees. The organization's equal employment opportunity officer wants to poll the opinions of a random sample of employees. To give adequate attention to the opinions of female employees, exactly how should the EEO officer sample from the given population? Be specific.

C.4. Suppose that you want to estimate the mean monthly gross income of all households in your local community. You decide to estimate this population parameter by calling 150 randomly selected residents and asking each individual to report the household's monthly income. Assume that you use the local phone directory as the frame in selecting the households to be included in your sample. What are some possible sources of error that might arise in your effort to estimate the population mean?

C.5. Provide an example of when you might want to take a stratified random sample instead of a simple random sample, and explain what the advantages of a stratified sample might be.

C.6. Provide an example of when you might want to take a cluster random sample instead of a simple random sample, and explain what the advantages of a cluster sample might be. Also, explain how you would choose the cluster sample.

C.7. Do you agree with the statement that nonresponse error can be overcome with larger samples? If you

agree, explain why. If you disagree, provide an example that backs up your opinion.

C.8. When pollsters take a random sample of about 1000 people to estimate the mean of some quantity over a population of millions of people, how is it possible for them to estimate the accuracy of the sample mean?

C.9. Suppose you want to estimate the population mean of some quantity when the population consists of millions of members (such as the population of all U.S. households). How is it possible that you can obtain a fairly accurate estimate, using the sample mean of only about 1000 randomly selected members?

C.10. What is the difference between a *standard deviation* and a *standard error*? Be precise.

C.11. Explain as precisely as possible what it means that the sample mean is an *unbiased* estimate of the population mean [as indicated in Equation (7.1)].

C.12. Explain the difference between the standard error formulas in equations (7.2) and (7.3). Why is Equation (7.3) the one necessarily used in real situations?

C.13. Explain as precisely as possible what Equation (7.4) means, and the reason for the 2 in the formula.

C.14. Explain as precisely as possible the role of the finite population correction. In which types of situations is it necessary? Is it necessarily used in the typical polls you see in the news?

C.15. In the wheel of fortune simulation with, say, three spins, many people mistakenly believe that the distribution of the average is the flat graph in Figure 7.9, that is, they believe the average of three spins is *uniformly* distributed between $0 and $1000. Explain intuitively why they are wrong.

C.16. Explain the difference between a point estimate for the mean and a confidence interval for the mean. Which provides more information?

C.17. Explain as precisely as possible what the central limit theorem says about averages.

C.18. Many people seem to believe that the central limit theorem "kicks in" only when n is at least 30. Why is this not necessarily true? When is such a large n necessary?

C.19. Suppose you are a pollster and are planning to take a sample that is very small relative to the population. In terms of estimating a population mean, can you say that a sample of size $9n$ is about 3 times as accurate as a sample of size n? Why or why not? Does the answer depend on the population size? For example, would it matter if the population size were 50 million instead of 10 million?

C.20. You saw in Equation (7.1) that the sample mean is an unbiased estimate of the population mean. However, some estimates of population parameters are biased. In such cases, there are two sources of error in estimating the population parameter: the bias and the standard error. To understand these, imagine a rifleman shooting at a bull's-eye. The rifleman could be aiming wrong and/or his shots could vary wildly from shot to shot. If he is aiming wrong but his shots are very consistent, what can you say about his bias and standard error? Answer the same question if he is correctly aiming at the bull's-eye but is very inconsistent. Can you say which of these two situations is worse?

CASE | 7.1 SAMPLING FROM DVD MOVIE RENTERS

The file **C07_01.xlsx** contains a large data set of 10,000 customer transactions for a fictional chain of video stores in the United States. Each row corresponds to a different customer and lists (1) a customer ID number (1–10,000), (2) the state where the customer lives, (3) the city where the customer lives, (4) the customer's gender, (5) the customer's favorite type of movie (drama, comedy, science fiction, or action), (6) the customer's next favorite type of movie, (7) the number of times the customer has rented movies in the past year, and (8) the total dollar amount the customer has spent on movie rentals during the past year. The data are sorted by state, then city, then gender. We assume that this data set represents the entire population of customers for this video chain. (Of course, national chains would have significantly larger customer populations, but this data set is large enough to illustrate the ideas.)

Imagine that only the data in columns A through D are readily available for this population. The company is interested in summary statistics of the data in columns E through H, such as the percentage of customers whose favorite movie type is drama or the average amount spent annually per customer, but it will have to do some work to obtain the data in columns E through H for any particular customer. Therefore, the company wants to perform sampling. The question is: What form—simple random sampling, systematic sampling, stratified sampling, cluster sampling, or even some type of multistage sampling—is most appropriate?

Your job is to investigate the possibilities and to write a report on your findings. For any sampling method, any sample size, and any quantity of interest (such as average dollar amount spent annually), you should be concerned with sampling cost and accuracy. One way to judge the latter is to generate several random samples from a particular method and calculate the mean and standard deviation of your point estimates from these samples. For example, you might generate 10 systematic samples, calculate the average amount spent (an $\overline{X}$) for each sample, and then calculate the mean and standard deviation of these 10 $\overline{X}$s. If your sampling method is accurate, the mean of the $\overline{X}$s should be close to the population average, and the standard deviation should be small. By doing this for several sampling methods and possibly several sample sizes, you can experiment to see what is most cost-efficient for the company. You can make any reasonable assumptions about the cost of sampling with any particular method.

CHAPTER

8

Confidence Interval Estimation

vitma/Shutterstock.com

ESTIMATING A COMPANY'S TOTAL TAXABLE INCOME

In Example 7.4 in the previous chapter, we illustrated how sampling can be used in auditing. We see another illustration of sampling in auditing in Example 8.5 of this chapter. In both examples, the point of the sampling is to discover some property (such as a mean or a proportion) from a large population of a company's accounts by examining a small fraction of these accounts and projecting the results to the population. An article by Press (1995) offers an interesting variation on this problem. He poses the question of how a government revenue agency should assess a business taxpayer's income for tax purposes on the basis of a sample audit of the company's business transactions. A sample of the company's transactions will indicate a taxable income for each sampled transaction. The methods of this chapter will be applied to the sample information to obtain a confidence interval for the total taxable income owed by the company.

Suppose for the sake of illustration that this confidence interval extends from $1,000,000 to $2,200,000 and is centered at $1,600,000. In other words, the government's best guess of the company's taxable income is $1,600,000, and the government is fairly confident that the true taxable income is between $1,000,000 and $2,200,000. How much tax should it assess the company? Press argues that the agency would like to maximize its revenue while minimizing the risk that the company will be assessed more than it really owes. This last assumption, that the government does not want to *overassess* the company, is crucial. By making several reasonable assumptions, he is able to argue that the agency should base the tax on the *lower* limit of the confidence interval, in this case, $1,000,000.[1]

On the other hand, if the agency were indifferent between overcharging and undercharging, then it would base the tax on the midpoint, $1,600,000, of the confidence interval. Using this strategy, the agency would overcharge in about half the cases and undercharge in the other half. This would certainly be upsetting to companies—it would appear that the agency is flipping a coin to decide whether to overcharge or undercharge.

If the government agency does indeed decide to base the tax on the *lower* limit of the confidence interval, Press argues that it can still increase its tax revenue—by increasing the sample size of the audit. When the sample size increases, the confidence interval shrinks in width, and the lower limit, which governs the agency's tax revenue, almost surely increases. But there is some point at which larger samples are not warranted, for the simple reason that larger samples cost more money to obtain. Therefore, there is an optimal size that will balance the cost of sampling with the desire to obtain more tax revenue. ■

8-1 INTRODUCTION

This chapter expands on the ideas from the previous chapter. Given an observed data set, we want to make inferences to some larger population. Two typical examples follow:

■ A mail-order company has accounts with thousands of customers. The company would like to infer the average time its customers take to pay their bills, so it randomly samples a relatively small number of its customers, sees how long these customers take to pay their bills, and draws inferences about the entire population of customers.

■ A manufacturing company is considering two compensation schemes to implement for its workers. It believes that these two different compensation schemes might provide different incentives and hence result in different worker productivity. To see whether this is true, the company randomly assigns groups of workers to the two different compensation schemes for a period of three months and observes their productivity. Then it attempts to infer whether any differences observed in the experiment can be generalized to the overall worker population.

In each of these examples, there is an unknown population parameter a company would like to estimate. In the mail-order example, the unknown parameter is the mean length of time customers take to pay their bills. Its true value could be discovered only by learning how long *every* customer in the entire population takes to pay its bills. This is not really possible, given the large number of customers. In the manufacturing example, the unknown parameter is a mean difference, the difference between the mean productivities with the two different compensation schemes. This mean difference could be discovered only by subjecting each worker to each compensation scheme and measuring their resulting productivities. This procedure would almost certainly be impossible from a practical standpoint. Therefore, the companies in these examples are likely to select

---

[1] In case this sounds overly generous on the government's part, the result is based on two important assumptions: (1) the confidence interval is a 90% confidence interval, and (2) the agency is 19 times more concerned about overassessing than about underassessing.

random samples and base their estimates of the unknown population parameters on the sample data.

The inferences discussed in this chapter are always based on an underlying probability model, which means that some type of random mechanism must generate the data. Two random mechanisms are generally used. The first involves sampling randomly from a larger population, as we discussed in the previous chapter. This is the mechanism responsible for generating the sample of customers in the mail-order example. Regardless of whether the sample is a simple random sample or a more complex random sample, such as a stratified sample, the fact that it is *random* allows us to use the rules of probability to make inferences about the population as a whole.

The second commonly used random mechanism is called a *randomized experiment*. The compensation scheme example just described is a typical randomized experiment. Here the company selects a set of subjects (employees), randomly assigns them to two different *treatment groups* (compensation schemes), and then compares some quantitative measure (productivity) across the groups. The fact that the subjects are *randomly* assigned to the two treatment groups is useful for two reasons. First, it allows us to rule out a number of factors that might have led to differences across groups. For example, assuming that males and females are randomly spread across the two groups, we can rule out gender as the cause of any observed group differences. Second, the random selection allows us to use the rules of probability to infer whether observed differences can be generalized to all employees.

We actually introduced 95% confidence intervals for the mean in the previous chapter. We generalize this method in the current chapter.

Generally, statistical inferences are of two types: *confidence interval estimation* and *hypothesis testing*. The first of these is the subject of the current chapter; hypothesis testing is discussed in the next chapter. They differ primarily in their point of view. For example, the mail-order company might sample 100 customers and find that they average 15.5 days before paying their bills. In confidence interval estimation, the data are used to obtain a point estimate and a **confidence interval** around this point estimate. In this example the point estimate is 15.5 days. It is a best guess for the mean bill-paying time in the entire customer population. Then, using the methods in this chapter, the company might find that a 95% confidence interval for the mean bill-paying time in the population is from 13.2 days to 17.8 days. The company is now 95% confident that the true mean bill-paying time in the population is within this interval.

Hypothesis testing takes a different point of view. Here we wish to check whether the observed data provide support for a particular hypothesis. In the compensation scheme example, suppose the manager believes that workers will have higher productivity if they are paid by salary than by an hourly wage. He runs the three-month randomized experiment described previously and finds that the salaried workers produce on average eight more parts per day than the hourly workers. Now he must make one of two conclusions. Either salaried workers are in general no more productive than hourly workers and the ones in the experiment just got lucky, or salaried workers really *are* more productive. The next chapter explains how to decide which of these conclusions is more reasonable.

There are only a few key ideas in this chapter, and the most important of these, *sampling distributions*, was introduced in the previous chapter. It is important to concentrate on these key ideas and not get bogged down in formulas or numerical calculations. Statistical software such as StatTools is generally available to take care of these calculations. The job of a businessperson is much more dependent on knowing which methods to use in which situations and how to interpret computer outputs than on memorizing and plugging into formulas.

8-2 SAMPLING DISTRIBUTIONS

As you will soon learn, most confidence intervals are of the form in Expression (8.1). For example, when estimating a population mean, the point estimate is the sample mean, the standard error is the sample standard deviation divided by the square root of the sample size, and the multiple is approximately equal to 2. To learn why it works this way, you must first understand sampling distributions. This knowledge will then be put to use in the next section.

Typical Form of Confidence Interval

$$\text{Point Estimate} \pm \text{Multiple} \times \text{Standard Error} \tag{8.1}$$

In the previous chapter, we introduced the sampling distribution of the sample mean $\overline{X}$ and saw how it was related to the central limit theorem. In general, whenever you make inferences about one or more population parameters, such as a mean or the difference between two means, you always base this inference on the sampling distribution of a point estimate, such as the sample mean. Although the *concepts* of point estimates and sampling distributions are no different from those in the previous chapter, there are some new details to learn.

We again begin with the sample mean $\overline{X}$. The central limit theorem states that if the sample size n is reasonably large, then for *any* population distribution, the sampling distribution of $\overline{X}$ is approximately normally distributed with mean μ and standard deviation $\sigma/\sqrt{n}$, where μ and σ are the population mean and standard deviation. An equivalent statement is that the standardized quantity Z defined in Equation (8.2) is approximately normal with mean 0 and standard deviation 1.

Standardized Z-Value

$$Z = \frac{\overline{X} - \mu}{\sigma/\sqrt{n}} \tag{8.2}$$

Typically, this fact is used to make inferences about an unknown population mean μ. There is one problem, however—the population standard deviation σ is virtually never known. This parameter, σ, is then called a *nuisance parameter*. Although it is typically not the parameter of primary interest, its value is needed for making inferences about the mean μ. The solution appears to be straightforward: Replace the nuisance parameter σ by its sample estimate s in the formula for Z and proceed from there. However, when σ is replaced by the sample standard deviation s, this introduces a new source of variability, and the sampling distribution is no longer normal. It is instead called the *t* **distribution**, a close relative of the normal distribution that appears in a variety of statistical applications.

8-2a The *t* Distribution

We first set the stage for this new sampling distribution. We are interested in estimating a population mean μ with a sample of size n. We assume the population distribution is normal with unknown standard deviation σ. We intend to base inferences on the standardized value of $\overline{X}$ from Equation (8.2), where σ is replaced by the sample standard deviation s, as shown in Equation (8.3). Then the standardized value in Equation (8.3) has a *t* distribution with $n - 1$ degrees of freedom.

The *degrees of freedom* is a numerical parameter of the t distribution that defines the precise shape of the distribution. Each time we encounter a t distribution, we will specify its degrees of freedom. In this particular sampling context, where we are basing inferences about μ on the sampling distribution of $\overline{X}$, the degrees of freedom turns out to be 1 less than the sample size n.

The t distribution looks very much like the standard normal distribution. It is bell-shaped and centered at 0. The only difference is that it is slightly more spread out, and this increase in spread is greater for *small* degrees of freedom. In fact, when n is large, so that the degrees of freedom is large, the t distribution and the standard normal distribution are practically indistinguishable. This is illustrated in Figure 8.1. With 5 degrees of freedom, it is possible to see the increased spread in the t distribution. With 30 degrees of freedom, the t and standard normal curves are practically the same curve.

Figure 8.1

The t and Standard Normal Distributions

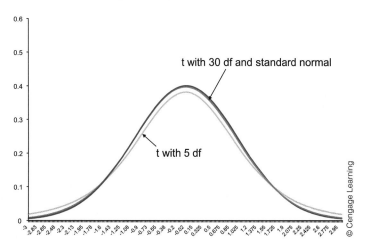

The t distribution and the standard normal distribution are practically the same when the degrees of freedom parameter is large.

The t-value in Equation (8.3) is very much like a typical Z-value such as in Equation (8.2). That is, the **t-value** represents the number of standard errors by which the sample mean differs from the population mean. For example, if a t-value is 2.5, the sample mean is 2.5 standard errors above the population mean. Or if a t-value is -2.5, the sample mean is 2.5 standard errors below the population mean. Also, t-values greater in magnitude than 3 are quite unexpected because of the same property of the normal distribution: It is very unlikely for a random value to be more than three standard deviations from its mean. (In this case the random value is a sample mean, and the standard deviation is the standard error of the mean.)

A **t-value** indicates the number of standard errors by which a sample mean differs from a population mean.

Because of this interpretation, t-values are perfect candidates for the *multiple* term in Expression (8.1), as you will soon see. First, however, we briefly examine some Excel® functions that are useful for working with the t distribution in Excel. If you are using StatTools for statistical inference, you will never really need these functions—so you might want to skip the rest of this section, at least for now.

Chapter 5 explained how to use Excel's NORMSDIST and NORMSINV functions to calculate probabilities or percentiles from the standard normal distribution. There are similar Excel functions for the *t* distribution: TDIST and TINV. Unfortunately, these functions are somewhat more difficult to master than their normal counterparts. The file **t Calculations.xlsx** spells out the possibilities (see Figure 8.2). The top three examples use the TDIST function, which finds the probability to the left or right of a given value. The bottom three examples use the TINV function, which finds the value with a given probability beyond it in one or both tails.

Figure 8.2 **Excel Functions for the *t* Distribution**

◢	A	B	C	D	E	F	G	H	I
1	Calculations for the t distribution								
2									
3	Sample size	30							
4	Degrees of freedom	29							
5									
6	One-tailed probabilities								
7	t-value	−2		Formulas			Formulas in Excel 2010 (or later)		
8	Probability in left tail	0.0275		=TDIST(−B7,B4,1)			=T.DIST(B7,B4,1)		
9									
10	t-value	2							
11	Probability in right tail	0.0275		=TDIST(B10,B4,1)			=T.DIST.RT(B10,B4)		
12									
13	Two-tailed probability								
14	t-value	2							
15	Probability in both tails	0.0549 ←		=TDIST(B14,B4,2)			=T.DIST.2T(B14,B4)		
16				Half of this probability is in each tail					
17	TINV calculations								
18	Probability in left tail	0.05							
19	t-value	−1.699		=-TINV(2*B18,B4)			=T.INV(B18,B4)		
20									
21	Probability in right tail	0.05							
22	t-value	1.699		=TINV(2*B21,B4)			=T.INV(1-B21,B4)		
23									
24	Probability in both tails	0.05 ←		Half of this probability is in each tail					
25	t-value	2.045		=TINV(B24,B4)			=T.INV.2T(B24,B4)		

© Cengage Learning

CHANGES IN EXCEL 2010

Chapter 5 discussed new statistical functions in Excel 2010. Except possibly for the replacement of CRITBINOM by BINOM.INV, these changes don't really seem to make much difference. However, the new functions definitely help with the *t* distribution. Before, the only available functions were TDIST and TINV, and because of the obscure way they work, everyone has had problems using them correctly. Therefore, Microsoft introduced five new functions in Excel 2010: T.DIST, T.DIST. RT, T.DIST.2T, T.INV, and T.INV.2T. As usual, a "DIST" function takes a value and returns a probability, whereas an "INV" function takes a probability and returns a value. Normally, these kinds of functions are written for left-hand tails (" < " problems), and this is the case for T.DIST and T.INV. However, T.DIST.RT lets you work with right-hand tails (" > " problems), and T.DIST.2T and T.INV.2T let you work with both tails. Figure 8.2 shows both the old and the new functions, and the **t Calculations** .xlsx file provides more details on their use. We strongly recommend the new functions if you have Excel 2010 or later. Again, however, you won't really need them if you are using StatTools.

In general, here are the technical details for using the TDIST function properly. (These are the obscure rules for the *old* TDIST function only. You can ignore these if you are using the new Excel 2010 functions.)

- Its first argument must be nonnegative.

- Unlike the NORMSDIST function, TDIST returns the probability to the *right* of the first argument (if the third argument is 1).

- The third argument of the TDIST function is either 1 or 2 and indicates the number of tails. By using 1 for this argument, you get the probability in the right-hand tail only. If you use 2 for the third argument, you obtain the probability of greater than the first argument or less than its negative.

The technical details for using the TINV function properly are as follows. (Again, these are for the *old* TINV function only.)

- The first argument is the total probability you want in both tails—half of this goes in the right-hand tail and half goes in the left-hand tail.

- Unlike the TDIST function, there is no third argument for the TINV function.

We agree that these functions, old or new, are somewhat difficult to learn. Fortunately, the StatTools add-in simplifies the process for most statistical inference applications. It does the *t* distribution calculations for you.

8-2b Other Sampling Distributions

The *t* distribution, a close relative of the normal distribution, is used to make inferences about a population mean when the population standard deviation is unknown. Throughout this chapter (and later chapters) you will see other contexts where the *t* distribution appears. The theme is always the same—one or more means are of interest, and one or more standard deviations are unknown.

The *t* (and normal) distributions are not the only sampling distributions you will encounter. Two other close relatives of the normal distribution that appear in various contexts are the *chi-square* and *F* distributions. These are used primarily to make inferences about variances (or standard deviations), as opposed to means. We omit the details of these distributions for now, but you will see them in later sections.

PROBLEMS

Note: Student solutions for problems whose numbers appear within a colored box are available for purchase at www.cengagebrain.com.

Level A

1. Calculate the following probabilities using Excel. (If you have Excel 2010 or later, we suggest using its new functions.)

a. $P(t_{10} \geq 1.75)$, where t_{10} has a *t* distribution with 10 degrees of freedom.

b. $P(t_{100} \geq 1.75)$, where t_{100} has a *t* distribution with 100 degrees of freedom. How do you explain the

difference between this result and the one obtained in part **a**?

c. $P(Z \geq 1.75)$, where *Z* is a standard normal random variable. Compare this result to the results obtained in parts **a** and **b**. How do you explain the differences in these probabilities?

d. $P(t_{20} \leq -0.80)$, where t_{20} has a *t* distribution with 20 degrees of freedom.

e. $P(t_3 \leq -0.80)$, where t_3 has a *t* distribution with 3 degrees of freedom. How do you explain the difference between this result and the result obtained in part **d**?

8-2 Sampling Distributions   **341**

2. Calculate the following quantities using Excel. (If you have Excel 2010 or later, we suggest using its new functions.)

   a. $P(-2.00 \leq t_{10} \leq 1.00)$, where t_{10} has a t distribution with 10 degrees of freedom.

   b. $P(-2.00 \leq t_{100} \leq 1.00)$, where t_{100} has a t distribution with 100 degrees of freedom. How do you explain the difference between this result and the one obtained in part **a**?

   c. $P(-2.00 \leq Z \leq 1.00)$, where Z is a standard normal random variable. Compare this result to the results obtained in parts **a** and **b**. How do you explain the differences in these probabilities?

   d. Find the 68th percentile of the t distribution with 20 degrees of freedom.

   e. Find the 68th percentile of the t distribution with 3 degrees of freedom. How do you explain

the difference between this result and the result obtained in part **d**?

3. Calculate the following quantities using Excel. (If you have Excel 2010 or later, we suggest using its new functions.)

   a. Find the value of x such that $P(t_{10} > x) = 0.75$, where t_{10} has a t distribution with 10 degrees of freedom.

   b. Find the value of y such that $P(t_{100} > y) = 0.75$, where t_{100} has a t distribution with 100 degrees of freedom. How do you explain the difference between this result and the result obtained in part **a**?

   c. Find the value of z such that $P(Z > z) = 0.75$, where Z is a standard normal random variable. Compare this result to the results obtained in parts **a** and **b**. How do you explain the differences in the values of x, y, and z?

8-3 CONFIDENCE INTERVAL FOR A MEAN

We now come to the main topic of this chapter: using properties of sampling distributions to construct confidence intervals. We assume that data have been generated by some random mechanism, either by observing a random sample from some population or by performing a randomized experiment. The goal is to infer the values of one or more population parameters such as the mean, the standard deviation, or a proportion from sample data. For each such parameter, you use the data to calculate a point estimate, which can be considered a best guess for the unknown parameter. You then calculate a confidence interval around the point estimate to measure its accuracy.

We begin by deriving a confidence interval for a population mean μ, and we discuss its interpretation. Although the particular details pertain to a specific parameter, the mean, the same ideas carry over to other parameters as well, as will be described in later sections. As usual, the sample $\overline{X}$ is used as the point estimate of μ.

To obtain a confidence interval for μ, you first specify a **confidence level**, usually 90%, 95%, or 99%. You then use the sampling distribution of the point estimate to determine the *multiple* of the standard error (SE) to go out on either side of the point estimate to achieve the given confidence level. If the confidence level is 95%, the value used most frequently in applications, the multiple is approximately 2. More precisely, it is a t-value. That is, a typical confidence interval for μ is of the form in Expression (8.4), where $SE(\overline{X}) = s/\sqrt{n}$.

Confidence Interval for Population Mean
$$\overline{X} \pm t\text{-multiple} \times SE\,(\overline{X}) \tag{8.4}$$

To obtain the correct t-multiple, let α be 1 minus the confidence level (expressed as a decimal). For example, if the confidence level is 90%, then $\alpha = 0.10$. Then the appropriate t-multiple is the value that cuts off probability $\alpha/2$ in each tail of the t distribution with $n - 1$ degrees of freedom. For example, if $n = 30$ and the confidence level is 95%, cell B25 of Figure 8.2 indicates that the correct t-value is 2.045. The corresponding 95% confidence interval for μ is then

$$\overline{X} \pm 2.045(s/\sqrt{n})$$

If the confidence level is instead 90%, the appropriate t-value is 1.699 (change the probability in cell B24 to 0.10 to see this), and the resulting 90% confidence interval is

$$\overline{X} \pm 1.699(s/\sqrt{n})$$

If the confidence level is 99%, the appropriate t-value is 2.756 (change the probability in cell B24 to 0.01 to see this), and the resulting 99% confidence interval is

$$\overline{X} \pm 2.756(s/\sqrt{n})$$

Confidence interval widths increase when you ask for higher confidence levels, but they tend to decrease when you use larger sample sizes.

Note that as the confidence level increases, the width of the confidence interval also increases. Because narrow confidence intervals are desirable, this presents a trade-off. You can either have less confidence and a narrow interval, or you can have more confidence and a wide interval. However, you can also take a larger sample. As n increases, the standard error $s/\sqrt{n}$ decreases, so the length of the confidence interval tends to decrease for *any* confidence level. (Why won't it decrease for sure? The larger sample *might* result in a larger value of s that could offset the increase in n.)

Example 8.1 illustrates confidence interval estimation for a population mean. It uses the One-Sample procedure in StatTools to perform the calculations. However, by examining the resulting Excel formulas, you can check that all it is really doing is (1) calculating the sample mean, (2) calculating the standard error of the sample mean, $s/\sqrt{n}$, (3) finding the appropriate t-multiple, and (4) combining these to form the confidence interval via Expression (8.4).

EXAMPLE 8.1 CUSTOMER RESPONSE TO A NEW SANDWICH

A fast-food restaurant recently added a new sandwich to its menu. To estimate the popularity of this sandwich, a random sample of 40 customers who ordered the sandwich were surveyed. Each of these customers was asked to rate the sandwich on a scale of 1 to 10, 10 being the best. The results of this survey appear in column B of Figure 8.4. (See the file **Satisfaction Ratings.xlsx**.) The manager wants to estimate the mean satisfaction rating over the entire population of customers by finding a 95% confidence interval. How should she proceed?

Objective   To use StatTools's One-Sample procedure to obtain a 95% confidence interval for the mean satisfaction rating of the new sandwich.

Solution

You need to use StatTools's One-Sample procedure on the Satisfaction variable. To do so, make sure a StatTools data set has been designated, select Confidence Interval from the StatTools Statistical Inference dropdown list, and select the Mean/Std. Deviation option. Then fill in the resulting dialog box as shown in Figure 8.3. In particular, select One-Sample Analysis as the Analysis type. (Other types will be used later in the chapter.) You should obtain the output shown in Figure 8.4. (*Note*: If you want to place the output next to the data, as shown here, select Settings from the StatTools ribbon, and, in the Report group, select either of the last two Placement options.)

Figure 8.3

Dialog Box for
Confidence Interval
for Mean

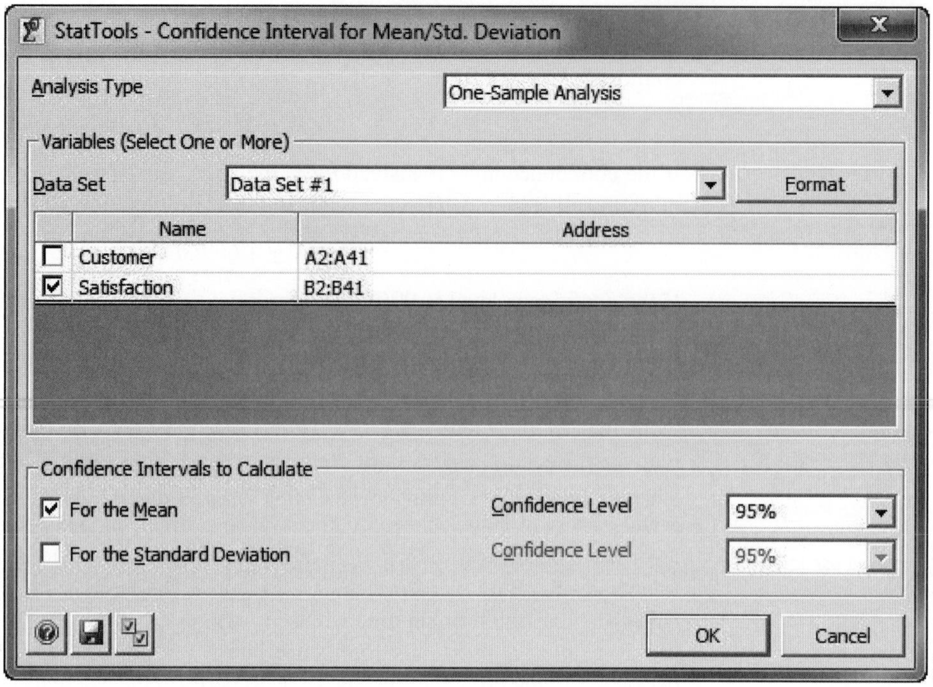

StatTools - Confidence Interval for Mean/Std. Deviation

Analysis Type   One-Sample Analysis

Variables (Select One or More)

Data Set   Data Set #1   Format

	Name	Address
☐	Customer	A2:A41
☑	Satisfaction	B2:B41

Confidence Intervals to Calculate

☑ For the Mean   Confidence Level   95%

☐ For the Standard Deviation   Confidence Level   95%

OK   Cancel

Figure 8.4

Analysis of New
Sandwich Data

	A	B	C	D	E
1	Customer	Satisfaction			Satisfaction
2	1	7		*Conf. Intervals (One-Sample)*	Data Set #1
3	2	5		Sample Size	40
4	3	5		Sample Mean	6.250
5	4	6		Sample Std Dev	1.597
6	5	8		Confidence Level (Mean)	95.0%
7	6	7		Degrees of Freedom	39
8	7	6		Lower Limit	5.739
9	8	7		Upper Limit	6.761
10	9	10			
11	10	7			
39	38	9			
40	39	5			
41	40	4			

The principal results are that (1) the best guess for the population mean rating is 6.250, the sample average in cell E4, and (2) a 95% confidence interval for the population mean rating extends from 5.739 to 6.761, as seen in cells E8 and E9. The manager can be 95% confident that the true mean rating over all customers who might try the sandwich is within this confidence interval.

The degrees of freedom for the t distribution is one less than the sample size, as shown in cell E7. The formulas for the confidence interval limits, in cells E8 and E9, are equivalent to the general formula in Expression (8.4), but they use special StatTools functions

To understand where these numbers come from, take a look at the formulas in column E.

to calculate the *t*-multiples. Note that StatTools doesn't display the standard error of the mean explicitly, but you can calculate it easily as the sample standard deviation in cell E5 divided by the square root of the sample size.

We stated previously that as the confidence level increases, the length of the confidence interval increases. You can convince yourself of this by entering different confidence levels such as 90% or 99% in cell E6. The lower and upper limits of the confidence interval in cells E8 and E9 will change automatically, getting closer together for the 90% level and farther apart for the 99% level. Just remember that you, the analyst, can choose the confidence level, but 95% is the level most commonly chosen.

Before leaving this example, we discuss the assumptions that lead to the confidence interval. First, you might question whether the sample is really a *random* sample—or whether it matters. Perhaps the manager used some random mechanism to select the customers to be surveyed. More likely, however, she simply surveyed 40 consecutive customers who tried the sandwich on a given day. This is called a *convenience sample* and is not really a *random* sample. However, unless there is some reason to believe that these 40 customers differ in some relevant aspect from the entire population of customers, it is probably safe to treat them as a random sample.

A second assumption is that the population distribution is *normal*. We made this assumption when we introduced the *t* distribution. Obviously, the population distribution *cannot* be exactly normal because it is concentrated on the 10 possible satisfaction ratings, and the normal distribution describes a continuum. However, this is probably not a problem for two reasons. First, confidence intervals based on the *t* distribution are *robust* to violations of normality. This means that the resulting confidence intervals are valid for any populations that are *approximately* normal. Second, the normal population assumption is less crucial for larger sample sizes because of the central limit theorem. A sample size of 40 should be large enough.

Finally, it is important to recognize what this confidence interval implies and what it doesn't imply. In the entire population of customers who ordered this sandwich, there is a distribution of satisfaction ratings. Some fraction rate it as 1, some rate it as 2, and so on. All we are trying to determine here is the *average* of all these ratings. Based on the analysis, the manager can be 95% confident that this (still unknown) average is between 5.739 and 6.761. However, this confidence interval doesn't tell her other characteristics of the population of ratings that might be of interest, such as the proportion of customers who rate the sandwich 6 or higher. It only provides information about the *mean* rating. Later in this chapter, you will see how to find a confidence interval for a proportion, which allows you to analyze another important characteristic of a population distribution. ∎

In the sandwich example, we said that the manager can be 95% confident that the true mean rating is between 5.739 and 6.761. What does this statement really mean? Contrary to what you might expect, it does *not* mean that the true mean lies between 5.739 and 6.761 with probability 0.95. Either the true mean is inside this interval or it is not. The true meaning of a 95% confidence interval is based on the *procedure* used to obtain it. Specifically, if you use this procedure on a large number of random samples, all from the same population, then approximately 95% of the resulting confidence intervals will be "good" ones that include the true mean, and the other 5% will be "bad" ones that do not include the true mean. Unfortunately, when you have only a single sample, as in the sandwich example, you have no way of knowing whether your confidence interval is one of the good ones or one of the bad ones, but you can be 95% confident that you obtained one of the good intervals.

This simulation is performed only to illustrate the true meaning of a "95% confidence interval." In any real situation, you obtain only a single random sample and the corresponding confidence interval.

Because this is such an important concept, we illustrate it in Figure 8.5 with simulation. (See the file **Confidence Interval Simulation Finished.xlsx**. There is no "unfinished" version of this file.) The data in column B are generated randomly from a normal distribution with the *known* values of μ and σ in cells B3 and B4. Next, StatTools's One-Sample Confidence Interval procedure is used to calculate a 95% confidence interval for the true value of μ, exactly as in the sandwich example. However, because the true value of μ is known, it is possible to record a 1 in cell H6 if the true mean is inside the interval and a 0 otherwise. The appropriate formula is

=IF(AND(B3>=D13,B3<=D14),1,0)

Finally, a data table can be used to replicate the simulated results 1000 times.[2] Specifically, the formula in G11 is

=G6

Then to build the data table in the range G11:H1011, leave the row input cell box empty and specify any blank cell as the column input cell. Finally, the AVERAGE function can be used in cell H7 to find the fraction of 1s in the range G12:G1011.

Figure 8.5 Simulation Demonstration of Confidence Intervals

	A	B	C	D	E	F	G	H
1	Interpretation of a "95% confidence interval"							
2								
3	Population mean	100						
4	Population stdev	20						
5								
6	Random sample			Random sample			Mean captured?	1
7	78.70		Conf. Intervals (One-Sample)	Data Set #1			% of CI's capturing mean	95.1%
8	111.72		Sample Size	30				
9	93.13		Sample Mean	93.74			Data table to replicate confidence interval	
10	74.28		Sample Std Dev	24.04			Replication	Mean captured?
11	75.31		Confidence Level (Mean)	95.0%			1	1
12	55.61		Degrees of Freedom	29			2	1
13	83.45		Lower Limit	84.76			3	1
14	82.48		Upper Limit	102.72			4	1
15	74.98						5	1
16	72.48		Graphical representation				6	1
17	113.06		Limit	Height			7	1
18	114.42		84.76	1			8	0
19	83.61		102.72	1			9	1
20	110.32						10	1
21	95.18		Mean	Height			11	1
22	111.87		100	1			12	1
23	55.45						13	1
24	118.47						14	1
25	114.64						15	1
26	77.27						16	1
27	76.21						17	1
28	64.16						18	1
29	95.07						19	1
30	128.13						20	1
31	100.43						21	1
32	141.25						22	1
33	146.15						23	1
34	94.14						24	1
35	109.04						25	1
36	61.14						26	1
37							27	1
38								

This simulation uses a *normal* population for illustration. But you could generate the random sample from another distribution (e.g., triangular) to see if the confidence intervals are still *valid*, i.e., if the % in cell H7 is about 95%.

(Chart legend: Confidence limits; Mean)

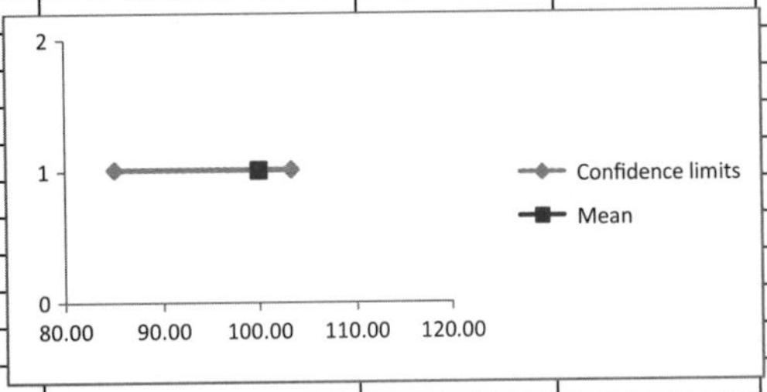

© Cengage Learning

[2]Depending on the speed of your PC, it can take a few seconds to simulate 1000 samples of size 30 in this data table. Therefore, it is a good idea to set the recalculation mode to "automatic except tables." (You can find this option under the Calculation Options dropdown menu on the Formulas ribbon.) That way, the data table recalculates only if you explicitly tell it to (by pressing the F9 key).

You can see that 948 of the simulated confidence intervals (each based on a *different* random sample of size 30) contain the true mean 100. In theory, 950 of the 1000 intervals should cover the true mean, and this is almost exactly what occurred. Of course, in a particular application you might unluckily obtain the fourth sample (in row 15). However, without knowing that the true mean is 100, you would have no way of knowing that you obtained a "bad" interval.

We also show this graphically in the file. (See Figure 8.5.) The small square in this graph is positioned at the known mean and never changes. The blue line represents a particular confidence interval. Put your cursor below this chart in, say, cell C35, and press the Delete key. (This forces a recalculation without recalculating the whole data table.) The position of the blue line will change. About 95% of the time, the blue line will straddle the small square—the confidence interval will include the true mean—but about 1 time out of 20, it will not. This also illustrates the meaning of a "95% confidence interval."

FUNDAMENTAL INSIGHT

True Meaning of a 95% Confidence Interval

Given the data in a particular sample, a 95% confidence interval for the mean will either include the (unknown) population mean or it won't. The true meaning of a 95% confidence interval is that if the same *procedure* is used on many different random samples, about 95% of the resulting confidence intervals will include the population mean, and only about 5% won't. Therefore, you can be 95% confident that any particular confidence interval you happen to get is a "good" one.

PROBLEMS

Level A

4. A manufacturing company's quality control personnel have recorded the proportion of defective items for each of 500 monthly shipments of one of the computer components that the company produces. The data are in the file **P07_07.xlsx**. The quality control department manager does not have sufficient time to review all of these data. Rather, she would like to examine the proportions of defective items for a sample of these shipments.

    a. Use StatTools to generate a simple random sample of size 25.

    b. Using the sample generated in part **a**, construct a 95% confidence interval for the mean proportion of defective items over all monthly shipments. Assume that the population consists of the proportion of defective items for each of the given 500 monthly shipments.

    c. Interpret the 95% confidence interval constructed in part **b**.

    d. Does the 95% confidence interval contain the actual population mean in this case? If not, explain why not. What proportion of many similarly constructed confidence intervals should include the true population mean?

5. The file **P08_05.xlsx** contains salary data on all NFL players in each of the years 2002 to 2009. Because this file contains all players for each of these years, you can calculate the *population mean* for each year

if *population* is defined as all NFL players that year. However, proceed as in the previous chapter to select a random sample of size 50 from the 2009 population. Based on this random sample, calculate a 95% confidence interval for the mean NFL total salary in 2009. Does it contain the population mean? Repeat this procedure several times until you find a random sample where the population mean is *not* included in the confidence interval.

6. The file **P08_06.xlsx** contains data on repetitive task times for each of two workers. John has been doing this task for months, whereas Fred has just started. Each time listed is the time (in seconds) to perform a routine task on an assembly line. The times shown are in chronological order.

    a. Find a 95% confidence interval for the mean time it takes John to perform the task. Do the same for Fred.

    b. Do you believe both of the confidence intervals in part **a** are valid and/or useful? Why or why not? Which of the two workers would you rather have, assuming that task time is the only issue?

7. The manager of a local fast-food restaurant is interested in improving the service provided to customers who use the restaurant's drive-up window. As a first step in this process, the manager asks an assistant to record the time (in seconds) it takes to serve a large number of customers at the final window in the facility's drive-up system. The file **P08_07.xlsx** contains a random sample of 200 service times during the busiest hour of the day.

a. Identify the relevant population.

b. Construct and interpret a 95% confidence interval for the mean service time of all customers arriving during the busiest hour of the day at this fast-food operation.

c. If the manager wants to improve service, at least during the busiest time of day, does this confidence interval provide useful information? What useful information does it *not* provide?

Level B

8. Continuing Problem 5, generate a random sample of 50 players for each of the eight years in the file **P08_05.xlsx**. For each of these samples, construct a 95% confidence interval for the mean total salary for that year. What is the confidence level that any particular one of these confidence intervals includes the population mean for that year? Is this the same confidence level that *all eight* of these confidence intervals include the respective population means? Why or why not?

9. The file **Confidence Interval Simulation.xlsx** generates observations randomly from a *normal* population. Suppose instead that each observation in column A is exponentially distributed with mean 10. (Refer to Section 5-6 for a brief explanation of the exponential distribution.) Unlike a normal distribution, an exponential distribution is very skewed to the right. A value from this distribution can be generated with the formula =−10*LN(RAND()). Rerun the simulation, still with sample size 30, with this exponential distribution. Are 95% confidence intervals still *valid*? That is, is the percentage in cell H7 approximately equal to 95%, as it should be? Press the F9 key a few times to check this.

10. Answer the questions in the previous problem when the population is a *mixture* of two normal distributions. Specifically, suppose each observation has a 65% chance of coming from a normal distribution with mean 100 and standard deviation 20, and a 35% chance of coming from a normal distribution with mean 200 and standard deviation 40. What is the mean of this mixture distribution? (*Hint*: Use an IF function to generate each random value in column A.)

8-4 CONFIDENCE INTERVAL FOR A TOTAL[3]

There are situations where a population mean is not the population parameter of most interest. A good example is the auditing example discussed in the previous chapter (Example 7.4). Rather than estimating the mean amount of receivables *per account*, the auditor might be more interested in the *total* amount of all receivables, summed over all accounts. In this section we provide a point estimate and a confidence interval for a population total.

First, we introduce some notation. Let T be a population total we want to estimate, such as the total of all receivables, and let $\hat{T}$ be a point estimate of T based on a simple random sample of size n from a population of size N. We first need a point estimate of T. For the population total T, it is reasonable to sum all of the values in the sample, denoted T_s, and then "project" this total to the population with Equation (8.5), where the second equality follows because the sample total T_s divided by the sample size n is the sample mean $\overline{X}$.

Point Estimate for Population Total

$$\hat{T} = \frac{N}{n}T_s = N\overline{X} \qquad (8.5)$$

Equation (8.5) is quite intuitive. For example, suppose there are 1000 accounts in the population, you sample 50 of them, and you observe a sample total of $5000. Then, because only 1/20 of the population was sampled, a natural estimate of the population total is $20 \times \$5000 = \$100,000$.

Like the sample mean $\overline{X}$, the estimate $\hat{T}$ has a sampling distribution. The mean and standard deviation of this sampling distribution are given in Equations (8.6) and (8.7), where σ is again the population standard deviation.

[3]This section can be omitted without any loss of continuity.

> **Mean and Standard Error of Point Estimate for Population Total**
>
> $$E(\hat{T}) = T \qquad \text{(8.6)}$$
> $$SE(\hat{T}) = N\sigma/\sqrt{n} \qquad \text{(8.7)}$$

Because σ is usually unknown, s is used instead of σ to obtain the approximate standard error of $\hat{T}$ given in Equation (8.8). The second equality follows because $s/\sqrt{n}$ is the standard error of $\overline{X}$.

> **Approximate Standard Error of Point Estimate for Population Total**
>
> $$SE(\hat{T}) = Ns/\sqrt{n} = N \times SE(\overline{X}) \qquad \text{(8.8)}$$

Note from Equation (8.6) that $\hat{T}$ is an unbiased estimate of the population total T. Therefore, it has no tendency to either overestimate or underestimate T.

From equations (8.5) and (8.8), the point estimate of T is the point estimate of the mean multiplied by N, and the standard error of this point estimate is the standard error of the sample mean multiplied by N. This has a very nice consequence. A confidence interval for T can be formed with the following two-step procedure:

1. Find a confidence interval for the sample mean in the usual way.

2. Multiply each endpoint of the confidence interval by the population size N.

We illustrate this procedure in Example 8.2.

EXAMPLE | **8.2 ESTIMATING TOTAL TAX REFUNDS**

The Internal Revenue Service would like to estimate the total net amount of refund due to a particular set of 1,000,000 taxpayers. Each taxpayer will either receive a refund, in which case the net refund is positive, or will have to pay an amount due, in which case the net refund is negative. Therefore the *total* net amount of refund is a natural quantity of interest; it is the net amount the IRS will have to pay out (or receive, if negative). Find a 95% confidence interval for this total using the refunds from a random sample of 500 taxpayers in the file **IRS Refunds.xlsx**.

Objective   To use StatTools's One-Sample Confidence Interval procedure, with an appropriate modification, to find a 95% confidence interval for the total (net) amount the IRS must pay out to these 1,000,000 taxpayers.

Solution

The solution appears in Figure 8.6 (with only part of the sample shown). Although there is no explicit StatTools procedure for dealing with population totals, you can take advantage of the close relationship between the confidence interval for a mean and the confidence interval for a total. First use StatTools to find a 95% confidence interval for the population mean. This output appears in rows 5–11. The average refund per taxpayer in the sample is slightly less than $300 (cell E6), and the standard error of this sample mean (not shown explicitly) is about $26. The confidence interval for the mean (in cells E10 and E11) extends from $244 to $346. This part of the output analyzes the average refund *per taxpayer*.

Figure 8.6

Confidence Interval for Population Total

	A	B	C	D	E
1	Customer	Refund		Population size	1000000
2	1	$70			
3	2	$1,190			Refund
4	3	$220		*Conf. Intervals (One-Sample)*	Data Set #1
5	4	−$280		Sample Size	500
6	5	$260		Sample Mean	$294.98
7	6	$370		Sample Std Dev	$581.31
8	7	$450		Confidence Level (Mean)	95.0%
9	8	$210		Degrees of Freedom	499
10	9	$1,150		Lower Limit	$243.90
11	10	$270		Upper Limit	$346.06
12	11	$470			
13	12	−$10		Confidence interval for population total	
14	13	−$160		Confidence level	95.0%
15	14	$2,430		Point estimate	$294,980,000
16	15	$140		Standard error	$25,997,048
17	16	−$190		Lower limit	$243,902,836
18	17	−$810		Upper limit	$346,057,164
19	18	−$20			
499	498	$190			
500	499	$1,840			
501	500	−$20			

© Cengage Learning

Next, project these results to the entire population. This is done in the range E15:E18 by multiplying each of the values in the previous paragraph by the population size, 1,000,000. The IRS can be 95% confident that it will need to pay out somewhere between 244 and 346 million dollars to these 1,000,000 taxpayers. ∎

PROBLEMS

Level A

11. The file **P02_16.xlsx** contains the number of arrivals at a turnpike tollbooth for each of four 5-minute intervals for each of 256 days. For this problem, assume that each column, such as arrivals from 8:00 AM to 8:05 AM, is a random sample of all arrivals from the corresponding hour of the day, such as 8:00 AM to 9:00 AM. Find a 95% confidence interval for the mean number of arrivals during each corresponding hour of the day, that is, one for 8:00 AM to 9:00 AM, one for 9:00 AM to 10:00 AM, and so on.

12. A lightbulb manufacturer wants to estimate the total number of defective bulbs contained in all of the boxes shipped by the company during the past week. Production personnel at this company have recorded the number of defective bulbs found in each of 50 randomly selected boxes shipped during the past week. These data are provided in the file **P08_12.xlsx.** Find a 95% confidence interval for the total number of defective bulbs contained in the 1000 boxes shipped by this company during the past week.

13. Auditors of a particular bank are interested in comparing the reported value of all 2265 customer savings account balances with their own findings regarding the actual value of such assets. Rather than reviewing the records of each savings account at the bank, the auditors decide to examine a representative sample of savings account balances. The population from which they will sample is given in the file **P08_13.xlsx.**
  a. Select 10 simple random samples, each consisting of 100 savings account balances from this population.
  b. For each sample generated in part **a**, construct a 95% confidence interval for the total value of all 2265 savings account balances within this bank. How many of them include the (known) population total?

Level B

14. Suppose you are gambling on a roulette wheel. Each time the wheel is spun, the result is one of the outcomes 0, 1, and so on through 36. Of these outcomes, 16 are red, 16 are black, and 1 is green. On each spin you bet $5 that a red outcome will occur and $1 that the green outcome will occur. If red occurs, you win a net $4. (You win $10 from red and nothing from green.) If green occurs, you win a net $24. (You win $30 from green and nothing from red.) If black occurs, you lose everything you bet for a loss of $6.

a. Use simulation to generate 20 plays from this strategy. Each play should indicate the net amount won or lost. Then, based on these 20 outcomes, find a 95% confidence interval for the total net amount won or lost from 1000 plays of the game. Would you conclude that this strategy is a winning one for you?

b. Repeat part **a**, but with slightly changed rules. Now your betting strategy is the same, but if red occurs, your net gain is $5 (you win $11 from red, nothing from green). Comment on whether this slight change makes much of a difference in the mean total from 1000 bets.

8-5 CONFIDENCE INTERVAL FOR A PROPORTION

How often have you heard on the evening news a survey finding such as, "52% of the public agree with the president's handling of the economy, with a sampling error of plus or minus 3%"? Surveys are often used to estimate proportions, such as the proportion of the public who agree with the president's handling of the economy. We will now discuss how to form a confidence interval for any population proportion p.

The basic procedure is very similar to the procedure for a population mean. It requires a point estimate, the standard error of this point estimate, and a multiple that depends on the confidence level. Then the confidence level has the same form as in Expression (8.1):

$$\text{point estimate} \pm \text{multiple} \times \text{standard error}$$

In the news example the point estimate is 52% and the "multiple × standard error" is 3%. Therefore, the confidence interval extends from 49% to 55%. Although the news show doesn't state the confidence level explicitly, it is 95% by convention. In words, they are 95% confident that the percentage of the public who agree with the president's handling of the economy is somewhere between 49% and 55%.

The theory that leads to this result is fairly straightforward. Let A be any property that members of a population either have or do not have. As examples, A might be the property that

- a person agrees with the president's handling of the economy
- a person has purchased a company's product at least once in the past three months
- the diameter of a part is within specification limits
- a customer's account is at least two months overdue
- a customer's rating of a new sandwich is at least 6 on a 10-point scale.

In each of these examples, let p be the proportion of the population with property A. From a random sample of size n, let $\hat{p}$ be the sample proportion of members with property A. For example, if 10 out of 50 sampled members have property A, then $\hat{p} = 10/50 = 0.2$. Then $\hat{p}$ is used as a point estimate of p.

It can be shown that for sufficiently large n, the sampling distribution of $\hat{p}$ is approximately *normal* with mean p and standard error $\sqrt{p(1-p)/n}$. Because p is the unknown parameter, $\hat{p}$ is substituted for p in this standard error to obtain the following approximate standard error of $\hat{p}$:

Standard Error of Sample Proportion

$$\text{SE}(\hat{p}) = \sqrt{\frac{\hat{p}(1-\hat{p})}{n}} \qquad\qquad \textbf{(8.9)}$$

Finally, the multiple used to obtain a confidence interval for p is a Z-value. (It is *not* a *t*-value.) It is the standard normal value that cuts off an appropriate probability in each tail. For example, the *z*-multiple for a 95% confidence interval is 1.96 because this value cuts off probability 0.025 in each tail of the standard normal distribution. In general, the confidence interval has the form in Expression (8.10):

Confidence Interval for a Proportion

$$\hat{p} \pm z\text{-multiple} \times \sqrt{\frac{\hat{p}(1 - \hat{p})}{n}} \qquad \textbf{(8.10)}$$

This confidence interval is based on the assumption of a large sample size. A rule of thumb for checking the validity of this assumption is the following. Let p_L and p_U be the lower and upper limits of the confidence interval. Then the sample size is sufficiently large—and the confidence interval is valid—if $np_L > 5$, $n(1 - p_L) > 5$, $np_U > 5$, and $n(1 - p_U) > 5$. Essentially, these mean that n should be reasonably large and the two values of p should not be too close to 0 or 1.

We illustrate the procedure in Example 8.3.

EXAMPLE | **8.3 ESTIMATING THE RESPONSE TO A NEW SANDWICH**

The fast-food manager from Example 8.1 has already sampled 40 customers to estimate the population mean rating of the restaurant's new sandwich. Recall that each rating is on a 1-to-10 scale, 10 being the best. The manager would now like to use the same sample to estimate the proportion of customers who rate the sandwich at least 6. Her thinking is that these are the customers who are likely to purchase the sandwich on subsequent visits.

Objective To illustrate the procedure for finding a confidence interval for the proportion of customers who rate the new sandwich at least 6 on a 10-point scale.

Solution

The solution appears in Figure 8.7. (See the file **Satisfaction Ratings.xlsx**.) It is first useful to create a 0/1 column that indicates whether a customer's rating is at least 6. To do this, enter the formula

=IF(B2>=6,1,0)

Figure 8.7

Confidence Interval for Proportion

	A	B	C	D	E	F
1	Customer	Satisfaction	At least 6?		Confidence interval based on column C	
2	1	7	1			At least 6?
3	2	5	0		Conf. Interval (Proportion)	Data Set #2
4	3	5	0		Category	1
5	4	6	1		Sample Size	40
6	5	8	1		Sample Proportion	0.625
7	6	7	1		Confidence Level	95.0%
8	7	6	1		Standard Error of Proportion	0.077
9	8	7	1		Lower Limit	0.475
10	9	10	1		Upper Limit	0.775
11	10	7	1			
12	11	9	1			
38	37	8	1			
39	38	9	1			
40	39	5	0			
41	40	4	0			

in cell C2 and copy it down. Next, designate a StatTools data set that includes this new column. (It can include columns A and B, but they are not relevant for the confidence interval.) Finally, select Confidence Interval from the Statistical Inference dropdown list, and select Proportion. Then fill out the dialog box as shown in Figure 8.8. Specifically, check the 1 in the Categories to Analyze section to analyze the proportion of 1s, not the proportion of 0s.

Figure 8.8

StatTools Dialog
Box for Confidence
Interval for
Proportion

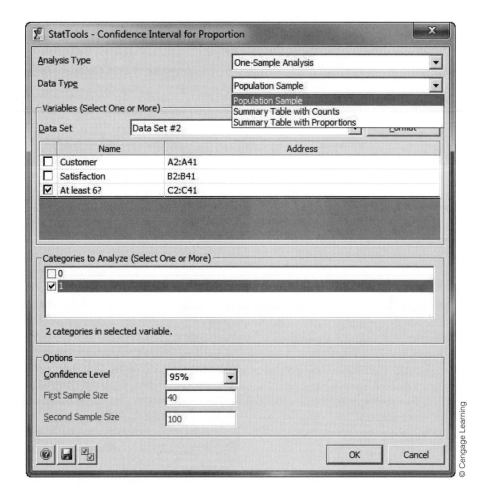

As the Data Type dropdown list indicates, the data for the confidence interval can be in three formats: (1) a sample of 0s and 1s, as in this example, (2) a summary table with counts, or (3) a summary table with proportions. These latter two options are also illustrated in the finished version of the **Satisfaction Ratings.xlsx** file. The reason for these options is that you could very easily start with a table of counts or proportions, rather than a long column of 0s and 1s. StatTools (version 5.5 and later) accommodates these possibilities.

Finally, using the confidence interval limits, $p_L = 0.475$ and $p_U = 0.775$, you can check the assumption of sufficiently large sample size. With $n = 40$, np_L, $n(1 - p_L)$, np_U, and $n(1 - p_U)$ are all well above 5, so that the validity of this confidence interval is established.

The output is fairly good news for the manager. Based on this sample of size 40, she can be 95% confident that the percentage of all customers who would rate the sandwich 6 or higher is somewhere between 47.5% and 77.5%. Of course, she realizes that this is a very wide interval, so there is still a lot of uncertainty about the *true* population proportion. To reduce the length of this interval, she would need to sample more customers—quite a few more customers. Typically, confidence intervals for proportions are fairly wide unless n is quite large. ∎

We explore this final statement a bit more. Referring again to news shows, you have probably noticed that they almost always quote a sampling error of plus or minus 3%. In words, the "plus or minus" part of their 95% confidence interval is 3%, or 0.03. How large a sample size must they use to achieve this? The "plus or minus" part of the confidence interval is 1.96 times the standard error of $\hat{p}$, so we must have

$$1.96 \times \sqrt{\hat{p}(1 - \hat{p})/n} = 0.03$$

Now, the quantity $\hat{p}(1 - \hat{p})$ is fairly constant for values of $\hat{p}$ between 0 and 1, provided that $\hat{p}$ isn't too close to 0 or 1. To get a reasonable estimate of the required n, we use $\hat{p} = 0.5$. Then we have

$$1.96 \times \sqrt{(0.5)(0.5)/n} = 0.03$$

Solving for n, we obtain $n = [(1.96)(0.5)/0.03]^2 \approx 1067$.

This is a rather remarkable result. To obtain a 95% confidence interval of this length for a population proportion, where the population consists of *millions* of people, only about 1000 people need to be sampled. The remarkable fact is that this small a sample can provide such accurate information about such a large population.

One of many business applications of confidence intervals for proportions is in auditing. Auditors typically use *attribute sampling* to check whether certain procedures are being followed correctly. The term "attribute" means that each item checked is done either correctly or incorrectly— there is no in-between. Examples of items not done correctly might include (1) an invoice copy that is not initialed by an accounting clerk, (2) an invoice quantity that does not agree with the quantity on the shipping document, (3) an invoice price that does not agree with the price on an authorized price list, and (4) an invoice with a clerical inaccuracy. Typically, an auditor focuses on one of these types of errors and then estimates the proportion of items with this type of error.

Because auditors are concerned primarily with how *large* the proportion of errors might be, they usually calculate *one-sided* confidence intervals for proportions. Instead of using sample data to find lower and upper limits p_L and p_U of a confidence interval, they automatically use $p_L = 0$ and then determine an upper limit p_U such that the 95% confidence interval is from 0 to p_U. A simple modification of the confidence interval in Expression (8.10) provides the result in Equation (8.11), where the z-multiple is chosen so that the entire probability (0.05 for a 95% interval) is in the right-hand tail. For a 95% confidence level, the relevant z-multiple is 1.645.

Upper Limit of a One-Sided Confidence Interval for a Proportion
$$p_U = \hat{p} + z\text{-multiple} \times \sqrt{\hat{p}(1 - \hat{p})/n} \qquad \textbf{(8.11)}$$

One further complication occurs, however. This formula for p_U relies on the large-sample approximation of the normal distribution to the binomial distribution. Auditors typically use an *exact* procedure to find p_U that is based directly on the binomial distribution. We illustrate how this is done in Example 8.4.

8.4 Auditing for Price Errors

An auditor wants to check the proportion of invoices that contain price errors—that is, prices that do not agree with those on an authorized price list. He checks 93 randomly sampled invoices and finds that two of them include price errors. What can he conclude, in terms of a one-sided 95% confidence interval, about the proportion of all invoices with price errors?

Objective   To find the upper limit of a one-sided 95% confidence interval for the proportion of errors in the context of attribute sampling in auditing.

Solution

The results appear in Figure 8.9, where StatTools has *not* been used because it does not include a procedure for one-sided confidence intervals. (See the file **One-Sided Confidence Interval.xlsx**.) The sample proportion is p = 2/93 = 0.0215 and the upper confidence limit based on the large-sample approximation is 0.046. This latter value is calculated in cell B14 with the formula

=B7+B13*SQRT(B7*(1-B7)/B5)

However, note that $np_U = 93(0.046) = 4.278$, which is less than 5. This indicates that the large-sample approximation might not be valid.

Figure 8.9

Analysis of Auditing Example

	A	B	C	D	E	F
1	An exact one-sided confidence interval in auditing					
2						
3	Confidence level	95%				
4	Number of errors	2				
5	Sample size	93				
6						
7	Sample proportion	0.0215				
8						
9	Exact upper confidence limit for p			Goal seek condition		
10	Upper limit	0.066		0.050	=	0.05
11						
12	Large-sample upper confidence limit for p					
13	z-multiple	1.645				
14	Upper limit	0.046				

© Cengage Learning

A more valid procedure, based on the binomial distribution, appears in row 10. It turns out that if p_U is the appropriate upper confidence limit, then p_U satisfies the equation

---

Formula for Upper Confidence Limit

$$P(X \leq k) = \alpha \qquad (8.12)$$

Here, X is binomially distributed with parameters n and p_U, k is the observed number of errors, and α is 1 minus the confidence level. There is no way to find p_U directly (by means of a formula) from Equation (8.12). However, you can use Excel's Goal Seek tool. First, enter *any* trial value of p_U in cell B10 and the binomial formula

=BINOMDIST(B4,B5,B10,1)

in cell D10. [This formula calculates $P(X \le k)$ from the trial value in cell B10.] Then use Goal Seek from the What-If Analysis dropdown menu on the Data ribbon, with cell D10 as the Set cell, 0.05 as the target value, and cell B10 as the Changing cell. (See Figure 8.10.)

Figure 8.10

Settings in Goal Seek Dialog Box

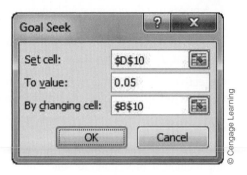

The resulting value of P_U is 0.066. This is considerably different (from the auditor's point of view) from the 0.046 value found from the large-sample approximation. It allows the auditor to state with 95% confidence that the percentage of invoices with price errors is no greater than 6.6%, based on the two errors out of 93 observed in the sample. ∎

PROBLEMS

Level A

15. A drugstore manager needs to purchase adequate supplies of various brands of toothpaste to meet the ongoing demands of its customers. In particular, the company is interested in estimating the proportion of its customers who favor the country's leading brand of toothpaste, Crest. The Data sheet of the file **P08_15.xlsx** contains the toothpaste brand preferences of 200 randomly selected customers, obtained recently through a customer survey. Find a 95% confidence interval for the proportion of all of the company's customers who prefer Crest toothpaste. How might the manager use this confidence interval for purchasing decisions?

16. The same data as in the previous problem are stored in a different format in the last two sheets of the file **P08_15.xlsx**.
   a. Use StatTools to find a 95% confidence interval for the proportion who favor Crest from the data in the Counts sheet. Using this same data on counts, calculate the confidence interval directly from the appropriate formulas, without using StatTools.
   b. Use StatTools to find a 95% confidence interval for the proportion who favor Crest from the data in the proportions sheet. Using this same data on proportions, calculate the confidence interval directly from the appropriate formulas, without using StatTools.

17. The employee benefits manager of a large public university would like to estimate the proportion of full-time employees who prefer adopting the first (plan A) of three available health care plans in the next annual enrollment period. A random sample of the university's employees and their tentative health care preferences are given in the file **P08_17.xlsx**.
   a. Find a 90% confidence interval for the proportion of all the university's employees who favor plan A.
   b. The file also includes the classification of each employee (administrative staff, support staff, or faculty). Find a separate 90% confidence interval for each of these groups for the proportion who favor plan A. How do these confidence intervals compare to one another? How do their lengths compare to the confidence interval in part **a**? Is this what you would expect? Explain.

18. A market research consultant hired by a leading soft-drink company wants to determine the proportion of consumers who favor its low-calorie brand over the leading low-calorie competitor in a particular geo-graphic region. A random sample of 250 consumers from the market under investigation is provided in the file **P08_18.xlsx**.
   a. Find a 90% confidence interval for the proportion of all consumers in this market who prefer the company's brand.
   b. The file contains the gender and age group for each customer in the sample. Find a separate 90% confidence for each gender for the proportion who prefer the company's brand. Then do the same

for each age group. Explain briefly how these confidence intervals compare to each other and to the confidence interval in part **a**.

Level B

19. Starting with the data from problem 17 in the file **P08_17.xlsx**, restructure the data so that you have a table of counts. Then use StatTools on the counts to answer the same questions as in problem 17.

20. Starting with the data from problem 18 in the file **P08_18.xlsx**, restructure the data so that you have a table of proportions. Then use StatTools on the proportions to answer the same questions as in problem 18.

8-6 CONFIDENCE INTERVAL FOR A STANDARD DEVIATION[4]

In Section 8-3 we focused primarily on estimation of a population *mean*. We had to deal with the population standard deviation σ in its role as a nuisance parameter. That is, we needed an estimate of σ to estimate the standard error of the sample mean. However, there are cases where the variability in the population, measured by σ, is of interest in its own right. We briefly describe a procedure for obtaining a confidence interval for σ in this section.

The theory is somewhat more complex than for the case of the mean. As you might expect, the sample standard deviation s is used as a point estimate of σ. However, the sampling distribution of s is not symmetric—in particular, it is not the normal distribution or the t distribution. Rather, the appropriate sampling distribution is a right-skewed distribution called the **chi-square distribution**. Like the t distribution, the chi-square distribution has a degrees of freedom parameter, which (for this procedure) is again $n - 1$.

Tables of the chi-square distribution, for selected degrees of freedom, appear in many statistics books, but the necessary information can be obtained more easily with Excel's CHIDIST and CHIINV functions. The CHIDIST function takes the form

$$=\textbf{CHIDIST}(v, df)$$

This function returns the probability to the *right* of value v when the degrees of freedom parameter is df. Similarly, the CHIINV function takes the form

$$=\textbf{CHIINV}(p, df)$$

This returns the value with probability p to the *right* of it when the degrees of freedom parameter is df.

CHANGES IN EXCEL 2010

These chi-square functions were changed considerably in Excel 2010. There are now CHISQ.DIST and CHISQ.INV functions for *left* tails, and CHISQ.DIST has a last "cum" argument just like NORM.DIST and T.DIST. Also, there are two functions, CHISQ.DIST.RT and CHISQ.INV.RT, for *right* tails.

We do not present the rather complex confidence interval formulas for σ. However, we point out that because of the skewness of the sampling distribution of s, a confidence interval for σ is *not* centered at s. That is, the confidence interval is *not* the point estimate plus or minus a multiple of a standard error. Instead, s is always closer to the left endpoint of the confidence interval than to the right endpoint, as indicated in Figure 8.11.

---

[4]This section can be omitted without any loss of continuity.

Figure 8.11

Confidence Interval
for Standard
Deviation

Lower limit   Sample stdev *s*   Upper limit
© Cengage Learning

The StatTools One-Sample Confidence Interval procedure enables you to obtain a confidence interval for a population standard deviation as easily as for a mean. We illustrate this in Example 8.5.

| EXAMPLE | **8.5 ANALYZING VARIABILITY IN DIAMETERS OF MACHINE PARTS** |

A machine produces parts that are supposed to have diameter 10 centimeters. However, due to inherent variability, some diameters are greater than 10 and some are less. The production supervisor is concerned about two things. First, he is concerned that the mean diameter is not what it should be, 10 centimeters. Second, he is worried about the extent of variability in the diameters. Even if the mean is on target, excessive variability implies that many of the parts will fail to meet specifications. To analyze the process, he randomly samples 50 parts during the course of a day and measures the diameter of each part to the nearest millimeter. The results are shown in columns A and B of Figure 8.12. (See the file **Part Diameters.xlsx**.) Should the supervisor be concerned about the results from this sample?

Figure 8.12   Analysis of Parts Data

	A	B	C	D	E	F	G	H	I
1	Part	Diameter			Diameter				
2	1	10.031		*Conf. Intervals (One-Sample)*	Data Set #1				
3	2	10.011		**Sample Size**	50				
4	3	10.003		**Sample Mean**	9.996				
5	4	10.025		**Sample Std Dev**	0.034				
6	5	10.048		**Confidence Level (Mean)**	95.0%				
7	6	10.014		**Degrees of Freedom**	49				
8	7	10.030		**Lower Limit**	9.986				
9	8	10.008		**Upper Limit**	10.005				
10	9	10.049		**Confidence Level (Std Dev)**	95.0%				
11	10	9.995		**Degrees of Freedom**	49				
12	11	9.965		**Lower Limit**	0 029				
13	12	10.003		**Upper Limit**	0.043				
14	13	9.959							
15	14	10.013		**Proportion of unusable parts**					
16	15	10.012		**Maximum deviation for usability**	0.065				
17	16	10.005		**Assumed mean**	10				
18	17	9.921		**Assumed standard deviation**	0.043				
19	18	9.930		**Proportion unusuable**	0.131				
20	19	9.990							
21	20	9.948		**Two-way data table for finding proportion unusable as a function of mean and stdev**					
22	21	10.077			Assumed standard deviation				
23	22	9.959			0.131	0.029	0.034	0.043	
24	23	10.000		Assumed mean	9.986	0.041	0.080	0.149	
25	24	9.998			9.996	0.025	0.060	0.130	
26	25	9.983			10.005	0.026	0.061	0.131	
27	26	9.995							
50	49	9.973							
51	50	9.970							

© Cengage Learning

Objective   To use StatTools's One-Sample Confidence Interval procedure to find a confidence interval for the standard deviation of part diameters, and to see how variability affects the proportion of unusable parts produced.

Solution

Because the manager is concerned about the mean *and* the standard deviation of diameters, it is useful to obtain 95% confidence intervals for both. This is easy to do with StatTools's One-Sample Confidence Interval procedure for Mean/Std. Deviation. Go through the same dialog box as before (see Figure 8.3), but now check the boxes for both confidence interval options—mean and standard deviation. The top part of the output in Figure 8.12 (through cell E9) provides a 95% confidence interval for the mean. This confidence interval extends from 9.986 cm to 10.005 cm. Therefore, there is probably not too much cause for concern about the mean. The supervisor can be fairly confident that the mean diameter of all parts is close to 10 cm.

The bottom part of the output (the range E10:E13) provides a 95% confidence interval for the standard deviation of diameters. This interval extends from 0.029 cm to 0.043 cm. Is this good news or bad news? It depends. Let's say that a part is unusable if its diameter is more than 0.065 cm from the target. Let's also assume that the true mean is right on target and that the standard deviation is at the *upper* end of the confidence interval, that is, $\sigma = 0.043$ cm. Finally, assume that the population distribution of diameters is normal. Then the calculation in cell E19 shows that 13.1% of the parts will be unusable. The formula in cell E19 is

=NORMDIST(10-E16,E17,E18,1)+(1-NORMDIST(10+E16,E17,E18,1))

It adds the normal probabilities of being below or above the usable range.

To pursue this analysis one step further, a two-way data table in the range E23:H26 is useful. The means used in column E are the lower confidence limit, the sample mean, and the upper confidence limit. Similarly, the assumed standard deviations used in row 23 are the lower confidence limit, the sample standard deviation, and the upper confidence limit. To form the table, enter the formula **=E19** in cell E23, highlight the range E23:H26, and create a data table with cells E18 and E17 as the row and column input cells.

Each value in the body of the data table is the resulting proportion of unusable parts. Obviously, a mean close to the target and a small standard deviation are best, but even this best-case scenario results in 2.5% unusable parts (see cell F25). However, a mean off target and a large standard deviation can lead to as many as 14.9% unusable parts (see cell H24). In any case, the message for the supervisor is clear—he must work to reduce the underlying variability in the process. This variability is hurting him much more than an off-target mean. ■

PROBLEMS

Level A

21. Senior management of a large consulting firm is concerned about a growing decline in the organization's weekly number of billable hours. Ideally, the organization expects each professional employee to spend *at least* 40 hours per week on work. The file **P08_21.xlsx** contains the work hours reported by a random sample of employees in a typical week.
   a. Find a 95% confidence interval for the *mean* number of hours worked by the company's employees in a typical week.
   b. Find a 95% confidence interval for the *standard deviation* of the number of hours worked by the company's employees in a typical week.

c. Given the target range of 40 to 60 hours of work per week, should senior management be concerned about the number of hours their employees are currently devoting to work? Explain how the answers to *both* parts **a** and **b** help to answer this question.

Level B

22. The file **P08_06.xlsx** contains data on repetitive task times for each of two workers. John has been doing this task for months, whereas Fred has just started.

Each time listed is the time (in seconds) to perform a routine task on an assembly line. The times shown are in chronological order.

a. Find a 95% confidence interval for the standard deviation of times for John. Do the same for Fred. What do these indicate?
b. Given that these times are listed chronologically, how useful are the confidence intervals in part **a**? Specifically, is there any evidence that the variation in times is changing over time for either of the two workers?

8-7 CONFIDENCE INTERVAL FOR THE DIFFERENCE BETWEEN MEANS

Statisticians call these general types of problems "comparison problems." They are among the most important types of problems tackled with statistical methods.

One of the most important applications of statistical inference is the comparison of two population means. There are many applications to business, including the following.

Applications of Comparisons of Means in Business

■ Men and women shop at a retail clothing store. The manager would like to know how much more (or less), on average, a woman spends on a typical purchase occasion than a man.

■ Two airline companies fly similar routes. A consumer organization would like to check how much the average delay differs between the two airlines, where delay is defined as the actual arrival time at the destination minus the scheduled arrival time.

■ A supermarket chain mails coupons for various products to a randomly selected subset of its customers in a particular city. Its other customers in this city receive no such coupons. The chain would like to check how much the average amount spent on these products differs between the two sets of customers over the next couple of months.

■ A computer company has a customer service center that responds to customers' questions and complaints. The center employs two types of people: those who have had a recent course in dealing with customers (but little actual experience) and those with a lot of experience dealing with customers (but no formal course). The company would like to know how these two types of employees differ with respect to the average number of customer complaints of poor service in the last six months.

■ A consulting company hires business students directly out of undergraduate school. The new hires all take a problem-solving test. They then go through an intensive three-month training program, after which they take another similar problem-solving test. The company wants to know how much the average test score improves after the training program.

■ A car dealership often deals with husband–wife pairs shopping for cars. To check whether husbands react differently than their wives to the sales presentation, husbands and wives are asked (separately) to rate the quality of the sales presentation. The dealership wants to know how much husbands differ from their wives in terms of average ratings.

Each of these examples deals with a difference between means from two populations. However, the first four examples differ in one important respect from the last two. In the last two examples, there is a natural *pairing* across the two samples. In the first of these, each employee takes a test before a course and then a test after the course, so that each employee is naturally paired with himself or herself. In the final example, husbands and wives are naturally paired with one another. There is no such pairing in the first four examples. Instead, we assume that the samples in these first four examples are chosen *independently* of one another. For statistical reasons we need to distinguish these two cases, *independent samples* and *paired samples*, in the discussion that follows.

8-7a Independent Samples

The framework for this situation is the following. We are interested in some quantity, such as dollars spent or airplane delay, for each of two populations. The population means are μ_1 and μ_2, and the population standard deviations are σ_1 and σ_2. We take random samples of sizes n_1 and n_2 (which need not be equal) from the populations to estimate the difference between means, $\mu_1 - \mu_2$. A point estimate of this difference is the natural one, the difference between sample means, $\overline{X}_1 - \overline{X}_2$. Starting with this estimate, we want to form a confidence interval for the unknown population mean difference, $\mu_1 - \mu_2$.

It can be shown mathematically that the appropriate sampling distribution of the difference between sample means is again the t distribution, now with $n_1 + n_2 - 2$ degrees of freedom.[5] Therefore, a confidence interval for $\mu_1 - \mu_2$ is given by Expression (8.13). The t-multiple is the value that cuts off the appropriate probability (depending on the confidence level) in each tail of the t distribution with $n_1 + n_2 - 2$ degrees of freedom. For example, if the confidence level is 95% and $n_1 = n_2 = 30$, the appropriate t-multiple is 2.002, which can be found in Excel with the function **TINV(0.05,58)** (or **T.INV(0.025,58)** in Excel 2010 or later). Of course, it is calculated automatically by StatTools.

Confidence Interval for Difference Between Means

$$\overline{X}_1 - \overline{X}_2 \pm t\text{-multiple} \times SE(\overline{X}_1 - \overline{X}_2)$$

(8.13)

The standard error, $SE(\overline{X}_1 - \overline{X}_2)$, is more involved. We must first make the assumption that the population standard deviations are equal, that is, $\sigma_1 = \sigma_2$. (We shortly present an alternative procedure for the situation where the population standard deviations are *not* equal.) Then an estimate of this common standard deviation is provided by the "pooled" estimate from both samples, labeled s_p.

Pooled Estimate of Common Standard Deviation

$$s_p = \sqrt{\frac{(n_1 - 1)s_1^2 + (n_2 - 1)s_2^2}{n_1 + n_2 - 2}}$$

Here, s_1 and s_2 are the sample standard deviations from the two samples. This pooled estimate is somewhere between s_1 and s_2, with the relative sample sizes determining its exact value. Then the standard error of $\overline{X}_1 - \overline{X}_2$ is given by Equation (8.14):

Standard Error of Difference Between Sample Means

$$SE(\overline{X}_1 - \overline{X}_2) = s_p\sqrt{\frac{1}{n_1} + \frac{1}{n_2}}$$

(8.14)

---

[5]This assumes that either the population distributions are normal or that the sample sizes are reasonably large, conditions that are at least approximately met in a wide variety of applications.

Fortunately, the StatTools Two-Sample Confidence Interval procedure takes care of these calculations, as illustrated in Example 8.6.

EXAMPLE	8.6 RELIABILITY OF TREADMILL MOTORS AT SURESTEP

SureStep Company manufactures high-quality treadmills for use in exercise clubs. SureStep currently purchases its motors for these treadmills from supplier A. However, it is considering a change to supplier B, which offers a slightly lower cost. The only question is whether supplier B's motors are as reliable as supplier A's. To check this, SureStep installs motors from supplier A on 30 of its treadmills and motors from supplier B on another 30 of its treadmills. It then runs these treadmills under typical conditions and, for each treadmill, records the number of hours until the motor fails. The data from this experiment appear in Figure 8.13. (See the file **Treadmill Motors.xlsx**.) What can SureStep conclude?

Figure 8.13 Analysis of Treadmill Motors Data

	A	B	C	D	E	F
1	Supplier A	Supplier B			**Supplier A**	**Supplier B**
2	1358	658		*Sample Summaries*	Data Set #1	Data Set #1
3	793	404		Sample Size	30	30
4	587	735		Sample Mean	748.80	655.67
5	608	457		Sample Std Dev	283.88	259.99
6	472	431				
7	562	658			**Equal**	**Unequal**
8	879	453		*Conf. Intervals (Difference of Means)*	Variances	Variances
9	575	488		Confidence Level	95.0%	95.0%
10	1293	522		Sample Mean Difference	93.13	93.13
11	1457	1247		Standard Error of Difference	70.281	70.281
12	705	1095		Degrees of Freedom	58	58
13	623	430		Lower Limit	−47.549	−47.549
14	725	726		Upper Limit	233.815	233.815
15	569	793				
16	424	498				
17	436	502		*Equality of Variances Test*		
18	1250	589		Ratio of Sample Variances	1.1923	
19	493	975		*p*-Value	0.6390	
20	485	808				
21	462	456				
22	765	731				
23	854	491				
24	634	487				
25	1109	503				
26	800	465				
27	883	1475				
28	522	508				
29	791	846				
30	684	732				
31	666	507				

Objective To use StatTools's Two-Sample Confidence Interval procedure to find a confidence interval for the difference between mean lifetimes of motors, and to see how this confidence interval can help SureStep choose the better supplier.

Solution

In any comparison problem it is a good idea to look initially at side-by-side box plots of the two samples. These appear in Figure 8.14. These show that (1) the distributions of times until failure are skewed to the right for each supplier, (2) the mean for supplier A is somewhat greater than the mean for supplier B, and (3) there are several mild outliers. There seems to be little doubt that supplier A's motors will last longer on average than supplier B's—or is there? A confidence interval for the mean difference allows you to see whether the differences apparent in the box plots can be generalized to *all* motors from the two suppliers.

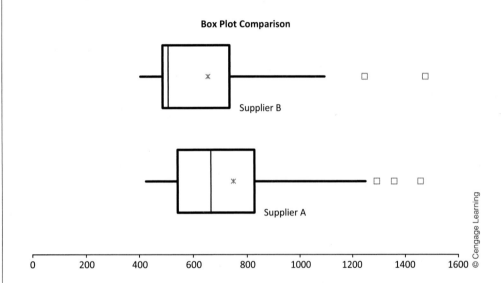

You can find this confidence interval by using the StatTools Two-Sample Confidence Interval procedure. To do so, select Confidence Interval and Mean/Std. Deviation from the StatTools Statistical Inference dropdown list, and fill in the resulting dialog box as shown in Figure 8.15. Specifically, make sure the Analysis Type dropdown list shows Two-Sample Analysis, and click on the Format button to make sure the Unstacked option is checked. You will then see the dialog box in Figure 8.16. By default, the difference analyzed will be "A minus B," but you can change it to "B minus A" by clicking the Reverse Order button. For now, click OK. This produces the output in Figure 8.13. The top part of the output summarizes the two samples. It shows that the sample means differ by approximately 93 hours and the sample standard deviations are of roughly the same magnitude.

*StatTools Tip: **Stacked versus Unstacked Data Sets***
The data are "unstacked" because there are separate columns for supplier A's times and supplier B's times. The Format button in the StatTools dialog box allows you to select the appropriate option: Stacked or Unstacked.

The confidence interval calculations appear in the range E9:E14. The difference between sample means is 93.133 hours, the standard error of the sample mean difference is 70.281 hours, and a 95% confidence interval for the mean difference extends from

Figure 8.15
Dialog Box for Two-Sample Procedure

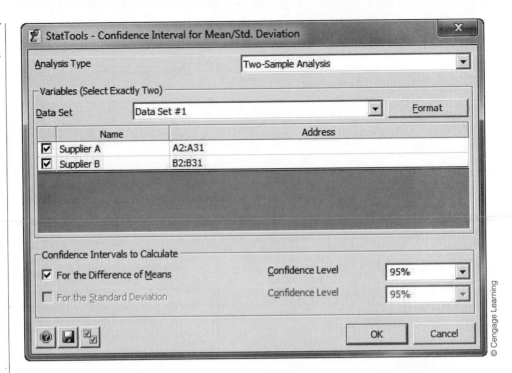

Figure 8.16
Dialog Box for Reversing the Difference

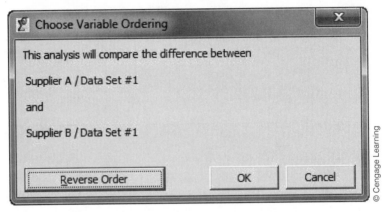

−47.549 to 233.815 hours. Not only is this interval quite wide, but it extends from a negative value to a positive value. If SureStep had to make a guess, it would say that supplier A's motors last longer on average than supplier B's. But because of the negative part of the confidence interval, there is still a possibility that the opposite is true.

Should SureStep continue with supplier A? This depends on the trade-off between the cost of the motors and warranty costs (and any other relevant costs). Because the warranty probably depends on whether a motor lasts a certain amount of time, warranty costs probably depend on a *proportion* (the proportion that fail before 500 hours, say) rather than a mean. Therefore, we postpone further discussion of this issue until we discuss differences between proportions in Section 8-8. ∎

Equal-Variance Assumption

This two-sample analysis makes the strong assumption that the standard deviations (or variances) of the two populations are equal. How can you tell if they are equal, and what do you do if they are clearly *not* equal?

To check whether they are equal, first look at the two sample standard deviations. If they are of widely different magnitudes, this certainly casts doubt on the equal-variance assumption. The sample standard deviations in the treadmill example, 283.88 and 259.98, are of similar magnitudes and present no clear evidence of unequal population variances. However, a statistical test for equality of two population variances is automatically shown at the bottom of the StatTools Two-Sample output. Because we have not yet discussed hypothesis testing, we postpone the discussion of this test for now. Suffice it to say that the test presents no evidence of unequal variances for this example.

If there is reason to believe that the population variances are unequal, then a slightly different procedure can be used to calculate a confidence interval for the difference between means. The appropriate standard error of $\overline{X}_1 - \overline{X}_2$ is now

$$\text{SE}(\overline{X}_1 - \overline{X}_2) = \sqrt{s_1^2/n_1 + s_2^2/n_2}$$

and the degrees of freedom used to find the t-multiple is given by a complex expression not shown here.

StatTools always calculates the results in both columns. When they are nearly the same, as they often are, it makes no practical difference which you quote.

StatTools's Two-Sample procedure automatically calculates the confidence interval under this unequal-variance assumption. For the treadmill example the results are in the range F9:F14 of Figure 8.13. In this example they are exactly the same as the results (in column E), which makes the equal-variance assumption. This is a consequence of equal sample sizes and roughly equal sample variances. In general, the two results differ appreciably only when the sample sizes *and* the sample variances differ considerably across samples. In any case, the appropriate results to use are those on the right (column F) if there is reason to suspect unequal population variances and those on the left (column E) otherwise.

FUNDAMENTAL INSIGHT

Role of Variances in Estimating the Difference between Means

It might be surprising that variances (or standard deviations) play such an important role in estimating the difference between means, but this is actually quite intuitive. If there is a lot of variability in the populations, it is more difficult to get accurate estimates of the population means, and hence the difference between the means. But if there is very little variability, it is much easier to estimate the means accurately.

We next examine customer waiting lines in a supermarket. We again make a comparison between two means, this time the mean number of customers in line during rush times versus normal times. There are two objectives in this example. First, it provides one more illustration of the two-sample procedure, now with unequal sample sizes. Perhaps more importantly, it illustrates that not all data sets come ready-made for performing a particular analysis. Some data manipulation is necessary before StatTools's Two-Sample procedure can be used. Indeed, this is sometimes the most time-consuming part of statistical analysis in real applications—getting the data ready for the analysis.

EXAMPLE | 8.7 CUSTOMER WAITING AT R&P SUPERMARKET

The manager of R&P Supermarket has collected a week's worth of data on customer arrivals, departures, and waiting. There are 48 observations per day, each taken at the end of a half-hour period. The data appear in the file **Customer Checkouts.xlsx**. The various times of day are listed in the Time Interval variable. (See Figure 8.17.) They include Morning Rush, Morning, Lunch Rush, Afternoon, Afternoon Rush, Evening, and Night. (The comment in cell C3 explains exactly which time intervals these refer to.) There is also a variable, End Waiting, that records the number of customers still being served or waiting in line at the end of each half-hour period.

Figure 8.17   Original Data for Supermarket Example

	A	B	C	D	E	F	G	H	I
1	Day	StartTime	TimeInterval	InitialWaiting	Arrivals	Departures	End Waiting	Checkers	Total Customers
2	Mon	8:00 AM	Morning rush	2	21	22	1	3	23
3	Mon	8:30 AM	Morning rush	1	25	18	8	3	26
4	Mon	9:00 AM	Morning	8	27	28	7	3	35
5	Mon	9:30 AM	Morning	7	21	23	5	3	28
6	Mon	10:00 AM	Morning	5	20	23	2	5	25
7	Mon	10:30 AM	Morning	2	36	31	7	5	38
8	Mon	11:00 AM	Morning	7	30	36	1	5	37
9	Mon	11:30 AM	Lunch rush	1	34	29	6	5	35
10	Mon	12:00 PM	Lunch rush	6	56	48	14	7	62
11	Mon	12:30 PM	Lunch rush	14	58	64	8	7	72
12	Mon	1:00 PM	Lunch rush	8	53	52	9	7	61
13	Mon	1:30 PM	Afternoon	9	30	36	3	5	39
14	Mon	2:00 PM	Afternoon	3	34	31	6	5	37

© Cengage Learning

The manager would like to check whether the average value of End Waiting differs during rush periods from normal, non-night periods. She is concerned that there might be excessive waiting during rush periods, in which case she might need to add more checkout people during these times. She plans to exclude the night period from the analysis because she knows from experience that customers very seldom need to wait during the night.

Objective   To use StatTools's Two-Sample Confidence Interval procedure to find a confidence interval for the difference between mean waiting times during the supermarket's rush periods versus its normal periods.

Solution

Starting with the data set in its original form, two main steps are required:

1. Rename the seven time intervals (Morning rush, Morning, and so on) so that there are only three: Rush, Normal, and Night.

2. Perform the statistical comparison between the End Waiting variables for the Rush and Normal periods.

The finished version of the file contains the results of step 1 in the Renamed Data sheet and the results of step 2 in this same sheet (next to the renamed data). If you want to follow along, hands-on, with the step-by-step procedure, you should use the "data only" version of the **Customer Checkouts.xlsx** file and perform the following steps.

Performing a Statistical Comparison between Variables

1. **Copy sheet.** Create a copy of the Data sheet by holding down the Ctrl key and dragging the Data sheet tab to the right. Double-click the new sheet tab and name it Renamed Data.

2. **Rename time intervals.** To rename the time intervals on the Renamed Data sheet, use Excel's Find and Replace feature. Click column C's tab to select the entire column, and then select Replace from the Find & Select dropdown menu on the Home ribbon. Type **Morning rush** in the "Find what:" box, type **Rush** in the "Replace with:" box, and click the Replace All button. Repeat this for the other time intervals

to be renamed. That is, replace Lunch rush and Afternoon rush by Rush, and replace Morning, Afternoon, and Evening by Normal. Figure 8.18 shows some of the results. (You could accomplish the same thing with a complex IF formula or a lookup table.)

Figure 8.18   Supermarket Data with Time Categories Renamed

	A	B	C	D	E	F	G	H	I
1	Day	Start Time	Time Interval	Initial Waiting	Arrivals	Departures	End Waiting	Checkers	Total Customers
2	Mon	8:00 AM	Rush	2	21	22	1	3	23
3	Mon	8:30 AM	Rush	1	25	18	8	3	26
4	Mon	9:00 AM	Normal	8	27	28	7	3	35
5	Mon	9:30 AM	Normal	7	21	23	5	3	28
6	Mon	10:00 AM	Normal	5	20	23	2	5	25
7	Mon	10:30 AM	Normal	2	36	31	7	5	38
8	Mon	11:00 AM	Normal	7	30	36	1	5	37
9	Mon	11:30 AM	Rush	1	34	29	6	5	35
10	Mon	12:00 PM	Rush	6	56	48	14	7	62
11	Mon	12:30 PM	Rush	14	58	64	8	7	72
12	Mon	1:00 PM	Rush	8	53	52	9	7	61

© Cengage Learning

3. **Create box plots.** Define a StatTools data set from the data on the Renamed Data sheet, and use StatTools's Box Plot procedure to create side-by-side box plots of the End Waiting variable. Select the Stacked option, and select Time Interval as the Cat variable and End Waiting as the Val variable. See Figure 8.19 for the box plots.

Figure 8.19

Box Plots for Supermarket Example

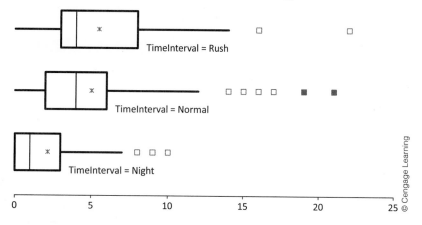

Box-Whisker Plot of Comparison of End Waiting/Data Set #1

© Cengage Learning

4. **Perform two-sample analysis.** Select Confidence Interval and Mean/Std. Deviation from the StatTools Statistical Inference dropdown list using the renamed data set. In the resulting dialog box, select the Stacked option, and again select Time Interval as the Cat variable and End Waiting as the Val variable. Because there are three categories for Time Interval, StatTools will ask you which two of these you want to base the difference on. Select Normal and Rush. StatTools then analyzes the difference "Normal minus Rush." If you checked the Analyze in Reverse Order option, StatTools would analyze the opposite difference, "Rush minus Normal." (See the StatTools dialog boxes in Figures 8.20 and 8.21.)

Figure 8.20
Two-Sample Dialog Box

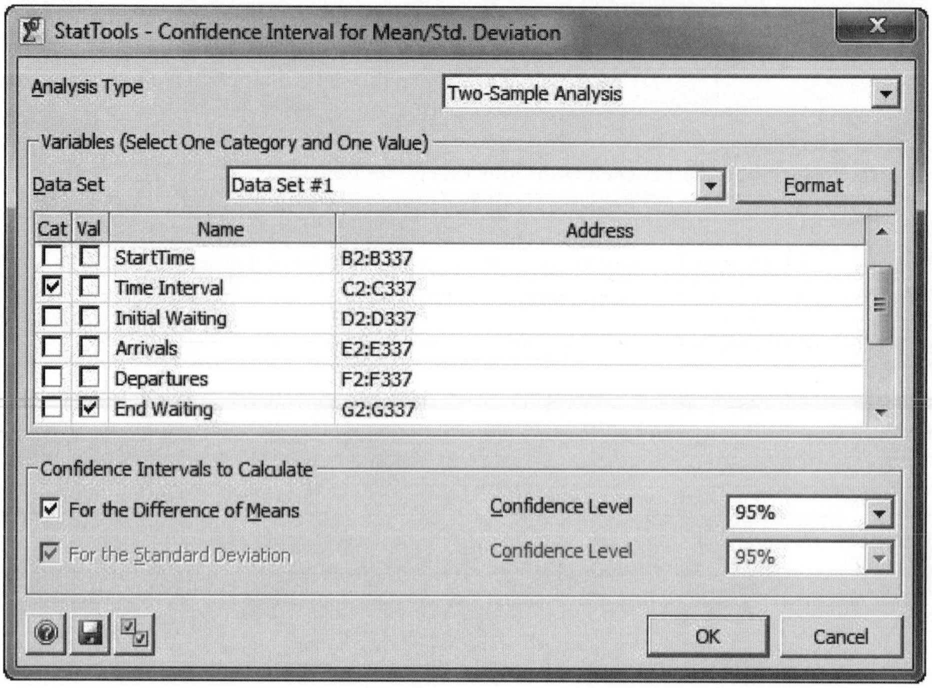

© Cengage Learning

Figure 8.21
Dialog Box for Selecting Two Categories of Interest

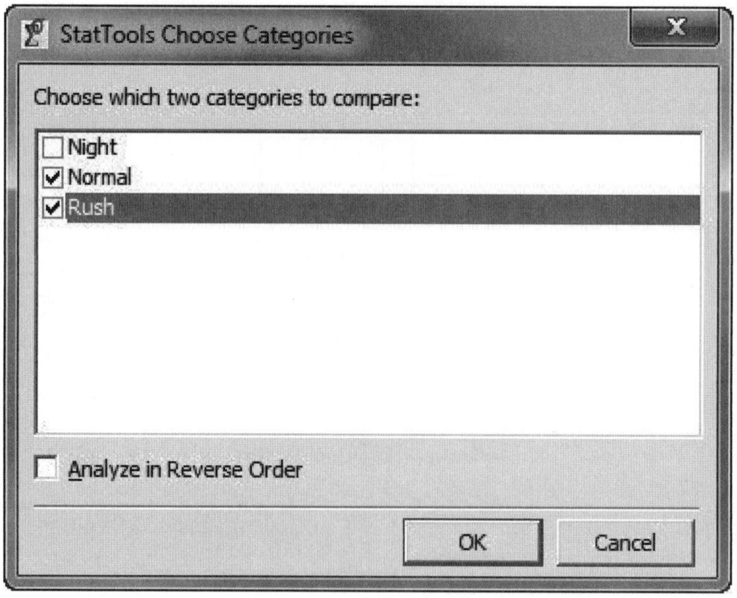

© Cengage Learning

The side-by-side box plots in Figure 8.19 show that (1) the distribution of End Waiting is skewed to the right for each time interval, with a number of outliers, and (2) the mean value of End Waiting is slightly larger for Rush than for Normal, with Night a distant third. Given the nature of the data, it should not really be surprising that the data are skewed to the right with a number of outliers. When the supermarket gets busy, waiting lines can really build. All it takes are a few really long checkout times to produce an excessively large value of End Waiting, and this is evidently what happened at R&P.

The output from the two-sample procedure appears in Figure 8.22. The sample means of End Waiting are 5.480 and 5.014 for the Rush and Normal periods, the sample standard deviations are 4.284 and 4.293, and these are based on sample sizes of 98 and 140 half-hour periods. These summary statistics provide some evidence of a difference between population means but very little evidence of different population variances. This latter statement means that the results in column L, not column M, are relevant (although the two are practically identical). A point estimate for the mean difference (Normal minus Rush) is −0.465, and a 95% confidence interval for this mean difference extends from −1.578 to 0.648.

Figure 8.22

Analysis of Supermarket Data

	K	L	M
1		EndWaiting (Normal)	EndWaiting (Rush)
2	Sample Summaries	Data Set #1	Data Set #1
3	Sample Size	140	98
4	Sample Mean	5.014	5.480
5	Sample Std Dev	4.293	4.284
6			
7		Equal	Unequal
8	Conf. Intervals (Difference of Means)	Variances	Variances
9	Confidence Level	95.0%	95.0%
10	Sample Mean Difference	−0.465	−0.465
11	Standard Error of Difference	0.565	0.565
12	Degrees of Freedom	236	209
13	Lower Limit	−1.578	−1.579
14	Upper Limit	0.648	0.648
15			
16			
17	Equality of Variances Test		
18	Ratio of Sample Variances	1.0042	
19	p-Value	0.9912	

© Cengage Learning

What can the manager conclude from this analysis? Should she add extra checkout people during rush periods? This is difficult to answer because it obviously involves a trade-off between the cost of extra checkout people and the "cost" of making customers wait in line. Also, there is no way of knowing, at least not from the present analysis, how much effect extra checkout people would have on waiting. However, the manager does know from this analysis that the mean difference between rush and normal periods is rather minor. Specifically, because the confidence interval extends from a negative value to a positive value, it is possible that the *true* mean difference is *positive*. That is, the mean for normal times could be *larger* than the mean for rush times. Therefore, the results of this analysis do not provide a strong incentive for the manager to change the current system. ∎

8-7b Paired Samples

When the samples to be compared are paired in some natural way, such as a pre-test and post-test for each person, or husband–wife pairs, there is a more appropriate form of analysis than the two-sample procedure. Consider the example where each new employee takes a test, then receives a three-month training course, and afterward takes another similar test. There is likely to be a fairly strong correlation between the pre-test and post-test scores. Employees who score relatively low on the first test are likely to score relatively low on the second test, and employees who score relatively high on the first test are likely to score relatively high on the second test. The two-sample procedure does not take this correlation into account and therefore ignores important information. The paired procedure described in this section, on the other hand, uses this information to advantage.

The procedure itself is very straightforward. It does not directly analyze two separate variables (pre-test scores and post-test scores, say); it analyzes their *differences*. For each pair in the sample, the difference between the two scores for the pair is calculated. Then a *one*-sample analysis, as in Section 8-3, is performed on these differences. Actually, StatTools's Paired-Sample procedure does the difference calculations *and* the ensuing one-sample analysis automatically, as described in Example 8.8.

EXAMPLE	8.8 HUSBAND AND WIFE REACTIONS TO SALES PRESENTATIONS

Stevens Honda-Buick automobile dealership often sells to husband-wife pairs. The manager would like to check whether the sales presentation is viewed any more or less favorably by the husbands than by the wives. If it is, then some new training might be recommended for its salespeople. To check for differences, a random sample of husbands and wives are asked (separately) to rate the sales presentation on a scale of 1 to 10, 10 being the most favorable rating. The results appear in Figure 8.23. (See the **Sales Presentation Ratings.xlsx** file.) What can the manager conclude from these data?

Figure 8.23

Data for Sales Presentation Example

	A	B	C
1	Pair	Husband	Wife
2	1	6	3
3	2	7	8
4	3	8	5
5	4	6	4
6	5	8	5
7	6	7	6
8	7	8	5
9	8	6	7
10	9	7	8
11	10	7	5
35	34	7	4
36	35	10	5

© Cengage Learning

Objective   To use StatTools's Paired-Sample Confidence Interval procedure to find a confidence interval for the mean difference between husbands' and wives' ratings of sales presentations.

Solution

We illustrate two ways to perform the analysis. Normally, you would use only the second of these, but the first sheds some light on the procedure. For the first method, make a copy of the Data sheet and name it OneSample. Then manually form a new variable in column D called Difference by entering the formula

=B2-C2

in cell D2 and copying it down column D. (See Figure 8.24.) This new variable is, for each couple, the husband's rating minus the wife's rating. After creating a StatTools data set for the data on this sheet, select Confidence Interval and Mean/Std. Deviation from the StatTools Statistical Inference dropdown list, select One-Sample Analysis as the Analysis

Type, and select the Difference variable. This produces the output shown in Figure 8.24. The sample mean Husband minus Wife difference is 1.629 and a 95% confidence interval for this difference extends from 1.057 to 2.200.

Figure 8.24 One-Sample Analysis of Differences for Sales Presentation Data

	A	B	C	D	E	F	G
1	Pair	Husband	Wife	Difference			Difference
2	1	6	3	3		Conf. Intervals (One-Sample)	OneSampleData
3	2	7	8	−1		Sample Size	35
4	3	8	5	3		Sample Mean	1.629
5	4	6	4	2		Sample Std Dev	1.664
6	5	8	5	3		Confidence Level (Mean)	95.0%
7	6	7	6	1		Degrees of Freedom	34
8	7	8	5	3		Lower Limit	1.057
9	8	6	7	−1		Upper Limit	2.200
10	9	7	8	−1			
11	10	7	5	2			
35	34	7	4	3			
36	35	10	5	5			

© Cengage Learning

To perform this analysis more efficiently, again make a copy of the Data sheet and name it PairedSample. After creating a StatTools data set for the data on this sheet, select Confidence Interval and Mean/Std. Deviation from the StatTools Statistical Inference dropdown, and fill in the resulting dialog box as shown in Figure 8.25. Specifically, select Paired-Sample Analysis as the Analysis Type. (As usual, you will then get a chance to

Figure 8.25

Dialog Box for Paired-Sample Analysis

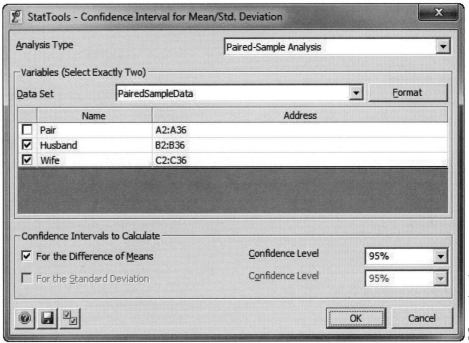

© Cengage Learning

reverse the order of the difference, but don't do so; let it remain "Husband minus Wife.") The resulting output appears in Figure 8.26. The results are exactly the same as before. This is because StatTools's Paired-Sample procedure performs a one-sample analysis on the differences—and it saves you the work of creating the differences.

Figure 8.26

Paired-Sample Analysis of Sales Presentation Data

◢	A	B	C	D	E	F
1	Pair	Husband	Wife			
2	1	6	3		Conf. Intervals (Paired-Sample)	Husband - Wife
3	2	7	8		Sample Size	35
4	3	8	5		Sample Mean	1.629
5	4	6	4		Sample Std Dev	1.664
6	5	8	5		Confidence Level	95.0%
7	6	7	6		Degrees of Freedom	34
8	7	8	5		Lower Limit	1.057
9	8	6	7		Upper Limit	2.200
10	9	7	8			
11	10	7	5			
35	34	7	4			
36	35	10	5			

© Cengage Learning

Figure 8.27 shows side-by-side box plots of the husband and wife scores. These box plots are not as useful here as in the two-sample procedure because you lose sight of which husbands are paired with which wives. A more useful box plot is of the differences, shown in Figure 8.28. Here it is apparent that the sample mean difference is positive, and even more importantly, the vast majority of husband scores are greater than the corresponding wife scores. There is little doubt that most husbands tend to react more favorably to the sales presentations than their wives. Perhaps the salespeople need to be somewhat more sensitive to their female customers.

Figure 8.27

Side-by-Side Box Plots for Sales Presentation Data

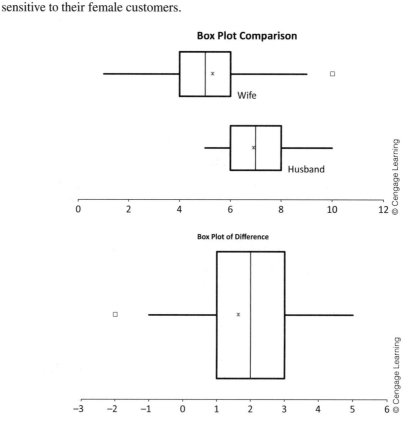

© Cengage Learning

Figure 8.28

Single Box Plot of Differences for Sales Presentation Data

© Cengage Learning

Before leaving this example, let's see what would have happened if the two-sample procedure had been used on the Husband and Wife variables. The results appear in Figure 8.29. Because there is a considerable difference between the sample standard deviations, the confidence interval output in column G, not column F, is relevant, although there is not much difference between them. The important point is that the resulting confidence interval for the mean difference extends from 0.895 to 2.362, which is somewhat *wider* than the confidence interval from the paired-sample procedure. This is typical. When the two-sample procedure is used in a situation where the paired-sample procedure is more appropriate, the data are not used as efficiently. The effect is that the standard error of the difference tends to be larger, and the resulting confidence interval tends to be wider.

Figure 8.29 Two-Sample Analysis of Sales Presentation Data

	A	B	C	D	E	F	G
1	Pair	Husband	Wife			**Husband**	**Wife**
2	1	6	3		*Sample Summaries*	TwoSampleData	TwoSampleData
3	2	7	8		Sample Size	35	35
4	3	8	5		Sample Mean	6.914	5.286
5	4	6	4		Sample Std Dev	1.222	1.792
6	5	8	5				
7	6	7	6			**Equal**	**Unequal**
8	7	8	5		*Conf. Intervals (Difference of Means)*	Variances	Variances
9	8	6	7		Confidence Level	95.0%	95.0%
10	9	7	8		Sample Mean Difference	1.629	1.629
11	10	7	5		Standard Error of Difference	0.367	0.367
12	11	6	3		Degrees of Freedom	68	60
13	12	5	4		Lower Limit	0.897	0.895
14	13	8	5		Upper Limit	2.360	2.362
15	14	7	8				
16	15	7	5				
17	16	7	6		*Equality of Variances Test*		
18	17	6	5		Ratio of Sample Variances	0.4649	
19	18	5	4		*p*-Value	0.0285	
20	19	6	5				
35	34	7	4				
36	35	10	5				

© Cengage Learning

Why is the paired-sample procedure appropriate here? It is *not* just because husbands and wives naturally come in pairs. It is because they tend to react similarly to one another. You can check that the correlation between the husbands' scores and their wives' scores is 0.442. (This can be found with Excel's CORREL function on the Husband and Wife variables.) This is far from a perfect correlation, but it is large enough to warrant using the paired-sample procedure. ∎

In general, the paired-sample procedure is appropriate when the samples are naturally paired in some way *and* there is a reasonably large positive correlation between the pairs. In this case the paired-sample procedure makes more efficient use of the data and generally results in narrower confidence intervals.

PROBLEMS

Level A

23. The director of a university's career development center is interested in comparing the starting annual salaries of male and female students who recently graduated from the university and commenced full-time employment. The director has formed pairs of male and female graduates with the same major and similar grade-point averages. Specifically, she has collected a random sample of 50 such pairs and has recorded the starting annual salary of each person. These data are provided in the file **P08_23.xlsx**. Find a 95% confidence interval for the mean difference between similar male and female graduates of this university. Interpret your result.

24. A real estate agent has collected a random sample of 75 houses that were recently sold in a suburban community. She is particularly interested in comparing the appraised value and recent selling price of the houses in this particular market. The data are provided in the file **P08_24.xlsx**. Using this sample data, find a 95% confidence interval for the mean difference between the appraised values and selling prices of the houses sold in this suburban community. Interpret the confidence interval for the real estate agent.

25. *The Wall Street Journal CEO Compensation Study* analyzed CEO pay from many U.S. companies with fiscal year 2008 revenue of at least $5 billion that filed their proxy statements between October 2008 and March 2009. The data are in the file **P02_30.xlsx**.
   a. Create a new column, Total, that is the sum of columns D and E.
   b. After combining Telecommunications and Technology into a single company type, there are nine company types. For each of these, find a 95% confidence interval for the difference between the mean of Total for that company type and mean of Total for all other company types. Comment on what these nine confidence intervals indicate about CEO pay in different industries.

Level B

26. The file **P02_35.xlsx** contains data from a survey of 500 randomly selected households.
   a. Separate the households in the sample by the location of their residence within the given community. For each of the four locations, use the sample information to find a 90% confidence interval for the mean annual income (sum of first income and second income) of all relevant households. Compare these four interval estimates. You might also consider generating box plots of the total income for households in each of the four locations.
   b. Find a 90% confidence interval for the difference between the mean annual income of all households in the first (i.e., SW) and second (i.e., NW) sectors of this community. Find similar 90% confidence intervals for the differences between the mean annual income levels of all households from all other pairs of locations (i.e., first and third, first and fourth, second and third, second and fourth, and third and fourth). Summarize your findings.

27. A company employs two shifts of workers. Each shift produces a type of gasket where the thickness is the critical dimension. The average thickness and the standard deviation of thickness for shift 1, based on a random sample of 30 gaskets, are 10.53 mm and 0.14 mm. The similar figures for shift 2, based on a random sample of 25 gaskets, are 10.55 mm and 0.17 mm. Let $\mu_1 - \mu_2$ be the mean difference in thickness between shifts 1 and 2.
   a. Using the formulas from this section, not StatTools, find a 95% confidence interval for $\mu_1 - \mu_2$.
   b. Based on your answer to part **a**, are you convinced that the gaskets from shift 2 are, on average, wider than those from shift 1? Why or why not?
   c. How would your answers to parts **a** and **b** change if the sample sizes were instead 300 and 250?

8-8 CONFIDENCE INTERVAL FOR THE DIFFERENCE BETWEEN PROPORTIONS

The final confidence interval we examine is a confidence interval for the difference between two population proportions. As in the previous section, this comparison procedure finds many real applications. Several potential business applications follow.

Applications of Comparisons of Proportions in Business

- When an appliance store is about to have a sale, it sometimes sends selected customers a mailing to notify them of the sale. On other occasions it includes a coupon for 5% off the sale price in these mailings. The store's manager would like to know whether the inclusion of coupons affects the proportion of customers who respond.

- A manufacturing company has two plants that produce identical products. The company wants to know how much the proportion of out-of-spec products differs across the two plants.

- A pharmaceutical company has developed a new over-the-counter sleeping pill. To judge its effectiveness, the company runs an experiment where one set of randomly chosen people takes the new pill and another set takes a placebo. (Neither set knows which type of pill they are taking.) The company judges the effectiveness of the new pill by comparing the proportions of people who fall asleep within a certain amount of time with the new pill and with the placebo.

- An advertising agency would like to check whether men are more likely than women to switch TV channels when a commercial comes on. The agency runs an experiment where the channel-switching behavior of randomly chosen men and women can be monitored, and it collects data on the proportion of viewers who switch channels on at least half of the commercial times. The agency then compares these proportions across gender.

The basic form of analysis in each of these examples is the same as in the two-sample analysis for differences between means. However, instead of comparing two means, we now compare two proportions.

Formally, let p_1 and p_2 represent the two unknown population proportions, and let $\hat{p}_1$ and $\hat{p}_2$ be the two sample proportions, based on samples of sizes n_1 and n_2. Then the point estimate of the difference between proportions, $p_1 - p_2$, is the difference between sample proportions, $\hat{p}_1 - \hat{p}_2$. If the sample sizes are reasonably large, then the sampling distribution of $\hat{p}_1 - \hat{p}_2$ is approximately normal.[6]

Therefore, a confidence interval for $p_1 - p_2$ is given by Expression (8.15). Here, the z-multiple is the usual value from the standard normal distribution that cuts off the appropriate probability in each tail (1.96 for a 95% confidence interval, for example). Also, the standard error of $\hat{p}_1 - \hat{p}_2$ is given by Equation (8.16).

Confidence Interval for Difference Between Proportions

$$\hat{p}_1 - \hat{p}_2 \pm z\text{-multiple} \times \text{SE}(\hat{p}_1 - \hat{p}_2)$$

(8.15)

Standard Error of Difference Between Sample Proportions

$$\text{SE}(\hat{p}_1 - \hat{p}_2) = \sqrt{\frac{\hat{p}_1(1 - \hat{p}_1)}{n_1} + \frac{\hat{p}_2(1 - \hat{p}_2)}{n_2}}$$

(8.16)

Example 8.9 illustrates this procedure and how it is implemented in StatTools.

---

[6]This large-sample assumption is valid as long as $n_i \hat{p}_i > 5$ and $n_i(1 - \hat{p}_i) > 5$ for $i = 1$ and $i = 2$.

8.9 Sales Response to Coupons for Discounts on Appliances

A n appliance store is about to have a big sale. It selects 300 of its best customers and randomly divides them into two sets of 150 customers each. It then mails a notice of the sale to all 300 customers but includes a coupon for an extra 5% off the sale price to the second set of customers only. As the sale progresses, the store keeps track of which of these customers purchase appliances. The resulting data appear in Figure 8.30. They are shown in three equivalent ways, as discussed below. (See the file **Coupon Effectiveness .xlsx**.) What can the store's manager conclude about the effectiveness of the coupons?

Figure 8.30 Equivalent Setups for Coupon Data

	A	B	C	D	E	F	G
1	Customer	Received coupon	Purchased		**Table of counts**		
2	1	Yes	Yes				
3	2	Yes	Yes		Category	Received coupon	Didn't receive coupon
4	3	Yes	Yes		Purchased	55	35
5	4	Yes	Yes		Didn't purchase	95	115
6	5	Yes	Yes		Sample sizes	150	150
7	6	Yes	Yes				
8	7	Yes	Yes		**Table of proportions**		
9	8	Yes	Yes				
10	9	Yes	Yes		Category	Received coupon	Didn't receive coupon
11	10	Yes	Yes		Purchased	0.3667	0.2333
12	11	Yes	Yes		Didn't purchase	0.6333	0.7667
13	12	Yes	Yes		Sample sizes	150	150
14	13	Yes	Yes				
299	298	No	No				
300	299	No	No				
301	300	No	No				

(Data Set #2 label points to cells F4:G4; Data Set #1 label in columns B–C near rows 11–12; Data Set #3 label points to cells F11:G12)

Objective To find a confidence interval for the difference between proportions of customers purchasing appliances with and without 5% discount coupons.

Solution

First, keep in mind the overall objective. From Figure 8.30 (cells F11 and G11), you can see that 36.67% of customers who received a coupon purchased something, as opposed to only 23.33% of those who didn't receive a coupon. The difference, $36.67\% - 23.33\% = 13.33\%$ (or 0.1333), is the quantity of interest. Specifically, the sample difference is 13.33%, and the objective is to find a confidence interval for this difference for the entire population. You could plug the data into Equations (8.15) and (8.16), but StatTools will do it for you. This is fairly simple once you understand how the difference between proportions procedure works in StatTools.

The data could be given as a table of counts (top right part of Figure 8.30), as a table of proportions (bottom right part of Figure 8.30), or as a long list of values (left part of Figure 8.30, with many hidden rows). StatTools allows all three setups, and they are discussed in detail in the finished version of the **Coupons Effectiveness.xlsx** file. For now, let's say the table of counts is available. Then the StatTools data set should be the top right shaded region in Figure 8.30. The Category variable indicates the two possible responses (purchased or didn't purchase), and the other two columns show how many customers purchased or didn't purchase in each of the two subpopulations (received coupon or didn't). Given this setup, the next step is to select Confidence Interval and Proportion from the Statistical Inference dropdown list and fill out the dialog box as shown in Figure 8.31. Once you click OK, you will have the chance to reverse the difference (switch from "Received coupon minus Didn't receive coupon" to the opposite), but don't make this switch here. (Also, note that the sample sizes at the bottom of this dialog box have been filled in. With the table of counts option, StatTools figures out the correct sample sizes, in this case 150 for each subpopulation.)

Figure 8.31

Dialog Box for Difference Between Proportions

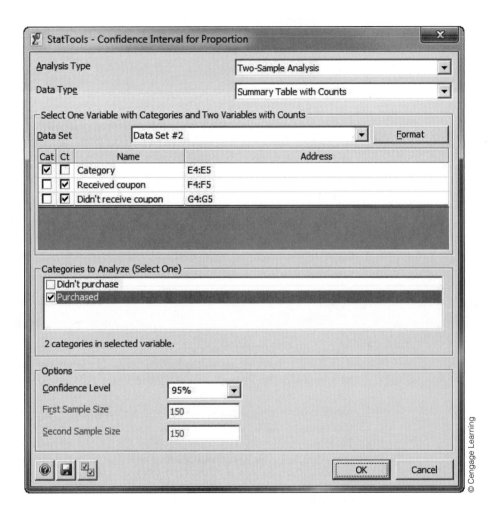

The output appears in Figure 8.32. It shows the sample difference between proportions, 0.133, and the standard error of this difference, 0.052. The 95% confidence interval for the difference is approximately plus or minus two standard errors from the sample difference. It extends from 0.031 to 0.236, or from 3.1 percentage points to 23.6 percentage points. This interval indicates how much higher the proportion of purchasers becomes when coupons are offered.

Figure 8.32

Confidence
Interval for
Difference Between
Proportions

	I	J	K
1			
2	*Analyzed Category*		
3	Proportion of Items in This Category	Yes	
4			
5			
6		Purchased (Yes)	Purchased (No)
7	*Sample Summaries*	Data Set #1	Data Set #1
8	Sample Size	150	150
9	Sample Proportion	0.367	0.233
10			
11			
12	*Conf. Interval (Difference Between Proportions)*		
13	Confidence Level	95.0%	
14	Difference Between Proportions	0.133	
15	Standard Error of Difference	0.052	
16	Lower Limit	0.031	
17	Upper Limit	0.236	

© Cengage Learning

This StatTools procedure is slightly more complicated than the others in this chapter, because the StatTools developers wanted to accommodate different data setups. The finished version of the **Coupon Effectiveness.xlsx** file provides more details on how the procedure works. We suggest that you mimic this file when you do it on your own. ∎

We now revisit Example 8.6, where SureStep Company is trying to decide which of two suppliers to buy its treadmill motors from. We now compare the two suppliers with regard to warranty costs by analyzing the difference between relevant proportions.

EXAMPLE **8.10 ANALYZING WARRANTIES ON TREADMILL MOTORS AT SURESTEP**

As before, SureStep Company is trying to decide whether to switch from supplier to supplier B for the motors in its treadmills. Let's suppose that each treadmill carries a three-month warranty on the motor. If the motor fails within three months, SureStep will supply the customer with a new motor at no cost. This includes installation of the new motor at SureStep's expense. Based on the normal usage at most exercise clubs, SureStep translates the three-month warranty period into approximately 500 hours of treadmill use. Therefore, using the data from Example 8.6 (in the **Treadmill Warranty.xlsx** file, the same data as in the **Treadmill Motors.xlsx** file), the company would like to compare the proportion of motors failing before 500 hours across the two suppliers.

Objective To find a confidence interval for the difference between proportions of motors failing within the warranty period for the two suppliers.

Solution

The data and StatTools output appear in Figure 8.33. The data in column A and B are first transformed to Yes/No values in columns C and D to see which motors fail within warranty. The typical formula in cell C2 is

=IF(A2 < 500, "Yes", "No")

Figure 8.33 Analysis of Treadmill Warranty Data

	A	B	C	D	E	F	G	H
1	Supplier A	Supplier B	Supplier A fail	Supplier B fail		*Analyzed Category*		
2	1358	658	No	No		**Proportion of Items in This Category**	Yes	
3	793	404	No	Yes				
4	587	735	No	No				
5	608	457	No	Yes			Supplier B fail	Supplier A fail
6	472	431	Yes	Yes		*Sample Summaries*	Data Set #1	Data Set #1
7	562	658	No	No		**Sample Size**	30	30
8	879	453	No	Yes		**Sample Proportion**	0.367	0.200
9	575	488	No	Yes				
10	1293	522	No	No				
11	1457	1247	No	No		*Conf. Interval (Difference Between Proportions)*		
12	705	1095	No	No		**Confidence Level**	95.0%	
13	623	430	No	Yes		**Difference Between Proportions**	0.167	
14	725	726	No	No		**Standard Error of Difference**	0.114	
15	569	793	No	No		**Lower Limit**	−0.057	
16	424	498	Yes	Yes		**Upper Limit**	0.391	
17	436	502	Yes	No				
18	1250	589	No	No				
30	684	732	No	No				
31	666	507	No	No				

The StatTools data set should include columns C and D (and it can also include columns A and B, but they aren't necessary). To obtain the confidence interval, select Confidence Interval and Proportion from the Statistical Inference dropdown list, and fill in the dialog box as shown in Figure 8.34. Note the Data Type is now Population Sample (long columns,

Figure 8.34
Dialog Box for Difference Between Proportions

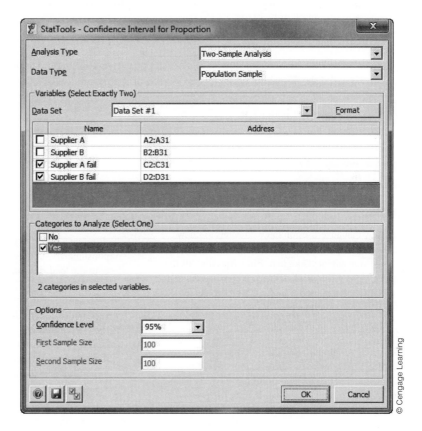

not just counts), and the Format is Unstacked (one column for Supplier A, another for Supplier B). Then reverse the difference, so that the output shows "B minus A."

The output shows that the point estimate of the difference in proportions is 0.167 and a 95% confidence interval for this difference extends from −0.057 to 0.391. Keep in mind that this difference is the proportion for supplier B minus the proportion for supplier A.

This is fairly convincing, but not conclusive, evidence that a higher proportion of supplier B motors will fail under warranty. It says that if 100 motors from each supplier were tested, as many as 39 more B motors than A motors might fail before 500 hours—but as many as five or six more A motors than B motors might fail before 500 hours. In other words, there is still some uncertainty about which supplier makes the more reliable motors, even though the weight of the evidence favors supplier A.

What does this mean in terms of costs? And should SureStep change suppliers? The confidence interval implies that more motors are likely to fail under warranty if SureStep changes to supplier B, but B's motors cost less. A cost analysis might go as follows. Suppose that each motor from supplier A costs SureStep $500, whereas supplier B offers them for $475 apiece. Let's follow 100 motors sent to exercise clubs for a period of three months. If they are from supplier A, they cost $500 apiece, and approximately 20% (see cell H5 in Figure 8.33) will fail within the warranty period. Each failure costs SureStep another $500, so the expected cost to SureStep is

$$\$500(100) + \$500(20\%)(100) = \$60,000$$

On the other hand, if these 100 motors come from supplier B, the unit cost is only $475, but approximately 36.7% of them will fail within the warranty period. Therefore, the expected cost is

$$= \$475(100) + \$475(36.7\%)(100) = \$64,933$$

Based on this analysis, the cheaper motors from supplier B are likely to cost more in the long run, so SureStep should probably not switch suppliers. (By the way, we omitted the cost of installing the motors from the analysis. This would have made supplier A look even better.) ■

PROBLEMS

Level A

28. A company that advertises on the Web wants to know which search engine its customers prefer as their primary search engine: Google or Bing. Specifically, the company wants to know whether the preference depends on the browser being used. The file **P08_28.xlsx** contains counts of 800 customers' favorite search engine, broken down by the browser used.
   a. Find a 95% confidence interval for the difference between two proportions: the proportion of Internet Explorer users whose favorite search engine is Google and the similar proportion of Firefox users.
   b. Repeat part **a**, replacing Google with Bing.
   c. Interpret the results in parts **a** and **b**. Do the search engine preferences seem to depend on the browser used?

29. A market research consultant hired by a leading soft-drink company is interested in estimating the difference between the proportions of female and male consumers who favor the company's low-calorie brand over the leading competitor's low-calorie brand in a particular geographical region. A random sample of 250 consumers from the market under investigation is provided in the file **P08_18.xlsx**. After separating the 250 randomly selected consumers by *gender*, find a 95% confidence interval for the difference between these two proportions. Of what value might this interval estimate be to marketing managers at the company?

Level B

30. The file **P02_35.xlsx** contains data from a survey of 500 randomly selected households. Researchers would like to use the available sample information to see whether home ownership rates vary by household *location*. For example, is there a nonzero difference between the proportions of individuals who own their homes (as opposed to those who rent their homes) in households located in the first (i.e., SW) and second (i.e., NW) sectors of this community? Use the given sample to find a 95% confidence interval that estimates this difference between proportions in home ownership rates for each pair of locations. Interpret and summarize your results. (The solution should include six confidence intervals.)

31. Continuing from problem 29, marketing managers at the soft-drink company have asked their market research consultant to explore further the difference between the proportions of women and men who prefer drinking their brand over the leading competitor. Specifically, the company's managers would like to know whether the difference between the proportions of female and male consumers who favor their brand varies by the *age* of the consumers. Use the same data as in problem 29 to assess whether estimates of this difference vary across the four given age categories: under 20, between 20 and 40, between 40 and 60, and over 60. Use a 95% confidence level for each of the *four* required confidence intervals. Summarize your findings. What recommendations would you make to the marketing managers in light of your findings?

8-9 SAMPLE SIZE SELECTION

In this section we discuss the most widely used methods for achieving a confidence interval of a specified length. Confidence intervals are a function of three things: (1) the data in the sample, (2) the confidence level, and (3) the sample size(s). We briefly discuss the role of the first two in terms of their effect on confidence interval length and then discuss the effect of sample size in more depth.

The data in the sample directly affect the length of a confidence interval through their sample standard deviation(s). It might appear that because of *random* sampling, you have no control over the sample data, but this is not entirely true. In the case of surveys from a population, there are random sampling plans that can reduce the amount of variability in the sample and hence reduce confidence interval length. Indeed, this is the primary reason for using the stratified sampling procedure discussed in the previous chapter.

Variance reduction is also possible in randomized experiments. There is a whole area of statistics called *experimental design* that suggests how to perform experiments to obtain the most information from a given amount of sample data. Although this is often aimed at scientific and medical research, it is also appropriate in business contexts. For example, the automobile dealership in Example 8.8 was wise to use *paired* husband–wife data rather than two independent samples of men and women. The pairing leads to a potential reduction in variability and hence a narrower confidence interval.

The *confidence level* has a clear effect on confidence interval length. As the confidence level increases, the length of the confidence interval increases as well. For example, a 99% confidence interval is always longer than a 95% confidence interval, assuming that they are both based on the same data. However, the confidence level is rarely used to control the length of the confidence interval. Instead, the confidence level choice is usually based on convention, and 95% is by far the most commonly used value. In fact, it is the default level built into most software packages, including StatTools. You can override this default (by choosing 90% or 99%, for example), but it is not common to do so simply to control confidence interval length.

The most obvious way to control confidence interval length is to choose the sample size(s) appropriately. In the rest of this section, you will learn how this can be done. For each parameter we discuss, the goal is to make the length of a confidence interval sufficiently narrow. Because each confidence interval discussed so far (with the exception of the confidence interval for a standard deviation) is a point estimate plus or minus some quantity, we focus on the "plus or minus" part, called the *half-length* of the interval.

(See Figure 8.35.) The usual approach is to specify the half-length B you would like to obtain. Then you find the sample size(s) necessary to achieve this half-length.

Figure 8.35

Half-Length of
Confidence Interval

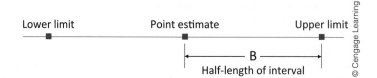

FUNDAMENTAL INSIGHT

Confidence Interval Length
The length of any confidence interval is influenced by three things: the sample size, the confidence level, and the variability in the population. The confidence level is typically set at 95%, and you have no control over the variability in the population (except possibly by choosing an appropriate experimental design). Therefore, the best way to control confidence interval length is through the choice of the sample size.

8-9a Sample Size Selection for Estimation of the Mean

We begin with a confidence interval for the mean. From Section 8-3, the relevant formula is

$$\overline{X} \pm t\text{-multiple} \times s/\sqrt{n}$$

The goal is to make the half-length of this interval equal to some prescribed value B. For example, if you want the confidence interval to be of the form $\overline{X} \pm 5$, you use $B = 5$. Actually, it is not possible to achieve this half-length B *exactly*, but you can come close.

By setting

$$t\text{-multiple} \times s/\sqrt{n} = B$$

and solving for n, the appropriate sample size is

$$n = \left(\frac{t\text{-multiple} \times s}{B}\right)^2$$

Keep in mind that the sample size must be determined before the data are observed.

Unfortunately, sample size selection must be done *before* a sample is observed. Therefore, no value of s is yet available. Also, because the t-multiple depends on n (through the degrees of freedom parameter), it is not clear which t-multiple to use.

The usual solution is to replace s by some reasonable estimate σ_{est} of the population standard deviation σ, and to replace the t-multiple with the corresponding z-multiple from the standard normal distribution. The latter replacement is justified because z-values and t-values are practically equal unless n is very small. The resulting **sample size formula** is given in Equation (8.17). This formula generally results in a noninteger value of n, in which case the practice is to round n up to the next larger integer.

Sample Size Formula for Estimating a Mean

$$n = \left(\frac{z\text{-multiple} \times \sigma_{est}}{B}\right)^2 \qquad\qquad \textbf{(8.17)}$$

Example 8.11, an extension of Example 8.1, shows how to implement Equation (8.17).

8.11 SAMPLE SIZE SELECTION FOR ESTIMATING REACTION TO A NEW SANDWICH

The fast-food manager in Example 8.1 surveyed 40 customers, each of whom rated a new sandwich on a scale of 1 to 10. Based on the data, a 95% confidence interval for the mean rating of all potential customers extended from 5.739 to 6.761, with a half-length of $(6.761 - 5.739)/2 = 0.511$. How large a sample would be needed to reduce this half-length to approximately 0.3?

Objective To find the sample size of customers required to achieve a sufficiently narrow confidence interval for the mean rating of the new sandwich.

Solution

Equation (8.17) for n uses three inputs: the z-multiple, which is 1.96 for a 95% confidence level; the prescribed confidence interval half-length B, which is 0.3 for this example; and an estimate σ_{est} of the standard deviation. This final quantity must be guessed, but based on the given sample of size 40, the observed sample standard deviation, 1.597, from Example 8.1 can be used. Therefore, Equation (8.17) yields

$$n = \left(\frac{1.96(1.597)}{0.3}\right)^2 = 108.86$$

which is rounded up to $n = 109$. The claim, then, is that if the manager surveys 109 customers, a 95% confidence interval will have approximate half-length 0.3. Its *exact* half-length will differ slightly from 0.3 because the standard deviation from the sample will almost surely not be exactly 1.597.

StatTools has a Sample Size Selection procedure that performs this sample size calculation and can be used anywhere in a spreadsheet. There doesn't even have to be a data set. Just select Sample Size Selection from the Statistical Inference dropdown list, select the parameter to analyze (in this case the mean), and enter the requested values. In this case the requested values are the confidence level (95%), the half-length of the interval (0.3), and an estimate of the standard deviation (1.597). (See Figure 8.36, where the choices on the right depend on which parameter is selected on the left.) This produces the output shown in Figure 8.37, which indicates that a sample size of 109 is required.

What if the manager is at the planning stage and doesn't have a "preliminary" sample of size 40? What standard deviation estimate should she use for σ_{est} (because the value 1.597 is no longer available)? This is not an easy question to answer, but because of the

Figure 8.36

Sample Size Selection Dialog Box

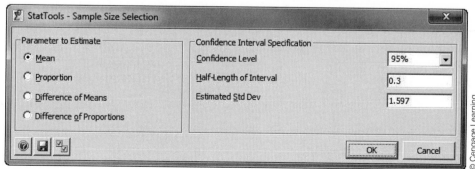

Figure 8.37

Sample Size for
Mean

	A	B
8	*Sample Size for Mean*	
9	Confidence Level	95.00%
10	Half-length of Interval	0.3
11	Std Dev (estimate)	1.597
12	Sample Size	109

role of σ_{est} in Equation (8.17), it is crucial for the determination of n. The manager basically has three choices: (1) she can base her estimate of the standard deviation on historical data, assuming relevant historical data are available; (2) she can take a small preliminary sample (of size 20, say) to get an estimate of the standard deviation; or (3) she can simply guess a value for the standard deviation. We do not recommend the third option, but there are cases in which it is the only feasible option available. ∎

We have demonstrated the use of Equation (8.17) for a sample mean. In the same way, it can also be used in the paired-sample procedure. In this case the resulting value of n refers to the number of *pairs* that should be included in the sample, and σ_{est} refers to an estimate of the standard deviation of the *differences* (Husband scores minus Wife scores, for example).

8-9b Sample Size Selection for Estimation of Other Parameters

The sample-size analysis for the mean carries over with very few changes to other parameters. We discuss three other parameters in this section: a *proportion*, the *difference between two means*, and the *difference between two proportions*. In each case the required confidence interval can be obtained by setting the half-length equal to a prescribed value B and solving for n.

There are two points worth mentioning. First, the confidence interval for the difference between means uses a t-multiple. As was done for the mean, this can be replaced by a z-multiple, which is perfectly acceptable in most situations. Second, the confidence intervals for differences between means or proportions require *two* sample sizes, one for each sample. The formulas below assume that each sample uses the *same* sample size, denoted by n.

The sample size formula for a proportion p is given by Equation (8.18). Here, p_{est} is an estimate of the population proportion p. A *conservative* value of n can be obtained by using $p_{est} = 0.5$. It is conservative in the sense that the sample size obtained by using $p_{est} = 0.5$ guarantees a confidence interval half-length no greater than B, regardless of the true value of p.

Sample Size Formula for Estimating a Proportion

$$n = \left(\frac{z\text{-multiple}}{B}\right)^2 p_{est}(1 - p_{est}) \qquad \textbf{(8.18)}$$

The sample size formula for the difference between means is given by Equation (8.19). Here, σ_{est} is an estimate of the standard deviation of *each* population, where we assume (as in Section 8-7a) that the two populations have a *common* standard deviation σ.

Sample Size Formula for Estimating the Difference Between Means

$$n = 2\left(\frac{z\text{-multiple} \times \sigma_{est}}{B}\right)^2$$

(8.19)

Finally, the sample size formula for the difference between proportions is given by Equation (8.20). Here, p_{1est} and p_{2est} are estimates of the two unknown population proportions p_1 and p_2. As in the case of a single proportion, a conservative value of n is obtained by using the estimates $p_{1est} = p_{2est} = 0.5$.

Sample Size Formula for Estimating the Difference Between Proportions

$$n = \left(\frac{z\text{-multiple}}{B}\right)^2 [p_{1est}(1 - p_{1est}) + p_{2est}(1 - p_{2est})]$$

(8.20)

EXAMPLE | **8.12 SAMPLE SIZE SELECTION FOR ESTIMATING THE PROPORTION WHO HAVE TRIED A NEW SANDWICH**

Suppose that the fast-food manager from the previous example wants to estimate the proportion of customers who have tried its new sandwich. She wants a 90% confidence interval for this proportion to have half-length 0.05. For example, if the sample proportion turns out to be 0.42, a 90% confidence interval should be (approximately) 0.42 ± 0.05. How many customers need to be surveyed?

Objective To find the sample size of customers required to achieve a sufficiently narrow confidence interval for the proportion of customers who have tried the new sandwich.

Solution

If the manager has no idea what the proportion is, she can use $p_{est} = 0.5$ in Equation (8.18) to obtain a conservative value of n. The appropriate z-multiple is now 1.645 because this value cuts off probability 0.05 in each tail of the standard normal distribution. (Remember that we are asking for a 90% confidence level, not the usual 95% level.) Therefore, the required value of n is

$$n = \left(\frac{1.645}{0.05}\right)^2 (0.5)(1 - 0.5) \simeq 271$$

On the other hand, if the manager is fairly sure that the proportion who have tried the new sandwich is around 0.3, she can use $p_{est} = 0.3$ instead. This time, use StatTools and enter the values 90% (confidence level), 0.05 (desired half-length), and 0.3 (estimate of the proportion). The resulting output is shown in Figure 8.38.

Figure 8.38

Sample Size for Proportion

	A	B
8	Sample Size for Proportion	
9	Confidence Level	90.00%
10	Half-length of Interval	0.05
11	Proportion (estimate)	0.3000
12	Sample Size	228

© Cengage Learning

These calculations indicate that if you have more specific information about the unknown proportion, you can use a smaller sample size—in this case 228 rather than 271. Also, note that we selected a 90% confidence level rather than the usual 95% level. There is a trade-off here. Using 90% rather than 95% obviously provides less confidence in the result, but it requires a smaller sample size. You can check that the required sample sizes for a 95% confidence level increase from the current values, 271 and 228, to 385 and 323, respectively. ∎

EXAMPLE 8.13 SAMPLE SIZE SELECTION FOR ANALYZING CUSTOMER COMPLAINTS

A computer company has a customer service center that responds to customers' questions and complaints. The center employs two types of people: those who have had a recent course in dealing with customers (but little actual experience) and those with a lot of experience dealing with customers (but no formal course). The company wants to estimate the difference between these two types of employees in terms of the average number of customer complaints regarding poor service in the last six months. The company plans to obtain information on a randomly selected sample of each type of employee, using equal sample sizes. How many employees should be in each sample to achieve a 95% confidence interval with approximate half-length 2?

Objective To see how many employees in each experimental group must be sampled to achieve a sufficiently narrow confidence interval for the difference between the mean numbers of complaints.

Solution

Equation (8.19) should be used with z-multiple 1.96 and $B = 2$. However, this formula also requires a value for σ_{est}, an estimate of the (assumed) common standard deviation for each group of employees, and there is no obvious estimate available. The manager might use the following argument. Based on a brief look at complaint data, he believes that some employees receive as few as 6 complaints over a six-month period, whereas others receive as many as 36 (about six per month). Now he can estimate σ_{est} by arguing that all observations are likely to be within three standard deviations of the mean, so that the range of data—minimum to maximum—is about six standard deviations. Therefore, he sets

$$6\sigma_{est} = 36 - 6 = 30$$

and obtains $\sigma_{est} = 5$. Using this value in Equation (8.19), the required sample size is

$$n = 2\left(\frac{1.96(5)}{2}\right)^2 \approx 49$$

The StatTools Sample Size Selection procedure confirms this value. Enter the values 95% (confidence level), 2 (desired half-length), and 5 (estimated standard deviation). The resulting output is shown in Figure 8.39.

Figure 8.39

Sample Size for Difference Between Means

	A	B
8	*Sample Size for Difference of Means*	
9	Confidence Level	95.00%
10	Half-length of Interval	2
11	Common Std Dev (estimate)	5
12	Sample Size	49

© Cengage Learning

Some analysts prefer the estimate

$$4\sigma_{est} = 36 - 6 = 30$$

that is, $\sigma_{est} = 7.5$, arguing that the quoted range (6 to 36) might not include "extreme" values and hence might extend to only *two* standard deviations on either side of the mean. By using this estimate of the standard deviation, you can check that the required sample size increases from 49 to 109. The important point here is that the estimate of the standard deviation can have a dramatic effect on the required sample size. (And don't forget that this size sample must be taken from *each* group of employees.) ∎

Example 8.14 illustrates what can happen when you ask for extremely accurate confidence intervals.

EXAMPLE	**8.14 SAMPLE SIZE SELECTION FOR ANALYZING PROPORTIONS OF OUT-OF-SPEC PRODUCTS**

A manufacturing company has two plants that produce identical products. The production supervisor wants to know how much the proportion of out-of-spec products differs across the two plants. He suspects that the proportion of out-of-spec products in each plant is in the range of 3% to 5%, and he wants a 99% confidence interval to have approximate half-length 0.005 (or 0.5%). How many items should he sample from each plant?

Objective To see how many products in each plant must be sampled to achieve a sufficiently narrow confidence interval for the difference between the proportions of out-of-spec products.

Solution

Equation (8.20) should be used with z-multiple 2.576 (the value that cuts off probability 0.005 in each tail of the standard normal distribution), $B = 0.005$, and $p_{1est} = p_{2est} = 0.05$. The reasoning for the latter is that the supervisor believes each proportion is around 3% to 5%, and the most conservative (largest) sample size corresponds to using the larger 5% value. Then the required sample size is

$$n = \left(\frac{2.576}{0.005}\right)^2 [0.05(0.95) + 0.05(0.95)] \simeq 25{,}213$$

This sample size (from *each* sample) is almost certainly prohibitive, so the supervisor realizes he must lower his goals. One way is to decrease the confidence level, say, from 99% to 95%. Another way is to increase the desired half-length from 0.005 to, say, 0.025. We implemented both of these changes in the StatTools Sample Size Selection procedure by entering the values 95% (confidence level), 0.025 (desired half-length), and 0.05 and 0.05 (estimates of the proportions). The resulting output is shown in Figure 8.40. Even now each required sample size is 584. Obviously, narrow confidence intervals for differences between proportions can require very large sample sizes. ∎

Figure 8.40

Sample Size for Difference Between Proportions

	A	B
8	*Sample Size for Difference of Proportions*	
9	Confidence Level	95.00%
10	Half-length of Interval	0.025
11	Proportion 1 (estimate)	0.0500
12	Proportion 2 (estimate)	0.0500
13	Sample Size	584

© Cengage Learning

Level A

32. Elected officials in a California city are preparing the annual budget for their community. They would like to estimate how much their constituents living in this city are typically paying each year in real estate taxes. Given that there are over 100,000 homeowners in this city, the officials have decided to sample a representative subset of taxpayers and study their tax payments.
    a. What sample size is required to generate a 95% confidence interval for the mean annual real estate tax payment with a half-length of $100? Assume that the best estimate of the population standard deviation σ is $535.
    b. If a random sample of the size from part **a** is selected and a 95% confidence interval for the mean is calculated from this sample, will the half-length of the confidence interval be equal to $100? Explain why or why not.
    c. Now suppose that the officials want to construct a 95% confidence interval with a half-length of $75. What sample size is required to achieve this objective? Again, assume that the best estimate of the population standard deviation σ is $535. Explain the difference between this result and the result from part **a**.

33. You have been assigned to determine whether more people prefer Coke or Pepsi. Assume that roughly half the population prefers Coke and half prefers Pepsi. How large a sample do you need to take to ensure that you can estimate, with 95% confidence, the proportion of people preferring Coke within 2% of the actual value?

34. You are trying to estimate the average amount a family spends on food during a year. In the past the standard deviation of the amount a family has spent on food during a year has been approximately $1000. If you want to be 99% sure that you have estimated average family food expenditures within $50, how many families do you need to survey?

35. In past years, approximately 20% of all U.S. families purchased potato chips at least once a month. You are interested in determining the fraction of all U.S. families that currently purchase potato chips at least once a month. How many families must you survey if you want to be 99% sure that your estimate of the relevant proportion is accurate within 2%?

36. Continuing Problem 32, suppose that the officials in this city want to estimate the proportion of taxpayers whose annual real estate tax payments exceed $2000.
    a. What sample size is required to generate a 99% confidence interval for this proportion with a half-length of 0.10? Assume for now that the relevant population proportion p is close to 0.50.
    b. Assume now that officials discover another source that suggests that approximately 30% of all property owners in this community pay more than $2000 annually in real estate taxes. What sample size is now required to generate the 99% confidence interval requested in part **a**?
    c. Why is there a difference between your answers to parts **a** and **b**?
    d. If a random sample of the size from part **a** is selected and a 99% confidence for the proportion is calculated from this sample, will the half-length of the confidence interval be equal to 0.10? Explain why or why not.

Level B

37. Continuing the previous problem, suppose that the officials in this city want to estimate the difference between the proportions, labeled p_1 and p_2, of taxpayers living in neighborhood 1 whose annual real estate tax payments exceed $2000 and the similar proportion for taxpayers living in neighborhood 2.
    a. What sample size (randomly selected from all taxpayers residing in each of neighborhoods 1 and 2) is required to generate a 90% confidence interval for this difference between proportions with a half-length of 0.10? Assume for now that p_1 and p_2 are both close to 0.5.
    b. We assumed that the two population proportions in part **a** are both close to 0.5. Use a two-way data table to find the required (common) sample size when each of the population proportions is allowed to vary from 0.1 to 0.9 in increments of 0.1. Comment on the sensitivity of the required sample size to the magnitudes of the population proportions.

8-10 CONCLUSION

When you want to estimate a population parameter from sample data, one of the most useful ways to do so is to report a point estimate and a corresponding confidence interval. This confidence interval provides a quick sense of where the true parameter lies. It essentially quantifies the amount of uncertainty in the point estimate. Obviously, narrow confidence intervals are desired. You have seen that the length of a confidence interval is determined by the variability in the data, the confidence level, usually set at 95%, and the sample size(s). You have also seen how sample size formulas can be used at the planning stage to achieve confidence intervals that are sufficiently narrow. Finally, you have seen how confidence intervals can be calculated from mathematical formulas or with statistical software such as StatTools. The advantage of software is that it enables you to concentrate on the important issues for business applications: which confidence intervals are appropriate, how to interpret them, and how to control their length.

Summary of Key Terms

Term	Explanation	Excel	Pages	Equation
Confidence interval	An interval that, with a stated level of confidence, captures a population parameter		337	8.1
t distribution	The sampling distribution of the standardized sample mean when the sample standard deviation is used in place of the population standard deviation	=TDIST(*value*,*df*, 1 or 2) =TINV(*prob*,*df*)	338	8.2
Confidence level	Percentage (usually 90%, 95%, or 99%) that indicates how confident you are that the interval captures the true population parameter		342	
Confidence interval for a mean	Interval that is likely to capture a population mean	StatTools/Statistical Inference/Confidence Interval	342	8.4
Confidence interval for a total	Interval that is likely to capture the total of all observations in a population	Can be derived from StatTools/Statistical Inference/Confidence Interval	348	
Confidence interval for a proportion	Interval that is likely to capture the proportion of all population members that satisfy a specified property	StatTools/Statistical Inference/Confidence Interval	352	8.10
Confidence interval for a standard deviation	Interval that is likely to capture a population standard deviation	StatTools/Statistical Inference/Confidence Interval	357	
Chi-square distribution	Skewed distribution useful for estimating standard deviations	=CHIDIST(*value*,*df*) =CHIINV(*prob*,*df*)	357	
Confidence interval for difference between means with independent samples	Interval that is likely to capture the difference between two population means when the samples are independent	StatTools/Statistical Inference/Confidence Interval	360–361	8.13, 8.14
Confidence interval for difference between means with paired samples	Interval that is likely to capture the difference between two population means when the samples are paired in a natural way	StatTools/Statistical Inference/Confidence Interval	369	
Confidence interval for difference between proportions	Interval that is likely to capture the difference between similarly defined proportions from two populations	StatTools/Statistical Inference/Confidence Interval	375	8.15, 8.16
Sample size formulas	Formulas that specify the sample size(s) required to obtain sufficiently narrow confidence intervals	StatTools/Statistical Inference/Sample Size Selection	382–385	8.17–8.20

PROBLEMS

Conceptual Questions

C.1. Under what conditions, if any, is it *not* correct to assume that the sampling distribution of the sample mean is approximately normally distributed?

C.2. When, if ever, is it appropriate to use the standard normal distribution as a substitute for the t distribution with $n - 1$ degrees of freedom in estimating a population mean?

C.3. "Assuming that all else remains constant, the length of a confidence interval for a population mean increases whenever the confidence level and sample size increase simultaneously." Is this statement true or false? Explain your choice.

C.4. Assuming that all else remains constant, what happens to the length of a 95% confidence interval for a population parameter when the sample size is reduced by half? You can assume that the resulting sample size is still quite large. Justify your answer.

C.5. "The probability is 0.99 that a 99% confidence interval contains the true value of the relevant population parameter." Is this statement true or false? Explain your choice.

C.6. Suppose you have a list of salaries of *all* professional athletes in a given sport in a given year. For example, you might have the salaries of all Major League Baseball players in 2012. Does it make sense to find a 95% confidence interval for the mean salary? If so, what is the relevant population?

C.7. Suppose that someone proposes a new way to calculate a 95% confidence interval for a mean. This could involve *any* arithmetic on the given data. For example, it *could* say to go out 1.75 interquartile ranges (IQRs) on either side of the median. What would it mean to say that this procedure produces *valid* 95% confidence intervals? How could you use simulation to check whether the procedure produces valid 95% confidence intervals?

C.8. The sample size formula for a confidence interval for the population mean requires an estimate of the population standard deviation. Intuitively, why is this the case? Specifically, why is the required sample size larger if the population standard deviation is larger?

C.9. Suppose a 95% confidence interval for a population mean has been calculated, and it extends from 123.7 to 155.2. Some people would then state, "The probability that the population mean is between 123.7 and 155.2 is 0.95." Why is this, strictly speaking, an invalid statement? How would you rephrase it to make it a valid statement?

C.10. Researchers often create multiple 95% confidence intervals based on a given data set. For example, if the variable of interest is home price and there are five neighborhoods in the population, they might create 10 confidence intervals, one for each difference between mean home prices for a given pair of neighborhoods. (There are 10 pairs.) Can they then conclude that there is 95% confidence that *all* 10 of their confidence intervals will include the corresponding population mean differences? Why or why not?

C.11. Based on a given random sample, suppose you calculate a 95% confidence interval for the following difference: the mean test score for students under 25 years old minus the mean test score for students at least 25 years old, and the confidence interval extends from −14.3 to 1.2. How would you interpret these results? Would you claim that older students, on average, score higher on this test? Would you claim that, on average, it is possible that the younger students score higher on this test?

Level A

38. A sample of 15 quality control managers with more than 20 years experience have an average salary of $68,000 and a sample standard deviation of $19,000.

   a. You can be 95% confident that the mean salary for all quality managers with at least 20 years of experience is between what two numbers? What assumption are you making about the distribution of salaries?

   b. What size sample is needed to ensure that you can estimate the population mean salary of all quality managers with more than 20 years of experience and have only one chance in 100 of being off by more than $500?

39. Political polls typically sample randomly from the U.S. population to investigate the percentage of voters who favor some candidate or issue. The number of people polled is usually on the order of 1000. Suppose that one such poll asks voters how they feel about the President's handling of environmental issues. The results show that 575 out of the 1280 people polled say they either approve or strongly approve of the President's handling. Find a 95% confidence interval for the proportion of the entire voter population who approve or strongly approve of the President's handling. If the same sample proportion were found in a sample twice as large—that is 1150 out of 2560—how would this affect the confidence interval? How would the confidence interval change if the confidence level were 90% instead of 95%?

40. Referring to the previous problem, you often hear the results of such a poll in the news. In fact, the newscasters usually report something such as, "44.9% of the population approve or strongly approve of the President's handling of the environment. The margin of error in this result is plus or minus 3%." Where does this 3% comes from? If the pollsters want the margin of error to be plus or minus 3%, how does this lead to a sample size of approximately 1000?

41. The widths of 100 elevator rails have been measured. The sample mean and standard deviation of the elevator rails are 2.05 inches and 0.01 inch.

   a. Find a 95% confidence interval for the average width of an elevator rail. Do you need to assume that the widths of elevator rails are normally distributed?

   b. How large a sample of elevator rails would you have to measure to ensure that you could estimate, with 95% confidence, the average diameter of an elevator rail within 0.01 inch?

42. You want to determine the percentage of Fortune 500 CEOs who think Indiana University (IU) deserves its current *Business Week* rating. You mail a questionnaire to all 500 CEOs and 100 respond. Exactly half of the respondents believe IU does deserve its ranking.

   a. Find a 95% confidence interval for the fraction of Fortune 500 CEOs who believe IU deserves its ranking.

   b. Suppose again that you want to estimate the fraction of Fortune 500 CEOs who believe IU deserves its ranking. Your goal is to have only a 5% chance of having your estimate be in error by more than 0.02. What size sample would you need to take? Is it possible to implement this result?

   c. Is the finite population correct (*fpc*) from the previous chapter relevant here? Why or why not?

43. The SEC requires companies to file annual reports concerning their financial status. It is impossible to audit every account receivable. Suppose an auditor audits a random sample of 49 accounts receivable invoices and finds a sample average of $128 and a sample standard deviation of $53.

   a. Find a 99% confidence interval for the mean size of an accounts receivable invoice. Does your answer require the sizes of the accounts receivable invoices to be normally distributed?

   b. How large a sample is required for you to be 99% sure that the estimate of the mean invoice size is accurate within $5?

44. An opinion poll surveyed 900 people and reported that 36% believe a certain governor broke campaign financing laws in his election campaign.

   a. Find a 95% confidence interval for the population proportion of people who believe the governor broke campaign financing laws. Does the result of the poll convince you that fewer than 38% of all U.S. citizens favor that viewpoint?

   b. Suppose 10,000 (not 900) people are surveyed and 36% believe that the governor broke campaign financing laws. Would you now be convinced that fewer than 38% of all U.S. citizens favor that viewpoint? Why is your answer different than in part **a**?

   c. How many people would you have to survey to be 99% confident that you can estimate to within 1% the fraction of people who believe the governor broke campaign financing laws?

45. The file **P08_07.xlsx** contains a random sample of 200 service times during the busiest hour of the day at a particular fast-food restaurant. Find a 95% confidence interval for each of the following population parameters. Then explain how each result might be useful to the manager of the restaurant in terms of improving service.

   a. The mean service time

   b. The standard deviation of service times

   c. The proportion of service times longer than 90 seconds

   d. The proportion of service times shorter than 60 seconds

46. We know that IQs are normally distributed with a mean of 100 and standard deviation of 15. Suppose you want to verify this, so you take 100 random samples of size four each and, for each sample, find a 95% confidence interval for the mean IQ. You expect that approximately 95 of these intervals will contain the true mean IQ (100) and approximately five of these intervals will not contain the true mean. Use simulation in Excel to see whether this is the case.

47. In Section 8-9, we gave a sample size formula for confidence interval estimation of a mean. If the confidence level is 95%, then because the z-multiple is about 2, this formula is essentially

$$n = \frac{4\sigma^2}{B^2}$$

However, this formula is based on the assumption that the sample size n will be small relative to the population size N. If this is *not* the case, the appropriate formula turns out to be

$$n = \frac{N\sigma^2}{\sigma^2 + (N-1)B^2/4}$$

(This is based on the same idea as the finite population correction from the previous chapter.) Now suppose you want to find a 95% confidence interval for a population mean. Based on preliminary (or historical) data, you believe that the population standard deviation is approximately 15. You want the confidence interval to have length 4. That is, you want the confidence interval to be of the form $\overline{X} \pm 2$. What sample size is required if $N = 400$? if $N = 800$? if $N = 10,000$? if $N = 100,000,000$? How would you summarize these findings in words?

48. Ritter Manufacturing Company has kept track of machine hours and overhead costs at its main manufacturing plant for the past 52 weeks. The data appear in the file **P08_48.xlsx**. Ritter has studied these data to understand the relationship between machine hours and overhead costs. Although the relationship is far from perfect, Ritter believes a fairly accurate prediction of overhead costs can be obtained from machine hours through the equation

Estimated Overhead = 746.5078 + 3.3175* Machine Hours

By substituting any observed value of Machine Hours into this equation, Ritter obtains an estimated value of Overhead, which is always somewhat different from the true value of Overhead. The difference is called the prediction error.

a. Find a 95% confidence interval for the mean prediction error. Do the same for the *absolute* prediction error. (*Hint*: For example, the prediction error in week 1, actual overhead minus predicted overhead, is –94.5303. The absolute prediction error is the absolute value, 94.5303.)

b. A close examination of the data suggests that week 45 is a possible outlier. Illustrate this by creating a box plot of the prediction errors. In what sense is week 45 an outlier? See whether week 45 has much effect on the confidence intervals from part **a** by recalculating these confidence intervals, this time with week 45 deleted. Discuss your findings briefly.

Problems 49 through 58 are related to the data in the file **P08_49.xlsx**. This file contains data on 400 customers' orders from ElecMart, a company that sells electronic appliances by mail order. (This same data set was used in Example 3.4 of Chapter 3.) You can consider the data as a random sample from all of ElecMart's orders.

49. Find a 95% confidence interval for the mean total cost of all customer orders. Then do this separately for each of the four regions. Create side-by-side box plots of total cost for the four regions. Does the positive skewness in these box plots invalidate the confidence interval procedure used?

50. Find a 95% confidence interval for the proportion of all customers whose order is for more than $100. Then do this separately for each of the three times of day.

51. Find a 95% confidence interval for the proportion of all customers whose orders contain at least three items *and* cost at least $100 total.

52. Find a 95% confidence interval for the difference between the mean amount of the highest cost item purchased for the High customer category and the similar mean for the Medium customer category. Do the same for the difference between the Medium and Low customer categories. Because of the way these customer categories are defined, you would probably expect these mean differences to be positive. Is this what the data indicate?

53. Of the subpopulation of customers who order in the evening, consider the proportion who are female. Similarly, of the subpopulation of customers who order in the morning, consider the proportion who are female. Find a 95% confidence interval for the difference between these two proportions.

54. Find a 95% confidence interval for the difference between the following two proportions: the proportion of female customers who order during the evening and the proportion of male customers who order during the evening.

55. Find a 95% confidence interval for the difference between the following means: the mean total order cost for West customers and the mean total order cost for Northeast customers. Do the same for the other combinations: West versus Midwest, West versus South, Northeast versus South, Northeast versus Midwest, and South versus Midwest.

56. Find a 95% confidence interval for the difference between the mean cost per item for female orders and the similar mean for males.

Level B

57. Let $p_{E,F}$ be the proportion of female orders that are paid for with the ElecMart credit card, and let $p_{E,M}$ be the similar proportion for male orders.

a. Find a 95% confidence interval for $p_{E,F}$; for $p_{E,M}$; and for the difference $p_{E,F} - p_{E,M}$.

b. Let $p_{E,F,Wd}$ be the proportion of female orders on weekdays that are paid for with the ElecMart credit card, and let $p_{E,F,We}$ be the similar proportion for weekends. Define $p_{E,M,Wd}$ and $p_{E,M,We}$ similarly for males. Find a 95% confidence interval for the difference $(p_{E,F,Wd} - p_{E,M,Wd}) - (p_{E,F,We} - p_{E,M,We})$. Interpret this difference in words. Why might it be of interest to ElecMart?

58. Suppose these 400 orders are a sample of the 4295 orders made during this time period, and suppose 2531 of these orders were placed by females. Find a 95% confidence interval for the total paid for all 4295

orders. Do the same for all 2531 orders placed by females. Do the same for all 1764 orders placed by males.

Problems 59 through 64 are related to the data in the file **P08_59.xlsx**. This file contains data on 91 billings from Rebco, a company that sells plumbing supplies to retailers. You can consider the data as a random sample from all of Rebco's billings.

59. Find a 95% confidence interval for the mean amount of all Rebco's bills. Do the same for each customer size separately.

60. Find a 95% confidence interval for the mean number of days it takes Rebco's customers (as a combined group) to pay their bills. Do the same for each customer size separately. Create a box plot for the variable Days, based on all 91 billings. Also, create side-by-side box plots for Days for the three separate customer sizes. Do any of these suggest problems with the validity of the confidence intervals?

61. Find a 95% confidence interval for the proportion of all large customers who pay bills of at least $1000 at least 15 days after they are billed.

62. Find a 95% confidence interval for the proportion of all bills paid within 15 days. Find a 95% confidence interval for the difference between the proportion of large customers who pay within 15 days and the similar proportion of medium-size customers. Find a 95% confidence interval for the difference between the proportion of medium-size customers who pay within 15 days and the similar proportion of small customers.

63. Suppose a bill is considered late if it is paid after 20 days. In this case its "lateness" is the number of days over 20. For example, a bill paid 23 days after billing has a lateness of 3, whereas a bill paid 18 days after billing has a lateness of 0. Find a 95% confidence interval for the mean amount of lateness for all customers. Find similar confidence intervals for each customer size separately. Why is the distribution of lateness certainly not normal? Do you think this matters for the validity of the confidence interval?

64. Suppose Rebco can earn interest at the rate of 0.011% daily on excess cash. The company realizes that it could earn extra interest if its customers paid their bills more promptly.
  a. Find a 95% confidence interval for the mean amount of interest it could gain if each of its customers paid exactly one day more promptly. Find similar confidence intervals for each customer class separately.
  b. Suppose these 91 billings represent a random sample of the 2792 billings Rebco generates during

the year. Find a 95% confidence interval for the total amount of extra interest it could gain by getting each of these 2792 billings to be paid two days more promptly.

65. The file **P08_65.xlsx** contains data on the first 100 customers who entered a two-teller bank on Friday. All variables in this file are times, measured in minutes.
  a. Find a 95% confidence interval for the mean amount of time a customer spends in service with a teller.
  b. The bank is most interested in mean waiting times because customers get upset when they have to spend a lot of time waiting in line. Use the usual procedure to calculate a 95% confidence interval for the mean waiting time per customer.
  c. Your answer in part **b** is not valid! (It is much too narrow. It makes you believe you have a much more accurate estimate of the mean waiting time than you really have.) We made two implicit assumptions when we stated the confidence interval procedure for a mean: (1) The individual observations come from the same distribution, and (2) the individual observations are probabilistically independent. Why are both of these, particularly (2), violated for the customer waiting times? [*Hint*: For (1), how do the first few customers differ from "typical" customers? For (2), if you are behind someone in line who has to wait a long time, what do you suspect about your own waiting time?]
  d. Following up on assumption (2) of part **c**, you might expect waiting times of successive customers to be *autocorrelated*, that is, correlated with each other. Large waiting times tend to be followed by large waiting times, and small by small. Check this with StatTools's Autocorrelation procedure in the Time Series & Forecasting group. An autocorrelation of a certain lag, say, lag 2, is the correlation in waiting times between a customer and the second customer behind her. Do these successive waiting times appear to be autocorrelated? (A *valid* confidence interval for the mean waiting time takes autocorrelations into account—but it is considerably more difficult to calculate.)

Problems 66 through 68 are related to the data in the file **P08_66.xlsx**. SoftBus Company sells PC equipment and customized software to small companies to help them manage their day-to-day business activities. Although SoftBus spends time with all customers to understand their needs, the customers are eventually on their own to use the equipment and software intelligently. To understand its customers better, SoftBus recently sent questionnaires to a large number of prospective customers. Key personnel—those who would be using the software—were asked to fill out the questionnaire. SoftBus received 82 usable responses, as shown in the file. You can assume that these employees represent a random sample of all of SoftBus's prospective customers.

66. Construct a histogram of the PC Knowledge variable. [Because there are only five possible responses (1–5), this histogram should have only five bars.] Repeat this separately for those who own a PC and those who do not. Then find a 95% confidence interval for the mean value of PC Knowledge for all of SoftBus's prospective customers; and of all its prospective customers who own PCs; and of all its prospective customers who do not own PCs. The PC Knowledge variable obviously can't be exactly normally distributed because it has only five possible values. Do you think this invalidates the confidence intervals? Explain your choice.

67. SoftBus believes it can afford to spend much less time with customers who own PCs and score at least 4 on PC Knowledge. Let's call these the "PC-savvy" customers. On the other hand, SoftBus believes it will have to spend a lot of time with customers who do not own a PC and score 2 or less on PC Knowledge. Let's call these the "PC-illiterate" customers.
   a. Find a 95% confidence interval for the proportion of all prospective customers who are PC-savvy. Find a similar interval for the proportion who are PC-illiterate.
   b. Repeat part **a** twice, once for the subpopulation of customers who have at least 12 years of experience and once for the subpopulation who have less than 12 years of experience.
   c. Again repeat part **a** twice, once for the subpopulation of customers who have no more than a high school diploma and once for the subpopulation who have more than a high school diploma.
   d. Find a 95% confidence interval for the difference between two proportions: the proportion of all customers with some college education who are PC-savvy and the similar proportion of all customers with no college education. Repeat this, substituting "PC-savvy" with "PC-illiterate."
   e. Discuss any insights you gain from parts **a** through **d** that might be of interest to SoftBus.

68. Following up on the previous problem, SoftBus believes its profit from each prospective customer depends on the customer's level of PC knowledge. It divides the customers into three classes: PC-savvy, PC-illiterate, and all others (where the first two classes are as defined in the previous problem). As a rough guide, SoftBus figures it can gain profit P1 from each PC-savvy customer, profit P_3 from each PC-illiterate customer, and profit P_2 from each of the others.
   a. What values of P_1, P_2, and P_3 seem reasonable? For example, would you expect $P_1 < P_2 < P_3$ or the opposite?
   b. Using any reasonable values for P_1, P_2, and P_3, find a 95% confidence interval for the mean profit per customer that SoftBus can expect to obtain.

Problems 69 through 72 are related to the data in the file **P08_69.xlsx**. Comfy Company sells medium-priced patio furniture through a mail-order catalog. It has operated primarily in the East but is now expanding to the Southwest. To get off to a good start, it plans to send potential customers a catalog with a discount coupon. However, Comfy is not sure how large a discount is needed to entice customers to buy. It experiments by sending catalogs to selected residents in six cities. Tucson and San Diego receive coupons for 5% off any furniture within the next two months, Phoenix and Santa Fe receive coupons for 10% off, and Riverside and Albuquerque receive coupons for 15% off.

69. Find a 95% confidence interval for the proportion of customers who will purchase at least one item if they receive a coupon for 5% off. Repeat for 10% off and for 15% off.

70. Find a 95% confidence interval for the proportion of customers who will purchase at least one item and pay at least $500 total if they receive a coupon for 5% off. Repeat for 10% off and for 15% off.

71. Comfy wonders whether the customers who receive larger discounts are buying more expensive items. Recalling that the value in the Total Paid column is *after* the discount, find a 95% confidence interval for the difference between the mean *original price per item* for customers who purchase something with the 5% coupon and the similar mean for customers who purchase something with the 10% coupon. Repeat with 5% and 10% replaced by 10% and 15%. What can you conclude?

72. Comfy wonders whether there are differences across pairs of cities that receive the *same* discount.
   a. Find a 95% confidence interval for the difference between the mean amount spent in Tucson and the similar mean in San Diego. (These means should include the "0 purchases.") Repeat this for the

difference between Phoenix and Santa Fe and then between Riverside and Albuquerque. Does city appear to make a difference?

b. Repeat part **a**, but instead of analyzing differences between means, analyze differences between proportions of customers who purchase something. Does city appear to make a difference?

Problems 73 through 76 are related to the data in the file **P08_73.xlsx**. Niyaki Company sells Blu-ray disc players through a number of retail stores. On one popular model, there is a standard warranty that covers parts for the first six months and labor for the first year. Customers are always asked whether they wish to purchase an extended service plan for $50 that extends the original warranty two more years—that is, to 30 months on parts and 36 months on service. To get a better understanding of warranty costs, the company has gathered data on 70 Blu-ray units purchased. This data is listed in the Data1 sheet of the file **P08_73 .xlsx**. The two costs in this sheet (columns D and E) are tracked only for repairs covered by warranty. [Otherwise, the customer bears the cost(s).]

73. Create a histogram of the time until first failure for this type of disc player. Then find a 95% confidence interval for the mean time until failure for this type of disc player. Does the shape of the histogram invalidate the confidence interval? Why or why not?

74. Find a 95% confidence interval for the proportion of customers who purchase the extended service plan. Find a 95% confidence interval for the proportion of all customers who would benefit by purchasing the extended service plan.

75. Find a 95% confidence interval for Niyaki's mean net warranty cost per unit sold (net of the $50 paid for the plan for those who purchase it). You can assume that this mean is for the *first* failure only; subsequent failures of the same units are ignored here.

76. This problem follows up on the previous two problems with the data in the Data2 sheet of the file. Here Niyaki did more investigation on the same 70 customers. It tracked subsequent failures and costs (if any) that occurred within the warranty period. (*Note*: Only two customers had three failures within the warranty period, and parts weren't covered for either on the third failure. Also, no one had more than three failures within the warranty period.)

a. With these data, find the confidence intervals requested in the previous two problems.

b. Suppose that Niyaki sold this Blu-ray model to 12,450 customers during the year. Find a 95%

confidence interval for its total net cost due to warranties from all of these sales.

77. The file **P08_77.xlsx** contains data on 856 customers who have either tried or not tried a company's new frozen lasagna dinner. (This data set was used in Example 3.5 in Chapter 3.) The manager of the company would like to compare the proportion of customers who have tried the lasagna across various subpopulations. For each of the following, find a 95% confidence interval for the difference between the proportions who have tried the lasagna for the two specified subpopulations. Explain briefly how the results help the manager to understand his customers. (*Hint*: One approach is to use pivot tables to get the count data you need.)

a. Those with weight under 190 versus those with weight at least 190

b. Females versus males

c. Those who live alone versus those who do not live alone

d. Those who live in a home or condo versus those who live in an apartment

e. Those who live in the South or West versus those who live in the East

f. Those who average five or more trips to the mall per month versus those who average fewer than five trips to the mall per month.

78. The formula for a 95% confidence interval for a mean (sample mean plus or minus approximately two standard errors) is so well-rooted in statistical theory and practice that you might not even consider other possibilities. However, many researchers and even practitioners favor a totally different method of calculating a 95% confidence interval for the mean. It is called the *bootstrap* method. Starting with a sample of size n, they generate many "bootstrap samples," calculate the sample mean of each, and report the 2.5 and 97.5 percentiles of these sample means as the endpoints of the confidence interval. Each bootstrap sample is a random sample of size n, with *replacement*, from the given data. That is, each member of a bootstrap sample is equally likely to be any of the original n data points. Implement this in Excel, starting with the sample of 50 salaries in the file **P08_78.xlsx**. Create at least 100 bootstrap samples. Compare the resulting bootstrap confidence interval with the one from StatTools (the traditional one). (*Hint*: The bootstrap samples can be generated quickly with a combination of the RANDBETWEEN and VLOOKUP functions.)

Harrigan University is a liberal arts university in the Midwest that attempts to attract the highest-quality students, especially from its region of the country. It has gathered data on 178 applicants who were accepted by Harrigan (a random sample from all acceptable applicants over the past several years). The data are in the file **C08_01.xlsx**. The variables are as follows:

- Accepted: whether the applicant accepts Harrigan's offer to enroll
- MainRival: whether the applicant enrolls at Harrigan's main rival university
- HSClubs: number of high school clubs applicant served as an officer
- HSSports: number of varsity letters applicant earned
- HSGPA: applicant's high school GPA
- HSPctile: applicant's percentile (in terms of GPA) in his or her graduating class
- HSSize: number of students in applicant's graduating class
- SAT: applicant's combined SAT score
- Combined Score: a combined score for the applicant used by Harrigan to rank applicants

The derivation of the combined score is a closely kept secret by Harrigan, but it is basically a weighted average of the various components of high school performance and SAT. Harrigan is concerned that it is not getting enough of the best students, and worse yet, that many of these best students are going to Harrigan's main rival. Solve the following problems and then, based on your analysis, comment on whether Harrigan appears to have a legitimate concern.

1. Find a 95% confidence interval for the proportion of all acceptable applicants who accept Harrigan's invitation to enroll. Do the same for all acceptable applicants with a combined score less than 330, with a combined score between 330 and 375, and then with a combined score greater than 375. (Note that 330 and 375 are approximately the first and third quartiles of the Combined Score variable.)

2. Find a 95% confidence interval for the proportion of all acceptable students with a combined score less than the median (356) who choose Harrigan's rival over Harrigan. Do the same for those with a combined score greater than the median.

3. Find 95% confidence intervals for the mean combined score, the mean high school GPA, and the mean SAT score of all acceptable students who accept Harrigan's invitation to enroll. Do the same for all acceptable students who choose to enroll elsewhere. Then find 95% confidence intervals for the differences between these means, where each difference is a mean for students enrolling at Harrigan minus the similar mean for students enrolling elsewhere.

4. Harrigan is interested (as are most schools) in getting students who are involved in extracurricular activities (clubs and sports). Does it appear to be doing so? Find a 95% confidence interval for the proportion of all students who decide to enroll at Harrigan who have been officers of at least two clubs. Find a similar confidence interval for those who have earned at least four varsity letters in sports.

5. The combined score Harrigan calculates for each student gives some advantage to students who rank highly in a *large* high school relative to those who rank highly in a small high school. Therefore, Harrigan wonders whether it is relatively more successful in attracting students from large high schools than from small high schools. Develop one or more confidence intervals for relevant parameters to shed some light on this issue.

CASE 8.2 EMPLOYEE RETENTION AT D&Y

Demand for systems analysts in the consulting industry is greater than ever. Graduates with a combination of business and computer knowledge—some even from liberal arts programs—are getting great offers from consulting companies. Once these people are hired, they frequently switch from one company to another as competing companies lure them away with even better offers. One consulting company, D&Y, has collected data on a sample of systems analysts with undergraduate degrees they hired several years ago. The data are in the file C08_02.xlsx. The variables are as follows:

- Starting Salary: employee's starting salary at D&Y
- On Road Pct: percentage of time employee has spent on the road with clients
- State Univ: whether the employee graduated from State University (D&Y's principal source of recruits)
- CIS Degree: whether the employee majored in Computer Information Systems (CIS) or a similar computer-related area
- Stayed 3 Years: whether the employee stayed at least three years with D&Y
- Tenure: tenure of employee at D&Y (months) if he or she moved before three years

D&Y is trying to learn everything it can about retention of these valuable employees. You can help by solving the following problems and then, based on your analysis, presenting a report to D&Y.

1. Although starting salaries are in a fairly narrow band, D&Y wonders whether they have anything to do with retention.

   b. Find a 95% confidence interval for the mean starting salary of all employees who stay at least three years with D&Y. Do the same for those who leave before three years. Then find a 95% confidence interval for the difference between these means.

   c. Among all employees whose starting salary is below the median ($37,750), find a 95% confidence interval for the proportion who stay with D&Y for at least three years. Do the same for the employees with starting salaries above the median. Then find a 95% confidence interval for the difference between these proportions.

2. D&Y wonders whether the percentage of time on the road might influence who stays and who leaves. Repeat the previous problem, but now do the analysis in terms of percentage of time on the road rather than starting salary. (The median percentage of time on the road is 54%.)

3. Find a 95% confidence interval for the mean tenure (in months) of all employees who leave D&Y within three years of being hired. Why is it not possible with the given data to find a confidence interval for the mean tenure at D&Y among *all* systems analysts hired by D&Y?

4. State University's students, particularly those in its nationally acclaimed CIS area, have traditionally been among the best of D&Y's recruits. But are they relatively hard to retain? Find one or more relevant confidence intervals to help you make an argument one way or the other.

CASE 8.3 DELIVERY TIMES AT SNOWPEA RESTAURANT

The SnowPea Restaurant is a Chinese carryout/delivery restaurant. Most of SnowPea's deliveries are within a 10-mile radius, but it occasionally delivers to customers more than 10 miles away. SnowPea employs a number of delivery people, four

of whom are relatively new hires. The restaurant has recently been receiving customer complaints about excessively long delivery times. Therefore, SnowPea has collected data on a random sample of deliveries by its four new delivery people during the peak dinner time. The data are in the file **C08_03.xlsx**. The variables are as follows:

- Deliverer: which person made the delivery
- Prep Time: time from when order was placed until delivery person started driving it to the customer
- Travel Time: time to drive from SnowPea to customer
- Distance: distance (miles) from SnowPea to customer

Solve the following problems and then, based on your analysis, write a report that makes reasonable recommendations to SnowPea management.

1. SnowPea is concerned that one or more of the new delivery people might be slower than others.

   a. Let μ_{Di} and μ_{Ti} be the mean delivery time and mean total time for delivery person i, where the total time is the sum of the delivery and prep times. Find 95% confidence intervals for each of these means for each delivery person. Although these might be interesting, give two reasons why they are not really fair measures for comparing the efficiency of the delivery people.

   b. Responding to the criticisms in part **a**, find a 95% confidence interval for the mean speed of delivery for each delivery person, where speed is measured as miles per hour during the trip from SnowPea to the customer. Then find 95% confidence intervals for the mean difference in speed between each pair of delivery people.

2. SnowPea would like to advertise that it can achieve a total delivery time of no more than M minutes for all customers within a 10-mile radius. On all orders that take more than M minutes, SnowPea will give the customers a $10 certificate on their next purchase.

   a. Assuming for now that the delivery people in the sample are representative of all

of SnowPea's delivery people, find a 95% confidence interval for the proportion of deliveries (within the 10-mile limit) that will be on time if $M = 25$ minutes; if $M = 30$ minutes; if $M = 35$ minutes.

   b. Suppose SnowPea makes 1000 deliveries within the 10-mile limit. For each of the values of M in part **a**, find a 95% confidence interval for the total dollar amount of certificates it will have to pay for being late.

3. The policy in the previous problem is simple to state and simple to administer. However, it is somewhat unfair to customers who live close to SnowPea—they will never get $10 certificates. A fairer, but more complex, policy is the following. SnowPea first analyzes the data and finds that total delivery times can be predicted fairly well with the equation

   Predicted Delivery Time $= 14.8 + 2.06*\text{Distance}$

   (This is based on regression analysis, the topic of Chapters 10 and 11.) Also, most of these predictions are within 5 minutes of the actual delivery times. Therefore, whenever SnowPea receives an order over the phone, it looks up the customer's address in its computerized geographical database to find distance, calculates the predicted delivery time based on this equation, rounds this to the nearest minute, adds 5 minutes, and guarantees this delivery time or else a $10 certificate. It does this for *all* customers, even those beyond the 10-mile limit.

   a. Assuming again that the delivery people in the sample are representative of all of SnowPea's delivery people, find a 95% confidence interval for the proportion of all deliveries that will be within the guaranteed total delivery time.

   b. Suppose SnowPea makes 1000 deliveries. Find a 95% confidence interval for the total dollar amount of certificates it will have to pay for being late.

Ralph Butts, manager of Woodland Operations for Intergalactica Papelco's Southeastern Region, had to decide this morning whether to approve the Bodfish Lot logging contract that was sitting on his desk. Accompanying the contract was a cruise report that gave Mr. Butts the results of a sample survey of the timber on the Bodfish Lot. Was there enough timber to make logging operations worthwhile?

The Pluto Mill of Intergalactica Papelco is located on the River Styxx in Median, Michigan. The scale of operations at Pluto is enormous. Just one of its several $500 million, football-field-long, four-story-high paper machines has the capability to produce a 20-mile-long, 16-foot-wide, 20-ton reel of paper every hour. Such a machine is run nonstop 24 hours a day for as many of the 365 days in the year that mill maintenance can keep the machine running within specified quality levels. In total, the Pluto Mill produces about 400,000 tons of white paper a year. Because it takes about a ton of wood to produce a ton of paper, a huge quantity of cordwood logs suitable for chipping and pulping must be supplied continually to keep the mill operating. Intergalactica Papelco runs a large-scale logistics, planning, and procurement operation to provide the Pluto Mill with the requisite species, quantity, and quality of wood in a timely fashion.

The Pluto Mill sits on 500 acres of land in the midst of a region in which the huge Intergalactica Papelco owns over a quarter of a million acres of forest. Although this wholly owned forest is the single largest supplier of wood to the mill, more than 60% of the wood used at Pluto is purchased from independent landowners and loggers under contract. Supplying contract wood dependably on such an enormous scale involves frequent purchasing decisions by the Intergalactica Woodlands Operations as to which independent woodlots have sufficient wood volume and quality to support economical logging operations. A prospective seller enters into a tentative agreement with Intergalactica on the basis of market price and a visual scan of the woodlot. The final decision about whether to proceed with the logging is usually based on sampling estimates of the total wood volume on the lot.

A case in point was the Bodfish Lot in Henryville, Arkansas, whose owner approached Intergalactica with a proposal for logging during the 1991 to 1992 season. Aerial photographs indicated that the land was sufficiently promising to warrant a "cruise" to estimate the total volume of wood. (*Cruising* is a term used in the forestry industry to describe a systematic procedure for estimating the quantity, quality, variety, and value of the wood on a plot of land. Indeed, standard cruising methods have been developed and disseminated by the U.S. Department of Agriculture and Forestry Service.) Estimation based on limited sampling is essential. Even for the modest-size Bodfish Lot, with 586 acres of forested land, it would be practically impossible to measure every tree on the lot.

For the Bodfish Lot cruise, it was decided to sample 89 distinct 1/7-acre plots for actual measurement. Although the plots were chosen systematically, the sample was, Intergalactica hoped, still effectively "random." Indeed, *no* consistent attempt was made to select the plots from areas of heavy tree growth, large-diameter trees, heavy spruce concentration, and so on. In fact, the opposite was true: The regular spacing of the sampling grid more or less guaranteed a good cross section of the entire lot. This was what is called in forestry industry jargon a "standard line plot cruise." The total lot was 700 acres in area. The plots were spaced at 8-chain intervals apart on a rectangular grid drawn in advance at the Intergalactica Woodlands Field Office at One Root mean Square in the town of Covariance, Illinois. The aerial photographs showed that, of the Bodfish Lot's 700 total acres, 586 acres were forested. The total volume estimate, to be done separately for each species, was to be based on the average for the 89 sampled plots on these 586 acres.

A circular area two-person cruise was then initiated. Typically, about 10 plots could be cruised in one day. The foresters counted the entire number of cordwood trees over 6 inches in diameter within each 1/7-acre circle. Then, back in the office in Covariance, the number of trees on each plot was entered into a computer according to species, diameter, and possible end product. The file **C08_04 .xlsx** contains this tabulation from the cruise notes

[7]This case was contributed by Peter Kolesar from Columbia University.

of the counts for spruce, hard maple, and beech of the number of cordwood trees on the 89 sampled plots. (In the actual database, 13 different species of trees were recorded, and Intergalactica would have decided which trees were more suitable for lumber, plywood, or pulping applications.)

With these data, Intergalactica now had to decide whether to contract to log the lot. Ralph Butts, manager of Woodlands Operations, knew that even though Intergalactica would pay on the basis of the weight received at the mill, he needed at least 31,000 cordwood size trees on the lot to make operations economical. More detailed knowledge of the amount of timber by species would help the Pluto Mill make the crucial blending decisions that affect the cost and quality of the resulting wood pulp.

This was just one of several hundred similiar contracts to be made over the coming year. Butts was concerned with the rising cost of cruising in the Southeastern Region. Was the Bodfish Lot cruise excessive, he wondered? Could he get by in the future with considerably smaller samples? Suppose that only one-half or one-quarter of the plots on Bodfish had been cruised?

Hypothesis Testing

ROBERT PARIGGER/EPA/Newscom

OFFICIAL SPONSORS OF THE OLYMPICS

Hypothesis testing is one of the most frequently used tools in academic research, including research in the area of business. Many studies pose interesting questions, stated as hypotheses, and then test these with appropriate statistical analysis of experimental data. One such study is reported in McDaniel and Kinney (1996). They investigate the effectiveness of "ambush marketing" in prominent sports events such as the Olympic Games. Many companies pay significant amounts of money, perhaps $10 million, to become official sponsors of the Olympics. Ambushers are their competitors, who pay no such fees but nevertheless advertise heavily during the Olympics, with the intention of linking their own brand image to the event in the minds of consumers. The question McDaniel and Kinney investigate is whether consumers are confused into thinking that the ambushers are the official sponsors.

At the time of the 1994 Winter Olympics in Lillehammer, Norway, the researchers ran a controlled experiment using 215 subjects ranging in age from 19 to 49 years old. Approximately half of the subjects—the "control group"—viewed a 20-minute tape of a women's skiing event in which several actual commercials for official sponsors in four product categories were interspersed. (The categories were fast food, automobile, credit card, and insurance; the official sponsors were McDonald's, Chrysler, VISA, and John Hancock.) The other half—the "treatment group"—watched the same tape but with commercials for competing ambushers. (The ambushers were Wendy's, Ford, American Express, and Northwestern Mutual, all of which advertised during the 1994 Olympics.) After watching the tape, each subject was asked to fill out a questionnaire. This questionnaire asked subjects to recall the official Olympics sponsors in each product category, to rate their attitudes toward the products, and to state their intentions to purchase the products.

McDaniel and Kinney tested several hypotheses. First, they tested the hypothesis that there would be *no* difference between the control and treatment groups in terms of which products they would recall as official Olympics sponsors. The experimental evidence allowed them to reject this hypothesis decisively. For example, the vast majority of the control group, who watched the McDonald's commercial, recalled McDonald's as being the official sponsor in the fast-food category. But a clear majority of the treatment group, who watched the Wendy's commercial, recalled Wendy's as being the official sponsor in this category. Evidently, Wendy's commercial was compelling.[1]

Because the ultimate objective of commercials is to increase purchases of a company's brand, the researchers also tested the hypothesis that viewers of official sponsor commercials would rate their intent to purchase that brand *higher* than viewers of ambusher commercials would rate their intent to purchase the ambusher brand. After all, isn't this why the official sponsors were paying large fees? However, except for the credit card category, the data did *not* support this hypothesis. VISA viewers did indeed rate their intent to use VISA higher than American Express viewers rated their intent to use American Express. But in the other three product categories, the ambusher brand came out *ahead* of the official brand in terms of intent to purchase (although the differences were not statistically significant).

There are at least two important messages this research should convey to business. First, if a company is going to spend a lot of money to become an official sponsor of an event such as the Olympic Games, it must create a more vivid link in the mind of consumers between its product and the event. Otherwise, the company might be wasting its money. Second, ambush marketing is very possibly a wise strategy. By seeing enough of the ambushers' commercials during the event, consumers get confused into thinking that the ambusher is an official sponsor. In addition, previous research in the area suggests that consumers do not view ambushers negatively for using an ambush strategy. ■

9-1 INTRODUCTION

When you want to make inferences about a population on the basis of sample data, you can perform the analysis in either of two ways. You can proceed as in the previous chapter, where you calculate a point estimate of a population parameter and then form a confidence interval around this point estimate. In this way you bring no preconceived ideas to the analysis but instead let the data speak for themselves in estimating the parameter's true value.

In contrast, an analyst often has a particular theory, or hypothesis, that he or she would like to test. This hypothesis might be that a new packaging design will produce more sales than the current design, that a new drug will have a higher cure rate for a given disease than any drug currently on the market, that people who smoke cigarettes are more susceptible to heart disease than nonsmokers, and so on. In this case the analyst typically collects sample data and checks whether the data provide enough evidence to support the hypothesis.

The hypothesis that the analyst is attempting to prove is called the **alternative hypothesis**. It is also frequently called the **research hypothesis**. The opposite of the alternative hypothesis is called the **null hypothesis**. It usually represents the current

Hypothesis testing is a form of decision making under uncertainty, where you decide which of two competing hypotheses to accept, based on sample data. However, in contrast to the methods discussed in Chapter 6, it is performed in a very specific way, as described in this chapter.

---

[1]Whereas the McDonald's commercial featured the five-ringed Olympics logo and had an Olympics theme, the Wendy's commercial used a humorous approach built around the company's founder, Dave Thomas, and his dream of winning gold in the Olympics bobsled competition.

thinking or status quo. That is, the null hypothesis is usually the accepted theory that the analyst is trying to *disprove*. In the previous examples the null hypotheses are:

- The new packaging design is no better than the current design.
- The new drug has a cure rate no higher than other drugs on the market.
- Smokers are no more susceptible to heart disease than nonsmokers.

The burden of proof is traditionally on the alternative hypothesis. It is up to the analyst to provide enough evidence in support of the alternative; otherwise, the null hypothesis will continue to be accepted. A slight amount of evidence in favor of the alternative is usually not enough. For example, if a slightly higher percentage of people are cured with a new drug in a sequence of clinical tests, this still might not be enough evidence to warrant introducing the new drug to the market. In general, we reject the null hypothesis—and accept the alternative—only if the results of the hypothesis test are *statistically significant*, a concept we will explain in this chapter.

> The **null hypothesis** is usually the current thinking, or status quo. The **alternative**, or **research, hypothesis** is usually the hypothesis a researcher wants to prove. The burden of proof is on the alternative hypothesis.

As you will see in this chapter, confidence interval estimation and hypothesis testing use data in much the same way and they often report basically the same results, only from different points of view. There continues to be a debate (largely among academic researchers) over which of these two procedures is more useful. We believe that in a business context, confidence interval estimation is more useful and enlightening than hypothesis testing. However, hypothesis testing continues to be a key aspect of statistical analysis. Indeed, statistical software packages routinely include the elements of standard hypothesis tests in their outputs. You will see this, for example, when you study regression analysis in Chapters 10 and 11. Therefore, it is essential to understand the fundamentals of hypothesis testing so that you can interpret this output intelligently.

9-2 CONCEPTS IN HYPOTHESIS TESTING

Before we plunge into the details of specific hypothesis tests, it is useful to discuss the *concepts* behind hypothesis testing. There are a number of concepts and statistical terms involved, all of which lead eventually to the key concept of statistical significance. Example 9.1 provides context for this discussion.

EXAMPLE | **9.1 A New Pizza Style at Pepperoni Pizza Restaurant**

The manager of Pepperoni Pizza Restaurant has recently begun experimenting with a new method of baking pepperoni pizzas. He personally believes that the new method produces a better-tasting pizza, but he would like to base the decision whether to switch from the old method to the new method on customer reactions. Therefore, he performs an experiment. For 100 randomly selected customers who order a pepperoni pizza for home delivery, he includes both an old-style and a free new-style pizza in the order. All he asks is that these customers rate the *difference* between pizzas on a −10 to +10 scale, where −10 means that they strongly favor the old style, $+10$ means they strongly favor the new style, and 0 means they are indifferent between the two styles. Once he gets the ratings from the customers, how should he proceed?

We begin by stating that Example 9.1 is used primarily to explain hypothesis-testing concepts. We do *not* mean to imply that the manager would, or should, use a hypothesis-testing procedure to decide whether to switch from the old method to the new method. First, hypothesis testing does not take costs into account. If the new method of making pizzas uses more expensive cheese, for example, then hypothesis testing would ignore this important aspect of the decision problem. Second, even if the costs of the two pizza-making methods are equivalent, the manager might base his decision on a simple point estimate and possibly a confidence interval. For example, if the sample mean rating is 1.8 and a 95% confidence interval for the mean rating extends from 0.3 to 3.3, this in itself should probably be enough evidence to make the manager switch to the new method.

We come back to these ideas—basically, that hypothesis testing is not necessarily the best procedure to use in a business decision-making context—throughout this chapter. However, with these caveats in mind, we discuss how the manager *might* proceed by using hypothesis testing. ∎

9-2a Null and Alternative Hypotheses

As we stated in the introduction to this chapter, the hypothesis the manager is trying to prove is called the alternative, or research, hypothesis, whereas the null hypothesis represents the status quo. In this example the manager would personally like to prove that the new method provides better-tasting pizza, so this becomes the alternative hypothesis. The opposite, that the old-style pizzas are at least as good as the new-style pizzas, becomes the null hypothesis. We assume he judges which of these is true on the basis of the mean rating over the entire customer population, labeled μ. If it turns out that $\mu \leq 0$, the null hypothesis is true. Otherwise, if $\mu > 0$, the alternative hypothesis is true.

Hypotheses for Pizza Example

Null hypothesis: $\mu \leq 0$

Alternative hypothesis: $\mu > 0$

where μ is the mean population rating

Usually, the null hypothesis is labeled H_0 and the alternative hypothesis is labeled H_a. Therefore, in our example they can be specified as $H_0: \mu \leq 0$ and $H_a: \mu > 0$. This is typical. The null and alternative hypotheses divide all possibilities into two nonoverlapping sets, exactly one of which must be true. In our case the mean rating is either less than or equal to 0, or it is positive. Exactly one of these possibilities *must* be true, and the manager intends to use sample data to learn which is true.

Traditionally, hypothesis testing has been phrased as a decision-making problem, where an analyst decides either to accept the null hypothesis or reject it, based on the sample evidence. In our example, accepting the null hypothesis means deciding that the new-style pizza is not really better than the old-style pizza and presumably discontinuing the new style. In contrast, rejecting the null hypothesis means deciding that the new-style pizza is indeed better than the old-style pizza and presumably switching to the new style.

9-2b One-Tailed Versus Two-Tailed Tests

The form of the alternative hypothesis can be either *one-tailed* or *two-tailed*, depending on what the analyst is trying to prove. The pizza manager's alternative hypothesis is **one-tailed** because he is hoping to prove that the customers' ratings are, on average, greater than 0. The only sample results that will lead to rejection of the null hypothesis are those in a particular direction, namely, those where the sample mean rating is *positive*. On the other hand, if the manager sets up his rating scale in the reverse order, so that *negative* ratings favor the new-style pizza, the test is still one-tailed, but now only negative sample means lead to rejection of the null hypothesis.

In contrast, a **two-tailed test** is one where results in either of two directions can lead to rejection of the null hypothesis. A slight modification of the pizza example where a two-tailed alternative might be appropriate is the following. Suppose the manager currently uses two methods for producing pepperoni pizzas. He is thinking of discontinuing one of these methods if it appears that customers, on average, favor one method over the other. Therefore, he runs the same experiment as before, but now the hypotheses he tests are $H_0: \mu = 0$ versus $H_a: \mu \neq 0$, where μ is again the mean rating across the customer population. In this case either a large positive sample mean *or* a large negative sample mean will lead to rejection of the null hypothesis—and presumably to discontinuing one of the production methods.

A **one-tailed alternative** is one that is supported only by evidence in a single direction.

A **two-tailed alternative** is one that is supported by evidence in either of two directions.

It is important to realize that the analyst, not the data, determines the type of alternative hypothesis. The hypothesis depends entirely on what the analyst wants to prove, and it should be formed before the data are collected.

Once the hypotheses are set up, it is easy to detect whether the test is one-tailed or two-tailed. One-tailed alternatives are phrased in terms of ">" or "<" whereas two-tailed alternatives are phrased in terms of "≠". The real question is whether to set up hypotheses for a particular problem as one-tailed or two-tailed. There is no *statistical* answer to this question. It depends entirely on what an analyst is trying to prove. If the pizza manager is trying to prove that the new-style pizza is better than the old-style pizza—only results on one side will lead to a switch—a one-tailed alternative is appropriate. However, if he is trying to decide whether to discontinue either of two existing production methods—where results on *either* side will lead to a switch—then a two-tailed alternative is appropriate.

9-2c Types of Errors

Regardless of whether the manager decides to accept or reject the null hypothesis, it *might* be the wrong decision. He might incorrectly reject the null hypothesis when it is true ($\mu \leq 0$), and he might incorrectly accept the null hypothesis when it is false ($\mu > 0$). In the tradition of hypothesis testing, these two types of errors have acquired the names *type I* and *type II errors*. In general, you commit a **type I error** when you incorrectly *reject* a null hypothesis that is true. You commit a **type II error** when you incorrectly *accept* a null hypothesis that is false. These ideas appear graphically in Figure 9.1.

The pizza manager commits a type I error if he concludes, based on sample evidence, that the new-style pizza is better (and switches to it) when in fact the entire customer

Figure 9.1

Types of Errors in Hypothesis Testing

		Truth	
		H_0 is true	H_a is true
Decision	Reject H_0	Type I error	No error
	Do not reject H_0	No error	Type II error

© Cengage Learning

population would, on average, favor the old-style pizza. In contrast, he commits a type II error if he concludes, again based on sample evidence, that the new style is no better (and discontinues it) when in fact the entire customer population would, on average, favor the new style.

> **Type I error:** Switching to new style when it is no better than old style
>
> **Type II error:** Staying with old style when new style is better

The traditional hypothesis-testing procedure favors caution in terms of rejecting the null hypothesis. The thinking is that if you reject the null hypothesis and it is really true, then you commit a type I error—which is bad. Given this rather conservative way of thinking, you are inclined to accept the null hypothesis unless the sample evidence provides *strong* support for the alternative hypothesis. Unfortunately, you can't have it both ways. By accepting the null hypothesis, you risk committing a type II error.

Type I errors are usually considered more costly, although this can lead to conservative decision making.

This is exactly the dilemma the pizza manager faces. If he wants to avoid a type I error (where he switches to the new style but really shouldn't), then he will require fairly convincing evidence from the survey that he *should* switch. If he observes *some* evidence to this effect, such as a sample mean rating of +1.5 and a 95% confidence interval that extends from −0.3 to +3.3, this evidence might not be strong enough to make him switch. However, if he decides not to switch, he risks committing a type II error.

9-2d Significance Level and Rejection Region

The analyst gets to choose the significance level α. It is traditionally chosen to be 0.05, but it is occasionally chosen to be 0.01 or 0.10.

The real question, then, is how strong the evidence in favor of the alternative hypothesis must be to reject the null hypothesis. Two approaches to this problem are commonly used. In the first, you prescribe the probability of a type I error that you are willing to tolerate. This type I error probability is usually denoted by α and is most commonly set equal to 0.05, although $\alpha = 0.01$ and $\alpha = 0.10$ are also frequently used. The value of α is called the **significance level** of the test. Then, given the value of α, you use statistical theory to determine a *rejection region*. If the sample evidence falls in the **rejection region**, you reject the null hypothesis; otherwise, you accept it. The rejection region is chosen precisely so that the probability of a type I error is at most α. Sample evidence that falls into the rejection region is called **statistically significant at the α level**. For example, if $\alpha = 0.05$, the evidence is statistically significant at the 5% level.

> The **rejection region** is the set of sample data that leads to the rejection of the null hypothesis.
>
> The **significance level**, α, determines the size of the rejection region. Sample results in the rejection region are called **statistically significant** at the α level.

It is important to understand the effect of varying α. If α is small, such as 0.01, the probability of a type I error is small. Therefore, a lot of sample evidence in favor of the alternative hypothesis is required before the null hypothesis can be rejected. Equivalently, the rejection region in this case is small. In contrast, when α is larger, such as 0.10, the rejection region is larger, and it is easier to reject the null hypothesis.

9-2e Significance from *p*-values

A second approach, and one that is currently more popular, is to avoid the use of a significance level α and instead simply report *how significant* the sample evidence is. This is done by means of a *p*-value. The idea is quite simple—and very important. Suppose in the pizza example that the true mean rating (if it could be observed) is $\mu = 0$. In other words, the customer population, on average, judges the two styles of pizza to be equal. Now suppose that the sample mean rating is +2.5. The manager has two options at this point. (Remember that he doesn't know that μ equals 0; he observes only the sample.) He can conclude that (1) the null hypothesis is true—the new-style pizza is not preferred over the old style—and he just observed an unusual sample, or (2) the null hypothesis is *not* true—customers do prefer the new-style pizza—and the sample he observed is a typical one for such customers.

The *p*-value of the sample quantifies this. The **p-value** is the probability of seeing a random sample *at least as extreme as the observed sample*, given that the null hypothesis is true. Here, "extreme" is relative to the null hypothesis. For example, a sample mean rating of +3.5 from the pizza customers is more extreme evidence than a sample mean rating of +2.5. Each provides some evidence against the null hypothesis, but the former provides stronger, more extreme evidence.

> The **p-value** of a sample is the probability of seeing a sample with at least as much evidence in favor of the alternative hypothesis as the sample actually observed. The smaller the *p*-value, the more evidence there is in favor of the alternative hypothesis.

Let's suppose that the pizza manager collects data from the 100 sampled customers and finds that the *p*-value for the sample is 0.03. This means that *if* the entire customer population, on average, judges the two types of pizza to be approximately equal, then only three random samples out of 100 would provide as much evidence in support of the new style as the observed sample. So should he conclude that the null hypothesis is true and he just happened to observe an unusual sample, or should he conclude that the null hypothesis is *not* true? There is no clear *statistical* answer to this question; it depends on how convinced the manager must be before switching. But we can say in general that smaller *p*-values indicate more evidence in support of the alternative hypothesis. If a *p*-value is sufficiently small, then almost any analyst will conclude that rejecting the null hypothesis (and accepting the alternative) is the more reasonable decision.

How small is a "small" *p*-value? This is largely a matter of semantics, but Figure 9.2 indicates the attitude of many analysts. A *p*-value less than 0.01 is regarded as convincing evidence that the alternative hypothesis is true. After all, fewer than one sample out of 100 would provide such support for the alternative hypothesis if it weren't true. If the *p*-value is between 0.01 and 0.05, there is strong evidence in favor of the alternative hypothesis. Unless the consequences of making a type I error are really serious, this is typically enough evidence to reject the null hypothesis.

Figure 9.2

Evidence in Favor of the Alternative Hypothesis

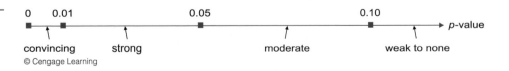

© Cengage Learning

The interval between 0.05 and 0.10 is a gray area. If a researcher is trying to prove a research hypothesis and observes a *p*-value between 0.05 and 0.10, she will probably be reluctant to publish her results as "proof" of the alternative hypothesis, but she will probably be encouraged to continue her research and collect more sample evidence. Finally, p-values larger than 0.10 are generally interpreted as weak evidence (or no evidence) in support of the alternative.

If you remember only one thing from this chapter, remember that a p-value measures how unlikely the observed sample results are, given that the null hypothesis is true. Therefore, a low p-value provides evidence for rejecting the null hypothesis and accepting the alternative.

There is a strong connection between the α-level approach and the p-value approach. Specifically, the null hypothesis can be rejected at a specified significance level α only if the p-value from the sample is less than or equal to α. Equivalently, the sample evidence is statistically significant at a given α level only if its p-value is less than or equal to α. For example, if the p-value from a sample is 0.03, the null hypothesis can be rejected at the 10% and the 5% significance levels but not at the 1% level. The p-value essentially states *how* significant a given sample is.

> Sample evidence is statistically significant at the α level only if the p-value is less than α.

The advantage of the p-value approach is that you don't have to choose a significance level α ahead of time. Because it is far from obvious what value of α to choose in any particular situation, this is certainly an advantage. Another compelling advantage is that p-values for standard hypothesis tests are included in virtually all statistical software output. In addition, all p-values can be interpreted in basically the same way: A small p-value provides support for the alternative hypothesis.

FUNDAMENTAL INSIGHT

Key Role of p-values

The single most important thing to remember from this chapter is the role of p-values. This is especially important because p-values are listed in virtually all outputs from statistical software. If a p-value is small, the result is statistically significant, meaning that the null hypothesis can be rejected in favor of the alternative.

Analysts don't always agree on how "small" a p-value needs to be—some say less than 0.01, some say less than 0.05, and some say less than 0.10. But just about all analysts agree that if a p-value is greater than 0.10, the result is *not* statistically significant, which means that there is not enough evidence to reject the null hypothesis.

9-2f Type II Errors and Power

A type II error occurs when the alternative hypothesis is true but there isn't enough evidence in the sample to reject the null hypothesis. This type of error is traditionally considered less important than a type I error, but it can lead to serious consequences in real situations. For example, in medical trials on a proposed new cancer drug, a type II error occurs if the new drug is really superior to existing drugs but experimental evidence is not sufficiently conclusive to warrant marketing the new drug. For patients suffering from cancer, this is obviously a serious error.

As we stated previously, the alternative hypothesis is typically the hypothesis a researcher wants to prove. If it is in fact true, the researcher wants to be able to reject the null hypothesis and hence avoid a type II error. The probability that she is able to do so is called the **power** of the test—that is, the power is 1 minus the probability of a type II error. There are several ways to achieve high power, the most obvious of which is to increase sample size. By sampling more members of the population, you are better able to see whether the alternative is really true and hence avoid a type II error if the alternative is indeed true. As in the previous chapter, there are formulas that specify the sample size required to achieve a certain power for a given set of hypotheses. We will not pursue these in this book, but you should be aware that they exist.

The **power** of a test is 1 minus the probability of a type II error. It is the probability of rejecting the null hypothesis when the alternative hypothesis is true.

9-2g Hypothesis Tests and Confidence Intervals

The results of hypothesis tests are often accompanied by confidence intervals. This provides two complementary ways to interpret the data. However, there is a more formal connection between the two, at least for two-tailed tests. Let α be the stated significance level of the test. We will state the connection for the most commonly used level, $\alpha = 0.05$, although it extends to any α value. The connection is that the null hypothesis can be rejected at the 5% significance level if and only if a 95% confidence interval does *not* include the hypothesized value of the parameter.

When using a confidence interval to perform a two-tailed hypothesis test, reject the null hypothesis if and only if the hypothesized value does *not* lie inside a confidence interval for the parameter.

As an example, consider the test of $H_0{:}\mu = 0$ versus $H_a{:}\mu \neq 0$. Suppose a 95% confidence interval for μ extends from 1.35 to 3.42, so that it does *not* include the hypothesized value 0. Then H_0 can be rejected at the 5% significance level, and the *p*-value from the sample must be less than 0.05. On the other hand, if a 95% confidence interval for μ extends, say, from -1.25 to 2.31 (negative to positive), the null hypothesis cannot be rejected at the 5% significance level, and the *p*-value must be greater than 0.05.

There is also a correspondence between one-tailed hypothesis tests and *one-sided* confidence intervals, but we will not pursue it here.

9-2h Practical versus Statistical Significance

We have stated that statistically significant results are those that produce sufficiently small *p*-values. In other words, **statistically significant results** are those that provide strong evidence in support of the alternative hypothesis. You frequently hear about studies, particularly in the medical sciences, that produce statistically significant results. For example, you might hear that mice injected with one kind of drug develop significantly more cancer cells than mice injected with a second kind of drug.

The point of this section is that such results are not necessarily significant in terms of *importance*. They might be significant only in the statistical sense. An example of what could happen is the following. An education researcher wants to see whether quantitative SAT scores differ, on average, across gender. He sets up the hypotheses $H_0{:}\mu_M = \mu_F$ versus $H_a{:}\mu_M \neq \mu_F$, where μ_M and μ_F are the mean quantitative SAT scores for males and females, respectively. He then randomly samples scores from 4000 males and 4000 females and finds the male and female sample averages to be 521 and 524. He also finds that the sample standard deviation for each group is about 50. Based on these numbers, the *p*-value for the sample data is approximately 0.007. (You will learn how to make this calculation later in the chapter.) Therefore, he claims that the results are significant proof that males do score differently (lower) than females.

If you read these results in a newspaper, your immediate reaction might be, "Who cares?" After all, the difference between 521 and 524 is not very large from a practical point of view. So why does the education researcher get to make his claim? The reasoning is as follows. In all likelihood, the means μ_M and μ_F are not *exactly* equal. There is bound to be some difference between genders over the entire population. If the researcher takes large enough samples—and 4000 is plenty large—he is almost certain to obtain enough evidence to "prove" that the means are not equal. That is, he will almost surely obtain *statistically* significant results. However, the difference he finds, as in the numbers we quoted, might be of little *practical* significance. No one really cares whether females score three points higher or lower than males. If the difference were on the order of 30 to 40 points, then the result would be more interesting.

As this example illustrates, there is always a possibility of statistical significance but not practical significance with large sample sizes. To be fair, we should also mention the opposite case, which typically occurs with small sample sizes. Here the results are sometimes not *statistically* significant even though the truth about the population(s), if it were known, would be of *practical* significance. Let's assume that a medical researcher wants to test whether a new form of treatment produces a higher cure rate for a deadly disease than the best treatment currently on the market. Due to expenses, the researcher is able to run a controlled experiment on only a relatively small number of patients with the disease. Unfortunately, the results of the experiment are inconclusive. They show some evidence that the new treatment works better, but the *p*-value for the test is only 0.25.

In the scientific community these results would not be enough to warrant a switch to the new treatment. However, it is certainly possible that the new treatment, if it were used on a large number of patients, would provide a "significant" improvement in the cure rate—where "significant" now means *practical* significance. In this type of situation, the researcher could easily fail to discover practical significance because the sample sizes are not large enough to detect it statistically.

From here on, when we use the term "significant," we mean *statistically* significant. However, you should always keep the ideas in this section in mind. A statistically significant result is not necessarily of practical importance. Conversely, a result that fails to be statistically significant is not necessarily one that should be ignored.

Extremely large samples can easily lead to statistically significant results that are not practically significant. In contrast, small samples can fail to produce statistically significant results that might indeed be practically significant.

9-3 HYPOTHESIS TESTS FOR A POPULATION MEAN

Now that we have covered the general concepts behind hypothesis testing and the principal sampling distributions (in the previous two chapters), the mechanics of hypothesis testing are fairly straightforward. We discuss in some detail how the procedure works for a population mean. Then in later sections we illustrate similar hypothesis tests for other parameters.

As with confidence intervals, the key to the analysis is the sampling distribution of the sample mean. Recall that if you subtract the true mean μ from the sample mean and divide the difference by the standard error $s/\sqrt{n}$, the result has a t distribution with $n - 1$ degrees of freedom. In a hypothesis-testing context, the true mean to use is the null hypothesis value, specifically, the borderline value between the null and alternative hypotheses. This value is usually labeled μ_0, where the subscript indicates that it is based on the *null* hypothesis.

To run the test, referred to as the **t test for a population mean**, you calculate the *test statistic* in Equation (9.1). This t-value indicates how many standard errors the sample mean is from the null value, μ_0. If the null hypothesis is true, or more specifically, if $\mu = \mu_0$, this test statistic has a t distribution with $n - 1$ degrees of freedom. The *p*-value for the test is the probability beyond the test statistic in both tails (for a two-tailed alternative) or in a single tail (for a one-tailed alternative) of the t distribution.

> **Test Statistic for Test of Mean**
>
> $$t\text{-value} = \frac{\overline{X} - \mu_0}{s/\sqrt{n}} \qquad (9.1)$$

We illustrate the procedure by continuing the pizza manager's problem in Example 9.1.

EXAMPLE | **9.1 A NEW PIZZA STYLE AT PEPPERONI PIZZA RESTAURANT (CONTINUED)**

Recall that the manager of Pepperoni Pizza Restaurant is running an experiment to test the hypotheses $H_0{:}\mu \leq 0$ versus $H_a{:}\mu > 0$, where μ is the mean rating in the entire customer population. Here, each customer rates the difference between an old-style pizza and a new-style pizza on a scale from -10 to $+10$, where negative ratings favor the old style and positive ratings favor the new style. The ratings for 40 randomly selected customers and several summary statistics appear in Figure 9.3. (See the file **Pizza Ratings.xlsx**.) Is there sufficient evidence from these sample data for the manager to reject H_0?

Figure 9.3

Data and Summary
Measures for Pizza
Example

	A	B
1	Customer	Rating
2	1	−7
3	2	7
4	3	−2
5	4	4
39	38	3
40	39	5
41	40	−6

© Cengage Learning

Objective To use a one-sample t test to see whether consumers prefer the new-style pizza to the old style.

Solution

From the summary statistics, we see that the sample mean is $\overline{X} = 2.10$ and the sample standard deviation is $s = 4.717$. This positive sample mean provides some evidence in favor of the alternative hypothesis, but given the rather large value of s and the box plot of ratings in Figure 9.4, which indicates a lot of negative ratings, does it provide *enough* evidence to reject H_0?

To run the test, you calculate the test statistic, using the borderline null hypothesis value $\mu_0 = 0$, and report how much probability is beyond it in the right tail of the appropriate t distribution. The *right* tail is appropriate because the alternative is one-tailed of the "greater than" variety. The test statistic is

$$t\text{-value} = \frac{2.10 - 0}{4.717/\sqrt{40}} = 2.816$$

Figure 9.4

Box Plot for Pizza
Data

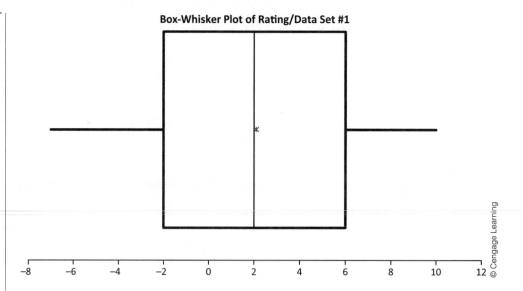

Box-Whisker Plot of Rating/Data Set #1

© Cengage Learning

This t-value indicates that the sample mean is slightly more than 2.8 standard errors to the right of the null value, 0. Intuitively, this provides a lot of evidence in favor of the alternative—it is quite unlikely to see a sample mean 2.8 standard errors to the right of a "true" mean. The probability beyond this value in the right tail of a t distribution with $n - 1 = 39$ degrees of freedom is approximately 0.004, which can be found in Excel® with the formula **=TDIST(2.816,39,1)**. (Recall that the first argument is the t-value, the second is the degrees of freedom, and the third is the number of tails. Better yet, recall that this value can be calculated in Excel 2010 and later versions with the more intuitive formula **=T.DIST.RT(2.816,39)**.)

This probability, 0.004, is the p-value for the test. It indicates that these sample results would be *very* unlikely if the null hypothesis were true. The manager has two choices at this point. He can conclude that the null hypothesis is true and he obtained a very unlikely sample, or he can conclude that the alternative hypothesis is true—and presumably switch to the new-style pizza. This second conclusion certainly appears to be the more reasonable choice.

Another way of interpreting the results of the test is in terms of traditional significance levels. The null hypothesis can be rejected at the 1% significance level because the p-value is less than 0.01. Of course, it can also be rejected at the 5% level or the 10% level because the p-value is also less than 0.05 and 0.10. But the p-value is the preferred way to report the results because it indicates exactly *how* significant these sample results are.

The StatTools One-Sample Hypothesis Test procedure can be used to perform this analysis easily, with the results shown in Figure 9.5. To use it, create a StatTools data set and select Hypothesis Test and then Mean/Std. Deviation from the StatTools Statistical Inference dropdown list. Then fill out the resulting dialog box as shown in Figure 9.6. In particular, make sure the Analysis Type is One-Sample Analysis and the Alternative Hypothesis Type is the "Greater Than" choice.

Most of the output in Figure 9.5 should be familiar: It mirrors the calculations we just did, and you can check the formulas in the output cells to ensure that you understand the procedure. Note the following. First, the value in cell E13, 0, is the null hypothesis value μ_0 at the borderline between H_0 and H_a; it is the value specified in the dialog box in Figure 9.6. Second, look at the note entered in cell D9. (This note isn't visible in Figure 9.5, but it can be seen in the completed file.) It reminds you that this test is based on the normality of the underlying population distribution and/or a sufficiently large sample

Figure 9.5

Hypothesis Test for
the Mean for the
Pizza Example

	D	E
8		Rating
9	*Hypothesis Test (One-Sample)*	Data Set #1
10	Sample Size	40
11	Sample Mean	2.100
12	Sample Std Dev	4.717
13	Hypothesized Mean	0
14	Alternative Hypothesis	>0
15	Standard Error of Mean	0.746
16	Degrees of Freedom	39
17	*t*-Test Statistic	2.8159
18	*p*-Value	0.0038
19	Null Hypoth. at 10% Significance	Reject
20	Null Hypoth. at 5% Significance	Reject
21	Null Hypoth. at 1% Significance	Reject

© Cengage Learning

Figure 9.6

One-Sample
Hypothesis Test
Dialog Box

© Cengage Learning

size. If these conditions are not satisfied (which is not a problem for this example), then other more appropriate tests are available. Finally, StatTools compares the *p*-value to the three traditional significance levels, 1%, 5%, and 10%, and interprets significance in terms of these. As indicated in cells E19, E20, and E21, the null hypothesis can be rejected in favor of the alternative at each of these three significance levels. ∎

Test Statistics and *p*-values

All hypothesis tests are implemented by calculating a test statistic from the data and seeing how far out this test statistic is in one or both tails of some well-known distribution. The details of this procedure might or might not be included in the output from statistical software, but the *p*-value is always included. The *p*-value specifies the probability in the tail (or tails) beyond the test statistic. In words, it measures how unlikely such an extreme value of the test statistic is if the null hypothesis is true.

Before leaving this example, we ask one last question. Should the manager switch to the new-style pizza on the basis of these sample results? We would probably recommend "yes." There is no indication that the new-style pizza costs any more to make than the old-style pizza, and the sample evidence is fairly convincing that customers, on average, prefer the new-style pizza. Therefore, unless there are reasons for not switching that we haven't mentioned here, we recommend the switch. However, if it costs more to make the new-style pizza (and its price is no higher), hypothesis testing is *not* the best way to perform the decision analysis. We return to this theme throughout this chapter.

Example 9.1 illustrates how to run and interpret any one-tailed hypothesis for the mean, assuming the alternative is of the "greater than" variety. If the alternative is still one-tailed but of the "less than" variety, there is virtually no change. We illustrate this in Figure 9.7, where the ratings have been reversed in sign. That is, each rating was multiplied by −1, so that negative ratings now favor the new-style pizza. The hypotheses are now $H_0: \mu \geq 0$ versus $H_a: \mu < 0$ because a negative mean now supports the new style. The only difference in running the analysis with StatTools is that you select the "Less Than" choice for the Alternative Analysis Type in the dialog box shown in Figure 9.6. As Figure 9.7 indicates, the test statistic is now the negative of the previous test statistic, −2.816, and the *p*-value, 0.004, is exactly the same. This is now the probability in the *left* tail of the *t* distribution, but the interpretation of the results is the same as before.

Figure 9.7

Hypothesis Test with Reverse Coding

	A	B	C	D	E
1	Customer	Rating			**Rating**
2	1	7		*Hypothesis Test (One-Sample)*	Data Set #2
3	2	−7		Sample Size	40
4	3	2		Sample Mean	−2.100
5	4	−4		Sample Std Dev	4.717
6	5	−7		Hypothesized Mean	0
7	6	−6		Alternative Hypothesis	<0
8	7	0		Standard Error of Mean	0.746
9	8	−2		Degrees of Freedom	39
10	9	−8		*t*-Test Statistic	−2.8159
11	10	−2		*p*-Value	0.0038
12	11	−3		Null Hypoth. at 10% Significance	Reject
13	12	4		Null Hypoth. at 5% Significance	Reject
14	13	−8		Null Hypoth. at 1% Significance	Reject
15	14	5			
40	39	−5			
41	40	6			

© Cengage Learning

The analysis of two-tailed tests for the mean is also quite similar to the analysis in Example 9.1. A typical two-tailed test is illustrated in Example 9.2.

9.2 MEASURING STUDENT REACTION TO A NEW TEXTBOOK

A large, required chemistry course at State University has been using the same textbook for a number of years. Over the years, the students have been asked to rate this textbook on 10-point scale, and the average rating has been stable at about 5.2. This year, the faculty decided to experiment with a new textbook. After the course, 50 randomly selected students were asked to rate this new textbook, also on a scale of 1 to 10. The results appear in column B of Figure 9.8. (See the file **Textbook Ratings.xlsx**.) Can we conclude that the students like this new textbook any more or less than the previous textbook?

Figure 9.8   Test of Two-Tailed Alternative

	A	B	C	D	E
1	Student	Rating		Mean rating of previous textbook	5.2
2	1	6			
3	2	3			**Rating**
4	3	6		*Hypothesis Test (One-Sample)*	**Data Set #1**
5	4	7		**Sample Size**	50
6	5	6		**Sample Mean**	5.680
7	6	10		**Sample Std Dev**	1.953
8	7	6		**Hypothesized Mean**	5.2
9	8	8		**Alternative Hypothesis**	<> 5.2
10	9	7		**Standard Error of Mean**	0.276
11	10	10		**Degrees of Freedom**	49
12	11	3		*t*-**Test Statistic**	1.738
13	12	6		*p*-**Value**	0.088
14	13	4		**Null Hypoth. at 10% Significance**	Reject
15	14	6		**Null Hypoth. at 5% Significance**	Don't Reject
16	15	8		**Null Hypoth. at 1% Significance**	Don't Reject
17	16	10			
18	17	5			**Rating**
19	18	4		*Conf. Intervals (One-Sample)*	**Data Set #1**
20	19	6		**Sample Size**	50
21	20	4		**Sample Mean**	5.680
22	21	6		**Sample Std Dev**	1.953
23	22	6		**Confidence Level (Mean)**	95.0%
24	23	4		**Degrees of Freedom**	49
25	24	5		**Lower Limit**	5.125
26	25	7		**Upper Limit**	6.235
27	26	8			
50	49	6			
51	50	5			

Objective   To use a one-sample *t* test, with a two-tailed alternative, to see whether students like the new textbook any more or less than the old textbook.

Solution

The first question is whether the test should be one-tailed or two-tailed. Of course, the faculty have chosen the new textbook with the expectation that it will be preferred by the students, but it is very possible that students will like it *less* than the previous textbook.

(Students are notoriously unpredictable in their acceptance of textbooks.) Therefore, we set this up as a two-tailed test—that is, the alternative hypothesis is that the mean rating of the new textbook is either less than *or* greater than the mean rating of the previous textbook. Formally, we write the hypotheses as $H_0: \mu = 5.2$ versus $H_a: \mu \neq 5.2$.

The test is run (and the StatTools One-Sample Hypothesis Test procedure can be used) almost exactly as with a one-tailed test. The only difference is that you specify the "Not Equal" choice for the Alternative Hypothesis Type, and the Null Hypothesis Value is now 5.2, the historical average rating. (See Figure 9.9.) The t-distributed test statistic is calculated in the same way as before:

$$t\text{-value} = \frac{\overline{X} - 5.2}{s/\sqrt{n}} = \frac{5.680 - 5.2}{1.953/\sqrt{50}} = 1.738$$

The p-value is then the probability beyond -1.738 in the left tail *and* beyond $+1.738$ in the right tail of a t distribution with $n - 1 = 49$ degrees of freedom. The effect is to double the one-tailed p-value. From the output (cell E13) in Figure 9.8, you can see that the two-tailed p-value is 0.088.

Figure 9.9

Dialog Box for Two-Tailed Hypothesis Test

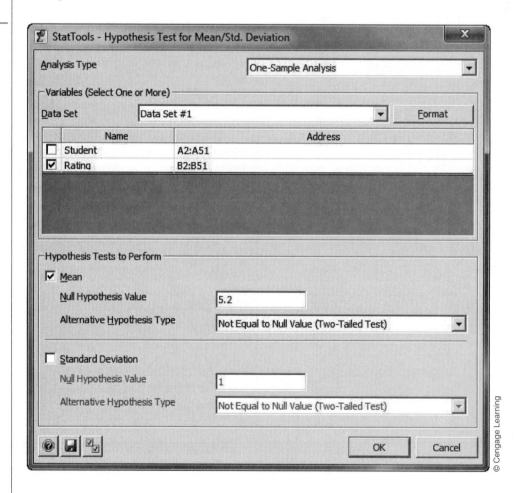

© Cengage Learning

This moderately small p-value provides some evidence, but not absolutely convincing evidence, that the mean rating of the new textbook is different from the old mean rating of 5.2. Specifically, the output indicates that the null hypothesis can be rejected at the 10% level, but not at the 5% or 1% levels. If the p-value were lower (which might occur if more students were sampled), the evidence would be more conclusive. As in Example 9.1, we can now ask whether the faculty should continue to use the new textbook. Here again, it is probably not a decision that hypothesis testing, at least by itself, should determine. The students *appear* to favor the new textbook, if only by a small margin. If the faculty also favor it, we see no reason for not switching to it.

Because this is a two-tailed test, you could also perform the test by appealing to confidence intervals. A 95% confidence interval for the mean rating of the new textbook, also shown in Figure 9.8, extends from 5.125 to 6.235. Because this interval *does* include the old mean rating of 5.2, the null hypothesis cannot be rejected at the 5% significance level. This is in agreement with the *p*-value of the test, which is greater than 0.05. However, you can check that a 90% confidence interval for the mean does *not* include 5.2. Therefore, the null hypothesis can be rejected at the 10% level. This too is in agreement with the *p*-value, which is less than 0.10. ∎

PROBLEMS

Note: Student solutions for problems whose numbers appear within a colored box are available for purchase at www.cengagebrain.com.

Level A

1. The file **P09_01.xlsx** contains a random sample of 100 lightbulb lifetimes. The company that produces these lightbulbs wants to know whether it can claim that its lightbulbs typically last more than 1000 burning hours.
   a. Identify the null and alternative hypotheses for this situation.
   b. Can this lightbulb manufacturer claim that its lightbulbs typically last more than 1000 hours at the 5% significance level? What about at the 1% significance level? Explain your answers.

2. A manufacturer is interested in determining whether it can claim that the boxes of detergent it sells contain, on average, more than 500 grams of detergent. The firm selects a random sample of 100 boxes and records the amount of detergent (in grams) in each box. The data are provided in the file **P09_02.xlsx**.
   a. Identify the null and alternative hypotheses for this situation.
   b. Is there statistical support for the manufacturer's claim? Explain.

3. A producer of steel cables wants to know whether the steel cables it produces have an average breaking strength of 5000 pounds. An average breaking strength of less than 5000 pounds would not be adequate, and to produce steel cables with an average breaking strength in excess of 5000 pounds would unnecessarily increase production costs. The producer collects a random sample of 64 steel cable pieces. The breaking strength for each of these cable pieces is recorded in the file **P09_03.xlsx**.
   a. Identify the null and alternative hypotheses for this situation.
   b. Using a 5% significance level, what statistical conclusion can the producer reach regarding the average breaking strength of its steel cables? Would the conclusion be any different at the 1% level? Explain your answers.

4. A U.S. Navy recruiting center knows from past experience that the heights of its recruits have traditionally been normally distributed with mean 69 inches. The recruiting center wants to test the claim that the average height of this year's recruits is greater than 69 inches. To do this, recruiting personnel take a random sample of 64 recruits from this year and record their heights. The data are provided in the file **P09_04.xlsx**.
   a. Identify the null and alternative hypotheses for this situation.
   b. On the basis of the available sample information, do the recruiters find support for the given claim at the 5% significance level? Explain.
   c. Use the sample data to construct a 95% confidence interval for the average height of this year's recruits. Based on this confidence interval, what conclusion should recruiting personnel reach regarding the given claim?

5. Suppose that you wish to test $H_0 : \mu \leq 10$ versus $H_a : \mu > 10$ at the $\alpha = 0.05$ significance level. Furthermore, suppose that you observe values of the sample mean and sample standard deviation when $n = 40$ that do *not* lead to the rejection of H_0. Is it true that you might reject H_0 if you observed the same values of the sample mean and sample standard deviation from a sample with $n > 40$? Why or why not?

Level B

6. A study is performed in a large southern town to determine whether the average weekly grocery bill per four-person family in the town is significantly different from the national average. A random sample of the weekly grocery bills of two-person families in this town is given in the file **P09_06.xlsx**. Assume the national average weekly grocery bill for a two-person family is $100.
   a. Identify the null and alternative hypotheses for this situation.
   b. Is the sample evidence statistically significant? If so, at what significance levels can you reject the null hypothesis?

c. For which values of the sample mean (i.e., average weekly grocery bill) would you reject the null hypothesis at the 1% significance level? For which values of the sample mean would you reject the null hypothesis at the 10% level?

7. An aircraft manufacturer needs to buy aluminum sheets with an average thickness of 0.05 inch. The manufacturer knows that significantly thinner sheets would be unsafe and considerably thicker sheets would be too heavy. A random sample of 100 sheets from a potential supplier is collected. The thickness of each sheet in this sample is measured (in inches) and recorded in the file **P09_07.xlsx**.

   a. Identify the null and alternative hypotheses for this situation.

b. Based on the results of an appropriate hypothesis test, should the aircraft manufacturer buy aluminum sheets from this supplier? Explain why or why not.

   c. For which values of the sample mean (i.e., average thickness) would the aircraft manufacturer decide to buy sheets from this supplier? Assume a significance level of 5% in answering this question.

8. Suppose that you observe a random sample of size n from a normally distributed population. If you are able to reject H_0:$\mu = \mu_0$ in favor of a two-tailed alternative hypothesis at the 10% significance level, is it true that you can definitely reject H_0 in favor of the appropriate one-tailed alternative at the 5% significance level? Why or why not?

9-4 HYPOTHESIS TESTS FOR OTHER PARAMETERS

Just as we developed confidence intervals for a variety of parameters, we can develop hypothesis tests for other parameters. They are based on the same sampling distributions discussed in the previous chapter, and they are run and interpreted exactly as the tests for the mean in the previous section. In each case the sample data are used to calculate a test statistic that has a well-known sampling distribution. Then a corresponding p-value measures the support for the alternative hypothesis. Beyond this, only the details change, as we illustrate in this section.

9-4a Hypothesis Tests for a Population Proportion

To test a population proportion p, recall that the sample proportion $\hat{p}$ has a sampling distribution that is approximately normal when the sample size is reasonably large. Specifically, the distribution of the standardized value

$$\frac{\hat{p} - p}{\sqrt{p(1 - p)/n}}$$

is approximately normal with mean 0 and standard deviation 1. This leads to the following **z test for a population proportion**.

Let p_0 be the borderline value of p between the null and alternative hypotheses. Then p_0 is substituted for p to obtain the test statistic in Equation (9.2). The p-value of the test is found by seeing how much probability is beyond this test statistic in the tail (or tails) of the standard normal distribution.[2] A rule of thumb for checking the large-sample assumption of this test is to check whether $np_0 > 5$ and $n(1 - p_0) > 5$.

Test Statistic for Test of Proportion

$$z\text{-value} = \frac{\hat{p} - p_0}{\sqrt{p_0(1 - p_0)/n}} \tag{9.2}$$

Example 9.3 illustrates this test of proportion.

[2]Do not confuse the unknown proportion p with the p-value of the test. They are logically different concepts and just happen, by tradition, to share the same letter p.

EXAMPLE | **9.3 CUSTOMER COMPLAINTS AT WALPOLE APPLIANCE COMPANY**

Walpole Appliance Company has a customer service department that handles customer questions and complaints. This department's processes are set up to respond quickly and accurately to customers who phone in their concerns. However, there is a sizable minority of customers who prefer to write letters. Traditionally, the customer service department has not been very efficient in responding to these customers.

Letter writers first receive a mailgram asking them to call customer service (which is exactly what letter writers wanted to avoid in the first place), and when they do call, the customer service representative who answers the phone typically has no knowledge of the customer's problem. As a result, the department manager estimates that 15% of letter writers have not obtained a satisfactory response within 30 days of the time their letters were first received. The manager's goal is to reduce this value by at least half, that is, to 7.5% or less.

To do so, she changes the process for responding to letter writers. Under the new process, these customers now receive a prompt and courteous form letter that responds to their problem. (This is possible because the vast majority of concerns can be addressed by one of several form letters.) Each form letter states that if the customer still has problems, he or she can call the department. The manager also files the original letters so that if customers do call back, the representative who answers will be able to find their letters quickly and respond intelligently. With this new process in place, the manager has tracked 400 letter writers and has found that only 23 of them are classified as "unsatisfied" after a 30-day period. Does it appear that the manager has achieved her goal?

Objective To use a test for a proportion to see whether the new process of responding to complaint letters results in an acceptably low proportion of unsatisfied customers.

Solution

The manager's goal is to reduce the proportion of unsatisfied customers after 30 days from 0.15 to 0.075 or less. Because the burden of proof is on her to "prove" that she has accomplished this goal, we set up the hypotheses as $H_0: p \geq 0.075$ versus $H_a: p < 0.075$, where p is the proportion of all letter writers who are still unsatisfied after 30 days. The sample proportion she has observed is $\hat{p} = 23/400 = 0.0575$. This is obviously less than 0.075, but is it *enough* less to reject the null hypothesis?

The test can be run with StatTools, as shown in Figure 9.10 and in the file **Customer Complaints.xlsx**. The trick is to arrange the data in one of the three formats for a StatTools proportions analysis, as described in Section 8-5 of the previous chapter. (Refer to the finished version of the file **Satisfaction Ratings.xlsx** in the previous chapter for more details.) For this example, the data are arranged as shown in the range A5:B7. This is the StatTools data set, a table of counts. Then you run the test by selecting Hypothesis Test/Proportion from the Statistical Inference dropdown list and filling in the dialog box as shown in Figure 9.11. The results of the test appear in column E of Figure 9.10. Specifically, the sample proportion is $23/400 = 0.058$, its standard error is 0.013, the test statistic is -1.329, and the p-value for the test is 0.092.

The p-value might not be as low as you expected—or as low as the manager would like. In spite of the fact that the sample proportion appears to be well below the target proportion of 0.075, the evidence in support of the alternative hypothesis is not overwhelming. In statistical terminology, the results are significant at the 10% level, but not at the 5% or 1% levels.

Figure 9.10 also shows a 95% confidence interval for the unknown proportion p. This confidence interval extends from 0.035 to 0.080. It includes the target value, 0.075, but just

Figure 9.10   Analysis of New Process for Letter Writers

	A	B	C	D	E	F
1	**Test of a proportion: responding to customer complaint letters**					**Count**
2					**Hypothesis Test (Proportion)**	**Data Set #1**
3	Target proportion with new procedure	0.075			Category	Number of unsatisfied customers
4					Sample Size	400
5	Category	Count			Sample Proportion	0.058
6	Number of unsatisfied customers	23			Hypothesized Proportion	0.075
7	Number of satisfied customers	377			Alternative Hypothesis	<0.075
8					Standard Error of Sample Proportion	0.013
9					z-Test Statistic	−1.3288
10					p-Value	0.0920
11					Null Hypoth. at 10% Significance	Reject
12					Null Hypoth. at 5% Significance	Don't Reject
13					Null Hypoth. at 1% Significance	Don't Reject
14						
15						**Count**
16					**Conf. Interval (Proportion)**	**Data Set #1**
17					Category	Number of unsatisfied customers
18					Sample Size	400
19					Sample Proportion	0.058
20					Confidence Level	95.0%
21					Standard Error of Proportion	0.012
22					Lower Limit	0.035
23					Upper Limit	0.080

© Cengage Learning

Figure 9.11

Dialog Box for a
Test of a Proportion

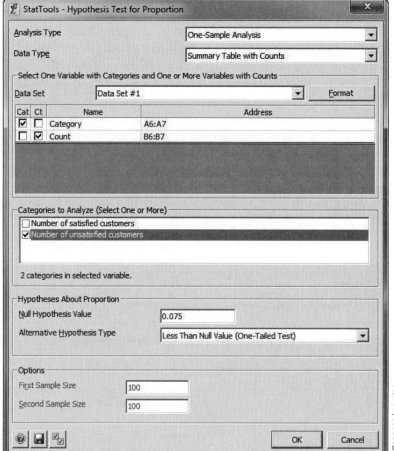

© Cengage Learning

barely. In this sense it also provides some support for the argument that the manager has indeed achieved her goal.[3]

Analysts might disagree on whether a hypothesis test or a confidence interval is the more appropriate way to present these results. However, we see them as complementary and do not necessarily favor one over the other. The bottom line is that they both provide some, but not totally conclusive, evidence that the manager has achieved her goal. ■

9-4b Hypothesis Tests for Differences between Population Means

This comparison problem—comparing two population means—is one of the most important problems analyzed with statistical methods. It can be analyzed with confidence intervals, hypothesis tests, or both.

We now discuss the comparison problem, where the **difference between two population means** is tested. As in the previous chapter, the form of the analysis depends on whether the two samples are independent or paired. For variety, we begin with the paired case.

If the samples are paired, then the test, referred to as the *t* **test for difference between means from paired samples**, proceeds exactly as in Section 9-3, using the differences as the single variable of analysis. That is, if $\overline{D}$ is the sample mean difference between n pairs, D_0 is the hypothesized difference (the borderline value between H_0 and H_a), and s_D is the sample standard deviation of the differences, then the test is based on the test statistic in Equation (9.3). If D_0 is the true mean difference, this test statistic has a t distribution with $n - 1$ degrees of freedom. The validity of the test also requires that n be reasonably large and/or the population of *differences* be approximately normally distributed.

Test Statistic for Paired Samples Test of Difference Between Means

$$t\text{-value} = \frac{\overline{D} - D_0}{s_D/\sqrt{n}}$$

(9.3)

In contrast, if the samples are independent, the test is referred to as the *t* **test for difference between means from independent samples**. If the population standard deviations are equal, the two-sample theory discussed in Section 8-7 is relevant. It leads to the test statistic in Equation (9.4). Here, $\overline{X}_1$ and $\overline{X}_2$ are the two sample means, D_0 is the hypothesized difference, n_1 and n_2 are the sample sizes, and s_p is the same pooled estimate of the common population standard deviation as in the previous chapter:

$$s_p = \sqrt{\frac{(n_1 - 1)s_1^2 + (n_2 - 1)s_1^2}{n_1 + n_2 - 2}}$$

If D_0 is the true mean difference, this test statistic has a t distribution with $n_1 + n_2 - 2$ degrees of freedom. The validity of this test again requires that the sample sizes be reasonably large and/or the populations be approximately normally distributed.

Test Statistic for Independent Samples Test of Difference Between Means

$$t\text{-value} = \frac{(\overline{X}_1 - \overline{X}_2) - D_0}{s_p\sqrt{1/n_1 + 1/n_2}}$$

(9.4)

---

[3]Note that the standard error in cell E10 for the hypothesis test uses the target proportion 0.075. In contrast, the standard error for the confidence interval in cell E23 uses the sample proportion 0.0575. The sampling distribution for a hypothesis test always uses the borderline value between H_0 and H_a. But because confidence intervals are not connected to any hypotheses, their standard errors must rely on sample data. In most cases the two standard errors are practically the same.

Fortunately, these formulas are implemented automatically by StatTools's procedures. Example 9.4 illustrates an example of the paired-sample *t* test.

EXAMPLE

9.4 Measuring the Effects of Traditional and New Styles of Soft-Drink Cans

Beer and soft-drink companies have become very concerned about the style of their cans. There are cans with fluted and embossed sides and cans with six-color graphics and holograms. Coca-Cola has even introduced a contoured can, shaped like the old-fashioned Coke bottle minus the neck. Evidently, these companies believe the style of the can makes a difference to consumers, which presumably translates into higher sales.

Assume that a soft-drink company is considering a style change to its current can, which has been the company's trademark for many years. To determine whether this new style is popular with consumers, the company runs a number of focus group sessions around the country. At each of these sessions, randomly selected consumers are allowed to examine the new and traditional styles, exchange ideas, and offer their opinions. Eventually, they fill out a form where, among other questions, they are asked to respond to the following items, each on a scale of 1 to 7, 7 being the best:

- Rate the attractiveness of the traditional-style can (AO).
- Rate the attractiveness of the new-style can (AN).
- Rate the likelihood that you would buy the product with the traditional-style can (WBO).
- Rate the likelihood that you would buy the product with the new-style can (WBN).

(A and WB stand for "attractiveness" and "would buy," and O and N stand for "old" and "new.") What can the company conclude from these data? (See the file **Soft-Drink Cans.xlsx**.) Are hypothesis tests appropriate?

Objective To use paired-sample *t* tests for differences between means to see whether consumers rate the attractiveness, and their likelihood to purchase, higher for a new-style can than for the traditional-style can.

Solution

First, it is a good idea to examine summary statistics for the data. The averages from each survey item are shown at the bottom of Figure 9.12. They indicate some support for the new-style

Figure 9.12

Data on Soft-Drink Cans

	A	B	C	D	E
1	Consumer	AO	AN	WBO	WBN
2	1	5	7	4	1
3	2	7	7	6	6
4	3	6	7	7	6
5	4	1	3	1	1
6	5	3	4	1	1
179	178	5	4	4	3
180	179	3	4	1	3
181	180	3	5	6	7
182					
183	Averages	4.41	4.95	3.86	4.34

© Cengage Learning

can. Also, you might expect the ratings for a given consumer to be correlated. This turns out to be the case, as shown by the relatively large positive correlations in Figure 9.13. These large positive correlations indicate that if you want to examine differences between survey items, a paired-sample procedure will make the most efficient use of the data. Of course, a paired-sample procedure also makes sense because each consumer answers each item on the form. (If this is confusing, think about the following alternative setup, where there are four *separate* groups of consumers. The first group responds to item 1 only, the second group responds to item 2 only, and so on. Then the responses to the various items are in no way paired, and an *independent-sample* procedure would be used instead. However, this experimental design is not as efficient as the paired design in terms of making the best use of a given amount of data.)

Figure 9.13

Correlations for Soft-Drink Can Data

	A	B	C	D	E
7		**AO**	**AN**	**WBO**	**WBN**
8	*Correlation Table*	Data Set #1	Data Set #1	Data Set #1	Data Set #1
9	AO	1.000			
10	AN	0.74 0	1.000		
11	WBO	0.746	0.595	1.000	
12	WBN	0.594	0.401	0.774	1.000

There are several differences of interest. The two most obvious are the difference between the attractiveness ratings of the two styles and the difference between the likelihoods of buying the two styles—that is, column B minus column C and column D minus column E. A third difference of interest is the difference between the attractiveness ratings of the new style and the likelihoods of buying the new can—that is, column C minus column E. This difference indicates whether *perceptions* of the new-style can are likely to translate into actual *sales*. Finally, a fourth difference that might be of interest is the difference between the third difference (column C minus column E) and the similar difference for the old style (column B minus column D). This checks whether the translation of perceptions into sales is any different for the two styles of cans.

All of these differences appear next to the original data in Figure 9.14. In terms of the original data, they are labeled as:

- Diff1: AO – AN
- Diff2: WBO – WBN
- Diff3: AN – WBN
- Diff4: AO – WBO
- Diff5: (AN – WBN) – (AO – WBO)

Figure 9.14 **Original and Difference Variables for Soft-Drink Can Data**

	A	B	C	D	E	F	G	H	I	J
1	Consumer	AO	AN	WBO	WBN	AO–AN	WBO–WBN	AN–WBN	AO–WBO	(AN–WBN)–(AO–WBO)
2	1	5	7	4	1	−2	3	6	1	5
3	2	7	7	6	6	0	0	1	1	0
4	3	6	7	7	6	−1	1	1	−1	2
5	4	1	3	1	1	−2	0	2	0	2
6	5	3	4	1	1	−1	0	3	2	1
179	178	5	4	4	3	1	1	1	1	0
180	179	3	4	1	3	−1	−2	1	2	−1
181	180	3	5	6	7	−2	−1	−2	−3	1

These differences have been calculated in columns F through J. (Actually, StatTools's Paired-Sample procedure generates the required differences internally when it tests these differences. We manually inserted the differences in Figure 9.14 so that you can see them explicitly.)

For each of the differences, Diff1, Diff2, Diff3, and Diff5, you can test the mean difference over all potential consumers with a paired-sample analysis. (You actually run the one-sample procedure on the difference variables.) Exactly as in the previous chapter, each difference variable is treated as a *single* sample and the same *t* test as in Section 9-3 is run on this sample. (This means that the differences in columns F through J of Figure 9.14 should be included in the StatTools data set.) In each case the hypothesized difference, D_0, is 0. The only question is whether to run one-tailed or two-tailed tests. We suggest that the tests for Diff1, Diff2, and Diff5 be two-tailed tests and that the test on Diff3 be a one-tailed test with the alternative of the "greater than" variety. The reasoning is that the company probably has little idea which way the differences Diff1, Diff2, and Diff5 will go (positive or negative), whereas it expects that Diff3 to be positive on average. That is, the company expects consumers' ratings of the attractiveness of the new design to be larger, on average, than their likelihoods of purchasing the product. However, any of these hypotheses could be run as one-tailed or two-tailed tests. It depends on the prior beliefs of the company. In any case, to change a one-tailed *p*-value to a two-tailed *p*-value, all you need to do is multiply by 2. Similarly, you can change two-tailed *p*-values to one-tailed *p*-values by dividing by 2.

The results from the four tests appear in Figures 9.15 and 9.16. (These outputs also include 99% confidence intervals for the corresponding mean differences.) You can obtain each output for Diff1, Diff2, and Diff3 by selecting Confidence Interval or Hypothesis Test

Figure 9.15   Analysis of Diff1 and Diff2 Variables

	A	B	C	D	E
7		AO–AN			WBO–WBN
8	**Conf. Intervals (One-Sample)**	Data Set #1		**Conf. Intervals (One-Sample)**	Data Set #1
9	Sample Size	180		Sample Size	180
10	Sample Mean	−0.539		Sample Mean	−0.478
11	Sample Std Dev	1.351		Sample Std Dev	1.347
12	Confidence Level (Mean)	99.0%		Confidence Level (Mean)	99.0%
13	Degrees of Freedom	179		Degrees of Freedom	179
14	Lower Limit	−0.801		Lower Limit	−0.739
15	Upper Limit	−0.277		Upper Limit	−0.216
16					
17		AO–AN			WBO–WBN
18	**Hypothesis Test (One-Sample)**	Data Set #1		**Hypothesis Test (One-Sample)**	Data Set #1
19	Sample Size	180		Sample Size	180
20	Sample Mean	−0.539		Sample Mean	−0.478
21	Sample Std Dev	1.351		Sample Std Dev	1.347
22	Hypothesized Mean	0		Hypothesized Mean	0
23	Alternative Hypothesis	<> 0		Alternative Hypothesis	<> 0
24	Standard Error of Mean	0.1007		Standard Error of Mean	0.1004
25	Degrees of Freedom	179		Degrees of Freedom	179
26	*t*-Test Statistic	−5.3514		*t*-Test Statistic	−4.7578
27	*p*-Value	< 0.0001		*p*-Value	< 0.0001
28	Null Hypoth. at 10% Significance	Reject		Null Hypoth. at 10% Significance	Reject
29	Null Hypoth. at 5% Significance	Reject		Null Hypoth. at 5% Significance	Reject
30	Null Hypoth. at 1% Significance	Reject		Null Hypoth. at 1% Significance	Reject

© Cengage Learning

Figure 9.16 Analysis of Diff3 and Diff5 Variables

◢	A	B	C	D	E
7		**AN–WBN**			**(AN–WBN)–(AO–WBO)**
8	*Conf. Intervals (One-Sample)*	Data Set #1		*Conf. Intervals (One-Sample)*	Data Set #1
9	Sample Size	180		Sample Size	180
10	Sample Mean	0.611		Sample Mean	0.061
11	Sample Std Dev	2.213		Sample Std Dev	2.045
12	Confidence Level (Mean)	99.0%		Confidence Level (Mean)	99.0%
13	Degrees of Freedom	179		Degrees of Freedom	179
14	Lower Limit	0.182		Lower Limit	−0.336
15	Upper Limit	1.041		Upper Limit	0.458
16					
17		**AN–WBN**			**(AN–WBN)–(AO–WBO)**
18	*Hypothesis Test (One-Sample)*	Data Set #1		*Hypothesis Test (One-Sample)*	Data Set #1
19	Sample Size	180		Sample Size	180
20	Sample Mean	0.611		Sample Mean	0.061
21	Sample Std Dev	2.213		Sample Std Dev	2.045
22	Hypothesized Mean	0		Hypothesized Mean	0
23	Alternative Hypothesis	>0		Alternative Hypothesis	<>0
24	Standard Error of Mean	0.1650		Standard Error of Mean	0.1524
25	Degrees of Freedom	179		Degrees of Freedom	179
26	*t*-Test Statistic	3.7046		*t*-Test Statistic	0.4010
27	*p*-Value	0.0001		*p*-Value	0.6889
28	Null Hypoth. at 10% Significance	Reject		Null Hypoth. at 10% Significance	Don't Reject
29	Null Hypoth. at 5% Significance	Reject		Null Hypoth. at 5% Significance	Don't Reject
30	Null Hypoth. at 1% Significance	Reject		Null Hypoth. at 1% Significance	Don't Reject

from the StatTools Statistical Inference dropdown list, used on the appropriate difference variable and the One-Sample analysis type.[4]

Results of the analysis of soft-drink can style

■ From the output for the Diff1 variable (AO – AN) in Figure 9.15, there is overwhelming evidence that consumers, on average, rate the attractiveness of the new design higher than the attractiveness of the current design. The *t*-distributed test statistic is −5.351, calculated as

$$\frac{-0.539 - 0}{0.101} = -5.351$$

The corresponding *p*-value for a two-tailed test of the mean difference is (to three decimal places) 0.000. A 99% confidence interval for the mean difference extends from −0.801 to −0.277. Note that this 99% confidence interval does *not* include the hypothesized value 0. This is consistent with the fact that the two-tailed *p*-value is less than 0.01. (Recall the relationship between confidence intervals and two-tailed hypothesis tests from Section 9-2g.)

■ The results are basically the same for the difference between consumers' likelihoods of buying the product with the two styles. (See the output for the Diff2 variable, WBO − WBN, in Figure 9.15.) Again, consumers are definitely more likely, on

---

[4]Because this can be a source of confusion, we repeat again that when you want to run a paired-sample analysis in StatTools, you can do it by creating the differences manually and then using the One-Sample option, or you can choose the Paired-Sample option and select the two original variables you want to compare, in which case StatTools creates the difference variable internally for you. The results are identical.

average, to buy the product with the new-style can. A 99% confidence interval for the mean difference extends from −0.739 to −0.216, which is again all negative.

■ The company's hypothesis that consumers' ratings of attractiveness of the new-style can are greater, on average, than their likelihoods of buying the product with this style can is confirmed. (See the output for the Diff3 variable, AN − WBN, in Figure 9.16.) The test statistic for this one-tailed test is 3.705 and the corresponding *p*-value is 0.000. A 99% confidence interval for the mean difference extends from 0.182 to 1.041, which is all positive.

■ There is no evidence that the difference between attractiveness ratings and the likelihood of buying is any different for the new-style can than for the current-style can. [See the output for the Diff5 variable, (AN − WBN) − (AO − WBO), in Figure 9.16.] The test statistic for a two-tailed test of this difference is 0.401 and the corresponding *p*-value, 0.689, isn't even close to any of the traditional significance levels. Furthermore, a 99% confidence interval for the mean difference extends from a negative value, −0.336, to a positive value 0.458.

These results are further supported by histograms of the difference variables, such as those shown in Figures 9.17 and 9.18. (Box plots could be used, but we prefer histograms

Figure 9.17

Histogram of the Diff1 Variable

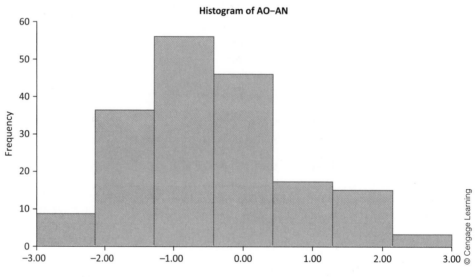

Figure 9.18

Histogram of the Diff5 Variable

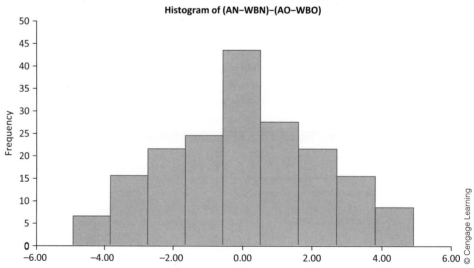

when the variables include only a few possible integer values.) The histogram of the Diff1 variable in Figure 9.17 shows many more negative differences than positive differences. This leads to the large negative test statistic and the all-negative confidence interval. In contrast, the histogram of the Diff5 variable in Figure 9.18 is almost perfectly symmetric around 0 and hence provides no evidence that the mean difference is *not* zero.

This example illustrates once again how hypothesis tests and confidence intervals provide complementary information, although the confidence intervals are arguably more useful here. The hypothesis test for the first difference, for example, shows that the average rating for the new style is undoubtedly larger than for the current style. This is useful information, but it is even more useful to know *how much* larger the average for the new style is. A confidence interval provides this information.

We conclude this example by recalling the distinction between practical significance and statistical significance. Due to the extremely low *p*-values, the results in Figure 9.15, for example, leave no doubt as to statistical significance. But this could be due to the large sample size. That is, if the true mean differences are even slightly different from 0, large samples will almost surely discover this and report small *p*-values. The soft-drink company, on the other hand, is more interested in knowing whether the observed differences are of any practical importance. This is not a statistical question. It is a question of what differences are important for the *business*. We suspect that the company would indeed be quite impressed with the observed differences in the sample—and might very well switch to the new-style can. ■

FUNDAMENTAL INSIGHT

Signficance and Sample Size in Tests of Differences

The contrast between statistical and practical significance is especially evident in tests of differences between means. If the sample sizes are relatively small, it is likely that no *statistical* significance will be found, even though the real difference between means, if they could be estimated more accurately with more data, might be *practically* significant. On the other hand, if the sample sizes are very large, then just about any difference between sample means is likely to be *statistically* significant, even though the real difference between means might be of no *practical* importance.

Example 9.5 illustrates the independent two-sample *t* test. You can tell that a paired-sample procedure is not appropriate because there is no attempt to match the observations in the two samples in any way. Indeed, this is obvious because the sample sizes are not equal.

EXAMPLE

9.5 PRODUCTIVITY DUE TO EXERCISE AT INFORMATRIX SOFTWARE COMPANY

Many companies have installed exercise facilities at their plants. The goal is not only to provide a bonus (free use of exercise equipment) for their employees, but to make the employees more productive by getting them in better shape. One such (fictional) company, Informatrix Software Company, installed exercise equipment on site a year ago. To check whether it has had a beneficial effect on employee productivity, the company gathered data on a sample of 80 randomly chosen employees, all between the ages of 30 and 40 and all with similar job titles and duties. The company observed which of these employees use the exercise facility regularly (at least three times per week on average). This group included 23 of the 80 employees in the sample. The other 57 employees were asked whether they exercise regularly elsewhere, and 6 of them replied that they do. The remaining 51, who admitted to being nonexercisers, were then compared to the combined group of 29 exercisers.

The comparison was based on the employees' productivity over the year, as rated by their supervisors. Each rating was on a scale of 1 to 25, 25 being the best. To increase the validity of the study, neither the employees nor the supervisors were told that a study was in progress. In particular, the supervisors did not know which employees were involved in the study or which were exercisers. The data from the study appear in Figure 9.19. (See the file **Exercise & Productivity.xlsx**.) Do these data support the company's (alternative) hypothesis that exercisers outperform nonexercisers on average? Can the company infer that any difference between the two groups is due to exercise?

Figure 9.19

Data for Study on Effectiveness of Exercise

	A	B	C
1	Employee	Exerciser	Rating
2	1	Yes	14
3	2	No	7
4	3	No	15
5	4	Yes	15
6	5	No	13
79	78	No	13
80	79	No	19
81	80	No	12

© Cengage Learning

Objective   To use a two-sample t test for the difference between means to see whether regular exercise increases worker productivity.

Solution

Side-by-side box plots are typically a good way to begin the analysis when comparing two populations.

To see whether there is any indication of a difference between the two groups, a good first step is to create side-by-side box plots of the Rating variable. These appear in Figure 9.20. Although there is a great deal of overlap between the two distributions, the distribution for

Figure 9.20

Box Plots for Exercise Data

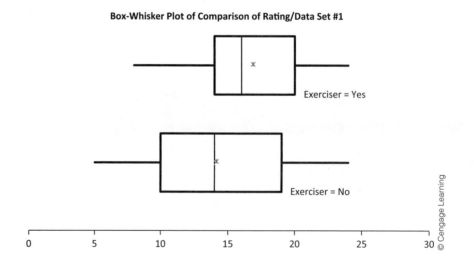

© Cengage Learning

the exercisers is somewhat to the right of that for the nonexercisers. Also, the variances of the two distributions appear to be roughly the same, although there is slightly more variation in the nonexerciser distribution.

A formal test of the mean difference uses the hypotheses $H_0: \mu_1 - \mu_2 \geq 0$ versus $H_a: \mu_1 - \mu_2 < 0$, where μ_1 and μ_2 are the mean ratings for the nonexerciser and exerciser populations. It makes sense to use a one-tailed test, with the alternative of the "less than" variety, because the company expects higher ratings, on average, for the exercisers. The output for this test, along with a 95% confidence interval for $\mu_1 - \mu_2$, appears in Figure 9.21. You can obtain the right part (the hypothesis test) by filling out the StatTools Hypothesis Test dialog box as shown in Figure 9.22. Specifically, select Two-Sample Analysis as the Analysis Type, click the Format button and make sure the Stacked option is checked, select

Figure 9.21

Analysis of Exercise Data

	A	B	C
7		Rating (No)	Rating (Yes)
8	*Sample Summaries*	Data Set #1	Data Set #1
9	Sample Size	51	29
10	Sample Mean	14.137	16.862
11	Sample Std Dev	5.307	4.103
12			
13		Equal	Unequal
14	*Conf. Intervals (Difference of Means)*	Variances	Variances
15	Confidence Level	95.0%	95.0%
16	Sample Mean Difference	−2.725	−2.725
17	Standard Error of Difference	1.141650904	1.064318358
18	Degrees of Freedom	78	71
19	Lower Limit	−4.99766642	−4.847004594
20	Upper Limit	−0.451961707	−0.602623533
21			
22		Equal	Unequal
23	*Hypothesis Test (Difference of Means)*	Variances	Variances
24	Hypothesized Mean Difference	0	0
25	Alternative Hypothesis	< 0	< 0
26	Sample Mean Difference	−2.725	−2.725
27	Standard Error of Difference	1.141650904	1.064318358
28	Degrees of Freedom	78	70
29	*t*-Test Statistic	−2.3867	−2.5601
30	*p*-Value	0.0097	0.0063
31	Null Hypoth. at 10% Significance	Reject	Reject
32	Null Hypoth. at 5% Significance	Reject	Reject
33	Null Hypoth. at 1% Significance	Reject	Reject
34			
35			
36	*Equality of Variances Test*		
37	Ratio of Sample Variances	1.6725	
38	*p*-Value	0.1454	

Figure 9.22

Dialog Box for Two-Sample Analysis

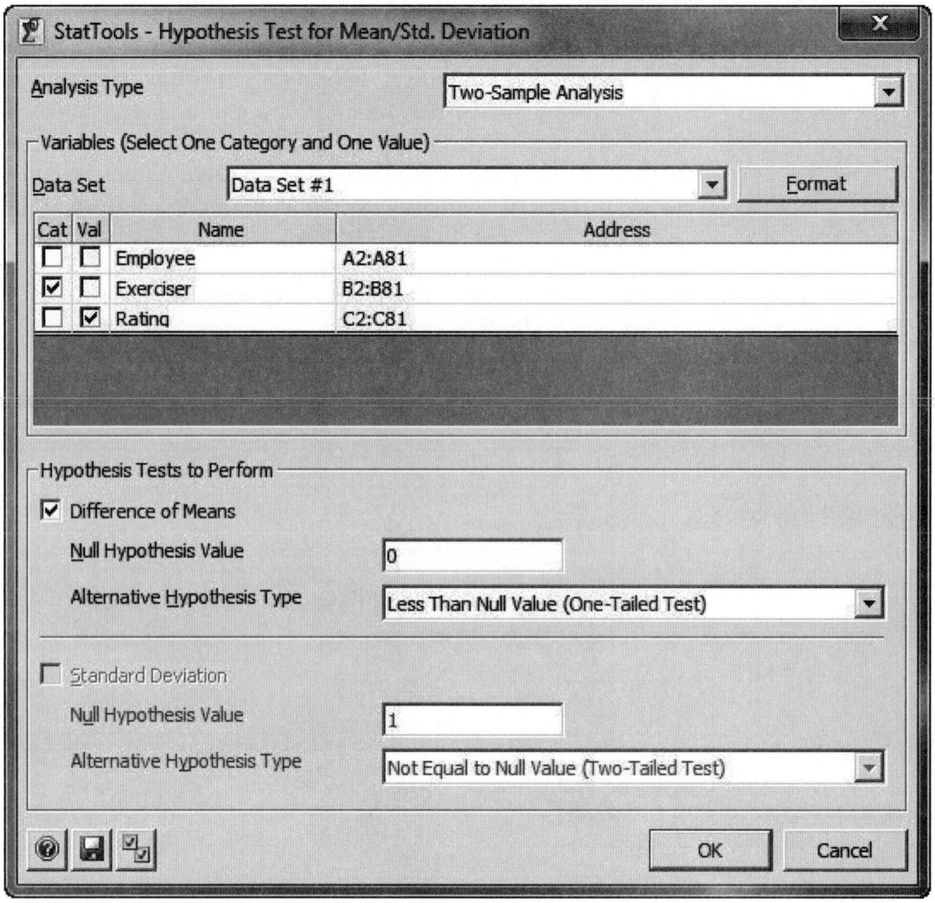

Exerciser as the "Cat" variable and Rating as the "Val" variable, and choose the "Less Than" Alternative Hypothesis Type.[5]

If the population standard deviations are at least approximately equal (and the values in cells B11 and C11 suggest that this assumption is plausible), the output in the range B37:B44 is relevant. It shows that the observed sample mean difference, −2.725, is indeed negative. That is, the exercisers in the sample outperformed the nonexercisers by 2.725 rating points on average. The output also shows that (1) the standard error of the sample mean difference is 1.142, (2) the test statistic is −2.387, and (3) the p-value for a one-tailed test is slightly less than 0.010. In words, the data provide enough evidence to reject the null hypothesis at the 1% significance level, as well as at the 5% and 10% levels. It is clear that exercisers perform better, in terms of mean ratings, than nonexercisers. A 95% confidence for this mean difference is all negative; it extends from −4.988 to −0.452.

This answers the first question we posed, but it doesn't answer the second. There is no way to be sure that the higher ratings for the exercisers are a direct result of exercise. It is possible that employees who exercise are naturally more ambitious and hard-working people, and that this extra drive is responsible for *both* their exercising and their higher ratings. This study is an *observational study*. The company observes two randomly selected groups of employees and analyzes the results. It does not explicitly control for other factors, such as personality, that might be responsible for differences in ratings. Therefore,

---

[5]The Stacked versus Unstacked issue is the same as you have seen before. The data in this file are stacked because there are two long columns that list a categorical variable, Exerciser, and a numerical variable, Rating.

the company can never be sure that there is a causal relationship between exercise and performance ratings. All the company can state is that exercisers appear, on average, to be more productive than nonexercisers—for whatever reason.

We are almost finished with this example, but not quite. What about the output in column C, and the test in rows 48 and 49? The test we just performed and the confidence interval we reported are based on the assumption of equal population standard deviations (or variances). As we discussed in Section 8-7a, if this assumption is violated, then a slightly different form of analysis should be performed, and its results are reported in column C. As you can see, the results are very similar to those in column B, although the *p*-value is slightly lower and the confidence interval is slightly narrower.

The test reported in rows 48 and 49 is a formal test of the hypothesis $H_0: \sigma_1^2/\sigma_2^2 = 1$ versus $H_a: \sigma_1^2/\sigma_2^2 \neq 1$, where the parameter being tested is the *ratio* of the two population variances. (The details behind this test are explained in the following subsection.) If this null hypothesis can be rejected on the basis of a low *p*-value in cell B49, then the equal-variance assumption is almost certainly *not* valid, and the output in column C should be used. Otherwise, the output in column B should be used. The *p*-value in cell B49, 0.1454, suggests that the evidence *against* equal population variances is far from overwhelming. Of course, the similarity of the outputs in columns B and C implies, especially from a practical point of view, that it doesn't really make much difference. In other examples it can be more critical. ■

StatTools Tip: *p-value for Test of Equal Variances*
If the p-value for the test of equal variances is small, use the right column (here column C) for testing the difference between means. Otherwise, use the (traditional) left column (here column B).

9-4c Hypothesis Test for Equal Population Variances

As we just explained, the two-sample procedure for a difference between population means depends on whether population variances are equal.[6] Therefore, it is natural to test first for equal variances. This test, referred to as the **F test for equality of two variances**, is phrased in terms of the *ratio* of population variances, σ_1^2/σ_2^2. The null hypothesis is that this ratio is 1 (equal variances), whereas the alternative is that it is not 1 (unequal variances). The test statistic for this test is the ratio of sample variances:

$$F\text{-value} = s_1^2/s_2^2$$

Assuming that the population variances are equal, this test statistic has an F distribution with $n_1 - 1$ and $n_2 - 1$ degrees of freedom.

The F distribution is a distribution of positive values and is always skewed to the right. It typically appears in tests of equal variances.

The **F distribution**, named after the famous statistician R. A. Fisher, is another sampling distribution that arises frequently in statistical studies. (It will appear again in the next two chapters on regression.) Because it always describes a ratio, there are two degrees of freedom parameters, one for the numerator and one for the denominator, and the numerator degrees of freedom is always quoted first.

Tables of the F distribution, for selected degrees of freedom, appear in many statistics books, but the necessary information can be obtained more easily with Excel's FDIST and FINV functions. The FDIST function takes the form

$$=\text{FSIDT}(v,df1,df2)$$

---

[6]The test in this section is traditionally stated in terms of variances, as we do here. It can also be stated in terms of standard deviations, because equal variances imply equal standard deviations and vice versa.

This function returns the probability to the *right* of value v when the degrees of freedom are $df1$ and $df2$. Similarly, the FINV function takes the form

=FINV(p,$df1$,$df2$)

It returns the value with probability p to the right of it when the degrees of freedom are $df1$ and $df2$.

CHANGES IN EXCEL 2010

These F functions were changed considerably in Excel 2010. There are now F.DIST and F.INV functions for *left* tails, and F.DIST has a last "cum" argument just like NORM.DIST, T.DIST, and CHISQ.DIST. Also, there are two functions, F.DIST.RT and F.INV.RT, for *right* tails.

When StatTools tests for equal variances, it first calculates the ratio of variances. (See cell B48 in Figure 9.20.) It then implements the F test to calculate the corresponding p-value (in cell B49). For our purposes, the most important thing is the p-value from the test. A small p-value provides strong evidence that the population variances are *not* equal. Otherwise, an equal-variance assumption is reasonable. The p-value for the exercise data, 0.1454, provides *some* evidence of unequal variances, but the evidence is certainly not overwhelming.

9-4d Hypothesis Tests for Differences between Population Proportions

One of the most common uses of hypothesis testing is to test whether two population proportions are equal. The following z **test for difference between proportions** can then be used. Let p_1 and p_2 be the two population proportions, and let $\hat{p}_1$ and $\hat{p}_2$ be the corresponding sample proportions, based on sample sizes n_1 and n_2. The goal is to test whether the sample proportions differ enough to conclude that the *population* proportions are not equal. As usual, a test on the difference $\hat{p}_1 - \hat{p}_2$, requires a standard error. If the null hypothesis is true, so that $p_1 = p_2$, then it can be shown that the standard error of $\hat{p}_1 - \hat{p}_2$ is given by Equation (9.5), where $\hat{p}_c$ is the pooled proportion from the two samples combined. For example, if $\hat{p}_1 = 20/85$ and $\hat{p}_2 = 34/115$, then $\hat{p}_c = (20 + 34)/(85 + 115) = 54/200$. The reason for using this pooled estimate is that if the null hypothesis is true and the two population proportions are equal, it makes sense to base an estimate of this common proportion on the *combined* sample of data.

Standard Error for Difference between Sample Proportions

$$\text{SE}(\hat{p}_1 - \hat{p}_2) = \sqrt{\hat{p}_c(1 - \hat{p}_c)(1/n_1 + 1/n_2)} \qquad \textbf{(9.5)}$$

Given this standard error, the rest is straightforward. Assuming that the sample sizes are reasonably large, the test statistic in Equation (9.6) has (approximately) a standard normal distribution. The test can be run with StatTools, as illustrated in Example 9.6.

Test Statistic for Difference between Proportions

$$z\text{-value} = \frac{\hat{p}_1 - \hat{p}_2}{\text{SE}(\hat{p}_1 - \hat{p}_2)} \qquad \textbf{(9.6)}$$

9.6 EMPLOYEE EMPOWERMENT AT ARMCO COMPANY

ArmCo Company, a large manufacturer of automobile parts, has several plants in the United States. For years, ArmCo employees have complained that their suggestions for improvements in the manufacturing processes have been ignored by upper management. In the spirit of employee empowerment, ArmCo management at the Midwest plant decided to initiate a number of policies to respond to employee suggestions. For example, a mailbox was placed in a central location, and employees were encouraged to drop suggestions into this box. No such initiatives were taken at the other ArmCo plants. As expected, there was a great deal of employee enthusiasm at the Midwest plant shortly after the new policies were implemented, but the question was whether life would revert to normal and the enthusiasm would dampen with time.

To check this, 100 randomly selected employees at the Midwest plant and 300 employees from other plants were asked to fill out a questionnaire six months after the implementation of the new policies at the Midwest plant. Employees were instructed to respond to each item on the questionnaire by checking either a "yes" box or a "no" box. Two specific items on the questionnaire were the following:

- Management at this plant is generally responsive to employee suggestions for improvements in the manufacturing processes.

- Management at this plant is more responsive to employee suggestions now than it used to be.

The results of the questionnaire for these two items appear in rows 5 and 6 of Figure 9.23. (See the file **Empowerment 1.xlsx**.) Does it appear that the policies at the

Figure 9.23   Results for Employee Empowerment Example

	A	B	C	D	E	F	G
1	Employee empowerment results						
2							
3	Item 1: Management responds				Item 2: Things have improved		
4	Category	Midwest	Other		Category	Midwest	Other
5	Yes	39	93		Yes	68	159
6	No	61	207		No	32	141
7	Totals	100	300		Totals	100	300
8							
9							
10	*Analyzed Category*				*Analyzed Category*		
11	Proportion of Items in This Category	Yes			Proportion of Items in This Category	Yes	
12							
13							
14		Midwest	Other			Midwest	Other
15	*Sample Summaries*	Data Set #1	Data Set #1		*Sample Summaries*	Data Set #2	Data Set #2
16	Sample Size	100	300		Sample Size	100	300
17	Sample Proportion	0.390	0.310		Sample Proportion	0.680	0.530
18							
19							
20	*Hypothesis Test (Difference Between Proportions)*				*Hypothesis Test (Difference Between Proportions)*		
21	Pooled Proportion	0.330			Pooled Proportion	0.568	
22	Difference Between Proportions	0.080			Difference Between Proportions	0.150	
23	Hypothesized Difference	0			Hypothesized Difference	0	
24	Alternative Hypothesis	> 0			Alternative Hypothesis	> 0	
25	Standard Error of Difference	0.054			Standard Error of Difference	0.057	
26	Test Statistic	1.4734			Test Statistic	2.6221	
27	*p*-Value	0.0703			*p*-Value	0.0044	
28	Null Hypoth. at 10% Significance	Reject			Null Hypoth. at 10% Significance	Reject	
29	Null Hypoth. at 5% Significance	Don't Reject			Null Hypoth. at 5% Significance	Reject	
30	Null Hypoth. at 1% Significance	Don't Reject			Null Hypoth. at 1% Significance	Reject	
31							
43	*Conf. Interval (Difference Between Proportions)*				*Conf. Interval (Difference Between Proportions)*		
44	Confidence Level	95.0%			Confidence Level	95.0%	
45	Difference Between Proportions	0.080			Difference Between Proportions	0.150	
46	Standard Error of Difference	0.056			Standard Error of Difference	0.055	
47	Lower Limit	−0.029			Lower Limit	0.043	
48	Upper Limit	0.189			Upper Limit	0.257	

Midwest plant are appreciated? Should ArmCo implement these policies in its other plants?

Objective   To use a test for the difference between proportions to see whether a program of accepting employee suggestions is appreciated by employees.

Solution

For either questionnaire item, let p_1 be the proportion of "yes" responses that would be obtained at the Midwest plant if the questionnaire were given to all of its employees, and define p_2 similarly for the other plants. Management certainly hopes to find a larger proportion of "yes" responses (to either item) at the Midwest plant than at the other plants, so the appropriate test is one-tailed, with the hypotheses set up as $H_0: p_1 - p_2 \leq 0$ versus $H_a: p_1 - p_2 > 0$. (These could also be written as $H_0: p_1 \leq p_2$ versus $H_0: p_1 > p_2$, but this has no effect on the test.)

Using the counts in rows 5 and 6, StatTools can run the test for differences between proportions. As with the test for a single proportion, you should recall the three possible StatTools data setups that were discussed in Section 8-8 of the previous chapter. (See the finished version of the file **Coupon Effectiveness.xlsx** from the previous chapter for more details.) For this example, the two relevant StatTools data sets are the tables of counts in the ranges A4:C6 and E4:G6. To run the test for the first item (whether management responds), select Hypothesis Test/Proportions from the Statistical Inference dropdown list and fill in the resulting dialog box as shown in Figure 9.24. This implies that the difference

Figure 9.24

Dialog Box for Testing Difference Between Proportions

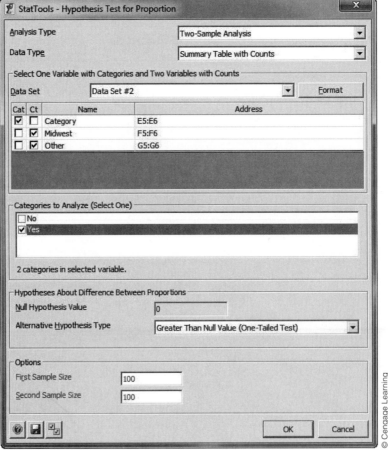

being tested is the difference between the proportion of "yes" votes in the Midwest and Other. When you click OK, you will see the dialog box in Figure 9.25. As it now stands, the difference will be Midwest minus Other. This is fine for this example, so click OK, but if you wanted Other minus Midwest, you would click the Reverse Order button. Of course, the test for the second item (whether things have improved) is performed similarly.

Figure 9.25

Dialog Box
for Reversing
Difference

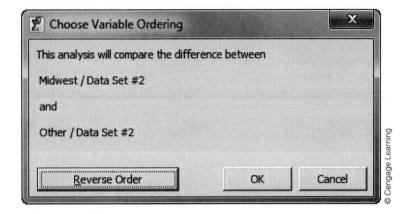

As shown in Figure 9.23, the *p*-values for the two tests (row 27) are 0.070 and 0.004. These results should be fairly good news for management. There is moderate, but not overwhelming, support for the hypothesis that management at the Midwest plant is more responsive than at the other plants, at least as perceived by employees. There is convincing support for the hypothesis that things have improved more at the Midwest plant than at the other plants. Corresponding 95% confidence intervals for the differences between proportions appear in rows 47 and 48. Because they are almost completely positive, they support the hypothesis-test findings. Moreover, they provide a range of plausible values for the differences between the population proportions.

The only real downside to these findings, from Midwest management's point of view, is the sample proportion $\hat{p}_1$ for the first item. Only 39% of the sampled employees at the Midwest plant believe that management generally responds to their suggestions, even though 68% believe things are better than they used to be. A reasonable conclusion by ArmCo management is that they are on the right track at the Midwest plant, and the policies initiated there ought to be initiated at other plants, but more must be done at *all* plants. ∎

PROBLEMS

Level A

9. In the past, 60% of all undergraduate students enrolled at State University earned their degrees within four years of matriculation. A random sample of 95 students from the class that matriculated in the fall of 2008 was recently selected to test whether there has been a change in the proportion of students who graduate within four years. Administrators found that 40 of these 95 students graduated in the spring of 2012 (i.e., four academic years after matriculation).

a. Given the sample outcome, find a 95% confidence interval for the relevant population proportion. Does this interval estimate suggest that there has been a change in the proportion of students who graduate within four years? Why or why not?

b. Suppose now that State University administrators want to test the claim made by faculty that the proportion of students who graduate within four years at State University has fallen *below* the historical value of 60% this year. Use this sample proportion to test their claim. Report a *p*-value and interpret it.

10. Suppose a well-known baseball player states that, at this stage of his career, he is a "300 hitter" or better. That is, he claims that he gets a hit in at least 30% of his at-bats. Over the next month of the baseball season, this player has 105 at-bats and gets 33 hits.

    a. Identify the null and alternative hypotheses from the player's point of view.

    b. Is there enough evidence from this month's data to reject the null hypothesis at the 5% significance level?

    c. We might raise two issues with this test. First, does the data come from a *random* sample from some population? Second, what is the relevant population? Discuss these issues. Do you think the test in part **b** is valid? Is it meaningful?

11. The director of admissions of a distinguished (i.e., top-20) MBA program is interested in studying the proportion of entering students in similar graduate business programs who have achieved a composite score on the Graduate Management Admissions Test (GMAT) in excess of 630. In particular, the admissions director believes that the proportion of students entering top-rated programs with such composite GMAT scores is now 50%. To test this hypothesis, he has collected a random sample of MBA candidates entering his program in the fall of 2012. He believes that these students' GMAT scores are indicative of the scores earned by their peers in his program and in competitors' programs. The GMAT scores for these 125 individuals are given in the Data 2012 sheet of the file **P09_11.xlsx**. (You can ignore the data in the Data 2002 sheet for now.) Test the admission director's claim at the 5% significance level and report your findings. Does your conclusion change when the significance level is increased to 10%?

12. A market research consultant hired by a leading soft-drink company wants to determine the proportion of consumers who favor its low-calorie drink over the leading competitor's low-calorie drink in a particular urban location. A random sample of 250 consumers from the market under investigation is provided in the file **P08_18.xlsx**.

    a. Find a 95% confidence interval for the proportion of all consumers in this market who prefer this company's drink over the competitor's. What does this confidence interval tell us?

    b. Does the confidence interval in part **a** support the claim made by one of the company's marketing managers that more than half of the consumers in this urban location favor its drink over the competitor's? Explain your answer.

    c. Comment on the sample size used in this study. Specifically, is the sample unnecessarily large? Is it too small? Explain your reasoning.

13. The CEO of a medical supply company is committed to expanding the proportion of highly qualified women in the organization's staff of salespersons. He claims that the proportion of women in similar sales positions across the country in 2012 is less than 50%. Hoping to find support for his claim, he directs his assistant to collect a random sample of salespersons employed by his company, which is thought to be representative of sales staffs of competing organizations in the industry. These data are listed in the Data 2012 sheet of the file **P09_13.xlsx**. (You can ignore the data in the Data 2007 sheet for now.) Test this manager's claim using the given sample data and report a *p*-value. Is there statistical support for his hypothesis that the proportion of women in similar sales positions across the country is less than 50%?

14. Management of a software development firm would like to establish a wellness program during the lunch hour to enhance the physical and mental health of its employees. Before introducing the wellness program, management must first be convinced that a sufficiently large majority of its employees are not already exercising at lunchtime. Specifically, it plans to initiate the program only if less than 40% of its personnel take time to exercise prior to eating lunch. To make this decision, management has surveyed a random sample of 100 employees regarding their midday exercise activities. The results of the survey are given in the Before sheet of the file **P09_14.xlsx**. Is there sufficient evidence at the 10% significance level for managers of this organization to initiate a corporate wellness program? Why or why not? What about at the 1% significance level?

15. The managing partner of a major consulting firm is trying to assess the effectiveness of expensive computer skills training given to all new entry-level professionals. In an effort to make such an assessment, she administers a computer skills test immediately before and after the training program to each of 40 randomly chosen employees. The pretraining and posttraining scores of these 40 individuals are recorded in the file **P09_15.xlsx**. Do the given sample data support the claim at the 10% significance level that the organization's training program is increasing the new employee's working knowledge of computing? What about at the 1% significance level?

16. A large buyer of household batteries wants to decide which of two equally priced brands to purchase. To do this, he takes a random sample of 100 batteries of each brand. The lifetimes, measured in hours, of the randomly chosen batteries are recorded in the file **P09_16.xlsx**.

    a. Using the given sample data, find a 95% confidence interval for the difference between the mean lifetimes of brand 1 and brand 2 batteries.

Based on this confidence interval, which brand would you advise the buyer to purchase? Would you even need a confidence interval to make this recommendation? Explain.

b. Repeat part **a** with a 99% confidence interval.

c. How are your results in parts **a** and **b** related to hypothesis testing? Be specific.

17. The managers of a chemical manufacturing plant want to determine whether recent safety training workshops have reduced the weekly number of reported safety violations at the facility. The management team has randomly selected weekly safety violation reports for each of 25 weeks prior to the safety training and 25 weeks after the safety workshops. These data are provided in the file **P09_17.xlsx**. Given this evidence, is it possible to conclude that the safety workshops have been effective in reducing the number of safety violations reported per week? Report a *p*-value and interpret your findings for the management team.

18. A real estate agent has collected a random sample of 75 houses that were recently sold in a suburban community. She is particularly interested in comparing the appraised value and recent selling price of the houses in this particular market. The values of these two variables for each of the 75 randomly chosen houses are provided in the file **P08_24.xlsx**. Using these sample data, test whether there is a statistically significant mean difference between the appraised values and selling prices of the houses sold in this suburban community. Report a *p*-value. For which levels of significance is it appropriate to conclude that *no* difference exists between these two values? Which is more appropriate, a one-tailed test or a two-tailed test? Explain your reasoning.

19. The owner of two submarine sandwich shops located in a particular city would like to know how the mean daily sales of the first shop (located in the downtown area) compares to that of the second shop (located on the southwest side of town). In particular, he would like to determine whether the mean daily sales levels of these two restaurants are essentially equal. He records the sales (in dollars) made at each location for 30 randomly chosen days. These sales levels are given in the file **P09_19.xlsx**. Find a 95% confidence level for the mean difference between the daily sales of restaurant 1 and restaurant 2. Based on this confidence interval, is it possible to conclude that there is a statistically significant mean difference at the 5% level of significance? Explain why or why not. Can you infer from this confidence interval whether there is a statistically significant mean difference at the 10% level? What about at the 1% level? Again, explain why or why not.

20. Suppose that an investor wants to compare the risks associated with two different stocks. One way to measure the risk of a given stock is to measure the variation in the stock's daily price changes. The investor obtains a random sample of 25 daily price changes for stock 1 and 25 daily price changes for stock 2. These data are provided in the file **P09_20.xlsx**. Explain why this investor can compare the risks associated with the two stocks by testing the null hypothesis that the variances of the stocks' price changes are equal. Perform this test, using a 10% significance level, and interpret the results.

21. A manufacturing company wants to determine whether there is a difference between the variance of the number of units produced per day by one machine operator and the similar variance for another machine operator. The file **P09_21.xlsx** contain the number of units produced by operator 1 and operator 2, respectively, on each of 25 days. Note that these two sets of days are not necessarily the same, so you can assume that the two samples are *independent* of one another.

a. Identify the null and alternative hypotheses in this situation.

b. Do these sample data indicate a statistically significant difference at the 10% level? Explain your answer. With your conclusion, which possible error could you be making, a type I or type II error?

c. At which significance levels could you *not* reject the null hypothesis?

22. A large buyer of household batteries wants to decide which of two equally priced brands to purchase. To do this, he takes a random sample of 100 batteries of each brand. The lifetimes, measured in hours, of the batteries are recorded in the file **P09_16.xlsx**. Before testing for the difference between the mean lifetimes of these two batteries, he must first determine whether the underlying population variances are equal.

a. Perform a test for equal population variances. Report a *p*-value and interpret its meaning.

b. Based on your conclusion in part **a**, which test statistic should be used in performing a test for the difference between population *means*? Perform this test and interpret the results.

23. Do undergraduate business students who major in finance earn, on average, higher annual starting salaries than their peers who major in marketing? Before addressing this question through a statistical hypothesis test, you should determine whether the variances of annual starting salaries of the two types of majors are equal. The file **P09_23.xlsx** contains (hypothetical) starting salaries of 50 randomly selected finance majors and 50 randomly chosen marketing majors.

a. Perform a test for equal population variances. Report a *p*-value and interpret its meaning.

b. Based on your conclusion in part **a**, which test statistic should you use in performing a test for the existence of a difference between population means? Perform this test and interpret the results.

24. The CEO of a medical supply company is committed to expanding the proportion of highly qualified women in the organization's large staff of salespersons. Given the recent hiring practices of his human resources director, he claims that the company has increased the proportion of women in sales positions throughout the organization between 2007 and 2012. Hoping to find support for his claim, he directs his assistant to collect random samples of the salespersons employed by the company in 2007 and 2012. These data are listed in the file **P09_13.xlsx**. Test the CEO's claim using the sample data and report a *p*-value. Is there statistical support for the claim that his strategy is effective?

25. The director of admissions of a top-20 MBA program is interested in studying the proportion of entering students in similar graduate business programs who have achieved a composite score on the Graduate Management Admissions Test (GMAT) in excess of 630. In particular, the admissions director believes that the proportion of students entering top-rated programs with such composite GMAT scores is higher in 2012 than it was in 2002. To test this hypothesis, he has collected random samples of MBA candidates entering his program in the fall of 2012 and in the fall of 2002. He believes that these students' GMAT scores are indicative of the scores earned by their peers in his program and in competitors' programs. The GMAT scores for the randomly selected students entering in each year are listed in the file **P09_11.xlsx**. Test the admission director's claim at the 5 significance level and report your findings. Does your conclusion change when the significance level is increased to 10%?

26. Managers of a software development firm have established a wellness program during the lunch hour to enhance the physical and mental health of their employees. Now, they would like to see whether the wellness program has increased the proportion of employees who exercise regularly during the lunch hour. To make this assessment, the managers surveyed a random sample of 100 employees about their noontime exercise habits *before* the wellness program was initiated. Later, *after* the program was initiated, *another* 100 employees were independently chosen and surveyed about their lunchtime exercise habits. The results of these two surveys are given in the file **P09_14.xlsx**.
  a. Find a 95% confidence interval for the difference in the proportions of employees who exercise regularly during their lunch hour before and after the implementation of the corporate wellness program.
  b. Does the confidence interval found in part **a** support the claim that the wellness program has increased the proportion of employees who exercise regularly during the lunch hour? If so, at which levels of significance is this claim supported?

  c. Would your results in parts **a** and **b** differ if the *same* 100 employees surveyed before the program were also surveyed after the program? Explain.

27. An Environmental Protection Agency official asserts that more than 80% of the plants in the northeast region of the United States meet air pollution standards. An antipollution advocate is not convinced by the EPA's claim. She takes a random sample of 64 plants in the northeast region and finds that 56 meet the federal government's pollution standards.
  a. Does the sample information support the EPA's claim at the 5% level of significance?
  b. For which values of the sample proportion (based on a sample size of 64) would the sample data support the EPA's claim, using a 5% significance level?
  c. Would the conclusion found in part **a** change if the sample proportion remained constant but the sample size increased to 124? Explain why or why not.

Level B

28. A television network decides to cancel one of its shows if it is convinced that less than 14% of the viewing public are watching this show.
  a. If a random sample of 1500 households with televisions is selected, what sample proportion values will lead to this show's cancellation, assuming a 5% significance level?
  b. What is the probability that this show will be cancelled if 13.4% of all viewing households are watching it? That is, what is the probability that a sample will lead to rejection of the null hypothesis? You can assume that 13.4% is the *population* proportion (even though it wouldn't be known to the network).

29. An economic researcher wants to know whether he can reject the null hypothesis, at the 10% significance level, that no more than 20% of the households in Pennsylvania make more than $70,000 per year.
  a. If 200 Pennsylvania households are chosen at random, how many of them would have to be earning more than $70,000 per year to allow the researcher to reject the null hypothesis?
  b. Assuming that the true proportion of *all* Pennsylvania households with annual incomes of at least $70,000 is 0.217, find the probability of *not* rejecting a *false* null hypothesis when the sample size is 200.

30. Senior partners of an accounting firm are concerned about recent complaints by some female managers that they are paid less than their male counterparts. In response to these charges, the partners ask their human resources director to record the salaries of female and male managers with equivalent education, work experience, and job performance. A random sample of these pairs of managers is provided in the file **P09_30.xlsx**. That is, each male-female pair is matched in terms of education, work experience, and job performance.

  a. Do these data support the claim made by the female managers? Report and interpret a *p*-value.

  b. Assuming a 5% significance level, which values of the sample mean difference between the female and male salaries would support the claim of discrimination against female managers?

31. Do undergraduate business students who major in finance earn, on average, higher annual starting salaries than their peers who major in marketing? Address this question through a statistical hypothesis test. The file **P09_23.xlsx** contains the (hypothetical) starting salaries of 50 randomly selected finance majors and 50 randomly selected marketing majors.

  a. Is it appropriate to perform a paired-comparison *t* test with these data? Explain why or why not.

  b. Perform an appropriate hypothesis test with a 5% significance level. Summarize your findings.

  c. How large would the difference between the mean starting salaries of finance and marketing majors have to be before you could conclude that finance majors earn more on average? Employ a 5% significance level in answering this question.

32. The file **P02_35.xlsx** contains data from a survey of 500 randomly selected households. Test for the existence of a significant difference between the mean debt levels of the households in the first (i.e., SW) and second (i.e., NW) sectors of this community. Perform similar hypothesis tests for the differences between the mean debt levels of households from all other pairs of locations (i.e., first and third, first and fourth, second and third, second and fourth, and third and fourth). Summarize your findings.

33. Elected officials in a Florida city are preparing the annual budget for their community. They want to determine whether their constituents living across town are typically paying the same amount in real estate taxes each year. Given that there are over 20,000 homeowners in this city, they have decided to sample a representative subset of taxpayers and thoroughly study their tax payments. A randomly selected set of 170 homeowners is given in the file **P09_33.xlsx**. Specifically, the officials want to test whether there is a difference between the mean real estate tax bill paid by residents of the *first* neighborhood of this town and each of the remaining five neighborhoods. That is, each *pair* referenced below is from neighborhood 1 and one of the other neighborhoods.

  a. Before conducting any hypothesis tests on the difference between various pairs of mean real estate tax payments, perform a test for

equal population variances for each pair of neighborhoods. For each pair, report a *p*-value and interpret its meaning.

  b. Based on your conclusions in part **a**, which test statistic should be used in performing a test for a difference between population means in each pair?

  c. Given your conclusions in part **b**, perform an appropriate test for the difference between mean real estate tax payments in each pair of neighborhoods. For each pair, report a *p*-value and interpret its meaning.

34. Suppose that you sample two normal populations independently. The variances of these two populations are σ_1^2 and σ_2^2. You take random samples of sizes n_1 and n_2 and observe sample variances of s_1^2 and s_2^2.

  a. If $n_1 = n_2 = 21$, how large must the fraction s_1/s_2 be before you can reject the null hypothesis that σ_1^2 is no greater than σ_2^2 at the 5% significance level?

  b. Answer part **a** when $n_1 = n_2 = 41$.

  c. If s_1 is 25% greater than s_2, approximately how large must n_1 and n_2 be if you are able to reject the null hypothesis in part **a** at the 5% significance level? Assume that n_1 and n_2 are equal.

35. Two teams of workers assemble automobile engines at a manufacturing plant in Michigan. Quality control personnel inspect a random sample of the teams' assemblies and judge each assembly to be acceptable or unacceptable. A random sample of 127 assemblies from team 1 shows 12 unacceptable assemblies. A similar random sample of 98 assemblies from team 2 shows 5 unacceptable assemblies.

  a. Find a 95% confidence interval for the difference between the proportions of unacceptable assemblies from the two teams.

  b. Based on the confidence interval found in part **a**, is there sufficient evidence to conclude, at the 5% significance level, that the two teams differ with respect to their proportions of unacceptable assemblies?

  c. For which values of the difference between these two sample proportions could you conclude that a statistically significant difference exists at the 5% level?

36. A market research consultant hired by a leading soft-drink company is interested in determining whether there is a difference between the proportions of female and male consumers who favor the company's low-calorie brand over the leading competitor's low-calorie brand in a particular urban location. A random sample of 250 consumers from the market under investigation is provided in the file **P08_18.xlsx**.

  a. After separating the 250 randomly selected consumers by gender, perform the statistical test and report a *p*-value. At which levels of α will the market research consultant conclude that there is essentially no difference between the proportions of female and male consumers who prefer this company's brand to the competitor's brand in this urban area?

b. Marketing managers at this company have asked their market research consultant to explore further the potential differences in the proportions of women and men who prefer drinking the company's brand to the competitor's brand. Specifically, the company's managers wants to know whether the potential difference between the proportions of female and male consumers who favor the company's brand varies by the age of the consumers. Using the same random sample of consumers as in part **a**, assess whether this difference varies across the four given age categories: under 20, between 20 and 40, between 40 and 60, and over 60. Specifically, run the test in part **a** four times, one for each age group. Are the results the same for each age group?

37. The employee benefits manager of a large public university wants to determine whether differences exist in the proportions of various groups of full-time employees who prefer adopting the second (i.e., plan B) of three available health care plans in the coming annual enrollment period. A random sample of the university's employees and their tentative health care preferences is given in the file **P08_17.xlsx**.

a. Perform tests for differences in the proportions of employees within respective classifications who favor plan B in the coming year. For instance, the first such test should examine the difference

between the proportion of administrative employees who favor plan B and the proportion of the support staff who prefer plan B.

b. Report a p-value for each of your hypothesis tests and interpret your results. How might the benefits manager use the information you have derived from these tests?

38. The file **P02_35.xlsx** contains data from a survey of 500 randomly selected households. Researchers would like to use the available sample information to test whether home ownership rates vary by household location. For example, is there a nonzero difference between the proportions of individuals who own their homes (as opposed to those who rent their homes) in households located in the first (i.e., SW) and second (i.e., NW) sectors of this community? Use the sample data to test for a difference in home ownership rates in these two sectors as well as for those of other pairs of household locations. In each test, use a 5% significance level. Interpret and summarize your results. (You should perform and interpret a total of six hypothesis tests.)

39. For testing the difference between two proportions, $\sqrt{\hat{p}_c(1 - \hat{p}_c)(1/n_1 + 1/n_2)}$ is used as the approximate standard error of $\hat{p}_1 - \hat{p}_2$, where $\hat{p}_c$ is the pooled sample proportion. Explain why this is reasonable when the null-hypothesized value of $p_1 - p_2$ is zero. Why would this not be a good approximation when the null-hypothesized value of $p_1 - p_2$ is a nonzero number? What would you recommend using for the standard error of $\hat{p}_1 - \hat{p}_2$ in that case?

9-5 TESTS FOR NORMALITY

In this section we discuss several **tests for normality**. As you have already seen, many statistical procedures are based on the assumption that population data are normally distributed. The tests in this section allow you to test this assumption. The null hypothesis is that the population is normally distributed, whereas the alternative is that the population distribution is not normal. Therefore, the burden of proof is on showing that the population distribution is *not* normal. Unless there is sufficient evidence to this effect, the normal assumption will continue to be accepted.

The first test we discuss is called a **chi-square goodness-of-fit test**. It is quite intuitive. A histogram of the sample data is compared to the *expected* bell-shaped histogram that would be observed if the data were normally distributed with the *same* mean and standard deviation as in the sample. If the two histograms are sufficiently similar, the null hypothesis of normality is accepted. Otherwise, it can be rejected.

The chi-square test for normality makes a comparison between the observed histogram and a histogram based on normality.

The test is based on a numerical measure of the difference between the two histograms. Let C be the number of categories in the histogram, and let O_i be the observed number of observations in category i. Also, let E_i be the expected number of observations in category i if the population were normal with the same mean and standard deviation as in the sample. Then the goodness-of-fit measure in Equation (9.7) is used as a test statistic.

If the null hypothesis of normality is true, this test statistic has (approximately) a chi-square distribution with $C - 3$ degrees of freedom. Because *large* values of the test statistic indicate a poor fit—the O_i's do not match up well with the E_i's—the p-value for the test is the probability to the right of the test statistic in the chi-square distribution with $C - 3$ degrees of freedom.

Test Statistic for Chi-Square Test of Normality

$$\chi^2\text{-value} = \sum_{i=1}^{C} (O_i - E_i)^2 / E_i \qquad\qquad (9.7)$$

(Here, χ is the Greek letter chi.)

Although it is possible to perform this test manually, it is certainly preferable to use StatTools, as illustrated in Example 9.7.

EXAMPLE | **9.7 DISTRIBUTION OF METAL STRIP WIDTHS IN MANUFACTURING**

A company manufactures strips of metal that are supposed to have width of 10 centimeters. For purposes of quality control, the manager plans to run some statistical tests on these strips. However, realizing that these statistical procedures assume normally distributed widths, he first tests this normality assumption on 90 randomly sampled strips. How should he proceed?

Objective To use the chi-square goodness-of-fit test to see whether a normal distribution of the metal strip widths is reasonable.

Solution

The sample data appear in Figure 9.26, where each width is measured to three decimal places. (See the file **Testing Normality.xlsx**.) A number of summary measures also appear.

Figure 9.26

Data for Testing Normality

	A	B	C	D	E
1	Part	Width			Width
2	1	9.990		*One Variable Summary*	Data Set #1
3	2	10.031		Mean	9.999
4	3	9.985		Std. Dev.	0.010
5	4	9.983		Median	9.998
6	5	10.004		Minimum	9.970
7	6	10.000		Maximum	10.031
8	7	9.992		Count	90
9	8	9.996		1st Quartile	9.993
10	9	9.997		3rd Quartile	10.006
11	10	9.993		5.00%	9.983
12	11	9.991		95.00%	10.014
13	12	9.991			
90	89	10.003			
91	90	9.996			

© Cengage Learning

To run the test, select Chi-Square Test from the StatTools Normality Tests dropdown list, which leads to basically the same dialog box as in StatTools's Histogram procedure. As with the Histogram procedure, you can specify the bins, or you can accept StatTools's default bins. For now, do the latter.[7] The resulting histograms in Figure 9.27 provide visual evidence of the goodness of fit. The left bars represent the observed frequencies (the O_is), and the right bars represent the expected frequencies for a normal distribution (the E_is). The normal fit to the data appears to be quite good.

Figure 9.27

Observed and Normal Histograms

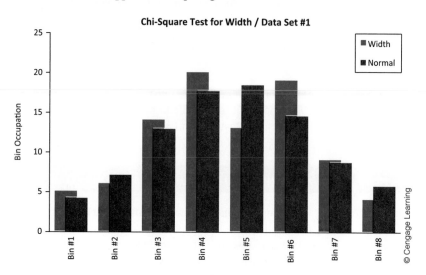

The output in Figure 9.28 confirms this statistically. Each value in column E is an E_i, calculated as the total number of observations multiplied by the normal probability of being in the corresponding category. Column F contains the individual $(O_i - E_i)^2/E_i$

Figure 9.28 Chi-Square Test of Normality

◢	A	B	C	D	E	F
7		Width				
8	*Chi-Square Test*	Data Set #1				
9	Mean	9.999256		Remember that the burden of proof is on showing that the distribution is *not* normal. The high *p*-value here indicates that there is not enough evidence to reject the null hypothesis of normality, and this finding is confirmed on the next two sheets.		
10	Std Dev	0.009728				
11	Chi-Square Stat.	4.2027				
12	*p*-Value	0.5206				
13						
14						
15	*Chi-Squared Bins*	BinMin	BinMax	Actual	Normal	Distance
16	Bin # 1	−Inf	9.983000	5	4.2630	0.1274
17	Bin # 2	9.983000	9.988167	6	7.1827	0.1948
18	Bin # 3	9.988167	9.993333	14	12.9751	0.0810
19	Bin # 4	9.993333	9.998500	20	17.7934	0.2736
20	Bin # 5	9.998500	10.003667	13	18.5249	1.6477
21	Bin # 6	10.003667	10.008833	19	14.6421	1.2970
22	Bin # 7	10.008833	10.014000	9	8.7859	0.0052
23	Bin # 8	10.014000	+Inf	4	5.8328	0.5759

[7]You might try defining the bins differently and rerunning the test. The category definitions *can* make a difference in the results. This is a disadvantage of the chi-square test.

terms, and cell B11 contains their sum, the chi-square test statistic. The corresponding *p*-value in cell B12 is 0.5206.

This large *p*-value provides no evidence whatsoever of non-normality. It implies that if this procedure were repeated on many random samples, each taken from a population known to be normal, a fit at least this poor would occur in over 50% of the samples. Stated differently, fewer than 50% of the fits would be *better* than the one observed here. Therefore, the manager can feel comfortable in making a normal assumption for this population. ∎

We make three comments about this chi-square procedure. First, the test *does* depend on which (and how many) bins you use for the histogram. Reasonable choices are likely to lead to the same conclusion, but this is not guaranteed. Second, the test is not very effective unless the sample size is large, say, at least 80 or 100. Only then can you begin to see the true shape of the histogram and judge accurately whether it is normal. Finally, the test tends to be *too* sensitive if the sample size is really large. In this case any little "bump" on the observed histogram is likely to lead to a conclusion of non-normality. This is one more example of practical versus statistical significance. With a large sample size you might be able to reject normality with a high degree of certainty, but the practical difference between the observed and normal histograms could very well be unimportant.

The Lilliefors test is based on a comparison of the cdf from the data and a normal cdf.

The chi-square test of normality is an intuitive one because it is based on histograms. However, it suffers from the first two points discussed in the previous paragraph. In particular, it is not as *powerful* as other available tests. This means that it is often unable to distinguish between normal and non-normal distributions, and hence it often fails to reject the null hypothesis of normality when it should be rejected. A more powerful test is called the *Lilliefors test*.[8] This test is based on the *cumulative distribution function* (cdf), which shows the probability of being less than or equal to any particular value. Specifically, the **Lilliefors test** compares two cdfs: the cdf from a normal distribution and the cdf corresponding to the given data. This latter cdf, called the *empirical cdf*, shows the fraction of observations less than or equal to any particular value. If the data come from a normal distribution, the normal and empirical cdfs should be quite close. Therefore, the Lilliefors test compares the *maximum vertical distance* between the two cdfs and compares it to specially tabulated values. If this maximum vertical distance is sufficiently large, the null hypothesis of normality can be rejected.

To run the Lilliefors test for the Width variable in Example 9.7, select Lilliefors Test from the StatTools Normality Tests dropdown list. StatTools then shows the numerical outputs in Figure 9.29 and the corresponding graph in Figure 9.30 of the normal

Figure 9.29

Lilliefors Test Results

◢	A	B
7		Width
8	*Lilliefors Test Results*	Data Set #1
9	Sample Size	90
10	Sample Mean	9.999256
11	Sample Std Dev	0.009728
12	Test Statistic	0.0513
13	CVal (15% Sig. Level)	0.0810
14	CVal (10% Sig. Level)	0.0856
15	CVal (5% Sig. Level)	0.0936
16	CVal (2.5% Sig. Level)	0.0998
17	CVal (1% Sig. Level)	0.1367

© Cengage Learning

[8]This is actually a special case of the more general and widely known *Kolmogorov-Smirnoff* (or K-S) test.

Figure 9.30

Normal and
Empirical
Cumulative
Distribution
Functions

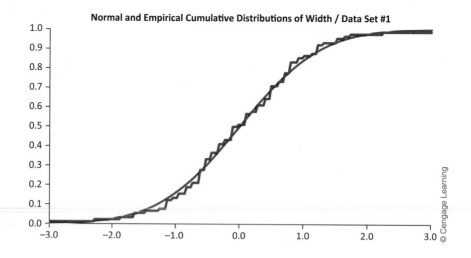

Normal and Empirical Cumulative Distributions of Width / Data Set #1

and empirical cdfs. The numeric output indicates that the maximum vertical distance between the two curves is 0.0513. It also provides a number of "CVal" values for comparison. If the test statistic is larger than any of these, the null hypothesis of normality can be rejected at the corresponding significance level. In this case, however, the test statistic is relatively small—not nearly large enough to reject the normal hypothesis at any of the usual significance levels. This conclusion agrees with the one based on the chi-square goodness-of-fit test (as well as the closeness of the two curves in Figure 9.30). Nevertheless, you should be aware that the two tests do not agree on *all* data sets.

If data are normally distributed, the points on the corresponding Q-Q plot should be close to a 45° line.

We conclude this section with a popular, but informal, test of normality. This is based on a plot called a **quantile-quantile** (or **Q-Q) plot**. Although the technical details for forming this plot are somewhat complex, it is basically a scatterplot of the standardized values from the data set versus the values that would be expected if the data were perfectly normally distributed (with the same mean and standard deviation as in the data set). If the data are, in fact, normally distributed, the points in this plot tend to cluster around a 45° line. Any large deviation from a 45° line signals some type of non-normality. Again, however, this is not a *formal* test of normality. A Q-Q plot is usually used only to obtain a general idea of whether the data are normally distributed and, if they are not, what type of non-normality exists. For example, if points on the right of the plot are well *above* a 45° line, this is an indication that the largest observations in the data set are larger than would be expected from a normal distribution. Therefore, these points might be high-end outliers and/or a signal of positive skewness.

To obtain a Q-Q plot for the Width variable in Example 9.7, select Q-Q Normal Plot from the StatTools Normality Tests dropdown list and check each option at the bottom of the dialog box. The Q-Q plot for the Width data in Example 9.7 appears in Figure 9.31. Although the points in this Q-Q plot do not all lie *exactly* on a 45° line, they are about as close to doing so as can be expected from real data. Therefore, there is no reason to question the normal hypothesis for these data—the same conclusion as from the chi-square and Lilliefors tests. (Note that in the StatTools Q-Q plot dialog box, you can elect to plot *standardized Q*-values. This option was used in Figure 9.31. The plot with *unstandardized Q*-values, not shown here, provides virtually the same information. The only difference is in the scale of the vertical axis.)

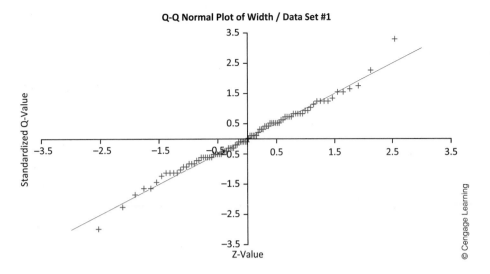

Figure 9.31

Q-Q Plot with
Standardized
Q-Values

PROBLEMS

Level A

40. The file **P02_11.xlsx** contains data on 148 houses sold in a certain suburban region.
   a. Create a histogram of the selling prices. Is there any visual evidence that the distribution of selling prices is *not* normal?
   b. Test the selling prices for normality using the chi-square test. Is there enough evidence at the 5% significance level to conclude that selling prices are *not* normally distributed? If so, what is there about the distribution that is not normal?
   c. Use the Lilliefors test and the Q-Q plot to check for normality of selling prices. Do these suggest the same conclusion as in part **b**? Explain.

41. The file **P09_33.xlsx** contains real estate taxes paid by a sample of 170 homeowners in a Florida city.
   a. Create a histogram of the taxes paid. Is there any visual evidence that the distribution of taxes paid is *not* normal?
   b. Test the taxes paid for normality using the chi-square test. Is there enough evidence at the 5% significance level to conclude that taxes paid are *not* normally distributed? If so, what is there about the distribution that is not normal?
   c. Use the Lilliefors test and the Q-Q plot to check for normality of taxes paid. Do these suggest the same conclusion as in part **b**? Explain.

42. The file **P09_42.xlsx** contains many years of monthly percentage changes in the Dow Jones Industrial Average (DJIA). (This is the same data set that was used for Example 2.6 in Chapter 2.)

   a. Create a histogram of the percentage changes in the DJIA. Is there any visual evidence that the distribution of the Dow percentage changes is *not* normal?
   b. Test the percentage changes of the DJIA for normality using the chi-square test. Is there enough evidence at the 5% significance level to conclude that the Dow percentage changes are *not* normally distributed? If so, what is there about the distribution that is not normal?
   c. Use the Lilliefors test and the Q-Q plot to check for normality of percentage changes. Do these suggest the same conclusion as in part **b**? Explain.
   d. Repeat parts **a–c**, but use data only from the years 1990 to 2011. Do you get the same results as for the full data set?

Level B

43. Will the chi-square test ever conclude, at the 5% significance level, that data are not normally distributed when you know that they are? Check this with simulation. Specifically, generate *n* normally distributed numbers with mean 100 and standard deviation 15. You can do this with the formula **=NORMINV(RAND(),100,12)**. Do *not* freeze them; keep them random. Then run the chi-square normality test on the random numbers. Because the chi-square results are linked to the data, you will get new chi-square results every time you press F9 to recalculate.
   a. Using *n* = 150, do you ever get a *p*-value less than 0.05? If so, what does such a *p*-value mean? Would you *expect* to get a few such *p*-values? Explain.

9-5 Tests for Normality **445**

b. Repeat part **a** using $n = 1000$. Do the results change in any qualitative way?

c. Repeat parts **a** and **b**, but use the Lilliefors test instead of the chi-square test. Do you get the same basic results?

44. Repeat the previous problem but with a *non*-normal population. Specifically, generate n random numbers from a fifty-fifty mixture of two normal distributions with respective means 90 and 110 and common standard deviation 10. You can do this with the formula **=IF(RAND()<0.5,NORMINV(RAND(),90,10), NORMINV(RAND(),110,10))** (This is *not* a normal distribution because it has two peaks.)

45. The file **P09_45.xlsx** contains measurements of ounces in randomly selected cans from a soft-drink filling machine. These cans reportedly contain 12 ounces, but because of natural variation, the actual amounts differ slightly from 12 ounces.

a. Can the company legitimately state that the amounts in cans are *normally* distributed?

b. *Assuming* that the distribution is normal with the mean and standard deviation found in this sample,

calculate the probability that at least half of the *next* 100 cans filled will contain less than 12 ounces.

c. If the test in part **a** indicated that the data are *not* normally distributed, how might you calculate the probability requested in part **b**?

46. The chi-square test for normality discussed in this section is far from perfect. If the sample is too small, the test tends to accept the null hypothesis of normality for any population distribution even remotely bell-shaped; that is, it is not *powerful* in detecting non-normality. On the other hand, if the sample is very large, it will tend to reject the null hypothesis of normality for *any* data set.[9] Check this by using simulation. First, simulate data from a normal distribution using a large sample size. Is there a good chance that the null hypothesis will (wrongly) be rejected? Then simulate data from a non-normal distribution (uniform, say, or the mixture in Problem 44) using a small sample size. Is there a good chance that the null hypothesis will (wrongly) not be rejected? Summarize your findings in a short report.

9-6 CHI-SQUARE TEST FOR INDEPENDENCE

The test we discuss in this section, like one of the tests for normality from the previous section, uses the name "chi-square." However, this test, called the **chi-square test for independence**, has an entirely different objective. It is used in situations where a population is categorized in two different ways. For example, people might be characterized by their smoking habits and their drinking habits. The question then is whether these two attributes are independent in a probabilistic sense. They are *independent* if information on a person's drinking habits is of no use in predicting the person's smoking habits (and vice versa). In this particular example, however, you might suspect that the two attributes are *dependent*. In particular, you might suspect that heavy drinkers are more likely (than non-heavy drinkers) to be heavy smokers, and you might suspect that nondrinkers are more likely (than drinkers) to be nonsmokers. The chi-square test for independence enables you to test this empirically.

Rejecting independence does not indicate the form of dependence. To see this, you must look more closely at the data.

The null hypothesis for this test is that the two attributes are independent. Therefore, statistically significant results are those that indicate some sort of dependence. As always, this puts the burden of proof on the alternative hypothesis of dependence. In the smoking–drinking example, you will continue to believe that smoking and drinking habits are unrelated—that is, independent—unless there is sufficient evidence from the data that they are dependent. Furthermore, even if you are able to conclude that they are dependent, the test itself does not indicate the *form* of dependence. It could be that heavy drinkers tend to be nonsmokers, and nondrinkers tend to be heavy smokers. Although this is unlikely, it is definitely a form of dependence. The only way you can decide which form of dependence exists is to look closely at the data.

The data for this test consist of *counts* in various combinations of categories. These are usually arranged in a rectangular *contingency table*, also called a *cross-tabs*, or, using

---

[9]Actually, all of the tests for normality suffer from this latter problem.

Excel terminology, a pivot table.[10] For example, if there are three smoking categories and three drinking categories, the table will have three rows and three columns, for a total of nine cells. The count in a cell is the number of observations in that particular combination of categories. Example 9.8 illustrates this data setup and the resulting analysis.

> The **chi-square test for independence** is based on the counts in a contingency (or cross-tabs) table. It tests whether the row variable is probabilistically independent of the column variable.

EXAMPLE

9.8 RELATIONSHIP BETWEEN DEMANDS FOR DESKTOPS AND LAPTOPS AT BIG OFFICE

Big Office, a chain of large office supply stores, sells a variety of Windows and Mac laptops. Company executives want to know whether the demands for these two types of computers are related in any way. They might act as complementary products, where high demand for Windows laptops accompanies high demand for Mac laptops (computers in general are hot), they might act as substitute products (demand for one takes away demand for the other), or their demands might be unrelated. Because of limitations in its information system, Big Office does not have the exact demands for these products. However, it does have daily information on categories of demand, listed in aggregate (that is, over all stores). These data appear in Figure 9.32. (See the file **Laptop Demand.xlsx**.) Each day's demand for each type of computer is categorized as Low, Medium Low, Medium High, or High. The table is based on 250 days, so that the counts add to 250. The individual counts show, for example, that demand was high for both Windows *and* Mac laptops on 11 of the 250 days. For convenience, the row and column totals are provided in the margins. Based on these data, can Big Office conclude that demands for these two products are independent?

Figure 9.32

Counts of Daily Demands for Windows and Mac Laptops

⁄	A	B	C	D	E	F	G
1	Counts on 250 days of demands at Big Office						
2							
3			Windows laptops				
4			Low	Medium Low	Medium High	High	
5	Mac laptops	Low	4	17	17	5	43
6		Medium Low	8	23	22	27	80
7		Medium High	16	20	14	20	70
8		High	10	17	19	11	57
9			38	77	72	63	250

© Cengage Learning

Objective To use the chi-square test of independence to test whether demand for Windows laptops is independent of demand for Mac laptops.

Solution

The idea of the test is to compare the actual counts in the table with what would be *expected* under independence. If the actual counts are sufficiently far from the expected counts, the

---

[10]As discussed in Chapter 3, statisticians have long used the terms *contingency table* and *cross-tabs* (interchangeably) for the tables we are discussing here. Pivot tables are more general—they can contain summary measures such as averages and standard deviations, not just counts. But when they contain counts, they are equivalent to contingency tables and cross-tabs.

null hypothesis of independence can be rejected. The *distance* measure used to check how far apart they are, shown in Equation (9.8), is essentially the same chi-square statistic used in the chi-square test for normality. Here, O_{ij} is the actual count in cell i,j (row i, column j), E_{ij} is the expected count for this cell assuming independence, and the sum is over all cells in the table. If this test statistic is sufficiently large, the independence hypothesis can be rejected. (We provide more details of the test shortly.)

Test Statistic for Chi-Square Test for Independence

$$\text{chi-square test statistic} = \sum_{ij}(O_{ij} - E_{ij})^2/E_{ij} \qquad (9.8)$$

What is expected under independence? The totals in row 9 indicate that demand for Windows laptops was low on 38 of the 250 days. Therefore, if you had to estimate the probability of low demand for Windows laptops, your estimate would be $38/250 = 0.152$. Now, if demands for the two products were independent, you should arrive at this *same* estimate from the data in any of rows 5 through 8. That is, a probability estimate for Windows laptops should be the same regardless of the demand for Mac laptops. The probability estimate of low Windows demand from row 5, for example, is $4/43 = 0.093$. Similarly, for rows 6, 7, and 8 it is $8/80 = 0.100$, $16/70 = 0.229$, and $10/57 = 0.175$, respectively. These calculations provide some evidence that Windows and Mac laptops act as *substitute* products—the probability of low Windows demand is larger when Mac demand is medium high or high than when it is low or medium low.

This reasoning is the basis for calculating the E_{ij}s. Specifically, it can be shown that the relevant formula for E_{ij} is given by Equation (9.9), where R_i is the row total in row i, C_j is the total in column j, and N is the number of observations. For example, E_{11} for these data is $43(38)/250 = 6.536$, which is slightly larger than the corresponding observed count, $O_{11} = 4$.

Expected Counts Assuming Row and Column Independence

$$E_{ij} = R_i C_j/N \qquad (9.9)$$

You can perform the calculations for the test easily with StatTools. This is one StatTools procedure that does *not* require a data set to be defined. You simply select Chi-Square Independence Test from the StatTools Statistical Inference dropdown list to obtain the dialog box shown in Figure 9.33. Here, you select the range of the contingency table. This range can include the row and column category labels (row 4 and column B), in which

Figure 9.33

Dialog Box for Chi-Square Test for Independence

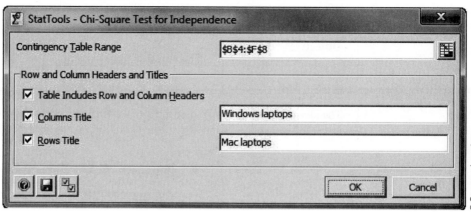

case you should check the top checkbox. The other two checkboxes, along with the titles, are used to provide labels for the resulting output.

The output appears in Figure 9.34. The top table (not shown here) repeats the counts from the original table. The next two tables show these counts as percentages of rows and percentages of columns, respectively. The expected counts and distances from actual to expected are shown next. They lead to the chi-square statistic and corresponding *p*-value at the bottom.

The *p*-value of the test, 0.045, can be interpreted in the usual way. Specifically, the null hypothesis of independence can be rejected at the 5% or 10% significance levels, but not at the 1% level. There is a fairly strong evidence that the demands for the two products are not independent.

If the alternative hypothesis of dependence is accepted, the output in Figure 9.34 can be used to examine its form. The two tables in rows 17 through 20 and rows 24 through 27 are especially helpful. If the demands *were* independent, the rows of this first table should

Tables of counts expressed as percentages of rows or of columns are useful for judging the form (and extent) of any possible dependence.

Figure 9.34 Output for Chi-Square Test

	A	B	C	D	E	F
15		Rows: Mac laptops / Columns: Windows laptops				
16	*Percentage of Rows*	Low	Medium Low	Medium High	High	
17	Low	9.30%	39.53%	39.53%	11.63%	100.00%
18	Medium Low	10.00%	28.75%	27.50%	33.75%	100.00%
19	Medium High	22.86%	28.57%	20.00%	28.57%	100.00%
20	High	17.54%	29.82%	33.33%	19.30%	100.00%
21						
22		Rows: Mac laptops / Columns: Windows laptops				
23	*Percentage of Columns*	Low	Medium Low	Medium High	High	
24	Low	10.53%	22.08%	23.61%	7.94%	
25	Medium Low	21.05%	29.87%	30.56%	42.86%	
26	Medium High	42.11%	25.97%	19.44%	31.75%	
27	High	26.32%	22.08%	26.39%	17.46%	
28		100.00%	100.00%	100.00%	100.00%	
29						
30		Rows: Mac laptops / Columns: Windows laptops				
31	*Expected Counts*	Low	Medium Low	Medium High	High	
32	Low	6.5360	13.2440	12.3840	10.8360	
33	Medium Low	12.1600	24.6400	23.0400	20.1600	
34	Medium High	10.6400	21.5600	20.1600	17.6400	
35	High	8.6640	17.5560	16.4160	14.3640	
36						
37		Rows: Mac laptops / Columns: Windows laptops				
38	*Distance from Expected*	Low	Medium Low	Medium High	High	
39	Low	0.9840	1.0652	1.7206	3.1431	
40	Medium Low	1.4232	0.1092	0.0469	2.3207	
41	Medium High	2.7002	0.1129	1.8822	0.3157	
42	High	0.2060	0.0176	0.4067	0.7878	
43						
44						
45	*Chi-Square Statistic*					
46	Chi-Square	17.2420				
47	*p*-Value	0.0451				

© Cengage Learning

9-6 Chi-Square Test for Independence **449**

be identical, and the columns of the second table should be identical. This is because each row in the first table shows the distribution of Windows demand for a given category of Mac demand, whereas each column in the second table shows the distribution of Mac demand for a given category of Windows demand. A close study of these percentages again provides some evidence that the two products act as substitutes, but the evidence is not overwhelming. ■

It is worth noting that the table of counts necessary for the chi-square test of independence can be a pivot table. For example, the pivot table in Figure 9.35 shows counts of the Married and Own Home attributes. (For Married, 1 means married, 0 means unmarried, and for Own Home, 1 means a home owner, 0 means not a home owner. This pivot table is based on the data in the **Catalog Marketing.xlsx** file from Chapter 2.) To see whether these two attributes are independent, the chi-square test would be performed on the table in the range B5:C6. You might want to check that the p-value for the test is 0.000 (to three decimals), so that Married and Own Home are *definitely* not independent.

Figure 9.35

Using a Pivot Table for a Chi-Square Test

Count	Column Labels		
Row Labels	0	1	Grand Total
0	307	191	498
1	177	325	502
Grand Total	484	516	1000

© Cengage Learning

PROBLEMS

Level A

47. The file **P08_49.xlsx** contains data on 400 orders placed to ElecMart company over a period of several months. For each order, the file lists the time of day, the type of credit card used, the region of the country where the customer resides, and others. (This is the same data set used in Example 3.4 of Chapter 3.) Use a chi-square test for independence to see whether the following variables are independent. If the variables appear to be related, discuss the form of dependence you see.
    a. Time and Region
    b. Region and Buy Category
    c. Gender and Card Type

48. The file **P08_18.xlsx** categorizes 250 randomly selected consumers on the basis of their gender, their age, and their preference for our brand or a competitor's brand of a low-calorie soft drink. Use a chi-square test for independence to see whether the drink preference is independent of gender, and then whether it is independent of age. If you find any dependence, discuss its nature.

49. The file **P02_11.xlsx** contains data on 148 houses that were recently sold. Two variables in this data set are

the selling price of the house and the number of bedrooms in the house. We want to use a chi-square test for independence to see whether these two variables are independent. However, this test requires *categorical* variables, and Selling Price is essentially continuous. Therefore, to run the test, first divide the prices into several categories: less than 120, 120 to 130, 130 to 140, and greater than 140. Then run the test and report your results.

Level B

50. The file **P03_50.xlsx** contains annual salaries for all NBA basketball players in each of five seasons.
    a. Using only the data for the most recent season (2008–2009), check whether there is independence between position and salary. To do this, first change any hyphenated position such as C-F to the first listed, in this case C. (Presumably, this is the player's primary position.) Then make Salary categorical with four categories: the first is all salaries below the first quartile, the second is all salaries from the first quartile to the median, and so on. Explain your findings.
    b. Repeat part **a** but with a Yes/No playoff team categorization instead of position. The playoff

teams in that season were Atlanta, Boston, Chicago, Cleveland, Dallas, Denver, Detroit, Houston, Los Angeles Lakers, Miami, New Orleans, Orlando, Philadelphia, Portland, San Antonio, and Utah.

51. The file **P09_51.xlsx** contains data on 1000 randomly selected Walmart customers. The data set includes demographic variables for each customer as well as their salaries and the amounts they have spent at Walmart during the past year.

   a. A lookup table in the file suggests a way to categorize the salaries. Use this categorization and chi-square tests of independence to see whether Salary is independent of (1) Age, (2) Gender, (3) Home, or (4) Married. Discuss any types of dependence you find.

   b. Repeat part **a**, replacing Salary with Amount Spent. First you must categorize Amount Spent. Create

four categories for Amount Spent based on the four quartiles. The first category is all values of Amount Spent below the first quartile of Amount Spent, the second category is between the first quartile and the median, and so on.

52. The file **C07_01.xlsx** (the file that accompanies the case for Chapter 7) contains data on close to 10,000 customers from several large cities in the United States. The variables include the customers' gender and their first choice among several types of movies. Perform chi-square tests of independence to test whether the following variables are related. If they are, discuss the form of dependence you see.

   a. State and First Choice
   b. City and First Choice
   c. Gender and First Choice

9-7 CONCLUSION

The concepts and procedures in this chapter form a cornerstone in both applied and theoretical statistics. Of particular importance is the interpretation of a p-value, especially because p-values are reported in virtually all statistical software packages. A p-value summarizes the evidence in support of an alternative hypothesis, which is usually the hypothesis an analyst is trying to prove. Small p-values provide support for the alternative hypothesis, whereas large p-values provide little or no support for it.

Although hypothesis testing continues to be an important tool for analysts, it is important to note its limitations, particularly in business applications. First, given a choice between a confidence interval for some population parameter and a test of this parameter, we generally favor the confidence interval. For example, a confidence interval not only indicates whether a mean difference is 0, but it also provides a plausible range for this difference. Second, many business *decision* problems cannot be handled adequately with hypothesis-testing procedures. Either they ignore important cost information or they treat the consequences of incorrect decisions (type I and type II errors) in an inappropriate way. Finally, the *statistical* significance at the core of hypothesis testing is sometimes quite different from the *practical* significance that is of most interest to business managers.

Summary of Key Terms

Term	Explanation	Excel	Pages	Equation
Null hypothesis	Hypothesis that represents the current thinking or status quo		403	
Alternative hypothesis	Typically, the hypothesis the analyst is trying to prove or research hypothesis		402	
One-tailed test	Test where values in only one direction will lead to rejection of the null hypothesis		405	
Two-tailed test	Test where values in both directions will lead to rejection of the null hypothesis		405	
Type I error	Error committed when null hypothesis is true but is rejected		405	

(continued)

Summary of Key Terms (*Continued*)

Term	Explanation	Excel	Pages	Equation
Type II error	Error committed when null hypothesis is false but is not rejected		405	
Significance level	The probability of a type I error an analyst chooses		406	
Rejection region	Sample results that lead to rejection of null hypothesis		406	
Statistically significant results	Sample results that lead to rejection of null hypothesis		409	
p-value	Probability of observing a sample result at least as extreme as the one actually observed		407	
Power	Probability of correctly rejecting the null when it is false		408	
t test for a population mean	Test for a mean from a single population	StatTools/Statistical Inference/Hypothesis Test	410	9.1
z test for a population proportion	Test for a proportion from a single population	StatTools/Statistical Inference/Hypothesis Test	418	9.2
t test for difference between means from paired samples	Test for the difference between two population means when samples are paired in a natural way	StatTools/Statistical Inference/Hypothesis Test	421	9.3
t test for difference between means from independent samples	Test for the difference between two population means when samples are independent	StatTools/Statistical Inference/Hypothesis Test	421	9.4
F test for equality of two variances	Test for equality of two population variances, used to check an assumption of two-sample *t* test for difference between means	StatTools/Statistical Inference/Hypothesis Test	431	
F distribution	Skewed distribution useful for testing equality of variances	= FDIST(*value, df1, df2*) = FINV(*prob, df1, df2*)	431	
z test for difference between proportions	Test for difference between similarly defined proportions from two populations	StatTools/Statistical Inference/Hypothesis Test	432	9.5, 9.6
Tests for normality	Tests to check whether a population is normally distributed; possibilities include chi-square test, Lilliefors test, and Q-Q plot	StatTools/Normality Tests	440	9.7
Chi-square test for independence	Test to check whether two attributes are probabilistically independent	StatTools/Statistical Inference/Chi-square Independence Test	446	9.8, 9.9

PROBLEMS

Conceptual Questions

C.1. Suppose you are testing the null hypothesis that a mean equals 75 versus a two-tailed alternative. If the true (but unknown) mean is 80, what kind of error *might* you make? When will you *not* make this error?

C.2. Suppose you hear the claim that a given test, such as the chi-square test for normality, is not very *powerful*. What exactly does this mean? If another test, such as the Lilliefors test, is claimed to be more powerful, how is it better than the less powerful test?

C.3. Explain exactly what it means for a test statistic to fall in the rejection region.

C.4. Give an example of when a one-sided test on a population mean would make more sense than a two-tailed test. Give an example of the opposite. In general, why do we say that there is no *statistical* way to decide whether a test should be run as a one-tailed test or a two-tailed test?

C.5. For any given hypothesis test, that is, for any specification of the null and alternative hypotheses, explain why you could make only a type I error or a type II error, but not both. When would you make a type I error? When would you make a type II error? Answer as generally as possible.

C.6. What are the null and alternative hypotheses in the chi-square or Lilliefors test for normality? Where is the burden of proof? Might you argue that it should go in the other direction? Explain.

C.7. We didn't discuss the role of sample size in this chapter as thoroughly as we did for confidence intervals in the previous chapter, but more advanced books do include sample size formulas for hypothesis testing. Consider the situation where you are testing the null hypothesis that a population mean is less than or equal to 100 versus a one-tailed alternative. A sample size formula might indicate the sample size needed to make the power at least 0.90 when the true mean is 103. What are the trade-offs here? Essentially, what is the advantage of a larger sample size?

C.8. Suppose that you wish to test a researcher's claim that the mean height in meters of a normally distributed population of rosebushes at a nursery has increased from its commonly accepted value of 1.60. To carry out this test, you obtain a random sample of size 150 from this population. This sample yields a mean of 1.80 and a standard deviation of 1.30. What are the appropriate null and alternative hypotheses? Is this a one-tailed or two-tailed test?

C.9. Suppose that you wish to test a manager's claim that the proportion of defective items generated by a particular production process has decreased from its long-run historical value of 0.30. To carry out this test, you obtain a random sample of 300 items produced through this process. The test indicates a *p*-value of 0.01. What exactly is this *p*-value telling you? At what levels of significance can you reject the null hypothesis?

C.10. Suppose that a 99% confidence interval for the proportion *p* of all Lakeside residents whose annual income exceeds 80,000 extends from 0.10 to 0.18. The confidence interval is based on a random sample of 150 Lakeside residents. Using this information and a 1% significance level, you wish to test $H_0: p = 0.08$ versus $H_a: p \neq 0.08$. Based on the given information, are you able to reject the null hypothesis? Why or why not?

C.11. Suppose that you are performing a one-tailed hypothesis test. "Assuming that everything else remains constant, a decrease in the test's level of significance (α) leads to a higher probability of rejecting the null hypothesis." Is this statement true or false? Explain your reasoning.

C.12. Can pleasant aromas help people work more efficiently? Researchers conducted an investigation to answer this question. Fifty students worked a paper-and-pencil maze ten times. On five attempts, the students wore a mask with floral scents. On the other five attempts, they wore a mask with no scent. The 10 trials were performed in random order and each used a different maze. The researchers found that the subjects took less time to complete the maze when wearing the scented mask. Is this an example of an *observational study* or a *controlled experiment*? Explain.

Level A

53. The file **P09_53.xlsx** contains the number of days 44 mothers spent in the hospital after giving birth (in the year 2005). Before health insurance rules were changed (the change was effective January 1, 2005), the average number of days spent in a hospital by a new mother was two days. For a 5% level of significance, do the data in the file indicate (the research hypothesis) that women are now spending less time in the hospital after giving birth than they were prior to 2005? Explain your answer in terms of the *p*-value for the test.

54. Eighteen readers took a speed-reading course. The file **P09_54.xlsx** contains the number of words that they could read before and after the course. Test the alternative hypothesis at the 5% significance level that reading speeds have increased, on average, as a result of the course. Explain your answer in terms of the *p*-value. Do you need to assume that reading speeds (before and after) are normally distributed? Why or why not?

55. Statistics have shown that a child 0 to 4 years of age has a 0.0002 probability of getting cancer in any given year. Assume that during each of the last seven years there have been 100 children ages 0 to 4 years whose parents work in a university's business school. Four of these children have gotten cancer. Use this evidence to test whether the incidence of childhood cancer among children ages 0 to 4 years whose parents work at this business school exceeds the national average. State your hypotheses and determine the appropriate *p*-value.

56. African Americans in a St. Louis suburb sued the city claiming they were discriminated against in school-teacher hiring. Of the city's population, 5.7% were African American; of 405 teachers in the school system, 15 were African American. Set up appropriate hypotheses and determine whether African Americans are underrepresented. Does your answer depend on whether you use a one-tailed or two-tailed test? In discrimination cases, the Supreme Court always uses a two-tailed test at the 5% significance level. (Source: U.S. Supreme Court Case, *Hazlewood v. City of St. Louis*)

57. We hear that teenagers in today's world spend too much time playing video games. Does this have a significant effect on the grades they earn at school? You could test by this dividing students into two groups, those whose current high school grade-point average (GPA) is 3.0 or above and those whose GPA is below 3.0. Then you could sample students from each of these groups, discover the numbers of hours per week spent playing video games, and run a test to see whether high-GPA students average less time playing video games than low-GPA students. Run such a test on the (fictional) data in the file **P09_57.xlsx** and report the results. If the results are significant, does this prove that too many hours spent playing video games *causes* lower GPAs? Explain.

58. Sixty people have rated a new beer on a taste scale of 0 to 100. Their ratings are in the file **P09_58.xlsx**. Marketing has determined that the beer will be a success if the average taste rating exceeds 75. Using a 5% significance level, is there sufficient evidence to conclude that the beer will be a success? Discuss your result in terms of a *p*-value. Assume ratings are at least approximately normally distributed.

59. Fifty people were asked to rate a competitive beer on a taste scale of 0 to 100. Another 50 people were asked to rate our beer on the same taste scale. The file **P09_59.xlsx** contains the results. Do these data provide sufficient evidence to conclude, at the 1% significance level, that people believe our beer tastes better than the competitor's? Assume ratings are at least approximately normally distributed. Would you reach the same conclusion if only the data from the first 10 people in each group were used?.

60. Callaway is thinking about entering the golf ball market. The company will make a profit if its market share is more than 20%. A market survey indicates that 140 of 624 golf ball purchasers will buy a Callaway golf ball.
  a. Is this enough evidence to persuade Callaway to enter the golf ball market?
  b. How would you make the decision if you were Callaway management? Would you use hypothesis testing?

61. Sales of a new product will be profitable if the average of sales per store exceeds 100 per week. The product was test-marketed for one week at 10 stores, with the results listed in the file **P09_61.xlsx**. Assume that sales at each store are at least approximately normally distributed.
  a. Is this enough evidence to persuade the company to market the new product?
  b. How would you make the decision if you were deciding whether to market the new product? Would you use hypothesis testing?

62. A recent study concluded that children born to mothers who take Prozac tend to have more birth defects than children born to mothers who do not take Prozac.
  a. What do you think the null and alternative hypotheses were for this study?
  b. If you were a spokesperson for Eli Lilly (the company that produces Prozac), how might you rebut the conclusions of this study?

Level B

63. Suppose that you are the state superintendent of Tennessee public schools. You want to know whether decreasing the class size in grades 1 through 3 will improve student performance. Explain how you would set up a test to determine whether decreased class size improves student performance. What hypotheses would you use in this experiment? (This was actually done and smaller class size did help, particularly with minority students.)

64. The file **P02_35.xlsx** contains data from a survey of 500 randomly selected households. Economic researchers would like to test for a significant difference between the mean annual income levels of the first household wage earners in the first (i.e., SW) and second (i.e., NW) sectors of this community. In fact, they intend to perform similar hypothesis tests for the differences between the mean annual income levels of the first household wage earners from all other pairs of locations (i.e., first and third, first and fourth, second and third, second and fourth, and third and fourth).
  a. Before conducting any hypothesis tests on the difference between various pairs of mean income levels, perform a test for equal population variances in each pair of locations. For each pair, report a *p*-value and interpret its meaning.
  b. Based on your conclusions in part **a**, which test statistic should be used in performing a test for the existence of a difference between population means?
  c. Given your conclusions in part **b**, perform a test for the existence of a difference in mean annual income levels in each pair of locations. For each pair, report a *p*-value and interpret its meaning.

65. A group of 25 husbands and wives were chosen randomly. Each person was asked to indicate the most he or she would be willing to pay for a new car (assuming each had decided to buy a new car). The results are shown in the file **P09_65.xlsx**. Can you accept the alternative hypothesis that the husbands are willing to spend more, on average, than the wives at the 5% significance level? What is the associated *p*-value? Is it appropriate to use a paired-sample or independent-sample test? Does it make a difference? Explain your reasoning.

66. A company is concerned with the high cholesterol levels of many of its employees. To help combat the problem, it opens an exercise facility and encourages its employees to use this facility. After a year, it chooses a random 100 employees who claim they use the facility regularly, and another 200 who claim they don't use it at all. The cholesterol levels of these 300 employees are checked, with the results shown in the file **P09_66.xlsx**.

   a. Is this sample evidence "proof" that the exercise facility, when used, tends to lower the mean cholesterol level? Phrase this as a hypothesis-testing problem and do the appropriate analysis. Do you feel comfortable that your analysis answers the question definitively (one way or the other)? Why or why not?

   b. Repeat part **a**, but replace "mean cholesterol level" with "percentage with level over 215." (The company believes that any level over 215 is dangerous.)

   c. What can you say about causality? Could you ever conclude from such a study that the exercise *causes* low cholesterol? Why or why not?

67. Suppose that you are trying to compare two populations on some variable (GMAT scores of men versus women, for example). Specifically, you are testing the null hypothesis that the means of the two populations are equal versus a two-tailed hypothesis. Are the following statements correct? Why or why not?

   a. A given difference (such as five points) between sample means from these populations will probably not be considered statistically significant if the sample sizes are small, but it will probably be considered statistically significant if the sample sizes are large.

   b. Virtually any difference between the population means will lead to statistically significant sample results if the sample sizes are sufficiently large.

68. Continuing the previous problem, analyze part **b** in Excel as follows. Start with hypothetical population mean GMAT scores for men and women, along with population standard deviations. Enter these at the top of a worksheet. You can make the two means as close as you like, but not identical. Simulate a sample of

men's GMAT scores with your mean and standard deviation in column A. Do the same for women in column B. The sample sizes do not have to be the same, but you can make them the same. Then run the test for the difference between two means. (The point of this problem is that if the population means are fairly close and you pick relatively small sample sizes, the sample mean differences probably won't be significant. If you find this, generate new samples of a larger sample size and redo the test. Now they might be significant. If not, try again with a still larger sample size. Eventually, you should get statistically significant differences.)

69. This problem concerns course scores (on a 0−100 scale) for a large undergraduate computer programming course. The class is composed of both underclassmen (freshmen and sophomores) and upperclassmen (juniors and seniors). Also, the students can be categorized according to their previous mathematical background from previous courses as "low" or "high" mathematical background. The data for these students are in the file **P09_69.xlsx**. The variables are:

- Score: score on a 0−100 scale
- Upper Class: 1 for an upperclassman, 0 otherwise
- High Math: 1 for a high mathematical background, 0 otherwise

For the following questions, assume that the students in this course represent a random sample from all college students who might take the course. This latter group is the population.

   a. Find a 90% confidence interval for the population mean score for the course. Do the same for the mean of all upperclassmen. Do the same for the mean of all upperclassmen with a high mathematical background.

   b. The professor believes he has enough evidence to "prove" the research hypothesis that upperclassmen score at least five points better, on average, than lowerclassmen. Do you agree? Answer by running the appropriate test.

   c. If a "good" grade is one that is at least 80, is there enough evidence to reject the null hypothesis that the fraction of good grades is the same for students with low math backgrounds as those with high math backgrounds? Which do you think is more appropriate, a one-tailed or two-tailed test? Explain your reasoning.

70. A cereal company wants to see which of two promotional strategies, supplying coupons in a local newspaper or including coupons in the cereal package itself, is more effective. (In the latter case, there is a label on the package indicating the presence of the coupon inside.) The company randomly chooses 80 Kroger's stores around the country—all of approximately the same size and overall sales volume—and promotes its cereal one way at 40 of these sites, and the other way at the other 40 sites. (All are at different geographical locations, so local newspaper ads for one of the sites should not affect sales at any other site.) Unfortunately, as in many business experiments, there is a factor beyond the company's control, namely, whether its main competitor at any particular site happens to be running a promotion of its own. The file **P09_70.xlsx** has 80 observations on three variables:

- Sales: number of boxes sold during the first week of the company's promotion
- Promotion Type: 1 if coupons are in local paper, 0 if coupons are inside box
- Competitor Promotion: 1 if main competitor is running a promotion, 0 otherwise

a. Based on all 80 observations, find (1) the difference in sample mean sales between stores running the two different promotional types (and indicate which sample mean is larger), (2) the standard error of this difference, and (3) a 90% confidence interval for the population mean difference.

b. Test whether the population mean difference is zero (the null hypothesis) versus a two-tailed alternative. State whether you should accept or reject the null hypothesis, and why.

c. Repeat part **b**, but now restrict the population to stores where the competitor is not running a promotion of its own.

d. Based on data from all 80 observations, can you accept the (alternative) hypothesis, at the 5% level, that the mean company sales drop by at least 30 boxes when the competitor runs its own promotion (as opposed to not running its own promotion)?

e. We often use the term *population* without really thinking what it means. For this problem, explain in words exactly what the population mean refers to. What is the relevant population?

71. There is a lot of concern about "salary compression" in universities. This is the effect of paying huge salaries to attract newly-minted Ph.D. graduates to university tenure-track positions and not having enough left in the budget to compensate tenured faculty as fully as they might deserve. In short, it is very possible for a new hire to make a larger salary than a person with many years of valuable experience. The file **P09_71.xlsx** contains (fictional but realistic) salaries for a sample of business school professors, some already tenured and some not yet through the tenure process. Formulate reasonable null and alternative hypotheses and then test them with this data set. Write a short report of your findings.

CASE 9.1 REGRESSION TOWARD THE MEAN

In Chapters 10 and 11, you will study regression, a method for relating one variable to other explanatory variables. However, the term *regression* has sometimes been used in a slightly different way, meaning "regression toward the mean." The example often cited is of male heights. If a father is unusually tall, for example, his son will typically be taller than average but not as tall as the father. Similarly, if a father is unusually short, the son will typically be shorter than average but not as short as the father. We say that the son's height tends to regress toward the mean. This case illustrates how regression toward the mean can occur.

Suppose a company administers an aptitude test to all of its job applicants. If an applicant scores below some value, he or she cannot be hired immediately but is allowed to retake a similar exam at a later time. In the interim the applicant can presumably study to prepare for the second exam. If we focus on the applicants who fail the exam the

first time and then take it a second time, we would probably expect them to score better on the second exam. One plausible reason is that they are more familiar with the exam the second time. However, we will rule this out by assuming that the two exams are sufficiently different from one another. A second plausible reason is that the applicants have studied between exams, which has a beneficial effect. However, we will argue that even if studying has *no beneficial effect whatsoever*, these applicants will tend to do better the second time around. The reason is regression toward the mean. All of these applicants scored unusually low on the first exam, so they will tend to regress toward the mean on the second exam—that is, they will tend to score higher.

You can employ simulation to demonstrate this phenomenon, using the following model. Assume that the scores of *all* potential applicants are normally distributed with mean μ and standard deviation σ. Because we are assuming that any studying between exams has no beneficial effect, this distribution of scores is the *same* on the second exam as on the first. An applicant fails the first exam if his or her score is below some cutoff value *L*. Now, we would certainly expect scores on the two exams to be positively correlated, with some correlation ρ. (This is the Greek letter "rho," often used for a population correlation.) That is, if everyone took both exams, applicants who scored high on the first would tend to score high on the second, and those who scored low on the first would tend to score low on the second. (This isn't regression to the mean, but simply that some applicants are better than others.)

Given this model, you can proceed by simulating many pairs of scores, one pair for each applicant. The scores for each exam should be normally distributed with parameters μ and σ, but the trick is to make them correlated. You can use our Binormal function to do this. (Binormal is short for *bivariate normal*.) This function is supplied in the file **C09_01.xlsm**. (Binormal is *not* a built-in

Excel function.) It takes a pair of means (both equal to μ), a pair of standard deviations (both equal to σ), and a correlation ρ as arguments, with the syntax **=BINORMAL (*means, stdevs, correlation*)**. To enter the formula, highlight two adjacent cells such as B5 and C5, type the formula, and press Ctrl+Shift+Enter. Then copy and paste to generate similar values for other applicants.

Once you have generated pairs of scores for many applicants, you should ignore all pairs except for those where the score on the first exam is less than *L*. (Sorting is suggested here, but freeze the random numbers first.) For these pairs, test whether the mean score on the second exam is *higher* than on the first, using a paired-samples test. If it is, you have demonstrated regression toward the mean. As you will probably discover, however, the results will depend on the values of the parameters you choose for μ, σ, ρ, and *L*. You should experiment with these. Assuming that you are able to demonstrate regression toward the mean, can you explain intuitively why it occurs?

CASE 9.2 Friday Effect in the Stock Market

Many people believe that there is a "Friday effect" in the stock market. They don't necessarily spell out exactly what they mean by this, but there is a sense that stock prices tend to be lower on Fridays than on other days. Because stock prices are readily available on the Web, it should be fairly easy to test this (alternative) hypothesis empirically.

Before collecting data and running a test, however, you must decide *exactly* which hypotheses you want to test because there are several possibilities. Formulate at least two sets of null/alternative hypotheses. Then gather some stock price data and test your hypotheses. Can you conclude that there is a statistically significant Friday effect in the stock market?

CASE 9.3 The Wichita Anti–Drunk Driving Advertising Campaign[11]

Each year drinking and driving behavior are estimated to be responsible for approximately 24,000 traffic fatalities in the United States. Data show that a preponderance of this problem is due to the behavior of young males. Indeed, a disproportionate number of traffic fatalities are young people between 15 and 24 years of age. Market research among young people has suggested that the

perverse behavior of driving automobiles while under the influence of alcoholic beverages might be reduced by a mass media communications/advertising program based on an understanding of the "consumer psychology" of young male drinking and driving. There is some precedent for this belief. Reduction in cigarette smoking over the last 25 years is often attributed in part to mass antismoking advertising

[11]This case was contributed by Peter Kolesar from Columbia University.

campaigns. There is also precedent for being less optimistic because past experimental campaigns against drunk driving have shown little success.

Between March and August of 1986, an anti–drinking and driving advertising campaign was conducted in the city of Wichita, Kansas. In this federally sponsored experiment, several carefully constructed messages were aired on television and radio and posted in newspapers and on billboards. Unlike earlier and largely ineffective campaigns that depended on donated talent and media time, this test was sufficiently funded to create impressive anti–drinking and driving messages, and to place them so that the targeted audience would be reached. The messages were pretested before the program and the final version won an OMNI advertising award.

To evaluate the effectiveness of this anti–drinking and driving campaign, researchers collected before and after data (preprogram and postprogram) of several types. In addition to data collection in Wichita, they also selected Omaha, Nebraska, as a control. Omaha, another midwestern city on the Great Plains, was arguably similar to Wichita, but was not subjected to such an advertising campaign. The following tables contain some of the data gathered by researchers to evaluate the impact of the program.

Table 9.1 contains background demographics on the test and control cities. Table 9.2 contains data obtained from telephone surveys of 18- to 24-year-old males in both cities. The surveys were done using a random telephone dialing technique. They had an 88% response rate during the preprogram survey and a 91% response rate during the postprogram survey. Respondents were asked whether they had driven under the influence of four or more alcoholic drinks, or six or more alcoholic drinks, at least once in the previous month. The preprogram data were collected in September 1985, and the postprogram data were collected in September 1986.

Table 9.1   Demographics for Wichita and Omaha

	Wichita	Omaha
Total population	411,313	483,053
Percentage 15–24 years	19.2	19.5
Race		
White	85	87
Black	8	9
Hispanic	4	2
Other	3	2
Percent high school graduates among those 18 years and older	75.4	79.9
Private car ownership	184,641	198,723

© Cengage Learning

Table 9.2   Telephone Survey of 18- to 24-Year-Old Males

	Wichita		Omaha	
	Before Program	After Program	Before Program	After Program
Respondents	205	221	203	157
Drove after 4 drinks	71	61	77	69
Drove after 6 drinks	42	37	45	38

© Cengage Learning

Table 9.3 contains counts of fatal or incapacitating accidents involving young people gathered from the Kansas and Nebraska traffic safety departments during the spring and summer months of 1985 (before program) and 1986 (during the program). The spring and summer months were defined to be the period from March to August. These data were taken by the research team as indicators of driving under the influence of alcohol. Researchers at first proposed to also gather data on the blood alcohol content of drivers involved in fatal accidents. However, traffic safety experts pointed out that such data are often inconsistent and incomplete because police at the scene of a fatal accident have more pressing duties to perform than to gather such data. On the other hand, it is well established that alcohol is implicated in a major proportion of nighttime traffic fatalities, and for that reason, the data also focus on accidents at night among two classes of young people: the group of accidents involving 18- to 24-year-old males as a driver, and the group of accidents involving 15- to 24-year-old males and/or females as a driver.

The categories of accidents recorded were as follows:

■ Total: total count of all fatal and incapacitating accidents in the indicated driver group

■ Single vehicle: single vehicle fatal and incapacitating accidents in the indicated driver group

■ Nighttime: nighttime (8 P.M. to 8 A.M.) fatal and incapacitating accidents in the indicated driver group

It was estimated that if a similar six-month advertising campaign were run nationally, it would cost about $25 million. The Commissioner of the U.S. National Highway Safety Commission had funded a substantial part of the study and needed to decide what, if anything, to do next.

Table 9.3 Average Monthly Number of Fatal and Incapacitating Accidents, March to August

Driver Group	Accident Type	Wichita 1985	Wichita 1986	Omaha 1985	Omaha 1986
18- to 24-year-old males	Total	68	55	41	40
	Single	13	13	13	14
	Night	36	35	25	26
15- to 24-year-old males and females	Total	117	97	59	57
	Single	22	17	16	20
	Night	56	52	34	38

© Cengage Learning

CASE 9.4 REMOVING VIOXX FROM THE MARKET

For years, the drug Vioxx, developed and marketed by Merck, was one of the blockbuster drugs on the market. One of a number of so-called Cox-2 anti-inflammatory drugs, Vioxx was considered by many people a miracle drug for alleviating the pain from arthritis and other painful afflictions. Vioxx was marketed heavily on television, prescribed by most physicians, and used by an estimated two million Americans.

All of that changed in October 2004, when the results of a large study were released. The study, which followed approximately 2600 subjects over a period of about 18 months, concluded that Vioxx use over a long period of time caused a significant increase in the risk of developing serious heart problems. Merck almost immediately pulled Vioxx from the American market and doctors stopped prescribing it. On the basis of the study, Merck faced not only public embarrassment but the prospect of huge financial losses.

More specifically, the study had 1287 patients use Vioxx for an 18-month period, and it had another 1299 patients use a placebo over the same

period. After 18 months, 45 of the Vioxx patients had developed serious heart problems, whereas only 25 patients on the placebo developed such problems.

Given these results, would you agree with the conclusion that Vioxx caused a *significant* increase in the risk of developing serious heart problems? First, answer this from a purely statistical point of view, where *significant* means statistically significant. What hypothesis should you test, and how should you run the test? When you run the test, what is the corresponding *p*-value? Next, look at it from the point of view of patients. If you were a Vioxx user, would these results cause you significant worry? After all, some of the subjects who took placebos also developed heart problems, and 45 might not be considered that much larger than 25. Finally, look at it from Merck's point of view. Are the results practically significant to the company? What does it stand to lose? Develop an estimate, no matter how wild it might be, of the financial losses Merck might incur. Just think of all of those American Vioxx users and what they might do.

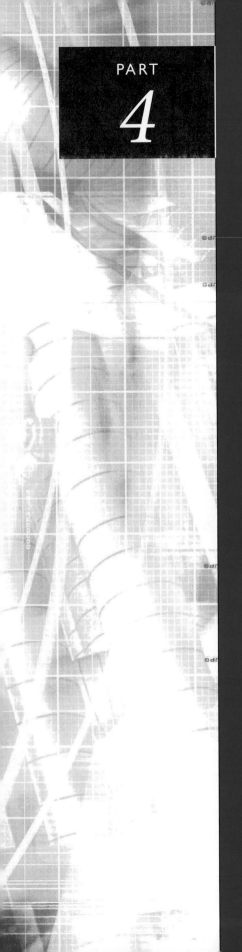

Regression Analysis: Estimating Relationships

Drew Myers/Corbis

SITE LOCATION OF LA QUINTA MOTOR INNS

Regression analysis is an extremely flexible tool that can aid decision making in many areas. Kimes and Fitzsimmons (1990) describe how it has been used by La Quinta Motor Inns, a moderately priced hotel chain oriented toward serving the business traveler, to help make site location decisions. Location is one of the most important decisions for a lodging firm. All hotel chains search for ideal locations and often compete against each other for the same sites. A hotel chain that can select good sites more accurately and quickly than its competition has a distinct competitive advantage.

Kimes and Fitzsimmons, academics hired by La Quinta to model its site location decision process, used regression analysis. They collected data on 57 mature inns belonging to La Quinta during a three-year business cycle. The data included profitability for each inn (defined as operating margin percentage—profit plus depreciation and interest expenses, divided by the total revenue), as well as a number of potential explanatory variables that could be used to predict profitability. These explanatory variables fell into five categories: competitive characteristics (such as number of hotel rooms in the vicinity and average room rates); demand generators (such as hospitals and office buildings within a 4-mile radius that might attract customers to the area); demo-graphic characteristics (such as local population, unemployment rate, and median family income); market awareness (such as years the inn has been open and state population per inn); and physical considerations (such as accessibility, distance to downtown, and sign visibility).

The analysts then determined which of these potential explanatory variables were most highly correlated (positively or negatively) with profitability and entered these variables into a regression equation for profitability. The estimated regression equation was

$$\text{Predicted Profitability} = 39.05 - 5.41\,\text{StatePop} + 5.81\,\text{Price}$$

$$-3.09\sqrt{\text{MedIncome}} + 1.75\,\text{ColStudents}$$

where *StatePop* is the state population (in 1000s) per inn, *Price* is the room rate for the inn, *MedIncome* is the median income (in $1000s) of the area, *ColStudents* is the number of college students (in 1000s) within four miles, and all variables in this equation are standardized to have mean 0 and standard deviation 1. This equation predicts that profitability will increase when room rate and the number of college students *increase* and when state population and median income *decrease*. The R^2 value (to be discussed in this chapter) was a respectable 0.51, indicating a reasonable predictive ability. Using good statistical practice, the analysts validated this equation by feeding it explanatory variable data on a set of *different* inns, attempting to predict profitability for these new inns. The validation was a success—the regression equation predicted profitability fairly accurately for this new set of inns.

La Quinta management, however, was not as interested in predicting the exact profitability of inns as in predicting which would be profitable and which would be unprofitable. A cutoff value of 35% for operating margin was used to divide the profitable inns from the unprofitable inns. (Approximately 60% of the inns in the original sample were profitable by this definition.) The analysts were still able to use the regression equation they had developed. For any prospective site, they used the regression equation to predict profitability, and if the predicted value was sufficiently high, they predicted that site would be profitable. They selected a decision rule—that is, how high was "sufficiently high"—from considerations of the two potential types of errors. One type of error, a false positive, was predicting that a site would be profitable when in fact it was headed for unprofitability. The opposite type of error, a false negative, was predicting that a site would be unprofitable (and rejecting the site) when in fact it would have been profitable. La Quinta management was more concerned about false positives, so it was willing to be conservative in its decision rule and miss a few potential opportunities for profitable sites.

Since the time of the study, La Quinta has implemented the regression model in spreadsheet form. For each potential site, it collects data on the relevant explanatory variables, uses the regression equation to predict the site's profitability, and applies the decision rule on whether to build. Of course, the model's recommendation is only that—a recommendation. Top management has the ultimate say on whether any site is used. As Sam Barshop, then chairman of the board and president of La Quinta Motor Inns stated, "We currently use the model to help us in our site-screening process and have found that it has raised the 'red flag' on several sites we had under consideration. We plan to continue using and updating the model in the future in our attempt to make La Quinta a leader in the business hotel market." ■

10-1 INTRODUCTION

Regression analysis is the study of relationships between variables. It is one of the most useful tools for a business analyst because it applies to so many situations. Some potential uses of regression analysis in business include the following:

- How do wages of employees depend on years of experience, years of education, and gender?

- How does the current price of a stock depend on its own past values, as well as the current and past values of a market index?

- How does a company's current sales level depend on its current and past advertising levels, the advertising levels of its competitors, the company's own past sales levels, and the general level of the market?

- How does the total cost of producing a batch of items depend on the total quantity of items that have been produced?

- How does the selling price of a house depend on such factors as the appraised value of the house, the square footage of the house, the number of bedrooms in the house, and perhaps others?

Each of these questions asks how a single variable, such as selling price or employee wages, depends on other relevant variables. If we can estimate this relationship, then we can not only better understand how the world operates, but we can also do a better job of predicting the variable in question. For example, we can not only understand how a company's sales are affected by its advertising, but we can also use the company's records of current and past advertising levels to predict future sales.

The branch of statistics that studies such relationships is called **regression analysis**, and it is the subject of this chapter and the next. Because of its generality and applicability, regression analysis is one of the most pervasive of all statistical methods in the business world. There are several ways to categorize regression analysis. One categorization is based on the overall purpose of the analysis. As suggested previously, there are two potential objectives of regression analysis: to understand how the world operates and to make predictions. Either of these objectives could be paramount in any particular application. If the variable in question is employee salary and we are using variables such as years of experience, level of education, and gender to explain salary levels, then the purpose of the analysis is probably to understand how the world operates—that is, to explain how the variables combine in any given company to determine salaries. More specifically, the purpose of the analysis might be to discover whether there is any gender discrimination in salaries, after allowing for differences in work experience and education level.

Regression can be used to understand how the world operates, and it can be used for prediction.

The primary objective of the analysis can also be prediction. A good example of this is when the variable in question is company sales, and variables such as advertising and past sales levels are used as explanatory variables. In this case it is certainly important for the company to know how the relevant variables impact its sales. But the company's primary objective is probably to predict *future* sales levels, given current and past values of the explanatory variables. A company could even use a regression model for a what-if analysis, where it predicts future sales for many conceivable patterns of advertising and then selects its advertising level on the basis of these predictions.

Fortunately, the same regression analysis enables us to solve both problems simultaneously. That is, it indicates how the world operates and it enables us to make predictions. So although the objectives of regression studies might differ, the same basic analysis always applies.

A second categorization of regression analysis is based on the type of data being analyzed. There are two basic types: cross-sectional data and time series data. *Cross-sectional data* are usually data gathered from approximately the same period of time from a population. The housing and wage examples mentioned previously are typical cross-sectional studies. The first concerns a sample of houses, presumably sold during a short period of time, such as houses sold in Florida during the first couple of months of 2012. The second concerns a sample of employees observed at a particular point in time, such as a sample of automobile workers observed at the beginning of 2013.

In contrast, *time series data* involve one or more variables that are observed at several, usually equally spaced, points in time. The stock price example mentioned previously fits this description. We observe the price of a particular stock and possibly the price of a market index at the beginning of every week, say, and then try to explain the movement of the stock's price through time.

Regression can be used to analyze cross-sectional data or time series data.

Regression analysis can be applied equally well to cross-sectional and time series data. However, there are technical reasons for treating time series data somewhat differently. The primary reason is that time series variables are usually related to their own past values. This property of many time series variables is called *autocorrelation*, and it adds complications to the analysis that we will discuss only briefly.

A third categorization of regression analysis involves the number of explanatory variables in the analysis. First, we need to introduce some terms. In every regression study there is a single variable that we are trying to explain or predict, called the **dependent variable** (also called the **response** variable or the **target** variable). To help explain or predict the dependent variable, we use one or more **explanatory variables** (also called **independent** variables or **predictor** variables).[1] If there is a single explanatory variable, the analysis is called **simple regression**. If there are several explanatory variables, it is called **multiple regression**.

> The **dependent** (or **response** or **target**) **variable** is the single variable being explained by the regression. The **explanatory** (or **independent** or **predictor**) **variables** are used to explain the dependent variable.

There are important differences between simple and multiple regression. The primary difference, as the name implies, is that simple regression is simpler. The calculations are simpler, the interpretation of output is somewhat simpler, and fewer complications can occur. We will begin with a simple regression example to introduce the ideas of regression. But simple regression is really just a special case of multiple regression, and there is little need to single it out for separate discussion—especially when computer software is available to perform the calculations in either case.

> A **simple regression** analysis includes a single explanatory variable, whereas **multiple regression** can include any number of explanatory variables.

"Linear" regression allows you to estimate linear relationships as well as some nonlinear relationships.

A final categorization of regression analysis is of linear versus nonlinear models. The only type of regression analysis we study here is *linear* regression. Generally, this means that the relationships between variables are *straight-line* relationships, whereas the term *nonlinear* implies curved relationships. By focusing on linear regression, it might appear that we are ignoring the many nonlinear relationships that exist in the business world. Fortunately, linear regression can often be used to estimate nonlinear relationships. As you will see, the term *linear regression* is more general than it appears. Admittedly, many of the relationships we study can be explained adequately by straight lines. But it is also true that many nonlinear relationships can be *linearized* by suitable mathematical transformations. Therefore, the only relationships we are ignoring in this book are those—and there are some—that cannot be transformed to linear. Such relationships can be studied, but only by advanced methods beyond the level of this book.

---

[1]The traditional terms used in regression are *dependent* and *independent* variables. However, because these terms can cause confusion with probabilistic independence, a completely different concept, there has been an increasing use of the terms *response* and *explanatory* (or *predictor*) variables. We tend to prefer the terms *dependent* and *explanatory*, but this is largely a matter of taste.

In this chapter we focus on line-fitting and curve-fitting; that is, on estimating equations that describe relationships between variables. We also discuss the interpretation of these equations, and we provide numerical measures that indicate the goodness of fit of the estimated equations. In the next chapter we extend the analysis to statistical inference of regression output.

10-2 SCATTERPLOTS: GRAPHING RELATIONSHIPS

A good way to begin any regression analysis is to draw one or more scatterplots. As discussed in Chapter 3, a scatterplot is a graphical plot of two variables, an X and a Y. If there is any relationship between the two variables, it is usually apparent from the scatterplot.

Example 10.1, which we will continue through the chapter, illustrates the usefulness of scatterplots. It is a typical example of cross-sectional data.

EXAMPLE | 10.1 SALES VERSUS PROMOTIONS AT PHARMEX

Pharmex is a chain of drugstores that operates around the country. To see how effective its advertising and other promotional activities are, the company has collected data from 50 randomly selected metropolitan regions. In each region it has compared its own promotional expenditures and sales to those of the leading competitor in the region over the past year. There are two variables:

- Promote: Pharmex's promotional expenditures as a percentage of those of the leading competitor
- Sales: Pharmex's sales as a percentage of those of the leading competitor

Note that each of these variables is an *index*, not a dollar amount. For example, if Promote equals 95 for some region, this indicates that Pharmex's promotional expenditures in that region are 95% as large as those for the leading competitor in that region. The company expects that there is a positive relationship between these two variables, so that regions with relatively larger expenditures have relatively larger sales. However, it is not clear what the nature of this relationship is. The data are listed in the file **Drugstore Sales.xlsx**. (See Figure 10.1 for a partial listing of the data.) What type of relationship, if any, is apparent from a scatterplot?

Figure 10.1

Data for Drugstore Example

▲	A	B	C	D	E	F	G
1	Region	Promote	Sales				
2	1	77	85				
3	2	110	103				
4	3	110	102		Each value is a percentage of		
5	4	93	109		what the leading competitor did.		
6	5	90	85				
7	6	95	103				
50	49	95	108				
51	50	96	87				

© Cengage Learning

Objective To use a scatterplot to examine the relationship between promotional expenses and sales at Pharmex.

Solution

First, recall from Chapter 3 that there are two ways to create a scatterplot in Excel®. You can use Excel's Chart Wizard to create a Scatter chart, or you can use the StatTools Scatterplot procedure. The advantages of the latter are that it is slightly easier to implement and it provides automatic formatting of the chart.

It is customary to put the explanatory variable on the horizontal axis and the dependent variable on the vertical axis. In this example the store believes large promotional expenditures tend to "cause" larger values of sales, so Sales is on the vertical axis and Promote is on the horizontal axis. The resulting scatterplot appears in Figure 10.2.

Figure 10.2

Scatterplot of Sales versus Promote

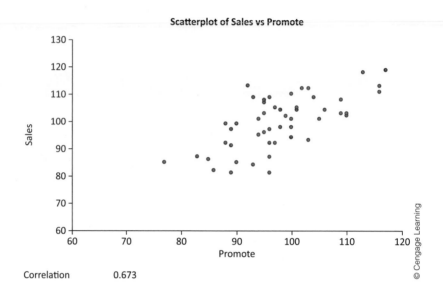

Correlation   0.673

Remember that a StatTools chart is really just an Excel chart. So you can manipulate it using Excel tools. For this scatterplot, we changed the scales of the axes so that the scatter fills up more of the chart area.

This scatterplot indicates that there is indeed a positive relationship between Promote and Sales—the points tend to rise from bottom left to top right—but the relationship is not perfect. If it were perfect, a given value of Promote would prescribe the value of Sales exactly. Clearly, this is not the case. For example, there are five regions with promotional values of 96 but all of them have different sales values. So the scatterplot indicates that while the variable Promote is helpful for predicting Sales, it does not lead to perfect predictions.

Note the correlation of 0.673 shown at the bottom of Figure 10.2. StatTools inserts this value automatically (if you request it) to indicate the strength of a *linear* relationship between the two variables. For now, just note that it is positive and its magnitude is moderately large. We will say more about correlations in the next section.

Finally, we briefly discuss causation. There is a tendency for an analyst (such as a drugstore manager) to say that larger promotional expenses *cause* larger sales values. However, unless the data are obtained in a carefully controlled experiment—which is certainly not the case here—you can never be absolutely sure about causation. One reason is that you can't always be sure which direction the causation goes. Does X cause Y, or does Y cause X? Another reason is that you can almost never rule out the possibility that some other variable is causing the variation in *both* of the observed variables. Although this is unlikely in this drugstore example, it is still a possibility. ■

Example 10.2 uses time series data to illustrate several other features of scatterplots. We will follow this example throughout the chapter as well.

EXAMPLE | **10.2 EXPLAINING OVERHEAD COSTS AT BENDRIX**

Bendrix Company manufactures various types of parts for automobiles. The manager of the factory wants to get a better understanding of overhead costs. These overhead costs include supervision, indirect labor, supplies, payroll taxes, overtime premiums, depreciation, and a number of miscellaneous items such as insurance, utilities, and janitorial and maintenance expenses. Some of these overhead costs are *fixed* in the sense that they do not vary appreciably with the volume of work being done, whereas others are *variable* and do vary directly with the volume of work. The fixed overhead costs tend to come from the supervision, depreciation, and miscellaneous categories, whereas the variable overhead costs tend to come from the indirect labor, supplies, payroll taxes, and overtime categories. However, it is not easy to draw a clear line between the fixed and variable overhead components.

The Bendrix manager has tracked total overhead costs for the past 36 months. To help explain these, he has also collected data on two variables that are related to the amount of work done at the factory. These variables are:

- Machine Hours: number of machine hours used during the month
- Production Runs: the number of separate production runs during the month

The first of these is a direct measure of the amount of work being done. To understand the second, we note that Bendrix manufactures parts in large batches. Each batch corresponds to a production run. Once a production run is completed, the factory must set up for the next production run. During this setup there is typically some downtime while the machinery is reconfigured for the part type scheduled for production in the next batch. Therefore, the manager believes that both of these variables could be responsible (in different ways) for variations in overhead costs. Do scatterplots support this belief?

Objective   To use scatterplots to examine the relationships among overhead, machine hours, and production runs at Bendrix.

Solution

The data appear in Figure 10.3. (See the **Overhead Costs.xlsx** file.) Each observation (row) corresponds to a single month. The goal is to find possible relationships between the Overhead variable and the Machine Hours and Production Runs variables, but because these are time series variables, you should also be on the lookout for any relationships between these variables and the Month variable. That is, you should also investigate any time series behavior in these variables.

This data set illustrates, even with a modest number of variables, how the number of potentially useful scatterplots can grow quickly. At the very least, you should examine the

Figure 10.3

Data for Bendrix
Overhead Example

◢	A	B	C	D
1	Month	Machine Hours	Production Runs	Overhead
2	1	1539	31	99798
3	2	1284	29	87804
4	3	1490	27	93681
5	4	1355	22	82262
6	5	1500	35	106968
34	33	1678	41	117183
35	34	1723	35	107828
36	35	1413	30	88032
37	36	1390	54	117943

© Cengage Learning

scatterplot between each potential explanatory variable (Machine Hours and Production Runs) and the dependent variable (Overhead). These appear in Figures 10.4 and 10.5. You can see that Overhead tends to increase as either Machine Hours increases or Production Runs increases. However, both relationships are far from perfect.

Figure 10.4

Scatterplot of
Overhead versus
Machine Hours

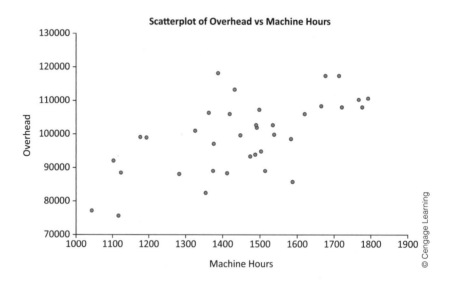

© Cengage Learning

Figure 10.5

Scatterplot of
Overhead versus
Production Runs

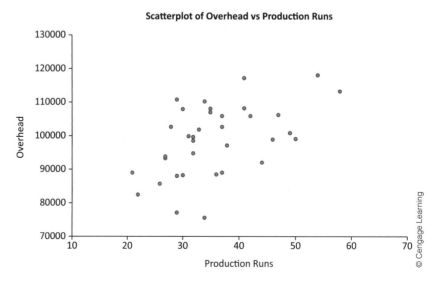

© Cengage Learning

To check for possible time series patterns, you can also create a time series graph for any of the variables. One of these, the time series graph for Overhead, is shown in Figure 10.6. It indicates a fairly random pattern through time, with no apparent upward trend or other obvious time series pattern. You can check that time series graphs of the Machine Hours and Production Runs variables also indicate no obvious time series patterns.

Finally, when there are multiple explanatory variables, you should check for relationships among them. The scatterplot of Machine Hours versus Production Runs appears in Figure 10.7. (Either variable could be chosen for the vertical axis.) This "cloud" of points indicates no relationship worth pursuing.

This is precisely the role of scatterplots: to provide a visual representation of relationships or the lack of relationships between variables.

Figure 10.6

Time Series Graph of Overhead versus Month

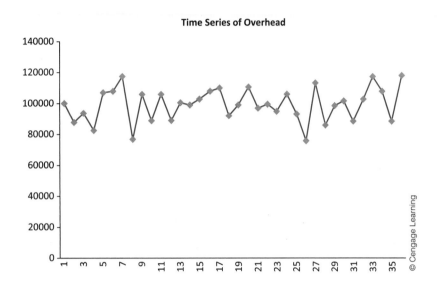

Figure 10.7

Scatterplot of Machine Hours versus Production Runs

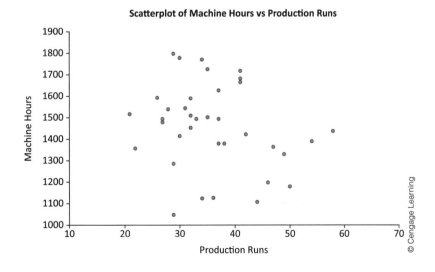

In summary, the Bendrix manager should continue to explore the positive relationship between Overhead and each of the Machine Hours and Production Runs variables. However, none of the variables appears to have any time series behavior, and the two potential explanatory variables do not appear to be related to each other. ∎

10-2a Linear versus Nonlinear Relationships

Scatterplots are extremely useful for detecting behavior that might not be obvious otherwise. We illustrate some of these in the next few subsections. First, the typical relationship you hope to see is a straight-line, or *linear*, relationship. This doesn't mean that all points lie on a straight line—this is too much to expect in business data—but that the points tend to cluster around a straight line. The scatterplots in Figures 10.2, 10.4, and 10.5 all exhibit linear relationships. At least, there is no obvious curvature.

The scatterplot in Figure 10.8, on the other hand, illustrates a relationship that is clearly nonlinear. The data in this scatterplot are 1990 data on more than 100 countries. The variables listed are life expectancy (of newborns, based on current mortality conditions) and GNP per capita. The obvious curvature in the scatterplot can be explained as follows. For poor countries, a slight increase in GNP per capita has a large effect on life expectancy. However, this effect decreases for wealthier countries. A straight-line relationship is definitely not appropriate for these data. However, as discussed previously, *linear* regression—after an appropriate transformation of the data—might still be applicable.

Figure 10.8

Scatterplot of Life Expectancy versus GNP per Capita

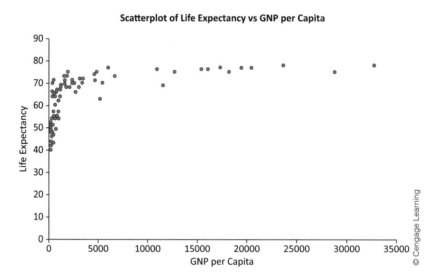

10-2b Outliers

Scatterplots are especially useful for identifying **outliers**, observations that lie outside the typical pattern of points. The scatterplot in Figure 10.9 shows annual salaries versus years of experience for a sample of employees at a particular company. There is a clear linear relationship between these two variables—for all employees except the point at the top right. A closer look at the data reveals that this one employee is the company CEO, whose salary is well above that of all the other employees.

> An **outlier** is an observation that falls outside of the general pattern of the rest of the observations.

Although scatterplots are good for detecting outliers, they do not necessarily indicate what you ought to do about any outliers you find. This depends entirely on the particular situation. If you are attempting to investigate the salary structure for typical employees at a company, then you should probably not include the company CEO. First, the CEO's salary is not determined in the same way as the salaries for typical employees. Second, if you do include the CEO in the analysis, it can greatly distort the results for the mass of typical

Figure 10.9

Scatterplot of Salary
versus Years of
Experience

Scatterplot of Salary vs Years Experience

employees. In other situations, however, it might *not* be appropriate to eliminate outliers just to make the analysis come out more nicely.

It is difficult to generalize about the treatment of outliers, but the following points are worth noting.

- If an outlier is clearly not a member of the population of interest, then it is probably best to delete it from the analysis. This is the case for the company CEO in Figure 10.9.

- If it isn't clear whether outliers are members of the relevant population, you can run the regression analysis with them and again without them. If the results are practically the same in both cases, then it is probably best to report the results with the outliers included. Otherwise, you can report both sets of results with a verbal explanation of the outliers.

10-2c Unequal Variance

Occasionally, there is a clear relationship between two variables, but the variance of the dependent variable depends on the value of the explanatory variable. Figure 10.10 illustrates a common example of this. It shows the amount spent at a mail-order company versus salary for the customers in the data set. There is a clear upward relationship, but the variability of amount spent increases as salary increases. This is evident from the *fan* shape. As you will see in the next chapter, this unequal variance violates one of the assumptions of linear regression analysis, and there are special techniques to deal with it.

10-2d No Relationship

A scatterplot can provide one other useful piece of information: It can indicate that there is *no* relationship between a pair of variables, at least none worth pursuing. This is usually the case when the scatterplot appears as a shapeless swarm of points, as illustrated in Figure 10.11. Here the variables are an employee performance score and the number of overtime hours worked in the previous month for a sample of employees. There is virtually no hint of a relationship between these two variables in this plot, and if these are the only two variables in the data set, the analysis can stop right here. Many people who use statistics evidently believe that a computer can perform magic on a set of numbers and find relationships that were completely hidden. Occasionally this is true, but when a scatterplot appears as in Figure 10.11, the variables are not related in any useful way, and that's all there is to it.

Figure 10.10

Unequal Variance of
Dependent Variable
in a Scatterplot

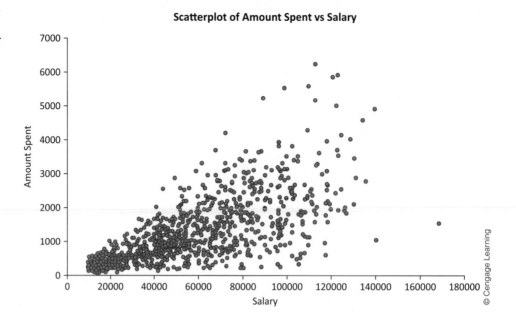

Scatterplot of Amount Spent vs Salary

Figure 10.11

An Example of
No Relationship

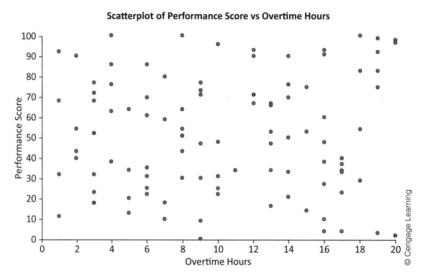

Scatterplot of Performance Score vs Overtime Hours

10-3 CORRELATIONS: INDICATORS OF LINEAR RELATIONSHIPS

Scatterplots provide graphical indications of relationships, whether they are linear, non-linear, or essentially nonexistent. **Correlations** are numerical summary measures that indicate the strength of linear relationships between pairs of variables.[2] A correlation between a pair of variables is a single number that summarizes the information in a scatterplot. A correlation can be very useful, but it has an important limitation: It measures the strength of *linear* relationships only. If there is a nonlinear relationship, as suggested by a scatterplot, the correlation can be completely misleading. With this important limitation in mind, let's look a bit more closely at correlations.

[2]This section includes some material from Chapter 3 that we repeat here for convenience.

The usual notation for a correlation between two variables X and Y is r_{XY}. (The subscripts can be omitted if the variables are clear from the context.) The formula for r_{XY} is given by Equation (10.1). Note that it is a sum of products in the numerator, divided by the product $s_X s_Y$ of the sample standard deviations of X and Y. This requires a considerable amount of computation, so correlations are almost always computed by software packages.

Formula for Correlation

$$r_{XY} = \frac{\Sigma(X_i - \overline{X})(Y_i - \overline{Y})/(n-1)}{s_X s_Y}$$

(10.1)

The numerator of Equation (10.1) is also a measure of association between two variables X and Y, called the **covariance** between X and Y. Like a correlation, a covariance is a single number that measures the strength of the linear relationship between two variables. By looking at the sign of the covariance or correlation—plus or minus—you can tell whether the two variables are positively or negatively related. The drawback to a covariance, however, is that its magnitude depends on the units in which the variables are measured.

The magnitude of a covariance is difficult to interpret because it depends on the units of measurement.

To illustrate, the covariance between Overhead and Machine Hours in the Bendrix manufacturing data set is 1,333,138. (It can be found with Excel's COVAR function or with StatTools.) However, if each overhead value is divided by 1000, so that overhead costs are expressed in thousands of dollars, and each value of Machine Hours is divided by 100, so that machine hours are expressed in hundreds of hours, the covariance decreases by a factor of 100,000 to 13.33138. This is in spite of the fact that the basic relationship between these variables has not changed and the revised scatterplot has exactly the same shape. For this reason it is difficult to interpret the magnitude of a covariance, and we concentrate instead on correlations.

Unlike covariances, correlations have the attractive property that they are completely unaffected by the units of measurement. The rescaling described in the previous paragraph has absolutely no effect on the correlation between Overhead and Machine Hours. In either case the correlation is 0.632. All correlations are between -1 and $+1$, inclusive. The sign of a correlation, plus or minus, determines whether the linear relationship between two variables is positive or negative. In this respect, a correlation is just like a covariance. However, the strength of the linear relationship between the variables is measured by the absolute value, or magnitude, of the correlation. The closer this magnitude is to 1, the stronger the linear relationship is.

A correlation close to -1 or $+1$ indicates a strong linear relationship. A correlation close to 0 indicates virtually no linear relationship.

A correlation equal to 0 or near 0 indicates practically no linear relationship. A correlation with magnitude close to 1, on the other hand, indicates a strong linear relationship. At the extreme, a correlation equal to -1 or $+1$ occurs only when the linear relationship is perfect—that is, when all points in the scatterplot lie on a straight line. Although such extremes practically never occur in business applications, large correlations greater in magnitude than 0.9, say, are not at all uncommon.

Looking back at the scatterplots for the Pharmex drugstore data in Figure 10.2, you can see that the correlation between Sales and Promote is positive—as the upward-sloping scatter of points suggests—and is equal to 0.673. This is a moderately large correlation. It confirms the pattern in the scatterplot, namely, that the points increase linearly from left to right but with considerable variation around any particular straight line.

Similarly, the scatterplots for the Bendrix manufacturing data in Figures 10.4 and 10.5 indicate moderately large positive correlations, 0.632 and 0.521, between Overhead and Machine Hours and between Overhead and Production Runs. However, the correlation indicated in Figure 10.7 between Machine Hours and Production Runs, −0.229, is quite small and indicates almost no relationship between these two variables.

Correlations can be misleading when variables are related nonlinearly.

You must be careful when interpreting the correlations in Figures 10.8 and 10.9. The scatterplot between life expectancy and GNP per capita in Figure 10.8 is obviously nonlinear, and correlations are relevant descriptors only for *linear* relationships. If anything, the correlation of 0.616 in this example tends to underestimate the true strength of the relationship—the nonlinear one—between life expectancy and GNP per capita. In contrast, the correlation between salary and years of experience in Figure 10.9 is large, 0.894, but it is not nearly as large as it would be if the outlier were omitted. (It is then 0.992.) This example illustrates the considerable effect a single outlier can have on a correlation.

An obvious question is whether a given correlation is "large." This is a difficult question to answer directly. Clearly, a correlation such as 0.992 is quite large—the points tend to cluster very closely around a straight line. Similarly, a correlation of 0.034 is quite small—the points tend to be a shapeless swarm. But there is a continuum of in-between values, as exhibited in Figures 10.2, 10.4, and 10.5. We give a more definite answer to this question when we examine the *square* of the correlation later in this chapter.

As for calculating correlations, there are two possibilities in Excel. To calculate a *single* correlation r_{XY} between variables X and Y, you can use Excel's CORREL function in the form

=**CORREL**(*X*-range,*Y*-range)

Alternatively, you can use StatTools to obtain a whole table of correlations between a set of variables.

Finally, we reiterate the important limitation of correlations (and covariances), namely, that they apply only to *linear* relationships. If a correlation is close to zero, you cannot automatically conclude that there is no relationship between the two variables. You should look at a scatterplot first. The chances are that the points are a shapeless swarm and that no relationship exists. But it is also possible that the points cluster around some curve. In this case the correlation is a misleading measure of the relationship.

10-4 SIMPLE LINEAR REGRESSION

Scatterplots and correlations are very useful for indicating linear relationships and the strengths of these relationships. But they do not actually *quantify* the relationships. For example, it is clear from the scatterplot of the Pharmex drugstore data that sales are related to promotional expenditures. But the scatterplot does not specify exactly what this relationship is. If the expenditure index for a given region is 95, what would you predict this region's sales index to be? Or if one region's expenditure index is 5 points higher than another's, how much larger would you predict the sales index of the former to be? To answer these questions, the relationship between the dependent variable Sales and the explanatory variable Promote must be quantified.

Remember that simple linear regression does not mean "easy"; it means only that there is a single explanatory variable.

In this section we answer these types of questions for simple linear regression, where there is a *single* explanatory variable. We do so by fitting a straight line through the scatterplot of the dependent variable Y versus the explanatory variable X and then basing the answers to the questions on the fitted straight line. But which straight line? We address this issue next.

10-4a Least Squares Estimation

The scatterplot between Sales and Promote, repeated in Figure 10.12, hints at a linear relationship between these two variables. It would not be difficult to draw a straight line through these points to produce a reasonably good fit. In fact, a possible linear fit is

Figure 10.12

Scatterplot with
Possible Linear Fit
Superimposed

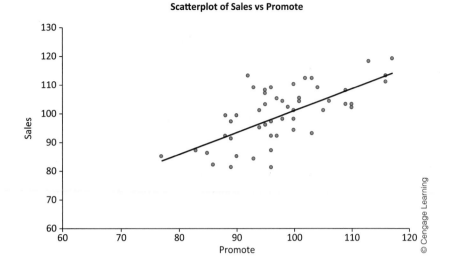

Scatterplot of Sales vs Promote

indicated in the graph. But we proceed more systematically than simply drawing lines free-hand. Specifically, we choose the line that makes the vertical distances from the points to the line as small as possible, as explained next.

Consider the magnified graph in Figure 10.13. Several points in the scatterplot are shown, along with a line drawn through them. Note that the vertical distance from the horizontal axis to any point, which is just the value of Sales for that point, can be decomposed into two parts: the vertical distance from the horizontal axis to the line, and the vertical distance from the line to the point. The first of these is called the **fitted value**, and the second is called the **residual**. The idea is very simple. By using a straight line to reflect the relationship between Sales and Promote, you expect a given Sales to be at the height of the line above any particular value of Promote. That is, you expect Sales to equal the fitted value.

A **fitted value** is the predicted value of the dependent variable. Graphically, it is the height of the line above a given explanatory value. The corresponding **residual** is the difference between the actual and fitted values of the dependent variable.

Figure 10.13

Fitted Values and
Residuals

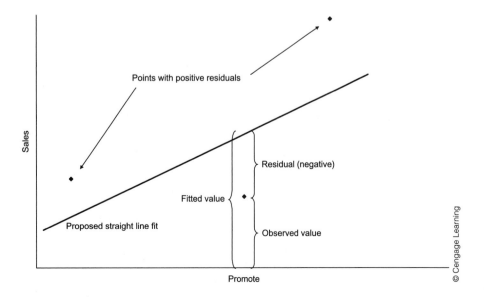

But the relationship is not perfect. Not all (perhaps not any) of the points lie exactly on the line. The differences are the residuals. They show how much the observed values differ from the fitted values. If a particular residual is positive, the corresponding point is above the line; if it is negative, the point is below the line. The only time a residual is zero is when the point lies directly on the line. The relationship between observed values, fitted values, and residuals is very general and is stated in Equation (10.2).

Fundamental Equation for Regression

$$\text{Observed Value} = \text{Fitted Value} + \text{Residual} \qquad \textbf{(10.2)}$$

We can now explain how to choose the best-fitting line through the points in the scatterplot. It is the line with the *smallest sum of squared residuals*. The resulting line is called the **least squares line**. Why do we use the sum of *squared* residuals? Why not minimize some other measure of the residuals? First, it is not appropriate to simply minimize the sum of the residuals. This is because the positive residuals would cancel the negative residuals. In fact, the least squares line has the property that the sum of the residuals is always exactly zero. To adjust for this, we could minimize the sum of the *absolute values* of the residuals, and this is a perfectly reasonable procedure. However, for technical and historical reasons, it is not the procedure usually chosen. The minimization of the sum of squared residuals is deeply rooted in statistical tradition, and it works well.

The **least squares line** is the line that minimizes the sum of the squared residuals. It is the line quoted in regression outputs.

The minimization problem itself is a calculus problem and is not discussed here. Virtually all statistical software packages perform this minimization automatically, so you do not need to be concerned with the technical details. However, we do provide the formulas for the least squares line.

Recall from basic algebra that the equation for any straight line can be written as

$$Y = a + bX$$

Here, a is the Y-intercept of the line, the value of Y when $X = 0$, and b is the slope of the line, the change in Y when X increases by one unit. Therefore, the least squares line is specified completely by its slope and intercept. These are given by equations (10.3) and (10.4).

Equation for Slope in Simple Linear Regression

$$b = \frac{\Sigma(X_i - \overline{X})(Y_i - \overline{Y})}{\Sigma(X_i - \overline{X})^2} = r_{XY}\frac{s_Y}{s_X} \qquad \textbf{(10.3)}$$

Equation for Intercept in Simple Linear Regression

$$a = \overline{Y} - b\overline{X} \qquad \textbf{(10.4)}$$

We have presented these formulas primarily for conceptual purposes, not for hand calculations—the software takes care of the calculations. From the formula on the right for b, you can see that it is closely related to the correlation between X and Y. Specifically, if the standard deviations, s_X and s_Y, of X and Y are kept constant, the slope b of the least squares line varies directly with the correlation between the two variables. The effect of the formula for a is not quite as interesting. It simply forces the least squares line to go through the point of sample means, $(\overline{X}, \overline{Y})$.

It is easy to obtain the least squares line in Excel with the StatTools Regression procedure. We illustrate this in the following continuations of Examples 10.1 and 10.2.

| EXAMPLE | 10.1 SALES VERSUS PROMOTIONS AT PHARMEX (CONTINUED) |

Find the least squares line for the Pharmex drugstore data, using Sales as the dependent variable and Promote as the explanatory variable.

Objective To use StatTools's Regression procedure to find the least squares line for sales as a function of promotional expenses at Pharmex.

Solution

To perform the analysis, select Regression from the StatTools Regression and Classification dropdown list. Then fill in the resulting dialog box as shown in Figure 10.14. Specifically, select Multiple as the Regression Type (this type is used for both single and multiple regression in StatTools), and select Promote as the single I variable and Sales as the single D variable. (Here, I and D stand for independent and dependent. Remember that there is always a *single D* variable, but in multiple regression there can be several I variables.) Note that there is an option to create several scatterplots involving the fitted values and residuals. We suggest checking the third option, as shown. Finally, there is an Include Prediction option. We will explain it in a later section. You can leave it unchecked for now.

Figure 10.14
Regression Dialog Box

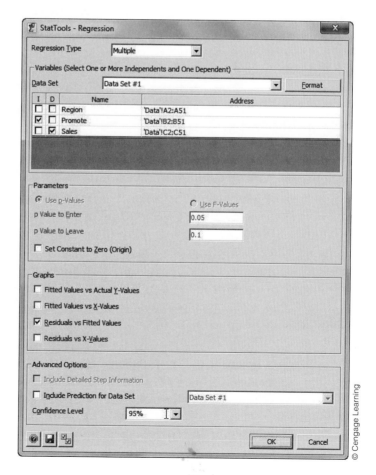

The regression output includes three parts. The first is the main regression output shown in Figure 10.15. The last two are a scatterplot of residuals and fitted values requested in the regression dialog box and a list of fitted values and residuals, a few of which are shown in Figure 10.16. (The list of fitted values and residuals is part of the output only if at least one of the optional scatterplots in the regression dialog box is selected.)

Figure 10.15

Regression Output for Drugstore Example

	A	B	C	D	E	F	G
7	Multiple Regression for Sales						
8		Multiple	R-Square	Adjusted	StErr of		
9	Summary	R		R-Square	Estimate		
10		0.6730	0.4529	0.4415	7.394732934		
11							
12		Degrees of	Sum of	Mean of	F-Ratio	p-Value	
13	ANOVA Table	Freedom	Squares	Squares			
14	Explained	1	2172.880392	2172.880392	39.7366	< 0.0001	
15	Unexplained	48	2624.739608	54.68207516			
16							
17		Coefficient	Standard	t-Value	p-Value	Confidence Interval 95%	
18	Regression Table		Error			Lower	Upper
19	Constant	25.12642006	11.8825852	2.1146	0.0397	1.234881256	49.01795886
20	Promote	0.762296485	0.120928454	6.3037	< 0.0001	0.519153532	1.005439438

Figure 10.16

Scatterplot and Partial List of Residuals versus Fitted Values

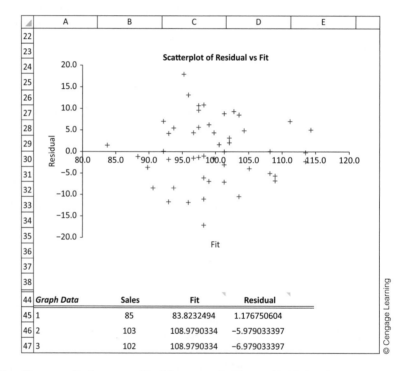

44	Graph Data	Sales	Fit	Residual
45	1	85	83.8232494	1.176750604
46	2	103	108.9790334	−5.979033397
47	3	102	108.9790334	−6.979033397

We will eventually interpret all of the output in Figure 10.15, but for now, we focus on only a small part of it. Specifically, the intercept and slope of the least squares line appear under the Coefficient label in cells B18 and B19. They imply that the equation for the least squares line is[3]

$$\text{Predicted Sales} = 25.1264 + 0.7623\text{Promote}$$

[3]We always report the left side of the estimated regression equation as the *predicted* value of the dependent variable. It is not the *actual* value of the dependent variable because the observations do not all lie on the estimated regression line.

*Excel Tip: **Built-in Excel Regression Functions***

The Regression procedure for simple regression uses special StatTools functions to calculate all of the regression output. However, it can also be generated from several built-in statistical functions available in Excel. These include the CORREL, RSQ, STEYX, INTERCEPT, SLOPE, and LINEST functions. For example, the slope and intercept of the least squares line can be calculated directly with the formulas

=SLOPE(Y-range,X-range)

and

=INTERCEPT(Y-range,X-range)

These formulas (with the appropriate X and Y ranges) can be entered anywhere in a spreadsheet to obtain the slope and intercept for a simple regression equation—no add-ins are necessary. The LINEST function can be used to find relevant output for a multiple regression. You can look up all of these functions in Excel's online help.

*Excel Tip: **Regression from Excel's Trendline Option***

As discussed in Chapter 3, you can also superimpose a trendline on a scatterplot by right-clicking any point on the chart and selecting Trendline. The line superimposed is indeed the least-squares regression line. In addition, you can ask for the equation of the line and its R^2 value (to be discussed shortly) to be added to the chart. However, this works only when there is a single X variable. There is no comparable trendline option for multiple regression.

In many applications, it makes no sense to have the explanatory variable(s) equal to zero. Then the intercept term has no practical or economic meaning.

The regression equation for this example can be interpreted as follows. The slope, 0.7623, indicates that the sales index tends to increase by about 0.76 for each one-unit increase in the promotional expenses index. Alternatively, if two regions are compared, where the second region spends one unit more than the first region, the predicted sales index for the second region is 0.76 larger than the sales index for the first region. The interpretation of the intercept is less important. It is literally the predicted sales index for a region that does no promotions. However, no region in the sample has anywhere near a zero promotional value. Therefore, in a situation like this, where the range of observed values for the explanatory variable does not include zero, it is best to think of the intercept term as simply an "anchor" for the least squares line that enables predictions of Y values for the range of observed X values.

A shapeless swarm of points in a scatterplot of residuals versus fitted values is typically good news. It means that no regression assumptions are violated.

A useful graph in almost any regression analysis is a scatterplot of residuals (on the vertical axis) versus fitted values. This scatterplot for the Pharmex data appears in Figure 10.16 (along with a few of the residuals and fitted values used to create the chart). You typically examine such a scatterplot for any obvious patterns. A good fit not only has small residuals, but it has residuals scattered *randomly* around zero with no apparent pattern. This appears to be the case for the Pharmex data. ∎

EXAMPLE   10.2 EXPLAINING OVERHEAD COSTS AT BENDRIX (CONTINUED)

The Bendrix manufacturing data set has two potential explanatory variables, Machine Hours and Production Runs. Eventually, we will estimate a regression equation with *both* of these variables included. However, if we include only one at a time, what do they tell us about overhead costs?

Objective   To use the StatTools Regression procedure to regress overhead expenses at Bendrix against machine hours and then against production runs.

Solution

The regression output for Overhead with Machine Hours as the single explanatory variable appears in Figure 10.17. The output when Production Runs is the only explanatory variable appears in Figure 10.18. The two least squares lines are therefore

$$\text{Predicted Overhead} = 48621 + 34.7\text{Machine Hours} \qquad \textbf{(10.5)}$$

and

$$\text{Predicted Overhead} = 75606 + 655.1\text{Production Runs} \qquad \textbf{(10.6)}$$

Figure 10.17

Regression Output for Overhead versus Machine Hours

	A	B	C	D	E	F	G
7	Multiple Regression for Overhead						
8		Multiple	R-Square	Adjusted	StErr of		
9	Summary	R		R-Square	Estimate		
10		0.6319	0.3993	0.3816	8584.739353		
11							
12		Degrees of	Sum of	Mean of	F-Ratio	p-Value	
13	ANOVA Table	Freedom	Squares	Squares			
14	Explained	1	1665463368	1665463368	22.5986	<0.0001	
15	Unexplained	34	2505723492	73697749.75			
16							
17		Coefficient	Standard	t-Value	p-Value	Confidence Interval 95%	
18	Regression Table		Error			Lower	Upper
19	Constant	48621.35463	10725.3327	4.5333	< 0.0001	26824.85615	70417.85312
20	Machine Hours	34.70223642	7.299902097	4.7538	< 0.0001	19.86705047	49.53742238

Figure 10.18

Regression Output for Overhead versus Production Runs

	A	B	C	D	E	F	G
7	Multiple Regression for Overhead						
8		Multiple	R-Square	Adjusted	StErr of		
9	Summary	R		R-Square	Estimate		
10		0.5205	0.2710	0.2495	9457.239463		
11							
12		Degrees of	Sum of	Mean of	F-Ratio	p-Value	
13	ANOVA Table	Freedom	Squares	Squares			
14	Explained	1	1130247999	1130247999	12.6370	0.0011	
15	Unexplained	34	3040938861	89439378.26			
16							
17		Coefficient	Standard	t-Value	p-Value	Confidence Interval 95%	
18	Regression Table		Error			Lower	Upper
19	Constant	75605.51571	6808.610629	11.1044	< 0.0001	61768.75415	89442.27728
20	Production Runs	655.0706602	184.2746779	3.5549	0.0011	280.5794579	1029.561862

© Cengage Learning

Clearly, these two equations are quite different, although each effectively breaks Overhead into a fixed component and a variable component. Equation (10.5) implies that the fixed component of overhead is about $48,621. Bendrix can expect to incur this amount even if zero machine hours are used. The variable component is the 34.7Machine Hours term. It implies that the expected overhead increases by about $35 for each extra machine hour. Equation (10.6), on the other hand, breaks overhead down into a fixed component of $75,606 and a variable component of about $655 per each production run.

The difference between these two equations can be attributed to the fact that neither tells the whole story. If the manager's goal is to split overhead into a fixed component and a variable component, the variable component should include *both* of the measures of work activity (and maybe others) to give a more complete explanation of overhead. We will explain how to do this when this example is reanalyzed with *multiple* regression. ∎

482 Chapter 10 Regression Analysis: Estimating Relationships

10-4b Standard Error of Estimate

We now examine fitted values and residuals to see how they lead to a useful summary measure for a regression equation. In a typical simple regression model, the expression $a + bX$ is the fitted value of Y. Graphically, it is the height of the estimated line above the value X. The fitted value is often denoted as $\hat{Y}$ (pronounced Y-hat):[4]

$$\hat{Y} = a + bX$$

Then a typical residual, denoted by e, is the difference between the observed value Y and the fitted value $\hat{Y}$. The following is a restatement of Equation (10.2):

$$e = Y - \hat{Y}$$

A few of the fitted values and associated residuals for the Pharmex drugstore example are shown in Figure 10.19. (Recall that these columns are inserted automatically by StatTools's Regression procedure when you request the optional scatterplot of residuals versus fitted values.)

Figure 10.19

Fitted Values and Residuals for Pharmex Example

	A	B	C	D
44	Graph Data	Sales	Fit	Residual
45	1	85	83.8232494	1.176750604
46	2	103	108.9790334	−5.979033397
47	3	102	108.9790334	−6.979033397
48	4	109	96.01999315	12.98000685
49	5	85	93.7331037	−8.733103699

© Cengage Learning

The magnitudes of the residuals provide a good indication of how useful the regression line is for predicting Y values from X values. However, because there are numerous residuals, it is useful to summarize them with a single numerical measure. This measure, called the **standard error of estimate** and denoted s_e, is essentially the standard deviation of the residuals. It is given by Equation (10.7).

Formula for Standard Error of Estimate

$$s_e = \sqrt{\frac{\Sigma e_i^2}{n - 2}} \qquad (10.7)$$

Actually, because the average of the residuals from a least squares fit is always zero, this is identical to the standard deviation of the residuals except for the denominator $n - 2$, not the usual $n - 1$. As you will see in more generality later on, the rule is to subtract the number of parameters being estimated from the sample size n to obtain the denominator. Here there are two parameters being estimated: the intercept a and the slope b.

The usual empirical rules for standard deviations can be applied to the standard error of estimate. For example, about two-thirds of the residuals are typically within one standard error of their mean (which is zero). Stated another way, about two-thirds of the observed

About two-thirds of the fitted $\hat{Y}$ values are typically within one standard error of the actual Y values. About 95% are within two standard errors.

---

[4]We can also write Predicted Y instead of $\hat{Y}$, but the latter notation is common in the statistics literature.

Y values are typically within one standard error of the corresponding fitted $\hat{Y}$ values. Similarly, about 95% of the observed Y values are typically within two standard errors of the corresponding fitted $\hat{Y}$ values.[5]

The standard error of estimate s_e is included in all StatTools regression outputs. Alternatively, it can be calculated directly with Excel's STEYX function (when there is only one X variable) in the form

=STEYX(Y-range,X-range)

In general, the standard error of estimate indicates the level of accuracy of predictions made from the regression equation. The smaller it is, the more accurate predictions tend to be.

The standard error for the Pharmex data appears in cell E9 of Figure 10.15. Its value, approximately 7.39, indicates the typical magnitude of error when using promotional expenses, via the regression equation, to predict sales. More specifically, if the regression equation is used to predict sales for many regions, about two-thirds of the predictions will be within 7.39 of the actual sales values, and about 95% of the predictions will be within two standard errors, or 14.78, of the actual sales values.

Is this level of accuracy good? One measure of comparison is the standard deviation of the sales variable, namely, 9.90. (This is obtained by the usual STDEV function applied to the observed sales values.) It can be interpreted as the standard deviation of the residuals around a *horizontal* line positioned at the mean value of Sales. This is the relevant regression line if there are no explanatory variables—that is, if Promote is ignored. In other words, it is a measure of the prediction error if the sample mean of Sales is used as the prediction for *every* region and Promote is ignored. Unfortunately, the standard error of estimate, 7.39, is not much less than 9.90. This means that the Promote variable adds a relatively small amount to prediction accuracy. Predictions with it are not much better than predictions without it. A standard error of estimate *well* below 9.90 would certainly be preferred.

The standard error of estimate can often be used to judge which of several potential regression equations is the most useful. In the Bendrix manufacturing example we estimated two regression lines, one using Machine Hours and one using Production Runs. From Figures 10.17 and 10.18, their standard errors are approximately $8585 and $9457. These imply that Machine Hours is a slightly better predictor of overhead. The predictions based on Machine Hours will tend to be slightly more accurate than those based on Production Runs. Of course, the predictions based on *both* predictors should yield even more accurate predictions, as you will see when we discuss multiple regression for this example.

10-4c The Percentage of Variation Explained: R-Square

We now discuss another important measure of the goodness of fit of the least squares line: R^2 (pronounced "R-square"). Along with the standard error of estimate s_e, it is the most frequently quoted measure in applied regression analysis. With a value always between 0 and 1, R^2 always has exactly the same interpretations: It is the *fraction of variation of the dependent variable explained by the regression line*. (It is often expressed as a percentage, so you hear about the *percentage* of variation explained by the regression line.)

R^2 is the percentage of variation of the dependent variable explained by the regression.

To see more precisely what this means, we look briefly into the derivation of R^2. In the previous section we suggested that one way to measure the regression equation's ability

[5]This requires that the residuals be at least approximately normally distributed, a requirement discussed in the next chapter.

to predict is to compare the standard error of estimate, s_e, to the standard deviation of the dependent variable, s_Y. The idea is that s_e is (essentially) the standard deviation of the residuals, whereas s_Y is the standard deviation of the residuals from a horizontal regression line at height $\overline{Y}$, the sample mean of the dependent variable. Therefore, if s_e is small compared to s_Y (that is, if s_e/s_Y is small), the regression line is evidently doing a good job in explaining the variation of the dependent variable.

The R^2 measure is based on this idea. It is defined by Equation (10.8). (This value is obtained automatically with StatTools's regression procedure, or it can be calculated with Excel's RSQ function when there is a single X variable.) Equation (10.8) indicates that when the residuals are small, R^2 will be close to 1, but when they are large, R^2 will be close to 0.

Formula for R^2

$$R^2 = 1 - \frac{\Sigma e_i^2}{\Sigma (Y_i - \overline{Y})^2} \tag{10.8}$$

R^2 measures the goodness of a linear fit. The better the linear fit is, the closer R^2 is to 1.

You can see from cell C9 of Figure 10.15 that the R^2 measure for the Pharmex drugstore data is 0.453. In words, the single explanatory variable Promote is able to explain only 45.3% of the variation in the Sales variable. This is not particularly good—the same conclusion we made when we based goodness of fit on s_e. There is still 54.7% of the variation left unexplained. Of course, we would like R^2 to be as close to 1 as possible. Usually, the only way to increase it is to use better and/or more explanatory variables.

Analysts often compare equations on the basis of their R^2 values. You can see from Figures 10.17 and 10.18 that the R^2 values using Machine Hours and Production Runs as single explanatory variables for the Bendrix overhead data are 39.9% and 27.1%, respectively. These provide one more piece of evidence that Machine Hours is a slightly better predictor of Overhead than Production Runs. Of course, they also suggest that the percentage of variation of Overhead explained could be increased by including *both* variables in a single equation. This is true, as you will see shortly.

In simple linear regression, R^2 is the square of the correlation between the dependent variable and the explanatory variable.

There is a good reason for the notation R^2. It turns out that R^2 is the square of the correlation between the observed Y values and the fitted $\hat{Y}$ values. This correlation appears in all regression outputs as the *multiple R*. For the Pharmex data it is 0.673, as seen in cell B9 of Figure 10.15. Aside from rounding, the square of 0.673 is 0.453, which is the R^2 value right next to it. In the case of simple linear regression, when there is only a single explanatory variable in the equation, the correlation between the Y variable and the fitted $\hat{Y}$ values is the same as the absolute value of the correlation between the Y variable and the explanatory X variable. For the Pharmex data you already saw that the correlation between Sales and Promote is indeed 0.673.

This interpretation of R^2 as the square of a correlation helps to clarify the issue of when a correlation is "large." For example, if the correlation between two variables Y and X is ± 0.8, the regression of Y on X will have an R^2 of 0.64; that is, the regression with X as the only explanatory variable will explain 64% of the variation in Y. If the correlation drops to ± 0.7, this percentage drops to 49%; if the correlation increases to ± 0.9, the percentage increases to 81%. The point is that before a single variable X can explain a large percentage of the variation in some other variable Y, the two variables must be highly correlated—in *either* a positive or negative direction.

PROBLEMS

Note: Student solutions for problems whose numbers appear within a colored box are available for purchase at www.cengagebrain.com.

Level A

1. Explore the relationship between the selling prices (Y) and the appraised values (X) of the 148 homes in the file **P02_11.xlsx** by estimating a simple linear regression model. Interpret the standard error of estimate s_e and R^2 and the least squares line for these data.
   a. Is there evidence of a *linear* relationship between the selling price and appraised value? If so, characterize the relationship. Is it positive or negative? Is it weak or strong?
   b. For which of the three remaining variables, the size of the home, the number of bedrooms, and the number of bathrooms, is the relationship with the home's selling price *stronger*? Justify your choice with additional simple linear regression models.

2. The file **P02_10.xlsx** contains midterm and final exam scores for 96 students in a corporate finance course. Each row contains the two exam scores for a given student, so you might expect them to be positively correlated.
   a. Create a scatterplot of the final exam score (Y) versus the midterm score (X). Based on the visual evidence, would you say that the scores for the two exams are strongly related? Is the relationship a linear one?
   b. Superimpose a trend line on the scatterplot, and use the option to display the equation and the R^2 value. What does this equation indicate in terms of predicting a student's final exam score from his or her midterm score? Be specific.
   c. Run a regression to confirm the trend-line equation from part **b**. What does the standard error of estimate say about the accuracy of the prediction requested in part **b**?

3. A company produces electric motors for use in home appliances. One of the company's production managers is interested in examining the relationship between inspection costs in a month (X) and the number of motors produced that month that were returned by dissatisfied customers (Y). He has collected the data in the file **P10_03.xlsx** for the past 36 months. Estimate a simple linear regression equation using the given data and interpret it for this production manager. Also, interpret s_e and R^2 for these data.

4. The owner of Original Italian Pizza restaurant chain wants to understand which variable most strongly influences the sales of his specialty deep-dish pizza. He has gathered data on the monthly sales of deep-dish pizzas at his restaurants and observations on other potentially relevant variables for each of his 15

outlets in central Indiana. These data are provided in the file **P10_04.xlsx**. Estimate a simple linear regression equation between the quantity sold (Y) and each of the following candidates for the best explanatory variable: average price of deep-dish pizzas, monthly advertising expenditures, and disposable income per household in the areas surrounding the outlets. Which variable is *most* strongly associated with the number of pizzas sold? Explain your choice.

5. The human resources manager of DataCom, Inc., wants to examine the relationship between annual salaries (Y) and the number of years employees have worked at DataCom (X). These data have been collected for a sample of employees and are given in columns B and C of the file **P10_05.xlsx**.
   a. Estimate the relationship between Y and X. Interpret the least squares line.
   b. How well does the estimated simple linear regression equation fit the given data? Provide evidence for your answer.

6. The file **P02_02.xlsx** contains information on over 200 movies that came out during 2006 and 2007.
   a. Create two scatterplots and corresponding correlations, one of Total US Gross (Y) versus 7-day Gross (X) and one of Total US Gross (Y) versus 14-day Gross (X). Based on the visual evidence, is it possible to predict the total U.S. gross of a movie from its first week's gross or its first two weeks' gross?
   b. Run two simple regressions corresponding to the two scatterplots in part **a**. Explain exactly what they tell you about the movie business. How accurate would the two predictions requested in part **a** tend to be? Be as specific as possible.

7. Examine the relationship between the average utility bills for homes of a particular size (Y) and the average monthly temperature (X). The data in the file **P10_07.xlsx** include the average monthly bill and temperature for each month of the past year.
   a. Use the given data to estimate a simple linear regression equation. Interpret the least squares line.
   b. How well does the estimated regression equation fit the given data? How might you do a better job of explaining the variation of the average utility bills for homes of a certain size?

8. The file **P10_08.xlsx** contains data on the top 200 professional golfers in 2011. (The same data set, covering multiple years, was used in Example 3.4 in Chapter 3.)
   a. Create a new variable, Earnings per Round, and the ratio of Earnings to Rounds. Then create five scatterplots and corresponding correlations, each with Earnings per Round on the Y axis. The X-axis

variables are those that most golf enthusiasts probably think are related to Earnings per Round: Yards/Drive, Driving Accuracy, Greens in Regulation, Putting Average, and Sand Save Pct. Comment on the results. Are any of these highly related to Earnings per Round? Do the correlations have the signs you would expect (positive or negative)?

b. For the two most highly correlated variables with Earnings per Round (positive or negative), run the regressions corresponding to the scatterplots. Explain exactly what they tell you about predicting Earnings per Round. How accurate do you think these predictions would be?

9. Management of a home appliance store wants to understand the growth pattern of the monthly sales of Blu-ray disc players over the past two years. The managers have recorded the relevant data in the file **P10_09.xlsx**. Have the sales of this product been growing linearly over the past 24 months? Using simple linear regression, explain why or why not.

10. Do the selling prices of houses in a given community vary systematically with their sizes (as measured in square feet)? Answer this question by estimating a simple regression equation where the selling price of the house is the dependent variable and the size of the house is the explanatory variable. Use the sample data given in the file **P10_10.xlsx**. Interpret your estimated equation and the associated R^2.

11. The file **P10_11.xlsx** contains annual observations of the American minimum wage since 1955. Has the minimum wage been growing at roughly a *constant* rate over this period? Use simple linear regression analysis to address this question. Explain the results you obtain. (You can ignore the data in column C for now.)

12. Based on the data in the file **P02_23.xlsx** from the U.S. Department of Agriculture, explore the relationship between the number of farms (X) and the average size of a farm (Y) in the United States. Specifically, estimate a simple linear regression equation and interpret it.

13. Estimate the relationship between monthly electrical power usage (Y) and home size (X) using the data in the file **P10_13.xlsx**. Interpret your results. How well does a simple linear regression equation explain the variation in monthly electrical power usage?

14. The file **P02_12.xlsx** includes data on the 50 top graduate programs in the United States, according to a recent *U.S. News & World Report* survey. Columns B, C, and D contain ratings: an overall rating, a rating by peer schools, and a rating by recruiters. The other columns contain data that might be related to these ratings.

a. Find a table of correlations between all of the numerical variables. From these correlations, which variables in columns E–L are most highly correlated with the various ratings?

b. For the Overall rating, run a regression using it as the dependent variable and the variable (from columns E–L) most highly correlated with it. Interpret this equation. Could you have guessed the value of R^2 before running the regression? Explain. What does the standard error of estimate indicate?

c. Repeat part **b** with the Peers rating as the dependent variable. Repeat again with the Recruiters rating as the dependent variable. Discuss any differences among the three regressions in parts **b** and **c**.

Level B

15. If you haven't already done Problem 6 on 2006–2007 movies, do it now. The scatterplots of Total US Gross versus 7-day Gross or 14-day Gross indicate some possible outliers at the right—the movies that did great during their first week or two. Identify these outliers (you can decide how many qualify) and move them out of the data set. Then redo Problem 6 without the outliers. Comment on whether you get very different results. Specifically, do these outliers affect the slope of either regression line? Do they affect the standard error of estimate or R^2?

10-5 MULTIPLE REGRESSION

In general, there are two possible approaches to obtaining improved fits in regression. The first is to examine a scatterplot of residuals for nonlinear patterns and then make appropriate modifications to the regression equation. We will discuss this approach later in the chapter. The second approach is much more straightforward: Add more explanatory variables to the regression equation. In the Bendrix manufacturing example, we deliberately included only a single explanatory variable in the equation at a time to keep the equations simple. But because scatterplots indicate that both explanatory variables are also related to Overhead, it makes sense to try including both in the regression equation. With any luck, the linear fit should improve.

When you include several explanatory variables in the regression equation, you move into the realm of *multiple* regression. Some of the concepts from simple regression carry over naturally to multiple regression, but some change considerably. The following list provides a starting point that we expand on throughout this section.

Characteristics of Multiple Regression

- Graphically, you are no longer fitting a *line* to a set of points. If there are exactly two explanatory variables, you are fitting a *plane* to the data in three-dimensional space. There is one dimension for the dependent variable and one for each of the two explanatory variables. Although you can imagine a flat plane passing through a swarm of points, it is difficult to graph this on a two-dimensional screen. And if there are more than two explanatory variables, you can only imagine the regression plane; drawing in four or more dimensions is impossible.

- The regression equation is still estimated by the least squares method—that is, by minimizing the sum of squared residuals. However, it is definitely not practical to implement this method by hand. A statistical software package such as StatTools is required.

- Simple regression is actually a special case of multiple regression—that is, an equation with a single explanatory variable can be considered a "multiple" regression equation. This explains why it is possible to use StatTools's Multiple Regression procedure for simple regression.

- There is a slope term for each explanatory variable in the equation. The interpretation of these slope terms is somewhat different than in simple regression, as explained in the following subsection.

- The standard error of estimate and R^2 summary measures are almost exactly as in simple regression, as explained in Section 10-5b.

- Many *types* of explanatory variables can be included in the regression equation, as explained in Section 10-6. To a large part, these are responsible for the wide applicability of multiple regression in the business world. However, the burden is on you to choose the *best* set of explanatory variables. This is generally not easy.

10-5a Interpretation of Regression Coefficients

A typical slope term measures the expected change in Y when the corresponding X increases by one unit.

If Y is the dependent variable and X_1 through X_k are the explanatory variables, then a typical multiple regression equation has the form shown in Equation (10.9), where a is again the Y-intercept, and b_1 through b_k are the slopes. Collectively, a and the bs in Equation (10.9) are called the **regression coefficients**. The intercept a is the expected value of Y when all of the Xs equal zero. (Of course, this makes sense only if it is practical for all of the Xs to equal zero, which is seldom the case.) Each slope coefficient is the expected change in Y when this particular X increases by one unit *and the other Xs in the equation remain constant*. For example, b_1 is the expected change in Y when X_1 increases by one unit and the other Xs in the equation, X_2 through X_k, remain constant.

General Multiple Regression Equation
$$\text{Predicted } Y = a + b_1X_1 + b_2X_2 + \cdots + b_kX_k \qquad \textbf{(10.9)}$$

This extra proviso, "when the other Xs in the equation remain constant," is crucial for the interpretation of the regression coefficients. In particular, it means that the estimates of the bs depend on which other Xs are included in the regression equation. We illustrate these ideas in the following continuation of Example 10.2.

EXAMPLE | **10.2 EXPLAINING OVERHEAD COSTS AT BENDRIX (CONTINUED)**

Estimate and interpret the equation for Overhead when both explanatory variables, Machine Hours and Production Runs, are included in the regression equation.

Objective To use StatTools's Regression procedure to estimate the equation for overhead costs at Bendrix as a function of machine hours and production runs.

Solution

To obtain the regression output, select Regression from the StatTools Regression and Classification dropdown list and fill out the resulting dialog box as shown in Figure 10.20. As before, choose the Multiple option, specify the single *D* variable and the two *I* variables, and check any optional graphs you want to see. (This time we have selected the first and third options.)

Figure 10.20

Multiple Regression Dialog Box

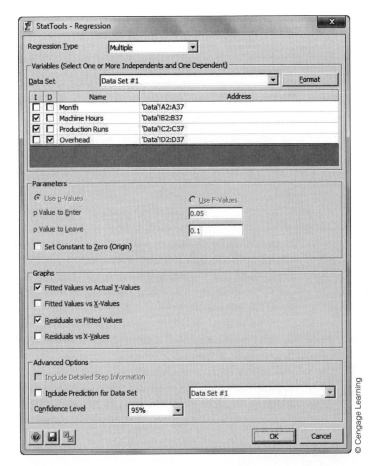

The main regression output appears in Figure 10.21. The coefficients in the range B18:B20 indicate that the estimated regression equation is

Predicted Overhead = 3997 + 43.54Machine Hours + 883.62Production Runs **(10.10)**

The interpretation of Equation (10.10) is that if the number of production runs is held constant, the overhead cost is expected to increase by $43.54 for each extra machine hour, and if the number of machine hours is held constant, the overhead cost is expected to increase by $883.62 for each extra production run. The Bendrix manager can interpret the intercept, $3997, as the fixed component of overhead. The slope terms involving Machine Hours and Production Runs are the variable components of overhead.

Figure 10.21

Multiple Regression Output for Bendrix Example

	A	B	C	D	E	F	G
7	Multiple Regression for Overhead						
8		Multiple	R-Square	Adjusted	StErr of		
9	Summary	R		R-Square	Estimate		
10		0.9308	0.8664	0.8583	4108.99309		
11							
12		Degrees of	Sum of	Mean of	F-Ratio	p-Value	
13	ANOVA Table	Freedom	Squares	Squares			
14	Explained	2	3614020661	1807010330	107.0261	< 0.0001	
15	Unexplained	33	557166199.1	16883824.22			
16							
17		Coefficient	Standard	t-Value	p-Value	Confidence Interval 95%	
18	Regression Table		Error			Lower	Upper
19	Constant	3996.678209	6603.650932	0.6052	0.5492	−9438.550632	17431.90705
20	Machine Hours	43.53639812	3.5894837	12.1289	< 0.0001	36.23353862	50.83925761
21	Production Runs	883.6179252	82.25140753	10.7429	< 0.0001	716.2761784	1050.959672

© Cengage Learning

It is interesting to compare Equation (10.10) with the separate equations for Overhead involving only a single variable each. From the previous section these are

$$\text{Predicted Overhead} = 48621 + 34.7\text{Machine Hours}$$

and

$$\text{Predicted Overhead} = 75606 + 655.1\text{Production Runs}$$

Note that the coefficient of Machine Hours has increased from 34.7 to 43.5 and the coefficient of Production Runs has increased from 655.1 to 883.6. Also, the intercept is now lower than either intercept in the single-variable equations. In general, it is difficult to guess the changes that will occur when more explanatory variables are included in the equation, but it is likely that changes *will* occur.

The estimated coefficient of any explanatory variable typically depends on which other explanatory variables are included in the equation.

The reasoning is that when Machine Hours is the only variable in the equation, Production Runs is *not* being held constant—it is being ignored—so in effect the coefficient 34.7 of Machine Hours indicates the effect of Machine Hours *and* the omitted Production Runs on Overhead. But when both variables are included, the coefficient 43.5 of Machine Hours indicates the effect of Machine Hours only, holding Production Runs constant. Because the coefficients of Machine Hours in the two equations have different *meanings*, it is not surprising that they have different numerical estimates. ∎

FUNDAMENTAL INSIGHT

Multiple Regression, Correlations, and Scatterplots

When there are multiple potential Xs for a regression on Y, it is useful to calculate correlations and scatterplots of Y versus each X. But remember that correlations and scatterplots are for *two variables only*; they do not necessarily tell the whole story. Sometimes, as in this overhead example, a multiple regression can turn out quite differently than might be expected from correlations and scatterplots alone. Specifically, the R^2 value for the multiple regression can be considerably smaller *or* larger than might be expected.

10-5b Interpretation of Standard Error of Estimate and R-Square

The multiple regression output in Figure 10.21 is very similar to simple regression output. In particular, cells C9 and E9 again show R^2 and the standard error of estimate s_e. Also, the square root of R^2 appears in cell B9. The interpretation of these quantities is almost exactly the same as in simple regression. The standard error of estimate is essentially the standard deviation of residuals, but it is now given by Equation (10.11), where n is the number of observations and k is the number of explanatory variables in the equation.

Formula for Standard Error of Estimate in Multiple Regression

$$s_e = \sqrt{\frac{\Sigma e_i^2}{n - k - 1}}$$

(10.11)

Fortunately, you can interpret s_e exactly as before. It is a measure of the typical prediction error when the multiple regression equation is used to predict the dependent variable. In this example, about two-thirds of the predictions should be within one standard error, or $4109, of the actual overhead cost. By comparing this with the standard errors from the single-variable equations for Overhead, $8585 and $9457, you can see that the multiple regression equation will tend to provide predictions that are more than twice as accurate as the single-variable equations—a big improvement.

The R^2 value is again the percentage of variation of the dependent variable explained by the combined set of explanatory variables. In fact, it even has the same formula as before [see Equation (10.8)]. For the Bendrix data you can see that Machine Hours and Production Runs combine to explain 86.6% of the variation in Overhead. This is a big improvement over the single-variable equations that were able to explain only 39.9% and 27.1% of the variation in Overhead. Remarkably, the combination of the two explanatory variables explains a larger percentage than the *sum* of their individual effects. This is not common, but this example shows that it is possible.

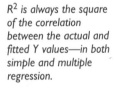

R^2 is always the square of the correlation between the actual and fitted Y values—in both simple and multiple regression.

The square root of R^2 shown in cell B9 of Figure 10.21 (the multiple R) is again the correlation between the fitted values and the observed values of the dependent variable. For the Bendrix data the correlation between them is 0.931, quite high. A graphical indication of this high correlation can be seen in one of the requested scatterplots, the plot of fitted versus observed values of Overhead. This scatterplot appears in Figure 10.22. If the

Figure 10.22

Scatterplot of Fitted Values versus Observed Values of Overhead

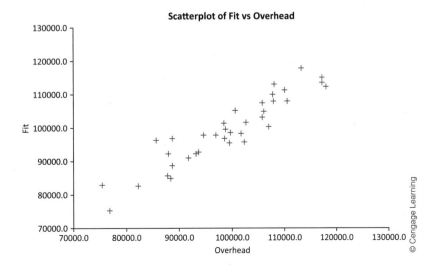

regression equation gave *perfect* predictions, all of the points in this plot would lie on a 45° line—each fitted value would *equal* the corresponding observed value. Although a perfect fit virtually never occurs, the closer the points are to a 45° line, the better the fit is, as indicated by R^2 or its square root.

Although the R^2 value is one of the most frequently quoted values from a regression analysis, it does have one serious drawback: R^2 can only *increase* when extra explanatory variables are added to an equation. This can lead to "fishing expeditions," where you keep adding variables to an equation, some of which have no conceptual relationship to the dependent variable, just to inflate the R^2 value. To avoid adding extra variables that do not really belong, an **adjusted R^2** value is typically listed in regression outputs. This adjusted value appears in cell D9 of Figure 10.21. Although it has no direct interpretation as "percentage of variation explained," it *can* decrease when unnecessary explanatory variables are added to an equation. Therefore, it serves as an index that you can monitor. If you add variables and the adjusted R^2 *decreases*, the extra variables are essentially not pulling their weight and should probably be omitted. We will say much more about this issue in the next chapter.

> **Adjusted R^2** is a measure that adjusts R^2 for the number of explanatory variables in the equation. It is used primarily to monitor whether extra explanatory variables really belong in the equation.

FUNDAMENTAL INSIGHT

R^2, Adjusted R^2, and Standard Error of Estimate

Sometimes a regression equation is "built" by successively adding explanatory variables to an equation. As more variables are added, it is a mathematical fact that R^2 *must* increase; it cannot decrease. However, the standard error of estimate *can* increase, and the adjusted R^2 *can* decrease, each signaling that the extra variables are not useful and should probably be omitted from the equation. In fact, the purpose of adjusted R^2 is to monitor whether the equation is getting better or worse as more variables are added.

PROBLEMS

Level A

16. A trucking company wants to predict the yearly maintenance expense (Y) for a truck using the number of miles driven during the year (X_1) and the age of the truck (X_2, in years) at the beginning of the year. The company has gathered the data given in the file **P10_16.xlsx**, where each observation corresponds to a particular truck.
    a. Estimate a multiple regression equation using the given data. Interpret each of the estimated regression coefficients. Why is the magnitude of the Miles Driven coefficient so much lower than the magnitude of the Age of Truck coefficient? Is it because Miles Driven is not as important in predicting Maintenance Expense?
    b. Interpret the standard error of estimate s_e and R^2 for these data.

17. DataPro is a small but rapidly growing firm that provides electronic data-processing services to commercial firms, hospitals, and other organizations. For each of the past 12 months, DataPro has tracked the number of contracts sold, the average contract price, advertising expenditures, and personal selling expenditures. These data are provided in the file **P10_17.xlsx**. Using the number of contracts sold as the dependent variable, estimate a multiple regression equation with three explanatory variables. Interpret each of the estimated regression coefficients, the standard error of estimate, and R^2.

18. An antique collector believes that the price received for a particular item increases with its age and with the number of bidders. The file **P10_18.xlsx** contains data on these three variables for 32 recently auctioned comparable items.
    a. Estimate a multiple regression equation using the given data. Interpret each of the estimated regression coefficients. Is the antique collector correct in believing that the price received for the item increases with its age and with the number of bidders?
    b. Interpret the standard error of estimate s_e and R^2. Does it appear that predictions of price from this equation will be very accurate?

19. Stock market analysts are continually looking for reliable predictors of stock prices. Consider the problem of modeling the price per share of electric utility stocks (Y). Two variables thought to influence this stock price are return on average equity (X_1) and annual dividend rate (X_2). The stock price, returns on equity, and dividend rates on a randomly selected day for 16 electric utility stocks are provided in the file **P10_19.xlsx**.
   a. Estimate a multiple regression equation using the given data. Interpret each of the estimated regression coefficients.
   b. Interpret the standard error of estimate s_e, R^2, and the adjusted R^2. Does it appear that predictions of price from this equation will be very accurate?

20. The manager of a commuter rail transportation system was recently asked by her governing board to determine which factors have a significant impact on the demand for rides in the large city served by the transportation network. The system manager collected data on variables thought to be possibly related to the number of weekly riders on the city's rail system. The file **P10_20.xlsx** contain these data.
   a. What do you expect the signs of the coefficients of the explanatory variables in this multiple regression equation to be? Why? (Answer this *before* running the regression.)
   b. Estimate a multiple regression equation using the given data. Interpret each of the estimated regression coefficients. Are the signs of the estimated coefficients consistent with your expectations in part **a**?
   c. What proportion of the total variation in the number of weekly riders is *not* explained by this estimated multiple regression equation?

21. Consider the enrollment data for *Business Week*'s top U.S. graduate business programs in the file **P10_21.xlsx**. Use the data in the MBA Data sheet to estimate a multiple regression equation to assess whether there is a relationship between the total number of full-time students (Enrollment) and the following explanatory variables: (a) the proportion of female students, (b) the proportion of minority students, and (c) the proportion of international students enrolled at these business schools.
   a. Interpret the coefficients of the estimated regression equation. Do any of these results surprise you? Explain.
   b. How well does the estimated regression equation fit the given data?

22. A regional express delivery service company recently conducted a study to investigate the relationship between the cost of shipping a package (Y), the package weight (X_1), and the distance shipped (X_2). Twenty packages were randomly selected from among the large number received for shipment, and a detailed analysis of the shipping cost was conducted for each

package. These sample observations are given in the file **P10_22.xlsx**.
   a. Estimate a simple linear regression equation involving shipping cost and package weight. Interpret the slope coefficient of the least squares line and the R^2 value.
   b. Add another explanatory variable, distance shipped, to the regression model in part **a**. Estimate and interpret this expanded equation. How does the R^2 value for this multiple regression equation compare to that of the simple regression equation in part **a**? Explain any difference between the two R^2 values. Interpret the *adjusted* R^2 value for the revised equation.

Level B

23. The owner of a restaurant in Bloomington, Indiana, has recorded sales data for the past 19 years. He has also recorded data on potentially relevant variables. The entire data set appears in the file **P10_23.xlsx**.
   a. Estimate a simple linear regression equation involving annual sales (the dependent variable) and the size of the population residing within 10 miles of the restaurant (the explanatory variable). Interpret the R^2 value.
   b. Add another explanatory variable—annual advertising expenditures—to the regression equation in part **a**. Estimate and interpret this expanded equation. How does the R^2 value for this equation compare to the equation in part **a**? Explain any difference between the two R^2 values. What, if anything, does the *adjusted* R^2 value for the revised equation indicate?
   c. Add one more explanatory variable to the multiple regression equation estimated in part **b**. In particular, estimate and interpret the coefficients of a multiple regression equation that includes the *previous* year's advertising expenditure. How does the inclusion of this third explanatory variable affect the R^2 and adjusted R^2 values, in comparison to the corresponding values for the equation of part **b**? Explain any changes in these values.

24. Continuing Problem 8 on the 2011 golfer data in the file **P10_08.xlsx**, the simple linear regressions for Earnings per Round were perhaps not as good as you expected. Explore several multiple regressions for Earnings per Round, using the variables in columns I–M and R. Proceed as follows.
   a. Create a table of correlations for these variables.
   b. Run a regression of Earnings per Round versus the most highly correlated variable (positive or negative) with Earnings per Round. Then run a second regression with the two most highly correlated variables with Earnings per Round. Then run a third with the three most highly correlated, and so on until all six explanatory variables are in the equation.

c. Comment on the changes you see from one equation to the next. Does the coefficient of a variable entered earlier change as you enter more variables? How much better do the equations get, in terms of standard error of estimate and R^2, as you enter more variables? Does adjusted R^2 ever indicate that an equation is *worse* than the one before it?

d. The bottom line is whether these variables, as a whole, do a very good job of predicting Earnings per Round. Would you say they do? Why or why not?

25. Using the sample data given in the file **P10_10.xlsx**, use multiple regression to predict the selling price of houses in a given community. Proceed as follows.

a. Add one explanatory variable at a time and estimate each regression equation along the way. Report and explain changes in the standard error of estimate s_e, R^2, and adjusted R^2 as each explanatory variable is added to the model. Does it matter in which order you add the variables? Try at least two different orderings to answer this question.

b. Interpret each of the estimated regression coefficients in the full equation, that is, the equation with all explanatory variables included.

c. What proportion of the total variation in the selling price is explained by the multiple regression equation that includes all four explanatory variables?

10-6 MODELING POSSIBILITIES

Once you move from simple to multiple regression, the floodgates open. All types of explanatory variables are potential candidates for inclusion in the regression equation. In this section we examine several new types of explanatory variables. These include dummy variables, interaction variables, and nonlinear transformations. The techniques in this section provide you with many alternative approaches to modeling the relationship between a dependent variable and potential explanatory variables. In many applications these techniques produce much better fits than you could obtain without them.

FUNDAMENTAL INSIGHT

Modeling Possibilities

As the title of this section suggests, these techniques are modeling *possibilities*. They provide a wide variety of explanatory variables to choose from. However, this does not mean that it is wise to include all or even many of these new types of explanatory variables in any particular regression equation. The

chances are that only a few, if any, will significantly improve the fit. Knowing which explanatory variables to include requires a great deal of practical experience with regression, as well as a thorough understanding of the data in its context. The material in this section should *not* be an excuse for a mindless fishing expedition.

10-6a Dummy Variables

Some potential explanatory variables are categorical and cannot be measured on a quantitative scale. However, these categorical variables are often related to the dependent variable, so you need a way to include them in a regression equation. The trick is to use **dummy variables**, also called **indicator** or **0–1** variables. Dummy variables are variables that indicate the category a given observation is in. If a dummy variable for a given category equals 1, the observation is in that category; if it equals 0, the observation is not in that category.

> A **dummy variable** is a variable with possible values 0 and 1. It equals 1 if the observation is in a particular category and 0 if it is not.

Categorical variables are used in two situations. The first and perhaps most common situation is when a categorical variable has only two categories. A good example of this is a gender variable that has the two categories "male" and "female." In this case only a *single* dummy variable is required, and you have the choice of assigning the 1s to either category. If the dummy variable is called Gender, you can code Gender as 1 for males and 0 for females, or you can code Gender as 1 for females and 0 for males. You just need to be consistent and specify explicitly which coding scheme you are using.

The other situation is when there are more than two categories. A good example of this is when you have quarterly time series data and you want to treat the quarter of the year as a categorical variable with four categories, 1 through 4. Then you can create four dummy variables, Q1 through Q4. For example, Q2 equals 1 for all second-quarter observations and 0 for all other observations. Although you can create four dummy variables, only three of them—*any* three—should be used in a regression equation, as we will explain shortly.

Example 10.3 illustrates how to create, use, and interpret dummy variables in regression analysis.

| EXAMPLE | **10.3 POSSIBLE GENDER DISCRIMINATION IN BANK SALARIES** |

Fifth National Bank of Springfield is facing a gender discrimination suit.[6] The charge is that its female employees receive substantially smaller salaries than its male employees. The bank's employee data are listed in the file **Bank Salaries.xlsx**. For each of its 208 employees, the data set includes the following variables:

- Education: education level, a categorical variable with categories 1 (finished high school), 2 (finished some college courses), 3 (obtained a bachelor's degree), 4 (took some graduate courses), 5 (obtained a graduate degree)
- Grade: a categorical variable indicating the current job level, the possible levels being 1 through 6 (6 is highest)
- Years1: years of experience with this bank
- Years2: number of years of work experience at another bank prior to working at Fifth National
- Age: employee's current age
- Gender: a categorical variable with values "Female" and "Male"
- PC Job: a categorical yes/no variable depending on whether the employee's current job is computer-related
- Salary: current annual salary

Figure 10.23 lists a few of the observations. Do these data provide evidence that there is discrimination against females in terms of salary?

Figure 10.23

Selected Data for Bank Example

⊿	A	B	C	D	E	F	G	H	I
1	Employee	Education	Grade	Years1	Years2	Age	Gender	PC Job	Salary
2	1	3	1	3	1	26	Male	No	$32,000
3	2	1	1	14	1	38	Female	No	$39,100
4	3	1	1	12	0	35	Female	No	$33,200
5	4	2	1	8	7	40	Female	No	$30,600
6	5	3	1	3	0	28	Male	No	$29,000
207	206	5	6	32	0	62	Male	No	$88,000
208	207	5	6	35	0	59	Male	No	$94,000
209	208	5	6	33	0	62	Female	No	$30,000

© Cengage Learning

[6]This example and the accompanying data set are based on a real case from 1995. Only the bank's name has been changed.

Objective To use the StatTools Regression procedure to analyze whether the bank discriminates against females in terms of salary.

Solution

A naive approach to this problem is to compare the average female salary to the average male salary. This can be done with a pivot table, as in Chapter 3, or with a more formal hypothesis test, as in Chapter 9. Using these methods, you can check that the average of all salaries is $39,922, the female average is $37,210, the male average is $45,505, and the difference between the male and female averages is statistically significant at any reasonable level of significance. In short, the females definitely earn less. But perhaps there is a reason for this. They might have lower education levels, they might have been hired more recently, and so on. The question is whether the difference between female and male salaries is still evident after taking these other attributes into account. This is a perfect task for regression.

The first task is to create dummy variables for the various categorical variables. You can do this manually with IF functions or you can use the StatTools Dummy procedure. To do it manually, create a dummy variable Female based on Gender in column J by entering the formula

=IF(F45="Female",1,0)

in cell J4, and copy it down. Note that females are coded as 1s and males as 0s. (Remember that the quotes are necessary when a text value is used in an IF function.)

The StatTools Dummy procedure is somewhat easier, especially when there are multiple categories. For example, to create five dummies for the education levels, select Dummy from the StatTools Data Utilities dropdown menu, select the Create One Dummy Variable for Each Distinct Category option, and select the Education variable to base the dummies on. This creates five dummy columns with variable names Education=1 through Education=5. (For simplicity, we renamed these dummies Educ1 through Educ5.) You could follow the same procedure to create six dummies, Grade=1 through Grade=6, for the job grade categories. (We also renamed these as Grade1 through Grade6.)

It is also possible to add dummies to effectively collapse categories.

Sometimes you might want to collapse several categories. For example, you might want to collapse the five education categories into three categories: 1, (2,3), and (4,5). The new second category includes employees who have taken undergraduate courses or have completed a bachelor's degree, and the new third category includes employees who have taken graduate courses or have completed a graduate degree. It is easy to do this. You can again use IF functions, or you can simply add the Educ2 and Educ3 columns to get the dummy for the new second category. Similarly, you add the Educ4 and Educ5 columns for the new third category. (Do you see why this works?)

Once the dummies have been created, you can run a regression analysis with Salary as the dependent variable, using any combination of numerical and dummy explanatory variables. However, there are two rules you must follow:

1. You shouldn't use any of the *original* categorical variables, such as Education, that the dummies are based on.

2. You should always use *one fewer dummy* than the number of categories for any categorical variable.

Always include one fewer dummy than the number of categories. The omitted dummy corresponds to the reference category.

This second rule is a technical one. If you violate it, the statistical software (StatTools or most other packages) will display an error message. For example, if you want to use education level as an explanatory variable, you should enter only four of the five dummies Educ1 through Educ5. *Any* four of these can be used. The omitted dummy then corresponds to the *reference* category. The interpretation of any dummy variable coefficient is relative to this reference category. When there are only two categories, as with the gender variable, the common procedure is to name the variable with the category, such as Female, that corresponds to the 1s. If you create the dummy variables manually, you probably will not even bother to create a dummy for males. In this case "Male" automatically becomes the reference category.

To explain dummy variables in regression, it is useful to proceed in several steps in this example. (After you get used to the procedure, you can combine all of these steps into a single step. Alternatively, you can use a stepwise procedure, as explained in the next chapter.) The first step is to estimate a regression equation with only one explanatory variable, Female. The output appears in Figure 10.24, and the resulting equation is

---

Predicted Salary Based on Gender Only
$$\text{Predicted Salary} = 45505 - 8296\text{Female} \qquad \textbf{(10.12)}$$

Figure 10.24 Output for Bank Example with a Single Explanatory Variable

▲	A	B	C	D	E	F	G
7	**Multiple Regression for Salary**						
8		**Multiple**	**R-Square**	**Adjusted**	**StErr of**		
9	**Summary**	**R**		**R-Square**	**Estimate**		
10		0.3465	0.1201	0.1158	10584.26048		
11							
12		**Degrees of**	**Sum of**	**Mean of**	**F-Ratio**	**p-Value**	
13	**ANOVA Table**	**Freedom**	**Squares**	**Squares**			
14	**Explained**	1	3149633845	3149633845	28.1151	< 0.0001	
15	**Unexplained**	206	23077473386	112026569.8			
16							
17		**Coefficient**	**Standard**	**t-Value**	**p-Value**	**Confidence Interval 95%**	
18	**Regression Table**		**Error**			**Lower**	**Upper**
19	**Constant**	45505.44118	1283.530115	35.4533	< 0.0001	42974.90165	48035.9807
20	**Female**	−8295.512605	1564.493318	−5.3024	< 0.0001	−11379.98419	−5211.041015

© Cengage Learning

To interpret regression equations with dummy variables, it is useful to rewrite the equation for each category.

To interpret this equation, recall that Female has only two possible values, 0 and 1. If you substitute Female=1 into Equation (10.12), you obtain

$$\text{Predicted Salary} = 45505 - 8296(1) = 37209$$

Because Female=1 corresponds to females, this equation simply indicates the predicted female salary. Similarly, if you substitute Female = 0 into Equation (10.12), you obtain

$$\text{Predicted Salary} = 45505 - 8296(0) = 45505$$

Because Female=0 corresponds to males, this equation indicates the predicted male salary. Therefore, the interpretation of the −8296 coefficient of the Female dummy variable is straightforward. It is the average female salary relative to the reference (male) category. In short, females get paid $8296 less on average than males.

However, Equation (10.12) tells only part of the story. It ignores all information except for gender. The next step is to expand this equation by adding the experience variables

Years1 and Years2. The output with the Female dummy variable and these two experience variables appears in Figure 10.25. The corresponding regression equation is

---

Predicted Salary Based on Experience and Gender

$$\text{Predicted Salary} = 35492 + 988\text{Years1} + 131\text{Years2} - 8080\text{Female} \quad \textbf{(10.13)}$$

Figure 10.25 Regression Output with Two Numerical Explanatory Variables Included

	A	B	C	D	E	F	G
7	**Multiple Regression for Salary**						
8		**Multiple**	**R-Square**	**Adjusted**	**StErr of**		
9	**Summary**	**R**		**R-Square**	**Estimate**		
10		0.7016	0.4923	0.4848	8079.397428		
11							
12		**Degrees of**	**Sum of**	**Mean of**	**F-Ratio**	**p-Value**	
13	**ANOVA Table**	**Freedom**	**Squares**	**Squares**			
14	**Explained**	3	12910668018	4303556006	65.9279	< 0.0001	
15	**Unexplained**	204	13316439212	65276662.81			
16							
17		**Coefficient**	**Standard**	**t-Value**	**p-Value**	**Confidence Interval 95%**	
18	**Regression Table**		**Error**			**Lower**	**Upper**
19	**Constant**	35491.66097	1341.021528	26.4661	< 0.0001	32847.62127	38135.70067
20	**Years1**	987.9936807	80.92814461	12.2083	< 0.0001	828.4308231	1147.556538
21	**Years2**	131.3379165	180.9229477	0.7259	0.4687	−225.3807836	488.0566166
22	**Female**	−8080.212123	1198.170124	−6.7438	< 0.0001	−10442.5973	−5717.82695

It is again useful to write Equation (10.13) in two forms: one for females (substituting Female=1) and one for males (substituting Female=0). After doing the arithmetic, they become

$$\text{Predicted Salary} = 27412 + 988\text{Years1} + 131\text{Years2}$$

and

$$\text{Predicted Salary} = 35492 + 988\text{Years1} + 131\text{Years2}$$

Except for the intercept term, these equations are identical. You can now interpret the coefficient −8080 of the Female dummy variable as the average salary disadvantage for females relative to males *after controlling for job experience*. Gender discrimination still appears to be a very plausible conclusion. However, note that the R^2 value is only 49.2%. Perhaps there is still more to the story.

The next step is to add education level to the equation by including four of the five education level dummies. Although *any* four could be used, we use Educ2 through Educ5, so that the lowest level becomes the reference category. (This should lead to *positive* coefficients for these dummies, which are easier to interpret.) The resulting output appears in Figure 10.26. The estimated regression equation is now

---

Predicted Salary Based on Experience, Education, and Gender

$$\text{Predicted Salary} = 26613 + 1033\text{Years1} + 362\text{Years2} - 4501\text{Female}$$
$$+ 160\text{Educ2} + 4765\text{Educ3} + 7320\text{Educ4} + 11770\text{Educ5} \quad \textbf{(10.14)}$$

Figure 10.26 Regression Output with Education Dummies Included

▲	A	B	C	D	E	F	G
7	**Multiple Regression for Salary**						
8		**Multiple**	**R-Square**	**Adjusted**	**StErr of**		
9	**Summary**	**R**		**R-Square**	**Estimate**		
10		0.8030	0.6449	0.6324	6824.373646		
11							
12		**Degrees of**	**Sum of**	**Mean of**	**F-Ratio**	**p-Value**	
13	**ANOVA Table**	**Freedom**	**Squares**	**Squares**			
14	**Explained**	7	16912692100	2416098871	51.8787	< 0.0001	
15	**Unexplained**	200	9314415131	46572075.65			
16							
17		**Coefficient**	**Standard**	**t-Value**	**p-Value**	**Confidence Interval 95%**	
18	**Regression Table**		**Error**			**Lower**	**Upper**
19	**Constant**	26613.35544	1794.143455	14.8335	< 0.0001	23075.49073	30151.22014
20	**Years1**	1032.930137	69.60252669	14.8404	< 0.0001	895.681177	1170.179096
21	**Years2**	362.2341784	158.1233928	2.2908	0.0230	50.43125717	674.0370996
22	**Female**	−4501.322074	1085.767439	−4.1458	< 0.0001	−6642.342787	−2360.301361
23	**Educ2**	160.241811	1656.011646	0.0968	0.9230	−3105.2413	3425.724921
24	**Educ3**	4764.556451	1473.434122	3.2336	0.0014	1859.09727	7670.015632
25	**Educ4**	7319.841017	2694.168528	2.7169	0.0072	2007.22027	12632.46176
26	**Educ5**	11770.20898	1510.213706	7.7937	< 0.0001	8792.224276	14748.19368

© Cengage Learning

Now there are two categorical variables involved, gender and education level. However, you can still write a separate equation *for each combination* of categories by setting the dummies to appropriate values. For example, the equation for females at education level 5 is found by setting Female and Educ5 equal to 1, and setting the other education dummies equal to 0. After combining terms, this equation is

$$\text{Predicted Salary} = 33882 + 1033\text{Years1} + 362\text{Years2}$$

The intercept 33882 is the intercept from Equation (10.14), 26613, plus the coefficients of Female and Educ5.

Equation (10.14) can be interpreted as follows. For either gender and any education level, the expected increase in salary for one extra year of experience with Fifth National is $1033; the expected increase in salary for one extra year of prior experience with another bank is $362. The coefficients of the education dummies indicate the average increase in salary an employee can expect relative to the reference (lowest) education level. For example, an employee with education level 4 can expect to earn $7320 more than an employee with education level 1, all else being equal. Finally, the key coefficient, −$4501 for females, indicates the average salary disadvantage for females relative to males, given that they have the same experience levels *and* the same education levels. Note that the R^2 value is now 64.5%, quite a bit larger than when the education dummies were not included. We appear to be getting closer to the truth. In particular, you can see that there appears to be gender discrimination in salaries, even after accounting for job experience and education level.

One further explanation for gender differences in salary might be job grade. Perhaps females tend to be in lower job grades, which would help explain why they get lower salaries on average. One way to check this is with a pivot table, as in Figure 10.27, with

Figure 10.27

Pivot Table of Job
Grade Counts for
Bank Data

	A	B	C	D
3	**Count of Employee**	**Gender** ▾		
4	**Grade** ▾	**Female**	**Male**	**Grand Total**
5	1	34.29%	17.65%	28.85%
6	2	20.71%	19.12%	20.19%
7	3	25.71%	10.29%	20.67%
8	4	12.14%	16.18%	13.46%
9	5	6.43%	17.65%	10.10%
10	6	0.71%	19.21%	6.73%
11	**Grand Total**	**100.00%**	**100.00%**	**100.00%**

© Cengage Learning

job grade in the row area, gender in the column area, and counts, displayed as percentages of columns in the values area. Clearly, females tend to be concentrated at the lower job grades. For example, 28.85% of all employees are at the lowest job grade, but 34.29% of all females are at this grade and only 17.65% of males are at this grade. The opposite is true at the higher job grades. This certainly helps to explain why females get lower salaries on average.

It is possible to go one step further to see the effect of job grade on salary. As with the education dummies, the lowest job grade is used as the reference category and only the five dummies for the other categories are included. Two other potential explanatory variables can be added to the equation: Age and PC, a dummy based on the PC Job categorical variable. The regression output for this equation with all variables appears in Figure 10.28.

As expected, the coefficients of the job grade dummies are all positive, and they increase as the job grade increases—it pays to be in the higher job grades. The effect of age appears to be minimal, and there appears to be a "bonus" of close to $5000 for having

Figure 10.28

Regression Output
with Other
Variables Added

	A	B	C	D	E	F	G
7	**Multiple Regression for Salary**						
8		**Multiple**	**R-Square** ▾	**Adjusted**	**StErr of**		
9	**Summary**	**R**		**R-Square**	**Estimate**		
10		0.8748	0.7652	0.7495	5633.856652		
11							
12		**Degrees of**	**Sum of**	**Mean of**	**F-Ratio**	**p-Value**	
13	**ANOVA Table**	**Freedom**	**Squares**	**Squares**			
14	Explained	13	20069481121	1543806240	48.6386	< 0.0001	
15	Unexplained	194	6157626110	31740340.77			
16							
17		**Coefficient**	**Standard**	**t-Value**	**p-Value**	**Confidence Interval 95%**	
18	**Regression Table**		**Error**			**Lower**	**Upper**
19	Constant	29391.72269	1581.602999	18.5835	< 0.0001	26272.37844	32511.06693
20	Years1	507.8146352	84.04315446	6.0423	< 0.0001	342.0590503	673.5702201
21	Years2	162.2517732	135.6045194	1.1965	0.2330	−105.1966176	429.700164
22	Female	−2562.880256	1007.981448	−2.5426	0.0118	−4550.889339	−574.8711733
23	Educ2	−471.2637566	1392.114233	−0.3385	0.7353	−3216.885461	2274.357948
24	Educ3	585.3660589	1302.869087	0.4493	0.6537	−1984.24034	3154.972458
25	Educ4	310.7013975	2393.063336	0.1298	0.8968	−4409.059723	5030.462518
26	Educ5	2739.040039	1586.853849	1.7261	0.0859	−390.6602872	5868.740365
27	Grade2	1569.386058	1182.368482	1.3273	0.1860	−762.5609114	3901.333027
28	Grade3	5212.847139	1258.521305	4.1420	< 0.0001	2730.70643	7694.987848
29	Grade4	8589.108489	1491.797843	5.7576	< 0.0001	5646.884038	11531.33294
30	Grade5	13652.49316	1869.021833	7.3046	< 0.0001	9966.282079	17338.70424
31	Grade6	23780.10768	2772.581866	8.5769	< 0.0001	18311.83448	29248.38087
32	PC	4914.624622	1469.165005	3.3452	0.0010	2017.038182	7812.211062

© Cengage Learning

a PC-related job. The R^2 value has now increased to 76.5%, and the penalty for being a female has decreased to $2555—still large but not as large as before.

The regression indicates that being in lower job grades implies lower salaries, but it doesn't explain why females are in the lower job grades in the first place.

However, even if this penalty, the coefficient of Female in this last equation, is considered "small," is it convincing evidence against the argument for gender discrimination? We believe the answer is no. We have used variations in job grades to reduce the penalty for being female. But the real question is why females are predominantly in the low job grades. Perhaps this is the real source of gender discrimination. Perhaps management is not advancing the females as quickly as it should, which naturally results in lower salaries for females. In a sense, job grade is not really an explanatory variable; it is a dependent variable.

We conclude this example for now, but we will say more about it in the next two subsections. ■

10-6b Interaction Variables

Consider the following regression equation for a dependent variable Y versus a numerical variable X and a dummy variable D. If the estimated equation is of the form

> **Generic Equation with No Interaction**
> $$\hat{Y} = a + b_1 X + b_2 D \tag{10.15}$$

then, as in the previous section, this equation can be written as two separate equations:

$$\hat{Y} = (a + b_2) + b_1 X$$

and

$$\hat{Y} = a + b_1 X$$

The first corresponds to $D = 1$, and the second corresponds to $D = 0$. The only difference between these two equations is the intercept term; the slope for each is b_1. Geometrically, they correspond to two *parallel* lines that are a vertical distance b_2 apart. For example, if D corresponds to gender, there is a female line and a parallel male line. The effect of X on Y is the same for females and males. When X increases by one unit, Y is expected to change by b_1 units for males or females.

In effect, when you include *only* a dummy variable in a regression equation, as in Equation (10.15), you are allowing the intercepts of the two lines to differ (by an amount b_2), but you are *forcing* the lines to be parallel. To be more realistic, you might want to allow them to have different slopes, in addition to possibly different intercepts. You can do this by including an **interaction variable**. Algebraically, an interaction variable is the *product* of two variables. Its inclusion allows the effect of one of the variables on Y to depend on the value of the other variable.

> An **interaction variable** is the product of two explanatory variables. You can include such a variable in a regression equation if you believe the effect of one explanatory variable on Y depends on the value of another explanatory variable.

Suppose you create the interaction variable XD (the product of X and D) and then estimate the equation

$$\hat{Y} = a + b_1 X + b_2 D + b_3 XD$$

As usual, this equation can be rewritten as two separate equations, depending on whether $D = 0$ or $D = 1$. If $D = 1$, terms can be combined to write

$$\hat{Y} = (a + b_2) + (b_1 + b_3)X$$

If $D = 0$, the dummy and interaction variables drop out and the equation becomes

$$\hat{Y} = a + b_1 X$$

The notation is not important. The important part is that the interaction term, $b_3 XD$, allows the slope of the regression line to differ between the two categories.

The following continuation of Example 10.3 illustrates one possible use of interaction variables.

EXAMPLE | **10.3 POSSIBLE GENDER DISCRIMINATION IN BANK SALARIES (CONTINUED)**

Earlier you estimated an equation for Salary using the numerical explanatory variables Years1 and Years2 and the dummy variable Female. If you drop the Years2 variable from this equation (for simplicity) and rerun the regression, you obtain the equation

Predicted Salary With No Interactions
$$\text{Predicted Salary} = 35824 + 981\,\text{Years1} - 8012\text{Female} \qquad \textbf{(10.16)}$$

The R^2 value for this equation is 49.1%. If an interaction variable between Years1 and Female is added to this equation, what is its effect?

Objective To use multiple regression with an interaction variable to see whether the effect of years of experience on salary is different across the two genders.

Solution

You first need to form an interaction variable that is the product of Years1 and Female. This can be done in two ways in Excel. You can do it manually with an Excel formula that multiplies the two variables involved, or you can use the Interaction option from the StatTools Data Utilities dropdown menu. For the latter, select the Two Numeric Variables option in the Interaction Between dropdown list, and select Female and Years1 as the variables to be used to create the interaction variable.[7]

Once the interaction variable has been created, you can include it in the regression equation in addition to the other variables in Equation (10.16). The multiple regression output appears in Figure 10.29. The estimated regression equation is

$$\text{Predicted Salary} = 30430 + 1528\,\text{Years1} + 4098\text{Female}$$
$$-1248\text{Interaction(Years1,Female)}$$

where Interaction(Years1,Female) is StatTools's default name for the interaction variable. As before, it is useful to write this as two separate equations, one for females and one for males. The female equation (Female=1, so that Interaction(Years1,Female) = Years1) is

$$\text{Predicted Salary} = (30430 + 4098) + (1528 - 1248)\text{Years1}$$
$$= 34528 + 280\text{Years1}$$

and the male equation (Female = 0, so that Interaction(Years1,Female) = 0) is

$$\text{Predicted Salary} = 30430 + 1528\,\text{Years1}$$

---

[7]See the StatTools online help for this data utility. It explains the various options for creating interaction variables.

Figure 10.29 Regression Output with an Interaction Variable

◢	A	B	C	D	E	F	G
7	**Multiple Regression for Salary**						
8		**Multiple**	**R-Square**	**Adjusted**	**StErr of**		
9	**Summary**	**R**		**R-Square**	**Estimate**		
10		0.7991	0.6386	0.6333	6816.298288		
11							
12		**Degrees of**	**Sum of**	**Mean of**	**F-Ratio**	**p-Value**	
13	**ANOVA Table**	**Freedom**	**Squares**	**Squares**			
14	Explained	3	16748875071	5582958357	120.1620	< 0.0001	
15	Unexplained	204	9478232160	46461922.35			
16							
17		**Coefficient**	**Standard**	**t-Value**	**p-Value**	**Confidence Interval 95%**	
18	**Regression Table**		**Error**			**Lower**	**Upper**
19	Constant	30430.02774	1216.574332	25.0129	< 0.0001	28031.35571	32828.69977
20	Years1	1527.761719	90.46033769	16.8887	< 0.0001	1349.40461	1706.118829
21	Female	4098.251879	1665.842019	2.4602	0.0147	813.7763213	7382.727436
22	Interaction(Years1,Female)	−1247.798369	136.6757036	−9.1296	< 0.0001	−1517.276508	−978.3202292

© Cengage Learning

Graphically, these equations appear as in Figure 10.30. The Y-intercept for the female line is slightly higher—females with no experience with Fifth National tend to start out slightly higher than males—but the slope of the female line is much smaller. That is, males tend to move up the salary ladder much more quickly than females. Again, this provides another argument, although a somewhat different one, for gender discrimination against females. Notice that the R^2 value with the interaction variable has increased from 49.1% to 63.9%. The interaction variable has definitely added to the explanatory power of the equation. ∎

Figure 10.30

Nonparallel Female and Male Salary Lines

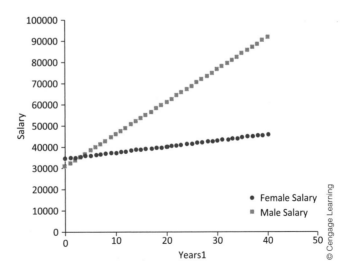

© Cengage Learning

Interpretation of Regression Coefficients

This example illustrates just one possible use of interaction variables. The product of *any* two variables, a numerical and a dummy variable, two dummy variables, or even two numerical variables, can be used. The trick is to interpret the results correctly, and the easiest way to do this is the way we have been doing it—by writing several separate equations and seeing how they differ. To illustrate one further possibility (among many), suppose you include the variables Years1, Female, and HighJob in the equation for Salary, along with interactions between Female and Years1 and between Female and HighJob. Here, HighJob is a new dummy variable that is 1 for job grades 4 to 6 and is 0 for job grades 1 to 3. The resulting equation is

---

Predicted Salary With Interactions

Predicted Salary = 28168 + 1261Years1 + 9242HighJob + 6601Female

−1224Interaction(Years1,Female) + 1564Interaction(Female,HighJob)   **(10.17)**

---

and the R^2 value is now 76.6%.

The interpretation of Equation (10.17) is quite a challenge because it is really composed of four separate equations, one for each combination of Female and HighJob. For females in the high job category, the equation becomes

$$\text{Predicted Salary} = (28168 + 9242 + 6601 + 1564) + (1261 - 1224)\text{Years1}$$
$$= 45575 + 37\text{Years1}$$

and for females in the low job category it is

$$\text{Predicted Salary} = (28168 + 6601) + (1261 - 1224)\text{Years1}$$
$$= 34769 + 37\text{Years1}$$

Similarly, for males in the high job category, the equation becomes

$$\text{Predicted Salary} = (28168 + 9242) + 1261\text{Years1}$$
$$= 37410 + 1261\text{Years1}$$

and for males in the low job category it is

$$\text{Predicted Salary} = 28168 + 1261\text{Years1}$$

Putting this into words, the various coefficients can be interpreted as follows.

- The intercept 28168 is the average *starting* salary (that is, with no experience at Fifth National) for males in the low job category.
- The coefficient 1261 of Years1 is the expected increase in salary per extra year of experience for males (in either job category).
- The coefficient 9242 of HighJob is the expected salary premium for males starting in the high job category instead of the low job category.
- The coefficient 6601 of Female is the expected starting salary premium for females relative to males, given that they start in the low job category.
- The coefficient −1224 of Interaction (Years1,Female) is the penalty per extra year of experience for females relative to males—that is, male salaries increase this much more than female salaries each year.
- The coefficient 1564 of Interaction(Female,HighJob) is the extra premium (in addition to the male premium) for females starting in the high job category instead of the low job category.

There are clearly pros and cons to adding interaction variables. On the plus side, they allow for more complex and interesting models, and they can lead to significantly better fits.

Interaction Variables

As this example indicates, interaction variables can make a regression quite difficult to interpret, and they are certainly not always necessary. However, without them, the effect of each X on Y is *independent* of the values of the other Xs. If you believe, for example, that the effect of years of experience on salary is different for males than it is for females, the *only* way to capture this behavior is to include an interaction variable between years of experience and gender.

On the minus side, they can become extremely difficult to interpret correctly. Therefore, we recommend that you add them only when there is good economic and statistical justification for doing so.

Postscript to Example 10.3

When regression analysis is used in a legal case, as it was in the bank gender discrimination example, it can uncover multiple versions of the "truth." That is, by including or omitting various variables, the resulting equations can imply quite different things about the issue in question, in this case, gender discrimination. If one side claims, for example, that the equation

$$\text{Predicted Salary} = 35492 + 988\,\text{Years1} + 131\,\text{Years2} - 8080\,\text{Female}$$

is the true equation for explaining how salaries are determined at the bank, it is ludicrous for them to claim that the bank literally does it this way. No one believes that bank executives sit down and say: "We will start everyone at \$35,492. Then we will add \$988 for every year of experience with our bank and \$131 for every year of prior work experience at another bank. Finally, we will subtract \$8080 from this total if the person is female." All the analysts can claim is that the given regression equation is consistent, to a greater or lesser extent, with the observed data. If a number of regression equations, such as the ones estimated in this example, all point to lower salaries for females after controlling for other factors, then it doesn't matter whether management is deliberately discriminating against females according to some preconceived formula; the regression analysis indicates that females *are* compensated less than males with the same qualifications. Without a smoking gun, it is very difficult for either side to *prove* anything, but regression analysis permits either side to present evidence that is most consistent with the data.

10-6c Nonlinear Transformations

The general linear regression equation has the form

$$\text{Predicted } Y = a + b_1 X_1 + b_2 X_2 + \cdots + b_k X_k$$

You typically include nonlinear transformations in a regression equation because of economic considerations or curvature detected in scatterplots.

It is *linear* in the sense that the right side of the equation is a constant plus a sum of products of constants and variables. However, there is no requirement that the dependent variable Y or the explanatory variables X_1 through X_k be the *original* variables in the data set. Most often they are, but they can also be transformations of original variables. You already saw one example of this in the previous section with interaction variables. They are not original variables but are instead products of original (or even transformed) variables. The software treats them in the same way as original variables; only the interpretation differs. In this section we look at several possible **nonlinear transformations** of variables. These are often used because of curvature detected in scatterplots. They can also arise because of economic considerations. That is, economic theory often leads to particular nonlinear transformations.

You can transform the dependent variable Y or any of the explanatory variables, the Xs. You can also do both. In either case there are a few nonlinear transformations that are typically used. These include the natural logarithm, the square root, the reciprocal, and the square. The purpose of each of these is usually to "straighten out" the points in a scatterplot. If several different transformations straighten out the data equally well, the one that is easiest to interpret is preferred.

We begin with Example 10.4, where only the X variable needs to be transformed.

EXAMPLE   **10.4 DEMAND VERSUS COST FOR ELECTRICITY**

Public Service Electric Company produces different quantities of electricity each month, depending on the demand. The file **Cost of Power.xlsx** lists the number of units of electricity produced (Units) and the total cost of producing these (Cost) for a 36-month period. The data appear in Figure 10.31. How can regression be used to analyze the relationship between Cost and Units?

Figure 10.31

Data for Electric Power Example

	A	B	C
1	Month	Cost	Units
2	1	45623	601
3	2	46507	738
4	3	43343	686
5	4	46495	736
6	5	47317	756
35	34	46295	667
36	35	45218	705
37	36	45357	637

© Cengage Learning

Objective   To see whether the cost of supplying electricity is a nonlinear function of demand, and, if it is, what form the nonlinearity takes.

Solution

A good place to start is with a scatterplot of Cost versus Units. This appears in Figure 10.32. It indicates a definite positive relationship and one that is nearly linear. However, there is also some evidence of curvature in the plot. The points increase slightly less rapidly as Units increases from left to right. In economic terms, there might be economies of scale, so that the marginal cost of electricity decreases as more units of electricity are produced.

Figure 10.32

Scatterplot of Cost versus Units for Electricity Example

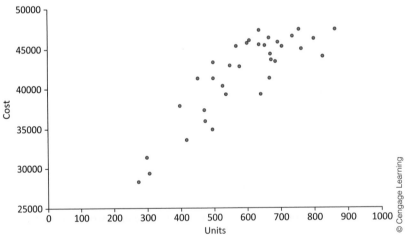

Scatterplot of Cost vs Units

© Cengage Learning

Nevertheless, you can first use regression to estimate a *linear* relationship between Cost and Units. The resulting regression equation is

$$\text{Predicted Cost} = 23651 + 30.53\text{Units}$$

The corresponding R^2 and s_e are 73.6% and $2734. It is always a good idea to request a scatterplot of the residuals versus the fitted values. This scatterplot is shown in Figure 10.33.

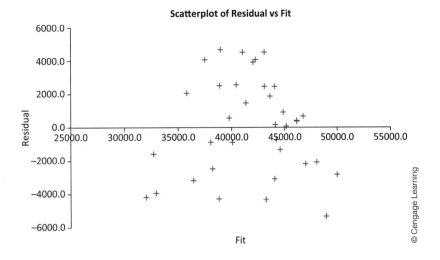

Figure 10.33
Residuals from a Straight-Line Fit

A scatterplot of residuals versus fitted values often indicates the need for a nonlinear transformation.

Note that the residuals to the far left and the far right are all negative, whereas the majority of the residuals in the middle are positive. Admittedly, the pattern is far from perfect—there are several negative residuals in the middle—but this plot certainly suggests nonlinear behavior.

This negative–positive–negative behavior of residuals suggests a *parabola*—that is, a **quadratic** relationship with the *square* of Units included in the equation. The next step is to create a new variable (Units)^2 in the data set. You can do this manually (with the formula **=C4^2** in cell D4, copied down) or by selecting Transform in the StatTools Data Utilities dropdown menu.[8] This latter method has the advantage that it allows you to transform several variables simultaneously. Then you can use multiple regression to estimate the equation for Cost with *both* explanatory variables, Units and (Units)^2, included. The resulting equation, as shown in Figure 10.34, is

> **Quadratic Equation for Predicted Cost**
> $$\text{Predicted Cost} = 5793 + 98.35\text{Units} - 0.0600(\text{Units})^2 \qquad \textbf{(10.18)}$$

Note that R^2 has increased to 82.2% and s_e has decreased to \$2281.

Figure 10.34
Regression Output with Squared Term Included

	A	B	C	D	E	F	G
7	**Multiple Regression for Cost**						
8		Multiple R	R-Square	Adjusted R-Square	StErr of Estimate		
9	*Summary*						
10		0.9064	0.8216	0.8108	2280.799771		
11							
12		Degrees of Freedom	Sum of Squares	Mean of Squares	F-Ratio	p-Value	
13	*ANOVA Table*						
14	Explained	2	790511518.3	395255759.1	75.9808	< 0.0001	
15	Unexplained	33	171667570.7	5202047.597			
16							
17		Coefficient	Standard Error	t-Value	p-Value	Confidence Interval 95%	
18	*Regression Table*					Lower	Upper
19	Constant	5792.798287	4763.058499	1.2162	0.2325	–3897.717092	15483.31367
20	Units	98.35039079	17.23690011	5.7058	< 0.0001	63.28165383	133.4191277
21	(Units)^2	–0.059972929	0.015066406	–3.9806	0.0004	–0.090625763	–0.029320096

[8]StatTools provides four nonlinear transformations: natural logarithm, square, square root, and reciprocal.

One way to see how this regression equation fits the scatterplot of Cost versus Units (in Figure 10.32) is to use Excel's Trendline option. To do so, activate the scatterplot, right-click on any point, select Add Trendline, and select the Polynomial type or order 2, that is, a quadratic. A graph of Equation (10.18) is superimposed on the scatterplot, as shown in Figure 10.35. It shows a reasonably good fit, plus an obvious curvature.

Figure 10.35

Quadratic Fit in Electricity Example

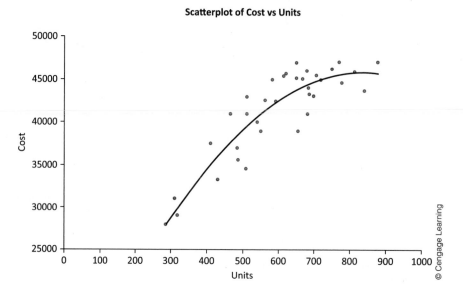

Scatterplot of Cost vs Units

The main downside to a quadratic regression equation, as in Equation (10.18), is that there is no easy way to interpret the coefficients of Units and (Units)^2. For example, you can't conclude from the 98.35 coefficient of Units that Cost increases by 98.35 dollars when Units increases by one. The reason is that when Units increases by one, (Units)^2 doesn't stay constant; it *also* increases. All you can say is that the terms in Equation (10.18) combine to explain the nonlinear relationship between units produced and total cost.

Excel's Trendline option allows you to super-impose a number of different curves on a scatterplot.

Note that the coefficient of (Units)^2, −0.0600, is a small negative value. First, the fact that it is negative makes the parabola bend downward. This produces the decreasing marginal cost behavior, where every extra unit of electricity incurs a smaller cost. Actually, the curve described by Equation (10.18) eventually goes *downhill* for large values of Units, but this part of the curve is irrelevant because the company evidently never produces such large quantities. Second, you should not be fooled by the small magnitude of this coefficient. Remember that it is the coefficient of Units *squared*, which is a large quantity. Therefore, the effect of the product −0.0600 (Units)^2 is sizable.

There is at least one other possibility you can examine. Rather than a quadratic fit, you can try a logarithmic fit. In this case you need to create a new variable, Log(Units), the natural logarithm of Units, and then regress Cost against the *single* variable Log(Units). To create the new variable, you can use a formula with Excel's LN function or you can use the Transform option from StatTools Data Utilities. Also, you can superimpose a logarithmic curve on the scatterplot of Cost versus Units by using Excel's Trendline feature with the logarithm option. This curve appears in Figure 10.36. To the naked eye, it appears to be similar, and about as good a fit, as the quadratic curve in Figure 10.35.

The resulting regression equation is

Logarithmic Equation for Predicted Cost

Predicted Cost = −63993 + 16654Log(Units)   **(10.19)**

Figure 10.36

Logarithmic Fit to
Electricity Data

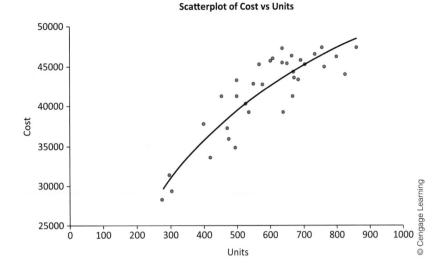

Scatterplot of Cost vs Units

© Cengage Learning

and the R^2 and s_e values are 79.8% and 2393. These latter values indicate that the logarithmic fit is not quite as good as the quadratic fit. However, the advantage of the logarithmic equation is that it is easier to interpret. In fact, one reason **logarithmic transformations** of variables are used so widely in regression analysis is that they are fairly easy to interpret.

In the present case, where the log of an *explanatory* variable is used, you can interpret its coefficient as follows. Suppose that Units increases by 1%, for example, from 600 to 606. Then Equation (10.19) implies that the expected Cost will increase by approximately $0.01(16654) = 166.54$ dollars. In words, every 1% increase in Units is accompanied by an expected $166.54 increase in Cost. Note that for larger values of Units, a 1% increase represents a larger absolute increase (from 700 to 707 instead of from 600 to 606, say). But each such 1% increase entails the *same* increase in Cost. This is another way of describing the decreasing marginal cost property. ∎

In general, if b is the coefficient of the log of X, the expected change in Y when X increases by 1% is approximately 0.01 times b.

The electricity example has shown two possible nonlinear transformations of the *explanatory* variable (or variables) that you can use. All you need to do is create the transformed Xs and run the regression. The interpretation of statistics such as R^2 and s_e is exactly the same as before; only the interpretation of the coefficients of the transformed Xs changes. It is also possible to transform the dependent variable Y. Now, however, you must be careful when interpreting summary statistics such as R^2 and s_e, as explained in the following examples.

Each of these examples transforms the dependent variable Y by taking its natural logarithm and then using the log of Y as the new dependent variable. This approach has been used in a wide variety of business applications. Essentially, it is often a good option when the distribution of Y is skewed to the right, with a few very large values and many small to medium values. The effect of the logarithm transformation is to spread the small values out and squeeze the large values together, making the distribution more symmetric. This is illustrated in Figures 10.37 and 10.38 for a hypothetical distribution of house hold incomes. The histogram of incomes in Figure 10.37 is clearly skewed to the right. However, the histogram of the natural log of income in Figure 10.38 is much more nearly symmetric—and, for technical reasons, more suitable for use as the dependent variable in regression.

A logarithmic transformation of Y is often useful when the distribution of Y values is skewed to the right.

Figure 10.37

Skewed Distribution
of Income

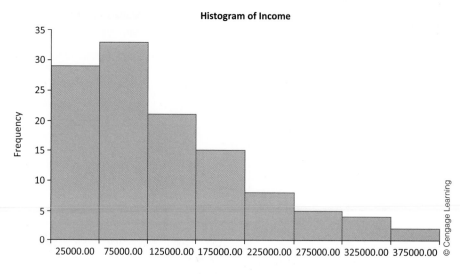

Figure 10.38

Symmetric
Distribution of
Log(Income)

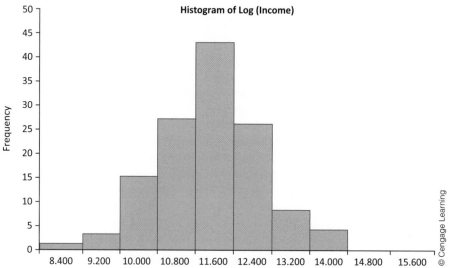

EXAMPLE | **10.3 POSSIBLE GENDER DISCRIMINATION IN BANK SALARIES (CONTINUED)**

Returning to the bank discrimination example, a glance at the distribution of salaries of the 208 employees shows some skewness to the right—a few employees make substantially more than the majority of employees. Therefore, it might make more sense to use the natural logarithm of Salary as the dependent variable, not Salary. If you do this, how can you interpret the results?

Objective To reanalyze the bank salary data, now using the logarithm of salary as the dependent variable.

Solution

All of the previous analyses with this data set could be repeated with Log(Salary) as the dependent variable. For the sake of discussion, we look only at the regression equation with Female and Years1 as explanatory variables. After creating the Log(Salary) variable and running the regression, the output in Figure 10.39 results. The estimated regression equation is

> **Prediction of Log Salary Based on Experience and Gender**
> Predicted Log(Salary) = 10.4907 + 0.0188Years1 − 0.1616Female **(10.20)**

The R^2 and s_e values are 42.4% and 0.1794. For comparison, when this same equation was estimated with Salary as the dependent variable, R^2 and s_e were 49.1% and 8.070.

Figure 10.39   Regression Output with Log of Salary as Dependent Variable

	A	B	C	D	E	F	G
7	**Multiple Regression for Log(Salary)**						
8		**Multiple**	**R-Square**	**Adjusted**	**StErr of**		
9	**Summary**	**R**		**R-Square**	**Estimate**		
10		0.6514	0.4243	0.4187	0.179361414		
11							
12		**Degrees of**	**Sum of**	**Mean of**	**F-Ratio**	**p-Value**	
13	**ANOVA Table**	**Freedom**	**Squares**	**Squares**			
14	**Explained**	2	4.861326452	2.430663226	75.5556	< 0.0001	
15	**Unexplained**	205	6.59495595	0.032170517			
16							
17		**Coefficient**	**Standard**	**t-Value**	**p-Value**	**Confidence Interval 95%**	
18	**Regression Table**		**Error**			**Lower**	**Upper**
19	**Constant**	10.49065238	0.027984265	374.8768	< 0.0001	10.4354785	10.54582626
20	**Years1**	0.018834989	0.001784364	10.5556	< 0.0001	0.01531693	0.022353049
21	**Female**	−0.161583066	0.026517	−6.0936	< 0.0001	−0.213864077	−0.109302055

© Cengage Learning

When the logarithm of Y is used in the regression equation, the interpretations of s_e and R^2 are different because the units of the dependent variable are completely different.

You must be careful when interpreting R^2 and s_e. Neither is directly comparable to the R^2 or s_e value with Salary as the dependent variable. Recall that R^2 in general is the percentage of the dependent variable explained by the regression equation. The problem here is that the two R^2 values are percentages explained of *different* dependent variables, Log(Salary) and Salary. The fact that one is smaller than the other (42.4% versus 49.1%) does not necessarily mean that it corresponds to a worse fit. They are simply not comparable.

The situation is much worse with s_e. Each s_e is a measure of a typical residual, but the residuals in the Log(Salary) equation are in log dollars, whereas the residuals in the Salary equation are in dollars. These units are completely different. For example, the log of $1000 is only 6.91. Therefore, it is no surprise that s_e for the Log(Salary) equation is *much* smaller than s_e for the Salary equation. If you want comparable standard error measures for the two equations, you should take antilogs of fitted values from the Log(Salary) equation to convert them back to dollars, subtract these from the original Salary values, and take the standard deviation of these "residuals." (The EXP function in Excel can be used to take antilogs.) You can check that the resulting standard deviation is 7774.[9] This is somewhat smaller than s_e from the Salary equation, an indication of a slightly better fit.

[9]To make the two "standard deviations" comparable, we use the denominator $n − 3$ in each.

Finally, it is fairly easy to interpret Equation (10.20) itself. When the dependent variable is $\text{Log}(Y)$ and a term on the right-hand side of the equation is of the form bX, then whenever X increases by one unit, the predicted value of Y changes by a constant *percentage*, and this percentage is approximately equal to b (written as a percentage). For example, if $b = 0.035$, then when X increases by one unit, the predicted value of Y increases by approximately 3.5%. Applied to Equation (10.20), this means that for each extra year of experience with Fifth National, an employee's salary can be expected to increase by about 1.88%. To interpret the Female coefficient, note that the only possible increase in Female is one unit (from 0 for male to 1 for female). When this occurs, the expected percentage *decrease* in salary is approximately 16.16%. In other words, Equation (10.20) implies that females can expect to make about 16% less than men for comparable years of experience. ∎

Any coefficient b can now be interpreted as the approximate percentage change in Y when the corresponding X increases by one unit.

We are not necessarily claiming that the bank data are fit better with Log(Salary) as the dependent variable than with Salary—it appears to be a virtual toss-up. However, the lessons from this example are important in general. They are as follows.

■ The R^2 values with Y and $\text{Log}(Y)$ as dependent variables are not directly comparable. They are percentages explained of *different* variables.

■ The s_e values with Y and $\text{Log}(Y)$ as dependent variables are usually of totally different magnitudes. To make the s_e from the log equation comparable, you need to go through the procedure described in the example so that the residuals are in *original* units.

■ To interpret any term of the form bX in the log equation, you should first express b as a percentage. For example, $b = 0.035$ becomes 3.5%. Then when X increases by one unit, the expected *percentage* change in Y is approximately this percentage b.

Remember these points, especially the third, when using the logarithm of Y as the dependent variable.

The log transformation of a dependent variable Y is used frequently. This is partly because it induces nice statistical properties (such as making the distribution of Y more symmetric). But an important advantage of this transformation is its ease of interpretation in terms of percentage changes.

Constant Elasticity Relationships

A particular type of nonlinear relationship that has firm grounding in economic theory is called a **constant elasticity relationship**. It is also called a **multiplicative relationship**. It has the form shown in Equation (10.21).

Formula for Multiplicative Relationship
$$\text{Predicted } Y = aX_1^{b_1}X_2^{b_2}\cdots X_k^{b_k} \qquad\qquad \textbf{(10.21)}$$

One property of this type of relationship is that the effect of a one-unit change in any X on Y depends on the levels of the other Xs in the equation. This is not true for the *additive* relationships of the form

$$\text{Predicted } Y = a + b_1X_1 + b_2X_2 + \cdots + b_kX_k$$

that we have been discussing. For additive relationships, when any X increases by one unit, the predicted value of Y changes by the corresponding b units, regardless of the levels of the other Xs. However, multiplicative relationships have the following nice property.

> In a **multiplicative** (or **constant elasticity**) **relationship**, the dependent variable is expressed as a *product* of explanatory variables raised to powers. When any explanatory variable X changes by 1%, the predicted value of the dependent variable changes by a constant *percentage*, regardless of the value of this X or the values of the other Xs.

The term *constant elasticity* comes from economics. Economists define the elasticity of Y with respect to X as the percentage change in Y that accompanies a 1% increase in X. Often this is in reference to a demand–price relationship. Then the *price elasticity* is the percentage decrease in demand when price increases by 1%. Usually, the elasticity depends on the current value of X. For example, the price elasticity when the price is \$35 might be different than when the price is \$50. However, if the relationship is of the form

$$\text{Predicted } Y = aX^b$$

then the elasticity is *constant*, the same for any value of X. In fact, it is approximately equal to the exponent b. For example, if Predicted $Y = 2X^{-1.5}$, the constant elasticity is approximately -1.5, so that when X increases by 1%, the predicted value of Y decreases by approximately 1.5%.

The constant elasticity for any X is approximately equal to the exponent of that X.

The constant elasticity property carries over to the multiple-X relationship in Equation (10.21). Then each exponent is the approximate elasticity for its X. For example, if Predicted $Y = 2X_1^{-1.5}X_2^{0.7}$, you can make the following statements:

- When X_1 increases by 1%, the predicted value of Y decreases by approximately 1.5%, regardless of the current values of X_1 and X_2.
- When X_2 increases by 1%, the predicted value of Y increases by approximately 0.7%, regardless of the current values of X_1 and X_2.

You can use linear regression to estimate the nonlinear relationship in Equation (10.21) by taking natural logarithms of *all* variables. Here two properties of logarithms are used: (1) the log of a product is the sum of the logs, and (2) the log of X^b is b times the log of X. Therefore, taking logs of both sides of Equation (10.21) gives

$$\text{Predicted } \text{Log}(Y) = \text{Log}(a) + b_1\text{Log}(X_1) + \cdots + b_k\text{Log}(X_k)$$

This equation is *linear* in the log variables $\text{Log}(X_1)$ through $\text{Log}(X_k)$, so you can estimate it in the usual way with multiple regression. You can then interpret the coefficients of the explanatory variables directly as elasticities. Example 10.5 illustrates the method.

FUNDAMENTAL INSIGHT

Using Logarithmic Transformations in Regression

If scatterplots suggest nonlinear relationships, there are an unlimited number of nonlinear transformations of Y and/or the Xs that could be tried in a regression analysis. The reason that logarithmic transformations are arguably the most frequently used nonlinear transformations, besides the fact that they often produce good fits, is that they can be interpreted naturally in terms of percentage changes. In real studies, this interpretability is an important advantage over other potential nonlinear transformations.

EXAMPLE | **10.5 FACTORS RELATED TO SALES OF DOMESTIC AUTOS**

The file **Car Sales.xlsx** contains annual data (1970–1999) on domestic auto sales in the United States. The data are listed in Figure 10.40. The variables are defined as

- Sales: annual domestic auto sales (in number of units)
- Price Index: consumer price index of transportation
- Income: real disposable income
- Interest: prime rate of interest

Our goal is to estimate and interpret a multiplicative (constant elasticity) relationship between Sales and Price Index, Income, and Interest.

Figure 10.40

Data for
Automobile
Demand Example

	A	B	C	D	E
1	Year	Sales	Price Index	Income	Interest
2	1970	7,115,270	37.5	2630	7.91%
3	1971	8,676,410	39.5	2745.3	5.72%
4	1972	9,321,310	39.9	2874.3	5.25%
5	1973	9,618,510	41.2	3072.3	8.03%
6	1974	7,448,340	45.8	3051.9	10.81%
7	1975	7,049,840	50.1	3108.5	7.86%
8	1976	8,606,860	55.1	3243.5	6.84%
29	1997	6,907,992	144.3	5854.5	8.44%
30	1998	6,756,804	141.6	6168.6	8.35%
31	1999	6,987,208	144.4	6320	8.00%

© Cengage Learning

Objective   To use logarithms of variables in a multiple regression to estimate a multiplicative relationship for automobile sales as a function of price, income, and interest rate.

Solution

The first step is to take natural logs of all four variables. (You can do this in one step with the StatTools Transform utility or you can use Excel's LN function.) Then you can run a multiple regression, with Log(Sales) as the dependent variable and Log(Price Index), Log(Income), and Log(Interest) as the explanatory variables. The resulting output is shown in Figure 10.41. The corresponding equation for Log(Quantity) is

$$\text{Predicted Log(Sales)} = 14.126 - 0.384\text{Log(Price Index)} + 0.388\text{Log(Income)} - 0.070\text{Log(Interest)}$$

If you like, you can convert this back to original variables, that is, back to multiplicative form, by taking antilogs. The result is

$$\text{Predicted Sales} = 1364048 \text{Price Index}^{-0.384}\text{Income}^{0.388}\text{Interest}^{-0.070}$$

The constant 1364048 is the antilog of 14.126 (and be calculated in Excel with the EXP function).

In either form the equation implies that the elasticities are approximately equal to -0.384, 0.388, and -0.070. When Price Index increases by 1%, the predicted value of Sales tends to decrease by about 0.384%; when Income increases by 1%, the predicted value of Sales tends to increase by about 0.388%; and when Interest increases by 1%, the predicted value of Sales tends to decrease by about 0.070%.

Does this multiplicative equation provide a better fit to the automobile data than an additive relationship? Without doing considerably more work, it is difficult to answer this question with any certainty. As discussed in the previous example, it is *not* sufficient to

Figure 10.41 Regression Output for Multiplicative Relationship

	A	B	C	D	E	F	G
7	*Multiple Regression for Log(Salary)*						
8		**Multiple**	**R-Square**	**Adjusted**	**StErr of**		
9	*Summary*	**R**		**R-Square**	**Estimate**		
10		0.6813	0.4642	0.4023	0.105266641		
11							
12		**Degrees of**	**Sum of**	**Mean of**	**F-Ratio**	**p-Value**	
13	*ANOVA Table*	**Freedom**	**Squares**	**Squares**			
14	Explained	3	0.249567792	0.083189264	7.5073	0.0009	
15	Unexplained	26	0.288107711	0.011081066			
16							
17		**Coefficient**	**Standard**	**t-Value**	**p-Value**	**Confidence Interval 95%**	
18	*Regression Table*		**Error**			**Lower**	**Upper**
19	Constant	14.1259673	1.983804217	7.1206	< 0.0001	10.04819933	18.20373526
20	Log(Price Index)	−0.383711347	0.209090516	−1.8351	0.0779	−0.813503058	0.046080364
21	Log(Income)	0.388137798	0.362078371	1.0720	0.2936	−0.356124953	1.132400549
22	Log(Interest)	−0.069849699	0.089314722	−0.7821	0.4412	−0.253438739	0.113739341

© Cengage Learning

compare R^2 and s_e values for the two fits. Again, the reason is that one has Log(Sales) as the dependent variable, whereas the other has Sales, so the R^2 and s_e measures aren't comparable. We simply state that the multiplicative relationship provides a reasonably good fit (for example, a scatterplot of its fitted values versus residuals shows no unusual patterns), and it makes sense economically. But the additive equation is arguably just about as good.

Before leaving this example, we note that the results for this data set are not quite as clear as they might appear. (This is often the case with real data.) First, the correlation between Sales and Income, or between Log(Sales) and Log(Income), is negative, not positive. However, because of multicollinearity, a topic discussed in the next chapter, the regression coefficient of Log(Income) is positive. Second, most of the behavior appears to be driven by the early years. If you rerun the analysis from 1980 on, you will discover almost no relationship between Sales and the other variables. ∎

One final example of a multiplicative relationship is the *learning curve* model. A **learning curve** relates the unit production time (or cost) to the cumulative volume of output since that production process first began. Empirical studies indicate that production times tend to decrease by a relatively constant *percentage* every time cumulative output doubles. To model this phenomenon, let Y be the time required to produce a unit of output, and let X be the *cumulative* amount of output that has been produced so far. If we assume that the relationship between Y and X is of the constant elasticity form

$$\text{Predicted } Y = aX^b$$

then it can be shown that whenever X doubles, the predicted value of Y decreases to a *constant percentage* of its previous value. This constant is often called the *learning rate*. For example, if the learning rate is 80%, then each doubling of cumulative production yields a 20% reduction in unit production time. It can be shown that the learning rate satisfies the equation

> *Equation for Learning Rate*
> $$b = \text{LN(learning rate)}/\text{LN}(2) \tag{10.22}$$

(where LN refers to the natural logarithm). So once you estimate b, you can use Equation (10.22) to estimate the learning rate.

Example 10.6 illustrates a typical application of the learning curve model.

EXAMPLE 10.6 THE LEARNING CURVE FOR PRODUCTION OF A NEW PRODUCT

Presario Company produces a variety of small industrial products. It has just finished producing 22 batches of a new product (new to Presario) for a customer. The file **Learning Curve.xlsx** contains the times (in hours) to produce each batch. These data are listed in Figure 10.42. Clearly, the times have tended to decrease as Presario has gained more experience in making the product. Does the multiplicative learning model apply to these data, and what does it imply about the learning rate?

Figure 10.42

Data for Learning Curve Example

	A	B	C	D
1	Batch	Time	Log(Batch)	Log(Time)
2	1	125.00	0	4.828313737
3	2	110.87	0.693147181	4.708358344
4	3	105.35	1.098612289	4.65728814
5	4	103.34	1.386294361	4.638024523
6	5	98.98	1.609437912	4.59491781
7	6	99.90	1.791759469	4.604169686
20	19	82.06	2.944438979	4.407450687
21	20	82.81	2.995732274	4.416548827
22	21	76.52	3.044522438	4.337552145
23	22	78.45	3.091042453	4.362461479

© Cengage Learning

Objective To use a multiplicative regression equation to estimate the learning rate for production time.

Solution

One way to check whether the multiplicative learning model is reasonable is to create the log variables Log(Time) and Log(Batch) in the usual way and then see whether a scatterplot of Log(Time) versus Log(Batch) is approximately *linear*. The multiplicative model implies that it should be. Such a scatterplot appears in Figure 10.43, along with a superimposed linear trend line. The fit appears to be quite good.

The relationship can be estimated by regressing Log(Time) on Log(Batch). The resulting equation is

$$\text{Predicted Log(Time)} = 4.834 - 0.155\text{Log(Batch)} \tag{10.23}$$

Figure 10.43

Scatterplot of Log Variables with Linear Trend Superimposed

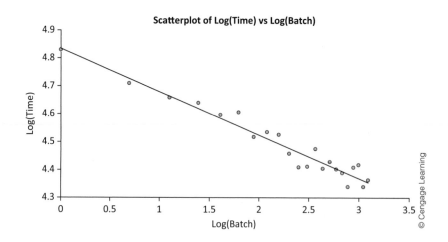

© Cengage Learning

There are a couple of ways to interpret this equation. First, because it is a constant elasticity relationship, the coefficient −0.155 can be interpreted as an elasticity. That is, when Batch increases by 1%, Time tends to decrease by approximately 0.155%.

Although this interpretation is correct, it is not as useful as the "doubling" interpretation discussed previously. Equation (10.22) states that the estimated learning rate satisfies

$$-0.155 = \text{LN(learning rate)}/\text{LN}(2)$$

Solving for the learning rate [multiply through by LN(2) and then take antilogs], you can see that it is 0.898, or approximately 90%. In words, whenever cumulative production doubles, the time to produce a batch decreases by about 10%.

Presario could use this regression equation to predict future production times. For example, suppose the customer places an order for 15 more batches of the same product. Note that Presario is already partway up the learning curve, that is, these batches are numbers 23 through 37, and the company already has experience producing the product. You can use Equation (10.23) to predict the log of production time for each batch. Then you can take their antilogs and sum them to obtain the total production time. The calculations are shown in rows 24 through 39 of Figure 10.44. You enter the batch numbers and calculate their logs in columns A and C. Then you substitute the values of Log(Batch) in column C into Equation (10.23) to obtain the predicted values of Log(Time) in column E. Finally, you use Excel's EXP function to calculate the antilogs of these predictions in column B, and you calculate their sum in cell B39. The total predicted time to finish the order is about 1115 hours. ∎

Figure 10.44

Using the Learning Curve Model for Predictions

	A	B	C	D	E	F
22	21	76.52	3.044522438	4.337552145		
23	22	78.45	3.091042453	4.362461479		
24	23	77.324	3.135494216	4.348009995		
25	24	76.816	3.17805383	4.341413654		
26	25	76.332	3.218875825	4.335086627		
27	26	75.869	3.258096538	4.329007785		
28	27	75.426	3.295836866	4.323158388		
29	28	75.003	3.33220451	4.317521744		
30	29	74.596	3.36729583	4.312082919		
31	30	74.205	3.401197382	4.306828497		
32	31	73.829	3.433987204	4.301746382		
33	32	73.466	3.465735903	4.296825631		
34	33	73.117	3.496507561	4.292056313		
35	34	72.779	3.526360525	4.287429384		
36	35	72.453	3.555348061	4.282936587		
37	36	72.137	3.583518938	4.278570366		
38	37	71.832	3.610917913	4.274323782		
39		1115.183	⟵———	Predicted time for next 15 batches		

PROBLEMS

Level A

26. In a study of housing demand, a county assessor is interested in developing a regression model to estimate the selling price of residential properties within her jurisdiction. She randomly selects 15 houses and records the selling price in addition to the following values: the size of the house (in square feet), the total number of rooms in the house, the age of the house, and an indication of whether the house has an attached garage. These data are stored in the file **P10_26.xlsx**.

    a. Estimate and interpret a multiple regression equation that includes the four potential explanatory variables. How do you interpret the coefficient of the Attached Garage variable?

b. Evaluate the estimated regression equation's goodness of fit.

c. Use the estimated equation to predict the sales price of a 3000-square-foot, 20-year-old home that has seven rooms but no attached garage. How accurate is your prediction?

27. A manager of boiler drums wants to use regression analysis to predict the number of worker-hours needed to erect the drums in future projects. Data for 36 randomly selected boilers have been collected. In addition to worker-hours (Y), the variables measured include boiler capacity, boiler design pressure, boiler type, and drum type. All of these measurements are listed in the file **P10_27.xlsx**.

a. Estimate an appropriate multiple regression equation to predict the number of worker-hours needed to erect boiler drums.

b. Interpret the estimated regression coefficients.

c. According to the estimated regression equation, what is the difference between the mean number of worker-hours required for erecting industrial and utility field boilers?

d. According to the estimated regression equation, what is the difference between the mean number of worker-hours required for erecting boilers with steam drums and those with mud drums?

e. Given the estimated regression equation, predict the number of worker-hours needed to erect a utility-field, steam-drum boiler with a capacity of 550,000 pounds per hour and a design pressure of 1400 pounds per square inch. How accurate is your prediction?

f. Given the estimated regression equation, predict the number of worker-hours needed to erect an industrial-field, mud-drum boiler with a capacity of 100,000 pounds per hour and a design pressure of 1000 pounds per square inch. How accurate is your prediction?

28. Suppose that a regional express delivery service company wants to estimate the cost of shipping a package (Y) as a function of cargo type, where cargo type includes the following possibilities: fragile, semifragile, and durable. Costs for 15 randomly chosen packages of approximately the same weight and same distance shipped, but of different cargo types, are provided in the file **P10_28.xlsx**.

a. Estimate an appropriate multiple regression equation to predict the cost of shipping a given package.

b. Interpret the estimated regression coefficients. You should find that the estimated intercept and slope of the equation are sample means. Which sample means are they?

c. According to the estimated regression equation, which cargo type is the *most* costly to ship? Which cargo type is the *least* costly to ship?

d. How well does the estimated equation fit the given sample data? How do you think the model's goodness of fit could be improved?

e. Given the estimated regression equation, predict the cost of shipping a package with semifragile cargo.

29. The file **P10_11.xlsx** contains annual observations (in column B) of the American minimum wage. The basic question here is whether the minimum wage has been growing at roughly a *constant* rate over this period.

a. Create a time series graph for these data. Comment on the observed behavior of the minimum wage over time.

b. Estimate a linear regression equation of the minimum wage versus time (the Year variable). What does the estimated slope indicate?

c. Analyze the residuals from the equation in part **b**. Are they essentially random? If not, return to part **b** and revise your equation appropriately. Then interpret the revised equation.

30. Estimate a regression equation that *adequately* estimates the relationship between monthly electrical power usage (Y) and home size (X) using the data in the file **P10_13.xlsx**. Interpret your results. How well does your model explain the variation in monthly electrical power usage?

31. An insurance company wants to determine how its annual operating costs depend on the number of home insurance (X_1) and automobile insurance (X_2) policies that have been written. The file **P10_31.xlsx** contains relevant information for 10 branches of the insurance company. The company believes that a multiplicative model might be appropriate because operating costs typically increase by a constant percentage as the number of either type of policy increases by a given percentage. Use the given data to estimate a multiplicative model for this insurance company. Interpret your results. Does a multiplicative model provide a good fit with these data? Answer by calculating the appropriate standard error of estimate and R^2 value, based on *original* units of the dependent variable.

32. Suppose that an operations manager is trying to determine the number of labor hours required to produce the ith unit of a certain product. Consider the data provided in the file **P10_32.xlsx**. For example, the second unit produced required 517 labor hours, and the 600th unit required 34 labor hours.

a. Use the given data to estimate a relationship between the total number of units produced and the labor hours required to produce the last unit in the total set. Interpret your findings.

b. Use your estimated relationship to predict the number of labor hours that will be needed to produce the 800th unit.

Level B

33. The human resources manager of DataCom, Inc., wants to predict the annual salaries of given employees using the potential explanatory variables in the file **P10_05.xlsx**.

   a. Estimate an appropriate multiple regression equation to predict the annual salary of a given DataCom employee using all of the data in columns C–H.

   b. Interpret the estimated regression coefficients.

   c. According to the estimated regression model, is there a difference between the mean salaries earned by male and female employees at DataCom? If so, how large is the difference? According to your equation, does this difference depend on the values of the other explanatory variables? Explain.

   d. According to the estimated regression model, is there a difference between the mean salaries earned by employees in the sales department and those in the advertising department at DataCom? If so, how large is the difference? According to your equation, does this difference depend on the values of the other explanatory variables? Explain.

   e. According to the estimated regression model, in which department are DataCom employees paid the *highest* mean salary (after controlling for other explanatory variables)? In which department are DataCom employees paid the *lowest* mean salary?

   f. Given the estimated regression model, predict the annual salary of a female employee who served in a similar department at another company for 10 years prior to coming to work at DataCom. This woman, a graduate of a four-year collegiate business program, has been supervising 12 subordinates in the purchasing department since joining the organization five years ago.

34. Does the rate of violent crime acts vary across different regions of the United States? Answer this with the (somewhat old) 1999 data in the file **P10_34.xlsx** as requested below.

   a. Estimate an appropriate regression model to explain the variation in violent crime rate across the four given regions of the United States. Interpret the estimated equation. Rank the four regions from highest to lowest according to their mean violent crime rate. Could you have done this without regression? Explain.

   b. How would you modify the regression model in part **a** to account for possible differences in the violent crime rate across the various subdivisions of the given regions? Estimate your revised regression equation and interpret your findings. Rank the nine subdivisions from highest to lowest according to their mean violent crime rate.

35. Continuing Problems 6 and 15 on the 2006–2007 movie data in the file **P02_02.xlsx**, create a new variable Total Revenue that is the sum of Total US Gross, International Gross, and US DVD Sales. How well can this new variable be predicted from the data in columns C–F? For Distributor, relabel the categories so that there are only two: Large Distributor and Small Distributor. The former is any distributor that had at least 12 movies in this period, and the latter is all the rest. For Genre, relabel the categories to be Comedy, Drama, Adventure, Action, Thriller/Suspense, and Other. (Other includes Black Comedy, Documentary, Horror, Musical, and Romantic Comedy.) Interpret the coefficients of the estimated regression equation. How would you explain the results to someone in the movie business? Do you think that predictions of total revenue from this regression equation will be very accurate? Why?

36. Continuing Problem 18, suppose that the antique collector believes that the *rate of increase* of the auction price with the age of the item will be driven upward by a large number of bidders. How would you revise the multiple regression equation developed previously to model this feature of the problem?

   a. Estimate your revised equation using the data in the file **P10_18.xlsx**.

   b. Interpret each of the estimated coefficients in your revised model.

   c. Does this revised model fit the given data better than the original multiple regression model? Explain why or why not.

37. Continuing Problem 19, revise the previous multiple regression equation to include an interaction term between the return on average equity (X_1) and annual dividend rate (X_2).

   a. Estimate your revised equation using the data provided in the file **P10_19.xlsx**.

   b. Interpret each of the estimated coefficients in your revised equation. In particular, how do you interpret the coefficient for the interaction term in the revised equation?

   c. Does this revised equation fit the given data better than the original multiple regression equation? Explain why or why not.

38. Continuing Problem 22, suppose that one of the managers of this regional express delivery service company is trying to decide whether to add an interaction term involving the package weight (X_1) and the distance shipped (X_2) in the previous multiple regression equation.

a. Why would the manager want to add such a term to the regression equation?

b. Estimate the revised equation using the data given in the file **P10_22.xlsx**.

c. Interpret each of the estimated coefficients in your revised equation. In particular, how do you interpret the coefficient for the interaction term in the revised equation?

d. Does this revised equation fit the data better than the original multiple regression equation? Explain why or why not.

10-7 VALIDATION OF THE FIT

The fit from a regression analysis is often overly optimistic. When you use the least squares procedure on a given set of data, all of the idiosyncrasies of the particular data set are exploited to obtain the best possible fit. However, there is no guarantee that the fit will be as good when the estimated regression equation is applied to *new* data. In fact, it usually isn't. This is particularly important when the goal is to use the regression equation to predict new values of the dependent variable. The usual situation is that you use a given data set to estimate a regression equation. Then you gather new data on the *explanatory* variables and use these, along with the already-estimated regression equation, to predict the new (but unknown) values of the dependent variable.

One way to see whether this procedure will be successful is to split the original data set into two subsets: one subset for estimation and one subset for validation. A regression equation is estimated from the first subset. Then the values of explanatory variables from the second subset are substituted into this equation to obtain predicted values for the dependent variable. Finally, these predicted values are compared to the *known* values of the dependent variable in the second subset. If the agreement is good, there is reason to believe that the regression equation will predict well for new data. This procedure is called **validating the fit**.

This validation procedure is fairly simple to perform in Excel. We illustrate it for the Bendrix manufacturing data in Example 10.2. (See the file **Overhead Costs Validation.xlsx**.) There we used 36 monthly observations to regress Overhead on Machine Hours and Production Runs. For convenience, the regression output is repeated in Figure 10.45. In particular, it shows an R^2 value of 86.6% and an s_e value of $4109.

Now suppose that this data set is from one of Bendrix's two plants. The company would like to predict overhead costs for the other plant by using data on machine hours and production runs at the other plant. The first step is to see how well the regression from Figure 10.45 fits data from the other plant. This validation on the 36 months of data is shown in Figure 10.46.

To obtain the results in this figure, proceed as follows.

> **FUNDAMENTAL INSIGHT**
>
> **Training and Validation Sets**
> This practice of *partitioning* a data set into a set for estimation and a set for validation is becoming much more common as larger data sets become available. It allows you to see how a given procedure such as regression works on a data set where you *know* the Ys. If it works well, you have more confidence that it will work well on a new data set where you do *not* know the Ys. This partitioning is a routine part of data mining, the exploration of large data sets. In data mining, the first data set is usually called the *training* set, and the second data set is called the *validation* or *testing* set.

Procedure for Validating Regression Results

1. **Copy old results.** Copy the results from the original regression to the ranges B5:D5 and B9:B10.

2. **Calculate fitted values and residuals.** The fitted values are now the predicted values of overhead for the other plant, based on the original regression equation. Find these by substituting the new values of Machine Hours and Production Runs into the original equation. Specifically, enter the formula

=$B$5+SUMPRODUCT($C$5:$D$5,B13:C13)

Figure 10.45 Multiple Regression Output for Bendrix Example

	A	B	C	D	E	F	G
7	**Multiple Regression for Overhead**						
8		**Multiple**	**R-Square**	**Adjusted**	**StErr of**		
9	**Summary**	**R**		**R-Square**	**Estimate**		
10		0.9308	0.8664	0.8583	4108.99309		
11							
12		**Degrees of**	**Sum of**	**Mean of**	**F-Ratio**	**p-Value**	
13	**ANOVA Table**	**Freedom**	**Squares**	**Squares**			
14	Explained	2	3614020661	1807010330	107.0261	< 0.0001	
15	Unexplained	33	557166199.1	16883824.22			
16							
17		**Coefficient**	**Standard**	**t-Value**	**p-Value**	**Confidence Interval 95%**	
18	**Regression Table**		**Error**			**Lower**	**Upper**
19	Constant	3996.678209	6603.650932	0.6052	0.5492	−9438.550632	17431.90705
20	Machine Hours	43.53639812	3.5894837	12.1289	< 0.0001	36.23353862	50.83925761
21	Production Runs	883.6179252	82.25140753	10.7429	< 0.0001	716.2761784	1050.959672

© Cengage Learning

Figure 10.46

Validation of
Bendrix Regression
Results

	A	B	C	D	E	F
1	**Validation data**					
2						
3	Coefficients from regression equation (based on original data)					
4	Constant	Machine Hours	Production Runs			
5	3996.6782	43.5364	883.6179			
6						
7	Comparison of summary measures					
8		Original	Validation			
9	R-square	0.8664	0.7733			
10	StErr of Est	4108.99	5256.50			
11						
12	Month	Machine Hours	Production Runs	Overhead	Fitted	Residual
13	1	1374	24	92414	85023	7391
14	2	1510	35	92433	100663	−8230
15	3	1213	21	81907	75362	6545
16	4	1629	27	93451	98775	−5324
17	5	1858	28	112203	109629	2574
46	34	1529	29	94325	96189	−1864
47	35	1389	47	98474	105999	−7525
48	36	1350	34	90857	92814	−1957

© Cengage Learning

in cell E13 and copy it down. Then calculate the residuals (prediction errors for the other plant) by entering the formula

=D13-E13

in cell F13 and copying it down.

3. **Calculate summary measures.** You can see how well the original equation fits the new data by calculating R^2 and s_e values. Recall that R^2 in general is the square of the correlation between observed and fitted values. Therefore, enter the formula

=CORREL(E13:E48,D13:D48)^2

in cell C9. The *se* value is essentially the average of the squared residuals, but it uses the denominator $n - 3$ (when there are two explanatory variables) rather than $n - 1$. Therefore, enter the formula

=SQRT(SUMSQ((F13:F48)/33)

Excel's SUMSQ function is often handy. It sums the squares of values in a range.

in cell C10.

The results in Figure 10.46 are typical. The validation results are usually not as good as the original results. The value of R^2 has decreased from 86.6% to 77.3%, and the value of s_e has increased from \$4109 to \$5257. Nevertheless, Bendrix might conclude that the original regression equation is adequate for making future predictions at either plant.

10-8 CONCLUSION

In this chapter we have illustrated how to fit an equation to a set of points and how to interpret the resulting equation. We have also discussed two measures, R^2 and s_e, that indicate the goodness of fit of the regression equation. Although the general technique is called *linear* regression, it can be used to estimate nonlinear relationships through suitable transformations of variables. We are not finished with our study of regression, however. In the next chapter we make some statistical assumptions about the regression model and then discuss the types of inferences that can be made from regression output. In particular, we discuss the accuracy of the estimated regression coefficients, the accuracy of predictions made from the regression equation, and the choice of explanatory variables to include in the regression equation.

Summary of Key Terms

Term	Symbol	Explanation	Excel	Page	Equation
Regression analysis		A general method for estimating the relationship between a dependent variable and one or more explanatory variables		465	
Dependent (or response) variable	Y	The variable being estimated or predicted in a regression analysis		466	
Explanatory (or independent) variables	$X_1, X_2,$ and so on	The variables used to explain or predict the dependent variable		466	
Simple regression		A regression model with a single explanatory variable	StatTools/Regression & Classification/ Regression	466	
Multiple regression		A regression model with any number of explanatory variables	StatTools/Regression & Classification/ Regression	466	
Correlation	r_{XY}	A measure of the strength of the linear relationship between two variables X and Y	**=CORREL (range1, range2)**, or StatTools/Summary Statistics/Correlation and Covariance	474	10.1

Term	Symbol	Explanation	Excel	Page	Equation
Fitted value		The predicted value of the dependent variable, found by substituting explanatory values into the regression equation		477	10.2
Residual		The difference between the actual and fitted values of the dependent variable		477	10.2
Least squares line		The regression equation that minimizes the sum of squared residuals	StatTools/Regression & Classification/ Regression	478	10.3, 10.4
Standard error of estimate	s_e	Essentially, the standard deviation of the residuals; indicates the magnitude of the prediction errors	StatTools/Regression & Classification/ Regression	483	10.7, 10.11
R-square	R^2	The percentage of variation in the response variable explained by the regression model	StatTools/Regression & Classification/ Regression	485	10.8
Adjusted R^2		A measure similar to R^2, but adjusted for the number of explanatory variables in the equation		492	
Regression coefficients	a, b_1, b_2, and so on	The constant and the coefficients of the explanatory variables in a regression equation	StatTools/Regression & Classification/ Regression	488	10.9
Dummy (or indicator) variables		Variables coded as 0 or 1, used to capture categorical variables in a regression analysis	StatTools/Data Utilities/ Dummy	494	
Interaction variables		Products of explanatory variables, used when the effect of one on the dependent variable depends on the value of the other	StatTools/Data Utilities/ Interaction	501	
Nonlinear transformations		Variables created to capture nonlinear relationships in a regression model	StatTools/Data Utilities/ Transform	505	
Quadratic relationship		A regression model with linear and squared explanatory variables	StatTools/Regression & Classification/ Regression	507	
Model with logarithmic transformations		A regression model using logarithms of Y and/or Xs	StatTools/Regression & Classification/ Regression	509	
Constant elasticity (or multiplicative) relationship		A relationship where predicted Y changes by a constant percentage when any X changes by 1%; requires logarithmic transformations	StatTools/Regression & relationship Classification/ Regression	512	10.21
Learning curve		A particular multiplicative relationship used to indicate how cost or time in production decreases over time	StatTools/Regression & Classification/ Regression	515	10.22
Validation of fit		Checks how well a regression model based on one sample predicts a related sample	StatTools/Regression & Classification/ Regression	520	

PROBLEMS

Conceptual Questions

C.1. Consider the relationship between yearly wine consumption (liters of alcohol from drinking wine, per person) and yearly deaths from heart disease (deaths per 100,000 people) in 19 developed countries. Suppose that you read a newspaper article in which the reporter states the following:

Researchers find that the correlation between yearly wine consumption and yearly deaths from heart disease is −0.84. Thus, it is reasonable to conclude that increased consumption of alcohol from wine causes fewer deaths from heart disease in industrialized societies.

Comment on the reporter's interpretation of the correlation in this situation.

C.2. "It is generally appropriate to delete all outliers in a data set that are apparent in a scatterplot." Do you agree with this statement? Explain.

C.3. How would you interpret the relationship between two numeric variables when the estimated least squares regression line for them is essentially *horizontal* (i.e., flat)?

C.4. Suppose that you generate a scatterplot of residuals versus fitted values of the dependent variable for an estimated regression equation. Furthermore, you find the correlation between the residuals and fitted values to be 0.829. Does this provide a good indication that the estimated regression equation is satisfactory? Explain why or why not.

C.5. Suppose that you have generated three alternative multiple regression equations to explain the variation in a particular dependent variable. The regression output for each equation can be summarized as follows:

	Equation 1	Equation 2	Equation 3
No. of Xs	4	6	9
R^2	0.76	0.77	0.79
Adjusted R^2	0.75	0.74	0.73

Which of these equations would you select as "best"? Explain your choice.

C.6. Suppose you want to investigate the relationship between a dependent variable Y and two potential explanatory variables X_1 and X_2. Is the R^2 value for the equation with both X variables included necessarily at least as large as the R^2 value from each equation with only a single X? Explain why or why not. Could the R^2 value for the equation with

both X variables included be *larger* than the sum of the R^2 values from the separate equations, each with only a single X included? Is there any intuitive explanation for this?

C.7. Suppose you believe that two variables X and Y are related, but you have no idea which way the causality goes. Does X cause Y or vice versa (or maybe even neither)? Can you tell by regressing Y on X and then regressing X on Y? Explain. Also, provide at least one real example where the direction of causality would be ambiguous.

C.8. Suppose you have two columns of monthly data, one on advertising expenditures and one on sales. If you use this data set, as is, to regress sales on advertising, will it adequately capture the behavior that advertising in one month doesn't really affect sales in *that* month but only in *future* months? What should you do, in terms of regression, to capture this timing effect?

C.9. Suppose you want to predict reading speed using, among other variables, the device the person is reading from. This device could be a regular book, an iPad, a Kindle, or others. Therefore, you create dummy variables for device. How, exactly, would you do it? If you use regular book as the reference category and another analyst uses, say, Kindle as the reference category, will you get the same regression results? Explain.

C.10. Explain the benefits of using natural logarithms of variables, either of Y or of the Xs, as opposed to other possible nonlinear functions, when scatterplots (or possibly economic considerations) indicate that nonlinearities should be taken into account. Explain exactly how you interpret regression coefficients if logs are taken only of Y, only of the Xs, or of both Y and the Xs.

C.11. The number of cars per 1000 people is known for virtually every country in the world. For many countries, however, per capita income is not known. How might you estimate per capita income for countries where it is unknown?

Level A

39. Many companies manufacture products that are at least partially produced using chemicals (e.g., paint, gasoline, and steel). In many cases, the quality of the finished product is a function of the temperature and pressure at which the chemical reactions take place. Suppose that a particular manufacturer wants to model the quality (Y) of a product as a function of the temperature (X_1) and the pressure (X_2) at which it is produced. The file **P10_39.xlsx** contains data obtained from a carefully designed experiment involving these variables. Note that the assigned quality score can range from a minimum of 0 to a maximum of 100 for each manufactured product.

    a. Estimate a multiple regression equation that includes the two given explanatory variables. Does the estimated equation fit the data well?

    b. Add an interaction term between temperature and pressure and run the regression again. Does the inclusion of the interaction term improve the model's goodness of fit?

    c. Interpret each of the estimated coefficients in the two equations. How are they different? How do you interpret the coefficient for the interaction term in the second equation?

40. A power company located in southern Alabama wants to predict the peak power load (i.e., the maximum amount of power that must be generated each day to meet demand) as a function of the daily high temperature (X). A random sample of 25 summer days is chosen, and the peak power load and the high temperature are recorded each day. The file **P10_40.xlsx** contains these observations.

    a. Create a scatterplot for these data. Comment on the observed relationship between Y and X.

    b. Estimate an appropriate regression equation to predict the peak power load for this power company. Interpret the estimated regression coefficients.

    c. Analyze the estimated equation's residuals. Do they suggest that the regression equation is adequate? If not, return to part **b** and revise your equation. Continue to revise the equation until the results are satisfactory.

    d. Use your final equation to predict the peak power load on a summer day with a high temperature of 100 degrees.

41. Management of a home appliance store would like to understand the growth pattern of the monthly sales of Blu-ray disc players over the past two years. Managers have recorded the relevant data in the file **P10_09.xlsx**.

    a. Create a scatterplot for these data. Comment on the observed behavior of monthly sales at this store over time.

    b. Estimate an appropriate regression equation to explain the variation of monthly sales over the given time period. Interpret the estimated regression coefficients.

    c. Analyze the estimated equation's residuals. Do they suggest that the regression equation is adequate? If not, return to part **b** and revise your equation. Continue to revise the equation until the results are satisfactory.

42. A small computer chip manufacturer wants to forecast monthly operating costs as a function of the number of units produced during a month. The company has collected the 16 months of data in the file **P10_42.xlsx**.

    a. Determine an equation that can be used to predict monthly production costs from units produced. Are there any outliers?

    b. How could the regression line obtained in part **a** be used to determine whether the company was efficient or inefficient during any particular month?

43. The file **P02_07.xlsx** includes data on 204 employees at the (fictional) company Beta Technologies.

    a. Create a recoded version of Education, where 0 or 2 is recoded as 1, 4 is recoded as 2, and 6 or 8 is recoded as 3. Then create dummy variables for these three categories.

    b. Use pivot tables to explore whether average salary depends on gender, and whether it depends on the recoded Education. Then use scatterplots to explore whether salary is related to age, prior experience, and Beta experience. Briefly state your results.

    c. Run a regression of salary versus gender, age, prior experience, Beta experience, and any two of the education dummies, and interpret the results.

    d. If any of the potential explanatory variables seems to be unrelated to salary, based on the results from part **b**, run one or more regressions without such a variable. Comment on whether it makes much of a difference in the regression outputs.

44. The file **P10_44.xlsx** contains data that relate the unit cost of producing a fuel pressure regulator to the cumulative number of fuel pressure regulators produced at an automobile production plant. For example, the 4000th unit cost $13.70 to produce.

    a. Fit a learning curve to these data.

    b. You would predict that doubling cumulative production reduces the cost of producing a regulator by what amount?

45. The *beta* of a stock is found by running a regression with the monthly return on a market index as the explanatory variable and the monthly return on the stock as the dependent variable. The beta of the stock is then the slope of this regression line.

    a. Explain why most stocks have a positive beta.

    b. Explain why a stock with a beta with absolute value greater than one is more volatile than the market index and a stock with a beta less than one (in absolute value) is less volatile than the market index.

    c. Use the data in the file **P10_45.xlsx** to estimate the beta for each of the four companies listed: Caterpillar, Goodyear, McDonalds, and Ford. Use the S&P 500 as the market index.

    d. For each of these companies, what percentage of the variation in its returns is explained by the variation in the market index? What percentage is unexplained by variation in the market index?

e. Verify (using Excel's COVAR and VARP functions) that the beta for each company is given by

$$\frac{\text{Covariance between Company and Market}}{\text{Variance of Market}}$$

Also, verify that the correlation between each company's returns and the market's returns is the square root of R^2.

46. Continuing the previous problem, explore whether the beta for these companies changes through time. For example, are the betas based on 1990s data different from those based on 2000s data? Or are data based on only five years of data different from those based on longer time periods?

47. The file **Catalog Marketing.xlsx** contains recent data on 1000 HyTex customers. (This is the same data set used in Example 2.7 in Chapter 2.)

a. Create a pivot table of average amount spent versus the number of catalogs sent. Is there any evidence that these two variables are related? Would it make sense to enter Catalogs, as is, in a regression equation for Amount Spent, or should dummies be used? Explain.

b. Create a pivot table of average amount spent versus History. Is there any evidence that these two variables are related? Would it make sense to enter History, as is, in a regression equation for Amount Spent, or should dummies be used? Explain.

c. Answer part **b** with History replaced by Age.

d. Base on your results from parts **a** through **c**, estimate an appropriate regression equation for Amount Spent, using the appropriate forms for Catalogs, History, and Age, plus the variables Gender, Own Home, Married, and Close. Interpret this equation and comment on its usefulness in predicting Amount Spent.

48. The file **P10_48.xlsx** contains monthly sales and price of a popular candy bar.

a. Describe the type of relationship between price and sales (linear/nonlinear, strong/weak).

b. What percentage of variation in monthly sales is explained by variation in price? What percentage is unexplained?

c. If the price of the candy bar is $1.05, predict monthly candy bar sales.

d. Use the regression output to determine the correlation between price and candy bar sales.

e. Are there any outliers?

49. The file **P10_49.xlsx** contains the amount of money spent advertising a product and the number of units sold for eight months.

a. Assume that the only factor influencing monthly sales is advertising. Fit the following three curves to these data: linear ($Y = a + bX$), exponential ($Y = ab^X$), and multiplicative ($Y = aX^b$). Which equation fits the data best?

b. Interpret the best-fitting equation.

c. Using the best-fitting equation, predict sales during a month in which $60,000 is spent on advertising.

50. A golf club manufacturer is trying to determine how the price of a set of clubs affects the demand for clubs. The file **P10_50.xlsx** contains the price of a set of clubs and the monthly sales.

a. Assume the only factor influencing monthly sales is price. Fit the following three curves to these data: linear ($Y = a + bX$), exponential ($Y = ab^X$), and multiplicative ($Y = aX^b$). Which equation fits the data best?

b. Interpret your best-fitting equation.

c. Using the best-fitting equation, predict sales during a month in which the price is $470.

51. The file **P03_55.xlsx** lists the average salary for each Major League Baseball (MLB) team from 2004 to 2011, along with the number of team wins in each of these years.

a. Rearrange the data so that there are four long columns: Team, Year, Salary, and Wins. There should be 8*30 values for each.

b. Create a scatterplot of Wins (Y) versus Salary (X). Is there any indication of a relationship between these two variables? Is it a linear relationship?

c. Run a regression of Wins versus Salary. What does it say, if anything, about teams buying their way to success?

52. Repeat the previous problem with the basketball data in the file **P03_56.xlsx**. (Now there will be 6*30 rows in the rearranged data set.)

53. Repeat Problem 51 with the football data in the file **P03_57.xlsx**. (Now there will be 8*32 rows in the rearranged data set.)

54. Baker Company wants to develop a budget to predict how overhead costs vary with activity levels. Management is trying to decide whether direct labor hours (DLH) or units produced is the better measure of activity for the firm. Monthly data for the preceding 24 months appear in the file **P10_54.xlsx**. Use regression analysis to determine which measure, DLH or Units (or both), should be used for the budget. How would the regression equation be used to obtain the budget for the firm's overhead costs?

55. The auditor of Kiely Manufacturing is concerned about the number and magnitude of year-end adjustments that are made annually when the financial statements of Kiely Manufacturing are prepared. Specifically, the auditor suspects that the management of Kiely Manufacturing is using discretionary write-offs to manipulate the reported net income.

To check this, the auditor has collected data from 25 companies that are similar to Kiely Manufacturing in terms of manufacturing facilities and product lines. The cumulative reported third-quarter income and the final net income reported are listed in the file **P10_55.xlsx** for each of these 25 companies. If Kiely Manufacturing reports a cumulative third-quarter income of $2,500,000 and a preliminary net income of $4,900,000, should the auditor conclude that the relationship between cumulative third-quarter income and the annual income for Kiely Manufacturing differs from that of the 25 companies in this sample? Explain why or why not.

56. The file **P10_56.xlsx** contains some interesting data on the U.S. presidential elections from 1880 through 2008. The variable definitions are on the Source sheet. The question is whether the Vote variable can be predicted very well from the other variables.
    a. Create pivot tables and/or scatterplots to check whether Vote appears to be related to the other variables. Comment on the results.
    b. Run a regression of Vote versus the other variables (not including Year). Do the coefficients go in the direction (positive or negative) you would expect? If you were going to use the regression equation to predict Vote for the 2012 election and you had the relevant data for the explanatory variables for 2012, how accurate do you think your prediction would be?

Level B

57. We stated in the beginning of the chapter that regression can be used to understand the way the world works. That is, you can look at the regression coefficients (their signs and magnitudes) to see the effects of the explanatory variables on the dependent variable. However, is it possible that apparently small changes in the data can lead to very different-looking equations? The file **P10_57.xlsx** lets you explore this question. Columns K–R contain data on over 100 (fictional) homes that were recently sold. The regression equation for this original data set is given in the range T15:U21. (It was found with StatTools in the usual way.) Columns C–I contain slight changes to the original data, with the amount of change determined by the adjustable parameters in row 2. (Look at the formulas in columns C–I to see how the original data have been changed randomly.) The regression equation for the changed data appears in the range T6:U12. It has been calculated through special matrix functions (not StatTools), so that it changes automatically when the random data change. (These require the 1 s in column B.) Experiment by pressing the F9 key or changing the adjustable parameters to see how much the two regression equations can differ. After

experimenting, briefly explain how you think housing pricing works—or can you tell?

58. The file **P02_35.xlsx** contains data from a survey of 500 randomly selected households. For this problem, use Monthly Payment as the dependent variable in several regressions, as explained below.
    a. Beginning with Family Size, iteratively add one explanatory variable and estimate the resulting regression equation to explain the variation in Monthly Payment. If adding any explanatory variable causes the *adjusted* R^2 measure to fall, do not include that variable in subsequent versions of the regression model. Otherwise, include the variable and consider adding the next variable in the set. Which variables are included in the final version of your regression model? (Add dummies for Location in a single step, and use Total Income rather than First Income and Second Income separately.)
    b. Interpret the final estimated regression equation you obtained through the process outlined in part **a**. Also, interpret the standard error of estimate s_e, R^2, and the adjusted R^2 for the final estimated model.

59. (This problem is based on an actual court case in Philadelphia.) In the 1994 congressional election, the Republican candidate outpolled the Democratic candidate by 400 votes (excluding absentee ballots). The Democratic candidate outpolled the Republican candidate by 500 absentee votes. The Republican candidate sued (and won), claiming that vote fraud must have played a role in the absentee ballot count. The Republican's lawyer ran a regression to predict (based on past elections) how the absentee ballot margin could be predicted from the votes tabulated on voting machines. Selected results are given in the file **P10_59.xlsx**. Show how this regression could be used by the Republican to "prove" his claim of vote fraud.

60. In the world of computer science, Moore's law is famous. Although there are various versions of this law, they all say something to the effect that computing power *doubles* every two years. Several researchers estimated this law with regression using real data in 2006. Their paper can be found online at http://download.intel.com/pressroom/pdf/computertrendsrelease.pdf. For example, one interesting chart appears on page S1, backed up with regression results on another page. What exactly do these results say about doubling every two years (or do they contradict Moore's law)?

61. (The data for this problem are fictitious, but they are not far off.) For each of the top 25 business schools, the file **P10_61.xlsx** contains the average salary of a professor. Thus, for Indiana University (number 15 in the rankings), the average salary is $46,000. Use this information and regression to show that IU is doing a great job with its available resources.

62. Suppose the correlation between the average height of parents and the height of their firstborn male child is 0.5. You are also told that:

■ The average height of all parents is 66 inches.

■ The standard deviation of the average height of parents is 4 inches.

■ The average height of all male children is 70 inches.

■ The standard deviation of the height of all male children is 4 inches.

If a mother and father are 73 and 80 inches tall, respectively, how tall do you predict their son to be? Explain why this is called "regression toward the mean."

63. Do increased taxes increase or decrease economic growth? The file **P10_63.xlsx** lists tax revenues as a percentage of gross domestic product (GDP) and the average annual percentage growth in GDP per capita for nine countries during the years 1970 through 1994. Do these data support or contradict the dictum of supply-side economics?

64. For each of the four data sets in the file **P10_64.xlsx**, calculate the least squares line. For which of these data sets would you feel comfortable in using the least squares line to predict Y?

65. Suppose you run a regression on a data set of Xs and Ys and obtain a least squares line of $Y = 12 - 3X$.
  a. If you double each value of X, what is the new least squares line?
  b. If you triple each value of Y, what is the new least squares line?
  c. If you add 6 to each value of X, what is the new least squares line?
  d. If you subtract 4 from each value of Y, what is the new least squares line?

66. The file **P10_66.xlsx** contains monthly cost accounting data on overhead costs, machine hours, and direct material costs. This problem will help you explore the meaning of R^2 and the relationship between R^2 and correlations.
  a. Create a table of correlations between the individual variables.
  b. If you ignore the two explanatory variables Machine Hours and Direct Material Cost and predict each Overhead Cost as the *mean* of Overhead Cost, then a typical "error" is Overhead Cost minus the mean of Overhead Cost. Find the sum of squared errors using this form of prediction, where the sum is over all observations.
  c. Now run three regressions: (1) Overhead Cost (OHCost) versus Machine Hours, (2) OHCost versus Direct Material Cost, and (3) OHCost versus both Machine Hours and Direct Material Cost. (The first two are simple regressions, the third is a multiple regression.) For each, find the sum of

squared residuals, and divide this by the sum of squared errors from part **b**. What is the relationship between this ratio and the associated R^2 for that equation? (Now do you see why R^2 is referred to as the percentage of variation explained?)
  d. For the first two regressions in part **c**, what is the relationship between R^2 and the corresponding correlation between the dependent and explanatory variable? For the third regression it turns out that the R^2 can be expressed as a complicated function of all three correlations in part **a**. That is, the function involves not just the correlations between the dependent variable and each explanatory variable, but also the correlation between the explanatory variables. Note that this R^2 is not just the sum of the R^2 values from the first two regressions in part **c**. Why do you think this is true, intuitively? However, R^2 for the multiple regression is still the square of a correlation—namely, the correlation between the observed and predicted values of OHCost. Verify that this is the case for these data.

67. The file **P10_67.xlsx** contains hypothetical starting salaries for MBA students directly after graduation. The file also lists their years of experience prior to the MBA program and their class rank in the MBA program (on a 0–100 scale).
  a. Estimate the regression equation with Salary as the dependent variable and Experience and Class Rank as the explanatory variables. What does this equation imply? What does the standard error of estimate s_e tell you? What about R^2?
  b. Repeat part **a**, but now include the interaction term Experience*Class Rank (the product) in the equation as well as Experience and Class Rank individually. Answer the same questions as in part **a**. What evidence is there that this extra variable (the interaction variable) is worth including? How do you interpret this regression equation? Why might you expect the interaction to be present in real data of this type?

68. In a study published in 1985 in *Business Horizons*, Platt and McCarthy employed multiple regression analysis to explain variations in compensation among the CEOs of large companies. (Although the data set is old, we suspect the results would be similar with more current data.) Their primary objective was to discover whether levels of compensations are affected more by short-run considerations—"I'll earn more now if my company does well in the short run"—or long-run considerations—"My best method for obtaining high compensation is to stay with my company for a long time." The study used as its dependent variable the total compensation for each of the 100 highest paid CEOs in 1981. This variable was defined as the sum of salary, bonuses, and other benefits (measured in $1000s).

The following potential explanatory variables were considered. To capture short-run effects, the average of the company's previous five years' percentage changes in earnings per share (EPS) and the projected percentage change in next year's EPS were used. To capture the long-run effect, age and years as CEO, two admittedly correlated variables, were used. Dummy variables for the CEO's background (finance, marketing, and so on) were also considered. Finally, the researchers considered several nonlinear and interaction terms based on these variables. The best-fitting equation was the following:

$$\text{Total Compensation} = -3943 + 898.7 \text{ Years as CEO}$$
$$+ 9.28 (\text{Years as CEO})^2 - 17.19 \text{ Years as CEO Age}$$
$$+ 88.27 \text{ Age} + 867.4 \text{ Finance}$$

(The last variable is a dummy variable, equal to 1 if the CEO had a finance background, 0 otherwise.) The corresponding R^2 was 19.4%.

a. Explain what this equation implies about CEO compensations.

b. The researchers drew the following conclusions. First, it appears that CEOs should indeed concentrate on long-run considerations—namely, those that keep them on their jobs the longest. Second, the absence of the short-run company-related variables from the equations helps to confirm the conjecture that CEOs who concentrate on earning the quick buck for their companies may not be acting in their best self-interest. Finally, the positive coefficient of the dummy variable may imply that financial people possess skills that are vitally important, and firms therefore outbid one another for the best financial talent. Based on the data given, do you agree with these conclusions?

c. Consider a CEO (other than those in the study) who has been in his position for 10 years and has a financial background. Predict his total yearly compensation (in $1000s) if he is 50 years old and then if he is 55 years old. Explain why the difference between these two predictions is not 5(88.27), where 88.27 is the coefficient of the Age variable.

69. Wilhoit Company has observed that there is a linear relationship between indirect labor expense and direct labor hours. Data for direct labor hours and indirect labor expense for 18 months are given in the file **P10_69.xlsx**. At the start of month 7, all cost categories in the Wilhoit Company increased by 10%, and they stayed at this level for months 7 through 12. Then at the start of month 13, another 10% across-the-board increase in all costs occurred, and the company operated at this price level for months 13 through 18.

a. Plot the data. Verify that the relationship between indirect labor expense and direct labor hours is approximately linear within each six-month period. Use regression (three times) to estimate the slope and intercept during months 1 through 6, during months 7 through 12, and during months 13 through 18.

b. Use regression to fit a straight line to all 18 data points simultaneously. What values of the slope and intercept do you obtain?

c. Perform a price level adjustment to the data and re-estimate the slope and intercept using all 18 data points. Assuming no cost increases for month 19, what is your prediction for indirect labor expense if there are 35,000 direct labor hours in month 19?

d. Interpret your results. What causes the difference in the linear relationship estimated in parts **b** and **c**?

70. Bohring Company manufactures a sophisticated radar unit that is used in a fighter aircraft built by Seaways Aircraft. The first 50 units of the radar unit have been completed, and Bohring is preparing to submit a proposal to Seaways Aircraft to manufacture the next 50 units. Bohring wants to submit a competitive bid, but at the same time, it wants to ensure that all the costs of manufacturing the radar unit are fully covered. As part of this process, Bohring is attempting to develop a standard for the number of labor hours required to manufacture each radar unit. Developing a labor standard has been a continuing problem in the past. The file **P10_70.xlsx** lists the number of labor hours required for each of the first 50 units of production. Bohring accountants want to see whether regression analysis, together with the concept of learning curves, can help solve the company's problem.

71. Sometimes it is instructive to generate random data that have a given relationship and then use regression on the generated data to see if the estimated regression is basically the same as that used to generate the data in the first place.

a. Let X be normally distributed with mean 100 and standard deviation 10, and let Y equal $100 + 5X$ plus a normally distributed random residual with mean 0 and standard deviation 40. Generate 50 observations.

b. Copy the random data and paste as values in another range of the worksheet. Then run the regression on the copy (the frozen values).

c. Repeat part **b** several times to see if you get basically the same regression results each time. That is, each run should be on a *different* set of frozen data.

d. Write a short report of your method and your findings.

10.1 QUANTITY DISCOUNTS AT FIRM CHAIR COMPANY

Firm Chair Company manufactures customized wood furniture and sells the furniture in large quantities to major furniture retailers. Jim Bolling has recently been assigned to analyze the company's pricing policy. He has been told that quantity discounts were usually given. For example, for one type of chair, the pricing changed at quantities of 200 and 400—that is, these were the price breaks, where the marginal cost of the next chair changed.

For this type of chair, the file **C10_01.xlsx** contains the quantity and total price to the customer for 81 orders. Use regression to help Jim discover the pricing structure that Firm Chair evidently used. (*Note:* A linear regression of Total Price versus Quantity will give you a "decent" fit, but you can do much better by introducing appropriate variables into the regression.)

10.2 HOUSING PRICE STRUCTURE IN MID CITY

Sales of single-family houses have been brisk in Mid City this year. This has especially been true in older, more established neighborhoods, where housing is relatively inexpensive compared to the new homes being built in the newer neighborhoods. Nevertheless, there are also many families who are willing to pay a higher price for the prestige of living in one of the newer neighborhoods. The file **C10_02.xlsx** contains data on 128 recent sales in Mid City. For each sale, the file shows the neighborhood (1, 2, or 3) in which the house is located, the number of offers made on the house, the square footage, whether the house is made primarily of brick, the number of bathrooms, the number of bedrooms, and the selling price. Neighborhoods 1 and 2 are more traditional

neighborhoods, whereas neighborhood 3 is a newer, more prestigious neighborhood.

Use regression to estimate and interpret the pricing structure of houses in Mid City. Here are some considerations.

1. Do buyers pay a premium for a brick house, all else being equal?

2. Is there a premium for a house in neighborhood 3, all else being equal?

3. Is there an *extra* premium for a brick house in neighborhood 3, in addition to the usual premium for a brick house?

4. For purposes of estimation and prediction, could neighborhoods 1 and 2 be collapsed into a single "older" neighborhood?

10.3 DEMAND FOR FRENCH BREAD AT HOWIE'S BAKERY

Howie's Bakery is one of the most popular bakeries in town, and the favorite at Howie's is French bread. Each day of the week, Howie's bakes a number of loaves of French bread, more or less according to a daily schedule. To maintain its fine reputation, Howie's gives away to charity any loaves

not sold on the day they are baked. Although this occurs frequently, it is also common for Howie's to run out of French bread on any given day—more demand than supply. In this case, no extra loaves are baked that day; the customers have to go elsewhere (or come back to Howie's the next day) for their

French bread. Although French bread at Howie's is always popular, Howie's stimulates demand by running occasional 10% off sales.

Howie's has collected data for 20 consecutive weeks, 140 days in all. These data are listed in the file **C10_03.xlsx**. The variables are Day (Monday–Sunday), Supply (number of loaves baked that day), On Sale (whether French bread is on sale that day), and Demand (loaves actually sold that day). Howie's would like you to see whether regression can be used successfully to estimate Demand from the other data in the file. Howie reasons that if these other variables can be used to predict Demand, then he might be able to determine his daily supply (number of loaves to bake) in a more cost-effective way.

How successful is regression with these data? Is Howie correct that regression can help him determine his daily supply? Is any information missing that would be useful? How would you obtain it? How would you use it? Is this extra information *really* necessary?

CASE 10.4 INVESTING FOR RETIREMENT

Financial advisors offer many types of advice to customers, but they generally agree that one of the best things people can do is invest as much as possible in tax-deferred retirement plans. Not only are the earnings from these investments exempt from income tax (until retirement), but the investment itself is tax-exempt. This means that if a person invests, say, $10,000 of his $100,000 income in a tax-deferred retirement plan, he pays income tax that year on only $90,000 of his income. This is probably the best method available to most people for avoiding tax payments. However, which group takes advantage of this attractive investment opportunity: everyone, people with low salaries, people with high salaries, or who?

The file **C10_04.xlsx** lets you investigate this question. It contains data on 194 (hypothetical) couples: number of dependent children, combined annual salary of husband and wife, current mortgage on home, average amount of other (nonmortgage) debt, and percentage of combined income invested in tax-deferred retirement plans (assumed to be limited to 15%, which is realistic). Using correlations, scatterplots, and regression analysis, what can you conclude about the tendency of this group of people to invest in tax-deferred retirement plans?

CHAPTER
11

Regression Analysis: Statistical Inference

izusek/Izabela Habur/iStockphoto.com

PREDICTING MOVIE REVENUES

In the opener for Chapter 3, we discussed the article by Simonoff and Sparrow (2000) that examined movie revenues for 311 movies released in 1998 and late 1997. We saw that movie revenues were related to several variables, including genre, Motion Picture Association of America (MPAA) rating, country of origin, number of stars in the cast, whether the movie was a sequel, and whether the movie was released during a few choice times. In Chapter 3, we were limited to looking at summary measures and charts of the data. Now that we are studying regression, we can look further into the analysis performed by Simonoff and Sparrow. Specifically, they examined whether these variables, plus others, are effective in predicting movie revenues.

The authors report the results from three multiple regression models. All of these used the logarithm of the total U.S. gross revenue from the film as the dependent variable. (They used the *logarithm* because the distribution of gross revenues is very positively skewed.) The first model used only the *prerelease* variables listed in the previous paragraph. The values of these variables were all known prior to the movie's release. Therefore, the purpose of this model was to see how well revenues could be predicted *before* the movie was released.

The second model used the variables from model 1, along with two variables that could be observed after the first week of the movie's release: the first weekend gross and the number of screens the movie opened on. (Actually, the logarithms of these latter two variables were used, again because of positive skewness. Also, the authors found it necessary to run two separate regressions at this stage—one for movies that opened on

532

10 or fewer screens, and another for movies that opened on more than 10 screens.) The idea here was that the success or failure of many movies depends to a large extent on how they do right after they are released. Therefore, it was expected that this information would add significantly to the predictive power of the regression model.

The third model built on the second by adding an additional explanatory variable: the number of Oscar nominations the movie received for key awards (Best Picture, Best Director, Best Actor, Best Actress, Best Supporting Actor, and Best Supporting Actress). This information is often not known until well after a movie's release, but it was hypothesized that Oscar nominations would lead to a significant increase in a movie's revenues, and that a regression model with this information could lead to very different predictions of revenue.

Simonoff and Sparrow found that the coefficients of the first regression model were in line with the box plots shown earlier in Figure 3.1 of Chapter 3. For example, the variables that measured the number of star actors and actresses were both positive and significant, indicating that star power tends to lead to larger revenues. However, the predictive power of this model was poor. Given its standard error of prediction (and taking into account that the *logarithm* of revenue was the dependent variable), the authors stated that "the predictions of total grosses for an individual movie can be expected to be off by as much as a multiplicative factor of 100 high or low." It appears that there is no way to predict which movies will succeed and which will fail based on prerelease data only.

The second model added considerable predictive power. The regression equations indicated that gross revenue is positively related to first weekend gross and negatively related to the number of opening screens, both of these variables being significant. As for prediction, the factor of 100 mentioned in the previous paragraph decreased to a factor of 10 (for movies with 10 or fewer opening screens) or 2 (for movies with more than 10 opening screens). This is still not perfect—predictions of total revenue made after the movie's first weekend can still be fairly far off—but this additional information about initial success certainly helps.

The third model added only slightly to the predictive power, primarily because so few of the movies (10 out of 311) received Oscar nominations for key awards. However, the predictions for those that did receive nominations increased considerably. For example, the prediction for the multiple Oscar nominee *Saving Private Ryan,* based on the second model, was 194.622 (millions of dollars). Its prediction based on the third model increased to a whopping 358.237. (Interestingly, the prediction for this movie from the first model was only 14.791, and its actual gross revenue was 216.119. Perhaps the reason *Saving Private Ryan* did not make as much as the third model predicted was that the Oscar nominations were announced about nine months after its release—too long after release to do much good.)

Simonoff and Sparrow then used their third model to predict gross revenues for 24 movies released in 1999—movies that were not in the data set used to estimate the regression model. They found that 21 out of 24 of the resulting 95% prediction intervals captured the actual gross revenues, which is about what would be expected. However, many of these prediction intervals were extremely wide, and several of the predictions were well above or below the actual revenues. The authors conclude by quoting Tim Noonan, a former movie executive: "Since predicting gross is extremely difficult, you have to serve up a [yearly] slate of movies and know that over time you'll have 3 or 4 to the left and 2 or 3 to the right. You must make sure you are doing things that mitigate your downside risk." ∎

11-1 INTRODUCTION

The previous chapter discussed how to fit a regression equation to a set of points by using the least squares method. The purpose of this regression equation is to provide a good fit to the points in the sample so that you can understand the relationship between a dependent variable and one or more explanatory variables. The entire emphasis of the discussion in the previous chapter was on finding a regression model that fits the observations in the sample. In this chapter we take a slightly different point of view. We assume that the observations in the sample are taken from some larger population. For example, the sample of 50 regions from the Pharmex drugstore example could represent a sample of all the regions where Pharmex does business. In this case, we might be interested in the relationship between variables in the entire population, not just in the sample.

There are two basic problems we discuss in this chapter. The first has to do with a *population regression model*. We want to infer its characteristics—that is, its intercept and slope term(s)—from the corresponding terms estimated by least squares. We also want to know which explanatory variables belong in the equation. There are typically a large number of *potential* explanatory variables, and it is often not clear which of these do the best job of explaining variation in the dependent variable. In addition, we would like to infer whether there is any population regression equation worth pursuing. It is possible that the potential explanatory variables provide very little explanation of the dependent variable.

The second problem we discuss in this chapter is *prediction*. We touched on the prediction problem in the previous chapter, primarily in the context of predicting the dependent variable for part of the sample held out for validation purposes. In reality, we had the values of the dependent variable for that part of the sample, so prediction was not really necessary. Now we go beyond the sample and predict values of the dependent variable for *new* observations. There is no way to check the accuracy of these predictions, at least not right away, because the values of the dependent variable are not yet known. However, it is possible to calculate prediction intervals to measure the accuracy of the predictions.

11-2 THE STATISTICAL MODEL

To perform statistical inference in a regression context, a **statistical model** is required; that is, we must first make several assumptions about the population. Throughout the analysis these assumptions remain exactly that—they are only assumptions, not facts. These assumptions represent an idealization of reality, and as such, they are never likely to be entirely satisfied for the population in any real study. From a practical point of view, all we can ask is that they represent a close approximation to reality. If this is the case, then the analysis in this chapter is valid. But if the assumptions are grossly violated, statistical inferences that are based on these assumptions should be viewed with suspicion. Although we can never be entirely certain of the validity of the assumptions, there are ways to check for gross violations, and we discuss some of these.

Regression Assumptions

- There is a population regression line. It joins the *means* of the dependent variable for all values of the explanatory variables. For any fixed values of the explanatory variables, the mean of the errors is zero.
- For any values of the explanatory variables, the variance (or standard deviation) of the dependent variable is a constant, the same for all such values.
- For any values of the explanatory variables, the dependent variable is normally distributed.
- The errors are probabilistically independent.

Because these assumptions are so crucial to the regression analysis that follows, it is important to understand exactly what they mean. Assumption 1 is probably the most important. It implies that for some set of explanatory variables, there is an exact linear relationship in the population between the *means* of the dependent variable and the values of the explanatory variables.

These explanatory variables could be original variables or variables you create, such as dummies, interactions, or nonlinear transformations.

To be more specific, let Y be the dependent variable, and assume that there are k explanatory variables, X_1 through X_k. Let $\mu_{Y|X_1, \ldots, X_k}$ be the mean of all Ys for any fixed values of the Xs. Then assumption 1 implies that there is an exact linear relationship between the mean $\mu_{Y|X_1, \ldots, X_k}$ and the Xs. That is, it implies that there are coefficients α and β_1 through β_k such that the following equation holds for all values of the Xs:

Population Regression Line Joining Means

$$\mu_{Y|X_1, \ldots, X_k} = \alpha + \beta_1 X_1 + \cdots + \beta_k X_k \qquad \textbf{(11.1)}$$

It is common to use Greek letters to denote population parameters and regular letters for their sample estimates.

In the terminology of the previous chapter, α is the intercept term, and β_1 through β_k are the slope terms. We use Greek letters for these coefficients to denote that they are *unobservable* population parameters. Assumption 1 implies the existence of a population regression equation and the corresponding α and βs. However, it tells us nothing about the *values* of these parameters. They still need to be estimated from sample data, using the least squares method to do so.

Equation (11.1) says that the *means* of the Ys lie on the population regression line. However, it is clear from a scatterplot that most *individual* Ys do not lie on this line. The vertical distance from any point to the line is called an **error**. The error for any point, labeled ε, is the difference between Y and $\mu_{Y|X_1, \ldots, X_k}$, that is,

$$Y = \mu_{Y|X_1, \ldots, X_k} + \varepsilon$$

By substituting the assumed linear form for $\mu_{Y|X_1, \ldots, X_k}$, we obtain Equation (11.2). This equation states that each value of Y is equal to a fitted part plus an error. The fitted part is the linear expression $\alpha + \beta_1 X_1 + \cdots + \beta_k X_k$. The error ε is sometimes positive, in which case the point is above the regression line, and sometimes negative, in which case the point is below the regression line. The last part of assumption 1 states that these errors average to zero in the population, so that the positive errors cancel the negative errors.

Population Regression Line with Error

$$Y = \alpha + \beta_1 X_1 + \cdots + \beta_k X_k + \varepsilon \qquad \textbf{(11.2)}$$

Note that an error ε is not quite the same as a residual e. An error is the vertical distance from a point to the (unobservable) population regression line. A residual is the vertical distance from a point to the *estimated* regression line. Residuals can be calculated from observed data; errors cannot.

Assumption 2 concerns variation around the population regression line. Specifically, it states that the variation of the Ys about the regression line is the *same*, regardless of the values of the Xs. A technical term for this property is **homoscedasticity**. A simpler term is **constant error variance**. In the Pharmex example (Example 10.1), constant error variance implies that the variation in Sales values is the same regardless of the value of Promote. As another example, recall the Bendrix manufacturing example (Example 10.2). There we related overhead costs (Overhead) to the number of machine hours (Machine Hours) and the number of production runs (Production Runs). Constant error variance implies that overhead costs vary just as much for small values of Machine Hours and Production Runs as for large values—or any values in between.

There are many situations where assumption 2 is questionable. The variation in Y often increases as X increases—a violation of assumption 2. We presented an example of this in Figure 10.10 (repeated here in Figure 11.1), which is based on customer spending at a mail-order company. This scatterplot shows the amount spent versus salary for a sample of the company's customers. Clearly, the variation in the amount spent increases as salary increases, which makes intuitive sense. Customers with small salaries have little disposable income, so they all tend to spend small amounts for mail-order items. Customers with large salaries have more disposable income. Some of them spend a lot of it on mail-order items and some spend only a little of it—hence, a larger variation. Scatterplots with this "fan" shape are not at all uncommon in real studies, and they exhibit a clear violation of assumption 2.[1] We say that the data in this graph exhibit **heteroscedasticity**, or more simply, **nonconstant error variance**. These terms are summarized in the following box.

Homoscedasticity means that the variability of Y values is the same for all X values.

Heteroscedasticity means that the variability of Y values is larger for some X values than for others.

Figure 11.1

Illustration of Nonconstant Error Variance

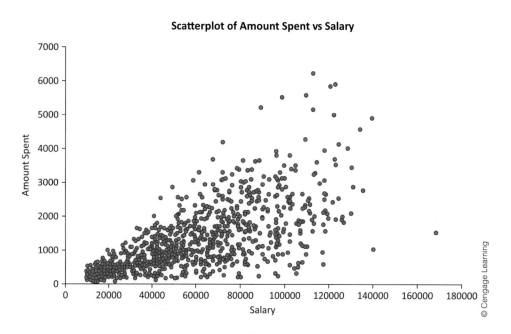

Scatterplot of Amount Spent vs Salary

The easiest way to detect nonconstant error variance is through a visual inspection of a scatterplot. You create a scatterplot of the dependent variable versus an explanatory variable X and see whether the points vary more for some values of X than for others. You can

---

[1]The fan shape in Figure 11.1 is probably the most common form of nonconstant error variance, but it is not the only possible form.

also examine the residuals with a residual plot, where residual values are on the vertical axis and some other variable (Y or one of the Xs) is on the horizontal axis. If the residual plot exhibits a fan shape or other evidence of nonconstant error variance, this also indicates a violation of assumption 2.

Assumption 3 is equivalent to stating that the errors are normally distributed. You can check this by forming a histogram (or a Q-Q plot) of the residuals. If assumption 3 holds, the histogram should be approximately symmetric and bell-shaped, and the points in the Q-Q plot should be close to a 45° line.[2] But if there is an obvious skewness, too many residuals more than, say, two standard deviations from the mean, or some other nonnormal property, this indicates a violation of assumption 3.

Finally, assumption 4 requires probabilistic independence of the errors. Intuitively, this assumption means that information on some of the errors provides no information on the values of other errors. For example, if you are told that the overhead costs for months 1 through 4 are all above the regression line (positive residuals), you cannot infer anything about the residual for month 5 if assumption 4 holds.

Assumption 4 (independence of residuals) is usually in doubt only for time series data.

For cross-sectional data there is generally little reason to doubt the validity of assumption 4 unless the observations are ordered in some particular way. For cross-sectional data assumption 4 is usually taken for granted. However, for time series data, assumption 4 is often violated. This is because of a property called *autocorrelation*. For now, we simply mention that one output given automatically in many regression packages is the *Durbin–Watson statistic*. The Durbin–Watson statistic is one measure of autocorrelation and thus it measures the extent to which assumption 4 is violated. We briefly discuss this Durbin–Watson statistic toward the end of this chapter and in the next chapter.

One other assumption is important for numerical calculations. No explanatory variable can be an *exact* linear combination of any other explanatory variables. Another way of stating this is that there should be no exact linear relationship between any set of explanatory variables. This would be violated, for example, if one variable were an exact multiple of another, or if one variable were equal to the sum of several other variables. More generally, the violation occurs if one of the explanatory variables can be written as a weighted sum of several of the others. This is called *exact multicollinearity*.

Exact multicollinearity means that at least one of the explanatory variables is redundant and is not needed in the regression equation.

If exact multicollinearity exists, it means that there is *redundancy* in the data. One of the Xs could be eliminated without any loss of information. Here is a simple example. Suppose that Machine Hours1 is machine hours measured in hours, and Machine Hours2 is machine hours measured in *hundreds* of hours. Then it is clear that these two variables contain exactly the same information, and either of them could (and should) be eliminated.

As another example, suppose that Ad1, Ad2, and Ad3 are the amounts spent on radio ads, television ads, and newspaper ads. Also, suppose that Total Ad is the amount spent on radio, television, and newspaper ads combined. Then there is an exact linear relationship among these variables:

$$\text{Total Ad} = \text{Ad1} + \text{Ad2} + \text{Ad3}$$

In this case there is no need to include Total Ad in the analysis because it contains no information that is not already contained in the variables Ad1, Ad2, and Ad3. Therefore, Total Ad should be eliminated from the analysis.

---

[2]A Q-Q (quantile-quantile) plot is used to detect nonnormality. It is available in StatTools from the Normality Tests dropdown list. Nonnormal data often produce a Q-Q plot that is close to a 45° line in the middle of the plot but deviates from this line in one or both of the tails.

StatTools Tip: StatTools Exact Relationship Warning

StatTools issues a warning if it detects an exact linear relationship between explanatory variables in a regression model.

Generally, it is fairly simple to spot an exact linear relationship such as these, and then to eliminate it by excluding the redundant variable from the analysis. However, if you do *not* spot the relationship and try to run the regression analysis with the redundant variable included, regression packages will typically respond with an error message. If the package interrupts the analysis with an error message containing the words "exact multicollinearity" or "linear dependence," you should look for a redundant explanatory variable. The message from StatTools in this case is shown in Figure 11.2. We got it by deliberately entering dummy variables from each category of a categorical variable—something we have warned you *not* to do.

Figure 11.2

Error Message
from StatTools
Indicating Exact
Multicollinearity

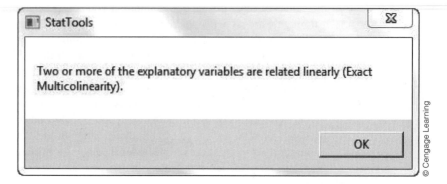

Although this problem can be a nuisance, it is usually caused by an oversight and can be fixed easily by eliminating a redundant variable. A more common and serious problem is *multicollinearity*, where explanatory variables are highly, but not exactly, correlated. A typical example is an employee's years of experience and age. Although these two variables are not equal for all employees, they are likely to be highly correlated. If they are both included as explanatory variables in a regression analysis, the software will not issue any error messages, but the estimates it produces can be unreliable and difficult to interpret. We will discuss multicollinearity in more detail later in this chapter.

11-3 INFERENCES ABOUT THE REGRESSION COEFFICIENTS

In this section we explain how to make inferences about the population regression coefficients from sample data. We begin by making the assumptions discussed in the previous section. In particular, the first assumption states that there is a population regression line. Equation (11.2) for this line is repeated here:

$$Y = \alpha + \beta_1 X_1 + \cdots + \beta_k X_k + \varepsilon$$

We refer to α and the βs collectively as the *regression coefficients*. Again, Greek letters are used to indicate that these quantities are unknown and unobservable. There is one other unknown constant in the model: the variance of the errors. Regression assumption 2 states that these errors have a constant variance, the same for all values of the Xs. We label this constant variance σ^2. Equivalently, the common standard deviation of the errors is σ.

This is how it looks in theory. There is a fixed set of explanatory variables, and given these variables, the problem is to estimate α, the βs, and σ. In practice, however, it is not usually this straightforward. In real regression applications the choice of relevant explanatory variables is almost never obvious. There are at least two guiding principles: relevance and data availability. You certainly want variables that are related to the dependent variable. The best situation is when there is an established economic or physical theory to guide you.

For example, economic theory suggests that the demand for a product (dependent variable) is related to its price (possible explanatory variable). But there are not enough established theories to cover every situation. You often have to use the available data, plus some trial and error, to determine a *useful* set of explanatory variables. In this sense, it is usually pointless to search for one single "true" population regression equation. Instead, you typically estimate several competing models, each with a different set of explanatory variables, and ultimately select one of them as being the most useful.

Typically, the most challenging part of a regression analysis is deciding which explanatory variables to include in the regression equation.

Deciding which explanatory variables to include in a regression equation is probably the most difficult part of any applied regression analysis. Available data sets frequently offer an overabundance of potential explanatory variables. In addition, it is possible and often useful to create new variables from original variables, such as their logarithms. So where do you stop? Is it best to include every conceivable explanatory variable that might be related to the dependent variable? One overriding principle is **parsimony**—explaining the most with the least. For example, if a dependent variable can be explained just as well (or nearly as well) with two explanatory variables as with 10 explanatory variables, the principle of parsimony says to use only two. Models with fewer explanatory variables are generally easier to interpret, so they are preferred whenever possible.

> The principle of **parsimony** is to explain the most with the least. It favors a model with fewer explanatory variables, assuming that this model explains the dependent variable almost as well as a model with additional explanatory variables.

Before you can determine which equation has the best set of explanatory variables, however, you must be able to estimate the unknown parameters for a given equation. That is, for a given set of explanatory variables X_1 through X_k, you must be able to estimate α, the βs, and σ. You learned how to find point estimates of these parameters in the previous chapter. The estimates of α and the βs are the least squares estimates of the intercept and slope terms. For example, the 36 months of overhead data in the Bendrix example were used to estimate the equation

Predicted Overhead = 3997 + 43.54Machine Hours + 883.62Production Runs

This implies that the least squares estimates of α, β_1, and β_2 are 3997, 43.54, and 883.62. Furthermore, because the residuals are really estimates of the errors, the standard error of estimate s_e is an estimate of σ. For the same overhead equation this estimate is $s_e = \$4109$.

You learned in Chapter 8 that there is more to statistical estimation than finding point estimates of population parameters. Each potential sample from the population typically leads to *different* point estimates. For example, if Bendrix estimates the equation for overhead from a different 36-month period (or possibly from another of its plants), the results will almost certainly be different. Therefore, we now discuss how these point estimates vary from sample to sample.

11-3a Sampling Distribution of the Regression Coefficients

The key idea is again sampling distributions. Recall that the sampling distribution of any estimate derived from sample data is the distribution of this estimate over all possible samples. This idea can be applied to the least squares estimate of a regression coefficient. For example, the sampling distribution of b_1, the least squares estimate of β_1, is the distribution of b_1s you would see if you observed many samples and ran a least squares regression on each of them.

Fortunately, mathematicians have derived the required sampling distributions. We state the main result as follows. Let β be any of the βs, and let b be the least squares estimate of β. If the regression assumptions hold, the standardized value $(b - \beta)/s_b$ has a t distribution with $n - k - 1$ degrees of freedom. Here, k is the number of explanatory variables included in the equation, and s_b is the estimated standard deviation of the sampling distribution of b.

Sampling Distribution of a Regression Coefficient

If the regression assumptions are valid, the standardized value

$$t = \frac{b - \beta}{s_b}$$

has a t distribution with $n - k - 1$ degrees of freedom.

This result has three important implications. First, the estimate b is *unbiased* in the sense that its mean is β, the true but unknown value of the slope. If bs were estimated from repeated samples, some would underestimate β and others would overestimate β, but on average they would be on target.

Second, the estimated standard deviation of b is labeled s_b. It is usually called the **standard error of a regression coefficient**, or more simply, the standard error of b. This standard error is related to the standard error of estimate s_e, but it is not the same. Generally, the formula for s_b is quite complicated, and it is not shown here, but its value is printed in all standard regression outputs. It measures how much the bs would vary from sample to sample. A small value of s_b is preferred—it means that b is a more accurate estimate of the true coefficient β.

Finally, the shape of the distribution of b is symmetric and bell-shaped. The relevant distribution is the t distribution with $n - k - 1$ degrees of freedom.

We have stated this result for a typical coefficient of one of the Xs. These are usually the coefficients of most interest. However, exactly the same result holds for the intercept term α. Now we illustrate how to use this result.

FUNDAMENTAL INSIGHT

Standard Errors in Regression

There are two quite different standard errors in regression outputs. The standard error of estimate, usually shown at the top of the output, is a measure of the error you are likely to make when you use the regression equation to predict a value of Y. In contrast, the standard errors of the coefficients measure the accuracy of the individual coefficients.

EXAMPLE | 11.1 EXPLAINING OVERHEAD COSTS AT BENDRIX

This example is a continuation of the Bendrix manufacturing example from the previous chapter. As before, the dependent variable is Overhead and the explanatory variables are Machine Hours and Production Runs. What inferences can be made about the regression coefficients?

Objective To use standard regression output to make inferences about the regression coefficients of machine hours and production runs in the equation for overhead costs.

Solution

The output from StatTools's Regression procedure is shown in Figure 11.3. (See the file **Overhead Costs.xlsx.**) This output is practically identical to regression outputs from all other statistical software packages. The estimates of the regression coefficients appear

Figure 11.3 Regression Output for Bendrix Example

▲	A	B	C	D	E	F	G
7	**Multiple Regression for Overhead**						
8		**Multiple**	**R-Square**	**Adjusted**	**StErr of**		
9	**Summary**	**R**		**R-Square**	**Estimate**		
10		0.9308	0.8664	0.8583	4108.99309		
11							
12		**Degrees of**	**Sum of**	**Mean of**	**F-Ratio**	**p-Value**	
13	**ANOVA Table**	**Freedom**	**Squares**	**Squares**			
14	Explained	2	3614020661	1807010330	107.0261	<0.0001	
15	Unexplained	33	557166199.1	16883824.22			
16							
17		**Coefficient**	**Standard**	**t-Value**	**p-Value**	**Confidence Interval 95%**	
18	**Regression Table**		**Error**			**Lower**	**Upper**
19	Constant	3996.678209	6603.650932	0.6052	0.5492	−9438.550632	17431.90705
20	Machine Hours	43.53639812	3.5894837	12.1289	<0.0001	36.23353862	50.83925761
21	Production Runs	883.6179252	82.25140753	10.7429	<0.0001	716.2761784	1050.959672

© Cengage Learning

under the label Coefficient in the range B18:B20. These values estimate the true, but unobservable, population coefficients. The next column, labeled Standard Error, shows the s_b values. Specifically, 3.589 is the standard error of the coefficient of Machine Hours, and 82.251 is the standard error of the coefficient of Production Runs.

Each b represents a point estimate of the corresponding β, based on this particular sample. The corresponding s_b indicates the accuracy of this point estimate. For example, the point estimate of β_1, the effect on Overhead of a one-unit increase in Machine Hours (when Production Runs is held constant), is 43.536. You can be about 95% confident that the true β_1 is within two standard errors of this point estimate, that is, from approximately 36.357 to 50.715. Similar statements can be made for the coefficient of Production Runs and the intercept (Constant) term. ■

As with any population parameter, the sample data can be used to obtain a **confidence interval for a regression coefficient**. For example, the preceding paragraph implies that an approximate 95% confidence interval for the coefficient of Machine Hours extends from approximately 36.357 to 50.715. More precisely, a confidence interval for any β is of the form

$$b \pm t\text{-multiple} \times s_b$$

where the t-multiple depends on the confidence level and the degrees of freedom (here $n - k - 1$). StatTools always provides these 95% confidence intervals for the regression coefficients automatically, as shown in the bottom right of Figure 11.3.

11-3b Hypothesis Tests for the Regression Coefficients and *p*-Values

There is another important piece of information in regression outputs: the t-values for the individual regression coefficients. These are shown in the "t-Value" column of the regression output in Figure 11.3. Each t-value is the ratio of the estimated coefficient to its standard error, as shown in Equation (11.3). Therefore, it indicates how many standard errors the regression coefficient is from zero. For example, the t-value for Machine Hours is about 12.13, so the regression coefficient of Machine Hours, 43.536, is more than 12 of its standard errors to the right of zero. Similarly, the coefficient of Production Runs is more than 10 of its standard errors to the right of zero.

---

t-value for Test of Regression Coefficient

$$t\text{-value} = b/s_b \tag{11.3}$$

A t-value can be used in an important **hypothesis test for a regression coefficient**. To motivate this test, suppose that you want to decide whether a particular explanatory variable belongs in the regression equation. A sensible criterion for making this decision is to check whether the corresponding regression coefficient is zero. If a variable's coefficient is zero, there is no point in including this variable in the equation because the zero coefficient will cancel its effect on the dependent variable.

The test for whether a regression coefficient is zero can be run by looking at the corresponding p-value: Reject the "equals zero" hypothesis if the p-value is small, say, less than 0.05.

Therefore, it is reasonable to test whether a variable's coefficient is zero. This is usually tested versus a *two-tailed* alternative. The null and alternative hypotheses are of the form $H_0:\beta = 0$ versus $H_a:\beta \neq 0$. If you can reject the null hypothesis and conclude that this coefficient is *not* zero, you then have an argument for including the variable in the regression equation. Conversely, if you cannot reject the null hypothesis, you might decide to eliminate this variable from the equation.

The t-value for a variable allows you to run this test easily. You simply compare the t-value in the regression output with a tabulated t-value and reject the null hypothesis only if the t-value from the computer output is greater in magnitude than the tabulated t-value.

Most statistical packages, including StatTools, make this test even easier to run by reporting the corresponding p-value for the test. This eliminates the need for finding the tabulated t-value. The p-value is interpreted exactly as in Chapter 9. It is the probability (in both tails) of the relevant t distribution beyond the listed t-value. For example, referring again to Figure 11.3, the t-value for Machine Hours is 12.13, and the associated p-value is less than 0.0001. This means that there is virtually no probability beyond the observed t-value. In words, you are still not exactly sure of the true coefficient of Machine Hours, but you are virtually sure it is not zero. The same can be said for the coefficient of Production Runs.

In practice, you typically run a multiple regression with several explanatory variables and scan their p-values. If the p-value of a variable is low, then this variable should be kept in the equation; if the p-value is high, you might consider eliminating this variable from the equation. In Section 11-5, we will discuss this *include/exclude decision* in greater depth and provide rules of thumb for the meaning of "low" and "high" p-values.

11-3c A Test for the Overall Fit: The ANOVA Table

The t-values for the regression coefficients allow you to see which of the potential explanatory variables are useful in explaining the dependent variable. But it is conceivable that *none* of these variables does a very good job. That is, it is conceivable that the entire group of explanatory variables explains only an insignificant portion of the variability of the dependent variable. Although this is the exception rather than the rule in most real applications, it can happen. An indication of this is that you obtain a very small R^2 value. Because R^2 is the square of the correlation between the observed values of the dependent variable and the fitted values from the regression equation, another indication of a lack of fit is that this correlation (the "multiple R") is small. In this section we state a formal procedure for testing the overall fit, or explanatory power, of a regression equation.

Suppose that the dependent variable is Y and the explanatory variables are X_1 through X_k. Then the proposed population regression equation is

$$Y = \alpha + \beta_1 X_1 + \cdots + \beta_k X_k + \varepsilon$$

To say that this equation has absolutely no explanatory power means that the same value of Y will be predicted regardless of the values of the Xs. In this case it makes no difference which values of the Xs are used, because they all lead to the same predicted value of Y. But the only way this can occur is if all of the βs are 0. So the formal hypothesis test in this section is $H_0: \beta_1 = \cdots = \beta_k = 0$ versus the alternative that at least one of the βs is not zero. If the null hypothesis can be rejected, as it can in the majority of applications, this means that the explanatory variables *as a group* provide at least some explanatory power. These hypotheses are summarized as follows.

> The null hypothesis is that all coefficients of the explanatory variables are zero. The alternative is that at least one of these coefficients is not zero.

At first glance it might appear that this null hypothesis can be tested by looking at the individual t-values. If they are all small (statistically insignificant), then the null hypothesis of no fit cannot be rejected; otherwise, it can be rejected. However, as you will see in the next section, it is possible, because of multicollinearity, to have small t-values even though the variables as a whole have *significant* explanatory power.

The correct approach is to use an F test. This is sometimes referred to as the ANOVA (analysis of variance) test because the elements for calculating the required F-value are shown in an **ANOVA table for regression**. In general, an ANOVA table analyzes different sources of variation. In the case of regression, the variation in question is the variation of the dependent variable Y. The *total variation* of this variable is the sum of squared deviations about the mean and is labeled *SST* (sum of squares total).

$$SST = \sum (Y_i - \overline{Y})^2$$

The ANOVA table splits this total variation into two parts, the part *explained* by the regression equation, and the part left *unexplained*. The unexplained part is the sum of squared residuals, usually labeled *SSE* (sum of squared errors):

$$SSE = \sum e_i^2 = \sum (Y_i - \hat{Y}_i)^2$$

The explained part is then the difference between the total and unexplained variation. It is usually labeled *SSR* (sum of squares due to regression):

$$SSR = SST - SSE$$

The F test is a formal procedure for testing whether the explained variation is large compared to the unexplained variation. Specifically, each of these sources of variation has an associated degrees of freedom (df). For the explained variation, $df = k$, which is the number of explanatory variables. For the unexplained variation, $df = n - k - 1$, the sample size minus the total number of coefficients (including the intercept term). The ratio of either sum of squares to its degrees of freedom is called a mean square, or *MS*. The two mean squares in this case are *MSR* and *MSE*, given by

$$MSR = \frac{SSR}{k}$$

and

$$MSE = \frac{SSE}{n - k - 1}$$

Note that *MSE* is the square of the standard error of estimate, that is,

$$MSE = s_e^2$$

Finally, the ratio of these mean squares is the required *F*-ratio for the test:

$$F\text{-ratio} = \frac{MSR}{MSE}$$

When the null hypothesis of no explanatory power is true, this *F*-ratio has an *F* distribution with *k* and $n - k - 1$ degrees of freedom. If the *F*-ratio is small, the explained variation is small relative to the unexplained variation, and there is evidence that the regression equation provides little explanatory power. But if the *F*-ratio is large, the explained variation is large relative to the unexplained variation, and you can conclude that the equation does have some explanatory power.

As usual, the *F*-ratio has an associated *p*-value that allows you to run the test easily. In this case the *p*-value is the probability to the *right* of the observed *F*-ratio in the appropriate *F* distribution. This *p*-value is reported in most regression outputs, along with the elements that lead up to it. If it is sufficiently small, less than 0.05, say, then you can conclude that the explanatory variables as a whole have at least some explanatory power.

Reject the null hypothesis—and conclude that these X variables have at least some explanatory power—if the F-value in the ANOVA table is large and the corresponding p-value is small.

Although this test is run routinely in most applications, there is often little doubt that the equation has some explanatory power; the only questions are how much, and which explanatory variables provide the best combination. In such cases the *F*-ratio from the ANOVA table is typically "off the charts" and the corresponding *p*-value is practically zero. On the other hand, *F*-ratios, particularly large ones, should not necessarily be used to choose between equations with different explanatory variables included.

For example, suppose that one equation with three explanatory variables has an *F*-ratio of 54 with an extremely small *p*-value—very significant. Also, suppose that another equation that includes these three variables plus a few more has an *F*-ratio of 37 and also has a very small *p*-value. (When we say small, we mean *small*. These *p*-values are probably listed as <0.0001.) Is the first equation better because its *F*-ratio is higher? Not necessarily. The two *F*-ratios imply only that both of these equations have a good deal of explanatory power. It is better to look at their s_e values (or adjusted R^2 values) and their *t*-values to choose between them.

The ANOVA table is part of the StatTools output for any regression run. It appeared for the Bendrix example in Figure 11.3, which is repeated for convenience in Figure 11.4. The ANOVA table is in rows 12 through 14. The degrees of freedom are in column B, the sums of squares are in column C, the mean squares are in column D, the *F*-ratio is in cell E13, and its associated *p*-value is in cell F13. As predicted, this *F*-ratio is "off the charts," and the *p*-value is practically zero.

This information wouldn't be much comfort for the Bendrix manager who is trying to understand the causes of variation in overhead costs. This manager already *knows* that machine hours and production runs are related positively to overhead costs—everyone in the company knows that. What he really wants is a set of explanatory variables that yields a high R^2 and a low s_e. The low *p*-value in the ANOVA tables does not guarantee these. All it guarantees is that Machine Hours and Production Runs are of *some* help in explaining variations in Overhead.

As this example indicates, the ANOVA table can be used as a screening device. If the explanatory variables do not explain a significant percentage of the variation in the dependent variable, then you can either discontinue the analysis or search for an entirely new set of explanatory variables. But even if the *F*-ratio in the ANOVA table is extremely significant (as it usually is), there is no guarantee that the regression equation provides a good enough fit for practical uses. This depends on other measures such as s_e and R^2.

Figure 11.4 Regression Output for Bendrix Example

	A	B	C	D	E	F	G
7	**Multiple Regression for Overhead**						
8		**Multiple**	**R-Square**	**Adjusted**	**StErr of**		
9	**Summary**	**R**		**R-Square**	**Estimate**		
10		0.9308	0.8664	0.8583	4108.99309		
11							
12		**Degrees of**	**Sum of**	**Mean of**	**F-Ratio**	**p-Value**	
13	**ANOVA Table**	**Freedom**	**Squares**	**Squares**			
14	**Explained**	2	3614020661	1807010330	107.0261	<0.0001	
15	**Unexplained**	33	557166199.1	16883824.22			
16							
17		**Coefficient**	**Standard**	**t-Value**	**p-Value**	**Confidence Interval 95%**	
18	**Regression Table**		**Error**			**Lower**	**Upper**
19	**Constant**	3996.678209	6603.650932	0.6052	0.5492	−9438.550632	17431.90705
20	**Machine Hours**	43.53639812	3.5894837	12.1289	<0.0001	36.23353862	50.83925761
21	**Production Runs**	883.6179252	82.25140753	10.7429	<0.0001	716.2761784	1050.959672

PROBLEMS

Note: Student solutions for problems whose numbers appear within a colored box are available for purchase at www.cengagebrain.com.

Level A

1. Explore the relationship between the selling prices (Y) and the appraised values (X) of the 148 homes in the file **P02_11.xlsx** by estimating a simple linear regression equation. Find a 95% confidence interval for the model's slope parameter (β_1). What does this confidence interval tell you about the relationship between Y and X for these data?

2. The owner of the Original Italian Pizza restaurant chain would like to predict the sales of his specialty, deep-dish pizza. He has gathered data on the monthly sales of deep-dish pizzas at his restaurants and observations on other potentially relevant variables for each of his 15 outlets in central Indiana. These data are provided in the file **P10_04.xlsx**.
  a. Estimate a multiple regression model between the quantity sold (Y) and the explanatory variables in columns C–E.
  b. Is there evidence of any violations of the key assumptions of regression analysis?
  c. Which of the variables in this equation have regression coefficients that are statistically different from zero at the 5% significance level?

  d. Given your findings in part **c**, which variables, if any, would you choose to remove from the equation estimated in part **a**? Why?

3. The file **P02_10.xlsx** contains midterm and final exam scores for 96 students in a corporate finance course. Based on a regression equation for the final exam score as a function of the midterm exam score, find a 95% confidence interval for the slope of the population regression line. State exactly what this confidence interval indicates.

4. A trucking company wants to predict the yearly maintenance expense (Y) for a truck using the number of miles driven during the year (X_1) and the age of the truck (X_2, in years) at the beginning of the year. The company has gathered the information given in the file **P10_16.xlsx**. Each observation corresponds to a particular truck.
  a. Estimate a multiple regression equation using the given data.
  b. Does autocorrelation appear to be a problem? What about multicollinearity? What about heteroscedasticity?
  c. Find 95% confidence intervals for the regression coefficients of X_1 and X_2. Based on these interval estimates, which variable, if any, would you choose to remove from the equation estimated in part **a**? Why?

5. Based on the data in the file **P02_23.xlsx** from the U.S. Department of Agriculture, explore the relationship between the number of farms (X) and the average size of a farm (Y) in the United States.

   a. Use the given data to estimate a simple linear regression model.

   b. Test whether there is sufficient evidence to conclude that the slope parameter (β_1) is *less than* zero. Use a 5% significance level.

   c. Based on your finding in part **b**, is it possible to conclude that a linear relationship exists between the number of farms and the average farm size during the given time period? Explain.

6. An antique collector believes that the price received for a particular item increases with its age and the number of bidders. The file **P10_18.xlsx** contains data on these three variables for 32 recently auctioned comparable items.

   a. Estimate an appropriate multiple regression model using the given data.

   b. Interpret the ANOVA table for this model. In particular, does this set of explanatory variables provide at least *some* power in explaining the variation in price? Report a *p*-value for this hypothesis test.

7. The file **P02_02.xlsx** contains information on over 200 movies that came out during 2006 and 2007. Run a regression of Total US Gross versus 7-day Gross, and then run a multiple regression of Total US Gross versus 7-day Gross and 14-day Gross. Report the 95% confidence interval for the coefficient of 7-day Gross in each equation. What exactly do these confidence intervals tell you about the effect of 7-day Gross on Total US Gross? Why are they not at all the same? What is the relevant population that this data set is a sample from?

8. The file **P10_10.xlsx** contains data on 150 homes that were sold recently in a particular community.

   a. Find a table of correlations between all of the variables. Do the correlations between Price and each of the other variables have the sign (positive or negative) you would expect? Explain briefly.

   b. Run a regression of Price versus Rooms. What does the 95% confidence interval for the coefficient of Rooms tell you about the effect of Rooms on Price for the entire population of such homes?

   c. Run a multiple regression of Price versus Home Size, Lot Size, Rooms, and Bathrooms. What is the 95% confidence interval for the coefficient of Rooms now? Why do you think it can be so different from the one in part **b**? Based on this regression, can you reject the null hypothesis that the population regression coefficient of Rooms is zero versus a two-tailed alternative? What does this mean?

9. Suppose that a regional express delivery service company wants to estimate the cost of shipping a package (Y) as a function of cargo type, where cargo

type includes the following possibilities: fragile, semifragile, and durable. Costs for 15 randomly chosen packages of approximately the same weight and same distance shipped, but of different cargo types, are provided in the file **P10_28.xlsx**.

   a. Estimate an appropriate multiple regression equation to predict the cost of shipping a given package.

   b. Interpret the ANOVA table for this model. In particular, do the explanatory variables included in your equation in part **a** provide at least *some* power in explaining the variation in shipping costs? Interpret the *p*-value for this hypothesis test.

10. The file **P10_05.xlsx** contains salaries for a sample of DataCom employees, along with several variables that might be related to salary. Run a multiple regression of Salary versus Years Employed, Years Education, Gender, and Number Supervised. For each of these variables, explain exactly what the results in the Coefficient, Standard Error, *t*-value, and *p*-value columns mean. Based on the results, can you reject the null hypothesis that the population coefficient of any of these variables is zero versus a two-tailed alternative at the 5% significance level? If you can, what would you probably do next in the analysis?

Level B

11. A multiple regression with 36 observations and three explanatory variables yields the ANOVA table in Table 11.1.

Table 11.1 ANOVA Table

	Degrees of Freedom	Sum of Squares
Explained		1211
Unexplained		
Total		2567

© Cengage Learning

   a. Complete this ANOVA table.

   b. Can you conclude at the 1% significance level that these three explanatory variables have *some* power in explaining variation in the dependent variable?

12. Suppose you find the ANOVA table shown in Table 11.2 for a simple linear regression.

Table 11.2 ANOVA Table

	Degrees of Freedom	Sum of Squares
Explained		52
Unexplained	87	
Total		1598

© Cengage Learning

   a. Find the correlation between X and Y, assuming that the slope of the least squares line is negative.

   b. Find the *p*-value for the test of the hypothesis of no explanatory power at all. What does it tell you in this particular case?

11-4 MULTICOLLINEARITY

Recall that the coefficient of any variable in a regression equation indicates the effect of this variable on the dependent variable, provided that the other variables in the equation remain constant. Another way of stating this is that the coefficient represents the effect of this variable on the dependent variable *in addition to* the effects of the other variables in the equation. In the Bendrix example, if Machine Hours and Production Runs are included in the equation for Overhead, the coefficient of Machine Hours indicates the *extra* amount Machine Hours explains about variation in Overhead, in addition to the amount already explained by Production Runs. Similarly, the coefficient of Production Runs indicates the extra amount Production Runs explains about variation in Overhead, in addition to the amount already explained by Machine Hours. Therefore, the relationship between an explanatory variable X and the dependent variable Y is not always accurately reflected in the coefficient of X; it depends on which *other* Xs are included or not included in the equation.

This is especially true when *multicollinearity* exists. By definition, **multicollinearity** is the presence of a fairly strong linear relationship between two or more explanatory variables, and it can make regression output difficult to interpret.

> **Multicollinearity** occurs when there is a fairly strong linear relationship among a set of explanatory variables.

Consider Example 11.2. It is a rather contrived example, but it is useful for illustrating the potential effects of multicollinearity.

EXAMPLE | 11.2 HEIGHT VERSUS FOOT LENGTH

We want to explain a person's height by means of foot length. The dependent variable is Height, and the explanatory variables are Right and Left, the length of the right foot and the length of the left foot, respectively. What can occur when Height is regressed on *both* Right and Left?

Objective   To illustrate the problem of multicollinearity when both foot length variables are used in a regression for height.

Solution

Clearly, there is no need to include both Right and Left in an equation for Height—either one of them suffices—but we include them both to make a point. It is likely that there is a large correlation between height and foot size, so you would expect this regression equation to do a good job. For example, the R^2 value will probably be large. But what about the coefficients of Right and Left? Here there is a problem. The coefficient of Right indicates the right foot's effect on Height in addition to the effect of the left foot. This additional effect is probably minimal. That is, after the effect of Left on Height has been taken into account, the extra information provided by Right is probably minimal. But it goes the other way also. The extra effect of Left, in addition to that provided by Right, is probably also minimal.

To show what can happen numerically, we used simulation to generate a hypothetical data set of heights and left and right foot lengths. We did this so that, except for random error, height is approximately 31.8 plus 3.2 times foot length (all expressed in inches). (See Figure 11.5 and the file **Heights Simulation.xlsx.** You can check the formulas in columns

Figure 11.5 One Example of Height versus Foot Length

	A	B	C	D	E	F	G	H	I	J
1	Parameters of foot size distribution				Parameters of regression, given generic foot size					
2	Mean	12.95			Intercept	31.8				
3	Stdev1	3.1			Slope	3.2				
4	Stdev2	0.2			StErr of Est	3.0				
5										
6	Generic foot size	Left	Right	Height			Correlations	Squares		
7	15.192	15.226	15.263	79.021		Left vs Right	0.997			
8	15.299	15.206	15.002	81.234		Left vs Height	0.949	0.900		
9	9.615	9.788	9.994	61.563		Right vs Height	0.943	0.889		
10	11.265	11.501	11.174	68.852						
11	11.728	11.412	11.468	72.973		Regression equation				
12	12.128	12.17	12.178	63.909		Variable	Coeff	StErr	t-value	p-value
13	11.59	11.532	11.731	71.372		Constant	32.621	1.449	22.518	0.0000
14	16.629	16.323	16.805	82.533		Left	4.586	1.323	3.465	0.0008
15	12.469	12.575	12.524	69.931		Right	−1.418	1.336	−1.062	0.2911
16	16.092	16.192	16.226	82.803		Sum of coeffs	3.168			
17	16.874	16.951	17.149	86.422						
18	16.312	16.604	16.391	86.157		SSE	980.393			
19	14.325	14.348	14.29	83.371		MSE	10.107			
20	13.279	13.344	13.251	69.753		StErr of est	3.179			
21	16.35	16.414	16.454	85.13						
22	12.82	12.606	12.742	75.441		R-square	0.901			
23	15.665	15.714	15.625	81.416		Multiple R	0.949			
24	11.79	11.752	11.984	68.128						
25	14.505	14.723	14.83	80.924						
105	8.614	8.389	8.867	58.185						
106	10.612	10.521	10.922	68.215						

A–D to see how we generated the data with the desired properties.) It is clear that the correlation between Height and either Right or Left is quite large, and the correlation between Right and Left is very close to 1 (see cells G7 to G9).

The regression output when both Right and Left are entered in the equation for Height appears at the bottom right in Figure 11.5. (We entered our own matrix formulas for the regression because we wanted them to be "live," unlike those in StatTools.) The output tells a somewhat confusing story. The multiple R and the corresponding R^2 are about as expected, given the correlations between Height and either Right or Left. In particular, the multiple R is close to the correlation between Height and either Right or Left. Also, the s_e value is quite good. It implies that predictions of height from this regression equation will typically be off by only about three inches.

Multicollinearity often causes regression coefficients to have the "wrong" sign, t-values to be too small, and p-values to be too large.

However, the coefficients of Right and Left are not at all what you might expect, given that the heights were generated as approximately 31.8 plus 3.2 times foot length. In fact, the coefficient of Right is the wrong sign—it is *negative*. Besides this "wrong" sign, the tip-off that there is a problem is that the t-value of Right is quite small and the corresponding p-value is quite large. Judging by this, you might conclude that Height and Right are either not related or are related negatively. But you know from the correlation in cell G9 that both of these conclusions are wrong. In contrast, the coefficient of Left has the "correct" sign, and its t-value and associated p-value do imply statistical significance. However, this happened by chance. Slight changes in the data could change the results completely—the coefficient of Right could become negative and insignificant, or both coefficients could become insignificant. For example, the random numbers in Figure 11.6, generated from the same model, lead to regression output where *neither* Right nor Left is statistically significant.

Figure 11.6

Another Example of Height versus Foot Length

	F	G	H	I	J
11	Regression equation				
12	Variable	Coeff	StErr	*t*-value	*p*-value
13	Constant	32.996	1.365	24.171	0.0000
14	Left	1.551	1.063	1.459	0.1477
15	Right	1.563	1.073	1.457	0.1484
16	Sum of coeffs	3.114			
17					
18	SSE	833.526			
19	MSE	8.593			
20	StErr of est	2.931			
21					
22	R-square	0.908			
23	Multiple *R*	0.953			

© Cengage Learning

Multicollinearity typically causes unreliable estimates of regression coefficients, but it does not generally cause poor predictions.

The problem is that although both Right and Left are clearly related to Height, it is impossible for the least squares method to distinguish their *separate* effects. Note that the regression equation does estimate the combined effect fairly well—the sum of the coefficients of Right and Left in cell G16 in both figures is close to the coefficient 3.2 that was used to generate the data. Also, the estimated intercept is pretty close to the intercept 31.8 that was used to generate the data. Therefore, the estimated equation will work well for predicting heights. It just does not produce reliable estimates of the individual coefficients of Right and Left. ■

This example illustrates an extreme form of multicollinearity, where two explanatory variables are very highly correlated. In general, there are various degrees of multicollinearity. In each of them, there is a linear relationship between two or more explanatory variables, and this relationship makes it difficult to estimate the individual effects of the *X*s on the dependent variable. The symptoms of multicollinearity can be "wrong" signs of the coefficients, smaller-than-expected *t*-values, and larger-than-expected (insignificant) *p*-values. In other words, variables that are really related to the dependent variable can look like they aren't related, based on their *p*-values. The reason is that their effects on *Y* are already explained by other *X*s in the equation.

Moderate to extreme multicollinearity poses a problem in many regression applications. Unfortunately, there are usually no easy remedies.

Sometimes multicollinearity is easy to spot and treat. For example, it would be silly to include both Right and Left foot length in the equation for Height. They are obviously very highly correlated and either one suffices in the equation for Height. One of them—either one—should be excluded from the equation. However, multicollinearity is not usually this easy to treat or even diagnose.

FUNDAMENTAL INSIGHT

Effect of Multicollinearity

Multicollinearity occurs when *X*s are highly correlated with one another, and it is a problem in many real regression applications. It prevents you from separating the influences of these *X*s on *Y*. In short, it prevents you from seeing clearly how the world works. However, multicollinearity is *not* a problem if you simply want to use a regression equation as a "black box" for predictions.

Suppose, for example, that you want to use regression to explain variations in salary. Three potentially useful explanatory variables are age, years of experience with the company, and years of experience in the industry. It is very likely that each of these is positively related to salary, and it is also very likely that they are very closely related to each other. However, it isn't clear which, if any, you should exclude from the regression equation. If you include all three, you are likely to find that at least one of them is insignificant (high p-value), in which case you might consider excluding it from the equation. If you do so, the s_e and R^2 values will probably not change very much—the equation will provide equally good predicted values—but the coefficients of the variables that remain in the equation could change considerably.

PROBLEMS

Level A

13. Using the data given in the file **P10_10.xlsx**, estimate a multiple regression equation to predict the price of houses in a given community. Employ all available explanatory variables. Is there evidence of multicollinearity in this model? Explain why or why not.

14. Consider the data for *Business Week*'s top U.S. MBA programs in the MBA Data sheet of the file **P10_21.xlsx**. Use these data to estimate a multiple regression model to assess whether there is a relationship between the enrollment and the following explanatory variables: (a) the percentage of international students, (b) the percentage of female students, (c) the percentage of Asian American students, (d) the percentage of minority students, and (e) the resident tuition and fees at these business schools.
   a. Determine whether each of the regression coefficients for the explanatory variables in this model is statistically different from zero at the 5% significance level. Summarize your findings.
   b. Is there evidence of multicollinearity in this model? Explain why or why not.

15. The manager of a commuter rail transportation system was recently asked by her governing board to determine the factors that have a significant impact on the demand for rides in the large city served by the transportation network. The system manager has collected data on variables that might be related to the number of weekly riders on the city's rail system. The file **P10_20.xlsx** contains these data.
   a. Estimate a multiple regression model using all of the available explanatory variables. Perform a test of significance for each of the model's regression coefficients. Are the signs of the estimated coefficients consistent with your expectations?
   b. Is there evidence of multicollinearity in this model? Explain why or why not. If multicollinearity is present, explain what you would do to remedy this problem.

Level B

16. The file **P10_05.xlsx** contains salaries for a sample of DataCom employees, along with several variables that might be related to salary.
   a. Estimate the relationship between Y (Salary) and X (Years Employed) using simple linear regression. (For this problem, ignore the other potential explanatory variables.) Is there evidence to support the hypothesis that the coefficient for the number of years employed is statistically different from zero at the 5% significance level?
   b. Estimate a multiple regression model to explain annual salaries of DataCom employees with X and X^2 as explanatory variables. Perform relevant hypothesis tests to determine the significance of the regression coefficients of these two variables. Summarize your findings.
   c. How do you explain your findings in part **b** in light of the results found in part **a**?

17. The owner of a restaurant in Bloomington, Indiana, has recorded sales data for the past 19 years. He has also recorded data on potentially relevant variables. The data appear in the file **P10_23.xlsx**.
   a. Estimate a multiple regression equation that includes annual sales as the dependent variable and the following explanatory variables: year, size of the population residing within 10 miles of the restaurant, annual advertising expenditures, and advertising expenditures in the *previous* year.
   b. Which of the explanatory variables have significant effects on sales at the 10% significance level? Do any of these results surprise you? Explain why or why not.
   c. Exclude all insignificant explanatory variables from the equation in part **a** and estimate the equation with the remaining variables. Comment on the significance of each remaining variable.
   d. Based on your analysis of this problem, does multicollinearity appear to be present in the original or revised versions of the model? Explain.

11-5 INCLUDE/EXCLUDE DECISIONS

In this section we make further use of the t-values of regression coefficients. In particular, we explain how they can be used to make **include/exclude decisions** for explanatory variables in a regression equation. Section 11-3 explained how a t-value can be used to test whether a population regression coefficient is zero. But does this mean that you should automatically include a variable if its t-value is significant and automatically exclude it if its t-value is insignificant? The decision is not always this simple.

The bottom line is that you are always trying to get the best fit possible, and the principle of parsimony suggests using the fewest number of variables. This presents a trade-off, where there not always easy answers. On the one hand, more variables certainly increase R^2, and they usually reduce the standard error of estimate s_e. On the other hand, fewer variables are better for parsimony. To help with the decision, we present several guidelines. These guidelines are not hard and fast rules, and they are sometimes contradictory. In real applications there are often several equations that are equally good for all practical purposes, and it is rather pointless to search for a single "true" equation.

FUNDAMENTAL INSIGHT

Searching for the "True" Regression Equation

Finding the best Xs (or the best form of the Xs) to include in a regression equation is undoubtedly the most difficult part of any real regression analysis. We offer two important things to keep in mind. First, it is rather pointless to search for the "true" regression equation. There are often several equations that, for all practical purposes, are equally *useful* for describing how the world works or making predictions. Second, the guidelines provided here for including and excluding variables are not ironclad rules. They typically involve choices at the margin, that is, between equations that are very similar and equally useful. In short, there is usually no single "correct answer."

Guidelines for Including/Excluding Variables in a Regression Equation

1. Look at a variable's t-value and its associated p-value. If the p-value is above some accepted significance level, such as 0.05, this variable is a candidate for exclusion.

2. Check whether a variable's t-value is less than 1 or greater than 1 in magnitude. If it is less than 1, then it is a mathematical fact that s_e will decrease (and adjusted R^2 will increase) if this variable is excluded from the equation. If it is greater than 1, the opposite will occur. Because of this, some statisticians advocate excluding variables with t-values less than 1 and including variables with t-values greater than 1.

3. Look at t-values and p-values, rather than correlations, when making include/exclude decisions. An explanatory variable can have a fairly high correlation with the dependent variable, but because of *other* variables included in the equation, it might not be needed. This would be reflected in a low t-value and a high p-value, and this variable could possibly be excluded for reasons of parsimony. This often occurs in the presence of multicollinearity.

4. When there is a group of variables that are in some sense logically related, it is sometimes a good idea to include all of them or exclude all of them. In this case, their individual t-values are less relevant. Instead, a "partial F test" (not discussed here) can be used to make the include/exclude decision.

5. Use economic and/or physical theory to decide whether to include or exclude variables, and put less reliance on t-values and/or p-values. Some variables might really *belong* in an equation because of their theoretical relationship with the dependent variable, and their low t-values, possibly the result of an unlucky sample, should not necessarily disqualify them from being in the equation. Similarly, a variable that has no economic or physical relationship with the dependent variable might have a

significant *t*-value just by chance. This does not necessarily mean that it should be included in the equation. You should not use a software package blindly to hunt for "good" explanatory variables. You should have some idea, before running the package, of which variables belong and which do not belong.

Again, these guidelines can give contradictory signals. Specifically, guideline 2 bases the include/exclude decision on whether the magnitude of the *t*-value is greater or less than 1. However, analysts who base the decision on statistical significance at the usual 5% level, as in guideline 1, typically exclude a variable from the equation unless its *t*-value is at least 2 (approximately). This latter approach is more stringent—fewer variables will be retained—but it is probably the more popular approach. However, either approach is likely to result in similar equations for all practical purposes.

In our experience, you should not agonize too much about whether to include or exclude a variable "at the margin." If you decide to exclude a variable that doesn't add much explanatory power, you get a somewhat cleaner equation, and you probably won't see any dramatic shifts in R^2 or s_e. On the other hand, if you decide to keep such a variable in the equation, the equation is less parsimonious and you have one more variable to interpret, but otherwise, there is no real penalty for including it.

We illustrate how these guidelines can be used in Example 11.3.

| EXAMPLE | **11.3 EXPLAINING SPENDING AMOUNTS AT HYTEX** |

The file **Catalog Marketing.xlsx** contains data on 1000 customers who purchased mail-order products from HyTex Company in the current year. (This is a slightly different version of the file that was used in Chapter 2.) HyTex is a direct marketer of stereo equipment, personal computers, and other electronic products. HyTex advertises entirely by mailing catalogs to its customers, and all of its orders are taken over the telephone. The company spends a great deal of money on its catalog mailings, and it wants to be sure that this is paying off in sales. For each customer there are data on the following variables:

- Age: age of the customer at the end of the current year
- Gender: coded as 1 for males, 0 for females
- Own Home: coded as 1 if customer owns a home, 0 otherwise
- Married: coded as 1 if customer is currently married, 0 otherwise
- Close: coded as 1 if customer lives reasonably close to a shopping area that sells similar merchandise, 0 otherwise
- Salary: combined annual salary of customer and spouse (if any)
- Children: number of children living with customer
- Previous Customer: coded as 1 if customer purchased from HyTex during the previous year, 0 otherwise
- Previous Spent: total amount of purchases made from HyTex during the previous year
- Catalogs: number of catalogs sent to the customer this year
- Amount Spent: total amount of purchases made from HyTex this year

Estimate and interpret a regression equation for Amount Spent based on all of these variables.

Objective   To see which potential explanatory variables are useful for explaining current year spending amounts at HyTex with multiple regression.

Solution

With this much data, 1000 observations, it is possible to set aside part of the data set for validation, as discussed in Section 10-7. Although any split can be used, we decided to base the regression on the first 750 observations and use the other 250 for validation. Therefore, you should select only the range through row 751 when defining the StatTools data set.

You can begin by entering all of the potential explanatory variables. The goal is then to exclude variables that aren't necessary, based on their t-values and p-values. The multiple regression output with all explanatory variables appears in Figure 11.7. It indicates a fairly good fit. The R^2 value is 74.7% and s_e is about \$491. Given that the actual amounts spent in the current year vary from a low of under \$50 to a high of over \$5500, with a median of about \$950, a typical prediction error of around \$491 is decent but not great.

From the p-value column, you can see that there are four variables, Age, Gender, Own Home, and Married, that have p-values well above 0.05. These are the obvious candidates for exclusion from the equation. You could rerun the equation with all four of these variables excluded, but it is a better practice to exclude one variable at a time. It is possible that when one of these variables is excluded, another one of them will become significant (the Right–Left foot phenomenon).

Figure 11.7   Regression Output with All Explanatory Variables Included

▲	A	B	C	D	E	F	G
7	Multiple Regression for Amount Spent						
8		Multiple	R-Square	Adjusted	StErr of		
9	Summary	R		R-Square	Estimate		
10		0.8643	0.7470	0.7435	491.4512858		
11							
12		Degrees of	Sum of	Mean of	F-Ratio	p-Value	
13	ANOVA Table	Freedom	Squares	Squares			
14	Explained	10	526916948.1	52691694.81	218.1631	<0.0001	
15	Unexplained	739	178486506.7	241524.3663			
16							
17		Coefficient	Standard	t-Value	p-Value	Confidence Interval 95%	
18	Regression Table		Error			Lower	Upper
19	Constant	197.3915241	85.86360421	2.2989	0.0218	28.82587637	365.9571719
20	Age	0.601445629	1.259639222	0.4775	0.6332	−1.871451979	3.074343236
21	Gender	−57.49239921	37.90222368	−1.5169	0.1297	−131.901259	16.91646056
22	Own Home	23.30677568	40.35588283	0.5775	0.5638	−55.91905687	102.5326082
23	Married	8.687679107	48.54347701	0.1790	0.8580	−86.61186861	103.9872268
24	Close	−418.7340829	45.23563466	−9.2567	<0.0001	−507.5397431	−329.9284227
25	Salary	0.017942797	0.001156152	15.5194	<0.0001	0.015673063	0.020212531
26	Children	−161.4874694	21.00318878	−7.6887	<0.0001	−202.7204941	−120.2544446
27	Previous Customer	−546.0081005	63.47937718	−8.6013	<0.0001	−670.6294978	−421.3867032
28	Previous Spent	0.268375232	0.052751039	5.0876	<0.0001	0.164815485	−0.371934979
29	Catalogs	43.94626919	2.861836645	15.3560	<0.0001	38.32797082	49.56456756

Actually, this did not happen. We first excluded the variable with the largest p-value, Married, and reran the regression. At this point, Age, Gender, and Own Home still had large p-values, so we excluded Age, the variable with the largest remaining p-value, and reran the regression. Next, we excluded Own Home, the variable with the largest remaining p-value, and finally, we excluded Gender because its p-value was still large. The resulting output appears in Figure 11.8. The R^2 and s_e values of 74.6% and $491 are almost the same as they were with all variables included, and all of the p-values are very small.

Figure 11.8 Regression Output with Insignificant Variables Excluded

	A	B	C	D	E	F	G
7	**Multiple Regression for Amount Spent**						
8		**Multiple**	**R-Square**	**Adjusted**	**StErr of**		
9	**Summary**	**R**		**R-Square**	**Estimate**		
10		0.8636	0.7458	0.7438	491.2282666		
11							
12		**Degrees of**	**Sum of**	**Mean of**	**F-Ratio**	**p-Value**	
13	**ANOVA Table**	**Freedom**	**Squares**	**Squares**			
14	**Explained**	6	526113683.9	87685613.98	363.3805	<0.0001	
15	**Unexplained**	743	179289770.9	241305.2099			
16							
17		**Coefficient**	**Standard**	**t-Value**	**p-Value**	**Confidence Interval 95%**	
18	**Regression Table**		**Error**			**Lower**	**Upper**
19	**Constant**	205.0935974	70.31522685	2.9168	0.0036	67.05342081	343.1337739
20	**Close**	−416.2462089	45.0846279	−9.2326	<0.0001	−504.7546341	−327.7377837
21	**Salary**	0.01796931	0.000904013	19.8773	<0.0001	0.016194587	0.019744033
22	**Children**	−161.1577008	20.48284328	−7.8679	<0.0001	−201.368839	−120.9465626
23	**Previous Customer**	−543.5948057	63.29880215	−8.5878	<0.0001	−667.8606044	−419.329007
24	**Previous Spent**	0.272368078	0.052536256	5.1844	<0.0001	0.1692309	0.375505256
25	**Catalogs**	43.80671576	2.854219252	15.3481	<0.0001	38.20342118	49.41001034

© Cengage Learning

Interpretation of Regression Equation

This final regression equation can be interpreted as follows:

- The coefficient of Close implies that an average customer living close to stores with this type of merchandise spent about $416 less than an average customer living far from such stores.

- The coefficient of Salary implies that, on average, about 1.8 cents of every extra salary dollar was spent on HyTex merchandise.

- The coefficient of Children implies that about $161 *less* was spent for every extra child living at home.

- The Previous Customer and Previous Spent terms are somewhat more difficult to interpret. First, both of these terms are zero for customers who didn't purchase from HyTex in the previous year. For those who did, the terms become

−544 + 0.27Previous Spent. The coefficient 0.27 implies that each extra dollar spent the previous year can be expected to contribute an extra 27 cents in the current year. The −544 literally means that if you compare a customer who didn't purchase from HyTex last year to another customer who purchased only a tiny amount, the latter is expected to spend about $544 less than the former this year. However, none of the latter customers were in the data set. A look at the data shows that of all customers who purchased from HyTex last year, almost all spent at least $100 and most spent considerably more. In fact, the median amount spent by these customers last year was about $900 (the median of all positive values for the Previous Spent variable). If you substitute this median value into the expression −544 + 0.27Previous Spent, you obtain −298. Therefore, this "median" spender from last year can be expected to spend about $298 less this year than the previous year nonspender.

■ The coefficient of Catalogs implies that each extra catalog can be expected to generate about $44 in extra spending.

We conclude this example with a couple of cautionary notes. First, if you validate this final regression equation on the other 250 customers, using the procedure from Section 10-7, you will find R^2 and s_e values of 73.2% and $490. These are very promising. They are very close to the values based on the original 750 customers. Second, we haven't tried all possibilities yet. We haven't tried nonlinear or interaction variables, nor have we looked at different coding schemes (such as treating Catalogs as a categorical variable and using dummy variables to represent it). Also, we haven't checked for non-constant error variance (Figure 11.1 is based on this data set) or looked at the potential effects of outliers. ■

PROBLEMS

Level A

18. The Undergraduate Data sheet of the file **P10_21.xlsx** contains information on 101 undergraduate business programs in the U.S., including various rankings by *Business Week*. Use multiple regression to explore the relationship between the median starting salary and the following set of potential explanatory variables: annual cost, full-time enrollment, faculty-student ratio, average SAT score, and average ACT score. Which explanatory variables should be included in a final version of this regression equation? Justify your choices. Is multicollinearity a problem? Why or why not?

19. A manager of boiler drums wants to use regression analysis to predict the number of worker-hours needed to erect the drums in future projects. Consequently, data for 36 randomly selected boilers were collected. In addition to worker-hours (Y), the variables measured include boiler capacity, boiler design pressure, boiler type, and drum type. All of these measurements are listed in the file **P10_27.xlsx**. Estimate an appropriate multiple regression model to predict the number of worker-hours needed to erect

given boiler drums using all available explanatory variables. Which explanatory variables should be included in a final version of this regression model? Justify your choices.

20. The file **P02_35.xlsx** contains data from a survey of 500 randomly selected households.
   a. In an effort to explain the variation in the size of the monthly home mortgage or rent payment, estimate a multiple regression equation that includes all of the potential household explanatory variables.
   b. Using the regression output, determine which of the explanatory variables should be excluded from the regression equation. Justify your choices.
   c. Do you obtain substantially different results if you combine First Income and Second Income into a Total Income variable and then use the latter as the only income explanatory variable?

21. The file **P02_07.xlsx** includes data on 204 employees at the (fictional) company Beta Technologies.
   a. Estimate a multiple regression equation to explain the variation in employee salaries at Beta

Technologies using all of the potential explanatory variables.

b. Using the regression output, determine which of the explanatory variables, if any, should be excluded from the regression equation. Justify your choices.

c. Regardless of your answer to part **b**, exclude the *least* significant variable (not counting the constant) and estimate the resulting equation. Would you conclude that this equation and the one from part **a** are equally good? Explain.

22. Stock market analysts are continually looking for reliable predictors of stock prices. Consider the problem of modeling the price per share of electric utility stocks (Y). Two variables thought to influence such a stock price are return on average equity (X_1) and annual dividend rate (X_2). The stock price, returns on equity, and dividend rates on a randomly selected day for 16 electric utility stocks are provided in the file **P10_19.xlsx**.

a. Estimate a multiple regression model using the given data. Include linear terms as well as an interaction term involving the return on average equity (X_1) and annual dividend rate (X_2).

b. Which of the three explanatory variables (X_1, X_2, and $X_1 X_2$) should be included in a final version of this regression model? Explain. Does your conclusion make sense in light of your knowledge of corporate finance?

11-6 STEPWISE REGRESSION[3]

Multiple regression represents an improvement over simple regression because it allows any number of explanatory variables to be included in the analysis. Sometimes, however, the large number of potential explanatory variables makes it difficult to know which variables to include. Many statistical packages provide some assistance by including automatic equation-building options. These options estimate a series of regression equations by successively adding (or deleting) variables according to prescribed rules. Generically, the methods are referred to as **stepwise regression**.

Before discussing how stepwise procedures work, consider a naive approach to the problem. You have already looked at correlation tables for indications of linear relationships. Why not simply include all explanatory variables that have large correlations with the dependent variable? There are two reasons for not doing this. First, although a variable is highly correlated with the dependent variable, it might also be highly correlated with other explanatory variables. Therefore, this variable might not be needed in the equation once the other explanatory variables have been included. This actually happens quite often.

Second, even if a variable's correlation with the dependent variable is small, its contribution when it is included with a number of other explanatory variables can be greater than anticipated. Essentially, this variable can have something unique to say about the dependent variable that none of the other variables provides, and this fact might not be apparent from the correlation table. This behavior doesn't happen as often, but it is possible.

For these reasons it is sometimes useful to let the software discover the best combination of variables by means of a stepwise procedure. There are a number of procedures for building equations in a stepwise manner, but they all share a basic idea. Suppose there is an existing regression equation and you want to add another variable to this equation from a set of variables not yet included. At this point, the variables already in the equation have explained a certain percentage of the variation of the dependent variable. The residuals represent the part still unexplained. Therefore, in choosing the next variable to enter the equation, you should pick the one that is most highly correlated with the current residuals. If none of the remaining variables is highly correlated

[3]This section can be omitted without any loss of continuity.

with the residuals, you might decide to quit. This is the essence of stepwise regression. However, besides adding variables to the equation, a stepwise procedure might delete a variable. This is sometimes reasonable because a variable entered early in the procedure might no longer be needed, given the presence of other variables that have entered subsequently.

Many statistical packages have three types of equation-building procedures: forward, backward, and stepwise. A *forward* procedure begins with no explanatory variables in the equation and successively adds one at a time until no remaining variables make a significant contribution. A *backward* procedure begins with *all* potential explanatory variables in the equation and deletes them one at a time until further deletion would do more harm than good. Finally, a true *stepwise* procedure is much like a forward procedure, except that it also considers possible deletions along the way. All of these procedures have the same basic objective—to find an equation with a small s_e and a large R^2 (or adjusted R^2). There is no guarantee that they will all produce exactly the same final equation, but in most cases their final results are very similar. The important thing to realize is that the equations estimated along the way, including the final equation, are estimated exactly as before—by least squares. Therefore, none of these procedures produces any new results. They merely take the burden off the user of having to decide ahead of time which variables to include in the equation.

StatTools implements each of the forward, backward, and stepwise procedures. To use them, select the dependent variable and a set of *potential* explanatory variables. Then specify the criterion for adding and/or deleting variables from the equation. This can be done in two ways, with an F-value or a p-value. We suggest using p-values because they are easier to understand, but either method is easy to use. In the p-value method, you select a p-value such as the default value of 0.05. If the regression coefficient for a potential entering variable would have a p-value less than 0.05 (if it were entered), then it is a candidate for entering (if the forward or stepwise procedure is used). The procedure selects the variable with the *smallest* p-value as the next entering variable. Similarly, if any currently included variable has a p-value greater than some value such as the default value of 0.10, then (with the stepwise and backward procedures) it is a candidate for leaving the equation. The methods stop when there are no candidates (according to their p-values) for entering or leaving the current equation.

Example 11.3 is a continuation of the HyTex mail-order example and illustrates these stepwise procedures.

Stepwise regression (and its variations) can be helpful in discovering a useful regression model, but it should not be used mindlessly.

FUNDAMENTAL INSIGHT

Stepwise Regression

The option to let the statistical software build the regression equation automatically makes the various versions of stepwise regression very popular with many users. However, keep in mind that it does nothing that can't be done with multiple regression, where the choice of Xs is specified manually. And sometimes a careful manual selection of the Xs to include is better than letting the software make the selection mindlessly. Stepwise regression has its place, but it shouldn't be a substitute for thoughtful analysis.

EXAMPLE | **11.3 EXPLAINING SPENDING AMOUNTS AT HYTEX (CONTINUED)**

The analysis of the HyTex mail-order data (for the first 750 customers in the data set) resulted in a regression equation that included all potential explanatory variables except for Age, Gender, Own Home, and Married. These were excluded because their t-values are large and their p-values are small (less than 0.05). Do forward, backward, and stepwise procedures produce the same regression equation for the amount spent in the current year?

Objective To use StatTools's Stepwise Regression procedure to analyze the HyTex data.

Solution

Each of these options is found in the StatTools Regression dialog box. It is just a matter of choosing the appropriate option from the Regression Type dropdown list. In each, specify Amount Spent as the dependent variable and select all of the other variables (besides Customer) as *potential* explanatory variables. Once you choose one of the stepwise types, the dialog box changes, as shown in Figure 11.9, to include a Parameters section and an "advanced" option to Include Detailed Step Information. We suggest the choices in Figure 11.9 for stepwise regression.

Figure 11.9

Dialog Box for
Stepwise Regression

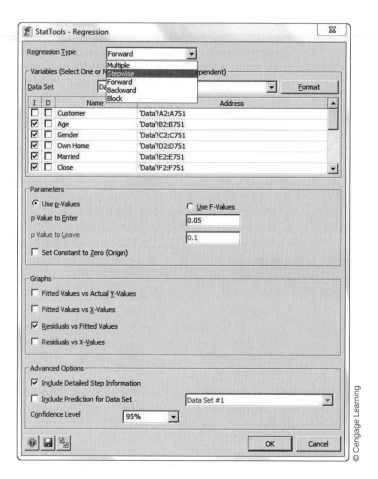

It turns out that each stepwise procedure (stepwise, forward, and backward) produces the same *final* equation that we obtained previously, with all variables except Age, Gender, Own Home, and Married included. This often happens, but not always. The stepwise and forward procedures add the variables in the order Salary, Catalogs, Close, Children, Previous Customer, and Previous Spent. The backward procedure, which starts with *all* variables in the equation, eliminates variables in the order Age, Married, Own Home, and Gender. A sample of the stepwise output appears in Figure 11.10. The variables that enter or exit the equation are listed at the bottom of the output. The usual regression output for the final equation also appears. Again, however, this final equation's output is *exactly* the same as when multiple regression is used with these particular variables. ∎

Figure 11.10   Regression Output from Stepwise Procedure

Stepwise Regression for Amount Spent

Summary	Multiple R	R-Square	Adjusted R-Square	StErr of Estimate
	0.8636	0.7458	0.7438	491.2282666

ANOVA Table	Degrees of Freedom	Sum of Squares	Mean of Squares	F-Ratio	p-Value
Explained	6	526113683.9	87685613.98	363.3805	<0.0001
Unexplained	743	179289770.9	241305.2099		

Regression Table	Coefficient	Standard Error	t-Value	p-Value	Confidence Interval 95% Lower	Upper
Constant	205.0935974	70.31522685	2.9168	0.0036	67.05342081	343.1337739
Salary	0.01796931	0.000904013	−19.8773	<0.0001	0.016194587	0.019744033
Catalogs	43.80671576	2.854219252	15.3481	<0.0001	38.20342118	49.41001034
Close	−416.2462089	45.0846279	−9.2326	<0.0001	−504.7546341	−327.7377837
Children	−161.1577008	20.48284328	−7.8679	<0.0001	−201.368839	−120.9465626
Previous Customer	−543.5948057	63.29880215	−8.5878	<0.0001	−667.8606044	−419.329007
Previous Spent	0.272368078	0.052536256	5.1844	<0.0001	0.1692309	0.375505256

Step Information	Multiple R	R-Square	Adjusted R-Square	StErr of Estimate	Enter or Exit
Salary	0.6837	0.4674	0.4667	708.6821053	Enter
Catalogs	0.7841	0.6148	0.6138	603.0853946	Enter
Close	0.8192	0.6710	0.6697	557.7263832	Enter
Children	0.8477	0.7187	0.7171	516.1356647	Enter
Previous Customer	0.8583	0.7366	0.7349	499.698203	Enter
Previous Spent	0.8636	0.7458	0.7438	491.2282666	Enter

Stepwise regression or any of its variations can be very useful for narrowing down the set of all possible explanatory variables to a set that is useful for explaining a dependent variable. However, these procedures should not be used as a substitute for thoughtful analysis. With the availability of such procedures in statistical software packages, there is sometimes a tendency to turn the analysis over to the computer and accept its output. A good analyst does not just collect as much data as possible, throw it into a software package, and blindly report the results. There should always be some rationale, whether it is based on economic theory, business experience, or common sense, for the variables that are used to explain a given dependent variable. A thoughtless use of stepwise regression can sometimes capitalize on chance to obtain an equation with a reasonably large R^2 but no useful or practical interpretation. It is very possible that such an equation will not generalize well to new data.

Finally, keep in mind that if one stepwise procedure produces slightly different outputs than another (for example, one might include a variable, the other might exclude it), the differences are typically very small and are not worth agonizing about. The two equations typically have very similar R^2 values and standard errors of estimate, and they typically produce very similar predictions. If anything, most analysts prefer the smaller equation because of parsimony, but they realize that the differences are "at the margin."

PROBLEMS

Level A

23. The Undergraduate Data sheet of the file **P10_21.xlsx** contains information on 101 undergraduate business programs in the U.S., including various rankings by *Business Week*. Use forward, backward, and stepwise regression analysis to explore the relationship between the median starting salary and the following set of potential explanatory variables: annual cost, full-time enrollment, faculty-student ratio, average SAT score, and average ACT score. Do these three methods all lead to the same regression equation? If not, do you think any of the final equations are substantially better than any of the others?

24. The file **P11_24.xlsx** contains data on the top 200 professional golfers in each of the years 2003–2011. (The same data set was used in Example 3.3 in Chapter 3.)

   a. Create one large data set in a new sheet called All Years that has the data for all nine years stacked on top of one other. (This is possible because the variables are the same in each year.) In this combined data set, create a new column called Earnings per Round, the ratio of Earnings to Rounds. Similarly, create three other new variables, Eagles per Round, Birdies per Round, and Bogies per Round.

   b. Using the data set from part **a**, run a forward regression of Earnings per Round versus the following potential explanatory variables: Age, Yards/Drive, Driving Accuracy, Greens in Regulation, Putting Average, Sand Save Pct, Eagles per Round, Birdies per Round, and Bogies per Round. Given the results, comment on what seems to be important on the professional tour in terms of earnings per round. For any variable that does *not* end up in the equation, is it omitted because it is not related to Earnings per Round or because its effect is explained by other variables in the equation?

   c. Repeat part **b** with backward regression. Do you get the same, or basically the same, results?

25. In a study of housing demand, a county assessor is interested in developing a regression model to estimate the selling price of residential properties within her jurisdiction. She randomly selects 15 houses and records the selling price in addition to the following values: the size of the house (in hundreds of square feet), the total number of rooms in the house, the age of the house, and an indication of whether the house has an attached garage. These data are listed in the file **P10_26.xlsx**.

   a. Use stepwise regression to decide which explanatory variables should be included in the assessor's statistical model. Use the p-value method with a cutoff value of 0.05 for entering and leaving. Summarize your findings.

   b. How do the results in part **a** change when the critical p-value for entering and leaving is increased to 0.10? Explain any differences between the regression equation obtained here and the one found in part **a**.

26. Continuing Problem 2 with the data in the file **P10_04.xlsx**, employ stepwise regression to evaluate your conclusions regarding the specification of a regression model to predict the sales of deep-dish pizza by the Original Italian Pizza restaurant chain. Use the p-value method with a cutoff value of 0.05 for entering and leaving. Compare your conclusions in Problem 2 with those derived from a stepwise regression.

Level B

27. How sensitive are stepwise regression results to small changes in the data? This problem allows you to explore this. The file **P11_27.xlsm** can be used to generate 100 randomly chosen observations from a given population. It contains macros that help you do this. Specifically, the means, standard deviations, and correlations for the population of 10 Xs and Y are given in rows 2–14. The macro has already been used to generate a "generic" row of data in row 16. It is done so that the Xs and Y are normally distributed with the given means, standard deviations, and correlations. Press the F9 key a few times to see how the data in row 16 change. There is also a button you can click. When you do so, the generic row 16 is copied to rows 20–119 to generate new random data, and the new random data are frozen. Click the button a few times to see how this works. Designate a StatTools data set in the range A19:L119 and run stepwise regression on the data. Then generate new data by clicking the button and run stepwise regression again. Repeat this a few times. Then explain the results. Do all of the stepwise regressions produce about the same results? Are they consistent with the parameters in the top section, particularly the correlations involving Y in row 14?

28. Repeat the previous problem at least once, using means, standard deviations, and correlations of your choice. The interesting thing you will discover is that you can't arbitrarily enter just any correlations between -1 and $+1$. For many choices, the generic row will exhibit #VALUE! errors. This means that no population could possibly have the correlations you entered. Try to find correlations that do *not* produce the #VALUE! errors.

11-7 OUTLIERS

In all of the regression examples so far, we have ignored the possibility of outliers. Unfortunately, outliers cannot be ignored in many real applications. They are often present, and they can often have a substantial effect on the results. In this section we briefly discuss outliers in the context of regression—how to detect them and what to do about them.

You probably tend to think of an **outlier** as an observation that has an extreme value for at least one variable. For example, if salaries in a data set are mostly in the $40,000 to $80,000 range, but one salary is $350,000, this observation is clearly an outlier with respect to salary. However, in a regression context outliers are not always this obvious. In fact, an observation can be considered an outlier for several reasons, and some types of outliers can be difficult to detect. An observation can be an outlier for one or more of the following reasons.

Potential Characteristics of an Outlier

Outliers can come in several forms, as indicated in this list.

- It has an extreme value for at least one variable.
- Its value of the dependent variable is much larger or smaller than predicted by the regression line, and its residual is abnormally large in magnitude. An example appears in Figure 11.11. The line in this scatterplot fits most of the points, but it misses badly on the one obvious outlier. This outlier has a large positive residual, but its Y value is not abnormally large. Its Y value is only large relative to points with the same X value that it has.

Figure 11.11

Outlier with a Large Residual

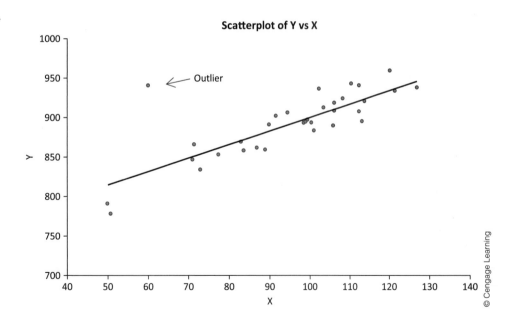

© Cengage Learning

- Its residual is not only large in magnitude, but this point "tilts" the regression line toward it. An example appears in Figure 11.12. The two lines shown are the regression lines with the outlier and without it. The outlier makes a big difference in the slope and intercept of the regression line. This type of outlier is called an **influential point**, for the obvious reason.

- Its values of individual explanatory variables are not extreme, but they fall outside the general pattern of the other observations. An example appears in Figure 11.13. Here, we assume that the two variables shown, Years (years of experience) and Rating (an employee's performance rating) are both explanatory variables for some other dependent variable (Salary) that isn't shown in the plot. The obvious outlier does not have an abnormal value of either Years or Rating, but it falls well outside the pattern of most employees.

Figure 11.12

Outlier That Tilts the Regression Line

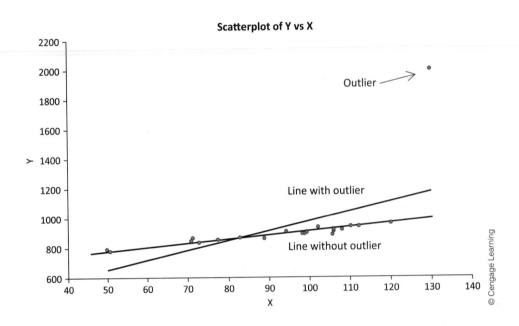

Figure 11.13

Outlier Outside the Pattern of Explanatory Variables

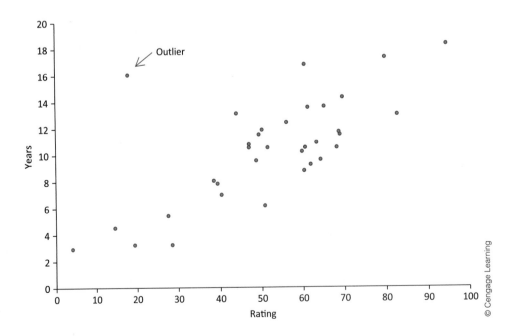

Once outliers have been identified, there is still the dilemma of what to do with them. In most cases the regression output will look "nicer" if you delete outliers, but this is not necessarily appropriate. If you can argue that the outlier isn't really a member of the relevant population, then it is appropriate and probably best to delete it. But if no such argument can be made, then it is not really appropriate to delete the outlier just to make the analysis come out better. Perhaps the best advice in this case is the advice we gave in the previous chapter: Run the analysis with the outliers and run it again without them. If the key outputs do not change much, then it does not really matter whether the outliers are included or not. If the key outputs change substantially, then report the results both with and without the outliers, along with a verbal explanation.

Example 11.4, a continuation of the bank discrimination example, illustrates this procedure.

| EXAMPLE | 11.4 POSSIBLE GENDER DISCRIMINATION IN BANK SALARIES |

Recall from Example 10.3 of the previous chapter that Fifth National Bank has 208 employees. The data for these employees are listed in the file **Bank Salaries.xlsx**. Are there any obvious outliers? In what sense are they outliers? Does it matter to the regression results, particularly those concerning gender discrimination, whether the outliers are removed?

Objective   To locate possible outliers in the bank salary data, and to see to what extent they affect the regression model.

Solution

There are several places to look for outliers. An obvious place is the Salary variable. The box plot in Figure 11.14 shows that there are several employees making substantially more in salary than most of the employees. You could consider these outliers and remove them, arguing perhaps that these are senior managers who shouldn't be included in the discrimination analysis. We leave it to you to check whether the regression results are any different with these high-salary employees than without them.

Figure 11.14

Box Plot of Salaries for Bank Data

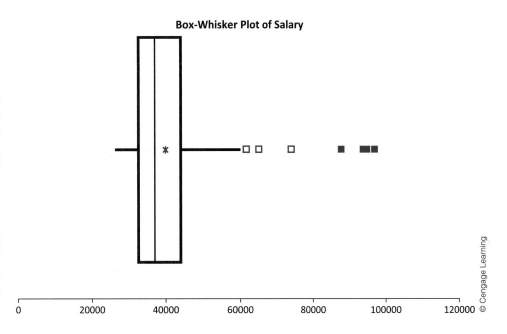

Box-Whisker Plot of Salary

© Cengage Learning

Another place to look is at a scatterplot of the residuals versus the fitted values. This type of plot (offered as an option by StatTools) shows points with abnormally large residuals. For example, we ran the regression with Female, Years1, Interaction(Years1, Female), and four education dummies, and we obtained the output and scatterplot in Figures 11.15 and 11.16. This scatterplot has several points that could be considered outliers, but we

Figure 11.15 Regression Output with Outlier Included

	A	B	C	D	E	F	G
7	**Multiple Regression for Salary**						
8		**Multiple**	**R-Square**	**Adjusted**	**StErr of**		
9	**Summary**	**R**		**R-Square**	**Estimate**		
10		0.8552	0.7314	0.7220	5935.253768		
11							
12		**Degrees of**	**Sum of**	**Mean of**	**F-Ratio**	**p-Value**	
13	**ANOVA Table**	**Freedom**	**Squares**	**Squares**			
14	Explained	7	19181659773	2740237110	77.7875	<0.0001	
15	Unexplained	200	7045447458	35227237.29			
16							
17		**Coefficient**	**Standard**	**t-Value**	**p-Value**	**Confidence Interval 95%**	
18	**Regression Table**		**Error**			**Lower**	**Upper**
19	Constant	24780.99621	1551.053232	15.9769	<0.0001	21722.4802	27839.51222
20	Years1	1456.387783	79.76132092	18.2593	<0.0001	1299.106735	1613.66883
21	Female	4898.656211	1454.087118	3.3689	0.0009	2031.347314	7765.965107
22	Educ2	546.5489826	1418.139175	0.3854	0.7004	−2249.874302	3342.972267
23	Educ3	3587.341305	1287.361495	2.7866	0.0058	1048.798035	6125.884576
24	Educ4	5862.894079	2346.570952	2.4985	0.0133	1235.69968	10490.08848
25	Educ5	9428.090372	1337.29233	7.0501	<0.0001	6791.088677	12065.09207
26	Interaction (Years1, Female)	−1029.858414	121.9237374	−8.4467	<0.0001	−1270.279372	−789.4374568

© Cengage Learning

Figure 11.16

Scatterplot of Residuals versus Fitted Values with Outlier Identified

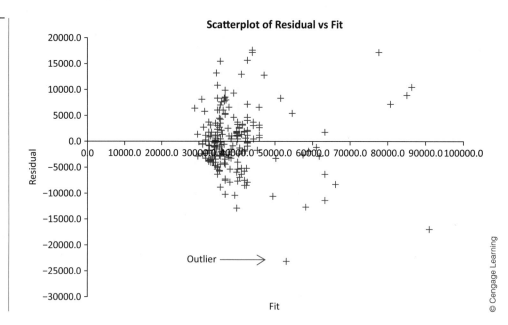

© Cengage Learning

focus on the point identified in the figure. The residual for this point is approximately −23,000. Given that s_e for this regression is approximately 5900, this residual is about four standard errors below zero—quite a lot. If you examine this point more closely, you will see that it corresponds to employee 208, who is a 62-year-old female employee in the highest job grade. She has 33 years of experience with Fifth National, she has a graduate degree, and she earns only $30,000. She is clearly an unusual employee, and there are probably special circumstances that can explain her small salary, although we can only guess at what they are.

In any case, if you delete this employee and rerun the regression with the same variables, you will obtain the output in Figure 11.17[4]. Now, recalling that gender discrimination is the key issue in this example, you can compare the coefficients of Female and Interaction (Years1, Female) in the two outputs. The coefficient of Female has dropped from 4899 to 3774. In words, the Y-intercept for the female regression line used to be about $4900 higher than for the male line; now it is only about $3800 higher. More importantly, the coefficient of Interaction (Years1, Female) has changed from −1030 to −858. This coefficient indicates how much less steep the female line for Salary versus Years1 is than the male line. So a change from −1030 to −858 indicates *less* discrimination against females now than before. In other words, this unusual female employee accounts for a good bit of the discrimination argument—although a strong argument still exists even without her. ∎

Figure 11.17 Regression Output with Outlier Excluded

	A	B	C	D	E	F	G
7	**Multiple Regression for Salary**						
8		**Multipe R**	**R-Square**	**Adjusted R-Square**	**StErr of Estimate**		
9	**Summary**						
10		0.8690	0.7551	0.7465	5670.502581		
11							
12		**Degrees of Freedom**	**Sum of Squares**	**Mean of Squares**	**F-Ratio**	**p-Value**	
13	**ANOVA Table**						
14	Explained	7	19729421790	2818488827	87.6543	<0.0001	
15	Unexplained	199	6398765306	32154599.53			
16							
17		**Coefficient**	**Standard Error**	**t-Value**	**p-Value**	**Confidence Interval 95%**	
18	**Regression Table**					Lower	Upper
19	Constant	24056.61632	1490.643417	16.1384	<0.0001	21117.13228	26996.10036
20	Years1	1449.596434	76.21848953	19.0190	<0.0001	1299.296884	1599.895983
21	Female	3774.31467	1411.666835	2.6737	0.0081	990.5690171	6558.060323
22	Educ2	777.5423804	1355.859612	0.5735	0.5670	−1896.153855	3451.238616
23	Educ3	4118.331691	1235.622784	3.3330	0.0010	1681.737257	6554.926125
24	Educ4	6366.633068	2244.710714	2.8363	0.0050	1940.161087	10793.10505
25	Educ5	10547.47488	1301.794181	8.1023	<0.0001	7980.393329	13114.55644
26	Interaction (Years1, Female)	−858.2021956	122.6128115	−6.9993	<0.0001	−1099.989332	−616.4150594

© Cengage Learning

[4]As it turns out, this employee is the last observation in the data set. An easy way to run the regression (with StatTools) without this employee is to redefine the StatTools data set so that it doesn't include this last row.

PROBLEMS

Level A

29. The file **P11.29.xlsx** contains data on the top 40 golfers in 2008. (It is a subset of the data examined in earlier chapters.) This was the year when Tiger Woods won the U.S. Open in June and then had year-ending surgery directly afterward. Using all 40 golfers, run a forward stepwise regression of Earnings per Round versus the potential explanatory variables in columns B–G. (Don't use Earnings in column H.) Then create a second data set that omits Tiger Woods and repeat the regression on this smaller data set. Are the results about the same? Explain the effect, if any, of the Tiger Woods outlier on the regression.

30. The file **P02_07.xlsx** includes data on 204 employees at the (fictional) company Beta Technologies.

   a. Run a forward stepwise regression of Annual Salary versus Gender, Age, Prior Experience, Beta Experience, and Education. Would you say this equation does a good job of explaining the variation in salaries?

   b. Add a new employee to the end of the data set, a top-level executive. The values of Gender through Annual Salary for this person are, respectively, 0, 56, 10, 15, 6, and $500,000. Run the regression in part **a** again, including this executive. Are the results much different? Is it "fair" to exclude this executive when analyzing the salary structure at this company?

Level B

31. Statistician Frank J. Anscombe created a data set to illustrate the importance of doing more than just examining the standard regression output. These data are provided in the file **P10_64.xlsx**.

   a. Regress Y_1 on X. How well does the estimated equation fit the data? Is there evidence of a linear relationship between Y_1 and X at the 5% significance level?

   b. Regress Y_2 on X. How well does the estimated equation fit the data? Is there evidence of a linear relationship between Y_2 and X at the 5% significance level?

   c. Regress Y_3 on X. How well does the estimated equation fit the data? Is there evidence of a linear relationship between Y_3 and X at the 5% significance level?

   d. Regress Y_4 on X_4. How well does the estimated equation fit the data? Is there evidence of a linear relationship between Y_4 and X_4 at the 5% significance level?

   e. Compare these four simple linear regression equations (1) in terms of goodness of fit and (2) in terms of overall statistical significance.

   f. How do you explain these findings, considering that each of the regression equations is based on a *different* set of variables?

   g. What role, if any, do outliers have on each of these estimated regression equations?

11-8 VIOLATIONS OF REGRESSION ASSUMPTIONS

Much of the theoretical research in the area of regression has dealt with violations of the regression assumptions discussed in Section 11-2. There are three issues: how to detect violations of the assumptions, what goes wrong if the violations are ignored, and what to do about them if they are detected. Detection is usually relatively easy. You can look at scatterplots, histograms, and time series graphs for visual signs of violations, and there are a number of numerical measures (many not covered here) that have been developed for diagnostic purposes. The second issue, what goes wrong if the violations are ignored, depends on the type of violation and its severity. The third issue is the most difficult to resolve. There are some relatively easy fixes and some that are well beyond the level of this book. In this section we briefly discuss some of the most common violations and a few possible remedies for them.

11-8a Nonconstant Error Variance

The second regression assumption states that the variance of the errors should be *constant* for all values of the explanatory variables. This is a lot to ask, and it is almost always violated to some extent. Fortunately, mild violations do not have much effect on the validity of the regression output, so you can usually ignore them.

A fan shape can cause an incorrect value for the standard error of estimate, so that confidence intervals and hypothesis tests for the regression coefficients are not valid.

However, one particular form of nonconstant error variance occurs fairly often and should be dealt with. This is the fan shape shown earlier in the scatterplot of Amount Spent versus Salary in Figure 11.1. As salaries increase, the variability of amounts spent also increases. Although this fan shape appears in the scatterplot of the dependent variable Amount Spent versus the explanatory variable Salary, it also appears in the scatterplot of residuals versus fitted values if you regress Amount Spent versus Salary. If you ignore this nonconstant error variance, the standard error of the regression coefficient of Salary is inaccurate, and a confidence interval for this coefficient or a hypothesis test concerning it can be misleading.

There are at least two ways to deal with this fan-shape phenomenon. The first is to use a different estimation method than least squares. It is called *weighted least squares*, and it is an option available in some statistical software packages. However, it is fairly advanced and it is not available with StatTools, so we will not discuss it here.

A logarithmic transformation of Y can sometimes cure the fan-shape problem.

The second method is simpler. When you see a fan shape, where the variability increases from left to right in a scatterplot, you can try a logarithmic transformation of the dependent variable. The reason this often works is that the logarithmic transformation squeezes the large values closer together and pulls the small values farther apart. The scatterplot of the log of Amount Spent versus Salary is in Figure 11.18. Clearly, the fan shape evident in Figure 11.1 is gone.

Figure 11.18

Scatterplot without Fan Shape

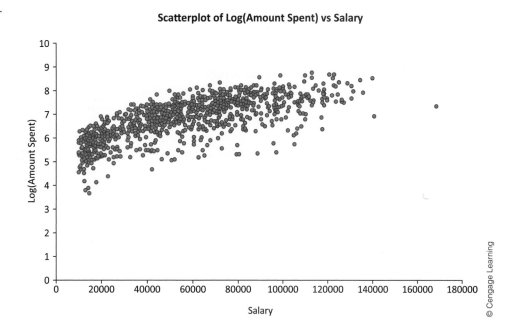

This logarithmic transformation is not a magical cure for all instances of nonconstant error variance. For example, it appears to have introduced some curvature into the plot in Figure 11.18. However, as we discussed in the previous chapter, when the distribution of the dependent variable is heavily skewed to the right, as it often is, the logarithmic transformation is worth exploring.

11-8b Nonnormality of Residuals

The third regression assumption states that the error terms are normally distributed. You can check this assumption fairly easily by forming a histogram of the residuals. You can even perform a formal test of normality of the residuals by using the procedures discussed in Section 9-5 of Chapter 9. However, unless the distribution of the residuals is severely nonnormal, the inferences made from the regression output are still approximately valid. In addition, one form of nonnormality often encountered is skewness to the right, and this can often be remedied by the same logarithmic transformation of the dependent variable that remedies nonconstant error variance.

11-8c Autocorrelated Residuals

The fourth regression assumption states that the error terms are probabilistically independent. This assumption is usually valid for cross-sectional data, but it is often violated for time series data. The problem with time series data is that the residuals are often correlated with nearby residuals, a property called **autocorrelation of residuals**. The most frequent type of autocorrelation is positive autocorrelation. For example, if residuals separated by one month are correlated—called *lag 1 autocorrelation*—in a positive direction, then an overprediction in January, say, will likely lead to an overprediction in February, and an underprediction in January will likely lead to an underprediction in February. If this autocorrelation is large, serious prediction errors can occur if it isn't dealt with appropriately.

A Durbin–Watson statistic below 2 signals that nearby residuals are positively correlated with one another.

A numerical measure has been developed to check for lag 1 autocorrelation. It is called the **Durbin–Watson statistic** (after the two statisticians who developed it), and it is quoted automatically in the regression output of many statistical software packages. The Durbin–Watson (DW) statistic is scaled to be between 0 and 4. Values close to 2 indicate very little lag 1 autocorrelation, values below 2 indicate positive autocorrelation, and values above 2 indicate negative autocorrelation.

Because *positive* autocorrelation is the usual culprit, the question becomes how much below 2 the DW statistic must be before you should react. There is a formal hypothesis test for answering this question, and a set of tables appears in some statistics texts. Without going into the details, we simply state that when the number of time series observations, n, is about 30 and the number of explanatory variables is fairly small, say, 1 to 5, then any DW statistic less than 1.2 should get your attention. If n increases to around 100, then you shouldn't be concerned unless the DW statistic is below 1.5.

If e_i is the ith residual, the formula for the DW statistic is

$$\text{DW} = \frac{\sum_{i=2}^{n}(e_i - e_{i-1})^2}{\sum_{i=1}^{n}e_i^2}$$

This is obviously not very attractive for hand calculation, so the StatDurbinWatson function is included in StatTools. To use it, run any regression and check the option to create a graph of residuals versus fitted values. This automatically creates columns of fitted values and residuals. Then enter the formula

=StatDurbinWatson(*ResidRange*)

in any cell, substituting the actual range of residuals for "ResidRange."

The following continuation of Example 11.1 with the Bendrix manufacturing data—the only time series data set we have analyzed with regression—checks for possible lag 1 autocorrelation.

EXAMPLE | **11.1 EXPLAINING OVERHEAD COSTS AT BENDRIX (CONTINUED)**

Is there any evidence of lag 1 autocorrelation in the Bendrix data when Overhead is regressed on Machine Hours and Production Runs?

Objective To use the Durbin–Watson statistic to check whether there is any lag 1 auto-correlation in the residuals from the Bendrix regression model for overhead costs.

Solution

You should run the usual multiple regression and check that you want a graph of residuals versus fitted values. The results are shown in Figure 11.19. The residuals are listed in column D. Each represents how much the regression overpredicts (if negative) or underpredicts (if positive) the overhead cost for that month. You can check for lag 1 autocorrelation in two ways, with the DW statistic and by examining the time series graph of the residuals in Figure 11.20.

The DW statistic is calculated in cell F45 of Figure 11.19 with the formula

=StatDurbinWatson(D45:D80)

(Remember that StatDurbinWatson is *not* a built-in Excel® function. It is available only if StatTools is loaded.) Based on our guidelines for DW values, 1.3131 suggests positive

---

Figure 11.19 Regression Output with Residuals and DW Statistic

⬜	A	B	C	D	E	F
45	*Graph Data*	**Overhead**	**Fit**	**Residual**		**Durbin-Watson for residuals**
46	1	99798	98391.35059	1406.649409		1.313
47	2	87804	85522.33322	2281.666779		
48	3	93681	92723.59538	957.4046174		
49	4	82262	82428.09201	−166.0920107		

© Cengage Learning

Figure 11.20

Time Series Graph of Residuals

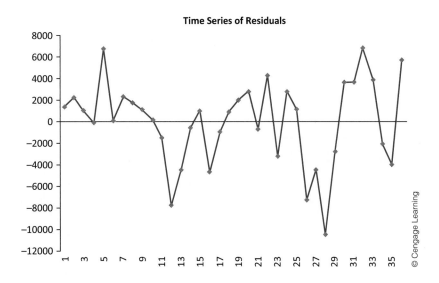

Time Series of Residuals

© Cengage Learning

autocorrelation—it is less than 2—but not enough to cause concern.[5] This general conclusion is supported by the time series graph. Serious autocorrelation of lag 1 would tend to show longer runs of residuals alternating above and below the horizontal axis—positives would tend to follow positives, and negatives would tend to follow negatives. There is some indication of this behavior in the graph but not an excessive amount. ∎

What should you do if the DW statistic signals significant autocorrelation? Unfortunately, the answer to this question would take us much more deeply into time series analysis than we can go in this book. Suffice it to say that time series analysis in the context of regression can become very complex, and there are no easy fixes for the autocorrelation that often occurs.

PROBLEMS

Level A

32. A company produces electric motors for use in home appliances. One of the company's production managers is interested in examining the relationship between the dollars spent per month in inspecting finished motor products (X) and the number of motors produced during that month that were returned by dissatisfied customers (Y). He has collected the data in the file **P10_03.xlsx** to explore this relationship for the past 36 months.
   a. Estimate a simple linear regression equation using the given data and interpret it. What does the ANOVA table indicate for this model?
   b. Examine the residuals of the regression equation. Do you see evidence of any violations of the regression assumptions?
   c. Conduct a Durbin–Watson test on the model's residuals. Interpret the result of this test.
   d. In light of your result in part **c**, do you recommend modifying the original regression model? If so, how would you revise it?

33. Examine the relationship between the average utility bills for homes of a particular size (Y) and the average monthly temperature (X). The data in the file **P10_07.xlsx** include

the average monthly bill and temperature for each month of the past year.
   a. Use the given data to estimate a simple linear regression equation. How well does the estimated regression model fit the given data? What does the ANOVA table indicate for this model?
   b. Examine the residuals of the regression equation. Do you see evidence of any violations of the regression assumptions?
   c. Conduct a Durbin–Watson test on the model's residuals. Interpret the result of this test.
   d. In light of your result in part **c**, do you recommend modifying the original regression model? If so, how would you revise it?

34. The manager of a commuter rail transportation system was recently asked by her governing board to predict the demand for rides in the large city served by the transportation network. The system manager has collected data on variables thought to be related to the number of weekly riders on the city's rail system. The file **P10_20.xlsx** contains these data.
   a. Estimate a multiple regression equation using all of the available explanatory variables. What does the ANOVA table indicate for this model?
   b. Is there evidence of auto correlated residuals in this model? Explain why or why not.

11-9 PREDICTION

Once you have estimated a regression equation from a set of data, you might want to use this equation to predict the value of the dependent variable for *new* observations. As an example, suppose that a retail chain is considering opening a new store in one of several proposed locations. It naturally wants to choose the location that will result in the largest revenues. The problem is that the revenues for the new locations are not yet known.

[5]A more formal test, using Durbin–Watson tables, supports this conclusion.

They can be observed only after stores are opened in these locations, and the chain cannot afford to open more than one store at the current time. An alternative is to use regression analysis. Using data from *existing* stores, the chain can run a regression of the dependent variable revenue on several explanatory variables such as population density, level of wealth in the vicinity, number of competitors nearby, ease of access given the existing roads, and so on.

Assuming that the regression equation has a reasonably large R^2 and, even more important, a reasonably small s_e, the chain can then use this equation to predict revenues for the proposed locations. Specifically, it will gather values of the explanatory variables for each of the proposed locations, substitute these into the regression equation, and look at the predicted revenue for each proposed location. All else being equal, the chain will probably choose the location with the highest predicted revenue.

As another example, suppose that you are trying to explain the starting salaries for undergraduate college students. You want to predict the *mean* salary of all graduates with certain characteristics, such as all male marketing majors from state-supported universities. To do this, you first gather salary data from a sample of graduates from various universities. Included in this data set are relevant explanatory variables for each graduate in the sample, such as the type of university, the student's major, GPA, years of work experience, and so on. You then use these data to estimate a regression equation for starting salary and substitute the relevant values of the explanatory variables into the regression equation to obtain the required prediction.

Regression can be used to predict Y for a single observation, or it can be used to predict the mean Y for many observations, all with the same X values.

These two examples illustrate two types of prediction problems in regression. The first problem, illustrated by the retail chain example, is the more common of the two. Here the objective is to predict the value of the dependent variable for one or more *individual* members of the population. In this specific example you are trying to predict the future revenue for several potential locations of the new store. In the second problem, illustrated by the salary example, the objective is to predict the *mean* of the dependent variable for all members of the population with certain values of the explanatory variables. In the first problem you are predicting an individual value; in the second problem you are predicting a mean.

The second problem is inherently easier than the first in the sense that the resulting prediction is bound to be more accurate. The reason is intuitive. Recall that the mean of the dependent variable for any fixed values of the explanatory variables lies on the population regression line. Therefore, if you can accurately estimate this line—that is, if you can accurately estimate the regression coefficients—you can accurately predict the required mean. In contrast, most individual points do *not* lie on the population regression line. Therefore, even if your estimate of the population regression line is perfectly accurate, you still cannot predict exactly where an individual point will fall.

Stated another way, when you predict a mean, there is a single source of error: the possibly inaccurate estimates of the regression coefficients. But when you predict an individual value, there are two sources of error: the inaccurate estimates of the regression coefficients and the inherent variation of individual points around the regression line. This second source of error often dominates the first.

We illustrate these comments in Figure 11.21. For the sake of illustration, the dependent variable is salary and the single explanatory variable is years of experience with the company. Let's suppose that you want to predict either the salary for a particular employee with 10 years of experience or the mean salary of all employees with 10 years of experience. The two lines in this graph represent the population regression line (which in reality is unobservable) and the estimated regression line. For each prediction problem the point prediction—the best guess—is the value above 10 on the estimated regression line. The error in predicting the mean occurs because the two lines in the graph are not the

Figure 11.21

**Prediction Errors
for an Individual
Value and a Mean**

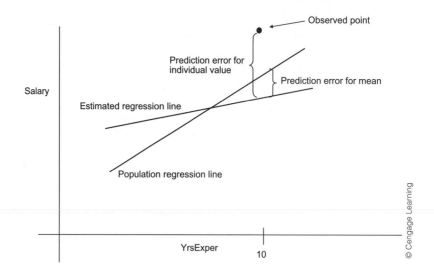

same—that is, the estimated line is not quite correct. The error in predicting the individual value (the point shown in the graph) occurs because the two lines are not the same and also because this point does not lie on the population regression line.

One general aspect of prediction becomes apparent by looking at this graph. If we let Xs denote the explanatory variables, predictions for values of the Xs close to their means are likely to be more accurate than predictions for Xs far from their means. In the graph, the mean of YrsExper is about 7. (This is approximately where the two lines cross.) Because the slopes of the two lines are different, they get farther apart as YrsExper gets farther away from 7 (on either side). As a result, predictions tend to become less accurate.

It is more difficult to predict for extreme Xs than for Xs close to the mean. Trying to predict for Xs beyond the range of the data set (extrapolation) is quite risky.

This phenomenon shows up as higher standard errors of prediction as the Xs get farther away from their means. However, for extreme values of the Xs, there is another problem. Suppose, for example, that all values of YrsExper in the data set are between 1 and 15, and you attempt to predict the salary for an employee with 25 years of experience. This is called *extrapolation*; you are attempting to predict beyond the limits of the sample.

The problem here is that there is no guarantee, and sometimes no reason to believe, that the relationship within the range of the sample is valid outside of this range. It is perfectly possible that the effect of years of experience on salary is considerably different in the 25-year range than in the range of the sample. If it is, then extrapolation is bound to yield inaccurate predictions. In general, you should avoid extrapolation whenever possible. If you really want to predict the salaries of employees with 25-plus years of experience, you should include some employees of this type in the original sample.

We now discuss how to make predictions and how to estimate their accuracy, both for individual values and for means. To keep it simple, we first assume that there is a single explanatory variable X. We choose a fixed "trial" value of X, labeled X_0, and predict the value of a single Y or the mean of all Ys when X equals X_0. For both prediction problems the **point prediction**, or best guess, is found by substituting into the right side of the estimated regression equation. Graphically, this is the height of the estimated regression line above X_0.

> To calculate a **point prediction**, substitute the given values of the Xs into the estimated regression equation.

To measure the accuracy of these point predictions, you calculate a standard error for each prediction. These **standard errors of prediction** can be interpreted in the usual way. For example, you are about 68% certain that the actual values will be within one standard error of the point predictions, and you are about 95% certain that the actual values will be within two standard errors of the point predictions. For the individual prediction problem, the standard error is labeled s_{ind} and is given by Equation (11.4). As indicated by the approximate equality on the right, when the sample size n is large and X_0 is fairly close to $\overline{X}$, the last two terms inside the square root are relatively small, and this standard error of prediction can be approximated by s_e, the standard error of estimate.

Standard Error of Prediction for a Single Y

$$s_{ind} = s_e \sqrt{1 + \frac{1}{n} + \frac{(X_0 - \overline{X})^2}{\sum_{i=1}^{n}(X_i - \overline{X})^2}} \simeq s_e \qquad (11.4)$$

For the prediction of the mean, the standard error is labeled s_{mean} and is given by Equation (11.5). Here, if X_0 is fairly close to $\overline{X}$, the last term inside the square root is relatively small, and this standard error of prediction is approximately equal to the expression on the right.

Standard Error of Prediction for the Mean Y

$$s_{mean} = s_e \sqrt{\frac{1}{n} + \frac{(X_0 - \overline{X})^2}{\sum_{i=1}^{n}(X_i - \overline{X})^2}} \simeq s_e / \sqrt{n} \qquad (11.5)$$

These standard errors can be used to calculate a 95% prediction interval for an individual value and a 95% confidence interval for a mean value. Exactly as in Chapter 8, you go out a t-multiple of the relevant standard error on either side of the point prediction. The t-multiple is the value that cuts off 0.025 probability in the right-hand tail of a t distribution with $n - 2$ degrees of freedom.

The term *prediction interval* (rather than confidence interval) is used for an individual value because an individual value of Y is not a population *parameter*; it is an individual point. However, the interpretation is basically the same. If you calculate a 95% prediction interval for many members of the population, you can expect their actual Y values to fall within the corresponding prediction intervals about 95% of the time.

To see how all of this can be implemented in Excel, we revisit the Bendrix example of predicting overhead expenses.

EXAMPLE | **11.1 PREDICTING OVERHEAD AT BENDRIX (CONTINUED)**

We have already used regression to analyze overhead expenses at Bendrix, based on 36 months of data. Suppose Bendrix expects the values of Machine Hours and Production Runs for the next three months to be 1430, 1560, 1520, and 35, 45, 40, respectively. What are their point predictions and 95% prediction intervals for Overhead for these three months?

Objective To predict Overhead at Bendrix for the next three months, given anticipated values of Machine Hours and Production Runs.

Solution

StatTools has the capability to provide predictions and 95% prediction intervals, but you must set up a second data set to capture the results. This second data set can be placed next to (or below) the original data set. It should have the same variable name headings, and it should include values of the explanatory variable to be used for prediction. (It can also have LowerLimit95 and UpperLimit95 headings, but these are optional and will be added by StatTools if they do not already exist.) For this example we called the original data set Original Data and the new data set Data for Prediction. The regression dialog box and results in Data for Prediction appear in Figures 11.22 and 11.23. In the dialog box, note that the Prediction option is checked, and the second data set is specified in the corresponding dropdown list.

Figure 11.22

Regression Dialog Box with Predictions Checked

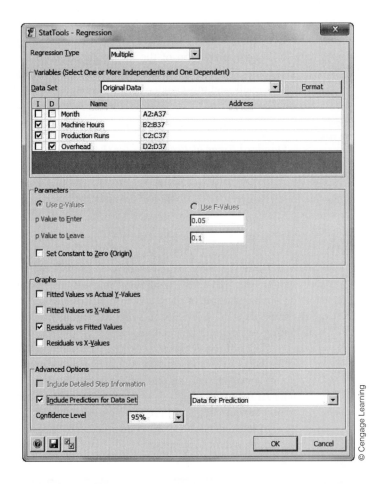

Figure 11.23

Prediction of Overhead

	F	G	H	I	J	K
1	Month	Machine Hours	Production Runs	Overhead	LowerLimit95	UpperLimit95
2	37	1430	35	97180.35	88700.80	105659.91
3	38	1560	45	111676.27	103002.95	120349.58
4	39	1520	40	105516.72	96993.16	114040.28

The text box in Figure 11.23 explains how the second data set range should be set up. Initially, you should enter the given values in the Month, Machine Hours, and Production Runs columns. Then when the regression is run (with the Prediction option checked), the values in the Overhead, LowerLimit95, and UpperLimit95 columns will be filled in. (Again, if you do not create LowerLimit95 and UpperLimit95 columns as part of the second data set, StatTools will do it for you.)

The Overhead values in column I are the point predictions for the next three months, and the LowerLimit95 and UpperLimit95 values in column J and K indicate the 95% prediction intervals. You can see from the wide prediction intervals how much uncertainty remains. The reason is the relatively large standard error of estimate, s_e. If you could halve the value of s_e, the length of the prediction interval would be only half as large. Contrary to what you might expect, this is not a sample size problem. That is, a larger sample size would probably *not* produce a smaller value of s_e. The problem is that Machine Hours and Production Runs are not perfectly correlated with Overhead. The only way to decrease s_e and get more accurate predictions is to find other explanatory variables that are more closely related to Overhead. ■

StatTools provides prediction intervals for individual values, as you have just seen, but it does not provide confidence intervals for the mean of Y, given a set of Xs. To obtain such a confidence interval, you can use Equation (11.5) to get the required standard error of prediction (for simple regression only), or you can approximate it by $s_e/\sqrt{n}$.

PROBLEMS

Level A

35. The file **P10_05.xlsx** contains salaries for a sample of DataCom employees, along with several variables that might be related to salary.
  a. Estimate an appropriate multiple regression equation to predict the annual salary of a given DataCom employee.
  b. Given the estimated regression model, predict the annual salary of a male employee who served in a similar department at another company for five years prior to coming to work at DataCom. This man, a graduate of a four-year collegiate business program, has been supervising six subordinates in the sales department since joining the organization seven years ago.
  c. Find a 95% prediction interval for the salary earned by the employee in part **b**.
  d. Find a 95% confidence interval for the mean salary earned by all DataCom employees sharing the characteristics provided in part **b**.
  e. How can you explain the difference between the widths of the intervals in parts **c** and **d**?

36. The owner of a restaurant in Bloomington, Indiana, has recorded sales data for the past 19 years. He has also recorded data on potentially relevant variables. The data appear in the file **P10_23.xlsx**.

  a. Estimate a regression equation for sales as a function of population, advertising in the current year, and advertising in the previous year. Can you expect predictions of sales in *future* years to be very accurate if they are based on this regression equation? Explain.
  b. The company would like to predict sales in the next year (year 20). It doesn't know what the population will be in year 20, so it assumes no change from year 19. Its planned advertising level for year 20 is $30,000. Find a prediction and a 95% prediction interval for sales in year 20.

37. A power company located in southern Alabama wants to predict the peak power load (i.e., Y, the maximum amount of power that must be generated each day to meet demand) as a function of the daily high temperature (X). A random sample of 25 summer days is chosen, and the peak power load and the high temperature are recorded on each day. The file **P10_40.xlsx** contain these observations.
  a. Use the given data to estimate a simple linear regression equation. How well does the regression equation fit the given data?
  b. Examine the residuals of the estimated regression equation. Do you see evidence of any violations of the assumptions regarding the errors of the regression model?
  c. Calculate the Durbin–Watson statistic on the model's residuals. What does it indicate?

d. Given your result in part **d**, do you recommend modifying the original regression model in this case? If so, how would you revise it?

e. Use the final version of your regression equation to predict the peak power load on a summer day with a high temperature of 90 degrees.

f. Find a 95% prediction interval for the peak power load on a summer day with a high temperature of 90 degrees.

g. Find a 95% confidence interval for the *average* peak power load on all summer days with a high temperature of 90 degrees.

11-10 CONCLUSION

In these two chapters on regression, you have seen how useful regression analysis can be for a variety of business applications and how statistical software such as StatTools enables you to obtain relevant output—both graphical and numerical—with very little effort. However, you have also seen that there are many concepts that you must understand well before you can use regression analysis appropriately. Given that user-friendly software is available, it is all too easy to generate enormous amounts of regression output and then misinterpret or misuse much of it.

At the very least, you should (1) be able to interpret the standard regression output, including statistics on the regression coefficients, summary measures such as R^2 and s_e, and the ANOVA table; (2) know what to look for in the many scatterplots available; (3) know how to use dummy variables, interaction terms, and nonlinear transformations to improve a fit; and (4) be able to spot clear violations of the regression assumptions. However, we haven't covered everything. Indeed, many entire books are devoted exclusively to regression analysis. Therefore, you should recognize when you *don't* know enough to handle a regression problem such as nonconstant error variance or autocorrelation appropriately. In this case, you should consult a statistical expert.

Summary of Key Terms

Term	Symbol	Explanation	Excel	Page	Equation
Statistical model		A theoretical model including several assumptions that must be satisfied, at least approximately, for inferences from regression output to be valid		534	11.1
Error	ε	The difference between the actual Y value and the predicted value from the population regression line		535	
Homoscedasticity (and heteroscedasticity)		Equal (and unequal) variance of the dependent variable for different values of the explanatory variables		535, 536	
Parsimony		The concept of explaining the most with the least		539	
Standard error of a regression coefficient	s_b	Measures how much the estimates of a regression coefficient vary from sample to sample	StatTools/Regression & Classification/Regression	540	
Confidence interval for a regression coefficient		An interval likely to contain the population regression coefficient	StatTools/Regression & Classification/Regression	541	
t-value for test of regression coefficient	t	The ratio of the estimate of a regression coefficient to its standard error, used to test whether the coefficient is 0	StatTools/Regression & Classification/Regression	542	11.3

(continued)

Term	Symbol	Explanation	Excel	Page	Equation
Hypothesis test for a regression coefficient		Typically, a two-tailed test, where the null hypothesis is that the regression coefficient is 0	StatTools/Regression & Classification/Regression	542	
ANOVA table for regression		Used to test whether the explanatory variables, as a whole, have any significant explanatory power	StatTools/Regression & Classification/Regression	543	
Multicollinearity		Occurs when there is a fairly strong linear relationship between explanatory variables		547	
Include/exclude decisions		Guidelines for deciding whether to include or exclude potential explanatory variables		551	
Stepwise regression		A class of automatic equation-building methods, where variables are added (or deleted) in order of their importance	StatTools/Regression & Classification/Regression	556	
Outliers		Observations that lie outside the general pattern of points and can have a substantial effect on the regression model		561	
Influential point		A point that can "tilt" the regression line		561	
Autocorrelation of residuals		Lack of independence in the series of residuals, especially relevant for time series data		568	
Durbin–Watson statistic		A measure of the autocorrelation between residuals, especially useful for time series data	**= StatDurbin Watson(range)**, a StatTools function	568	
Point prediction		The predicted value of Y from the regression equation		572	
Standard errors of prediction	s_{ind}, s_{mean}	Measures of the accuracy of prediction when predicting Y for an individual observation, or predicting the mean of all Y's, for fixed values of the explanatory variables	StatTools/Regression & Classification/Regression	573	11.4, 11.5

PROBLEMS

Conceptual Questions

C.1. Suppose a regression output produces the following 99% confidence interval for one of the regression coefficients: $[-32.47, -16.88]$. Given this information, should an analyst reject the null hypothesis that this population regression coefficient is equal to zero? Explain your answer.

C.2. Explain why it is not possible to estimate a linear regression model that contains *all* dummy variables associated with a particular categorical explanatory variable.

C.3. Suppose you have a data set that includes *all* of the professional athletes in a given sport over a given period of time, such as *all* NFL football players during the 2008–2010 seasons, and you use regression to estimate a variable of interest. Are the inferences discussed in this chapter relevant? Recall that we have been assuming that the data represent a random sample of some larger population. In this sports example, what is the larger population—or is there one?

C.4. Distinguish between the test of significance of an individual regression coefficient and the ANOVA test. When, if ever, are these two statistical tests essentially equivalent?

C.5. Which of these intervals based on the same estimated regression equation with fixed values of the explanatory variables would be *wider*: (1) a 95% prediction interval for an individual value of Y or (2) a 95% confidence interval for the mean value of Y? Explain your answer. How do you interpret the wider of these two intervals in words?

C.6. Regression outputs from virtually all statistical packages look the same. In particular, the section on coefficients lists the coefficients, their standard errors, their t-values, their p-values, and (possibly) 95% confidence intervals for them. Explain how all of these are related.

C.7. If you are building a regression equation in a forward stepwise manner, that is, by adding one variable at a time, explain why it is useful to monitor the adjusted R^2 and the standard error of estimate. Why is it not as useful to monitor R^2?

C.8. You run a regression with two explanatory variables and notice that the p-value in the ANOVA table is extremely small but the p-values of both explanatory variables are larger than 0.10. What is the probable reason? Can you conclude that neither explanatory variable does a good job in predicting the dependent variable?

C.9. Why are outliers sometimes called *influential* observations? What *could* happen to the slope of a regression of Y versus a single X when an outlier is included versus when it is not included? Will this necessarily happen when a point is an outlier? Answer by giving a couple of examples.

C.10. The Durbin-Watson test is for detecting lag 1 autocorrelation in the residuals. Which values of DW signal *positive* autocorrelation? If you observe such a DW value but ignore it, what might go wrong with predictions based on the regression equation? Specifically, if the data are time series data, and your goal is to predict the next six months, what might go wrong with the predictions?

Level A

38. For 12 straight weeks you have observed the sales (in number of cases) of canned tomatoes at Mr. D's super-market. Each week you kept track of the following:

- Was a promotional notice placed in all shopping carts for canned tomatoes?

- Was a coupon given for canned tomatoes?
- Was a price reduction (none, 1, or 2 cents off) given?

The file **P11_38.xlsx** contains these data.

a. Use multiple regression to determine how these factors influence sales.

b. Discuss how you can tell whether autocorrelation, heteroscedasticity, or multicollinearity might be a problem.

c. Predict sales of canned tomatoes during a week in which Mr. D's uses a shopping cart notice, a coupon, and a one-cent price reduction.

39. The file **P11_39.xlsx** contains quarterly data on pork sales. Price is in dollars per hundred pounds, quantity sold is in billions of pounds, per capita income is in dollars, U.S. population is in millions, and GDP is in billions of dollars.

a. Use the data to develop a regression equation that could be used to predict the quantity of pork sold during future periods. Discuss how you can tell whether heteroscedasticity, autocorrelation, or multicollinearity might be a problem.

b. Suppose that during each of the next two quarters, price is 45, U.S. population is 240, GDP is 2620, and per capita income is 10,000. (These are in the units described previously.) Predict the quantity of pork sold during each of the next two quarters.

40. The file **P11_40.xlsx** contains monthly sales for a photography studio and the price charged per portrait during each month. Use regression to estimate an equation for predicting the current month's sales from last month's sales and the current month's price.

a. If the price of a portrait during month 21 is $30, predict month 21 sales.

b. Discuss how you can tell whether autocorrelation, multicollinearity, or heteroscedasticity might be a problem.

41. The file **P11_41.xlsx** contains data on a motel chain's revenue and advertising. Note that column C is simply column B "pushed down" a row.

a. If the goal is to get the best-fitting regression equation for Revenue, which of the Advertising variables should be used? Or is it better to use both?

b. Using the best-fitting equation from part **a**, make predictions for the motel chain's revenues during the next four quarters. Assume that advertising during each of the next four quarters is $50,000.

c. Does autocorrelation of the residuals from the best-fitting equation appear to be a problem?

42. The file **P11_42.xlsx** contains the quarterly revenues (in millions of dollars) of a utility company for a seven-year period. The goal is to use these data to build a multiple regression model that can be used to forecast future revenues.

a. Which variables should be included in the regression? Explain your rationale for including or excluding variables. (Look at a time series graph for clues.)

b. Interpret the coefficients of your final equation.

c. Make a forecast for revenues during the next quarter, quarter 29. Also, estimate the probability that revenue in the next quarter will be at least $150 million. (*Hint*: Use the standard error of prediction and the fact that the errors are approximately normally distributed.)

43. The belief that larger majorities for a president in a presidential election help the president's party increase its representation in the House and Senate is called the *coattail* effect. The file **P11_43.xlsx** lists the percentage by which each president since 1948 won the election and the number of seats in the House and Senate gained (or lost) during each election by the elected president's party. Are these data consistent with the idea of presidential coattails?

44. When potential workers apply for a job that requires extensive manual assembly of small intricate parts, they are initially given three different tests to measure their manual dexterity. The ones who are hired are then periodically given a performance rating on a 0 to 100 scale that combines their speed and accuracy in performing the required assembly operations. The file **P11_44.xlsx** lists the test scores and performance ratings for a randomly selected group of employees. It also lists their seniority (months with the company) at the time of the performance rating.

a. Look at a matrix of correlations. Can you say with certainty (based only on these correlations) that the R^2 value for the regression will be at least 35%? Why or why not?

b. Is there any evidence (from the correlation matrix) that multicollinearity will be a problem? Why or why not?

c. Run the regression of Performance Rating versus all four explanatory variables. List the equation, the value of R^2, and the value of s_e. Do all of the coefficients have the signs (negative or positive) you would expect? Briefly explain.

d. Referring to the equation in part **c**, if a worker (outside of the 80 in the sample) has 15 months of seniority and test scores of 57, 71, and 63, find a prediction and an approximate 95% prediction interval for this worker's Performance Rating score.

e. One of the *t*-values for the coefficients in part **c** is less than 1. Explain briefly why this occurred. Does it mean that this variable is not related to Performance Rating?

f. Arguably, the three test measures provide overlapping (or redundant) information. For the

sake of parsimony (explaining "the most with the least"), it might be sensible to regress Performance Rating versus only two explanatory variables, Seniority and Average Test, where Average Test is the average of the three test scores—that is, Average Test = (Test1 + Test2 + Test3)/3. Run this regression and report the same measures as in part **c**: the equation itself, R^2, and s_e. Can you argue that this equation is just as good as the equation in part **c**? Explain briefly.

45. Nicklaus Electronics manufactures electronic components used in the computer and space industries. The annual rate of return on the market portfolio and the annual rate of return on Nicklaus Electronics stock for the last 36 months are listed in the file **P11_45.xlsx**. The company wants to calculate the *systematic risk* of its common stock. (It is systematic in the sense that it represents the part of the risk that Nicklaus shares with the market as a whole.) The rate of return Y_t in period *t* on a security is hypothesized to be related to the rate of return m_t on a market portfolio by the equation

$$Yt = \alpha + \beta m_t + \varepsilon_t$$

Here, α is the risk-free rate of return, β is the security's systematic risk, and ε_t is an error term. Estimate the systematic risk of the common stock of Nicklaus Electronics. Would you say that Nicklaus stock is a risky investment? Why or why not?

46. The auditor of Kaefer Manufacturing uses regression analysis during the analytical review stage of the firm's annual audit. The regression analysis attempts to uncover relationships that exist between various account balances. Any such relationship is subsequently used as a preliminary test of the reasonableness of the reported account balances. The auditor wants to determine whether a relationship exists between the balance of accounts receivable at the end of the month and that month's sales. The file **P11_46.xlsx** contains data on these two accounts for the last 36 months. It also shows the sales levels two months before month 1.

a. Is there any statistical evidence to suggest a relationship between the monthly sales level and accounts receivable?

b. Referring to part **a**, would the relationship be described any better by including this month's sales and the previous month's sales (called *lagged sales*) in the equation for accounts receivable? What about adding the sales from more than a month ago to the equation? For this problem, why might it make accounting sense to include lagged sales variables in the equation? How do you interpret their coefficients?

c. During month 37, which is a fiscal year-end month, the sales were $1,800,000. The reported accounts receivable balance was $3,000,000. Does this reported amount seem consistent with past experience? Explain.

47. A company gives prospective managers four separate tests for judging their potential. For a sample of 30 managers, the test scores and the subsequent job effectiveness ratings (Rating) given one year later are listed in the file **P11_47.xlsx**.

    a. Look at scatterplots and the table of correlations for these five variables. Does it appear that a multiple regression equation for Rating, with the test scores as explanatory variables, will be successful? Can you foresee any problems in obtaining accurate estimates of the individual regression coefficients?

    b. Estimate the regression equation that includes all four test scores, and find 95% confidence intervals for the coefficients of the explanatory variables. How can you explain the negative coefficient of Test3, given that the correlation between Rating and Test3 is positive?

    c. Can you reject the null hypothesis that these test scores, as a whole, have no predictive ability for job effectiveness at the 1% level? Why or why not?

    d. If a new prospective manager has test scores of 83, 74, 65, and 77, what do you predict his job effectiveness rating will be in one year? What is the standard error of this prediction?

48. Confederate Express is attempting to determine how its monthly shipping costs depend on the number of units shipped during a month. The file **P11_48.xlsx** contains the number of units shipped and total shipping costs for the last 15 months.

    a. Use regression to determine a relationship between units shipped and monthly shipping costs.

    b. Plot the errors for the predictions in order of time sequence. Is there any unusual pattern?

    c. You have now been told that there was a trucking strike during months 11 through 15, and you believe that this might have influenced shipping costs. How can the analysis in part **a** be modified to account for the effects of the strike? After accounting for the effects of the strike, does the unusual pattern in part **b** disappear?

49. The file **P11_49.xlsx** contains monthly data on fatal automobile crashes in the U.S. in each of eight three-hour intervals. Suppose you didn't have the data on the midnight to 3AM time interval. How well could multiple regression be used to predict the data for this interval? Which time intervals are most useful in this prediction? Is multicollinearity a problem?

Level B

50. You want to determine the variables that influence bus usage in major American cities. For 24 cities, the following data are listed in the file **P11_50.xlsx**:

    - Bus travel (annual, in thousands of hours)
    - Income (average per capita income)
    - Population (in thousands)
    - Land area (in square miles)

    a. Use these data to fit the multiplicative equation

    $$BusTravel = \alpha Income^{\beta_1} Population^{\beta_2} LandArea^{\beta_3}$$

    b. Are all variables significant at the 5% level?

    c. Interpret the estimated values of β_1, β_2, and β_3.

51. The file **P11_51.xlsx** contains data on 80 managers at a large (fictitious) corporation. The variables are Salary (current annual salary), Years Experience (years of experience in the industry), Years Here (years of experience with this company), and Mgt Level (current level in the company, coded 1 to 4). You want to regress Salary on the potential explanatory variables. What is the best way to do so? Specifically, how should you handle Mgt Level? Should you include both Years Experience and Years Here or only one of them, and if only one, which one? Present your results, and explain them and your reasoning behind them.

52. A toy company has assigned you to analyze the factors influencing the sales of its most popular doll. The number of these dolls sold during the last 23 years is given in the file **P11_52.xlsx**. The following factors are thought to influence sales of these dolls:

    - Was there a recession?
    - Were the dolls on sale at Christmas?
    - Was there an upward trend over time?

    a. Determine an equation that can be used to predict annual sales of these dolls. Make sure that all variables in your equation are significant at the 10% level.

    b. Interpret the coefficients in your equation.

    c. Are there any outliers?

    d. Is heteroscedasticity or autocorrelation of residuals a problem?

    e. During the current year (year 24), a recession is predicted and the dolls will be put on sale at Christmas. There is a 1% chance that sales of the dolls will exceed what value? You can assume here that heteroscedasticity and autocorrelation are *not* a problem. (*Hint*: Use the standard error of prediction and the fact that the errors are approximately normally distributed.)

53. The file **P11_53.xlsx** shows the "yield curve" (at monthly intervals). For example, in January 1985 the annual rate on a three-month T-bill was 7.76% and the annual rate on a 30-year government bond was 11.45%. Use regression to determine which interest rates tend to move together most closely. (Source: International Investment and Exchange Database. Developed by Craig Holden, Indiana University School of Business.)

54. The Keynesian school of macroeconomics believes that increased government spending leads to increased growth. The file **P11_54.xlsx** contains the following annual data:

- Government spending as percentage of GDP (gross domestic product)
- Percentage annual growth in annual GDP

Are these data consistent with the Keynesian school of economics? (Source: *Wall Street Journal*.)

55. The June 1997 issue of *Management Accounting* gave the following rule for predicting your current salary if you are a managerial accountant. Take $31,865. Next, add $20,811 if you are top management, add $3604 if you are senior management, or subtract $11,419 if you are entry management. Then add $1105 for every year you have been a managerial accountant. Add $7600 if you have a master's degree or subtract $12,467 if you have no college degree. Add 11,257 if you have a professional certification. Finally, add $8667 if you are male.

   a. How do you think the journal derived this method of predicting an accountant's current salary? Be specific.

   b. How could a managerial accountant use this information to determine whether he or she is significantly underpaid?

56. A business school committee was charged with studying admissions criteria to the school. Until that time, only juniors were admitted. Part of the committee's task was to see whether freshman courses would be equally good predictors of success as freshman and sophomore courses combined. Here, we take "success" to mean doing well in I-core (the integrated core, a combination of the junior level finance, marketing, and operations courses, F301, M301, and P301). The file **P11_56.xlsx** contains data on 250 students who had just completed I-core. For each student, the file lists their grades in the following courses:

- M118 (freshman)—finite math
- M119 (freshman)—calculus
- K201 (freshman)—computers
- W131 (freshman)—writing
- E201, E202 (sophomore)—micro- and macroeconomics
- L201 (sophomore)—business law
- A201, A202 (sophomore)—accounting
- E270 (sophomore)—statistics
- I-core (junior)—finance, marketing, and operations

Except for I-core, each value is a grade point for a specific course (such as 3.7 for an A−). For I-core, each value is the average grade point for the three courses comprising I-core.

   a. The I-core grade point is the eventual dependent variable in a regression analysis. Look at the correlations between all variables. Is multicollinearity likely to be a problem? Why or why not?

   b. Run a multiple regression using all of the potential explanatory variables. Now, eliminate the variables as follows. (This is a reasonable variation of the procedures discussed in the chapter.) Look at 95% confidence intervals for their coefficients (as usual, not counting the intercept term). Any variable whose confidence interval contains the value zero is a candidate for exclusion. For all such candidates, eliminate the variable with the *t*-value lowest in magnitude. Then rerun the regression, and use the same procedure to possibly exclude another variable. Keep doing this until 95% confidence intervals of the coefficients of all remaining variables do *not* include zero. Report this final equation, its R^2 value, and its standard error of estimate s_e.

   c. Give a quick summary of the properties of the final equation in part **b**. Specifically, (1) do the variables have the "correct" signs, (2) which courses tend to be the best predictors, (3) are the predictions from this equation likely to be much good, and (4) are there any obvious violations of the regression assumptions?

   d. Redo part **b**, but now use as your potential explanatory variables only courses taken in the freshman year. As in part **b**, report the final equation, its R^2, and its standard error of estimate s_e.

   e. Briefly, do you think there is enough predictive power in the freshman courses, relative to the freshman and sophomore courses combined, to change to a sophomore admit policy? (Answer only on the basis of the regression results; don't get into other merits of the argument.)

57. The file **P11_57.xlsx** has (somewhat old) data on several countries. The variables are listed here.

- Country: name of country
- GNP per Capita: GNP per capita
- Population Growth: average annual percentage change in population, 1980–1990
- Calories: daily per capita calorie content of food used for domestic consumption
- Life Expectancy: average life expectancy of newborns given current mortality conditions
- Fertility: births per woman given current fertility rates

With data such as these, cause and effect are difficult to determine. For example, does low Life Expectancy cause GNP per Capita to be low, or vice versa? Therefore, the purpose of this problem is to experiment with the following sets of dependent and explanatory variables. In each case, look at scatterplots (and use economic reasoning) to find and estimate the best form of the equation, using only linear and logarithmic variables. Then interpret precisely what each equation is saying.

   a. Dependent: Life Expectancy; Explanatories: Calories, Fertility

   b. Dependent: Life Expectancy; Explanatories: GNP per Capita, Population Growth

   c. Dependent: GNP per Capita; Explanatories: Population Growth, Calories, Fertility

58. Suppose that an economist has been able to gather data on the relationship between demand and price for a particular product. After analyzing scatterplots and using economic theory, the economist decides to estimate an equation of the form $Q = aP^b$, where Q is quantity demanded and P is price. An appropriate regression analysis is then performed, and the estimated parameters turn out to be $a = 1000$ and $b = -1.3$. Now consider two scenarios: (1) the price increases from \$10 to \$12.50; (2) the price increases from \$20 to \$25.

   a. Do you predict the percentage decrease in demand to be the same in scenario 1 as in scenario 2? Why or why not?

   b. What is the predicted percentage decrease in demand in scenario 1? What about scenario 2? Be as exact as possible. (*Hint*: Remember from economics that an elasticity shows directly what happens for a "small" percentage change in price. These changes aren't that small, so you'll have to do some calculating.)

59. A human resources analyst believes that in a particular industry, the wage rate (\$/hr) is related to seniority by an equation of the form $W = ae^{bS}$, where W equals wage rate and S equals seniority (in years). However, the analyst suspects that both parameters, a and b, might depend on whether the workers belong to a union. Therefore, the analyst gathers data on a number of workers, both union and nonunion, and estimates the following equation with regression:

$$\ln(W) = 2.14 + 0.027S + 0.12U + 0.006SU$$

Here $\ln(W)$ is the natural log of W, U is 1 for union workers and 0 for nonunion workers, and SU is the product of S and U.

   a. According to this model, what is the predicted wage rate for a nonunion worker with 0 years of seniority? What is it for a union worker with 0 years of seniority?

   b. Explain exactly what this equation implies about the predicted effect of seniority on wage rate for a nonunion worker and for a union worker.

60. A company has recorded its overhead costs, machine hours, and labor hours for the past 60 months. The data are in the file **P11_60.xlsx**. The company decides to use regression to explain its overhead hours linearly as a function of machine hours and labor hours. However, recognizing good statistical practice, it decides to estimate a regression equation for the first 36 months and then validate this regression with the data from the last 24 months. That is, it will substitute the values of machine and labor hours from the last 24 months into the regression equation that is based on the first 36 months and see how well it does.

   a. Run the regression for the first 36 months. Explain briefly why the coefficient of labor hours is not significant.

   b. For this part, use the regression equation from part **a** with both variables still in the equation (even though one was insignificant). Fill in the fitted and residual columns for months 37 through 60. Then do relevant calculations to see whether the R^2 (or multiple R) and the standard error of estimate s_e are as good for these 24 months as they are for the first 36 months. Explain your results briefly. (*Hint*: Remember the meaning of the multiple R and the standard error of estimate.)

61. Pernavik Dairy produces and sells a wide range of dairy products. Because most of the dairy's costs and prices are set by a government regulatory board, most of the competition between the dairy and its competitors takes place through advertising. The controller of Pernavik has developed the sales and advertising levels for the last 52 weeks. These appear in the file **P11_61.xlsx**. Note that the advertising levels for the three weeks prior to week 1 are also listed. The controller wonders whether Pernavik is spending too much money on advertising. He argues that the company's contribution-margin ratio is about 10%. That is, 10% of each sales dollar goes toward covering fixed costs. This means that each advertising dollar has to generate at least \$10 of sales or the advertising is not cost-effective. Use regression to determine whether advertising dollars are generating this type of sales response. (*Hint*: It is very possible that the sales value in any week is affected not only by advertising this week, but also by advertising levels in the past one, two, or three weeks. These are called *lagged* values of advertising. Try regression models with lagged values of advertising included, and see whether you get better results.)

62. Pierce Company manufactures drill bits. The production of the drill bits occurs in lots of 1000 units. Due to the intense competition in the industry and the correspondingly low prices, Pierce has undertaken a study of the manufacturing costs of each of the products it manufactures. One part of this study concerns the overhead costs associated with producing the drill bits. Senior production personnel have determined that the number of lots produced, the direct labor hours used, and the number of production runs per month might help to explain the behavior of overhead costs. The file **P11_62.xlsx** contains the data on these variables for the past 36 months.

a. How well can you can predict overhead costs on the basis of these variables with a linear regression equation? Why might you be disappointed with the results?

b. A production supervisor believes that labor hours and the number of production run setups affect overhead because Pierce uses a lot of supplies when it is working on the machines and because the machine setup time for each run is charged to overhead. As he says, "When the rate of production increases, we use overtime until we can train the additional people that we require for the machines. When the rate of production falls, we incur idle time until the surplus workers are transferred to other parts of the plant. So it would seem to me that there will be an additional overhead cost whenever the level of production changes. I would also say that because of the nature of this rescheduling process, the bigger the change in production, the greater the effect of the change in production on the increase in overhead." How might you use this information to find a better regression equation than in part **a**? (*Hint*: Develop a new explanatory variable, and assume that the number of lots produced in the month preceding month 1 was 5964.)

63. Danielson Electronics manufactures color television sets for sale in a highly competitive marketplace. Recently Ron Thomas, the marketing manager of Danielson Electronics, has been complaining that the company is losing market share because of a poor-quality image, and he has asked that the company's major product, the 25-inch console model, be redesigned to incorporate a higher quality level. The company general manager, Steve Hatting, is considering the request to improve the product quality but is not convinced that consumers will be willing to pay the additional expense for improved quality. As the company controller, you are in charge of determining the cost-effectiveness of improving the quality of the television sets. With the help of the marketing staff, you have obtained a summary of the average retail price of the company's television set and the prices of 29 competitive sets. In addition, you have obtained from *The Shoppers' Guide*, a magazine that evaluates and reports on various consumer products, a quality rating of the television sets produced by Danielson Electronics and its competitors. The file

P11_63.xlsx summarizes these data. According to *The Shoppers' Guide*, the quality rating, which varies from 0 to 10 (10 being the highest level of quality), considers such factors as the quality of the picture, the frequency of repair, and the cost of repairs. Discussions with the product design group suggest that the cost of manufacturing this type of television set is $125 + Q^2$, where Q is the quality rating.

a. Regress Average Price versus Quality Rating. Does the regression equation imply that customers are willing to pay a premium for quality? Explain.

b. Given the results from part **a**, is there **a** preferred level of quality for this product? Assume that the quality level will affect only the price charged and not the level of sales of the product.

c. How might you answer part **b** if the level of sales is also affected by the quality level (or alternatively, if the level of sales is affected by price)?

64. The file **P11_64.xlsx** contains data on gasoline consumption and several economic variables. The variables are gasoline consumption for passenger cars (Gas Used), service station price excluding taxes (Station Price), retail price of gasoline including state and federal taxes (Retail Price), Consumer Price Index for all items (CPI), Consumer Price Index for public transportation (CPIT), number of registered passenger cars (Cars), average miles traveled per gallon (MPG), and real per capita disposable income (Income).

a. Regress Gas Used linearly versus CPIT, Cars, MPG, Income, and Deflated Price, where Deflated Price is the deflated retail price of gasoline (Retail Price divided by CPI). What signs would you expect the coefficients to have? Do they have these signs? Which of the coefficients are statistically significant at the 5% significance level?

b. Suppose the government makes the claim that for every one cent of tax on gasoline, there will be a $1 billion increase in tax revenue. Use the estimated equation in part **a** to support or refute the government's claim.

65. On October 30, 1995, the citizens of Quebec went to the polls to decide the future of their province. They were asked to vote "Yes" or "No" on whether Quebec, a predominantly French-speaking province, should secede from Canada and become a sovereign country. The "No" side was declared the winner, but only by a thin margin. Immediately following the vote, however, allegations began to surface that the result was closer than it should have been. [Source: Cawley and Sommers (1996)]. In particular, the ruling separatist Parti Québécois, whose job was to decide which ballots were rejected, was accused by the "No" voters of systematic electoral fraud by voiding thousands of "No" votes in the predominantly allophone and anglophone electoral divisions of Montreal. (An *allophone* refers to someone

whose first language is neither English nor French. An *anglophone* refers to someone whose first language is English.)

Cawley and Sommers examined whether electoral fraud had been committed by running a regression, using data from the 125 electoral divisions in the October 1995 referendum. The dependent variable was REJECT, the percentage of rejected ballots in the electoral division. The explanatory variables were as follows:

- ALLOPHONE: percentage of allophones in the electoral division
- ANGLOPHONE: percentage of anglophones in the electoral division
- REJECT94: percentage of rejected votes from that electoral division during a similar referendum in 1994
- LAVAL: dummy variable equal to 1 for electoral divisions in the Laval region, 0 otherwise
- LAV_ALL: interaction (i.e., product) of LAVAL and ALLOPHONE

The estimated regression equation (with *t*-values in parentheses) is

$$\text{Predicted REJECT} = 1.112 + \underset{(5.68)}{\,} \underset{(4.34)}{0.020 \text{ ALLOPHONE}}$$

$$+ \underset{(0.12)}{0.001 \text{ ANGLOPHONE}} + \underset{(2.64)}{0.223 \text{ REJECT94}}$$

$$- \underset{(-8.61)}{3.773 \text{ LAVAL}} + \underset{(15.62)}{0.387 \text{ LAV\_ALL}}$$

The R^2 value was 0.759. Based on this analysis, Cawley and Sommers state that, "The evidence presented here suggests that there were voting irregularities in the October 1995 Quebec referendum, especially in Laval." Discuss how they came to this conclusion.

66. Suppose you are trying to explain variations in salaries for technicians in a particular field of work. The file **P11_66.xlsx** contains annual salaries for 200 technicians. It also shows how many years of experience each technician has, as well as his or her education level. There are four education levels, as explained in the comment in cell D1. Three suggestions are put forth for the relationship between Salary and these two explanatory variables:

- You should regress Salary linearly versus the two given variables, Experience and Education.
- All that really matters in terms of education is whether the person got a college degree or not. Therefore, you should regress Salary linearly versus Experience and a dummy variable indicating whether he or she got a college degree.
- Each level of education might result in different jumps in salary. Therefore, you should regress Salary linearly versus Experience and dummy variables for the different education levels.

a. Run the indicated regressions for each of these three suggestions. Then (1) explain what each equation is saying and how the three are different (focus here on the coefficients), (2) which you prefer, and (3) whether (or how) the regression results in your preferred equation contradict the average salary results shown in the Pivot Table sheet of the file.

b. Consider the four workers shown on the Prediction sheet of the file. (These are four new workers, not among the original 200.) Using your preferred equation, calculate a predicted salary and a 95% prediction interval for each of these four workers.

c. It turns out (you don't have to check this) that the interaction between years of experience and education level is *not* significant for this data set. In general, however, argue why you might expect an interaction between them for salary data of technical workers. What form of interaction would you suspect? (There is not necessarily one right answer, but argue convincingly one way or the other for a positive or a negative interaction.)

67. The file **P03_55.xlsx** contains baseball data on all MLB teams from during the years 2004–2011. For each year and team, the total salary and the number of (regular-season) wins are listed.

a. Rearrange the data so that there are six columns: Team, Year, Salary Last Year, Salary This Year, Wins Last Year, and Wins This Year. You don't need rows for 2004 rows, because the data for 2003 isn't available for Salary Last Year and Wins Last Year. Your ending data set should have 7*30 rows of data.

b. Run a multiple regression for Wins This Year versus the other variables (besides Team). Then run a forward stepwise regression with these same variables. Compare the two equations, and explain exactly what the coefficients of the equation from the forward method imply about wins.

c. The Year variable *should* be insignificant. Is it? Why would it be contradictory for the "true" coefficient of Year to be anything other than zero?

d. Statistical inference from regression equations is all about inferring from the given data to a larger population. Does it make sense to talk about a larger population in this situation? If so, what is the larger population?

68. Do the previous problem, but use the basketball data on all NBA teams in the file **P03_56.xlsx**.

69. Do the previous problem, but use the football data on all NFL teams in the file **P03_57.xlsx**.

70. The file **P03_65.xlsx** contains basketball data on all NBA teams for five seasons. The SRS (simple rating system) variable is a measure of how good a team is in any given year. (It is explained in more detail in the comment in cell F3.)

a. Given the explanation of SRS, it makes sense to use multiple regression, with PTS and O_PTS as the explanatory variables, to predict SRS. Do you get a good fit?

b. Suppose instead that the goal is to predict Wins. Try multiple regression, using the variables in columns G–AH or variables calculated from them. For example, instead of FG and FGA, you could try FG/FGA, the fraction of attempted field goals made. You will have to guard against exact multicollinearity. For example, PTS can be calculated exactly from FG, 3P, and FT. This is a good time to use some form of stepwise regression. How well is your best equation able to predict Wins?

71. Do the preceding problem, but now use the football data in the file **P03_66.xlsx**. (This file contains offensive and defensive ratings in the OSRS and DSRS variables, but you can ignore them for this problem. Focus only on the SRS rating in part **a**.)

72. The file **P03_63.xlsx** contains 2009 data on R&D expenses and many financial variables for 85 U.S. publicly traded companies in the computer and electronic product manufacturing industry. The question is whether R&D expenses can be predicted from any combination of the potential variables. Use scatterplots, correlations (possibly on nonlinear transformations of variables) to search for promising relationships. Eventually, find a regression that seems to provide the best explanatory power for R&D expenses. Interpret this best equation and indicate how good a fit it provides.

CASE 11.1 ARTSY CORPORATION[6]

Artsy Corporation has been sued in U.S. Federal Court on charges of sex discrimination in employment under Title VII of the Civil Rights Act of 1964.[7] The litigation at contention here is a class-action lawsuit brought on behalf of all females who were employed by the company, or who had applied for work with the company, between 1979 and 1987. Artsy operates in several states, runs four quite distinct businesses, and has many different types of employees. The allegations of the plaintiffs deal with issues of hiring, pay, promotions, and other "conditions of employment."

In such large class-action employment discrimination lawsuits, it has become common for statistical evidence to play a central role in the determination of guilt or damages. In an interesting twist on typical legal procedures, a precedent has developed in these cases that plaintiffs may make a prima facie case purely in terms of circumstantial statistical evidence. If that statistical evidence is reasonably strong, the burden of proof shifts to the defendants to rebut the plaintiffs' statistics with other data, other analyses of the same data, or nonstatistical testimony. In practice, statistical arguments often dominate the proceedings of such Equal Employment Opportunity (EEO) cases. Indeed, in this case the statistical data used as evidence filled numerous computer tapes, and the supporting statistical analysis comprised thousands of pages of

printouts and reports. We work here with a typical subset that pertains to one contested issue at one of the company's locations.

The data in the file **C11_01.xlsx** relate to the pay of 256 employees on the hourly payroll at one of the company's production facilities. The data include an identification number (ID) that would identify the person by name or social security number; the person's gender (Gender), where 0 denotes female and 1 denotes male; the person's job grade in 1986 (Grade); the length of time (in years) the person had been in that job grade as of December 31, 1986 (Time in Grade); and the person's weekly pay rate as of December 31, 1986 (Rate). These data permit a statistical examination of one of the issues in the case—fair pay for female employees. We deal with one of three pay classes of employees—those on the biweekly payroll at one of the company's locations at Pocahantas, Maine.

The plaintiffs' attorneys have proposed settling the pay issues in the case for this group of female employees for a "back pay" lump payment to female employees of 25% of their pay during the period 1979 to 1987. It is your task to examine the data statistically for evidence in favor of, or against,

[6]This case was contributed by Peter Kolesar from Columbia University.

[7]Artsy is an actual corporation, and the data given in this case are real, but the name has been changed to protect the firm's true identity.

the charges. You are to advise the lawyers for the company on how to proceed. Consider the following issues as they have been laid out to you by the attorneys representing the firm:

1. Overall, how different is pay by gender? Are the differences in pay statistically significant? Does a statistical significance test have meaning in a case like this? If so, how should it be performed? Lay out as succinctly as possible the arguments that you anticipate the plaintiffs will make with this data set.

2. The company wishes to argue that a legitimate explanation of the pay-rate differences may be the difference in job grades. (In this analysis, we will tacitly assume that each person's job grade is, in fact, appropriate for him or her, even though the plaintiffs' attorneys have charged that females have been unfairly kept in the lower grades. Other statistical data, not available here, are used in that analysis.) The lawyers ask, "Is there a relatively easy way to understand, analyze, and display the pay differences by job grade? Is it easy enough that it could be presented to an average jury without confusing them?" Again, use the data to anticipate the possible arguments of the plaintiffs. To what extent does job grade appear to explain the pay-rate differences between the genders? Propose and carry out appropriate hypothesis tests or confidence intervals to check whether the difference in pay between genders is statistically significant within each of the grades.

3. In the actual case, the previous analysis suggested to the attorneys that differences in pay rates are due, at least in part, to differences in job grades. They had heard that in another EEO case, the dependence of pay rate on job grade had been investigated with regression analysis. Perform a simple linear regression of pay rate on job grade for them. Interpret the results fully. Is the regression significant? How much of the variability in pay does job grade account for? Carry out a full check of the quality of your regression. What light does this shed on the pay fairness issue? Does it help or hurt the company? Is it fair to the female employees?

4. It is argued that seniority within a job grade should be taken into account because the company's written pay policy explicitly calls for the consideration of this factor. How different are times in grade by gender? Are they enough to matter?

5. Artsy's legal team wants an analysis of the simultaneous influence of grade and time in grade on pay. Perform a multiple regression of pay rate versus grade and time in grade. Is the regression significant? How much of the variability in pay rates is explained by this model? Will this analysis help your clients? Could the plaintiffs effectively attack it? Consider residuals in your analysis of these issues.

6. Organize your analyses and conclusions in a brief report summarizing your findings for your client, Artsy Corporation. Be complete but succinct. Be sure to advise them on the settlement issue. Be as forceful as you can be in arguing "the Artsy Case" without misusing the data or statistical theory. Apprise your client of the risks they face, by showing them the forceful and legitimate counterargument the female plaintiffs could make.

CASE | 11.2 HEATING OIL AT DUPREE FUELS COMPANY[8]

Dupree Fuels Company is facing a difficult problem. Dupree sells heating oil to residential customers. Given the amount of competition in the industry, both from other home heating oil suppliers and from electric and natural gas utilities, the price of the oil supplied and the level of service are critical in determining a company's success. Unlike electric and natural gas customers, oil customers are exposed to the risk of running out of fuel. Home heating oil suppliers therefore have to guarantee that the customer's oil tank will not be allowed to run dry. In fact, Dupree's service pledge is,

[8]Case Studies 11.2 through 11.4 are based on problems from *Advanced Management Accounting*, 2nd edition, by Robert S. Kaplan and Anthony A. Atkinson, 1989, Upper Saddle River, NJ: Prentice Hall. We thank them for allowing us to adapt their problems.

"50 free gallons on us if we let you run dry." Beyond the cost of the oil, however, Dupree is concerned about the perceived reliability of his service if a customer is allowed to run out of oil.

To estimate customer oil use, the home heating oil industry uses the concept of a *degree-day*, equal to the difference between the average daily temperature and 68 degrees Fahrenheit. So if the average temperature on a given day is 50, the degree-days for that day will be 18. (If the degree-day calculation results in a negative number, the degree-day number is recorded as 0.) By keeping track of the number of degree-days since the customer's last oil fill, knowing the size of the customer's oil tank, and estimating the customer's oil consumption as a function of the number of degree-days, the oil supplier can estimate when the customer is getting low on fuel and then resupply the customer.

Dupree has used this scheme in the past but is disappointed with the results and the computational burdens it places on the company. First, the system requires that a consumption-per-degree-day figure be estimated for each customer to reflect that customer's consumption habits, size of home, quality of home insulation, and family size. Because Dupree has more than 1500 customers, the computational burden of keeping track of all of these customers is enormous. Second, the system is crude and unreliable. The consumption per degree-day for each customer is computed by dividing the oil consumption during the preceding year by the degree-days during the preceding year. Customers have tended to use less fuel than estimated during the colder months and more fuel than estimated during the warmer months. This means that Dupree is making more deliveries

than necessary during the colder months and customers are running out of oil during the warmer months.

Dupree wants to develop a consumption estimation model that is practical and more reliable. The following data are available in the file **C11_02.xlsx**:

- The number of degree-days since the last oil fill and the consumption amounts for 40 customers.

- The number of people residing in the homes of each of the 40 customers. Dupree thinks that this might be important in predicting the oil consumption of customers using oil-fired water heaters because it provides an estimate of the hot-water requirements of each customer. Each of the customers in this sample uses an oil-fired water heater.

- An assessment, provided by Dupree sales staff, of the home type of each of these 40 customers. The home type classification, which is a number between 1 and 5, is a composite index of the home size, age, exposure to wind, level of insulation, and furnace type. A low index implies a lower oil consumption per degree-day, and a high index implies a higher consumption of oil per degree-day. Dupree thinks that the use of such an index will allow them to estimate a consumption model based on a sample data set and then to apply the same model to predict the oil demand of each of his customers.

Use regression to see whether a statistically reliable oil consumption model can be estimated from the data.

<hr>

CASE 11.3 DEVELOPING A FLEXIBLE BUDGET AT THE GUNDERSON PLANT

The Gunderson Plant manufactures the industrial product line of FGT Industries. Plant management wants to be able to get a good, yet quick, estimate of the manufacturing overhead costs that can be expected each month. The easiest and simplest method to accomplish this task is to develop a flexible budget formula for the manufacturing overhead costs. The plant's accounting staff has suggested that simple linear regression be used to

determine the behavior pattern of the overhead costs. The regression data can provide the basis for the flexible budget formula. Sufficient evidence is available to conclude that manufacturing overhead costs vary with direct labor hours. The actual direct labor hours and the corresponding manufacturing overhead costs for each month of the last three years have been used in the linear regression analysis.

The three-year period contained various occurrences not uncommon to many businesses. During the first year, production was severely curtailed during two months due to wildcat strikes. In the second year, production was reduced in one month because of material shortages, and increased significantly (scheduled overtime) during two months to meet the units required for a one-time sales order. At the end of the second year, employee benefits were raised significantly as the result of a labor agreement. Production during the third year was not affected by any special circumstances. Various members of Gunderson's accounting staff raised some issues regarding the historical data collected for the regression analysis. These issues were as follows.

- Some members of the accounting staff believed that the use of data from all 36 months would provide a more accurate portrayal of the cost behavior. While they recognized that any of the monthly data could include efficiencies and inefficiencies, they believed these efficiencies and inefficiencies would tend to balance out over a longer period of time.
- Other members of the accounting staff suggested that only those months that were considered normal should be used so that the regression would not be distorted.

- Still other members felt that only the most recent 12 months should be used because they were the most current.
- Some members questioned whether historical data should be used at all to form the basis for a flexible budget formula.

The accounting department ran two regression analyses of the data—one using the data from all 36 months and the other using only the data from the last 12 months. The information derived from the two linear regressions is shown below (t-values shown in parentheses). The 36-month regression is

$$OH_t = 123,810 + 1.60\,DLH_t, \quad R^2 = 0.32$$
$$ {}_{(1.64)}$$

The 12-month regression is

$$OH_t = 109,020 + 3.00\,DLH_t, \quad R^2 = 0.48$$
$$ {}_{(3.01)}$$

Questions

1. Which of the two results (12 months versus 36 months) would you use as a basis for the flexible budget formula?
2. How would the four specific issues raised by the members of Gunderson's accounting staff influence your willingness to use the results of the statistical analyses as the basis for the flexible budget formula? Explain your answer.

CASE   11.4 FORECASTING OVERHEAD AT WAGNER PRINTERS

Wagner Printers performs all types of printing, including custom work, such as advertising displays, and standard work, such as business cards. Market prices exist for standard work, and Wagner Printers must match or better these prices to get the business. The key issue is whether the existing market price covers the cost associated with doing the work. On the other hand, most of the custom work must be priced individually. Because all custom work is done on a job-order basis, Wagner routinely keeps track of all the direct labor and direct materials costs associated with each job. However, the overhead for each job must be estimated. The overhead is applied to each job using a predetermined (normalized) rate based on estimated overhead and labor hours. Once

the cost of the prospective job is determined, the sales manager develops a bid that reflects both the existing market conditions and the estimated price of completing the job.

In the past, the normalized rate for overhead has been computed by using the historical average of overhead per direct labor hour. Wagner has become increasingly concerned about this practice for two reasons. First, it hasn't produced accurate forecasts of overhead in the past. Second, technology has changed the printing process, so that the labor content of jobs has been decreasing, and the normalized rate of overhead per direct labor hour has steadily been increasing. The file C11_04.xlsx shows the overhead data that Wagner has collected for its shop for the past

52 weeks. The average weekly overhead for the last 52 weeks is $54,208, and the average weekly number of labor hours worked is 716. Therefore, the normalized rate for overhead that will be used in the upcoming week is about $76(= 54208/716) per direct labor hour.

Questions

1. Determine whether you can develop a more accurate estimate of overhead costs.

2. Wagner is now preparing a bid for an important order that may involve a considerable amount of repeat business. The estimated requirements for this project are 15 labor hours, 8 machine hours, $150 direct labor cost, and $750 direct material cost. Using the existing approach to cost estimation, Wagner has estimated the cost for this job as $2040(= 150 + 750 + (76 \times 15))$. Given the existing data, what cost would you estimate for this job?

Blend Images/Jon Feingersh/the Agency Collection/Getty Images

REVENUE MANAGEMENT AT HARRAH'S CHEROKEE CASINO & HOTEL

Real applications of forecasting are almost never done in isolation. They are typically one part—a crucial part—of an overall quantitative solution to a business problem. This is certainly the case at Harrah's Cherokee Casino & Hotel in North Carolina, as explained in an article by Metters et al. (2008). This particular casino uses revenue management (RM) on a daily basis to increase its revenue from its gambling customers. As customers call to request reservations at the casino's hotel, the essential problem is to decide which reservations to accept and which to deny. The idea is that there is an opportunity cost from accepting early requests from lower-valued customers because higher-valued customers might request the same rooms later on.

As the article explains, there are several unique features about casinos, and this casino in particular, that make a quantitative approach to RM successful. First, the detailed behaviors of customers can be tracked, via electronic cards they use while placing bets in the electronic gambling machines, so that the casino can create a large database of individual customers' gambling patterns. This allows the casino to segment the customers into different groups, based on how much they typically bet in a given night. For example, one segment might contain all customers who bet between $500 and $600 per night. When a customer calls for a room reservation and provides his card number, the casino can immediately look up his information in the database and see which segment he is in.

A second reason for the successful use of RM is that customers differ substantially in the price they are willing to pay for the same commodity, a stay at the casino's hotel. Actually, many don't pay anything for the room or the food—these are frequently complimentary from the casino—but they pay by losing money at gambling. Some customers typically gamble thousands of dollars per night while others gamble much less. (This is quite different from the disparities in other hotels or in air travel, where a business traveler might pay twice as much as a vacationer, but not much more.) Because some customers are much more valuable than others, there are real opportunity costs from treating all customers alike.

A third reason for the success of RM at this casino is that the casino can afford to hold out for the best-paying customers until the last minute. The reason is that a significant percentage of the customers from all segments wait until the last minute to make their reservations. In fact, they often make them while driving, say, from Atlanta to the casino. Therefore, the casino can afford to deny requests for reservations to lower-valued customers made a day or two in advance, knowing that last-minute reservations, very possibly from higher-valued customers, will fill up the casino's rooms. Indeed, the occupancy rate is virtually always 98% or above.

The overall RM solution includes (1) data collection and customer segmentation, as explained above, (2) forecasting demand for reservations from each customer segment, (3) a linear programming (LP) optimization model that is run frequently to decide which reservations to accept, and (4) a customer relationship management model to entice loyal customers to book rooms on nights with lower demand. The forecasting model is very similar to the Winters' exponential smoothing model discussed in this chapter. Specifically, the model uses the large volume of historical data to forecast customer demand by each customer segment for any particular night in the future. These forecasts include information about time-related or seasonal patterns (weekends are busier, for example) and any special events that are scheduled. Also, the forecasts are updated daily as the night in question approaches. These forecasts are then used in an LP optimization model to determine which requests to approve. For example, the LP model might indicate that, given the current status of bookings and three nights to go, requests for rooms on the specified night should be accepted only for the four most valuable customer segments. As the given night approaches and the number of booked rooms changes, the LP model is rerun many times and provides staff with the necessary information for real-time decisions. (By the way, a customer who is refused a room at the casino is often given a free room at another nearby hotel. After all, this customer can still be valuable enough to offset the price of the room at the other hotel.)

It is difficult to measure the effect of this entire RM system because it has always been in place since the casino opened. But there is no doubt that it is effective. Despite the fact that it serves no alcohol and has only electronic games, not the traditional gaming tables, the casino has nearly full occupancy and returns a 60% profit margin on gross revenue—double the industry norm. ■

12-1 INTRODUCTION

Many decision-making applications depend on a forecast of some quantity. Here are several examples.

Examples of Forecasting Applications

- When a service organization, such as a fast-food restaurant, plans its staffing over some time period, it must forecast the customer demand as a function of time. This might be done at a very detailed level, such as the demand in successive 15-minute periods, or at a more aggregate level, such as the demand in successive weeks.

- When a company plans its ordering or production schedule for a product it sells to the public, it must forecast the customer demand for this product so that it can stock appropriate quantities—neither too many nor too few.
- When an organization plans to invest in stocks, bonds, or other financial instruments, it typically attempts to forecast movements in stock prices and interest rates.
- When government officials plan policy, they attempt to forecast movements in macroeconomic variables such as inflation, interest rates, and unemployment.

Unfortunately, forecasting is a very difficult task, both in the short run and in the long run. Typically, forecasts are based on historical data. Analysts search for patterns or relationships in the historical data, and then make forecasts. There are two problems with this approach. The first is that it is not always easy to uncover historical patterns or relationships. In particular, it is often difficult to separate the noise, or random behavior, from the underlying patterns. Some forecasts can even overdo it, by attributing importance to patterns that are in fact random variations and are unlikely to repeat themselves.

The second problem is that there are no guarantees that past patterns will continue in the future. A new war could break out somewhere in the world, a company's competitor could introduce a new product into the market, the bottom could fall out of the stock market, and so on. Each of these shocks to the system being studied could drastically alter the future in a highly unpredictable way. This partly explains why forecasts are almost always wrong. Unless they have inside information to the contrary, analysts must assume that history will repeat itself. But we all know that history does *not* always repeat itself. Therefore, there are many famous forecasts that turned out to be way off the mark, even though the analysts made reasonable assumptions and used standard forecasting techniques. Nevertheless, forecasts are required throughout the business world, so fear of failure is no excuse for not giving it our best effort.

12-2 FORECASTING METHODS: AN OVERVIEW

There are many forecasting methods available, and all practitioners have their favorites. To say the least, there is little agreement among practitioners or academics as to the best forecasting method. The methods can generally be divided into three groups: (1) *judgmental* methods, (2) *extrapolation* (or *time series*) methods, and (3) *econometric* (or *causal*) methods. The first of these is basically nonquantitative and will not be discussed here; the last two are quantitative. In this section we describe extrapolation and econometric methods in some generality. In the rest of the chapter, we go into more detail, particularly about the extrapolation methods.

12-2a Extrapolation Models

Extrapolation models are quantitative models that use past data of a time series variable—and nothing else, except possibly time itself—to forecast future values of the variable. The idea is that past movements of a variable, such as company sales or U.S. exports to Japan, can be used to forecast future values of the variable. Many extrapolation models are available, including trend-based regression, autoregression, moving averages, and exponential smoothing. Some of these models are relatively simple, both conceptually and in terms of the calculations required, whereas others are quite complex. Also, as the names imply, some of these models use the same regression methods from the previous two chapters, whereas others do not.

All of these extrapolation models search for *patterns* in the historical series and then extrapolate these patterns into the future. Some try to track long-term upward or downward trends and then project these. Some try to track the seasonal patterns (such as sales up in

November and December, down in other months) and then project these. Basically, the more complex the model the more closely it tries to track historical patterns. Researchers have long believed that good forecasting models should be able to track the ups and downs—the zigzags on a graph—of a time series. This has led to voluminous research and increasingly complex methods. But is complexity always better?

Surprisingly, empirical evidence shows that complexity is *not* always better. This is documented in a quarter-century review article by Armstrong (1986) and an article by Schnarrs and Bavuso (1986). They document a number of empirical studies on literally thousands of time series forecasts where complex models fared no better, and sometimes even worse, than simple models. In fact, the Schnarrs and Bavuso article presents evidence that a naive forecast from a "random walk" model sometimes outperforms all of the more sophisticated extrapolation models. This naive model forecasts that next period's value will be the same as this period's value. So if today's closing stock price is 51.375, it forecasts that tomorrow's closing stock price will be 51.375. This model is certainly simple, and it sometimes works quite well. We discuss random walks in more detail in Section 12-5.

The evidence in favor of simpler models is not accepted by everyone, particularly not those who have spent years investigating complex models, and complex models continue to be studied and used. However, there is a very plausible reason why simple models can provide reasonably good forecasts. The whole goal of extrapolation models is to extrapolate historical patterns into the future. But it is often difficult to determine which patterns are real and which represent noise—random ups and downs that are not likely to repeat themselves. Also, if something important changes (a competitor introduces a new product or there is an oil embargo, for example), it is certainly possible that historical patterns will change. A potential problem with complex models is that they can track a historical series *too* closely. That is, they sometimes track patterns that are really noise. Simpler models, on the other hand, track only the most basic underlying patterns and therefore can be more flexible and accurate in forecasting the future.

12-2b Econometric Models

Econometric models, also called causal or regression-based models, use regression to forecast a time series variable by using other explanatory time series variables. For example, a company might use a causal model to regress future sales on its advertising level, the population income level, the interest rate, and possibly others. In one sense, regression analysis involving time series variables is similar to the regression analysis discussed in the previous two chapters. The same least squares approach and the same multiple regression software can be used in many time series regression models. In fact, several examples and problems in the previous two chapters used time series data.

However, causal regression models for time series data present new mathematical challenges that go well beyond the level of this book. To get a glimpse of the potential difficulties, suppose a company wants to use a regression model to forecast its monthly sales for some product, using two other time series variables as predictors: its monthly advertising levels for the product and its main competitor's monthly advertising levels for a competing product. The resulting regression equation has the form

---

Prediction from Regression Equation

$$\text{Predicted } Y_t = a + b_1 X_{1t} + b_2 X_{2t} \tag{12.1}$$

Here, Y_t is the company's sales in month t, and X_{1t} and X_{2t} are, respectively, the company's and the competitor's advertising levels in month t. This regression model might provide some useful results, but there are some issues that must be faced.

One issue is that the appropriate "lags" for the regression equation must be determined. Do sales this month depend only on advertising levels *this* month, as specified in Equation (12.1), or also on advertising levels in the previous month, the previous two months, and so on? A second issue is whether to include lags of the *sales* variable in the regression equation as explanatory variables. Presumably, sales in one month might depend on the level of sales in previous months (as well as on advertising levels). A third issue is that the two advertising variables can be autocorrelated and cross-correlated. *Autocorrelation* means correlated with itself. For example, the company's advertising level in one month might depend on its advertising levels in previous months. *Cross-correlation* means being correlated with a lagged version of another variable. For example, the company's advertising level in one month might be related to the competitor's advertising levels in previous months, or the competitor's advertising in one month might be related to the company's advertising levels in previous months.

These are difficult issues, and the way in which they are addressed can make a big difference in the usefulness of the regression model. We will examine several regression-based models in this chapter, but we won't discuss situations such as the one just described, where one time series variable Y is regressed on one or more time series of Xs. [Pankratz (1991) is a good reference for these latter types of models. Unfortunately, the level of mathematics is considerably beyond the level in this book.]

12-2c Combining Forecasts

There is one other general forecasting method that is worth mentioning. In fact, it has attracted a lot of attention in recent years, and many researchers believe that it has potential for increasing forecast accuracy. The method is simple—it combines two or more forecasts to obtain the final forecast. The reasoning behind this method is also simple: The forecast errors from different forecasting methods might cancel one another. The forecasts that are combined can be of the same general type—extrapolation forecasts, for example—or they can be of different types, such as judgmental and extrapolation.

The *number* of forecasts to combine and the *weights* to use in combining them have been the subject of several research studies. Although the findings are not entirely consistent, it appears that the marginal benefit from each individual forecast after the first two or three is minor. Also, there is not much evidence to suggest that the simplest weighting scheme—weighting each forecast equally, that is, averaging them—is any less accurate than more complex weighting schemes.

12-2d Components of Time Series Data

In Chapter 2 we discussed time series graphs, a useful graphical way of displaying time series data. We now use these time series graphs to help explain and identify four important components of a time series. These components are called the *trend* component, the *seasonal* component, the *cyclic* component, and the *random* (or *noise*) component.

We start by looking at a very simple time series. This is a time series where every observation has the same value. Such a series is shown in Figure 12.1. The graph in this figure shows time (t) on the horizontal axis and the observed values (Y) on the vertical axis. We assume that Y is measured at regularly spaced intervals, usually days, weeks, months, quarters, or years, with Y_t being the value of the observation at time period t. As indicated in Figure 12.1, the individual observation points are usually joined by straight lines to make any patterns in the time series more apparent. Because all observations in this time series are equal, the resulting time series graph is a horizontal line. We refer to this time series as the *base* series. We will now illustrate more interesting time series built from this base series.

Figure 12.1

The Base Series

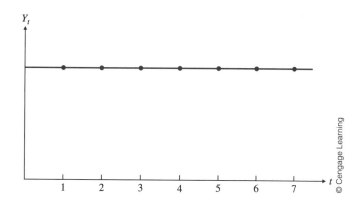

If the observations increase or decrease regularly through time, we say that the time series has a **trend**. The graphs in Figure 12.2 illustrate several possible trends. The *linear* trend in Figure 12.2a occurs if a company's sales increase by the same amount from period to period. This constant per period change is then the slope of the linear trend line. The curve in Figure 12.2b is an *exponential* trend. It occurs in a business such as the personal computer business, where sales have increased at a tremendous rate (at least during the 1990s, the boom years). For this type of curve, the *percentage* increase in Y_t from period to period remains constant. The curve in Figure 12.2c is an *S-shaped* trend. This type of trend is appropriate for a new product that takes a while to catch on, then exhibits a rapid increase in sales as the public becomes aware of it, and finally tapers off to a fairly constant level because of market saturation. The series in Figure 12.2 all represent *upward* trends. Of course, there are *downward* trends of the same types.

Figure 12.2   Series with Trends

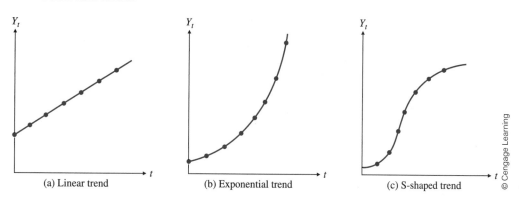

(a) Linear trend   (b) Exponential trend   (c) S-shaped trend

Many time series have a seasonal component, that is, they exhibit **seasonality**. For example, a company's sales of swimming pool equipment increase every spring, then stay relatively high during the summer, and then drop off until next spring, at which time the yearly pattern repeats itself. An important aspect of the seasonal component is that it tends to be predictable from one year to the next. That is, the *same* seasonal pattern tends to repeat itself every year.

Figure 12.3 illustrates two possible seasonal patterns. In Figure 12.3a there is nothing but the seasonal component. That is, if there were no seasonal variation, the series would be the base series in Figure 12.1. Figure 12.3b illustrates a seasonal pattern superimposed on a linear trend line.

The third component of a time series is the **cyclic component**. By studying past movements of many business and economic variables, it becomes apparent that there are

Figure 12.3

Series with
Seasonality

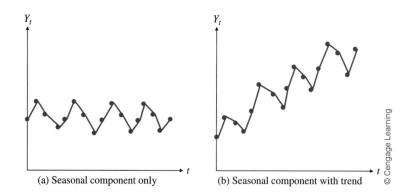

(a) Seasonal component only

(b) Seasonal component with trend

© Cengage Learning

business cycles that affect many variables in similar ways. For example, during a recession housing sales generally go down, unemployment goes up, stock prices go down, and so on. But when the recession is over, all of these variables tend to move in the opposite direction. Unfortunately, the cyclic component is more difficult to predict than the seasonal component. The reason is that seasonal variation is much more regular. For example, swimming pool supplies sales *always* start to increase during the spring. Cyclic variation, on the other hand, is more irregular because the length of the business cycle varies, sometimes considerably. A further distinction is that the length of a seasonal cycle is generally one year; the length of a business cycle is generally longer than one year and its actual length is difficult to predict.

The graphs in Figure 12.4 illustrate the cyclic component of a time series. In Figure 12.4a cyclic variation is superimposed on the base series in Figure 12.1. In Figure 12.4b this same cyclic variation is superimposed on the series in Figure 12.3b. The resulting graph has trend, seasonal variation, and cyclic variation.

Figure 12.4

Series with Cyclic
Component

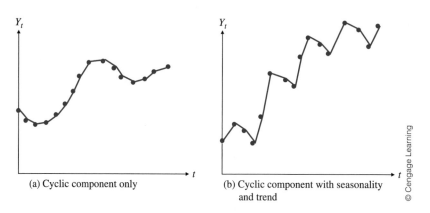

(a) Cyclic component only

(b) Cyclic component with seasonality
and trend

© Cengage Learning

The final component in a time series is called **random variation**, or simply **noise**. This unpredictable component gives most time series graphs their irregular, zigzag appearance. Usually, a time series can be determined only to a certain extent by its trend, seasonal, and cyclic components. Then other factors determine the rest. These other factors may be inherent randomness, unpredictable "shocks" to the system, the unpredictable behavior of human beings who interact with the system, and possibly others. These factors combine to create a certain amount of unpredictability in almost all time series.

Figures 12.5 and 12.6 show the effect that noise can have on a time series graph. The graph on the left of each figure shows the random component only, superimposed on the base series. Then on the right of each figure, the random component is superimposed on the trend-with-seasonal-component graph from Figure 12.3b. The difference

Figure 12.5

Series with Noise

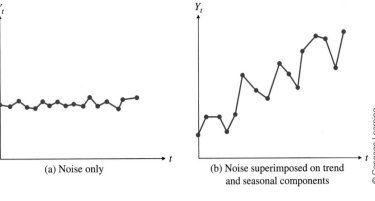

(a) Noise only

(b) Noise superimposed on trend and seasonal components

© Cengage Learning

Figure 12.6

Series with More Noise

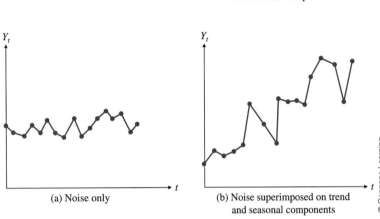

(a) Noise only

(b) Noise superimposed on trend and seasonal components

© Cengage Learning

between Figures 12.5 and 12.6 is the relative magnitude of the noise. When it is small, as in Figure 12.5, the other components emerge fairly clearly; they are not disguised by the noise. But if the noise is large in magnitude, as in Figure 12.6, the noise makes it very difficult to distinguish the other components.

12-2e Measures of Accuracy

We now introduce some notation and discuss aspects common to most forecasting methods. In general, we let Y denote the variable of interest. Then Y_t denotes the observed value of Y at time t. Typically, the first observation (the most distant one) corresponds to period $t = 1$, and the last observation (the most recent one) corresponds to period $t = T$, where T denotes the number of historical observations of Y. The periods themselves might be days, weeks, months, quarters, years, or any other convenient unit of time.

Suppose that Y_{t-k} has just been observed and you want to make a "k-period-ahead" forecast; that is, you want to use the information through time $t - k$ to forecast Y_t. The resulting forecast is denoted by $F_{t-k,t}$. The first subscript indicates the period in which the forecast is made, and the second subscript indicates the period being forecast. As an example, if the data are monthly and September 2012 corresponds to $t = 67$, then a forecast of Y_{69}, the value in November 2012, would be labeled $F_{67,69}$. The **forecast error** is the difference between the actual value and the forecast. It is denoted by E with appropriate subscripts. Specifically, the forecast error associated with $F_{t-k,t}$ is

$$E_{t-k,t} = Y_t - F_{t-k,t}$$

This double-subscript notation is necessary to specify when the forecast is being made and which period is being forecast. However, the former is often clear from context. Therefore, to simplify the notation, we usually drop the first subscript and write F_t and E_t to denote the forecast of Y_t and the error in this forecast.

You first develop a model to fit the historical data. Then you use this model to forecast the future.

There are actually two steps in any forecasting procedure. The first step is to build a model that fits the historical data well. The second step is to use this model to forecast the future. Most of the work goes into the first step. For any trial model you see how well it "tracks" the known values of the time series. Specifically, the one-period-ahead forecasts, F_t (or more precisely, $F_{t-1,t}$) are calculated from the model, and these are compared to the known values, Y_t, for each t in the historical time period. The goal is to find a model that produces small forecast errors, E_t. Presumably, if the model tracks the *historical* data well, it will also forecast *future* data well. Of course, there is no guarantee that this is true, but it is often a reasonable assumption.

A model that makes any one of these error measures small tends to make the other two small as well.

Forecasting software packages typically report several summary measures of the forecast errors. The most important of these are **MAE (mean absolute error)**, **RMSE (root mean square error)**, and **MAPE (mean absolute percentage error)**. These are defined in Equations (12.2), (12.3), and (12.4). Fortunately, models that make any one of these measures small tend to make the others small, so you can choose whichever measure you want to minimize. In the following formulas, N denotes the number of terms in each sum. This value is typically slightly less than T, the number of historical observations, because it is usually not possible to provide a forecast for each historical period.

Mean Absolute Error

$$\text{MAE} = \left(\sum_{t=1}^{N} |E_t| \right)/N \tag{12.2}$$

Root Mean Square Error

$$\text{RMSE} = \sqrt{\left(\sum_{t=1}^{N} E_t^2 \right)/N} \tag{12.3}$$

Mean Absolute Percentage Error

$$\text{MAPE} = 100\% \times \left(\sum_{t=1}^{N} |E_t/Y_t| \right)/N \tag{12.4}$$

RMSE is similar to a standard deviation in that the errors are squared; because of the square root, it is in the same units as those of the forecast variable. The MAE is similar to the RMSE, except that absolute values of errors are used instead of squared errors. The MAPE is probably the most easily understood measure because it does not depend on the units of the forecast variable; it is always stated as a percentage. For example, the statement that the forecasts are off on average by 2% has a clear meaning, even if you do not know the units of the variable being forecast.

Some forecasting software packages choose the best model from a given class (such as the best exponential smoothing model) by minimizing MAE, RMSE, or MAPE. However, small values of these measures guarantee only that the model tracks the *historical* observations well. There is still no guarantee that the model will forecast *future* values accurately.

One other measure of forecast errors is the *average* of the errors. (It is not reported by StatTools, but it is easy to calculate.) Recall from the regression chapters that the residuals from any regression equation, which are analogous to forecast errors, always average to zero. This is a mathematical property of the least-squares method. However, there is no such guarantee for forecasting errors based on nonregression methods. For example, it is very possible that most of the forecast errors, and the corresponding average, are *negative*. This would imply a *bias*, where the forecasts tend to be too high. Or the average of the forecast errors could be *positive*, in which case the forecasts tend to be too low. If you choose an "appropriate" forecasting method, based on the evidence from a time series graph, this type of bias is not likely to be a problem, but it is easy to check. Furthermore, if a company realizes that its forecasting method produces forecasts that are consistently, say, 5% below the actual values, it could simply multiply its forecasts by 1/0.95 to remove the bias.

We now examine a number of useful forecasting models. You should be aware that more than one of these models can be appropriate for any particular time series data. For example, a random walk model and an autoregression model could be equally effective for forecasting stock price data. (Remember also that forecasts from more than one model can be combined to obtain a possibly better forecast.) We try to provide some insights into choosing the best type of model for various types of time series data, but ultimately the choice depends on the experience of the analyst.

FUNDAMENTAL INSIGHT

Extrapolation and Noise

There are two important things to remember about extrapolation methods. First, by definition, all such methods try to extrapolate historical patterns into the future. If history doesn't essentially repeat itself, for whatever reason, these methods are doomed to fail. In fact, if you *know* that something has changed fundamentally, you probably should not use an extrapolation method. Second, it does no good to track noise and then forecast it into the future. For this reason, most extrapolation methods try to smooth out the noise, so that the underlying pattern is more apparent.

12-3 TESTING FOR RANDOMNESS

All forecasting models have the general form shown in Equation (12.5). The fitted value in this equation is the part calculated from past data and any other available information (such as the season of the year), and it is used as a forecast for Y. The residual is the forecast error, the difference between the observed value of Y and its forecast:

Typical Forecasting Equation
$$Y_t = \text{Fitted Value} + \text{Residual} \qquad (12.5)$$

In a time series context the terms residual *and* forecast error *are used interchangeably.*

For time series data, there is a residual for each historical period, that is, for each value of t. We want this time series of residuals to be random noise, as discussed in Section 12-2d. The reason is that if this series of residuals is not noise, it can be modeled further. For example, if the residuals trend upwardly, the forecasting model can be modified to include this trend component in the *fitted* value. The point is that the fitted value should include all components of the original series that can possibly be forecast, and the leftover residuals should be unpredictable noise.

We now discuss ways to determine whether a time series of residuals is random noise (which we usually abbreviate to "random"). The simplest method, but not always a reliable one, is to examine time series graphs of residuals visually. Nonrandom patterns are sometimes easy to detect. For example, the time series graphs in Figures 12.7 through 12.11 illustrate some common nonrandom patterns. In Figure 12.7, there is an upward trend. In Figure 12.8, the variance increases through time (larger zigzags to the right). Figure 12.9 exhibits seasonality, where observations in certain months are consistently larger than those in other months. There is a meandering pattern in Figure 12.10, where large observations

Figure 12.7

A Series with Trend

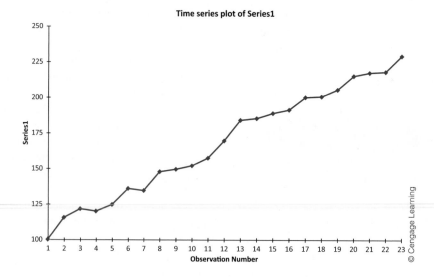

Figure 12.8

A Series with
Increasing Variance
Through Time

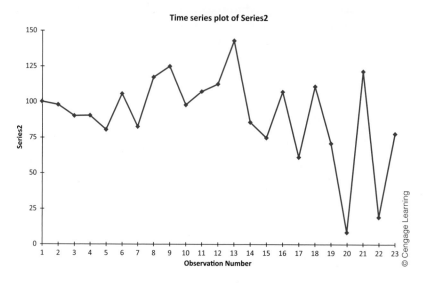

Figure 12.9

A Series with
Seasonality

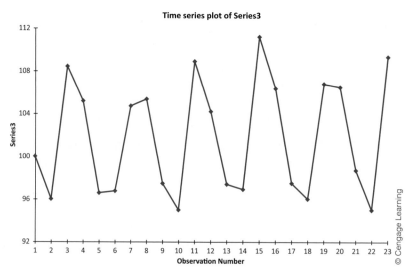

Figure 12.10

A Series That
Meanders

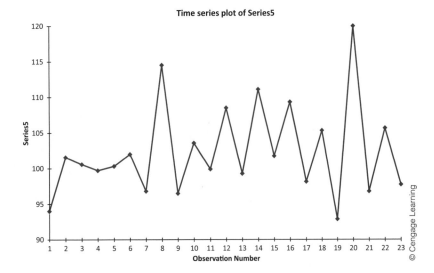

Figure 12.11

A Series That
Oscillates
Frequently

tend to be followed by other large observations, and small observations tend to be followed by other small observations. Finally, Figure 12.11 illustrates the opposite behavior, where there are *too many* zigzags—large observations tend to follow small observations and vice versa. None of the time series in these figures is random.

12-3a The Runs Test

It is not always easy to detect randomness or the lack of it from the visual inspection of a graph. Therefore, we discuss two quantitative methods that test for randomness. The first is called the *runs test*. You first choose a base value, which could be the average value of the series, the median value, or even some other value. Then a **run** is defined as a consecutive series of observations that remain on one side of this base level. For example, if the base level is 0 and the series is 1, 5, 3, –3, –2, –4, –1, 3, 2, there are three runs: 1, 5, 3; –3, –2, –4, –1; and 3, 2. The idea behind the runs test is that a random series should have a number of runs that is neither too large nor too small. If the series has too few runs, it could be trending (as in Figure 12.7) or it could be meandering (as in Figure 12.10). If the series has too many runs, it is zigzagging too often (as in Figure 12.11).

This runs test can be used on any time series, not just a series of residuals.

> The **runs test** is a formal test of the null hypothesis of randomness. If there are too many or too few runs in the series, the null hypothesis of randomness can be rejected.

We do not provide the mathematical details of the runs test, but we illustrate how it is implemented in StatTools in Example 12.1.

| EXAMPLE | **12.1 FORECASTING MONTHLY STEREO SALES** |

Monthly sales for a chain of stereo retailers are listed in the file **Stereo Sales.xlsx**. They cover the period from the beginning of 2009 to the end of 2012, during which there was no upward or downward trend in sales and no clear seasonality. This behavior is apparent in the time series graph of sales in Figure 12.12. Therefore, a simple forecast model of sales is to use the *average* of the series, 182.67, as a forecast of sales for each month. Do the resulting residuals represent random noise?

Figure 12.12

Time Series Graph of Stereo Sales

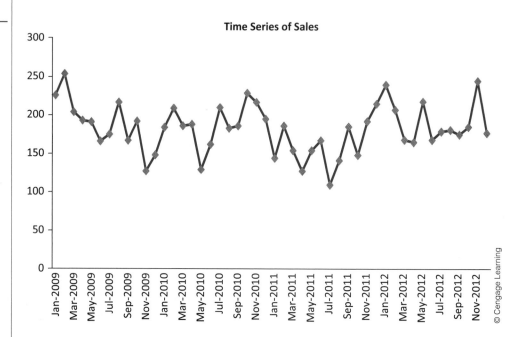

Objective   To use StatTools's Runs Test procedure to check whether the residuals from this simple forecasting model represent random noise.

Solution

The residuals for this forecasting model are found by subtracting the average, 182.67, from each observation. Therefore, the plot of the residuals, shown in Figure 12.13, has exactly the same shape as the plot of sales. The only difference is that it is shifted down by 182.67 and has mean 0. The runs test can now be used to check whether there are too many or too few runs around the base value of 0 in this residual plot. To do so, select Runs Test for Randomness from the StatTools Time Series and Forecasting dropdown, choose Residual as the variable to analyze, and choose Mean of Series as the cutoff value. (This corresponds to the horizontal line at 0 in Figure 12.13.) The resulting output in shown in Figure 12.14.

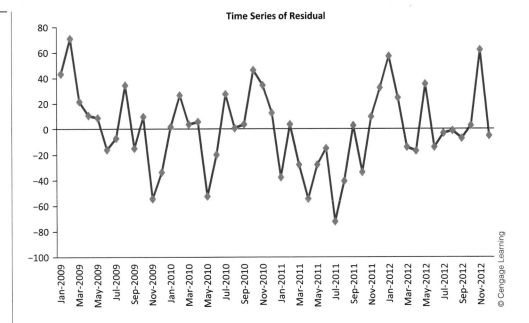

Figure 12.13

Time Series Graph of Residuals

Figure 12.14

Runs Test for Randomness

◢	A	B
7		Residual
8	*Runs Test for Randomness*	Data Set #1
9	Observations	48
10	Below Mean	22
11	Above Mean	26
12	Number of Runs	20
13	Mean	0.00
14	E(R)	24.8333
15	StdDev(R)	3.4027
16	Z-Value	−1.4204
17	P-Value (two-tailed)	0.1555

© Cengage Learning

The important elements of this output are the following:

- The number of observed runs is 20, in cell J12.
- The number of runs *expected* under an assumption of randomness is 24.833, in cell J14. (This follows from a probability argument not shown here.) Therefore, the series of residuals has too *few* runs. Positive values tend to follow positive values, and negative values tend to follow negative values.

A small p-value in the runs test provides evidence of nonrandomness.

- The z-value in cell J16, −1.42, indicates how many standard errors the observed number of runs is below the expected number of runs. The corresponding p-value indicates how extreme this z-value is. It can be interpreted just like other p-values for hypothesis tests. If it is small, say, less than 0.05, then the null hypothesis of randomness can be rejected. In this case, the conclusion is that the series of residuals is not random noise. However, the p-value for this example is only 0.1555. Therefore, there is not convincing evidence of nonrandomness in the residuals. In other words, it is reasonable to conclude that the residuals represent noise. ■

12-3b Autocorrelation

Like the runs test, autocorrelations can be calculated for any time series, not just a series of residuals.

In this section we discuss another way to check for randomness of a time series of residuals—we examine the **autocorrelations** of the residuals. The "auto" means that successive observations are correlated with one another. For example, in the most common form of autocorrelation, *positive* autocorrelation, large observations tend to follow large observations, and small observations tend to follow small observations. In this case the runs test is likely to pick it up because there will be fewer runs than expected. Another way to check for the same nonrandomness is to calculate the autocorrelations of the time series.

> An **autocorrelation** is a type of correlation used to measure whether values of a time series are related to their own past values.

To understand autocorrelations, it is first necessary to understand what it means to *lag* a time series. This concept is easy to illustrate in a spreadsheet. We again use the monthly stereo sales data in the **Stereo Sales.xlsx** file. To lag by one month, you simply "push down" the series by one row. See column D of Figure 12.15. Note that there is a blank cell at the top of the lagged series (in cell D2). You can continue to push the series down one row at a time to obtain other lags. For example, the lag 3 version of the series appears in column F. Now there are three missing observations at the top. Note that in December 2009, say, the first, second, and third lags correspond to the observations in November 2009, October 2009, and September 2009, respectively. That is, lags are simply previous observations, removed by a certain number of periods from the present time. These lagged columns can be obtained by copying and pasting the original series or by selecting Lag from the StatTools Data Utilities dropdown menu.

Figure 12.15

Lags for Stereo Sales

	A	B	C	D	E	F
1	Month	Sales	Residual	Lag1(Residual)	Lag2(Residual)	Lag3(Residual)
2	Jan-2009	226	43.333			
3	Feb-2009	254	71.333	43.333		
4	Mar-2009	204	21.333	71.333	43.333	
5	Apr-2009	193	10.333	21.333	71.333	43.333
6	May-2009	191	8.333	10.333	21.333	71.333
7	Jun-2009	166	−16.667	8.333	10.333	21.333
8	Jul-2009	175	−7.667	−16.667	8.333	10.333
9	Aug-2009	217	34.333	−7.667	−16.667	8.333
10	Sep-2009	167	−15.667	34.333	−7.667	−16.667

© Cengage Learning

FUNDAMENTAL INSIGHT

Role of Autocorrelation in Time Series Analysis

Due to the introductory nature of this book, we do not discuss autocorrelation in much detail. However, it is the key to many forecasting methods, especially more complex methods. This is not surprising. Autocorrelations essentially specify how observations in nearby time periods are related, so this information is often useful in forecasting. However, it is not at all obvious how to use this information—hence the complexity of some forecasting methods.

Then the autocorrelation of lag k, for any integer k, is essentially the correlation between the original series and the lag k version of the series. For example, in Figure 12.15 the lag 1 autocorrelation is the correlation between the observations in columns C and D. Similarly, the lag 2 autocorrelation is the correlation between the observations in columns C and E.[1]

---

[1] We ignore the exact details of the calculations here. Just be aware that the formula for autocorrelations that is usually used differs slightly from the correlation formula in Chapter 3. Fortunately, the difference is very slight and of no practical importance.

We have shown the lagged versions of Sales in Figure 12.15, and we have explained autocorrelations in terms of these lagged variables, to help motivate the concept of auto-correlation. However, you can use StatTools's Autocorrelation procedure directly, *without* forming the lagged variables, to calculate autocorrelations. This is illustrated in the following continuation of Example 12.1.

EXAMPLE

12.1 FORECASTING MONTHLY STEREO SALES (CONTINUED)

The runs test on the stereo sales data suggests that the pattern of sales is not completely random. There is some tendency for large values to follow large values, and for small values to follow small values. Do autocorrelations support this evidence?

Objective To examine the autocorrelations of the residuals from the forecasting model for evidence of nonrandomness.

Solution

To answer this question, you can use StatTools's Autocorrelation procedure, found on the StatTools Time Series and Forecasting dropdown list. It requires you to specify the time series variable (Residual), the number of lags you want (the StatTools default value was accepted here), and whether you want a chart of the autocorrelations. This chart is called a **correlogram**. The resulting autocorrelations and correlogram appear in Figure 12.16. A typical autocorrelation of lag k indicates the relationship between observations k periods

Figure 12.16

Correlogram and Autocorrelations of Residuals

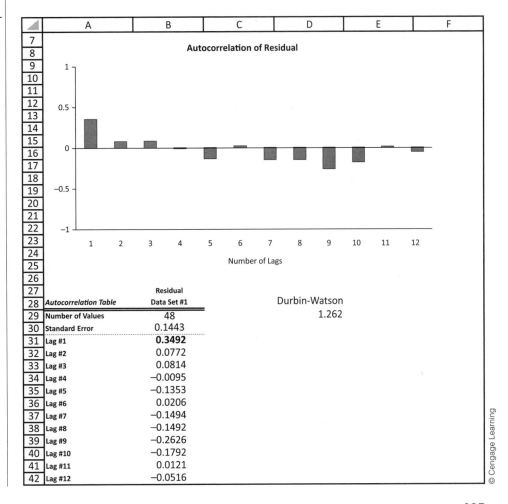

	Residual		Durbin-Watson
	Data Set #1		
Autocorrelation Table			
Number of Values	48		1.262
Standard Error	0.1443		
Lag #1	**0.3492**		
Lag #2	0.0772		
Lag #3	0.0814		
Lag #4	−0.0095		
Lag #5	−0.1353		
Lag #6	0.0206		
Lag #7	−0.1494		
Lag #8	−0.1492		
Lag #9	−0.2626		
Lag #10	−0.1792		
Lag #11	0.0121		
Lag #12	−0.0516		

apart. For example, the autocorrelation of lag 3, 0.0814, indicates that there is very little relationship between residuals separated by three months.

How large is a "large" autocorrelation? Under the assumption of randomness, it can be shown that the standard error of any autocorrelation is approximately $1/\sqrt{T}$, in this case $1/\sqrt{48} = 0.1443$. (Recall that T denotes the number of observations in the series.) If the series is random, then only an occasional autocorrelation will be larger than two standard errors in magnitude. Therefore, any autocorrelation that *is* larger than two standard errors in magnitude is worth your attention. All significantly nonzero autocorrelations are bold-faced in the StatTools output. For this example, the only "large" autocorrelation for the residuals is the first, or lag 1, autocorrelation of 0.3492. The fact that it is *positive* indicates once again that there is some tendency for large residuals to follow large residuals and for small to follow small. The autocorrelations for other lags are less than two standard errors in magnitude and can safely be ignored. ∎

Typically, you can ask for autocorrelations up to as many lags as you like. However, there are several practical considerations to keep in mind. First, it is common practice to ask for no more lags than 25% of the number of observations. For example, if there are 48 observations, you should ask for no more than 12 autocorrelations (lags 1 to 12). (StatTools chooses this number of lags if you accept its Auto setting.)

Second, the first few lags are typically the most important. Intuitively, if there is any relationship between successive observations, it is likely to be between nearby observations. The June 2012 observation is more likely to be related to the May 2012 observation than to the October 2011 observation. Sometimes there is a fairly large spike in the correlogram at some large lag, such as lag 9. However, this can often be dismissed as a random blip unless there is some obvious reason for its occurrence. A similarly large autocorrelation at lag 1 or 2 is usually taken more seriously. The one exception to this is a *seasonal* lag. For example, an autocorrelation at lag 12 for monthly data corresponds to a relationship between observations a year apart, such as May 2012 and May 2011. If this autocorrelation is significantly large, it probably should not be ignored.

As discussed briefly in the previous chapter, one measure of the lag 1 autocorrelation, often the most important autocorrelation, is provided by the Durbin-Watson (DW) statistic. (See Section 11-8c.) This statistic can be calculated with the StatTools function StatDurbinWatson. Its value for the residuals in this example is 1.262, as shown in Figure 12.16. The DW statistic is always between 0 and 4. A DW value of 2 indicates *no* lag 1 autocorrelation, a DW value less than 2 indicates *positive* autocorrelation, and a DW value greater than 2 indicates *negative* autocorrelation. The current DW value, 1.262, is considerably less than 2, another indication that the lag 1 autocorrelation of the residuals is positive and possibly significant. There are tables of significance levels for DW statistics (how much less than 2 must DW be to be significant?), but they are not presented here.

Autocorrelation analysis is somewhat advanced. However, it is the basis for many useful forecasting methods.

We will not examine autocorrelations much further in this book. However, many advanced forecasting techniques are based largely on the examination of the autocorrelation structure of time series. This autocorrelation structure indicates how a series is related to its own past values through time, which can be very valuable information for forecasting *future* values.

PROBLEMS

Note: Student solutions for problems whose numbers appear within a colored box are available for purchase at www.cengagebrain.com.

Level A

1. The file **P12_01.xlsx** contains the monthly number of airline tickets sold by a travel agency. Is this time series

random? Perform a runs test and find a few autocorrelations to support your answer.

2. The file **P12_02.xlsx** contains the weekly sales at a local bookstore for each of the past 25 weeks. Is this time series *random*? Perform a runs test and find a few autocorrelations to support your answer.

3. The number of employees on the payroll at a food-processing plant is recorded at the start of each month. These data are provided in the file **P12_03.xlsx**. Perform a runs test and find a few autocorrelations to determine whether this time series is random.

4. The quarterly numbers of applications for home mortgage loans at a branch office of Northern Central Bank are recorded in the file **P12_04.xlsx**. Perform a runs test and find a few autocorrelations to determine whether this time series is random.

5. The number of reported accidents at a manufacturing plant located in Flint, Michigan, was recorded at the start of each month. These data are provided in the file **P12_05.xlsx**. Is this time series *random*? Perform a runs test and find a few autocorrelations to support your answer.

6. The file **P12_06.xlsx** contains the weekly sales at the local outlet of West Coast Video Rentals for each of the past 36 weeks. Perform a runs test and find a few autocorrelations to determine whether this time series is random.

Level B

7. Determine whether the RAND() function in Excel actually generates a random stream of numbers.

Generate at least 100 random numbers to test their randomness with a runs test and with autocorrelations. Summarize your findings.

8. Use a runs test and calculate autorrelations to decide whether the random series explained in each part of this problem (**a–c**) are random. For each part, generate at least 100 random numbers in the series.
   a. A series of independent normally distributed values, each with mean 70 and standard deviation 5.
   b. A series where the first value is normally distributed with mean 70 and standard deviation 5, and each succeeding value is normally distributed with mean equal to the *previous* value and standard deviation 5. (For example, if the fourth value is 67.32, then the fifth value will be normally distributed with mean 67.32.)
   c. A series where the first value, Y_1, is normally distributed with mean 70 and standard deviation 5, and each succeeding value, Y_t, is normally distributed with mean $(1 + a_t)Y_{t-1}$ and standard deviation $5(1 + a_t)$, where the a_t values are independent and normally distributed with mean 0 and standard deviation 0.2. (For example, if $Y_{t-1} = 67.32$ and $a_t = -0.2$, then Y_t will be normally distributed with mean $0.8(67.32) = 53.856$ and standard deviation $0.8(5) = 4$.)

12-4 REGRESSION-BASED TREND MODELS

Many time series follow a long-term trend except for random variation. This trend can be upward or downward. A straightforward way to model this trend is to estimate a regression equation for Y_t, using time t as the *single* explanatory variable. In this section we discuss the two most frequently used trend models, *linear* trend and *exponential* trend.

12-4a Linear Trend

A linear trend means that the time series variable changes by a constant *amount* each time period. The relevant equation is Equation (12.6), where, as in previous regression equations, a is the intercept, b is the slope, and e_t is an error term.[2]

Linear Trend Model

$$Y_t = a + bt + e_t \qquad\qquad (12.6)$$

The interpretation of b is that it represents the expected change in the series from one period to the next. If b is positive, the trend is upward; if b is negative, the trend is downward. The intercept term a is less important. It literally represents the expected value of the series at time $t = 0$. If time t is coded so that the first observation corresponds to $t = 1$, then a is where the series was one period before the observations began. However, it is possible that time is coded in another way. For example, if the data are annual, starting in 1997, the

---

[2]It is traditional in the regression literature to use Greek letters for population parameters and Roman letters for estimates of them. However, we decided to use only Roman letters in the regression sections of this chapter. For a book at this level, they are less intimidating.

first value of t might be entered as 1997, which means that the intercept a then corresponds to a period 1997 years earlier. Clearly, its value should not be taken literally in this case.

As always, a graph of the time series is a good place to start. It indicates whether a **linear trend** is likely to provide a good fit. Generally, the graph should rise or fall at approximately a constant rate through time, without too much random variation. But even if there is a lot of random variation—a lot of zigzags—a linear trend to the data might still be a good starting point. Then the *residuals* from this trend line, which should have no remaining trend, could possibly be modeled by some other method in this chapter.

EXAMPLE | 12.2 MONTHLY U.S. POPULATION

The file **US Population.xlsx** contains monthly population data for the United States from January 1952 to December 2011 (in thousands). During this period, the population has increased steadily from about 156 million to about 313 million. The time series graph of these data appears in Figure 12.17. How well does a linear trend fit these data? Are the residuals from this fit random?

Figure 12.17   Time Series Graph of U.S. Population

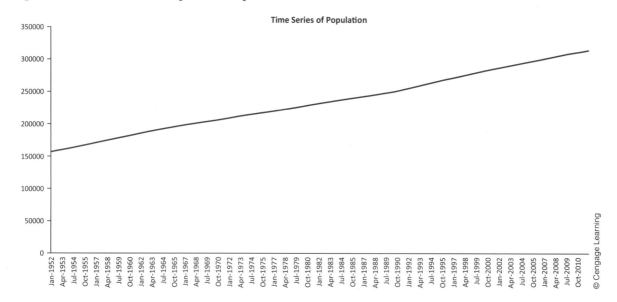

Objective   To fit a linear trend line to monthly population and examine its residuals for randomness.

Solution

The graph in Figure 12.17 indicates a clear upward trend with little or no curvature. Therefore, a linear trend is certainly plausible. To estimate it with regression, a *numeric* time variable is needed—labels such as Jan-52 will not do. This time variable appears in column C of the data set, using the consecutive values 1 through 720. You can then run a simple regression of Population versus Time, with the results shown in Figure 12.18. The estimated linear trend line is

$$\text{Forecast Population} = 156731.5 + 212.71 \text{Time}$$

Figure 12.18

Regression Output for Linear Trend

	A	B	C	D	E	F	G
7	Multiple Regression for Population						
8		Multiple		Adjusted	StErr of		
9	Summary	R	R-Square	R-Square	Estimate		
10		0.9983	0.9966	0.9966	2575.965942		
11							
12		Degrees of	Sum of	Mean of			
13	ANOVA Table	Freedom	Squares	Squares	F-Ratio	p-Value	
14	Explained	1	1.40729E+12	1.40729E+12	212081.9743	<0.0001	
15	Unexplained	718	4764361185	6635600.536			
16							
17		Coefficient	Standard	t-Value	p-Value	Confidence Interval 95%	
18	Regression Table		Error			Lower	Upper
19	Constant	156731.5457	192.2013402	815.4550	<0.0001	156354.2019	157108.8895
20	Time	212.7082296	0.461883464	460.5236	<0.0001	211.801426	213.6150331

This equation implies that the population tends to increase by 212.71 thousand per month. (The 156731.5 value in this equation is the predicted population at time 0; that is, December 1951.) To use this equation to forecast future population values, substitute later values of Time into the regression equation, so that each future forecast is 212.71 larger than the previous forecast. For example, the forecast for January 2012 is

$$\text{Forecast Population Jan-2012} = 156731.5 + 212.71(721) = 310094$$

As described in Chapter 2, Excel® provides an easier way to obtain this trend line. Once the graph in Figure 12.17 is constructed, you can use Excel's Trendline tool. To do so, right-click any point on the chart and select Add Trendline. This provides several types of trend lines to choose from, and the linear option works well for this example. You can also check the options to show the regression equation and its R^2 value on the chart, as shown in Figure 12.19. This superimposed trend line indicates a very good fit.

Figure 12.19 Time Series Graph with Linear Trend Superimposed

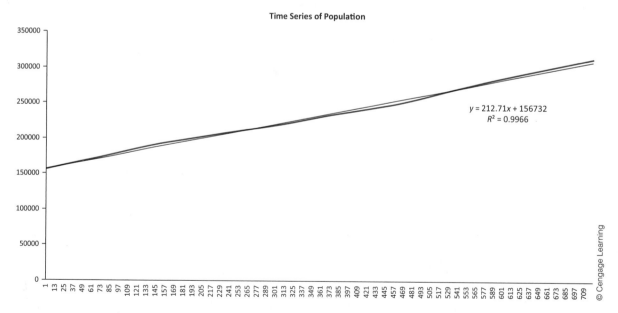

$y = 212.71x + 156732$
$R^2 = 0.9966$

© Cengage Learning

However, the fit is not perfect, as the plot of the residuals in Figure 12.20 indicates. These residuals tend to meander, staying negative for a while, then positive, then negative, and then positive. You can check that the runs test for these residuals produces a z-value of -26.63, with a corresponding p-value of 0.000, and that its first 32 autocorrelations are significantly positive. In short, these residuals are definitely *not* random noise, and they

12-4 Regression-Based Trend Models **609**

Figure 12.20

Time Series Graph
of Residuals

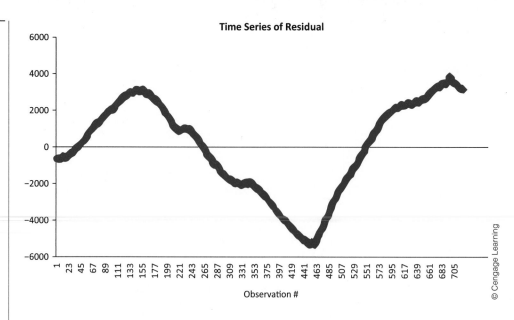

Time Series of Residual

Observation #

© Cengage Learning

could be modeled further. However, we will not pursue this analysis here. In fact, it is not at all obvious how the autocorrelations of the residuals *could* be exploited to get a better forecast model. ∎

12-4b Exponential Trend

An exponential trend for Y is equivalent to a linear trend for the logarithm of Y.

In contrast to a linear trend, an exponential trend is appropriate when the time series changes by a constant *percentage* (as opposed to a constant dollar amount) each period. Then the appropriate regression equation is Equation (12.7), where c and b are constants, and u_t represents a *multiplicative* error term.

Exponential Trend Model

$$Y_t = ce^{bt}u_t \tag{12.7}$$

Equation (12.7) is useful for understanding how an exponential trend works, as we will discuss, but it is not useful for estimation. For that, a *linear* equation is required. Fortunately, linearity can be achieved by taking natural logarithms of both sides of Equation (12.7). (The key, as usual, is that the logarithm of a product is the sum of the logarithms.) The result appears in Equation (12.8), where $a = \ln(c)$ and $e_t = \ln(u_t)$. This equation represents a *linear* trend, but the dependent variable is now the logarithm of the original Y_t. This implies the following important fact: If a time series exhibits an exponential trend, then a plot of its logarithm should be approximately linear.

Equivalent Linear Trend for Logarithm of Y

$$\ln(Y_t) = a + bt + e_t \tag{12.8}$$

Because the software performs the calculations, your main responsibility is to interpret the final result. This is fairly easy. It can be shown that the coefficient b (expressed as a percentage) is approximately the percentage change per period. For example, if $b = 0.05$, the series is increasing by approximately 5% per period.[3] On the other hand, if $b = -0.05$, the series is decreasing by approximately 5% per period.

---

[3]More precisely, this percentage change is $e^b - 1$. For example, when $b = 0.05$, this is $e^b - 1 = 5.13\%$.

An exponential trend can be estimated with the StatTools Regression procedure, but only after the log transformation has been made on Y_t. We illustrate this in Example 12.3.

12.3 QUARTERLY PC DEVICE SALES

The file **PC Device Sales.xlsx** contains quarterly sales data (in millions of dollars) for a large PC device manufacturer from the first quarter of 1999 through the fourth quarter of 2013. Are the company's sales growing exponentially through this entire period?

Objective To estimate the company's exponential growth and to see whether it has been maintained during the entire period from 1999 until the end of 2013.

Solution

We first estimate and interpret an exponential trend for the years 1999 through 2008. Then we see how well the projection of this trend into the future fits the data after 2008. The time series graph through 2008 appears in Figure 12.21. You can use Excel's Trendline tool, with the Exponential option, to superimpose an exponential trend line and the corresponding equation on this plot. The fit is evidently quite good. Equivalently, Figure 12.22 illustrates the time series of log sales for this same period, with a *linear* trend line superimposed. Its fit is equally good.

Figure 12.21

Time Series Graph of Sales with Exponential Trend Superimposed

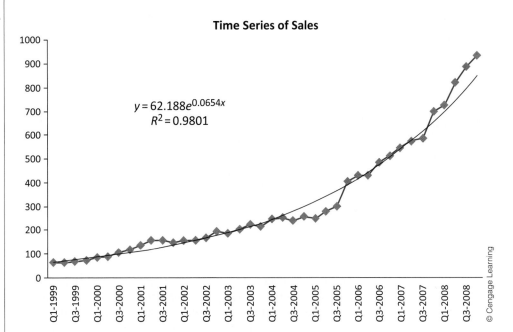

You can also use the StatTools Regression procedure to estimate this exponential trend, as shown in Figure 12.23. To produce this output, you must first add a time variable in column C (with values 1 through 40) and make a logarithmic transformation of Sales in column D. Then you can regress Log(Sales) on Time (using the data through 2008 only) to obtain the regression output. Note that its two coefficients are the same as those shown for the linear trend in Figure 12.22. If you take the antilog of the constant 4.130 (with the formula **=EXP(B19)**), you will obtain the constant *multiple* shown in Figure 12.21. It corresponds to the constant c in Equation (12.7).

What does it all mean? The estimated Equation (12.7) is

$$\text{Forecast Sales} = 62.188e^{0.0654t}$$

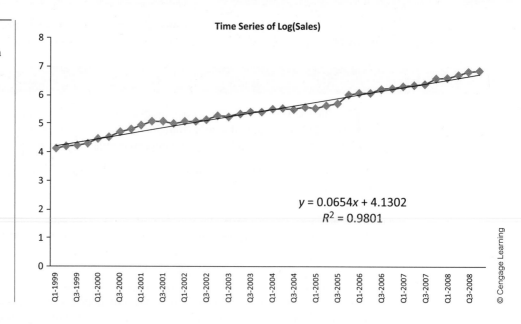

Figure 12.22

Time Series Graph of Log Sales with Linear Trend Superimposed

Time Series of Log(Sales)

$y = 0.0654x + 4.1302$
$R^2 = 0.9801$

© Cengage Learning

Figure 12.23   Regression Output for Estimating Exponential Trend

	A	B	C	D	E	F	G
7	Multiple Regression for Log(Sales)						
8		Multiple	R-Square	Adjusted	StErr of		
9	Summary	R		R-Square	Estimate		
10		0.9900	0.9801	0.9796	0.1104546		
11							
12		Degrees of	Sum of	Mean of	F-Ratio	p-Value	
13	ANOVA Table	Freedom	Squares	Squares			
14	Explained	1	22.82336019	22.82336019	1870.7337	<0.0001	
15	Unexplained	38	0.463608308	0.012200219			
16							
17		Coefficient	Standard	t-Value	p-Value	Confidence Interval 95%	
18	Regression Table		Error			Lower	Upper
19	Constant	4.130161863	0.035594182	116.0347	<0.0001	4.058105209	4.202218517
20	Time	0.065437423	0.001512935	43.2520	<0.0001	0.062374647	0.068500199

© Cengage Learning

The most important constant in this equation is the coefficient of Time, $b = 0.0654$. Expressed as a percentage, this coefficient implies that the company's sales increased by approximately 6.54% per quarter throughout this 10-year period. (The constant multiple, $c = 62.188$, is the forecast of sales at time 0; that is, quarter 4 of 1998.) To use this equation for forecasting the future, substitute later values of Time into the regression equation, so that each future forecast is about 6.54% larger than the previous forecast. For example, the forecast of the second quarter of 2009 is

$$\text{Forecast Sales in Q2-09} = 62.188e^{0.0654(42)} = 971.20$$

Has this exponential growth continued beyond 2008? It has *not,* due possibly to slumping sales in the computer industry or increased competition from other manufacturers. You can check this by creating the Forecast column in Figure 12.24 (by substituting into the regression equation for the entire period through Q4–13). You can then use StatTools to create a time series graph of the two series Sales and Forecast, shown in Figure 12.25. It is clear that sales in the forecast period did not exhibit nearly the 6.54% growth observed in the estimation period. As the company clearly realizes, nothing this good lasts forever.

Figure 12.24

Creating Forecasts of Sales

	A	B	C	D	E
1	Quarter	Sales	Time	Log(Sales)	Forecast
2	Q1-1999	61.14	1	4.113166316	66.39351
3	Q2-1999	64.07	2	4.159976236	70.88343
4	Q3-1999	66.18	3	4.192378302	75.67699
5	Q4-1999	72.76	4	4.287166354	80.79472
6	Q1-2000	84.70	5	4.439115602	86.25853
54	Q1-2012	1466.92	53	7.290920244	1994.892
55	Q2-2012	1465.41	54	7.289890346	2129.799
56	Q3-2012	1592.03	55	7.37276521	2273.828
57	Q4-2012	1700.33	56	7.438577629	2427.598
58	Q1-2013	1689.69	57	7.432300359	2591.767
59	Q2-2013	1796.50	58	7.493595607	2767.037
60	Q3-2013	1822.91	59	7.508189404	2954.161
61	Q4-2013	1898.27	60	7.548698224	3153.938

© Cengage Learning

Figure 12.25 Time Series Graph of Forecasts Superimposed on Sales for the Entire Period

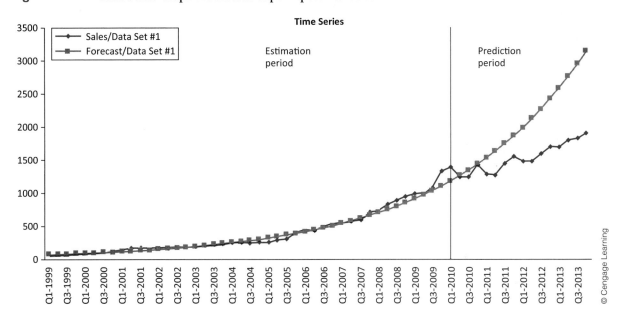

© Cengage Learning

Before leaving this example, we comment briefly on the standard error of estimate shown in cell E10 of Figure 12.23. This value, 0.1105, is in *log* units, not original dollar units. Therefore, it is a totally misleading indicator of the forecast errors that might be made from the exponential trend equation. To obtain more meaningful measures, you should first obtain the forecasts of sales, as explained previously. Then you can easily obtain any of the three forecast error measures discussed previously. The results appear in Figure 12.26.

Figure 12.26 Measures of Forecast Errors

	A	B	C	D	E	F	G	H	I	J	K	L
1	Quarter	Sales	Time	Log(Sales)	Forecast	SqError	AbsError	AbsPctError		Measures of forecast error		
2	Q1-1999	61.14	1	4.113166316	66.39351	27.59935	5.253508	0.085925881		RMSE	33.69	
3	Q2-1999	64.07	2	4.159976236	70.88343	46.42284	6.813431	0.106343544		MAE	23.08	
4	Q3-1999	66.18	3	4.192378302	75.67699	90.19279	9.496989	0.143502396		MAPE	8.30%	
5	Q4-1999	72.76	4	4.287166354	80.79472	64.55665	8.034715	0.110427639				
6	Q1-2000	84.70	5	4.439115602	86.25853	2.429023	1.558532	0.018400619				

© Cengage Learning

The squared errors, absolute errors, and absolute percentage errors are first calculated with the formulas =(B2-E2)^2, =ABS(B2-E2), and =G2/B2 in cells F2, G2, and H2, which are then copied down. The error measures (for the data through 2008 only) then appear in cells K2, K3, and K4. The corresponding formulas for RMSE, MAE, and MAPE are straightforward. RMSE is the square root of the average of the squared errors in column F, and MAE and MAPE are the averages of the values in columns G and H, respectively. The latter is particularly simple to interpret. Forecasts for the 10-year estimation period were off, on average, by 8.30%. (Of course, as you can check, forecasts for the quarters *after* 2008 were off by much more.) ■

Whenever you observe a time series that is increasing at an increasing rate (or decreasing at a decreasing rate), an exponential trend model is worth trying. The key to the analysis is to regress the *logarithm* of the time series variable versus time (or use Excel's Trendline tool). The coefficient of time, written as a percentage, is then the approximate percentage increase (if positive) or decrease (if negative) per period.

PROBLEMS

Level A

9. The file **P12_01.xlsx** contains the monthly number of airline tickets sold by a travel agency.
   a. Does a linear trend appear to fit these data well? If so, estimate and interpret the linear trend model for this time series. Also, interpret the R^2 and s_e values.
   b. Provide an indication of the typical forecast error generated by the estimated model in part **a**.
   c. Is there evidence of some seasonal pattern in these sales data? If so, characterize the seasonal pattern.

10. The file **P12_10.xlsx** contains the daily closing prices of Walmart stock during 2011. Does a linear or exponential trend fit these data well? If so, estimate and interpret the best trend model for this time series. Also, interpret the R^2 and s_e values.

11. The file **P12_11.xlsx** contains monthly values of the U.S. national debt (in dollars) from 1993 to early 2010. Fit an exponential growth curve to these data. Write a short report to summarize your findings. If the U.S. national debt continues to rise at the exponential rate you find, approximately what will its value be at the end of 2020?

12. The file **P12_12.xlsx** contains five years of monthly data on sales (number of units sold) for a particular company. The company suspects that except for random noise, its sales are growing by a constant *percentage* each month and will continue to do so for at least the near future.
   a. Explain briefly whether the plot of the series visually supports the company's suspicion.
   b. Fit the appropriate regression model to the data. Report the resulting equation and state explicitly what it says about the percentage growth per month.

   c. What are the RMSE and MAPE for the forecast model in part **b**? In words, what do they measure? Considering their magnitudes, does the model seem to be doing a good job?
   d. In words, how does the model make forecasts for future months? Specifically, given the forecast value for the last month in the data set, what simple arithmetic could you use to obtain forecasts for the next few months?

13. The file **P12_13.xlsx** contains quarterly data on GDP. (The data are expressed in billions of chained 2005 dollars, and they are seasonally adjusted.)
   a. Look at a time series plot of GDP. Does it suggest an exponential relationship; an exponential relationship?
   b. Use regression to estimate an exponential relationship between GDP and Time (starting with 1 for Q1-1966). Interpret this equation. Would you say that the fit is good?
   c. How would the exponential fit differ if you included only the data through the end of year 2007?

Level B

14. The file **P03_30.xlsx** gives monthly exchange rates (units of local currency per U.S. dollar) for nine currencies. Technical analysts believe that by charting past changes in exchange rates, it is possible to predict future changes of exchange rates. After analyzing the autocorrelations for these data, do you believe that technical analysis has potential?

15. The unit sales of a new drug for the first 25 months after its introduction to the marketplace are recorded in the file **P12_15.xlsx**.

a. Estimate a linear trend equation using the given data. How well does the linear trend fit these data? Are the residuals from this linear trend model *random*?

b. If the residuals from this linear trend model are *not* random, propose another regression-based trend model that more adequately explains the long-term trend in this time series. Estimate the alternative model(s) using the given data. Check the residuals from the model(s) for randomness. Summarize your findings.

c. Given the best estimated model of the trend in this time series, interpret R^2 and s_e.

12-5 THE RANDOM WALK MODEL

Random series are sometimes building blocks for other time series models. The model we now discuss, the **random walk model**, is an example of this. In a random walk model, the series itself is not random. However, its *differences*—that is, the changes from one period to the next—are random. This type of behavior is typical of stock price data (as well as various other time series data). For example, the graph in Figure 12.27 shows monthly closing prices for a manufacturer's stock from January 2006 through April 2012. (See the file **Stock Prices.xlsx**.) This series is not random, as can be seen from its gradual upward trend at the beginning and the general meandering behavior throughout. (Although the runs test and autocorrelations are not shown for the series itself, they confirm that the series is not random. There are significantly *fewer* runs than expected, and the autocorrelations are significantly *positive* for many lags.)

Figure 12.27

Time Series Graph of Stock Prices

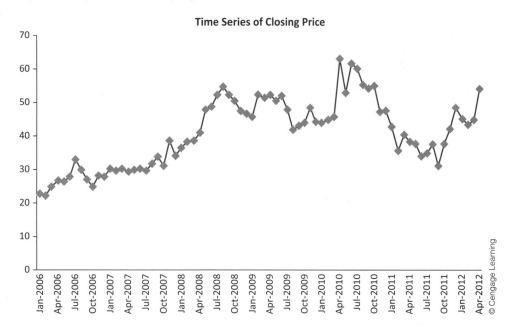

If it were April 2012, and you were asked to forecast the company's prices for the next few months, it is intuitive that you would not use the average of the historical values as your forecast. This forecast would tend to be too low because of the upward trend. Instead, you might base your forecast on the most recent observation. This is exactly what the random walk model does.

Equation (12.9) for the random walk model is given as follows, where m (for mean difference) is a constant and e_t is a random series (noise) with mean 0 and a standard deviation that remains *constant* through time.

> **Random Walk Model**
>
> $$Y_t = Y_{t-1} + m + e_t \qquad (12.9)$$

If we let $DY_t = Y_t - Y_{t-1}$, the change in the series from time t to time $t-1$ (where D stands for difference), then the random walk model can be rewritten as in Equation (12.10). This implies that the differences form a random series with mean m and a constant standard deviation. An estimate of m is the average of the differences, labeled $\overline{Y}_D$, and an estimate of the standard deviation is the sample standard deviation of the differences, labeled s_D.

Difference Form of Random Walk Model
$$DY_t = m + e_t \tag{12.10}$$

In words, a series that behaves according to this random walk model has random differences, and the series tends to trend upward (if $m > 0$) or downward (if $m < 0$) by an amount m each period. If you are standing in period t and want to forecast Y_{t+1}, then a reasonable forecast is given by Equation (12.11). That is, you add the estimated trend to the current observation to forecast the next observation.

One-Step-Ahead Forecast for Random Walk Model
$$F_{t+1} = Y_t + \overline{Y}_D \tag{12.11}$$

We illustrate this method in Example 12.4.

EXAMPLE	**12.4 RANDOM WALK MODEL OF STOCK PRICES**

The monthly closing prices of the manufacturing company's stock from January 2006 through April 2012, shown in Figure 12.27, indicate some upward trend. (See the file **Stock Prices.xlsx**.) Does this series follow a random walk model with an upward trend? If so, how should future values of these stock prices be forecast?

Objective   To check whether the company's monthly closing prices follow a random walk model with an upward trend and to see how future prices can be forecast.

Solution

We have already seen that the closing price series itself is not random, due to the upward trend. To check for the adequacy of a random walk model, a series of *differences* is required. Each value in the differenced series is that month's closing price minus the previous month's closing price. You can calculate this series easily with an Excel formula, or you can generate it automatically by selecting Difference from the StatTools Data Utilities dropdown menu. (When asked for the *number* of difference variables, accept the default value of 1.) This differenced series appears in column C of Figure 12.28. This figure also shows the mean and standard deviation of the differences, 0.418 and 4.245, which are used in forecasting. Finally, this figure shows several autocorrelations of the differences, only one of which is (barely) significant. A runs test for the differences, not shown here, has a large p-value, which supports the conclusion that the differences are random.

The plot of the differences appears in Figure 12.29. A visual inspection of the plot also supports the conclusion of random differences, although these differences do not vary around a mean of 0. Rather, they vary around a mean of 0.418. This positive value measures the upward trend—the closing prices increase, on average, by 0.418 per month. Finally, the variability in this figure is fairly constant (except for the two wide swings in 2010). Specifically, the zigzags do not tend to get appreciably wider through time. Therefore, it

Figure 12.28

Differences of Closing Prices

	A	B	C	D	E	F
1	Month	Closing Price	Difference1(Closing Price)			Difference1(Closing Price)
2	Jan-2006	22.595			One Variable Summary	Data Set #1
3	Feb-2006	22.134	−0.461		Mean	0.418
4	Mar-2006	24.655	2.521		Std. Dev.	4.245
5	Apr-2006	26.649	1.994		Count	75
6	May-2006	26.303	−0.346			
7	Jun-2006	27.787	1.484			Difference1(Closing Price)
8	Jul-2006	32.705	4.918		Autocorrelation Table	Data Set #1
9	Aug-2006	29.745	−2.96		Number of Values	75
10	Sep-2006	26.741	−3.004		Standard Error	0.1155
11	Oct-2006	24.852	−1.889		Lag #1	−0.2435
12	Nov-2006	28.050	3.198		Lag #2	0.1348
13	Dec-2006	27.847	−0.203		Lag #3	−0.0049
14	Jan-2007	30.040	2.193		Lag #4	−0.0507
15	Feb-2007	29.680	−0.36		Lag #5	0.0696
16	Mar-2007	30.139	0.459		Lag #6	0.0009
17	Apr-2007	29.276	−0.863		Lag #7	−0.0630
18	May-2007	29.703	0.427		Lag #8	−0.0295
19	Jun-2007	30.017	0.314		Lag #9	0.0496
20	Jul-2007	29.687	−0.33		Lag #10	−0.1728
21	Aug-2007	31.765	2.078		Lag #11	−0.0334
22	Sep-2007	33.788	2.023		Lag #12	−0.0554
23	Oct-2007	30.942	−2.846			
76	Mar-2012	44.853	1.451			
77	Apr-2012	53.947	9.094			

© Cengage Learning

Figure 12.29

Time Series Graph of Differences

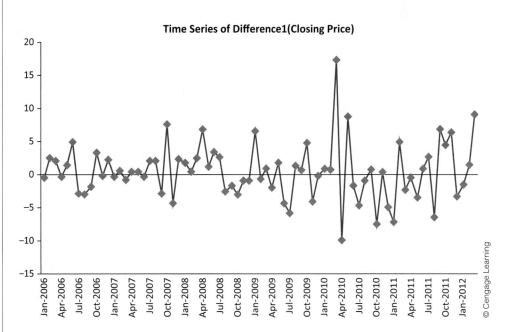

Time Series of Difference1(Closing Price)

© Cengage Learning

is reasonable to conclude that the random walk model with an upward drift fits this series fairly well.

To forecast future closing prices, simply multiply the mean difference by the number of periods ahead, and add this to the final closing price (53.947 in April 2012). For example, a forecast of the closing price for September 2012 is:

$$\text{Forecast Closing Price for 9/12} = 53.947 + 0.418(5) = 56.037$$

As a rough measure of the accuracy of this forecast, you can use the standard deviation of the differences, 4.245. Specifically, it can be shown that the standard error for forecasting k periods ahead is the standard deviation of the differences multiplied by the square root of k. In this case, the standard error is 9.492. As usual, you can be 95% confident that the actual closing price in September will be no more than two standard errors from the forecast. Unfortunately, this results in a wide interval—from about 37 to 75. This reflects the fact that it is very difficult to make accurate forecasts, especially long-range forecasts, for a series with this much variability. ∎

PROBLEMS

Level A

16. The file **P12_16.xlsx** contains the daily closing prices of American Express stock during 2011.

    a. Use the random walk model to forecast the closing price of this stock on the next trading day.

    b. You can be about 95% certain that the forecast made in part **a** will be off by no more than how many dollars?

17. The closing value of the AMEX Airline Index for each trading day during 2011 is given in the file **P12_17.xlsx**.

    a. Use the random walk model to forecast the closing price of this stock on the next trading day.

    b. You can be about 68% certain that the forecast made in part **a** will be off by no more than how many dollars?

18. The file **P12_18.xlsx** contains the daily closing prices of Chevron stock during 2011.

    a. Use the random walk model to forecast the closing price of this stock on the next trading day.

    b. You can be about 99.7% certain that the forecast made in part **a** will be off by no more than how many dollars?

19. The closing value of the Dow Jones Industrial Average for each trading day during 2010 and 2011 is provided in the file **P12_19.xlsx**.

    a. Use the random walk model to forecast the closing price of this index on the next trading day. Is a random walk model justified with these data?

    b. Would it be wise to use the random walk model to forecast the closing price of this index for a trading day approximately *one month* after the next trading day? Explain why or why not.

20. Continuing the previous problem, the *monthly* closing values of the Dow Jones Industrial Average are listed in the file **P11_20.xlsx**. Answer the same questions as in the previous problem, but now for months instead of days.

21. The closing price of a share of JP Morgan Chase stock for each trading day during 2011 is recorded in the file **P12_21.xlsx**.

    a. Use the random walk model to forecast the closing price of this stock on each of the next 10 trading days.

    b. You can be about 68% certain that the last forecast made in part **a** will be off by no more than how many dollars?

22. The purpose of this problem is to get you used to the concept of autocorrelation in a time series. You could do this with any time series, but here you should use the series of Walmart daily stock prices in the file **P12_10.xlsx**.

    a. First, do it the quick way. Use the Autocorrelation procedure in StatTools to get a list of autocorrelations and a corresponding correlogram of the closing prices. You can choose the number of lags.

    b. Now do it the more time-consuming way. Create columns of lagged versions of Closing Price—3 or 4 lags will suffice. Next, look at scatterplots of Closing Price versus its first few lags. If the autocorrelations are large, you should see fairly tight scatters—that's what autocorrelation is all about. Also, generate a correlation matrix to see the correlations between Closing Price and its first few lags. These should be approximately the same as the autocorrelations from part **a**. (Autocorrelations are calculated slightly differently than regular correlations, which accounts for any slight discrepancies you might notice—but these discrepancies should be minor.)

    c. Create the first differences of Closing Price in a new column. (You can do this manually with formulas, or you can use StatTools's Difference procedure on the Data Utilities menu.) Now repeat parts **a** and **b** with the differences instead of the original closing prices—that is, examine the autocorrelations of the differences. They should be small, and the scatterplots of the differences versus lags of the differences should be shapeless swarms. This illustrates what happens when the differences of a time series variable have insignificant autocorrelations.

    d. Write a short report of your findings.

Level B

23. Consider a random walk model with the following equation: $Y_t = Y_{t-1} + 500 + e_t$, where e_t is a normally distributed random series with mean 0 and standard deviation 10.

a. Use Excel to simulate a time series that behaves according to this random walk model.

b. Use the time series you constructed in part **a** to forecast the next observation.

24. The file **P12_24.xlsx** contains the daily closing prices of Procter & Gamble stock from the beginning of July 2010 to the end of June 2011. Use only the 2010 data to estimate the trend component of the random walk model. Next, use the estimated random walk model to forecast the behavior of the time series for the 2011 dates in the series. Comment on the accuracy of the generated forecasts over this period. How could you improve the forecasts as you progress through the 2011 trading days?

12-6 MOVING AVERAGES FORECASTS

Perhaps the simplest and one of the most frequently used extrapolation models is the **moving averages model**. To implement this model, you first choose a **span**, the number of terms in each moving average. Let's say the data are monthly and you choose a span of six months. Then the forecast of next month's value is the average of the values of the last six months. For example, you average January to June to forecast July, you average February to July to forecast August, and so on. This procedure is the reason for the term *moving averages*.

> A **moving average** is the average of the observations in the past few periods, where the number of terms in the average is the **span**.

A moving averages model with a span of 1 is a random walk model with no trend.

The role of the span is important. If the span is large—say, 12 months—then many observations go into each average, and extreme values have relatively little effect on the forecasts. The resulting series of forecasts will be much smoother than the original series. (For this reason, the moving average method is called a *smoothing* method.) In contrast, if the span is small—say, three months—then extreme observations have a larger effect on the forecasts, and the forecast series will be much less smooth. In the extreme, if the span is 1, there is no smoothing effect at all. The method simply forecasts next month's value to be the same as the current month's value. This is often called the *naive* forecasting model. It is a special case of the random walk model with the mean difference equal to 0.

What span should you use? This requires some judgment. If you believe the ups and downs in the series are random noise, then you don't want future forecasts to react too quickly to these ups and downs, and you should use a relatively large span. But if you want to track every little zigzag—under the belief that each up or down is predictable—then you should use a smaller span. You shouldn't be fooled, however, by a plot of the (smoothed) forecast series superimposed on the original series. This graph will almost always look better when a small span is used, because the forecast series will appear to track the original series better. Does this mean it will always provide better future forecasts? Not necessarily. There is little point in tracking random ups and downs closely if they represent unpredictable noise.

Example 12.5 illustrates the use of moving averages.

EXAMPLE | **12.5 HOUSES SOLD IN THE UNITED STATES**

The file **House Sales.xlsx** contains monthly data on the number of new one-family houses sold in the U.S. (in thousands) from January 1991 through December 2011. (These data, available from the U.S. Census Bureau Web site, are listed as SAAR, seasonally adjusted at an annual rate.)[4] A time series graph of the data appears in Figure 12.30. Housing sales were steadily trending upward until about the beginning of 2006, but then the bottom fell out of the housing market. Does a moving averages model fit this series well? What span should be used?

[4]We discuss seasonal adjustment in Section 12-8. Government data are often reported in seasonally adjusted form, with the seasonality removed, to make any trends more apparent.

Figure 12.30 Time Series Plot of Monthly House Sales

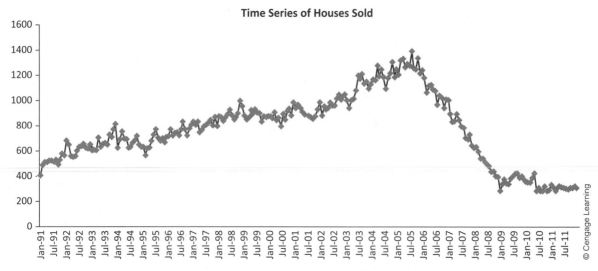

Objective To see whether a moving averages model with an appropriate span fits the housing sales data and to see how StatTools implements this method.

Solution

Although the moving averages method is quite easy to implement in Excel—you just form an average of the appropriate span and copy it down—it can be tedious. It is much easier to implement with StatTools. Actually, the StatTools forecasting procedure is fairly general in that it allows you to forecast with several methods, either with or without taking seasonality into account. Because this is your first exposure to this procedure, we will go through it in some detail in this example. In later examples, we will mention some of its other capabilities.

To use the StatTools Forecasting procedure, select Forecast from the StatTools Time Series and Forecasting dropdown list. This brings up the dialog box in Figure 12.31, which has three tabs in its bottom section. The Time Scale tab, shown in Figure 12.31, allows you

Figure 12.31

Forecast Dialog Box with Time Scale Tab Visible

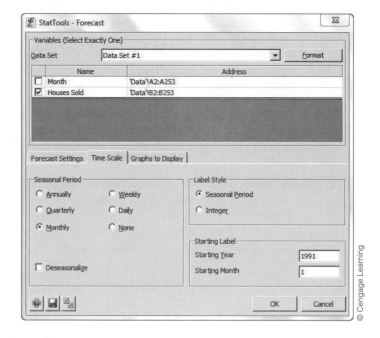

to select the time period. The Forecast Settings tab, shown in Figure 12.32, allows you to select a forecasting method. Finally, the Graphs to Display tab, not shown here, allows you to select several optional time series graphs. For now, fill out the dialog box sections as shown and select the Forecast Overlay option in the Graphs to Display tab. In particular, note from Figure 12.32 that the moving averages method is being used with a span of 3, and it will generate forecasts for the next 12 months.

Figure 12.32

Forecast Dialog Box with Forecast Settings Tab Visible

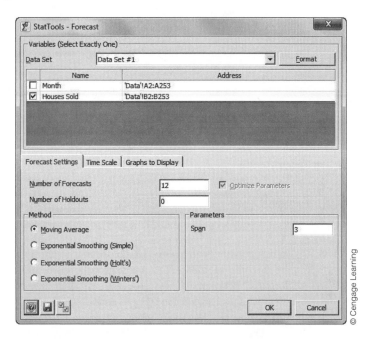

Another option in Figure 12.32 is that you can elect to "hold out" a subset of the series for validation purposes. If you hold out several periods at the end of the series for validation, any model that is built is estimated only for the non-holdout observations, and summary measures are reported for the non-holdout and holdout subsets separately. For now, don't use a holdout period.

The output consists of several parts, as shown in Figures 12.33 through 12.36. We actually ran the analysis twice, once for a span of 3 and once for a span of 12. These figures show the comparison. (We also obtained output for a span of 6, with results fairly similar to those for a span of 3.) First, the summary measures MAE, RMSE, and MAPE of the forecast errors are shown in Figure 12.33. As you can see, the forecasts using a span of 3 are considerably more accurate. For example, they are off by about 5.73% on average, whereas the similar measure with a span of 12 is 9.07%.

The essence of the forecasting method is very simple and is captured in column C of Figure 12.34 for a span of 3 (with many hidden rows). Each value in the historical period

Figure 12.33 Moving Averages Summary Output

◢	A	B	C	D	E	F	G
7	*Moving Averages Forecasts for Houses Sold*					*Moving Averages Forecasts for Houses Sold*	
8	*Forecasting Constant*					*Forecasting Constant*	
9	Span	3				Span	12
10							
11							
12	*Moving Averages*					*Moving Averages*	
13	Mean Abs Err	40.28				Mean Abs Err	62.25
14	Root Mean Sq Err	52.22				Root Mean Sq Err	82.26
15	Mean Abs Per% Err	5.37%				Mean Abs Per% Err	9.07%

Figure 12.34   Moving Averages Detailed Output

	A	B	C	D	E	F	G	H	I
40	*Forecasting Data*	House Sold	Forecast	Error		*Forecasting Data*	House Sold	Forecast	Error
41	Jan-1991	401.00				Jan-1991	401.00		
42	Feb-1991	482.00				Feb-1991	482.00		
43	Mar-1991	507.00				Mar-1991	507.00		
289	Sep-2011	302.00	296.00	6.00		Sep-2011	302.00	302.00	0.00
290	Oct-2011	307.00	295.67	11.33		Oct-2011	307.00	300.83	6.17
291	Nov-2011	314.00	299.67	14.33		Nov-2011	314.00	302.92	11.08
292	Dec-2011	307.00	307.67	−0.67		Dec-2011	307.00	305.17	1.83
293	Jan-2012		309.33			Jan-2012		303.17	
294	Feb-2012		310.11			Feb-2012		302.60	
295	Mar-2012		308.81			Mar-2012		304.40	
296	Apr-2012		309.42			Apr-2012		304.35	
297	May-2012		309.45			May-2012		303.38	
298	Jun-2012		309.23			Jun-2012		302.99	
299	Jul-2012		309.37			Jul-2012		302.99	
300	Aug-2012		309.35			Aug-2012		303.66	
301	Sep-2012		309.31			Sep-2012		304.79	
302	Oct-2012		309.34			Oct-2012		305.03	
303	Nov-2012		309.33			Nov-2012		304.86	
304	Dec-2012		309.33			Dec-2012		304.10	

in this column is an average of the three preceding values in column B. The forecast errors are then just the differences between columns B and C. For the future periods, the forecast formulas in column C use observations when they are available. If they are not available, previous forecasts are used. For example, the forecast for February 2012 is the average of the *observed* values in November and December 2011 and the *forecast* value in January 2012.

The graphs in Figures 12.35 and 12.36 show the behavior of the forecasts. The forecast series with span 3 follows the ups and downs of the actual series fairly closely, and when the series starts going down, the moving averages track the turnaround fairly well. In contrast, the 12-month moving average series is much smoother. This is probably a good feature when the series is trending upward—there is no sense in tracking the noise—but

Figure 12.35

Moving Averages
Forecasts with
Span 3

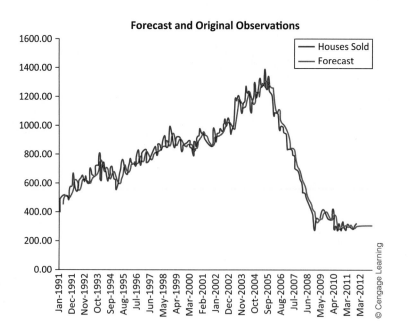

Forecast and Original Observations

Figure 12.36

Moving Averages
Forecasts with
Span 12

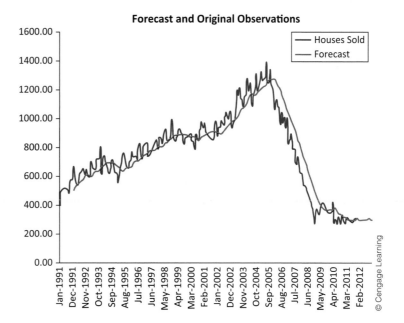

Forecast and Original Observations

when the series suddenly starts downward, the moving averages consistently lag behind. That is, the forecasts in this latter period are consistently too high. (This same behavior occurs for a span of 6, but the forecasts are not as biased in the latter part of the series as with a span of 12.)

One interesting feature of the moving average method is that *future* forecasts tend to be quite flat. This is apparent in the last two figures, but you can check that if we had used only the data through 2008, where the series was still trending downward, the forecasts for 2009 would still be fairly constant; they would *not* continue to decrease. This is a basic property of moving average forecasts: *future* forecasts tend to be close to the last few values of the series. ∎

The moving average method we have presented is the simplest of a group of moving average methods used by professional forecasters. We *smoothed* exactly once; that is, we took moving averages of several observations at a time and used these as forecasts. More complex methods smooth more than once, basically to get rid of random noise. They take moving averages, then moving averages of these moving averages, and so on for several stages. This can become quite complex, but the objective is quite simple—to smooth the data so that underlying patterns are easier to see.

PROBLEMS

Level A

25. The file **P12_16.xlsx** contains the daily closing prices of American Express stock during 2011.
   a. Using a span of 3, forecast the price of this stock for the next trading day with the moving average method. How well does this method with span 3 forecast the known observations in this series?
   b. Repeat part **a** with a span of 10.
   c. Which of these two spans appears to be more appropriate? Justify your choice.

26. The closing value of the AMEX Airline Index for each trading day during 2011 is given in the file **P12_17.xlsx**.
   a. How well does the moving average method track this series when the span is 4; when the span is 12?
   b. Using the more appropriate span, forecast the closing value of this index on the next trading day with the moving average method.

27. The closing value of the Dow Jones Industrial Average for each trading day during 2010 and 2011 is provided in the file **P12_19.xlsx**.

a. Using a span of 2, forecast the price of this index on the next trading day with the moving average method. How well does the moving average method with span 2 forecast the known observations in this series?

b. Repeat part **a** with a span of 5; with a span of 15.

c. Which of these three spans appears to be most appropriate? Justify your choice.

28. The file **P12_10.xlsx** contains the daily closing prices of Walmart stock during 2011. Use the moving average method with a carefully chosen span to forecast this time series for the next three trading days. Defend your choice of the span used.

29. The Consumer Confidence Index (CCI) attempts to measure people's feelings about general business conditions, employment opportunities, and their own income prospects. The file **P02_20.xlsx** contains the annual average values of the CCI. Use the moving average method with a carefully chosen span to forecast this time series in the next two years. Defend your choice of the span used.

Level B

30. The file **P02_28.xlsx** contains total monthly U.S. retail sales data. While holding out the final six months of observations for validation purposes, use the method of moving averages with a carefully chosen span to forecast U.S. retail sales in the next year. Comment on the performance of your model. What makes this time series more challenging to forecast?

31. Consider a random walk model with the following equation: $Y_t = Y_{t-1} + e_t$, where e_t is a random series with mean 0 and standard deviation 1. Specify a moving average model that is equivalent to this random walk model. In particular, what is the appropriate span in the equivalent moving average model? What is the smoothing effect of this span?

12-7 EXPONENTIAL SMOOTHING FORECASTS

There are two possible criticisms of the moving averages method. First, it puts equal weight on each value in a typical moving average. Many analysts would argue that if next month's forecast is to be based on the previous 12 months' observations, more weight should be placed on the more recent observations. The second criticism is that the moving averages method requires a lot of data storage. This is particularly true for companies that routinely make forecasts of hundreds or even thousands of items. If 12-month moving averages are used for 1000 items, then 12,000 values are needed for next month's forecasts. This may or may not be a concern, given today's inexpensive computer storage.

Exponential smoothing is a method that addresses both of these criticisms. It bases its forecasts on a weighted average of past observations, with more weight on the more recent observations, and it requires very little data storage. In addition, it is not difficult for most business people to understand, at least conceptually. Therefore, this method is used widely in the business world, particularly when frequent and automatic forecasts of many items are required.

There are many variations of exponential smoothing. The simplest is appropriately called *simple* exponential smoothing. It is relevant when there is no pronounced trend or seasonality in the series. If there is a trend but no seasonality, *Holt's* method is applicable. If, in addition, there is seasonality, *Winters'* method can be used. This does not exhaust the types of exponential smoothing models—researchers have invented many other variations—but these three models will suffice for us.

> **Simple exponential smoothing** is appropriate for a series with no pronounced trend or seasonality. **Holt's method** is appropriate for a series with trend but no seasonality. **Winters' method** is appropriate for a series with seasonality (and possibly trend).

In this section we examine simple exponential smoothing and Holt's method for trend. Then in the next section we examine Winters' method for seasonal models.

12-7a Simple Exponential Smoothing

The level is an estimate of where the series would be if it were not for random noise.

We now examine simple exponential smoothing in some detail. We first introduce two new terms. Every exponential model has at least one **smoothing constant**, which is always a number between 0 and 1. Simple exponential smoothing has a single smoothing constant denoted by α. (Its role is discussed shortly.) The second new term is L_t, called the *level* of the series at time t. This value is not observable but can only be estimated. Essentially, it is an estimate of where the series would be at time t if there were no random noise. Then the simple exponential smoothing method is defined by the following two equations, where F_{t+k} is the forecast of Y_{t+k} made at time t:

Simple Exponential Smoothing Formulas

$$L_t = \alpha Y_t + (1 - \alpha)L_{t-1} \tag{12.12}$$

$$F_{t+k} = L_t \tag{12.13}$$

Even though you usually don't have to substitute into these equations manually, you should understand what they say. Equation (12.12) shows how to update the estimate of the level. It is a weighted average of the current observation, Y_t, and the previous level, L_{t-1}, with respective weights α and $1 - \alpha$. Equation (12.13) shows how forecasts are made. It says that the k-period-ahead forecast, F_{t+k}, made of Y_{t+k} in period t is the most recently estimated level, L_t. This is the *same* for any value of $k \geq 1$. The idea is that in simple exponential smoothing, you believe that the series is not really going anywhere. So as soon as you estimate where the series ought to be in period t (if it weren't for random noise), you forecast that this is where it will be in any future period.

The smoothing constant α is analogous to the span in moving averages. There are two ways to see this. The first way is to rewrite Equation (12.12), using the fact that the forecast error, E_t, made in forecasting Y_t at time $t - 1$ is $Y_t - F_t = Y_t - L_{t-1}$. Using algebra, Equation (12.12) can be rewritten as Equation (12.14).

Equivalent Formula for Simple Exponential Smoothing

$$L_t = L_{t-1} + \alpha E_t \tag{12.14}$$

This equation says that the next estimate of the level is adjusted from the previous estimate by adding a multiple of the most recent forecast error. This makes sense. If the previous forecast was too high, then E_t is negative, and the estimate of the level is adjusted downward. The opposite is true if the previous forecast was too low. However, Equation (12.14) says that the method does not adjust by the entire magnitude of E_t, but only by a fraction of it. If α is small, say, $\alpha = 0.1$, the adjustment is minor; if α is close to 1, the adjustment is large. So if you want the method to react quickly to movements in the series, you should choose a large α; otherwise, you should choose a small α.

Another way to see the effect of α is to substitute recursively into the equation for L_t. By performing some algebra, you can verify that L_t satisfies Equation (12.15), where the sum extends back to the first observation at time $t = 1$.

Another Equivalent Formula for Simple Exponential Smoothing

$$L_t = \alpha Y_t + \alpha(1 - \alpha)Y_{t-1} + \alpha(1 - \alpha)^2 Y_{t-2} + \alpha(1 - \alpha)^3 Y_{t-3} + \cdots \tag{12.15}$$

Equation (12.15) shows how the exponentially smoothed forecast is a weighted average of previous observations. Furthermore, because $1 - \alpha$ is less than 1, the weights on the Ys decrease from time t backward. If α is close to 0, then $1 - \alpha$ is close to 1 and the weights decrease very slowly. In other words, observations from the distant past continue to have a large influence on the next forecast. This means that the graph of the forecasts will be relatively smooth, just as with a large span in the moving averages method. But if α is close to 1, the weights decrease rapidly, and only very recent observations have much influence on the next forecast. In this case forecasts react quickly to sudden changes in the series. This is equivalent to a small span in moving averages.

Small smoothing constants provide forecasts that respond slowly to changes in the series. Large smoothing constants do the opposite.

What value of α should you use? There is no universally accepted answer to this question. Some practitioners recommend always using a value around 0.1 or 0.2. Others recommend experimenting with different values of α until a measure such as RMSE or MAPE is minimized. Some packages even have an optimization feature to find this optimal value of α. (This is the case with StatTools.) But just as we discussed in the moving averages section, the value of α that tracks the historical series most closely does not necessarily guarantee the most accurate *future* forecasts.

FUNDAMENTAL INSIGHT

Smoothing Constants in Exponential Smoothing

All versions of exponential smoothing—and there are more than are discussed here—use one or more smoothing constants between 0 and 1. To make any such method produce smoother forecasts,

and hence react less quickly to noise, you should use smaller smoothing constants, such as 0.1 or 0.2. When larger smoothing constants are used, the historical forecasts might appear to track the actual series fairly closely, but they might just be tracking random noise.

EXAMPLE | 12.5 HOUSES SOLD IN THE UNITED STATES (CONTINUED)

Previously, we used the moving averages method to forecast monthly housing sales in the U.S. (See the **House Sales.xlsx** file.) How well does simple exponential smoothing work with this data set? What smoothing constant should be used?

Objective To see how well a simple exponential smoothing model, with an appropriate smoothing constant, fits the housing sales data, and to see how StatTools implements this method.

Solution

You can use StatTools to implement the simple exponential smoothing model, specifically equations (12.12) and (12.13). You do this again by selecting Forecast from the StatTools Time Series and Forecasting dropdown list. Specifically, you fill in the forecast dialog box essentially as with moving averages, except that you select the simple exponential smoothing option in the Forecast Settings tab (see Figure 12.37). You should also choose a smoothing constant (0.2 was chosen here, but any other value could be chosen) or you can elect to find an optimal smoothing constant (we didn't optimize for this example, at least not yet).

The results appear in Figures 12.38 (with many hidden rows) and 12.39. The heart of the method takes place in columns C, D, and E of Figure 12.38. Column C calculates the smoothed levels (L_t) from Equation (12.12), column D calculates the forecasts (F_t) from Equation (12.13), and column E calculates the forecast errors (E_t) as the observed values minus the forecasts. Although the Excel formulas do not appear in the figure, you can examine them in the StatTools output.

Every exponential smoothing method requires *initial* values, in this case the initial smoothed level in cell C41. There is no way to calculate this value, L_1, from Equation (12.12)

Figure 12.37
Forecast Settings for Exponential Smoothing

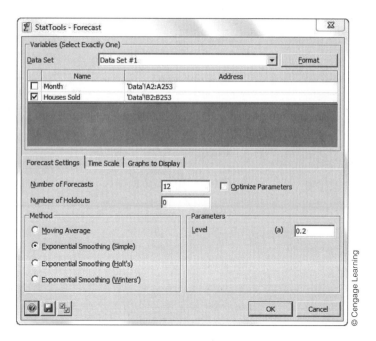

Figure 12.38
Simple Exponential Smoothing Output

	A	B	C	D	E
7	*Simple Exponential Smoothing Forecasts for Houses Sold*				
8	*Forecasting Constant*				
9	Level (Alpha)	0.200			
10					
11					
12	*Simple Exponential*				
13	Mean Abs Err	51.72			
14	Root Mean Sq Err	67.52			
15	Mean Abs Per% Err	7.61%			
16					
40	*Forecasting Data*	Houses Sold	Level	Forecast	Error
41	Jan-1991	401.00	401.00		
42	Feb-1991	482.00	417.20	401.00	81.00
43	Mar-1991	507.00	435.16	417.20	89.80
289	Sep-2011	302.00	301.79	301.73	0.27
290	Oct-2011	307.00	302.83	301.79	5.21
291	Nov-2011	314.00	305.06	302.83	11.17
292	Dec-2011	307.00	305.45	305.06	1.94
293	Jan-2012			305.45	
294	Feb-2012			305.45	
295	Mar-2012			305.45	
296	Apr-2012			305.45	
297	May-2012			305.45	
298	Jun-2012			305.45	
299	July-2012			305.45	
300	Aug-2012			305.45	
301	Sep-2012			305.45	
302	Oct-2012			305.45	
303	Nov-2012			305.45	
304	Dec-2012			305.45	

© Cengage Learning

Figure 12.39

Graph of Forecasts
from Simple
Exponential
Smoothing

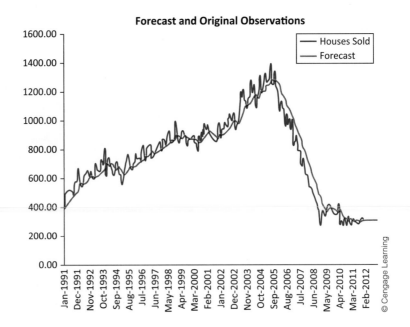

because the *previous* value, L_0, is unknown. Different implementations of exponential smoothing initialize in different ways. StatTools initializes by setting L_1 equal to Y_1 (in cell B41). The effect of initializing in different ways is usually minimal because any effect of early data is usually washed out as forecasts are made into the future. In the present example, values from 1991 have little effect on forecasts for 2012 and beyond.

Note that the 12 future forecasts (rows 293 down) are all equal to the last calculated smoothed level, the one for December 2011 in cell C292. The fact that these remain constant is a consequence of the assumption behind *simple* exponential smoothing, namely, that the series is not really going anywhere. Therefore, the last smoothed level is the best available indication of future values of the series.

Figure 12.39 shows the forecast series superimposed on the original series. You can see the obvious smoothing effect of a relatively small α level. The forecasts don't track the series very well, but if the various zigzags in the original series are really random noise, then perhaps the forecasts shouldn't try to track these random ups and downs too closely. That is, perhaps a forecast series that emphasizes the basic underlying pattern is preferred. However, notice that once the series starts going downhill, the forecasts never quite catch up. This is the same behavior you saw with a span of 12 for moving averages.

In the next subsection, Holt's method is used on this series to see whether it captures the trend better than simple exponential smoothing.

You can see several summary measures of the forecast errors in Figure 12.38. The RMSE and MAE indicate that the forecasts from this model are typically off by a magnitude of about 52 to 68 thousand, and the MAPE indicates that they are off by about 7.6%. (These are similar to the errors obtained earlier with moving averages with span 12.) These are fairly sizable errors. One way to reduce the errors is to use a different smoothing method. We will try this in the next subsection with Holt's method. Another way to reduce the errors is to use a different smoothing constant. There are two methods you can use. First, you can simply enter different values in the smoothing constant cell in the Forecast sheet. All formulas, including those for MAE, RMSE, and MAPE, will update automatically.

Second, you can check the Optimize Parameters option in the Forecast dialog box shown in Figure 12.37. This automatically runs an optimization algorithm (not Solver, by the way) to find the smoothing constant that minimizes RMSE. (StatTools is programmed to minimize RMSE. However, you could try minimizing MAPE, say, by using Excel's Solver add-in.) When this optimization option is used for the housing data, the results in Figure 12.40 are obtained (from a smoothing constant of 0.680). The corresponding MAE, RMSE, and MAPE are 38.1, 49.0, and 5.36%, respectively—better than before. This larger smoothing constant produces a less smooth forecast curve and slightly better error measures. However, there is no guarantee that *future* forecasts made with this optimal smoothing constant will be any better than with a smoothing constant of 0.2. ∎

Figure 12.40

Graph of Forecasts with an Optimal Smoothing Constant

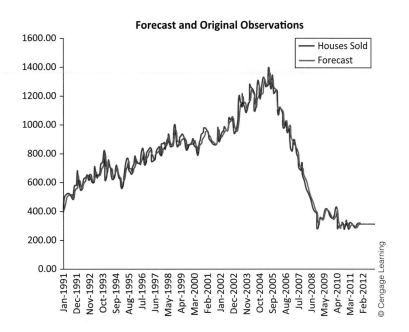

12-7b Holt's Model for Trend

The trend term in Holt's method estimates the change from one period to the next.

The simple exponential smoothing model generally works well if there is no obvious trend in the series. But if there is a trend, this method consistently lags behind it. For example, if the series is constantly increasing, simple exponential smoothing forecasts will be consistently low. Holt's method rectifies this by dealing with trend explicitly. In addition to the level of the series, L_t, Holt's method includes a trend term, T_t, and a corresponding smoothing constant β. The interpretation of L_t is exactly as before. The interpretation of T_t is that it represents an estimate of the *change* in the series from one period to the next. The equations for Holt's model are as follows.

Formulas for Holt's Exponential Smoothing Method

$$L_t = \alpha Y_t + (1 - \alpha)(L_{t-1} + T_{t-1}) \qquad \textbf{(12.16)}$$

$$T_t = \beta(L_t - L_{t-1}) + (1 - \beta)T_{t-1} \qquad \textbf{(12.17)}$$

$$F_{t+k} = L_t + kT_t \qquad \textbf{(12.18)}$$

These equations are not as bad as they look. (And don't forget that the software does all of the calculations for you.) Equation (12.16) says that the updated level is a weighted average of the current observation and the previous level plus the estimated change. Equation (12.17) says that the updated trend is a weighted average of the difference between two consecutive levels and the previous trend. Finally, Equation (12.18) says that the k-period-ahead forecast made in period t is the estimated level plus k times the estimated change per period.

Everything we said about α for simple exponential smoothing applies to both α and β in Holt's model. The new smoothing constant β controls how quickly the method reacts to observed changes in the trend. If β is small, the method reacts slowly. If it is large, the method reacts more quickly. Of course, there are now two smoothing constants to select. Some practitioners suggest using a small value of α (0.1 to 0.2, say) and setting β equal to α. Others suggest using an optimization option (available in StatTools) to select the optimal smoothing constants. We illustrate the possibilities in the following continuation of the housing sales example.

EXAMPLE | **12.5 HOUSES SOLD IN THE UNITED STATES (CONTINUED)**

We again examine the monthly data on housing sales in the U.S. In the previous subsection, we saw that simple exponential smoothing, even with an optimal smoothing constant, does only a fair job of forecasting housing sales. Given that there is an upward trend and then a downward trend in housing sales over this period, Holt's method might be expected to perform better. Does it? What smoothing constants are appropriate?

Objective   To see whether Holt's method, with appropriate smoothing constants, captures the trends in the housing sales data better than simple exponential smoothing (or moving averages).

Solution

You implement Holt's method in StatTools almost exactly as for simple exponential smoothing. The only difference is that you can now choose *two* smoothing constants, as shown in Figure 12.41. They can have different values, but they have both been chosen to be 0.2 for this example.

Figure 12.41

Dialog Box for Holt's Method

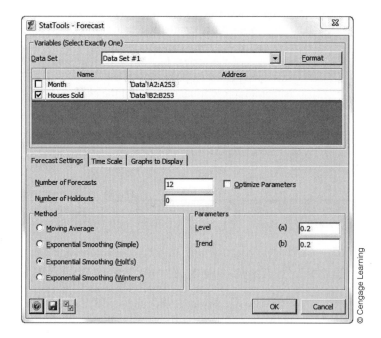

© Cengage Learning

The StatTools outputs in Figures 12.42 and 12.43 are also very similar to the simple exponential smoothing outputs. The only difference is that there is now a trend column, column D, in the numerical output. You can check that the formulas in columns C, D, and E implement equations (12.16), (12.17), and (12.18). As before, an initialization is required in row 42. These require values of L_1 and T_1 to get the method started. Different implementations of Holt's method obtain these initial values in slightly different ways, but the effect is fairly minimal in most cases. (You can check cells C42 and D42 to see how StatTools does it.[5])

Figure 12.42 Output from Holt's Method

	A	B	C	D	E	F
7	Holt's Exponential Smoothing Forecasts for Houses Sold					
8	Forecasting Constants					
9	Level (Alpha)	0.200				
10	Trend (Beta)	0.200				
11						
12						
13	Holt's Exponential					
14	Mean Abs Err	41.50				
15	Root Mean Sq Err	53.86				
16	Mean Abs Per% Err	6.11%				
17						
41	Forecasting Data	Houses Sold	Level	Trend	Forecast	Error
42	Jan-1991	401.00	401.00	−0.37		
43	Feb-1991	482.00	416.90	2.88	400.63	81.37
44	Mar-1991	507.00	437.23	6.37	419.78	87.22
290	Sep-2011	302.00	289.85	−0.78	286.81	15.19
291	Oct-2011	307.00	292.65	−0.07	289.07	17.93
292	Nov-2011	314.00	296.87	0.79	292.59	21.41
293	Dec-2011	307.00	299.53	1.16	297.66	9.34
294	Jan-2012				300.69	
295	Feb-2012				301.85	
296	Mar-2012				303.02	
297	Apr-2012				304.18	
298	May-2012				305.34	
299	Jun-2012				306.51	
300	Jul-2012				307.67	
301	Aug-2012				308.83	
302	Sep-2012				310.00	
303	Oct-2012				311.16	
304	Nov-2012				312.32	
305	Dec-2012				313.48	

The error measures for this implementation of Holt's method are slightly better than for simple exponential smoothing, but these measures are fairly sensitive to the smoothing constants. Therefore, a second run of Holt's method was performed, using the Optimize Parameters option. This resulted in somewhat better results and the forecasts shown in Figure 12.44. The optimal smoothing constants are $\alpha = 0.679$ and $\beta = 0.000$, and the MAE, RMSE, and MAPE values are identical to those from simple exponential smoothing

[5]The initial trend in cell D42 (the first period) is the final observation minus the initial observation, all divided by the number of observations. This is the average change over the entire time period. This might not be the best way to initialize, as suggested by the literature, and StatTools might be rewritten in a future version to initialize with the average change over the first two years. This would give it a better chance to *learn* how a trend changes over time.

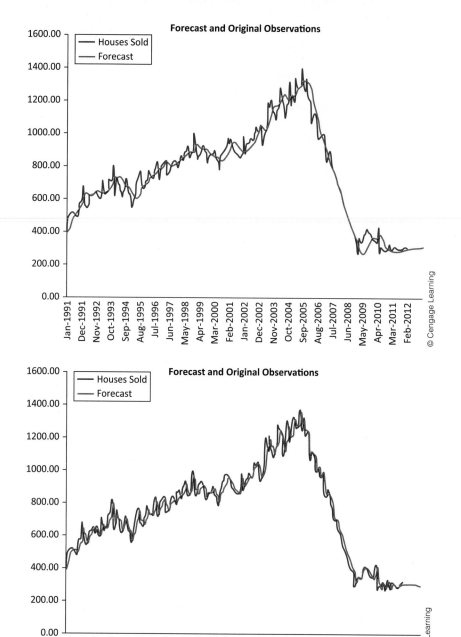

Figure 12.43

Forecasts from Holt's Method with Nonoptimal Smoothing Constants

Figure 12.44

Forecasts from Holt's Method with Optimal Smoothing Constants

with an optimal smoothing constant. Note that the zero smoothing constant for trend doesn't mean that there is no trend. It just means that the *initial* estimate of trend, the average change from the first time period to the last, is kept throughout. For this particular time series, despite the upward trend and the downward trend, the series ends very close to where it started. Therefore, the initial trend estimate is about zero, and future forecasts with the optimal smoothing constants are essentially flat. However, you can check that if a larger smoothing constant for trend is used, say 0.4, future forecasts will exhibit the slight upward trend evident in 2011. Based on a look at the graph and common sense, we would suggest smoothing constants of about 0.2 for this series.

You should not conclude from this example that Holt's method is never superior to simple exponential smoothing. Holt's method is often able to react quickly to a sudden upswing or downswing in the data, whereas simple exponential smoothing typically has a delayed reaction to such a change. ■

PROBLEMS

Level A

32. Consider the airline ticket data in the file **P12_01.xlsx.**
    a. Create a time series chart of the data. Based on what you see, which of the exponential smoothing models do you think should be used for forecasting? Why?
    b. Use simple exponential smoothing to forecast these data, using no holdout period and requesting 12 months of future forecasts. Use the default smoothing constant of 0.1.
    c. Repeat part **b**, optimizing the smoothing constant. Does it make much of an improvement?
    d. Write a short report to summarize your results.

33. Consider the applications for home mortgages data in the file **P12_04.xlsx.**
    a. Create a time series chart of the data. Based on what you see, which of the exponential smoothing models do you think should be used for forecasting? Why?
    b. Use simple exponential smoothing to forecast these data, using no holdout period and requesting four quarters of future forecasts. Use the default smoothing constant of 0.1.
    c. Repeat part **b**, optimizing the smoothing constant. Does it make much of an improvement?
    d. Write a short report to summarize your results.

34. Consider the American Express closing price data in the file **P12_16.xlsx.**
    a. Create a time series chart of the data. Based on what you see, which of the exponential smoothing models do you think should be used for forecasting? Why?
    b. Use Holt's exponential smoothing to forecast these data, using no holdout period and requesting 20 days of future forecasts. Use the default smoothing constants of 0.1.
    c. Repeat part **b**, optimizing the smoothing constants. Does it make much of an improvement?
    d. Repeat parts **a** and **b**, this time using a holdout period of 50 days.
    e. Write a short report to summarize your results.

35. Consider the poverty level data in the file **P02_44.xlsx.**
    a. Create a time series chart of the data. Based on what you see, which of the exponential smoothing models do you think should be used for forecasting? Why?

    b. Use simple exponential smoothing to forecast these data, using no holdout period and requesting three years of future forecasts. Use the default smoothing constant of 0.1.
    c. Repeat part **b**, optimizing the smoothing constant. Make sure you request a chart of the series with the forecasts superimposed. Does the Optimize Parameters option make much of an improvement?
    d. Write a short report to summarize your results. Considering the chart in part **c**, would you say the forecasts are adequate?

Problems 36 through 38 ask you to apply the exponential smoothing formulas. These do not require StatTools. In fact, they do not even require Excel. You can do them with a calculator (or with Excel).

36. An automobile dealer is using Holt's method to forecast weekly car sales. Currently, the level is estimated to be 50 cars per week, and the trend is estimated to be six cars per week. During the current week, 30 cars are sold. After observing the current week's sales, forecast the number of cars three weeks from now. Use $\alpha = \beta = 0.3$.

37. You have been assigned to forecast the number of aircraft engines ordered each month from an engine manufacturing company. At the end of February, the forecast is that 100 engines will be ordered during April. Then during March, 120 engines are actually ordered.
    a. Using $\alpha = 0.3$, determine a forecast (at the end of March) for the number of orders placed during April and during May. Use simple exponential smoothing.
    b. Suppose that MAE = 16 at the end of March. At the end of March, the company can be 68% sure that April orders will be between what two values, assuming normally distributed forecast errors? (*Hint*: It can be shown that the standard deviation of forecast errors is approximately 1.25 times MAE.)

38. Simple exponential smoothing with $\alpha = 0.3$ is being used to forecast sales of SLR (single lens reflex) cameras at an appliance store. Forecasts are made on a monthly basis. After August camera sales are observed, the forecast for September is 100 cameras.
    a. During September, 120 cameras are sold. After observing September sales, what is the forecast

for October camera sales? What is the forecast for November camera sales?

b. It turns out that June sales were recorded as 10 cameras. Actually, however, 100 cameras were sold in June. After correcting for this error, what is the forecast for October camera sales?

Level B

39. Holt's method assumes an *additive* trend. For example, a trend of five means that the level will increase by five units per period. Suppose that there is actually a *multiplicative* trend. For example, if the current estimate of the level is 50 and the current estimate of the trend is 1.2, the forecast of demand increases by 20% per period. So the forecast demand for next period is 50(1.2) and forecast demand for two periods in the future is $50(1.2)^2$. If you want to use a multiplicative trend in Holt's method, you should use equations of the form:

$$L_t = \alpha Y_t + (1 - \alpha)(I)$$
$$T_t = \beta(II) + (1 - \beta)T_{t-1}$$

a. What should (*I*) and (*II*) be?

b. Suppose you are working with monthly data and month 12 is December, month 13 is January, and so on. Also suppose that $L_{12} = 100$ and $T_{12} = 1.2$, and you observe $Y_{13} = 200$. At the end of month 13, what is the forecast for Y_{15}? Assume $\alpha = \beta = 0.5$ and a multiplicative trend.

40. A version of simple exponential smoothing can be used to predict the outcome of sporting events. To illustrate, consider pro football. Assume for simplicity that all games are played on a neutral field. Before each day of play, assume that each team has a rating. For example, if the rating for the Bears is +10 and the rating for the Bengals is +6, the Bears are predicted to beat the Bengals by $10 - 6 = 4$ points. Suppose that the Bears play the Bengals and win by 20 points. For this game, the model underpredicted the Bears' performance by $20 - 4 = 16$ points. Assuming that the best α for pro football is 0.10, the Bears' rating will increase by $16(0.1) = 1.6$ points and the Bengals' rating will decrease by 1.6 points. In a rematch, the Bears will then be favored by $(10 + 1.6) - (6 - 1.6) = 7.2$ points.

a. How does this approach relate to the equation $L_t = L_{t-1} + \alpha E_t$?

b. Suppose that the home field advantage in pro football is three points; that is, home teams tend to outscore equally rated visiting teams by an average of three points a game. How could the home field advantage be incorporated into this system?

c. How might you determine the *best* α for pro football?

d. How could the ratings for each team at the beginning of the season be chosen?

e. Suppose this method is used to predict pro football (16-game schedule), college football (11-game schedule), college basketball (30-game schedule), and pro basketball (82-game schedule). Which sport do you think will have the smallest optimal α? Which will have the largest optimal α? Why?

f. Why might this approach yield poor forecasts for major league baseball?

12-8 SEASONAL MODELS

Some time series software packages have special types of graphs for spotting seasonality, but we won't discuss these here.

So far we have said practically nothing about seasonality. Seasonality is the consistent month-to-month (or quarter-to-quarter) differences that occur each year. (It could also be the day-to-day differences that occur each week.) For example, there is seasonality in beer sales—high in the summer months, lower in other months. Toy sales are also seasonal, with a huge peak in the months preceding Christmas. In fact, if you start thinking about time series variables that you are familiar with, the majority of them probably have some degree of seasonality.

How can you tell whether there is seasonality in a time series? The easiest way is to check whether a graph of the time series has a *regular* pattern of ups and/or downs in particular months or quarters. Although random noise can sometimes mask such a pattern, the seasonal pattern is usually fairly obvious. (We have also included the file **Check for Seasonality.xlsx** in the finished examples folder. It indicates one possible way to check for seasonality.)

As you saw with the housing sales data, government agencies often perform part of the second method for us—that is, they deseasonalize the data.

There are basically three methods for dealing with seasonality. First, you can use Winters' exponential smoothing model. It is similar to simple exponential smoothing and Holt's method, except that it includes another component (and smoothing constant) to capture seasonality. Second, you can *deseasonalize* the data, then use any forecasting method to model the deseasonalized data, and finally "reseasonalize" these forecasts. Finally, you can use multiple regression with dummy variables for the seasons. We discuss all three of these methods in this section.

Seasonal models are usually classified as *additive* or *multiplicative*. Suppose that the series contains monthly data, and that the average of the 12 monthly values for a typical year is 150. An **additive** model finds seasonal indexes, one for each month, that are *added* to the monthly average, 150, to get a particular month's value. For example, if the index for March is 22, then a typical March value is $150 + 22 = 172$. If the seasonal index for September is -12, then a typical September value is $150 - 12 = 138$. A **multiplicative** model also finds seasonal indexes, but they are *multiplied* by the monthly average to get a particular month's value. Now if the index for March is 1.3, a typical March value is $150(1.3) = 195$. If the index for September is 0.9, then a typical September value is $150(0.9) = 135$.

In an **additive seasonal model**, an appropriate seasonal index is added to a base forecast. These indexes, one for each season, typically average to 0.

In a **multiplicative seasonal model**, a base forecast is multiplied by an appropriate seasonal index. These indexes, one for each season, typically average to 1.

Either an additive or a multiplicative model can be used to forecast seasonal data. However, because multiplicative models are somewhat easier to interpret (and have worked well in applications), we focus on them. Note that the seasonal index in a multiplicative model can be interpreted as a percentage. Using the figures in the previous paragraph as an example, March tends to be 30% above the monthly average, whereas September tends to be 10% below it. Also, the seasonal indexes in a multiplicative model typically average to 1. Software packages usually ensure that this happens.

12-8a Winters' Exponential Smoothing Model

We now turn to Winters' exponential smoothing model. It is very similar to Holt's model—it again has level and trend terms and corresponding smoothing constants α and β—but it also has seasonal indexes and a corresponding smoothing constant γ (gamma). This new smoothing constant controls how quickly the method reacts to observed changes in the seasonality pattern. If γ is small, the method reacts slowly. If it is large, the method reacts more quickly. As with Holt's model, there are equations for updating the level and trend terms, and there is one extra equation for updating the seasonal indexes. For completeness, we list these equations, but they are clearly too complex for hand calculation and are best left to the software. In Equation (12.21), S_t refers to the multiplicative seasonal index for period t. In equations (12.19), (12.21), and (12.22), M refers to the number of seasons ($M = 4$ for quarterly data, $M = 12$ for monthly data).

Formulas for Winters' Exponential Smoothing Model

$$L_t = \alpha \frac{Y_t}{S_{t-M}} + (1 - \alpha)(L_{t-1} + T_{t-1}) \tag{12.19}$$

$$T_t = \beta(L_t - L_{t-1}) + (1 - \beta)T_{t-1} \tag{12.20}$$

$$S_t = \gamma \frac{Y_t}{L_t} + (1 - \gamma)S_{t-M} \tag{12.21}$$

$$F_{t+k} = (L_t + kT_t)S_{t+k-M} \tag{12.22}$$

To see how the forecasting in Equation (12.22) works, suppose you have observed data through June and you want a forecast for the coming September, that is, a three-month-ahead forecast. (In this case t refers to June and $t + k = t + 3$ refers to September.) The method first adds 3 times the current trend term to the current level. This gives a forecast for September that would be appropriate if there were no seasonality. Next, it multiplies this forecast by the most recent estimate of September's seasonal index (the one from the previous September) to get the forecast for September. Of course, the software does all of the calculations, but this is basically what it is doing. We illustrate the method Example 12.6.

| EXAMPLE | 12.6 QUARTERLY SOFT DRINK SALES |

The data in the **Soft Drink Sales.xlsx** file represent quarterly sales (in millions of dollars) for a large soft drink company from quarter 1 of 1997 through quarter 4 of 2012. There has been an upward trend in sales during this period, and there is also a fairly regular seasonal pattern, as shown in Figure 12.45. Sales in the warmer quarters, 2 and 3, are consistently higher than in the colder quarters, 1 and 4. How well can Winters' method track this upward trend and seasonal pattern?

Figure 12.45

Time Series Graph of Soft Drink Sales

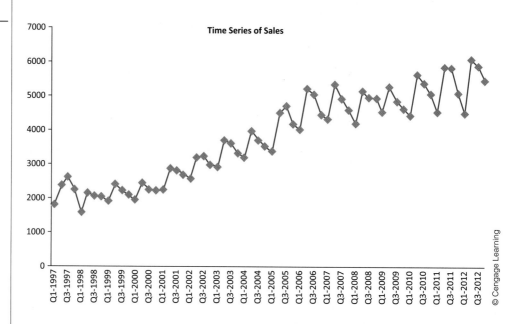

Objective To see how well Winters' method, with appropriate smoothing constants, can forecast the company's seasonal soft drink sales.

Solution

To use Winters' method with StatTools, you proceed exactly as with any of the other exponential smoothing methods. However, for a change (and because there are so many years of data), you can use StatTools's option of holding out some of the data for validation. Specifically, fill out the Time Scale tab in the Forecast dialog box as shown in Figure 12.46. Then fill in the Forecast Settings tab of this dialog box as shown in Figure 12.47, selecting Winters' method, basing the model on the data through Q4-2010, holding out eight quarters of data (Q1-2011 through Q4-2012), and forecasting four quarters into the future (all of 2013). Note that when you choose Winters' method in Figure 12.47, the Deseasonalize option in Figure 12.46 is automatically disabled. It wouldn't make sense to deseasonalize

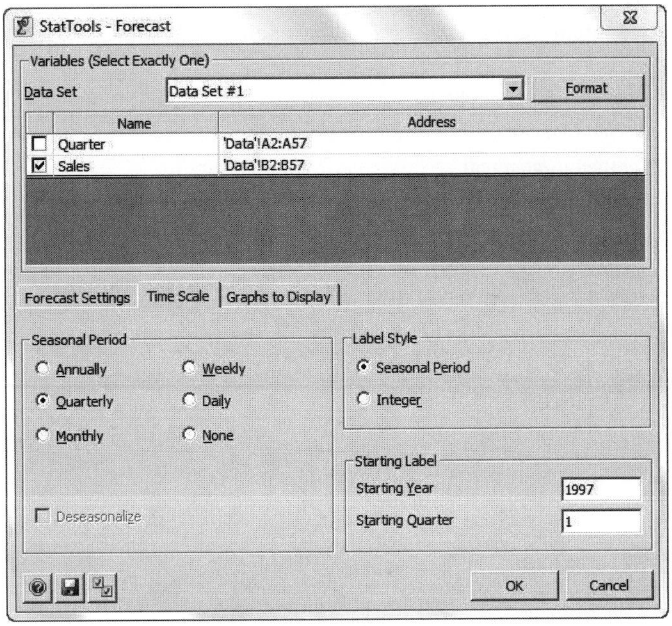

Figure 12.46

Time Scale Settings for Soft Drink Sales

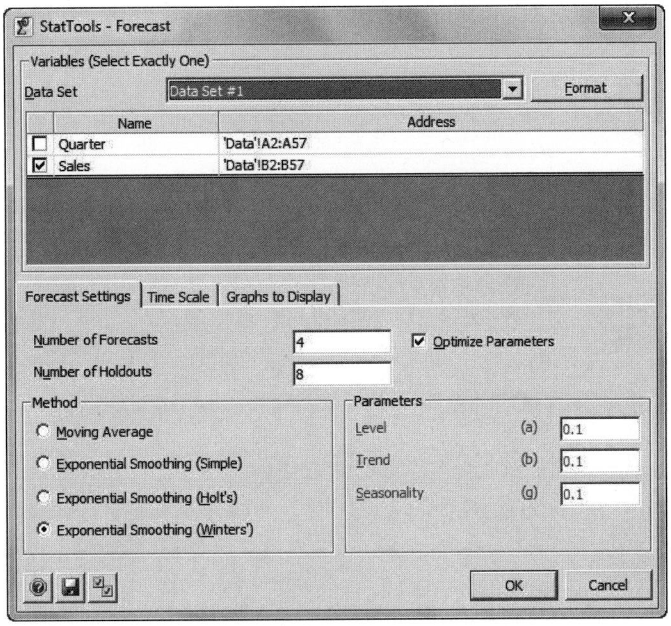

Figure 12.47

Forecast Settings for Soft Drink Sales

You can check that if three years of data are held out, the MAPE for the holdout period increases quite a lot. It is common for the fit to be considerably better in the estimation period than in the holdout period.

and use Winters' method; you do one or the other. Also, you can optimize the smoothing constants as is done here, but this is optional.

Parts of the output are shown in Figure 12.48. The following points are worth noting: (1) The optimal smoothing constants (those that minimize RMSE) are $\alpha = 1.0$, $\beta = 0.0$, and $\gamma = 0.0$. Intuitively, these mean that the method reacts immediately to changes in level, but it never reacts to changes in the trend or the seasonal pattern. (2) Aside from seasonality, the series is trending upward at a rate of 56.65 per quarter (see column D). This is the initial estimate of trend and, because β is 0, it never changes. (3) The seasonal pattern stays constant throughout this 14-year period. The seasonal indexes, shown in column E, are 0.88, 1.10, 1.05, and 0.96. For example, quarter 1 is 12% below the yearly average, and quarter 2 is 10% above the yearly average. (4) The forecast series tracks the actual series quite well during

Figure 12.48 Output from Winters' Method for Soft Drink Sales

	A	B	C	D	E	F	G
7	Winters' Exponential Smoothing Forecasts for Sales						
8	Forecasting Constants (Optimized)						
9	Level (Alpha)	1.000					
10	Trend (Beta)	0.000					
11	Season (Gamma)	0.000					
12							
13		Estimation	Holdouts				
14	Winters' Exponential	Period	Period				
15	Mean Abs Err	123.23	123.65				
16	Root Mean Sq Err	166.71	158.65				
17	Mean Abs Per% Err	3.86%	2.48%				
18							
42	Forecasting Data	Sales	Level	Trend	Season	Forecast	Error
43	Q1-1997	1807.37	2052.06	56.65	0.88		
44	Q2-1997	2355.32	2136.61	56.65	1.10	2324.57	30.75
45	Q3-1997	2591.83	2461.52	56.65	1.05	2309.37	282.46
46	Q4-1997	2236.39	2320.05	56.65	0.96	2427.36	−190.97
95	Q1-2010	4431.36	5031.31	56.65	0.88	4284.47	146.89
96	Q2-2010	5602.21	5082.00	56.65	1.10	5608.78	−6.57
97	Q3-2010	5349.85	5080.87	56.65	1.05	5410.69	−60.84
98	Q4-2010	5036.00	5224.40	56.65	0.96	4952.25	83.75
99	Q1-2011	4534.61				4651.32	−116.71
100	Q2-2011	5836.17				5884.09	−47.92
101	Q3-2011	5818.28				5679.93	138.35
102	Q4-2011	5070.42				5254.42	−184.00
103	Q1-2012	4497.47				4850.90	−353.43
104	Q2-2012	6075.52				6133.88	−58.36
105	Q3-2012	5868.67				5918.52	−49.85
106	Q4-2012	5432.24				5472.85	−40.61
107	Q1-2013					5050.47	
108	Q2-2013					6383.67	
109	Q3-2013					6157.11	
110	Q4-2013					5691.27	

the non-holdout period. For example, MAPE is 3.86%, meaning that the forecasts are off by about 4% on average. Surprisingly, MAPE for the holdout period is even lower, at 2.48%.

The plot of the forecasts superimposed on the original series, shown in Figure 12.49, indicates that Winters' method clearly picks up the seasonal pattern and the upward trend and projects both of these into the future. In later examples, we will investigate whether other seasonal forecasting methods can do this effectively.

One final comment is that you are not obligated to find the *optimal* smoothing constants. Some analysts suggest using more "typical" values such as $\alpha = \beta = 0.2$ and $\gamma = 0.5$. (It is customary to choose γ larger than α and β because each season's seasonal index gets updated only once per year.) To see how these smoothing constants affect the

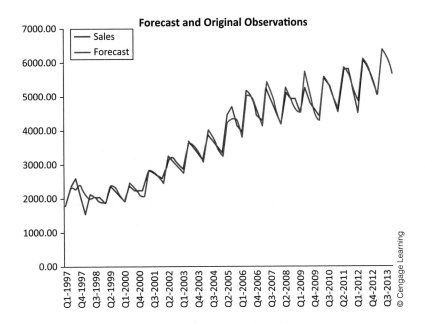

Figure 12.49

Graph of Forecasts from Winters' Method

results, you can substitute their values in the range B9:B11 of Figure 12.48. As expected, MAE, RMSE, and MAPE all get somewhat worse (they increase to 185, 236, and 5.78%, respectively, for the estimation period), but a plot of the forecasts superimposed on the original sales data still indicates a very good fit. ∎

The three exponential smoothing methods we have examined are not the only ones available. For example, there are linear and quadratic models available in some software packages. These are somewhat similar to Holt's model except that they use only a single smoothing constant. There are also adaptive exponential smoothing models, where the smoothing constants themselves are allowed to change over time. Although these more complex models have been studied thoroughly in the academic literature and are used by some practitioners, they typically offer only marginal gains in forecast accuracy over the models we have examined.

12-8b Deseasonalizing: The Ratio-to-Moving-Averages Method

You have probably seen references to time series data that have been **deseasonalized**. (Web sites often use the abbreviations SA and NSA for seasonally adjusted and nonseasonally adjusted.) The reason why data are often published in deseasonalized form is that readers can then spot trends more easily. For example, if you see a time series of sales that has not been deseasonalized, and it shows a large increase from November to December, you might not be sure whether this represents a real increase in sales or a seasonal phenomenon (Christmas sales). However, if this increase is really just a seasonal effect, the deseasonalized version of the series will show no such increase in sales.

Government economists and statisticians have a variety of sophisticated methods for deseasonalizing time series data, but they are typically variations of the **ratio-to-moving-averages method** described here. This method is applicable when seasonality is multiplicative, as described in the previous section. The goal is to find the seasonal indexes, which can then be used to deseasonalize the data. For example, if the estimated index for June is 1.3, this means that June's values are typically about 30% larger than the average for all months. Therefore, June's value is *divided* by 1.3 to obtain the (smaller) deseasonalized value. Similarly, if February's index is 0.85, then February's values are 15% below the average for all months, so February's value is divided by 0.85 to obtain the (larger) deseasonalized value.

> To **deseasonalize** an observation (assuming a multiplicative model of seasonality), *divide* it by the appropriate seasonal index.

To find the seasonal index for June 2012 (or any other month) in the first place, you essentially divide June's observation by the average of the 12 observations surrounding June. (This is the reason for the term *ratio* in the name of the method.) There is one minor problem with this approach. June 2012 is not exactly in the middle of any 12-month sequence. If you use the 12 months from January 2012 to December 2012, June 2012 is in the *first* half of the sequence; if you use the 12 months from December 2011 to November 2012, June 2012 is in the *last* half of the sequence. Therefore, you can compromise by averaging the January-to-December and December-to-November averages. This is called a *centered* average. Then the seasonal index for June is June's observation divided by this centered average. The following equation shows more specifically how it works.

$$\text{Jun2012 index} = \frac{\text{Jun2012}}{\left(\dfrac{\text{Dec2011} + \ldots + \text{Nov2012}}{12} + \dfrac{\text{Jan2012} + \ldots + \text{Dec2012}}{12}\right)/2}$$

The only remaining question is how to combine all of the indexes for any specific month such as June. After all, if the series covers several years, the procedure produces several June indexes, one for each year. The usual way to combine them is to average them. This single average index for June is then used to deseasonalize *all* of the June observations.

Once the seasonal indexes are obtained, each observation is divided by its seasonal index to deseasonalize the data. The deseasonalized data can then be forecast by *any* of the methods we have described (other than Winters' method, which wouldn't make much sense). For example, Holt's method or the moving averages method could be used to forecast the deseasonalized data. Finally, the forecasts are "reseasonalized" by *multiplying* them by the seasonal indexes.

As this description suggests, the method is not meant for hand calculations. However, it is straightforward to implement in StatTools, as we illustrate in the following continuation of Example12.6.

EXAMPLE	**12.6 QUARTERLY SOFT DRINK SALES (CONTINUED)**

We return to the soft drink sales data. (See the file **Soft Drink Sales.xlsx**.) Is it possible to obtain the same forecast accuracy with the ratio-to-moving-averages method as with Winters' method?

Objective   To use the ratio-to-moving-averages method to deseasonalize the soft drink data and then forecast the deseasonalized data.

Solution

The answer to this question depends on which forecasting method is used to forecast the *deseasonalized* data. The ratio-to-moving-averages method only provides a means for deseasonalizing the data and providing seasonal indexes. Beyond this, any method can be used to forecast the deseasonalized data, and some methods typically work better than others. For this example, we actually compared two possibilities: the moving averages method with a span of four quarters, and Holt's exponential smoothing method optimized, but the results are shown only for the latter. Because the deseasonalized series still has a clear upward trend, Holt's method should do well, and the moving averages forecasts should tend to lag behind the trend. This is exactly what occurred. For example, the values of MAPE for the two methods are 6.11% (moving averages) and 3.86% (Holt's). (To make a fair comparison with the Winters' method output for these data, an eight-quarter holdout period was again used). The MAPE values reported are for the non-holdout period.)

To implement this latter method in StatTools, proceed exactly as before, but this time check the Deseasonalize option in the Time Scale tab of the Forecast dialog box. (See Figure 12.50.) Note that when the Holt's option is checked, this Deseasonalize option is enabled. When you check this option, you get a larger selection of optional charts in the Graphs to Display tab. You can ask to see charts of the deseasonalized data and/or the original "reseasonalized" data.

Figure 12.50

Checking the Deseasonalizing Option

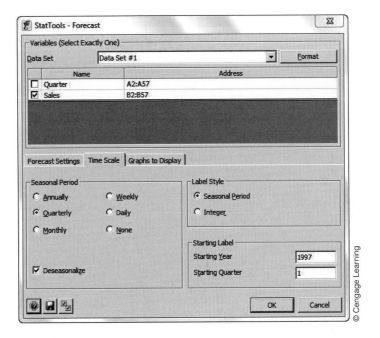

Selected outputs are shown in Figures 12.51 through 12.54. Figures 12.51 and 12.52 show the numerical output. In particular, Figure 12.52 shows the seasonal indexes from the ratio-to-moving averages method in column C. These are virtually identical to the seasonal indexes found with Winters' method, although the methods are mathematically different. Column D contains the deseasonalized sales (column B divided by column C), columns E

Figure 12.51

Summary Measures for Forecast Errors

⬚	A	B	C	D	E
7	*Holt's Exponential Smoothing Forecasts For Sales*				
8	*Forecasting Constants (Optimized)*				
9	Level (Alpha)	1.000			
10	Trend (Beta)	0.000			
11					
12		**Estimation**	**Holdouts**	**Deseason**	**Deseason**
13	*Holt's Exponential*	**Period**	**Period**	**Estimate**	**Holdouts**
14	Mean Abs Err	123.23	123.65	124.26	130.24
15	Root Mean Sq Err	166.71	158.65	169.38	173.56
16	Mean Abs Per% Err	3.86%	2.48%	3.86%	2.48%

© Cengage Learning

Figure 12.52 Ratio-to-Moving-Averages Output

	A	B	C	D	E	F	G	H	I	J
62	**Forecasting Data**	**Sales**	**Index**	**Sales**	**Level**	**Trend**	**Forecast**	**Errors**	**Forecast**	**Errors**
63	Q1-1997	1807.37	0.88	2052.06	2052.06	56.65				
64	Q2-1997	2355.32	1.10	2136.61	2136.61	56.65	2108.71	27.89	2324.57	30.75
65	Q3-1997	2591.83	1.05	2461.52	2461.52	56.65	2193.26	268.26	2309.37	282.46
66	Q4-1997	2236.39	0.96	2320.05	2320.05	56.65	2518.17	−198.11	2427.36	−190.97
67	Q1-1998	1549.14	0.88	1758.87	1758.87	56.65	2376.70	−617.83	2093.30	−544.16
68	Q2-1998	2105.79	1.10	1910.25	1910.25	56.65	1815.52	94.73	2001.37	104.42
117	Q3-2010	5349.85	1.05	5080.87	5080.87	56.65	5138.64	−57.78	5410.69	−60.84
118	Q4-2010	5036.00	0.96	5224.40	5224.40	56.65	5137.52	86.88	4952.25	83.75
119	Q1-2011	4534.61	0.88	5148.54			5281.05	−132.51	4651.32	−116.71
120	Q2-2011	5836.17	1.10	5294.23			5337.70	−43.47	5884.09	−47.92
121	Q3-2011	5818.28	1.05	5525.74			5394.35	131.40	5679.93	138.35
122	Q4-2011	5070.42	0.96	5260.11			5451.00	−190.89	5254.42	−184.00
123	Q1-2012	4497.47	0.88	5106.37			5507.64	−401.27	4850.90	−353.43
124	Q2-2012	6075.52	1.10	5511.35			5564.29	−52.94	6133.88	−58.36
125	Q3-2012	5868.67	1.05	5573.60			5620.94	−47.34	5918.52	−49.85
126	Q4-2012	5432.24	0.96	5635.46			5677.59	−42.13	5472.85	−40.61
127	Q1-2013		0.88				5734.24		5050.47	
128	Q2-2013		1.10				5790.89		6383.67	
129	Q3-2013		1.05				5847.54		6157.11	
130	Q4-2013		0.96				5904.19		5691.27	

through H implement Holt's method on the deseasonalized data, and columns I and J are the "reseasonalized" forecasts and errors.

The deseasonalized data, with forecasts superimposed, appear in Figure 12.53. Here you see only the smooth upward trend with no seasonality, which Holt's method is able

Figure 12.53

Forecast Graph of Deseasonalized Series

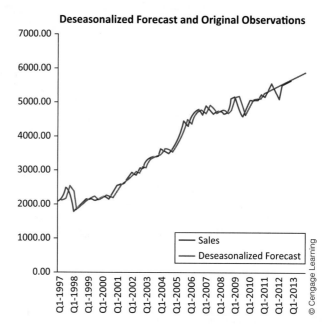

to track very well. Then Figure 12.54 shows the results of reseasonalizing. Again, the forecasts track the actual sales data very well. In fact, you can see that the summary measures of forecast errors (in Figure 12.51, range B14:B16) are quite comparable to those from Winters' method. The reason is that both arrive at virtually the same seasonal pattern. ■

Figure 12.54

Forecast Graph
of Reseasonalized
(Original) Series

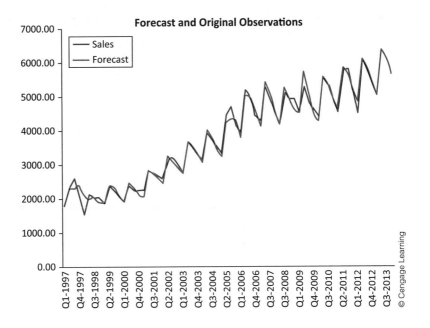

Forecast and Original Observations

12-8c Estimating Seasonality with Regression

We now examine a regression approach to forecasting seasonal data that uses **dummy variables** for the seasons. Depending on how you write the regression equation, you can create either an additive or a multiplicative seasonal model.

As an example, suppose that the data are quarterly data with a possible linear trend. Then you can create dummy variables Q_1, Q_2, and Q_3 for the first three quarters (using quarter 4 as the reference quarter) and estimate the additive equation

$$\text{Forecast } Y_t = a + bt + b_1Q_1 + b_2Q_2 + b_3Q_3$$

Then the coefficients of the dummy variables, b_1, b_2 and b_3, indicate how much each quarter differs from the reference quarter, quarter 4, and the coefficient b represents the trend.

For example, if the estimated equation is

$$\text{Forecast } Y_t = 130 + 25t + 15Q_1 + 5Q_2 - 20Q_3$$

the average increase from one quarter to the next is 25 (the coefficient of t). This is the trend effect. However, quarter 1 averages 15 units higher than quarter 4, quarter 2 averages 5 units higher than quarter 4, and quarter 3 averages 20 units lower than quarter 4. These coefficients indicate the seasonality effect.

As discussed in Chapter 10, it is also possible to estimate a *multiplicative* model using dummy variables for seasonality (and possibly time for trend). Then you would estimate the equation

$$\text{Forecast } Y_t = ae^{bt}e^{b_1Q_1}e^{b_2Q_2}e^{b_3Q_3}$$

or, after taking logs,

$$\text{Forecast Log } Y_t = \text{Log } a + bt + b_1Q_1 + b_2Q_2 + b_3Q_3$$

One advantage of this approach is that it provides a model with *multiplicative* seasonal factors. It is also fairly easy to interpret the regression output, as illustrated in the following continuation of the soft drink sales example.

EXAMPLE | 12.6 QUARTERLY SOFT DRINK SALES (CONTINUED)

Returning to the soft drink sales data (see the file **Soft Drink Sales.xlsx**), does a regression approach provide forecasts that are as accurate as those provided by the other seasonal methods in this chapter?

Objective To use a multiplicative regression equation, with dummy variables for seasons and a time variable for trend, to forecast soft drink sales.

Solution

We illustrate the multiplicative approach, although an additive approach is also possible. Figure 12.55 illustrates the data setup. Besides the Sales and Time variables, you need to create dummy variables for three of the four quarters and a Log(Sales) variable. You can then use multiple regression, with Log(Sales) as the dependent variable, and Time, Q1, Q2, and Q3 as the explanatory variables.

Figure 12.55

Data Setup for Multiplicative Model with Dummies

	A	B	C	D	E	F	G
1	Quarter	Sales	Time	Q1	Q2	Q3	Log(Sales)
2	Q1-1997	1807.37	1	1	0	0	7.499628029
3	Q2-1997	2355.32	2	0	1	0	7.764431878
4	Q3-1997	2591.83	3	0	0	1	7.860119469
5	Q4-1997	2236.39	4	0	0	0	7.712618238
6	Q1-1998	1549.14	5	1	0	0	7.345455217
7	Q2-1998	2105.79	6	0	1	0	7.652445973
8	Q3-1998	2041.32	7	0	0	1	7.621351936
9	Q4-1998	2021.01	8	0	0	0	7.611352665
10	Q1-1999	1870.46	9	1	0	0	7.533939669
11	Q2-1999	2390.56	10	0	1	0	7.779282927

© Cengage Learning

The regression output appears in Figure 12.56. (Again, to make a fair comparison with previous methods, the regression is based only on the data through quarter 4 of 2010. That

Figure 12.56 Regression Output for Multiplicative Model

	A	B	C	D	E	F	G
7	**Multiple Regression for Log(Sales)**						
8		**Multiple**	**R-Square**	**Adjusted**	**StErr of**		
9	**Summary**	**R**		**R-Square**	**Estimate**		
10		0.9661	0.9333	0.9281	0.096531736		
11							
12		**Degrees of**	**Sum of**	**Mean of**	**F-Ratio**	**p-Value**	
13	**ANOVA Table**	**Freedom**	**Squares**	**Squares**			
14	Explained	4	6.649640636	1.662410159	178.4013	< 0.0001	
15	Unexplained	51	0.475237175	0.009318376			
16							
17		**Coefficient**	**Standard**	**t-Value**	**p-Value**	**Confidence Interval 95%**	
18	**Regression Table**		**Error**			**Lower**	**Upper**
19	Constant	7.481383962	0.035236299	212.3204	< 0.0001	7.410644139	7.552123785
20	Time	0.020616712	0.000799999	25.7709	< 0.0001	0.019010647	0.022222777
21	Q1	−0.075770747	0.036564416	−2.0723	0.0433	−0.149176877	−0.002364618
22	Q2	0.139348297	0.036520632	3.8156	0.0004	0.066030069	0.212666525
23	Q3	0.088093474	0.036494336	2.4139	0.0194	0.014828038	0.161358911

© Cengage Learning

is, the last eight quarters are again held out. This means that the StatTools data set should extend only through row 57.) Of particular interest are the coefficients of the explanatory variables. Recall that for a log-dependent variable, these coefficients can be interpreted as *percentage* changes in the original sales variable. Specifically, the coefficient of Time means that deseasonalized sales increase by about 2.1% per quarter. Also, the coefficients of Q1, Q2, and Q3 mean that sales in quarters 1, 2, and 3 are, respectively, about 7.6% below, 14.0% above, and 8.8% above sales in the reference quarter, quarter 4. This pattern is quite comparable to the pattern of seasonal indexes you saw in previous models for these data.

To compare the forecast accuracy of this method to earlier models, you must perform several steps manually. (See Figure 12.57 for reference.) First, calculate the forecasts in column H by entering the formula

=EXP(Regression!$B$19+MMULT(Data!C2:F2,Regression!$B$20:$B$23))

in cell H2 and copying it down. (This formula assumes the regression output is in a sheet named Regression. It uses Excel's MMULT function to sum the products of explanatory values and regression coefficients. You can replace this by "writing out" the sum of products if you like. The formula then takes EXP of the resulting sum to convert the log sales value back to the original sales units.) Next, calculate the absolute errors, squared errors, and absolute percentage errors in columns I, J, and K, and summarize them in the usual way, both for the estimation period and the holdout period, in columns N and O.

Figure 12.57   **Forecast Errors and Summary Measures**

	A	B	C	D	E	F	G	H	I	J	K	L	M	N	O
1	Quarter	Sales	Time	Q1	Q2	Q3	Log(Sales)	Forecast	SqError	AbsError	PctAbsError		Error measures		
2	Q1-1997	1807.37	1	1	0	0	7.499628029	1679.464	16359.97	127.9061	0.070769173			Estimation	Holdout
3	Q2-1997	2355.32	2	0	1	0	7.764431878	2125.932	52618.75	229.3878	0.097391339		RMSE	340.38	1076.50
4	Q3-1997	2591.83	3	0	0	1	7.860119469	2061.785	280947.3	530.0446	0.204505939		MAE	269.72	1056.10
5	Q4-1997	2236.39	4	0	0	0	7.712618238	1927.253	95565.85	309.1373	0.138230484		MAPE	7.68%	19.82%
6	Q1-1998	1549.14	5	1	0	0	7.345455217	1823.835	75457.41	274.6951	0.177321046				
7	Q2-1998	2105.79	6	0	1	0	7.652445973	2308.683	41165.59	202.893	0.096350086				
8	Q3-1998	2041.32	7	0	0	1	7.621351936	2239.022	39086.06	197.702	0.096850054				

Note that these summary measures are considerably larger for this regression model than for the previous seasonality models, especially in the holdout period. You can get some idea why the holdout period does so poorly by looking at the plot of observations versus forecasts in Figure 12.58. The multiplicative regression model with Time included

Figure 12.58

Graph of Forecasts for Multiplicative Model

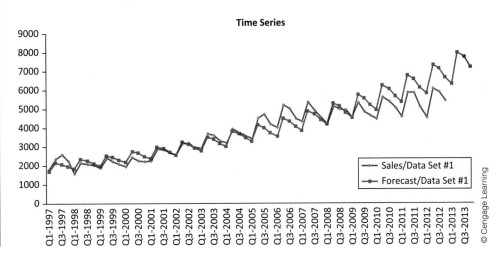

really implies *exponential* growth (as in Section 12-4b), with seasonality superimposed. However, this company's sales growth tapered off in the last couple of years and did not keep up with the exponential growth curve. In short, the dummy variables do a good job of tracking seasonality, but the underlying exponential trend curve outpaces actual sales. It is reasonable to conclude that this regression model is *not* as good for forecasting this company's sales as Winters' method or Holt's method on the deseasonalized data.

This method of detecting seasonality by using dummy variables in a regression equation is always an option. The other variables included in the regression equation could be time t, lagged versions of Y_t, and/or current or lagged versions of other explanatory variables. These variables would capture any time series behavior other than seasonality. Just remember that there is always one less dummy variable than the number of seasons. If the data are quarterly, then three dummies are needed; if the data are monthly, then 11 dummies are needed. If the coefficients of any of these dummies turn out to be statistically insignificant, they can be omitted from the equation. Then the omitted terms are effectively combined with the reference season. For example, if the Q_1 term were omitted, then quarters 1 and 4 would essentially be combined and treated as the reference season, and the other two seasons would be compared to them through their dummy variable coefficients. ∎

PROBLEMS

Level A

41. University Credit Union is open Monday through Saturday. Winters' method is being used (with $\alpha = \beta = \gamma = 0.5$) to predict the number of customers entering the bank each day. After incorporating the arrivals on Monday, October 16, the seasonal indexes are: Monday, 0.90; Tuesday, 0.70; Wednesday, 0.80; Thursday, 1.1; Friday, 1.2; Saturday, 1.3. Also, the current estimates of level and trend are 200 and 1. On Tuesday, October 17, 182 customers enter the bank. At the close of business on October 17, forecast the number of customers who will enter the bank on each of the next six business days.

42. A local bank is using Winters' method with $\alpha = 0.2$, $\beta = 0.1$, and $\gamma = 0.5$ to forecast the number of customers served each day. The bank is open Monday through Friday. At the end of the previous week, the following seasonal indexes have been estimated: Monday, 0.80; Tuesday, 0.90; Wednesday, 0.95; Thursday, 1.10; Friday, 1.25. Also, the current estimates of level and trend are 20 and 1. After observing that 30 customers are served by the bank on this Monday, forecast the number of customers who will be served on each of the next five business days.

43. Suppose that Winters' method is used to forecast quarterly U.S. retail sales (in billions of dollars). At the end of the first quarter of 2012, the seasonal indexes are: quarter 1, 0.90; quarter 2, 0.95; quarter 3, 0.95; quarter 4, 1.20. Also, the current estimates of level and trend are 300 and 30. During the second quarter of 2012, retail sales are $360 billion. Assume $\alpha = 0.2$, $\beta = 0.4$, and $\gamma = 0.5$.

a. At the end of the second quarter of 2012, develop a forecast for retail sales during the third and fourth quarters of 2012.

b. At the end of the second quarter of 2012, develop a forecast for the first and second quarter of 2013.

44. The file **P02_55.xlsx** contains monthly retail sales of beer, wine, and liquor at U.S. liquor stores.

a. Is seasonality present in these data? If so, characterize the seasonality pattern and then deseasonalize this time series using the ratio-to-moving-average method.

b. If you decided to deseasonalize this time series in part **a**, forecast the deseasonalized data for each month of the next year using the moving average method with an appropriate span.

c. Does Holt's exponential smoothing method, with optimal smoothing constants, outperform the moving average method employed in part **b**? Demonstrate why or why not.

45. Continuing the previous problem, how do your responses to the questions change if you employ Winters' method to handle seasonality in this time series? Explain. Which forecasting method do you prefer, Winters' method or one of the methods used in the previous problem? Defend your choice.

46. The file **P12_46.xlsx** contains monthly time series data for total U.S. retail sales of building materials, garden equipment, and supplies dealers.

a. Is seasonality present in these data? If so, characterize the seasonality pattern and then deseasonalize this time series using the ratio-to-moving-average method.

b. If you decided to deseasonalize this time series in part **a**, forecast the deseasonalized data for each month of the next year using the moving average method with an appropriate span.

c. Does Holt's exponential smoothing method, with optimal smoothing constants, outperform the moving average method employed in part **b**? Demonstrate why or why not.

47. The file **P12_47.xlsx** consists of the monthly retail sales levels of U.S. gasoline service stations.

a. Is there a seasonal pattern in these data? If so, how do you explain this seasonal pattern? Also, if necessary, deseasonalize these data using the ratio-to-moving-average method.

b. Forecast this time series for the first four months of the next year using the most appropriate method for these data. Defend your choice of forecasting method.

48. The number of employees on the payroll at a food processing plant is recorded at the start of each month. These data are provided in the file **P12_03.xlsx**.

a. Is there a seasonal pattern in these data? If so, how do you explain this seasonal pattern? Also, if necessary, deseasonalize these data using the ratio-to-moving-average method.

b. Forecast this time series for the first four months of the next year using the most appropriate method. Defend your choice of forecasting method.

49. The file **P12_49.xlsx** contains total monthly U.S. retail sales data. Compare the effectiveness of Winters' method with that of the ratio-to-moving-average method in deseasonalizing this time series. Using the deseasonalized time series generated by each of these two methods, forecast U.S. retail sales with the most appropriate method. Defend your choice of forecasting method.

50. Suppose that a time series consisting of six years (2007–2012) of quarterly data exhibits obvious seasonality. In fact, assume that the seasonal indexes turn out to be 0.75, 1.45, 1.25, and 0.55.

a. If the last four observations of the series (the four quarters of 2012) are 2502, 4872, 4269, and 1924, calculate the deseasonalized values for the four quarters of 2012.

b. Suppose that a plot of the deseasonalized series shows an upward linear trend, except for some random noise. Therefore, you estimate a linear regression equation for this series versus time and obtain the following equation:

Predicted deseasonalized value = 2250 + 51Quarter

Here the time variable Quarter is coded so that Quarter = 1 corresponds to first quarter 2007, Quarter = 24 corresponds to fourth quarter 2012, and the others fall in between. Forecast the actual (not deseasonalized) values for the four quarters of 2013.

51. The file **P12_51.xlsx** contains monthly data on the number of nonfarm hires in the U.S. since 2000.

a. What evidence is there that seasonality is important in this series? Find seasonal indexes (by any method you like) and state briefly what they mean.

b. Forecast the next 12 months by using a linear trend on the seasonally adjusted data. State briefly the steps you use to obtain this type of forecast. Then give the final RMSE, MAPE, and forecast for the next month. Show numerically how you could replicate this forecast (i.e., explain in words how the package uses its estimated model to get the next month's forecast).

52. Quarterly sales for a department store over a six-year period are given in the file **P12_52.xlsx**.

a. Use multiple regression to develop an equation that can be used to predict future quarterly sales. (*Hint*: Use dummy variables for the quarters and a time variable for the quarter number, 1 to 24.)

b. Letting Y_t be the sales during quarter t, discuss how to estimate the following equation for this series.

$$Y_t = ab_1^t b_2^{X_1} b_3^{X_2} b_4^{X_3}$$

Here X_1 is a dummy for first quarters, X_2 is a dummy for second quarters, and X_3 is a dummy for third quarters.

c. Interpret the results from part **b**.

d. Which model appears to yield better predictions for sales, the one in part **a** or the one in part **b**?

53. A shipping company is attempting to determine how its shipping costs for a month depend on the number of units shipped during a month. The number of units shipped and total shipping cost for the last 15 months are given in the file **P12_53.xlsx**.

a. Determine a relationship between units shipped and monthly shipping cost.

b. Plot the errors for the predictions in order of time sequence. Is there any unusual pattern?

c. It turns out that there was a trucking strike during months 11 through 15, and you believe that this might have influenced shipping costs. How can the answer to part **a** be modified to account for the effect of the strike? After accounting for this effect, does the unusual pattern in part **b** disappear?

Level B

54. Consider a monthly series of air conditioner (AC) sales. In the discussion of Winters' method, a monthly seasonality of 0.80 for January, for example, means that during January, AC sales are expected to be 80% of the sales during an average month. An alternative approach to modeling seasonality, called an *additive model*, is to let the seasonality factor for each month represent how far above average AC sales are during the current month. For instance, if $S_{Jan} = -50$, then AC sales during January are expected to be 50 fewer than AC sales during an average month. (This is 50 ACs, not 50%.) Similarly, if $S_{\text{July}} = 90$, then AC sales during July are expected to be 90 more than AC sales during an average month. Let

S_t = Seasonality for month t after observing month t demand

L_t = Estimate of level after observing month t demand

T_t = Estimate of trend after observing month t demand

Then the Winters' method equations given in the text should be modified as follows:

$$L_t = \alpha(I) + (1 - \alpha)(L_{t-1} + T_{t-1})$$
$$T_t = \beta(L_t - L_{t-1}) + (1 - \beta)T_{t-1}$$
$$S_t = \gamma(II) + (1 - \gamma)S_{t-12}$$

a. What should (*I*) and (*II*) be?
b. Suppose that month 13 is January, $L_{12} = 30$, $T_{12} = -3$, $S_1 = -50$, and $S_2 = -20$. Let $\alpha = \gamma = \beta = 0.5$. Suppose 12 ACs are sold during month 13. At the end of month 13, what is the forecast for AC sales during month 14 using this additive model?

55. Winters' method assumes a multiplicative seasonality but an additive trend. For example, a trend of 5 means that the level will increase by five units per period. Suppose that there is actually a *multiplicative* trend. Then (ignoring seasonality) if the current estimate of the level is 50 and the current estimate of the trend is 1.2, the forecast of demand increases by 20% per period. So the forecast demand for the next period is 50(1.2) and forecast demand for two periods in the future is 50(1.2)^2. If you want to use a multiplicative trend in Winters' method, you should use the following equations (assuming a period is a month):

$$L_t = \alpha\left(\frac{Y_t}{S_{t-12}}\right) + (1 - \alpha)(I)$$
$$T_t = \beta(II) + (I - \beta)T_{t-1}$$
$$S_t = \gamma\left(\frac{Y_t}{L_t}\right) + (1 - \gamma)S_{t-12}$$

a. What should (*I*) and (*II*) be?
b. Suppose that you are working with monthly data and month 12 is December, month 13 is January, and so on. Also, suppose that $L_{12} = 100$, $T_{12} = 1.2$, $S_1 = 0.90$, $S_2 = 0.70$, and $S_3 = 0.95$. If you have just observed $Y_{13} = 200$, what is the forecast for Y_{15} using $\alpha = \beta = \gamma = 0.5$ and a multiplicative trend?

56. Consider the file **P12_49.xlsx**, which contains total monthly U.S. retail sales data. Does a regression approach for estimating seasonality provide forecasts that are as accurate as those provided by (a) Winters' method and (b) the ratio-to-moving-average method? Compare the summary measures of forecast errors associated with each method for deseasonalizing this time series. Summarize the results of these comparisons.

57. The file **P12_46.xlsx** contains monthly time series data for total U.S. retail sales of building materials, garden equipment, and supplies dealers. Does a regression approach for estimating seasonality provide forecasts that are as accurate as those provided by (a) Winters' method and (b) the ratio-to-moving-average method? Compare the summary measures of forecast errors associated with each method for deseasonalizing the given time series. Summarize the results of these comparisons.

12-9 CONCLUSION

We have covered a lot of ground in this chapter. Because forecasting is such an important activity in business, it has received a tremendous amount of attention by both academics and practitioners. All of the methods discussed in this chapter—and more—are actually used, often on a day-to-day basis. There is really no point in arguing which of these methods is best. All of them have their strengths and weaknesses. The most important point is that when they are applied properly, they have all been found to be useful in real business situations.

Summary of Key Terms

Term	Explanation	Excel	Page	Equation
Extrapolation models	Forecasting models where only past values of a variable (and possibly time itself) are used to forecast future values		592	
Econometric models	Forecasting models based on regression, where other time series variables are used as explanatory variables (also called causal or regression-based models)		593	

(continued)

Term	Explanation	Excel	Page	Equation
Trend	A systematic increase or decrease of a time series variable through time		595	
Seasonality	A regular pattern of ups and downs based on the season of the year, typically months or quarters		595	
Cyclic component	An irregular pattern of ups and downs caused by business cycles		596	
Noise (or random variation)	The unpredictable ups and downs of a time series variable		596	
Forecast error	The difference between the actual value and the forecast		597	
Mean absolute error (MAE)	The average of the absolute forecast errors	StatTools/Time Series & Forecasting/Forecast	598	12.2
Root mean square error (RMSE)	The square root of the average of the squared forecast errors	StatTools/Time Series & Forecasting/Forecast	598	12.3
Mean absolute percentage error (MAPE)	The average of the absolute percentage forecast errors	StatTools/Time Series & Forecasting/Forecast	598	12.4
Runs test	A test of whether the forecast errors are random noise	StatTools/Time Series & Forecasting/ Runs Test for Randomness	602	
Autocorrelations	Correlations of a time series variable with lagged versions of itself	StatTools/Time Series & Forecasting/ Autocorrelation	604	
Correlogram	A bar chart of autocorrelations at different lags	StatTools/Time Series & Forecasting/ Autocorrelation	605	
Linear trend model	A regression model where a time series variable changes by a constant amount each time period	StatTools/Regression & Classification/ Regression	607	12.6
Exponential trend model	A regression model where a time series variable changes by a constant percentage each time period	StatTools/Regression & Classification/ Regression	610	12.7
Random walk model	A model indicating that the differences between adjacent observations of a time series variable are constant except for random noise		615	12.9–12.11
Moving averages model	A forecasting model where the average of several past observations is used to forecast the next observation	StatTools/Time Series & Forecasting/Forecast	619	
Span	The number of observations in each average of a moving averages model	StatTools/Time Series & Forecasting/Forecast	619	
Exponential smoothing models	A class of forecasting models where forecasts are based on weighted averages of previous observations, giving more weight to more recent observations	StatTools/Time Series & Forecasting/Forecast	624	
Smoothing constants	Constants between 0 and 1 that prescribe the weight attached to previous observations and hence the smoothness of the series of forecasts	StatTools/Time Series & Forecasting/Forecast	624	

(continued)

Summary of Key Terms   (*Continued*)

Term	Explanation	Excel	Page	Equation
Simple exponential smoothing	An exponential smoothing model useful for time series with no prominent trend or seasonality	StatTools/Time Series & Forecasting/Forecast	624	12.12–12.15
Holt's method	An exponential smoothing model useful for time series with trend but no seasonality	StatTools/Time Series & Forecasting/Forecast	624	12.16–12.18
Winters' method	An exponential smoothing model useful for time series with seasonality (and possibly trend)	StatTools/Time Series & Forecasting/Forecast	624	12.19–12.22
Additive seasonal model	A model where a seasonal index is added to a base forecast (indexes typically average to 0)		635	
Multiplicative seasonal model	A model where a seasonal index is multiplied by a base forecast (indexes typically average to 1)		635	
Deseasonalizing	A method for removing the seasonal component from a time series	StatTools/Time Series & Forecasting/Forecast	639	
Ratio-to-moving-averages method	A method for deseasonalizing a time series, so that some other method can then be used to forecast the deseasonalized series	StatTools/Time Series & Forecasting/Forecast	639	
Dummy variables for seasonality	A regression-based method for forecasting seasonality, where dummy variables are used for the seasons	StatTools/Regression & Classification/Regression	643	

PROBLEMS

Conceptual Questions

C.1. "A truly random series will likely have a very small number of runs." Is this statement true or false? Explain your choice.

C.2. Distinguish between a *correlation* and an *autocorrelation.* How are these measures similar? How are they different?

C.3. Under what conditions would you prefer a simple exponential smoothing model to the moving averages method for forecasting a time series?

C.4. Is it more appropriate to use an *additive* or a *multiplicative* model to forecast seasonal data? Summarize the difference(s) between these two types of seasonal models.

C.5. Suppose that monthly data on some time series variable exhibits a clear upward trend but no seasonality. You decide to use moving averages, with any appropriate span. Will there tend to be a systematic bias in your forecasts? Explain why or why not.

C.6. Suppose that monthly data on some time series variable exhibits obvious seasonality. Can you use moving averages, with any appropriate span, to track the seasonality well? Explain why or why not.

C.7. Suppose that quarterly data on some time series variable exhibits obvious seasonality, although the seasonal pattern varies somewhat from year to year. Which method do you believe will work best: Winters' method or regression with dummy variables for quarters (and possibly a time variable for trend)? Why?

C.8. Most companies that use (any version of) exponential smoothing use fairly small smoothing constants such as 0.1 or 0.2. Explain why they don't tend to use larger values.

Level A

58. The file **P12_58.xlsx** contains monthly data on consumer revolving credit (in millions of dollars) through credit unions.
- **a.** Use these data to forecast consumer revolving credit through credit unions for the next 12 months. Do it in two ways. First, fit an exponential trend to the series. Second, use Holt's method with optimized smoothing constants.

b. Which of these two methods appears to provide the best forecasts? Answer by comparing their MAPE values.

59. The file **P12_69.xlsx** contains revenue (in millions of dollars) for Procter & Gamble.

a. Use these data to predict Procter & Gamble revenue for each of the next two years. You need consider only a linear and exponential trend, but you should justify the equation you choose.

b. Use your answer from part **a** to explain how your predictions of Procter & Gamble revenue increase from year to year.

c. Are there any outliers?

d. You can be approximately 95% sure that Procter & Gamble revenue in the year following next year will be between what two values?

60. The file **P12_60.xlsx** lists annual revenues (in millions of dollars) for Nike. Forecast the company's revenue in each of the next two years with a linear or exponential trend. Are there any outliers in your predictions for the observed period?

61. The file **P12_61.xlsx** contains annual data on carbon dioxide (CO_2) levels from 1959 through 2012, measured at the Mauna Loa Observatory in Hawaii. Fit linear, exponential, and quadratic (polynomial of order 2) trends to these data. In terms of MAD, which fit is best? Using the best fit, forecast CO_2 levels for the next 10 years.

62. The file **P12_62.xlsx** contains data on a motel chain's revenue and advertising.

a. Use these data and multiple regression to make predictions of the motel chain's revenues during the next four quarters. Assume that advertising during each of the next four quarters is $50,000. (*Hint:* Try using advertising, lagged by one quarter, as an explanatory variable.)

b. Use simple exponential smoothing to make predictions for the motel chain's revenues during the next four quarters.

c. Use Holt's method to make forecasts for the motel chain's revenues during the next four quarters.

d. Use Winters' method to determine predictions for the motel chain's revenues during the next four quarters.

e. Which of these forecasting methods would you expect to be the most accurate for these data?

63. The file **P12_63.xlsx** contains data on monthly U.S. permits for new housing units (in thousands of houses).

a. Using Winters' method, find values of α, β, and γ that yield an RMSE as small as possible. Does this method track the housing crash in recent years?

b. Although we have not discussed autocorrelation for smoothing methods, good forecasts derived from smoothing methods should exhibit no substantial autocorrelation in their forecast errors. Is this true for the forecasts in part **a**?

c. At the end of the observed period, what is the forecast of housing sales during the next few months?

64. Let Y_t be the sales during month t (in thousands of dollars) for a photography studio, and let P_t be the price charged for portraits during month t. The data are in the file **P11_45.xlsx**. Use regression to fit the following model to these data:

$$Y_t = a + b_1 Y_{t-1} + b_2 P_t + e_t$$

This equation indicates that last month's sales and the current month's price are explanatory variables. The last term, e_t, is an error term.

a. If the price of a portrait during month 21 is $10, what would you predict for sales in month 21?

b. Does there appear to be a problem with autocorrelation of the residuals?

Level B

65. The file **P12_65.xlsx** contains five years of monthly data for a particular company. The first variable is Time (1 to 60). The second variable, Sales1, contains data on sales of a product. Note that Sales1 increases linearly throughout the period, with only a minor amount of noise. (The third variable, Sales2, is discussed and used in the next problem.) For this problem use the Sales1 variable to see how the following forecasting methods are able to track a linear trend.

a. Forecast this series with the moving average method with various spans such as 3, 6, and 12. What can you conclude?

b. Forecast this series with simple exponential smoothing with various smoothing constants such as 0.1, 0.3, 0.5, and 0.7. What can you conclude?

c. Now repeat part **b** with Holt's exponential smoothing method, again for various smoothing constants. Can you do significantly better than in parts **a** and **b**?

d. What can you conclude from your findings in parts **a**, **b**, and **c** about forecasting this type of series?

66. The Sales2 variable in the file from the previous problem was created from the Sales1 variable by multiplying by monthly seasonal factors. Basically, the summer months are high and the winter months are low. This might represent the sales of a product that has a linear trend and seasonality.

a. Repeat parts **a**, **b**, and **c** from the previous problem to see how well these forecasting methods can deal with trend *and* seasonality.

b. Now use Winters' method, with various values of the three smoothing constants, to forecast the series. Can you do much better? Which smoothing constants work well?

c. Use the ratio-to-moving-average method, where you first deseasonalize the series and then forecast (by any appropriate method) the deseasonalized series.

Does this perform as well as, or better than, Winters' method?

d. What can you conclude from your findings in parts **a**, **b**, and **c** about forecasting this type of series?

67. The file **P12_67.xlsx** contains monthly time series data on corporate bond yields. These are averages of daily figures, and each is expressed as an annual rate. The variables are:

- Yield AAA: average yield on AAA bonds
- Yield BAA: average yield on BAA bonds

If you examine either Yield variable, you will notice that the autocorrelations of the series are not only large for many lags, but that the lag 1 autocorrelation of the *differences* is significant. This is very common. It means that the series is not a random walk and that it is probably possible to provide a better forecast than the naive forecast from the random walk model. Here is the idea. The large lag 1 autocorrelation of the differences means that the differences are related to the first lag of the differences. This relationship can be estimated by creating the difference variable and a lag of it, then regressing the former on the latter, and finally using this information to forecast the original Yield variable.

a. Verify that the autocorrelations are as described, and form the difference variable and the first lag of it. Call these DYield and L1DYield (where D means difference and L1 means first lag).

b. Run a regression with DYield as the dependent variable and L1DYield as the single explanatory variable. In terms of the original variable Yield, this equation can be written as

$$\text{Yield}_t - \text{Yield}_{t-1} = a + b(\text{Yield}_{t-1} - \text{Yield}_{t-2})$$

Solving for Yield_t is equivalent to the following equation that can be used for forecasting:

$$\text{Yield}_t = a + (1 + b)\text{Yield}_{t-1} - b\text{Yield}_{t-2}$$

Try it—that is, try forecasting the next month from the known last two months' values. How might you forecast values two or three months from the last observed month? (*Hint*: If you do not have an *observed* value to use in the right side of the equation, use a forecast value.)

c. The autocorrelation structure led us to the equation in part **b**. That is, the autocorrelations of the original series took a long time to die down, so we looked at the autocorrelations of the differences, and the large spike at lag 1 led to regressing DYield on L1DYield. In turn, this ultimately led to an equation for Yield_t in terms of its first two lags. Now see what you would have obtained if you had tried regressing

Yield$_t$ on its first two lags in the first place—that is, if you had used regression to estimate the equation

$$\text{Yield}_t = a + b_1\text{Yield}_{t-1} + b_2\text{Yield}_{t-2}$$

When you use multiple regression to estimate this equation, do you get the same equation as in part **b**?

68. The file **P12_68.xlsx** lists monthly and annual values of the average surface air temperature of the earth (in degrees Celsius). (Actually, the data are indexes, relative to the period 1951–1980 where the average temperature was about 14 degrees Celsius. So if you want the actual temperatures, you can add 14 to all values.) A look at the time series shows a gradual upward trend, starting with negative values and ending with (mostly) positive values. This might be used to support the claim of global warming. For this problem, use only the annual averages in column N.

a. Is this series a random walk? Explain.

b. Regardless of your answer in part **a**, use a random walk model to forecast the next value (2010) of the series. What is your forecast, and what is an approximate 95% forecast interval, assuming normally distributed forecast errors?

c. Forecast the series in three ways: (i) simple exponential smoothing ($\alpha = 0.35$), (ii) Holt's method ($\alpha = 0.5$, $\beta = 0.1$), and (iii) simple exponential smoothing ($\alpha = 0.3$) on trend-adjusted data, that is, the residuals from regressing linearly versus time. (These smoothing constants are close to optimal.) For each of these, list the MAPE, the RMSE, and the forecast for next year. Also, comment on any "problems" with forecast errors from any of these three approaches. Finally, compare the qualitative features of the three forecasting methods. For example, how do their short-run or longer-run forecasts differ? Is any one of the methods clearly superior to the others?

d. Does your analysis predict convincingly that global warming has been occurring? Explain.

69. The file **P12_69.xlsx** contains data on mass layoff events in all industries in the U.S. (See the file for an explanation of how mass layoff events are counted.) There are two versions of the data: nonseasonally adjusted and seasonally adjusted. Presumably, seasonal factors can be found by dividing the nonseasonally adjusted values by the seasonally adjusted values. For example, the seasonal factor for April 1995 is 1431/1492=0.959. How well can you replicate these seasonal factors with appropriate StatTools analyses?

CASE 12.1 ARRIVALS AT THE CREDIT UNION

The Eastland Plaza Branch of the Indiana University Credit Union was having trouble getting the correct staffing levels to match customer arrival patterns. On some days, the number of tellers was too high relative to the customer traffic, so that tellers were often idle. On other days, the opposite occurred. Long customer waiting lines formed because the relatively few tellers could not keep up with the number of customers. The credit union manager, James Chilton, knew that there was a problem, but he had little of the quantitative training he believed would be necessary to find a better staffing solution. James figured that the problem could be broken down into three parts. First, he needed a reliable forecast of each day's number of customer arrivals. Second, he needed to translate these forecasts into staffing levels that would make

an adequate trade-off between teller idleness and customer waiting. Third, he needed to translate these staffing levels into individual teller work assignments—who should come to work when.

The last two parts of the problem require analysis tools (queueing and scheduling) that we have not covered. However, you can help James with the first part—forecasting. The file C12_01.xlsx lists the number of customers entering this credit union branch each day of the past year. It also lists other information: the day of the week, whether the day was a staff or faculty payday, and whether the day was the day before or after a holiday. Use this data set to develop one or more forecasting models that James could use to help solve his problem. Based on your model(s), make any recommendations about staffing that appear reasonable.

CASE 12.2 FORECASTING WEEKLY SALES AT AMANTA

Amanta Appliances sells two styles of refrigerators at more than 50 locations in the Midwest. The first style is a relatively expensive model, whereas the second is a standard, less expensive model. Although weekly demand for these two products is fairly stable from week to week, there is enough variation to concern management at Amanta. There have been relatively unsophisticated attempts to forecast weekly demand, but they haven't been very successful. Sometimes demand (and the corresponding sales) are lower than forecast, so that inventory costs are high. Other times the forecasts are too low. When this happens and on-hand inventory is not sufficient to meet customer demand, Amanta requires expedited shipments to keep customers happy—and this nearly wipes out Amanta's profit margin on the expedited units.[6] Profits at Amanta would almost certainly increase if demand could be forecast more accurately.

Data on weekly sales of both products appear in the file C12_02.xlsx. A time series chart of the two sales variables indicates what Amanta management expected—namely, there is no evidence of any upward or downward trends or of any seasonality. In fact, it might appear that each series is an unpredictable sequence of random ups and downs. But is this really true? Is it possible to forecast either series, with some degree of accuracy, with an extrapolation method (where only past values of *that* series are used to forecast current and future values)? Which method appears to be best? How accurate is it? Also, is it possible, when trying to forecast sales of one product, to somehow incorporate current or past sales of the *other* product in the forecast model? After all, these products might be "substitute" products, where high sales of one go with low sales of the other, or they might be complementary products, where sales of the two products tend to move in the *same* direction.

[6]Because Amanta uses expediting when necessary, its sales each week are equal to its customer demands. Therefore, the terms "demand" and "sales" are used interchangeably.

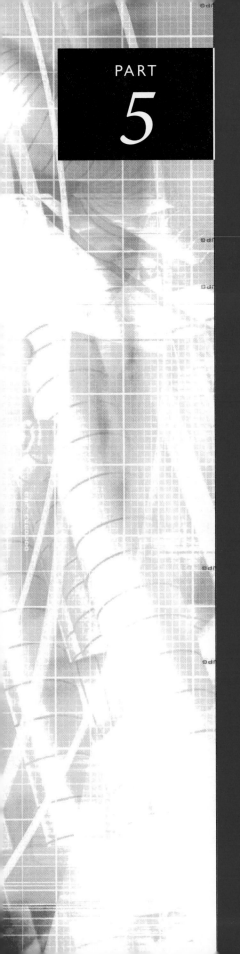

Introduction to Optimization Modeling

Bloomberg/Contributor/Getty Images

OPTIMIZING MANUFACTURING OPERATIONS AT GE PLASTICS

The General Electric Company (GE) is a global organization that must deliver products to its customers anywhere in the world in the right quantity, at the right time, and at a reasonable cost. One arm of GE is GE Plastics (GEP), a $5 billion business that supplies plastics and raw materials to such industries as automotive, appliance, computer, and medical equipment. (GEP has now been reorganized into GE Advanced Materials [GEAM].) As described in Tyagi et al. (2004), GEP practiced a "pole-centric" manufacturing approach, making each product in the geographic area (Americas, Europe, or Pacific) where it was to be delivered. However, it became apparent in the early 2000s that this approach was leading to higher distribution costs and mismatches in capacity as more of GEP's demand was originating in the Pacific region. Therefore, the authors of the article were asked to develop a global optimization model to aid GEP's manufacturing planning. Actually, GEP consists of seven major divisions, distinguished primarily by the capability of their products to withstand heat. The fastest growing of these divisions, the high performance polymer (HPP) division, was chosen as the pilot for the new global approach.

All GEP divisions operate as two-echelon manufacturing systems. The first echelon consists of resin plants, which convert raw material stocks into resins and ship them to the second echelon, the finishing plants. These latter plants combine the resins with additives to produce various grades of the end products. Each physical plant consists of several "plant lines" that operate independently, and each of these plant lines is capable of producing multiple products. All end products are then shipped to GE Polymerland warehouses throughout the world. GE Polymerland is a wholly owned subsidiary that acts as the commercial front for GEP. It handles all customer sales and deliveries from its network of distribution centers and warehouses in more than 20 countries. Because of its experience with customers, GE Polymerland is able to aid the GEP divisions in their planning processes by supplying forecasts of demands and prices for the various products in the various global markets. These forecasts are key inputs to the optimization model.

The optimization model itself attempts to maximize the total contribution margin over a planning horizon, where the contribution margin equals revenues minus the sum of manufacturing, material, and distribution costs. There are demand constraints, manufacturing capacity constraints, and network flow constraints. The decision variables include (1) the amount of resin produced at each resin plant line that will be used at each finishing plant line, and (2) the amount of each end product produced at each finishing plant line that will be shipped to each geographic region. The completed model has approximately 3100 decision variables and 1100 constraints and is completely linear. It was developed and solved in Excel (using LINGO, a commercial optimization solver, not Excel's Solver add-in), and execution time is very fast—about 10 seconds.

The demand constraints are handled in an interesting way. The authors of the study constrain manufacturing to produce no more than the forecasted demands, but they do not force manufacturing to meet these demands. Ideally, manufacturing would meet demands exactly. However, because of its rapid growth, capacity at HPP in 2002 appeared (at the time of the study) to be insufficient to meet the demand in 2005 and later years. The authors faced this challenge in two ways. First, in cases where demand exceeds capacity, they let their model of maximizing total contribution margin determine which demands to satisfy. The least profitable demands are simply not met. Second, the authors added a new resin plant to their model that would come on line in the year 2005 and provide much needed capacity. They ran the model several times for the year 2005 (and later years), experimenting with the location of the new plant. Although some of the details are withheld in the article for confidentiality reasons, the authors indicate that senior management approved the investment of a Europe-based plant that would cost more than $200 million in plant and equipment. This plant was planned to begin operations in 2005 and ramp up to full production capacity by 2007.

The decision support system developed in the study has been a success at the HPP division since its introduction in 2002. Although the article provides no specific dollar gains from the use of the model, it is noteworthy that the other GEP divisions are adopting similar models for their production planning. ■

13-1 INTRODUCTION

In this chapter, we introduce spreadsheet optimization, one of the most powerful and flexible methods of quantitative analysis. The specific type of optimization we will discuss here is **linear programming** (LP). LP is used in all types of organizations, often on a daily basis, to solve a wide variety of problems. These include problems in labor scheduling, inventory management, selection of advertising media, bond trading, management of cash flows, operation of an electrical utility's hydroelectric system, routing of delivery vehicles, blending in oil refineries, hospital staffing, and many others. The goal of this chapter is to introduce the basic elements of LP: the types of problems it can solve, how LP problems can be modeled in Excel®, and how Excel's powerful Solver add-in can be used to find optimal solutions. Then in the next chapter we will examine a variety of LP applications, and we will also look at applications of integer and nonlinear programming, two important extensions of LP.

13-2 INTRODUCTION TO OPTIMIZATION

Before we discuss the details of LP modeling, it is useful to discuss optimization in general. All optimization problems have several common elements. They all have *decision variables*, the variables whose values the decision maker is allowed to choose. Either directly or indirectly, the values of these variables determine such outputs as total cost, revenue, and profit. Essentially, they are the variables a company or organization must know to function properly; they determine everything else. All optimization problems have an *objective function* (**objective**, for short) to be optimized—maximized or minimized.[1] Finally, most optimization problems have **constraints** that must be satisfied. These are usually physical, logical, or economic restrictions, depending on the nature of the problem. In searching for the values of the decision variables that optimize the objective, only those values that satisfy all of the constraints are allowed.

Excel uses its own terminology for optimization, and we will use it as well. Excel refers to the decision variables as the **changing cells**. These cells must contain numbers that are allowed to change freely; they are *not* allowed to contain formulas. Excel refers to the objective as the **objective cell**. There can be only one objective cell, which could contain profit, total cost, total distance traveled, or others, and it must be related through formulas to the changing cells. When the changing cells change, the objective cell should change accordingly.[2]

The **changing cells** contain the values of the decision variables.

The **objective cell** contains the objective to be minimized or maximized.

The **constraints** impose restrictions on the values in the changing cells.

Finally, there must be appropriate cells and cell formulas that operationalize the constraints. For example, one constraint might indicate that the amount of labor used can be no more than the amount of labor available. In this case there must be cells for each of these two quantities, and typically at least one of them (probably the amount of labor used) will be related through formulas to the changing cells. Constraints can come in a variety of forms. One very common form is **nonnegativity**. This type of constraint states that changing cells must have nonnegative (zero or positive) values. Nonnegativity constraints are usually included for physical reasons. For example, it is impossible to produce a negative number of automobiles.

Nonnegativity constraints imply that changing cells must contain nonnegative values.

Typically, most of your effort goes into the model development step.

There are basically two steps in solving an optimization problem. The first step is the *model development* step. Here you decide what the decision variables are, what the objective is, which constraints are required, and how everything fits together. If you are developing an algebraic model, you must derive the correct algebraic expressions. If you are developing a spreadsheet model, the focus of this book, you must relate all variables with appropriate cell formulas. In particular, you must ensure that your model contains formulas that relate the changing cells to the objective cell and formulas that

---

[1] Actually, some optimization models are *multicriteria* models that try to optimize several objectives simultaneously. However, we will not discuss multicriteria models in this book.
[2] Some optimization add-ins, such as the Evolver add-in in the Palisade suite, refer to the decision variables as the *adjustable cells* and the objective as the *target cell*.

operationalize the constraints. This model development step is where most of your effort goes.

The second step in any optimization model is to *optimize*. This means that you must systematically choose the values of the decision variables that make the objective as large (for maximization) or small (for minimization) as possible and cause all of the constraints to be satisfied. Some terminology is useful here. Any set of values of the decision variables that satisfies all of the constraints is called a **feasible solution**. The set of all feasible solutions is called the **feasible region**. In contrast, an **infeasible solution** is a solution that violates at least one constraint. Infeasible solutions are disallowed. The desired feasible solution is the one that provides the best value—minimum for a minimization problem, maximum for a maximization problem—of the objective. This solution is called the **optimal solution**.

A **feasible solution** is a solution that satisfies all of the constraints.

The **feasible region** is the set of all feasible solutions.

An **infeasible solution** violates at least one of the constraints and is disallowed.

The **optimal solution** is the feasible solution that optimizes the objective.

An algorithm is basically a plan of attack. It is a prescription for carrying out the steps required to achieve some goal, such as finding an optimal solution. An algorithm is typically translated into a computer program that does the work.

Although most of your effort typically goes into the model development step, much of the published research in optimization has been about the optimization step. Algorithms have been devised for searching through the feasible region to find the optimal solution. One such algorithm is called the **simplex method**. It is used for *linear* models. There are other more complex algorithms used for other types of models (those with integer decision variables and/or nonlinearities).

We will not discuss the details of these algorithms. They have been programmed into Excel's **Solver** add-in. All you need to do is develop the model and then tell Solver what the objective cell is, what the changing cells are, what the constraints are, and what type of model (linear, integer, or nonlinear) you have. Solver then goes to work, finding the best feasible solution with the appropriate algorithm. You should appreciate that if you used a trial-and-error procedure, even a clever and fast one, it could take hours, weeks, or even years to complete. However, by using the appropriate algorithm, Solver typically finds the optimal solution in a matter of seconds.

Before concluding this discussion, we mention that there is really a *third* step in the optimization process: **sensitivity analysis**. You typically choose the most likely values of input variables, such as unit costs, forecasted demands, and resource availabilities, and then find the optimal solution for these particular input values. This provides a single "answer." However, in any realistic situation, it is wishful thinking to believe that all of the input values you use are exactly correct. Therefore, it is useful—indeed, mandatory in most applied studies—to follow up the optimization step with what-if questions. What if the unit costs increased by 5%? What if forecasted demands were 10% lower? What if resource availabilities could be increased by 20%? What effects would such changes have on the optimal solution? This type of sensitivity analysis can be done in an informal manner or it can be highly structured. Fortunately, as with the optimization step itself, good software allows you to obtain answers to various what-if questions quickly and easily.

13-3 A TWO-VARIABLE PRODUCT MIX MODEL

We begin with a very simple two-variable example of a *product mix* problem. This is a type of problem frequently encountered in business where a company must decide its product mix—how much of each of its potential products to produce—to maximize its net profit. You will see how to model this problem algebraically and then how to model it in Excel.

You will also see how to find its optimal solution with Solver. Next, because it contains only two decision variables, you will see how it can be solved graphically. Although this graphical solution is not practical for most realistic problems, it provides useful insights into general LP models. The final step is then to ask a number of what-if questions about the completed model.

EXAMPLE	13.1 ASSEMBLING AND TESTING COMPUTERS

PC Tech company assembles and then tests two models of computers, Basic and XP. For the coming month, the company wants to decide how many of each model to assemble and then test. No computers are in inventory from the previous month, and because these models are going to be changed after this month, the company doesn't want to hold any inventory after this month. It believes the most it can sell this month are 600 Basics and 1200 XPs. Each Basic sells for $300 and each XP sells for $450. The cost of component parts for a Basic is $150; for an XP it is $225. Labor is required for assembly and testing. There are at most 10,000 assembly hours and 3000 testing hours available. Each labor hour for assembling costs $11 and each labor hour for testing costs $15. Each Basic requires five hours for assembling and one hour for testing, and each XP requires six hours for assembling and two hours for testing. PC Tech wants to know how many of each model it should produce (assemble and test) to maximize its net profit, but it cannot use more labor hours than are available, and it does not want to produce more than it can sell.

Objective To use LP to find the best mix of computer models that stays within the company's labor availability and maximum sales constraints.

Solution

In all optimization models, you are given a variety of numbers—the inputs—and you are asked to make some decisions that optimize an objective, while satisfying all constraints. We summarize this information in a table such as Table 13.1. We believe it is a good idea to create such a table before diving into the modeling details. In particular, you always need to identify the appropriate decision variables, the appropriate objective, and the constraints, and you should always think about the relationships between them. Without a clear idea of these elements, it is almost impossible to develop a correct algebraic or spreadsheet model.

Tables such as this one serve as a bridge between the problem statement and the ultimate spreadsheet (or algebraic) model.

Table 13.1 Variables and Constraints for Two-Variable Product Mix Model

Input variables	Hourly labor costs, labor availabilities, labor required for each computer, costs of component parts, unit selling prices, and maximum sales
Decision variables (changing cells)	Number of each computer model to produce (assemble and test)
Objective cell	Total net profit
Other calculated variables	Labor of each type used
Constraints	Labor used ≤ Labor available, Number produced ≤ Maximum sales

© Cengage Learning

The decision variables in this product mix model are fairly obvious. The company must decide two numbers: how many Basics to produce and how many XPs to produce. Once these are known, they can be used, along with the problem inputs, to calculate the number of computers sold, the labor used, and the revenue and cost. However, as you will see with other models in this chapter and the next chapter, determining the decision variables is not always this obvious.

An Algebraic Model

In the traditional *algebraic* solution method, you first identify the decision variables.[3] In this small problem they are the numbers of computers to produce. We label these x_1 and x_2, although any other labels would do. The next step is to write expressions for the total net profit and the constraints in terms of the xs. Finally, because only nonnegative amounts can be produced, explicit constraints are added to ensure that the xs are nonnegative. The resulting **algebraic model** is

$$\text{Maximize } 80x_1 + 129x_2$$

subject to:

$$5x_1 + 6x_2 \le 10000$$
$$x_1 + 2x_2 \le 3000$$
$$x_1 \le 600$$
$$x_2 \le 1200$$
$$x_1, x_2 \ge 0$$

To understand this model, consider the objective first. Each Basic produced sells for \$300, and the total cost of producing it, including component parts and labor, is $150 + 5(11) + 1(15) = \$220$, so the profit margin is \$80. Similarly, the profit margin for an XP is \$129. Each profit margin is multiplied by the number of computers produced, and these products are then summed over the two computer models to obtain the total net profit.

The first two constraints are similar. For example, each Basic requires five hours for assembling and each XP requires six hours for assembling, so the first constraint says that the total hours required for assembling is no more than the number available, 10,000. The third and fourth constraints are the maximum sales constraints for Basics and XPs. Finally, negative amounts cannot be produced, so nonnegativity constraints on x_1 and x_2 are included.

Many commercial optimization packages require, as input, an algebraic model of a problem. If you ever use one of these packages, you will be required to think algebraically.

For many years all LP problems were modeled this way in textbooks. In fact, many commercial LP computer packages are still written to accept LP problems in essentially this format. Since around 1990, however, a more intuitive method of expressing LP problems has become popular. This method takes advantage of the power and flexibility of spreadsheets. Actually, LP problems could always be *modeled* in spreadsheets, but now with the addition of Solver, spreadsheets have the ability to *solve*—that is, optimize—LP problems as well. We use Excel's Solver for all examples in this book.[4]

A Graphical Solution

This graphical approach works only for problems with two decision variables.

When there are only two decision variables in an LP model, as there are in this product mix model, you can solve the problem graphically. Although this **graphical solution** approach is not practical in most realistic optimization models—where there are many more than two decision variables—the graphical procedure illustrated here still yields important insights for general LP models.

---

[3]This is not a book about algebraic models; the main focus is on *spreadsheet* modeling. However, we present algebraic models of the examples in this chapter for comparison with the corresponding spreadsheet models.
[4]The Solver add-in built into Excel was developed by a third-party software company, Frontline Systems. This company develops much more powerful versions of Solver for commercial sales, but its standard version built into Microsoft Office suffices for us. More information about Solver software offered by Frontline can be found at www.solver.com.

Recall from algebra that any line of the form $ax_1 + bx_2 = c$ has slope $-a/b$. This is because it can be put into the slope − intercept form $x_2 = c/b - (a/b)x_1$.

In general, if the two decision variables are labeled x_1 and x_2, then the steps of the method are to express the constraints and the objective in terms of x_1 and x_2, graph the constraints to find the feasible region [the set of all pairs (x_1, x_2) satisfying the constraints, where x_1 is on the horizontal axis and x_2 is on the vertical axis], and then move the objective through the feasible region until it is optimized.

To do this for the product mix problem, note that the constraint on assembling labor hours can be expressed as $5x_1 + 6x_2 \leq 10000$. To graph this, consider the associated equality (replacing $\leq$ with =) and find where the associated line crosses the axes. Specifically, when $x_1 = 0$, then $x_2 = 10000/6 = 1666.7$; and when $x_2 = 0$, then $x_1 = 10000/5 = 2000$. This provides the line labeled "assembling hour constraint" in Figure 13.1. It has slope $-5/6 = -0.83$. The set of all points that satisfy the assembling hour constraint includes the points on this line plus the points *below* it, as indicated by the arrow drawn from the line. [The feasible points are below the line because the point $(0, 0)$ is obviously below the line, and $(0, 0)$ clearly satisfies the assembly hour constraint.] Similarly, the testing hour and maximum sales constraints can be graphed as shown in the figure. The points that satisfy all three of these constraints and are nonnegative comprise the feasible region, which is below the heavier lines in the figure.

Figure 13.1

Graphical Solution to Two-Variable Product Mix Problem

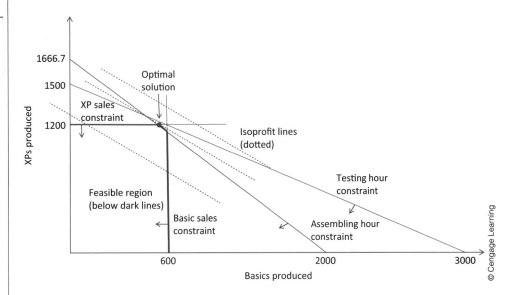

To see which feasible point maximizes the objective, it is useful to draw a sequence of lines where, for each, the objective is a constant. A typical line is of the form $80x_1 + 129x_2 = c$, where c is a constant. Any such line has slope $-80/129 = -0.620$, regardless of the value of c. This line is steeper than the testing hour constraint line (slope -0.5), but not as steep as the assembling hour constraint line (slope -0.83). The idea now is to move a line with this slope up and to the right, making c larger, until it just barely touches the feasible region. The last feasible point that it touches is the optimal point.

Several lines with slope -0.620 are shown in Figure 13.1. The middle dotted line is the one with the largest net profit that still touches the feasible region. The associated optimal point is clearly the point where the assembling hour and XP maximum sales lines intersect. You will eventually find (from Solver) that this point is $(560,1200)$, but even if you didn't have the Solver add-in, you could find the coordinates of this point by solving two equations (the ones for assembling hours and XP maximum sales) in two unknowns.

Again, the graphical procedure illustrated here can be used only for the simplest of LP models, those with two decision variables. However, the type of behavior pictured in

Although limited in use, the graphical approach yields the important insight that the optimal solution to any LP model is a corner point of a polygon. This limits the search for the optimal solution and makes the simplex method possible.

Figure 13.1 generalizes to *all* LP problems. In general, all feasible regions are (the multidimensional versions of) polygons. That is, they are bounded by straight lines (actually *hyperplanes*) that intersect at several *corner points*. There are five corner points in Figure 13.1, three of which are on the axes. [One of them is (0,0).] When the dotted objective line is moved as far as possible toward better values, the last feasible point it touches is one of the corner points. The actual corner point it last touches is determined by the slopes of the objective and constraint lines. Because there are only a finite number of corner points, it suffices to search among this finite set, not the infinite number of points in the entire feasible region.[5] This insight is largely responsible for the efficiency of the simplex method for solving LP problems.

FUNDAMENTAL INSIGHT

Geometry of LP Models and the Simplex Method

The feasible region in any LP model is always a multi-dimensional version of a polygon, and the objective is always a hyperplane, the multidimensional version of a straight line. The objective should always be moved as far as possible in the maximizing or minimizing direction until it just touches the edge of the feasible region.

Because of this geometry, the optimal solution is always a corner point of the polygon. The simplex method for LP works so well because it can search through the finite number of corner points extremely efficiently and recognize when it has found the best corner point. This rather simple insight, plus its clever implementation in software packages, has saved companies many, many millions of dollars in the past 50 years.

A Spreadsheet Model

We now turn our focus to *spreadsheet* modeling. There are many ways to develop an LP **spreadsheet model**. Everyone has his or her own preferences for arranging the data in the various cells. We do not provide exact prescriptions, but we do present enough examples to help you develop good habits. The common elements in all LP spreadsheet models are the inputs, changing cells, objective cell, and constraints.

- **Inputs.** All numerical inputs—that is, all numeric data given in the statement of the problem—should appear somewhere in the spreadsheet. Our convention is to color all of the input cells blue. We also try to put most of the inputs in the upper left section of the spreadsheet. However, we sometimes violate this latter convention when certain inputs fit more naturally somewhere else.

- **Changing cells.** Instead of using variable names, such as x, spreadsheet models use a set of designated cells for the decision variables. The values in these changing cells can be changed to optimize the objective. The values in these cells must be allowed to vary freely, so there should *not* be any formulas in the changing cells. To designate them clearly, our convention is to color them red.

- **Objective cell.** One cell, called the objective cell, contains the value of the objective. Solver systematically varies the values in the changing cells to optimize the value in the objective cell. This cell must be linked, either directly or indirectly, to the changing cells by formulas. Our convention is to color the objective cell gray.[6]

---

[5]This is not entirely true. If the objective line is exactly parallel to one of the constraint lines, there can be *multiple optimal solutions*—a whole line segment of optimal solutions. Even in this case, however, at least one of the optimal solutions is a corner point.

[6]Our blue/red/gray color scheme shows up very effectively on a color monitor. For users of previous editions who are used to colored *borders*, we find that it is easier in Excel 2007 and in later versions to color the cells rather than put borders around them.

> Color all input cells blue (appears light blue on the printed page).
>
> Color all of the changing cells red (appears deep blue on the printed page).
>
> Color the objective cell gray.

- **Constraints.** Excel does not show the constraints directly on the spreadsheet. Instead, they are specified in a Solver dialog box, to be discussed shortly. For example, a set of related constraints might be specified by

  B16:C16<=B18:C18

  This implies two separate constraints. The value in B16 must be less than or equal to the value in B18, and the value in C16 must be less than or equal to the value in C18. We will always assign range names to the ranges that appear in the constraints. Then a typical constraint might be specified as

  Number_to_produce<=Maximum_sales

  This is much easier to read and understand. (If you find that range names take too long to create, you certainly do not have to use them. Solver models work fine with cell addresses only.)

- **Nonnegativity.** Normally, the decision variables—that is, the values in the changing cells—must be nonnegative. These constraints do not need to be written explicitly; you simply check an option in the Solver dialog box to indicate that the changing cells should be nonnegative. Note, however, that if you want to constrain any *other* cells to be nonnegative, you must specify these constraints explicitly.

Overview of the Solution Process

As mentioned previously, the complete solution of a problem involves three stages. In the model development stage you enter all of the inputs, trial values for the changing cells, and formulas relating these in a spreadsheet. This stage is the most crucial because it is here that all of the ingredients of the model are included and related appropriately. In particular, the spreadsheet *must* include a formula that relates the objective to the changing cells, either directly or indirectly, so that if the values in the changing cells vary, the objective value varies accordingly. Similarly, the spreadsheet must include formulas for the various constraints (usually their left sides) that are related directly or indirectly to the changing cells.

After the model is developed, you can proceed to the second stage—invoking Solver. At this point, you formally designate the objective cell, the changing cells, the constraints, and selected options, and you tell Solver to find the *optimal* solution. If the first stage has been done correctly, the second stage is usually very quick and straightforward.

The third stage is sensitivity analysis. Here you see how the optimal solution changes (if at all) as selected inputs are varied. This often provides important insights about the behavior of the model.

We now illustrate this procedure for the product mix problem in Example 13.1.

Where Do the Numbers Come From?

Textbooks typically state a problem, including a number of input values, and proceed directly to a solution—without saying where these input values might come from. However, finding the correct input values can sometimes be the most difficult step in a real-world situation. (Recall that finding the necessary data is step 2 of the overall modeling process, as discussed in Chapter 1.) There are a variety of inputs in PC Tech's problem, some easy to find and others more difficult. Here are some ideas on how they might be obtained.

- The unit costs in rows 3, 4, and 10 should be easy to obtain. (See Figure 13.2.) These are the going rates for labor and the component parts. Note, however, that the labor costs are probably regular-time rates. If the company wants to consider overtime hours, then the overtime rate (and labor hours availability during overtime) would be necessary, and the model would need to be modified.

Figure 13.2   Two-Variable Product Mix Model with an Infeasible Solution

	A	B	C	D	E	F	G
1	**Assembling and testing computers**				**Range names used:**		
2					Hours_available	=Model!$D$21:$D$22	
3	Cost per labor hour assembling	$11			Hours_used	=Model!$B$21:$B$22	
4	Cost per labor hour testing	$15			Maximum_sales	=Model!$B$18:$C$18	
5					Number_to_produce	=Model!$B$16:$C$16	
6	Inputs for assembling and testing a computer				Total_profit	=Model!$D$25	
7		Basic	XP				
8	Labor hours for assembly	5	6				
9	Labor hours for testing	1	2				
10	Cost of component parts	$150	$225				
11	Selling price	$300	$450				
12	Unit margin	$80	$129				
13							
14	Assembling, testing plan (# of computers)						
15		Basic	XP				
16	Number to produce	600	1200				
17		<=	<=				
18	Maximum sales	600	1200				
19							
20	Constraints (hours per month)	Hours used		Hours available			
21	Labor availability for assembling	10200	<=	10000			
22	Labor availability for testing	3000	<=	3000			
23							
24	Net profit ($ this month)	Basic	XP	Total			
25		$48,000	$154,800	$202,800			

- The resource usages in rows 8 and 9, often called *technological coefficients*, should be available from the production department. These people know how much labor it takes to assemble and test these computer models.
- The unit selling prices in row 11 have actually been *chosen* by PC Tech's management, probably in response to market pressures and the company's own costs.
- The maximum sales values in row 18 are probably forecasts from the marketing and sales department. These people have some sense of how much they can sell, based on current outstanding orders, historical data, and the prices they plan to charge.
- The labor hour availabilities in rows 21 and 22 are probably based on the current workforce size and possibly on new workers who could be hired in the short run. Again, if these are regular-time hours and overtime is possible, the model would have to be modified to include overtime.

Developing the Spreadsheet Model

Developing the Product Mix 1 Model

The spreadsheet model appears in Figure 13.2. (See the file **Product Mix 1.xlsx**.) To develop this model, use the following steps.

1. **Inputs.** Enter all of the inputs from the statement of the problem in the shaded cells as shown.

2. **Range names.** Create the range names shown in columns E and F. Our convention is to enter enough range names, but not to go overboard. Specifically, we enter enough range names so that the setup in the Solver dialog box, to be explained shortly, is entirely in terms of range names. Of course, you can add more range names if you like (or you can omit them altogether). The following tip indicates a quick way to create range names.

Excel Tip: Shortcut for Creating Range Names
Select a range such as A16:C16 that includes nice labels in column A and the range you want to name in columns B and C. Then, from the Formulas ribbon, select Create from Selection and accept the default. You automatically get the labels in cells A16 as the range name for the range B16:C16. (Note that if the label contains spaces, they are replaced by underscores in the range name.) This shortcut illustrates the usefulness of adding concise but informative labels next to ranges you want to name.

3. **Unit margins.** Enter the formula

    =B11−B8*$B$3−B9*$B$4−B10

    in cell B12 and copy it to cell C12 to calculate the unit profit margins for the two models. (Enter relative/absolute addresses that allow you to copy whenever possible.)

At this stage, it is pointless to try to outguess the optimal solution. Any values in the changing cells will suffice.

4. **Changing cells.** Enter any two values for the changing cells in the Number_to_ produce range. Any trial values can be used initially; Solver eventually finds the optimal values. Note that the two values shown in Figure 13.2 cannot be optimal because they use more assembling hours than are available. However, you do not need to worry about satisfying constraints at this point; Solver takes care of this later on.

5. **Labor hours used.** To operationalize the labor availability constraints, you must calculate the amounts used by the production plan. To do this, enter the formula

    =SUMPRODUCT(B8:C8,Number_to_produce)

    in cell B21 for assembling and copy it to cell B22 for testing. This formula is a short-cut for the following fully written out formula:

    =B8*B16+C8*C16

The "linear" in linear programming is all about sums of products. Therefore, the SUMPRODUCT function is natural and should be used whenever possible.

The SUMPRODUCT function is very useful in spreadsheet models, especially LP models, and you will see it often. Here, it multiplies the number of hours per computer by the number of computers for each model and then sums these products over the two models. When there are only two products in the sum, as in this example, the SUMPRODUCT formula is not really any simpler than the written-out formula. However, imagine that there are 50 models. Then the SUMPRODUCT formula is *much* simpler to enter (and read). For this reason, use it whenever possible. Note that each range in this function, B8:C8 and Number_to_produce, is a one-row, two-column range. It is important in the SUMPRODUCT function that the two ranges be exactly the same size and shape.

6. **Net profits.** Enter the formula

    =B12*B16

    in cell B25, copy it to cell C25, and sum these to get the total net profit in cell D25. This latter cell is the objective to maximize. Note that if you didn't care about the net profits for the two *individual* models, you could calculate the total net profit with the formula

    =SUMPRODUCT(B12:C12,Number_to_produce)

As you see, the SUMPRODUCT function appears once again. It and the **SUM** function are the most used functions in LP models.

Experimenting with Possible Solutions

The next step is to specify the changing cells, the objective cell, and the constraints in a Solver dialog box and then instruct Solver to find the optimal solution. However, before you do this, it is instructive to try a few guesses in the changing cells. There are two reasons for doing so. First, by entering different sets of values in the changing cells, you can confirm that the formulas in the other cells are working correctly. Second, this experimentation can help you to develop a better understanding of the model.

For example, the profit margin for XPs is much larger than for Basics, so you might suspect that the company will produce only XPs. The most it can produce is 1200 (maximum sales), and this uses fewer labor hours than are available. This solution appears in Figure 13.3. However, you can probably guess that it is far from optimal. There are still many labor hours available, so the company could use them to produce some Basics and make more profit.

Figure 13.3

Two-Variable Product Mix Model with a Suboptimal Solution

◢	A	B	C	D
14	Assembling, testing plan (# of computers)			
15		Basic	XP	
16	Number of produce	0	1200	
17		<=	<=	
18	Maximum sales	600	1200	
19				
20	Constraints (hours per month)	Hours used		Hours available
21	Labor availability for assembling	7200	<=	10000
22	Labor availability for testing	2400	<=	3000
23				
24	Net profit ($ this month)	Basic	XP	Total
25		$0	$154,800	$154,800

© Cengage Learning

You can continue to try different values in the changing cells, attempting to get as large a total net profit as possible while staying within the constraints. Even for this small model with only two changing cells, the optimal solution is not totally obvious. You can only imagine how much more difficult it is when there are hundreds or even thousands of changing cells and many constraints. This is why software such as Excel's Solver is required. Solver uses a quick and efficient algorithm to search through all feasible solutions (or more specifically, all corner points) and eventually find the optimal solution. Fortunately, it is quite easy to use, as we now explain.

Using Solver

To invoke Excel's Solver, select Solver from the Data ribbon. (If there is no such item on your PC, you need to *load* Solver. To do so in Excel 2010 and later versions, click the File button, then Options, then Add-Ins, and then Go at the bottom of the dialog box. (In Excel 2007, you click the Office button and then Excel Options.) This shows you the list of available add-ins. If there is a Solver Add-in item in the list, check it to load Solver. If there is no such item, you need to rerun the Microsoft Office installer and elect to install Solver. It should be included in a typical install, but some people elect not to install it the first time around.) The dialog box in Figure 13.4 appears.[7] It has three important sections that you must fill in: the objective cell, the changing cells, and the constraints. For the product mix problem, you can fill these in by typing cell references or you can point, click, and drag the appropriate ranges in the usual way. Better yet, if there are any named ranges, these range names appear instead of cell addresses when you drag the ranges. In fact, for reasons of readability, our convention is to use only range names, not cell addresses, in this dialog box.

Figure 13.4
Solver Dialog Box
(in Excel 2010)

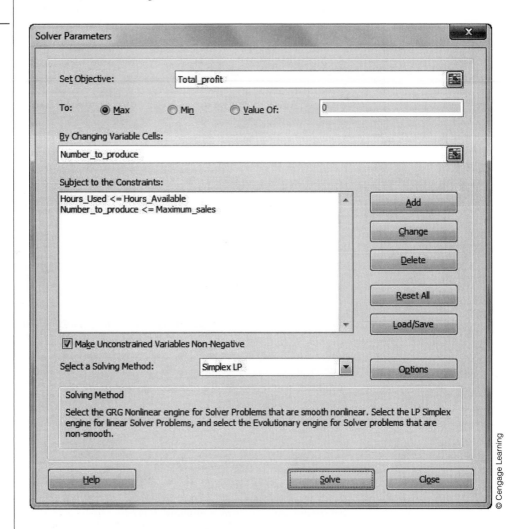

Excel Tip: Range Names in Solver Dialog Box
Our usual procedure is to use the mouse to select the relevant ranges for the Solver dialog box. Fortunately, if these ranges have already been named, the range names will automatically replace the cell addresses.

1. **Objective.** Select the Total_profit cell as the objective cell, and click the Max option. (Actually, the default option is Max.)

2. **Changing cells.** Select the Number_to_produce range as the changing cells.

---

[7]This is the new Solver dialog box, starting in Excel 2010. It is more convenient than similar dialog boxes in previous versions because the typical settings now all appear in a *single* dialog box. In previous versions you have to click the Options button to complete the typical settings.

3. **Constraints.** Click the Add button to bring up the dialog box in Figure 13.5. Here you specify a typical constraint by entering a cell reference or range name on the left, the type of constraint from the dropdown list in the middle, and a cell reference, range name, or numeric value on the right. Use this dialog box to enter the constraint

Number_to_produce<=Maximum_sales

(*Note:* You can type these range names into the dialog box, or you can drag them in the usual way. If you drag them, the cell addresses shown in the figure eventually change into range names if range names exist.) Then click the Add button and enter the constraint

Hours_used<=Hours_available

Then click OK to get back to the Solver dialog box. The first constraint says to produce no more than can be sold. The second constraint says to use no more labor hours than are available.

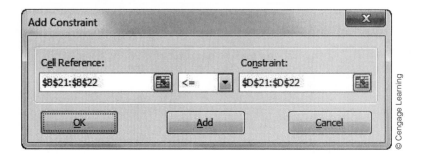

Figure 13.5

Add Constraint Dialog Box

© Cengage Learning

Excel Tip: Inequality and Equality Labels in Spreadsheet Models

The <= signs in cells B17:C17 and C21:C22 (see Figure 13.2 or Figure 13.3) are not a necessary part of the Excel model. They are entered simply as labels in the spreadsheet and do not substitute for entering the constraints in the Add Constraint dialog box. However, they help to document the model, so we include them in all of the examples. In fact, you should try to plan your spreadsheet models so that the two sides of a constraint are in nearby cells, with "gutter" cells in between where you can attach labels like <=, >=, or =. This convention tends to make the resulting spreadsheet models much more readable.

Solver Tip: Entering Constraints in Groups

Constraints typically come in groups. Beginners often enter these one at a time, such as B16 <= B18 and C16 <= C18, in the Solver dialog box. This can lead to a long list of constraints, and it is time-consuming. It is better to enter them as a group, as in B16:C16 <= B18:C18. This is not only quicker, but it also takes advantage of range names you have created. For example, this group ends up as Number_to_produce<=Maximum_Sales.

Checking the Non-Negative option ensures only that the changing cells will be nonnegative.

4. **Nonnegativity.** Because negative production quantities make no sense, you must tell Solver *explicitly* to make the changing cells nonnegative. To do this, check the Make Unconstrained Variables Non-Negative option shown in Figure 13.4. This automatically ensures that all changing cells are nonnegative. (In previous versions of Solver, you have to click the Options button and then check the Assume Non-Negative option in the resulting dialog box.)

5. **Linear model.** There is one last step before clicking the Solve button. As stated previously, Solver uses one of several numerical algorithms to solve various types of models. The models discussed in this chapter are all *linear* models. (We will discuss the

properties that distinguish linear models shortly.) Linear models can be solved most efficiently with the simplex method. To instruct Solver to use this method, make sure Simplex LP is selected in the Select a Solving Method dropdown list in Figure 13.4. (In previous versions of Solver, you have to click the Options button and then check the Assume Linear Model option in the resulting dialog box. In fact, from now on, if you are using a pre-2010 version of Excel and we instruct you to use the Simplex LP method, you should check the Assume Linear Model option. In contrast, if we instruct you to use a nonlinear algorithm, you should uncheck the Assume Linear Model option.)

6. **Optimize.** Click the Solve button in the dialog box in Figure 13.4. At this point, Solver does its work. It searches through a number of possible solutions until it finds the optimal solution. (You can watch the progress on the lower left of the screen, although for small models the process is virtually instantaneous.) When it finishes, it displays the message shown in Figure 13.6. You can then instruct it to return the values in the changing cells to their original (probably nonoptimal) values or retain the optimal values found by Solver. In most cases you should choose the latter. For now, click OK to keep the Solver solution. You should see the solution shown in Figure 13.7.

Figure 13.6

Solver Results Message

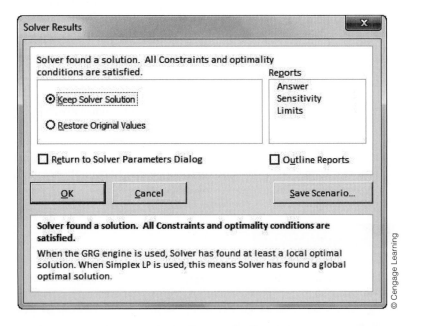

Figure 13.7

Two-Variable Product Mix Model with the Optimal Solution

	A	B	C	D
14	Assembling, testing plan (# of computers)			
15		Basic	XP	
16	Number of produce	560	1200	
17		<=	<=	
18	Maximum sales	600	1200	
19				
20	Constraints (hours per month)	Hours used		Hours available
21	Labor availability for assembling	10000	<=	10000
22	Labor availability for testing	2960	<=	3000
23				
24	Net profit ($ this month)	Basic	XP	Total
25		$44,800	$154,800	$199,600

Solver Tip: Messages from Solver
Actually, the message in Figure 13.6 is the one you hope for. However, in some cases Solver is not able to find an optimal solution, in which case one of several other messages appears. We discuss two of these later in the chapter.

Discussion of the Solution

This solution says that PC Tech should produce 560 Basics and 1200 XPs. This plan uses all available labor hours for assembling, has a few leftover labor hours for testing, produces as many XPs as can be sold, and produces a few less Basics than could be sold. No plan can provide a net profit larger than this one—that is, without violating at least one of the constraints.

The solution in Figure 13.7 is typical of solutions to optimization models in the following sense. Of all the inequality constraints, some are satisfied exactly and others are not. In this solution the XP maximum sales and assembling labor constraints are met exactly. Each of these is called a **binding constraint**. However, the Basic maximum sales and testing labor constraints do *not* hold as equalities. Each of these is called a **nonbinding constraint**. You can think of the binding constraints as bottlenecks. They are the constraints that prevent the objective from being improved. If it were not for the binding constraints on maximum sales and labor, PC Tech could obtain an even larger net profit.

> An inequality constraint is **binding** if the solution makes it an equality. Otherwise, it is **nonbinding**.

In a typical optimal solution, you should usually pay particular attention to two aspects of the solution. First, you should check which of the changing cells are *positive* (as opposed to 0). Generically, these are the "activities" that are done at a positive level. In a product mix model, they are the products included in the optimal mix. Second, you should check which of the constraints are binding. Again, these represent the bottlenecks that keep the objective from improving. ∎

FUNDAMENTAL INSIGHT

Binding and Nonbinding Constraints

Most optimization models contain constraints expressed as inequalities. In an optimal solution, each such constraint is either binding (holds as an equality) or nonbinding. It is extremely important to identify the binding constraints because they are the constraints that prevent the objective from improving. A typical constraint is on the availability of a resource. If such a constraint is binding, the objective could typically improve by having more of that resource. But if such a resource constraint is nonbinding, more of that resource would not improve the objective at all.

13-4 SENSITIVITY ANALYSIS

Indeed, many analysts view the "finished" model as a starting point for many what-if questions. We agree.

Having found the optimal solution, it might appear that the analysis is complete. But in real LP applications the solution to a *single* model is hardly ever the end of the analysis. It is almost always useful to perform a sensitivity analysis to see how (or if) the optimal solution changes as one or more inputs vary. We illustrate systematic ways of doing so in this section. Actually, we discuss two approaches. The first uses an optional sensitivity report that Solver offers. The second uses an add-in called SolverTable that one of the authors (Albright) developed.

13-4a Solver's Sensitivity Report

Sensitivity for the Product Mix 1 Model

When you run Solver, the dialog box in Figure 13.6 offers you the option to obtain a sensitivity report.[8] This report is based on a well-established theory of sensitivity analysis in optimization models, especially LP models. This theory was developed around algebraic models that are arranged in a "standardized" format. Essentially, all such algebraic models look alike, so the same type of sensitivity report applies to all of them. Specifically, they have an objective function of the form $c_1x_1 + \cdots + c_nx_n$, where n is the number of decision variables, the cs are constants, and the xs are the decision variables, and each constraint can be expressed as $a_1x_1 + \cdots + a_nx_n \le b$, $a_1x_1 + \cdots + a_nx_n \ge b$, or $a_1x_1 + \cdots + a_nx_n = b$, where the as and bs are constants. **Solver's sensitivity report** performs two types of sensitivity analysis: (1) on the coefficients of the objective, the cs, and (2) on the right sides of the constraints, the bs.

We illustrate the typical analysis by looking at the sensitivity report for PC Tech's product mix model in Example 13.1. For convenience, the algebraic model is repeated here.

$$\text{Maximize } 80x_1 + 129x_2$$

subject to:

$$5x_1 + 6x_2 \le 10000$$
$$x_1 + 2x_2 \le 3000$$
$$x_1 \le 600$$
$$x_2 \le 1200$$
$$x_1, x_2 \ge 0$$

On this Solver run, a sensitivity report is requested in Solver's final dialog box. (See Figure 13.6.) The sensitivity report appears on a new worksheet, as shown in Figure 13.8.[9] It contains two sections. The top section is for sensitivity to changes in the two coefficients, 80 and 129, of the decision variables in the objective. Each row in this section indicates how the optimal solution changes if one of these coefficients changes. The bottom section is for the sensitivity to changes in the right sides, 10000 and 3000, of the labor constraints.

Figure 13.8

Solver Sensitivity Results

	Cell	Name	Final Value	Reduced Cost	Objective Coefficient	Allowable Increase	Allowable Decrease
6	Variable Cells						
9	$B$16	Number to produce Basic	560	0	80	27.5	80
10	$C$16	Number to produce XP	1200	33	129	1E+30	33

	Cell	Name	Final Value	Shadow Price	Constraint R.H. Side	Allowable Increase	Allowable Decrease
12	Constraints						
15	$B$21	Labor availability for assembling Used	10000	16	10000	200	2800
16	$B$22	Labor availability for testing Used	2960	0	3000	1E+30	40

© Cengage Learning

[8]It also offers Answer and Limits reports. We don't find these particularly useful, so we will not discuss them here.
[9]If your table looks different from ours, make sure you chose the simplex method (or checked Assume Linear Model in pre-2010 versions of Solver). Otherwise, Solver uses a nonlinear algorithm and produces a different type of sensitivity report.

Each row of this section indicates how the optimal solution changes if one of these availabilities changes. (The maximum sales constraints represent a special kind of constraint—*upper bounds* on the changing cells. Upper bound constraints are handled in a special way in the Solver sensitivity report, as described shortly.)

Now let's look at the specific numbers and their interpretation. In the first row of the top section, the *allowable increase* and *allowable decrease* indicate how much the coefficient of profit margin for Basics in the objective, currently 80, could change before the optimal product mix would change. If the coefficient of Basics stays within this allowable range, from 0 (decrease of 80) to 107.5 (increase of 27.5), the optimal product mix—the set of values in the changing cells—does not change at all. However, outside of these limits, the optimal mix between Basics and XPs *might* change.

To see what this implies, change the selling price in cell B11 from 300 to 299, so that the profit margin for Basics decreases to $79. This change is well within the allowable decrease of 80. If you rerun Solver, you will obtain the *same* values in the changing cells, although the objective value will decrease. Next, change the value in cell B11 to 330. This time, the profit margin for Basics increases by 30 from its original value of $300. This change is outside the allowable increase, so the solution might change. If you rerun Solver, you will indeed see a change—the company now produces 600 Basics and fewer than 1200 XPs.

The *reduced costs* in the second column indicate, in general, how much the objective coefficient of a decision variable that is currently 0 or at its upper bound must change before that variable changes (becomes positive or decreases from its upper bound). The interesting variable in this case is the number of XPs, currently at its upper bound of 1200. The reduced cost for this variable is 33, meaning that the number of XPs will stay at 1200 unless the profit margin for XPs decreases by at least $33. Try it. Starting with the original inputs, change the selling price for XPs to $420, a change of less than $33. If you rerun Solver, you will find that the optimal plan still calls for 1200 XPs. Then change the selling price to $410, a change of more than $33 from the original value. After rerunning Solver, you will find that *fewer* than 1200 XPs are in the optimal mix.

The **reduced cost** for any decision variable with value 0 in the optimal solution indicates how much better that coefficient must be before that variable enters at a positive level. The reduced cost for any decision variable at its upper bound in the optimal solution indicates how much worse its coefficient must be before it will decrease from its upper bound. The reduced cost for any variable between 0 and its upper bound in the optimal solution is irrelevant.

Now turn to the bottom section of the report in Figure 13.8. Each row in this section corresponds to a constraint, although upper bound constraints on changing cells are omitted in this section. To have this part of the report make economic sense, the model should be developed as has been done here, where the right side of each constraint is a numeric constant (not a formula). Then the report indicates how much these right-side constants can change before the optimal solution changes. To understand this more fully, the concept of a shadow price is required. A **shadow price** indicates the change in the objective when a right-side constant changes.

The term **shadow price** is an economic term. It indicates the change in the optimal value of the objective when the right side of some constraint changes by one unit.

A shadow price is reported for each constraint. For example, the shadow price for the assembling labor constraint is 16. This means that if the right side of this constraint increases by one hour, from 10000 to 10001, the optimal value of the objective will increase by $16. It works in the other direction as well. If the right side of this constraint *decreases* by one hour, from 10000 to 9999, the optimal value of the objective will decrease by $16. However, as the right side continues to increase or decrease, this $16 change in the objective might not continue. This is where the reported allowable increase and allowable decrease are relevant. As long as the right side increases or decreases within its allowable limits, the same shadow price of 16 still applies. Beyond these limits, however, a different shadow price might apply.

You can prove this for yourself. First, increase the right side of the assembling labor constraint by 200 (exactly the allowable increase), from 10000 to 10200, and rerun Solver. (Don't forget to reset other inputs to their original values.) You will see that the objective indeed increases by 16(200)=$3200, from $199,600 to $202,800. Now increase this right side by one more hour, from 10200 to 10201 and rerun Solver. You will observe that the objective doesn't increase at all. This means that the shadow price beyond 10200 is *less than* 16; in fact, it is zero. This is typical. When a right side increases beyond its allowable increase, the new shadow price is typically less than the original shadow price (although it doesn't always fall to zero, as in this example).

The idea is that a constraint "costs" the company by keeping the objective from being better than it would be. A shadow price indicates how much the company would be willing to pay (in units of the objective) to "relax" a constraint. In this example, the company would be willing to pay $16 for each extra assembling hour. This is because such a change would increase the net profit by $16. But beyond a certain point—200 hours in this example—further relaxation of the constraint does no good, and the company is not willing to pay for any further increases.

The constraint on testing hours is slightly different. It has a shadow price of zero. In fact, the shadow price for a nonbinding constraint is always zero, which makes sense. If the right side of this constraint is changed from 3000 to 3001, nothing at all happens to the optimal product mix or the objective value; there is just one more unneeded testing hour. However, the allowable decrease of 40 indicates that something *does* change when the right side reaches 2960. At this point, the constraint becomes binding—the testing hours used equal the testing hours available—and beyond this, the optimal product mix starts to change. By the way, the allowable increase for this constraint, shown as 1+E30, means that it is essentially infinite. The right side of this constraint can be increased above 3000 indefinitely, and absolutely nothing will change in the optimal solution.

The Effect of Constraints on the Objective

If a constraint is added or an existing constraint becomes more constraining (for example, less of some resource is available), the objective can only get worse; it can never improve. The easiest way to understand this is to think of the feasible region. When a constraint is added or an existing constraint becomes more constraining, the feasible region shrinks, so some solutions that were feasible before, maybe even the optimal solution, are no longer feasible. The opposite is true if a constraint is deleted or an existing constraint becomes less constraining. In this case, the objective can only improve; it can never get worse. Again, the idea is that when a constraint is deleted or an existing constraint becomes less constraining, the feasible region expands. In this case, all solutions that were feasible before are still feasible, and there are some additional feasible solutions available.

13-4b SolverTable Add-In

Solver's sensitivity report is almost impossible to unravel for some models. In these cases SolverTable is preferable because of its easily interpreted results.

The reason Solver's sensitivity report makes sense for the product mix model is that the spreadsheet model is virtually a direct translation of a standard algebraic model. Unfortunately, given the flexibility of spreadsheets, this is not always the case. We have seen many perfectly good spreadsheet models—and have developed many ourselves— that are structured quite differently from their standard algebraic-model counterparts. In these cases, we have found Solver's sensitivity report to be more confusing than useful. Therefore, Albright developed an Excel add-in called SolverTable. **SolverTable** allows you to ask sensitivity questions about any of the input variables, not just coefficients of the objective and right sides of constraints, and it provides straightforward answers.

The SolverTable add-in is on this textbook's Web site (see the Preface for instructions on how to access it).[10] To install it, simply copy the SolverTable files to a folder on your hard drive. These files include the add-in itself (the .xlam file) and the online help files. To load SolverTable, you can proceed in one of two ways:

1. Open the **SolverTable.xlam** file just as you open any other Excel file.

2. Go to the add-ins list in Excel (click the File button, then Options, then Add-Ins, then Go) and check the SolverTable item. If it isn't in the list, Browse for the **SolverTable.xlam** file.

The advantage of the second option is that if SolverTable is checked in the add-ins list, it will open automatically every time you open Excel (and you can always uncheck it if you don't want it to open automatically).

The SolverTable add-in was developed to mimic Excel's built-in data table tool. Recall that data tables allow you to vary one or two inputs in a spreadsheet model and see instantaneously how selected outputs change. SolverTable is similar except that it runs Solver for every new input (or pair of inputs), and the current version also provides automatic charts of the results. There are two ways it can be used.

- **One-way table.** A one-way table means that there is a *single* input cell and *any number* of output cells. That is, there can be a single output cell or multiple output cells.

- **Two-way table.** A two-way table means that there are *two* input cells and one or more output cells. (You might recall that an Excel two-way data table allows only *one* output. SolverTable allows more than one. It creates a separate table for each output as a function of the two inputs.)

---

[10]It is also available from the Free Downloads link on the authors' Web site at www.kelley.iu.edu/albrightbooks. Actually, there are several versions of SolverTable available, each for a particular version of Solver. The one described in the text is for Solver in Excel 2007 or 2010 (or later). This Web site contains more information about these versions, as well as possible updates to SolverTable.

We illustrate some of the possibilities for the product mix example. Specifically, we check how sensitive the optimal production plan and net profit are to (1) changes in the selling price of XPs, (2) the number of labor hours of both types available, and (3) the maximum sales of the two models.

We assume that the model has been formulated and optimized, as shown in Figure 13.7, and that the SolverTable add-in has been loaded. To run SolverTable, click the Run SolverTable button on the SolverTable ribbon. You will be asked whether there is a Solver model on the active sheet. (Note that the *active* sheet at this point should be the sheet containing the model. If it isn't, click Cancel and then activate this sheet.) You are then given the choice between a one-way or a two-way table. For the first sensitivity question, choose the one-way option. You will see the dialog box in Figure 13.9. For the sensitivity analysis on the XP selling price, fill it in as shown. Note that ranges can be entered as cell addresses or range names. Also, multiple ranges in the Outputs box must be separated by commas.

We chose the input range from 350 to 550 in increments of 25 fairly arbitrarily. You can choose any desired range of input values.

Excel Tip: *Selecting Multiple Ranges*

If you need to select multiple output ranges, the trick is to keep your finger on the Ctrl key as you drag the ranges. This automatically enters the separating comma(s) for you. Actually, the same trick works for selecting multiple changing cell ranges in Solver's dialog box. It even works for entering multiple range arguments in any Excel function.

Figure 13.9

SolverTable
One-Way Dialog
Box

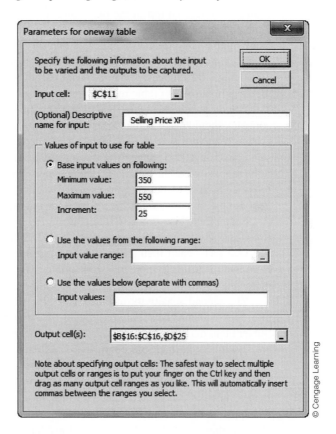

When you click OK, Solver solves a separate optimization problem for each of the nine rows of the table and then reports the requested outputs (number produced and net profit) in the table, as shown in Figure 13.10. It can take a while, depending on the speed of your computer and the complexity of the model, but everything is automatic. However,

Figure 13.10

SolverTable Results for Varying XP Price

	A	B	C	D	E	F	G
3	Selling Price XP (cell $C$11) values along side, output cell(s) along top						
4		Number_to_produce_1	Number_to_produce_2	Total_profit	Increase in profit		
5	$350	600	1166.667	$81,833			
6	$375	600	1166.667	$111,000	$29,167		
7	$400	600	1166.667	$140,167	$29,167		
8	$425	560	1200	$169,600	$29,433		
9	$450	560	1200	$199,600	$30,000		
10	$475	560	1200	$229,600	$30,000		
11	$500	560	1200	$259,600	$30,000		
12	$525	560	1200	$289,600	$30,000		
13	$550	560	1200	$319,600	$30,000		

if you want to update this table—by using different XP selling prices in column A, for example—you must repeat the procedure. Note that if the requested outputs are included in named ranges, the range names are used in the SolverTable headings. For example, the label Number_to_produce_1 indicates that this output is the first cell in the Number_to_produce range. The label Total_profit indicates that this output is the *only* cell in the Total_profit range. (If a requested output is not part of a named range, its cell address is used as the label in the SolverTable results.)

The outputs in this table show that when the selling price of XPs is relatively low, the company should make as many Basics as it can sell and a few less XPs, but when the selling price is relatively high, the company should do the opposite. Also, the net profit increases steadily through this range. You can calculate these changes (which are not part of the SolverTable output) in column E. The increase in net profit per every extra $25 in XP selling price is close to, but not always exactly equal to, $30,000. (These increases, calculated in column E, are not part of the SolverTable output.)

SolverTable also produces the chart in Figure 13.11. There is a dropdown list in cell K4 where you can choose any of the SolverTable outputs. (We selected the net profit, cell D25.) The chart then shows the data for that column from the table in Figure 13.10. Here there is a steady increase (slope about $30,000) in net profit as the XP selling price increases.

The second sensitivity question asks you to vary two inputs, the two labor availabilities, simultaneously. This requires a two-way SolverTable, so you should fill in the SolverTable dialog box as shown in Figure 13.12. Here two inputs and two input ranges are specified, and multiple output cells are again allowed. An output table is generated for *each* of the output cells, as shown in Figure 13.13. (To save space, the results for the second output are hidden.) For example, the top table shows how the optimal number of Basics varies as the two labor availabilities vary. Comparing the columns of this top table, it is apparent that the optimal number of Basics becomes increasingly sensitive to the available assembling hours as the number of available testing hours increases. The SolverTable output also includes two charts (not shown here) that let you graph any row or any column of any of these tables.

The third sensitivity question, involving maximum sales of the two models, reveals the flexibility of SolverTable. Instead of letting these two inputs vary independently in a

Figure 13.11

Associated
SolverTable Chart
for Net Profit

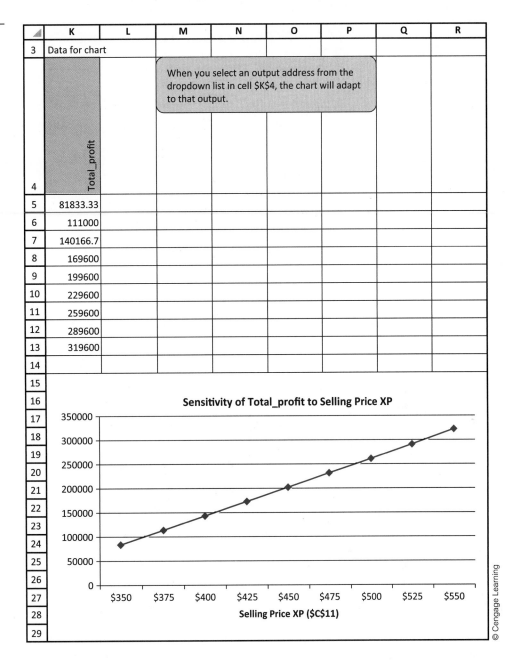

When you select an output address from the dropdown list in cell $K$4, the chart will adapt to that output.

	K	L	M	N	O	P	Q	R
3	Data for chart							
4	Total_profit							
5	81833.33							
6	111000							
7	140166.7							
8	169600							
9	199600							
10	229600							
11	259600							
12	289600							
13	319600							
14								

Sensitivity of Total_profit to Selling Price XP

Selling Price XP ($C$11)

© Cengage Learning

two-way SolverTable, it is possible to let both of them vary according to a *single* percentage change. For example, if this percentage change is 10%, both maximum sales increase by 10%. The trick is to modify the model so that one percentage-change cell drives changes in both maximum sales. The modified model appears in Figure 13.14. Starting with the original model, enter the original values, 600 and 1200, in new cells, E18 and F18. (Do *not* copy the range B18:C18 to E18:F18. This would make the right side of the constraint E18:F18, which is not the desired behavior.) Then enter any percentage change in cell G18. Finally, enter the formula

=E18*(1+$G$18)

Figure 13.12

SolverTable
Two-Way Dialog
Box

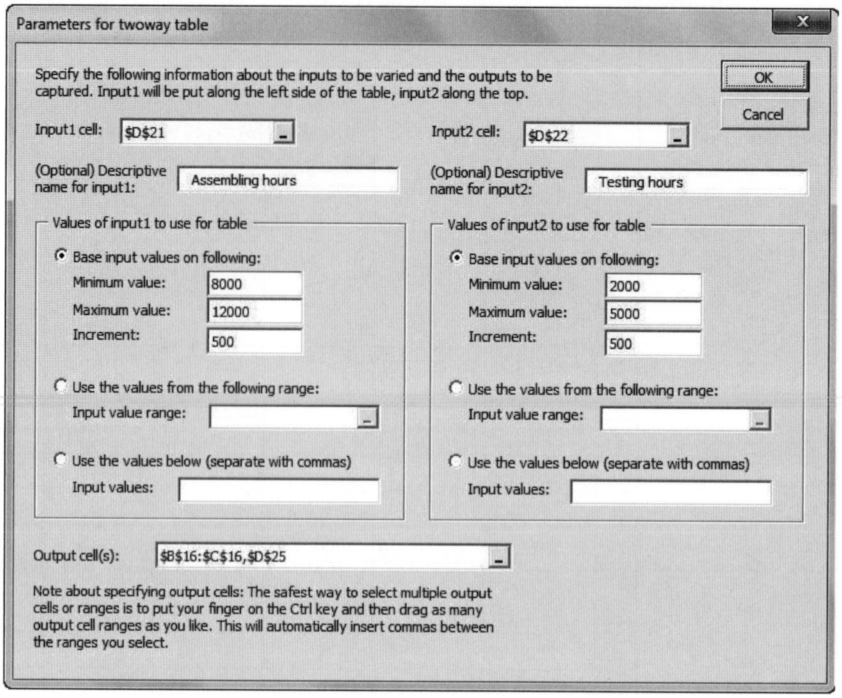

Parameters for twoway table

Specify the following information about the inputs to be varied and the outputs to be captured. Input1 will be put along the left side of the table, input2 along the top.

Input1 cell: `$D$21`   Input2 cell: `$D$22`

(Optional) Descriptive name for input1: Assembling hours

(Optional) Descriptive name for input2: Testing hours

Values of input1 to use for table

⦿ Base input values on following:
  Minimum value: 8000
  Maximum value: 12000
  Increment: 500

○ Use the values from the following range:
  Input value range:

○ Use the values below (separate with commas)
  Input values:

Values of input2 to use for table

⦿ Base input values on following:
  Minimum value: 2000
  Maximum value: 5000
  Increment: 500

○ Use the values from the following range:
  Input value range:

○ Use the values below (separate with commas)
  Input values:

OK

Cancel

Output cell(s): `$B$16:$C$16,$D$25`

Note about specifying output cells: The safest way to select multiple output cells or ranges is to put your finger on the Ctrl key and then drag as many output cell ranges as you like. This will automatically insert commas between the ranges you select.

© Cengage Learning

Figure 13.13

Two-Way
SolverTable Results

	A	B	C	D	E	F	G	H	I	J
3	Assembling hours (cell $D$21) values along side, Testing hours (cell $D$22) values along top, output cell in corner									
4	Number_to_produce_1	2000	2500	3000	3500	4000	4500	5000		
5	8000	600	250	160	160	160	160	160		
6	8500	600	500	260	260	260	260	260		
7	9000	600	600	360	360	360	360	360		
8	9500	600	600	460	460	460	460	460		
9	10000	600	600	560	560	560	560	560		
10	10500	600	600	600	600	600	600	600		
11	11000	600	600	600	600	600	600	600		
12	11500	600	600	600	600	600	600	600		
13	12000	600	600	600	600	600	600	600		
14										
15	Number_to_produce_2	2000	2500	3000	3500	4000	4500	5000		
16	8000	700	1125	1200	1200	1200	1200	1200		
17	8500	700	1000	1200	1200	1200	1200	1200		
18	9000	700	950	1200	1200	1200	1200	1200		
19	9500	700	950	1200	1200	1200	1200	1200		
20	10000	700	950	1200	1200	1200	1200	1200		
21	10500	700	950	1200	1200	1200	1200	1200		
22	11000	700	950	1200	1200	1200	1200	1200		
23	11500	700	950	1200	1200	1200	1200	1200		
24	12000	700	950	1200	1200	1200	1200	1200		
25										
26	Total_profit	2000	2500	3000	3500	4000	4500	5000		
27	8000	$138,300	$165,125	$167,600	$167,600	$167,600	$167,600	$167,600		
28	8500	$138,300	$169,000	$175,600	$175,600	$175,600	$175,600	$175,600		
29	9000	$138,300	$170,550	$183,600	$183,600	$183,600	$183,600	$183,600		
30	9500	$138,300	$170,550	$191,600	$191,600	$191,600	$191,600	$191,600		
31	10000	$138,300	$170,550	$199,600	$199,600	$199,600	$199,600	$199,600		
32	10500	$138,300	$170,550	$202,800	$202,800	$202,800	$202,800	$202,800		
33	11000	$138,300	$170,550	$202,800	$202,800	$202,800	$202,800	$202,800		
34	11500	$138,300	$170,550	$202,800	$202,800	$202,800	$202,800	$202,800		
35	12000	$138,300	$170,550	$202,800	$202,800	$202,800	$202,800	$202,800		

© Cengage Learning

Figure 13.14

Modified Model
for Simultaneous
Changes

◢	A	B	C	D	E	F	G
17		<=	<=		Original values		% change in both
18	Maximum sales	600	1200		600	1200	0%
19							
20	Constraints (hours per month)	Hours used		Hours available			
21	Labor availability for assembling	10000	<=	10000			
22	Labor availability for testing	2960	<=	3000			
23							
24	Net profit ($ this month)	Basic	XP	Total			
25		$44,800	$154,800	$199,600			

The trick here is to let the *single* value in cell G18 drive both values in cells B18 and C18 from their original values.

© Cengage Learning

in cell B18 and copy it to cell C18. Now a one-way SolverTable can be used with the percentage change in cell G18 to drive two different inputs simultaneously. Specifically, the SolverTable dialog box should be set up as in Figure 13.15, with the corresponding results in Figure 13.16.

Figure 13.15

SolverTable
One-Way Dialog
Box

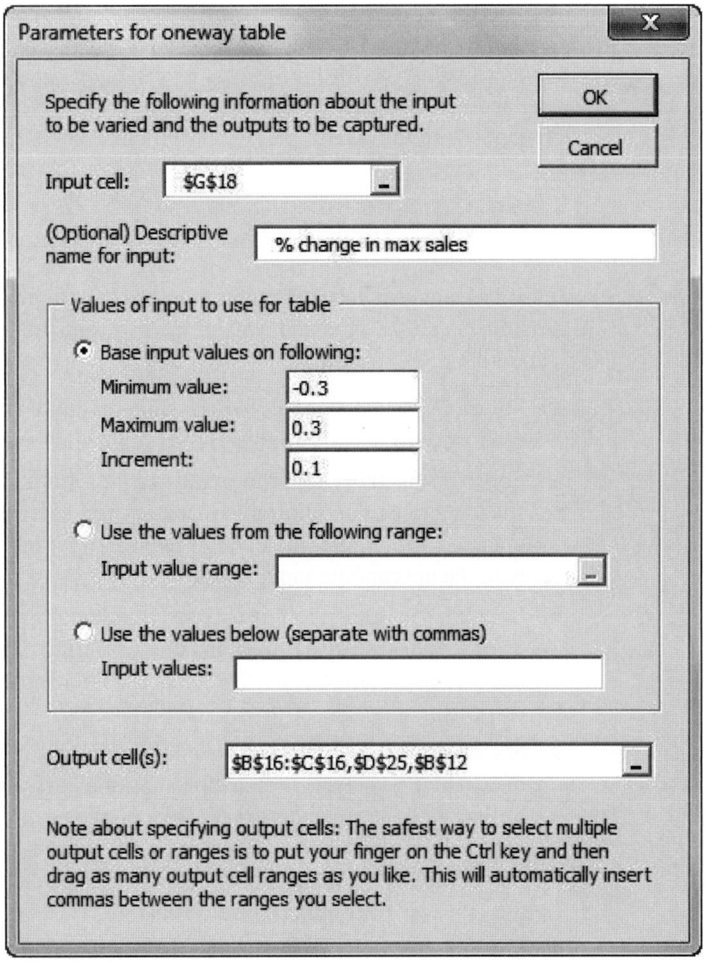

Parameters for oneway table

Specify the following information about the input to be varied and the outputs to be captured.

OK

Cancel

Input cell: $G$18

(Optional) Descriptive name for input: % change in max sales

Values of input to use for table

◉ Base input values on following:

Minimum value: -0.3

Maximum value: 0.3

Increment: 0.1

○ Use the values from the following range:

Input value range:

○ Use the values below (separate with commas)

Input values:

Output cell(s): $B$16:$C$16,$D$25,$B$12

Note about specifying output cells: The safest way to select multiple output cells or ranges is to put your finger on the Ctrl key and then drag as many output cell ranges as you like. This will automatically insert commas between the ranges you select.

© Cengage Learning

You should always scan these sensitivity results to see if they make sense. For example, if the company can sell 20% or 30% more of both models, it makes no more profit than if it can sell only 10% more. The reason is labor availability. By this point, there isn't enough labor to produce the increased demand.

It is always possible to run a sensitivity analysis by changing inputs manually in the spreadsheet model and rerunning Solver. The advantages of SolverTable, however, are that

Figure 13.16

Sensitivity to Percentage Change in Maximum Sales

	A	B	C	D	E	F	G
3	% change in max sales (cell $G$18) values along side, output cell(s) along top						
4		Number_to_produce_1	Number_to_produce_2	Total_profit	$B$12		
5	−30%	420	840	$141,960	$80		
6	−20%	480	960	$162,240	$80		
7	−10%	540	1080	$182,520	$80		
8	0%	560	1200	$199,600	$80		
9	10%	500	1250	$201,250	$80		
10	20%	500	1250	$201,250	$80		
11	30%	500	1250	$201,250	$80		

it enables you to perform a *systematic* sensitivity analysis for any selected inputs and outputs, and it keeps track of the results in a table and associated chart(s). You will see other applications of this useful add-in later in this chapter and in the next chapter.

13-4c Comparison of Solver's Sensitivity Report and SolverTable

Sensitivity analysis in optimization models is extremely important, so it is important that you understand the pros and cons of the two tools in this section. Here are some points to keep in mind.

- Solver's sensitivity report focuses only on the coefficients of the objective and the right sides of the constraints. SolverTable allows you to vary *any* of the inputs.

- Solver's sensitivity report provides very useful information through its reduced costs, shadow prices, and allowable increases and decreases. This same information can be obtained with SolverTable, but it requires a bit more work and some experimentation with the appropriate input ranges.

- Solver's sensitivity report is based on changing only one objective coefficient or one right side at a time. This one-at-a-time restriction prevents you from answering certain questions directly. SolverTable is much more flexible in this respect.

- Solver's sensitivity report is based on a well-established mathematical theory of sensitivity analysis in linear programming. If you lack this mathematical background—as many users do—the outputs can be difficult to understand, especially for somewhat "nonstandard" spreadsheet formulations. In contrast, SolverTable's outputs are straightforward. You can vary one or two inputs and see directly how the optimal solution changes.

- Solver's sensitivity report is not even available for integer-constrained models, and its interpretation for nonlinear models is more difficult than for linear models. SolverTable's outputs have the same interpretation for any type of optimization model.

- Solver's sensitivity report comes with Excel. SolverTable is a separate add-in that is not included with Excel—but it is included with this book and is freely available from the Free Downloads link at the authors' Web site, www.kelley.iu.edu/albrightbooks. Because the SolverTable software essentially automates Solver, which has a number of its own idiosyncrasies, some users have had problems with SolverTable on their PCs. We have tried to document these on our Web site, and we are hoping that the revised Solver in Excel 2010 helps to alleviate these problems.

In summary, each of these tools can be used to answer certain questions. We tend to favor SolverTable because of its flexibility, but in the optimization examples in this chapter and the next chapter, we will illustrate both tools to show how each can provide useful information.

13-5 PROPERTIES OF LINEAR MODELS

Linear programming is an important subset of a larger class of models called **mathematical programming models**.[11] All such models select the levels of various activities that can be performed, subject to a set of constraints, to maximize or minimize an objective such as total profit or total cost. In PC Tech's product mix example, the activities are the numbers of PCs to produce, and the purpose of the model is to find the levels of these activities that maximize the total net profit subject to specified constraints.

In terms of this general setup—selecting the optimal levels of activities—there are three important properties that LP models possess that distinguish them from general mathematical programming models: *proportionality*, *additivity*, and *divisibility*. We discuss these properties briefly in this section.

13-5a Proportionality

Proportionality means that if the level of any activity is multiplied by a constant factor, the contribution of this activity to the objective, or to any of the constraints in which the activity is involved, is multiplied by the same factor. For example, suppose that the production of Basics is cut from its optimal value of 560 to 280—that is, it is multiplied by 0.5. Then the amounts of labor hours from assembling and from testing Basics are both cut in half, and the net profit contributed by Basics is also cut in half.

Proportionality is a perfectly valid assumption in the product mix model, but it is often violated in certain types of models. For example, in various *blending* models used by petroleum companies, chemical outputs vary in a nonlinear manner as chemical inputs are varied. If a chemical input is doubled, say, the resulting chemical output is not necessarily doubled. This type of behavior violates the proportionality property, and it requires *nonlinear* optimization, which we discuss briefly in the next chapter.

13-5b Additivity

The **additivity** property implies that the sum of the contributions from the various activities to a particular constraint equals the total contribution to that constraint. For example, if the two PC models use, respectively, 560 and 2400 testing hours (as in Figure 13.7), then the total number used in the plan is the *sum* of these amounts, 2960 hours. Similarly, the additivity property applies to the objective. That is, the value of the objective is the *sum* of the contributions from the various activities. In the product mix model, the net profits from the two PC models add up to the total net profit. The additivity property implies that the contribution of any decision variable to the objective or to any constraint is *independent* of the levels of the other decision variables.

---

[11]The word *programming* in linear programming or mathematical programming has nothing to do with computer programming. It originated with the British term *programme*, which is essentially a plan or a schedule of operations.

13-5c Divisibility

The **divisibility** property simply means that both integer and noninteger levels of the activities are allowed. In the product mix model, we got integer values in the optimal solution, 560 and 1200, just by luck. For slightly different inputs, they could easily have been fractional values. In general, if you want the levels of some activities to be integer values, there are two possible approaches: (1) You can solve the LP model without integer constraints, and if the solution turns out to have fractional values, you can attempt to round them to integer values; or (2) you can explicitly constrain certain changing cells to contain integer values. The latter approach, however, requires *integer programming*, which we discuss briefly in the next chapter. At this point, we simply state that integer-constrained problems are *much* more difficult to solve than problems without integer constraints.

13-5d Discussion of Linear Properties

The previous discussion of these three properties, especially proportionality and additivity, is fairly abstract. How can you recognize whether a model satisfies proportionality and additivity? This is easy if the model is described algebraically. In this case the objective must be of the form

$$a_1x_1 + a_2x_2 + \cdots + a_nx_n$$

where n is the number of decision variables, the as are constants, and the xs are decision variables. This expression is called a *linear combination* of the xs. Also, each constraint must be equivalent to a form where the left side is a linear combination of the xs and the right side is a constant. For example, the following is a typical linear constraint:

$$3x_1 + 7x_2 - 2x_3 \leq 50$$

It is not quite so easy to recognize proportionality and additivity—or the lack of them—in a spreadsheet model, because the logic of the model is typically embedded in a series of cell formulas. However, the ideas are the same. First, the objective cell must ultimately (possibly through a series of formulas in intervening cells) be a sum of products of constants and changing cells, where a "constant" means that it does not depend on changing cells. Second, each side of each constraint must ultimately be either a constant or a sum of products of constants and changing cells. This explains why linear models contain so many SUM and SUMPRODUCT functions.

It is usually easier to recognize when a model is *not* linear. Two particular situations that lead to nonlinear models are when (1) there are products or quotients of expressions involving changing cells or (2) there are nonlinear functions, such as squares, square roots, or logarithms, that involve changing cells. These are typically easy to spot, and they guarantee that the model is nonlinear.

Real-life problems are almost never exactly linear. However, linear approximations often yield very useful results.

Whenever you model a real problem, you usually make some simplifying assumptions. This is certainly the case with LP models. The world is frequently *not* linear, which means that an entirely realistic model typically violates some or all of the three properties in this section. However, numerous successful applications of LP have demonstrated the usefulness of linear models, even if they are only *approximations* of reality. If you suspect that the violations are serious enough to invalidate a linear model, you should use an integer or nonlinear model, as we illustrate in the next chapter.

In terms of Excel's Solver, if the model is linear—that is, if it satisfies the proportionality, additivity, and divisibility properties—you should check the Simplex option (or the Assume Linear Model option in pre-2010 versions of Excel). Then Solver uses the simplex method, a very efficient method for a linear model, to solve the problem. Actually, you can check the Simplex option even if the divisibility property is violated—that is, for linear models with integer-constrained variables—but Solver then embeds the simplex method in a more complex algorithm in its solution procedure.

13-5e Linear Models and Scaling[12]

In some cases you might be sure that a model is linear, but when you check the Simplex option (or the Assume Linear Model option) and then solve, you get a Solver message to the effect that the conditions for linearity are not satisfied. This can indicate a logical error in your formulation, so that the proportionality and additivity conditions are indeed not satisfied. However, it can also indicate that Solver erroneously *thinks* the linearity conditions are not satisfied, which is typically due to roundoff error in its calculations—not any error on your part. If the latter occurs and you are convinced that the model is correct, you can try *not* using the simplex method to see whether that works. If it does not, you should consult your instructor. It is possible that the non-simplex algorithm employed by Solver simply cannot find the solution to your problem.

In any case, it always helps to have a *well-scaled* model. In a well-scaled model, all of the numbers are roughly the same magnitude. If the model contains some very large numbers—100,000 or more, say—and some very small numbers—0.001 or less, say—it is *poorly scaled* for the methods used by Solver, and roundoff error is far more likely to be an issue, not only in Solver's test for linearity conditions but in all of its algorithms.

You can decrease the chance of getting an incorrect "Conditions for Assume Linear Model are not satisfied" message by changing Solver's Precision setting.

If you believe your model is poorly scaled, there are three possible remedies. The first is to check the Use Automatic Scaling option in Solver. (It is found by clicking on the Options button in the main Solver dialog box.) This might help and it might not; we have had mixed success. (Frontline Systems, the company that develops Solver, has told us that the only drawback to checking this box is that the solution procedure can be slower.) The second option is to redefine the units in which the various quantities are defined. Finally, you can change the Precision setting in Solver's Options dialog box to a larger number, such 0.00001 or 0.0001. (The default has five zeros.)

Excel Tip: *Rescaling a Model*
Suppose you have a whole range of input values expressed, say, in dollars, and you would like to reexpress them in thousands of dollars, that is, you would like to divide each value by 1000. There is a simple copy/paste way to do this. Enter the value 1000 in some unused cell and copy it. Then select the range you want to rescale, and from the Paste dropdown menu, select Paste Special and then the Divide option. No formulas are required; your original values are automatically rescaled (and you can then delete the 1000 cell). You can use this same method to add, subtract, or multiply by a constant.

13-6 INFEASIBILITY AND UNBOUNDEDNESS

Infeasibility and Unboundedness

In this section we discuss two of the things that can go wrong when you invoke Solver. Both of these might indicate that there is a mistake in the model. Therefore, because mistakes are common in LP models, you should be aware of the error messages you might encounter.

13-6a Infeasibility

A perfectly reasonable model can have no feasible solutions because of too many constraints.

The first problem is **infeasibility**. Recall that a solution is *feasible* if it satisfies all of the constraints. Among all of the feasible solutions, you are looking for the one that optimizes the objective. However, it is possible that there are no feasible solutions to the model. There

[12]This section might seem overly technical. However, when you develop a model that you are sure is linear and Solver then tells you it doesn't satisfy the linear conditions, you will appreciate this section.

are generally two reasons for this: (1) there is a mistake in the model (an input was entered incorrectly, such as a $\leq$ symbol instead of $\geq$) or (2) the problem has been so constrained that there are no solutions left. In the former case, a careful check of the model should find the error. In the latter case, you might need to change, or even eliminate, some of the constraints.

To show how an infeasible problem could occur, suppose in PC Tech's product mix problem you change the maximum sales constraints to *minimum* sales constraints (and leave everything else unchanged). That is, you change these constraints from $\leq$ to $\geq$. If Solver is then used, the message in Figure 13.17 appears, indicating that Solver cannot find a feasible solution. The reason is clear: There is no way, given the constraints on labor hours, that the company can produce these minimum sales values. The company's only choice is to set at least one of the minimum sales values lower. In general, there is no fool-proof way to remedy the problem when a "no feasible solution" message appears. Careful checking and rethinking are required.

Figure 13.17

No Feasible Solution Message

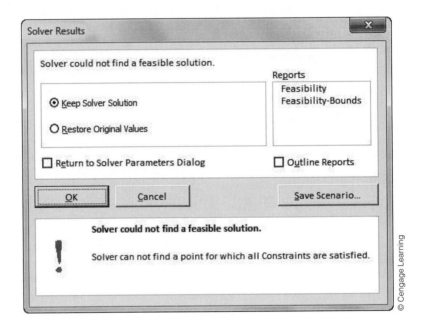

13-6b Unboundedness

A second type of problem is **unboundedness**. In this case, the model has been formulated in such a way that the objective is unbounded—that is, it can be made as large (or as small, for minimization problems) as you like. If this occurs, you have probably entered a wrong input or forgotten some constraints. To see how this could occur in the product mix problem, suppose that you change *all* constraints to be $\leq$ instead of $\geq$. Now there is no upper bound on available labor hours or the number of PCs the company can sell. If you make these changes in the model and then use Solver, the message in Figure 13.18 appears, stating that the objective cell does not converge. In other words, the total net profit can grow without bound.

Except in very rare situations, if Solver informs you that your model is unbounded, you have made an error.

13-6c Comparison of Infeasibility and Unboundedness

Infeasibility and unboundedness are quite different in a practical sense. It is quite possible for a reasonable model to have no feasible solutions. For example, the marketing department might impose several constraints, the production department might add some

Figure 13.18

Unbounded
Solution Message

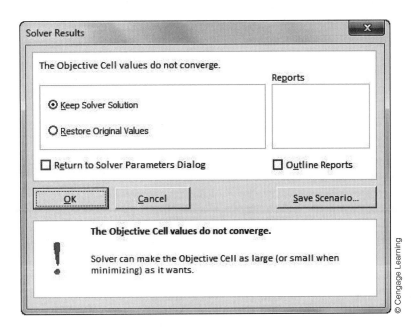

more, the engineering department might add even more, and so on. Together, they might constrain the problem so much that there are no feasible solutions left. The only way out is to change or eliminate some of the constraints. An unboundedness problem is quite different. There is no way a realistic model can have an unbounded solution. If you get the message shown in Figure 13.18, then you must have made a mistake: You entered an input incorrectly, you omitted one or more constraints, or there is a logical error in your model.

PROBLEMS

Note: Student solutions for problems whose numbers appear within a colored box are available for purchase at www.cengagebrain.com.

Level A

1. Other sensitivity analyses besides those discussed could be performed on the product mix model. Use SolverTable to perform each of the following. In each case keep track of the values in the changing cells and the objective cell, and discuss your findings.

  a. Let the selling price for Basics vary from $220 to $350 in increments of $10.

  b. Let the labor cost per hour for assembling vary from $5 to $20 in increments of $1.

  c. Let the labor hours for testing a Basic vary from 0.5 to 3.0 in increments of 0.5.

  d. Let the labor hours for assembling and testing an XP vary independently, the first from 4.5 to 8.0 and the second from 1.5 to 3.0, both in increments of 0.5.

2. In PC Tech's product mix problem, assume there is another PC model, the VXP, that the company can produce in addition to Basics and XPs. Each VXP requires eight hours for assembling, three hours for testing, $275 for component parts, and sells for $560. At most 50 VXPs can be sold.

  a. Modify the spreadsheet model to include this new product, and use Solver to find the optimal product mix.

  b. You should find that the optimal solution is *not* integer-valued. If you round the values in the changing cells to the nearest integers, is the resulting solution still feasible? If not, how might you obtain a feasible solution that is at least close to optimal?

3. Continuing the previous problem, perform a sensitivity analysis on the selling price of VXPs. Let this price vary from $500 to $650 in increments of $10, and keep track of the values in the changing cells and the objective cell. Discuss your findings.

4. Again continuing problem 2, suppose that you want to force the optimal solution to be integers. Do this in Solver by adding a new constraint. Select the changing cells for the left side of the constraint, and in the middle dropdown list, select the "int" option (for "integer"). How does the optimal integer solution compare to the optimal noninteger solution in problem 2? Are the changing cell values rounded versions of those in problem 2? Is the objective value more or less than in problem 2?

5. If all of the inputs in PC Tech's product mix problem are nonnegative (as they should be for any realistic version of the problem), are there any input values such that the resulting model has no feasible solutions? (Refer to the graphical solution.)

6. There are five corner points in the feasible region for the product mix problem. We identified the coordinates of one of them: (560, 1200). Identify the coordinates of the others.
   a. Only one of these other corner points has positive values for both changing cells. Discuss the changes in the selling prices of either or both models that would be necessary to make this corner point optimal.
   b. Two of the other corner points have one changing cell value positive and the other zero. Discuss the changes in the selling prices of either or both

models that would be necessary to make either of these corner points optimal.

Level B

7. Using the graphical solution of the product mix model as a guide, suppose there are only 2800 testing hours available. How do the answers to the previous problem change? (Is the previous solution still optimal? Is it still feasible?)

8. Again continuing problem 2, perform a sensitivity analysis where the selling prices of Basics and XPs simultaneously change by the same percentage, but the selling price of VXPs remains at its original value. Let the percentage change vary from −25% to 50% in increments of 5%, and keep track of the values in the changing cells and the total profit. Discuss your findings.

9. Consider the graphical solution to the product mix problem. Now imagine that another constraint— *any* constraint—is added. Which of the following three things are possible: (1) the feasible region shrinks; (2) the feasible region stays the same; (3) the feasible region expands? Which of the following three things are possible: (1) the optimal value in objective cell decreases; (2) the optimal value in objective cell stays the same; (3) the optimal value in objective cell increases? Explain your answers. Do they hold just for this particular model, or do they hold in general?

13-7 A LARGER PRODUCT MIX MODEL

The problem we examine in this section is a direct extension of the product mix model in the previous section. There are two modifications. First, the company makes eight computer models, not just two. Second, testing can be done on either of two lines, and these two lines have different characteristics.

EXAMPLE | **13.2 PRODUCING COMPUTERS AT PC TECH**

As in the previous example, PC Tech must decide how many of each of its computer models to assemble and test, but there are now eight available models, not just two. Each computer must be assembled and then tested, but there are now two lines for testing. The first line tends to test faster, but its labor costs are slightly higher, and each line has a certain number of hours available for testing. Any computer can be tested on either line. The inputs for the model are same as before: (1) the hourly labor costs for assembling and testing, (2) the required labor hours for assembling and testing any computer model, (3) the cost of component parts for each model, (4) the selling prices for each model, (5) the maximum sales for each model, and (6) labor availabilities. These input values are listed in the file **Product Mix 2.xlsx**. As before, the company wants to determine the product mix that maximizes its total net profit.

Objective   To use LP to find the mix of computer models that maximizes total net profit and stays within the labor hour availability and maximum sales constraints.

Where Do the Numbers Come From?

The same comments as in Example 13.1 apply here.

Solution

Table 13.2 lists the variables and constraints for this model. You must choose the number of computers of each model to produce on each line, the sum of which cannot be larger than the maximum that can be sold. This choice determines the labor hours of each type used and all revenues and costs. No more labor hours can be used than are available.

Table 13.2   Variables and Constraints for Larger Product Mix Model

Input variables	Hourly labor costs, labor availabilities, labor required for each computer, costs of component parts, unit selling prices, and maximum sales
Decision variables (changing cells)	Numbers of computer of each model to test on each line
Objective cell	Total net profit
Other calculated variables	Number of each computer model produced, hours of labor used for assembling and for each line of testing
Constraints	Computers produced $\leq$ Maximum sales Labor hours used $\leq$ Labor hours available

© Cengage Learning

It is probably not immediately obvious what the changing cells should be for this model (at least not before you look at Table 13.2). You might think that the company simply needs to decide how many computers of each model to produce. However, because of the two testing lines, this is not enough information. The company must also decide how many of each model to test *on each line*. For example, suppose they decide to test 100 model 4s on line 1 and 300 model 4s on line 2. This means they will need to assemble (and ultimately sell) 400 model 4s. In other words, given the detailed plan of how many to test on each line, everything else is determined. But without the detailed plan, there is not enough information to complete the model. This is the type of reasoning you must go through to determine the appropriate changing cells for any LP model.

An Algebraic Model

We will not spell out the algebraic model for this expanded version of the product mix model because it is so similar to the two-variable product mix model. However, we will say that it is larger, and hence probably more intimidating. Now we need decision variables of the form x_{ij}, the number of model j computers to test on line i, and the total net profit and each labor availability constraint will include a long SUMPRODUCT formula involving these variables. Instead of focusing on these algebraic expressions, we turn directly to the spreadsheet model.

Developing the Spreadsheet Model

Developing the Product Mix 2 Model

The spreadsheet in Figure 13.19 illustrates the solution procedure for PC Tech's product mix problem. (See the file **Product Mix 2.xlsx**.) The first stage is to develop the spreadsheet model step by step.

1. **Inputs.** Enter the various inputs in the blue ranges. Again, remember that our convention is to color all input cells blue. Enter only *numbers*, not formulas, in input cells. They should always be numbers directly from the problem statement. (In this case, we supplied them in the spreadsheet template.)

Figure 13.19 Larger Product Mix Model with Infeasible Solution

	A	B	C	D	E	F	G	H	I	J
1	**Assembling and testing computers**									
2										
3	Cost per labor hour assembling	$11								
4	Cost per labor hour testing, line 1	$19								
5	Cost per labor hour testing, line 2	$17								
6										
7	Inputs for assembling and testing a computer									
8		Model 1	Model 2	Model 3	Model 4	Model 5	Model 6	Model 7	Model 8	
9	Labor hours for assembly	4	5	5	5	5.5	5.5	5.5	6	
10	Labor hours for testing, line 1	1.5	2	2	2	2.5	2.5	2.5	3	
11	Labor hours for testing, line 2	2	2.5	2.5	2.5	3	3	3.5	3.5	
12	Cost of component parts	$150	$225	$225	$225	$250	$250	$250	$300	
13	Selling price	$350	$450	$460	$470	$500	$525	$530	$600	
14	Unit margin, tested on line 1	$128	$132	$142	$152	$142	$167	$172	$177	
15	Unit margin, tested on line 2	$122	$128	$138	$148	$139	$164	$160	$175	
16										
17	Assembling, testing plan (# of computers)									
18		Model 1	Model 2	Model 3	Model 4	Model 5	Model 6	Model 7	Model 8	
19	Number tested on line 1	0	0	0	0	0	500	1000	800	
20	Number tested on line 2	0	0	0	1250	0	0	0	0	
21	Total computers produced	0	0	0	1250	0	500	1000	800	
22		<=	<=	<=	<=	<=	<=	<=	<=	
23	Maximum sales	1500	1250	1250	1250	1000	1000	1000	800	
24										
25	Constraints (hours per month)	Hours used		Hours available						
26	Labor availability for assembling	19300	<=	20000						
27	Labor availability for testing, line 1	6150	<=	5000						
28	Labor availability for testing, line 2	3125	<=	6000						
29										
30	Net profit ($ per month)	Model 1	Model 2	Model 3	Model 4	Model 5	Model 6	Model 7	Model 8	Totals
31	Tested on line 1	$0	$0	$0	$0	$0	$83,500	$172,000	$141,600	$397,100
32	Tested on line 2	$0	$0	$0	$184,375	$0	$0	$0	$0	$184,375
33										$581,475
34										
35	**Range names used:**									
36	Hours_available	=Model!$D$26:$D$28								
37	Hours_used	=Model!$B$26:$B$28								
38	Maximum_sales	=Model!$B$23:$I$23								
39	Number_tested_on_line_1	=Model!$B$19:$I$19								
40	Number_tested_on_line_2	=Model!$B$20:$I$20								
41	Total_computers_produced	=Model!$B$21:$I$21								
42	Total_profit	=Model!$J$33								

2. **Range names.** Name the ranges indicated. According to our convention, there are enough named ranges so that the Solver dialog box contains only range names, no cell addresses. Of course, you can name additional ranges if you like. (Note that you can again use the range-naming shortcut explained in the Excel tip for the previous example. That is, you can take advantage of labels in adjacent cells, except for the Profit cell.)

3. **Unit margins.** Note that two rows of these are required, one for each testing line, because the costs of testing on the two lines are not equal. To calculate them, enter the formula

=B$13-$B$3*B$9-$B$4*B10-B$12

in cell B14 and copy it to the range B14:I15.

4. **Changing cells.** As discussed above, the changing cells are the red cells in rows 19 and 20. You do *not* have to enter the values shown in Figure 13.19. You can use any trial values initially; Solver will eventually find the *optimal* values. Note that the four values shown in Figure 13.19 cannot be optimal because they do not satisfy all of the constraints. Specifically, this plan uses more labor hours for assembling than are available. However, you do not need to worry about satisfying constraints at this point; Solver will take care of this later.

5. **Labor used.** Enter the formula

   =SUMPRODUCT(B9:E9,Total_computers_produced)

   in cell B26 to calculate the number of assembling hours used. Similarly, enter the formulas

   =SUMPRODUCT(B10:I10,Number_tested_on_line_1)

   and

   =SUMPRODUCT(B11:I11,Number_tested_on_line_2)

   in cells B27 and B28 for the labor hours used on each testing line.

   Excel Tip: Copying Formulas with Range Names
   When you enter a range name in an Excel formula and then copy the formula, the range name reference acts like an absolute reference. Therefore, it wouldn't work to copy the formula in cell B27 to cell B28. However, this would work if range names hadn't been used. This is one potential disadvantage of range names that you should be aware of.

6. **Revenues, costs, and profits.** The area from row 30 down shows the summary of monetary values. Actually, only the total profit in cell J33 is needed, but it is also useful to calculate the net profit from each computer model on each testing line. To obtain these, enter the formula

   =B14*B19

   in cell B31 and copy it to the range B31:I32. Then sum these to obtain the totals in column J. The total in cell J33 is the objective to maximize.

Experimenting with Other Solutions

Before going any further, you might want to experiment with other values in the changing cells. However, it is a real challenge to guess the optimal solution. It is tempting to fill up the changing cells corresponding to the largest unit margins. However, this totally ignores their use of the scarce labor hours. If you can guess the optimal solution to this model, you are better than we are!

Using Solver

The Solver dialog box should be filled out as shown in Figure 13.20. (Again, note that there are enough named ranges so that only range names appear in this dialog box.) Except that this model has two rows of changing cells, the Solver setup is identical to the one in Example 13.1.

Discussion of the Solution

You typically gain insights into a solution by checking which constraints are binding

When you click on Solve, you obtain the optimal solution shown in Figure 13.21. The optimal plan is to produce computer models 1, 4, 6, and 7 only, some on testing line 1 and others on testing line 2. This plan uses all of the available labor hours for assembling and testing on line 1, but about 1800 of the testing line 2 hours are not used. Also, maximum sales are achieved only for computer models 1, 6, and 7. This is typical of

Figure 13.20
Solver Dialog Box

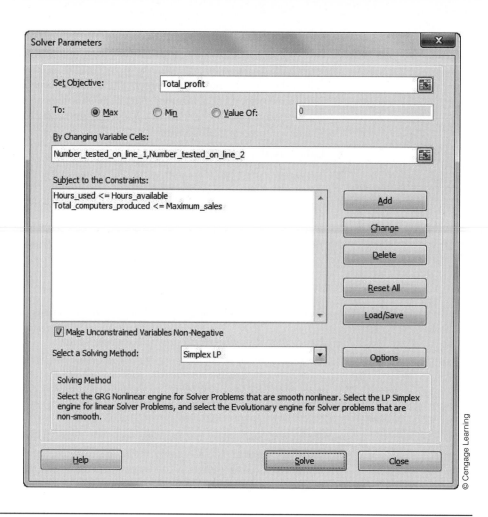

Figure 13.21 Optimal Solution to Larger Product Mix Model

	A	B	C	D	E	F	G	H	I	J
17	Assembling, testing plan (# of computers)									
18		Model 1	Model 2	Model 3	Model 4	Model 5	Model 6	Model 7	Model 8	
19	Number tested on line 1	1500	0	0	125	0	0	1000	0	
20	Number tested on line 2	0	0	0	475	0	1000	0	0	
21	Total computers produced	1500	0	0	600	0	1000	1000	0	
22		<=	<=	<=	<=	<=	<=	<=	<=	
23	Maximum sales	1500	1250	1250	1250	1000	1000	1000	800	
24										
25	Constraints (hours per month)	Hours used		Hours available						
26	Labor availability for assembling	20000	<=	20000						
27	Labor availability for testing, line 1	5000	<=	5000						
28	Labor availability for testing, line 2	4187.5	<=	6000						
29										
30	Net profit ($ per month)	Model 1	Model 2	Model 3	Model 4	Model 5	Model 6	Model 7	Model 8	Totals
31	Tested on line 1	$191,250	$0	$0	$19,000	$0	$0	$172,000	$0	$382,250
32	Tested on line 2	$0	$0	$0	$70,063	$0	$163,500	$0	$0	$233,563
33										$615,813

© Cengage Learning

an LP solution. Some of the constraints are met exactly—they are binding—whereas others contain a certain amount of "slack." The binding constraints prevent PC Tech from earning an even higher profit.

Excel Tip: Roundoff Error

Because of the way numbers are stored and calculated on a computer, the optimal values in the changing cells and elsewhere can contain small roundoff errors. For example, the value that really appears in cell E20 on one of our Excel 2007 PCs is 475.000002015897, not exactly 475. For all practical purposes, this number can be treated as 475, and we have formatted it as such in the spreadsheet. (We have been told that roundoff in Solver results should be less of a problem in Excel 2010 and later.)

Sensitivity Analysis

If you want to experiment with different inputs to this problem, you can simply change the inputs and then rerun Solver. The second time you use Solver, you do not have to specify the objective and changing cells or the constraints. Excel remembers all of these settings and saves them when you save the file.

You can also use SolverTable to perform a more systematic sensitivity analysis on one or more input variables. One possibility appears in Figure 13.22, where the number of available assembling labor hours is allowed to vary from 18,000 to 25,000 in increments of 1000, and the numbers of computers produced and profit are designated as outputs. There are several ways to interpret the output from this sensitivity analysis. First, you can look at columns B through I to see how the product mix changes as more assembling labor hours become available. For assembling labor hours from 18,000 to 23,000, the only thing that changes is that more model 4s are produced. Beyond 23,000, however, the company starts to produce model 3s and produces fewer model 7s. Second, you can see how extra labor hours add to the total profit. Note exactly what this increased profit means. For example, when labor hours increase from 20,000 to 21,000, the model requires that the company must *pay* $11 apiece for these extra hours (if it uses them). But the *net* effect is that profit increases by $29,500, or $29.50 per extra hour. In other words, the labor cost increases by $11,000 [=$11(1000)], but this is more than offset by the increase in revenue that comes from having the extra labor hours.

As column J illustrates, it is worthwhile for the company to obtain extra assembling labor hours, even though it has to pay for them, because its profit increases. However, the

---

Figure 13.22 Sensitivity to Assembling Labor Hours

⬜	A	B	C	D	E	F	G	H	I	J
3	Assembling labor (cell $D$26) values along side, output cell(s) along top									
4		Total_computers_produced_1	Total_computers_produced_2	Total_computers_produced_3	Total_computers_produced_4	Total_computers_produced_5	Total_computers_produced_6	Total_computers_produced_7	Total_computers_produced_8	Total_profit
5	18000	1500	0	0	200	0	1000	1000	0	$556,813
6	19000	1500	0	0	400	0	1000	1000	0	$586,313
7	20000	1500	0	0	600	0	1000	1000	0	$615,813
8	21000	1500	0	0	800	0	1000	1000	0	$645,313
9	22000	1500	0	0	1000	0	1000	1000	0	$674,813
10	23000	1500	0	0	1200	0	1000	1000	0	$704,313
11	24000	1500	0	700	1250	0	1000	500	0	$724,750
12	25000	1500	0	1250	1250	0	1000	60	0	$727,170

increase in profit per extra labor hour—the *shadow price* of assembling labor hours—is not constant. In the top part of the table, it is $29.50 (per extra hour), but it then decreases to $20.44 and then $2.42. The accompanying SolverTable chart of column J illustrates this decreasing shadow price through its decreasing slope.

Finally, you can gain additional insight from Solver's sensitivity report, shown in Figure 13.23. However, you have to be very careful in interpreting this report. Unlike Example 13.1, there are no upper bound (maximum sales) constraints on the *changing cells*. The maximum sales constraints are on the total computers produced (row 21 of the model), not the changing cells. Therefore, the only nonzero reduced costs in the top part of the table are for changing cells currently at zero (not those at their upper bounds as in the previous example). Each nonzero reduced cost indicates how much the profit margin for this activity would have to change before this activity would be profitable. Also, there is a row in the bottom part of the table for each constraint, *including* the maximum sales constraints. The interesting values are again the shadow prices. The first two indicate the amount the company would pay for an extra assembling or line 1

Figure 13.23   Solver's Sensitivity Report

	A	B	C	D	E	F	G	H
6		Variable Cells						
7				Final	Reduced	Objective	Allowable	Allowable
8		Cell	Name	Value	Cost	Coefficient	Increase	Decrease
9		$B$19	Number tested on line 1 Model 1	1500	0	127.5	1E+30	2.125
10		$C$19	Number tested on line 1 Model 2	0	−20	132	20	1E+30
11		$D$19	Number tested on line 1 Model 3	0	−10	142	10	1E+30
12		$E$19	Number tested on line 1 Model 4	125	0	152	2.833	1.7
13		$F$19	Number tested on line 1 Model 5	0	−25.875	142	25.875	1E+30
14		$G$19	Number tested on line 1 Model 6	0	−2.125	167	2.125	1E+30
15		$H$19	Number tested on line 1 Model 7	1000	0	172	1E+30	4.125
16		$I$19	Number tested on line 1 Model 8	0	−6.75	177	6.75	1E+30
17		$B$20	Number tested on line 2 Model 1	0	−2.125	122	2.125	1E+30
18		$C$20	Number tested on line 2 Model 2	0	−20	127.5	20	1E+30
19		$D$20	Number tested on line 2 Model 3	0	−10	137.5	10	1E+30
20		$E$20	Number tested on line 2 Model 4	475	0	147.5	1.136	2.083
21		$F$20	Number tested on line 2 Model 5	0	−23.75	138.5	23.75	1E+30
22		$G$20	Number tested on line 2 Model 6	1000	0	163.5	1E+30	1.25
23		$H$20	Number tested on line 2 Model 7	0	−6.375	160	6.375	1E+30
24		$I$20	Number tested on line 2 Model 8	0	−2.5	174.5	2.5	1E+30
25								
26		Constraints						
27				Final	Shadow	Constraint	Allowable	Allowable
28		Cell	Name	Value	Price	R.H. Side	Increase	Decrease
29		$B$26	Labor availability for assembling Hours used	20000	29.5	20000	3250	2375
30		$B$27	Labor availability for testing, line 1 Hours used	5000	2.25	5000	950	250
31		$B$28	Labor availability for testing, line 2 Hours used	4187.5	0	6000	1E+30	1812.5
32		$B$21	Total computers produced Model 1	1500	6.125	1500	166.667	812.5
33		$C$21	Total computers produced Model 2	0	0	1250	1E+30	1250
34		$D$21	Total computers produced Model 3	0	0	1250	1E+30	1250
35		$E$21	Total computers produced Model 4	600	0	1250	1E+30	650
36		$F$21	Total computers produced Model 5	0	0	1000	1E+30	1000
37		$G$21	Total computers produced Model 6	1000	1.25	1000	431.818	590.909
38		$H$21	Total computers produced Model 7	1000	4.125	1000	100	590.909
39		$I$21	Total computers produced Model 8	0	0	800	1E+30	800

© Cengage Learning

testing labor hour. (Does the 29.5 value look familiar? Compare it to the SolverTable results above.) The shadow prices for all *binding* maximum sales constraints indicate how much more profit the company could make if it could increase its demand by one computer of that model.

The information in this sensitivity report is all relevant and definitely provides some insights if studied carefully. However, this really requires you to know the exact rules Solver uses to create this report. That is, it requires a fairly in-depth knowledge of the theory behind LP sensitivity analysis, more than we have provided here. Fortunately, we believe the same basic information—and more—can be obtained in a more intuitive way by creating several carefully chosen SolverTable reports. ∎

PROBLEMS

Level A

Note: All references to the product mix model in the following problems are to the larger *product mix model in this section.*

10. Modify PC Tech's product mix model so that there is no maximum sales constraint. (This is easy to do in the Solver dialog box. Just highlight the constraint and click on the Delete button.) Does this make the problem unbounded? Does it change the optimal solution at all? Explain its effect.

11. In the product mix model it makes sense to change the maximum sales constraint to a "minimum sales" constraint, simply by changing the direction of the inequality. Then the input values in row 23 can be considered customer demands that must be met. Make this change and rerun Solver. What do you find? What do you find if you run Solver again, this time making the values in row 23 one-quarter of their current values?

12. Use SolverTable to run a sensitivity analysis on the cost per assembling labor hour, letting it vary from $5 to $20 in increments of $1. Keep track of the computers produced in row 21, the hours used in the range B26:B28, and the total profit. Discuss your findings. Are they intuitively what you expected?

13. Create a two-way SolverTable for the product mix model, where total profit is the only output and the two inputs are the testing line 1 hours and testing line 2 hours available. Let the former vary from 4000 to 6000 in increments of 500, and let the latter vary from 3000 to 5000 in increments of 500. Discuss the changes in profit you see as you look across the various rows of the table. Discuss the changes in profit you see as you look down the various columns of the table.

14. Model 8 has fairly high profit margins, but it isn't included at all in the optimal mix. Use SolverTable, along with some experimentation on the correct range,

to find the (approximate) selling price required for model 8 before it enters the optimal product mix.

Level B

15. Suppose that you want to increase *all three* of the resource availabilities in the product mix model simultaneously by the same percentage. You want this percentage to vary from −25% to 50% in increments of 5%. Modify the spreadsheet model slightly so that this sensitivity analysis can be performed with a *one-way* SolverTable, using the percentage change as the single input. Keep track of the computers produced in row 21, the hours used in the range B26:B28, and the total profit. Discuss the results.

16. Some analysts complain that spreadsheet models are difficult to resize. You can be the judge of this. Suppose the current product mix problem is changed so that there is an extra resource, packaging labor hours, and two additional PC models, 9 and 10. What additional input data are required? What modifications are necessary in the spreadsheet model (including range name changes)? Make up values for any extra required input data and incorporate these into a modified spreadsheet model. Then optimize with Solver. Do you conclude that it is easy to resize a spreadsheet model? (By the way, it turns out that algebraic models are typically *much* easier to resize.)

17. In Solver's sensitivity report for the product mix model, the allowable decrease for available assembling hours is 2375. This means that something happens when assembling hours fall to $20,000 − 2375 = 17,625$. See what this means by first running Solver with 17,626 available hours and then again with 17,624 available hours. Explain how the two solutions compare to the original solution and to each other.

13-8 A MULTIPERIOD PRODUCTION MODEL

The product mix examples illustrate a very important type of LP model. However, LP models come in many forms. For variety, we now present a quite different type of model that can also be solved with LP. (In the next chapter we provide other examples, linear and otherwise.) The distinguishing feature of the following model is that it relates decisions made during several time periods. This type of problem occurs when a company must make a decision now that will have ramifications in the future. The company does not want to focus completely on the short run and forget about the long run.

EXAMPLE	13.3 PRODUCING FOOTBALLS AT PIGSKIN

Pigskin Company produces footballs. Pigskin must decide how many footballs to produce each month. The company has decided to use a six-month planning horizon. The forecasted monthly demands for the next six months are 10,000, 15,000, 30,000, 35,000, 25,000, and 10,000. Pigskin wants to meet these demands on time, knowing that it currently has 5000 footballs in inventory and that it can use a given month's production to help meet the demand for that month. (For simplicity, we assume that production occurs during the month, and demand occurs at the end of the month.) During each month there is enough production capacity to produce up to 30,000 footballs, and there is enough storage capacity to store up to 10,000 footballs at the end of the month, after demand has occurred. The forecasted production costs per football for the next six months are $12.50, $12.55, $12.70, $12.80, $12.85, and $12.95, respectively. The holding cost per football held in inventory at the end of any month is figured at 5% of the production cost for that month. (This cost includes the cost of storage and also the cost of money tied up in inventory.) The selling price for footballs is not considered relevant to the production decision because Pigskin will satisfy all customer demand exactly when it occurs—at whatever the selling price is. In other words, total revenue for the planning horizon is *fixed*, regardless of production decisions. Therefore, Pigskin wants to determine the production schedule that minimizes the total production and holding costs.

Objective   To use LP to find the production schedule that meets demand on time and minimizes total production and inventory holding costs.

Where Do the Numbers Come From?

The input values for this problem are not all easy to find. Here are some thoughts on where they might be obtained. (See Figure 13.24.)

- The initial inventory in cell B4 should be available from the company's database system or from a physical count.

- The unit production costs in row 8 would probably be estimated in two steps. First, the company might ask its cost accountants to estimate the current unit production cost. Then it could examine historical trends in costs to estimate inflation factors for future months.

- The holding cost percentage in cell B5 is typically difficult to determine. Depending on the type of inventory being held, this cost can include storage and handling, rent, property taxes, insurance, spoilage, and obsolescence. It can also include capital costs—the cost of money that could be used for other purposes.

- The demands in row 18 are probably forecasts made by the marketing and sales department. They might be "seat-of-the-pants" forecasts, or they might be the result of a formal quantitative forecasting procedure as discussed in Chapter 12. Of course, if there are already some orders on the books for future months, these are included in the demand figures.
- The production and storage capacities in rows 14 and 22 are probably supplied by the production department. They are based on the size of the workforce, the available machinery, availability of raw materials, and physical space.

Solution

The variables and constraints for this model are listed in Table 13.3. There are two keys to relating these variables. First, the months cannot be treated independently. This is because the ending inventory in one month is the beginning inventory for the next month. Second, to ensure that demand is satisfied on time, the amount on hand after production in each month must be at least as large as the demand for that month. This constraint must be included explicitly in the model.

Table 13.3 Variables and Constraints for Production/Inventory Planning Model

Input variables	Initial inventory, unit holding cost percentage, unit production costs, forecasted demands, production and storage capacities
Decision variables (changing cells)	Monthly production quantities
Objective cell	Total cost
Other calculated variables	Units on hand after production, ending inventories, monthly production and inventory holding costs
Constraints	Units on hand after production ≥ Demand (each month) Units produced ≤ Production capacity (each month) Ending inventory ≤ Storage capacity (each month)

© Cengage Learning

When you model this type of problem, you must be very specific about the *timing* of events. In fact, depending on the assumptions you make, there can be a variety of potential models. For example, when does the demand for footballs in a given month occur: at the beginning of the month, at the end of the month, or continually throughout the month? The same question can be asked about production in a given month. The answers to these two questions indicate how much of the production in a given month can be used to help satisfy the demand in that month. Also, are the maximum storage constraint and the holding cost based on the *ending* inventory in a month, the *average* amount of inventory in a month, or the *maximum* inventory in a month? Each of these possibilities is reasonable and could be implemented.

By modifying the timing assumptions in this type of model, alternative—and equally realistic—models with very different solutions can be obtained.

To simplify the model, we assume that (1) all production occurs at the beginning of the month, (2) all demand occurs *after* production, so that all units produced in a month can be used to satisfy that month's demand, and (3) the storage constraint and the holding cost are based on *ending* inventory in a given month. (You are asked to modify these assumptions in the problems.)

An Algebraic Model

In the traditional algebraic model, the decision variables are the *production quantities* for the six months, labeled P_1 through P_6. It is also convenient to let I_1 through I_6 be the corresponding *end-of-month inventories* (after demand has occurred).[13] For example, I_3 is the number of footballs left over at the end of month 3. Therefore, the obvious constraints are on production and inventory storage capacities: $P_j \leq 30000$ and $I_j \leq 10000$ for $1 \leq j \leq 6$.

In addition to these constraints, *balance* constraints that relate the Ps and Is are necessary. In any month the inventory from the previous month plus the current production equals the current demand plus leftover inventory. If D_j is the forecasted demand for month j, the balance equation for month j is

$$I_{j-1} + P_j = D_j + I_j$$

The balance equation for month 1 uses the known beginning inventory, 5000, for the previous inventory (the I_{j-1} term). By putting all variables (Ps and Is) on the left and all known values on the right (a standard LP convention), these balance constraints can be written as

$$
\begin{aligned}
P_1 - I_1 &= 1000 - 5000 \\
I_1 + P_2 - I_2 &= 15000 \\
I_2 + P_3 - I_3 &= 30000 \\
I_3 + P_4 - I_4 &= 35000 \\
I_4 + P_5 - I_5 &= 25000 \\
I_5 + P_6 - I_6 &= 10000
\end{aligned}
$$

(13.1)

As usual, there are nonnegativity constraints: all Ps and Is must be nonnegative.

What about meeting demand on time? This requires that in each month the inventory from the preceding month plus the current production must be at least as large as the current demand. But take a look, for example, at the balance equation for month 3. By rearranging it slightly, it becomes

$$I_3 = I_2 + P_3 - 30000$$

Now, the nonnegativity constraint on I_3 implies that the right side of this equation, $I_2 + P_3 - 30000$, is also nonnegative. But this implies that demand in month 3 is covered—the beginning inventory in month 3 plus month 3 production is at least 30000. Therefore, the nonnegativity constraints on the Is *automatically* guarantee that all demands will be met on time, and no other constraints are needed. Alternatively, the constraint can be written directly as $I_2 + P_3 \geq 30000$. In words, the amount on hand after production in month 3 must be at least as large as the demand in month 3. The spreadsheet model takes advantage of this interpretation.

Finally, the objective to minimize is the sum of production and holding costs. It is the sum of unit production costs multiplied by Ps, plus unit holding costs multiplied by Is.

Developing the Spreadsheet Model

Developing the Production Planning Model

The spreadsheet model of Pigskin's production problem is shown in Figure 13.24. (See the file **Production Scheduling.xlsx**.) The main feature that distinguishes this model from the product mix model is that some of the constraints, namely, the balance equations (13.1),

[13]This example illustrates a subtle difference between algebraic and spreadsheet models. It is often convenient in algebraic models to define "decision variables," in this case the Is, that are really determined by other decision variables, in this case the Ps. In spreadsheet models, however, we typically define the changing cells as the smallest set of variables that must be chosen—in this case the production quantities. Then values that are determined by these changing cells, such as the ending inventory levels, can be calculated with spreadsheet formulas.

are built into the spreadsheet itself by means of formulas. This means that the only changing cells are the production quantities. The ending inventories shown in row 20 are *determined* by the production quantities and equations (13.1). As you see, the decision variables in an algebraic model (the *P*s and *I*s) are not *necessarily* the same as the changing cells in an equivalent spreadsheet model. (The only changing cells in the spreadsheet model correspond to the *P*s.)

Figure 13.24   Production Planning Model with a Suboptimal Solution

▲	A	B	C	D	E	F	G	H
1	Multiperiod production model							
2								
3	Input data							
4	Initial inventory	5000						
5	Holding cost as % of prod cost	5%						
6								
7	Month	1	2	3	4	5	6	
8	Production cost/unit	$12.50	$12.55	$12.70	$12.80	$12.85	$12.95	
9								
10	Production plan							
11	Month	1	2	3	4	5	6	
12	Units produced	15000	15000	30000	30000	25000	10000	
13		<=	<=	<=	<=	<=	<=	
14	Production capacity	30000	30000	30000	30000	30000	30000	
15								
16	On hand after production	20000	25000	40000	40000	30000	15000	
17		>=	>=	>=	>=	>=	>=	
18	Demand	10000	15000	30000	35000	25000	10000	
19								
20	Ending inventory	10000	10000	10000	5000	5000	5000	
21		<=	<=	<=	<=	<=	<=	
22	Storage capacity	10000	10000	10000	10000	10000	10000	
23								
24	Summary of costs							
25	Month	1	2	3	4	5	6	Totals
26	Production costs	$187,500	$188,250	$381,000	$384,000	$321,250	$129,500	$1,591,500
27	Holding costs	$6,250	$6,275	$6,350	$3,200	$3,213	$3,238	$28,525
28	Totals	$193,750	$194,525	$387,350	$387,200	$324,463	$132,738	$1,620,025
29								
30	Range names used							
31	Demand	=Model!$B$18:$G$18						
32	Ending_inventory	=Model!$B$20:$G$20						
33	On_hand_after_production	=Model!$B$16:$G$16						
34	Production_capacity	=Model!$B$14:$G$14						
35	Storage_capacity	=Model!$B$22:$G$22						
36	Total_Cost	=Model!$H$28						
37	Units_produced	=Model!$B$12:$G$12						

To develop the spreadsheet model in Figure 13.24, proceed as follows.

1. **Inputs.** Enter the inputs in the blue cells. Again, these are all entered as *numbers* directly from the problem statement. (Unlike some spreadsheet modelers who prefer to put all inputs in the upper left corner of the spreadsheet, we enter the inputs wherever they fit most naturally. Of course, this takes some planning before diving in.)

2. **Name ranges.** Name the ranges indicated. Note that all but one of these (Total_cost) can be named easily with the range-naming shortcut, using the labels in column A.

In multiperiod problems, there is often one formula for the first period and a slightly different (copyable) formula for all other periods.

3. **Production quantities.** Enter *any* values in the range Units_produced as production quantities. As always, you can enter values that you believe are good, maybe even optimal. This is not crucial, however, because Solver eventually finds the *optimal* production quantities.

4. **On-hand inventory.** Enter the formula

   =B4+B12

   in cell B16. This calculates the first month's on-hand inventory after production (but before demand). Then enter the typical formula

   =B20+C12

   for on-hand inventory after production in month 2 in cell C16 and copy it across row 16.

5. **Ending inventories.** Enter the formula

   =B16-B18

   for ending inventory in cell B20 and copy it across row 20. This formula calculates ending inventory in the current month as on-hand inventory before demand minus the demand in that month.

6. **Production and holding costs.** Enter the formula

   =B8*B12

   in cell B26 and copy it across to cell G26 to calculate the monthly production costs. Then enter the formula

   =$B$5*B8*B20

   in cell B27 and copy it across to cell G27 to calculate the monthly holding costs. Note that these are based on monthly ending inventories. Finally, calculate the cost totals in column H with the SUM function.

Using Solver

To use Solver, fill out the main dialog box as shown in Figure 13.25. The logic behind the constraints is straightforward. The constraints are that (1) the production quantities cannot exceed the production capacities, (2) the on-hand inventories after production must be at least as large as demands, and (3) ending inventories cannot exceed storage capacities. Check the Non-Negative option and select the Simplex LP method, and then click Solve.

Discussion of the Solution

The optimal solution from Solver appears in Figure 13.26. The solution can be interpreted best by comparing production quantities to demands. In month 1, Pigskin should produce just enough to meet month 1 demand (taking into account the initial inventory of 5000). In month 2, it should produce 5000 more footballs than month 2 demand, and then in month 3 it should produce just enough to meet month 3 demand, while still carrying the extra 5000 footballs in inventory from month 2 production. In month 4, Pigskin should finally use these 5000 footballs, along with the maximum production amount, 30,000, to meet month 4 demand. Then in months 5 and 6 it should produce exactly enough to meet these months' demands. The total cost is $1,535,563, most of which is production cost.

You can often improve your intuition by trying to reason why Solver's solution is indeed optimal.

Could you have guessed this optimal solution? Upon reflection, it makes perfect sense. Because the monthly holding costs are large relative to the differences in monthly production costs, there is little incentive to produce footballs before they are needed to take advantage of a "cheap" production month. Therefore, Pigskin Company produces foot

Figure 13.25
Solver Dialog Box for Production Planning Model

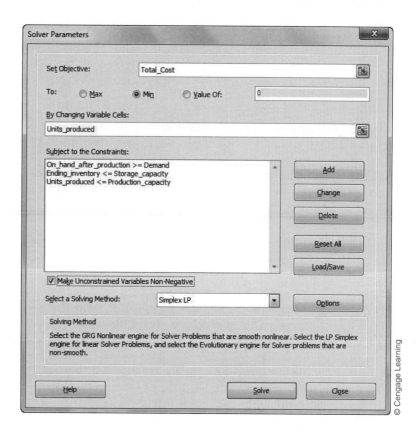

Figure 13.26   Optimal Solution for Production Planning Model

▲	A	B	C	D	E	F	G	H
10	**Production plan**							
11	Month	1	2	3	4	5	6	
12	Units produced	5000	20000	30000	30000	25000	10000	
13		<=	<=	<=	<=	<=	<=	
14	Production capacity	30000	30000	30000	30000	30000	30000	
15								
16	On hand after production	10000	20000	35000	35000	25000	10000	
17		>=	>=	>=	>=	>=	>=	
18	Demand	10000	15000	30000	35000	25000	10000	
19								
20	Ending inventory	0	5000	5000	0	0	0	
21		<=	<=	<=	<=	<=	<=	
22	Storage capacity	10000	10000	10000	10000	10000	10000	
23								
24	**Summary of costs**							
25	Month	1	2	3	4	5	6	Totals
26	Production costs	$62,500	$251,000	$381,000	$384,000	$321,250	$129,500	$1,529,250
27	Holding costs	$0	$3,138	$3,175	$0	$0	$0	$6,313
28	Totals	$62,500	$254,138	$384,175	$384,000	$321,250	$129,500	$1,535,563

balls in the month when they are needed—when possible. The only exception to this rule is the 20,000 footballs produced during month 2 when only 15,000 are needed. The extra 5000 footballs produced in month 2 are needed, however, to meet the month 4 demand of

35,000, because month 3 production capacity is used entirely to meet the month 3 demand. Thus month 3 capacity is not available to meet the month 4 demand, and 5000 units of month 2 capacity are used to meet the month 4 demand.

FUNDAMENTAL INSIGHT

Multiperiod Optimization Problems and Myopic Solutions

Many optimization problems are of a multiperiod nature, where a sequence of decisions must be made over time. When making the *first* of these decisions, the one for this week or this month, say, it is usually best to include future decisions in the model,

as has been done here. If you ignore future periods and make the initial decision based only on the first period, the resulting decision is called *myopic* (short-sighted). Myopic decisions are occasionally optimal, but not very often. The idea is that if you act now in a way that looks best in the short run, it might lead you down a strategically unattractive path for the long run.

Sensitivity Analysis

If you want Solver Table to keep track of a quantity that is not in your model, you need to create it with an appropriate formula in a new cell.

SolverTable can now be used to perform a number of interesting sensitivity analyses. We illustrate two possibilities. First, note that the most inventory ever carried at the end of a month is 5000, although the storage capacity each month is 10,000. Perhaps this is because the holding cost percentage, 5%, is fairly large. Would more ending inventory be carried if this holding cost percentage were lower? Or would even less be carried if it were higher? You can check this with the SolverTable output shown in Figure 13.27. Now the single input cell is cell B5, and the *single* output is the maximum ending inventory ever held, which you can calculate in cell B31 with the formula

=MAX(Ending_inventory)

As the SolverTable results indicate, the storage capacity limit is reached only when the holding cost percentage falls to 1%. (This output doesn't indicate which month or how many months the ending inventory is at the upper limit.) On the other hand, even when the holding cost percentage reaches 10%, the company still continues to hold a maximum ending inventory of 5000.

Figure 13.27

Sensitivity of Maximum Inventory to Holding Cost

▲	A	B	C	D	E	F	G
3	Holding cost pct (cell $B$5) values along side, output cell(s) along top						
4		Max_Inventory					
5	1%	10000					
6	2%	5000					
7	3%	5000					
8	4%	5000					
9	5%	5000					
10	6%	5000					
11	7%	5000					
12	8%	5000					
13	9%	5000					
14	10%	5000					

© Cengage Learning

A second possible sensitivity analysis is suggested by the way the optimal production schedule would probably be implemented. The optimal solution to Pigskin's model specifies the production level for each of the next six months. In reality, however, the company would probably implement the model's recommendation only for the *first* month. Then at the beginning of the second month, it would gather new forecasts for the *next* six months, months 2 through 7, solve a new six-month model, and again implement the model's recommendation for the first of these months, month 2. If the company continues in this manner, we say that it is following a six-month **rolling planning horizon**.

The question, then, is whether the assumed demands (really, forecasts) toward the end of the planning horizon have much effect on the optimal production quantity in month 1. You would hope not, because these forecasts could be quite inaccurate. The two-way Solver table in Figure 13.28 shows how the optimal month 1 production quantity varies with the forecasted demands in months 5 and 6. (We let each vary by plus or minus 20% from its current value.) As you can see, if the errors in the forecasted demands for months 5 and 6 remain fairly small, the optimal month 1 production quantity remains at 5000. This is good news. It means that the optimal production quantity in month 1 is fairly insensitive to the possibly inaccurate forecasts for months 5 and 6.

Figure 13.28

Sensitivity of Month 1 Production to Demand in Months 5 and 6

⊿	A	B	C	D	E	F	G	H
1	Two-way analysis for Solver model in Model worksheet							
2								
3	Month 5 demand (cell $F$18) values along side, Month 6 demand (cell $G$18) values along top							
4	Units_produced_1	8000	9000	10000	11000	12000		
5	20000	5000	5000	5000	5000	5000		
6	22000	5000	5000	5000	5000	5000		
7	24000	5000	5000	5000	5000	5000		
8	26000	5000	5000	5000	5000	5000		
9	28000	5000	5000	5000	5000	5000		
10	30000	5000	5000	5000	5000	5000		

© Cengage Learning

Solver's sensitivity report for this model is not shown here, but it is included in the finished version of the file. The bottom part of this report is relevant for changes in the storage capacity and changes in demand. In contrast, the top part of the report is virtually impossible to unravel. This is because the objective coefficients of the decision variables are each based on *multiple* inputs. (Each is a combination of unit production costs and the holding cost percentage.) Therefore, if you want to know how the solution will change if you change a single unit production cost or the holding cost percentage, this report does not answer your question. This is one case where a sensitivity analysis with SolverTable is much more straightforward and intuitive. It allows you to change *any* of the model's inputs and directly see the effects on the solution.

Modeling Issues

We assume that Pigskin uses a six-month planning horizon. Why six months? In multiperiod models such as this, the company has to make forecasts about the future, such as the level of customer demand. Therefore, the length of the planning horizon is usually the length of time for which the company can make reasonably accurate forecasts. Here, Pigskin evidently believes that it can forecast up to six months from now, so it uses a six-month planning horizon. ∎

PROBLEMS

Level A

18. Can you guess the results of a sensitivity analysis on the initial inventory in the Pigskin model? See if your guess is correct by using SolverTable and allowing the initial inventory to vary from 0 to 10,000 in increments of 1000. Keep track of the values in the changing cells and the objective cell.

19. Modify the Pigskin model so that there are eight months in the planning horizon. You can make up reasonable values for any extra required data. Don't forget to modify range names. Then modify the model again so that there are only four months in the planning horizon. Do either of these modifications change the optimal production quantity in month 1?

20. As indicated by the algebraic formulation of the Pigskin model, there is no real need to calculate inventory on hand after production and constrain it to be greater than or equal to demand. An alternative is to calculate ending inventory directly and constrain it to be nonnegative. Modify the current spreadsheet model to do this. (Delete rows 16 and 17, and calculate ending inventory appropriately. Then add an *explicit* nonnegativity constraint on ending inventory.)

21. In one modification of the Pigskin problem, the maximum storage constraint and the holding cost are based on the *average* inventory (not ending inventory) for a given month, where the average inventory is defined as the sum of beginning inventory and ending inventory, divided by 2, and beginning inventory is *before* production or demand. Modify the Pigskin model with this new assumption, and use Solver to find the optimal solution. How does this change the optimal production schedule? How does it change the optimal total cost?

Level B

22. Modify the Pigskin spreadsheet model so that except for month 6, demand does not have to be met on time. The only requirement is that all demand must be met eventually by the end of month 6. How does this change the optimal production schedule? How does it change the optimal total cost?

23. Modify the Pigskin spreadsheet model so that demand in any of the first five months must be met no later than a month late, whereas demand in month 6 must be met on time. For example, the demand in month 3 can be met partly in month 3 and partly in month 4. How does this change the optimal production schedule? How does it change the optimal total cost?

24. Modify the Pigskin spreadsheet model in the following way. Assume that the timing of demand and production are such that only 70% of the production in a given month can be used to satisfy the demand in that month. The other 30% occurs too late in that month and must be carried as inventory to help satisfy demand in later months. How does this change the optimal production schedule? How does it change the optimal total cost? Then use SolverTable to see how the optimal production schedule and optimal cost vary as the percentage of production usable for this month's demand (now 70%) is allowed to vary from 20% to 100% in increments of 10%.

13-9 A COMPARISON OF ALGEBRAIC AND SPREADSHEET MODELS

To this point you have seen algebraic optimization models and corresponding spreadsheet models. How do they differ? If you review the two product mix examples in this chapter, we believe you will agree that (1) the algebraic models are quite straightforward and (2) the spreadsheet models are almost direct translations into Excel of the algebraic models. In particular, each algebraic model has a set of *x*s that corresponds to the changing cell range in the spreadsheet model. In addition, each objective and each left side of each constraint in the spreadsheet model corresponds to a linear expression involving *x*s in the algebraic model.

However, the Pigskin production planning model is quite different. The spreadsheet model includes one set of changing cells, the production quantities, and everything else is related to these through spreadsheet formulas. In contrast, the algebraic model has *two* sets of variables, the *P*s for the production quantities and the *I*s for the ending inventories, and together these constitute the *decision variables*. These two sets of variables must then be related algebraically, and this is done through a series of *balance equations*.

This is a typical situation in algebraic models, where one set of variables (the production quantities) corresponds to the *real* decision variables, and other sets of variables, along with extra equations or inequalities, are introduced to capture the logic. We believe— and this belief is reinforced by many years of teaching experience—that this extra level of abstraction makes algebraic models much more difficult for typical users to develop and comprehend. It is the primary reason we have decided to focus almost exclusively on spreadsheet models in this book.

13-10 A DECISION SUPPORT SYSTEM

If your job is to develop an LP spreadsheet model to solve a problem such as Pigskin's production problem, then you will be considered the "expert" in LP. Many people who need to use such models, however, are *not* experts. They might understand the basic ideas behind LP and the types of problems it is intended to solve, but they will not know the details. In this case it is useful to provide these users with a **decision support system** (DSS) that can help them solve problems without having to worry about technical details.

We will not teach you in this book how to build a full-scale DSS, but we will show you what a typical DSS looks like and what it can do.[14] (We consider only DSSs built around spreadsheets. There are many other platforms for developing DSSs that we will not consider.) Basically, a spreadsheet-based DSS contains a spreadsheet model of a problem, such as the one in Figure 13.26. However, as a user, you will probably never even see this model. Instead, you will see a front end and a back end. The front end allows you to select input values for your particular problem. The user interface for this front end can include several features, such as buttons, dialog boxes, toolbars, and menus—the things you are used to seeing in Windows applications. The back end will then produce a report that explains the solution in nontechnical terms.

Developing a Decision Support System

We illustrate a DSS for a slight variation of the Pigskin problem in the file **Decision Support.xlsm**. This file has three sheets. When you open the file, you see the Explanation sheet shown in Figure 13.29. It contains two buttons, one for setting up the problem (getting the user's inputs) and one for solving the problem (running Solver). When you click the Set Up Problem button, you are asked for the inputs: the initial inventory, the forecasted demands for each month, and others. An example appears in Figure 13.30. These input boxes should be self-explanatory, so that all you need to do is enter the values you want to try. (To speed up the process, the inputs from the previous run are shown by default.) After you have entered all of these inputs, you can take a look at the Model sheet. This sheet contains a spreadsheet model similar to the one in Figure 13.26 but with the inputs you just entered.

Now go back to the Explanation sheet and click the Find Optimal Solution button. This automatically sets up the Solver dialog box and runs Solver. There are two possibilities.

Figure 13.29

Explanation Sheet for DSS

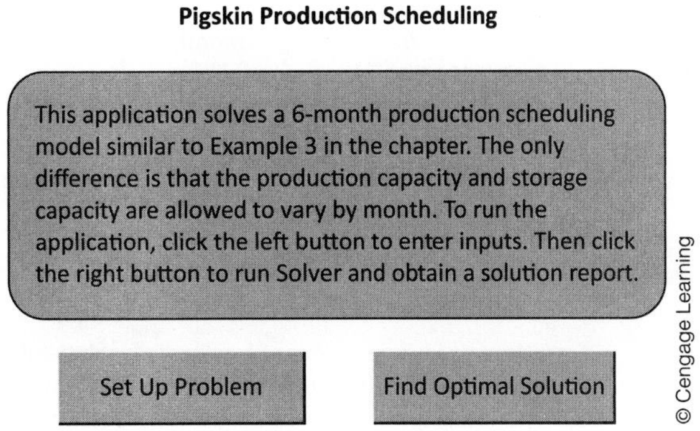

Pigskin Production Scheduling

This application solves a 6-month production scheduling model similar to Example 3 in the chapter. The only difference is that the production capacity and storage capacity are allowed to vary by month. To run the application, click the left button to enter inputs. Then click the right button to run Solver and obtain a solution report.

Set Up Problem   Find Optimal Solution

© Cengage Learning

---

[14]For readers interested in learning more about this DSS, the Premium Online Content Web site includes notes about its development in the file **Developing the Decision Support Application.docx**, under Chapter 13 Example Files. If you are interested in learning more about spreadsheet DSSs in general, Albright has written the book *VBA for Modelers*, now in its fourth edition. It contains a primer on the VBA language and presents many applications and instructions for creating DSSs with VBA.

Figure 13.30

Dialog Box for
Obtaining User
Inputs

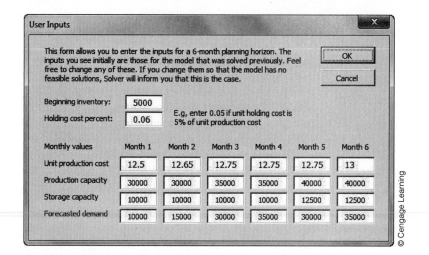

First, it is possible that there is no feasible solution to the problem with the inputs you
entered. In this case you see a message to this effect, as in Figure 13.31. In most cases,
however, the problem has a feasible solution. In this case you see the Report sheet, which
summarizes the optimal solution in nontechnical terms. Part of one sample output appears
in Figure 13.32.

Figure 13.31

Indication of No
Feasible Solutions

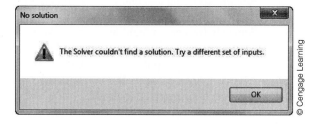

Figure 13.32   Optimal Solution Report

Summary of optimal solution

Planning horizon (months)	6
Total production cost	$1,918,500.00
Total holding cost	$0.00
Total cost	$1,918,500.00

Solve Another Problem

Monthly schedule

Month 1

Units		Dollars	
Start with	5000		
Produce	5000	Production cost	$62,500.00
Demand is	10000		
End with	0	Holding cost	$0.00

Month 2

Units		Dollars	
Start with	0		
Produce	15000	Production cost	$189,750.00
Demand is	15000		
End with	0	Holding cost	$0.00

Month 3

Units		Dollars	
Start with	0		
Produce	30000	Production cost	$382,500.00
Demand is	30000		
End with	0	Holding cost	$0.00

After studying this report, you can then click the Solve Another Problem button, which takes you back to the Explanation sheet so that you can solve a new problem. All of this is done automatically with Excel macros. These macros use Microsoft's Visual Basic for Applications (VBA) programming language to automate various tasks. In most professional applications, nontechnical people need only to enter inputs and look at reports. Therefore, the Model sheet and VBA code will most likely be hidden and protected from end users.

13-11 CONCLUSION

This chapter has provided a good start to LP modeling—and to optimization modeling in general. You have learned how to develop three basic LP spreadsheet models, how to use Solver to find their optimal solutions, and how to perform sensitivity analyses with Solver's sensitivity reports or with the SolverTable add-in. You have also learned how to recognize whether a mathematical programming model satisfies the linear assumptions. In the next chapter you will see a variety of other optimization models, but the three basic steps of model development, Solver optimization, and sensitivity analysis remain the same.

Summary of Key Terms

Term	Explanation	Excel	Page
Linear programming	Refers to optimization models with a linear objective and linear constraints, often abbreviated as LP		658
Objective	The value, such as profit, to be optimized in an optimization model		659
Constraints	Conditions that must be satisfied in an optimization model		659
Changing cells	Cells that contain the values of the decision variables	Specify in Solver dialog box	659
Objective cell	Cell that contains the value of the objective	Specify in Solver dialog box	659
Nonnegativity constraints	Constraints that require the decision variables to be nonnegative, usually for physical reasons		659
Feasible solution	A solution that satisfies all of the constraints		660
Feasible region	The set of all feasible solutions		660
Infeasible solution	A solution that doesn't satisfy all of the constraints		660
Optimal solution	The feasible solution that has the best value of the objective		660
Solver	Add-in that ships with Excel for performing optimization, developed by Frontline Systems	Solver on Data ribbon	660
Simplex method	An efficient algorithm for finding the optimal solution in a linear programming model		660
Sensitivity analysis	Seeing how the optimal solution changes as various input values change		660

(*continued*)

Summary of Key Terms (*Continued*)

Term	Explanation	Excel	Page
Algebraic model	A model that expresses the constraints and the objective algebraically		662
Graphical solution	Shows the constraints and objective graphically so that the optimal solution can be identified; useful only when there are two decision variables		662
Spreadsheet model	A model that uses spreadsheet formulas to express the logic of the model		664
Binding constraint	A constraint that holds as an equality		672
Nonbinding constraint	An inequality constraint where there is a difference between the two sides of the inequality		672
Solver's sensitivity report	Report available from Solver that shows sensitivity to objective coefficients and right sides of constraints	Available in Solver dialog box after Solver runs	673
Reduced cost	Amount the objective coefficient of a variable currently equal to zero must change before it is optimal for that variable to be positive (or the amount the objective of a variable currently at its upper bound must change before that variable decreases from its upper bound)		674
Shadow price	The change in the objective for a change in the right side of a constraint; indicates amount a company would pay for more of a scarce resource		674
SolverTable	Add-in developed by Albright that performs sensitivity analysis to any inputs and reports results in tabular and graphical form	SolverTable ribbon	676
Selecting multiple ranges	Useful when changing cells, e.g., are in noncontiguous ranges	Pressing Ctrl key, drag ranges, one after the other	677
Mathematical programming model	Any optimization model, whether linear, integer, or nonlinear		683
Proportionality, additivity, divisibility	Properties of optimization model that result in a linear programming model		683, 684
Infeasibility	Condition where a model has no feasible solutions		685
Unboundedness	Condition where there is no limit to the objective; almost always a sign of an error in the model		686
Rolling planning horizon	Multiperiod model where only the decision in the first period is implemented, and then a new multiperiod model is solved in succeeding periods		703
Decision support system	User-friendly system where an end user can enter inputs to a model and see outputs, but need not be concerned with technical details		705

PROBLEMS

Conceptual Questions

C.1. Suppose you use Solver to find the optimal solution to a maximization model. Then you remember that you omitted an important constraint. After adding the constraint and running Solver again, is the optimal value of the objective guaranteed to decrease? Why or why not?

C.2. Consider an optimization model with a number of resource constraints. Each indicates that the amount of the resource used cannot exceed the amount available. Why is the shadow price of such a resource constraint always zero when the amount used in the optimal solution is *less than* the amount available?

C.3. If you add a constraint to an optimization model, and the previously optimal solution satisfies the new constraint, will this solution still be optimal with the new constraint added? Why or why not?

C.4. Why is it generally necessary to add nonnegativity constraints to an optimization model? Wouldn't Solver automatically choose nonnegative values for the changing cells?

C.5. Suppose you have a *linear* optimization model where you are trying to decide which products to produce to maximize profit. What does the additive assumption imply about the profit objective? What does the proportionality assumption imply about the profit objective? Be as specific as possible. Can you think of any *reasonable* profit functions that would *not* be linear in the amounts of the products produced?

C.6. In a typical product mix model, where a company must decide how much of each product to produce to maximize profit, discuss possible situations where there might not be any feasible solutions. Could these be realistic? If you had such a situation in your company, how might you proceed?

C.7. In a typical product mix model, where a company must decide how much of each product to produce to maximize profit, there are sometimes customer demands for the products. We used upper-bound constraints for these: Don't produce more than you can sell. Would it be realistic to have lower-bound constraints instead: Produce at least as much as is demanded? Would it be realistic to have both (where the upper bounds are greater than the lower bounds)? Would it be realistic to have equality constraints: Produce exactly what is demanded?

C.8. In a typical production scheduling model like Pigskin's, if there are no production capacity constraints—the company can produce as much as it needs in any time period—but there are storage capacity constraints and demand must be met on time, is it possible that there will be no feasible solutions? Why or why not?

C.9. In a production scheduling problem like Pigskin's, suppose the company must produce *several* products to meet customer demands. Would it suffice to solve a separate model for each product, as we did for Pigskin, or would one big model for all products be necessary? If the latter, discuss what this big model might look like.

C.10. In any optimization model such as those in this chapter, we say that the model is unbounded (and Solver will indicate as such) if there is no limit to the value of the objective. For example, if the objective is profit, then for any dollar value, no matter how large, there is a feasible solution with profit at least this large. In the real world, why are there never any unbounded models? If you run Solver on a model and get an "unbounded" message, what should you do?

Level A

25. A chemical company manufactures three chemicals: A, B, and C. These chemicals are produced via two production processes: 1 and 2. Running process 1 for an hour costs $400 and yields 300 units of A, 100 units of B, and 100 units of C. Running process 2 for an hour costs $100 and yields 100 units of A and 100 units of B. To meet customer demands, at least 1000 units of A, 500 units of B, and 300 units of C must be produced daily.

   a. Use Solver to determine a daily production plan that minimizes the cost of meeting the company's daily demands.

   b. Confirm graphically that the daily production plan from part **a** minimizes the cost of meeting the company's daily demands.

   c. Use SolverTable to see what happens to the decision variables and the total cost when the hourly processing cost for process 2 increases in increments of $0.50. How large must this cost increase be before the decision variables change? What happens when it continues to increase beyond this point?

26. A furniture company manufactures desks and chairs. Each desk uses four units of wood, and each chair uses three units of wood. A desk contributes $400 to profit, and a chair contributes $250. Marketing restrictions require that the number of chairs produced be at least twice the number of desks produced. There are 2000 units of wood available.

a. Use Solver to maximize the company's profit.

b. Confirm graphically that the solution in part **a** maximizes the company's profit.

c. Use SolverTable to see what happens to the decision variables and the total profit when the availability of wood varies from 1000 to 3000 in 100-unit increments. Based on your findings, how much would the company be willing to pay for each extra unit of wood over its current 2000 units? How much profit would the company lose if it lost any of its current 2000 units?

27. A farmer in Iowa owns 450 acres of land. He is going to plant each acre with wheat or corn. Each acre planted with wheat yields $2000 profit, requires three workers, and requires two tons of fertilizer. Each acre planted with corn yields $3000 profit, requires two workers, and requires four tons of fertilizer. There are currently 1000 workers and 1200 tons of fertilizer available.

a. Use Solver to help the farmer maximize the profit from his land.

b. Confirm graphically that the solution from part **a** maximizes the farmer's profit from his land.

c. Use SolverTable to see what happens to the decision variables and the total profit when the availability of fertilizer varies from 200 tons to 2200 tons in 100-ton increments. When does the farmer discontinue producing wheat? When does he discontinue producing corn? How does the profit change for each 10-ton increment?

28. During the next four months, a customer requires, respectively, 500, 650, 1000, and 700 units of a commodity, and no backlogging is allowed (that is, the customer's requirements must be met on time). Production costs are $50, $80, $40, and $70 per unit during these months. The storage cost from one month to the next is $20 per unit (assessed on ending inventory). It is estimated that each unit on hand at the end of month 4 can be sold for $60. Assume there is no beginning inventory.

a. Determine how to minimize the net cost incurred in meeting the demands for the next four months.

b. Use SolverTable to see what happens to the decision variables and the total cost when the initial inventory varies from 0 to 1000 in 100-unit increments. How much lower would the total cost be if the company started with 100 units in inventory, rather than none? Would this same cost decrease occur for every 100-unit increase in initial inventory?

29. A company faces the following demands during the next three weeks: week 1, 2000 units; week 2, 1000 units; week 3, 1500 units. The unit production costs during each week are as follows: week 1, $130; week 2, $140; week 3, $150. A holding cost of $20 per unit

is assessed against each week's ending inventory. At the beginning of week 1, the company has 500 units on hand. In reality, not all goods produced during a month can be used to meet the current month's demand. To model this fact, assume that only half of the goods produced during a week can be used to meet the current week's demands.

a. Determine how to minimize the cost of meeting the demand for the next three weeks.

b. Revise the model so that the demands are of the form $D_t + kC_t$, where D_t is the original demand (from above) in month t, k is a given factor, and C_t is an amount of change in month t demand. Develop the model in such a way that you can use SolverTable to analyze changes in the amounts produced and the total cost when k varies from 0 to 10 in 1-unit increments, for any fixed values of the Cs. For example, try this when $C_1 = 200$, $C_2 = 500$, and $C_3 = 300$. Describe the behavior you observe in the table. Can you find any reasonable Cs that induce *positive* production levels in week 3?

30. Maggie Stewart loves desserts, but due to weight and cholesterol concerns, she has decided that she must plan her desserts carefully. There are two possible desserts she is considering: snack bars and ice cream. After reading the nutrition labels on the snack bar and ice cream packages, she learns that each serving of a snack bar weighs 37 grams and contains 120 calories and 5 grams of fat. Each serving of ice cream weighs 65 grams and contains 160 calories and 10 grams of fat. Maggie will allow herself no more than 450 calories and 25 grams of fat in her daily desserts, but because she loves desserts so much, she requires at least 120 grams of dessert per day. Also, she assigns a "taste index" to each gram of each dessert, where 0 is the lowest and 100 is the highest. She assigns a taste index of 95 to ice cream and 85 to snack bars (because she prefers ice cream to snack bars).

a. Use Solver to find the daily dessert plan that stays within her constraints and maximizes the total taste index of her dessert.

b. Confirm graphically that the solution from part **a** maximizes Maggie's total taste index.

c. Use a two-way Solver table to see how the optimal dessert plan varies when the calories per snack bar and per ice cream vary. Let the former vary from 80 to 200 in increments of 10, and let the latter vary from 120 to 300 in increments of 10.

31. For a telephone survey, a marketing research group needs to contact at least 600 wives, 480 husbands, 400 single adult males, and 440 single adult females. It costs $3 to make a daytime call and (because of higher labor costs) $5 to make an evening call. The file **P13_31.xlsx** lists the results that can be expected. For example, 30% of all daytime calls are answered by a wife, 15% of all evening calls are answered by a single male, and 40% of all daytime calls are not answered at all. Due to limited staff, at most 40% of all phone calls can be evening calls.

    a. Determine how to minimize the cost of completing the survey.

    b. Use SolverTable to investigate changes in the unit cost of either type of call. Specifically, investigate changes in the cost of a daytime call, with the cost of an evening call fixed, to see when (if ever) *only* daytime calls or *only* evening calls will be made. Then repeat the analysis by changing the cost of an evening call and keeping the cost of a daytime call fixed.

32. A furniture company manufactures tables and chairs. Each table and chair must be made entirely out of oak or entirely out of pine. A total of 15,000 board feet of oak and 21,000 board feet of pine are available. A table requires either 17 board feet of oak or 30 board feet of pine, and a chair requires either 5 board feet of oak or 13 board feet of pine. Each table can be sold for $800, and each chair for $300.

    a. Determine how the company can maximize its revenue.

    b. Use SolverTable to investigate the effects of simultaneous changes in the selling prices of the products. Specifically, see what happens to the total revenue when the selling prices of oak products and the selling prices of pine products are allowed to vary (independently) by as much as plus or minus 30%, in increments of 10%, from their original values. Revise your model from the previous problem so that you can use SolverTable to investigate these changes. Can you conclude that total revenue changes *linearly* within this range?

33. A manufacturing company makes two products. Each product can be made on either of two machines. The time (in hours) required to make each product on each machine is listed in the file **P13_33.xlsx**. Each month, 500 hours of time are available on each machine. Each month, customers are willing to buy up to the quantities of each product at the prices also given in the same file. The company's goal is to maximize the revenue obtained from selling units during the next two months.

    a. Determine how the company can meet this goal. Assume that it will not produce any units in a month that it cannot sell in that month.

    b. Use SolverTable to see what happens if customer demands for each product in each month simultaneously change by as much as plus or minus 30%, in increments of 10%, from their current values. Revise the model so that you can use SolverTable to investigate the effect of these changes on total revenue. Does revenue

change in a linear manner over this range? Can you explain intuitively why it changes in the way it does?

34. There are three factories on the Momiss River. Each emits two types of pollutants, labeled P_1 and P_2, into the river. If the waste from each factory is processed, the pollution in the river can be reduced. It costs $1500 to process a ton of factory 1 waste, and each ton processed reduces the amount of P_1 by 0.10 ton and the amount of P_2 by 0.45 ton. It costs $1000 to process a ton of factory 2 waste, and each ton processed reduces the amount of P_1 by 0.20 ton and the amount of P_2 by 0.25 ton. It costs $2000 to process a ton of factory 3 waste, and each ton processed reduces the amount of P_1 by 0.40 ton and the amount of P_2 by 0.30 ton. The state wants to reduce the amount of P_1 in the river by at least 30 tons and the amount of P_2 by at least 40 tons.

    a. Use Solver to determine how to minimize the cost of reducing pollution by the desired amounts. Are the LP assumptions (proportionality, additivity, divisibility) reasonable in this problem?

    b. Use SolverTable to investigate the effects of increases in the minimal reductions required by the state. Specifically, see what happens to the amounts of waste processed at the three factories and the total cost if both requirements (currently 30 and 40 tons, respectively) are increased by the *same* percentage. Revise your model so that you can use SolverTable to investigate these changes when the percentage increase varies from 10% to 100% in increments of 10%. Do the amounts processed at the three factories and the total cost change in a linear manner?

Level B

35. A company manufactures two types of trucks. Each truck must go through the painting shop and the assembly shop. If the painting shop were completely devoted to painting type 1 trucks, 800 per day could be painted, whereas if the painting shop were completely devoted to painting type 2 trucks, 700 per day could be painted. If the assembly shop were completely devoted to assembling truck 1 engines, 1500 per day could be assembled, whereas if the assembly shop were completely devoted to assembling truck 2 engines, 1200 per day could be assembled. It is possible, however, to paint *both* types of trucks in the painting shop. Similarly, it is possible to assemble both types in the assembly shop. Each type 1 truck contributes $1000 to profit; each type 2 truck contributes $1500. Use Solver to maximize the company's profit. (*Hint*: One approach, but not the only approach, is to try a graphical procedure first and then deduce the constraints from the graph.)

36. A company manufactures mechanical heart valves from the heart valves of pigs. Different heart operations require valves of different sizes. The company purchases pig valves from three different suppliers. The cost and size mix of the valves purchased from each supplier are given in the file **P13_36.xlsx**. Each month, the company places an order with each supplier. At least 500 large, 300 medium, and 300 small valves must be purchased each month. Because of the limited availability of pig valves, at most 500 valves per month can be purchased from each supplier.

   a. Use Solver to determine how the company can minimize the cost of acquiring the needed valves.

   b. Use SolverTable to investigate the effect on total cost of increasing its minimal purchase requirements each month. Specifically, see how the total cost changes as the minimal purchase requirements of large, medium, and small valves all increase from their original values by the *same* percentage. Revise your model so that SolverTable can be used to investigate these changes when the percentage increase varies from 2% to 20% in increments of 2%. Explain intuitively what happens when this percentage is at least 16%.

37. A company that builds sailboats wants to determine how many sailboats to build during each of the next four quarters. The demand during each of the next four quarters is as follows: first quarter, 160 sailboats; second quarter, 240 sailboats; third quarter, 300 sailboats; fourth quarter, 100 sailboats. The company must meet demands on time. At the beginning of the first quarter, the company has an inventory of 40 sailboats. At the beginning of each quarter, the company must decide how many sailboats to build during that quarter. For simplicity, assume that sailboats built during a quarter can be used to meet demand for that quarter. During each quarter, the company can build up to 160 sailboats with regular-time labor at a total cost of $1600 per sailboat. By having employees work overtime during a quarter, the company can build additional sailboats with overtime labor at a total cost of $1800 per sailboat. At the end of each quarter (after production has occurred and the current quarter's demand has been satisfied), a holding cost of $80 per sailboat is incurred.

   a. Determine a production schedule to minimize the sum of production and inventory holding costs during the next four quarters.

   b. Use SolverTable to see whether any changes in the $80 holding cost per sailboat could induce the company to carry more or less inventory. Revise your model so that SolverTable can be used to investigate the effects on ending inventory during the four-quarter period of systematic changes in

the unit holding cost. (Assume that even though the unit holding cost changes, it is still constant over the four-quarter period.) Are there any (nonnegative) unit holding costs that would induce the company to hold *more* inventory than it holds when the holding cost is $80? Are there any unit holding costs that would induce the company to hold *less* inventory than it holds when the holding cost is $80?

38. During the next two months an automobile manufacturer must meet (on time) the following demands for trucks and cars: month 1, 400 trucks and 800 cars; month 2, 300 trucks and 300 cars. During each month at most 1000 vehicles can be produced. Each truck uses two tons of steel, and each car uses one ton of steel. During month 1, steel costs $700 per ton; during month 2, steel is projected to cost $800 per ton. At most 2500 tons of steel can be purchased each month. (Steel can be used only during the month in which it is purchased.) At the beginning of month 1, 100 trucks and 200 cars are in the inventory. At the end of each month, a holding cost of $200 per vehicle is assessed. Each car gets 20 miles per gallon (mpg), and each truck gets 10 mpg. During each month, the vehicles produced by the company must average at least 16 mpg.

   a. Determine how to meet the demand and mileage requirements at minimum total cost.

   b. Use SolverTable to see how sensitive the total cost is to the 16 mpg requirement. Specifically, let this requirement vary from 14 mpg to 18 mpg in increments of 0.25 mpg. Explain intuitively what happens when the requirement is greater than 17 mpg.

39. A textile company produces shirts and pants. Each shirt requires two square yards of cloth, and each pair of pants requires three square yards of cloth. During the next two months the following demands for shirts and pants must be met (on time): month 1, 1000 shirts and 1500 pairs of pants; month 2, 1200 shirts and 1400 pairs of pants. During each month the following resources are available: month 1, 9000 square yards of cloth; month 2, 6000 square yards of cloth. In addition, cloth that is available during month 1 and is not used can be used during month 2. During each month it costs $8 to produce an article of clothing with regular-time labor and $16 with overtime labor. During each month a total of at most 2500 articles of clothing can be produced with regular-time labor, and an unlimited number of articles of clothing can be produced with overtime labor. At the end of each month, a holding cost of $3 per article of clothing is incurred.

   a. Determine how to meet demands for the next two months (on time) at minimum cost. Assume that

100 shirts and 200 pairs of pants are already in inventory at the beginning of month 1.

b. Use a two-way SolverTable to investigate the effect on total cost of two *simultaneous* changes. The first change is to allow the ratio of overtime to regular-time production cost (currently $16/$8 = 2) to decrease from 20% to 80% in increments of 20%, while keeping the regular time cost at $8. The second change is to allow the production capacity *each* month (currently 2500) to decrease by 10% to 50% in increments of 10%. The idea here is that less regular-time capacity is available, but overtime becomes relatively cheaper. Is the net effect on total cost positive or negative?

40. Each year, a shoe manufacturing company faces demands (which must be met on time) for pairs of shoes as shown in the file **P13_40.xlsx**. Employees work three consecutive quarters and then receive one quarter off. For example, a worker might work during quarters 3 and 4 of one year and quarter 1 of the next year. During a quarter in which an employee works, he or she can produce up to 500 pairs of shoes. Each worker is paid $5000 per quarter. At the end of each quarter, a holding cost of $10 per pair of shoes is incurred.

a. Determine how to minimize the cost per year (labor plus holding) of meeting the demands for shoes. To simplify the model, assume that at the end of each year, the ending inventory is 0. (You can assume that a given worker gets the *same* quarter off during each year.)

b. Suppose the company can pay a flat fee for a training program that increases the productivity of all of its workers. Use SolverTable to see how much the company would be willing to pay for a training program that increases worker productivity from 500 pairs of shoes per quarter to P pairs of shoes per quarter, where P varies from 525 to 700 in increments of 25.

41. A small appliance manufacturer must meet (on time) the following demands: quarter 1, 3000 units; quarter 2, 2000 units; quarter 3, 4000 units. Each quarter, up to 2700 units can be produced with regular-time labor, at a cost of $40 per unit. During each quarter, an unlimited number of units can be produced with overtime labor, at a cost of $60 per unit. Of all units produced, 20% are unsuitable and cannot be used to meet demand. Also, at the end of each quarter, 10% of all units on hand spoil and cannot be used to meet any future demands. After each quarter's demand is satisfied and spoilage is accounted for, a cost of $15 per unit in ending inventory is incurred.

a. Determine how to minimize the total cost of meeting the demands of the next three quarters.

Assume that 1000 usable units are available at the beginning of quarter 1.

b. The company wants to know how much money it would be worth to decrease the percentage of unsuitable items and/or the percentage of items that spoil. Write a short report that provides relevant information. Base your report on three uses of SolverTable: (1) where the percentage of unsuitable items decreases and the percentage of items that spoil stays at 10%, (2) where the percentage of unsuitable items stays at 20% and the percentage of items that spoil decreases, and (3) where both percentages decrease. Does the sum of the separate effects on total cost from the first two tables equal the combined effect from the third table? Include an answer to this question in your report.

42. A pharmaceutical company manufactures two drugs at Los Angeles and Indianapolis. The cost of manufacturing a pound of each drug depends on the location, as indicated in the file **P13_42.xlsx**. The machine time (in hours) required to produce a pound of each drug at each city is also shown in this table. The company must produce at least 1000 pounds per week of drug 1 and at least 2000 pounds per week of drug 2. It has 500 hours per week of machine time at Indianapolis and 400 hours per week at Los Angeles.

a. Determine how the company can minimize the cost of producing the required drugs.

b. Use SolverTable to determine how much the company would be willing to pay to purchase a combination of A extra hours of machine time at Indianapolis and B extra hours of machine time at Los Angeles, where A and B can be any positive multiples of 10 up to 50.

43. A company manufactures two products on two machines. The number of hours of machine time and labor depends on the machine and product as shown in the file **P13_43.xlsx**. The cost of producing a unit of each product depends on which machine produces it. These unit costs also appear in the same file. There are 200 hours available on each of the two machines, and there are 400 labor hours available total. This month at least 200 units of product 1 and at least 240 units of product 2 must be produced. Also, at least half of the product 1 requirement must be produced on machine 1, and at least half of the product 2 requirement must be produced on machine 2.

a. Determine how the company can minimize the cost of meeting this month's requirements.

b. Use SolverTable to see how much the "at least half" requirements are costing the company. Do this by changing *both* of these requirements from "at least half" to "at least x percent," where x can be any multiple of 5% from 0% to 50%.

Shelby Shelving is a small company that manufactures two types of shelves for grocery stores. Model S is the standard model; model LX is a heavy-duty version. Shelves are manufactured in three major steps: stamping, forming, and assembly. In the stamping stage, a large machine is used to stamp (i.e., cut) standard sheets of metal into appropriate sizes. In the forming stage, another machine bends the metal into shape. Assembly involves joining the parts with a combination of soldering and riveting. Shelby's stamping and forming machines work on both models of shelves. Separate assembly departments are used for the final stage of production.

The file **C13_01.xlsx** contains relevant data for Shelby. (See Figure 13.33.) The hours required on each machine for each unit of product are shown in the range B5:C6 of the Accounting Data sheet. For example, the production of one model S shelf requires 0.25 hour on the forming machine. Both the stamping and forming machines can operate for 800 hours each month. The model S assembly department has a monthly capacity of 1900 units. The model LX assembly department has a monthly capacity of only 1400 units. Currently Shelby is producing and selling 400 units of model S and 1400 units of model LX per month.

Figure 13.33   Data for Shelby Case

	A	B	C	D	E	F	G	H	I
1	Shelby Shelving Data for Current Production Schedule								
2									
3	Machine requirements (hours per unit)					Given monthly overhead cost data			
4		Model S	Model LX				Fixed	Variable S	Variable LX
5	Stamping	0.3	0.3			Stamping	$125,000	$80	$90
6	Forming	0.25	0.5			Forming	$95,000	$120	$170
7						Model S Assembly	$80,000	$165	$0
8		Model S	Model LX			Model LX Assembly	$85,000	$0	$185
9	Current monthly production	400	1400						
10						Standard costs of the shelves -- *based on the current production levels*			
11	Hours spent in departments						Model S	Model LX	
12		Model S	Model LX	Totals		Direct materials	$1,000	$1,200	
13	Stamping	120	420	540		Direct labor:			
14	Forming	100	700	800		Stamping	$35	$35	
15						Forming	$60	$90	
16	Percentages of time spent in departments					Assembly	$80	$85	
17		Model S	Model LX			Total direct labor	$175	$210	
18	Stamping	22.2%	77.8%			Overhead Allocation			
19	Forming	12.5%	87.5%			Stamping	$149	$159	
20						Forming	$150	$229	
21	Unit selling price	$1,800	$2,100			Assembly	$365	$246	
22						Total overhead	$664	$635	
23	Assembly capacity	1900	1400			Total cost	$1,839	$2,045	

© Cengage Learning

Model S shelves are sold for $1800, and model LX shelves are sold for $2100. Shelby's operation is fairly small in the industry, and management at Shelby believes it cannot raise prices beyond these levels because of the competition. However, the marketing department believes that Shelby can sell as much as it can produce at these prices. The costs of production are summarized in the Accounting Data sheet. As usual, values in blue cells are given, whereas other values are calculated from these.

Management at Shelby just met to discuss next month's operating plan. Although the shelves are selling well, the overall profitability of the company is a concern. The plant's engineer suggested that the current production of model S shelves be cut back. According to him, "Model S shelves are sold for $1800 per unit, but our costs are $1839. Even though we're selling only 400 units a month, we're losing money on each one. We should decrease production of model S." The controller disagreed. He said that the problem was the model S assembly department trying to absorb a large overhead with a small production volume. "The model S units are making a contribution to overhead. Even though production doesn't cover all of the fixed costs, we'd be worse off with lower production."

Your job is to develop an LP model of Shelby's problem, then run Solver, and finally make a recommendation to Shelby management, with a short verbal argument supporting the engineer or the controller.

Notes on Accounting Data Calculations

The fixed overhead is distributed using activity-based costing principles. For example, at current production levels, the forming machine spends 100 hours on model S shelves and 700 hours on model LX shelves.

The forming machine is used 800 hours of the month, of which 12.5% of the time is spent on model S shelves and 87.5% is spent on model LX shelves. The $95,000 of fixed overhead in the forming department is distributed as $11,875 ($= 95,000 \times 0.125$) to model S shelves and $83,125 ($= 95,000 \times 0.875$) to model LX shelves. The fixed overhead per unit of output is allocated as $29.69 ($= 11,875/400$) for model S and $59.38 ($= 83,125/1400$) for model LX. In the calculation of the standard overhead cost, the fixed and variable costs are added together, so that the overhead cost for the forming department allocated to a model S shelf is $149.69 ($= 29.69 + 120$, shown in cell G20 rounded up to $150). Similarly, the overhead cost for the forming department allocated to a model LX shelf is $229.38 ($= 59.38 + 170$, shown in cell H20 rounded down to $229).

<table>
<tr><td>CASE</td><td>13.2 SONOMA VALLEY WINES[15]</td></tr>
</table>

After graduating from business school, George Clark went to work for a Big Six accounting firm in San Francisco. Because his hobby has always been wine making, when he had the opportunity a few years later he purchased five acres plus an option to buy 35 additional acres of land in Sonoma Valley in Northern California. He plans eventually to grow grapes on that land and make wine with them. George knows that this is a big undertaking and that it will require more capital than he has at present. However, he figures that if he persists, he will be able to leave accounting and live full time from his winery earnings by the time he is 40.

Because wine making is capital-intensive and because growing commercial-quality grapes with a full yield of five tons per acre takes at least eight years, George is planning to start small. This is necessitated by both his lack of capital and his inexperience in wine making on a large scale, although he has long made wine at home. His plan is first to plant the grapes on his land to get the vines started. Then he needs to set up a small trailer where he can live on weekends while he installs the irrigation system and does the required work to the vines, such as pruning and fertilizing. To help maintain a positive cash flow during the first few years, he also plans to buy grapes

from other nearby growers so he can make his own label wine. He proposes to market it through a small tasting room that he will build on his land and keep open on weekends during the spring–summer season.

To begin, George is going to use $10,000 in savings to finance the initial purchase of grapes from which he will make his first batch of wine. He is also thinking about going to the Bank of Sonoma and asking for a loan. He knows that if he goes to the bank, the loan officer will ask for a business plan; so he is trying to pull together some numbers for himself first. This way he will have a rough notion of the profitability and cash flows associated with his ideas before he develops a formal plan with a pro forma income statement and balance sheet. He has decided to make the preliminary planning horizon two years and would like to estimate the profit over that period. His most immediate task is to decide how much of the $10,000 should be allocated to purchasing grapes for the first year and how much to purchasing grapes for the second year. In addition, each year he must decide how much he should allocate to purchasing grapes to make his favorite

[15]This case was written by William D. Whisler, California State University, Hayward.

Petite Syrah and how much to purchasing grapes to make the more popular Sauvignon Blanc that seems to have captured the attention of a wider market during the last few years in California.

In the first year, each bottle of Petite Syrah requires $0.80 worth of grapes and each bottle of Sauvignon Blanc uses $0.70 worth of grapes. For the second year, the costs of the grapes per bottle are $0.75 and $0.85, respectively.

George anticipates that his Petite Syrah will sell for $8.00 a bottle in the first year and for $8.25 in the second year, while his Sauvignon Blanc's price remains the same in both years at $7.00 a bottle.

Besides the decisions about the amounts of grapes purchased in the two years, George must make estimates of the sales levels for the two wines during the two years. The local wine-making association has told him that marketing is the key to success in any wine business; generally, demand is directly proportional to the amount of effort spent on marketing. Thus, since George cannot afford to do any market research about sales levels due to his lack of capital, he is pondering how much money he should spend to promote each wine each year. The wine-making association has given him a rule of thumb that relates estimated demand to the amount of money spent on advertising. For instance, they estimate that for each dollar spent in the first year promoting the Petite Syrah, a demand for five bottles will be created; and for each dollar spent in the second year, a demand for six bottles will result. Similarly, for each dollar spent on advertising for the Sauvignon Blanc in the first year, up to eight bottles can be sold; and for each dollar spent in the second year, up to ten bottles can be sold.

The initial funds for the advertising will come from the $10,000 savings. Assume that the cash earned from wine sales in the first year is available in the second year.

A personal concern George has is that he maintains a proper balance of wine products so that he will be well positioned to expand his marketing capabilities when he moves to the winery and makes it his full-time job. Thus, in his mind it is important to ensure that the number of bottles of Petite Syrah sold each year falls in the range between 40% and 70% of the overall number of bottles sold.

Questions

1. George needs help to decide how many grapes to buy, how much money to spend on advertising, how many bottles of wine to sell, and how much profit he can expect to earn over the two-year period. Develop a spreadsheet LP model to help him.

2. Solve the linear programming model formulated in Question 1.

The following questions should be attempted only after Questions 1 and 2 have been answered correctly.

3. After showing the business plan to the Bank of Sonoma, George learns that the loan officer is concerned about the market prices used in estimating the profits—recently it has been forecasted that Chile and Australia will be flooding the market with high-quality, low-priced white wines over the next couple of years. In particular, the loan officer estimates that the price used for the Sauvignon Blanc in the second year is highly speculative and realistically might be only half the price George calculated. Thus, the bank is nervous about lending the money because of the big effect such a decrease in price might have on estimated profits. What do you think?

4. Another comment the loan officer of the Bank of Sonoma has after reviewing the business plan is: "I see that you do have an allowance in your calculations for the carryover of inventory of unsold wine from the first year to the second year, but you do not have any cost associated with this. All companies must charge something for holding inventory, so you should redo your plans to allow for this." If the holding charges are $0.10 per bottle per year, how much, if any, does George's plan change?

5. The president of the local grape growers' association mentions to George that there is likely to be a strike soon over the unionization of the grape workers. (Currently they are not represented by any union.) This means that the costs of the grapes might go up by anywhere from 50% to 100%. How might this affect George's plan?

6. Before taking his business plan to the bank, George had it reviewed by a colleague at the accounting firm where he works. Although his friend was excited about the plan and its prospects, he was dismayed to learn that George had not used present value in determining his profit. "George, you are an accountant and must know that money has a time value; and although you are only doing a two-year planning problem, it still is important to calculate the present value profit." George replies, "Yes, I know all about present value. For big investments over long time periods, it is important to consider. But in this case, for a small investment and only a two-year time period, it really doesn't matter." Who is correct, George or his colleague? Why? Use an 8% discount factor in answering this question. Does the answer change if a 6% or 10% discount rate is used? Use a spreadsheet to determine the coefficients of the objective function for the different discount rates.

7. Suppose that the Bank of Sonoma is so excited about the prospects of George's wine-growing business that they offer to lend him an extra $10,000 at their best small business rate—28% plus a 10% compensating balance.[16] Should he accept the bank's offer? Why or why not?

8. Suppose that the rule of thumb George was given by the local wine-making association is incorrect. Assume that the number of bottles of Petite Syrah sold in the first and second years is at most four for each dollar spent on advertising. And likewise for the Sauvignon Blanc, assume that it can be at most only five in years 1 and 2.

9. How much could profits be increased if George's personal concerns (that Petite Syrah sales should account for between 40% and 70% of overall sales) are ignored?

---

[16]The compensating balance requirement means that only $9,000 of the $10,000 loan is available to George; the remaining $1,000 remains with the bank.

Juanmonino/iStockphoto.com

PRODUCTION, INVENTORY, AND DISTRIBUTION AT KELLOGG

The Kellogg Company is the largest cereal producer in the world and is a leading producer of convenience foods. Its worldwide sales in 1999 were nearly $7 billion. Kellogg's first product in 1906 was Corn Flakes, and it developed a variety of ready-to-eat cereals over the years, including Raisin Bran, Rice Krispies, Corn Pops, and others. Although the company continues to develop and market new cereals, it has also gone into convenience foods, such as Pop-Tarts and Nutri-Grain cereal bars, and has also entered the health-food market. Kellogg produces hundreds of products and sells thousands of stock-keeping units (SKUs). Managing production, inventory, and distribution of these—that is, the daily operations—in a cost-effective manner is a challenge.

By the late 1980s, Kellogg realized that the increasing scale and complexity of its operations required optimization methods to coordinate its daily operations in a centralized manner. As described in Brown et al. (2001), a team of management scientists developed an optimization software system called KPS (Kellogg Planning System). This system was originally intended for operational (daily and weekly) decisions, but it expanded into a system for making tactical (longer-range) decisions about issues such as plant budgets, capacity expansion, and consolidation. By the turn of the century, KPS had been in use for about a decade. Operational decisions made by KPS reduced production, inventory, and distribution costs by approximately $4.5 million per year. Better yet, the tactical side of KPS recently suggested a consolidation of production capacity that saved the company approximately $35–40 million annually.

Kellogg operates five plants in the United States and Canada, has seven distribution centers (DCs) in such areas as Los Angeles and Chicago, and has about 15 co-packers, companies that contract to produce or pack some of Kellogg's products. Customer demands are seen at the DCs and the plants. In the cereal business alone, Kellogg has to coordinate the packaging, inventorying, and distributing of 600 SKUs at about 27 locations with a total of about 90 production lines and 180 packaging lines. This requires a tremendous amount of day-to-day coordination to meet customer demand at a low cost. The KPS operational system that guides operational decisions is essentially a large linear programming (LP) model that takes as its inputs the forecasted customer demands for the various products and specifies what should be produced, held, and shipped on a daily basis. The resulting model is similar to the Pigskin model of football production discussed in the previous chapter, except that it is *much* larger.

Specifically, for each week of its 30-week planning horizon, the model specifies (1) how much of each product to make on each production line at each facility; (2) how much of each SKU to pack on each packaging line at each facility; (3) how much inventory of each SKU to hold at each facility; and (4) how much of each SKU to ship from each location to other locations. In addition, the model has to take constraints into account. For example, the production within a given plant in a week cannot exceed the processing line capacity in that plant. LP models such as Kellogg's tend to be very large—thousands of decision variables and hundreds or thousands of constraints—but the algorithms Kellogg uses are capable of optimizing such models very quickly. Kellogg runs its KPS model each Sunday morning and uses its recommendations in the ensuing week.

The KPS system illustrates a common occurrence when companies turn to management science for help. As stated earlier, the system was originally developed for making daily operational decisions. Soon, however, the company developed a tactical version of KPS for long-range planning on the order of 12 to 24 months. The tactical model is similar to the operational model except that time periods are now months, not days or weeks, and other considerations must be handled, such as limited product shelf lives. The point is, however, that when companies such as Kellogg become comfortable with management science methods in one part of their operations, they often look for other areas to apply similar methods. As with Kellogg, such methods can save the company millions of dollars. ■

14-1 INTRODUCTION

In a survey of Fortune 500 firms, 85% of those responding said that they use LP. In this chapter we discuss some of the LP models that are most often applied to real-world applications. Some typical examples include:

- scheduling bank clerks for check encoding
- optimizing the operation of an oil refinery
- planning dairy production at a creamery
- scheduling production of products at a fiberglass manufacturer
- optimizing a Wall Street firm's bond portfolio.

Actually, these problems are just a sampling of the types of problems we will model in this chapter. There are two basic goals in this chapter. The first is to illustrate some of the many real applications that can take advantage of LP. You will see that these applications cover a wide range, from oil production to worker scheduling to cash management. The second goal is to increase your facility in modeling LP problems on a spreadsheet. We present a few principles that will help you model a wide variety of problems. The best way to learn, however, is to see many examples and work through numerous problems. In short, mastering the art of LP spreadsheet modeling takes hard work and practice. You will have plenty of opportunity to do both with the material in this chapter.

Although a wide variety of problems can be formulated as *linear* programming models, there are some that cannot. Either they require *integer* variables or they are *nonlinear* in the decision variables. We include examples of integer programming and nonlinear programming models in this chapter, just to give you a taste of what is involved.[1] You will see that the modeling process for these types of problems is not much different than for LP problems. Once the models are formulated, Excel's Solver can be used to solve them. Then SolverTable can be used to perform sensitivity analysis. However, we point out that these integer and nonlinear models are inherently more difficult to solve. Solver must use more complex algorithms and is not always guaranteed to find the optimal solution. As long as you are aware of this, you will see that Solver provides the power to solve a great variety of realistic business problems.

Although there is a tremendous amount of theory behind the *algorithms* that solve these problems, the modeling process itself is fairly straightforward and is learned best by seeing a variety of examples. Therefore, we proceed in this chapter by modeling (and then solving) a diverse class of problems that arise in business. The exercises scattered throughout the chapter provide even more examples of how LP and its integer and nonlinear extensions can be applied.

All of these models can benefit from sensitivity analysis, either done formally with the SolverTable add-in or informally by changing one or more inputs and rerunning Solver. To keep the chapter from getting too long, we present only a few of the many possible sensitivity analyses. However, we stress that in real applications, model development is just the beginning of the overall analysis. It is then usually followed by extensive sensitivity analysis.

14-2 WORKER SCHEDULING MODELS

Many organizations use **worker scheduling models** to schedule employees to provide adequate service. Example 14.1 illustrates how to use LP, possibly with integer constraints, to schedule employees on a daily basis.

EXAMPLE | **14.1 POSTAL EMPLOYEE SCHEDULING**

A post office requires different numbers of full-time employees on different days of the week. The number of full-time employees required each day is given in Table 14.1. Union rules state that each full-time employee must work five consecutive days and then receive two days off. For example, an employee who works Monday to Friday must be off on Saturday and Sunday. The post office wants to meet its daily requirements using only full-time employees. Its objective is to minimize the number of full-time employees on its payroll.

Table 14.1 Employee Requirements for Post Office

Day of Week	Minimum Number of Employees Required
Monday	17
Tuesday	13
Wednesday	15
Thursday	19
Friday	14
Saturday	16
Sunday	11

© Cengage Learning

---

[1]Besides the nonlinear models discussed in this chapter, which can be solved with Solver's GRG nonlinear algorithm, there is an even more difficult class of nonlinear models called *nonsmooth* models. Although we will not discuss nonsmooth models, we can recommend Solver's Evolutionary algorithm for these difficult models. (This is available only in the version of Solver introduced in Excel® 2010.) These nonsmooth problems can also be solved with the Evolver add-in, part of Palisade's DecisionTools® Suite.

Objective To develop an LP model that relates five-day shift schedules to daily numbers of employees available, and to use Solver on this model to find a schedule that uses the fewest number of employees and meets all daily workforce requirements.

Where Do the Numbers Come From?

In real employee-scheduling problems, much of the work involves forecasting and queueing analysis to obtain worker requirements. This must be done before an optimal schedule can be found.

The only inputs needed for this problem are the minimum employee requirements in Table 14.1, but these are not easy to obtain. They would probably be obtained through a combination of two quantitative techniques: forecasting (Chapter 12) and queueing analysis (not covered in this book). The post office would first use historical data to forecast customer and mail arrival patterns throughout a typical week. It would then use queueing analysis to translate these arrival patterns into worker requirements on a daily basis. Actually, we have kept the problem relatively simple by considering only *daily* requirements. In a realistic setting, the organization might forecast worker requirements on an hourly or even a 15-minute basis.

Solution

The variables and constraints for this problem appear in Table 14.2. The trickiest part is identifying the appropriate decision variables. You might think that the decision variables should be the numbers of employees working on the various days of the week. Clearly, these values must eventually be determined. However, it is not enough to specify, say, that 18 employees are working on Monday. The problem is that this doesn't indicate when these 18 employees start their five-day shifts. Without this knowledge, it is impossible to implement the five-consecutive-day, two-day-off requirement. (If you don't believe this, try developing your own model with the wrong decision variables. You will eventually reach a dead end.)

Table 14.2   Variables and Constraints for Postal Scheduling Problem

Input variables	Minimum required number of workers each day
Decision variables (changing cells)	Number of employees working each of the five-day shifts (defined by their first day of work)
Objective cell	Total number of employees on the payroll
Other calculated variables	Number of employees working each day
Constraints	Employees working $\geq$ Employees required

© Cengage Learning

The key to this model is choosing the correct changing cells.

The trick is to define the decision variables as the numbers of employees working each of the seven possible five-day shifts. By knowing these values, the other output variables can be calculated. For example, the number working on Thursday is the sum of those who begin their five-day shifts on Sunday, Monday, Tuesday, Wednesday, and Thursday.

FUNDAMENTAL INSIGHT

Choosing the Changing Cells

The changing cells, which are really just the decision variables, should always be chosen so that their values determine all required outputs in the model. In other words, their values should tell the company exactly how to run its business. Sometimes the choice of changing cells is obvious, but in many cases (as in this worker scheduling model), the proper choice of changing cells takes some deeper thinking about the problem. An improper choice of changing cells typically leads to a dead end, where their values do not supply enough information to calculate required outputs or implement certain constraints.

Note that this is a "wraparound" problem. We assume that the daily requirements in Table 14.1 and the worker schedules continue week after week. So, for example, the employees assigned to the Thursday through Monday shift always wrap around from one week to the next on their five-day shift.

Developing the Worker Scheduling Model

Developing the Spreadsheet Model

The spreadsheet model for this problem is shown in Figure 14.1. (See the file **Worker Scheduling.xlsx**.) To develop this model, proceed as follows.

Figure 14.1   Worker Scheduling Model with Optimal Solution

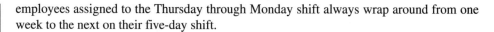

◢	A	B	C	D	E	F	G	H	I	J	K
1	Worker scheduling model								Range names used		
2									Employees_available	=Model!$B$23:$H$23	
3	Decision variables: number of employees starting their five-day shift on various days								Employees_required	=Model!$B$25:$H$25	
4	Mon	1.33							Employees_Starting	=Model!$B$4:$B$10	
5	Tue	3.33							Total_employees	=Model!$B$28	
6	Wed	2.00									
7	Thu	7.33									
8	Fri	0.00									
9	Sat	3.33									
10	Sun	5.00									
11											
12	Result of decisions: number of employees working on various days (along top) who started their shift on various days (along side)										
13		Mon	Tue	Wed	Thu	Fri	Sat	Sun			
14	Mon	1.33	1.33	1.33	1.33	1.33					
15	Tue		3.33	3.33	3.33	3.33	3.33				
16	Wed			2.00	2.00	2.00	2.00	2.00			
17	Thu	7.33			7.33	7.33	7.33	7.33			
18	Fri	0.00	0.00			0.00	0.00	0.00			
19	Sat	3.33	3.33	3.33			3.33	3.33			
20	Sun	5.00	5.00	5.00	5.00			5.00			
21											
22	Constraint on worker availabilities										
23	Employees available	17.00	13.00	15.00	19.00	14.00	16.00	17.67			
24		>=	>=	>=	>=	>=	>=	>=			
25	Employees required	17	13	15	19	14	16	11			
26											
27	Objective to maximize										
28	Total employees	22.33									

1. **Inputs and range names.** Enter the number of employees needed on each day of the week (from Table 14.1) in the blue cells, and create the range names shown.

2. **Employees beginning each day.** Enter *any* trial values for the number of employees beginning work on each day of the week in the Employees_starting range. These beginning days determine the possible five-day shifts. For example, the employees in cell B4 work Monday through Friday.

3. **Employees on hand each day.** The key to this solution is to realize that the numbers in the Employees_starting range—the changing cells—do not represent the number of workers who will show up each day. As an example, the number in cell B4 represent those who start on Monday work Monday through Friday. Therefore, enter the formula

   =$B$4

   in cell B14 and copy it across to cell F14. Proceed similarly for rows 15–20, being careful to take "wraparounds" into account. For example, the workers starting on Thursday work Thursday through Sunday, plus Monday. Then calculate the total number who are available on each day by entering the formula

   =SUM(B14:B20)

   in cell B23 and copying it across to cell H23.

Excel Tip: ***CTRL+Enter Shortcut***
You often enter a typical formula in a cell and then copy it. One way to do this efficiently is to select the entire range, here B23:H23. Then enter the typical formula, here ***=SUM(B14:B20)***, *and press* ***Ctrl+Enter***. *This has the same effect as copying, but it is slightly quicker.*

4. **Total employees.** Calculate the total number of employees in cell B28 with the formula

=SUM(Employees_starting)

Note that there is no double-counting in this sum. For example, the employees in cells B4 and B5 are *not* the same people.

At this point, you might want to experiment with the numbers in the changing cell range to see whether you can guess an optimal solution (without looking at Figure 14.1). It is not that easy. Each worker who starts on a given day works the next four days as well, so when you find a solution that meets the minimal requirements for the various days, you usually have a few more workers available on some days than are needed.

Using Solver

Invoke Solver and fill out its main dialog box as shown in Figure 14.2. (You don't need to include the integer constraints yet. They will be discussed shortly.) Make sure you check the Non-Negative option and select the Simplex LP method.

Figure 14.2
Solver Dialog Box for Worker Scheduling Model

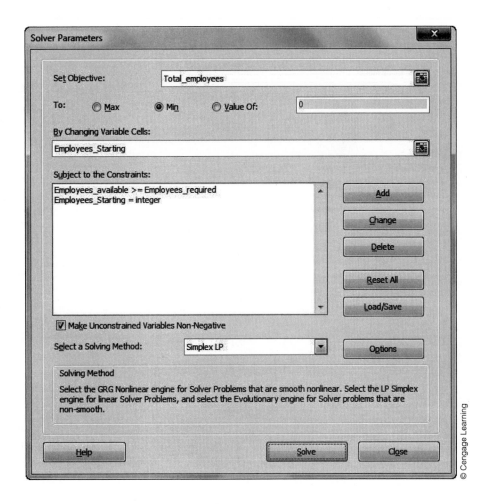

Discussion of the Solution

The optimal solution shown in Figure 14.1 has one drawback: It requires the number of employees starting work on some days to be a fraction. Because part-time employees are not allowed, this solution is unrealistic. However, it is simple to add an integer constraint on the changing cells. This integer constraint appears in Figure 14.2. (To create this integer constraint in Solver's Add Constraint dialog box, select the Employees_starting for the left side, and select "int" in the middle dropdown list. The word "integer" will automatically appear in the right side of the constraint.) With this integer constraint, the optimal solution appears in Figure 14.3.

Technical Tip: Solver Tolerance Setting

Set Solver's Tolerance to zero to ensure that you get the optimal integer solution. Be aware, however, that this can incur significant extra computing time for larger models.

When working with integer constraints, you should be aware of Solver's Tolerance setting. The idea is as follows. As Solver searches for the best integer solution, it is often able to find a "good" solution fairly quickly, but it often has to spend a lot of time finding slightly better solutions. A nonzero tolerance setting allows it to quit early. The default tolerance setting is 5 (percent). This means that if Solver finds a feasible solution that is guaranteed to have an objective value no more than 5% from the optimal value, it will quit and report this good solution (which might even be the optimal solution). Therefore, if you keep this default tolerance value, your integer solutions will sometimes not be optimal, but they will be close. If you want to ensure that you get an optimal solution, you can change the Solver tolerance value to zero. (In Excel® 2010 and later versions, click the Options button, and then under the All Methods tab, uncheck Ignore Integer Constraints and enter a value, the tolerance, in the Integer Optimality [%] box. In previous versions, click the Options button and enter a value in the Tolerance box.)

Figure 14.3   Optimal Integer Solution to Worker Scheduling Model

	A	B	C	D	E	F	G	H	I	J	K
1	Worker scheduling model								Range names used		
2									Employees_available	=Model!$B$23:$H$23	
3	Decision variables: number of employees starting their five-day shift on various days								Employees_required	=Model!$B$25:$H$25	
4	Mon	6							Employees_Starting	=Model!$B$4:$B$10	
5	Tue	6							Total_employees	=Model!$B$28	
6	Wed	0									
7	Thu	7									
8	Fri	0									
9	Sat	4									
10	Sun	0									
11											
12	Result of decisions: number of employees working on various days (along top) who started their shift on various days (along side)										
13		Mon	Tue	Wed	Thu	Fri	Sat	Sun			
14	Mon	6	6	6	6	6					
15	Tue		6	6	6	6	6				
16	Wed			0	0	0	0	0			
17	Thu	7			7	7	7	7			
18	Fri	0	0			0	0	0			
19	Sat	4	4	4			4	4			
20	Sun	0	0	0	0			0			
21											
22	Constraint on worker availabilities										
23	Employees available	17	16	16	19	19	17	11			
24		>=	>=	>=	>=	>=	>=	>=			
25	Employees required	17	13	15	19	14	16	11			
26											
27	Objective to maximize										
28	Total employees	23									

© Cengage Learning

The changing cells in the optimal solution indicate the numbers of workers who start their five-day shifts on the various days. You can then look at the *columns* of the B14:H20 range to see which employees are working on any given day. This optimal solution is typical in scheduling problems. Due to a labor constraint—each employee must work five consecutive days and then have two days off—it is typically impossible to meet the minimum employee requirements exactly. To ensure that there are enough employees available on busy days, it is necessary to have more than enough on hand on light days.

Multiple optimal solutions have different values in the changing cells, but they all have the same objective value.

Another interesting aspect of this problem is that when you solve it, you might get a *different* schedule that is still optimal—that is, a solution that still uses a total of 23 employees and meets all constraints. This is a case of **multiple optimal solutions**, not at all uncommon in LP problems. In fact, it is typically good news for a manager, who can then choose among the optimal solutions using other, possibly nonquantitative criteria. The finished version of the file discusses how you can use Solver to locate different optimal solutions from those in Figures 14.1 and 14.3.

Sensitivity Analysis

To run some sensitivity analyses with SolverTable, you need to modify the original model slightly to incorporate the effect of the input being varied.

The most obvious type of sensitivity analysis in this example is to analyze the effect of worker requirements on the optimal solution. Specifically, let's suppose the number of employees needed on each day of the week increases by two, four, or six. How does this change the total number of employees needed? You can answer this with SolverTable, but you must first modify the model slightly, as shown in Figure 14.4. The problem is that we want to increase *each* of the daily minimal required values by the same amount. The trick is to enter the original requirements in row 12, enter a trial value for the extra number required per day in cell K12, enter the formula **=B12+$K$12** in cell B27, and then copy this formula across to cell H27. Now you can use the one-way SolverTable option, using the Extra cell as the single input, letting it vary from 0 to 6 in increments of 2, and specifying the Total_employees cell as the single output cell.

Figure 14.4   Modified Worker Scheduling Model

◢	A	B	C	D	E	F	G	H	I	J	K
12	Employees required (original values)	17	13	15	19	14	16	11		Extra required each day	0
13											
14	Result of decisions: number of employees working on various days (along top) who started their shift on various days (along side)										
15		Mon	Tue	Wed	Thu	Fri	Sat	Sun			
16	Mon	2	2	2	2	2					
17	Tue		3	3	3	3	3				
18	Wed			3	3	3	3	3		Note how the original model has	
19	Thu	7			7	7	7	7		been modified so that the extra	
20	Fri	0	0			0	0	0		value in cell K12 drives all of the	
21	Sat	4	4	4			4	4		requirements in row 27.	
22	Sun	4	4	4	4			4			
23											
24	Constraint on worker availabilities										
25	Employees available	17	13	16	19	15	17	18			
26		>=	>=	>=	>=	>=	>=	>=			
27	Employees required	17	13	15	19	14	16	11			

© Cengage Learning

The results appear in Figure 14.5. When the requirement increases by two each day, only two extra employees are necessary (scheduled appropriately). However, when the requirement increases by four each day, *more* than four extra employees are necessary. The same is true when the requirement increases by six each day. This might surprise you at first, but there is an intuitive reason: Each extra worker works only five days of the week.

Note that we did not use Solver's sensitivity report here for two reasons. First, Solver does not offer a sensitivity report for models with integer constraints. Second, even if the integer constraints are deleted, Solver's sensitivity report does not answer questions about *multiple* input changes, as we have asked here. It is used for questions about one-at-a-time changes to inputs, such as a change to a *specific* day's worker requirement. In this sense, SolverTable is a more flexible tool.

Figure 14.5 Sensitivity to Number of Extra Workers Required per Day

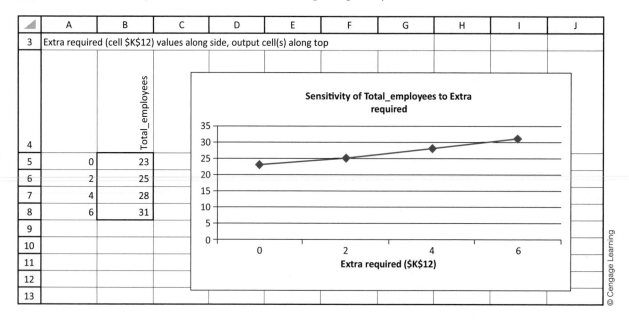

Modeling Issues

Heuristic solutions are often close to optimal, but they are never guaranteed to be optimal.

- The postal employee scheduling example is called a *static* scheduling model because we assume that the post office faces the same situation each week. In reality, demands change over time, workers take vacations in the summer, and so on, so the post office does not face the same situation each week. A *dynamic* scheduling model (not covered here) is necessary for such problems.

- In a weekly scheduling model for a supermarket or a fast-food restaurant, the number of decision variables can grow quickly and optimization software such as Solver will have difficulty finding an optimal solution. In such cases, heuristic methods (essentially clever trial-and-error algorithms) have been used to find good solutions to the problem. For example, Love and Hoey (1990) indicate how this was done for a particular staff scheduling problem.

- Our model can easily be expanded to handle part-time employees, the use of overtime, and alternative objectives such as maximizing the number of weekend days off received by employees. You are asked to explore such extensions in the problems. ∎

PROBLEMS

Note: Student solutions for problems whose numbers appear within a colored box are available for purchase at www.cengagebrain.com.

Level A

1. Modify the post office model so that employees are paid $10 per hour on weekdays and $15 per hour on weekends. Change the objective so that you now minimize the weekly payroll. (You can assume that each employee works eight hours per day.) Is the previous optimal solution still optimal?

2. How much influence can the worker requirements for one, two, or three days have on the weekly schedule in the post office example? You are asked to explore this in the following questions.
   a. Let Monday's requirements change from 17 to 25 in increments of 1. Use SolverTable to see how the total number of employees changes.
   b. Suppose the Monday and Tuesday requirements can each, independently of one another, increase from 1 to 8 in increments of 1. Use a two-way SolverTable to see how the total number of employees changes.

c. Suppose the Monday, Tuesday, and Wednesday requirements each increase by the *same* amount, where this increase can be from 1 to 8 in increments of 1. Use a one-way SolverTable to investigate how the total number of employees changes.

3. In the post office example, suppose that each full-time employee works eight hours per day. Thus, Monday's requirement of 17 workers can be viewed as a requirement of 8(17) = 136 hours. The post office can meet its daily labor requirements by using both full-time and part-time employees. During each week a full-time employee works eight hours a day for five consecutive days, and a part-time employee works four hours a day for five consecutive days. A full-time employee costs the post office $15 per hour, whereas a part-time employee (with reduced fringe benefits) costs the post office only $10 per hour. Union requirements limit part-time labor to 25% of weekly labor requirements.

a. Modify the model as necessary, and then use Solver to minimize the post office's weekly labor costs.

b. Use SolverTable to determine how a change in the part-time labor limitation (currently 25%) influences the optimal solution.

Level B

4. In the post office example, suppose the employees want more flexibility in their schedules. They want to be allowed to work five consecutive days followed by two days off *or* to work three consecutive days followed by a day off followed by two consecutive days followed by another day off. Modify the original model (with integer constraints) to allow this flexibility. Might this be a good deal for management as well as labor? Explain.

5. In the post office example, suppose that the post office can force employees to work one day of overtime each week on the day immediately following this five-day shift. For example, an employee whose regular shift is Monday to Friday can also be required to work on Saturday. Each employee is paid $100 a day for each of the first five days worked during a week and $135 for the overtime day (if any). Determine how the post office can minimize the cost of meeting its weekly work requirements.

6. Suppose the post office has 28 full-time employees and is not allowed to fire any of them or hire more. Determine a schedule that maximizes the number of weekend days off received by these employees.

14-3 BLENDING MODELS

In many situations, various inputs must be blended to produce desired outputs. In many of these situations, **blending models** can be used to find the optimal combination of outputs as well as the mix of inputs that are used to produce the desired outputs. The following are some typical examples of blending problems.

Inputs	Outputs
Meat, filler, water	Different types of sausage
Various types of oil	Heating oil, gasolines, aviation fuels
Carbon, iron, molybdenum	Different types of steels
Different types of pulp	Different kinds of recycled paper

Example 14.2 illustrates how to model a typical blending problem in Excel. Although this example is small relative to blending problems in real applications, it is still probably too complex for you to guess the optimal solution.

EXAMPLE | 14.2 BLENDING OIL PRODUCTS AT CHANDLER OIL

Chandler Oil has 5000 barrels of crude oil 1 and 10,000 barrels of crude oil 2 available. Chandler sells gasoline and heating oil. These products are produced by blending the two crude oils together. Each barrel of crude oil 1 has a "quality level" of 10 and each barrel of crude oil 2 has a quality level of 5.[2] Gasoline must have an average quality level of at least 8, whereas heating oil must have an average quality level of at least 6. Gasoline sells for $75 per barrel, and heating oil sells for $60 per barrel. We assume that demand for heating oil and gasoline is unlimited, so that all of Chandler's production can be sold. Chandler wants to maximize its revenue from selling gasoline and heating oil.

[2]To avoid being overly technical, we use the generic term *quality level*. In real oil blending, qualities of interest might be octane rating, viscosity, and others.

Objective   To develop an LP model for finding the revenue-maximizing plan that meets quality constraints and stays within limits on crude oil availabilities.

Where Do the Numbers Come From?

Most of the inputs for this problem should be easy to obtain.

- The selling prices for outputs are dictated by market pressures.
- The availabilities of inputs are based on crude supplies from the suppliers.
- The quality levels of crude oils are known from chemical analysis, whereas the required quality levels for outputs are specified by Chandler, probably in response to competitive or regulatory pressures.

Solution

In typical blending problems, the correct decision variables are the amounts of each input blended into each output.

The variables and constraints required for this blending model are listed in Table 14.3. The key is the selection of the appropriate decision variables. You might think it is sufficient to specify the amounts of the two crude oils used and the amounts of the two products produced. However, this is not enough. The problem is that this information doesn't tell Chandler how to *make* the outputs from the inputs. The company instead needs to have a blending plan: how much of each input to use in the production of a barrel of each output. Once you understand that this blending plan is the basic decision, all other output variables follow in a straightforward manner.

Table 14.3   Variables and Constraints for Blending Model

Input variables	Unit selling prices, availabilities of inputs, quality levels of inputs, required quality levels of outputs
Decision variables (changing cells)	Barrels of each input used to produce each output
Objective cell	Revenue from selling gasoline and heating oil
Other calculated variables	Barrels of inputs used, barrels of outputs produced (and sold), quality obtained and quality required for outputs
Constraints	Barrels of inputs used ≤ Barrels available Quality of outputs obtained ≥ Quality required

© Cengage Learning

Developing the Blending Model

Developing the Spreadsheet Model

The spreadsheet model for this problem appears in Figure 14.6. (See the file **Blending Oil.xlsx**.) To set it up, proceed as follows.

1. **Inputs and range names.** Enter the unit selling prices, quality levels for inputs, required quality levels for outputs, and availabilities of inputs in the blue cells. Then name the ranges as indicated.

2. **Inputs blended into each output.** As discussed, the quantities Chandler must specify are the barrels of each input used to produce each output. Enter *any* trial values for these quantities in the Blending_plan range. For example, the value in cell B16 is the amount of crude oil 1 used to make gasoline and the value in cell C16 is the amount of crude oil 1 used to make heating oil. The Blending_plan range contains the changing cells.

From here on, the solutions shown are optimal. However, remember that you can start with any solution. It doesn't even have to be feasible.

3. **Inputs used and outputs sold.** Calculate the row sums (in column D) and column sums (in row 18) of the Blending_plan range. There is a quick way to do this. Select both the row and column where the sums will go (select one, then hold down the Ctrl key and select the other), and click the AutoSum (Σ) button on the Home ribbon. This creates SUM formulas in the selected cells.

Figure 14.6 Oil Blending Model

	A	B	C	D	E	F	G
1	**Chandler oil blending model**					**Range names used**	
2						Barrels_available	=Model!$F$16:$F$17
3	**Monetary inputs**	Gasoline	Heating oil			Barrels_sold	=Model!$B$18:$C$18
4	Selling price/barrel	$75	$60			Barrels_used	=Model!$D$16:$D$17
5						Blending_plan	=Model!$B$16:$C$17
6	**Quality level per barrel of crudes**					Quality_points_obtained	=Model!$B$22:$C$22
7	Crude oil 1	10				Quality_points_required	=Model!$B$24:$C$24
8	Crude oil 2	5				Revenue	=Model!$B$27
9							
10	**Required quality level per barrel of product**						
11		Gasoline	Heating oil				
12		8	6				
13							
14	**Blending plan (barrels of crudes in each product)**						
15		Gasoline	Heating oil	Barrels used		Barrels available	
16	Crude oil 1	3000	2000	5000	<=	5000	
17	Crude oil 2	2000	8000	10000	<=	10000	
18	Barrels sold	5000	10000				
19							
20	**Constraints on quality**						
21		Gasoline	Heating oil				
22	Quality points obtained	40000	60000				
23		>=	>=				
24	Quality points required	40000	60000				
25							
26	**Objective to maximize**						
27	Revenue	$975,000					

© Cengage Learning

4. **Quality achieved.** Keep track of the quality level of gasoline and heating oil in the Quality_points_obtained range as follows. Begin by calculating for each output the number of quality points (QP) in the inputs used to produce this output:

QP in gasoline = 10 * Oil 1 in gasoline + 5 * Oil 2 in gasoline

QP in heating oil = 10 * Oil 1 in heating oil + 5 * Oil 2 in heating oil

The gasoline quality constraint is then

$$\text{QP in gasoline} \geq 8 * \text{Gasoline sold} \quad\quad (14.1)$$

Similarly, the heating oil quality constraint is

$$\text{QP in heating oil} \geq 6 * \text{Heating oil sold} \quad\quad (14.2)$$

To implement Inequalities (14.1) and (14.2), calculate the QP for gasoline in cell B22 with the formula

=SUMPRODUCT(B16:B17, $B$7:$B$8)

and copy this formula to cell C22 to generate the QP for heating oil.

5. **Quality required.** Calculate the required quality points for gasoline and heating oil in cells B24 and C24. Specifically, determine the required quality points for gasoline in cell B24 with the formula

=B12*B18

and copy this formula to cell C24 for heating oil.

6. **Revenue.** Calculate the total revenue in cell B27 with the formula

=SUMPRODUCT(B4:C4,B18:C18)

Using Solver

To solve Chandler's problem with Solver, fill out the main Solver dialog box as shown in Figure 14.7. As usual, check the Non-Negative option and select the Simplex LP method before optimizing. You should obtain the optimal solution shown in Figure 14.6.

Figure 14.7

Solver Dialog Box for Blending Model

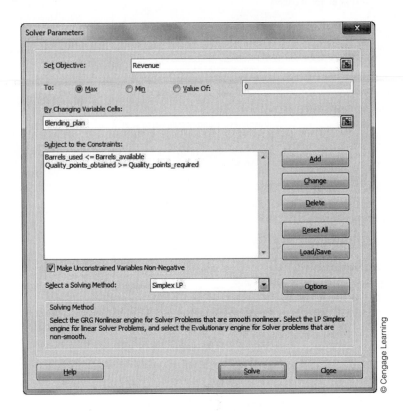

Discussion of the Solution

The optimal solution implies that Chandler should make 5000 barrels of gasoline with 3000 barrels of crude oil 1 and 2000 barrels of crude oil 2. The company should also make 10,000 barrels of heating oil with 2000 barrels of crude oil 1 and 8000 barrels of crude oil 2. With this blend, Chandler will obtain a revenue of $975,000. As stated previously, this problem is sufficiently complex to defy intuition. Clearly, gasoline is more profitable per barrel than heating oil, but given the crude availability and the quality constraints, it turns out that Chandler should sell twice as much heating oil as gasoline. This would have been very difficult to guess ahead of time.

Sensitivity Analysis

We perform two typical sensitivity analyses on this blending model. In each, we see how revenue and the amounts of the outputs produced (and sold) vary. In the first analysis, we use the unit selling price of gasoline as the input and let it vary from $50 to $90 in increments of $5. The SolverTable results appear in Figure 14.8. Two things are of interest. First, as the price of gasoline increases from $55 to $65, Chandler starts producing gasoline and less heating oil, exactly as you would expect. Second, the revenue can only increase or stay the same, as the changes in column E (calculated manually) indicate.

Figure 14.8

Sensitivity to the Selling Price of Gasoline

	A	B Barrels_sold_1	C Barrels_sold_2	D Revenue	E Increase	F	G
3	Selling price gasoline (cell $B$4) values along side, output cell(s) along top						
5	$50	0	15000	$900,000			
6	$55	0	15000	$900,000	$0		
7	$60	5000	10000	$900,000	$0		
8	$65	5000	10000	$925,000	$25,000		
9	$70	5000	10000	$950,000	$25,000		
10	$75	5000	10000	$975,000	$25,000		
11	$80	5000	10000	$1,000,000	$25,000		
12	$85	5000	10000	$1,025,000	$25,000		
13	$90	5000	10000	$1,050,000	$25,000		

In the second sensitivity analysis, we vary the availability of crude 1 from 2000 barrels to 20,000 barrels in increments of 1000 barrels. The resulting SolverTable output appears in Figure 14.9. These results make sense if you analyze them carefully. First, the revenue increases, but at a decreasing rate, as more crude 1 is available. This is a common occurrence in LP models. As more of a resource is made available, revenue can only increase or remain the same, but each extra unit of the resource produces less (or at least no more) revenue than the previous unit. Second, the amount of gasoline produced increases, whereas the amount of heating oil produced decreases. Here's why: Crude 1 has a higher quality than crude 2, and gasoline requires higher quality. Gasoline also sells for a higher price. Therefore, as more crude 1 is available, Chandler can produce more gasoline, receive more revenue, and still meet quality standards.

Figure 14.9

Sensitivity to the Availability of Crude 1

	A	B Barrels_sold_1	C Barrels_sold_2	D Revenue	E Increase	F	G	H
3	Barrels available crude 1 (cell $F$16) values along side, output cell(s) along top							
5	2000	0	10000	$600,000				
6	3000	1000	12000	$795,000	$195,000			
7	4000	3000	11000	$885,000	$90,000			
8	5000	5000	10000	$975,000	$90,000			
9	6000	7000	9000	$1,065,000	$90,000			
10	7000	9000	8000	$1,155,000	$90,000			
11	8000	11000	7000	$1,245,000	$90,000			
12	9000	13000	6000	$1,335,000	$90,000			
13	10000	15000	5000	$1,425,000	$90,000			
14	11000	17000	4000	$1,515,000	$90,000			
15	12000	19000	3000	$1 605,000	$90,000			
16	13000	21000	2000	$1,695,000	$90,000			
17	14000	23000	1000	$1,785,000	$90,000			
18	15000	25000	0	$1,875,000	$90,000			
19	16000	26000	0	$1,950,000	$75,000			
20	17000	27000	0	$2,025,000	$75,000			
21	18000	28000	0	$2,100,000	$75,000			
22	19000	29000	0	$2,175,000	$75,000			
23	20000	30000	0	$2,250,000	$75,000			

© Cengage Learning

Could these sensitivity questions also be answered with Solver's sensitivity report, shown in Figure 14.10? Consider the sensitivity to the change in the price of gasoline. The first and third rows of the top table in this report are for sensitivity to the objective coefficients of decision variables involving gasoline. The problem is that when the price of gasoline changes, *both* of these coefficients change. The reason is that the objective includes the sum of these two decision variables, multiplied by the unit price of gasoline. However, Solver's sensitivity report is valid only for one-at-a-time coefficient changes. Therefore, it cannot answer our question.

Figure 14.10 **Sensitivity Report for Blending Model**

A	B	C	D	E	F	G	H
6	Adjustable Cells						
7			Final	Reduced	Objective	Allowable	Allowable
8	Cell	Name	Value	Cost	Coefficient	Increase	Decrease
9	$B$16	Crude oil 1 Gasoline	3000	0	75	175	25
10	$C$16	Crude oil 1 Heating oil	2000	0	60	25	175
11	$B$17	Crude oil 2 Gasoline	2000	0	75	262.5	18.75
12	$C$17	Crude oil 2 Heating oil	8000	0	60	18.75	43.75
13							
14	Constraints						
15			Final	Shadow	Constraint	Allowable	Allowable
16	Cell	Name	Value	Price	R.H. Side	Increase	Decrease
17	$D$16	Crude oil 1 Barrels used	5000	90	5000	10000	2500
18	$D$17	Crude oil 2 Barrels used	10000	53	10000	10000	6666.666667
19	$B$22	Quality points obtained Gasoline	40000	−7	0	5000	20000
20	$C$22	Quality points obtained Heating oil	60000	−7	0	10000	6666.666667

© Cengage Learning

In contrast, the first row of the bottom table in Figure 14.10 complements the SolverTable sensitivity analysis on the availability of crude 1. It shows that if the availability increases by no more than 10,000 barrels or decreases by no more than 2500 barrels, the shadow price remains $90 per barrel—that is, the same $90,000 increase in profit per 1000 barrels in Figure 14.9. Beyond that range, the sensitivity report indicates only that the shadow price will change. The SolverTable results indicate *how* it changes. For example, when crude 1 availability increases beyond 15,000 barrels, the SolverTable results indicate that the shadow price decreases to $75 per barrel.

A Caution About Blending Constraints

Before concluding this example, we discuss why the model is linear. The key is the implementation of the quality constraints, shown in Inequalities (14.1) and (14.2). To keep a model linear, each side of an inequality constraint must be a constant, the product of a constant and a variable, or a sum of such products. If the quality constraints are implemented as in Inequalities (14.1) and (14.2), the constraints are indeed linear. However, it is arguably more natural to rewrite this type of constraint by dividing through by the amount sold. For example, the modified gasoline constraint becomes

$$\frac{\text{QP in gasoline}}{\text{Gasoline sold}} \geq 8 \qquad\qquad \textbf{(14.3)}$$

Although this form of the constraint is perfectly valid—and is possibly more natural to many people—it suffers from two drawbacks. First, it makes the model nonlinear. This is because the left side is no longer a sum of products; it involves a quotient. We prefer linear models whenever possible. Second, suppose it turns out that Chandler's optimal solution calls for *no* gasoline at all. Then Inequality (14.3) involves division by zero, and this causes an error in Excel. Because of these two drawbacks, it is best to "clear denominators" in all such blending constraints.

FUNDAMENTAL INSIGHT

Clearing Denominators

Some constraints, particularly those that arise in blending models, are most naturally expressed in terms of ratios. For example, the percentage of sulfur in a product is a ratio: (amount of sulfur in product)/(total amount of product). This ratio could then be constrained to be less than or equal to 6%, say. This is a perfectly valid way to express the constraint, but it has the undesirable effect of making the model nonlinear. The fix is simple. To make the model linear, multiply through by the denominator of the ratio. This has the added benefit of ensuring that division by zero will not occur.

Modeling Issues

In reality, a company using a blending model would run the model periodically (each day, say) and set production on the basis of the current inventory of inputs and the current forecasts of demands and prices. Then the forecasts and the input levels would be updated, and the model would be run again to determine the next day's production. ∎

PROBLEMS

Level A

7. Use SolverTable in Chandler's blending model to see whether, by increasing the selling price of gasoline, you can get an optimal solution that produces only gasoline, no heating oil. Then use SolverTable again to see whether, by increasing the selling price of heating oil, you can get an optimal solution that produces only heating oil, no gasoline.

8. Use SolverTable in Chandler's blending model to find the shadow price of crude oil 1—that is, the amount Chandler would be willing to spend to acquire more crude oil 1. Does this shadow price change as Chandler keeps getting more of crude oil 1? Answer the same questions for crude oil 2.

9. How sensitive is the optimal solution (barrels of each output sold and profit) to the required quality points? Answer this by running a two-way SolverTable with these three outputs. You can choose the values of the two inputs to vary.

10. In Chandler's blending model suppose there is a chemical ingredient called C1 that both gasoline and heating oil need. At least 3% of every barrel of gasoline must be C1, and at least 5% of every barrel of heating oil must be C1. Suppose that 4% of all crude oil 1 is C1 and 6% of all crude oil 2

is C1. Modify the model to incorporate the constraints on C1, and then optimize. Don't forget to clear denominators.

11. In the current version of Chandler's blending model, a barrel of any input results in a barrel of output. However, in a real blending problem there can be losses. Suppose a barrel of input results in only a fraction of a barrel of output. Specifically, each barrel of either crude oil used for gasoline results in only 0.95 barrel of gasoline, and each barrel of either crude used for heating oil results in only 0.97 barrel of heating oil. Modify the model to incorporate these losses and then find the optimal solution.

Level B

12. We warned you about clearing denominators in the quality constraints. This problem indicates what happens if you don't do so.
   a. Implement the quality constraints as indicated in Inequality (14.3). Then run Solver with the simplex method. What happens? What if you run Solver with the GRG nonlinear method?
   b. Repeat part **a**, but increase the selling price of heating oil to $120 per barrel. What happens now?

14-4 LOGISTICS MODELS

In many situations a company produces products at locations called *origins* and ships these products to customer locations called *destinations*. Typically, each origin has a limited capacity that it can ship, and each destination must receive a required quantity of the product. **Logistics models** can be used to determine the minimum-cost shipping method for satisfying customer demands.

14-4a Transportation Models

We begin by assuming that the only possible shipments are those directly from an origin to a destination. That is, no shipments between origins or between destinations are allowed. Such a problem has traditionally been called a *transportation problem*.

EXAMPLE | **14.3 SHIPPING CARS FROM PLANTS TO REGIONS**

Grand Prix Automobile Company manufactures automobiles in three plants and then ships them to four regions of the country. The plants can supply the amounts listed in the right column of Table 14.4. The customer demands by region are listed in the bottom row of this table, and the unit costs of shipping an automobile from each plant to each region are listed in the middle of the table. Grand Prix wants to find the lowest-cost shipping plan for meeting the demands of the four regions without exceeding the capacities of the plants.

Table 14.4 **Input Data for Grand Prix Example**

	Region 1	Region 2	Region 3	Region 4	Capacity
Plant 1	131	218	266	120	450
Plant 2	250	116	263	278	600
Plant 3	178	132	122	180	500
Demand	450	200	300	300	

© Cengage Learning

Objective To develop an LP model for finding the least-cost way of shipping the automobiles from plants to regions, staying within plant capacities and meeting regional demands.

Where Do the Numbers Come From?

A typical transportation problem requires three sets of numbers: capacities (or supplies), demands (or requirements), and unit shipping (and possibly production) costs.

- The *capacities* indicate the most each plant can supply in a given amount of time—a month, say—under current operating conditions. In some cases it might be possible to increase the "base" capacities, by using overtime, for example. In such cases the model could be modified to determine the amounts of additional capacity to use (and pay for).

- The customer *demands* are typically estimated from some type of forecasting model (as discussed in Chapter 12). The forecasts are often based on historical customer demand data.

- The *unit shipping costs* come from a transportation cost analysis—what does it really cost to send a single automobile from any plant to any region? This is not an easy question to answer, and it requires an analysis of the best mode of transportation (such as railroad, ship, or truck). However, companies typically have the required data. Actually, the unit "shipping" cost can also include the unit production cost at each plant. However, if this cost is the same across all plants, as we are tacitly assuming here, it can be omitted from the model.

Solution

The variables and constraints required for this model are listed in Table 14.5. The company must decide exactly the number of autos to send from each plant to each region—a shipping plan. Then it can calculate the total number of autos sent out of each plant and the total number received by each region.

Table 14.5 Variables and Constraints for Transportation Model

Input variables	Plant capacities, regional demands, unit shipping costs
Decision variables (changing cells)	Number of autos sent from each plant to each region
Objective cell	Total shipping cost
Other calculated variables	Number sent out of each plant, number sent to each region
Constraints	Number sent out of each plant ≤ Plant capacity Number sent to each region ≥ Region demand

Representing Transportation in a Network Model

In a transportation problem all flows go from left to right—from origins to destinations. You will see more complex network structures in the next subsection.

A network diagram of this model appears in Figure 14.11. This diagram is typical of network models. It consists of nodes and arcs. A *node*, indicated by a circle, generally represents a geographical location. In this case the nodes on the left correspond to plants, and the nodes on the right correspond to regions. An *arc*, indicated by an arrow, generally represents a route for getting a product from one node to another. Here, the arcs all go from a plant node to a region node—from left to right.

Figure 14.11

Network Representation of Transportation Model

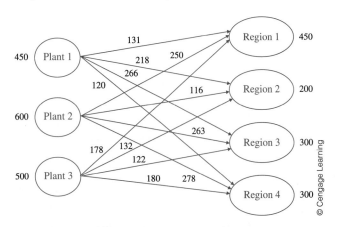

© Cengage Learning

The problem data fit nicely on such a diagram. The capacities are placed next to the plant nodes, the demands are placed next to the region nodes, and the unit shipping costs are placed on the arcs. The decision variables are usually called *flows*. They represent the amounts shipped on the various arcs. Sometimes (although not in this problem), there are upper limits on the flows on some or all of the arcs. These upper limits, called *arc capacities*, can also be shown on the diagram.[3]

Developing the Spreadsheet Model

Developing the Transportation Model

The spreadsheet model appears in Figure 14.12. (See the file **Transportation 1.xlsx**.) To develop this model, perform the following steps.

1. **Inputs.**[4] Enter the unit shipping costs, plant capacities, and region demands in the blue cells.

2. **Shipping plan.** Enter any trial values for the shipments from plants to regions in the Shipping_plan range. These are the changing cells. Note that this rectangular range is exactly the same shape as the range where the unit shipping costs are entered. This is a natural model design, and it simplifies the formulas in the following steps.

---

[3]There can even be lower limits, other than zero, on certain flows, but we don't consider any such constraints here.
[4]From here on, we might not remind you about creating range names, but we will continue to list our suggested range names on the spreadsheets.

14-4 Logistics Models **735**

Figure 14.12 Transportation Model

▲	A	B	C	D	E	F	G	H	I	J	K
1	Grand Prix transportation model								Range names used:		
2									Capacity	=Model!$I$13:$I$15	
3	Unit shipping costs								Demand	=Model!$C$18:$F$18	
4			To						Shipping_Plan	=Model!$C$13:$F$15	
5			Region 1	Region 2	Region 3	Region 4			Total_cost	=Model!$B$21	
6	From	Plant 1	$131	$218	$266	$120			Total_received	=Model!$C$16:$F$16	
7		Plant 2	$250	$116	$263	$278			Total_shipped	=Model!$G$13:$G$15	
8		Plant 3	$178	$132	$122	$180					
9											
10	Shipping plan, and constraints on supply and demand										
11			To								
12			Region 1	Region 2	Region 3	Region 4	Total shipped		Capacity		
13	From	Plant 1	150	0	0	300	450	<=	450		
14		Plant 2	100	200	0	0	300	<=	600		
15		Plant 3	200	0	300	0	500	<=	500		
16		Total received	450	200	300	300					
17			>=	>=	>=	>=					
18		Demand	450	200	300	300					
19											
20	Objective to minimize										
21	Total cost	$176,050									

© Cengage Learning

3. **Numbers shipped from plants.** To calculate the amount shipped out of each plant in the range G13:G15, select this range and click the AutoSum (Σ) button.

4. **Amounts received by regions.** Similarly, calculate the amount shipped to each region in the range C16:F16 by selecting the range and clicking the AutoSum button.

5. **Total shipping cost.** Calculate the total cost of shipping power from the plants to the regions in the Total_cost cell with the formula

   =SUMPRODUCT(C6:F8,Shipping_plan)

   This formula sums all products of unit shipping costs and amounts shipped. You now see the benefit of placing unit shipping costs and amounts shipped in similar-size rectangular ranges—you can then use the SUMPRODUCT function.

Using Solver

Invoke Solver with the settings shown in Figure 14.13. As usual, check the Non-Negative option and select the Simplex LP method before optimizing.

Discussion of the Solution

It is typical in transportation models, especially large models, that only a relatively few of the possible routes are used.

The Solver solution appears in Figure 14.12 and is illustrated graphically in Figure 14.14. The company incurs a total shipping cost of $176,050 by using the shipments listed in Figure 14.14. Except for the six routes shown, no other routes are used. Most of the shipments occur on the low-cost routes, but this is not always the case. For example, the route from plant 2 to region 1 is relatively expensive, and it is used. On the other hand, the route from plant 3 to region 2 is relatively cheap, but it is not used. A good shipping plan tries to use cheap routes, but it is constrained by capacities and demands.

Note that the available capacity is not all used. The reason is that total capacity is 1550, whereas total demand is only 1250. Even though the demand constraints are of the "≥" type, there is clearly no reason to send the regions more than they request because it only increases shipping costs. Therefore, the optimal plan sends them the minimal amounts they request and no more. In fact, the demand constraints could have been modeled as "=" constraints, and Solver would have found exactly the same solution.

Figure 14.13

Solver Dialog Box
for Transportation
Model

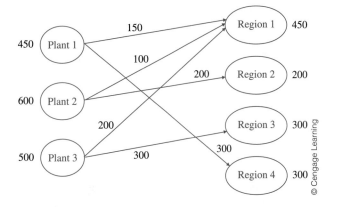

Solver Parameters

Se_t Objective: Total_cost

To: ○ Max ● Mi_n ○ _Value Of: 0

_By Changing Variable Cells:

Shipping_Plan

_Subject to the Constraints:

Total_shipped <= Capacity
Total_received >= Demand

Add
_Change
_Delete
_Reset All
Load/Save

☑ Ma_ke Unconstrained Variables Non-Negative

_Select a Solving Method: Simplex LP O_ptions

Solving Method
Select the GRG Nonlinear engine for Solver Problems that are smooth nonlinear. Select the LP Simplex engine for linear Solver Problems, and select the Evolutionary engine for Solver problems that are non-smooth.

Help _Solve C_lose

© Cengage Learning

Figure 14.14

Graphical
Representation of
Optimal Solution

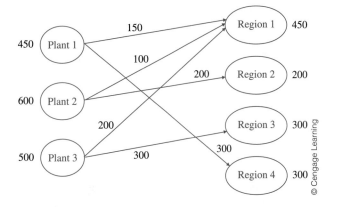

Sensitivity Analysis

There are many sensitivity analyses you could perform on the basic transportation model. For example, you could vary any one of the unit shipping costs, capacities, or demands. The effect of any such change in a single input is captured nicely in Solver's sensitivity report, shown in Figure 14.15. The top part indicates the effects of changes in the unit shipping costs. The results here are typical. For all routes with positive flows, the corresponding reduced cost is zero, whereas for all routes not currently being used, the reduced cost indicates how much *less* the unit shipping cost would have to be before the company would start shipping along that route. For example, if the unit shipping cost from plant 2 to region 3 decreased by more than $69, this route would become attractive.

Figure 14.15

Solver's Sensitivity Report for Transportation Model

	A	B	C	D	E	F	G	H
6		Adjustable Cells						
7				Final	Reduced	Objective	Allowable	Allowable
8		Cell	Name	Value	Cost	Coefficient	Increase	Decrease
9		$C$13	Plant 1 Region 1	150	0	131	119	13
10		$D$13	Plant 1 Region 2	0	221	218	1E+30	221
11		$E$13	Plant 1 Region 3	0	191	266	1E+30	191
12		$F$13	Plant 1 Region 4	300	0	120	13	239
13		$C$14	Plant 2 Region 1	100	0	250	39	72
14		$D$14	Plant 2 Region 2	200	0	116	88	116
15		$E$14	Plant 2 Region 3	0	69	263	1E+30	69
16		$F$14	Plant 2 Region 4	0	39	278	1E+30	39
17		$C$15	Plant 3 Region 1	200	0	178	13	69
18		$D$15	Plant 3 Region 2	0	88	132	1E+30	88
19		$E$15	Plant 3 Region 3	300	0	122	69	194
20		$F$15	Plant 3 Region 4	0	13	180	1E+30	13
21								
22		Constraints						
23				Final	Shadow	Constraint	Allowable	Allowable
24		Cell	Name	Value	Price	R.H. Side	Increase	Decrease
25		$G$13	Plant 1 Total shipped	450	−119	450	100	150
26		$G$14	Plant 2 Total shipped	300	0	600	1E+30	300
27		$G$15	Plant 3 Total shipped	500	−72	500	100	200
28		$C$16	Total received Region 1	450	250	450	300	100
29		$D$16	Total received Region 2	200	116	200	300	200
30		$E$16	Total received Region 3	300	194	300	200	100
31		$F$16	Total received Region 4	300	239	300	150	100

The bottom part of this report is useful because of its shadow prices. For example, plants 1 and 3 are currently shipping all of their capacity, so the company would benefit from having more capacity at these plants. In particular, the report indicates that each extra unit of capacity at plant 1 is worth $119, and each extra unit of capacity at plant 3 is worth $72. However, because the allowable increase for each of these is 100, you know that after an increase in capacity of 100 at either plant, further increases will probably be worth less than the current shadow prices.

The key to this sensitivity analysis is to modify the model slightly before running SolverTable.

One interesting analysis that cannot be performed with Solver's sensitivity report is to keep shipping costs and capacities constant and allow all of the demands to change by a certain percentage (positive or negative). To perform this analysis, use SolverTable, with the varying percentage as the single input. Then keep track of the total cost and any particular amounts shipped of interest. The key to doing this correctly is to modify the model slightly, as illustrated in the previous chapter and Example 14.1, before running SolverTable. The appropriate modifications appear in the third sheet of the finished version of the **Transportation 1.xlsx** file. Then run SolverTable, allowing the percentage change in all demands to vary from −20% to 30% in increments of 5%, and keep track of total cost. As the table in Figure 14.16 shows, the total shipping cost increases at an increasing rate as the demands increase. However, at some point the problem has no feasible solutions. As soon as the total demand is greater than the total capacity, it is impossible to meet all demand.

An Alternative Model

The transportation model in Figure 14.12 is a very natural one. In the graphical representation in Figure 14.11, note that all arcs go from left to right, that is, from plants to regions. Therefore, the rectangular range of shipments allows you to calculate shipments out of plants as row sums and shipments into regions as column sums. In anticipation of later models in this chapter, however, where the graphical network

738 Chapter 14 Optimization Models

Figure 14.16

Sensitivity Analysis to Percentage Changes in All Demands

	A	B	C	D	E	F	G	H
3	% change in demands (cell $I$10) values along side, output cell(s) along top							
4		Total_cost	Increase					
5	–20%	$130,850						
6	–15%	$140,350	$9,500					
7	–10%	$149,850	$9,500					
8	–5%	$162,770	$12,920					
9	0%	$176,050	$13,280					
10	5%	$189,330	$13,280					
11	10%	$202,610	$13,280					
12	15%	$215,890	$13,280					
13	20%	$229,170	$13,280					
14	25%	Not feasible						
15	30%	Not feasible						

can be more complex, we present an alternative model of the transportation problem. (See the file **Transportation 2.xlsx**.)

First, it is useful to introduce some additional network terminology. Recall that flows are the amounts shipped on the various arcs. The direction of the arcs indicates which way the flows are allowed to travel. An arc pointed into a node is called an *inflow*, whereas an arrow pointed out of a node is called an *outflow*. In the basic transportation model, all outflows originate from suppliers, and all inflows go toward demanders. However, general networks can have both inflows and outflows for any given node.

With this general structure in mind, the typical network model has one changing cell per arc. It indicates how much (if any) to send along that arc in the direction of the arrow. Therefore, it is often useful to model network problems by listing all of the arcs and their corresponding flows in one long list. Then constraints can be indicated in a separate section of the spreadsheet. Specifically, for each node in the network, there is a **flow balance constraint**. These flow balance constraints for the basic transportation model are simply the supply and demand constraints already discussed, but they can be more general for other network models, as will be discussed in the next subsection.

Although this model is possibly less natural than the original model, it generalizes better to other logistics models.

The alternative model of the Grand Prix problem appears in Figure 14.17. The plant and region indexes and the associated unit shipping costs are entered manually in the range

Figure 14.17 Alternative Form of Transportation Model

	A	B	C	D	E	F	G	H	I	J	K	L	M
1	Grand Prix transportation model: a more general network formulation										Range names used:		
2											Capacity	=Model!$I$6:$I$8	
3	Network structure and flows					Flow balance constraints					Demand	=Model!$I$12:$I$15	
4	Origin	Destination	Unit cost	Flow		Capacity constraints					Destination	=Model!$B$5:$B$16	
5	1	1	131	150		Plant	Outflow		Capacity		Flow	=Model!$D$5:$D$16	
6	1	2	218	0		1	450	<=	450		Inflow	=Model!$G$12:$G$15	
7	1	3	266	0		2	300	<=	600		Origin	=Model!$A$5:$A$16	
8	1	4	120	300		3	500	<=	500		Outflow	=Model!$G$6:$G$8	
9	2	1	250	100							Total_Cost	=Model!$B$19	
10	2	2	116	200		Demand constraints							
11	2	3	263	0		Region	Inflow		Demand				
12	2	4	278	0		1	450	>=	450				
13	3	1	178	200		2	200	>=	200				
14	3	2	132	0		3	300	>=	300				
15	3	3	122	300		4	300	>=	300				
16	3	4	180	0									
17													
18	Objective to minimize												
19	Total Cost	$176,050											

A5:C16. Each row in this range corresponds to an arc in the network. For example, row 12 corresponds to the arc from plant 2 to region 4, with unit shipping cost $278. Then the changing cells for the flows are in column D. (If there were arc capacities, they could be placed to the right of the flows.)

The flow balance constraints are conceptually straightforward. Each cell in the Outflow and Inflow ranges in column G contains the appropriate sum of flows. For example, cell G6, the outflow from plant 1, represents the sum of cells D5 through D8, whereas cell G12, the inflow to plant 1, represents the sum of cells D5, D9, and D13. Fortunately, there is an easy way to enter these summation formulas.[5] The trick is to use Excel's built-in SUMIF function, in the form **=SUMIF(compareRange,criterion,sumRange)**. For example, the formula in cell G6 is

=SUMIF(Origin,F6,Flow)

This formula compares the plant number in cell F6 to the Origin range in column A and sums all flows where they are equal—that is, it sums all flows out of plant 1. This formula can be copied down to cell G8 to obtain the flows out of the other plants. For flows into regions, the similar formula in cell G12 for the flow into region 1 is

=SUMIF(Destination,F12,Flow)

and this can be copied down to cell G15 for flows into the other regions. In general, the SUMIF function finds all cells in the first argument that satisfy the criterion in the second argument and then sums the corresponding cells in the third argument. It is a very handy function—and not just for network modeling.

Excel Function: SUMIF

The SUMIF function is useful for summing values in a certain range if cells in a related range satisfy a given condition. It has the syntax =SUMIF(compareRange,criterion,sumRange), where compareRange and sumRange are similar-size ranges. This formula checks each cell in compareRange to see whether it satisfies the criterion. If it does, it adds the corresponding value in sumRange to the overall sum. For example, =SUMIF(A12:A13,1,D12:D23) sums all values in the range D12:D23 where the corresponding cell in the range A12:A23 has the value 1.

This use of the SUMIF function, along with the list of origins, destinations, unit costs, and flows in columns A through D, is the key to the model. The rest is straightforward. The total cost is a SUMPRODUCT of unit costs and flows, and the Solver dialog box is set up as shown in Figure 14.18.

The alternative network model not only accommodates more general networks, but it is more efficient because it has fewer changing cells.

This alternative model generalizes nicely to other network problems. Essentially, it shows that all network models look alike. There is an additional benefit from this alternative model. Suppose that flows from certain plants to certain regions are not allowed. (Maybe no roads exist.) It is not easy to disallow such routes in the original model. One option is to allow the "disallowed" routes but to impose extremely large unit shipping costs on them. This works, but it is wasteful because it adds changing cells that do not really belong in the model. However, the alternative network model simply omits arcs that are not allowed. For example, if the route from plant 2 to region 4 is not allowed, you simply omit the data in the range A12:D12. This creates a model with exactly as many changing cells as allowable arcs. This additional benefit can be very valuable when the number of potential arcs in the network is huge—even though the vast majority of them are disallowed—which is exactly the situation in many large network models.

---

[5]Try entering these formulas as simple sums even for a 3 × 4 transportation model, and you will see why the SUMIF function is so handy.

Figure 14.18
Solver Dialog Box
for Alternative
Transportation
Model

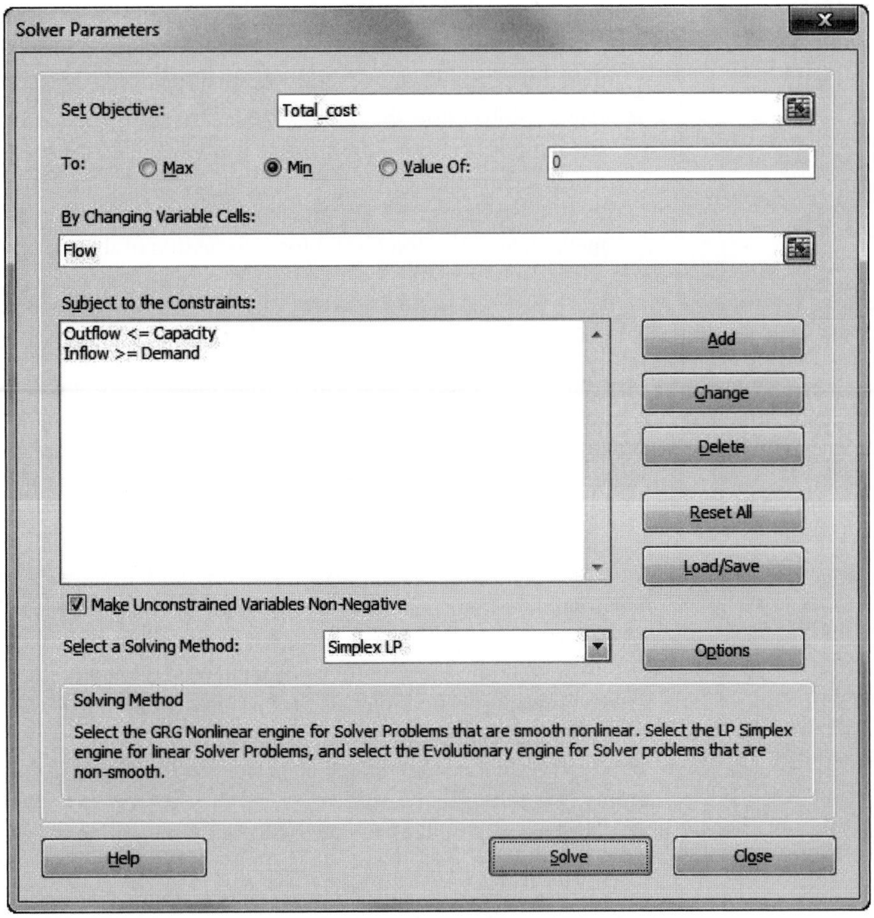

Figure 14.18 Solver Dialog Box for Alternative Transportation Model

We do not necessarily recommend this more general network model for simple transportation problems. In fact, it is probably less natural than the original model in Figure 14.12. However, it paves the way for the more complex network problems discussed next.

Modeling Issues

Depending on how you treat the demand constraints, you can get several varieties of the basic transportation model.

■ The customer demands in typical transportation problems can be handled in one of two ways. First, you can think of these forecasted demands as minimal requirements that must be sent to the customers. This is how regional demands were treated here. Alternatively, you could consider the demands as maximal sales quantities, the most each region can sell. Then you would constrain the amounts sent to the regions to be less than or equal to the forecasted demands. Whether the demand constraints are expressed as "≥" or "≤" (or even "=") constraints depends on the context of the problem—do the dealers need at least this many, do they need exactly this many, or can they sell only this many?

■ If all the supplies and demands for a transportation problem are integers, the optimal Solver solution automatically has integer-valued shipments. Explicit integer constraints are not required. This is a very important benefit. It means that the "fast" simplex method can be used rather than much slower integer algorithms.

■ Shipping costs are often nonlinear (and "nonsmooth") due to quantity discounts. For example, if it costs $3 per item to ship up to 100 items between locations and $2 per item for each additional item, the proportionality assumption of LP is violated and the resulting transportation model is nonlinear. Shipping problems that involve quantity discounts are generally quite difficult to solve.

- Excel's Solver uses the simplex method to solve transportation problems. There is a streamlined version of the simplex method, called the *transportation simplex method*, that is much more efficient than the ordinary simplex method for transportation problems. Large transportation problems are usually solved with the transportation simplex method. See Winston (2003) for a discussion of the transportation simplex method. ∎

14-4b Other Logistics Models

The objective of many real-world network models is to ship goods from one set of locations to another at minimum cost, subject to various constraints. There are many variations of these models. The simplest models include a single product that must be shipped via one mode of transportation (truck, for example) in a particular period of time. More complex models—and much larger ones—can include multiple products, multiple modes of transportation, and/or multiple time periods. We discuss one such problem in this section.

Basically, the general logistics problem is like the transportation problem except for two possible differences. First, arc capacities are often imposed on some or all of the arcs. These become simple upper-bound constraints in the model. Second and more significant, there can be inflows *and* outflows associated with any node. Nodes are generally categorized as origins, destinations, and transshipment points. An *origin* is a location that starts with a certain supply (or possibly a capacity for supplying). A *destination* is the opposite; it requires a certain amount to end up there. A *transshipment point* is a location where goods simply pass through.

The best way to think of these categories is in terms of net inflow and net outflow. The *net inflow* for any node is defined as total inflow minus total outflow for that node. The *net outflow* is the negative of this, total outflow minus total inflow. Then an origin is a node with positive net outflow, a destination is a node with positive net inflow, and a transshipment point is a node with net outflow (and net inflow) equal to 0. It is important to realize that inflows are sometimes allowed to origins, but their *net* outflows are positive. Similarly, outflows from destinations are sometimes allowed, but their *net* inflows are positive. For example, if Cincinnati and Memphis are manufacturers (origins) and Dallas and Phoenix are retail locations (destinations), then it is possible that flow could go from Cincinnati to Memphis to Dallas to Phoenix.

There are typically two types of constraints in logistics models (besides nonnegativity of flows). The first type represents the arc capacity constraints, which are simple upper bounds on the arc flows. The second type represents the **flow balance constraints**, one for each node. For an origin, this constraint is typically of the form **Net Outflow = Capacity** or possibly **Net Outflow ≤ Capacity**. For a destination, it is typically of the form **Net Inflow >= Demand** or possibly **Net Inflow = Demand**. For a transshipment point, it is of the form **Net Inflow = 0** (which is equivalent to **Net Outflow = 0**).

It is easy to visualize these constraints in a graphical representation of the network by simply examining the flows on the arrows leading into and out of the various nodes. We illustrate a typical logistics model in Example 14.4.

> ### FUNDAMENTAL INSIGHT
>
> #### Flow Balance Constraints
> All network optimization models have some form of flow balance constraints at the various nodes of the network. This flow balance relates the amount that enters the node to the amount that leaves the node. In many network models, the simple structure of these flow balance constraints guarantees that the optimal solutions have integer values. It also enables specialized network versions of the simplex method to solve the huge network models typically encountered in real logistics applications.

EXAMPLE | **14.4 PRODUCING AND SHIPPING TOMATO PRODUCTS AT REDBRAND**

RedBrand Company produces a tomato product at three plants. This product can be shipped directly to the company's two customers or it can first be shipped to the company's two warehouses and then to the customers. Figure 14.19 is a network representation of RedBrand's problem. Nodes 1, 2, and 3 represent the plants (these are the origins, denoted by S for supplier), nodes 4 and 5 represent the warehouses (these are the transshipment points, denoted by T), and nodes 6 and 7 represent the customers (these are the destinations, denoted by D). Note that some shipments are allowed among plants, among warehouses, and among customers. Also, some arcs have arrows on both ends. This means that flow is allowed in either direction.

Figure 14.19

Graphical Representation of Logistics Model

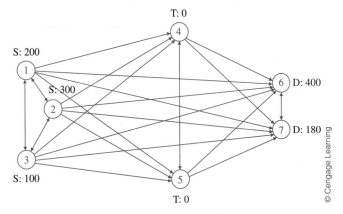

The cost of producing the product is the same at each plant, so RedBrand is concerned with minimizing the total shipping cost incurred in meeting customer demands. The production capacity of each plant (in tons per year) and the demand of each customer are shown in Figure 14.19. For example, plant 1 (node 1) has a capacity of 200, and customer 1 (node 6) has a demand of 400. In addition, the cost (in thousands of dollars) of shipping a ton of the product between each pair of locations is listed in Table 14.6, where a blank indicates that RedBrand cannot ship along that arc. We also assume that at most 200 tons of the product can be shipped between any two nodes. This is the common arc capacity. RedBrand wants to determine a minimum-cost shipping schedule.

Table 14.6 Shipping Costs for RedBrand Example (in $1000s)

From node	To node						
	1	2	3	4	5	6	7
1		5.0	3.0	5.0	5.0	20.0	20.0
2	9.0		9.0	1.0	1.0	8.0	15.0
3	0.4	8.0		1.0	0.5	10.0	12.0
4					1.2	2.0	12.0
5				0.8		2.0	12.0
6							1.0
7						7.0	

Objective   To develop an LP model for finding the minimum-cost way to ship the tomato product from suppliers to customers, possibly through warehouses, so that customer demands are met and supplier capacities are not exceeded.

Where Do the Numbers Come From?

The network configuration itself would come from geographical considerations—which routes are physically possible (or sensible) and which are not. The numbers would be derived as in the Grand Prix automobile example. (See Example 14.3 for further discussion.)

Solution

The variables and constraints for RedBrand's model are listed in Table 14.7. The key to the model is handling the flow balance constraints. You will see exactly how to implement these when we give step-by-step instructions for developing the spreadsheet model. However, it is not enough, say, to specify that the flow out of plant 2 is less than or equal to the capacity of plant 2. The reason is that there might also be flow *into* plant 2 (from another plant). Therefore, the correct flow balance constraint for plant 2 is that the flow out of it must be less than or equal to its capacity plus any flow into it. Equivalently, the *net* outflow from plant 2 must be less than or equal to its capacity.

Table 14.7 Variables and Constraints for RedBrand Model

Input variables	Plant capacities, customer demands, unit shipping costs on allowable arcs, common arc capacity
Decision variables (changing cells)	Shipments on allowed arcs
Objective cell	Total cost
Other calculated variables	Flows into and out of nodes
Constraints	Flow on each arc ≤ Common arc capacity Flow balance at each node

Developing the Spreadsheet Model

To set up the spreadsheet model, proceed as follows. (See Figure 14.20 and the file **RedBrand Logistics 1.xlsx**. Also, refer to the network in Figure 14.19.)

Figure 14.20 Logistics Model

	A	B	C	D	E	F	G	H	I	J	K
1	RedBrand shipping model										
2											
3	Inputs										
4	Common arc capacity	200									
5											
6	Network structure, flows, and arc capacity constraints							Node balance constraints			
7	Origin	Destination	Unit Cost	Flow		Arc Capacity		Plant constraints			
8	1	2	5	0	<=	200		Node	Plant net outflow		Plant capacity
9	1	3	3	180	<=	200		1	180	<=	200
10	1	4	5	0	<=	200		2	300	<=	300
11	1	5	5	0	<=	200		3	100	<=	100
12	1	6	20	0	<=	200					
13	1	7	20	0	<=	200		Warehouse constraints			
14	2	1	9	0	<=	200		Node	Warehouse net outflow		Required
15	2	3	9	0	<=	200		4	0	=	0
16	2	4	1	120	<=	200		5	0	=	0
17	2	5	1	0	<=	200					
18	2	6	8	180	<=	200		Customer constraints			
19	2	7	15	0	<=	200		Node	Customer net inflow		Customer demand
20	3	1	0.4	0	<=	200		6	400	>=	400
21	3	2	8	0	<=	200		7	108	>=	180
22	3	4	1	80	<=	200					
23	3	5	0.5	200	<=	200		Range names used			
24	3	6	10	0	<=	200		Arc_Capacity	=Model!$F$8:$F$33		
25	3	7	12	0	<=	200		Customer_demand	=Model!$K$20:$K$21		
26	4	5	1.2	0	<=	200		Customer_net_inflow	=Model!$I$20:$I$21		
27	4	6	2	200	<=	200		Destination	=Model!$B$8:$B$33		
28	4	7	12	0	<=	200		Flow	=Model!$D$8:$D$33		
29	5	4	0.8	0	<=	200		Origin	=Model!$A$8:$A$33		
30	5	6	2	200	<=	200		Plant_capacity	=Model!$K$9:$K$11		
31	5	7	12	0	<=	200		Plant_net_outflow	=Model!$I$9:$I$11		
32	6	7	1	180	<=	200		Total_cost	=Model!$B$36		
33	7	6	7	0	<=	200		Unit_Cost	=Model!$C$8:$C$33		
34								Warehouse_net_outflow	=Model!$I$15:$I$16		
35	Objective to minimize										
36	Total cost	$3,260									

1. **Origins and destinations.** Enter the node numbers (1 to 7) for the origins and destinations of the various arcs in the range A8:B33. Note that the disallowed arcs are not entered in this list.

2. **Input data.** Enter the unit shipping costs (in thousands of dollars), the common arc capacity, the plant capacities, and the customer demands in the blue cells. Again, only the nonblank entries in Table 14.6 are used to fill the column of unit shipping costs.

3. **Flows on arcs.** Enter *any* initial values for the flows in the range D8:D33. These are the changing cells.

4. **Arc capacities.** To indicate a common arc capacity for all arcs, enter the formula

   =$B$4

   in cell F8 and copy it down column F.

5. **Flow balance constraints.** Nodes 1, 2, and 3 are supply nodes, nodes 4 and 5 are transshipment points, and nodes 6 and 7 are demand nodes. Therefore, set up the left sides of the flow balance constraints appropriately for these three cases. Specifically, enter the net *outflow* for node 1 in cell I9 with the formula

   =SUMIF(Origin,H9,Flow)-SUMIF(Destination,H9,Flow)

   and copy it down to cell I11. This formula subtracts flows into node 1 from flows out of node 1 to obtain net outflow for node 1. Next, copy this *same* formula to cells I15 and I16 for the warehouses. (Remember that, for transshipment nodes, the left side of the constraint can be net outflow *or* net inflow, whichever you prefer. The reason is that if net outflow is zero, net inflow must also be zero.) Finally, enter the net *inflow* for node 6 in cell I20 with the formula

   =SUMIF(Destination,H20,Flow)-SUMIF(Origin,H20,Flow)

   and copy it to cell I21. This formula subtracts flows out of node 6 from flows into node 6 to obtain the net inflow for node 6.

6. **Total shipping cost.** Calculate the total shipping cost (in thousands of dollars) in cell B36 with the formula

   =SUMPRODUCT(Unit_cost,Flow)

We generally prefer positive numbers on the right sides of constraints. This is why we calculate net outflows for origins and net inflows for destinations.

Using Solver

The Solver dialog box should be set up as in Figure 14.21. The objective is to minimize total shipping costs, subject to the three types of flow balance constraints and the arc capacity constraints.

Discussion of the Solution

The optimal solution in Figure 14.20 indicates that RedBrand's customer demand can be satisfied with a shipping cost of $3,260,000. This solution appears graphically in Figure 14.22. Note in particular that plant 1 produces 180 tons (under capacity) and ships it all to plant 3, not directly to warehouses or customers. Also, note that all shipments from the warehouses go directly to customer 1. Then customer 1 ships 180 tons to customer 2. We purposely chose unit shipping costs (probably unrealistic ones) to produce this type of behavior, just to show that it *can* occur. As you can see, the costs of shipping from plant 1 directly to warehouses or customers are relatively large compared to the cost of shipping directly to plant 3. Similarly, the costs of shipping from plants or warehouses directly to

Figure 14.21
Solver Dialog Box for Logistics Model

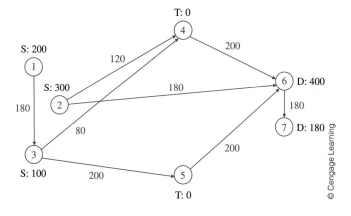

Solver Parameters

Se_t Objective: | Total_cost |

To: ○ Ma_x ● Mi_n ○ _Value Of: | 0 |

_By Changing Variable Cells:
| Flow |

Su_bject to the Constraints:
```
Customer_net_inflow >= Customer_demand
Flow <= Arc_Capacity
Plant_net_outflow <= Plant_capacity
Warehouse_net_outflow = 0
```

Add
Change
Delete
Reset All
Load/Save

☑ Ma_ke Unconstrained Variables Non-Negative

S_elect a Solving Method: | Simplex LP | ▼ | Options

Solving Method

Select the GRG Nonlinear engine for Solver Problems that are smooth nonlinear. Select the LP Simplex engine for linear Solver Problems, and select the Evolutionary engine for Solver problems that are non-smooth.

Help   Solve   Close

© Cengage Learning

Figure 14.22
Optimal Flows for Logistics Model

© Cengage Learning

customer 2 are prohibitive. Therefore, RedBrand ships to customer 1 and lets customer 1 forward some of its shipment to customer 2.

Sensitivity Analysis

How much effect does the arc capacity have on the optimal solution? Currently, three of the arcs with positive flow are at the arc capacity of 200. You can use SolverTable to see how sensitive this number and the total cost are to the arc capacity[6]. In this case the single

---

[6]Note that Solver's sensitivity report would not answer our question. This report is useful only for one-at-a-time changes in inputs, and here we are simultaneously changing the upper limit for *each* flow. However, this report (its bottom section) can be used to assess the effects of changes in plant capacities or customer demands.

input cell for SolverTable is cell B4, which is varied from 150 to 300 in increments of 25. Two quantities are designated as outputs: total cost and the number of arcs at arc capacity. As before, if you want to keep track of an output that does not already exist, you can create it with an appropriate formula in a new cell before running SolverTable. Specifically, you can enter the formula **=COUNTIF(Flow,B4)** in an unused cell. This formula counts the arcs with flow equal to arc capacity. (See the finished version of the file for a note about this formula.)

Excel Function: COUNTIF

The COUNTIF function counts the number of values in a given range that satisfy some criterion. The syntax is **=COUNTIF(range, criterion)***. For example, the formula* **=COUNTIF(D8:D33,150)** *counts the number of cells in the range D8:D33 that contain the value 150. This formula could also be entered as* **=COUNTIF(D8:D33,"=150")***. Similarly, the formula* **=COUNTIF(D8:D33,">=100")** *counts the number of cells in this range with values greater than or equal to 100.*[7]

The SolverTable output in Figure 14.23 is what you would expect. As the arc capacity decreases, more flows bump up against it, and the total cost increases. But even when the arc capacity is increased to 300, two flows are constrained by it. In this sense, even this large an arc capacity costs RedBrand money.

Figure 14.23
Sensitivity to Arc Capacity

◢	A	B	C	D	E	F	G
3	Common arc capacity (cell $B$4) values along side, output cell(s) along top						
4		Total_cost	Arcs_at_capacity				
5	150	$4,120	5				
6	175	$3,643	6				
7	200	$3,260	3				
8	225	$2,998	3				
9	250	$2,735	3				
10	275	$2,473	3				
11	300	$2,320	2				

© Cengage Learning

Modeling Issues

- There are many variations of this basic logistics model. Two variations are illustrated in the files **RedBrand Logistics 2 Finished.xlsx** and **RedBrand Logistics 3 Finished.xlsx**. In the first variation, two products compete for the same arc capacity. In the second, there is shrinkage at the warehouses due to spoiling.

---

[7]The COUNTIF and SUMIF functions are limited in that they allow only one condition, such as ">=10". For this reason, Microsoft added two new functions in Excel 2007, COUNTIFS and SUMIFS, that allow multiple conditions. You can learn about them in online help.

- Excel's Solver uses the simplex method to solve logistics models. However, the simplex method can be simplified dramatically for these types of models. The simplified version of the simplex method, called the *network simplex method*, is much more efficient than the ordinary simplex method. Specialized computer codes have been written to implement the network simplex method, and all large logistics problems are solved by using the network simplex method. This is fortunate because real logistics models tend to be extremely large. See Winston (2003) for a discussion of this method.

- If the given supplies and demands for the nodes are integers and all arc capacities are integers, the logistics model always has an optimal solution with all integer flows. Again, this is very fortunate for large problems—you get integer solutions "for free" without having to use an integer programming algorithm. Note, however, that this "integers for free" benefit is guaranteed only for the basic logistics model, as in the original RedBrand model. When the model is modified in certain ways, such as by adding a shrinkage factor, the optimal solution is no longer guaranteed to be integer-valued. ∎

PROBLEMS

Level A

13. In the original Grand Prix example, the total capacity of the three plants is 1550, well above the total customer demand. Would it help to have 100 more units of capacity at plant 1? What is the most Grand Prix would be willing to pay for this extra capacity? Answer the same questions for plant 2 and for plant 3. Explain why extra capacity can be valuable even though the company already has more total capacity than it requires.

14. The optimal solution to the original Grand Prix problem indicates that with a unit shipping cost of $132, the route from plant 3 to region 2 is evidently too expensive—no autos are shipped along this route. Use SolverTable to see how much this unit shipping cost would have to be reduced before some autos would be shipped along this route.

15. In the RedBrand example, suppose the plants cannot ship to each other and the customers cannot ship to each other. Modify the model appropriately, and rerun Solver. How much does the total cost increase because of these disallowed routes?

16. Modify the RedBrand example so that all flows must be from plants to warehouses and from warehouses to customers. Disallow all other arcs. How much does this restriction cost RedBrand, relative to the original optimal shipping cost?

17. In the RedBrand example, the costs for shipping from plants or warehouses to customer 2 were purposely made high so that it would be optimal to ship to customer 1 and then let customer 1 ship to customer 2. Use SolverTable appropriately to do the following. Decrease the unit shipping costs from plants and warehouses to customer 1, all by the same amount, until it is no longer optimal for customer 1 to ship to customer 2. Describe what happens to the optimal shipping plan at this point.

18. In the RedBrand example the arc capacity is the same for all allowable arcs. Modify the model so that each arc has its own arc capacity. You can make up the arc capacities.

19. Continuing the previous problem, make the problem even more general by allowing upper bounds (arc capacities) *and* lower bounds for the flows on the allowable arcs. Some of the upper bounds can be very large numbers, effectively indicating that there is no arc capacity for these arcs, and the lower bounds can be zero or positive. If they are positive, they indicate that some positive flow must occur on these arcs. Modify the model appropriately to handle these upper and lower bounds. You can make up the upper and lower bounds.

20. Suppose in the original Grand Prix example that the routes from plant 2 to region 1 and from plant 3 to region 3 are not allowed. (Perhaps there are no railroad lines for these routes.) How would you modify the original model (Figure 14.12) to rule out these routes? How would you modify the alternative model (Figure 14.17) to do so? Discuss the pros and cons of these two approaches.

21. The RedBrand two-product model in the file **RedBrand Logistics 2 Finished.xlsx** assumes that the unit shipping costs are the same for both products. Modify the model so that each product has its own unit shipping costs. You can assume that the original unit shipping costs apply to product 1, and you can make up new unit shipping costs for product 2.

Level B

22. Here is a problem to challenge your intuition. In the original Grand Prix example, reduce the capacity of plant 2 to 300. Then the total capacity is equal to the total demand. Rerun Solver on the modified model. You should find that the optimal solution uses all capacity and exactly meets all demands with a total cost of $176,050. Now increase the capacity of plant 1 and the demand at region 2 by one automobile each, and optimize again. What happens to the optimal total cost? How can you explain this "more for less" paradox?

23. Continuing the previous problem (with capacity 300 at plant 2), suppose you want to see how much extra capacity and extra demand you can add to plant 1 and region 2 (the same amount to each) before the total shipping cost stops decreasing and starts increasing. Use SolverTable appropriately to find out. (You will probably need to use some trial and error on the range of input values.) Can you explain intuitively what causes the total cost to stop decreasing and start increasing?

24. Modify the original Grand Prix example by increasing the demand at each region by 200, so that total demand is well above total plant capacity. However, now interpret these "demands" as "maximum sales," the most each region can accommodate, and change the "demand" constraints to become "≤" constraints, not "≥" constraints. How does the optimal solution change? Does it make realistic sense? If not, how might you change the model to obtain a realistic solution?

25. Modify the original Grand Prix example by increasing the demand at each region by 200, so that total demand is well above total plant capacity. This means that some demands cannot be supplied. Suppose there is a unit "penalty" cost at each region for not supplying an automobile. Let these unit penalty costs be $600, $750, $625, and $550 for the four regions. Develop a model to minimize the sum of shipping costs and penalty costs for unsatisfied demands. (*Hint*: Introduce a fourth plant with plenty of capacity, and set its unit shipping costs to the regions equal to the unit penalty costs. Then interpret an auto shipped from this fictitious plant to a region as a unit of demand not satisfied.)

26. How difficult is it to expand the RedBrand model? Answer this by adding a new plant, two new warehouses, and three new customers, and modify the spreadsheet model appropriately. You can make up the required input data. Would you conclude that these types of spreadsheet models scale easily?

27. In the RedBrand model with shrinkage in the file **RedBrand Logistics 3 Finished.xlsx**, change the assumptions. Now instead of assuming that there is some shrinkage at the warehouses, assume that there is shrinkage in delivery along each *route*. Specifically, assume that a certain percentage of the units sent along each arc perish in transit—from faulty refrigeration, for example—and this percentage can differ from one arc to another. Modify the model appropriately to take this type of behavior into account. You can make up the shrinkage factors, and you can assume that arc capacities apply to the amounts originally shipped, not to the amounts after shrinkage. (Make sure your input data permit a *feasible* solution. After all, if there is too much shrinkage, it will be impossible to meet demands with available plant capacity. Increase the plant capacities if necessary.)

28. Consider a modification of the RedBrand model where there are *N* plants, *M* warehouses, and *L* customers. Assume that the only allowable arcs are from plants to warehouses and from warehouses to customers. If *all* such arcs are allowable— all plants can ship to all warehouses and all warehouses can ship to all customers—how many changing cells are in the spreadsheet model? Keeping in mind that Excel's Solver can handle at most 200 changing cells, provide some combinations of *N*, *M*, and *L* that barely stay within Solver's limit.

29. Continuing the previous problem, develop a sample model with your own choices of *N*, *M*, and *L* that barely stay within Solver's limit. You can make up any input data. The important point here is the layout and formulas of the spreadsheet model.

14-5 AGGREGATE PLANNING MODELS

In this section, we extend the production planning model discussed in Example 13.3 of the previous chapter to include a situation where the number of workers available influences the possible production levels. We allow the workforce level to be modified each period through the hiring and firing of workers. Such models, where we determine workforce levels and production schedules for a multiperiod time horizon, are called **aggregate planning models**. There are many variations of aggregate planning models, depending on the detailed assumptions made. We consider a fairly simple version and then ask you to modify it in the problems.

EXAMPLE | **14.5 WORKER AND PRODUCTION PLANNING AT SURESTEP**

During the next four months SureStep Company must meet (on time) the following demands for pairs of shoes: 3000 in month 1; 5000 in month 2; 2000 in month 3; and 1000 in month 4. At the beginning of month 1, 500 pairs of shoes are on hand, and SureStep has 100 workers. A worker is paid $1500 per month. Each worker can work up to 160 hours a month before he or she receives overtime. A worker can work up to 20 hours of overtime per month and is paid $13 per hour for overtime labor. It takes four hours of labor and $15 of raw material to produce a pair of shoes. At the beginning of each month, workers can be hired or fired. Each hired worker costs $1600, and each fired worker costs $2000. At the end of each month, a holding cost of $3 per pair of shoes left in inventory is incurred. Production in a given month can be used to meet that month's demand. SureStep wants to use LP to determine its optimal production schedule and labor policy.

Objective To develop an LP spreadsheet model that relates workforce and production decisions to monthly costs, and to find the minimum-cost solution that meets forecasted demands on time and stays within limits on overtime hours and production capacity.

Where Do the Numbers Come From?

There are a number of required inputs for this type of problem. Some, including initial inventory, holding costs, and demands, are similar to requirements for Example 13.3 in the previous chapter, so we won't discuss them again here. Others might be obtained as follows.

- The data on the current number of workers, the regular hours per worker per month, the regular hourly wage rates, and the overtime hourly rate, should be well known. The maximum number of overtime hours per worker per month is probably either the result of a policy decision by management or a clause in the workers' contracts.

- The costs for hiring and firing a worker are not trivial. The hiring cost includes training costs and the cost of decreased productivity due to the fact that a new worker must learn the job. The firing cost includes severance costs and costs due to loss of morale. Neither the hiring nor the firing cost would be simple to estimate accurately, but the human resources department should be able to estimate their values.

- The unit production cost is a combination of two inputs: the raw material cost per pair of shoes and the labor hours per pair of shoes. The raw material cost is the going rate from the supplier(s). The labor per pair of shoes represents the "production function"—the average labor required to produce a unit of the product. The operations managers should be able to supply this number.

Solution

The key to this model is choosing the correct changing cells—the decision variables that determine all outputs.

The variables and constraints for this aggregate planning model are listed in Table 14.8. As you see, there are a lot of variables to keep track of. In fact, the most difficult aspect of modeling this problem is knowing which variables the company gets to choose—the decision variables—and which variables are *determined* by these decisions. It should be clear that the company gets to choose the number of workers to hire and fire and the number of shoes to produce. Also, because management sets only an upper limit on overtime hours, it gets to decide how many overtime hours to use within this limit. But once it decides the values of these variables, everything else is determined. We will show how these are determined through detailed cell formulas, but you should mentally go through the list of "Other calculated variables" in the table and deduce how they are determined by the decision variables. Also, you should convince yourself that the three constraints listed are the ones, and the only ones, that are required.

Table 14.8   Variables and Constraints for Aggregate Planning Model

Input variables	Initial inventory of shoes, initial number of workers, number and wage rate of regular hours, maximum number and wage rate of overtime hours, hiring and firing costs, data for unit production and holding costs, forecasted demands
Decision variables (changing cells)	Monthly values for number of workers hired and fired, number of shoes produced, and overtime hours used
Objective cell	Total cost
Other calculated variables	Monthly values for workers on hand before and after hiring/firing, regular hours available, maximum overtime hours available, total production hours available, production capacity, inventory on hand after production, ending inventory, and various costs
Constraints	Overtime labor hours used ≤ Maximum overtime hours Production ≤ Capacity Inventory on hand after production ≥ Demand

© Cengage Learning

Developing the Spreadsheet Model

Developing the Basic Aggregate Planning Model

The spreadsheet model appears in Figure 14.24. (See the file **Aggregate Planning 1.xlsx**.) It can be developed as follows.

1. **Inputs and range names.** Enter the input data and create the range names listed.

2. **Production, hiring, and firing plan.** Enter *any* trial values for the number of pairs of shoes produced each month, the overtime hours used each month, the workers hired each month, and the workers fired each month. These four ranges, in rows 18, 19, 23, and 30, comprise the changing cells.

This is common in multiperiod problems. You usually have to relate a beginning value in one period to an ending value from the previous period.

3. **Workers available each month.** In cell B17 enter the initial number of workers available with the formula

   =B5

   Because the number of workers available at the beginning of any other month (before hiring and firing) is equal to the number of workers from the previous month, enter the formula

   =B20

Figure 14.24 Aggregate Planning Model

	A	B	C	D	E	F	G	H / I
1	SureStep aggregate planning model						Range names used:	
2							Forecasted_demand	=Model!$B$36:$E$36
3	Input data						Inventory_after_production	=Model!$B$34:$E$34
4	Initial inventory of shoes	500					Maximum_overtime_labor_hours_available	=Model!$B$25:$E$25
5	Initial number of workers	100					Overtime_labor_hours_used	=Model!$B$23:$E$23
6	Regular hours/worker/month	160					Production_capacity	=Model!$B$32:$E$32
7	Maximum overtime hours/worker/month	20					Shoes_produced	=Model!$B$30:$E$30
8	Hiring cost/worker	$1,600					Total_cost	=Model!$F$46
9	Firing cost/worker	$2,000					Workers_fired	=Model!$B$19:$E$19
10	Regular wages/worker/month	$1,500					Workers_hired	=Model!$B$18:$E$18
11	Overtime wage rate/hour	$13						
12	Labor hours/pair of shoes	4						
13	Raw material cost/pair of shoes	$15						
14	Holding cost/pair of shoes in inventory/month	$3						
15								
16	Worker plan	Month 1	Month 2	Month 3	Month 4			
17	Workers from previous month	100	94	93	50			
18	Workers hired	0	0	0	0			
19	Workers fired	6	1	43	0			
20	Workers available after hiring and firing	94	93	50	50			
21								
22	Regular-time hours available	15040	14880	8000	8000			
23	Overtime labor hours used	0	80	0	0			
24		<=	<=	<=	<=			
25	Maximum overtime labor hours available	1880	1860	1000	1000			
26								
27	Total hours for production	15040	14960	8000	8000			
28								
29	Production plan	Month 1	Month 2	Month 3	Month 4			
30	Shoes Produced	3760	3740	2000	1000			
31		<=	<=	<=	<=			
32	Production capacity	3760	3740	2000	2000			
33								
34	Inventory after production	4260	5000	2000	1000			
35		>=	>=	>=	>=			
36	Forecasted demand	3000	5000	2000	1000			
37	Ending inventory	1260	0	0	0			
38								
39	Monetary outputs	Month 1	Month 2	Month 3	Month 4	Totals		
40	Hiring cost	$0	$0	$0	$0	$0		
41	Firing cost	$12,000	$2,000	$86,000	$0	$100,000		
42	Regular-time wages	$141,000	$139,500	$75,000	$75,000	$430,500		
43	Overtime wages	$0	$1,040	$0	$0	$1,040		
44	Raw material cost	$56,400	$56,100	$30,000	$15,000	$157,500		
45	Holding cost	$3,780	$0	$0	$0	$3,780		
46	Totals	$213,180	$198,640	$191,000	$90,000	$692,820	←——— Objective to minimize	

in cell C17 and copy it to the range D17:E17. Then calculate the number of workers available in month 1 (after hiring and firing) in cell B20 with the formula

=B17+B18-B19

and copy this formula to the range C20:E20 for the other months.

4. **Overtime capacity.** Because each available worker can work up to 20 hours of overtime in a month, enter the formula

=$B$7*B20

in cell B25 and copy it to the range C25:E25.

In Example 13.3 from the previous chapter, production capacities were given inputs. Now they are based on the size of the workforce, which itself is a decision variable.

5. **Production capacity.** Because each worker can work 160 regular-time hours per month, calculate the regular-time hours available in month 1 in cell B22 with the formula

=$B$6*B20

and copy it to the range C22:E22 for the other months. Then calculate the total hours available for production in cell B27 with the formula

=SUM(B22:B23)

752 Chapter 14 Optimization Models

and copy it to the range C27:E27 for the other months. Finally, because it takes four hours of labor to make a pair of shoes, calculate the production capacity in month 1 with the formula

=B27/$B$12

in cell B32 and copy it to the range C32:E32.

6. **Inventory each month.** Calculate the inventory after production in month 1 (which is available to meet month 1 demand) with the formula

=B4+B30

in cell B34. For any other month, the inventory after production is the previous month's ending inventory plus that month's production, so enter the formula

=B37+C30

in cell C34 and copy it to the range D34:E34. Then calculate the month 1 ending inventory in cell B37 with the formula

=B34-B36

and copy it to the range C37:E37.

7. **Monthly costs.** Calculate the various costs shown in rows 40 through 45 for month 1 by entering the formulas

=$B$8*B18

=$B$9*B19

=$B$10*B20

=$B$11*B23

=$B$13*B30

=$B$14*B37

in cells B40 through B45. Then copy the range B40:B45 to the range C40:E45 to calculate these costs for the other months.

8. **Totals.** In row 46 and column F, use the SUM function to calculate cost totals, with the value in F46 being the overall total cost to minimize.

*Excel Tip: **Calculating Row and Column Sums with AutoSum***
A common operation in spreadsheet models is to calculate row and column sums for a rectangular range, as we did for costs in step 8. There is a very quick way to do this. Select the row and column where the sums will go (remember to press the Ctrl key to select nonadjacent ranges) and click the AutoSum (Σ) button. This enters all of the sums automatically. It even calculates the "grand sum" in the corner (cell F46 in the example) if this cell is part of the selection.

Using Solver

The Solver dialog box should be filled in as shown in Figure 14.25. Note that the changing cells include four separate named ranges. To enter these in the dialog box, drag the four ranges, keeping your finger on the Ctrl key. (Alternatively, you can drag a range, type a comma, drag a second range, type another comma, and so on.) As usual, you should also check the Non-Negative option and select the Simplex LP method before optimizing.

Note that there are integer constraints on the numbers hired and fired. You could also constrain the numbers of shoes produced to be integers. However, integer constraints

Figure 14.25
Solver Dialog Box
for Aggregate
Planning Model

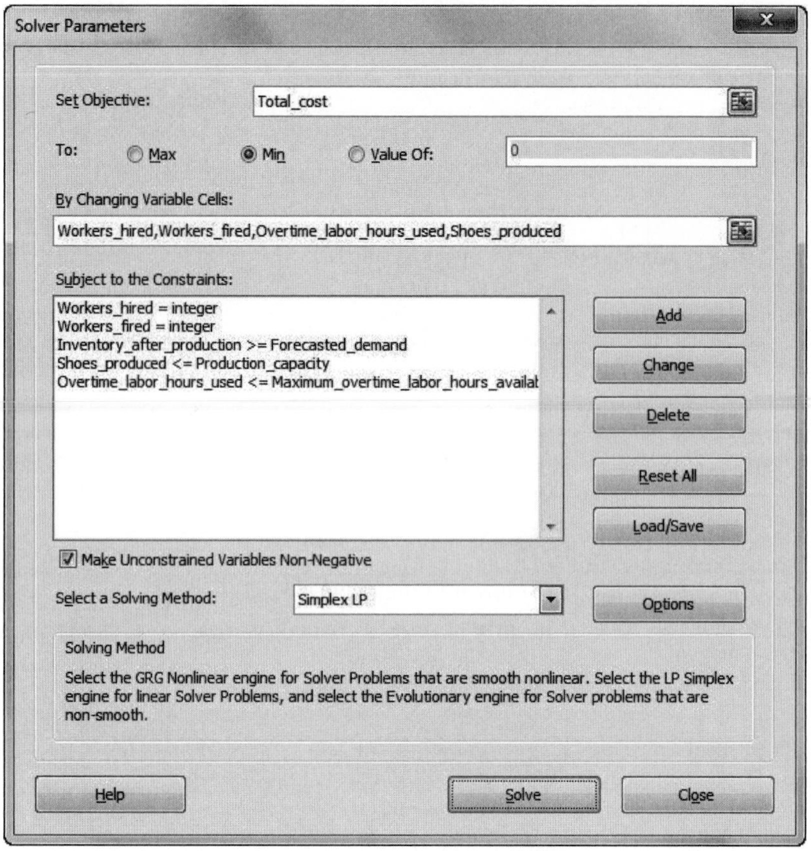

typically require longer solution times. Therefore, it is often best to omit such constraints, especially when the optimal values are fairly large, such as the production quantities in this model. If the solution then has noninteger values, you can usually round them to integers for a solution that is at least close to the optimal integer solution.

Discussion of the Solution

The optimal solution is given in Figure 14.24. Observe that SureStep should never hire any workers, and it should fire six workers in month 1, one worker in month 2, and 43 workers in month 3. Eighty hours of overtime are used, but only in month 2. The company produces over 3700 pairs of shoes during each of the first 2 months, 2000 pairs in month 3, and 1000 pairs in month 4. A total cost of $692,820 is incurred. The Solver solution will recommend overtime hours only when regular-time production capacity is exhausted. This is because overtime labor is more expensive.

Because integer constraints make a model more difficult to solve, use them sparingly—only when they are really needed.

Again, you would probably not force the number of pairs of shoes produced each month to be an integer. It makes little difference whether the company produces 3760 or 3761 pairs of shoes during a month, and forcing each month's shoe production to be an integer can greatly increase the time Solver needs to find an optimal solution. On the other hand, it is somewhat more important to ensure that the number of workers hired and fired each month is an integer, given the relatively small numbers of workers involved.

Finally, if you want to ensure that Solver finds the optimal solution in a problem where some or all of the changing cells must be integers, you should go into Options (in the Solver dialog box) and set the tolerance to zero. (This is the Integer Optimality setting starting in Excel 2010.) Otherwise, Solver might stop when it finds a solution that is only *close* to optimal.

Sensitivity Analysis

There are many possible sensitivity analyses for this SureStep model. We illustrate one of them with SolverTable, where we see how the overtime hours used and the total cost vary with the overtime wage rate.[8] The results appear in Figure 14.26. As you can see, when the wage rate is really low, the company uses considerably more overtime hours, whereas when it is sufficiently large, the company uses no overtime hours. It is not surprising that the company uses much more overtime when the overtime rate is $7 or $9 per hour. The *regular*-time wage rate is $9.375 per hour (=1500/160). Of course, the company would never pay *less* per hour for overtime than for regular time.

Figure 14.26
Sensitivity to Overtime Wage Rate

	A	B	C	D	E	F	G
3	Overtime rate (cell $B$11) values along side, output cell(s) along top						
4		Overtime_labor_hours_used_1	Overtime_labor_hours_used_2	Overtime_labor_hours_used_3	Overtime_labor_hours_used_4	Total_cost	
5	$7	1620	1660	0	0	$684,755	
6	$9	80	1760	0	0	$691,180	
7	$11	0	80	0	0	$692,660	
8	$13	0	80	0	0	$692,820	
9	$15	0	80	0	0	$692,980	
10	$17	0	80	0	0	$693,140	
11	$19	0	0	0	0	$693,220	
12	$21	0	0	0	0	$693,220	

© Cengage Learning

The Rolling Planning Horizon Approach

In reality, an aggregate planning model is usually implemented via a rolling planning horizon. To illustrate, we assume that SureStep works with a four-month planning horizon. To implement the SureStep model in the rolling planning horizon context, we view the demands as forecasts and solve a four-month model with these forecasts. However, the company would implement only the month 1 production and work scheduling recommendation. Thus (assuming that the numbers of workers hired and fired in a month must be integers) the company would hire no workers, fire six workers, and produce 3760 pairs of shoes with regular-time labor in month 1. Next, the company would observe month 1's actual demand. Suppose it is 2950. Then SureStep would begin month 2 with 1310 (= 4260 − 2950) pairs of shoes and 94 workers. It would now enter 1310 in cell B4 and 94 in cell B5 (referring to Figure 14.24). Then it would replace the demands in the Demand range with the updated forecasts for the *next* four months. Finally, SureStep would rerun Solver and use the production levels and hiring and firing recommendations in column B as the production level and workforce policy for month 2.

---

[8]Solver's sensitivity report isn't even available here because of the integer constraints.

Model with Backlogging Allowed

The term "backlogging" means that the customer's demand is met at a later date. The term "back-ordering" means the same thing.

Developing the Aggregate Planning Backlogging Model

In many situations, backlogging of demand is allowed—that is, customer demand can be met at a later date. We now show how to modify the SureStep model to include the option of backlogging demand. We assume that at the end of each month a cost of $20 is incurred for each unit of demand that remains unsatisfied at the end of the month. This is easily modeled by allowing a month's ending inventory to be negative. For example, if month 1's ending inventory is −10, a shortage cost of $200 (and no inventory holding cost) is incurred. To ensure that SureStep produces any shoes at all, we constrain the ending inventory in month 4 to be nonnegative. This implies that all demand is *eventually* satisfied by the end of the four-month planning horizon. We now need to modify the monthly cost calculations to incorporate costs due to backlogging.

There are actually several modeling approaches to this backlogging problem. We show the most natural approach in Figure 14.27. (See the file **Aggregate Planning 2.xlsx**.)

Figure 14.27 Nonlinear Aggregate Planning Model Using IF Functions

	A	B	C	D	E	F	G	H	I	J
40	**Monetary outputs**	Month 1	Month 2	Month 3	Month 4	Totals				
41	Hiring cost	$0	$0	$0	$0	$0				
42	Firing cost	$12,000	$2,000	$110,000	$0	$124,000				
43	Regular-time wages	$141,000	$139,500	$57,000	$57,000	$394,500				
44	Overtime wages	$0	$0	$0	$0	$0				
45	Raw material cost	$56,400	$55,800	$22,800	$22,500	$157,500				
46	Holding cost	$3,780	$0	$0	$0	$3,780				
47	Shortage cost	$0	$400	$10,000	$0	$10,400				
48	Totals	$213,180	$197,700	$199,800	$79,500	$690,180	← Objective to minimize			

Note the use of IF functions in rows 46 and 47 to capture the holding and shortage costs. These IF functions make the model nonlinear (and "nonsmooth"), and Solver can't handle these functions in a predictable manner. It was just lucky here! Try changing the unit shortage cost in cell B15 to $40 and rerun Solver. Then you won't be so lucky – Solver will converge to a solution that is pretty far from optimal.

To begin, enter the per-unit monthly shortage cost in cell B15. (A new row was inserted for this cost input.) Note in row 38 how the ending inventory in months 1 through 3 can be positive (leftovers) or negative (shortages). You can account correctly for the resulting costs with IF functions in rows 46 and 47. For holding costs, enter the formula

=IF(B38>0,$B$14*B38,0)

in cell B46 and copy it across. For shortage costs, enter the formula

=IF(B38<0,−$B$15*B38,0)

in cell B47 and copy it across. (The minus sign makes this a *positive* cost.)

Although these formulas accurately compute holding and shortage costs, the IF functions make the objective cell a *nonlinear* function of the changing cells, and Solver's GRG nonlinear algorithm must be used, as indicated in Figure 14.28.[9] (How do you know the model is nonlinear? Although there is a mathematical reason, it is easier to try running Solver with the simplex algorithm. Solver will then *inform* you that the model is nonlinear.)

We ran Solver with this setup from a variety of initial solutions in the changing cells, and it always found the optimal solution. But we were lucky. When certain functions, including IF, MIN, MAX, and ABS, are used to relate the objective cell to the changing cells, the resulting model becomes not only nonlinear but *nonsmooth*. Essentially, nonsmooth functions can have sharp edges or discontinuities. Solver's GRG nonlinear algorithm can handle "smooth" nonlinearities, as you will see in Section 14-8, but it has trouble with nonsmooth functions. Sometimes it gets lucky, as it did here, and other times it finds a

---

[9]GRG stands for generalized reduced gradient. This is a technical term for the mathematical algorithm used. The other algorithm available in Solver (starting with Excel 2010) is the Evolutionary algorithm. It can handle IF functions, but we will not discuss this algorithm here.

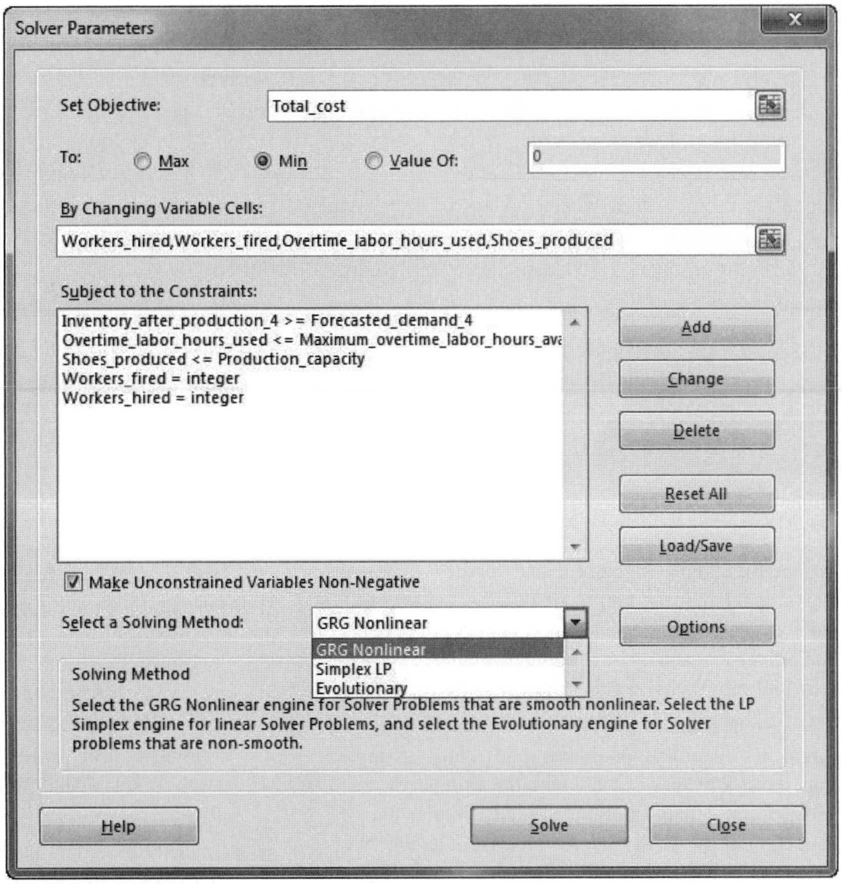

Figure 14.28
Solver Dialog
Box for the
GRG Nonlinear
Algorithm

Solver Parameters

Se_t Objective: | Total_cost |

To: ○ Max ● Mi_n ○ _V_alue Of: | 0 |

_B_y Changing Variable Cells:

| Workers_hired,Workers_fired,Overtime_labor_hours_used,Shoes_produced |

S_u_bject to the Constraints:

Inventory_after_production_4 >= Forecasted_demand_4
Overtime_labor_hours_used <= Maximum_overtime_labor_hours_ava
Shoes_produced <= Production_capacity
Workers_fired = integer
Workers_hired = integer

Add

_C_hange

_D_elete

Reset All

Load/Save

☑ Ma_k_e Unconstrained Variables Non-Negative

S_e_lect a Solving Method: | GRG Nonlinear ▼ |

GRG Nonlinear
Simplex LP
Evolutionary

O_p_tions

Solving Method

Select the GRG Nonlinear engine for Solver Problems that are smooth nonlinear. Select the LP Simplex engine for linear Solver Problems, and select the Evolutionary engine for Solver problems that are non-smooth.

Help   _S_olve   Cl_o_se

© Cengage Learning

nonoptimal solution that is not even close to the optimal solution. For example, we changed the unit shortage cost from $20 to $40 and reran Solver. Starting from a solution where all changing cells contain zero, Solver stopped at a solution with total cost $726,360, even though the optimal solution has total cost $692,820. So we weren't so lucky this time.

The moral is that you should avoid these nonsmooth functions in optimization models if at all possible. If you *do* use them, as we have done here, you should run Solver several times, starting from different initial solutions. There is still no guarantee that you will get the optimal solution, but you will see more evidence of how Solver is progressing. (Alternatively, you can use Frontline Systems's Evolutionary Solver, which became available in Excel's Solver in Excel 2010. You can also use the Evolver add-in, part of Palisade's DecisionTools® Suite.)

Solver Tip: Nonsmooth Functions
There is nothing inherently wrong with using IF, MIN, MAX, ABS, and other nonsmooth functions in spreadsheet optimization models. The problem is that Solver's GRG nonlinear algorithm cannot handle these functions in a predictable manner.

There are sometimes alternatives to using IF, MIN, MAX, and ABS functions that make a model linear. Unfortunately, these alternatives are often far from intuitive, and we will not cover them here. (If you are interested, we have included the "linearized" version of the backlogging model in the file **Aggregate Planning 3 Finished.xlsx**.) ∎

PROBLEMS

Level A

30. Extend SureStep's original (no backlogging) aggregate planning model from four to six months. Try several different values for demands in months 5 and 6, and run Solver for each. Is your optimal solution for the *first* four months the same as the one in the example?

31. The current solution to SureStep's no-backlogging aggregate planning model does quite a lot of firing. Run a one-way SolverTable with the firing cost as the input variable and the numbers fired as the outputs. Let the firing cost increase from its current value to double that value in increments of $400. Do high firing costs eventually induce the company to fire fewer workers?

32. SureStep is currently getting 160 regular-time hours from each worker per month. This is actually calculated from 8 hours per day times 20 days per month. For this, they are paid $9.375 per hour (=1500/160). Suppose workers can change their contract so that they have to work only 7.5 hours per day regular time—everything above this becomes overtime—and their regular-time wage rate increases to $10 per hour. They will still work 20 days per month. Does this change the optimal no-backlogging solution?

33. Suppose SureStep could begin a machinery upgrade and training program to increase its worker productivity. This program would result in the following values of labor hours per pair of shoes over the next four months: 4, 3.9, 3.8, and 3.8. How much would this new program be worth to SureStep, at least for this four-month planning horizon with no backlogging? How might you evaluate the program's worth *beyond* the next four months?

Level B

34. In the current no-backlogging problem, SureStep doesn't hire any workers, and it uses almost no overtime. This is evidently because of low demand. Change the demands to 6000, 8000, 5000, and 3000, and rerun Solver. Is there now any hiring and/or overtime? With this new demand pattern, explore the trade-off between hiring and overtime by running a two-way SolverTable. As inputs, use the hiring cost per worker and the maximum overtime hours allowed per worker per month, varied over reasonable ranges. As outputs, use the total number of workers hired over the four months and the total number of overtime hours used over the four months. Discuss the results.

35. In the SureStep no-backlogging problem, change the demands so that they become 6000, 8000, 5000, and 3000. Also, change the problem slightly so that newly hired workers take six hours to produce a pair of shoes during their first month of employment. After that, they take only four hours per pair of shoes. Modify the model appropriately, and use Solver to find the optimal solution.

36. You saw that the "natural" way to model SureStep's backlogging problem, with IF functions, leads to a nonsmooth model that Solver has difficulty handling. There is another version of the problem that is also difficult for Solver. Suppose SureStep wants to meet all demands on time (no backlogging), but it wants to keep its employment level as constant over time as possible. To induce this, it charges a cost of $1000 each month on the absolute difference between the beginning number of workers and the number after hiring and firing—that is, the absolute difference between the values in rows 17 and 20 of the original spreadsheet model. Implement this extra cost in the model in the "natural" way, using the ABS function. Using demands of 6000, 8000, 5000, and 3000, see how well Solver does in solving this nonsmooth model. Try several initial solutions, and see whether Solver gets the same optimal solution from each of them.

14-6 FINANCIAL MODELS

The majority of optimization examples described in management science textbooks are in the area of operations: scheduling, blending, logistics, aggregate planning, and others. This is probably warranted, because many of the most successful management science applications in the real world have been in these areas. However, optimization and other management science methods have also been applied successfully in a number of financial areas, and they deserve recognition. In this section we begin the discussion with two typical applications of LP in finance. The first involves investment strategy. The second involves pension fund management.

EXAMPLE   **14.6 FINDING AN OPTIMAL INVESTMENT STRATEGY AT BARNEY-JONES**

At the present time, the beginning of year 1, Barney-Jones Investment Corporation has $100,000 to invest for the next four years. There are five possible investments, labeled A through E. The timing of cash outflows and cash inflows for these investments is somewhat irregular. For example, to take part in investment A, cash must be invested at the beginning of year 1, and for every dollar invested, there are returns of $0.50 and $1.00 at the beginnings of years 2 and 3. Information for the other investments follows, where all returns are per dollar invested:[10]

- Investment B: Invest at the beginning of year 2, receive returns of $0.50 and $1.00 at the beginnings of years 3 and 4
- Investment C: Invest at the beginning of year 1, receive return of $1.20 at the beginning of year 2
- Investment D: Invest at the beginning of year 4, receive return of $1.90 at the beginning of year 5
- Investment E: Invest at the beginning of year 3, receive return of $1.50 at the beginning of year 4

We assume that any amounts can be invested in these strategies and that the returns are the same for each dollar invested. However, to create a diversified portfolio, Barney-Jones wants to limit the amount put into any investment to $75,000. The company wants an investment strategy that maximizes the amount of cash on hand at the beginning of year 5. At the beginning of any year, it can invest only cash on hand, which includes returns from previous investments. Any cash not invested in any year can be put in a short-term money market account that earns 3% annually.

Objective   To develop an LP model that relates investment decisions to total ending cash, and to use Solver to find the strategy that maximizes ending cash and invests no more than a given amount in any one investment.

Where Do the Numbers Come From?

There is no mystery here. We assume that the terms of each investment are spelled out, so that Barney-Jones knows exactly when money must be invested and what the amounts and timing of returns will be. Of course, this would not be the case for many real-world

---

[10]You might criticize this model for assuming *known* returns in future years. If the returns are actually uncertain with given probability distributions, the RISKOptimizer tool in @RISK (part of Palisade's DecisionTools Suite) can be used to find the investment strategy that maximizes the *expected* return. However, we won't discuss this possibility here.

investments, such as money put into the stock market, where considerable uncertainty is involved. We consider one such example of investing with uncertainty when we study portfolio optimization in Section 14-8.

Solution

There are often multiple equivalent ways to state a constraint. You can choose the one that is most natural for you.

The variables and constraints for this investment model are listed in Table 14.9. On the surface, this problem appears to be very straightforward. You must decide how much to invest in the available investments at the beginning of each year, using only the cash available. If you try modeling this problem without our help, however, we suspect that you will have some difficulty. It took us a few tries to get a model that is easy to read and generalizes to other similar investment problems. Note that the second constraint in the table can be expressed in two ways. It can be expressed as shown, where the cash on hand *after* investing is nonnegative, or it can be expressed as "cash invested in any year must be less than or equal to cash on hand at the beginning of that year." These are equivalent. The one you choose is a matter of taste.

Table 14.9 Variables and Constraints for Investment Model

Input variables	Timing of investments and returns, initial cash, maximum amount allowed in any investment, money market rate on cash
Decision variables (changing cells)	Amounts to invest in investments
Objective cell	Ending cash at the beginning of year 5
Other calculated variables	Cash available at the beginning of years 2–4
Constraints	Amount in any investment ≤ Max investment amount Cash on hand after investing each year ≥ 0

© Cengage Learning

Developing the Spreadsheet Model

Developing the Investment Model

Note how the two input tables allow you to create copyable SUMPRODUCT formulas for cash outflows and inflows. Careful spreadsheet planning can often greatly simplify the necessary formulas.

The spreadsheet model for this investment problem appears in Figure 14.29. (See the file **Investing.xlsx**.) To set up this spreadsheet, proceed as follows.

1. **Inputs and range names.** As usual, enter the given inputs in the blue cells and name the ranges indicated. Pay particular attention to the two shaded tables. This is probably the first model you have encountered where model development is affected significantly by the way you enter the inputs, specifically, the information about the investments. We suggest separating cash outflows from cash inflows, as shown in the two ranges B11:F14 and B19:F23. The top table indicates when investments can be made, where $0.00 indicates no possible investment, and $1.00 indicates a dollar of investment. The bottom table then indicates the amounts and timing of returns per dollar invested.

2. **Investment amounts.** Enter *any* trial values in the Dollars_invested range. This range contains the changing cells. Also put a link to the maximum investment amount per investment by entering the formula

    =$B$5

    in cell B28 and copying it across.

3. **Cash balances and flows.** The key to the model is the section in rows 32 through 36. For each year, you need to calculate the beginning cash held from the previous year, the returns from investments that are due in that year, the investments made in that year, and cash balance after investments. Begin by entering the initial cash in cell B32 with the formula

    =B4

Figure 14.29 Investment Model

	A	B	C	D	E	F	G	H	I	J
1	Investments with irregular timing of returns							Range names used		
2								Cash_after_investing	=Model!$E$32:$E$35	
3	Inputs							Dollars_invested	=Model!$B$26:$F$26	
4	Initial amount to invest	$100,000						Final_cash	=Model!$B$38	
5	Maximum per investment	$75,000						Maximum_per_investment	=Model!$B$28:$F$28	
6	Interest rate on cash	3%								
7										
8	Cash outlays on investments (all incurred at beginning of year)									
9		Investment								
10	Year	A	B	C	D	E				
11	1	$1.00	$0.00	$1.00	$0.00	$0.00				
12	2	$0.00	$1.00	$0.00	$0.00	$0.00				
13	3	$0.00	$0.00	$0.00	$0.00	$1.00				
14	4	$0.00	$0.00	$0.00	$1.00	$0.00				
15										
16	Cash returns from investments (all incurred at beginning of year)									
17		Investment								
18	Year	A	B	C	D	E				
19	1	$0.00	$0.00	$0.00	$0.00	$0.00				
20	2	$0.50	$0.00	$1.20	$0.00	$0.00				
21	3	$1.00	$0.50	$0.00	$0.00	$0.00				
22	4	$0.00	$1.00	$0.00	$0.00	$1.50				
23	5	$0.00	$0.00	$0.00	$1.90	$0.00				
24										
25	Investment decisions									
26	Dollars invested	$64,286	$75,000	$35,714	$75,000	$75,000				
27		<=	<=	<=	<=	<=				
28	Maximum per investment	$75,000	$75,000	$75,000	$75,000	$75,000				
29										
30	Constraints on cash balance									
31	Year	Beginning cash	Returns from investments	Cash invested	Cash after investing					
32	1	$100,000	$0	$100,000	$0	>=	0			
33	2	$0	$75,000	$75,000	-$0	>=	0			
34	3	-$0	$101,786	$75,000	$26,786	>=	0			
35	4	$27,589	$187,500	$75,000	$140,089	>=	0			
36	5	$144,292	$142,500							
37										
38	Final cash	$286,792	←	Objective to maximize : final cash at beginning of year 5						

© Cengage Learning

Moving across, calculate the return due in year 1 in cell C32 with the formula

=SUMPRODUCT(B19:F19,Dollars_invested)

Admittedly, no returns come due in year 1, but this formula can be copied down column C for other years. Next, calculate the total amount invested in year 1 in cell D32 with the formula

=SUMPRODUCT(B11:F11,Dollars_invested)

Now find the cash balance after investing in year 1 in cell E32 with the formula

=B32+C32-D32

The only other required formula is the formula for the cash available at the beginning of year 2. Because any cash not invested earns 3% interest, enter the formula

=E32*(1+$B$6)

in cell B33. This formula, along with those in cells C32, D32, and E32, can now be copied down. (The zeros in column G are entered manually as a reminder of the nonnegativity constraint on cash after investing.)

4. **Ending cash.** The ending cash at the beginning of year 5 is the sum of the amount in the money market and any returns that come due in year 5. Calculate this sum with the formula

=SUM(B36:C36)

Always look at the Solver solution for signs of implausibility. This can often help you spot an error in your model.

in cell B38. (*Note:* Here is the type of error to watch out for. We originally failed to calculate the return in cell C36 and mistakenly used the beginning cash in cell B36 as the objective cell. We realized our error when the optimal solution called for no money in investment D, which is clearly an attractive investment. The moral is that you can often catch errors by looking at the *plausibility* of the outputs.)

Review of the Model

Take a careful look at this model and how it has been set up. There are undoubtedly alternative ways to model this problem, but the attractive feature of this model is the way the tables of inflows and outflows in rows 11 through 14 and 19 through 23 create *copyable* formulas for returns and investment amounts in columns C and D of rows 32 through 35. In fact, this same model setup, with only minor modifications, will work for *any* set of investments, regardless of the timing of investments and their returns. This is a quality you should strive for in your spreadsheet models: generalizability.

Using Solver

To find the optimal investment strategy, fill in the main Solver dialog box as shown in Figure 14.30. Note that the explicit nonnegativity constraint is necessary, even though the Non-Negative option is checked. Again, this is because the Non-Negative option covers only the changing cells. If you want other output cells to be nonnegative, you must add such constraints explicitly.

Figure 14.30

Solver Dialog Box for Investment Model

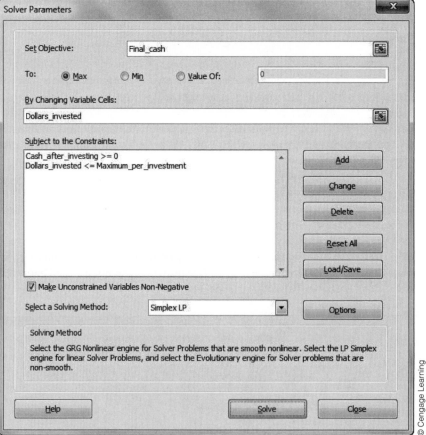

Discussion of the Results

The optimal solution appears in Figure 14.29. Let's follow the cash. The company spends all of its cash in year 1 on the two available investments, A and C ($64,286 in A, $35,714 in C). A total of $75,000 in returns from these investments is available in year 2, and all of this is invested in investment B. At the beginning of year 3, a total of $101,786 is available from investment A and B returns, and $75,000 of this is invested in investment E. This leaves $26,786 for the money market, which grows to $27,589 at the beginning of year 4. In addition, returns totaling $187,500 from investments B and E come due in year 4. Of this total cash of $215,089, $75,000 is invested in investment D, and the rest, $140,089, is put in the money market. The return from investment D, $142,500, plus the money available from the money market, $144,292, equals the final cash in the objective cell, $286,792.

Sensitivity Analysis

A close look at the optimal solution in Figure 14.29 indicates that Barney-Jones is penalizing itself by imposing a maximum of $75,000 per investment. This upper limit is forcing the company to put cash into the money market fund, despite this fund's low rate of return. Therefore, a natural sensitivity analysis is to see how the optimal solution changes as this maximum value changes. You can perform this sensitivity analysis with a one-way SolverTable, shown in Figure 14.31.[11] The maximum in cell B5 is the input cell, varied from $75,000 to $225,000 in increments of $25,000, and the optimal changing cells and objective cell are outputs. As you can see, the final cash (column G) grows steadily as the maximum allowable investment amount increases. This is because the company can take greater advantage of the attractive investments and put less in the money market account.

Figure 14.31
Sensitivity of Optimal Solution to Maximum Investment Amount

	A	B	C	D	E	F	G
3	Max per investment (cell $B$5) values along side, output cell(s) along top						
4		Dollars_invested_1	Dollars_invested_2	Dollars_invested_3	Dollars_invested_4	Dollars_invested_5	Final_cash
5	$75,000	$64,286	$75,000	$35,714	$75,000	$75,000	$286,792
6	$100,000	$61,538	$76,923	$38,462	$100,000	$100,000	$320,731
7	$125,000	$100,000	$50,000	$0	$125,000	$125,000	$353,375
8	$150,000	$100,000	$50,000	$0	$150,000	$125,000	$375,125
9	$175,000	$100,000	$50,000	$0	$175,000	$125,000	$396,875
10	$200,000	$100,000	$50,000	$0	$200,000	$125,000	$418,625
11	$225,000	$100,000	$50,000	$0	$225,000	$125,000	$440,375

© Cengage Learning

To perform sensitivity on an output variable not calculated explicitly in your spreadsheet model, calculate it in some unused portion of the spreadsheet before running SolverTable.

You can go one step further with the two-way SolverTable in Figure 14.32. Now both the maximum investment amount and the money market rate are inputs, and the maximum amount ever put in the money market fund is the single output. Because this latter amount is not calculated in the spreadsheet model, you need to calculate it with the formula **=MAX(Cash_after_investing)** in an unused cell before using it as the output cell for SolverTable. In every case, even with a large maximum investment amount and a low

---

[11]Because Solver's sensitivity reports do not help answer our specific sensitivity questions in this example or the next example, we discuss only SolverTable results.

Figure 14.32 Sensitivity of Maximum in Money Market to Two Inputs

⬛	A	B	C	D	E	F	G	H	I
3	Interest on cash (cell $B$6) values along side, Max per investment (cell $B$5) values along top, output cell in corner								
4	Maximum_in_money_market	$75,000	$100,000	$125,000	$150,000	$175,000	$200,000	$225,000	
5	0.5%	$139,420	$126,923	$112,500	$87,500	$62,500	$37,500	$12,500	
6	1.0%	$139,554	$126,923	$112,500	$87,500	$62,500	$37,500	$12,500	
7	1.5%	$139,688	$126,923	$112,500	$87,500	$62,500	$37,500	$12,500	
8	2.0%	$139,821	$126,923	$112,500	$87,500	$62,500	$37,500	$12,500	
9	2.5%	$139,955	$126,923	$112,500	$87,500	$62,500	$37,500	$12,500	
10	3.0%	$140,089	$126,923	$112,500	$87,500	$62,500	$37,500	$12,500	
11	3.5%	$140,223	$126,923	$112,500	$87,500	$62,500	$37,500	$12,500	
12	4.0%	$140,357	$126,923	$112,500	$87,500	$62,500	$37,500	$12,500	
13	4.5%	$140,491	$126,923	$112,500	$87,500	$62,500	$37,500	$12,500	

© Cengage Learning

money market rate, the company puts *some* money into the money market account. The reason is simple. Even when the maximum investment amount is $225,000, the company evidently has more cash than this to invest at some point (probably at the beginning of year 4). Therefore, it will have to put some of it in the money market. ∎

Example 14.7 illustrates a common situation where fixed payments are due in the future and current funds must be allocated and invested so that their returns are sufficient to make the payments. We place this in a pension fund context.

EXAMPLE | 14.7 MANAGING A PENSION FUND AT ARMCO

James Judson is the financial manager in charge of the company pension fund at Armco Incorporated. James knows that the fund must be sufficient to make the payments listed in Table 14.10. Each payment must be made on the first day of each year. James is going to finance these payments by purchasing bonds. It is currently the beginning of year 1, and three bonds are available for immediate purchase. The prices and coupons for the bonds are as follows. (All coupon payments arrive in time to meet the pension payments for the year in which they arrive.)

- Bond 1 costs $980 and yields a $60 coupon in years 2 through 5 and a $1060 payment on maturity in year 6.
- Bond 2 costs $970 and yields a $65 coupon in years 2 through 11 and a $1065 payment on maturity in year 12.
- Bond 3 costs $1050 and yields a $75 coupon in years 2 through 14 and a $1075 payment on maturity in year 15.

Table 14.10 Payments for Pension Example

Year	Payment	Year	Payment	Year	Payment
1	$11,000	6	$18,000	11	$25,000
2	$12,000	7	$20,000	12	$30,000
3	$14,000	8	$21,000	13	$31,000
4	$15,000	9	$22,000	14	$31,000
5	$16,000	10	$24,000	15	$31,000

© Cengage Learning

James must decide how much cash to allocate (from company coffers) to meet the initial $11,000 payment and buy enough bonds to make future payments. He knows that any excess cash on hand can earn an annual rate of 4% in a fixed-rate account. How should he proceed?

Objective To develop an LP model that relates initial allocation of money and bond purchases to future cash availabilities, and to minimize the initialize allocation of money required to meet all future pension fund payments.

Where Do the Numbers Come From?

As in the previous financial example, the inputs are fairly easy to obtain. A pension fund has known liabilities that must be met in future years, and information on bonds and fixed-rate accounts is widely available.

Solution

The variables and constraints required for this pension fund model are listed in Table 14.11. When modeling this problem, there is a new twist that involves the money James must allocate now for his funding problem. It is clear that he must decide how many bonds of each type to purchase now (note that no bonds are purchased in the *future*), but he must also decide how much money to allocate from company coffers. This allocated money has to cover the initial pension payment this year *and* the bond purchases. In addition, James wants to find the *minimum* allocation that will suffice. Therefore, this initial allocation serves two roles in the model. It is a decision variable *and* it is the objective to minimize. In terms of spreadsheet modeling, it is perfectly acceptable to make the objective cell one of the changing cells, and this is done here. You will not see this in many models—because the objective typically involves a linear combination of several decision variables—but it is occasionally the most natural way to proceed.

Table 14.11 Variables and Constraints for Pension Model

Input variables	Pension payments, information on bonds, fixed interest rate on cash
Decision variables (changing cells)	Cash to allocate now, numbers of bonds to purchase now
Object cell	Cash to allocate now (minimize)
Other calculated variables	Cash available to meet pension payments each year
Constraints	Cash available for payments ≥ Payment amounts

© Cengage Learning

FUNDAMENTAL INSIGHT

The Objective as a Changing Cell

In all optimization models, the objective cell has to be a function of the changing cells, that is, the objective value should change as values in the changing cells change. It is perfectly consistent with this requirement to have the objective cell *be* one of the changing cells. This doesn't occur in very many optimization models, but it is sometimes useful, even necessary.

Developing the Pension Fund Model

Developing the Spreadsheet Model

The completed spreadsheet model is shown in Figure 14.33. (See the file **Pension Fund Management.xlsx**.) You can create it with the following steps.

Figure 14.33 Pension Fund Management Model

	A	B	C	D	E	F	G	H	I	J	K	L	M	N	O	P
1	Pension fund management															
2																
3	Costs (year 1) and income (in years 2–15) from bonds															
4	Year	1	2	3	4	5	6	7	8	9	10	11	12	13	14	15
5	Bond 1	$980	$60	$60	$60	$60	$1,060									
6	Bond 2	$970	$65	$65	$65	$65	$65	$65	$65	$65	$65	$65	$1,065			
7	Bond 3	$1,050	$75	$75	$75	$75	$75	$75	$75	$75	$75	$75	$75	$75	$75	$1,075
8																
9	Interest rate	4.0%														
10																
11	Number of bonds to purchase now															
12	Bond 1	73.69														
13	Bond 2	77.21														
14	Bond 3	28.84														
15																
16	Cash allocated	$197,768	←—— Objective to minimize, also a changing cell													
17																
18	Constraints to meet payments															
19	Year	1	2	3	4	5	6	7	8	9	10	11	12	13	14	15
20	Cash available	$20,376	$21,354	$21,332	$19,228	$16,000	$85,298	$77,171	$66,639	$54,646	$41,133	$25,000	$84,390	$58,728	$31,000	$31,000
21		>=	>=	>=	>=	>=	>=	>=	>=	>=	>=	>=	>=	>=	>=	>=
22	Pension payment	$11,000	$12,000	$14,000	$15,000	$16,000	$18,000	$20,000	$21,000	$22,000	$24,000	$25,000	$30,000	$31,000	$31,000	$31,000
23																
24	Range names used:															
25	Bonds_purchased	=Model!$B$12:$B$14														
26	Cash_allocated	=Model!$B$16														
27	Cash_available	=Model!$B$20:$P$20														
28	Pension_payment	=Model!$B$22:$P$22														

Note (pointing to cell B16): The value in cell B16 is the cash allocated to make the current payment and buy bonds now. It is both a changing cell and the target cell to minimize.

© Cengage Learning

Always document your spreadsheet conventions as clearly as possible.

1. **Inputs and range names.** Enter the given data and name the ranges as indicated. Note that the bond costs in the range B5:B7 have been entered as *positive* quantities. Some financial analysts might prefer that they be entered as negative numbers, indicating outflows. It doesn't really matter, however, as long as you are careful with the Excel formulas later on.

2. **Cash allocated and bonds purchased.** As discussed previously, the cash allocated in year 1 and the numbers of bonds purchased are both decision variables, so enter *any* values for these in the Cash_allocated and Bonds_purchased ranges. Note that the color-coding convention for the Cash_allocated cell has to be modified. Because it is both a changing cell and the objective cell, we colored it red but added a note to emphasize that it is the objective to minimize.

3. **Cash available to make payments.** In the current year, the only cash available is the money initially allocated minus cash used to purchase bonds. Calculate this quantity in cell B20 with the formula

   =Cash_allocated-SUMPRODUCT(Bonds_purchased,B5:B7)

   For all other years, the cash available comes from two sources: excess cash invested at the fixed interest rate the year before and payments from bonds. Calculate this quantity for year 1 in cell C20 with the formula

   =(B20-B22)*(1+$B$9)+SUMPRODUCT(Bonds_purchased,C5:C7)

   and copy it across row 20 for the other years.

   As you can see, this model is fairly straightforward to develop once you understand the role of the amount allocated in cell B16. However, we have often given this problem as an assignment to our students, and many fail to deal correctly with the amount allocated. (They usually forget to make it a changing cell.) So make sure you understand what we have done, and why we have done it this way.

Using Solver

The main Solver dialog box should be filled out as shown in Figure 14.34. Once again, notice that the Cash_allocated cell is both the objective cell and one of the changing cells.

Figure 14.34
Solver Dialog Box for Pension Fund Model

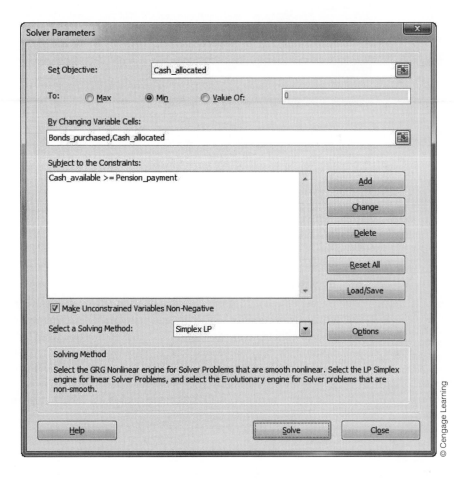

Discussion of the Solution

The optimal solution appears in Figure 14.33. You might argue that the numbers of bonds purchased should be constrained to integer values. We tried this and the optimal solution changed very little: The optimal numbers of bonds to purchase changed to 74, 79, and 27, and the optimal money to allocate increased to $197,887. With this integer solution, shown in Figure 14.35, James sets aside $197,887 initially. Any less than this would not work—he couldn't make enough from bonds to meet future pension payments. All but $20,387 of this (see cell B20) is spent on bonds, and of the $20,387, $11,000 is used to make the current pension payment. After this, the amounts in row 20, which are always sufficient to make the payments in row 22, are composed of returns from bonds and cash, with interest, from the previous year. Even more so than in previous examples, there is no way to guess this optimal solution. The timing of bond returns and the irregular pension payments make a spreadsheet optimization model absolute necessary.

Figure 14.35   Optimal Integer Solution for Pension Fund Model

	A	B	C	D	E	F	G	H	I	J	K	L	M	N	O	P
1	Pension fund management															
2																
3	Costs (year 1) and income (in year 2–15) from bonds															
4	Year	1	2	3	4	5	6	7	8	9	10	11	12	13	14	15
5	Bond 1	$980	$60	$60	$60	$60	$1,060									
6	Bond 2	$970	$65	$65	$65	$65	$65	$65	$65	$65	$65	$65	$1,065			
7	Bond 3	$1,050	$75	$75	$75	$75	$75	$75	$75	$75	$75	$75	$75	$75	$75	$1,075
8																
9	Interest rate	4.0%														
10																
11	Number of bonds to purchase now															
12	Bond 1	74.00														
13	Bond 2	79.00														
14	Bond 3	27.00														
15																
16	Cash allocated	$197,887	←	Objective to minimize, also a changing cell												
17																
18	Constraints to meet payments															
19	Year	1	2	3	4	5	6	7	8	9	10	11	12	13	14	15
20	Cash available	$20,387	$21,363	$21,337	$19,231	$16,000	$85,600	$77,464	$66,923	$54,919	$41,396	$25,252	$86,422	$60,704	$32,917	$31,019
21		>=	>=	>=	>=	>=	>=	>=	>=	>=	>=	>=	>=	>=	>=	>=
22	Pension payment	$11,000	$12,000	$14,000	$15,000	$16,000	$18,000	$20,000	$21,000	$22,000	$24,000	$25,000	$30,000	$31,000	$31,000	$31,000
23																
24	Range names used:															
25	Bonds_purchased	=Model!$B$12:$B$14														
26	Cash_allocated	=Model!$B$16														
27	Cash_available	=Model!$B$20:$P$20														
28	Pension payment	=Model!$B$22:$P$22														

Sensitivity Analysis

Constraints always have the potential to penalize the objective to some extent. SolverTable is a perfect tool for finding the magnitude of this penalty.

Because the bond information and pension payments are evidently fixed, there is only one obvious direction for sensitivity analysis: on the fixed interest rate in cell B9. We tried this, allowing this rate to vary from 2% to 6% in increments of 0.5% and keeping track of the optimal changing cells, including the objective cell. The results appear in Figure 14.36 (without the integer constraints). They indicate that as the interest rate increases, James can get by with fewer bonds of types 1 and 2, and he can allocate less money for the problem. The reason is that he is making more interest on excess cash. ∎

Figure 14.36

Sensitivity to Fixed Interest Rate

	A	B	C	D	E	F	G
3	Interest rate (cell $B$9) values along side, output cell(s) along top						
4		Bonds_purchased_1	Bonds_purchased_2	Bonds_purchased_3	Money_allocated		
5	2.0%	77.12	78.71	28.84	$202,010		
6	2.4%	76.41	78.40	28.84	$201,145		
7	2.8%	75.72	78.10	28.84	$200,288		
8	3.2%	75.03	77.80	28.84	$199,439		
9	3.6%	74.36	77.50	28.84	$198,600		
10	4.0%	73.69	77.21	28.84	$197,768		
11	4.4%	73.04	76.92	28.84	$196,946		
12	4.8%	72.40	76.63	28.84	$196,131		
13	5.2%	71.77	76.34	28.84	$195,325		
14	5.6%	71.15	76.06	28.84	$194,527		
15	6.0%	70.54	75.78	28.84	$193,737		

PROBLEMS

Level A

37. Modify the Barney-Jones investment problem so that there is a minimum amount that must be put into any investment, although this minimum can vary by investment. For example, the minimum amount for investment A might be $0, whereas the minimum amount for investment D might be $50,000. These minimum amounts should be inputs; you can make up any values you like. Run Solver on your modified model.

38. In the Barney-Jones investment problem, increase the maximum amount allowed in any investment to $150,000. Then run a one-way sensitivity analysis to the money market rate on cash. Capture one output variable: the maximum amount of cash ever put in the money market account. You can choose any reasonable range for varying the money market rate.

39. We claimed that our model for Barney-Jones is generalizable. Try generalizing it to the case where there are two more potential investments, F and G. Investment F requires a cash outlay in year 2 and returns $0.50 in *each* of the next four years. Investment G requires a cash outlay in year 3 and returns $0.75 in each of years 5, 6, and 7. Modify the model as necessary, making the objective the final cash after year 7.

40. In our Barney-Jones spreadsheet model, we ran investments across columns and years down rows. Many financial analysts prefer the opposite. Modify the spreadsheet model so that years go across columns and investments go down rows. Run Solver to ensure that your modified model is correct. (We suggest three possible ways to do this, and you can experiment to see which you prefer. First, you could start over on a blank worksheet. Second, you could use Copy and then Paste Special with the Transpose option. Third, you could use Excel's TRANSPOSE function.)

41. In the pension fund problem, suppose there is a fourth bond, bond 4. Its unit cost in year 1 is $1020, it returns coupons of $70 in years 2 through 7 and a payment of $1070 in year 8. Modify the model to incorporate this extra bond, and reoptimize. Does the solution change— that is, should James purchase any of bond 4?

42. In the pension fund problem, suppose there is an upper limit of 60 on the number of bonds of any particular type that can be purchased. Modify the model to incorporate this extra constraint and then optimize. How much more money does James need to allocate initially?

43. In the pension fund problem, suppose James has been asked to see how the optimal solution will change if the required payments in years 8 through 15 all increase by the same percentage, where this percentage could be anywhere from 5% to 25%. Use an appropriate one-way SolverTable to help him out, and write a memo describing the results.

44. Our pension fund model is streamlined, perhaps too much. It does all of the calculations concerning cash flows in row 20. James decides he would like to break these out into several rows of calculations: Beginning cash (for year 1, this is the amount allocated; for other years, it is the unused cash, plus interest, from the previous year), Amount spent on bonds (positive in year 1 only), Amount received from bonds (positive for years 2 through 15 only), Cash available for making pension fund payments, and, below the Pension payment row, Cash left over (amount invested in the fixed interest rate). Modify the model by inserting these rows, enter the appropriate formulas, and run Solver. You should obtain the same result, but you get more detailed information.

Level B

45. Suppose the investments in the Barney-Jones problem sometimes require cash outlays in more than one year. For example, a $1 investment in investment B might require $0.25 to be spent in year 1 and $0.75 to be spent in year 2. Does the current model easily accommodate such investments? Try it with some cash outlay data you can make up, run Solver, and interpret your results.

46. In the pension fund problem, you know that if the amount of money allocated initially is *less* than the amount found by Solver, James will not be able to meet all of the pension fund payments. Use the current model to demonstrate that this is true. To do so, enter a value less than the optimal value in cell B16. Then run Solver, but remove the Cash_allocated cell as a changing cell and as the objective cell. (If there is no objective cell, Solver simply tries to find a solution that satisfies all of the constraints.) What do you find?

47. Continuing the previous problem in a slightly different direction, continue to use the Cash_allocated cell as a changing cell, but add a constraint that it must be less than or equal to any value, such as $195,000, that is *less* than its current optimal value. With this constraint, James will again not be able to meet all of the pension fund payments. Create a new objective cell to minimize the total amount of payments not met. The easiest way to do this is with IF functions. Unfortunately, this makes the model nonsmooth, and Solver might have trouble finding the optimal solution. Try it and see.

14-7 INTEGER OPTIMIZATION MODELS

In this section you will learn how to model some problems by using 0–1 variables (and possibly other integer variables) as changing cells. A **0–1 variable**, or **binary variable**, is a variable that must equal 0 or 1. Usually a 0–1 variable corresponds to an activity that is or is not undertaken. If the 0–1 variable corresponding to the activity equals 0, the activity is not undertaken; if it equals 1, the activity is undertaken.

Optimization models in which some or all of the variables must be integers are known as **integer programming (IP) models**. You have already seen examples of integer constraints in the discussion of scheduling workers, aggregate planning, and pension fund management. This section illustrates some of methods that are needed to formulate IP models of complex situations. You should be aware that Solver typically has a much harder time solving an IP problem than an LP problem. In fact, Solver is unable to solve some IP problems, even when they have an optimal solution. The reason is that these problems are inherently difficult, no matter what software package is used. However, as you will see in this section, your ability to model complex problems increases tremendously when you are able to use IP, particularly with 0–1 variables.

FUNDAMENTAL INSIGHT

Difficulty of Integer Programming Models

You might suspect that IP models would be *easier* to solve than LP models. After all, there are only a finite number of feasible integer solutions in an IP model, whereas there are infinitely many feasible (integer and noninteger) solutions in an LP model. However, exactly the opposite is true. IP models are *much* more difficult than LP models. All IP algorithms try to perform an efficient search through the typically huge number of feasible integer solutions. General-purpose algorithms such as branch and bound can be very effective for modest-size problems, but they can fail (or require extremely long computing times) on the large problems often faced in real applications. In such cases, analysts must develop special-purpose optimization algorithms, or perhaps even heuristics, to find "good," but not necessarily optimal, solutions.

14-7a Capital Budgeting Models

Perhaps the simplest types of IP models are **capital budgeting models**. Example 14.8 perfectly illustrates the go/no-go decisions inherent in many IP models.

| EXAMPLE | **14.8 SELECTING INVESTMENTS AT TATHAM** |

Tatham Company is considering seven investments. The cash required for each investment and the net present value (NPV) each investment adds to the firm are listed in Table 14.12. The cash available for investment is $15,000. Tatham wants to find the investment policy that maximizes its NPV. The crucial assumption here is that if Tatham wishes to take part in any of these investments, it must go all the way. It cannot, for example, go

Table 14.12   Data for Capital Budgeting Example

Investment	Cash Required	NPV
1	$5000	$16,000
2	$2500	$8000
3	$3500	$10,000
4	$6000	$19,500
5	$7000	$22,000
6	$4500	$12,000
7	$3000	$7500

halfway in investment 1 by investing $2500 and realizing an NPV of $8000. In fact, if partial investments were allowed, LP could be used; IP wouldn't be necessary.

Objective   To use a binary IP model to find the set of investments that stays within budget and maximizes total NPV.

Where Do the Numbers Come From?

The initial required cash and the available budget are easy to obtain. It is undoubtedly harder to obtain the NPV for each investment. This requires a time sequence of anticipated cash inflows from the investments and a discount factor. Simulation might even be used to estimate these NPVs. In any case, this is exactly what many financial analysts do: estimate the NPVs for potential investments.

Solution

The variables and constraints required for this model are listed in Table 14.13. The most important part is that the decision variables must be binary, where a 1 means an investment is undertaken and a 0 means it is not. These variables cannot have fractional values such as 0.5, because partial investments are not allowed—the company has to go all the way or not at all. Note that the binary restriction is specified in the second row, not the last row. This is done throughout the chapter. However, when you set up the Solver dialog box, you need to add explicit binary constraints in the constraints section.

Table 14.13   Variables and Constraints for Capital Budgeting Model

Input variables	Initial cash required for investments, NPVs from investments, budget
Decision variables (changing cells)	Whether to invest (binary variables)
Objective cell	Total NPV
Other calculated variables	Total initial cash invested
Constraints	Total initial cash invested ≤ Budget

© Cengage Learning

Developing the Spreadsheet Model

Developing the Capital Budgeting Model

To form the spreadsheet model, which is shown in Figure 14.37, proceed as follows. (See the file **Capital Budgeting 1.xlsx**.)

Figure 14.37   Capital Budgeting Model

	A	B	C	D	E	F	G	H
1	Tatham capital budgeting model							
2								
3	Input data on potential investments							
4	Investment	1	2	3	4	5	6	7
5	Investment cost	$5,000	$2,500	$3,500	$6,500	$7,000	$4,500	$3,000
6	NPV	$16,000	$8,000	$10,000	$19,500	$22,000	$12,000	$7,500
7	NPV per investment dollar	3.20	3.20	2.86	3.25	3.14	2.67	2.50
8								
9	Decisions: whether to invest							
10	Investment levels	1	1	0	0	1	0	0
11								
12	Budget constraints							
13		Amount invested		Budget				
14		$14,500	<=	$15,000				
15								
16	Objective to maximize							
17	Total NPV	$46,000						
18								
19	Range names used:							
20	Amount_invested	=Model!$B$14						
21	Budget	=Model!$D$14						
22	Investment_levels	=Model!$B$10:$H$10						
23	Total_NPV	=Model!$B$17						

© Cengage Learning

1. **Inputs.** Enter the initial cash requirements, the NPVs, and the budget in the input cells.

2. **0–1 values for investments.** Enter *any* trial 0–1 values for the investments in the Investment_levels range. (Actually, you can even enter fractional values such as 0.5 in these cells. The Solver constraints will eventually force them to be 0 or 1.)

3. **Cash invested.** Calculate the total cash invested in cell B14 with the formula

   =SUMPRODUCT(B5:H5,Investment_levels)

A SUMPRODUCT formula, where one of the ranges consists of 0s and 1s, really just sums the values in the other range that "match up" with the 1s.

   Note that this formula sums the costs *only* for those investments with binary variables equal to 1. To see this, think how the SUMPRODUCT function works when one of its ranges is a range of 0s and 1s. It effectively sums the cells in the other range corresponding to the 1s.

4. **NPV contribution.** Calculate the NPV contributed by the investments in cell B17 with the formula

   =SUMPRODUCT(B6:H6, Investment_levels)

   Again, this sums only the NPVs of the investments with binary variables equal to 1.

Using Solver

Solver makes it easy to specify binary constraints. Simply select the "bin" option.

The Solver dialog box appears in Figure 14.38. The goal is to maximize the total NPV, subject to staying within the budget. However, the changing cells must be *constrained* to be binary. Fortunately, Solver makes this simple, as shown in the dialog box in Figure 14.39. You add a constraint with Investments in the left box and choose the "bin" option in the middle box. The "binary" in the right box is then added automatically. Note that if *all* changing cells are binary, you do not need to check Solver's Non-Negative option (because 0 and 1 are certainly nonnegative), but you should still select the Simplex LP method.

Figure 14.38

Solver Dialog Box for Capital Budgeting Model

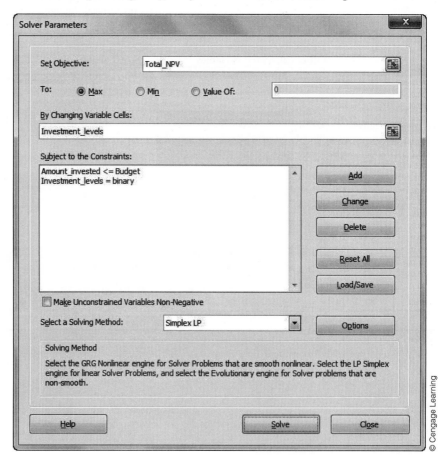

© Cengage Learning

Figure 14.39

Specifying a Binary
Constraint

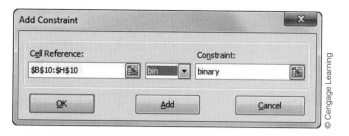

Discussion of the Solution

The optimal solution in Figure 14.37 indicates that Tatham can obtain a maximum NPV of $46,000 by selecting investments 1, 2, and 5. These three investments consume only $14,500 of the available budget, with $500 left over. However, this $500 is not enough—because of the "investing all the way" requirement—to invest in any of the remaining investments.

If Tatham's investments are ranked on the basis of NPV per dollar invested (see row 7 of Figure 14.37), the ranking from best to worst is 4, 1, 2, 5, 3, 6, 7. Using your economic intuition, you might expect the investments to be chosen in this order—until the budget runs out. However, the optimal solution does not do this. It selects the second-, third-, and fourth-best investments, but it omits the best one. To understand why it does this, imagine investing in the order from best to worst, according to row 7, until the budget allows no more. By the time you have invested in investments 4, 1, and 2, you will have consumed $13,500 of the budget, and the remainder, $1500, is not sufficient to invest in any of the rest. This strategy provides an NPV of only $43,500. A smarter strategy, the optimal solution from Solver, gains you an extra $2500 in NPV.

Sensitivity Analysis

SolverTable can be used on models with binary variables exactly as in previous models. For example, to see how the total NPV varies as the budget increases, select the Budget cell as the single input cell, allow it to vary from $15,000 to $25,000 in increments of $1000, and designate the binary variables, the amount of the budget used, and the total NPV as outputs. The results are given in Figure 14.40. Clearly, Tatham can achieve a larger

Figure 14.40   Sensitivity to Budget

	A	B	C	D	E	F	G	H	I	J	K
3	Budget (cell $D$14) values along side, output cell(s) along top										
4		Investment_levels_1	Investment_levels_2	Investment_levels_3	Investment_levels_4	Investment_levels_5	Investment_levels_6	Investment_levels_7	Amount_invested	Total_NPV	Increase
5	$15,000	1	1	0	0	1	0	0	$14,500	$46,000	
6	$16,000	0	1	0	1	1	0	0	$15,500	$49,500	$3,500
7	$17,000	1	1	1	1	0	0	0	$17,000	$53,500	$4,000
8	$18,000	1	0	0	1	1	0	0	$18,000	$57,500	$4,000
9	$19,000	0	1	1	1	1	0	0	$19,000	$59,500	$2,000
10	$20,000	0	1	0	1	1	1	0	$20,000	$61,500	$2,000
11	$21,000	1	1	0	1	1	0	0	$20,500	$65,500	$4,000
12	$22,000	1	0	1	1	1	0	0	$21,500	$67,500	$2,000
13	$23,000	1	0	0	1	1	1	0	$22,500	$69,500	$2,000
14	$24,000	1	1	1	1	1	0	0	$24,000	$75,500	$6,000
15	$25,000	1	1	0	1	1	1	0	$25,000	$77,500	$2,000

NPV with a larger budget, but as the numbers and the chart show, each extra $1000 of budget does *not* have the same effect on total NPV. The first $1000 increase to the budget adds $3500 to total NPV, the next two $1000 increases add $4000 each, the next two $1000 increases add $2000 each, and so on. Note also how the selected investments vary quite a lot as the budget increases. This somewhat strange behavior is due to the "lumpiness" of the inputs and the all-or-nothing nature of the problem.

Effect of Solver Tolerance Setting

When the Tolerance setting is 5% instead of 0%, Solver's solution might not be optimal, but it will be close.

To illustrate the effect of the Solver Tolerance setting, compare the SolverTable results in Figure 14.41 with those in Figure 14.40. (Again, remember that this is the Integer Optimality setting starting in Excel 2010.) Each is for the Tatham capital budgeting model, but Figure 14.41 uses Solver's default tolerance of 5%, whereas Figure 14.40 uses a tolerance of 0%. The three shaded cells in Figure 14.41 indicate *lower* total NPVs than the corresponding cells in Figure 14.40. In these three cases, Solver stopped short of finding the true optimal solutions because it found solutions within the 5% tolerance and then quit.

Figure 14.41 Results with Tolerance at 5%

	A	B	C	D	E	F	G	H	I	J
3	Budget (cell$ D$14) values along side, output cell(s) along top									
4		Investment_levels_1	Investment_levels_2	Investment_levels_3	Investment_levels_4	Investment_levels_5	Investment_levels_6	Investment_levels_7	Amount_invested	Total_NPV
5	$15,000	1	1	0	0	1	0	0	$14,500	$46,000
6	$16,000	0	1	0	1	1	0	0	$15,500	$49,500
7	$17,000	1	1	1	1	0	0	0	$17,000	$53,500
8	$18,000	1	0	0	1	1	0	0	$18,000	$57,500
9	$19,000	0	1	1	1	1	0	0	$19,000	$59,500
10	$20,000	1	0	1	0	1	1	0	$20,000	$60,000
11	$21,000	1	1	0	1	1	0	0	$20,500	$65,500
12	$22,000	1	1	0	1	1	0	0	$20,500	$65,500
13	$23,000	0	1	0	1	1	1	1	$23,000	$69,000
14	$24,000	1	1	1	1	1	0	0	$24,000	$75,500
15	$25,000	1	1	0	1	1	1	0	$25,000	$77,500

© Cengage Learning

FUNDAMENTAL INSIGHT

Recognizing the Optimal Integer Solution

IP algorithms often find a very good integer solution very quickly. So why do they sometimes run so long? This is due to the *implicit enumeration* aspect of the algorithms. They have difficulty ruling out large numbers of potential solutions until they have searched all regions of the solution space. In other words, they have difficulty recognizing that they might have found the optimal solution because there are many potential solutions they haven't yet explored. When you run Solver on a reasonably large IP model, watch the status bar. Often a very good *incumbent* solution, the best solution found so far, is found within seconds, but then Solver spins its wheels for minutes or even hours trying to verify that this solution is optimal. This is why the default tolerance setting in Solver is 5%, not 0%.

774 Chapter 14 Optimization Models

Modeling Issues

- Capital budgeting models with multiple periods can also be handled. Figure 14.42 shows one possibility. (See the **Capital Budgeting 2 Finished.xlsx** file.) The costs in rows 5 and 6 are *both* incurred if any given investment is selected. Now there are two budget constraints, one in each year, but otherwise the model is exactly as before. Note that some investments could have a cost of 0 in year 1 and a positive cost in year 2. This would mean that these investments are undertaken in year 2 rather than year 1. Also, it would be easy to modify the model to incorporate costs in years 3, 4, and so on.

Figure 14.42 A Two-Period Capital Budgeting Model

▲	A	B	C	D	E	F	G	H
1	Tatham two-period capital budgeting model							
2								
3	Input data on potential investments							
4	Investment	1	2	3	4	5	6	7
5	Year 1 cost	$5,000	$2,500	$3,500	$6,500	$7,000	$4,500	$3,000
6	Year 2 cost	$2,000	$1,500	$2,000	$0	$500	$1,500	$0
7	NPV	$16,000	$8,000	$10,000	$20,000	$22,000	$12,000	$8,000
8								
9	Decisions: whether to invest							
10	Investment levels	1	1	0	1	0	0	0
11								
12	Budget constraints							
13		Amount invested		Budget				
14		$14,000	<=	$14,000				
15		$3,500	<=	$4,500				
16								
17	Objective to maximize							
18	Total NPV	$44,000						

- If Tatham could choose a *fractional* amount of an investment, then you could maximize its NPV by deleting the binary constraint. The optimal solution to the resulting LP model has a total NPV of $48,714. All of investments 1, 2, and 4, and 0.214 of investment 5 are chosen. Note that there is no way to round the changing cell values from this LP solution to obtain the optimal IP solution. Sometimes the solution to an IP model *without* the integer constraints bears little resemblance to the optimal IP solution.

- Any IP involving binary variables with only one constraint is called a *knapsack problem*. Think of the problem faced by a hiker going on an overnight hike. For example, imagine that the hiker's knapsack can hold only 34 pounds, and she must choose which of several available items to take on the hike. The benefit derived from each item is analogous to the NPV of each project, and the weight of each item is analogous to the cash required by each investment. The single constraint is analogous to the budget constraint—that is, only 34 pounds can fit in the knapsack. In a knapsack problem, the goal is to get the most value in the knapsack without overloading it. ∎

14-7b Fixed-Cost Models

Fixed-cost models are used when a fixed cost is incurred if an activity is undertaken at *any positive* level. This cost is independent of the level of the activity and is known as a **fixed cost** (or fixed charge). Here are three examples of fixed costs:

- Construction of a warehouse incurs a fixed cost that is the same whether the warehouse is used at partial or full capacity.

- A cash withdrawal from a bank incurs a fixed cost, independent of the size of the withdrawal, due to the time spent at the bank.

- A machine that is used to make several products must be set up for the production of each product. Regardless of the number of units of a product the company produces, the same fixed cost (lost production due to the setup time) is incurred.

In these examples a fixed cost is incurred if an activity is undertaken at any positive level, and zero fixed cost is incurred if the activity is not undertaken at all. Although it might not be obvious, this feature makes the problem inherently *nonlinear,* which means that a straightforward application of LP is not possible. However, Example 14.9 illustrates how a clever use of binary variables results in a *linear* model.

FUNDAMENTAL INSIGHT

Binary Variables for Modeling

Binary variables are often used to transform a nonlinear model into a linear (integer) model. For example, a fixed cost is not a linear function of the level of some activity; it is either incurred or it isn't incurred. This type of all-or-nothing behavior is difficult for nonlinear algorithms to handle. However, this behavior can often be handled easily by using binary variables to make the model linear. Still, large models with many binary variables can be difficult to solve. One approach is to solve the model without integer constraints and then round fractional values to the nearest integer (0 or 1). Unfortunately, this approach is typically not very good because the rounded solution is often infeasible. Even if it is feasible, its objective value can be considerably worse than the optimal objective value.

EXAMPLE | 14.9 TEXTILE MANUFACTURING AT GREAT THREADS

Great Threads Company is capable of manufacturing shirts, shorts, pants, skirts, and jackets. Each type of clothing requires Great Threads to acquire the appropriate type of machinery. The machinery needed to manufacture each type of clothing must be rented at the weekly rates shown in Table 14.14. This table also lists the amounts of cloth and labor required per unit of clothing, as well as the selling price and the unit variable cost for each type of clothing. There are 4000 labor hours and 4500 square yards (sq yd) of cloth available in a given week. The company wants to find a solution that maximizes its weekly profit.

Table 14.14 Data for Great Threads Example

	Rental Cost	Labor Hours	Cloth (sq yd)	Selling Price	Unit Variable Cost
Shirts	$1500	2.0	3.0	$35	$20
Shorts	$1200	1.0	2.5	$40	$10
Pants	$1600	6.0	4.0	$65	$25
Skirts	$1500	4.0	4.5	$70	$30
Jackets	$1600	8.0	5.5	$110	$35

© Cengage Learning

Objective To develop a linear model with binary variables that can be used to maximize the company's profit, correctly accounting for fixed costs and staying within resource availabilities.

Where Do the Numbers Come From?

Except for the fixed costs, this is the same basic problem as the product mix problem (Examples 13.1 and 13.2) in Chapter 13. Therefore, the same discussion there about input variables applies here. As for the fixed costs, they are the given rental rates for the machinery.

Solution

The variables and constraints required for this model are listed in Table 14.15. Note that the cost of producing x shirts during a week is 0 if $x = 0$, but it is $1500 + 20x$ if $x > 0$. This

Table 14.15 Variables and Constraints for Fixed-Cost Model

Input variables	Fixed rental costs, resource usages (labor hours, cloth) per unit of clothing, selling prices, unit variable costs, resource availabilities
Decision variables (changing cells)	Whether to produce any of each clothing (binary), how much of each clothing to produce
Objective cell	Profit
Other calculated variables	Resources used, upper bounds on amounts to produce, total revenue, total variable cost, total fixed cost
Constraints	Amount produced ≤ Logical upper bound (capacity) Resources used ≤ Resources available

cost structure violates the proportionality assumption (discussed in the previous chapter) that is needed for a linear model. If proportionality were satisfied, the cost of making, say, 10 shirts would be double the cost of making five shirts. However, because of the fixed cost, the total cost of making five shirts is $1600, and the cost of making 10 shirts is only $1700. This violation of proportionality requires you to use binary variables to obtain a *linear* model. Specifically, these binary variables model the fixed costs correctly, as explained in detail here.

Developing the Fixed Cost Manufacturing Model

Developing the Spreadsheet Model

The spreadsheet model, shown in Figure 14.43, can now be developed as follows. (See the file **Fixed Cost Manufacturing.xlsx**.)

Figure 14.43 Fixed-Cost Clothing Model

▲	A	B	C	D	E	F	G	H	I	J
1	Great Threads fixed cost clothing model							**Range names used:**		
2								Logical_upper_limit	=Model!$B$18:$F$18	
3	**Input data on products**							Produce_any?	=Model!$B$14:$F$14	
4		Shirts	Shorts	Pants	Skirts	Jackets		Profit	=Model!$B$29	
5	Labor hours/unit	2	1	6	4	8		Resource_available	=Model!$D$22:$D$23	
6	Cloth (sq.yd.)/unit	3	2.5	4	4.5	5.5		Resource_used	=Model!$B$22:$B$23	
7								Units_produced	=Model!$B$16:$F$16	
8	Selling price/unit	$35	$40	$65	$70	$110				
9	Variable cost/unit	$20	$10	$25	$30	$35				
10	Fixed cost for equipment	$1,500	$1,200	$1,600	$1,500	$1,600				
11										
12	**Production plan, constraints on capacity**									
13		Shirts	Shorts	Pants	Skirts	Jackets				
14	Rent equipment	0	1	0	0	1				
15										
16	Units produced	0	965.52	0	0	379.31				
17		<=	<=	<=	<=	<=				
18	Logical upper bound	0.00	1800.00	0.00	0.00	500.00				
19										
20	**Constraints on resources**									
21		Resource used		Available						
22	Labor hours	4000.00	<=	4000						
23	Cloth	4500.00	<=	4500						
24										
25	**Monetary outputs**									
26	Revenue	$80,345								
27	Variable cost	$22,931								
28	Fixed cost for equipment	$2,800								
29	Profit	$54,614	←	Objective to maximize						

1. **Inputs.** Enter the given inputs.

2. **Binary values for clothing types.** Enter *any* trial values for the binary variables for the various clothing types in the Rent_equipment range. For example, a 1 in cell C14 implies that *some* shorts are produced. More importantly, it implies that the machinery for making shorts is rented and its fixed cost is incurred.

3. **Production quantities.** Enter *any* trial values for the numbers of the various clothing types produced in the Units_produced range. At this point you could enter "illegal" values, such as 0 in cell B14 and a positive value in cell B16. This is illegal because it implies that the company produces some shirts but doesn't incur the fixed cost of the machinery for shirts. However, Solver will eventually disallow such illegal combinations.

4. **Labor and cloth used.** In cell B22 enter the formula

   =SUMPRODUCT(B5:F5,Units_produced)

   to calculate total labor hours, and copy this to cell B23 for cloth.

5. **Effective capacities.** Here is the tricky part of the model. You need to ensure that if any of a given type of clothing is produced, then its binary variable equals 1. This ensures that the model incurs the fixed cost of renting the machine for this type of clothing. You could easily implement these constraints with IF statements. For example, to implement the constraint for shirts, you could enter the following formula in cell B14:

   =IF(B16>0,1,0)

   However, Solver is unable to deal with IF functions predictably. Therefore, the fixed-cost constraints are modeled in a different way, as follows:

   $$\text{Shirts produced} \leq \text{Maximum capacity} \times (0\text{--}1 \text{ variable for shirts}) \qquad \textbf{(14.4)}$$

   There are similar inequalities for the other types of clothing.

   Here is the logic behind Inequality (14.4). If the 0–1 variable for shirts is 0, the right side of the inequality is 0, which means that the left side must be 0—no shirts can be produced. That is, if the binary variable for shirts is 0, so that no fixed cost for shirts is incurred, then Inequality (14.4) does not allow Great Threads to "cheat" and produce a positive number of shirts. On the other hand, if the binary variable for shirts is 1, the inequality is certainly true and is essentially redundant. It simply states that the number of shirts produced must be no greater than the *maximum* number that could be produced. Inequality (14.4) rules out the one case that needs to be ruled out—namely, that Great Threads produces shirts but avoids the fixed cost.

   To implement Inequality (14.4), a maximum capacity is required. To obtain this, suppose the company puts all of its resources into producing shirts. Then the number of shirts that can be produced is limited by the smaller of

   $$\frac{\text{Available labor hours}}{\text{Labor hours per shirt}}$$

   and

   $$\frac{\text{Available square yards of cloth}}{\text{Square yards of cloth per shirt}}$$

   Therefore, the smaller of these—the most limiting—can be used as the maximum needed in Inequality (14.4).

   To implement this logic, calculate the effective capacity for shirts in cell B18 with the formula

   =B14*MIN($D$22/B5,$D$23/B6)

Then copy this formula to the range C16:F16 for the other types of clothing.[12] By the way, this MIN formula causes no problems for Solver because it does not involve *changing* cells, only input cells.

6. **Monetary values.** Calculate the total sales revenue and the total variable cost by entering the formula

=SUMPRODUCT(B8:F8, Units_produced)

in cell B26 and copying it to cell B27. Then calculate the total fixed cost in cell B28 with the formula

=SUMPRODUCT(B10:F10, Rent_equipment)

Note that this formula sums the fixed costs only for those products with binary variables equal to 1. Finally, calculate the total profit in cell B29 with the formula

=B26-B27-B28

Using Solver

The Solver dialog box is shown in Figure 14.44. The goal is to maximize profit, subject to using no more labor hours or cloth than are available, and ensure that production is less than or equal to *effective* capacity. The key is that this effective capacity is zero if none of a given type of clothing is produced. As usual, check the Non-Negative option, and set the tolerance to zero (under the Options button). Importantly, note that by using binary changing cells, the resulting model is *linear*, which means that the simplex algorithm can be used.

Figure 14.44
Solver Dialog Box for Fixed-Cost Model

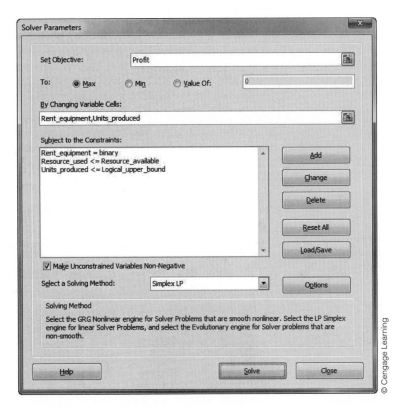

---

[12]Why not set the upper limit on shirts equal to a huge number like 1,000,000? The reason is that Solver works most efficiently when the upper limit is as tight—that is, as low—as possible. A tighter upper limit means fewer potential feasible solutions for Solver to search through.

Although Solver finds the optimal solution automatically, you should understand the effect of the logical upper-bound constraint on production. It rules out a solution such as the one shown in Figure 14.45. This solution calls for a positive production level of pants but does not incur the fixed cost of the pants equipment. The logical upper-bound constraint rules this out because it prevents a positive value in row 16 if the corresponding binary value in row 14 is 0. In other words, if the company wants to produce some pants, the constraint in Inequality (14.4) forces the associated binary variable to be 1, thus incurring the fixed cost for pants.

Figure 14.45

An Illegal (and Nonoptimal) Solution

	A	B	C	D	E	F
12	Production plan, constraints on capacity					
13		Shifts	Shorts	Pants	Skirts	Jackets
14	Rent equipment	0	1	0	1	1
15						
16	Units produced	0	965.52	450	0	379.31
17		<=	<=	<=	<=	<=
18	Logical upper bound	0.00	1800.00	0.00	1000.00	500.00

Note that Inequality (14.4) does *not* rule out the situation you see for skirts, where the binary value is 1 and the production level is 0. However, Solver will never choose this type of solution as optimal. Solver recognizes that the binary value in this case can be changed to 0, so that the fixed cost for skirt equipment is not incurred.

Discussion of the Solution

The optimal solution appears in Figure 14.43. It indicates that Great Threads should produce about 966 shorts and 379 jackets, but no shirts, pants, or skirts. The total profit is $54,614. Note that the binary variables for shirts, pants, and skirts are all 0, which forces production of these products to be 0. However, the binary variables for shorts and jackets, the products that are produced, are 1. This ensures that the fixed cost of producing shorts and jackets is included in the total cost.

It might be helpful to think of this solution as occurring in two stages. In the first stage Solver determines which products to produce—in this case, shorts and jackets only. Then in the second stage, Solver decides how *many* shorts and jackets to produce. If you knew that the company plans to produce shorts and jackets only, you could then ignore the fixed costs and determine the best production quantities with the same types of product mix models discussed in the previous chapter. Of course, these two stages—deciding which products to produce and how many of each to produce—are interrelated, and Solver considers both of them in its solution process.

As always, adding constraints can only make the objective worse. In this case, it means decreased profit.

The Great Threads management might not be very excited about producing shorts and jackets only. Suppose the company wants to ensure that at least three types of clothing are produced at positive levels. One approach is to add another constraint—namely, that the sum of the binary values in row 14 is greater than or equal to 3. You can check, however, that when this constraint is added and Solver is rerun, the binary variable for skirts becomes 1, but no skirts are produced. Shorts and jackets are more profitable than skirts, so only shorts and jackets are produced. (See Figure 14.46.) The new constraint forces

Figure 14.46   Fixed-Cost Model with Extra Constraint

	A	B	C	D	E	F	G	H	I
12	Production plan, constraints on capacity								
13		Shirts	Shorts	Pants	Skirts	Jackets	Sum		Required
14	Rent equipment	0	1	0	1	1	3	>=	3
15									
16	Units produced	0	965.52	0	0	379.31			
17		<=	<=	<=	<=	<=			
18	Logical upper bound	0.00	1800.00	0.00	1000.00	500.00			

Great Threads to rent an extra piece of machinery (for skirts), but it doesn't force the company to use it. To force the company to produce some skirts, you would also need to add a constraint on the value in E16, such as E16 > = 100. Any of these additional constraints will cost Great Threads money, but if, as a matter of policy, the company wants to produce more than two types of clothing, this is its only option.

Sensitivity Analysis

Because the optimal solution currently calls for only shorts and jackets to be produced, an interesting sensitivity analysis is to see how much incentive is required for other products to be produced. One way to model this is to increase the selling price for a nonproduced product such as skirts in a one-way SolverTable. The results of this, keeping track of all binary variables and profit, are shown in Figure 14.47. When the selling price for skirts is $85 or less, the company continues to produce only shorts and jackets. However, when the selling price is $90 or greater, the company stops producing shorts and jackets and produces *only* skirts. You can check that the optimal production quantity of skirts is 1000 when the selling price of skirts is any value $90 or above. The only reason that the profits in Figure 14.47 increase from row 9 down is that the revenues from these 1000 skirts increase.

Figure 14.47

Sensitivity of Binary Variables to Selling Price of Skirts

	A	B	C	D	E	F	G
3	Skirt price (cell $E$8) values along side, output cell(s) along top						
4		Rent_equipment_1	Rent_equipment_2	Rent_equipment_3	Rent_equipment_4	Rent_equipment_5	Profit
5	$70	0	1	0	0	1	$54,614
6	$75	0	1	0	0	1	$54,614
7	$80	0	1	0	0	1	$54,614
8	$85	0	1	0	0	1	$54,614
9	$90	0	0	0	1	0	$58,500
10	$95	0	0	0	1	0	$63,500
11	$100	0	0	0	1	0	$68,500

© Cengage Learning

A Model with IF Functions

In case you are still not convinced that the binary variable approach is required, and you think IF functions could be used instead, take a look at the last sheet in the finished version of the file. The resulting model *looks* the same as in Figure 14.43, but it incorporates the following changes:

■ The binary range is no longer part of the changing cells range. Instead, the formula =IF(B16>0,1,0) is entered in cell B14 and copied across to cell F14. Logically, this probably appears more natural. If a production quantity is positive, a 1 is entered in row 14, which means that the fixed cost is incurred.

■ The effective capacities are calculated in row 18 with IF functions. Specifically, the formula =IF(B16>0,MIN($D$22/B5,$D$23/B6),0) is entered in cell B18 and copied across to cell F18.

■ The Solver dialog box is modified as shown in Figure 14.48. The Rent_equipment range is not part of the changing cells range, and there is no binary constraint. The simplex method cannot be used because the IF functions make the model nonlinear.

Figure 14.48

Solver Dialog Box When IF Functions Are Used

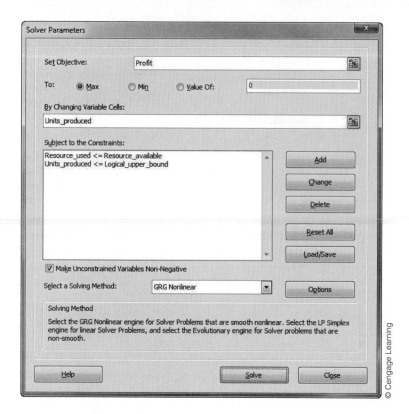

© Cengage Learning

When we ran Solver on this modified model, we found inconsistent results, depending on the initial production quantities entered in row 16. For example, when we entered initial values all equal to 0, the Solver solution was exactly that—all 0s. Of course, this solution is *terrible* because it leads to a profit of $0. However, when we entered initial production quantities all equal to 100, Solver found the correct optimal solution, the same as in Figure 14.43. Was this just lucky? To check, we tried another initial solution, where the production quantities for shorts and jackets were 0, and the production quantities for shirts, pants, and skirts were all 500. In this case Solver found a solution where only skirts are produced. Of course, we know this is not optimal.

Actually, the problem with using the GRG Nonlinear method indicated in Figure 14.48 is that this model is "nonsmooth," and the GRG Nonlinear method doesn't work well on nonsmooth models. Starting in Excel 2010, there is another option—the Evolutionary method. This method works well on nonsmooth models, but it guarantees only an approximately optimal solution, and it is relatively slow. It is not discussed further in this book.

In any case, the IF-function approach is not the way to go. Its success depends on the initial values in the changing cells, and this requires good guesses. The binary approach ensures that Solver finds the correct solution. ∎

14-7c Set-Covering Models

In a **set-covering model**, each member of a given set (set 1) must be "covered" by an acceptable member of another set (set 2). The objective in a set-covering problem is to minimize the number of members in set 2 necessary to cover all the members in set 1. For example, set 1 might consist of all the cities in a county and set 2 might consist of the cities in which a fire station is located. A member of set 2 covers, or handles the needs of, a city in set 1 if the fire station is located within, say, 10 minutes of the city. The goal is to

782 Chapter 14 Optimization Models

minimize the number of fire stations needed to cover all cities. Set-covering models have been applied to areas as diverse as airline crew scheduling, truck dispatching, political redistricting, and capital investment. Example 14.10 is a typical set-covering model.

EXAMPLE	**14.10 HUB LOCATION AT WESTERN AIRLINES**

Western Airlines has decided that it wants to design a hub system in the United States. Each hub is used for connecting flights to and from cities within 1000 miles of the hub. Western runs flights among the following cities: Atlanta, Boston, Chicago, Denver, Houston, Los Angeles, New Orleans, New York, Pittsburgh, Salt Lake City, San Francisco, and Seattle. The company wants to determine the smallest number of hubs it will need to cover all of these cities, where a city is "covered" if it is within 1000 miles of at least one hub. Table 14.16 lists the cities that are within 1000 miles of other cities.

Table 14.16   Data for Western Airlines Set-Covering Example

	Cities Within 1000 Miles
Atlanta (AT)	AT, CH, HO, NO, NY, PI
Boston (BO)	BO, NY, PI
Chicago (CH)	AT, CH, NY, NO, PI
Denver (DE)	DE, SL
Houston (HO)	AT, HO, NO
Los Angeles (LA)	LA, SL, SF
New Orleans (NO)	AT, CH, HO, NO
New York (NY)	AT, BO, CH, NY, PI
Pittsburgh (PI)	AT, BO, CH, NY, PI
Salt Lake City (SL)	DE, LA, SL, SF, SE
San Francisco (SF)	LA, SL, SF, SE
Seattle (SE)	SL, SF, SE

Objective   To develop a binary model to find the minimum number of hub locations that can cover all cities.

Where Do the Numbers Come From?

Western has evidently made a policy decision that its hubs will cover cities within a 1000-mile radius. Then the cities covered by any hub location can be found from a map. (In a later sensitivity analysis, we explore how the solution changes when the allowable coverage distance varies.)

Solution

The variables and constraints for this set-covering model are listed in Table 14.17. The model is straightforward. There is a binary variable for each city to indicate whether a hub is located there. Then the number of hubs that cover each city is constrained to be at least one. There are no monetary costs in this version of the problem. The goal is to minimize the number of hubs.

Table 14.17   Variables and Constraints for Set-Covering Model

Input variables	Cities within 1000 miles of one another
Decision variables (changing cells)	Locations of hubs (binary)
Objective cell	Number of hubs
Other calculated variables	Number of hubs covering each city
Constraints	Number of hubs covering a city ≥ 1

Developing the Hub Location Model

Developing the Spreadsheet Model

The spreadsheet model for Western is shown in Figure 14.49. (See the file **Locating Hubs 1.xlsx**.) It can be developed as follows.

Figure 14.49 Set-Covering Model

	A	B	C	D	E	F	G	H	I	J	K	L	M	N	O	P	Q
1	Western Airlines hub location model																
2																	
3	Input data: which cities are covered by which potential hubs														Range names used:		
4		Potential hub													Hubs_covered_by	=Model!$B$25:$B$36	
5	City	AT	BO	CH	DE	HO	LA	NO	NY	PI	SL	SF	SE		Total_hubs	=Model!$B$39	
6	AT	1	0	1	0	1	0	1	1	1	0	0	0		Use_as_hub	=Model!$B$21:$M$21	
7	BO	0	1	0	0	0	0	0	1	1	0	0	0				
8	CH	1	0	1	0	0	0	1	1	1	0	0	0				
9	DE	0	0	0	1	0	0	0	0	0	1	0	0				
10	HO	1	0	0	0	1	0	1	0	0	0	0	0				
11	LA	0	0	0	0	0	1	0	0	0	1	1	0				
12	NO	1	0	1	0	1	0	1	0	0	0	0	0				
13	NY	1	1	1	0	0	0	0	1	1	0	0	0				
14	PI	1	1	1	0	0	0	0	1	1	0	0	0				
15	SL	0	0	0	1	0	1	0	0	0	1	1	1				
16	SF	0	0	0	0	0	1	0	0	0	1	1	1				
17	SE	0	0	0	0	0	0	0	0	0	1	1	1				
18																	
19	Decisions: which cities to use as hubs																
20		AT	BO	CH	DE	HO	LA	NO	NY	PI	SL	SF	SE				
21	Use as hub	1	1	0	0	0	0	0	0	0	1	0	0				
22																	
23	Constraints that each city must be covered by at least one hub																
24	City	Hubs covered by		Required			Number of hubs each city must be covered by										
25	AT	1	>=	1			1										
26	BO	1	>=	1													
27	CH	1	>=	1													
28	DE	1	>=	1													
29	HO	1	>=	1													
30	LA	1	>=	1													
31	NO	1	>=	1													
32	NY	2	>=	1													
33	PI	2	>=	1													
34	SL	1	>=	1													
35	SF	1	>=	1													
36	SE	1	>=	1													
37																	
38	Objective to minimize																
39	Total hubs	3															

Note that there are multiple optimal solutions to this model, all of which require a total of 3 hubs. You might get a different solution from the one shown here, depending on your starting solution.

1. **Inputs.** Enter the information from Table 14.16 in the input cells. A 1 in a cell indicates that the column city covers the row city, whereas a 0 indicates that the column city does not cover the row city. For example, the three 1s in row 7 indicate that Boston, New York, and Pittsburgh are the only cities within 1000 miles of Boston.

2. **Binary values for hub locations.** Enter *any* trial values of 0s or 1s in the Use_as_hub range to indicate which cities are used as hubs. These are the changing cells.

3. **Cities covered by hubs.** Calculate the total number of hubs within 1000 miles of Atlanta in cell B25 with the formula

    =SUMPRODUCT(B6:M6,Use_as_hub)

    For any binary values in the changing-cells range, this formula sums the number of hubs that cover Atlanta. Then copy this to the rest of the Hubs_covered_by range. Note that a value in the Hubs_covered_by range can be 2 or greater. This indicates that a city is within 1000 miles of multiple hubs.

4. **Number of hubs.** Calculate the total number of hubs used in cell B39 with the formula

    =SUM(Use_as_hub)

© Cengage Learning

Using Solver

The completed Solver dialog box is shown in Figure 14.50. The goal is to minimize the total number of hubs, subject to covering each city by at least one hub and ensuring that the changing cells are binary.

Figure 14.50

Solver Dialog Box for Set-Covering Model

Discussion of the Solution

Figure 14.51 is a graphical representation of the optimal solution, where the double ovals indicate hub locations and the large circles indicate ranges covered by the hubs. (These large

Figure 14.51

Graphical Solution to Set-Covering Model

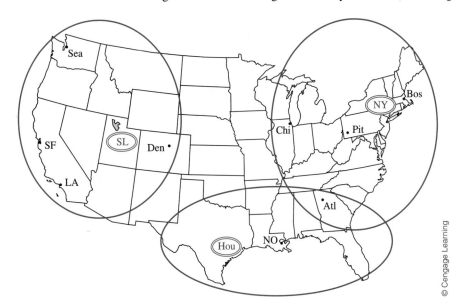

circles are not drawn to scale. In reality, they should be circles of radius 1000 miles centered at the hubs.) Three hubs—in Houston, New York, and Salt Lake City—are needed.[13] Would you have guessed this? The Houston hub covers Houston, Atlanta, and New Orleans. The New York hub covers Atlanta, Pittsburgh, Boston, New York, and Chicago. The Salt Lake City hub covers Denver, Los Angeles, Salt Lake City, San Francisco, and Seattle. Note that Atlanta is the only city covered by two hubs; it can be serviced by New York or Houston.

Sensitivity Analysis

An interesting sensitivity analysis for Western's problem is to see how the solution is affected by the mile limit. Currently, a hub can service all cities within 1000 miles. What if the limit were 800 or 1200 miles, say? To answer this question, you must first collect data on actual distances among all of the cities. Once you have a table of these distances, you can build the binary table, corresponding to the range B6:M17 in Figure 14.49, with IF functions. The modified model appears in Figure 14.52. (See the file **Locating Hubs 2.xlsx**.)

Figure 14.52 Modified Hub Location Model

Western Airlines hub location model with distances

Input data

Mile limit	1000

Range names used:

Hubs_covered_by	=Model!$B$28:$B$39
Total_hubs	=Model!$B$42
Use_as_hub	=Model!$B$24:$M$24

Distance from each city to each other city

	AT	BO	CH	DE	HO	LA	NO	NY	PI	SL	SF	SE
AT	0	1037	674	1398	789	2182	479	841	687	1878	2496	2618
BO	1037	0	1005	1949	1804	2979	1507	222	574	2343	3095	2976
CH	674	1005	0	1008	1067	2054	912	802	452	1390	2142	2013
DE	1398	1949	1008	0	1019	1059	1273	1771	1411	504	1235	1307
HO	789	1804	1067	1019	0	1538	356	1608	1313	1438	1912	2274
LA	2182	2979	2054	1059	1538	0	1883	2786	2426	715	379	1131
NO	479	1507	912	1273	356	1883	0	1311	1070	1738	2249	2574
NY	841	222	802	1771	1608	2786	1311	0	368	2182	2934	2815
PI	687	574	452	1411	1313	2426	1070	368	0	1826	2578	2465
SL	1878	2343	1390	504	1438	715	1738	2182	1826	0	752	836
SF	2496	3095	2142	1235	1912	379	2249	2934	2578	752	0	808
SE	2618	2976	2013	1307	2274	1131	2574	2815	2465	836	808	0

Which cities are covered by which potential hubs with this mile limit

City	Potential hub											
	AT	BO	CH	DE	HO	LA	NO	NY	PI	SL	SF	SE
AT	1	0	1	0	1	0	1	1	1	0	0	0
BO	0	1	0	0	0	0	0	1	1	0	0	0
CH	1	0	1	0	0	0	1	1	1	0	0	0
DE	0	0	0	1	0	0	0	0	0	1	0	0
HO	1	0	0	0	1	0	1	0	0	0	0	0
LA	0	0	0	0	0	1	0	0	0	1	1	0
NO	1	0	1	0	1	0	1	0	0	0	0	0
NY	1	1	1	0	0	0	0	1	1	0	0	0
PI	1	1	1	0	0	0	0	1	1	0	0	0
SL	0	0	0	1	0	1	0	0	0	1	1	1
SF	0	0	0	0	0	1	0	0	0	1	1	1
SE	0	0	0	0	0	0	0	0	0	1	1	1

Decisions: which cities to use as hubs

	AT	BO	CH	DE	HO	LA	NO	NY	PI	SL	SF	SE
Use as hub	0	0	0	0	1	0	0	1	0	1	0	0

Constraints that each city must be covered by atleast one hub

City	Hubs covered by		Required
AT	2	>=	1
BO	1	>=	1
CH	1	>=	1
DE	1	>=	1
HO	1	>=	1
LA	1	>=	1
NO	1	>=	1
NY	1	>=	1
PI	1	>=	1
SL	1	>=	1
SF	1	>=	1
SE	1	>=	1

Note: There are multiple optimal solutions to this model problem, so don't be surprised if you don't get exactly the same hub locations as shown here.

Objective to minimize

Total hubs	3

The typical formula in P9 is **=IF(B9<=$B$4,1,0)**, which is then copied to the rest of the P9:AA20 range.[14] You can then run SolverTable, selecting cell B4 as the single input cell, letting it vary from 800 to 1200 in increments of 100, and designating the hub locations and

---

[13] There are multiple optimal solutions for this model, all requiring three hubs, so you might obtain a different solution from ours.

[14] We have warned you about using IF functions in Solver models. However, the current use affects only the *inputs* to the problem, not quantities that depend on the changing cells. Therefore, it causes no problems.

© Cengage Learning

the number of hubs as outputs. The SolverTable results in Figure 14.53 show the effect of the mile limit. When this limit is lowered to 800 miles, four hubs are required, but when it is increased to 1100 or 1200, only two hubs are required. Note that the solution shown for the 1000-mile limit is different from the previous solution in Figure 14.49, but it still requires three hubs. (This is a case of multiple optimal solutions.) ∎

Figure 14.53   **Sensitivity to Mile Limit**

	A	B	C	D	E	F	G	H	I	J	K	L	M	N
3	Mile limit (cell $B$4) values along side, output cell(s) along top													
4		Use_as_hub_1	Use_as_hub_2	Use_as_hub_3	Use_as_hub_4	Use_as_hub_5	Use_as_hub_6	Use_as_hub_7	Use_as_hub_8	Use_as_hub_9	Use_as_hub_10	Use_as_hub_11	Use_as_hub_12	Total_hubs
5	800	1	1	0	0	0	0	0	0	0	1	0	1	4
6	900	1	1	0	0	0	0	0	0	0	1	0	0	3
7	1000	1	1	0	0	0	0	0	0	0	1	0	0	3
8	1100	0	0	1	0	0	0	0	0	0	1	0	0	2
9	1200	0	0	1	0	0	1	0	0	0	0	0	0	2

© Cengage Learning

PROBLEMS

Level A

48. Solve the following modifications of the capital budgeting model in Figure 14.37. (Solve each part independently of the others.)

   a. Suppose that at most two of projects 1 through 5 can be selected.

   b. Suppose that if investment 1 is selected, then investment 3 must also be selected.

   c. Suppose that at least one of investments 6 and 7 *must* be selected.

   d. Suppose that investment 2 can be selected only if *both* investments 1 and 3 are selected.

49. In the capital budgeting model in Figure 14.37, we supplied the NPV for each investment. Suppose instead that you are given only the streams of cash inflows from each investment shown in the file **P14_49.xlsx**. This file also shows the cash requirements and the budget. You can assume that (1) all cash outflows occur at the beginning of year 1; (2) all cash inflows occur at the ends of their respective years; and (3) the company uses a 10% discount rate for calculating its NPVs. Which investments should the company make?

50. Solve the previous problem using the input data in the file **P14_50.xlsx**.

51. Solve Problem 49 with the extra assumption that the investments can be grouped naturally as follows: 1–4, 5–8, 9–12, 13–16, and 17–20.

   a. Find the optimal investments when at most one investment from each group can be selected.

   b. Find the optimal investments when at least one investment from each group must be selected. (If the budget isn't large enough to permit this, increase the budget to a larger value.)

52. In the capital budgeting model in Figure 14.37, investment 4 has the largest ratio of NPV to cash requirement, but it is not selected in the optimal solution. How much NPV is lost if Tatham is *forced* to select investment 4? Answer by solving a suitably modified model.

53. As it currently stands, investment 7 in the capital budgeting model in Figure 14.37 has the lowest ratio of NPV to cash requirement, 2.5. Keeping this same ratio, can you change the cash requirement and NPV for investment 7 in such a way that it *is* selected in the optimal solution? Does this lead to any general insights? Explain.

54. Expand the capital budgeting model in Figure 14.37 so that there are now 20 possible investments. You can make up the data on cash requirements, NPVs, and the budget. However, use the following guidelines:

   ▪ The cash requirements and NPVs for the various investments can vary widely, but the ratio of NPV to cash requirement should be between 2.5 and 3.5 for each investment.

   ▪ The budget should allow somewhere between 5 and 10 of the investments to be selected.

55. Suppose in the capital budgeting model in Figure 14.37 that each investment requires $2000 during year 2 and only $5000 is available for investment during year 2.

a. Assuming that available money uninvested at the end of year 1 cannot be used during year 2, what combination of investments maximizes NPV?

b. Suppose that any uninvested money at the end of year 1 *can* be used for investment in year 2. Does your answer to part **a** change?

56. How difficult is it to expand the Great Threads model to accommodate another type of clothing? Answer by assuming that the company can also produce sweatshirts. The rental cost for sweatshirt equipment is $1100, the variable cost per unit and the selling price are $15 and $45, respectively, and each sweatshirt requires one labor hour and 3.5 square yards of cloth.

57. Referring to the previous problem, if it is optimal for the company to produce sweatshirts, use SolverTable to see how much larger the fixed cost of sweatshirt machinery would have to be before the company would *not* produce any sweatshirts. However, if the solution to the previous problem calls for no sweatshirts to be produced, use SolverTable to see how much lower the fixed cost of sweatshirt machinery would have to be before the company *would* start producing sweatshirts.

58. In the Great Threads model, the production quantities in row 16 were not constrained to be integers. Presumably, any fractional values could be safely rounded to integers. See whether this is true. Constrain these quantities to be integers and then run Solver. Are the optimal integer values the same as the rounded fractional values in Figure 14.43?

59. In the optimal solution to the Great Threads model, the labor hour and cloth constraints are both binding—the company is using all it has.

a. Use SolverTable to see what happens to the optimal solution when the amount of available cloth increases from its current value. (You can choose the range of input values to use.) Capture all of the changing cells, the labor hours and cloth used, and the profit as outputs. The real issue here is whether the company can profitably use more cloth when it is already constrained by labor hours.

b. Repeat part **a**, but reverse the roles of labor hours and cloth. That is, use the available labor hours as the input for SolverTable.

60. In the optimal solution to the Great Threads model, no pants are produced. Suppose Great Threads has an order for 300 pairs of pants that *must* be produced. Modify the model appropriately and use Solver to find the new optimal solution. (Is it enough to put a lower bound of 300 on the production quantity in cell D16? Will this automatically force the binary value in cell D14 to be 1? Explain.) How much profit does the company lose because of having to produce pants?

61. In the original Western Airlines set-covering model in Figure 14.49, we assumed that each city must be covered by at least one hub. Suppose that for added flexibility in flight routing, Western requires that each city must be covered by at least two hubs. How do the model and optimal solution change?

62. In the original Western Airlines set-covering model in Figure 14.49, we used the number of hubs as the objective to minimize. Suppose instead that there is a fixed cost of locating a hub in any city, where these fixed costs can vary across cities. Make up some reasonable fixed costs, modify the model appropriately, and use Solver to find the solution that minimizes the sum of fixed costs.

63. Set-covering models such as the original Western Airlines model in Figure 14.49 often have multiple optimal solutions. See how many alternative optimal solutions you can find. Of course, each must use three hubs because we know this is optimal. (*Hint*: Use various initial values in the changing cells and then run Solver repeatedly.)[15]

64. How hard is it to expand a set-covering model to accommodate new cities? Answer this by modifying the model in Figure 14.52. (See the file **Locating Hubs 2.xlsx**.) Add several cities that must be served: Memphis, Dallas, Tucson, Philadelphia, Cleveland, and Buffalo. You can look up the distances from these cities to each other and to the other cities in a reference book (or on the Web), or you can make up approximate distances.

a. Modify the model appropriately, assuming that these new cities must be covered *and* are candidates for hub locations.

b. Modify the model appropriately, assuming that these new cities must be covered but are *not* candidates for hub locations.

Level B

65. The models in this section are often called *combinatorial* models because each solution is a combination of the various 0s and 1s, and there are only a finite number of such combinations. For the capital budgeting model in Figure 14.37, there are seven investments, so there are $2^7 = 128$ possible solutions (some of which are infeasible). This is a fairly large number, but not *too* large. Solve the model *without* Solver by listing all 128 solutions. For each, calculate the total cash requirement and total NPV for the model. Then manually choose the one that stays within the budget and has the largest NPV.

66. Make up an example, as described in Problem 54, with 20 possible investments. However, do it so that the ratios of NPV to cash requirement are in a very

---

[15]One of our colleagues at Indiana University, Vic Cabot, now deceased, worked for years trying to develop a general algorithm (not just trial and error) for finding *all* alternative optimal solutions to optimization models. It turns out that this is a very difficult problem—and one that Vic never completely solved.

tight range, from 3.0 to 3.2. Then use Solver to find the optimal solution when the Solver tolerance is set to its default value of 5%, and record the solution. Next, solve again with the tolerance set to zero. Do you get the same solution? Try this on a few more instances of the model, where you keep tinkering with the inputs. The question is whether the tolerance matters in these types of narrow-range problems.

67. In the Great Threads model, we found an upper bound on production of any clothing type by calculating the amount that could be produced if *all* of the resources were devoted to this clothing type.
   a. What if you instead use a very large value such as 1,000,000 for this upper bound? Try it and see whether you get the same optimal solution.
   b. Explain why *any* such upper bound is required. Exactly what role does it play in the model?

68. In the last sheet of the finished version of the Fixed Cost Manufacturing file, we illustrated one way to model the Great Threads problem with IF functions, but saw that this approach doesn't work. Try a slightly different approach here. Eliminate the binary variables in row 14 altogether, and eliminate the upper bounds in row 18 and the corresponding upper bound constraints in the Solver dialog box. (The only constraints are now on resource availability.) However, use IF functions to calculate the total fixed cost of renting equipment, so that if the amount of any clothing type is positive, then its fixed cost is added to the total fixed cost. Is Solver able to handle this model? Does it depend on the initial values in the changing cells? (Don't forget to use Solver's nonlinear algorithm, not the simplex method.)

14-8 NONLINEAR OPTIMIZATION MODELS

In many optimization models the objective and/or the constraints are nonlinear functions of the decision variables. Such an optimization model is called a **nonlinear programming (NLP) model**. In this section we discuss how to use Excel's Solver to find optimal solutions to NLP models. We then discuss a couple of interesting applications, including the important portfolio optimization model.

14-8a Basic Ideas of Nonlinear Optimization

FUNDAMENTAL INSIGHT

Local Optimal Solution Versus Global Optimal Solution

Nonlinear objective functions can behave in many ways that make them difficult to optimize. In particular, they can have local optimal solutions that are not globally optimal, and nonlinear optimization algorithms can stop at such local optimal solutions. The important property of linear objectives that makes the simplex method so successful—namely, that the optimal solution is a corner point—doesn't hold for nonlinear objectives. Now any point in the feasible region can conceivably be optimal. This not only makes the search for the optimal solution more difficult, but it also makes it much more difficult to recognize whether a promising solution (a local optimum) is indeed the global optimum. This is why researchers have spent so much effort trying to obtain conditions that, when true, guarantee that a local optimum must be a global optimum. Unfortunately, these conditions are often difficult to check.

When you solve an LP model with Solver, you are guaranteed that the solution obtained is an optimal solution. When you solve an NLP model, however, it is very possible that Solver will obtain a suboptimal solution. This is because a nonlinear function can have *local* optimal solutions that are not the *global* optimal solution. A **local optimal solution** is one that is better than all nearby points, whereas the **global optimum** is the one that beats all points in the entire feasible region. If there are indeed one or more local optimal solutions that are not globally optimal, then it is entirely possible that Solver will stop at one of them. Unfortunately, this is not what you want; you want the global optimum.

There are mathematical conditions that guarantee the Solver solution is indeed the global optimum. However, these conditions are difficult to understand, and they are often difficult to check. A much simpler approach is to run Solver several times, each time with different starting values in the changing cells. In general, if Solver obtains the same optimal solution in all cases, you can be fairly confident—but still not absolutely sure—that Solver has found the global optimal solution. On the other hand, if you try different starting values for the changing cells and obtain several different solutions, you should keep the best solution found so far. That is, you should keep the solution with the lowest objective value (for a minimization problem) or the highest objective value (for a maximization problem).

14-8b Managerial Economics Models

Many problems in economics are nonlinear but can be solved with Solver. Example 14.11 illustrates one such peak-load pricing example.

<hr>

EXAMPLE | **14.11 PEAK-LOAD PRICING AT FLORIDA POWER AND LIGHT**

Florida Power and Light (FPL) faces demands during both peak-load and off-peak times. FPL must determine the price per kilowatt hour (kwh) to charge during both peak-load and off-peak periods. The daily demand for power during each period (in kwh) is related to price as follows:

$$D_p = 60 - 0.5P_p + 0.1P_o \qquad \textbf{(14.5)}$$

$$D_o = 40 - P_o + 0.1P_p \qquad \textbf{(14.6)}$$

Here, D_p and P_p are demand and price during peak-load times, and D_o and P_o are demand and price during off-peak times. Note that these demand functions are *linear* in the prices. Also, note from the signs of the coefficients that an increase in the peak-load price decreases the demand for power during the peak-load period but *increases* the demand for power during the off-peak period. Similarly, an increase in the price for the off-peak period decreases the demand for the off-peak period but *increases* the demand for the peak-load period. In economic terms, this implies that peak-load power and off-peak power are *substitutes* for one another. In addition, assume that it costs FPL $10 per day to maintain one kwh of capacity. The company wants to determine a pricing strategy and a capacity level that maximize its daily profit.

Objective To use a nonlinear model to determine prices and capacity when there are two different daily usage patterns, peak-load and off-peak.

Where Do the Numbers Come From?

A cost accountant should be able to estimate the unit cost of capacity. The difficult task is to estimate the demand functions in Equations (14.5) and (14.6). This requires either sufficient historical data on prices and demands (for both peak-load and off-peak periods) or educated guesses from management.

Solution

The variables and constraints for this model are listed in Table 14.18. The company must decide on two prices, and it must determine the amount of capacity to maintain. Because this capacity level, once determined, is relevant for peak-load and off-peak periods, it must be large enough to meet demands for both periods. This is the reasoning behind the constraint.

Due to the relationships between the demand and price variables, it is not at all obvious what FPL should do. The pricing decisions determine demand, and larger demand requires larger capacity, which costs money. In addition, revenue is price multiplied by demand, so it is not clear whether price should be low or high to increase revenue.

Table 14.18   Variables and Constraints for Peak-Load Pricing Model

Input variables	Parameters of demand functions, unit cost of capacity
Decision variables (changing cells)	Peak-load and off-peak prices, capacity
Objective cell	Profit
Other calculated variables	Peak-load and off-peak demands, revenue, cost of capacity
Constraints	Demands ≤ Capacity

© Cengage Learning

Developing the Peak-Load Pricing Model

Developing the Spreadsheet Model

The spreadsheet model appears in Figure 14.54. (See the file **Peak-Load Pricing.xlsx**.) It can be developed as follows.

Figure 14.54   Peak-Load Pricing Model

	A	B	C	D	E	F	G	H
1	Florida Power & Light peak-load pricing model					Range names used:		
2						Capacity	=Model!$B$15	
3	**Input data**					Common_Capacity	=Model!$B$21:$C$21	
4	Coefficients of demand functions					Demands	=Model!$B$19:$C$19	
5		Constant	Peak price	Off-peak price		Prices	=Model!$B$13:$C$13	
6	Peak-load demand	60	−0.5	0.1		Profit	=Model!$B$26	
7	Off-peak demand	40	0.1	−1				
8								
9	Cost of capacity/kwh	$10						
10								
11	**Decisions**							
12		Peak-load	Off-peak					
13	Prices	$70.31	$26.53					
14								
15	Capacity	27.50						
16								
17	**Constraints on demand**							
18		Peak-load	Off-peak					
19	Demand	27.50	20.50					
20		<=	<=					
21	Capacity	27.50	27.50					
22								
23	**Monetary summary**							
24	Revenue	$2,477.30						
25	Cost of capacity	$275.00						
26	Profit	$2,202.30						

© Cengage Learning

1. **Inputs.** Enter the parameters of the demand functions and the cost of capacity in the input cells.

2. **Prices and capacity level.** Enter *any* trial prices (per kwh) for peak-load and off-peak power in the Prices range, and enter *any* trial value for the capacity level in the Capacity cell. These are the three values FPL has control over, so they are the changing cells.

3. **Demands.** Calculate the demand for the peak-load period by substituting into Equation (14.5). That is, enter the formula

   =B6+SUMPRODUCT(Prices,C6:D6)

   in cell B19. Similarly, enter the formula

   =B7+SUMPRODUCT(Prices,C7:D7)

   in cell C19 for the off-peak demand.

4. **Copy capacity.** To indicate the capacity constraints, enter the formula

=Capacity

in cells B21 and C21. The reason for creating these links is that the two demand cells in row 19 must be paired with two capacity cells in row 21, so that the Solver constraints can be specified appropriately. (Solver doesn't allow you to have a "two versus one" constraint like B19:C19 <= B15.)

5. **Monetary values.** Calculate the daily revenue, cost of capacity, and profit in the corresponding cells with the formulas

=SUMPRODUCT(Demands,Prices)

=Capacity*B9

and

=B24-B25

Using Solver

The complete Solver dialog box is shown in Figure 14.55. The goal is to maximize profit by setting appropriate prices and capacity and ensuring that demand never exceeds capacity. Most importantly, the Simplex LP method cannot be used; you must select the GRG Nonlinear method instead. This is because prices are multiplied by demands to calculate revenues, and demands are *functions* of prices. Therefore, profit is a nonlinear function of the prices.

Figure 14.55
Solver Dialog Box for Peak-Load Pricing Model

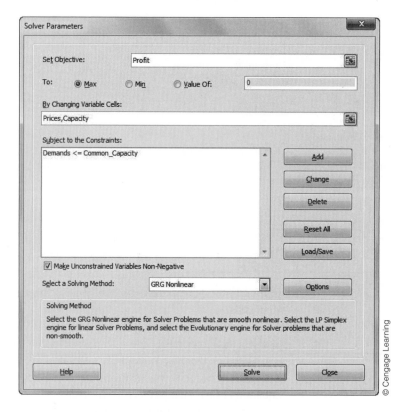

© Cengage Learning

Discussion of the Solution

The Solver solution in Figure 14.54 indicates that FPL should charge $70.31 per kwh during the peak-load period and $26.53 during the off-peak period. These prices generate demands of 27.5 (peak-load) and 20.5 (off-peak), so that a capacity of 27.5 kwh is required. The cost of this capacity is $275. When this is subtracted from the revenue of $2477.30, the daily profit becomes $2202.30.

Varying the changing cells slightly from their optimal values sometimes provides insight into the optimal solution.

To gain some insight into this solution, consider what happens if FPL changes the peak-load price slightly from its optimal value of $70.31. If FPL decreases the price to $70, say, you can check that the peak-load demand increases to 27.65 kwh and the off-peak demand decreases to 20.47 kwh. The net effect is that revenue increases slightly, to $2478.78. However, the peak-load demand is now greater than capacity, so FPL must increase its capacity from 27.50 to 27.65 kwh. This costs an extra $1.50, which more than offsets the increase in revenue. A similar chain of effects occurs if FPL increases the peak price to $71. In this case, peak-load demand decreases, off-peak demand increases, and total revenue decreases. Although FPL can get by with lower capacity, the net effect is slightly less profit. Fortunately, Solver evaluates all of these trade-offs when it finds the optimal solution.

Is the Solver Solution Optimal?

It is not difficult to show that the constraints for this model are linear and the objective is a *concave* function. This is enough to guarantee that there are no local maxima that are not globally optimal. In short, this guarantees that the Solver solution is optimal.

Sensitivity Analysis

To gain even more insight, SolverTable can be used to see the effects of changing the unit cost of capacity, which are allowed to vary from $5 to $15 in increments of $1. The results appear in Figure 14.56. They indicate that as the cost of capacity increases, the peak-load price increases, the off-peak price stays constant, the amount of capacity decreases, and profit decreases. The latter two effects are probably intuitive, but we challenge you to explain the effects on price. In particular, why does the peak-load price *increase*, and why doesn't the off-peak price increase as well? ∎

Figure 14.56

Sensitivity to Cost of Capacity

	A	B	C	D	E	F
3	Capacity cost (cell $B$9) values along side, output cell(s) along top					
4		Prices_1	Prices_2	Capacity	Profit	
5	$5	$67.81	$26.53	28.75	$2,342.92	
6	$6	$68.31	$26.53	28.50	$2,314.30	
7	$7	$68.81	$26.53	28.25	$2,285.92	
8	$8	$69.31	$26.53	28.00	$2,257.80	
9	$9	$69.81	$26.53	27.75	$2,229.92	
10	$10	$70.31	$26.53	27.50	$2,202.30	
11	$11	$70.81	$26.53	27.25	$2,174.92	
12	$12	$71.31	$26.53	27.00	$2,147.80	
13	$13	$71.81	$26.53	26.75	$2,120.92	
14	$14	$72.31	$26.53	26.50	$2,094.30	
15	$15	$72.81	$26.53	26.25	$2,067.92	

© Cengage Learning

14-8c Portfolio Optimization Models

Given a set of investments, how do financial analysts determine the portfolio that has the lowest risk and yields a high expected return? This question was answered by Harry Markowitz in the 1950s. For his work on this and other investment topics, he received the Nobel Prize in economics in 1991. The ideas discussed in this section are the basis for most methods of *asset allocation* used by Wall Street firms. For example, **portfolio optimization models** are used to determine the percentage of assets to invest in stocks, gold, and Treasury bills. Before proceeding, however, you need to learn about some important formulas involving the expected value and variance of sums of random variables.

Weighted Sums of Random Variables

Let R_i be the (random) return earned during a year on a dollar invested in investment i. For example, if $R_i = 0.10$, a dollar invested at the beginning of the year grows to $1.10 by the end of the year, whereas if $R_i = -0.20$, a dollar invested at the beginning of the year decreases in value to $0.80 by the end of the year. We assume that n investments are available. Let x_i be the fraction of our money invested in investment i. We assume that $x_1 + x_2 + \cdots + x_n = 1$, so that all of our money is invested. (To prevent shorting a stock—that is, selling shares we don't own—we assume that $x_i \geq 0$.) Then the annual return on our investments is given by the random variable R_p, where

$$R_p = R_1 x_1 + R_2 x_2 + \cdots + R_n x_n$$

(The subscript p on R_p stands for "portfolio.")

Let μ_i be the expected value (also called the mean) of R_i, let σ_i^2 be the variance of R_i (so that σ_i is the standard deviation of R_i), and let ρ_{ij} be the correlation between R_i and R_j. To do any work with investments, you must understand how to use the following formulas, which relate the data for the individual investments to the expected return and the variance of return for a *portfolio* of investments.

Expected value of $R_p = \mu_1 x_1 + \mu_2 x_2 + \cdots + \mu_n x_n$	**(14.7)**
Variance of $R_p = \sigma_1^2 x_1^2 + \sigma_2^2 x_2^2 + \cdots + \sigma_n^2 x_n^2 + \Sigma_{ij} \rho_{ij} \sigma_i \sigma_j x_i x_j$	**(14.8)**

The latter summation in Equation (14.8) is over all pairs of investments. The quantities in Equations (14.7) and (14.8) are extremely important in portfolio selection because of the risk–return trade-off investors need to make. All investors want to choose portfolios with high return, measured by the expected value in Equation (14.7), but they also want portfolios with low risk, usually measured by the variance in Equation (14.8).

Equation (14.8) can be rewritten slightly by using *covariances* instead of correlations. The covariance between two stock returns is another measure of the relationship between the two returns, but unlike a correlation, it is *not* scaled to be between –1 and +1. This is because covariances are affected by the units in which the returns are measured. Although a covariance is a somewhat less intuitive measure than a correlation, it is used so frequently by financial analysts that we use it here as well. If c_{ij} is the estimated covariance between stocks i and j, then $c_{ij} = r_{ij} s_i s_j$. (Here, r is an estimated correlation, and s is an estimated standard deviation.) Using this equation and the fact that the correlation between any stock and itself is 1, we can also write $c_{ii} = s_i^2$ for each stock i. Therefore, an equivalent form of Equation (14.8) is the following Example (14.9):

Estimated variance of $R_p = \Sigma_{i,j} c_{ij} x_i x_j$	**(14.9)**

This allows you to calculate the portfolio variance very easily with Excel's matrix functions, as explained next.

Matrix Functions in Excel

Matrix Multiplication in Excel

Equation (14.9) for the variance of portfolio return looks intimidating, particularly if there are many potential investments. Fortunately, two built-in Excel matrix functions, MMULT and TRANSPOSE, simplify the calculation. In this subsection we illustrate how to use these two functions. Then in the next subsection we use them in the portfolio selection model.

A *matrix* is a rectangular array of numbers. The matrix is an $i \times j$ matrix if it consists of i rows and j columns. For example,

$$A = \begin{pmatrix} 1 & 2 & 3 \\ 4 & 5 & 6 \end{pmatrix}$$

is a 2×3 matrix, and

$$B = \begin{pmatrix} 1 & 2 \\ 3 & 4 \\ 5 & 6 \end{pmatrix}$$

is a 3×2 matrix. If the matrix has only a single row, it is called a *row vector*. Similarly, if it has only a single column, it is called a *column vector*.

If matrix A has the same number of columns as matrix B has rows, it is possible to calculate the *matrix product* of A and B, denoted AB. The entry in row i, column j of the product AB is obtained by summing the products of the values in row i of A with the corresponding values in column j of B. If A is an $i \times k$ matrix and B is a $k \times j$ matrix, the product AB is an $i \times j$ matrix.

For example, if

$$A = \begin{pmatrix} 1 & 2 & 3 \\ 2 & 4 & 5 \end{pmatrix}$$

and

$$B = \begin{pmatrix} 1 & 2 \\ 3 & 4 \\ 5 & 6 \end{pmatrix}$$

then AB is the following 2×2 matrix:

$$AB = \begin{pmatrix} 1(1) + 2(3) + 3(5) & 1(2) + 2(4) + 3(6) \\ 2(1) + 4(3) + 5(5) & 2(2) + 4(4) + 5(6) \end{pmatrix} = \begin{pmatrix} 22 & 28 \\ 39 & 50 \end{pmatrix}$$

The Excel MMULT function performs matrix multiplication in a single step. The spreadsheet in Figure 14.57 indicates how to multiply matrices of different sizes. (See the file **Matrix Multiplication.xlsx**.) For example, to multiply matrix 1 by matrix 2 (which is possible because matrix 1 has three columns and matrix 2 has three rows), select the range B13:C14, type the formula

=MMULT(B4:D5,B7:C9)

and press Ctrl+Shift+Enter (all three keys at once). Note that you should select a range with two rows and two columns because matrix 1 has two rows and matrix 2 has two columns.

The matrix multiplication in cell B24 indicates that (1) it is possible to multiply three matrices together by using MMULT twice, and (2) the TRANSPOSE function can be used to convert a column vector to a row vector (or vice versa), if necessary. Here, you want to multiply Column 1 by the product of Matrix 3 and Column 1. However, Column 1 is 3×1, and Matrix 3 is 3×3, so Column 1 multiplied by Matrix 3 doesn't work. Instead, you must transpose Column 1 to make it 1×3. Then the result of multiplying all three together is a 1×1 matrix (a number). It can be calculated by selecting cell B24, typing the formula

=MMULT(TRANSPOSE(I4:I6),MMULT(B17:D19,I4:I6))

and pressing Ctrl+Shift+Enter. This formula uses MMULT twice because MMULT can multiply only *two* matrices at a time.

Figure 14.57 Examples of Matrix Multiplication in Excel

	A	B	C	D	E	F	G	H	I	J	K	L	M	N
1	Matrix multiplication in Excel													
2														
3	Typical multiplication of two matrices							Multiplication of a matrix and a column						
4	Matrix 1	1	2	3				Column 1	2					
5		2	4	5					3					
6									4					
7	Matrix 2	1	2											
8		3	4					Matrix 1 times Column 1, with formula =MMULT(B4:D5,I4:I6)						
9		5	6					Select range with 2 rows, 1 column, enter formula, press Ctrl+Shift+Enter						
10									20					
11	Matrix 1 times Matrix 2, with formula =MMULT(B4:D5,B7:C9)								36					
12	Select range with 2 rows, 2 columns, enter formula, press Ctrl+Shift+Enter.													
13		22	28					Multiplication of a row and a matrix						
14		39	50					Row 1	4	5				
15														
16	Multiplication of a quadratic form (row times matrix times column)							Row 1 times Matrix 1, with formula =MMULT(I14:J14,B4:D5)						
17	Matrix 3	2	1	3				Select range with 1 row, 3 columns, enter formula, press Ctrl+Shift+Enter						
18		1	–1	0										
19		3	0	4					14	28	37			
20								Multiplication of a row and a column						
21	Transpose of Column 1 times Matrix 3 times Column 1							Row 2	1	6	3			
22	Formula is =MMULT(TRANSPOSE(I4:I6),MMULT(B17:D19,I4:I6))													
23	Select range with 1 row, 1 column, enter formula, press Ctrl+Shift+Enter							Row 2 times Column 1, with formula =MMULT(I22:K22,I4:I6)						
24		123						Select range with 1 row, 1 column, enter formula, press Ctrl+Shift+Enter						
25									32					
26	Notes on quadratic form example:													
27	Two MMULT's are required because MMULT works on only two ranges at a time.													
28	TRANSPOSE is needed to change a column into a row.													

© Cengage Learning

Excel Function: MMULT

The MMULT and TRANSPOSE functions are useful for matrix operations. They are called array functions because they operate on an entire range, not just a single cell. The MMULT function multiplies two matrices and has the syntax =MMULT(range1,range2), *where range1 must have as many columns as range2 has rows. To use this function, select a range that has as many rows as range1 and as many columns as range2, type the formula, and press Ctrl+Shift+Enter. The resulting formula will have curly brackets around it in the Excel formula bar. You should not type these curly brackets. Excel enters them automatically to remind you that this is an array formula.*

The Portfolio Selection Model

Most investors have two objectives in forming portfolios: to obtain a large expected return and to obtain a small variance (to minimize risk). The problem is inherently nonlinear because the portfolio variance is nonlinear in the investment amounts. The most common way of handling this two-objective problem is to specify a minimal required expected return and then minimize the variance subject to the constraint on the expected return. Example 14.12 illustrates how to do this.

EXAMPLE 14.12 PORTFOLIO OPTIMIZATION AT PERLMAN & BROTHERS

The investment company Perlman & Brothers intends to invest a given amount of money in three stocks. From past data, the means and standard deviations of annual returns have been estimated as shown in Table 14.19. The correlations between the annual returns on the stocks are listed in Table 14.20. The company wants to find a minimum-variance portfolio that yields an expected annual return of at least 0.12 (that is, 12%).

Table 14.19 Estimated Means and Standard Deviations of Stock Returns

Stock	Mean	Standard Deviation
1	0.14	0.20
2	0.11	0.15
3	0.10	0.08

Table 14.20 Estimated Correlations between Stock Returns

Combination	Correlation
Stocks 1 and 2	0.6
Stocks 1 and 3	0.4
Stocks 2 and 3	0.7

Objective   To use NLP to find the portfolio that minimizes the risk, measured by portfolio variance, subject to achieving an expected return of at least 12%.

Where Do the Numbers Come From?

Financial analysts typically estimate the required means, standard deviations, and correlations for stock returns from historical data. However, you should be aware that there is no guarantee that these estimates, based on *historical* return data, are relevant for *future* returns. If analysts have new information about the stocks, they should incorporate this new information into their estimates.

Solution

The variables and constraints for this model are listed in Table 14.21. One interesting aspect of this model is that it is *not* necessary to specify the amount of money invested—it could be $100, $1000, $1,000,000, or any other amount. The model determines the *fractions* of this amount to invest in the various stocks, and these fractions are then relevant for any investment amount. The only requirement is that the fractions should sum to 1, so that all of the money is invested. Besides this, the fractions are constrained to be *nonnegative* to prevent shorting stocks.[16] Finally, the expected portfolio return is constrained to be at least as large as a specified expected return, such as 12%.

Table 14.21 Variables and Constraints for Portfolio Optimization Model

Input variables	Means, standard deviations, and correlations for stock returns, minimum required expected portfolio return
Decision variables (changing cells)	Fractions invested in the various stocks
Objective cell	Portfolio variance (minimize)
Other calculated variables	Covariances between stock returns, total fraction of money invested, expected portfolio return
Constraints	Total fraction invested = 1 Expected portfolio return ≥ Minimum required expected portfolio return

Developing the Portfolio Selection Model

Developing the Spreadsheet Model

The individual steps are now listed. (See Figure 14.58 and the file **Portfolio Selection.xlsx**.)

---

[16]If you want to allow shorting, do not check the Non-Negative option in the Solver dialog box.

Figure 14.58 Portfolio Optimization Model

	A	B	C	D	E	F	G	H	I
1	Portfolio selection model					Range names used:			
2						Actual_return	=Model!$B$23		
3	Stock input data					Fractions_to_invest	=Model!$B$15:$D$15		
4		Stock 1	Stock 2	Stock 3		Portfolio_variance	=Model!$B$25		
5	Mean return	0.14	0.11	0.1		Required_return	=Model!$D$23		
6	StDev of return	0.2	0.15	0.08		Total_invested	=Model!$B$19		
7									
8	Correlations	Stock 1	Stock 2	Stock 3		Covariances	Stock 1	Stock 2	Stock 3
9	Stock 1	1	0.6	0.4		Stock 1	0.04	0.018	0.0064
10	Stock 2	0.6	1	0.7		Stock 2	0.018	0.0225	0.0084
11	Stock 3	0.4	0.7	1		Stock 3	0.0064	0.0084	0.0064
12									
13	Investment decisions								
14		Stock 1	Stock 2	Stock 3					
15	Fractions to invest	0.500	0.000	0.500					
16									
17	Constraint on investing everything								
18		Total invested		Required value					
19		1.00	=	1					
20									
21	Constraint on expected portfolio return								
22		Actual return		Required return					
23		0.12	>=	0.12					
24									
25	Portfolio variance	0.0148							
26	Portfolio stdev	0.1217							

© Cengage Learning

1. **Inputs.** Enter the inputs in the input cells. These include the estimates of means, standard deviations, and correlations, as well as the required expected return.

2. **Fractions invested.** Enter *any* trial values in the Fractions_to_invest range for the fractions of Perlman's money placed in the three investments. Then sum these with the SUM function in cell B19.

3. **Expected annual return.** Use Equation (14.7) to calculate the expected annual return in cell B23 with the formula

   =SUMPRODUCT(B5:D5,Fractions_to_invest)

4. **Covariance matrix.** Equation (14.9) is used to calculate the portfolio variance. To do this, you must first calculate a matrix of covariances. Using the general formula for covariance, $c_{ij} = r_{ij}s_is_j$ (which holds even when $i = j$, because $r_{ii} = 1$), these can be calculated from the inputs by using lookups. Specifically, enter the formula

   =HLOOKUP($F9,$B$4:$D$6,3)*B9*HLOOKUP(G$8,$B$4:$D$6,3)

   in cell G9, and copy it to the range G9:I11. (Note that the term B9 captures the relevant correlation. The two HLOOKUP terms capture the appropriate standard deviations.)

5. **Portfolio variance.** Although the mathematical details are not presented here, it can be shown that the summation in Equation (14.9) is the product of three matrices: a row of fractions invested multiplied by the covariance matrix multiplied by a column of fractions invested. To calculate it, enter the formula

   =MMULT(Fractions_to_invest,MMULT(G9:I11,TRANSPOSE(Fractions_to_invest)))

   in cell B25 and press Ctrl+Shift+Enter. (Remember that Excel puts curly brackets around this formula. You should *not* type these curly brackets.) Note that this formula uses two MMULT functions. Again, this is because MMULT can multiply only two matrices at a time. The formula first multiplies the last two matrices and then multiplies this product by the first matrix.

6. **Portfolio standard deviation.** Most financial analysts talk in terms of portfolio *variance*. However, it is probably more intuitive to talk about portfolio *standard deviation* because it is in the same units as the returns. Calculate the standard deviation in cell B26 with the formula

=SQRT(Portfolio_variance)

Actually, either cell B25 or B26 can be used as the objective cell to minimize. Minimizing the square root of a function is equivalent to minimizing the function itself.

Using Solver

The completed Solver dialog box is shown in Figure 14.59. The constraints specify that the expected return must be at least as large as the minimal required return, and all of the company's money must be invested. The changing cells are constrained to be nonnegative (to avoid short selling), but because of the squared terms in the variance formula, you must select the GRG Nonlinear method.

Figure 14.59

Solver Dialog Box for Portfolio Model

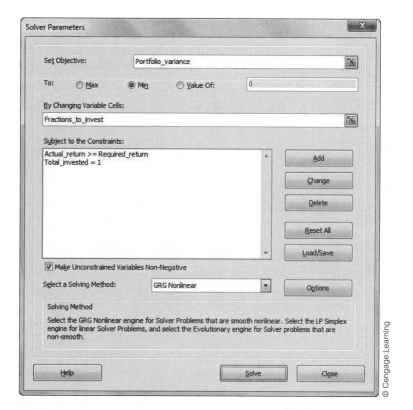

© Cengage Learning

Discussion of the Solution

The solution in Figure 14.58 indicates that the company should put half of its money in each of stocks 1 and 3, and it should not invest in stock 2 at all. This might be somewhat surprising, given that the ranking of riskiness of the stocks is 1, 2, 3, with stock 1 being the most risky but also having the highest expected return. However, the correlations play an important role in portfolio selection, so you can usually not guess the optimal portfolio on the basis of the means and standard deviations of stock returns alone.

The portfolio standard deviation of 0.1217 can be interpreted in a probabilistic sense. Specifically, if stock returns are approximately *normally* distributed, the actual portfolio return will be within one standard deviation of the expected return with probability about

0.68, and the actual portfolio return will be within two standard deviations of the expected return with probability about 0.95. Given that the expected return is 0.12, this implies a lot of risk—two standard deviations below this mean is a *negative* return (or loss) of slightly more than 12%.

Is the Solver Solution Optimal?

The constraints for this model are linear, and it can be shown that the portfolio variance is a *convex* function of the investment fractions. This is sufficient to guarantee that the Solver solution is indeed optimal.

Sensitivity Analysis

This model begs for a sensitivity analysis on the minimum required return. When the company requires a larger expected return, it must assume a larger risk. This behavior is illustrated in Figure 14.60, where SolverTable has been used with cell D23 as the single input

Figure 14.60 The Efficient Frontier

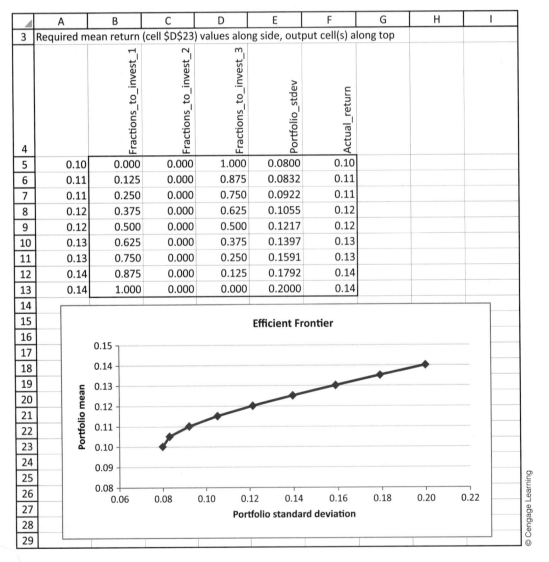

	A	B	C	D	E	F
3	Required mean return (cell $D$23) values along side, output cell(s) along top					
4		Fractions_to_invest_1	Fractions_to_invest_2	Fractions_to_invest_3	Portfolio_stdev	Actual_return
5	0.10	0.000	0.000	1.000	0.0800	0.10
6	0.11	0.125	0.000	0.875	0.0832	0.11
7	0.11	0.250	0.000	0.750	0.0922	0.11
8	0.12	0.375	0.000	0.625	0.1055	0.12
9	0.12	0.500	0.000	0.500	0.1217	0.12
10	0.13	0.625	0.000	0.375	0.1397	0.13
11	0.13	0.750	0.000	0.250	0.1591	0.13
12	0.14	0.875	0.000	0.125	0.1792	0.14
13	0.14	1.000	0.000	0.000	0.2000	0.14

cell, varied from 0.10 to 0.14 in increments of 0.005. Note that values outside this range are of little interest. Stock 3 has the minimum expected return, 0.10, and stock 1 has the highest expected return, 0.14, so no portfolio can have an expected return outside of this range.

The results indicate that the company should put more and more into risky stock 1 as the required return increases—and stock 2 continues to be unused. The accompanying scatter chart (with the option to "connect the dots") shows the risk–return trade-off. As the company assumes more risk, as measured by portfolio standard deviation, the expected return increases, but at a decreasing rate.

The curve in this chart is called the *efficient frontier*. Points on the efficient frontier can be achieved by appropriate portfolios. Points below the efficient frontier can be achieved, but they are not as good as points on the efficient frontier because they have a lower expected return for a given level of risk. In contrast, points above the efficient frontier are unachievable—the company cannot achieve this high an expected return for a given level of risk.

Modeling Issues

- Typical real-world portfolio selection problems involve a large number of potential investments, certainly many more than three. This admittedly requires more input data, particularly for the correlation matrix, but the basic model does not change at all. In particular, the matrix formula for portfolio variance is exactly the same. This shows the power of using Excel's matrix functions. Without them, the formula for portfolio variance would be a long, involved sum.

- If Perlman is allowed to short a stock, the fraction invested in that stock is allowed to be negative. To implement this, you can eliminate the nonnegativity constraints on the changing cells.

- An alternative objective might be to minimize the probability that the portfolio loses money. This possibility is illustrated in one of the problems. ∎

PROBLEMS

Level A

69. In the peak-load pricing model, the demand functions have positive and negative coefficients of prices. The negative coefficients indicate that as the price of a product increases, demand for *that* product decreases. The positive coefficients indicate that as the price of a product increases, demand for the *other* product increases.
    a. Increase the magnitudes of the negative coefficients from –0.5 and –1 to –0.7 and –1.2, and rerun Solver. Are the changes in the optimal solution intuitive? Explain.
    b. Increase the magnitudes of the positive coefficients from 0.1 and 0.1 to 0.3 and 0.3, and rerun Solver. Are the changes in the optimal solution intuitive? Explain.
    c. Make the changes in parts **a** and **b** simultaneously and rerun Solver. What happens now?

70. In the peak-load pricing model, we assumed that the capacity level is a decision variable. Assume now that capacity has already been set at 30 kwh. (Note that the cost of capacity is now a sunk cost, so it is irrelevant to the decision problem.) Change the model appropriately and run Solver. Then use SolverTable to see how sensitive the optimal solution is to the capacity level, letting it vary over some relevant range. Does it appear that the optimal prices will be set so that demand is always equal to capacity for at least one of the two periods of the day?

71. For each of the following, answer whether it makes sense to multiply the matrices of the given sizes. In each case where it makes sense, demonstrate an example in Excel, where you make up the numbers.
    a. AB, where A is 3×4 and B is 4×1
    b. AB, where A is 1×4 and B is 4×1
    c. AB, where A is 4×1 and B is 1×4
    d. AB, where A is 1×4 and B is 1×4
    e. ABC, where A is 1×4, B is 4×4, and C is 4×1
    f. ABC, where A is 3×3, B is 3×3, and C is 3×1
    g. $A^T B$, where A is 4×3 and B is 4×3, and A^T denotes the transpose of A

72. Add a new stock, stock 4, to the portfolio optimization model. Assume that the estimated mean and standard deviation of return for stock 4 are 0.125 and 0.175, respectively. Also, assume the correlations between stock 4 and the original three stocks are 0.3, 0.5, and 0.8. Run Solver on the modified model, where the required expected portfolio return is again 0.12. Is stock 4 in the optimal portfolio? Then run SolverTable as in the example. Is stock 4 in any of the optimal portfolios on the efficient frontier?

73. In the portfolio optimization model, stock 2 is not in the optimal portfolio. Use SolverTable to see whether it ever enters the optimal portfolio as its correlations with stocks 1 and 3 vary. Specifically, use a two-way SolverTable with two inputs, the correlations between stock 2 and stocks 1 and 3, each allowed to vary from 0.1 to 0.9 in increments of 0.1. Capture as outputs the three changing cells. Discuss the results. (*Note*: You will have to change the model slightly. For example, if you use cells B10 and C11 as the two SolverTable input cells, you will have to ensure that cells C9 and D10 change accordingly. This is easy. Just put formulas in these latter two cells.)

74. The stocks in the portfolio optimization model are all *positively* correlated. What happens when they are *negatively* correlated? Answer for each of the following scenarios. In each case, two of the three correlations are the negatives of their original values. Discuss the differences between the optimal portfolios in these three scenarios.

   a. Change the signs of the correlations between stocks 1 and 2 and between stocks 1 and 3. (Here, stock 1 tends to go in a different direction from stocks 2 and 3.)

   b. Change the signs of the correlations between stocks 1 and 2 and between stocks 2 and 3. (Here, stock 2 tends to go in a different direction from stocks 1 and 3.)

   c. Change the signs of the correlations between stocks 1 and 3 and between stocks 2 and 3. (Here, stock 3 tends to go in a different direction from stocks 1 and 2.)

75. The file **P14_75.xlsx** contains historical monthly returns for 28 companies. For each company, calculate the estimated mean return and the estimated variance of return. Then calculate the estimated correlations between the companies' returns. Note that "return" here means *monthly* return. (*Hint*: Use StatTools's Summary Statistics capabilities.)

76. This problem continues using the data from the previous problem. The file **P14_76.xlsx** includes all of the previous data. It also contains fractions in row 3 for creating a portfolio. These fractions are currently all equal to 1/28, but they can be changed to any values you like, so long as they continue to sum to 1. For any such fractions, find the estimated mean, variance, and standard deviation of the resulting portfolio return.

Level B

77. Continuing the previous problem, find the portfolio that achieves an expected monthly return of at least 0.01 (1%) and minimizes portfolio variance. Then use SolverTable to sweep out the efficient frontier. Create a chart of this efficient frontier from your SolverTable results. What are the relevant lower and upper limits on the required expected monthly return?

78. In many cases you can assume that the portfolio return is at least approximately *normally* distributed. Then you can use Excel's NORMDIST function as in Chapter 5 to calculate the probability that the portfolio return is negative. The relevant formula is **=NORMDIST(0,*mean*,*stdev*,1)**, where *mean* and *stdev* are the expected portfolio return and standard deviation of portfolio return, respectively.

   a. Modify the portfolio optimization model slightly, and then run Solver to find the portfolio that achieves at least a 0.12 (12%) expected return and minimizes the probability of a negative return. Do you get the same optimal portfolio as before? What is the probability that the return from this portfolio will be negative?

   b. Using the model in part **a**, create a chart of the efficient frontier. However, this time put the probability of a negative return on the horizontal axis.

14-9 CONCLUSION

This chapter has led you through spreadsheet optimization models of many diverse problems. No standard procedure can be used to model all problems. However, there are several keys to most models.

- First, determine the changing cells. For example, in blending problems it is important to realize that the changing cells are the amounts of inputs used to produce outputs, and in worker scheduling problems such as the post office example, it is important to realize that the changing cells are the number of people who start their five-day shift each day of the week.

- Set up the model so that you can easily calculate what you wish to maximize or minimize (usually profit or cost). For example, in the aggregate planning model it is a good idea to calculate total cost by calculating the monthly cost of the various activities in separate rows and then summing the subtotals.

- Set up the model so that the relationships between the cells in the spreadsheet and the constraints of the problem are readily apparent. For example, in the post office scheduling model it is convenient to calculate the number of people working each day of the week adjacent to the minimum required number of people for each day of the week.

- Optimization models do not always fall into ready-made categories. A model might involve a combination of the ideas discussed in the production scheduling, blending, and aggregate planning examples. In fact, many real applications are not strictly analogous to any of the models we have discussed. However, exposure to the models in this chapter should give you the insights you need to solve a wide variety of interesting problems.

Summary of Key Terms

Term	Explanation	Page
Worker scheduling models	Models for choosing the staffing levels to meet workload requirements	720
Multiple optimal solutions	Situation where several solutions obtain the same optimal objective value	725
Blending models	Models where inputs must be mixed in the right proportions to produce outputs	727
Logistics models	Models where goods must be shipped from one set of locations to another at minimal cost	733
Flow balance constraint	Constraint that relates the flow into a node and the flow out of the node	739
Aggregate planning models	Models where workforce levels and production levels must be set to meet customer demand	750
Integer programming (IP) models	Models where at least some of the decision variables must be integers	770
Binary variable	Integer variable that must be 0 or 1; used to indicate whether an activity takes place	770
Capital budgeting models	Models where a subset of investment activities is chosen from a set of possible activities	770
Fixed-cost models	Models where fixed costs are incurred for various activities if they are done at *any* positive level	775
Set-covering models	Models where members of one set must be selected to cover services to members of another set	782
Nonlinear programming (NLP) models	Models where either the objective function or the constraints (or both) are nonlinear functions of the decision variables	789
Global optimum	Solution that is the best in the entire feasible region	789
Local optimal solution	Solution that is better than all nearby solutions (but might not be optimal globally)	789
Portfolio optimization models	Models that attempt to find the portfolio of securities that achieves the best balance between risk and return	794

PROBLEMS

Conceptual Exercises

C.1. The worker scheduling model in this chapter was purposely made small (only seven changing cells). What would make a similar problem for a company like McDonald's much harder? What types of constraints would be required? How many changing cells (approximately) might there be?

C.2. Explain why it is problematic to include a constraint such as the following in an LP model for a blending problem:

$$\frac{\text{Total octane in gasoline 1 blend}}{\text{Barrels of gasoline 1 blended daily}} \geq 10$$

C.3. "It is essential to constrain all shipments in a transportation problem to have integer values to ensure that the optimal LP solution consists entirely of integer-valued shipments." Is this statement true or false? Why?

C.4. What is the relationship between transportation models and more general logistics models? Explain how these two types of linear optimization models are similar and how they are different.

C.5. Unlike the small logistics models presented here, real-world logistics problems can be huge. Imagine the global problem a company like FedEx faces each day. Describe as well as you can the types of decisions and constraints it has. How large (number of changing cells, number of constraints) might such a problem be?

C.6. Suppose that you formulate and solve an integer programming model with a cost-minimization objective. Assume that the optimal solution yields an objective cell value of $500,000. Now, consider the same linear optimization model without the integer restrictions. That is, suppose that you drop the requirement that the changing cells be integer-valued and reoptimize with Solver. How does the optimal objective cell value for this modified model (called the *LP relaxation* of the IP model) compare to the original total cost value of $500,000? Explain your answer.

C.7. The portfolio optimization model presented here is the standard model: minimize the variance (or standard deviation) of the portfolio, as a measure of risk, for a given required level of expected return. In general, the goal is to keep risk low and expected return high. Can you think of other ways to model the problem to achieve these basic goals? Is high variability all *bad* risk?

Level A

79. A bus company believes that it will need the following numbers of bus drivers during each of the next five years: 60 drivers in year 1; 70 drivers in year 2; 50 drivers in year 3; 65 drivers in year 4; 75 drivers in year

5. At the beginning of each year, the bus company must decide how many drivers to hire or fire. It costs $4000 to hire a driver and $2000 to fire a driver. A driver's salary is $45,000 per year. At the beginning of year 1 the company has 50 drivers. A driver hired at the beginning of a year can be used to meet the current year's requirements and is paid full salary for the current year.
   a. Determine how to minimize the bus company's salary, hiring, and firing costs over the next five years.
   b. Use SolverTable to determine how the total number hired, total number fired, and total cost change as the unit hiring and firing costs *each* increase by the same percentage.

80. A pharmaceutical company produces the drug NasaMist from four chemicals. Today, the company must produce 1000 pounds of the drug. The three active ingredients in NasaMist are A, B, and C. By weight, at least 8% of NasaMist must consist of A, at least 4% of B, and at least 2% of C. The cost per pound of each chemical and the amount of each active ingredient in one pound of each chemical are given in the file **P14_80.xlsx**. It is necessary that at least 100 pounds of chemical 2 and at least 450 pounds of chemical 3 be used.
   a. Determine the cheapest way of producing today's batch of NasaMist.
   b. Use SolverTable to see how much the percentage of requirement of A is really costing the company. Let the percentage required vary from 6% to 12%.

81. A bank is attempting to determine where to invest its assets during the current year. At present, $500,000 is available for investment in bonds, home loans, auto loans, and personal loans. The annual rates of return on each type of investment are known to be the following: bonds, 6%; home loans, 8%; auto loans, 5%; personal loans, 10%. To ensure that the bank's portfolio is not too risky, the bank's investment manager has placed the following three restrictions on the bank's portfolio:
   - The amount invested in personal loans cannot exceed the amount invested in bonds.
   - The amount invested in home loans cannot exceed the amount invested in auto loans.
   - No more than 25% of the total amount invested can be in personal loans.

   Help the bank maximize the annual return on its investment portfolio.

82. A fertilizer company blends silicon and nitrogen to produce two types of fertilizers. Fertilizer 1 must be at least 40% nitrogen and sells for $70 per pound. Fertilizer 2 must be at least 70% silicon and sells for $40 per pound. The company can purchase up to 8000 pounds of nitrogen at $15 per pound and up to 10,000 pounds of silicon at $10 per pound.

   a. Assuming that all fertilizer produced can be sold, determine how the company can maximize its profit.

   b. Use SolverTable to explore the effect on profit of changing the minimum percentage of nitrogen required in fertilizer 1.

   c. Suppose the availabilities of nitrogen and silicon both increase by the same percentage from their current values. Use SolverTable to explore the effect of this change on profit.

83. LP models are used by many Wall Street firms to select a desirable bond portfolio. The following is a simplified version of such a model. A company is considering investing in four bonds; $1 million is available for investment. The expected annual return, the worst-case annual return on each bond, and the *duration* of each bond are given in the file **P14_83.xlsx**. (The duration of a bond is a measure of the bond's sensitivity to interest rates.) The company wants to maximize the expected return from its bond investments, subject to three constraints:

   ■ The worst-case return of the bond portfolio must be at least 8%.

   ■ The average duration of the portfolio must be at most 6. For example, a portfolio that invests $600,000 in bond 1 and $400,000 in bond 4 has an average duration of $[600,000(3) + 400,000(9)]/1,000,000 = 5.4$

   ■ Because of diversification requirements, at most 40% of the total amount invested can be invested in a single bond.

   Determine how the company can maximize the expected return on its investment.

84. At the beginning of year 1, you have $10,000. Investments A and B are available; their cash flows are shown in the file **P14_84.xlsx**. Assume that any money not invested in A or B earns interest at an annual rate of 2%.

   a. Determine how to maximize your cash on hand at the beginning of year 4.

   b. Use SolverTable to determine how a change in the year 2 return for investment A changes the optimal solution to the problem.

   c. Use SolverTable to determine how a change in the year 3 return of investment B changes the optimal solution to the problem.

85. An oil company produces two types of gasoline, G1 and G2, from two types of crude oil, C1 and C2. G1 is allowed to contain up to 4% impurities, and G2 is allowed to contain up to 3% impurities. G1 sells for $48 per barrel, whereas G2 sells for $72 per barrel. Up to 4200 barrels of G1 and up to 4300 barrels of G2 can be sold. The cost per barrel of each crude, their availability, and the level of impurities in each crude are listed in the file **P14_85.xlsx**. Before blending the

crude oil into gas, any amount of each crude can be "purified" for a cost of $3.00 per barrel. Purification eliminates half of the impurities in the crude oil.

   a. Determine how to maximize profit.

   b. Use SolverTable to determine how an increase in the availability of C1 affects the optimal profit.

   c. Use SolverTable to determine how an increase in the availability of C2 affects the optimal profit.

   d. Use SolverTable to determine how a change in the profitability of G2 changes profitability and the types of gas produced.

86. The government is auctioning off oil leases at two sites: 1 and 2. At each site 10,000 acres of land are to be auctioned. Cliff Ewing, Blake Barnes, and Alexis Pickens are bidding for the oil. Government rules state that no bidder can receive more than 40% of the land being auctioned. Cliff has bid $10,000 per acre for site 1 land and $20,000 per acre for site 2 land. Blake has bid $9000 per acre for site 1 land and $22,000 per acre for site 2 land. Alexis has bid $11,000 per acre for site 1 land and $19,000 per acre for site 2 land.

   a. Determine how to maximize the government's revenue.

   b. Use SolverTable to see how changes in the government's rule on 40% of all land being auctioned affect the optimal revenue. Why can the optimal revenue not decrease if this percentage required increases? Why can the optimal revenue not increase if this percentage required decreases?

87. An automobile company produces cars in Los Angeles and Detroit and has a warehouse in Atlanta. The company supplies cars to customers in Houston and Tampa. The costs of shipping a car between various points are listed in the file **P14_87.xlsx**, where a blank means that a shipment is not allowed. Los Angeles can produce up to 1100 cars, and Detroit can produce up to 2900 cars. Houston must receive 2400 cars, and Tampa must receive 1500 cars.

   a. Determine how to minimize the cost of meeting demands in Houston and Tampa.

   b. Modify the answer to part **a** if shipments between Los Angeles and Detroit are not allowed.

   c. Modify the answer to part **a** if shipments between Houston and Tampa are allowed at a cost of $5 per car.

88. An oil company produces oil from two wells. Well 1 can produce up to 150,000 barrels per day, and well 2 can produce up to 200,000 barrels per day. It is possible to ship oil directly from the wells to the company's customers in Los Angeles and New York. Alternatively, the company could transport oil to the ports of Mobile and Galveston and then ship it by tanker to New York or Los Angeles, respectively. Los Angeles requires 160,000 barrels per day, and New York requires 140,000 barrels per day. The costs of shipping 1000 barrels between various locations are shown in the file **P14_88.xlsx**, where a blank indicates shipments that are not allowed. Determine how to minimize the transport costs in meeting the oil demands of Los Angeles and New York.

89. Based on Bean et al. (1987). Boris Milkem's firm owns six assets. The expected selling price (in millions of dollars) for each asset is given in the file **P14_89.xlsx**. For example, if asset 1 is sold in year 2, the firm receives $20 million. To maintain a regular cash flow, Milkem must sell at least $20 million of assets during year 1, at least $30 million worth during year 2, and at least $35 million worth during year 3. Determine how Milkem can maximize his total revenue from assets sold during the next three years.

90. This problem is based on Sonderman and Abrahamson (1985). In treating a brain tumor with radiation, physicians want the maximum amount of radiation possible to bombard the tissue containing the tumors. The constraint is, however, that there is a maximum amount of radiation that normal tissue can handle without suffering tissue damage. Physicians must therefore decide how to aim the radiation so as to maximize the radiation that hits the tumor tissue subject to the constraint of not damaging the normal tissue. As a simple example of this situation, suppose there are six types of radiation beams (beams differ in where they are aimed and their intensity) that can be aimed at a tumor. The region containing the tumor has been divided into six regions: three regions contain tumors and three contain normal tissue. The amount of radiation delivered to each region by each type of beam is shown in the file **P14_90.xlsx**. If each region of normal tissue can handle at most 60 units of radiation, which beams should be used to maximize the total amount of radiation received by the tumors?

91. A leading hardware company produces three types of computers: Pear computers, Apricot computers, and Orange computers. The relevant data are given in the file **P14_91.xlsx**. The equipment cost is a fixed cost; it is incurred if any of this type of computer is produced. A total of 30,000 chips and 12,000 hours of labor are available. The company wants to produce at least two types of computers.
  a. Determine how the company can maximize its profit.
  b. For any computer type *not* in the optimal product mix, use SolverTable to find how much larger its unit margin would have to be before it would enter the optimal product mix.

92. A food company produces tomato sauce at five different plants. The tomato sauce is then shipped to one of three warehouses, where it is stored until it is shipped to one of the company's four customers. All of the inputs for the problem are given in the file **P14_92.xlsx**, as follows:
  ■ The plant capacities (in tons)
  ■ The cost per ton of producing tomato sauce at each plant and shipping it to each warehouse

■ The cost of shipping a ton of sauce from each warehouse to each customer
■ The customer requirements (in tons) of sauce
■ The fixed annual cost of operating each plant and warehouse.

The company must decide which plants and warehouses to open, and which routes from plants to warehouses and from warehouses to customers to use. All customer demand must be met. A given customer's demand can be met from more than one warehouse, and a given plant can ship to more than one warehouse.
  a. Determine the minimum-cost method for meeting customer demands.
  b. Use SolverTable to see how a change in the capacity of plant 1 affects the total cost.
  c. Use SolverTable to see how a change in the customer 2 demand affects the total cost.

93. You are given the following means, standard deviations, and correlations for the annual return on three potential investments. The means are 0.12, 0.15, and 0.20. The standard deviations are 0.20, 0.30, and 0.40. The correlation between stocks 1 and 2 is 0.65, between stocks 1 and 3 is 0.75, and between stocks 2 and 3 is 0.41. You have $100,000 to invest and can invest no more than half of your money in any single investment. Determine the minimum-variance portfolio that yields an expected annual return of at least 0.14.

94. You have $50,000 to invest in three stocks. Let R_i be the random variable representing the annual return on $1 invested in stock i. For example, if $R_i = 0.12$, then $1 invested in stock i at the beginning of a year is worth $1.12 at the end of the year. The means are $E(R_1) = 0.14$, $E(R_2) = 0.11$, and $E(R_3) = 0.10$. The variances are $Var\ R_1 = 0.20$, $Var\ R_2 = 0.08$, and $Var\ R_3 = 0.18$. The correlations are $r_{12} = 0.8$, $r_{13} = 0.7$, and $r_{23} = 0.9$. Determine the minimum-variance portfolio that attains an expected annual return of at least 0.12.

Level B

95. The risk index of an investment can be obtained by taking the absolute values of percentage changes in the value of the investment for each year and averaging them. Suppose you are trying to determine the percentages of your money to invest in T-bills, gold, and stocks. The file **P14_95.xlsx** lists the annual returns (percentage changes in value) for these investments for the years 1968 through 1988. Let the risk index of a portfolio be the weighted average of the risk indices of these investments, where the weights are the fractions of the portfolio assigned to the investments. Suppose that the amount of each investment must be between 20% and 50% of the total invested. You would like the risk index of your portfolio to equal 0.15, and your goal is to maximize the expected return on your

portfolio. Determine the maximum expected return on your portfolio, subject to the stated constraints. Use the average return earned by each investment during the years 1968 through 1988 as your estimate of expected return. (If you like, you can try this problem with more recent data, but the model will be exactly the same.)

96. Broker Sonya Wong is currently trying to maximize her profit in the bond market. Four bonds are available for purchase and sale at the bid and ask prices shown in the file **P14_96.xlsx**. Sonya can buy up to 1000 units of each bond at the ask price or sell up to 1000 units of each bond at the bid price. During each of the next three years, the person who sells a bond will pay the owner of the bond the cash payments listed in the same file. Sonya's goal is to maximize her revenue from selling bonds minus her payment for buying bonds, subject to the constraint that after each year's payments are received, her current cash position (due only to cash payments from bonds and not purchases or sales of bonds) is nonnegative. Note that her current cash position can depend on past coupons and that cash accumulated at the end of each year earns 2.5% annual interest. Determine how to maximize net profit from buying and selling bonds, subject to the constraints previously described. Why do you think we limit the number of units of each bond that can be bought or sold?

97. A financial company is considering investing in three projects. If it fully invests in a project, the realized cash flows (in millions of dollars) will be as listed in the file **P14_97.xlsx**. For example, project 1 requires a cash outflow of $3 million today and returns $5.5 million three years from now. The company currently has $2 million in cash. At each time point (0, 6, 12, 18, 24, and 30 months from now), the company can, if desired, borrow up to $2 million at 3.5% interest (per six months). Leftover cash earns 3% interest (per six months). For example, if after borrowing and investing at the current time, the company has $1 million, it will receive $30,000 in interest six months from now. The company's goal is to maximize cash on hand after cash flows three years from now are accounted for. What investment and borrowing strategy should it use? Assume that the company can invest in a fraction of a project. For example, if it invests in one-half of project 3, it has cash outflows of –$1 million now and six months from now.

98. You are a CFA (chartered financial analyst). An overextended client has come to you because she needs help paying off her credit card bills. She owes the amounts on her credit cards listed in the file **P14_98 .xlsx**. The client is willing to allocate up to $5000 per month to pay off these credit cards. All cards must be paid off within 36 months. The client's goal is to minimize the total of all her payments. To solve this problem, you must understand how interest on a loan works. To illustrate, suppose the client pays $5000 on Saks during month 1. Then her

Saks balance at the beginning of month 2 is 20,000 – [5000 – 0.005(20,000)]. This follows because she incurs 0.005(20,000) in interest charges on her Saks card during month 1. Help the client solve her problem. Once you have solved this problem, give an intuitive explanation of the solution found by Solver.

99. A food company produces two types of turkey cutlets for sale to fast-food restaurants. Each type of cutlet consists of white meat and dark meat. Cutlet 1 sells for $4 per pound and must consist of at least 70% white meat. Cutlet 2 sells for $3 per pound and must consist of at least 60% white meat. At most 6000 pounds of cutlet 1 and 2000 pounds of cutlet 2 can be sold. The two types of turkey used to manufacture the cutlets are purchased from a turkey farm. Each type 1 turkey costs $10 and yields five pounds of white meat and two pounds of dark meat. Each type 2 turkey costs $8 and yields three pounds of white meat and three pounds of dark meat. Determine how the company can maximize its profit.

100. Each hour from 10 A.M. to 7 P.M., a bank receives checks and must process them. Its goal is to process all checks the same day they are received. The bank has 13 check processing machines, each of which can process up to 500 checks per hour. It takes one worker to operate each machine. The bank hires both full-time and part-time workers. Full-time workers work 10 A.M. to 6 P.M., 11 A.M. to 7 P.M., or noon to 8 P.M. and are paid $160 per day. Part-time workers work either 2 P.M. to 7 P.M. or 3 P.M. to 8 P.M. and are paid $75 per day. The numbers of checks received each hour are listed in the file **P14_100.xlsx**. In the interest of maintaining continuity, the bank believes that it must have at least three full-time workers under contract. Develop a work schedule that processes all checks by 8 P.M. and minimizes daily labor costs.

101. An oil company has oil fields in San Diego and Los Angeles. The San Diego field can produce up to 500,000 barrels per day, and the Los Angeles field can produce up to 400,000 barrels per day. Oil is sent from the fields to a refinery, either in Dallas or in Houston. (Assume that each refinery has unlimited capacity.) To refine 100,000 barrels costs $700 at Dallas and $900 at Houston. Refined oil is shipped to customers in Chicago and New York. Chicago customers require 400,000 barrels per day, and New York customers require 300,000 barrels per day. The costs of shipping 100,000 barrels of oil (refined or unrefined) between cities are shown in the file **P14_101.xlsx**.
   a. Determine how to minimize the total cost of meeting all demands.
   b. If each refinery had a capacity of 380,000 barrels per day, how would you modify the model in part **a**?

102. An electrical components company produces capacitors at three locations: Los Angeles, Chicago, and New York. Capacitors are shipped from these locations to public utilities in five regions of the country: northeast

(NE), northwest (NW), midwest (MW), southeast (SE), and southwest (SW). The cost of producing and shipping a capacitor from each plant to each region of the country is given in the file **P14_102.xlsx**. Each plant has an annual production capacity of 100,000 capacitors. Each year, each region of the country must receive the following number of capacitors: NE, 55,000; NW, 50,000; MW, 60,000; SE, 60,000; SW, 45,000. The company believes that shipping costs are too high, and it is therefore considering building one or two more production plants. Possible sites are Atlanta and Houston. The costs of producing a capacitor and shipping it to each region of the country are given in the same file. It costs $3 million (in current dollars) to build a new plant, and operating each plant incurs a fixed cost (in addition to variable shipping and production costs) of $50,000 per year. A plant at Atlanta or Houston will have the capacity to produce 100,000 capacitors per year. Assume that future demand patterns and production costs will remain unchanged. If costs are discounted at a rate of 12% per year, how can the company minimize the net present value (NPV) of all costs associated with meeting current and future demands?

103. Based on Bean et al. (1988). The owner of a shopping mall has 10,000 square feet of space to rent and wants to determine the types of stores that should occupy the mall. The minimum number and maximum number of each type of store and the square footage of each type are given in the file **P14_103.xlsx**. The annual profit made by each type of store depends on the number of stores of that type in the mall. This dependence is given in the same file, where all profits are in units of $10,000. For example, if there are two department stores in the mall, each department store will earn $210,000 profit per year.

Each store pays 5% of its annual profit as rent to the owner of the mall. Determine how the owner of the mall can maximize its rental income.

104. It is currently the beginning of 2010. A city (labeled C for convenience) is trying to sell municipal bonds to support improvements in recreational facilities and highways. The face values (in thousands of dollars) of the bonds and the due dates at which principal comes due are listed in the file **P14_104.xlsx**. (The due dates are the *beginnings* of the years listed.) An underwriting company (U) wants to underwrite C's bonds. A proposal to C for underwriting this issue consists of the following: (1) an interest rate, 3%, 4%, 5%, 6%, or 7%, for each bond, where coupons are paid annually, and (2) an up-front premium paid by U to C. U has determined the set of fair prices (in thousands of dollars) for the bonds listed in the same file. For example, if U underwrites bond 2 maturing in 2013 at 5%, it will charge C $444,000 for that bond. U is constrained to use at most three different interest rates. U wants to make a profit of at least $46,000, where its profit is equal to the sale price of the bonds minus the face value of the bonds minus the premium U pays to C. To maximize the chance that U will get C's business, U wants to minimize the total cost of the bond issue to C, which is equal to the total interest on the bonds minus the premium paid by U. For example, if the year 2015 bond (bond 1) is issued at a 4% rate, then C must pay two years of coupon interest: $2(0.04)(\$700,000) = \$56,000$. What assignment of interest rates to each bond and up-front premiums ensure that U will make the desired profit (assuming it gets the contract) and maximize the chance of U getting C's business? To maximize this chance, you can assume that U minimizes the net cost to C, that is, the cost of its coupon payments minus the premium from U to C.

CASE 14.1 GIANT MOTOR COMPANY

This problem deals with strategic planning issues for a large company.[17] The main issue is planning the company's production capacity for the coming year. At issue is the overall level of capacity and the type of capacity—for example, the degree of *flexibility* in the manufacturing system. The main tool used to aid the company's planning process is a mixed integer programming model. A *mixed* integer program has both integer and continuous variables.

Problem Statement

Giant Motor Company (GMC) produces three lines of cars for the domestic (U.S.) market: Lyras, Libras, and Hydras. The Lyra is a relatively inexpensive

subcompact car that appeals mainly to first-time car owners and to households using it as a second car for commuting. The Libra is a sporty compact car that is sleeker, faster, and roomier than the Lyra. Without any options, the Libra costs slightly more than the Lyra; additional options increase the price further. The Hydra is the luxury car of the GMC line. It is significantly more expensive than the Lyra and Libra, and it has the highest profit margin of the three cars.

---

[17]The idea for this case came from Eppen, Martin, and Schrage, "A Scenario Approach to Capacity Planning." *Operations Research* 37, no. 4 (July–August 1989): 517–527.

Retooling Options for Capacity Expansion

Currently GMC has three manufacturing plants in the United States. Each plant is dedicated to producing a single line of cars. In its planning for the coming year, GMC is considering the retooling of its Lyra and/or Libra plants. Retooling either plant would represent a major expense for the company. The retooled plants would have significantly increased production capacities. Although having greater *fixed* costs, the retooled plants would be more efficient and have lower *marginal* production costs—that is, higher *marginal* profit contributions. In addition, the retooled plants would be *flexible*: They would have the capability of producing more than one line of cars.

The characteristics of the current plants and the retooled plants are given in Table 14.22. The retooled Lyra and Libra plants are prefaced by the word *new*. The fixed costs and capacities in Table 14.22 are given on an annual basis. A dash in the profit margin section indicates that the plant cannot manufacture that line of car. For example, the new Lyra plant would be capable of producing both Lyras and Libras but not Hydras. The new Libra plant would be capable of producing any of the three lines of cars. Note, however, that the new Libra plant has a slightly lower profit margin for producing Hydras than the Hydra plant does. The flexible new Libra plant is capable of producing the luxury Hydra model but is not quite as efficient as the current Hydra plant that is dedicated to Hydra production.

The fixed costs are annual costs that are incurred by GMC independent of the number of cars that are produced by the plant. For the current plant configurations, the fixed costs include property taxes, insurance, payments on the loan that was taken out to construct the plant, and so on. If a plant is retooled, the fixed costs will include the previous fixed costs plus the additional cost of the renovation. The additional renovation cost will be an annual cost representing the cost of the renovation amortized over a long period.

Demand for GMC Cars

Short-term demand forecasts have been very reliable in the past and are expected to be reliable in the future. (Longer-term forecasts are not so accurate.) The demand for GMC cars for the coming year is given in Table 14.23.

Table 14.23 Demand for GMC Cars

	Demand (in 1000s)
Lyra	1400
Libra	1100
Hydra	800

A quick comparison of plant capacities and demands in Tables 14.22 and 14.23 indicates that GMC is faced with insufficient capacity. Partially offsetting the lack of capacity is the phenomenon of *demand diversion*. If a potential car buyer walks into a GMC dealer showroom wanting to buy a Lyra but the dealer is out of stock, frequently the salesperson can convince the customer to purchase the better Libra car, which is in stock. Unsatisfied demand for the Lyra is said to be *diverted* to the Libra. Only rarely in this situation can the salesperson convince the customer to switch to the luxury Hydra model.

From past experience GMC estimates that 30% of unsatisfied demand for Lyras is diverted to demand for Libras and 5% to demand for Hydras. Similarly, 10% of unsatisfied demand for Libras is diverted to demand for Hydras. For example, if the demand for Lyras is 1,400,000 cars, then the unsatisfied demand will be 400,000 if no capacity is added. Out of this unsatisfied demand, 120,000 (= 400,000 × 0.3) will materialize as demand for Libras, and 20,000 (= 400,000 × 0.05) will materialize as demand for Hydras. Similarly, if the demand for Libras is 1,220,000 cars (1,100,000 original demand plus 120,000 demand diverted from Lyras), then the unsatisfied demand for Lyras would be 420,000 if no capacity is added. Out of this unsatisfied demand, 42,000 (= 420,000 × 0.1) will materialize as demand

Table 14.22 Plant Characteristics

	Lyra	Libra	Hydra	New Lyra	New Libra
Capacity (in 1000s)	1000	800	900	1600	1800
Fixed cost (in $millions)	2000	2000	2600	3400	3700
Profit Margin by Car Line (in $1000s)					
Lyra	2	—	—	2.5	2.3
Libra	—	3	—	3.0	3.5
Hydra	—	—	5	—	4.8

for Hydras. All other unsatisfied demand is lost to competitors. The pattern of demand diversion is summarized in Table 14.24.

Questions

GMC wants to decide whether to retool the Lyra and Libra plants. In addition, GMC wants to determine its production plan at each plant in the coming year. Based on the previous data, develop a mixed integer programming model (some variables integer-constrained, some not) for solving GMC's production planning–capacity expansion problem for the coming year. According to the optimal solution, what should GMC do? How sensitive is the optimal solution to key inputs? The file **C14_01.xlsx** gets you started.

CASE 14.2 GMS Stock Hedging

Kate Torelli, a security analyst for LionFund, has identified a gold-mining stock (ticker symbol GMS) as a particularly attractive investment. Torelli believes that the company has invested wisely in new mining equipment. Furthermore, the company has recently purchased mining rights on land that has high potential for successful gold extraction. Torelli notes that gold has underperformed in the stock market for the last decade and believes that the time is ripe for a large increase in gold prices. In addition, she reasons that conditions in the global monetary system make it likely that investors may once again turn to gold as a safe haven in which to park assets. Finally, supply and demand conditions have improved to the point where there could be significant upward pressure on gold prices.

GMS is a highly leveraged company, so it is quite a risky investment by itself. Torelli is mindful of a passage from the annual report of a competitor, Baupost, which has an extraordinarily successful investment record: "Baupost has managed a decade of consistently profitable results despite, and perhaps in some respect due to, consistent emphasis on the avoidance of downside risk. We have frequently carried both high cash balances and costly market hedges. Our results are particularly satisfying when considered in the light of this sustained risk aversion." She would therefore like to *hedge* the stock purchase—that is, reduce the risk of an investment in GMS stock.

Currently GMS is trading at $100 per share. Torelli has constructed seven scenarios for the price of GMS stock one month from now. These scenarios and corresponding probabilities are shown in Table 14.25.

To hedge an investment in GMS stock, Torelli can invest in other securities whose prices tend to move in the direction opposite to that of GMS stock. In particular, she is considering over-the-counter put options on GMS stock as potential hedging instruments. The value of a put option increases as the price of the underlying stock decreases. For example, consider a put option with a strike price of $100 and a time to expiration of one month. This means that the owner of the put has the right to sell GMS stock at $100 per share one month in the future. Suppose that the price of GMS falls to $80 at that time. Then the holder of the put option can exercise the option and receive $20 (= 100 − 80). If the price of GMS falls to $70, the option would be worth $30 (= 100 − 70). However, if the price of GMS rises to $100 or more, the option expires worthless.

Table 14.25 Scenarios and Probabilities for GMS Stock in 1 Month

© Cengage Learning

	Scenario 1	Scenario 2	Scenario 3	Scenario 4	Scenario 5	Scenario 6	Scenario 7
Probability	0.05	0.10	0.20	0.30	0.20	0.10	0.05
GMS stock price($)	150	130	110	100	90	80	70

Table 14.26 Put Option Prices (Today) for GMS Case Study

	Put Option A	Put Option B	Put Option C
Strike Price($)	90	100	110
Option Price($)	2.20	6.40	12.50

Torelli called an options trader at a large investment bank for quotes. The prices for three European-style put options are shown in Table 14.26. (A European put can be exercised only at the expiration date, not before.) Torelli wishes to invest $10 million in GMS stock and put options.

Questions

1. Based on Torelli's scenarios, what is the expected return of GMS stock? What is the standard deviation of the return of GMS stock?

2. After a cursory examination of the put option prices, Torelli suspects that a good strategy is to buy one put option A for each share of GMS stock purchased. What are the mean and standard deviation of return for this strategy?

3. Assuming that Torelli's goal is to minimize the standard deviation of the portfolio return, what is the optimal portfolio that invests all $10 million? (For simplicity, assume that fractional numbers of stock shares and put options can be purchased. Assume that the amounts invested in each security must be nonnegative. However,

the number of options purchased need *not* equal the number of shares of stock purchased.) What are the expected return and standard deviation of return of this portfolio? How many shares of GMS stock and how many of each put option does this portfolio correspond to?

4. Suppose that short selling is permitted—that is, the nonnegativity restrictions on the portfolio weights are removed. Now what portfolio minimizes the standard deviation of return?

(*Hint*: A good way to attack this problem is to create a table of security returns, as indicated in Table 14.27, where only a few of the table entries are shown. To correctly calculate the standard deviation of portfolio return, you will need to incorporate the scenario probabilities. If r_i is the portfolio return in scenario i, and p_i is the probability of scenario i, then the standard deviation of portfolio return is

$$\sqrt{\sum_{i=1}^{7} P_i(r_i - \mu)^2}$$

where $\mu = \sum_{i=1}^{7} p_i r_i$ is the expected portfolio return.)

Table 14.27 Table of Security Returns

	GMS Stock	Put Option A	Put Option B	Put Option C
Scenario 1			−100%	
2	30%			
⋮				
7				220%

CHAPTER 15

Introduction to Simulation Modeling

Caro/Alamy

DEVELOPING BOARDING STRATEGIES AT AMERICA WEST

Management science often attempts to solve problems that we all experience. One such problem is the boarding process for airline flights. As customers, we all hate to wait while travelers boarding ahead of us store their luggage and block the aisles. But this is also a big problem for the airlines. Airlines lose money when their airplanes are on the ground, so they have a real incentive to reduce the turnaround time from when a plane lands until it departs on its next flight. Of course, the turnaround time is influenced by several factors, including passenger deplaning, baggage unloading, fueling, cargo unloading, airplane maintenance, cargo loading, baggage loading, and passenger boarding. Airlines try to perform all of these tasks as efficiently as possible, but passenger boarding is particularly difficult to shorten. Although the airlines want passengers to board as quickly as possible, they don't want to use measures that might antagonize their passengers.

One study by van den Briel et al. (2005) indicates how a combination of management science methods, including simulation, was used to make passenger boarding more efficient at America West Airlines. America West (which merged with US Airways in 2006) was a major U.S. carrier based in Phoenix, Arizona. It served more destinations nonstop than any other airline. The airline's fleet consisted of Airbus A320s, Airbus A319s, Boeing 757s, Boeing 737s, and Airbus A318s.

At the time of the study, airlines used a variety of boarding strategies, but the predominant strategy was the back-to-front (BF) strategy where, after boarding first-class passengers and passengers with special needs, the rest of the passengers are boarded in groups, starting with rows in the back of the plane. As the authors suspected (and most of us have experienced), this strategy still results in significant congestion. Within a given section of the plane (the back, say), passengers storing luggage in overhead compartments can block an aisle. Also, people in the aisle or middle seat often need to get back into the aisle to let window-seat passengers be seated. The authors developed an integer programming (IP) model to minimize the number of such aisle blockages. The decision variables determined which groups of seats should be boarded in which order. Of course, the BF strategy was one possible feasible solution, but it turned out to be a suboptimal solution. The IP model suggested that the best solution was an outside-in (OI) strategy, where groups of passengers in window seats board first, then groups in the middle seats, and finally groups in aisle seats, with all of these groups going essentially in a back-to-front order.

The authors recognized that their IP model was at best an idealized model of how passengers actually behave. Its biggest drawback is that it ignores the inherent randomness in passenger behavior. Therefore, they followed up their optimization model with a simulation model. As they state, "We used simulation to validate the analytical model and to obtain a finer level of detail." This validation of an approximate or idealized analytical model is a common use for simulation. To make the simulation as realistic as possible, they used two cameras, one inside the plane and one inside the bridge leading to the plane, to tape customer behavior. By analyzing the tapes, they were able to estimate the required inputs to their simulation model, such as the time between passengers, walking speed, blocking time, and time to store luggage in overhead compartments. After the basic simulation model was developed, it was used as a tool to evaluate various boarding strategies suggested by the IP model. It also allowed the authors to experiment with changes to the overall boarding process that might be beneficial. For example, reducing congestion *inside* the airplane is not very helpful if the gate agent at the entrance to the bridge processes passengers too slowly. Their final recommendation, based on a series of simulation experiments, was to add a second gate agent (there had been only one before) and to board passengers in six groups using an OI strategy. The simulation model suggested that this could reduce the boarding time by about 37%.

The authors' recommendations were implemented first as a pilot project and then systemwide. The pilot results were impressive, with a 39% reduction in boarding times. By September 2003, the new boarding strategies had been implemented in 80% of America West's airports, with a decrease in departure delays as much as 60.1%. Besides this obvious benefit to the airline, customers also appear to be happier. Now they can easily understand when to queue up for boarding, and they experience less blocking after they get inside the plane. ■

15-1 INTRODUCTION

A **simulation model** is a computer model that imitates a real-life situation. It is like other mathematical models, but it explicitly incorporates uncertainty in one or more input variables. When you run a simulation, you allow these random input variables to take on various values, and you keep track of any resulting output variables of interest. In this way, you are able to see how the outputs vary as a function of the varying inputs.

The fundamental advantage of a simulation model is that it provides an entire distribution of results, not simply a single bottom-line result. As an example, suppose an automobile manufacturer is planning to develop and market a new model car. The company is ultimately interested in the net present value (NPV) of the cash flows from this car over the next 10 years. However, there are many uncertainties surrounding this car, including the yearly customer demands for it, the cost of developing it, and others. The company could develop a spreadsheet model for the 10-year NPV, using its *best guesses* for these uncertain quantities. It could then report the NPV based on these best guesses. However, this analysis would be incomplete and probably misleading—there is no guarantee that the NPV based on best-guess inputs is representative of the NPV that will actually occur. It is much better to treat the uncertainty explicitly with a simulation model. This involves entering probability distributions for the uncertain quantities and seeing how the NPV varies as the uncertain quantities vary.

Each different set of values for the uncertain quantities is a scenario. Simulation allows the company to generate many scenarios, each leading to a particular NPV. In the end, it sees a whole distribution of NPVs, not a single best guess. The company can see what the NPV will be on average, and it can also see worst-case and best-case results.

These approaches are summarized in Figures 15.1 and 15.2. Figure 15.1 indicates that the deterministic (nonsimulation) approach, using best guesses for the uncertain inputs, is generally *not* the appropriate method. It leads to the "flaw of averages," as we will discuss later in the chapter. The problem is that the outputs from the deterministic model are often not representative of the true outputs. The appropriate method is shown in Figure 15.2. Here the uncertainty is modeled explicitly with random inputs, and the end result is a probability distribution for each of the important outputs.

Figure 15.1
Inappropriate Deterministic Model

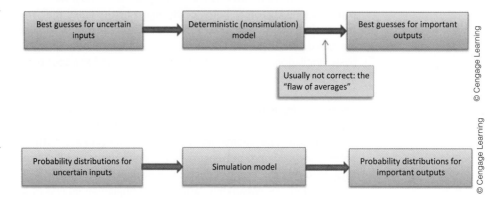

Figure 15.2
Appropriate Simulation Model

Simulation models are also useful for determining how sensitive a system is to changes in operating conditions. For example, the operations of a supermarket could be simulated. Once the simulation model has been developed, it could then be run (with suitable modifications) to ask a number of what-if questions. For example, if the supermarket experiences a 20% increase in business, what will happen to the average time customers must wait for service?

A huge benefit of computer simulation is that it enables managers to answer these types of what-if questions without actually changing (or building) a physical system. For example, the supermarket might want to experiment with the number of open registers to see the effect on customer waiting times. The only way it can *physically* experiment with more registers than it currently owns is to purchase more equipment. Then if it determines that this equipment is not a good investment—customer waiting times do not decrease appreciably—the company is stuck with expensive equipment it doesn't need. Computer simulation is a much less expensive alternative. It provides the company with an electronic replica of what would happen *if* the new equipment were purchased. Then, if the simulation indicates that the new equipment is worth the cost, the company can be confident that purchasing it is the right decision. Otherwise, it can abandon the idea of the new equipment *before* the equipment has been purchased.

Spreadsheet simulation modeling is quite similar to the other modeling applications in this book. You begin with input variables and then relate these with appropriate Excel® formulas to produce output variables of interest. The main difference is that simulation uses *random* numbers to drive the whole process. These random numbers are generated with special functions that we will discuss in detail. Each time the spreadsheet recalculates, all of the random numbers change. This provides the ability to model the logical process once and then use Excel's recalculation ability to generate many different scenarios. By collecting the data from these scenarios, you can see the most likely values of the outputs and the best-case and worst-case values of the outputs.

In this chapter we begin by illustrating spreadsheet models that can be developed with built-in Excel functionality. However, because simulation is such an important tool for analyzing real problems, add-ins to Excel have been developed to streamline the process of developing and analyzing simulation models. Therefore, we then introduce @RISK, one of the most popular simulation add-ins. This add-in not only augments the simulation capabilities of Excel, but it also enables you to analyze models much more quickly and easily.

The purpose of this chapter is to introduce basic simulation concepts, show how simulation models can be developed in Excel, and demonstrate the capabilities of @RISK. Then in the next chapter, armed with the necessary simulation tools, we will explore a variety of simulation models.

Before proceeding, you might ask whether simulation is really used in the business world. The answer is a resounding "yes." The chapter opener described an airline example, and many other examples can be found online. For example, if you visit www.palisade.com, you will see descriptions of interesting @RISK applications from companies that regularly use this add-in. Simulation has always been a powerful tool, but until the introduction of Excel add-ins such as @RISK, it had limited use for several reasons. It typically required specialized software that was either expensive or difficult to learn, or it required tedious computer programming. Fortunately, in the past two decades, spreadsheet simulation, together with Excel add-ins such as @RISK, has put this powerful methodology in the hands of the masses—people like you and the companies you are likely to work for. Many businesses now understand that there is no longer any reason to ignore uncertainty; they can model it directly with spreadsheet simulation.

15-2 PROBABILITY DISTRIBUTIONS FOR INPUT VARIABLES

In spreadsheet simulation models, input cells can contain random numbers. Any output cells then vary as these random inputs change.

In this section we discuss the building blocks of spreadsheet simulation models: **probability distributions for input variables** that capture uncertainty. All spreadsheet simulation models are similar to the spreadsheet models from previous chapters. They have a number of cells that contain values of input variables. The other cells then contain formulas that embed the logic of the model and eventually lead to the output variable(s) of interest. The primary difference between the spreadsheet models you have developed so far and simulation models is that at least one of the input variable cells in a simulation model contains *random* numbers. Each time the spreadsheet recalculates, the random numbers change, and the new random values of the inputs produce new values of the outputs. This is the essence of simulation—it enables you to see how outputs vary as random inputs change.

Excel Tip: *Recalculation Key*
The easiest way to make a spreadsheet recalculate is to press the **F9 key**. *This is often called the "recalc" key.*

Technically speaking, input cells do not contain random numbers; they contain *probability distributions*. In general, a probability distribution indicates the possible values of a variable and the probabilities of these values. As a very simple example, you might indicate by an appropriate formula (to be described later) that you want a probability distribution with possible values 50 and 100, and corresponding probabilities 0.7 and 0.3. If you force the sheet to recalculate repeatedly and watch this input cell, you will see the value 50 about 70% of the time and the value 100 about 30% of the time. No other values besides 50 and 100 will appear.

When you enter a given probability distribution in a random input cell, you are describing the possible values and the probabilities of these values that you believe mirror reality. There are many probability distributions to choose from, and you should always attempt to choose an *appropriate* distribution for each specific problem. This is not necessarily an easy task. Therefore, we address it in this section by answering several key questions:

- What types of probability distributions are available, and why do you choose one probability distribution rather than another in an actual simulation model?
- Which probability distributions can you use in simulation models, and how do you invoke them with Excel formulas?

In later sections we address one additional question: Does the choice of input probability distribution really matter—that is, are the *outputs* from the simulation sensitive to this choice?

FUNDAMENTAL INSIGHT

Basic Elements of Spreadsheet Simulation

A spreadsheet simulation model requires three elements: (1) a method for entering random quantities from specified probability distributions in input cells, (2) the usual types of Excel formulas for relating outputs to inputs, and (3) the ability to make the spreadsheet recalculate many times and capture the resulting outputs for statistical analysis. Excel has some capabilities for performing these steps, but Excel add-ins such as @RISK provide much better tools for automating the process.

15-2a Types of Probability Distributions

Imagine a toolbox that contains the probability distributions you know and understand. As you obtain more experience in simulation modeling, you will naturally add probability distributions to your toolbox that you can then use in future simulation models. We begin by adding a few useful probability distributions to this toolbox. However, before adding any specific distributions, it is useful to provide a brief review of some important general characteristics of probability distributions.[1] These include the following distinctions:

- Discrete versus continuous
- Symmetric versus skewed
- Bounded versus unbounded
- Nonnegative versus unrestricted

FUNDAMENTAL INSIGHT

Choosing Probability Distributions for Uncertain Inputs

In simulation models, it is important to choose *appropriate* probability distributions for all uncertain inputs. These choices can strongly affect the results.

Unfortunately, there are no "right answers." You need to choose the probability distributions that best encode your uncertainty, and this is not necessarily easy. However, the properties discussed in this section provide you with useful guidelines for making reasonable choices.

---

[1]This review is brief because the material was covered in Chapters 2, 4, and 5.

Discrete Versus Continuous

A probability distribution is *discrete* if it has a finite number of possible values.[2] For example, if you throw two dice and look at the sum of the faces showing, there are only 11 discrete possibilities: the integers 2 through 12. In contrast, a probability distribution is *continuous* if its possible values are essentially a continuum. An example is the amount of rain that falls during a month in Indiana. It could be any decimal value from 0 to, say, 15 inches.

The graph of a discrete distribution is a series of spikes, as shown in Figure 15.3.[3] The height of each spike is the probability of the corresponding value.

Figure 15.3

A Typical Discrete Probability Distribution

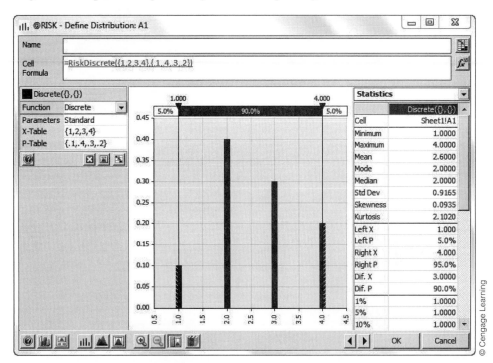

The heights above a density function are not probabilities, but they still indicate relative likelihoods of the possible values.

In contrast, a continuous distribution is characterized by a *density function*, a smooth curve as shown in Figure 15.4. There are two important properties of density functions. Recall from Chapter 5 that the height of the density function above any value indicates the relative likelihood of that value, and probabilities can be calculated as areas under the curve.

Sometimes it is convenient to treat a discrete probability distribution as continuous, and vice versa. For example, consider a student's random score on an exam that has 1000 possible points. If the grader scores each exam to the nearest integer, then even though the score is really discrete with many possible integer values, it is probably more convenient to model its distribution as a continuum. Continuous probability distributions are typically more intuitive and easier to work with than discrete distributions in cases such as this, where there are many possible values. In contrast, continuous distributions are sometimes *discretized* for simplicity.

Symmetric Versus Skewed

A probability distribution can either be symmetric or skewed to the left or right. Figures 15.4, 15.5, and 15.6 provide examples of each of these. You typically choose between a symmetric and skewed distribution on the basis of realism. For example, if you want to model a student's score on a 100-point exam, you will probably choose a left-skewed distribution.

---

[2]Actually, it is possible for a discrete variable to have a *countably infinite* number of possible values, such as all the nonnegative integers 0, 1, 2, and so on. However, this is not an important distinction for practical applications.
[3]This figure and several later figures have been captured from Palisade's @RISK add-in.

Figure 15.4

A Typical
Continuous
Probability
Distribution

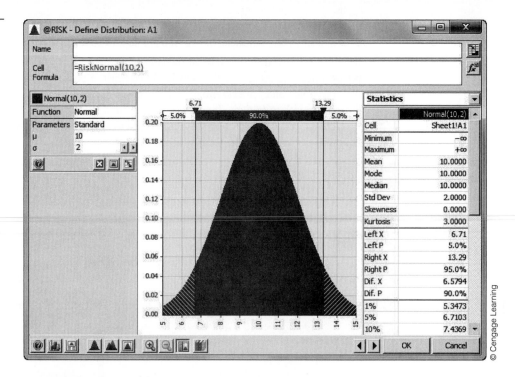

Figure 15.5

A Positively
Skewed Probability
Distribution

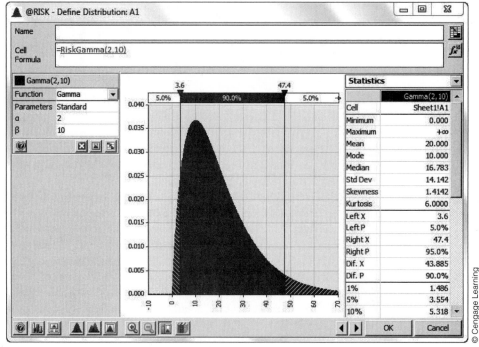

This is because a few poorly prepared students typically "pull down the curve." On the other hand, if you want to model the time it takes to serve a customer at a bank, you will probably choose a right-skewed distribution. This is because most customers take only a minute or two, but a few customers take a long time. Finally, if you want to model the monthly return on a stock, you might choose a distribution symmetric around zero, reasoning that the stock return is just as likely to be positive as negative and there is no obvious reason for skewness in either direction.

Figure 15.6

A Negatively Skewed Probability Distribution

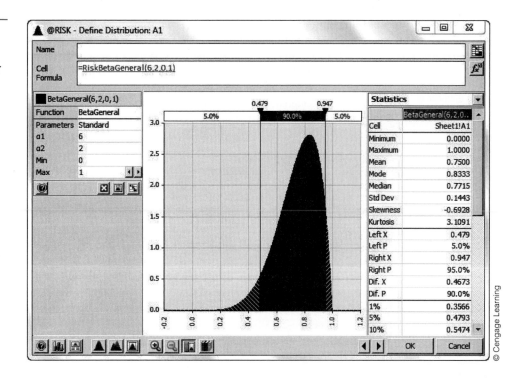

Bounded Versus Unbounded

A probability distribution is *bounded* if there are values *A* and *B* such that no possible value can be less than *A* or greater than *B*. The value *A* is then the *minimum* possible value, and the value *B* is the *maximum* possible value. The distribution is *unbounded* if there are no such bounds. Actually, it is possible for a distribution to be bounded in one direction but not the other. As an example, the distribution of scores on a 100-point exam is bounded between 0 and 100. In contrast, the distribution of the amount of damages Mr. Jones submits to his insurance company in a year is bounded on the left by 0, but there is no natural upper bound. Therefore, you might model this amount with a distribution that is bounded by 0 on the left but is unbounded on the right. Alternatively, if you believe that no damage amount larger than $20,000 can occur, you could model this amount with a distribution that is bounded in both directions.

Nonnegative versus Unrestricted

One important special case of bounded distributions is when the only possible values are *nonnegative*. For example, if you want to model the random cost of manufacturing a new product, you know for sure that this cost must be nonnegative. There are many other such examples. In such cases, you should model the randomness with a probability distribution that is bounded below by 0. This rules out negative values that make no practical sense.

15-2b Common Probability Distributions

Now that you know the *types* of probability distributions available, you can add some common probability distributions to your toolbox. The file **Probability Distributions.xlsx** was developed to help you learn and explore these. Each sheet in this file illustrates a particular probability distribution. It describes the general characteristics of the distribution, indicates how you can generate random numbers from the distribution either with Excel's built-in

Think of the **Probability Distributions.xlsx** *file as a "dictionary" of the most commonly used distributions. Keep it handy for reference.*

functions or with @RISK functions, and it includes histograms of these distributions from simulated data to illustrate their shapes.[4]

A family of distributions has a common name, such as "normal." Each member of the family is specified by one or more numerical parameters.

It is important to realize that each of the following distributions is really a *family* of distributions. Each member of the family is specified by one or more parameters. For example, there is not a *single* normal distribution; there is a normal distribution for each possible mean and standard deviation you specify. Therefore, when you try to find an appropriate input probability distribution in a simulation model, you first have to choose an appropriate family, and then you have to select the appropriate parameters for that family.

Uniform Distribution

The **uniform distribution** is the "flat" distribution illustrated in Figure 15.7. It is bounded by a minimum and a maximum, and all values between these two extremes are equally likely. You can think of this as the "I have no idea" distribution. For example, a manager might realize that a building cost is uncertain. If she can state only that, "I know the cost will be between $20,000 and $30,000, but other than this, I have no idea what the cost will be," then a uniform distribution from $20,000 to $30,000 is a natural choice. However, even though some people do use the uniform distribution in such cases, these situations are arguably not very common or realistic. If the manager really thinks about it, she can probably provide more information about the uncertain cost, such as, "The cost is more likely to be close to $25,000 than to either of the extremes." Then some distribution other than the uniform is more appropriate.

Figure 15.7
Uniform Distribution

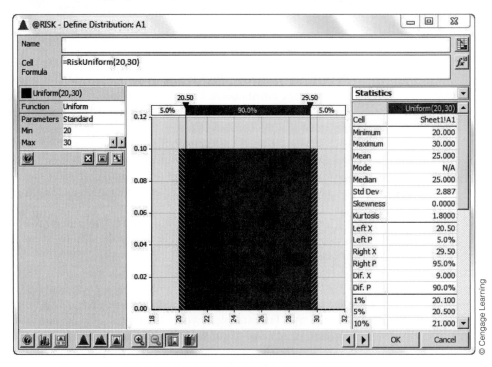

© Cengage Learning

Regardless of whether the uniform distribution is an appropriate candidate as an input distribution, it is important for another reason. All simulation software packages, including Excel, are capable of generating random numbers uniformly distributed between 0 and 1.

---

[4]In later sections of this chapter, and all through the next chapter, we discuss much of @RISK's functionality. For this section, the only functionality we use is @RISK's collection of functions, such as RISKNORMAL and RISKTRIANG, for generating random numbers from various probability distributions. You can skim the details of these functions for now and refer back to them as necessary in later sections.

These are the building blocks of most simulated random numbers, in that random numbers from other probability distributions are generated from them.

The RAND function is Excel's "building block" function for generating random numbers.

In Excel, you can generate a random number between 0 and 1 by entering the formula

=RAND()

in any cell. (The parentheses to the right of RAND indicate that this is an Excel function with no arguments. These parentheses must be included.)

Excel Function: RAND

RAND and RANDBETWEEN Functions

To generate a random number equally likely to be anywhere between 0 and 1, enter the formula **=RAND()** *into any cell. Press the F9 key, or recalculate in any other way, to make it change randomly.*

In addition to being between 0 and 1, the numbers created by this function have two properties that you would expect "random" numbers to have.

- **Uniform property.** Each time you enter the RAND function in a cell, all numbers between 0 and 1 have the same chance of occurring. This means that approximately 10% of the numbers generated by the RAND function will be between 0.0 and 0.1; 10% of the numbers will be between 0.65 and 0.75; 60% of the numbers will be between 0.20 and 0.80; and so on. This property explains why the random numbers are said to be *uniformly distributed* between 0 and 1.

- **Independence property.** Different random numbers generated by **=RAND()** formulas are *probabilistically independent*. This implies that when you generate a random number in cell A5, say, it has no effect on the values of any other random numbers generated in the spreadsheet. For example, if one call to the RAND function yields a large random number such as 0.98, there is no reason to suspect that the next call to RAND will yield an abnormally small (or large) random number; it is unaffected by the value of the first random number.

Excel Function: RANDBETWEEN

Besides the RAND function, there is one other function built into Excel that generates random numbers, the RANDBETWEEN function. It takes two integer arguments, as in **=RANDBETWEEN(1,6),** *and returns a random integer between these values (including the endpoints) so that all such integers are equally likely. The function was introduced in Excel 2007. (It was actually available in previous versions of Excel, but only if the Analysis Toolpak add-in was loaded.)*

To illustrate the RAND function, open a new workbook, enter the formula **=RAND()** in cell A4, and copy it to the range A4:A503. This generates 500 random numbers. Figure 15.8 displays a possible set of values. However, when you try this on your PC, you will undoubtedly obtain *different* random numbers. This is an inherent characteristic of simulation—no two answers are ever exactly alike. Now press the recalc (F9) key. All of the random numbers will change. In fact, each time you press the F9 key or do anything to make your spreadsheet recalculate, all of the cells containing the RAND function will change.

A histogram of the 500 random numbers appears in Figure 15.9. (Again, if you try this on your PC, the shape of your histogram will not be identical to the one shown in Figure 15.9, because it will be based on *different* random numbers.) From property 1, you would expect *equal* numbers of observations in the 10 categories. Obviously, the heights of the bars are *not* exactly equal, but the differences are due to chance—not to a faulty random number generator.

Figure 15.8

Uniformly
Distributed
Random Numbers
Generated by the
RAND Function

	A	B
1	**500 random numbers from RAND function**	
2		
3	Random #	
4	0.904839687	
5	0.110071803	
6	0.578533474	
7	0.40186657	
8	0.166471441	
9	0.455926747	
10	0.775722777	
501	0.331800254	
502	0.762717161	
503	0.396541369	

© Cengage Learning

Figure 15.9

Histogram of
the 500 Random
Numbers Generated
by the RAND
Function

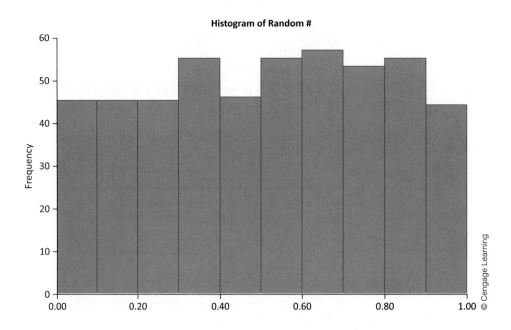

© Cengage Learning

Technical Note: **Pseudo-random Numbers**

The "random" numbers generated by the RAND function (or by the random number generator in any simulation software package) are not really random. They are sometimes called pseudo-random numbers. *Each successive random number follows the previous random number by a complex arithmetic operation. If you happen to know the details of this arithmetic operation, you can predict ahead of time exactly which random numbers will be generated by the RAND function. This is quite different from using a "true" random mechanism, such as spinning a wheel, to get the next random number—a mechanism that would be impractical to implement on a computer. Mathematicians and computer scientists have studied many ways to produce random numbers that have the two properties we just discussed, and they have developed many competing random number generators such as the RAND function in Excel. The technical details need not concern you. The important point is that these random number generators produce numbers that appear to be random and are useful for simulation modeling.*

It is simple to generate a uniformly distributed random number with a minimum and maximum other than 0 and 1. For example, the formula

=200+100*RAND( )

generates a number uniformly distributed between 200 and 300. (Make sure you see why.) Alternatively, you can use the @RISK formula[5]

=RISKUNIFORM(200,300)

You can take a look at this and other properties of the uniform distribution on the Uniform sheet in the **Probability Distributions.xlsx** file. (See Figure 15.10.)

Figure 15.10

Properties of Uniform Distribution

◢	A	B	C	D	E	F
1	**Uniform distribution**					
2						
3	**Characteristics**					
4	Continuous					
5	Symmetric					
6	Bounded in both directions					
7	Not necessarily positive (depends on bounds)					
8						
9	**Parameters**					
10	MinVal	50				
11	MaxVal	100				
12						
13	**Excel**		**Example**			
14	=MinVal + (MaxVal–MinVal)*RAND()		54.242387			
15						
16	**@RISK**					
17	=RISKUNIFORM(MinVal,MaxVal)		83.456018			

This is a flat distribution between two values, labeled here MinVal and MaxVal. Note that if MinVal=0 and MaxVal=1, then you can just use Excel's RAND function.

@RISK Function: RISKUNIFORM

To generate a random number from any uniform distribution, enter the formula **=RISKUNIFORM(MinVal,MaxVal)** *in any cell. Here, MinVal and MaxVal are the minimum and maximum possible values. Note that if MinVal is 0 and MaxVal is 1, this function is equivalent to Excel's RAND function.*

Freezing Random Numbers

The automatic recalculation of random numbers can be useful sometimes and annoying at other times. There are situations when you want the random numbers to stay fixed—that is, you want to **freeze random numbers** at their current values. The following three-step method does this.

1. Select the range that you want to freeze, such as A4:A503 in Figure 15.8.
2. Press Ctrl+c to copy this range.

Random numbers that have been frozen do not change when you press the F9 key.

3. With the same range still selected, select the Paste Values option from the Paste drop-down menu on the Home ribbon. This procedure pastes a copy of the range onto itself, except that the entries are now numbers, not formulas. Therefore, whenever the spreadsheet recalculates, these numbers do not change.

Each sheet in the **Probability Distributions.xlsx** file has a list of 500 random numbers that have been frozen. The histograms in the sheets are based on the frozen random numbers.

---

[5]As we have done with other Excel functions, we capitalize the @RISK functions, such as RISKUNIFORM, in the text. However, this is not necessary when you enter the formulas in Excel.

15-2 Probability Distributions for Input Variables **823**

However, we encourage you to enter "live" random numbers in column B over the frozen ones and see how the histogram changes when you press F9.

15-2c Using @RISK to Explore Probability Distributions

Exploring Distributions with @RISK

The **Probability Distributions.xlsx** file illustrates a few frequently used probability distributions, and it shows the formulas required to generate random numbers from these distributions. Another option is to use Palisade's @RISK add-in, which allows you to experiment with probability distributions with its **@RISK random functions**. Essentially, it allows you to see the shapes of various distributions and to calculate probabilities for them, all in a user-friendly graphical interface.

To run @RISK, click the Windows Start button, go to the Programs tab, locate the Palisades DecisionTools® Suite, and select @RISK. After a few seconds, you will see the welcome screen, which you can close. At this point, you should have an @RISK tab and corresponding ribbon. (You won't see the Project button unless you have Microsoft Project installed on your computer.) Select a blank cell in your worksheet, and then click the Define Distributions button on the @RISK ribbon (see Figure 15.11). You will see one of several galleries of distributions, depending on the tab you select. For example, Figure 15.12 shows the gallery of common distributions. Highlight one of the distributions and click Select Distribution. For example, choose the uniform distribution and enter 75 and 150 as the Min and Max parameters. You will see the shape of the distribution and a list of summary measures to the right, as shown in Figure 15.13. For example, it indicates that the mean and standard deviation of this uniform distribution are 112.5 and 21.65.

Figure 15.11 @RISK Ribbon

Figure 15.12

Gallery of Common Distributions

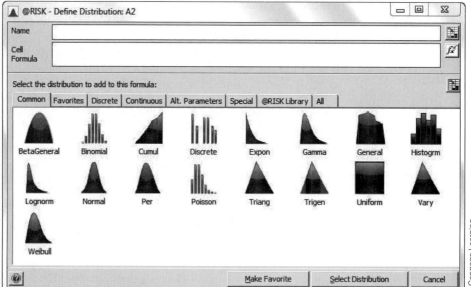

Figure 15.13

Uniform
Distribution
(from @RISK)

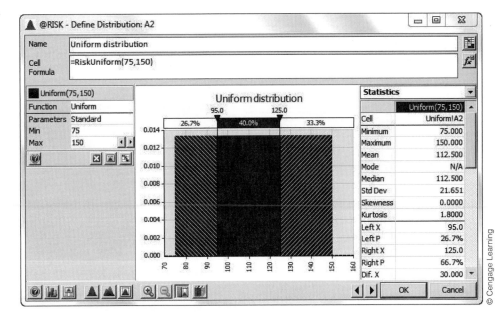

Everything in this window is interactive. Suppose you want to find the probability that a value from this distribution is less than 95. You can drag the left-hand "slider" in the diagram (the vertical line with the triangle at the top) to the position 95, as shown in Figure 15.13. You see immediately that the left-hand probability is 0.267. Similarly, if you want the probability that a value from this distribution is greater than 125, you can drag the right-hand slider to the position 125 to see that the required probability is 0.3333. (Rather than sliding, you can enter the numbers, such as 95 and 125, directly into the areas above the sliders.)

The interactive capabilities of @RISK's Define Distributions window, with its sliders, make it perfect for finding probabilities or percentiles for any given distribution.

You can also enter probabilities instead of values. For example, if you want the value such that there is probability 0.10 to the left of it—the 10th percentile—you can enter 10% in the left space above the chart. You will see that the corresponding value is 82.5. Similarly, if you want the value such that there is probability 0.10 to the right of it, you can enter 10% in the right space above the chart, and you will see that the corresponding value is 142.5.

The Define Distributions window in @RISK is quick and easy. We urge you to use it and experiment with some of its options. By the way, you can click the third button from the left at the bottom of the window to copy the chart into an Excel worksheet. However, you then lose the interactive capabilities, such as moving the sliders.

Discrete Distribution

A **discrete distribution** is useful for many situations, either when the uncertain quantity is not really continuous (the number of televisions demanded, for example) or when you want a discrete approximation to a continuous variable. All you need to specify are the possible values and their probabilities, making sure that the probabilities sum to 1. Because of this flexibility in specifying values and probabilities, discrete distributions can have practically any shape.

@RISK's way of generating a discrete random number is much simpler and more intuitive than Excel's method, which requires cumulative probabilities and a lookup function.

As an example, suppose a manager estimates that the demand for a particular brand of television during the coming month will be 10, 15, 20, or 25, with respective probabilities 0.1, 0.3, 0.4, and 0.2. This typical discrete distribution is illustrated in Figure 15.14.

The Discrete sheet of the **Probability Distributions.xlsx** file indicates how to work with a discrete distribution. (See Figure 15.15.) As you can see, there are two quite different ways to generate a random number from this distribution. We discuss the Excel way in detail in Section 15-4. For now, we simply mention that this is one case (of many) where

Figure 15.14

Discrete Distribution (from @RISK)

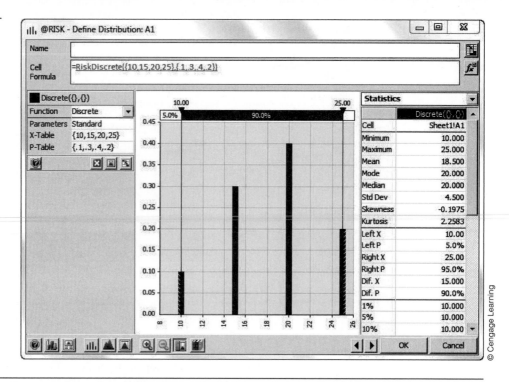

Figure 15.15 Properties of a Discrete Distribution

◢	A	B	C	D	E	F	G	H
1	**General discrete distribution**							
2								
3	**Characteristics**				This can have any shape, depending on the list of possible values and their probabilities.			
4	Discrete							
5	Can be symmetric or skewed (or bumpy, i.e., basically any shape)							
6	Bounded in both directions							
7	Not necessarily positive (depends on possible values)							
8								
9	**Parameters**				Lookup table required for Excel method			
10		Values	Probabilities		CumProb	Value		
11		10	0.1		0	10		
12		15	0.3		0.1	15		
13		20	0.4		0.4	20		
14		25	0.2		0.8	25		
15								
16	**Excel**		Example					
17	=VLOOKUP(RAND(),LookupTable,2)		25					
18								
19	**@RISK**							
20	=RISKDISCRETE(Values,Probs)		15					

Generating Random Numbers with Excel Functions

it is much easier to generate random numbers with @RISK functions than with built-in Excel functions. Assuming that @RISK is loaded, all you need to do is enter the function RISKDISCRETE with two arguments, a list of possible values and a list of their probabilities, as in

=**RISKDISCRETE(B11:B14,C11:C14)**

The Excel way, which requires cumulative probabilities and a lookup table, takes more work and is harder to remember.

@RISK Function: *RISKDISCRETE*

To generate a random number from any discrete probability distribution, enter the formula **=RISKDISCRETE(valRange,probRange)** *into any cell. Here valRange is the range where the possible values are stored, and probRange is the range where their probabilities are stored.*

The selected input distributions for any simulation model reflect historical data and an analyst's best judgment as to what will happen in the future.

At this point, a relevant question is why a manager would choose this particular discrete distribution. First, it is clearly an approximation. After all, if it is possible to have demands of 20 and 25, it should also be possible to have demands between these values. Here, the manager approximates a discrete distribution with *many* possible values—all integers from 0 to 50, say—with a discrete distribution with a few well-chosen values. This is fairly common in simulation modeling. Second, where do the probabilities come from? They are probably a blend of historical data (perhaps demand was near 15 in 30% of previous months) and the manager's subjective feelings about demand *next* month.

Normal Distribution

Normally distributed random numbers will almost certainly be within three standard deviations of the mean.

The *normal distribution* is the familiar bell-shaped curve that was discussed in detail in Chapter 5. (See Figure 15.16.) It is useful in simulation modeling as a continuous input distribution. However, it is *not* always the most appropriate distribution. It is symmetric, which can be a drawback when a skewed distribution is more realistic. Also, it allows negative values, which are not appropriate in many situations. For example, the demand for televisions cannot be negative. Fortunately, this possibility of negative values is often not a problem. Suppose you generate a normally distributed random number with mean 100 and standard deviation 20. Then, as you should recall from Chapter 5, there is almost no chance

Figure 15.16

Normal Distribution (from @RISK)

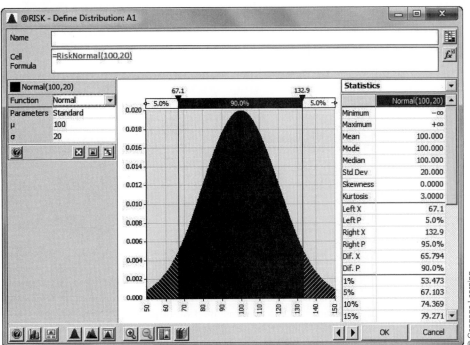

© Cengage Learning

of having values more than three standard deviations to the left of the mean, and this rules out negative values for all practical purposes.

A tip-off that a normal distribution might be an appropriate candidate for an input variable is a statement such as, "We believe the most likely value of demand is 100, and the chances are about 95% that demand will be no more than 40 units on either of side of this most likely value." Because a normally distributed value is within two standard deviations of its mean with probability 0.95, this statement translates easily to a mean of 100 and a standard deviation of 20. This does not imply that a normal distribution is the *only* candidate for the distribution of demand, but the statement naturally leads to this distribution.

The Normal sheet in the **Probability Distributions.xlsx** file indicates how you can generate normally distributed random numbers in Excel, either with or without @RISK. (See Figure 15.17.) This is one case where an add-in is not really necessary. The formula

=NORMINV(RAND(),*Mean,Stdev*)

always works. Still, this is not as easy to remember as @RISK's formula

=RISKNORMAL,(*Mean,Stdev*)

@RISK Function: RISKNORMAL

To generate a normally distributed random number, enter the formula =RISKNORMAL *(Mean,Stdev) in any cell. Here, Mean and Stdev are the mean and standard deviation of the normal distribution.*

Figure 15.17   Properties of the Normal Distribution

	A	B	C	D	E	F
1	Normal distribution					
2				This is the familiar bell-shaped curve, defined by two parameters: the mean and the standard deviation.		
3	Characteristics					
4	Continuous					
5	Symmetric (bell-shaped)					
6	Unbounded in both directions					
7	Is both positive and negative					
8						
9	Parameters					
10	Mean	100				
11	Stdev	10				
12						
13	Excel		Example			
14	=NORMINV(RAND(),Mean,Stdev)		77.53722541			
15						
16	@RISK					
17	=RISKNORMAL(Mean,Stdev)		90.71065954			

© Cengage Learning

Triangular Distribution

A triangular distribution is a good choice in many simulation models because it can have a variety of shapes and its parameters are easy to understand.

The **triangular distribution** is somewhat similar to the normal distribution in that its density function rises to some point and then falls, but it is more flexible and intuitive than the normal distribution. Therefore, it is an excellent candidate for many continuous input variables. The shape of a triangular density function is literally a triangle, as shown in Figure 15.18. It is specified by three easy-to-understand parameters: the minimum possible value, the most likely value, and the maximum possible value. The high point of the

Figure 15.18

Triangular
Distribution (from
@RISK)

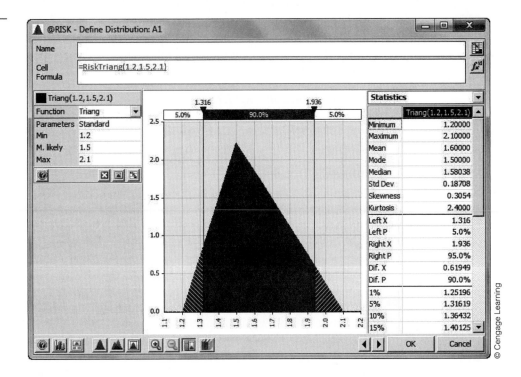

triangle is above the most likely value. Therefore, if a manager states, "We believe the most likely development cost is \$1.5 million, and we don't believe the development cost could possibly be less than \$1.2 million or greater than \$2.1 million," the triangular distribution with these three parameters is a natural choice. As in this numerical example, note that the triangular distribution can be skewed if the mostly likely value is closer to one extreme than another. Of course, it can also be symmetric if the most likely value is right in the middle.

The Triangular sheet of the **Probability Distributions.xlsx** file indicates how to generate random values from this distribution. (See Figure 15.19.) As you can see, there is no way to do it with native Excel (at least not without a macro). However, it is easy with @RISK, using the RISKTRIANG function, as in

=RISKTRIANG(B10,B11,B12)

Figure 15.19

Properties of
the Triangular
Distribution

	A	B	C	D	E	F	G
1	**Triangular distribution**						
2							
3	**Characteristics**						
4	Continuous						
5	Can be Symmetric or skewed in either direction						
6	Bounded in both directions						
7	Not necessarily positive (depends on bounds)						
8							
9	**Parameters**						
10	Min	50					
11	MostLikely	85					
12	Max	100					
13							
14	**Excel**						
15	There is no easy way to do it except by writing a macro.						
16							
17	**@RISK**		**Example**				
18	=RISKTRIANG(Min,MostLikely,Max)		64.12779617				

The density of this distribution is literally a triangle. The "top" of the triangle is above the most likely value, and the base of the triangle extends from the minimum value to the maximum value. It is intuitive for users because the three parameters have a natural meaning.

© Cengage Learning

This function takes three arguments: the minimum value, the most likely value, and the maximum value—in this order and separated by commas. You will see this function in many of our examples. Just remember that it has an abbreviated spelling: RISKTRIANG, not RISKTRIANGULAR.

@RISK Function: RISKTRIANG

To generate a random number from a triangular distribution, enter the formula =RISKTRIANG(MinVal,MLVal,MaxVal) in any cell. Here, MinVal is the minimum possible value, MLVal is the most likely value, and MaxVal is the maximum value.

Binomial Distribution

The *binomial distribution* is a discrete distribution that was discussed extensively in Chapter 5. Recall that the binomial distribution applies to a very specific situation: when a number of independent and identical trials occur, and each trial results in a *success* or *failure*. Then the binomial random number is the number of successes in these trials. The two parameters of this distribution, n and p, are the number of trials and the probability of success on each trial.

A random number from a binomial distribution indicates the number of successes in a certain number of identical trials.

As an example, suppose an airline company sells 170 tickets for a flight and estimates that 80% of the people with tickets will actually show up for the flight. How many people will actually show up? It is tempting to state that *exactly* 80% of 170, or 136 people, will show up, but this neglects the inherent randomness. A more realistic way to model this situation is to say that each of the 170 people, independently of one another, will show up with probability 0.8. Then the number of people who actually show up is binomially distributed with $n = 170$ and $p = 0.8$. (This assumes independent behavior across passengers, which might not be the case, for example, if whole families either show up or don't.) This distribution is illustrated in Figure 15.20.

Figure 15.20

Binomial Distribution (from @RISK)

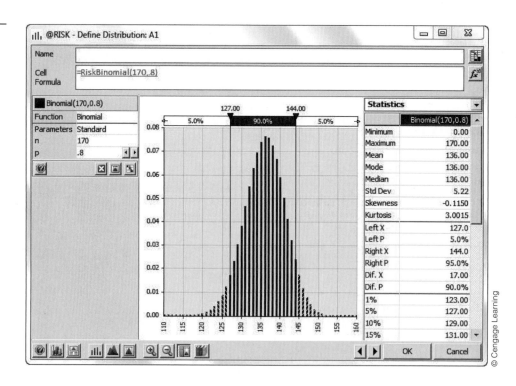

The Binomial sheet of the **Probability Distributions.xlsx** file indicates how to generate random numbers from this distribution. (See Figure 15.21.) Although it is possible to do this with Excel using the built-in CRITBINOM function and the RAND function, it is not very intuitive or easy to remember. (Starting in Excel 2010, CRITBINOM can be replaced by BINOM.INV.) Clearly, the @RISK way is preferable. In the airline example, you would generate the number who show up with the formula

=RISKBINOMIAL(170,0.8)

Note that the histogram in this figure is approximately bell-shaped. This is no accident. When the number of trials *n* is reasonably large and *p* isn't too close to 0 or 1, the binomial distribution can be well approximated by the normal distribution.

Figure 15.21   **Properties of the Binomial Distribution**

◢	A	B	C	D	E	F	G	H
1	**Binomial distribution**							
2								
3	**Characteristics**							
4	Discrete							
5	Can be symmetric or skewed			This distribution is of the number of "successes" in a given number of identical, independent trials, when the probability of success is constant on each trial.				
6	Bounded below by 0, bounded above by Ntrials							
7	Nonnegative							
8								
9	**Parameters**							
10	NTrials	170						
11	PSuccess	0.8						
12								
13	**Excel**		**Example**		Alternatively in Excel 2010			
14	=CRITBINOM(NTrials,PSuccess,RAND())		141		=BINOM.INV(Ntrials,Psuccess,RAND())			
15								
16	**@RISK**							
17	=RISKBINOMIAL(NTrials,PSuccess)		133					

© Cengage Learning

@RISK Function: RISKBINOMIAL
To generate a random number from a binomial distribution, enter the formula ***=RISKBINOMIAL(NTrials,PSuccess)*** *in any cell. Here, NTrials is the number of trials, and PSuccess is the probability of a success on each trial.*

It is natural to ask which distribution to use for a given uncertain quantity such as the price of oil, the demand for laptops, and so on. Admittedly, the choices we make in later examples are sometimes for convenience. However, in real business situations the choice is not always clear-cut, and it can make a difference in the results. Stanford professor Sam Savage and two of his colleages discuss this choice in a series of two articles on "Probability Management." (These articles are available online at http://lionhrtpub.com/orms/orms-2-06/frprobability.html and http://lionhrtpub.com/orms/orms-4-06/frprobability.html.) They argue that with the increasing importance of simulation models in today's business world, input distributions should not only be chosen carefully, but they should be kept and maintained as important corporate assets. They shouldn't just be chosen in some ad hoc fashion every time they are needed. For example, if the price of oil is an important input in many of a company's decisions, then experts within the company should assess an appropriate distribution for the price of oil and modify it as necessary when new information arises. The authors even suggest a new company position, Chief Probability Officer, to control access to the company's probability distributions.

So as you are reading these final two chapters, keep Savage's ideas in mind. The choice of probability distributions for inputs is not easy, yet neither is it arbitrary. The choice *can* make a difference in the results. This is the reason why you want as many families of probability distributions in your toolbox as possible. You then have more flexibility to choose a distribution that is appropriate for your situation.

PROBLEMS

Note: Student solutions for problems whose numbers appear within a colored box are available for purchase at www.cengagebrain.com.

Level A

1. Use the RAND function and the Copy command to generate a set of 100 random numbers.
   a. What fraction of the random numbers are smaller than 0.5?
   b. What fraction of the time is a random number less than 0.5 followed by a random number greater than 0.5?
   c. What fraction of the random numbers are larger than 0.8?
   d. Freeze these random numbers. However, instead of pasting them over the original random numbers, paste them onto a new range. Then press the F9 recalculate key. The original random numbers should change, but the pasted copy should remain the same.

2. Use Excel's functions (not @RISK) to generate 1000 random numbers from a normal distribution with mean 100 and standard deviation 10. Then freeze these random numbers.
   a. Calculate the mean and standard deviation of these random numbers. Are they approximately what you would expect?
   b. What fraction of these random numbers are within k standard deviations of the mean? Answer for $k = 1$; for $k = 2$; for $k = 3$. Are the answers close to what they should be (according to the empirical rules you learned in Chapters 2 and 5)?
   c. Create a histogram of the random numbers using 10 to 15 categories of your choice. Does this histogram have approximately the shape you would expect?

3. Use @RISK's Define Distributions tool to show a uniform distribution from 400 to 750. Then answer the following questions.
   a. What are the mean and standard deviation of this distribution?
   b. What are the 5th and 95th percentiles of this distribution?

   c. What is the probability that a random number from this distribution is less than 450?
   d. What is the probability that a random number from this distribution is greater than 650?
   e. What is the probability that a random number from this distribution is between 500 and 700?

4. Use @RISK's Define Distributions tool to draw a normal distribution with mean 500 and standard deviation 100. Then answer the following questions.
   a. What is the probability that a random number from this distribution is less than 450?
   b. What is the probability that a random number from this distribution is greater than 650?
   c. What is the probability that a random number from this distribution is between 500 and 700?

5. Use @RISK's Define Distributions tool to show a triangular distribution with parameters 300, 500, and 900. Then answer the following questions.
   a. What are the mean and standard deviation of this distribution?
   b. What are the 5th and 95th percentiles of this distribution?
   c. What is the probability that a random number from this distribution is less than 450?
   d. What is the probability that a random number from this distribution is greater than 650?
   e. What is the probability that a random number from this distribution is between 500 and 700?

6. Use @RISK's Define Distributions tool to show a binomial distribution that results from 50 trials with probability of success 0.3 on each trial, and use it to answer the following questions.
   a. What are the mean and standard deviation of this distribution?
   b. You have to be more careful in interpreting @RISK probabilities with a discrete distribution such as this binomial. For example, if you move the left slider to 11, you find a probability of 0.139 to the left of it. But is this the probability of "less than 11" or "less than or equal to 11"? One way to check is to use

Excel's BINOMDIST function. Use this function to interpret the 0.139 value from @RISK.

c. Using part **b** to guide you, use @RISK to find the probability that a random number from this distribution will be greater than 17. Check your answer by using the BINOMDIST function appropriately in Excel.

7. Use @RISK's Define Distributions tool to draw a triangular distribution with parameters 200, 300, and 600. Then superimpose a normal distribution on this drawing, choosing the mean and standard deviation to match those from the triangular distribution. (Click the Add Overlay button at the bottom of the window and then choose the distribution to superimpose.)

a. What are the 5th and 95th percentiles for these two distributions?

b. What is the probability that a random number from the triangular distribution is less than 400? What is this probability for the normal distribution?

c. Experiment with the sliders to answer questions similar to those in part **b**. Would you conclude that these two distributions differ most in the extremes (right or left) or in the middle? Explain.

8. We all hate to keep track of small change. By using random numbers, it is possible to eliminate the need for change and give the store and the customer a fair deal. This problem indicates how it could be done.

a. Suppose that you buy something for $0.20. How could you use random numbers (built into the cash register system) to decide whether you should pay $1.00 or nothing?

b. If you bought something for $9.60, how would you use random numbers to eliminate the need for change?

c. In the long run, why is this method fair to both the store and the customers? Would you personally (as a customer) be willing to abide by such a system?

Level B

9. A company is about to develop and then market a new product. It wants to build a simulation model for the entire process, and one key uncertain input is the development cost. For each of the following scenarios, choose an appropriate distribution together with its parameters, justify your choice in words, and use @RISK's Define Distributions tool to show your chosen distribution.

a. Company experts have no idea what the distribution of the development cost is. All they can state is "we are 95% sure it will be at least $450,000, and we are 95% sure it will be no more than $650,000."

b. Company experts can still make the same statement as in part **a**, but now they can also state: "We believe the distribution is symmetric, reasonably bell-shaped, and its most likely value is about $550,000."

c. Company experts can still make the same statement as in part **a**, but now they can also state: "We believe the distribution is skewed to the right, and its most likely value is about $500,000."

10. Continuing the preceding problem, suppose that another key uncertain input is the development time, which is measured in an *integer* number of months. For each of the following scenarios, choose an appropriate distribution together with its parameters, justify your choice in words, and use @RISK's Define Distributions tool to show your chosen distribution.

a. Company experts believe the development time will be from 6 to 10 months, but they have absolutely no idea which of these will result.

b. Company experts believe the development time will be from 6 to 10 months. They believe the probabilities of these five possible values will increase linearly to a most likely value at 8 months and will then decrease linearly.

c. Company experts believe the development time will be from 6 to 10 months. They believe that 8 months is twice as likely as either 7 months or 9 months and that either of these latter possibilities is three times as likely as either 6 months or 10 months.

15-3 SIMULATION AND THE FLAW OF AVERAGES

To help motivate simulation modeling in general, we present a simple example in this section. It will clearly show the distinction between Figure 15.1 (a deterministic model with best-guess inputs) and Figure 15.2 (an appropriate simulation model). In doing so, it will illustrate a pitfall called the "flaw of averages" that you should always try to avoid.[6]

[6]As far as we know, the term "flaw of averages" was coined by Sam Savage, the same Stanford professor quoted earlier.

EXAMPLE | **15.1 ORDERING CALENDARS AT WALTON BOOKSTORE**

The Flaw of Averages

In August, Walton Bookstore must decide how many of next year's nature calendars to order. Each calendar costs the bookstore $7.50 and sells for $10. After January 1, all unsold calendars will be returned to the publisher for a refund of $2.50 per calendar. Walton believes that the number of calendars it can sell by January 1 follows some probability distribution with mean 200. Walton believes that ordering to the average demand, that is, ordering 200 calendars, is a good decision. Is it?

Objective To illustrate the difference between a deterministic model with a best guess for uncertain inputs and a simulation model that incorporates uncertainty explicitly.

Where Do the Numbers Come From?

The monetary values are straightforward. The mean demand is probably an estimate based on historical demands for similar calendars.

Solution

A deterministic model appears in Figure 15.22. (See the file **Walton Bookstore 1.xlsx**.) Assuming the best guess for demand, Walton orders to this average value, and it appears that the company's best guess for profit is $500. (The formulas in cells B16:F16 are straight-forward. Anticipating that the order quantity and demand will not always be equal, they are **=B9, =B5*MIN(B9,B12), =B4*B12, =B6*MAX(B12-B9,0)**, and **=C16-D16+E16.**) Before reading further, do you believe that the *average* profit will be $500 when uncertainty in demand is introduced explicitly (and the company still orders 200 calendars)? Think what happens to profit when demand is less than 200 and when it is greater than 200. Are these two cases symmetric?

Figure 15.22
Deterministic
Model

	A	B	C	D	E	F
1	Walton's bookstore - deterministic model					
2						
3	Cost data					
4	Unit cost	$7.50				
5	Unit price	$10.00				
6	Unit refund	$2.50				
7						
8	Uncertain quantity					
9	Demand (average shown)	200				
10						
11	Decision variable					
12	Order quantity	200				
13						
14	Profit model					
15		Demand	Revenue	Cost	Refund	Profit
16		200	$2,000.00	$1,500.00	$0.00	$500.00

© Cengage Learning

We now contrast this with a simulation model where the demand in cell B9 is replaced by a random number. For this example, we assume that demand is *normally* distributed with mean 200 and standard deviation 40, although these specific assumptions are not crucial for the qualitative aspects of the example. All you need to do is enter the formula **=ROUND(RISKNORMAL(200,40),0)** in cell B9, where the ROUND function has been used to round to the nearest integer. Now the model appears as in Figure 15.23.

Figure 15.23

Simulation Model

	A	B	C	D	E	F
1	Walton's bookstore - simulation model					
2						
3	**Cost data**					
4	Unit cost	$7.50				
5	Unit price	$10.00				
6	Unit refund	$2.50				
7						
8	**Uncertain quantity (assumed normal with mean 200, stdev 40)**					
9	Demand (random)	254				
10						
11	**Decision variable**					
12	Order quantity	200				
13						
14	**Profit model**					
15		Demand	Revenue	Cost	Refund	Profit
16		254	$2,000.00	$1,500.00	$0.00	$500.00

© Cengage Learning

The random demand in cell B9 is now live, as are its dependents in row 16, so each time you press the F9 key, you get a new demand and associated profit. (This assumes that the @RISK "dice" button is toggled to orange, its "random" setting. More will be said about this setting later in the chapter.) Do you get about $500 in profit on average? Absolutely not! The situation isn't symmetric. The *largest* profit you can get is $500, which occurs about half the time, whenever demand is greater than 200. A typical such situation appears in the figure, where the excess demand of 63 is simply lost. However, when demand is less than 200, the profit is *less than* $500, and it keeps decreasing as demand decreases.

We ran @RISK with 1000 iterations (which will be explained in detail in Section 15-5) and found the resulting histogram of 1000 simulated profits shown in Figure 15.24. The large spike on the right is due to the cases where demand is 200 or more and profit is $500. All the little spikes to the left are where demand is less than 200 and profit is less than $500,

Figure 15.24

Histogram of Simulated Profits

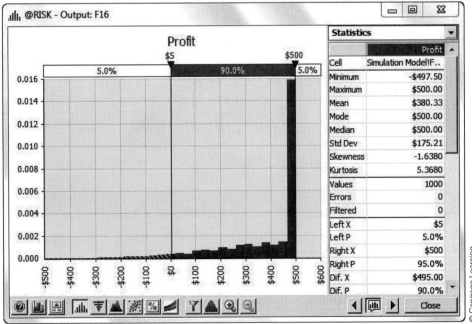

© Cengage Learning

sometimes considerably less. You can see on the right that the *mean* profit, the average of the 1000 simulated profits, is only about $380, well less than the $500 suggested by the deterministic model.

The point of this simple example is that a deterministic model can be very misleading. In particular, the output from a deterministic model that uses best guesses for uncertain inputs is *not* necessarily equal to, or even close to, the average of the outputs from a simulation. This is exactly what "the flaw of averages" means. ∎

FUNDAMENTAL INSIGHT

The Flaw of Averages

If a model contains uncertain inputs, it can be very misleading to build a deterministic model by using the *means* of the inputs to predict an output.

The resulting output value can be considerably different—lower *or* higher—than the mean of the output values obtained from running a simulation with uncertainty incorporated explicitly.

15-4 SIMULATION WITH BUILT-IN EXCEL TOOLS

In this section, we show how spreadsheet simulation models can be developed and analyzed with Excel's built-in tools without using add-ins. As you will see, this is certainly possible, but it presents two problems. First, the @RISK functions illustrated in the **Probability Distributions.xlsx** file are not available. You are able to use only Excel's RAND function and transformations of it to generate random numbers from various probability distributions. (You can also use the RANDBETWEEN function, but except for special cases, this doesn't help much.) Second, there is a bookkeeping problem. Once you build an Excel model with output cells linked to appropriate random input cells, you can press the F9 key as often as you like to see how the outputs vary. However, there is no quick way to keep track of these output values and summarize them. This bookkeeping feature is the real strength of a simulation add-in such as @RISK. It can be done with Excel, usually with data tables, but the summarization of the resulting data is completely up to the user—you. Therefore, we strongly recommend that you use the "Excel-only" method described in this section only if you don't have an add-in such as @RISK.

To illustrate the Excel-only procedure, we continue to analyze the calendar problem from Example 15.1. This general problem occurs when a company (such as a news vendor) must make a one-time purchase of a product (such as a newspaper) to meet customer demands for a certain period of time. If the company orders too few newspapers, it will lose potential profit by not having enough on hand to satisfy its customers. If it orders too many, it will have newspapers left over at the end of the day that, at best, can be sold at a loss. More generally, the problem is to match supply to an uncertain demand, a very common problem in business. In much of the rest of this chapter, we will discuss variations of this problem, generally referred to as the *newsvendor* problem.

EXAMPLE | **15.2 SIMULATING WITH EXCEL ONLY AT WALTON BOOKSTORE**

Recall that Walton Bookstore must decide how many of next year's nature calendars to order. Each calendar costs the bookstore $7.50 and sells for $10. After January 1, all unsold calendars will be returned to the publisher for a refund of $2.50 per calendar. In this version, we assume that demand for calendars (at the full price) is given by the probability distribution shown in Table 15.1. Walton wants to develop a simulation model to help it decide how many calendars to order.

Table 15.1 Probability Distribution of Demand for Walton Example

Demand	Probability
100	0.30
150	0.20
200	0.30
250	0.15
300	0.05

Objective To use built-in Excel tools—including the RAND function and data tables, but no add-ins—to simulate profit for several order quantities and ultimately choose the "best" order quantity.

Where Do the Numbers Come From?

The numbers in Table 15.1 are the key to the simulation model. They are discussed in more detail next.

Solution

We first discuss the probability distribution in Table 15.1. It is a discrete distribution with only five possible values: 100, 150, 200, 250, and 300. In reality, it is clear that other values of demand are possible. For example, there could be demand for exactly 187 calendars. In spite of its apparent lack of realism, we use this discrete distribution for two reasons. First, its simplicity is a nice feature to get you started with simulation modeling. Second, discrete distributions are often used in real business simulation models. Even though the discrete distribution is only an *approximation* to reality, it can still provide important insights into the actual problem.

As for the probabilities listed in Table 15.1, they are typically drawn from historical data or (if historical data are lacking) educated guesses. In this case, the manager of Walton Bookstore has presumably looked at demands for calendars in previous years, and he has used any information he has about the market for next year's calendars to estimate, for example, that the probability of a demand for 200 calendars is 0.30. The five probabilities in this table *must* sum to 1. Beyond this requirement, they should be as reasonable and consistent with reality as possible.

It is important to realize that this is really a decision problem under uncertainty. Walton must choose an order quantity *before* knowing the demand for calendars. Unfortunately, Solver cannot be used because of the uncertainty.[7] Therefore, we develop a simulation model for any *fixed* order quantity. Then we run this simulation model with various order quantities to see which one appears to be best.

Developing the Simulation Model

Developing the Walton Model with Excel Tools Only

Now we discuss the ordering model. For any fixed order quantity, we show how Excel can be used to simulate 1000 replications (or any other number of replications). Each replication is an independent replay of the events that occur. To illustrate, suppose you want to simulate profit if Walton orders 200 calendars. Figure 15.25 illustrates the results obtained by simulating 1000 independent replications for this order quantity. (See the file **Walton Bookstore 2.xlsx**.) Note that there are many hidden rows in Figure 15.25. To develop this model, use the following steps.

---

[7]Palisade Corporation has developed a tool called RISKOptimizer that can be used for optimization in a simulation model. It is included in @RISK, but we will not discuss it here.

Figure 15.25 Walton Bookstore Simulation Model

	A	B	C	D	E	F	G	H	I	J
1	Simulation of Walton's bookstore									
2										
3	Cost data			Demand distribution						
4	Unit cost	$7.50			Cum Prob	Demand	Probability			
5	Unit price	$10.00		0.00	100	0.30				
6	Unit refund	$2.50		0.30	150	0.20				
7				0.50	200	0.30				
8	Decision variable			0.80	250	0.15				
9	Order quantity	200		0.95	300	0.05				
10										
11	Summary measures for simulation below									
12	Average profit	$204.13		95% confidence interval for expected profit						
13	Stdev of profit	$328.04		Lower limit	$183.79					
14	Minimum profit	−$250.00		Upper limit	$224.46					
15	Maximum profit	$500.00			$40.66					
16					2754.8222					
17	Simulation								Distribution of profit	
18	Replication	Random #	Demand	Revenue	Cost	Refund	Profit		Value	Frequency
19	1	0.2249	100	$1,000	$1,500	$250	−$250		−250	299
20	2	0.6693	200	$2,000	$1,500	$0	$500		125	191
21	3	0.4164	150	$1,500	$1,500	$125	$125		500	510
22	4	0.7562	200	$2,000	$1,500	$0	$500			
23	5	0.1581	100	$1,000	$1,500	$250	−$250			
1016	998	0.5055	200	$2,000	$1,500	$0	$500			
1017	999	0.2457	100	$1,000	$1,500	$250	−$250			
1018	1000	0.3484	150	$1,500	$1,500	$125	$125			

© Cengage Learning

1. **Inputs.** Enter the cost data in the range B4:B6, the probability distribution of demand in the range E5:F9, and the proposed order quantity, 200, in cell B9. Pay particular attention to the way the probability distribution is entered (and compare to the Discrete sheet in the **Probability Distributions.xlsx** file). Columns E and F contain the possible demand values and the probabilities from Table 15.1. It is also necessary (see step 2 for the reasoning) to have the cumulative probabilities in column D. To obtain these, first enter the value 0 in cell D5. Then enter the formula

   =F5+D5

   in cell D6 and copy it to the range D7:D9.

2. **Generate random demands.** The key to the simulation is the generation of the customer demands in the range B19:B1018 from the random numbers generated by the RAND function and the probability distribution of demand. Here is how it works. The interval from 0 to 1 is split into five segments: 0.0 to 0.3 (length 0.3), 0.3 to 0.5 (length 0.2), 0.5 to 0.8 (length 0.3), 0.8 to 0.95 (length 0.15), and 0.95 to 1.0 (length 0.05). Note that these lengths are the probabilities of the various demands. Then a demand is associated with each random number, depending on which interval the random number falls in. For example, if a random number is 0.5279, this falls in the third interval, so it is associated with the third possible demand value, 200.

   To implement this procedure, you use a VLOOKUP function based on the range D5:F9 (named LookupTable). This table has the cumulative probabilities in column D and the possible demand values in column E. In fact, the whole purpose of the cumulative probabilities in column D is to allow the use of the VLOOKUP function. To generate the simulated demands, enter the formula

   =VLOOKUP(RAND(),LookupTable,2)

This rather cumbersome procedure for generating a discrete random number is not necessary when you use @RISK.

in cell B19 and copy it to the range B20:B1018. This formula compares any RAND value to the values in D5:D9 and returns the appropriate demand from E5:E9. (In the file, you will note that random cells are colored green. This coloring convention is not required, but we use it consistently to identify the random cells.)

This step is the key to the simulation, so make sure you understand exactly what it entails. The rest is bookkeeping, as indicated in the following steps.

3. **Revenue.** Once the demand is known, the number of calendars sold is the smaller of the demand and the order quantity. For example, if 150 calendars are demanded, 150 will be sold. But if 250 are demanded, only 200 can be sold (because Walton orders only 200). Therefore, to calculate the revenue in cell C19, enter the formula

=Unit_price*MIN(B19,Order_quantity)

4. **Ordering cost.** The cost of ordering the calendars does not depend on the demand; it is the unit cost multiplied by the number ordered. Calculate this cost in cell D19 with the formula

=Unit_cost*Order_quantity

5. **Refund.** If the order quantity is greater than the demand, there is a refund of $2.50 for each calendar left over; otherwise, there is no refund. Therefore, calculate the refund in cell E19 with the formula

=Unit_refund*MAX(Order_quantity-B19,0)

For example, if demand is 150, then 50 calendars are left over, and this MAX is 50, the larger of 50 and 0. However, if demand is 250, then no calendars are left over, and this MAX is 0, the larger of −50 and 0. (This calculation could also be accomplished with an IF function instead of a MAX function.)

6. **Profit.** Calculate the profit in cell F19 with the formula

=C19+E19-D19

7. **Copy to other rows.** This is a "one-line" simulation, where all of the logic is captured in a single row, row 19. For one-line simulations, you can replicate the logic with new random numbers very easily by copying down. Copy row 19 down to row 1018 to generate 1000 replications.

8. **Summary measures.** Each profit value in column F corresponds to one randomly generated demand. You usually want to see how these vary from one replication to another. First, calculate the average and standard deviation of the 1000 profits in cells B12 and B13 with the formulas

=AVERAGE(F19:F1018)

and

=STDEV(F19:F1018)

Similarly, calculate the smallest and largest of the 1000 profits in cells B14 and B15 with the MIN and MAX functions.

9. **Confidence interval for mean profit.** Calculate a 95% confidence interval for the mean profit in cells E13 and E14 with the formulas

=B12−1.96*B13/SQRT(1000)

and

=B12+1.96*B13/SQRT(1000)

(See the next section on confidence intervals within this example for details.)

10. **Distribution of simulated profits.** There are only three possible profits, −$250, $125, or $500 (depending on whether demand is 100, 150, or at least 200—see the following discussion). You can use the COUNTIF function to count the number of times each of these possible profits is obtained. To do so, enter the formula

=COUNTIF($F$19:$F$1018,H19)

in cell I19 and copy it down to cell I21.

Checking Logic with Deterministic Inputs

It can be difficult to check whether the logic in your model is correct, because of the random numbers. The reason is that you usually get different output values, depending on the particular random numbers generated. Therefore, it is sometimes useful to enter well-chosen *fixed* values for the random inputs, just to see whether your logic is correct. We call these *deterministic checks*. In the present example, you might try several fixed demands, at least one of which is *less than* the order quantity and at least one of which is *greater than* the order quantity. For example, if you enter a fixed demand of 150, the revenue, cost, refund, and profit should be $1500, $1500, $125, and $125, respectively. Or if you enter a fixed demand of 250, these outputs are $2000, $1500, $0, and $500. There is no randomness in these values; every correct model should get these same values. If your model doesn't get these values, there must be a logic error in your model that has nothing to do with random numbers or simulation. Of course, you should fix any such logical errors before reentering the *random* demand and running the simulation.

You can make a similar check by keeping the random demand, repeatedly pressing the F9 key, and watching the outputs for the different random demands. For example, if the refund is not $0 every time demand exceeds the order quantity, you know you have a logical error in at least one formula. The advantage of deterministic checks is that you can compare your results with those of other users, using *agreed-upon test values* of the random quantities. You should all get exactly the same outputs.

Discussion of the Simulation Results

At this point, it is a good idea to stand back and see what you have accomplished. First, in the body of the simulation, rows 19 through 1018, you randomly generated 1000 possible demands and the corresponding profits. Because there are only five possible demand values (100, 150, 200, 250, and 300), there are only five possible profit values: −$250, $125, $500, $500, and $500. Also, note that for the order quantity 200, the profit is $500 regardless of whether demand is 200, 250, or 300. (Make sure you understand why.) A tally of the profit values in these rows, including the hidden rows, indicates that there are 299 rows with profit equal to −$250 (demand 100), 191 rows with profit equal to $125 (demand 150), and 500 rows with profit equal to $500 (demand 200, 250, or 300). The average of these 1000 profits is $204.13, and their standard deviation is $328.04. (Again, however, remember that your answers will probably differ from these because of different random numbers.)

For this particular model, the output distribution is also discrete: There are only three possible profits for an order quantity of 200

Typically, a simulation model should capture one or more output variables, such as profit. These output variables depend on random inputs, such as demand. The goal is to estimate the probability distributions of the outputs. In the Walton simulation the estimated probability distribution of profit is

$$P(\text{Profit} = -\$250) = 299/1000 = 0.299$$

$$P(\text{Profit} = \$125) = 191/1000 = 0.191$$

$$P(\text{Profit} = \$500) = 500/1000 = 0.500$$

The estimated mean of this distribution is \$204.13 and the estimated standard deviation is \$328.04. It is important to realize that if the entire simulation is run again with *different* random numbers (such as the ones you might have generated on your PC), the answers will probably be slightly different. This is the primary reason for the confidence interval in cells E13 and E14. This interval expresses the remaining uncertainty about the *mean* of the profit distribution. Your best guess for this mean is the average of the 1000 profits you happened to observe. However, because the corresponding confidence interval is somewhat wide, from \$183.79 to \$224.46, you are not at all sure of the *true* mean of the profit distribution. You are only 95% confident that the true mean is within this interval. If you run this simulation again with different random numbers, the average profit might be somewhat different from the average profit you observed, \$204.13, and the other summary statistics will probably also be different. (For illustration, we pressed the F9 key five times and got the following average profits: \$213.88, \$206.00, \$212.75, \$219.50, and \$189.50. So this is truly a case of "answers will vary.")

Notes about Confidence Intervals

The confidence interval provides a measure of accuracy of the mean profit, as estimated from the simulation.

It is common in computer simulations to estimate the mean of some distribution by the average of the simulated observations. The usual practice is then to accompany this estimate with a **confidence interval,** which indicates the accuracy of the estimate. You should recall from Chapter 8 that to obtain a confidence interval for the mean, you start with the estimated mean and then add and subtract a multiple of the *standard error* of the estimated mean. If the estimated mean (that is, the average) is $\overline{X}$, the confidence interval is given in the following formula.

Confidence Interval for the Mean
$$\overline{X} \pm (\text{Multiple} \times \text{Standard Error of } \overline{X})$$

We repeat these basic facts about confidence intervals from Chapter 8 here for your convenience.

The standard error of $\overline{X}$ is the standard deviation of the observations divided by the square root of *n*, the number of observations:

Standard Error of $\overline{X}$
$$s/\sqrt{n}$$

Here, s is the symbol for the standard deviation of the observations. You can obtain it with the STDEV function in Excel.

The *multiple* in the confidence interval formula depends on the confidence level and the number of observations. If the confidence level is 95%, for example, the multiple is very close to 2, so a good guideline is to go out two standard errors on either side of the average to obtain an approximate 95% confidence interval for the mean.

> **Approximate 95% Confidence Interval for the Mean**
> $$\overline{X} \pm 2s/\sqrt{n}$$

To be more precise, if n is reasonably large, which is almost always the case in simulations, the central limit theorem implies that the correct multiple is the number from the standard normal distribution that cuts off probability 0.025 in each tail. This is a famous number in statistics: 1.96. Because 1.96 is very close to 2, it is acceptable for all practical purposes to use 2 instead of 1.96 in the confidence interval formula. (Note that you should use a different multiple if you want a 90% or a 99% confidence level rather than a 95% level.)

The idea is to choose the number of iterations large enough so that the resulting confidence interval will be sufficiently narrow.

Analysts often plan a simulation so that the confidence interval for the mean of some important output will be sufficiently narrow. The reasoning is that narrow confidence intervals imply more precision about the estimated mean of the output variable. If the confidence level is fixed at some value such as 95%, the only way to narrow the confidence interval is to simulate more replications. Assuming that the confidence level is 95%, the following value of n is required to ensure that the resulting confidence interval will have a half-length approximately equal to some specified value B:

> **Sample Size Determination**
> $$n = \frac{4 \times (\text{Estimated standard deviation})^2}{B^2}$$

This formula requires an estimate of the standard deviation of the output variable. For example, in the Walton simulation the 95% confidence interval with $n = 1000$ has half-length ($\$224.46 - \$183.79)/2 = \$20.33$. Suppose that you want to reduce this half-length to $\$12.50$—that is, you want $B = \$12.50$. You do not know the exact standard deviation of the profit distribution, but you can estimate it from the simulation as $\$328.04$. Therefore, to obtain the required confidence interval half-length B, you need to simulate n replications, where

$$n = \frac{4(328.04)^2}{12.50^2} \approx 2755$$

(When this formula produces a noninteger, it is common to round upward.) The claim, then, is that if you rerun the simulation with 2755 replications rather than 1000 replications, the half-length of the 95% confidence interval for the mean profit will be close to $\$12.50$.

Finding the Best Order Quantity

You are not yet finished with the Walton example. So far, the simulation has been run for only a single order quantity, 200. Walton's ultimate goal is to find the *best* order quantity. Even this statement must be clarified. What does "best" mean? As in Chapter 6, one possibility is to use the *expected* profit—that is, EMV—as the optimality criterion, but other characteristics of the profit distribution could influence the decision. You can obtain the required outputs with a data table. Specifically, you can use a data table to rerun the simulation for other order quantities. This data table and a corresponding chart are shown in Figure 15.26. (This is still part of the finished version of the **Walton Bookstore 2.xlsx** file.)

Figure 15.26   Data Table for Walton Bookstore Simulation

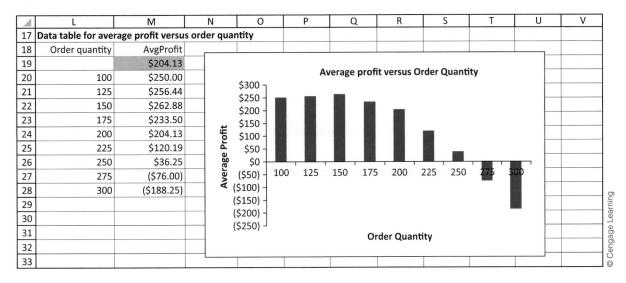

	L	M	N	O	P	Q	R	S	T	U	V
17	Data table for average profit versus order quantity										
18	Order quantity	AvgProfit									
19		$204.13									
20	100	$250.00									
21	125	$256.44									
22	150	$262.88									
23	175	$233.50									
24	200	$204.13									
25	225	$120.19									
26	250	$36.25									
27	275	($76.00)									
28	300	($188.25)									
29											
30											
31											
32											
33											

To optimize in simulation models, try various values of the decision variable(s) and run the simulation for each of them.

To create this table, enter the trial order quantities shown in the range L20: L28, enter the link **=B12** to the average profit in cell M19, and select the data table range L19: M28. Then select Data Table from the What-If Analysis dropdown list on the Data ribbon, specifying that the column input cell is B9. (See Figure 15.25.) Finally, construct a column chart of the average profits in the data table. Note that an order quantity of 150 appears to maximize the average profit. Its average profit of $262.88 is slightly higher than the average profits from nearby order quantities and much higher than the profit gained from an order of 200 or more calendars. However, again keep in mind that this is a simulation, so that all of these average profits depend on the particular random numbers generated. If you rerun the simulation with different random numbers, it is conceivable that some other order quantity could be best.

Excel Tip: *Calculation Settings with Data Tables*

Sometimes you will create a data table and the values will be constant the whole way down. This could mean you did something wrong, but more likely it is due to a calculation setting. To check, go to the Formulas ribbon and click the Calculation Options dropdown arrow. If it isn't Automatic (the default setting), you need to click the Calculate Now (or The key to simulating many replications in Excel (without an add-in) is to use a data table with any blank cell as the column input cell. Calculate Sheet) button or press the F9 key to make the data table calculate correctly. (The Calculate Now and F9 key recalculate everything in your workbook. The Calculate Sheet option recalculates only the active sheet.) Note that the Automatic Except for Data Tables setting is there for a reason. Data tables, especially those based on complex simulations, can take a lot of time to recalculate, and with the default setting, this recalculation occurs every time anything changes in your workbook. So the Automatic Except for Data Tables setting is handy to prevent data tables from recalculating until you force them to by pressing the F9 key or clicking one of the Calculate buttons.

Using a Data Table to Repeat Simulations

The Walton simulation is a particularly simple one-line simulation model. All of the logic—generating a demand and calculating the corresponding profit—can be captured in a single row. Then to replicate the simulation, you can simply copy this row down as far as you like. Many simulation models are significantly more complex and require more than one row to capture the logic. Nevertheless, they still result in one or more output quantities (such as profit) that you want to replicate. We now illustrate another method of **replicating with Excel tools only** that is more general (still using the Walton example). It uses a data table to generate the replications. Refer to Figure 15.27 and the file **Walton Bookstore 3.xlsx**.

Figure 15.27

Using a Data
Table to Simulate
Replications

	A	B	C	D	E	F
17	Simulation					
18		Demand	Revenue	Cost	Refund	Profit
19		100	$1,000	$1,500	$250	−$250
20						
21	Data table for replications, each shows profit from that replication					
22	Replication	Profit				
23		−$250				
24	1	$125				
25	2	$125				
26	3	$500				
27	4	$500				
28	5	$500				
1021	998	$500				
1022	999	$500				
1023	1000	$500				

© Cengage Learning

Through row 19, this model is exactly like the previous model. That is, it uses the given data at the top of the spreadsheet to construct a typical "prototype" of the simulation in row 19. This time, however, do not copy row 19 down. Instead, form a data table in the range A23:B1023 to replicate the basic simulation 1000 times. In column A, list the replication numbers, 1 to 1000. Next, enter the formula =F19 in cell B23. This forms a link to the profit from the prototype row for use in the data table. Then create a data table and enter *any blank cell* (such as C23) as the column input cell. (No row input cell is necessary, so its box should be left empty.) This tricks Excel into repeating the row 19 calculations 1000 times, each time with a new random number, and reporting the profits in column B of the data table. (If you wanted to see other simulated quantities, such as revenue, for each replication, you could add extra output columns to the data table.)

Excel Tip: How Data Tables Work

The key to simulating
many replications
in Excel (without an
addin) is to use a data
table with any blank
cell as the column
input cell.

To understand this procedure, you must understand exactly how data tables work. When you create a data table, Excel takes each value in the left column of the data table (here, column A), substitutes it into the cell designated as the column input cell, recalculates the spreadsheet, and returns the output value (or values) you have requested in the top row of the data table (such as profit). It might seem silly to substitute each replication number from column A into a blank cell such as cell C23, but this part is really irrelevant. The important part is the recalculation. Each recalculation leads to a new random demand and corresponding profit, and these profits are the quantities you want to keep track of. Of course, this means that you should not freeze the quantity in cell B19 before forming the data table. The whole point of the data table is to use a different random number for each replication, and this will occur only if the random demand in row 19 is "live."

Using a Two-Way Data Table

You can carry this method one step further to see how the profit depends on the order quantity. Here you use a two-way data table with the replication number along the side and possible order quantities along the top. See Figure 15.28 and the file **Walton Bookstore 4.xlsx**.

Figure 15.28   Using a Two-Way Data Table for the Simulation Model

	A	B	C	D	E	F	G	H	I	J
17	Simulation									
18		Demand	Revenue	Cost	Refund	Profit				
19		300	$2,000	$1,500	$0	$500				
20										
21	Data table showing profit for replications with various order quantities									
22	Replication			Order quantity						
23	$500.00	100	125	150	175	200	225	250	275	300
24	1	$250	$313	$375	$438	−$250	0	625	−625	375
25	2	$250	$125	$0	$438	$125	0	625	500	−750
26	3	$250	$313	$375	$438	−$250	0	−500	−250	0
27	4	$250	$313	$0	$250	$500	562.5	−500	125	−375
28	5	$250	$125	$375	$438	$125	0	−500	−625	375
1021	998	$250	$313	$375	−$125	$500	375	−125	500	−375
1022	999	$250	$313	$375	$438	$500	375	625	125	−750
1023	1000	$250	$125	$375	−$125	$500	0	250	125	−750

© Cengage Learning

Now the data table range is A23:J1023, and the driving formula in cell A23 is again the link **=F19**. The column input cell should again be *any blank cell*, and the row input cell should be B9 (the order quantity). Each cell in the body of the data table shows a simulated profit for a particular replication and a particular order quantity, and each is based on a *different* random demand.

By averaging the numbers in each column of the data table (see row 14), you can see which is the best order quantity. It is also helpful to construct a column chart of these averages, as in Figure 15.29. Now, however, assuming you have not frozen anything, the data table and the corresponding chart will change each time you press the F9 key. It turns out that 150 is *usually* the best order quantity, but depending on the random numbers generated, it is not always best (as is illustrated in the chart). ■

Figure 15.29

Column Chart of Average Profits for Different Order Quantities

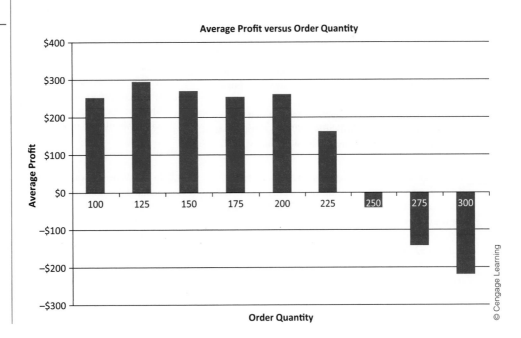

© Cengage Learning

By now you should appreciate the usefulness of data tables in spreadsheet simulations. They allow you to take a prototype simulation and replicate its key results as often as you like. This method makes summary statistics (over the entire group of replications) and corresponding charts fairly easy to obtain. Nevertheless, it takes some work to create the data tables and charts. In the next section you will see how the @RISK add-in does a lot of this work for you.

PROBLEMS

Level A

11. Suppose you own an expensive car and purchase auto insurance. This insurance has a $1000 deductible, so that if you have an accident and the damage is less than $1000, you pay for it out of your pocket. However, if the damage is greater than $1000, you pay the first $1000 and the insurance pays the rest. In the current year there is probability 0.025 that you will have an accident. If you have an accident, the damage amount is normally distributed with mean $3000 and standard deviation $750.

   a. Use Excel to simulate the amount you have to pay for damages to your car. This should be a one-line simulation, so run 5000 iterations by copying it down. Then find the average amount you pay, the standard deviation of the amounts you pay, and a 95% confidence interval for the average amount you pay. (Note that many of the amounts you pay will be 0 because you have no accidents.)

   b. Continue the simulation in part **a** by creating a two-way data table, where the row input is the deductible amount, varied from $500 to $2000 in multiples of $500. Now find the average amount you pay, the standard deviation of the amounts you pay, and a 95% confidence interval for the average amount you pay for each deductible amount.

   c. Do you think it is reasonable to assume that damage amounts are *normally* distributed? What would you criticize about this assumption? What might you suggest instead?

12. In August of the current year, a car dealer is trying to determine how many cars of the next model year to order. Each car ordered in August costs $20,000. The demand for the dealer's next year models has the probability distribution shown in the file **P15_12.xlsx**. Each car sells for $25,000. If demand for next year's cars exceeds the number of cars ordered in August, the dealer must reorder at a cost of $22,000 per car. Excess cars can be disposed of at $17,000 per car. Use simulation to determine how many cars to order in August. For your optimal order quantity, find a 95% confidence interval for the expected profit.

13. In the Walton Bookstore example, suppose that Walton receives no money for the first 50 excess calendars returned but receives $2.50 for every calendar after the first 50 returned. Does this change the optimal order quantity?

14. A sweatshirt supplier is trying to decide how many sweatshirts to print for the upcoming NCAA basketball championships. The final four teams have emerged from the quarterfinal round, and there is now a week left until the semifinals, which are then followed in a couple of days by the finals. Each sweatshirt costs $10 to produce and sells for $25. However, in three weeks, any leftover sweatshirts will be put on sale for half price, $12.50. The supplier assumes that the demand for his sweatshirts during the next three weeks (when interest in the tournament is at its highest) has the distribution shown in the file **P15_14.xlsx**. The residual demand, after the sweatshirts have been put on sale, has the distribution also shown in this file. The supplier, being a profit maximizer, realizes that every sweatshirt sold, even at the sale price, yields a profit. However, he also realizes that any sweatshirts produced but not sold (even at the sale price) must be thrown away, resulting in a $10 loss per sweatshirt. Analyze the supplier's problem with a simulation model.

Level B

15. In the Walton Bookstore example with a discrete demand distribution, explain why an order quantity other than one of the possible demands cannot maximize the expected profit. (*Hint*: Consider an order of 190 calendars, for example. If this maximizes expected profit, then it must yield a higher expected profit than an order of 150 or 100. But then an order of 200 calendars must also yield a larger expected profit than 190 calendars. Why?)

15-5 INTRODUCTION TO THE @RISK

Spreadsheet simulation modeling has become extremely popular in recent years, both in the academic and corporate communities. Much of the reason for this popularity is due to simulation add-ins such as @**RISK**. There are two primary advantages to using such an add-in. First, an add-in gives you easy access to many probability distributions you might want to use in your simulation models. You already saw in Section 15-2 how the RISKDISCRETE, RISKNORMAL, and RISKTRIANG functions, among others, are easy to use and remember. Second, an add-in allows you to perform simulations much more easily than is possible with Excel alone. To replicate a simulation in Excel, you typically need to build a data table. Then you have to calculate summary statistics, such as averages, standard deviations, and percentiles, with built-in Excel functions. If you want graphs to enhance the analysis, you have to create them. In short, you have to perform a number of time-consuming steps for each simulation. Simulation add-ins such as @RISK perform much of this work automatically.

@RISK provides a number of functions for simulating from various distributions, and it takes care of all the bookkeeping in spreadsheet simulations. Excel simulations without @RISK require much more work for the user.

Although we will focus only on @RISK in this book, it is not the only simulation add-in available for Excel. Two worthy competitors are Crystal Ball, developed by Decisioneering (www.decisioneering.com) and Risk Solver Platform, developed by Frontline Systems, the developer of Solver (www.frontsys.com). Both Crystal Ball and Risk Solver Platform have much of the same functionality as @RISK. However, the authors have a natural bias for @RISK—we have been permitted by its developer, Palisade Corporation (www.palisade .com), to provide the academic version free with this book. If it were not included, you would have to purchase it from Palisade at a fairly steep price. Indeed, Microsoft Office does not include @RISK, Crystal Ball, Risk Solver Platform, or any other simulation add-in—you must purchase them separately.

15-5a @RISK Features

Here is an overview of some of @RISK's features. We will discuss all of these in more detail in this section.

- @RISK contains a number of functions such as RISKNORMAL and RISKDISCRETE that make it easy to generate observations from a wide variety of probability distributions. You saw some of these in Section 15-2.

- You can designate any cell or range of cells in your simulation model as *output cells*. When you run the simulation, @RISK automatically keeps summary measures (averages, standard deviations, percentiles, and others) from the values generated in these output cells across the replications. It also creates graphs such as histograms based on these values. In other words, @RISK takes care of tedious bookkeeping operations for you.

- @RISK has a special function, **RISKSIMTABLE**, that allows you to run the same simulation several times, using a different value of some key input variable each time. This input variable is often a decision variable. For example, suppose that you would like to simulate an inventory ordering policy (as in the Walton Bookstore example). Your ultimate purpose is to compare simulation outputs across a number of possible order quantities such as 100, 150, 200, 250, and 300. If you use an appropriate formula involving the RISKSIMTABLE function, the entire simulation is performed for each of these order quantities separately—with one click of a button. You can then compare the outputs to choose the best order quantity.

15-5b Loading @RISK

To build simulation models with @RISK, you need to have Excel open with @RISK added in. The first step, if you have not already done so, is to install the Palisade DecisionTools suite with its Setup program. Then you can load @RISK by clicking the Windows Start button, selecting the Programs group, selecting the Palisade DecisionTools group, and selecting the @RISK item. If Excel is already open, this loads @RISK inside Excel. If Excel is not yet open, this launches Excel and @RISK simultaneously.[8] After @RISK is loaded, you see an @RISK tab and the corresponding @RISK ribbon in Figure 15.30.[9]

Figure 15.30   @RISK Ribbon

© Cengage Learning

15-5c @RISK Models with a Single Random Input Variable

The majority of the work (and thinking) goes into developing the model. Setting up @RISK and then running it are relatively easy.

In the remainder of this section we will illustrate some of @RISK's functionality by revisiting the Walton Bookstore example. The next chapter demonstrates the use of @RISK in a number of interesting simulation models. Throughout this discussion, you should keep one very important idea in mind. The development of a simulation model is basically a two-step procedure. The first step is to build the model itself. This step requires you to enter all of the logic that transforms inputs (including @RISK functions such as RISKDISCRETE) into outputs (such as profit). This is where most of the work and thinking go, exactly as in models from previous chapters, and @RISK cannot do this for you. It is *your* job to enter the formulas that link inputs to outputs appropriately. However, once this logic has been incorporated, @RISK takes over in the second step. It automatically replicates your model, with different random numbers on each replication, and it reports any summary measures that you request in tabular or graphical form. Therefore, @RISK greatly decreases the amount of busy work you need to do, but it is not a magic bullet.

We begin by analyzing an example with a single random input variable.

EXAMPLE   **15.3 USING @RISK AT WALTON BOOKSTORE**

Recall that Walton Bookstore buys calendars for $7.50, sells them at the regular price of $10, and gets a refund of $2.50 for all calendars that cannot be sold. In contrast to Example 15.2, assume now that Walton estimates a triangular probability distribution for demand, where the minimum, most likely, and maximum values of demand are 100, 175, and 300, respectively. The company wants to use this probability distribution, together with @RISK, to simulate the profit for any particular order quantity, with the ultimate goal of finding the best order quantity.

This is the same Walton Bookstore model as before, except that a triangular distribution for demand is used.

Objective   To learn about @RISK's basic functionality by revisiting the Walton Bookstore problem.

---

[8]We have had the best luck when we (1) close other applications we are not currently using, and (2) launch Excel and @RISK together by starting @RISK. However, you can also start @RISK *after* Excel is already running.
[9]If you have been using a previous version of @RISK, you will see some changes in the version 6.0 we are using here. However, the basic functionality and the user interface are essentially the same.

Where Do the Numbers Come From?

The monetary values are the same as before. The parameters of the triangular distribution of demand are probably Walton's best subjective estimates, possibly guided by its experience with previous calendars. As in many simulation examples, the triangular distribution is chosen for simplicity. In this case, the manager would need to estimate only three quantities: the minimum possible demand, the maximum possible demand, and the most likely demand.

Solution

We use this example to illustrate important features of @RISK. We first show how it helps you to implement an appropriate input probability distribution for demand. Then we show how it can be used to build a simulation model for a specific order quantity and generate outputs from this model. Finally, we show how the RISKSIMTABLE function enables you to simultaneously generate outputs from several order quantities so that you can choose the optimal order quantity.

Developing the Simulation Model

Developing the Walton Model with @RISK

The spreadsheet model for profit is essentially the same model developed previously *without* @RISK, as shown in Figure 15.31. (See the file **Walton Bookstore 5.xlsx**.) There are only a few new things to be aware of.

Figure 15.31   Simulation Model with a Fixed Order Quantity

	A	B	C	D	E	F	G	H	I	J
1	Simulation of Walton's Bookstore using @RISK							Range names used:		
2								Order_quantity	=Model!$B$9	
3	Cost data			Demand distribution - triangular				Profit	=Model!$F$13	
4	Unit cost	$7.50		Minimum	100			Unit_cost	=Model!$B$4	
5	Unit price	$10.00		Most likely	175			Unit_price	=Model!$B$5	
6	Unit refund	$2.50		Maximum	300			Unit_refund	=Model!$B$6	
7										
8	Decision variable									
9	Order quantity	200								
10										
11	Simulation									
12		Demand	Revenue	Cost	Refund	Profit				
13		267	$2,000	$1,500	$0	$500				
14										
15	Summary measures of profit from @RISK - based on 1000 iterations									
16	Minimum	−$242.50								
17	Maximum	$500.00								
18	Average	$337.48								
19	Standard deviation	$189.02								
20	5th percentile	−$47.50								
21	95th percentile	$500.00								
22	P(profit <= 300)	0.360								
23	P(profit > 400)	0.514								

1. **Input distribution.** To generate a random demand, enter the formula

   =ROUND(RISKTRIANG(E4,E5,E6),0)

   in cell B13 for the random demand. This uses the RISKTRIANG function to generate a demand from the triangular distribution. (As before, our convention is to color random input cells green.) Excel's ROUND function is used to round demand to the nearest integer. Recall from the discussion in Section 15-3 that Excel has no built-in functions to generate random numbers from a triangular distribution, but this is easy with @RISK.

2. **Output cell.** When the simulation runs, you want @RISK to keep track of profit. In @RISK's terminology, you need to designate the Profit cell, F13, as an *output cell*. To do this, select cell F13 and then click the Add Output button on the @RISK ribbon. (See Figure 15.30.) This adds **RISKOUTPUT(*"label"*)+** to the cell's formula. (Here, "label" is a label that @RISK uses for its reports. In this case it makes sense to use "Profit" as the label.) The formula in cell F13 changes from

=C13+E13-D13

to

=RISKOUTPUT("Profit")+C13+E13-D13

The RISKOUTPUT function indicates that a cell is an output cell, so that @RISK will keep track of its values throughout the simulation.

The plus sign following **RISKOUTPUT** does *not* indicate addition. It is simply @RISK's way of indicating that you want to keep track of the value in this cell (for reporting reasons) as the simulation progresses. Any number of cells can be designated in this way as output cells. They are typically the "bottom line" values of primary interest. Our convention is to color such cells gray for emphasis.

3. **Summary functions.** There are several places where you can store @RISK results. One of these is to use @RISK statistical functions to place results in your model worksheet. @RISK provides several functions for summarizing output values. Some of these are illustrated in the range B16:B23 of Figure 15.31. They contain the formulas

These @RISK summary functions allow you to show simulation results on the same sheet as the model. However, they are totally optional.

=RISKMIN(F13)

=RISKMAX(F3)

=RISKMEAN(F13)

=RISKSTDDEV(F13)

=RISKPERCENTILE(F13,0.05)

=RISKPERCENTILE(F13,0.95)

=RISKTARGET(F13,300)

and

=1-RISKTARGET(F13,400)

The values in these cells are not meaningful until you run the simulation (so do not be alarmed if they contain errors when you open the file). However, once the simulation runs, these formulas capture summary statistics of profit. For example, RISKMEAN calculates the average of the 1000 simulated profits, RISKPERCENTILE finds the value such that the specified percentage of simulated profits are less than or equal to this value, and RISKTARGET finds the percentage of simulated profits less than or equal to the specified value. Although these same summary statistics also appear in other @RISK reports, it is handy to have them in the same worksheet as the model. (You can find a list of all @RISK statistical functions from the Simulation Result group in the Insert Function dropdown list on the @RISK ribbon.)

@RISK FEATURE: Color Coding
One very handy feature that was added to @RISK 6.0 late in its development (after much of this book was developed) is its optional color coding. You will find this option in the Help group of the @RISK ribbon. It is a toggle. If it is toggled off, you see our blue/red/gray/green coloring. If it is toggled on, you see @RISK's color coding: blue for random

New Color Coding Feature

input cells, red for output cells, green for statistical functions, and yellow for decision cells (for RISKOptimizer models). You can change the coloring scheme if you prefer.

Running the Simulation

After you develop the model, the rest is straightforward. The procedure is always the same: (1) specify simulation settings, (2) run the simulation, and (3) examine the results.

Simulation and Application Settings in @RISK

1. **Simulation settings.** You must first choose some simulation settings. To do so, the buttons on the left in the Simulation group (see Figure 15.32) are useful. We typically do the following:

   - Set Iterations to a number such as 1000. (@RISK calls replications "iterations.") Any number can be used, but because the academic version of @RISK allows only 1000 uninterrupted iterations, we typically choose 1000.

   - Set Simulations to 1. In a later section, we will explain why you might want to request multiple simulations.

   - The "dice" button is a toggle for what appears in your worksheet. If it is orange (Random), all random cells appear random (they change when you press the F9 key). If it is white (Static), only the *means* appear in random input cells and the F9 key has no effect. We tend to prefer the Monte Carlo setting, but both settings have exactly the same effect when you run the simulation.

   - Many more settings are available by clicking the Simulation Settings button to the left of the "dice" button, but the ones we mentioned should suffice. In addition, more permanent settings can be chosen from Application Settings in the Utilities dropdown list on the @RISK ribbon. You can experiment with these, but the only one we like to change is the Place Reports In setting in the Reports group. The default is to place reports in a new workbook. If you like the reports to be in the same workbook as your model, you can change this setting to Active Workbook.

Figure 15.32

Simulation Group on @RISK Ribbon

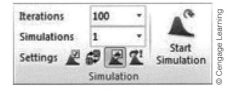

Leave Latin Hyper-cube sampling on. It produces more accurate results.

Latin Hypercube vs Monte Carlo Sampling

@RISK TECHNICAL ISSUES: *Latin Hypercube Sampling and Mersenne Twister Generator*

*Two settings you shouldn't change are the Sampling Type and Generator settings (available from the Simulation Settings button and then the Sampling tab). They should remain at the default Latin Hypercube and Mersenne Twister settings. The Mersenne Twister is one of many algorithms for generating random numbers, and it has been shown to have very good statistical properties. (Not all random number generators do.) **Latin Hypercube sampling** is a more efficient way of sampling than the other option (Monte Carlo) because it produces a more accurate estimate of the output distribution. In fact, we were surprised how accurate it is. In repeated runs of this model, always using different random numbers, we virtually always got a mean profit within a few pennies of $337.50. It turns out that this is the true mean profit for this input distribution of demand. Amazingly, simulation estimates it correctly—almost exactly—on virtually every run. Unfortunately, this means that a confidence interval for the mean, based on @RISK's outputs and the usual confidence* *interval formula (which assumes Monte Carlo sampling), is much wider (more pessimistic) than it should be. Therefore, we do not even calculate such confidence intervals from here on. However, it is not impossible. The accompanying video explains a method called Batch Means for calculating confidence intervals when Latin Hypercube sampling is used.*

2. **Run the simulation.** To run the simulation, click the Start Simulation button on the @RISK ribbon. When you do so, @RISK repeatedly generates a random number for each random input cell, recalculates the worksheet, and keeps track of all output cell values. You can watch the progress at the bottom left of the screen. Also, if the Automatically Show Output Graph button (to the right of the dice button) is toggled to orange, you will see a histogram of the currently selected input or output cell being built as the simulation runs. If you find this annoying, you can toggle this button to white.

3. **Examine the results.** The big questions are (1) which results you want and (2) where you want them. @RISK provides a lot of possibilities, and we mention the most frequently used.

   - You can ask for summary measures in your model worksheet by using the @RISK statistical functions, such as RISKMEAN, discussed earlier.

   - The quickest way to get results is to select an input or output cell (we chose the profit cell, F13) and then click the Browse Results button in the Results group of the @RISK ribbon. (See Figure 15.33.) This provides an interactive histogram of the selected value, as shown in Figure 15.34. You can move the sliders on this

For a quick histogram of an output or input, select the output or input cell and click @RISK's Browse Results button.

Figure 15.33

Results Group on @RISK Ribbon

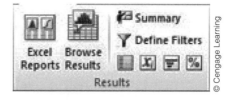

Figure 15.34

Interactive Histogram of Profit Output

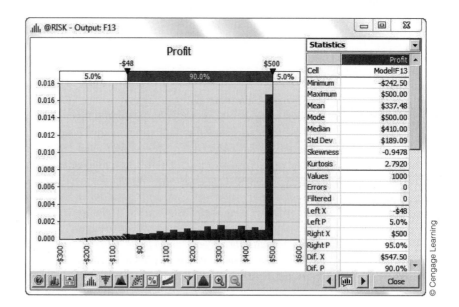

histogram to see probabilities of various outcomes. Note that the window you see from Browse Results is temporary—it goes away when you click Close. You can make a permanent copy of the chart by clicking the third button from the left (see the bottom of Figure 15.34) and choosing one of the copy options.

@RISK Tip: Percentiles Displayed on Charts

When we displayed the chart in Figure 15.34 the first time, it had the right slider on 500 but showed 5% to the right of it. By default, @RISK puts the sliders at the 5th and 95th percentiles, so that 5% is on either side of them. For this example, 500 is indeed the 95th percentile (why?), but the picture is a bit misleading because there is no chance of a profit greater than 500. When we manually moved the right slider away from 500 and back again, it displayed as in Figure 15.34, correctly indicating that there is no probability to the right of 500.

@RISK Tip: Saving Graphs and Tables

When you run a simulation with @RISK and then save your file, it asks whether you want to save your graphs and tables. We suggest that you save them. This makes your file slightly larger, but when you reopen it, the temporary graphs and tables, such as the histogram in Figure 15.34, are still available. Otherwise, you will have to rerun the simulation.

For a quick (and customizable) report of the results, click @RISK's Summary button.

■ You can click the Summary button (again, see Figure 15.33) to see the window in Figure 15.35 with the summary measures for Profit. In general, this report shows the summary for *all* designated inputs and outputs. By default, this Results Summary window shows a mini histogram for each output and a number of numerical summary measures. However, it is easy to customize. If you right-click anywhere on this table and choose Columns for Table, you can check or uncheck various options. For most of the later screenshots in this book, we elected *not* to show the Error column, but instead to show the standard deviation column.

Figure 15.35   Summary Table of Profit Output

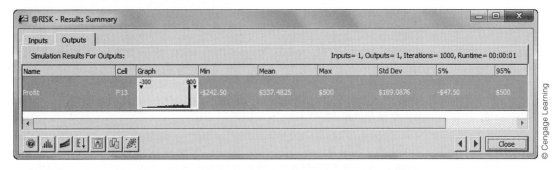

If you want permanent copies of the simulation results, click on @RISK's Excel Reports buttons and check the reports you want. They will be placed in new worksheets.

■ You can click the Excel Reports button (again, see Figure 15.33) to choose from a number of reports that are placed on new worksheets. This is a good option if you want permanent (but non-interactive) copies of reports in your workbook. As an example, Figure 15.36 shows part of the Quick Reports option you can request. It has the same information as the summary report in Figure 15.35, plus a lot more.

Discussion of the Simulation Results

The strength of @RISK is that it keeps track of any outputs you designate and then allows you to show the corresponding results as graphs or tables, in temporary windows or in permanent worksheets. As you have seen, @RISK provides several options for displaying results, and we encourage you to explore the possibilities. However, don't lose sight of the overall goal: to see how outputs vary as random inputs vary, and to generate reports that

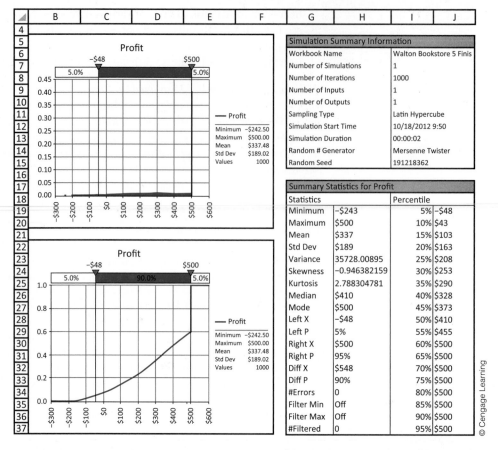

Figure 15.36
@RISK Quick Report

	Simulation Summary Information	
Workbook Name	Walton Bookstore 5 Finis	
Number of Simulations	1	
Number of Iterations	1000	
Number of Inputs	1	
Number of Outputs	1	
Sampling Type	Latin Hypercube	
Simulation Start Time	10/18/2012 9:50	
Simulation Duration	00:00:02	
Random # Generator	Mersenne Twister	
Random Seed	191218362	

Profit
Minimum −$242.50
Maximum $500.00
Mean $337.48
Std Dev $189.02
Values 1000

Summary Statistics for Profit			
Statistics		Percentile	
Minimum	−$243	5%	−$48
Maximum	$500	10%	$43
Mean	$337	15%	$103
Std Dev	$189	20%	$163
Variance	35728.00895	25%	$208
Skewness	−0.946382159	30%	$253
Kurtosis	2.788304781	35%	$290
Median	$410	40%	$328
Mode	$500	45%	$373
Left X	−$48	50%	$410
Left P	5%	55%	$455
Right X	$500	60%	$500
Right P	95%	65%	$500
Diff X	$548	70%	$500
Diff P	90%	75%	$500
#Errors	0	80%	$500
Filter Min	Off	85%	$500
Filter Max	Off	90%	$500
#Filtered	0	95%	$500

tell the story most effectively. For this particular example, the results in Figures 15.31, 15.34, 15.35, and 15.36 allow you to conclude the following:

- The smallest simulated profit (out of 1000) was −$235, the largest was $500, the average was $337.50, and the standard deviation of the 1000 profits was $189.05. Of all simulated profits, 5% were −$47.50 or below, 95% were $500 or above, 36% were less than or equal to $300, and 51.5% were larger than $400. (See Figure 15.31. These results are also available from the summary table in Figure 15.35 or the quick report in Figure 15.36.)

- The profit distribution for this particular order quantity is extremely skewed to the left, with a large bar at $500. (See Figure 15.34.) Do you see why? It is because profit is exactly $500 if demand is greater than or equal to the order quantity, 200. In other words, the probability that profit is $500 equals the probability that demand is at least 200. (This probability is 0.4.) Lower demands result in decreasing profits, which explains the gradual decline in the histogram from right to left.

Using RISKSIMTABLE

Walton's ultimate goal is to choose an order quantity that provides a large average profit. You could rerun the simulation model several times, each time with a different order quantity in the order quantity cell, and compare the results. However, this has two drawbacks. First, it takes a lot of time and work. The second drawback is more subtle. Each time you run the simulation, you get a *different* set of random demands. Therefore, one of the order quantities could win the contest just by luck. For a fairer comparison, it is better to test each order quantity on the *same* set of random demands.

The RISKSIMTABLE function allows you to run several simulations at once—one for each value of some variable (often a decision variable).

The RISKSIMTABLE function in @RISK enables you to obtain a fair comparison quickly and easily. This function is illustrated in Figure 15.37. (See the file **Walton Bookstore 6.xlsx**.) There are two modifications to the previous model. First, the order quantities to test are listed in row 9. (We chose these as representative order quantities. You could change, or add to, this list.) Second, instead of entering a *number* in cell B9, you enter the *formula*

=RISKSIMTABLE(D9:H9)

Note that the list does not need to be entered in the spreadsheet (although it is a good idea to do so). You could instead enter the formula

=RISKSIMTABLE({150,175,200,225,250})

where the list of numbers must be enclosed in curly brackets. In either case, the worksheet displays the first member of the list, 150, and the corresponding calculations for this first order quantity. However, the model is now set up to run the simulation for *all* order quantities in the list.

Figure 15.37   Model with a RISKSIMTABLE Function

	A	B	C	D	E	F	G	H	I	J	K
1	Simulation of Walton's Bookstore using @RISK								Range names used:		
2									Order_quantity	=Model!$B$9	
3	Cost data			Demand distribution - triangular					Profit	=Model!$F$13	
4	Unit cost	$7.50		Minimum	100				Unit_cost	=Model!$B$4	
5	Unit price	$10.00		Most likely	175				Unit_price	=Model!$B$5	
6	Unit refund	$2.50		Maximum	300				Unit_refund	=Model!$B$6	
7											
8	Decision variable			Order quantities to try							
9	Order quantity	150		150	175	200	225	250			
10											
11	Simulated quantities										
12		Demand	Revenue	Cost	Refund	Profit					
13		109	$1,090	$1,125	$103	$68					
14											
15	Summary measures of profit from @RISK - based on 1000 iterations for each simulation										
16	Simulation	1	2	3	4	5					
17	Order quantity	150	175	200	225	250					
18	Minimum	$22.50	–$102.50	–$227.50	–$352.50	–$477.50					
19	Maximum	$375.00	$437.50	$500.00	$562.50	$625.00					
20	Average	$354.19	$367.23	$337.57	$270.37	$175.08					
21	Standard deviation	$58.92	$121.82	$189.03	$246.99	$286.94					
22	5th percentile	$202.50	$77.50	–$47.50	–$172.50	–$297.50					
23	95th percentile	$375.00	$437.50	$500.00	$562.50	$625.00					

To implement this, only one setting needs to be changed. As before, enter 1000 for the number of iterations, but also enter 5 for the number of simulations. @RISK then runs five simulations of 1000 iterations each, one simulation for each order quantity in the list, and it uses the *same* 1000 random demands for each simulation. This provides a fair comparison.

@RISK Function: RISKSIMTABLE

To run several simulations all at once, enter the formula =RISKSIMTABLE(InputRange) in any cell. Here, InputRange refers to a list of the values to be simulated, such as various order quantities. Before running the simulation, make sure the number of simulations is set to the number of values in the InputRange list.

You can again get results from the simulation in various ways. Here are some possibilities.

- You can enter the same @RISK statistical functions in cells in the model work sheet, as shown in rows 18–23 of Figure 15.37. The trick is to realize that each such function has an optional last argument that specifies the simulation number. For example, the formulas in cells C20 and C22 are

=RISKMEAN($F$13,C16)

and

=RISKPERCENTILE($F$13,0.05,C16)

Remember that the results in these cells are meaningless (or show up as errors) until you run the simulation.

- You can select the profit cell and click the Browse Results button to see a histogram of profits, as shown in Figure 15.38. By default, the histogram shown is for the *first* simulation, where the order quantity is 150. However, if you click the red histogram button with the pound sign, you can select any of the simulations. As an example, Figure 15.39 shows the histogram of profits for the fifth simulation, where the order quantity is 250. (Do you see why these two histograms are so different? When the order quantity is 150, there is a high probability of selling out, so the spike on the right is large. But the probability of selling out with an order quantity of 250 is much lower, so its spike on the right is much less dominant.)

Figure 15.38

Histogram of Profit with Order Quantity 150

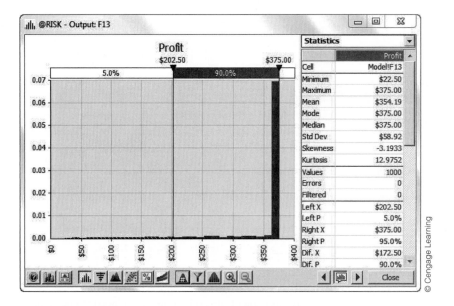

- You can click the Summary button to get the results from all simulations shown in Figure 15.40. (These results match those in Figure 15.37.)
- You can click the Excel Reports button to get any of a number of reports on permanent worksheets. Again, Quick Reports is a good choice. This produces several graphs and summary measures for each simulation, each on a different worksheet. This provides a lot of information with almost no work.

For this particular example, the results in Figures 15.37–15.40 are illuminating. You can see that an order quantity of 175 provides the largest *mean* profit. However, is this necessarily the optimal order quantity? This depends on the company's attitude toward risk. Certainly, larger order quantities incur more risk (their histograms are more spread out, their 5th and 95th percentiles are more extreme), but they also have more upside potential.

Figure 15.39

Histogram of Profit
with Order Quantity
250

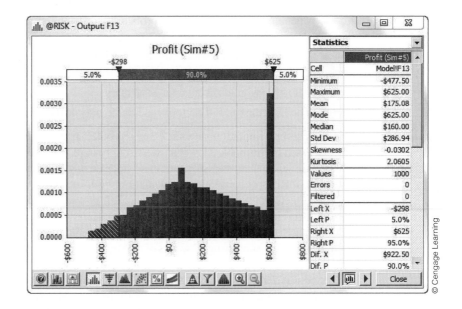

Figure 15.40   Summary Report for All Five Simulations

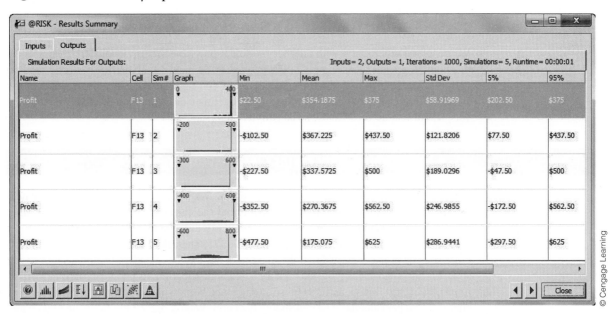

On the other hand, a smaller order quantity, while having a somewhat smaller mean, might
be preferable because of less variability. It is *not* an easy choice, but at least the simulation
results provide plenty of information for making the decision. ∎

15-5d Some Limitations of @RISK

The academic version of @RISK included with the book has some limitations you should
be aware of. (The commercial version of @RISK doesn't have these limitations. Also, the
exact limitations could change as newer academic versions become available.)

- The simulation model must be contained in a single workbook with at most four
  worksheets, and each worksheet is limited to 300 rows and 100 columns.

- The number of @RISK input probability distribution functions, such as RISKNORMAL, is limited to 100.

- The number of unattended iterations is limited to 1000. You can request more than 1000, but you have to click a button after each 1000 iterations.

- All @RISK graphs contain a watermark.

- The Distribution Fitting tool can handle only 150 observations.

To avoid potential problems, close all other workbooks when running an @RISK model.

The first limitation shouldn't cause problems, at least not for the fairly small models discussed in this book. However, we strongly urge you to close all other workbooks when you are running an @RISK simulation model, *especially* if they also contain @RISK functions. @RISK does a lot of recalculation, both in your active worksheet and in all other worksheets or workbooks that are open. So if you are experiencing extremely slow simulations, this is probably the reason.

The second limitation can be a problem, especially in multiperiod problems. For example, if you are simulating 52 weeks of a year, and each week requires two random inputs, you are already over the 100-function limit. One way to get around this is to use built-in Excel functions for random inputs rather than @RISK functions whenever possible. For example, if you want to simulate the flip of a fair coin, the formula **=IF(RAND()<0.5,"Heads","Tails")** works just as well as the formula **=IF(RISKUNIFORM(0, 1)<0.5,"Heads","Tails")**, but the former doesn't count against the 100-function limit.

15-5e @RISK Models with Several Random Input Variables

We conclude this section with another modification of the Walton Bookstore example. To this point, there has been a single random variable, demand. Often there are several random variables, each reflecting some uncertainty, and you want to include each of these in the simulation model. Example 15.4 illustrates how this can be done, and it also illustrates a very useful feature of @RISK, its sensitivity analysis.

EXAMPLE | **15.4 ADDITIONAL UNCERTAINTY AT WALTON BOOKSTORE**

As in the previous Walton Bookstore example, Walton needs to place an order for next year's calendar. We continue to assume that the calendars sell for $10 and customer demand for the calendars at this price is triangularly distributed with minimum value, most likely value, and maximum value equal to 100, 175, and 300. However, there are now two other sources of uncertainty. First, the maximum number of calendars Walton's supplier can supply is uncertain and is modeled with a triangular distribution. Its parameters are 125 (minimum), 200 (most likely), and 250 (maximum). Once Walton places an order, the supplier will charge $7.50 per calendar *if* he can supply the entire Walton order. Otherwise, he will charge only $7.25 per calendar. Second, unsold calendars can no longer be returned to the supplier for a refund. Instead, Walton will put them on sale for $5 apiece after January 1. At that price, Walton believes the demand for leftover calendars is triangularly distributed with parameters 0, 50, and 75. Any calendars *still* left over, say, after March 1, will be thrown away. Walton again wants to use simulation to analyze the resulting profit for various order quantities.

Objective   To develop and analyze a simulation model with multiple sources of uncertainty using @RISK, and to introduce @RISK's sensitivity analysis features.

Where Do the Numbers Come From?

As in Example 15.3, the monetary values are straightforward, and the parameters of the triangular distributions are probably educated guesses, possibly based on experience with previous calendars.

Solution

As always, the first step is to develop the model. Then you can run the simulation with @ RISK and examine the results.

The Walton Model with Multiple Uncertain Inputs

Developing the Simulation Model

The completed model is shown in Figure 15.41. (See the file **Walton Bookstore 7.xlsx**.) The model itself requires a bit more logic than the previous Walton model. It can be developed with the following steps.

Figure 15.41   @RISK Simulation Model with Three Random Inputs

	A	B	C	D	E	F	G	H	I	J	K	L	M
1	Simulation of Walton's Bookstore using @RISK										Range names used:		
2											Order_quantity	=Model!$B$10	
3	Cost data			Demand distribution: triangular							Profit	=Model!$J$14	
4	Unit cost 1	$7.50			Regular price	Sale price		Supply distribution: triangular			Regular_price	=Model!$B$6	
5	Unit cost 2	$7.25		Minimum	100	0		Minimum	125		Sale_price	=Model!$B$7	
6	Regular price	$10.00		Most likely	175	50		Most likely	200		Unit_cost_1	=Model!$B$4	
7	Sale price	$5.00		Maximum	300	75		Maximum	250		Unit_cost_2	=Model!$B$5	
8													
9	Decision variable			Order quantities to try									
10	Order quantity	150		150	175	200	225	250					
11													
12	Simulated quantities					At regular price		At sale price					
13		Maximum supply	Actual supply	Cost	Reg Demand	Reg Revenue	Left over	Sale Demand	Sale Revenue	Profit			
14		225	150	$1,125	161	$1,500	0	37	$0	$375			
15													
16	Summary measures of profit from @RISK - based on 1000 iterations for each simulation												
17	Simulation	1	2	3	4	5							
18	Order quantity	150	175	200	225	250							
19	Minimum	$55.00	–$132.50	–$320.00	–$347.50	–$356.50							
20	Maximum	$409.75	$478.50	$547.25	$613.25	$665.50							
21	Average	$361.54	$389.87	$395.81	$397.93	$400.90							
22	Standard deviation	$42.99	$94.73	$147.42	$173.14	$176.12							
23	5th percentile	$265.00	$167.50	$65.00	–$12.50	–$9.75							
24	95th percentile	$375.00	$459.25	$530.75	$574.75	$594.00							

© Cengage Learning

---

1. **Random inputs.** There are three random inputs in this model: the maximum supply the supplier can provide Walton, the customer demand when the selling price is $10, and the customer demand for sale-price calendars. Generate these in cells B14, E14, and H14 (using the ROUND function to obtain integers) with the RISKTRIANG function. Specifically, the formulas in cells B14, E14, and H14 are

   =ROUND(RISKTRIANG(I5,I6,I7),0)

   =ROUND(RISKTRIANG (E5,E6,E7),0)

   and

   =ROUND(RISKTRIANG (F5,F6,F7),0)

   Note that the formula in cell H14 generates the random *potential* demand for calendars at the sale price, even though there might not be any calendars left to put on sale.

2. **Actual supply.** The number of calendars supplied to Walton is the smaller of the number ordered and the maximum the supplier is able to supply. Calculate this value in cell C14 with the formula

   =MIN(B14,Order_quantity)

3. **Order cost.** Walton gets the reduced price, $7.25, if the supplier cannot supply the entire order. Otherwise, Walton must pay $7.50 per calendar. Therefore, calculate the total order cost in cell D14 with the formula (using the obvious range names)

   =IF(B14>=Order_quantity,Unit_cost_1,Unit_cost_2)*C14

4. **Other quantities.** The rest of the model is straightforward. Calculate the revenue from regular-price sales in cell F14 with the formula

    =Regular_price*MIN(C14,E14)

    Calculate the number left over after regular-price sales in cell G14 with the formula

    =MAX(C14-E14,0)

    Calculate the revenue from sale-price sales in cell I14 with the formula

    =Sale_price*MIN(G14,H14)

    Finally, calculate profit in cell J14 with the formula

    =F14+I14-D14

    Then designate this cell as an @RISK output cell. If you like, you can also designate other cells (the revenue cells, for example) as output cells.

5. **Order quantities.** As before, enter the following RISKSIMTABLE formula in cell B10 so that Walton can try different order quantities:

    =RISKSIMTABLE(D10:H10)

Running the Simulation

On each iteration, @RISK generates a new set of random inputs and calculates the corresponding output(s).

As usual, the next steps are to specify the simulation settings (we chose 1000 iterations and 5 simulations), and run the simulation. It is important to realize what @RISK does when it runs a simulation when there are several random input cells. In each iteration, @RISK generates a random value for each input variable *independently*. In this example, it generates a maximum supply in cell B14 from one triangular distribution, it generates a regular-price demand in cell E14 from another triangular distribution, and it generates a sale-price demand in cell H14 from a third triangular distribution. With these input values, it then calculates profit. For each order quantity, it then iterates this procedure 1000 times and keeps track of the corresponding profits.[10]

Discussion of the Simulation Results

Selected results are listed in Figure 15.41 (at the bottom), and the profit histogram for an order quantity of 200 is shown in Figure 15.42. (The histograms for the other order quantities are similar to what you have seen before, with more skewness to the left and a larger spike to the right as the order quantity decreases.) For this particular order quantity, the results indicate an average profit of about $396, a 5th percentile of $65, a 95th percentile of $531, and a distribution of profits that is again skewed to the left.

Sensitivity Analysis

We now demonstrate a feature of @RISK that is particularly useful when there are several random input cells. This feature lets you see which of these inputs has the most effect on an output cell. To perform this analysis, select the profit cell, J14, and click the Browse Results button. You will see a histogram of profit, as we have already discussed, with a number of buttons at the bottom of the window. Click the red button with the pound sign to select a simulation. We chose #3, where the order quantity is 200. Then click the "tornado" button (the fifth button from the left) and choose Change in Output Mean. This produces the chart in Figure 15.43. (The Regression and Correlation options produce similar results, and you can choose any of them if you prefer.)

[10]It is also possible to *correlate* the inputs, as we demonstrate in the next section.

Figure 15.42

Histogram of
Simulated Profits
for Order Quantity
200

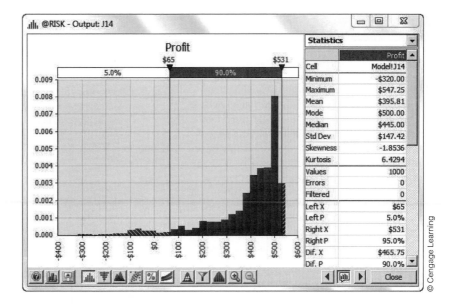

Figure 15.43

Tornado Graph for
Sensitivity Analysis

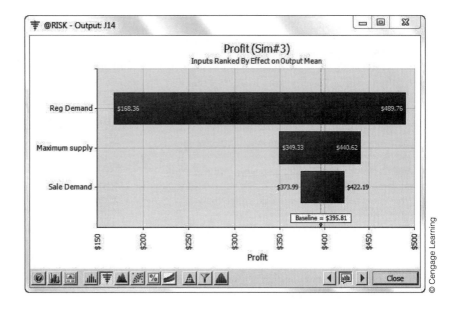

*A tornado chart
indicates which of the
random inputs have
large effects on an
output.*

This figure shows graphically and numerically how each of the random inputs affects profit: the longer the bar, the stronger the relationship between that input and profit. Specifically, each bar shows how the mean profit varies as each input varies over its range (and the other inputs are held constant). In this sense, you can see that the regular-price demand has by far the largest effect on profit. The other two inputs, maximum supply and sale-price demand, have much smaller effects. Identifying important input variables is important for real applications. If a random input has a large effect on an important output, then it is probably worth the time and money to learn more about this input and possibly reduce the amount of uncertainty involving it. ∎

PROBLEMS

Level A

16. If you add several normally distributed random numbers, the result is normally distributed, where the mean of the sum is the sum of the individual means, and the variance of the sum is the sum of the individual variances. (Remember that variance is the square of standard deviation.) This is a difficult result to prove mathematically, but it is easy to demonstrate with simulation. To do so, run a simulation where you add three normally distributed random numbers, each with mean 100 and standard deviation 10. Your single output variable should be the sum of these three numbers. Verify with @RISK that the distribution of this output is approximately normal with mean 300 and variance 300 (hence, standard deviation $\sqrt{300} = 17.32$).

17. In Problem 11 from the previous section, we stated that the damage amount is normally distributed. Suppose instead that the damage amount is triangularly distributed with parameters 500, 1500, and 7000. That is, the damage in an accident can be as low as $500 or as high as $7000, the most likely value is $1500, and there is definite skewness to the right. (It turns out, as you can verify in @RISK, that the mean of this distribution is $3000, the same as in Problem 11.) Use @RISK to simulate the amount you pay for damage. Run 5000 iterations. Then answer the following questions. In each case, explain how the indicated event would occur.
    a. What is the probability that you pay a positive amount but less than $750?
    b. What is the probability that you pay more than $600?
    c. What is the probability that you pay exactly $1000 (the deductible)?

18. Continuing the previous problem, assume, as in Problem 11, that the damage amount is *normally* distributed with mean $3000 and standard deviation $750. Run @RISK with 5000 iterations to simulate the amount you pay for damage. Compare your results with those in the previous problem. Does it appear to matter whether you assume a triangular distribution or a normal distribution for damage amounts? Why isn't this a totally fair comparison? (*Hint*: Use @RISK's Define Distributions tool to find the standard deviation for the triangular distribution.)

19. In Problem 12 of the previous section, suppose that the demand for cars is normally distributed with mean 100 and standard deviation 15. Use @RISK to determine the "best" order quantity—in this case, the one with the largest mean profit. Using the statistics and/or graphs from @RISK, discuss whether this order quantity would be considered best by the car dealer. (The point is that a decision maker can use more than just *mean* profit in making a decision.)

20. Use @RISK to analyze the sweatshirt situation in Problem 14 of the previous section. Do this for the discrete distributions given in the problem. Then do it for normal distributions. For the normal case, assume that the regular demand is normally distributed with mean 9800 and standard deviation 1300 and that the demand at the reduced price is normally distributed with mean 3800 and standard deviation 1400.

Level B

21. Although the normal distribution is a reasonable input distribution in many situations, it does have two potential drawbacks: (1) it allows negative values, even though they may be extremely improbable, and (2) it is a symmetric distribution. Many situations are modeled better with a distribution that allows only positive values and is skewed to the right. Two of these that have been used in many real applications are the gamma and lognormal distributions. @RISK enables you to generate observations from each of these distributions. The @RISK function for the gamma distribution is RISKGAMMA, and it takes two arguments, as in **=RISKGAMMA(3,10)**. The first argument, which must be positive, determines the shape. The smaller it is, the more skewed the distribution is to the right; the larger it is, the more symmetric the distribution is. The second argument determines the scale, in the sense that the product of it and the first argument equals the mean of the distribution. (The mean in this example is 30.) Also, the product of the second argument and the square root of the first argument is the standard deviation of the distribution. (In this example, it is $\sqrt{3}(10) = 17.32$.) The @RISK function for the lognormal distribution is RISKLOGNORM. It has two arguments, as in **=RISKLOGNORM(40,10)**. These arguments are the mean and standard deviation of the distribution. Rework Example 15.2 for the following demand distributions. Do the simulated outputs have any different qualitative properties with these skewed distributions than with the triangular distribution used in the example?
    a. Gamma distribution with parameters 2 and 85
    b. Gamma distribution with parameters 5 and 35
    c. Lognormal distribution with mean 170 and standard deviation 60

15-6 THE EFFECTS OF INPUT DISTRIBUTIONS ON RESULTS

In Section 15-2, we discussed input distributions. The randomness in input variables causes the variability in the output variables. We now briefly explore whether the choice of input distribution(s) makes much difference in the distribution of an output variable such as profit. This is an important question. If the choice of input distributions doesn't matter much, then you do not need to agonize over this choice. However, if it *does* make a difference, then you have to be more careful about choosing an appropriate input distribution for any particular situation. Unfortunately, it is impossible to answer the question definitively. The best we can say in general is, "It depends." Some models are more sensitive to changes in the shape or parameters of input distributions than others. Still, the issue is worth exploring.

We discuss two types of sensitivity analysis in this section. First, we check whether the shape of the input distribution matters. In the Walton Bookstore example, we assumed a triangularly distributed demand with some skewness. Are the results basically the same if a symmetric distribution such as the normal distribution is used instead? Second, we check whether the *independence* of input variables that have been assumed implicitly to this point is crucial to the output results. Many random quantities in real situations are *not* independent; they are positively or negatively correlated. Fortunately, @RISK enables you to build correlation into a model. We analyze the effect of this correlation.

15-6a Effect of the Shape of the Input Distribution(s)

We first explore the effect of the shape of the input distribution(s). As Example 15.5 indicates, if parameters that allow for a fair comparison are used, the shape can have a relatively minor effect.

EXAMPLE	**15.5 EFFECT OF DEMAND DISTRIBUTION AT WALTON BOOKSTORE**

We continue to explore the demand for calendars at Walton Bookstore. We keep the same unit cost, unit price, and unit refund for leftovers as in Example 15.3. However, in that example we assumed a triangular distribution for demand with parameters 100, 175, and 300. Assuming that Walton orders 200 calendars, is the distribution of profit affected if a *normal* distribution of demand is used instead?

Objective To see whether a triangular distribution with some skewness gives the same profit distribution as a normal distribution for demand.

Where Do the Numbers Come From?

The numbers here are the same as in Example 15.3. However, as discussed next, the parameters of the normal distribution are chosen to provide a fair comparison with the triangular distribution used earlier.

Solution

For a fair comparison of alternative input distributions, the distributions should have (at least approximately) equal means and standard deviations.

It is important in this type of analysis to make a fair comparison. When you select a normal distribution for demand, you must choose a mean and standard deviation for this distribution. Which values should you choose? It seems only fair to choose the *same* mean and standard deviation that the triangular distribution has. To find the mean and standard deviation for a triangular distribution with given minimum, most likely, and maximum values, you can take advantage of @RISK's Define Distributions tool. Select any blank cell, click on the Define Distributions button, select the triangular distribution, and enter the parameters 100, 175, and 300. You will see that the mean and standard deviation are 191.67 and 41.248, respectively. Therefore, for a fair comparison you should use a normal distribution with mean 191.67 and standard deviation 41.248. In fact, @RISK allows you to see a comparison of these two distributions, as in Figure 15.44. To get this chart, click the Add Overlay button, select the normal distribution from the gallery, and enter 191.67 and 41.248 as its mean and standard deviation.

Figure 15.44

Triangular and Normal Distributions for Demand

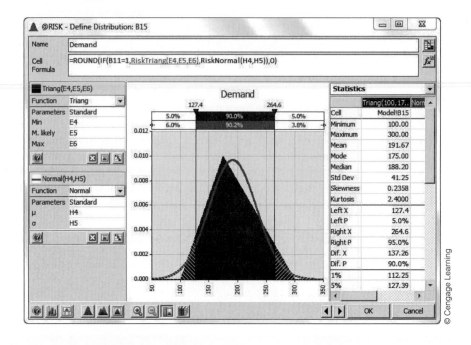

Developing the Simulation Model

The logic in this model is almost exactly the same as before. (See Figure 15.45 and the file **Walton Bookstore 8.xlsx**.) However, a clever use of the RISKSIMTABLE function allows you to run two simulations at once, one for the triangular distribution and one for the corresponding normal distribution. The following two steps are required.

1. **RISKSIMTABLE function.** It is useful to index the two distributions as 1 and 2. To indicate that you want to run the simulation with both of them, enter the formula

   =RISKSIMTABLE({1,2})

   in cell B11. Note that when you enter actual numbers in this function, rather than cell references, you must put curly brackets around the list.

2. **Demand.** When the value in cell B11 is 1, the demand distribution is triangular. When it is 2, the distribution is normal. Therefore, enter the formula

   =ROUND(IF(B11=1,RISKTRIANG(E4,E5,E6),RISKNORMAL(H4,H5)),0)

   in cell B15. The effect is that the first simulation will use the triangular distribution, and the second will use the normal distribution.

Running the Simulation

The only @RISK setting to change is the number of simulations. It should now be set to 2, the number of values in the RISKSIMTABLE formula. Other than this, you run the simulation exactly as before.

The Walton Model with Alternative Input Distributions

Look for ways to use the RISKSIMTABLE function. It can really improve efficiency because it runs several simulations at once.

Figure 15.45　@RISK Model for Comparing Two Input Distributions

	A	B	C	D	E	F	G	H	I	J	K	L	M
1	Simulation of Walton's Bookstore using @RISK - two possible demand distributions										Range names used:		
2											Order_quantity	=Model!$B$9	
3	Cost data			Demand distribution 1 - triangular			Demand distribution 2 - normal				Profit	=Model!$F$15	
4	Unit cost	$7.50		Minimum	100		Mean	191.67			Unit_cost	=Model!$B$4	
5	Unit price	$10.00		Most likely	175		Stdev	41.248			Unit_price	=Model!$B$5	
6	Unit refund	$2.50		Maximum	300						Unit_refund	=Model!$B$6	
7													
8	Decision variable												
9	Order quantity	200											
10													
11	Demand distribution to use	1	←	Formula is = RiskSimtable({1,2})									
12													
13	Simulated quantities												
14		Demand	Revenue	Cost	Refund	Profit							
15		167	$1,670	$1,500	$83	$253							
16													
17	Summary measures of profit from @RISK - based on 1000 iterations for each simulation												
18	Simulation	1	2										
19	Distribution	Triangular	Normal										
20	Minimum	−$235.00	−$700.00										
21	Maximum	$500.00	$500.00										
22	Average	$337.51	$342.80										
23	Standard deviation	$188.98	$202.09										
24	5th percentile	−$47.50	−$70.00										
25	95th percentile	$500.00	$500.00										

Discussion of the Simulation Results

The comparison is shown numerically in Figure 15.46 and graphically in Figure 15.47. As you can see, there is more chance of really low profits when the demand distribution is normal, but each simulation results in the same maximum profit. Both of these statements make sense. The normal distribution, being unbounded on the left, allows for very low demands, and these occasional low demands result in very low profits. On the other side, Walton's maximum profit is $500 regardless of the input distribution (provided that it allows demands greater than the order quantity). This occurs when Walton's sells all it orders, in which case excess demand has no effect on profit. Note that the mean profits for the two distributions differ by only about $5.

Figure 15.46　Summary Results for Comparison Model

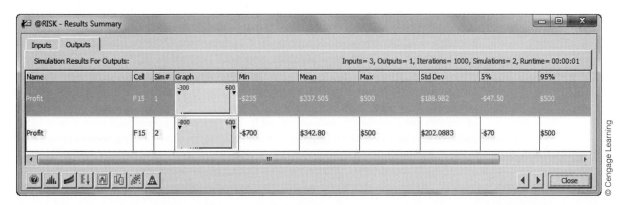

It is probably safe to conclude that the profit distribution in this model is not greatly affected by the choice of demand distribution, at least not when (1) the candidate input distributions have the same mean and standard deviation, and (2) their shapes are not *too* dissimilar. We would venture to guess that this general conclusion about insensitivity

Figure 15.47   Graphical Results for Comparison Model

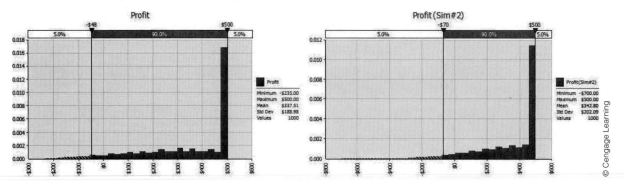

of output distributions to shapes of input distributions can be made in many simulation models. However, it is always worth checking, as we have done here, especially when there is a lot of money at stake. ∎

FUNDAMENTAL INSIGHT

Shape of the Output Distribution

Predicting the shape of the output distribution from the shape(s) of the input distribution(s) is difficult. For example, normally distributed inputs don't necessarily produce normally distributed outputs. It is also difficult to predict how sensitive the shape of the output distribution is to the shape(s) of the input

distribution(s). For example, normally and triangularly distributed inputs (with the same means and standard deviations) are likely to lead to similar output distributions, but there could be differences, say, in the tails of the output distributions. In any case, you should examine the *entire* output distribution carefully, not just a few of its summary measures.

15-6b Effect of Correlated Input Variables

Input variables in real-world problems are often correlated, which makes the material in this section particularly important.

Until now, all of the random numbers generated with @RISK functions have been probabilistically independent. This means, for example, that if a random value in one cell is much larger than its mean, the random values in other cells are completely unaffected. They are no more likely to be abnormally large or small than if the first value had been average or below average. Sometimes, however, independence is unrealistic. In such cases, **correlated inputs** are more appropriate. If they are positively correlated, then large numbers will tend to go with large numbers, and small with small. If they are negatively correlated, then large will tend to go with small and small with large. As an example, you might expect daily stock price changes for two companies in the same industry to be positively correlated. If the price of one oil company increases, you might expect the price of another oil company to increase as well. You can create correlated inputs in @RISK with the **RISKCORRMAT function**, as we illustrate in the following continuation of the Walton example.

EXAMPLE | **15.6 CORRELATED DEMANDS FOR TWO CALENDARS AT WALTON BOOKSTORE**

Suppose that Walton Bookstore must order two different calendars. To simplify the example, we assume that the calendars each have the same unit cost, unit selling price, and unit refund value as in previous examples. Also, we assume that each has a triangularly distributed demand with parameters 100, 175, and 300. However, we now assume they are "substitute" products, so that their demands are negatively correlated. This simply means that if a customer buys one, the customer is not likely to buy the other. Specifically, we assume a correlation of −0.9 between the two demands. How do these correlated inputs affect the distribution of profit, as compared to the situation where the demands are uncorrelated (correlation 0) or very *positively* correlated (correlation 0.9)?

Objective   To see how @RISK enables us to simulate correlated demands, and to see the effect of correlated demands on profit.

Where Do the Numbers Come From?

The only new input here is the correlation. It is probably negative because the calendars are substitute products, but it is a difficult number to estimate accurately. This is a good candidate for a sensitivity analysis.

Solution

The key to building in correlation is @RISK's RISKCORRMAT (correlation matrix) function. To use this function, you must include a correlation matrix in the model, as shown in the range J5:K6 of Figure 15.48. (See the file **Walton Bookstore 9.xlsx**.) A correlation matrix must always have 1s along its diagonal (because a variable is always perfectly correlated with itself) and the correlations between variables elsewhere. Also, the matrix must be symmetric, so that the correlations above the diagonal are a mirror image of those below it. (You can enforce this by entering the formula **=J6** in cell K5. Alternatively, @RISK allows you to enter the correlations only below the diagonal, or only above the diagonal, and it then infers the mirror images.)

Figure 15.48   Simulation Model with Correlated Demands

	A	B	C	D	E	F	G	H	I	J	K
1	Simulation of Walton's Bookstore using @RISK - correlated demands										
2											
3	Cost data - same for each product			Demand distribution for each product- triangular					Correlation matrix between demands		
4	Unit cost	$7.50		Minimum	100					Product 1	Product 2
5	Unit price	$10.00		Most likely	175				Product 1	1	−0.9
6	Unit refund	$2.50		Maximum	300				Product 2	−0.9	1
7											
8	Decision variables						Note RISKSIMTABLE		Possible correlations to try		
9	Order quantity 1	200					function in cell J6.			−0.9	0	0.9
10	Order quantity 2	200									
11									Range names used:		
12	Simulated quantities								Order_quantity_1	=Model!$B$9	
13		Demand	Revenue	Cost	Refund	Profit			Order_quantity_2	=Model!$B$10	
14	Product 1	192	$1,920	$1,500	$20	$440			Profit	=Model!$F$16	
15	Product 2	192	$1,920	$1,500	$20	$440			Unit_cost	=Model!$B$4	
16	Totals	384	$3,840	$3,000	$40	$880			Unit_price	=Model!$B$5	
17									Unit_refund	=Model!$B$6	
18	Summary measures of profit from @RISK - based on 1000 iterations										
19	Simulation	1	2	3							
20	Correlation	−0.9	0	0.9							
21	Minimum	$272.50	−$245.00	−$425.00							
22	Maximum	$1,000.00	$1,000.00	$1,000.00							
23	Average	$675.04	$675.04	$675.04							
24	Standard deviation	$157.59	$262.33	$365.23							
25	5th percentile	$392.50	$205.00	−$80.00							
26	95th percentile	$925.00	$1,000.00	$1,000.00							

The RISKCORRMAT function is "tacked on" as an extra argument to a typical random @RISK function.

To enter random values in any cells that are correlated, you start with a typical @RISK formula, such as

=RISKTRIANG(E4,E5,E6)

Then you add an extra argument, the RISKCORRMAT function, as follows:

=RISKTRIANG(E4,E5,E6,RISKCORRMAT(J5:K6,1))

The first argument of the RISKCORRMAT function is the correlation matrix range. The second is an index of the variable. In this example, the first calendar demand has index 1 and the second has index 2.

@RISK Function: RISKCORRMAT

*This function enables you to correlate two or more input variables. The function has the form **RISKCORRMAT(CorrMat,Index)**, where CorrMat is a matrix of correlations and Index is an index of the variable being correlated to others. For example, if there are three correlated variables, Index is 1 for the first variable, 2 is for the second, and 3 is for the third. The RISKCORRMAT function is not entered by itself. Rather, it is entered as the last argument of a random @RISK function, such as **=RISKTRIANG(10,15,30,RISKCORRMAT(CorrMat,2))**.*

The Walton Model with Correlated Demands

Developing the Simulation Model

Armed with this knowledge, the simulation model in Figure 15.48 is straightforward and can be developed as follows.

1. **Inputs.** Enter the inputs in the blue ranges in columns B and E.

2. **Correlation matrix.** For the correlation matrix in the range J5:H6, enter 1s on the diagonal, and enter the formula

   =J6

   in cell K5 (or leave cell K5 blank). Then enter the formula

   =RISKSIMTABLE(I9:K9)

   in cell J6. This allows you to simultaneously simulate negatively correlated demands, uncorrelated demands, and positively correlated demands.

3. **Order quantities.** Assume for now that the company orders the *same* number of each calendar, 200, so enter this value in cells B9 and B10. However, the simulation is set up so that you can experiment with any order quantities in these cells, including unequal values.

Correlations in @RISK Models

4. **Correlated demands.** Generate correlated demands by entering the formula

   =ROUND(RISKTRIANG(E4,E5,E6,RISKCORRMAT(J5:K6,1)),0)

   in cell B14 for demand 1 and the formula

   =ROUND(RISKTRIANG(E4,E5,E6,RISKCORRMAT(J5:K6,2)),0)

   in cell B15 for demand 2. The only difference between these is the index of the variable being generated. The first has index 1; the second has index 2.

5. **Other formulas.** The other formulas in rows 14 and 15 are identical to ones developed in previous examples, so they aren't presented again here. The quantities in row 16 are simply sums of rows 14 and 15. Also, the only @RISK output we designated is the total profit in cell F16, but you can designate others as output cells if you like.

Running the Simulation

You should set up and run @RISK exactly as before. For this example, set the number of iterations to 1000 and the number of simulations to 3 (because three different correlations are being tested).

Discussion of the Simulation Results

Selected numerical and graphical results are shown in Figures 15.49 and 15.50. You will probably be surprised to see that the *mean* total profit is the same, regardless of the correlation. This is no coincidence. In each of the three simulations, @RISK uses the *same* random numbers but "shuffles" them in different orders to get the correct correlations. This means that averages are unaffected. (The idea is that the average of the numbers 30, 26, and 48 is the same as the average of the numbers 48, 30, and 26.)

Figure 15.49 Summary Results for Correlated Model

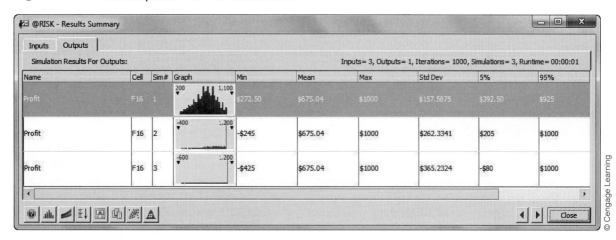

Figure 15.50 Graphical Results for Correlated Model

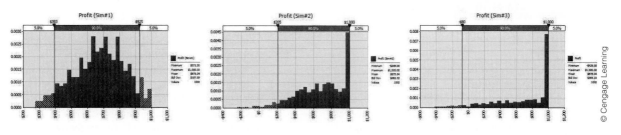

However, the correlation has a definite effect on the *distribution* of total profit. You can see this in Figure 15.49, for example, where the standard deviation of total profit increases as the correlation goes from negative to zero to positive. This same increase in variability is apparent in the histograms in Figure 15.50. Do you see intuitively why this increase in variability occurs? It is basically the "Don't put all of your eggs in one basket" effect. When the correlation is negative, high demands for one product tend to cancel low demands for the other product, so extremes in profit are rare. However, when the correlation is positive, high demands for the two products tend to go together, as do low demands. These make extreme profits on either end much more likely.

This same phenomenon would occur if you simulated an investment portfolio containing two stocks. When the stocks are positively correlated, the portfolio is much riskier (more variability) than when they are negatively correlated. Of course, this is the reason for diversifying a portfolio.

Modeling Issues

With the RISKCORRMAT function, you can correlate random numbers from any distributions.

We illustrated the RISKCORRMAT function for triangularly distributed values. However, it can be used with any of @RISK's distributions by tacking on RISKCORRMAT as a last argument. You can even mix them. For example, assuming CMat is the range name for a 2×2 correlation matrix, you could enter the formulas

=RISKNORMAL(10,2,RISKCORRMAT(CMat,1))

and

=RISKUNIFORM(100,200,RISKCORRMAT(CMat,2))

into any two cells. When you run the simulation, @RISK generates a sequence of normally distributed random numbers based on the first formula and another sequence of uniformly distributed random numbers based on the second formula. Then it shuffles them in some complex way until their correlation is approximately equal to the specified correlation in the correlation matrix. ■

FUNDAMENTAL INSIGHT

Correlated Inputs

When you enter random inputs in an @RISK simulation model and then run the simulation, each iteration generates *independent* values for the random inputs. If you know or suspect that some of the inputs are positively or negatively correlated, you should build this correlation structure into the model explicitly with the RISKCORRMAT function. This function might not change the mean of an output, but it can definitely affect the variability and shape of the output distribution.

PROBLEMS

Level A

22. Fizzy Company produces six-packs of soda cans. Each can is supposed to contain at least 12 ounces of soda. If the total weight in a six-pack is less than 72 ounces, Fizzy is fined $100 and receives no sales revenue for the six-pack. Each six-pack sells for $3.00. It costs Fizzy $0.02 per ounce of soda put in the cans. Fizzy can control the mean fill rate of its soda-filling machines. The amount put in each can by a machine is normally distributed with standard deviation 0.10 ounce.

  a. Assume that the weight of each can in a six-pack has a 0.8 correlation with the weight of the other cans in the six-pack. What mean fill quantity maximizes expected profit per six-pack? Try mean fill rates from 12.00 to 12.35 in increments of 0.05.

  b. If the weights of the cans in the six-pack are probabilistically independent, what mean fill quantity maximizes expected profit per six-pack? Try the same mean fill rates as in part **a.**

  c. How can you explain the difference in the answers to parts **a** and **b**?

23. When you use @RISK's correlation feature to generate correlated random numbers, how can you verify that they are correlated? Try the following. Use the RISKCORRMAT function to generate two normally distributed random numbers, each with mean 100 and standard deviation 10, and with correlation 0.7. To run a simulation, you need an output variable, so sum these two numbers and designate the sum as an output variable. Now run @RISK with 500 iterations. Click on @RISK's Excel Reports button and check the Simulation Data option to see the actual simulated data.

  a. Use Excel's CORREL function to calculate the correlation between the two input variables.

It should be close to 0.7. Then create a scatterplot of these two input variables. The plot should indicate a definite positive relationship.

b. Are the two input variables correlated with the output? Use Excel's CORREL function to find out. Interpret your results intuitively.

24. Repeat the previous problem, but make the correlation between the two inputs equal to −0.7. Explain how the results change.

25. Repeat Problem 23, but now make the second input variable triangularly distributed with parameters 50, 100, and 500. This time, verify not only that the correlation between the two inputs is approximately 0.7, but also that the shapes of the two input distributions are approximately what they should be: normal for the first and triangular for the second. Do this by creating histograms in Excel. The point is that you can use @RISK's RISKCORRMAT function to correlate random numbers from *different* distributions.

26. Suppose you are going to invest equal amounts in three stocks. The annual return from each stock is normally distributed with mean 0.01 (1%) and standard deviation 0.06. The annual return on your portfolio, the output variable of interest, is the average of the three stock returns. Run @RISK, using 1000 iterations, on each of the following scenarios.

a. The three stock returns are highly correlated. The correlation between each pair is 0.9.

b. The three stock returns are practically independent. The correlation between each pair is 0.1.

c. The first two stocks are moderately correlated. The correlation between their returns is 0.4. The third stock's return is negatively correlated with the other two. The correlation between its return and each of the first two is −0.8.

d. Compare the portfolio distributions from @RISK for these three scenarios. What do you conclude?

e. You might think of a fourth scenario, where the correlation between each *pair* of returns is a large negative number such as −0.8. But explain intuitively why this makes no sense. Try to run the simulation with these negative correlations and see what happens.

27. The effect of the shapes of input distributions on the distribution of an output can depend on the output function. For this problem, assume there are 10 input variables. The goal is to compare the case where these 10 inputs each have a normal distribution with mean 1000 and standard deviation 250 to the case where they each have a triangular distribution with parameters 600, 700, and 1700. (You can check with @RISK's Define Distributions window that even though this triangular distribution is very skewed, it has the same mean and approximately the same standard deviation as the normal distribution.) For each of the following outputs, run two @RISK simulations, one with the normally distributed inputs and one with the triangularly distributed inputs, and comment on the differences between the resulting output distributions. For each simulation run 1000 iterations.

a. Let the output be the *average* of the inputs.

b. Let the output be the *maximum* of the inputs.

c. Calculate the average of the inputs. Then the output is the minimum of the inputs if this average is less than 1000; otherwise, the output is the maximum of the inputs.

Level B

28. The Business School at State University currently has three parking lots, each containing 155 spaces. Two hundred faculty members have been assigned to each lot. On a peak day, an average of 70% of all lot 1 parking sticker holders show up, an average of 72% of all lot 2 parking sticker holders show up, and an average of 74% of all lot 3 parking sticker holders show up.

a. Given the current situation, estimate the probability that on a peak day, at least one faculty member with a sticker will be unable to find a spot. Assume that the number who show up at each lot is independent of the number who show up at the other two lots. Compare two situations: (1) each person can park only in the lot assigned to him or her, and (2) each person can park in any of the lots (pooling). (*Hint*: Use the RISKBINOMIAL function.)

b. Now suppose the numbers of people who show up at the three lots are highly correlated (correlation 0.9). How are the results different from those in part **a**?

15-7 CONCLUSION

Simulation has traditionally not received the attention it deserves in management science courses. The primary reason for this has been the lack of easy-to-use simulation software. Now, with Excel's built-in simulation capabilities, plus powerful and affordable add-ins such as @RISK, simulation is receiving its rightful emphasis. The world is full of uncertainty, which is what makes simulation so valuable. Simulation models provide important insights that are missing in models that do not incorporate uncertainty explicitly.

In addition, simulation models are relatively easy to understand and develop. Therefore, we suspect that simulation models (together with optimization models) will soon be the primary emphasis of many management science courses—if they are not already. In this chapter we have illustrated the basic ideas of simulation, how to perform simulation with Excel built-in tools, and how @RISK greatly enhances Excel's basic capabilities. In the next chapter we will build on this knowledge to develop and analyze simulation models in a variety of business areas.

Summary of Key Terms

Term	Explanation	Excel	Pages
Simulation model	Model with random inputs that affect one or more outputs, where the randomness is modeled explicitly		813
F9 key	The "recalc" key, used to make a spreadsheet recalculate	Press the F9 key	815
Probability distributions for input variables	Specification of the possible values and their proba bilities for random input variables; these distributions must be specified in any simulation model		815
Uniform distribution	The flat distribution, where all values in a bounded continuum are equally likely		820
RAND function	Excel's built-in random number generator; generates uniformly distributed random numbers between 0 and 1	=RAND()	831
RANDBETWEEN function	Excel's built-in function for generating equally likely random integers over an indicated range	=RANDBETWEEN (*min,max*)	821
Freeze random numbers	Change "volatile" random numbers into "fixed" numbers	Copy range, paste it onto itself with the Paste Values option	823
@RISK random functions	A set of functions, including RISKNORMAL and RISKTRIANG, for generating random numbers from various distributions	=RISKNORMAL (*mean,stdev*) or =RISKTRIANG (*min,mostlikely,max*), for example	824
Discrete distribution	A general distribution where a discrete number of possible values and their probabilities are specified		825
Triangular distribution	Literally a triangle-shaped distribution, specified by a minimum value, a most likely value, and a maximum value		828
Replicating with Excel tools only	Useful when an add-in such as @RISK is not available	Develop simulation model, use a data table with any blank column input cell to replicate one or more outputs	844
@RISK	A powerful simulation add-in developed by Palisade	@RISK ribbon	847
RISKSIMTABLE function	Used to run an @RISK simulation model for several values of some variable, often a decision variable	=RISKSIMTABLE (*list*)	864

Term	Explanation	Excel	Pages
RISKOUTPUT function	Used to indicate that a cell contains an output that will be tracked by @RISK	=RISKOUTPUT ("Profit") +Revenue-Cost, for example	850
Latin Hypercube sampling	An efficient way of simulating random numbers for a simulation model, where the results are more accurate than with other sampling methods		851
RISKCORRMAT function	Used to correlate two or more random input variables	=RISKNORMAL (100,10, RISKCORRMAT (CorrMat, 2)), for example	866
Correlated inputs	Random quantities, such as returns from stocks in the same industry, that tend to go together (or possibly go in opposite directions from one another)		867

PROBLEMS

Conceptual Questions

C.1. You are making several runs of a simulation model, each with a different value of some decision variable (such as the order quantity in the Walton calendar model), to see which decision value achieves the largest mean profit. Is it possible that one value beats another simply by random luck? What can you do to minimize the chance of a "better" value losing out to a "poorer" value?

C.2. If you want to replicate the results of a simulation model with Excel functions only, not @RISK, you can build a data table and let the column input cell be any blank cell. Explain why this works.

C.3. Suppose you simulate a gambling situation where you place many bets. On each bet, the distribution of your net winnings (loss if negative) is highly skewed to the left because there are some possibilities of really large losses but not much upside potential. Your only simulation output is the *average* of the results of all the bets. If you run @RISK with many iterations and look at the resulting histogram of this output, what will it look like? Why?

C.4. You plan to simulate a portfolio of investments over a multiyear period, so for each investment (which could be a particular stock or bond, for example), you need to simulate the change in its value for each of the years. How would you simulate these changes in a realistic way? Would you base it on historical data? What about correlations? Do you think the changes for different investments in a particular year would

be correlated? Do you think changes for a particular investment in different years would be correlated? Do you think correlations would play a significant role in your simulation in terms of realism?

C.5. Big Hit Video must determine how many copies of a new video to purchase. Assume that the company's goal is to purchase a number of copies that maximizes its expected profit from the video during the next year. Describe how you would use simulation to shed light on this problem. Assume that each time a video is rented, it is rented for one day.

C.6. Many people who are involved in a small auto accident do not file a claim because they are afraid their insurance premiums will be raised. Suppose that City Farm Insurance has three rates. If you file a claim, you are moved to the next higher rate. How might you use simulation to determine whether a particular claim should be filed?

C.7. A building contains 1000 lightbulbs. Each bulb lasts at most five months. The company maintaining the building is trying to decide whether it is worthwhile to practice a "group replacement" policy. Under a group replacement policy, all bulbs are replaced every T months (where T is to be determined). Also, bulbs are replaced when they burn out. Assume that it costs $0.05 to replace each bulb during a group replacement and $0.20 to replace each burned-out bulb if it is replaced individually. How would you use simulation to determine whether a group replacement policy is worthwhile?

C.8. Why is the RISKCORRMAT function necessary? How does @RISK generate random inputs by default, that is, when RISKCORRMAT is not used?

C.9. Consider the claim that normally distributed inputs in a simulation model are bound to lead to normally distributed outputs. Do you agree or disagree with this claim? Defend your answer.

C.10. It is very possible that when you use a correlation matrix as input to the RISKCORRMAT function in an @RISK model, the program will inform you that this is an invalid correlation matrix. Provide an example of an obviously invalid correlation matrix involving at least three variables, and explain why it is invalid.

C.11. When you use a RISKSIMTABLE function for a decision variable, such as the order quantity in the Walton model, explain how this provides a "fair" comparison across the different values tested.

C.12. Consider a situation where there is a cost that is either incurred or not. It is incurred only if the value of some random input is less than a specified cutoff value. Why might a simulation of this situation give a very different average value of the cost incurred than a deterministic model that treats the random input as *fixed* at its mean? What does this have to do with the "flaw of averages"?

Level A

29. Six months before its annual convention, the American Medical Association must determine how many rooms to reserve. At this time, the AMA can reserve rooms at a cost of $150 per room. The AMA believes the number of doctors attending the convention will be normally distributed with a mean of 5000 and a standard deviation of 1000. If the number of people attending the convention exceeds the number of rooms reserved, extra rooms must be reserved at a cost of $250 per room.

    a. Use simulation with @RISK to determine the number of rooms that should be reserved to minimize the expected cost to the AMA. Try possible values from 4100 to 4900 in increments of 100.

    b. Redo part **a** for the case where the number attending has a triangular distribution with minimum value 2000, maximum value 7000, and most likely value 5000. Does this change the substantive results from part a?

30. You have made it to the final round of the show *Let's Make a Deal*. You know that there is a $1 million prize behind either door 1, door 2, or door 3. It is equally likely that the prize is behind any of the three doors. The two doors without a prize have nothing behind them. You randomly choose door 2. Before you see

whether the prize is behind door 2, host Monty Hall opens a door that has no prize behind it. Specifically, suppose that before door 2 is opened, Monty reveals that there is no prize behind door 3. You now have the opportunity to switch and choose door 1. Should you switch? Simulate this situation 1000 times. For each replication use an @RISK function to generate the door that leads to the prize. Then use another @RISK function to generate the door that Monty will open. Assume that Monty plays as follows: Monty knows where the prize is and will open an empty door, but he cannot open door 2. If the prize is really behind door 2, Monty is equally likely to open door 1 or door 3. If the prize is really behind door 1, Monty must open door 3. If the prize is really behind door 3, Monty must open door 1.

31. A new edition of a very popular textbook will be published a year from now. The publisher currently has 2000 copies on hand and is deciding whether to do another printing before the new edition comes out. The publisher estimates that demand for the book during the next year is governed by the probability distribution in the file **P15_31.xlsx**. A production run incurs a fixed cost of $10,000 plus a variable cost of $15 per book printed. Books are sold for $130 per book. Any demand that cannot be met incurs a penalty cost of $20 per book, due to loss of goodwill. Up to 500 of any leftover books can be sold to Barnes & Noble for $35 per book. The publisher is interested in maximizing expected profit. The following print-run sizes are under consideration: 0 (no production run) to 16,000 in increments of 2000. What decision would you recommend? Use simulation with 1000 replications. For your optimal decision, the publisher can be 90% certain that the actual profit associated with remaining sales of the current edition will be between what two values?

32. A hardware company sells a lot of low-cost, high-volume products. For one such product, it is equally likely that annual unit sales will be low or high. If sales are low (60,000), the company can sell the product for $10 per unit. If sales are high (100,000), a competitor will enter and the company will be able to sell the product for only $8 per unit. The variable cost per unit has a 25% chance of being $6, a 50% chance of being $7.50, and a 25% chance of being $9. Annual fixed costs are $30,000.

    a. Use simulation to estimate the company's expected annual profit.

    b. Find a 95% interval for the company's annual profit, that is, an interval such that about 95% of the actual profits are inside it.

    c. Now suppose that annual unit sales, variable cost, and unit price are equal to their respective *expected* values—that is, there is no uncertainty.

Determine the company's annual profit for this scenario.

d. Can you conclude from the results in parts **a** and **c** that the expected profit from a simulation is equal to the profit from the scenario where each input assumes its expected value? Explain.

33. W. L. Brown, a direct marketer of women's clothing, must determine how many telephone operators to schedule during each part of the day. W. L. Brown estimates that the number of phone calls received each hour of a typical eight-hour shift can be described by the probability distribution in the file **P15_33.xlsx**. Each operator can handle 15 calls per hour and costs the company $20 per hour. Each phone call that is not handled is assumed to cost the company $6 in lost profit. Considering the options of employing 6, 8, 10, 12, 14, or 16 operators, use simulation to determine the number of operators that minimizes the expected hourly cost (labor costs plus lost profits).

34. Assume that all of a company's job applicants must take a test, and that the scores on this test are normally distributed. The *selection ratio* is the cutoff point used by the company in its hiring process. For example, a selection ratio of 20% means that the company will accept applicants for jobs who rank in the top 20% of all applicants. If the company chooses a selection ratio of 20%, the average test score of those selected will be 1.40 standard deviations above average. Use simulation to verify this fact, proceeding as follows.

a. Show that if the company wants to accept only the top 20% of all applicants, it should accept applicants whose test scores are at least 0.842 standard deviation above average. (No simulation is required here. Just use the appropriate Excel normal function.)

b. Now generate 1000 test scores from a normal distribution with mean 0 and standard deviation 1. The average test score of those selected is the average of the scores that are at least 0.842. To determine this, use Excel's DAVERAGE function. To do so, put the heading Score in cell A3, generate the 1000 test scores in the range A4:A1003, and name the range A3:A1003 Data. In cells C3 and C4, enter the *labels* Score and >0.842. (The range C3:C4 is called the *criterion range*.) Then calculate the average of all applicants who will be hired by entering the formula **=DAVERAGE(Data, "Score", C3:C4)** in any cell. This average should be close to the theoretical average, 1.40. This formula works as follows. Excel finds all observations in the Data range that satisfy the criterion described in the range C3:C4 (Score>0.842). Then it averages the values in the Score column (the second argument of DAVERAGE) corresponding to these entries.

See online help for more about Excel's database "D" functions.

c. What information would the company need to determine an optimal selection ratio? How could it determine the optimal selection ratio?

35. Lemington's is trying to determine how many Jean Hudson dresses to order for the spring season. Demand for the dresses is assumed to follow a normal distribution with mean 400 and standard deviation 100. The contract between Jean Hudson and Lemington's works as follows. At the beginning of the season, Lemington's reserves x units of capacity. Lemington's must take delivery for at least $0.8x$ dresses and can, if desired, take delivery on up to x dresses. Each dress sells for $160 and Hudson charges $50 per dress. If Lemington's does not take delivery on all x dresses, it owes Hudson a $5 penalty for each unit of reserved capacity that is unused. For example, if Lemington's orders 450 dresses and demand is for 400 dresses, Lemington's will receive 400 dresses and owe Jean 400($50) + 50($5). How many units of capacity should Lemington's reserve to maximize its expected profit?

36. Dilbert's Department Store is trying to determine how many Hanson T-shirts to order. Currently the shirts are sold for $21, but at later dates the shirts will be offered at a 10% discount, then a 20% discount, then a 40% discount, then a 50% discount, and finally a 60% discount. Demand at the full price of $21 is believed to be normally distributed with mean 1800 and standard deviation 360. Demand at various discounts is assumed to be a multiple of full-price demand. These multiples, for discounts of 10%, 20%, 40%, 50%, and 60% are, respectively, 0.4, 0.7, 1.1, 2, and 50. For example, if full-price demand is 2500, then at a 10% discount customers would be willing to buy 1000 T-shirts. The unit cost of purchasing T-shirts depends on the number of T-shirts ordered, as shown in the file **P15_36.xlsx**. Use simulation to determine how many T-shirts the company should order. Model the problem so that the company first orders some quantity of T-shirts, then discounts deeper and deeper, as necessary, to sell all of the shirts.

Level B

37. The annual return on each of four stocks for each of the next five years is assumed to follow a normal distribution, with the mean and standard deviation for each stock, as well as the correlations between stocks, listed in the file **P15_37.xlsx**. You believe that the stock returns for these stocks in a given year are correlated, according to the correlation matrix given, but you believe the returns in different years are uncorrelated. For example, the returns for stocks 1 and 2 in year 1 have correlation 0.55, but the correlation between the return of stock 1 in year 1 and the return of stock 1 in year 2 is 0, and the correlation between the return of stock 1 in year 1 and the return of stock 2 in year 2 is also 0. The file has the formulas you might expect for this situation in the range C20:G23. You can check how the RISKCORRMAT function has been used in these formulas. Just so that there is an @RISK output cell, calculate the average of all returns in cell B25 and designate it as an @RISK output. (This cell is not really important for the problem, but it is included because @RISK requires at least one output cell.)

a. Using the model exactly as it stands, run @RISK with 1000 iterations. The question is whether the correlations in the simulated data are close to what they should be. To check this, go to @RISK's Report Settings and check the Input Data option before you run the simulation. This gives you all of the simulated returns on a new sheet. Then calculate correlations for all pairs of columns in the resulting Inputs Data Report sheet. (StatTools can be used to create a matrix of all correlations for the simulated data.) Comment on whether the correlations are different from what they should be.

b. Recognizing that this is a common situation (correlation within years, no correlation across years), @RISK allows you to model it by adding a *third* argument to the RISKCORRMAT function: the year index in row 19 of the P15_37.xlsx file. For example, the RISKCORRMAT part of the formula in cell C20 becomes **=RISKNORMAL($B5,$C5, RISKCORRMAT ($B$12:$E$15,$B20,C$19))**. Make this change to the formulas in the range C20:G23, rerun the simulation, and redo the correlation analysis in part **a**. Verify that the correlations between inputs are now more in line with what they should be.

38. It is surprising (but true) that if 23 people are in the same room, there is about a 50% chance that at least two people will have the same birthday. Suppose you want to estimate the probability that if 30 people are in the same room, at least two of them will have the same birthday. You can proceed as follows.

a. Generate random birthdays for 30 different people. Ignoring the possibility of a leap year, each person has a 1/365 chance of having a given birthday (label the days of the year 1 to 365). You can use the RANDBETWEEN function to generate birthdays.

b. Once you have generated 30 people's birthdays, how can you tell whether at least two people have the same birthday? One way is to use Excel's RANK function. (You can learn how to use this function in Excel's online help.) This function returns the rank of a number relative to a given group of numbers. In the case of a tie, two numbers are given the same rank. For example, if the set of

numbers is 4, 3, 2, 5, the RANK function returns 2, 3, 4, 1. (By default, RANK gives 1 to the *largest* number.) If the set of numbers is 4, 3, 2, 4, the RANK function returns 1, 3, 4, 1.

c. After using the RANK function, you should be able to determine whether at least two of the 30 people have the same birthday. What is the (estimated) probability that this occurs?

39. United Electric (UE) sells refrigerators for $400 with a one-year warranty. The warranty works as follows. If any part of the refrigerator fails during the first year after purchase, UE replaces the refrigerator for an average cost of $100. As soon as a replacement is made, another one-year warranty period begins for the customer. If a refrigerator fails outside the warranty period, we assume that the customer immediately purchases another UE refrigerator. Suppose that the amount of time a refrigerator lasts follows a normal distribution with a mean of 1.8 years and a standard deviation of 0.3 year.

a. Estimate the average profit per year UE earns from a customer.

b. How could the approach of this problem be used to determine the optimal warranty period?

40. A Flexible Savings Account (FSA) plan allows you to put money into an account at the beginning of the calendar year that can be used for medical expenses. This amount is not subject to federal tax. As you pay medical expenses during the year, you are reimbursed by the administrator of the FSA until the money is exhausted. From that point on, you must pay your medical expenses out of your own pocket. On the other hand, if you put more money into your FSA than the medical expenses you incur, this extra money is lost to you. Your annual salary is $80,000 and your federal income tax rate is 30%.

a. Assume that your medical expenses in a year are normally distributed with mean $2000 and standard deviation $500. Build an @RISK model in which the output is the amount of money left to you after paying taxes, putting money in an FSA, and paying any extra medical expenses. Experiment with the amount of money put in the FSA, using a RISKSIMTABLE function.

b. Rework part **a**, but this time assume a gamma distribution for your annual medical expenses. Use 16 and 125 as the two parameters of this distribution. These imply the same mean and standard deviation as in part **a**, but the distribution of medical expenses is now skewed to the right, which is probably more realistic. Using simulation, see whether you should now put more or less money in an FSA than in the symmetric case in part **a**.

41. At the beginning of each week, a machine is in one of four conditions: 1 = excellent; 2 = good; 3 = average;

4 = bad. The weekly revenue earned by a machine in state 1, 2, 3, or 4 is $100, $90, $50, or $10, respectively. After observing the condition of the machine at the beginning of the week, the company has the option, for a cost of $200, of instantaneously replacing the machine with an excellent machine. The quality of the machine deteriorates over time, as shown in the file **P15_41.xlsx**. Four maintenance policies are under consideration:

- Policy 1: Never replace a machine.
- Policy 2: Immediately replace a bad machine.
- Policy 3: Immediately replace a bad or average machine.
- Policy 4: Immediately replace a bad, average, or good machine.

Simulate each of these policies for 50 weeks (using at least 250 iterations each) to determine the policy that maximizes expected weekly profit. Assume that the machine at the beginning of week 1 is excellent.

42. Simulation can be used to illustrate a number of results from statistics that are difficult to understand with nonsimulation arguments. One is the famous *central limit theorem*, which says that if you sample enough values from *any* population distribution and then average these values, the resulting average will be approximately normally distributed. Confirm this by using @RISK with the following population distributions (run a separate simulation for each): (a) discrete with possible values 1 and 2 and probabilities 0.2 and 0.8; (b) exponential with mean 1 (use the RISKEXPON function with the single argument 1); (c) triangular with minimum, most likely, and maximum values equal to 1, 9, and 10. (Note that each of these distributions is very skewed.) Run each simulation with 10 values in each average, and run 1000 iterations to simulate 1000 averages. Create a histogram of the averages to see whether it is indeed bell-shaped. Then repeat, using 30 values in each average. Are the histograms based on 10 values qualitatively different from those based on 30?

43. In statistics we often use observed data to test a hypothesis about a population or populations. The basic method uses the observed data to calculate a test statistic (a single number), as discussed in Chapter 9. If the magnitude of this test statistic is sufficiently large, the null hypothesis is rejected in favor of the research hypothesis. As an example, consider a researcher who believes teenage girls sleep longer than teenage boys on average. She collects observations on $n = 40$ randomly selected girls and $n = 40$ randomly selected boys. (Each observation is the average sleep time over several nights for a given person.) The averages are $\overline{X}_1 = 7.9$ hours for the girls and $\overline{X}_2 = 7.6$ hours for the boys. The standard deviation of the 40

observations for girls is $s_1 = 0.5$ hour; for the boys it is $s_2 = 0.7$ hour. The researcher, consulting Chapter 9, then calculates the test statistic

$$\frac{\overline{X}_1 - \overline{X}_2}{\sqrt{s_1^2/40 + s_2^2/40}} = \frac{7.9 - 7.6}{\sqrt{0.25/40 + 0.49/40}} = 2.206$$

Based on the fact that 2.206 is "large," she claims that her research hypothesis is confirmed—girls do sleep longer than boys.

You are skeptical of this claim, so you check it out by running a simulation. In your simulation you assume that girls and boys have the *same* mean and standard deviation of sleep times in the entire population, say, 7.7 and 0.6. You also assume that the distribution of sleep times is normal. Then you repeatedly simulate observations of 40 girls and 40 boys from this distribution and calculate the test statistic. The question is whether the observed test statistic, 2.206, is "extreme." If it is larger than most or all of the test statistics you simulate, then the researcher is justified in her claim; otherwise, this large a statistic could have happened easily by chance, even if the girls and boys have identical population means. Use @RISK to see which of these possibilities occurs.

44. A technical note in the discussion of @RISK indicated that Latin Hypercube sampling is more efficient than Monte Carlo sampling. This problem allows you to see what this means. The file **P15_44.xlsx** gets you started. There is a single output cell, B5. You can enter any random value in this cell, such as **RISKNORMAL(500,100)**. There are already @RISK statistical formulas in rows 9–12 to calculate summary measures of the output for each of 10 simulations. On the @RISK ribbon, click on the button to the left of the "dice" button to bring up the Simulation Settings dialog box, click on the Sampling tab, and make sure the Sampling Type is Latin Hypercube. Run 10 simulations with at least 1000 iterations each, and then paste the results in rows 9–12 as *values* in rows 17–20. Next, get back in Simulations Settings and change the Sampling Type to Monte Carlo, run the 10 simulations again, and paste the results in rows 9–12 as values into rows 23–26. For each row, 17–20 and 23–26, summarize the 10 numbers in that row with AVERAGE and STDEV. What do you find? Why do we say that Latin Hypercube sampling is more efficient? (Thanks to Harvey Wagner at University of North Carolina for suggesting this problem.)

45. We are continually hearing reports on the nightly news about natural disasters—droughts in Texas, hurricanes in Florida, floods in California, and so on. We often hear that one of these was the "worst in over 30 years," or some such statement. Are natural disasters getting worse these days, or does it just appear so? How might you use simulation to answer this question? Here is one possible approach. Imagine that there are N areas of the country (or the world) that tend to have, to some extent, various types of weather phenomena each year. For example, hurricanes are always a potential problem for Florida, and fires are always a potential problem in southern California. You might model the severity of the problem for any area in any year by a normally distributed random number with mean 0 and standard deviation 1, where negative values are interpreted as good years and positive values are interpreted as bad years. (We suggest the normal distribution, but there is no reason other distributions couldn't be used instead.) Then you could simulate such values for all areas over a period of several years and keep track, say, of whether any of the areas have worse conditions in the current year than they have had in the past several years, where "several" could be 10, 20, 30, or any other number of years you want to test. What might you keep track of? How might you interpret your results?

CASE   15.1 SKI JACKET PRODUCTION

Egress, Inc., is a small company that designs, produces, and sells ski jackets and other coats. The creative design team has labored for weeks over its new design for the coming winter season. It is now time to decide how many ski jackets to produce in this production run. Because of the lead times involved, no other production runs will be possible during the season. Predicting ski jacket sales months in advance of the selling season can be quite tricky. Egress has been in operation for only three years, and its ski jacket designs were quite successful in two of those years. Based on realized sales from the last three years, current economic conditions, and professional judgment, 12 Egress employees have independently estimated demand for their new design for the upcoming season. Their estimates are listed in Table 15.2.

Table 15.2   Estimated Demands

14,000	16,000
13,000	8000
14,000	5000
14,000	11,000
15,500	8000
10,500	15,000

To assist in the decision on the number of units for the production run, management has gathered the data in Table 15.3. Note that S is the price Egress charges retailers. Any ski jackets that do not sell during the season can be sold by Egress to discounters for V per jacket. The fixed cost of plant

Table 15.3   Monetary Values

Variable production cost per unit (C):	$80
Selling price per unit (S):	$100
Salvage value per unit (V):	$30
Fixed production cost (F):	$100,000

and equipment is F. This cost is incurred regardless of the size of the production run.

Questions

1. Egress management believes that a normal distribution is a reasonable model for the unknown demand in the coming year. What mean and standard deviation should Egress use for the demand distribution?

2. Use a spreadsheet model to simulate 1000 possible outcomes for demand in the coming year. Based on these scenarios, what is the expected profit if Egress produces $Q = 7800$ ski jackets? What is the expected profit if Egress produces $Q = 12,000$ ski jackets? What is the standard deviation of profit in these two cases?

3. Based on the same 1000 scenarios, how many ski jackets should Egress produce to maximize expected profit? Call this quantity Q.

4. Should Q equal mean demand or not? Explain.

5. Create a histogram of profit at the production level Q. Create a histogram of profit when the production level Q equals mean demand. What is the probability of a loss greater than $100,000 in each case?

Management of Ebony, a leading manufacturer of bath soap, is trying to control its inventory costs. The weekly cost of holding one unit of soap in inventory is $30 (one unit is 1000 cases of soap). The marketing department estimates that weekly demand averages 120 units, with a standard deviation of 15 units, and is reasonably well modeled by a normal distribution. If demand exceeds the amount of soap on hand, those sales are *lost*—that is, there is no backlogging of demand. The production department can produce at one of three levels: 110, 120, or 130 units per week. The cost of changing the production level from one week to the next is $3000.

Management would like to evaluate the following production policy. If the current inventory is less than $L = 30$ units, they will produce 130 units in the next week. If the current inventory is greater than $U = 80$ units, they will produce 110 units in the next week. Otherwise, Ebony will continue at the previous week's production level.

Ebony currently has 60 units of inventory on hand. Last week's production level was 120.

Questions

1. Develop a simulation model for 52 weeks of operation at Ebony. Graph the inventory of soap over time. What is the total cost (inventory cost plus production change cost) for the 52 weeks?

2. Run the simulation for 500 iterations to estimate the average 52-week cost with values of U ranging from 30 to 80 in increments of 10. Keep $L = 30$ throughout.

3. Report the sample mean and standard deviation of the 52-week cost under each policy. Using the simulated results, is it possible to construct *valid* 90% confidence intervals for the average 52-week cost for each value of U? In any case, graph the average 52-week cost versus U. What is the best value of U for $L = 30$?

4. What other production policies might be useful to investigate?

CHAPTER
16

Simulation Models

Stuart Pearce/Alamy

MERRILL LYNCH IMPROVES LIQUIDITY RISK MANAGEMENT FOR REVOLVING CREDIT LINES

The Merrill Lynch banking group comprises several Merrill Lynch affiliates, including Merrill Lynch Bank USA (ML Bank USA). (Its parent company is Bank of America.) ML Bank USA has assets of more than $60 billion (as of June 30, 2005, when the following article was written, closer to $70 billion by 2010). The bank acts as an intermediary, accepting deposits from Merrill Lynch retail customers and using the deposits to fund loans and make investments. One way ML Bank USA uses these assets is to provide revolving credit lines to institutional and large corporate borrowers. Currently, it has a portfolio of about $13 billion in credit-line commitments with more than 100 companies. When it makes these commitments, it must be aware of the liquidity risk, defined as the ability to meet all cash obligations when due. In other words, if a borrower asks for funds as part of its revolving credit-line agreement, the bank must have the funds available to honor the request, typically on the same day the request is made. This liquidity requirement poses a huge risk to the bank. The bank must keep enough cash or liquid investments (i.e., investments that can be converted to cash quickly) in reserve to honor its customers' requests whenever they occur. If the bank knew when, and in what quantities, these requests would occur, it could manage its cash reserves more prudently, essentially holding a smaller amount in liquid investments for credit requests and investing the rest in other more illiquid and profitable investments.

Duffy et al. (2005) discuss their role as members of Merrill Lynch's Banking Group and Management Science Group in developing a model to manage the liquidity risk for ML Bank USA's revolving credit lines. The revolving credit lines give borrowers access to a specified amount of cash on demand for short-term funding needs in return for a fee paid to the bank. The bank also earns an interest rate on advances that compensates it for the liquidity and other risks it takes. These credit lines are therefore profitable for the bank, but they are not the borrowers' primary sources of funding. Customers typically use these credit lines to retire maturing commercial paper (available at cheaper interest rates) during the process of rolling it over (i.e., attempting to reissue new commercial paper notes), and/or when their credit rating falls. The essence of the problem is that when a customer's credit ratings (measured by the Moody rating scale, for example) fall, the customers are less likely to obtain funds from cheaper sources such as commercial paper, so they then tend to rely on their credit lines from ML Bank USA and other banks. This poses problems for ML Bank USA. It must honor its commitments to the borrowers, as spelled out in the credit-line agreements, but customers with low credit ratings are the ones most likely to default on their loans.

Two other aspects of the problem are important. First, the credit-line agreements often have a "term-out" option, which allows the borrower to use funds for an additional period after expiration, typically for one year. A customer who is experiencing financial difficulties and has seen its credit rating fall is the type most likely to use its term-out option. Second, movements in credit ratings for customers in the same industry or even in different industries tend to be positively correlated because they can all be affected by movements in their industry or the overall economy. This increases the liquidity risk for ML Bank USA because it increases the chance that poor economic conditions will lead many customers to request additional credit.

The authors built a rather complex simulation model to track the demand for usage of these credit facilities. The model simulates monthly credit-line usage for each customer over a five-year period. During this period, some credit lines are renewed, some expire and are not renewed, and some customers exercise their term-out options. The model has several significant features: (1) it models the probabilistic changes in credit ratings for its customers, where a customer's credit rating can move from one level to another level in a given month with specified probabilities; (2) these probabilities are chosen in such a way that movements in credit ratings are positively correlated across customers; and (3) expert-system business rules are used to determine whether the company will renew or terminate expiring lines of credit and whether customers will exercise their term-out options. For example, a typical rule is that the bank does not renew a credit line if the borrower's credit rating is below a certain threshold.

The authors developed a user-friendly Excel-based system to run their model. It actually invokes and executes the simulation behind the scenes in a simulation package called Arena. Users of the system can change many of the parameters of the model, such as the business-rule cutoffs, to customize the simulation.

The model has helped ML Bank USA manage its revolving credit lines. The output of the model provides a scientific and robust measure of liquidity risk that the bank has confidence in—and therefore uses. The model has led to two tangible financial benefits. First, the model reduced the bank's liquidity requirement from 50% to 20% of outstanding commitments, thus freeing up about $4 billion of liquidity for other profitable illiquid investments. Second, during the first 21 months after the system was implemented, the bank's portfolio expanded from $8 billion in commitments and 80 customers to $13 billion and more than 100 customers. The bank continues to use the model for its long-range planning. ∎

16-1 INTRODUCTION

In the previous chapter, we introduced most of the important concepts for developing and analyzing spreadsheet simulation models. We also discussed many of the features available in the powerful simulation add-in, @RISK, that you receive with this book. Now we apply the tools to a wide variety of problems that can be analyzed with simulation. For convenience, we group the applications into four general areas: (1) operations models, (2) financial models, (3) marketing models, and (4) games of chance. The only overriding theme in this chapter is that simulation models can yield important insights in all of these areas. You do not need to cover all of the models in this chapter or cover them in any particular order. You can cover the ones of most interest to you in practically any order.

16-2 OPERATIONS MODELS

Whether we are discussing the operations of a manufacturing or a service company, there is likely to be uncertainty that can be modeled with simulation. In this section, we look at examples of bidding for a government contract (uncertainty in the bids by competitors), warranty costs (uncertainty in the time until failure of an appliance), and drug production (uncertainty in the yield and timing).

16-2a Bidding for Contracts

In situations where a company must bid against competitors, simulation can often be used to determine the company's optimal bid. Usually the company does not know what its competitors will bid, but it might have an idea about the range of the bids its competitors will choose. In this section, we show how to use simulation to determine a bid that maximizes the company's expected profit.

EXAMPLE | **16.1 BIDDING FOR A GOVERNMENT CONTRACT**

Miller Construction Company must decide whether to make a bid on a construction project. Miller believes it will cost the company $10,000 to complete the project (if it wins the contract), and it will cost $350 to prepare a bid. However, there is uncertainty about each of these. Upon further reflection, Miller assesses that the cost to complete the project has a triangular distribution with minimum, most likely, and maximum values $9000, $10,000, and $15,000. Similarly, Miller assesses that the cost to prepare a bid has a triangular distribution with parameters $300, $350, and $500. (Note the skewness in these distributions. Miller recognizes that cost overruns are much more likely than cost underruns.) Four potential competitors are going to bid against Miller. The lowest bid wins the contract, and the winner is then given the winning bid amount to complete the project. Based on past history, Miller believes that each potential competitor will bid, independently of the others, with probability 0.5. Miller also believes that each competitor's bid will be a multiple of its (Miller's) most likely cost to complete the project, where this multiple has a triangular distribution with minimum, most likely, and maximum values 0.9, 1.3, and 1.8, respectively. If Miller decides to prepare a bid, its bid amount will be a multiple of $500 in the range $10,500 to $15,000. The company wants to use simulation to determine which strategy to use to maximize its expected profit.

Objective To simulate the profit to Miller from any particular bid, and to see which bid amount is best.

Where Do the Numbers Come From?

We already discussed this type of bidding problem in Chapter 6. The new data required here are the parameters of the distributions of Miller's costs, those of the competitors' bids, and the probability that a given competitor will place a bid. Triangular distributions are chosen for simplicity, although Miller could try other types of distributions. The parameters of these distributions are probably educated guesses, possibly based on previous contracts and bidding experience against these same competitors. The probability that a given competitor will place a bid can be estimated from these same competitors' bidding history.

Solution

The logic is straightforward. You first simulate the number of competitors who will bid and then simulate their bids. Then for any bid Miller makes, you see whether Miller wins the contract, and if so, what its profit is.

Developing the Simulation Model

Government Contract Bidding Model

The simulation model appears in Figure 16.1. (See the file **Contract Bidding.xlsx**.) It can be developed with the following steps. (Note that this model does not check the possibility of Miller not bidding at all. But this case is easy. If Miller opts not to bid, the profit is a certain $0.)

Recall that the RISKSIMTABLE function allows you to run a separate simulation for each value in its list.

1. **Inputs.** Enter the inputs in the blue cells.

2. **Miller's bid.** You can test all of Miller's possible bids simultaneously with the RISKSIMTABLE function. To set up for this, enter the formula

    =RISKSIMTABLE(D16:M16)

Figure 16.1   Bidding Simulation Model

⟋	A	B	C	D	E	F	G	H	I	J	K	L	M
1	Bidding for a contract												
2													
3	Inputs												
4	Miller's costs, triangular distributed	Min	Most likely	Max									
5	Cost to prepare a bid	$300	$350	$500									
6	Cost to complete project	$9,000	$10,000	$15,000									
7													
8	Number of potential competitors	4											
9	Probability a given competitor bids	0.5											
10													
11	Parameters of triangular distributions for each competitor's bid (expressed as multiple of Miller's most likely cost to complete project)												
12	Min	0.9											
13	Most likely	1.3											
14	Max	1.8											
15				Possible bids for Miller									
16	Miller's bid	$10,500		$10,500	$11,000	$11,500	$12,000	$12,500	$13,000	$13,500	$14,000	$14,500	$15,000
17													
18	Simulation												
19	Miller's cost to prepare a bid	$416											
20	Miller's cost to complete project	$10,618											
21	Number of competing bids	2											
22	Competitor index	1	2	3	4								
23	Competitors' bids	$13,697	$12,816										
24	Minimum competitor bid	$12,816											
25													
26	Miller wins bid? (1 if yes, 0 if no)	1											
27	Miller's profit	–$534											

© Cengage Learning

in cell B16. As with all uses of this function, the spreadsheet shows the simulated values for the *first* bid, $10,500. However, when you run the simulation, you see outputs for all of the bids.

3. **Miller's costs.** Generate Miller's cost to prepare a bid in cell B19 with the formula

   =RISKTRIANG(B5,C5,D5)

   Then copy this to cell B20 to generate Miller's cost to complete the project.

4. **Competitors and their bids.** First, generate the random number of competitors who bid. This has a binomial distribution with four trials and probability of "success" equal to 0.5 for each trial, so enter the formula

   =RISKBINOMIAL(B8,B9)

   in cell B21. Then generate random bids for the competitors who bid in row 23 by entering the formula

   =IF(B22<=$B$21,RISKTRIANG($B$12,$B$13,$B$14)*$C$6,"")

   in cell B23 and copying across. This generates a random bid for all competitors who bid, and it enters a blank for those who don't. (Remember that the random value is the *multiple* of Miller's most likely cost to complete the project.) Calculate the smallest of these (if there are any) in cell B24 with the formula

   =IF(B21>=1,MIN(B23:E23),"")

   Of course, Miller will not see these other bids until it has submitted its own bid.

5. **Win contract?** See whether Miller wins the bid by entering the formula

   =IF(OR(B16<B24,B21=0),1,0)

   in cell B26. Here, 1 means that Miller wins the bid, and 0 means a competitor wins the bid. Of course, if there are no competing bids, Miller wins for sure. Then designate this cell as an @RISK output cell. Recall that to designate a cell as an @RISK output cell, you select the cell and then click on the Add Output button on @RISK's ribbon. You can then label this output appropriately. We used the label Wins Bid.

6. **Miller's profit.** If Miller submits a bid, the bid cost is lost for sure. Beyond that, the profit to Miller is the bid amount minus the cost of completing the project if the bid is won. Otherwise, Miller makes nothing. So enter the formula

   =IF(B26=1,B16-B20,0)−B19

   in cell B27. Then designate this cell as an additional @RISK output cell. (We named it Profit.)

Running the Simulation

Set the number of iterations to 1000, and set the number of simulations to 10 because there are 10 bid amounts Miller wants to test.

Discussion of the Simulation Results

The summary results appear in Figure 16.2. For each simulation—that is, each bid amount—there are two outputs: 1 or 0 to indicate whether Miller wins the contract and Miller's profit. The only interesting results for the 0–1 output are in the Mean column, which shows the fraction of iterations that resulted in 1s. So you can see, for example, that if Miller bids $12,000 (simulation #4), the probability of winning the bid is estimated to be about 0.6. This probability clearly decreases as Miller's bid increases.

Figure 16.2 Summary Results for Bidding Simulation

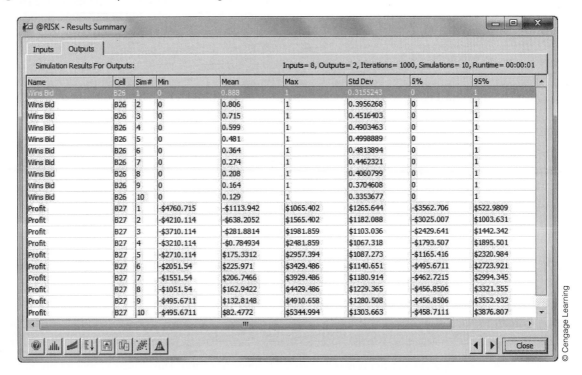

@RISK - Results Summary

Inputs | Outputs

Simulation Results For Outputs:

Inputs= 8, Outputs= 2, Iterations= 1000, Simulations= 10, Runtime= 00:00:01

Name	Cell	Sim#	Min	Mean	Max	Std Dev	5%	95%
Wins Bid	B26	1	0	0.888	1	0.3155243	0	1
Wins Bid	B26	2	0	0.806	1	0.3956268	0	1
Wins Bid	B26	3	0	0.715	1	0.4516403	0	1
Wins Bid	B26	4	0	0.599	1	0.4903463	0	1
Wins Bid	B26	5	0	0.481	1	0.4998889	0	1
Wins Bid	B26	6	0	0.364	1	0.4813894	0	1
Wins Bid	B26	7	0	0.274	1	0.4462321	0	1
Wins Bid	B26	8	0	0.208	1	0.4060799	0	1
Wins Bid	B26	9	0	0.164	1	0.3704608	0	1
Wins Bid	B26	10	0	0.129	1	0.3353677	0	1
Profit	B27	1	-$4760.715	-$1113.942	$1065.402	$1265.644	-$3562.706	$522.9809
Profit	B27	2	-$4210.114	-$638.2052	$1565.402	$1182.088	-$3025.007	$1003.631
Profit	B27	3	-$3710.114	-$281.8814	$1981.859	$1103.036	-$2429.641	$1442.342
Profit	B27	4	-$3210.114	-$0.784934	$2481.859	$1067.318	-$1793.507	$1895.501
Profit	B27	5	-$2710.114	$175.3312	$2957.394	$1087.273	-$1165.416	$2320.984
Profit	B27	6	-$2051.54	$225.971	$3429.486	$1140.651	-$495.6711	$2723.921
Profit	B27	7	-$1551.54	$206.7466	$3929.486	$1180.914	-$462.7215	$2994.345
Profit	B27	8	-$1051.54	$162.9422	$4429.486	$1229.365	-$456.8506	$3321.355
Profit	B27	9	-$495.6711	$132.8148	$4910.658	$1280.508	-$456.8506	$3552.932
Profit	B27	10	-$495.6711	$82.4772	$5344.994	$1303.663	-$458.7111	$3876.807

Close

© Cengage Learning

In terms of net profit, if you concentrate only on the Mean column, a bid amount of $13,000 (simulation #6) is the best. But as the other numbers in this figure indicate, the mean doesn't tell the whole story. For example, if Miller bids $13,000, it could win the bid but still lose a considerable amount of money because of cost overruns. The histogram of profit in Figure 16.3 indicates this more clearly. It shows that in spite of the positive mean, most outcomes are negative.

Figure 16.3

Histogram of Profit with $13,000 Bid

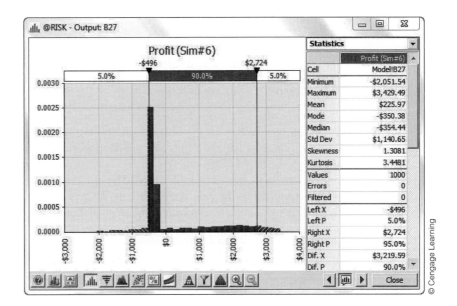

@RISK - Output: B27

Profit (Sim#6)

-$496 | $2,724

5.0% | 90.0% | 5.0%

Statistics	
	Profit (Sim#6)
Cell	Model!B27
Minimum	-$2,051.54
Maximum	$3,429.49
Mean	$225.97
Mode	-$350.38
Median	-$354.44
Std Dev	$1,140.65
Skewness	1.3081
Kurtosis	3.4481
Values	1000
Errors	0
Filtered	0
Left X	-$496
Left P	5.0%
Right X	$2,724
Right P	95.0%
Dif. X	$3,219.59
Dif. P	90.0%

Close

© Cengage Learning

So what should Miller do? If it doesn't bid at all, its profit is a certain $0. If Miller is an *expected* profit maximizer, then the fact that several of the means in Figure 16.2 are positive indicates that bidding is better than not bidding, with a bid of $13,000 being the best bid. However, potential cost overruns and the corresponding losses are certainly a concern. Depending on Miller's degree of risk aversion, the company might decide to (1) not bid at all, or (2) bid higher than $13,000 to minimize its worse loss. Still, we would caution Miller not to be *too* conservative. Rather than focusing on the Min (worst case) column in Figure 16.2, we would suggest focusing on the 5% column. This shows *nearly* how bad things could get (5% of the time it would be worse than this), and this 5th percentile remains fairly constant for higher bids. ■

16-2b Warranty Costs

When you buy a new product, it usually carries a warranty. A typical warranty might state that if the product fails within a certain period such as one year, you will receive a new product at no cost, and it will carry the *same* warranty. However, if the product fails after the warranty period, you have to bear the cost of replacing the product. Due to random lifetimes of products, we need a way to estimate the warranty costs (to the manufacturer) of a product. Example 16.2 illustrates how this can be accomplished with simulation.

EXAMPLE	16.2 WARRANTY COSTS FOR A CAMERA

Yakkon Company sells a popular camera for $400. This camera carries a warranty such that if the camera fails within 1.5 years, the company gives the customer a new camera for free. If the camera fails after 1.5 years, the warranty is no longer in effect. Every replacement camera carries exactly the same warranty as the original camera, and the cost to the company of supplying a new camera is always $225. Use simulation to estimate, for a given sale, the number of replacements under warranty and the NPV of profit from the sale, using a discount rate of 8%.

Objective   To use simulation to estimate the number of replacements under warranty and the total NPV of profit from a given sale.

Where Do the Numbers Come From?

The warranty information is a policy decision made by the company. The hardest input to estimate is the probability distribution of the lifetime of the product. We discuss this next.

Solution

The gamma distribution is a popular distribution, especially when you want a right-skewed distribution of a nonnegative quantity.

The only randomness in this problem concerns the time until failure of a new camera. Yakkon could estimate the distribution of time until failure from historical data. This would probably indicate a right-skewed distribution, as shown in Figure 16.4. If you look through the list of distributions available in @RISK under Define Distributions, you will see several with this same basic shape. The one shown in Figure 16.4 is a commonly used distribution called the *gamma distribution*. We will use a gamma distribution in this example, although other choices such as the triangular are certainly possible.

Selecting a Gamma Distribution

You can learn about distributions from @RISK's Define Distribution window.

The **gamma distribution** is characterized by two parameters, α and β. These determine its shape and location. It can be shown that the mean and standard deviation are $\mu = \alpha\beta$ and $\sigma = \sqrt{\alpha}\beta$. Alternatively, for any desired values of the mean and standard deviation,

Figure 16.4
Right-Skewed
Gamma
Distribution

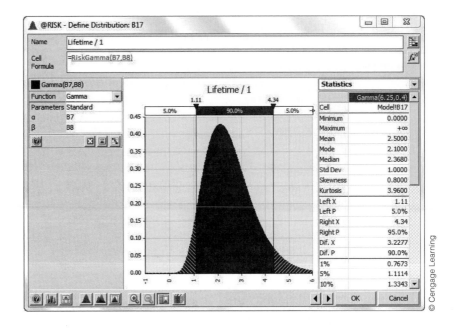

Warranty Cost Model

these equations can be solved for α and β, which leads to $\alpha = \mu^2/\sigma^2$ and $\beta = \sigma^2/\mu$. So, for example, if you want a gamma distribution with mean 2.5 and standard deviation 1 (which in this example would be based on camera lifetime data from the past), you should choose $\alpha = 2.5^2/1^2 = 6.25$ and $\beta = 1^2/2.5 = 0.4$. These are the values shown in Figure 16.4 and the ones used for this example. The values in the figure (from @RISK) imply that the probability of failure before 1.5 years is about 0.15, so that the probability of failure out of warranty is about 0.85.

Developing the Simulation Model

The simulation model appears in Figure 16.5. (See the file **Warranty Costs.xlsx**.) The particular random numbers in this figure indicate an example (a rather unusual one) where there are two failures within warranty. However, because the lifetime of the second replacement (cell D17) is greater than 1.5, the company incurs only two replacement costs, as shown in cells B19 and C19. The model can be developed with the following steps.

1. **Inputs.** Enter the inputs in the blue cells.

2. **Parameters of gamma distribution.** As discussed previously, if you enter a desired mean and standard deviation (in cells B5 and B6), you have to calculate the parameters of the gamma distribution. Do this by entering the formulas

   =B5^2/B6^2

   and

   =B6^2/B5

   in cells B7 and B8.

3. **Lifetimes and times of failures.** Generate at most five lifetimes and corresponding times of failures. (Why only five? You could generate more, but it is extremely unlikely that this same customer would experience more than five failures within warranty, so five suffices.) As soon as a lifetime is greater than 1.5, the warranty period, no further lifetimes are required; instead, "NA" can be recorded in row 17. With this in mind, enter the formulas

Figure 16.5

Warranty
Simulation Model

▲	A	B	C	D	E	F
1	**Warranty costs for camera**					
2						
3	**Inputs**					
4	Parameters of time to failure distribution of any new camera (Gamma)					
5	Desired mean	2.5				
6	Desired stdev	1				
7	Implied alpha	6.250				
8	Implied beta	0.400				
9						
10	Warranty period	1.5				
11	Cost of new camera (to customer)	$400				
12	Replacement cost (to company)	$225				
13	Discount rate	8%				
14						
15	**Simulation of new camera and its replacements (if any)**					
16	Camera	1	2	3	4	5
17	Lifetime	1.272	1.253	2.432	NA	NA
18	Time of failure	1.272	2.525	4.958	NA	NA
19	Cost to company	225	225	0	0	0
20	Discounted cost	204.02	185.26	0.00	0.00	0.00
21						
22	Failures within warranty	2				
23	NPV of profit from customer	($214.28)				

© Cengage Learning

=RISKGAMMA(B7,B8)

=IF(B17<B10,RISKGAMMA(B7,B8),"NA")

and

=IF(C17="NA","NA",IF(C17<$B$10,RISKGAMMA($B$7,$B$8),"NA"))

in cells B17, C17, and C17, and copy the latter formula to cells E17 and F17. These formulas guarantee that once "NA" is recorded in a cell, all cells to its right will also contain "NA." To get the actual times of failures, relative to time 0 when the customer originally purchases the camera, enter the formulas

=B17

and

=IF(C17="NA","NA",B18+C17)

in cells B18 and C18, and copy the latter across row 18. These values will be used for the NPV calculation because this requires the exact timing of cash flows.

@RISK Function: RISKGAMMA
To generate a random number from the gamma distribution, use the RISKGAMMA function in the form **=RISKGAMMA(alpha,beta)**. *The mean and standard deviation of this distribution are* $\mu = \alpha\beta$ *and* $\sigma = \sqrt{\alpha\beta}$. *Equivalently,* $\alpha = \mu^2/\sigma^2$ *and* $\beta = \sigma^2/\mu$.

4. **Costs and discounted costs.** In row 19, enter the replacement cost ($185) or 0, depending on whether a failure occurs within warranty, and in row 20 discount these costs back to time 0, using the failure times in row 18. To do this, enter the formulas

Excel's NPV function can be used only for cash flows that occur at the ends of the respective years. Otherwise, you have to discount cash flows manually.

$$=IF(B17<B10,B12,0)$$

and

$$=IF(C17="NA",0,IF(C17<\$B\$10,\$B\$12,0))$$

in cells B19 and C19, and copy this latter formula across row 19. Then enter the formula

$$=IF(B19>0,B19/(1+\$B\$13)^\wedge B18,0)$$

in cell B20 and copy it across row 20. This formula uses the well-known fact that the present value of a cash flow at time t is the cash flow multiplied by $1/(1 + r)^t$, where r is the discount rate.

5. **Outputs.** Calculate two outputs, the number of failures within warranty and the NPV of profit, with the formulas

$$=COUNTIF(B19:F19,">0")$$

and

$$=B11-B12-SUM(B20:F20)$$

in cells B22 and B23. Then designate these two cells as @RISK output cells. Note that the NPV is the margin from the sale (undiscounted) minus the sum of the discounted costs from replacements under warranty.

Running the Simulation

The @RISK setup is typical. Run 1000 iterations of a *single* simulation (because there is no RISKSIMTABLE function).

Discussion of the Simulation Results

The @RISK summary statistics and histograms for the two outputs appear in Figures 16.6, 16.7, and 16.8. They show a fairly clear picture. About 85% of the time, there are no failures under warranty and the company makes a profit of $175, the margin from the camera sale. However, there is about a 12.7% chance of exactly one failure under warranty, in which case the company's NPV of profit will be an approximate $50 loss (before discounting). Additionally, there is about a 2.3% chance that there will be even more failures under warranty, in which case the loss will be even greater. Note that in our 1000 iterations, the maximum number of failures under warranty was four, and the maximum net loss was $534.03. On average, the NPV of profit was $138.54.

These results indicate that Yakkon is not suffering terribly from warranty costs. However, there are several ways the company could decrease the effects of warranty costs. First, it could increase the price of the camera. Second, it could decrease the warranty

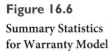

Figure 16.6

Summary Statistics for Warranty Model

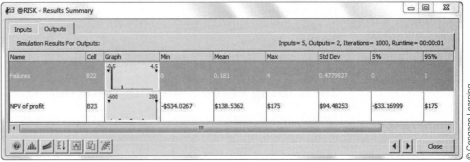

Figure 16.7

Histogram of
Number of Failures

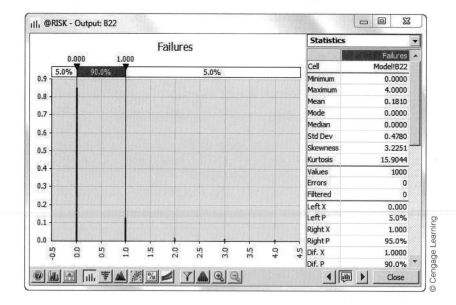

Figure 16.8

Histogram of NPV
of Profit

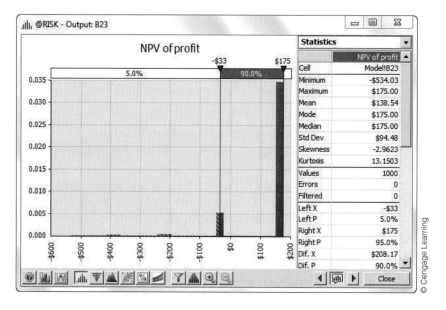

period, say, from 1.5 years to 1 year. Third, it could change the terms of the warranty. For example, it could stipulate that if the camera fails within a year, the customer gets a new camera for free, whereas if the time to failure is between 1 and 1.5 years, the customer pays some pro rata share of the replacement cost. Finally, it could try to sell the customer an extended warranty—at a hefty price. We ask you to explore these possibilities in the problems. ∎

16-2c Drug Production with Uncertain Yield

In many manufacturing settings, products are produced in batches, and the usable *yields* from these batches are uncertain. This is particularly true in the drug industry. Example 16.3 illustrates how a drug manufacturer can take this uncertainty into account when planning production.

EXAMPLE | **16.3 TRYING TO MEET AN ORDER DUE DATE AT WOZAC**

Wozac Company is a drug manufacturer. Wozac has recently accepted an order from its best customer for 8000 ounces of a new miracle drug, and Wozac wants to plan its production schedule to meet the customer's promised delivery date of December 1. There are three sources of uncertainty that make planning difficult. First, the drug must be produced in batches, and there is uncertainty in the time required to produce a batch, which could be anywhere from 5 to 11 days. This uncertainty is described by the discrete distribution in Table 16.1. Second, the yield (usable quantity) from any batch is uncertain. Based on historical data, Wozac believes the yield can be modeled by a triangular distribution with minimum, most likely, and maximum values equal to 600, 1000, and 1100 ounces, respectively. Third, all batches must go through a rigorous inspection once they are completed. The probability that a typical batch passes inspection is only 0.8. With probability 0.2, the batch fails inspection, and *none* of it can be used to help fill the order. Wozac wants to use simulation to help decide how many days prior to the due date it should begin production.

Table 16.1 Distribution of Days to Complete a Batch

Days	Probability
5	0.05
6	0.10
7	0.20
8	0.30
9	0.20
10	0.10
11	0.05

© Cengage Learning

Objective   To use simulation to determine when Wozac should begin production for this order so that there is a high probability of completing it by the due date.

Where Do the Numbers Come From?

The important inputs here are the probability distributions of the time to produce a batch, the yield from a batch, and the inspection result. The probabilities we have assumed would undoubtedly be based on previous production data. For example, the company might have observed that about 80% of all batches in the past passed inspection. Of course, a *discrete* distribution is natural for the number of days to produce a batch, and a *continuous* distribution is appropriate for the yield from a batch.

Solution

The idea is to simulate successive batches—their days to complete, their yields, and whether they pass inspection—and keep a running total of the usable ounces obtained so far. IF functions can then be used to check whether the order is complete or another batch is required. You need to simulate only as many as batches as are required to meet the order, and you should keep track of the days required to produce all of these batches. In this way, you can "back up" to see when production must begin to meet the due date. For example, if the simulation indicates that the order takes 96 days to complete, then production must begin on August 27, 96 days before the due date. (For simplicity, the model assumes that production occurs seven days a week.)

Developing the Simulation Model

Drug Production Model

The completed model appears in Figure 16.9. (See the file **Drug Production.xlsx**.) It can be developed as follows.

Figure 16.9 Drug Production Simulation Model

	A	B	C	D	E	F	G	H	I	J	K	L	M	N
1	Planning production of a drug													
2														
3	Input section						Distribution of days needed to produce a batch (discrete)				Range names used			
4	Ounces required	8000					Days	Probability			Batches_required		=Model!$I$15	
5	Due date	1-Dec					5	0.05			Days_to_complete		=Model!$I$16	
6							6	0.10			Due_date		=Model!$B$5	
7	Distribution of yield (ounces) from each batch (triangular)						7	0.20			Probabilty_pass		=Model!$B$11	
8		Min	Most likely	Max			8	0.30			Ounces_required		=Model!$B$4	
9		600	1000	1100			9	0.20						
10							10	0.10						
11	Prob of passing inspection	0.8					11	0.05						
12														
13								Outputs						
14	Simulation model							Batches required	11					
15	Batch	Days	Yield	Pass?	CumYield	Enough?		Days to complete	91					
16	1	9	941.6	Yes	941.6	Not yet		Day to start	1-Sep					
17	2	8	848.1	Yes	1789.7	Not yet								
18	3	7	911.6	Yes	2701.3	Not yet		Statistical summary measures						
19	4	9	872.8	No	2701.3	Not yet		Max batches reqd	11			Probability of meeting due date		
20	5	10	1027.5	Yes	3728.8	Not yet						Start date	Probability	
21	6	7	922.1	Yes	4651.0	Not yet		Avg days reqd	91	1-Sep		15-Jul	1.000	
22	7	10	968.7	Yes	5619.7	Not yet		Min days reqd	91	1-Sep		1-Aug	1.000	
23	8	5	943.0	Yes	6562.7	Not yet		Max days reqd	91	1-Sep		15-Aug	1.000	
24	9	10	987.5	No	6562.7	Not yet		5th perc days reqd	91	1-Sep		1-Sep	1.000	
25	10	8	1039.4	Yes	7602.2	Not yet		95th perc days reqd	91	1-Sep		15-Sep	1.000	
26	11	8	957.5	Yes	8559.6	Yes								
27	12													
28	13													
29	14													
30	15													
31	16													
32	17													
33	18													
34	19													
35	20													
36	21													
37	22													
38	23													
39	24													
40	25													

1. **Inputs.** Enter all of the inputs in the blue cells.

2. **Batch indexes.** You do not know ahead of time how many batches will be required to fill the order. There should be enough rows in the simulation to cover the worst case that is likely to occur. After some experimentation, it is apparent that 25 batches are almost surely enough. Therefore, enter the batch indexes 1 through 25 in column A of the simulation section. (If 25 were not enough, you could always add more rows.) The idea, then, is to fill the *entire* range B16:F40 with formulas. However, you can use appropriate IF functions in these formulas so that if enough has already been produced to fill the order, blanks are inserted in the remaining cells. For example, the scenario shown in Figure 16.9 is one where 11 batches were required, so blanks appear below row 26.

3. **Days for batches.** Simulate the days required for batches in column B. To do this, enter the formulas

   =RISKDISCRETE(G6:G12,H6:H12)

   and

   =IF(OR(F16="Yes",F16=""),"",RISKDISCRETE($G$6:$G$12,$H$6:$H$12))

   in cell B16 and B17, and copy the latter formula down to cell B40. Note how the IF function enters a blank in this cell if either of two conditions is true: the order was just completed in the previous batch or it has been completed for some time. Similar logic appears in later formulas.

4. **Batch yields.** Simulate the batch yields in column C. To do this, enter the formulas

=RISKTRIANG(B9,C9,D9)

and

=IF(OR(F16="Yes",F16=""),"",RISKTRIANG($B$9,$C$9,$D$9))

in cells C16 and C17, and copy the latter formula down to cell C40.

5. **Pass inspection?** Check whether each batch passes inspection with the formulas

=IF(RAND()<Probability_pass,"Yes","No")

and

=IF(OR(F16="Yes",F16=""),"",IF(RAND()<Probability_pass,"Yes","No"))

in cells D16 and D17, and copy the latter formula down to cell D40. Note that you could use @RISK's RISKUNIFORM(0,1) function instead of RAND(), but there is no real advantage to doing so. They are essentially equivalent. (Besides, the academic version of @RISK imposes an upper limit of 100 @RISK input functions per model, so it is often a good idea to substitute built-in Excel® functions when possible.)

6. **Order filled?** To keep track of the cumulative usable production and whether the order has been filled in columns E and F, first enter the formulas

=IF(D16="Yes",C16,0)

and

=IF(E16>=Ounces_required,"Yes","Not yet")

in cells E16 and F16 for batch 1. Then enter the general formulas

=IF(OR(F16="Yes",F16=""),"",IF(D17="Yes",C17+E16,E16))

and

=IF(OR(F16="Yes",F16=""),"",IF(E17>=Ounces_required,"Yes","Not yet"))

in cells E17 and F17, and copy them down to row 40. Note that the entry in column F is "Not yet" if the order is not yet complete. In the row that completes the order, it changes to "Yes," and then it is blank in succeeding rows.

7. **Outputs.** Calculate the batches and days required in cells I15 and I16 with the formulas

=COUNT(B16:B40)

and

=SUM(B16:B40)

These are the two cells used as output cells for @RISK, so designate them as such. Also, calculate the day the order should be started to just meet the due date in cell I17 with the formula

=Due_date−I16

This formula uses date subtraction to find an elapsed time. (Again, the assumption is that production occurs every day of the week.)

You can use Excel's RAND function inside an IF function to simulate whether some event occurs.

Date subtraction in Excel allows you to calculate the number of days between two given dates.

This completes the simulation model development. The other entries in columns H through J are explained shortly.

Running the Simulation

Set the number of iterations to 1000 and the number of simulations to 1, and then run the simulation as usual.

Discussion of the Simulation Results

After running the simulation, you can obtain the histograms of the number of batches required and the number of days required in Figures 16.10 and 16.11.

How should Wozac use this information? The key questions are how many batches will be required and (2) when production should start. To answer these questions, it is helpful to use several of @RISK's statistical functions. Recall that these functions can be entered directly into the Excel model worksheet. (Also, recall that they provide useful information only *after* the simulation has been run.) These functions provide no new information you don't already have from other @RISK windows, but they allow you to see (and manipulate) this information directly in the spreadsheet.

For the first question, enter the formula

=RISKMAX(Batches_required)

in cell I20. (Refer to Figure 16.9.) It shows that the worst case from the 1000 iterations, in

Figure 16.10

Histogram of Batches Required

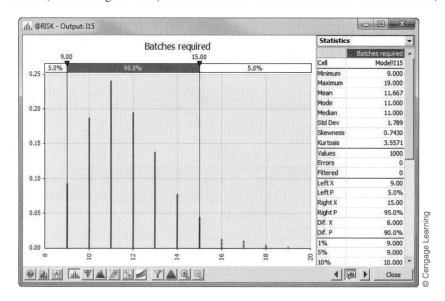

Figure 16.11

Histogram of Days
Required

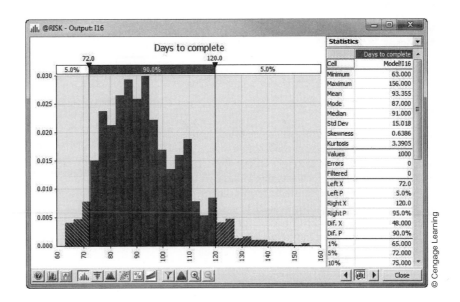

terms of batches required, is 19 batches. (If this maximum were 25, you would add more rows to the simulation model and run the simulation again.)

You can answer the second question in two ways. First, you can calculate summary measures for days required and then back up from the due date. This is done in the range I22:J26. The formulas in column I are

=INT(RISKMEAN(Days_to_complete))

=RISKMIN(Days_to_complete)

=RISKMAX(Days_to_complete)

=RISKPERCENTILE(Days_to_complete,0.05)

and

=RISKPERCENTILE(Days_to_complete,0.95)

(The first uses the INT function to produce an integer.) You can then subtract each of these from the due date to obtain the potential starting dates in column J. Wozac should realize the pros and cons of these starting dates. For example, if the company wants to be 95% sure of meeting the due date, it should start production on August 3. In contrast, if Wozac starts production on September 20, there is only a 5% chance of meeting the due date.

Alternatively, you can get a more direct answer to the question by using @RISK's RISKTARGET function. This allows you to find the probability of meeting the due date for *any* starting date, such as the trial dates in the range L22:L26. To do it, enter the formula

=RISKTARGET(Days_to_complete,Due_date-L22)

in cell M22 and copy it down. This function returns the fraction of iterations where the (random) value in the first argument is less than or equal to the (fixed) value in the second argument. For example, you can see that 83.3% of the iterations have a value of days required less than or equal to 108, the number of days from August 15 to the due date.

What is our recommendation to Wozac? We suggest going with the 95th percentile— begin production on August 3. Then there is only a 5% chance of failing to meet the due date. But the table in the range L22:M26 also provides useful information. For each potential starting date, Wozac can see the probability of meeting the due date. ∎

Using @RISK summary functions such as RISKMEAN, RISKPERCENTILE, and others enables you to capture simulation results in the same work-sheet as the simulation model. These functions do not provide relevant results until the simulation is run.

Note: Student solutions for problems whose numbers appear within a colored box are available for purchase at www.cengagebrain.com.

Level A

1. In Example 16.1, the possible profits vary from negative to positive for each of the 10 possible bids examined.
   a. For each of these, use @RISK's RISKTARGET function to find the probability that Miller's profit is positive. Do you believe these results should have any bearing on Miller's choice of bid?
   b. Use @RISK's RISKPERCENTILE function to find the 10th percentile for each of these bids. Can you explain why the percentiles have the values you obtain?

2. If the number of competitors in Example 16.1 doubles, how does the optimal bid change?

3. Referring to Example 16.1, if the average bid for each competitor stays the same, but their bids exhibit less variability, does Miller's optimal bid increase or decrease? To study this question, assume that each competitor's bid, expressed as a multiple of Miller's cost to complete the project, follows each of the following distributions.
   a. Triangular with parameters 1.0, 1.3, and 2.4
   b. Triangular with parameters 1.2, 1.3, and 2.2
   c. Use @RISK's Define Distributions window to check that the distributions in parts **a** and **b** have the same mean as the original triangular distribution in the example, but smaller standard deviations. What is the common mean? Why is it not the same as the most likely value, 1.3?

4. In Example 16.2, the gamma distribution was used to model the skewness to the right of the lifetime distribution. Experiment to see whether the triangular distribution could have been used instead. Let its minimum value be 0, and choose its most likely and maximum values so that this triangular distribution has approximately the same mean and standard deviation as the gamma distribution in the example. (Use @RISK's Define Distributions window and trial and error to do this.) Then run the simulation and comment on similarities or differences between your outputs and the outputs in the example.

5. See how sensitive the results in Example 16.2 are to the following changes. For each part, make the change indicated, run the simulation, and comment on any differences between your outputs and the outputs in the example.
   a. The cost of a new camera is increased to $450.
   b. The warranty period is decreased to one year.
   c. The terms of the warranty are changed. If the camera fails within one year, the customer gets a new camera for free. However, if the camera fails between 1 year and 1.5 years, the customer pays a pro rata share of the new camera, increasing linearly from 0 to full price. For example, if it fails at 1.2 years, which is 40% of the way from 1 to 1.5, the customer pays 40% of the full price.
   d. The customer pays $50 up front for an extended warranty. This extends the warranty to three years. This extended warranty is just like the original, so that if the camera fails within three years, the customer gets a new camera for free.

6. In Example 16.3, we commented on the 95th percentile on days required in cell I26 and the corresponding date in cell J26. If the company begins production on this date, then it is 95% sure to complete the order by the due date. We found this date to be August 3. Do you always get this answer? Find out by (1) running the simulation 10 more times, each with 1000 iterations, and finding the 95th percentile and corresponding date in each, and (2) running the simulation once more, but with 10,000 iterations. Comment on the difference between simulations (1) and (2) in terms of accuracy. Given these results, when would you recommend that production should begin?

7. In Example 16.3, suppose you want to run five simulations, where the probability of passing inspection is varied from 0.6 to 1.0 in increments of 0.1. Use the RISKSIMTABLE function appropriately to do this. Comment on the effect of this parameter on the key outputs. In particular, does the probability of passing inspection have a large effect on when production should start? (*Note*: When this probability is low, it might be necessary to produce more than 25 batches, the maximum built into the model. Check whether this maximum should be increased.)

16-3 FINANCIAL MODELS

There are many financial applications where simulation can be applied. Future cash flows, future stock prices, and future interest rates are some of the many uncertain variables financial analysts must deal with. In every direction they turn, they see uncertainty. In this section, we analyze a few typical financial applications that can benefit from simulation modeling.

16-3a Financial Planning Models

Many companies, such as GM, Eli Lilly, Procter & Gamble, and Pfizer, use simulation in their capital budgeting and financial planning processes. Simulation can be used to model the uncertainty associated with future cash flows. In particular, simulation can be used to answer questions such as the following:

- What are the mean and variance of a project's net present value (NPV)?
- What is the probability that a project will have a negative NPV?
- What are the mean and variance of a company's profit during the next fiscal year?
- What is the probability that a company will have to borrow more than $2 million during the next year?

Example 16.4 illustrates how simulation can be used to evaluate the financial success of a new car.

EXAMPLE | **16.4 DEVELOPING A NEW CAR AT GF AUTO**

General Ford (GF) Auto Corporation is developing a new model of compact car. This car is assumed to generate sales for the next five years. GF has gathered information about the following quantities through focus groups with the marketing and engineering departments.

- **Fixed cost of developing car.** This cost is assumed to $700 million. The fixed cost is incurred at the beginning of year 1, before any sales are recorded.
- **Margin per car.** This is the unit selling price minus the variable cost of producing a car. GF assumes that in year 1, the margin will be $4000. Every other year, GF assumes the margin will decrease by 4%.[1]
- **Sales.** The demand for the car is the uncertain quantity. In its first year, GF assumes sales—number of cars sold—will be triangularly distributed with parameters 50,000, 75,000, and 85,000. Every year after that, the company assumes that sales will decrease by some percentage, where this percentage is triangularly distributed with parameters 5%, 8%, and 10%. GF also assumes that the percentage decreases in successive years are independent of one another.
- **Depreciation and taxes.** The company will depreciate its development cost on a straight-line basis over the lifetime of the car. The corporate tax rate is 40%.
- **Discount rate.** GF figures its cost of capital at 10%.

Given these assumptions, GF wants to develop a simulation model that will evaluate its NPV of after-tax cash flows for this new car over the five-year time horizon.

Objective To simulate the cash flows from the new car model, from the development time to the end of its life cycle, so that GF can estimate the NPV of after-tax cash flows from this car.

Where Do the Numbers Come From?

There are many inputs to this problem. As we indicated, they are probably obtained from experts within the company and from focus groups of potential customers.

---

[1]The margin decreases because the company assumes variable costs tend to increase through time, whereas selling prices tend to remain fairly constant through time.

Solution

This model is like most financial multiyear spreadsheet models. The completed model extends several years to the right, but most of the work is for the first year or two. From that point, you can copy to the other years to complete the model.

New Car Development Model

Developing the Simulation Model

The simulation model for GF appears in Figure 16.12. (See the file **New Car Development. xlsx.**) It can be formed as follows.

Figure 16.12 GF Auto Simulation Model

	A	B	C	D	E	F	G
1	New car simulation						
2							
3	Inputs			Parameters of triangular distributions			
4	Fixed development cost	$700,000,000			Min	Most likely	Max
5	Year 1 contribution	$4,000		Year 1 sales	50000	75000	85000
6	Annual decrease in contribution	4%		Annual decay rate	5%	8%	10%
7	Tax rate	40%					
8	Discount rate	10%					
9							
10	Simulation						
11	End of year	1	2	3	4	5	
12	Unit sales	71222	67092	62910	57205	52469	
13	Unit contribution	$4,000	$3,840	$3,686	$3,539	$3,397	
14	Revenue minus variable cost	$284,888,275	$257,633,834	$231,910,837	$202,444,276	$178,256,819	
15	Depreciation	$140,000,000	$140,000,000	$140,000,000	$140,000,000	$140,000,000	
16	Before tax profit	$144,888,275	$117,633,834	$91,910,837	$62,444,276	$38,256,819	
17	After tax profit	$86,932,965	$70,580,300	$55,146,502	$37,466,566	$22,954,092	
18	Cash flow	$226,932,965	$210,580,300	$195,146,502	$177,466,566	$162,954,092	
19							
20	NPV of cash flows	$49,346,179					

© Cengage Learning

1. **Inputs.** Enter the various inputs in the blue cells.

2. **Unit sales.** Generate first-year sales in cell B12 with the formula

   =RISKTRIANG(E5,F5,G5)

   Then generate the reduced sales in later years by entering the formula

   =B12*(1−RISKTRIANG($E$6,$F$6,$G$6))

   in cell C12 and copying it across row 12. Note that each sales figure is a random fraction of the *previous* sales figure.

3. **Contributions.** Calculate the unit contributions in row 13 by entering the formulas

   =B5

   and

   =B13*(1−$B$6)

   in cells B13 and C13, and copying the latter across. Then calculate the contributions in row 14 as the product of the corresponding values in rows 12 and 13.

4. **Depreciation.** Calculate the depreciation each year in row 15 as the development cost in cell B4 divided by 5. This is exactly what "straight-line depreciation" means.

Depreciation is
subtracted to get
before-tax profit, but
it is then added back
after taxes have been
deducted.

5. **Before-tax and after-tax profits.** To calculate the before-tax profit in any year, subtract the depreciation from total contribution, so each value in row 16 is the difference between the corresponding values in rows 14 and 15. The reason is that depreciation isn't taxed. To calculate the after-tax profits in row 17, multiply each before-tax profit by one minus the tax rate in cell B7. Finally, each cash flow in row 18 is the sum of the corresponding values in rows 15 and 17. Here depreciation is added back to get the cash flow.

6. **NPV.** Calculate the NPV of cash flows in cell B20 with the formula

$$=-B4+NPV(B8,B18:F18)$$

and designate it as an @RISK output cell (the only output cell). Here, we are assuming that the development cost is incurred right now, so that it isn't discounted, and that all other cash flows occur at the ends of the respective years. This allows the NPV function to be used directly.

Running the Simulation

Set the number of iterations to 1000 and the number of simulations to 1, and then run the simulation as usual.

Discussion of the Simulation Results

After running @RISK, you obtain the histogram in Figure 16.13. These results are somewhat comforting, but also a cause of concern for GF. On the bright side, the mean NPV is about $31.5 million, and there is some chance that the NPV could go well above that figure, even up to almost $150 million. However, there is also a dark side, as shown by the two sliders in the histogram. One slider has been placed over an NPV of 0. As the histogram indicates, there is about a 71% chance of a positive NPV, but there is about a 29% chance of it being negative. The second slider has been positioned at its default 5th percentile setting. Financial analysts often call this percentile the **value at risk at the 5% level**, or **VaR 5%**, because it indicates nearly the worst possible outcome. From this simulation, you can see that GF's VaR 5% is approximately a $68.2 million loss.

Figure 16.13
Histogram of NPV

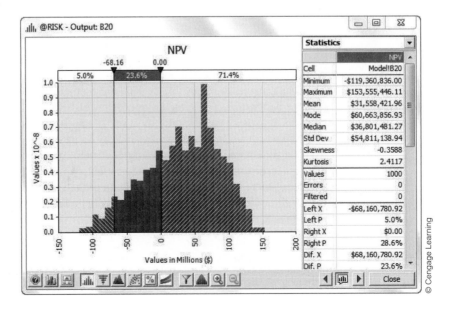

> The **value at risk at the 5% level,** or **VaR 5%**, is the 5th percentile of a distribution, and it is often used in financial models. It indicates nearly the worst possible outcome.

Financial analysts typically look at VaR 5% to see how bad— or more precisely, almost how bad— things could get.

What is most responsible for this huge variability in NPV, the variability in first-year sales or the variability in annual sales decreases? This can be answered with @RISK's tornado chart, which lets you see which random inputs have the most effect on a specified output. (See Figure 16.14.) To get this chart, click on the tornado button below the histogram in Figure 16.13 and select the Change in Output Mean option. This chart answers the question emphatically. Variability in first-year sales is by far the largest influence on NPV. It is very highly correlated with NPV. The annual decreases in sales are not unimportant, but they have much less effect on NPV. If GF wants to get a more favorable NPV distribution, it should do all it can to boost first-year sales—and make the first-year sales distribution less variable.

Figure 16.14
Tornado Chart for NPV

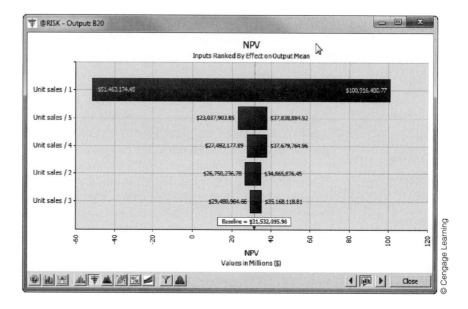

Before finishing this example, we revisit the flaw of averages. What if GF used a deterministic model to estimate NPV? Would the results match those from the simulation? We tried this two ways, once by entering the *most likely values* of the inputs instead of the random numbers, and once by entering the *means* instead of the random numbers. The results appear in Figure 16.15. (The mean of a triangular distribution is the average of its three parameters. These means appear in cells H5 and H6.) Now there are no random numbers in rows 12 and 24, only most likely values or means. The difference between the two NPVs is huge. In this case, the NPV by using means is very close to the mean NPV from the simulation, about $31 million. But if the company used most likely values for the inputs in its deterministic model, which certainly seems sensible, the NPV would be off by a factor of more than two, another variation of the flaw of averages. Besides this problem, neither deterministic model provides even a hint that the company has about a 29% chance of a negative NPV.[2] ∎

If you create a deterministic model using the most likely values of the uncertain inputs, you can possibly get an output value that is nowhere near the mean of that output.

[2]It turns out that the NPV in this model is *linear* in the two random inputs. When an output is linear in the inputs, the deterministic model using means of inputs *always* gives the correct mean output, so that the flaw of averages in the form from the previous chapter does not occur. Even so, a deterministic model still provides no indication of how bad or how good things could get.

Figure 16.15   Deterministic Models

⊿	A	B	C	D	E	F	G	H
1	**New car simulation**							
2								
3	**Inputs**			Parameters of triangular distributions				
4	Fixed development cost	$700,000,000			Min	Most likely	Max	Mean
5	Year 1 contribution	$4,000		Year 1 sales	50000	75000	85000	70000
6	Annual decrease in contribution	4%		Annual decay rate	5%	8%	10%	7.67%
7	Tax rate	40%						
8	Discount rate	10%						
9								
10	**Using most likely values for uncertain inputs**							
11	End of year	1	2	3	4	5		
12	Unit sales	75000	69000	63480	58402	53729		
13	Unit contribution	$4,000	$3,840	$3,686	$3,539	$3,397		
14	Revenue minus variable cost	$300,000,000	$264,960,000	$234,012,672	$206,679,992	$182,539,769		
15	Depreciation	$140,000,000	$140,000,000	$140,000,000	$140,000,000	$140,000,000		
16	Before tax profit	$160,000,000	$124,960,000	$94,012,672	$66,679,992	$42,539,769		
17	After tax profit	$96,000,000	$74,976,000	$56,407,603	$40,007,995	$25,523,861		
18	Cash flow	$236,000,000	$214,976,000	$196,407,603	$180,007,995	$165,523,861		
19								
20	NPV of cash flows	$65,500,687						
21								
22	**Using means for uncertain inputs**							
23	End of year	1	2	3	4	5		
24	Unit sales	70000	64633	59678	55103	50878		
25	Unit contribution	$4,000	$3,840	$3,686	$3,539	$3,397		
26	Revenue minus variable cost	$280,000,000	$284,192,000	$219,997,389	$195,005,685	$172,853,040		
27	Depreciation	$140,000,000	$140,000,000	$140,000,000	$140,000,000	$140,000,000		
28	Before tax profit	$140,000,000	$108,192,000	$79,997,389	$55,005,685	$32,853,040		
29	After tax profit	$84,000,000	$64,915,200	$47,998,433	$33,003,411	$19,711,824		
30	Cash flow	$224,000,000	$204,915,200	$187,998,433	$173,003,411	$159,711,824		
31								
32	NPV of cash flows	$31,565,909						

© Cengage Learning

FUNDAMENTAL INSIGHT

The Mean Isn't Everything

Many discussions of simulation focus on the *mean* of some output variable. This makes sense, given the importance of EMV for decision making, as discussed in Chapter 6. After all, EMV is just the mean of a monetary output. However, analysts in many areas, including finance, are often at least as interested in the extreme values of an output distribution. For example, the VaR 5% discussed in this example indicates nearly how bad things could get if unlucky outcomes occur. If large amounts of money are at stake, particularly potential losses, companies might not want to play the averages by focusing only on the mean. They should be aware of potential disasters as well. Of course, simulation also shows the bright side, the extremes on the right that could occur if lucky outcomes occur. Managers shouldn't be so conservative that they focus only on the negative outcomes and ignore the upside potential.

16-3b   Cash Balance Models

All companies track their cash balance over time. As specific payments come due, companies sometimes need to take out short-term loans to keep a minimal cash balance. Example 16.5 illustrates one such application.

16.5 MAINTAINING A MINIMAL CASH BALANCE AT ENTSON

Entson Company believes that its monthly sales during the period from November of the current year to July of next year are normally distributed with the means and standard deviations given in Table 16.2. Each month Entson incurs fixed costs of $250,000. In March taxes of $150,000 and in June taxes of $50,000 must be paid. Dividends of $50,000 must also be paid in June. Entson estimates that its receipts in a given month are a weighted sum of sales from the current month, the previous month, and two months ago, with weights 0.2, 0.6, and 0.2. In symbols, if R_t and S_t represent receipts and sales in month t, then

$$R_t = 0.2S_{t-2} + 0.6S_{t-1} + 0.2S_t \qquad \textbf{(16.1)}$$

The materials and labor needed to produce a month's sales must be purchased one month in advance, and the cost of these averages to 80% of the product's sales. For example, if sales in February are $1,500,000, then the February materials and labor costs are $1,200,000, but these must be paid in January.

Table 16.2 Monthly Sales (in Thousands of Dollars) for Entson

	Nov.	Dec.	Jan.	Feb.	Mar.	Apr.	May	Jun.	Jul.
Mean	1500	1600	1800	1500	1900	2600	2400	1900	1300
Standard Deviation	70	75	80	80	100	125	120	90	70

© Cengage Learning

At the beginning of January, Entson has $250,000 in cash. The company wants to ensure that each month's ending cash balance never falls below $250,000. This means that Entson might have to take out short-term (one-month) loans. For example, if the ending cash balance at the end of March is $200,000, Entson will take out a loan for $50,000, which it will then pay back (with interest) one month later. The interest rate on a short-term loan is 1% per month. At the beginning of each month, Entson earns interest of 0.5% on its cash balance. The company wants to use simulation to estimate the maximum loan it will need to take out to meet its desired minimum cash balance. Entson also wants to analyze how its loans will vary over time, and it wants to estimate the total interest paid on these loans.

Objective   To simulate Entson's cash flows and the loans the company must take out to meet a minimum cash balance.

Where Do the Numbers Come From?

Although there are many monetary inputs in the problem statement, they should all be easily accessible. Of course, Entson chooses the minimum cash balance of $250,000 as a matter of company policy.

Solution

There is a considerable amount of bookkeeping in this simulation, so it is a good idea to list the events in chronological order that occur each month. We assume the following:

■ Entson observes its beginning cash balance.
■ Entson receives interest on its beginning cash balance.

- Receipts arrive and expenses are paid (including payback of the previous month's loan, if any, with interest).
- If necessary, Entson takes out a short-term loan.
- The final cash balance is observed, which becomes next month's beginning cash balance.

Cash Balance Model

Developing the Simulation Model

The completed simulation model appears in Figure 16.16. (See the file **Cash Balance. xlsx.**) It requires the following steps.

1. **Inputs.** Enter the inputs in the blue cells. Note that loans are simulated (in row 42) only for the period from January to June of next year. However, sales figures are

Figure 16.16 Cash Balance Simulation Model

	A	B	C	D	E	F	G	H	I	J
1	Entson cash balance simulation									
2				All monetary values are in $1000s.						
3	**Inputs**									
4	Distribution of monthly sales (normal)									
5		Nov	Dec	Jan	Feb	Mar	Apr	May	Jun	Jul
6	Mean	1500	1600	1800	1500	1900	2600	2400	1900	1300
7	St Dev	70	75	80	80	100	125	120	90	70
8										
9	Monthly fixed stock			250	250	250	250	250	250	
10	Tax, dividend expenses			0	0	150	0	0	100	
11										
12	Receipts in any month are of form: A*(sales from 2 months ago)+B*(previous month's sales)+C*(current month's sales), where:									
13		A	B	C						
14		0.2	0.6	0.2						
15										
16	Cost of materials and labor for next month, spent this month, is a percentage of product's sales from next month, where the percentage is:									
17		80%								
18										
19	Initial cash in January	250								
20	Minimum cash balance	250								
21										
22	Monthly interest rates									
23	Interest rate on loan	1.0%								
24	Interest rate on cash	0.5%								
25										
26	**Simulation**									
27		Nov	Dec	Jan	Feb	Mar	Apr	May	Jun	Jul
28	Actual sales	1490.137	1550.547	1754.154	1442.131	2000.628	2596.001	2446.630	1981.397	1302.150
29										
30	Cash, receipts									
31	Beginning cash balance			250.000	426.732	250.000	250.000	250.000	250.000	
32	Interest on cash balance			1.250	2.134	1.250	1.250	1.250	1.250	
33	Receipts			1579.186505	1651.027757	1616.234701	2008.002889	2447.051859	2383.457375	
34	Costs									
35	Fixed costs			250	250	250	250	250	250	
36	Tax, dividend expenses			0	0	150	0	0	100	
37	Material, labor expenses			1153.705	1600.502	2076.800	1957.304	1585.117	1041.720	
38	Loan payback (principle)				0.000	20.609	880.131	1086.983	484.668	0.000
39	Loan payback (interest)				0.000	0.206	8.801	10.870	4.847	0.000
40										
41	Cash balance before loan			426.732	229.391	−630.131	−836.983	−234.668	753.472	
42	Loan amount (if any)			0.000	20.609	880.131	1086.983	484.668	0.000	
43	Final cash balance			426.732	250.000	250.000	250.000	250.000	753.472	
44										
45	Maximum loan	1086.983								
46	Total interest on loans	24.724								

© Cengage Learning

required (in row 28) in November and December of the current year to generate receipts for January and February. Also, July sales are required for next year to generate the material and labor costs paid in June.

2. **Actual sales.** Generate the sales in row 28 by entering the formula

=RISKNORMAL(B6,B7)

in cell B28 and copying across.

3. **Beginning cash balance.** For January of next year, enter the cash balance with the formula

=B19

in cell D31. Then for the other months enter the formula

=D43

in cell E31 and copy it across row 31. This reflects that the beginning cash balance for one month is the final cash balance from the previous month.

4. **Incomes.** Entson's incomes (interest on cash balance and receipts) are entered in rows 32 and 33. To calculate these, enter the formulas

=$B$24*D31

and

=SUMPRODUCT($B$14:$D$14,B28:D28)

in cells D32 and D33 and copy them across rows 32 and 33. This latter formula, which is based on Equation (16.1), multiplies the fixed weights in row 14 by the relevant sales and adds these products to calculate receipts.

5. **Expenses.** Entson's expenses (fixed costs, taxes and dividends, material and labor costs, and payback of the previous month's loan) are entered in rows 35 through 39. Calculate these by entering the formulas

=D9

=D10

=$B$17*E28

=D42

and

=D42*$B$23

in cells D35, D36, D37, E38, and E39, respectively, and copying these across rows 35 through 39. (For the loan payback, we are assuming that no loan payback is due in January.)

The loan amounts are determined by the random cash inflows and outflows and the fact that Entson's policy is to maintain a minimum cash balance.

6. **Cash balance before loan.** Calculate the cash balance before the loan (if any) by entering the formula

=SUM(D31:D33)−SUM(D35:D39)

in cell D41 and copying it across row 41.

7. **Amount of loan.** If the value in row 41 is below the minimum cash balance ($250,000), Entson must borrow enough to bring the cash balance up to this minimum. Otherwise, no loan is necessary. Therefore, enter the formula

$$=MAX(\$B\$20-D41,0)$$

in cell D42 and copy it across row 42. (You could use an IF function, rather the MAX function, to accomplish the same result.)

8. **Final cash balance.** Calculate the final cash balance by entering the formula

$$=D41+D42$$

in cell D43 and copying it across row 43.

9. **Maximum loan, total interest.** Calculate the maximum loan from January to June in cell B45 with the formula

$$=MAX(D42:I42)$$

Then calculate the total interest paid on all loans in cell B46 with the formula

$$=SUM(E39:J39)$$

An @RISK output range, as opposed to a single output cell, allows you to obtain a summary chart that shows the whole simulated range at once. This range is typically a time series.

10. **Output range.** In the usual way, designate cells B45 and B46 as output cells. Also, designate the entire range of loans, D42:I42, as an output range. To do this, highlight this range and click on the @RISK Add Output button. It will ask you for a name of the output. We suggest "Loans." Then a typical formula in this range, such as the formula for cell E42, will be

$$=RISKOUTPUT("Loans",2)+MAX(\$B\$20-E41,0)$$

This indicates that cell E42 is the second cell in the Loans output range.

Running the Simulation

Set the number of iterations to 1000 and the number of simulations to 1. Then run the simulation in the usual way.

Discussion of the Simulation Results

After running the simulation, you will obtain the summary results in Figure 16.17. They indicate that the maximum loan varies considerably, from a low of about $433,000 to a high of about $1,530,000. The average is about $952,700. You can also see that Entson is spending close to $20,000 on average in interest on the loans, although the actual amounts vary considerably from one iteration to another.

Figure 16.17
Summary Measures for Cash Balance Simulation

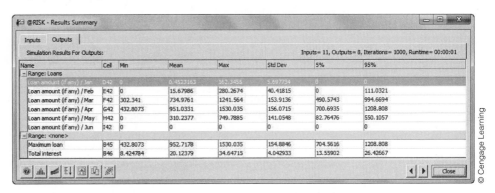

You can also gain insights from the summary trend chart of the series of loans, shown in Figure 16.18. To obtain this chart, click on the third button at the bottom of the Results Summary window in Figure 16.17. (This button is also available in any histogram window.) This chart clearly shows how the loans vary through time. The middle line is the

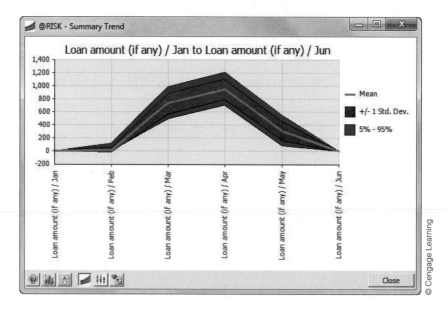

Figure 16.18
Summary Chart
of Loans Through
Time

expected loan amount. The inner bands extend to one standard deviation on either side of the mean, and the outer bands extend to the 5th and 95th percentiles. (@RISK lets you customize these bands in a number of ways by right-clicking on the chart.) You can see that the largest loans are required in March and April.

Is it intuitively clear why the required loans peak in March and April? After all, why should Entson need money in months when its sales tend to be relatively high? There are two factors working here. First, Entson has to pay its costs early. For example, it has to pay 80% of its April sales for labor and material expenses in March. Second, most of its receipts arrive late. For example, 80% of its receipts from sales in March are not received until *after* March. Therefore, the answer to the question is that the timing and amounts of loans are fairly complex. Of course, this is why Entson goes to the trouble of building a simulation model. ■

16-3c Investment Models

Individual investors typically want to choose investment strategies that meet some pre-specified goal. Example 16.6 is typical. Here, a person wants to meet a retirement goal, starting at an early age.

| EXAMPLE | **16.6 INVESTING FOR RETIREMENT** |

Attorney Sally Evans has just begun her career. At age 25, she has 40 years until retirement, but she realizes that now is the time to start investing. She plans to invest $1000 at the beginning of each of the next 40 years. Each year, she plans to put fixed percentages—the same each year—of this $1000 into stocks, Treasury bonds (T-bonds), and Treasury bills (T-bills). However, she is not sure which percentages to use. (We call these percentages *investment weights*.) She does have historical annual returns from stocks, T-bonds, and T-bills from 1946 to 2007. These are listed in the file **Retirement Planning. xlsx**. This file also includes inflation rates for these years. For example, for 1993 the annual returns for stocks, T-bonds, and T-bills were 9.99%, 18.24%, and 2.90%, respectively, and the inflation rate was 2.75%. Sally would like to use simulation to help decide what investment weights to use, with the objective of achieving a large investment value, in *today's* dollars, at the end of 40 years.

Objective To use simulation to estimate the value of Sally's future investments, in today's dollars, from several investment strategies in T-bills, T-bonds, and stocks.

Where Do the Numbers Come From?

Historical returns and inflation rates, such as those quoted here, are widely available on the Web.

Solution

You can simulate future scenarios by randomly choosing past scenarios, giving higher probabilities to more recent scenarios.

The most difficult modeling aspect is settling on a way to use historical returns and inflation factors to generate *future* values of these quantities. We suggest using a *scenario* approach. You can think of each historical year as a possible scenario, where the scenario specifies the returns and inflation factor for that year. Then for any future year, you randomly choose one of these scenarios. It seems intuitive that more recent scenarios ought to have a greater chance of being chosen. To implement this idea, you can give a weight (not to be confused with the investment weights) to each scenario, starting with weight 1 for 2007. Then the weight for any year is a *damping factor* multiplied by the weight from the next year. For example, the weight for 1996 is the damping factor multiplied by the weight for 1997. To change these weights to probabilities, you can divide each weight by the sum of all the weights. The damping factor illustrated here is 0.98. Others could be used instead, and it is not clear which produces the most realistic results. (This is an important question for financial research.)

Without a package like RiskOptimizer, you cannot find the "best" set of investment weights, but the simulation model lets you experiment with various sets of weights.

The other difficult part of the solution is choosing "good" investment weights. This is really an optimization problem: find three weights that add to 1 and produce the largest mean final cash. Palisade has another software package, RiskOptimizer, that solves this type of optimization–simulation problem. However, the example illustrates several sets of weights, where some percentage is put into stocks and the remainder is split evenly between T-bonds and T-bills, and see which does best. You can try other sets if you like.

Developing the Simulation Model

Investing for Retirement Model

The historical data and the simulation model (each with some rows hidden) appear in Figures 16.19 and 16.20. (Again, see the **Retirement Planning.xlsx** file.) It can be developed as follows.

1. **Inputs.** Enter the data in the blue regions of Figures 16.19 and 16.20.

Figure 16.19 Historical Data, Inputs, and Probabilities

◢	A	B	C	D	E	F	G
3	Historical data and probabilities						
4	Year	T-Bills	T-Bonds	Stocks	Inflation	ProbWts	Probability
5	1946	0.0035	−0.0010	−0.0807	0.1817	0.2916	0.0082
6	1947	0.0050	−0.0263	0.0571	0.0901	0.2976	0.0083
7	1948	0.0081	0.0340	0.0550	0.0271	0.3036	0.0085
8	1949	0.0110	0.0645	0.1879	−0.0180	0.3098	0.0087
9	1950	0.0120	0.0006	0.3171	0.0579	0.3161	0.0089
62	2003	0.0180	0.0038	0.2841	0.0227	0.9224	0.0258
63	2004	0.0218	0.0449	0.1070	0.0268	0.9412	0.0264
64	2005	0.0431	0.0287	0.0485	0.0339	0.9604	0.0269
65	2006	0.0488	0.0196	0.1563	0.0324	0.9800	0.0274
66	2007	0.0548	0.0488	0.1021	0.0285	1.0000	0.0280
67					Sums -->	35.7115	1.0000

Figure 16.20 Retirement Simulation Model

	I	J	K	L	M	N	O	P	Q
3	Inputs								
4	Damping factor	0.98				Range names used			
5	Yearly investment	$1,000				LTable1	=Model!$I$10:$L$12		
6	Planning horizon	40	years			LTable2	=Model!$A$5:$E$66		
7						Weights	=Model!$J$16:$L$16		
8	Alternative sets of weights to test								
9	Index	T-Bills	T-Bonds	Stocks					
10	1	0.10	0.10	0.80					
11	2	0.20	0.20	0.60					
12	3	0.30	0.30	0.40					
13									
14	Weights used								
15	Index	T-Bills	T-Bonds	Stocks					
16	1	0.10	0.10	0.80					
17									
18	Output from simulation below								
19	Final cash (today's dollars)		$93,814						
20									
21					Column offset for lookup2				
22	Simulation model			2	3	4	5		
23	Future year	Beginning cash	Scenario	T-Bills	T-Bonds	Stocks	Inflation	Ending cash	Deflator
24	1	$1,000	1965	1.0393	1.0073	1.1245	1.0192	1104	0.981
25	2	2104	1976	1.0508	1.1675	1.2384	1.0481	2552	0.936
26	3	3552	1966	1.0476	1.0365	0.8994	1.0335	3296	0.906
27	4	4296	1989	1.0837	1.1811	1.3149	1.0465	5491	0.866
28	5	6491	1997	1.0491	1.0994	1.3186	1.0170	8242	0.851
59	36	282303	1984	1.0985	1.1543	1.0627	1.0395	303600	0.225
60	37	304600	1981	1.1471	1.0185	0.9509	1.0894	297680	0.206
61	38	298680	1988	1.0635	1.0967	1.1681	1.0442	343631	0.197
62	39	344631	1997	1.0491	1.0994	1.3186	1.0170	437589	0.194
63	40	438589	1988	1.0635	1.0967	1.1681	1.0442	504596	0.186

2. **Weights.** The investment weights used for the model are in rows 10 through 12. (For example, the first set puts 80% in stocks and 10% in each of T-bonds and T-bills.) You can simulate all three sets of weights simultaneously with a RISKSIMTABLE and VLOOKUP combination as follows. First, enter the formula

   =RISKSIMTABLE({1,2,3})

   in cell I16. Then enter the formula

   =VLOOKUP($I$16,LTable1,2)

   in cell J16 and copy it to cells K16 and L16. Then modify the formulas in these latter two cells, changing the last argument of the VLOOKUP to 3 and 4, respectively. For example, the formula in cell L16 should end up as

   =VLOOKUP($I$16,LTable1,4)

   The effect is that you can run three simulations, one for each set of weights in rows 10 through 12.

3. **Probabilities.** Enter value 1 in cell F66. Then enter the formula

   =$J$4*F66

908   Chapter 16   Simulation Models

in cell F65 and copy it *up* to cell F5. Sum these values with the SUM function in cell F67. Then to convert them to probabilities (numbers that add to 1), enter the formula

=F5/$F$67

in cell G5 and copy it down to cell G66. Note how the probabilities for more recent years are considerably larger. When scenarios are selected randomly, recent years will have a greater chance of being chosen. (The SUM formula in cell G67 confirms that the probabilities sum to 1.)

4. **Scenarios.** Moving to the model in Figure 16.20, the goal is to simulate 40 scenarios in columns K through O, one for each year of Sally's investing. To do this, enter the formulas

=RISKDISCRETE($A$5:$A$66,$G$5:$G$66)

and

=1+VLOOKUP($K24,LTable2,L$22)

in cells K24 and L24, and copy this latter formula to the range M24:O24. Then copy all of these formulas down to row 63. Make sure you understand how the RISKDISCRETE and VLOOKUP functions combine to achieve the goal. (Also, check the list of range names used at the top of Figure 16.20.) The RISKDISCRETE randomly generates a year from column A, using the probabilities in column G. Then the VLOOKUP captures the data from this year. (You add 1 to the VLOOKUP to get a value such as 1.08, rather than 0.08.) This is the key to the simulation. (By the way, do you see why Excel's RANDBETWEEN function isn't used to generate the years in column K? The reason is that this function makes all possible years equally likely, and the goal is to make more recent years *more* likely.)

5. **Beginning, ending cash.** The bookkeeping part is straightforward. Begin by entering the formula

=J5

in cell J24 for the initial investment. Then enter the formulas

=J24*SUMPRODUCT(Weights,L24:N24)

and

=$J$5+P24

in cells P24 and J25 for ending cash in the first year and beginning cash in the second year. The former shows how the beginning cash grows in a given year. You should think it through carefully. The latter implies that Sally reinvests her previous money, plus she invests an additional $1000. Copy these formulas down columns J and P.

6. **Deflators.** You eventually need to deflate future dollars to today's dollars. The proper way to do this is to calculate deflators (also called deflation factors). Do this by entering the formula

=1/O24

in cell Q24. Then enter the formula

=Q24/O25

in cell Q25 and copy it down. The effect is that the deflator for future year 20, say, in cell Q43, is 1 divided by the product of all 20 inflation factors up through that year.

(This is similar to discounting for the time value of money, but the relevant discount rate, now the inflation rate, varies from year to year.)

7. **Final cash.** Calculate the final value *in today's dollars* in cell K19 with the formula

=P63*Q63

Then designate this cell as an @RISK output cell.

Running the Simulation

Set the number of iterations to 1000 and the number of simulations to 3 (one for each set of investment weights to be tested). Then run the simulation as usual.

Discussion of the Simulation Results

Summary results appear in Figure 16.21. The first simulation, which invests the most heavily in stocks, is easily the winner. Its mean final cash, slightly more than $153,000 in today's dollars, is much greater than the means for the other two sets of weights. The first simulation also has a *much* larger upside potential (its 95th percentile is close to $360,000), and even its downside is slightly better than the others: Its 5th percentile is the best, and its minimum is only slightly worse than the minimum for the other sets of weights.

Figure 16.21
Summary Results for Retirement Simulation

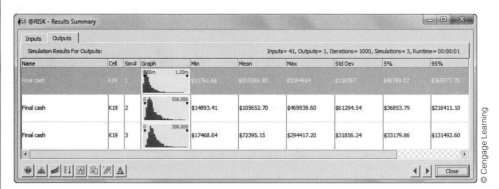

Nevertheless, the histogram for simulation 1 (put 80% in stocks), shown in Figure 16.22, indicates a lot of variability—and skewness—in the distribution of final cash. As in

Figure 16.22
Histogram of Final Cash with 80% in Stocks

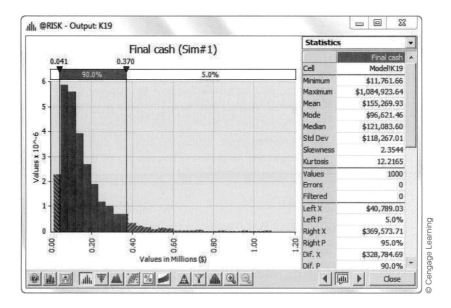

Example 16.4, the concept of value at risk (VaR) is useful. Recall that VaR 5% is defined as the 5th percentile of a distribution and is often the value investors worry about. Perhaps Sally should rerun the simulation with different investment weights, with an eye on the weights that increase her VaR 5%. Right now it is slightly more than $40,000—not too good considering that she invests $40,000 total. She might not like the prospect of a 5% chance of ending up with no more than this. We also encourage you to try running this simulation with other investment weights, both for the 40-year horizon and (after modifying the spreadsheet model slightly) for shorter time horizons such as 10 or 15 years. Even though the stock strategy appears to be best for a long horizon, it is not necessarily guaranteed to dominate for a shorter time horizon. ∎

PROBLEMS

Level A

8. Rerun the new car simulation from Example 16.4, but now introduce uncertainty into the fixed development cost. Let it be triangularly distributed with parameters $600 million, $650million, and $850 million. (You can check that the mean of this distribution is $700 million, the same as the cost given in the example.) Comment on the differences between your output and those in the example. Would you say these differences are important for the company?

9. Rerun the new car simulation from Example 16.4, but now use the RISKSIMTABLE function appropriately to simulate discount rates of 5%, 7.5%, 10%, 12.5%, and 15%. Comment on how the outputs change as the discount rate decreases from the value used in the example, 10%.

10. In the cash balance model from Example 16.5, the timing is such that some receipts are delayed by one or two months, and the payments for materials and labor must be made a month in advance. Change the model so that all receipts are received immediately, and payments made this month for materials and labor are 80% of sales *this* month (not next month). The period of interest is again January through June. Rerun the simulation, and comment on any differences between your outputs and those from the example.

11. In the cash balance model from Example 16.5, is the $250,000 minimum cash balance requirement really "costing" the company very much? Answer this by rerunning the simulation with minimum required cash balances of $50,000, $100,000, $150,000, and $200,000. Use the RISKSIMTABLE function to run all simulations at once. Comment on the outputs from these simulations. In particular, comment on whether the company appears to be better off with a lower minimum cash balance.

12. Run the retirement model from Example 16.6 with a damping factor of 1.0 (instead of 0.98), again using the same three sets of investment weights. Explain in words what it means, in terms of the simulation, to have a damping factor of 1. Then comment on the differences, if any, between your simulation results and those in the example.

13. The simulation output from Example 16.6 indicates that an investment heavy in stocks produces the best results. Would it be better to invest *entirely* in stocks? Answer this by rerunning the simulation. Is there any apparent downside to this strategy?

14. Modify the model from Example 16.6 so that you use only the years 1975 to 2007 of historical data. Run the simulation for the same three sets of investment weights. Comment on whether your results differ in any important way from those in the example.

15. Referring to the retirement example in Example 16.6, rerun the model for a planning horizon of 10 years; 15 years; 25 years. For each, which set of investment weights maximizes the VaR 5% (the 5th percentile) of final cash in today's dollars? Does it appear that a portfolio heavy in stocks is better for long horizons but not for shorter horizons?

Level B

16. Change the new car simulation from Example 16.4 as follows. It is the same as before for years 1 through 5, including depreciation through year 5. However, the car might sell through year 10. Each year *after* year 5, the company examines sales. If fewer than 45,000 cars were sold that year, there is a 50% chance the car won't be sold after that year. Modify the model and run the simulation. Keep track of two outputs: NPV (through year 10) and the number of years of sales.

17. *Based on Kelly (1956).* You currently have $100. Each week you can invest any amount of money you currently have in a risky investment. With probability 0.4, the amount you invest is tripled (e.g., if you invest $100, you increase your asset position by $300), and,

with probability 0.6, the amount you invest is lost. Consider the following investment strategies:

- Each week, invest 10% of your money.
- Each week, invest 30% of your money.
- Each week, invest 50% of your money.

Use @RISK to simulate 100 weeks of each strategy 1000 times. Which strategy appears to be best in terms of the maximum growth rate? (In general, if you can multiply your investment by M with probability p and lose your investment with probability $q = 1 - p$, you should invest a fraction $[p(M - 1) - q]/(M - 1)$ of your money each week. This strategy maximizes the expected growth rate of your fortune and is known as the *Kelly criterion*.) (*Hint*: If an initial wealth of I dollars grows to F dollars in 100 weeks, the weekly growth rate, labeled r, satisfies $F = (1 + r)^{100}*I$, so that $r = (F/I)^{1/100} - 1$.)

18. Amanda has 30 years to save for her retirement. At the beginning of each year, she puts $5000 into her retirement account. At any point in time, all of Amanda's retirement funds are tied up in the stock market. Suppose the annual return on stocks follows a normal distribution with mean 12% and standard deviation 25%. What is the probability that at the end of 30 years, Amanda will have reached her goal of having $1,000,000 for retirement? Assume that if Amanda reaches her goal *before* 30 years, she will stop investing. (*Hint*: Each year you should keep track of Amanda's beginning cash position—for year 1, this is $5000—and Amanda's ending cash position. Of course, Amanda's ending cash position for a given year is a function of her beginning cash position and the return on stocks for that year. To estimate the probability that Amanda meets her goal, use an IF statement that returns 1 if she meets her goal and 0 otherwise.)

19. In the financial world, there are many types of complex instruments called derivatives that *derive* their value from the value of an underlying asset. Consider the following simple derivative. A stock's current price is $80 per share. You purchase a derivative whose value to you becomes known a month from now. Specifically, let P be the price of the stock in a month. If P is between $75 and $85, the

derivative is worth nothing to you. If P is less than $75, the derivative results in a loss of $100*(75 - P)$ dollars to you. (The factor of 100 is because many derivatives involve 100 shares.) If P is greater than $85, the derivative results in a gain of $100*(P - 85)$ dollars to you. Assume that the distribution of the change in the stock price from now to a month from now is normally distributed with mean $1 and standard deviation $8. Let EMV be the expected gain/loss from this derivative. It is a weighted average of all the possible losses and gains, weighted by their likelihoods. (Of course, any loss should be expressed as a negative number. For example, a loss of $1500 should be expressed as -$1500.) Unfortunately, this is a difficult probability calculation, but EMV can be estimated by an @RISK simulation. Perform this simulation with at least 1000 iterations. What is your best estimate of EMV?

20. Suppose you currently have a portfolio of three stocks, A, B, and C. You own 500 shares of A, 300 of B, and 1000 of C. The current share prices are $42.76, $81.33, and $58.22, respectively. You plan to hold this portfolio for at least a year. During the coming year, economists have predicted that the national economy will be awful, stable, or great with probabilities 0.2, 0.5, and 0.3, respectively. Given the state of the economy, the returns (one-year percentage changes) of the three stocks are independent and normally distributed. However, the means and standard deviations of these returns depend on the state of the economy, as indicated in the file **P16_20.xlsx**.

   a. Use @RISK to simulate the value of the portfolio and the portfolio return in the next year. How likely is it that you will have a negative return? How likely is it that you will have a return of at least 25%?

   b. Suppose you had a crystal ball where you could predict the state of the economy with certainty. The stock returns would still be uncertain, but you would know whether your means and standard deviations come from row 6, 7, or 8 of the file **P16_20.xlsx**. If you learn, with certainty, that the economy is going to be *great* in the next year, run the appropriate simulation to answer the same questions as in part **a**. Repeat this if you learn that the economy is going to be *awful*. How do these results compare with those in part **a**?

16-4 MARKETING MODELS

There are plenty of opportunities for marketing departments to use simulation. They face uncertainty in the brand-switching behavior of customers, the entry of new brands into the market, customer preferences for different attributes of products, the effects of advertising on sales, and so on. We examine some interesting marketing applications of simulation in this section.

16-4a Models of Customer Loyalty

What is a loyal customer worth to a company? This is an extremely important question for companies. (It is an important part of customer relationship management, or CRM, currently one of the hottest topics in marketing.) Companies know that if customers become dissatisfied with the company's product, they are likely to switch and never return. Marketers refer to this customer loss as **churn**. The loss in profit from churn can be large, particularly because long-standing customers tend to be more profitable in any given year than new customers. Example 16.7 uses a reasonable model of customer loyalty and simulation to estimate the worth of a customer to a company. It is based on the excellent discussion of customer loyalty in Reichheld (1996).

EXAMPLE | 16.7 THE LONG-TERM VALUE OF A CUSTOMER AT CCAMERICA

CCAmerica is a credit card company that does its best to gain customers and keep their business in a highly competitive industry. The first year a customer signs up for service typically results in a loss to the company because of various administrative expenses. However, after the first year, the profit from a customer is typically positive, and this profit tends to increase through the years. The company has estimated the mean profit from a typical customer to be as shown in column B of Figure 16.23. (See the file **Customer Loyalty.xlsx**.) For example, the company expects to lose $40 in the customer's first year but to gain $87 in the fifth year—provided that the customer stays loyal that long. For modeling purposes, we assume that the *actual* profit from a customer in the customer's *n*th year of service is *normally* distributed with mean shown in Figure 16.23 and standard deviation equal to 10% of the mean. At the end of each year, the customer leaves the company, never to return, with probability 0.15, the *churn rate*. Alternatively, the customer

Figure 16.23

Mean Profit as a Function of Years as Customer

	A	B
10	Year	Mean Profit(if still here)
11	1	−40.00
12	2	66.00
13	3	72.00
14	4	79.00
15	5	87.00
16	6	92.00
17	7	96.00
18	8	99.00
19	9	103.00
20	10	106.00
21	11	111.00
22	12	116.00
23	13	120.00
24	14	124.00
25	15	130.00
26	16	137.00
27	17	142.00
28	18	148.00
29	19	155.00
30	20	161.00
39	29	161.00
40	30	161.00

© Cengage Learning

stays with probability 0.85, the *retention rate*. The company wants to estimate the NPV of the net profit from any such customer who has just signed up for service at the beginning of year 1, at a discount rate of 15%, assuming that the cash flow occurs in the middle of the year.[3] It also wants to see how sensitive this NPV is to the retention rate.

Objective   To use simulation to find the NPV of a customer and to see how this varies with the retention rate.

Where Do the Numbers Come From?

The numbers in Figure 16.23 are undoubtedly averages, based on the historical records of many customers. To build in randomness for any *particular* customer, we need a probability distribution around the numbers in this figure. We arbitrarily chose a normal distribution centered on the historical average and a standard deviation of 10% of the average. These are educated guesses. Finally, the churn rate is a number very familiar to marketing people, and it can also be estimated from historical customer data.

Solution

The idea is to keep simulating profits (or a loss in the first year) for the customer until the customer churns. We simulate 30 years of potential profits, but this could be varied.

Developing the Simulation Model

Customer Loyalty Model

The simulation model appears in Figure 16.24. It can be developed with the following steps.

1. **Inputs.** Enter the inputs in the blue cells.

2. **Retention rate.** Although an 85% retention rate was given in the statement of the problem, it is useful to investigate retention rates from 75% to 95%, as shown in column D. To run a separate simulation for each of these, enter the formula

   =RISKSIMTABLE(D4:D8)

   in cell B4.

Figure 16.24   Customer Loyalty Model

	A	B	C	D	E	F	G	H	I	J
1	Customer loyalty model in the credit card industry									
2										
3	Inputs			Retention rates to try						
4	Retention rate	0.75		0.75	0.80	0.85	0.90	0.95		
5	Discount rate	0.15								
6	Stdev % of mean	10%								
7										
8										
9	Estimated means			Simulation			Outputs			
10	Year	Mean Profit (if still here)	Quits at end of year?	Actual profit	Discounted profit		NPV	$76.13		
11	1	−40.00	No	−37.87	−35.32		Years loyal	3		
12	2	66.00	No	68.56	55.59					
13	3	72.00	Yes	79.22	55.86		Means			
14	4	79.00		0.00	0.00		Simulation	Retention rate	NPV	Years loyal
15	5	87.00		0.00	0.00		1	0.75	$97.29	3.99
16	6	92.00		0.00	0.00		2	0.80	$136.75	5.08
17	7	96.00		0.00	0.00		3	0.85	$179.30	6.61
18	8	99.00		0.00	0.00		4	0.90	$242.51	9.33
19	9	103.00		0.00	0.00		5	0.95	$369.72	16.18
20	10	106.00		0.00	0.00					
21	11	111.00		0.00	0.00					
38	28	161.00		0.00	0.00					
39	29	161.00		0.00	0.00					
40	30	161.00		0.00	0.00					

© Cengage Learning

---

[3]This assumption makes the NPV calculation slightly more complex, but it is probably more realistic than the usual assumption that cash flows occur at the *ends* of the years.

As usual, Excel's RAND function can be used inside an IF statement to determine whether a given event occurs.

3. **Timing of churn.** In column C, use simulation to discover when the customer churns. This column will contain a sequence of No values, followed by a Yes, and then a sequence of blanks (or all No values if the customer never churns). To generate these, enter the formulas

=IF(RAND()<1−B4,"Yes","No")

and

=IF(OR(C11="",C11="Yes"),"",IF(RAND()<1−$B$4,"Yes","No"))

in cells C11 and C12, and copy the latter formula down column C. Study these formulas carefully to see how the logic works. Note that they do not rely on @RISK functions. Excel's RAND function can be used any time you want to simulate whether or not an event occurs.

Careful discounting is required if cash flows occur in the middle of a year.

4. **Actual and discounted profits.** Profits (or a loss in the first year) occur as long as there is not a blank in column C. Therefore, simulate the actual profits by entering the formula

=IF(C11<>"",RISKNORMAL(B11,$B$6*ABS(B11)),0)

in cell D11 and copying it down. (The absolute value function, ABS, is required in case any of the cash flows are negative. A normal distribution cannot have a *negative* standard deviation.) Then discount these appropriately in column E by entering the formula

=D11/(1+$B$5)^(A11−0.5)

in cell E11 and copying it down. Note how the exponent of the denominator accounts for the cash flow in the *middle* of the year.

5. **Outputs.** Keep track of two outputs, the total NPV and the number of years the customer stays with the company. Calculate the NPV in cell H10 by summing the discounted values in column E. (They have already been discounted, so the NPV function is not needed.) To find the number of years the customer is loyal, count the number of No values plus the number of Yes values, that is, all nonblanks. Calculate this in cell H11 with the formula

=COUNTIF(C11:C40,"No")+COUNTIF(C11:C40,"Yes")

Finally, designate both of cells H10 and H11 as @RISK output cells.

Running the Simulation

Set the number of iterations to 1000 and the number of simulations to 5 (one for each potential retention rate). Then run the simulation as usual. (Actually, we ran 5000 iterations for each simulation, just to get more stable results.)

Discussion of the Simulation Results

Varying the retention rate can have a large impact on the value of a customer.

Summary results for all five retention rates and the histogram for an 85% retention rate appear in Figures 16.25 and 16.26. The histogram indicates that there is a 15.9% chance that the NPV will be negative, whereas the chance that it will be above $300 is 25.5%. You can also see from the summary measures that the mean NPV and the mean number of years loyal are quite sensitive to the retention rate.

To follow up on this observation, you can use the RISKMEAN function to capture the means in columns I and J of the model sheet and then create a line chart of them as a function of the retention rate. (See Figure 16.27.) This line chart shows the rather dramatic effect the retention rate can have on the value of a customer. For example, if it increases from the current 85% to 90%, the mean NPV increases by about 35%. If it increases from

Figure 16.25

Summary Results for Customer Loyalty Model

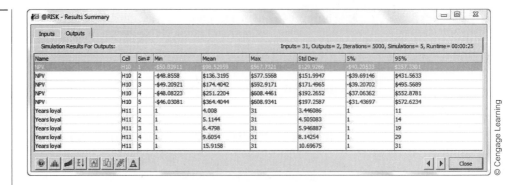

Name	Cell	Sim#	Min	Mean	Max	Std Dev	5%	95%
NPV	H10	1	-$50.83911	$98.52959	$567.7321	$129.9266	-$40.20533	$357.3301
NPV	H10	2	-$48.8558	$136.3195	$577.5568	$151.9947	-$39.69146	$431.5633
NPV	H10	3	-$49.20921	$174.4042	$592.9171	$171.4965	-$39.20702	$495.5689
NPV	H10	4	-$48.08223	$251.2204	$608.4461	$192.2652	-$37.06362	$552.8781
NPV	H10	5	-$46.03081	$364.4044	$608.9341	$197.2587	-$31.43697	$572.6234
Years loyal	H11	1	1	4.008	31	3.446086	1	11
Years loyal	H11	2	1	5.1144	31	4.505083	1	14
Years loyal	H11	3	1	6.4798	31	5.946887	1	19
Years loyal	H11	4	1	9.6054	31	8.14254	1	29
Years loyal	H11	5	1	15.9158	31	10.69675	1	31

Figure 16.26

Histogram of NPV for an 85% Retention Rate

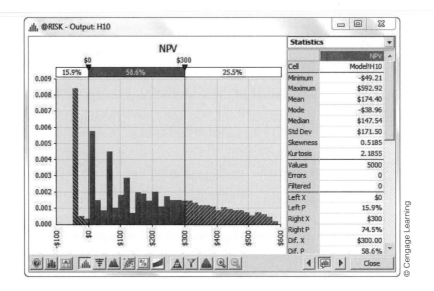

Figure 16.27

Sensitivity of Outputs to the Retention Rate

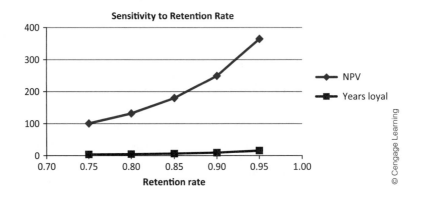

85% to 95%, the mean NPV increases by about 97%. In the other direction, if the retention rate decreases from 85% to 80%, the mean NPV decreases by about 30%. This is why credit card companies are so anxious to keep their customers. ∎

Example 16.8 is a variation of the previous example. We now investigate the effect of offering a customer an incentive to remain loyal.

16.8 THE VALUE OF A FREE MAINTENANCE AGREEMENT

Companies value loyal customers, and they sometimes go to great lengths to keep their customers loyal. This example investigates whether one such plan is worth its cost. We consider a nationwide company called Jamesons, which sells electronic appliances. Specifically, we will focus on sales of DVD players. To attract customers, the company is considering giving customers a free maintenance agreement with each purchase of a DVD player. The unit profit without free maintenance is currently $20. The company believes this will decrease to $16 with free maintenance. Their thinking is that about 4% of customers will actually use the free maintenance, and for each such customer, the company will lose about $100. Hence the average decrease in profit per purchaser is about $4.

Prior to this year, 50,000 customers were loyal to Jamesons and 100,000 customers were loyal to their competitors. (Loyalty is defined in terms of where the customer bought his or her last DVD player.) There are a number of uncertain quantities, and we assume they are all triangularly distributed. Their parameters (minimum, most likely, and maximum) are as follows. (1) The percentage of the 150,000 customers who purchase a DVD player in any given year has parameters 20%, 25%, and 40%. (2) The annual percentage change in unit profit has parameters 3%, 5%, and 6%. (3) In any year, the percentage of Jamesons' loyal customers who remain loyal has parameters 56%, 60%, and 66% if there is no free maintenance, and they increase to 60%, 64%, and 70% with free maintenance. (4) Similarly, the percentage of the competitors' loyal customers who switch to Jamesons has parameters 27%, 30%, and 34% if there is no free maintenance, and they increase to 32%, 35%, and 39% with free maintenance. These inputs are listed in the file **Free Maintenance.xlsx** and are shown in Figure 16.28.

Figure 16.28 Inputs for Free Maintenance Example

	A	B	C	D	E	F	G	H	I	J	K	L
1	Free maintenance agreement - is it worth it?											
2												
3	Common inputs					Inputs that depend on policy						
4	Loyal customers in previous year						Not free	Free				
5	To our brand	50000				Unit profit	$20	$16				
6	To their brand	100000										
7						% of our loyal customers who remain loyal (triangular distribution)						
8	% of potential customers who purchase in any year (triangular distribution)					Minimum	56%	60%				
9	Minimum	20%				Most likely	60%	64%				
10	Most likely	25%				Maximum	66%	70%				
11	Maximum	40%										
12						% of their loyal customers who switch to us (triangular distribution)						
13	Annual % growth in profit contribution (triangular distribution)					Minimum	27%	32%				
14	Minimum	3%				Most likely	30%	35%				
15	Most likely	5%				Maximum	34%	39%				
16	Maximum	6%										
17												
18	Discount rate	10%										

Jamesons is hoping that the decrease in unit profit from the free maintenance agreement will be more than offset by the higher loyalty percentages. Using a 15-year planning horizon, does the NPV of profits with a 10% discount rate confirm the company's hopes?

Objective   To use simulation to see whether it makes sense for Jamesons to give a free maintenance agreement to DVD player purchasers.

Where Do the Numbers Come From?

In the previous example, we discussed the switching rates, which would be estimated from extensive customer data. The other data in the problem statement are straightforward to obtain.

Solution

The solution strategy is to compare two simulations, one without free maintenance and one with it. Because they are so similar, you can use RISKSIMTABLE to run both simulations. We make one assumption that is common in marketing but might not be intuitive. We assume that only *purchasers* in a given year have any chance of switching loyalty in the next year. For example, if a customer is loyal to Jamesons and doesn't purchase a DVD player in a given year, this customer is automatically loyal to Jamesons in the next year.

Developing the Simulation Model

Free Maintenance Agreement Model

The completed simulation model appears in Figure 16.29. (Again, see the first finished version of the file **Free Maintenance.xlsx**.) It can be developed with the following steps.

Figure 16.29 Free Maintenance Simulation Model

	A	B	C	D	E	F	G	H	I	J	K	L	M	N	O	P	Q
20	Simulation																
21	Index of simulation	1															
22																	
23	Year	0	1	2	3	4	5	6	7	8	9	10	11	12	13	14	15
24	% loyal to us who purchase	38.3%	25.6%	27.1%	28.7%	28.7%	25.0%	27.3%	25.1%	23.3%	27.8%	25.2%	26.6%	33.9%	39.2%	23.8%	27.6%
25	% loyal to them who purchase	31.5%	22.3%	34.5%	31.7%	24.5%	24.1%	35.5%	27.1%	24.5%	32.7%	22.1%	28.0%	35.8%	26.9%	34.2%	28.5%
26	% who stay loyal to us		62.0%	65.2%	63.5%	60.6%	57.1%	59.6%	62.7%	62.1%	60.5%	60.7%	60.0%	65.4%	57.3%	63.3%	62.5%
27	% who switch loyalty to us		29.9%	28.9%	30.7%	27.7%	28.6%	29.3%	27.8%	29.8%	30.1%	30.8%	31.8%	30.8%	32.7%	32.9%	31.8%
28	Customers loyal to us	50000	52152	53813	58706	60075	58982	59451	62353	63505	64049	65723	65029	66380	66572	64391	67964
29	Customers loyal to them	100000	97848	96187	91294	89925	91018	90549	87647	86495	85951	84277	84971	83620	83428	85609	82036
30	Purchases of our product		13376	14566	16853	17239	14766	16213	15624	14800	17781	16549	17269	22520	26128	15348	18781
31	% change in unit profit			4.70%	3.87%	3.82%	4.56%	4.83%	5.01%	4.78%	5.78%	4.05%	5.14%	4.87%	4.73%	4.79%	4.62%
32	Unit profit		$20.00	$20.94	$21.75	$22.58	$23.61	$24.75	$25.99	$27.24	$28.81	$29.98	$31.52	$33.06	$34.62	$36.28	$37.96
33	Profit contribution		$267,525	$305,020	$366,531	$389,279	$348,649	$401,308	$406,096	$403,103	$512,298	$496,126	$544,329	$744,457	$904,563	$556,793	$712,849
34																	
35	NPV	$3,291,826															

© Cengage Learning

1. **Inputs.** Enter the given data in the blue cells.
2. **Maintenance decision.** The current "no free maintenance" policy is labeled simulation #1 and the proposed "free maintenance" policy is labeled simulation #2, so enter the formula

   =RISKSIMTABLE({1,2})

   in cell B21.
3. **Percentages who purchase.** We assume that each year a random percentage of Jamesons' loyal customers and a random percentage of the competitors' loyal customers purchase a DVD player. Each of these is generated from the triangular distribution in rows 9–11 (see Figure 16.28), so enter the formula

   =RISKTRIANG($B$9,$B$10,$B$11)

   in the range B24:Q25.
4. **Percentage who stay or become loyal.** Each year a random percentage of the customers previously loyal to Jamesons remain loyal, and a random percentage of the competitors' previously loyal customers switch loyalty to Jamesons. Also, the distributions of these random percentages depend on the company's maintenance policy. Therefore, enter the formula

   =IF($B$21=1,RISKTRIANG($G$8,$G$9,$G$10),RISKTRIANG($H$8,$H$9,$H$10))

   in cell C26, enter the formula

=IF($B$21=1,RISKTRIANG($G$13,$G$14,$G$15),RISKTRIANG($H$13,$H$14,$H$15))

in cell C27, and copy these across their rows.

5. **Numbers of loyal customers.** Create links to cells B5 and B6 in cells B28 and B29. Then, remembering that only *purchasers* in a given year can switch loyalty, calculate the number of customers loyal to Jamesons in year 1 with the formula

=B28*((1-B24)+B24*C26)+B29*B25*C27

in cell C28 and copy it across row 28. Similarly, calculate the number of customers loyal to the competitors in year 1 with the formula

=B29*((1-B25)+B25*(1-C27))+B28*B24*(1-C26)

in cell C29 and copy it across row 29. These are basic bookkeeping formulas. Jamesons' loyal customers are those who (1) were loyal and didn't purchase, (2) were loyal, purchased, and stayed loyal, and (3) weren't loyal, purchased, and switched loyalty. Similar logic holds for the competitors' loyal customers.

6. **Purchasers at Jamesons.** Calculate the number of purchasers at Jamesons in year 1 with the formula

=C24*C28

in cell C30 and copy it across row 30.

7. **Monetary outcomes.** These are straightforward. Start by entering the formula

=IF($B$21=1,G5,H5)

for unit profit in year 1 in cell C32. Then enter the formulas

=RISKTRIANG($B$14,$B$15,$B$16)

=C32*(1+D31)

and

=C32*C30

in cells D31, D32, and C33, respectively, and copy them across their rows. Finally, calculate the NPV with the formula

=NPV(B18,C33:Q33)

in cell B35, and designate this as an @RISK output cell.

Running the Simulation

Set up @RISK to run 1000 iterations and 2 simulations, one for each maintenance decision to be tested. Then run the simulation as usual.

Discussion of the Simulation Results

The summary measures for the two simulations appear in Figure 16.30. Using the current inputs, the free maintenance initiative does not look good. Every measure, except possibly the

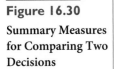

Figure 16.30

Summary Measures for Comparing Two Decisions

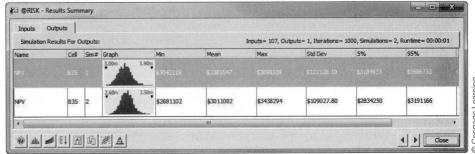

© Cengage Learning

standard deviation, is worse with the free maintenance agreement than without it. Evidently, the increase in loyal customers does *not* compensate for the decrease in unit profit. If Jamesons is reasonably confident about the inputs for this model, it should scrap the free maintenance idea. However, it might want to perform some sensitivity analysis on the decrease in unit profit or the increase in loyalty percentages (or both) to see when the free maintenance agreement starts looking attractive. We tried two possibilities. First, if the decrease in unit profit is only $2, not $4, and everything else remains the same, the two mean NPVs are very close, so the free maintenance agreement might be worth trying. Second, if the decrease in unit profit remains at $4, but all of the input percentages in the ranges H8:H10 and H13:H15 increase by five percentage points, the mean NPV with the free maintenance agreement is still considerably lower than the mean NPV without it. Evidently, the company can't take this big a hit in its profit margin unless it can convince a *lot* more customers to stay or become loyal.

There is an interesting modeling issue in this example. For each of the random quantities, we have generated a new random value each year. Would it be better to generate one random number from each triangular distribution and use it for each year? Would it make a difference in the results? The modified simulation appears in Figure 16.31. (You can see the details in the second finished version of the **Free Maintenance.xlsx** file.) The only random quantities are in rows 22–26. As is evident in the rows below them, these random numbers are used for each of the years. The summary measures from this simulation appear in Figure 16.32. If we are interested in comparing the *mean* NPV with no free maintenance versus free maintenance, we get about the same comparison in either model. The main difference between Figures 16.30 and 16.32 is the variability. Are you surprised that the models with more random numbers in Figure 16.30 have much smaller standard deviations than those in Figure 16.32? Evidently, there is an averaging effect. When different random numbers are used for each year, the highs and lows tend to cancel out, resulting in lower variability in NPV.

Figure 16.31   Modified Simulation Model

	A	B	C	D	E	F	G	H	I	J	K	L	M	N	O	P	Q
20	Simulation																
21	Index of simulation	1															
22	% loyal to us who purchase each year	24.8%															
23	% not loyal to us who purchase each year	25.4%															
24	% growth each year	4.4%															
25	% who stay loyal each year	58.5%	63.6%														
26	% who switch to us each year	30.8%	35.2%														
27																	
28	Year	0	1	2	3	4	5	6	7	8	9	10	11	12	13	14	15
29	% loyal to us who purchase	24.8%	24.8%	24.8%	24.8%	24.8%	24.8%	24.8%	24.8%	24.8%	24.8%	24.8%	24.8%	24.8%	24.8%	24.8%	24.8%
30	% loyal to them who purchase	25.4%	25.4%	25.4%	25.4%	25.4%	25.4%	25.4%	25.4%	25.4%	25.4%	25.4%	25.4%	25.4%	25.4%	25.4%	25.4%
31	% who stay loyal to us		58.5%	58.5%	58.5%	58.5%	58.5%	58.5%	58.5%	58.5%	58.5%	58.5%	58.5%	58.5%	58.5%	58.5%	58.5%
32	% who switch loyalty to us		30.8%	30.8%	30.8%	30.8%	30.8%	30.8%	30.8%	30.8%	30.8%	30.8%	30.8%	30.8%	30.8%	30.8%	30.8%
33	Customers loyal to us	50000	52666	54847	56634	58096	59292	60272	61074	61730	62268	62708	63068	63363	63604	63801	63963
34	Customers loyal to them	100000	97334	95153	93366	91904	90708	89728	88926	88270	87732	87292	86932	86637	86396	86199	86037
35	Purchases of our product		13080	13622	14066	14429	14726	14969	15169	15332	15465	15574	15664	15737	15797	15846	15886
36	% change in unit profit		4.41%	4.41%	4.41%	4.41%	4.41%	4.41%	4.41%	4.41%	4.41%	4.41%	4.41%	4.41%	4.41%	4.41%	4.41%
37	Unit profit		$20.00	$20.88	$21.80	$22.76	$23.77	$24.82	$25.91	$27.06	$28.25	$29.49	$30.80	$32.15	$33.57	$35.05	$36.60
38	Profit contribution		$261,605	$284,460	$306,679	$328,472	$350,026	$371,503	$393,050	$414,798	$436,864	$459,356	$482,371	$506,001	$530,332	$555,443	$581,412
39																	
40	NPV	$2,881,662															

© Cengage Learning

Figure 16.32

Summary Results for Modified Model

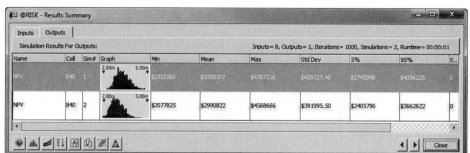

© Cengage Learning

Regardless of which version is more realistic (and an argument can be made for either), an advantage of the model with only a few random numbers is that you can use @ RISK's tornado chart to see which source of randomness has the most effect on NPV. This tornado chart appears in Figure 16.33. (It is for simulation #2 with free maintenance agreement, but the chart for simulation #1 is virtually the same.) Perhaps surprisingly, it is not the switching behavior that drives NPV; it is driven more by the percentage of customers who purchase. As this example illustrates, it is sometimes an advantage to keep the models simple. Key insights are then more apparent than when there is more complexity. ∎

Figure 16.33
Tornado Chart
for NPV

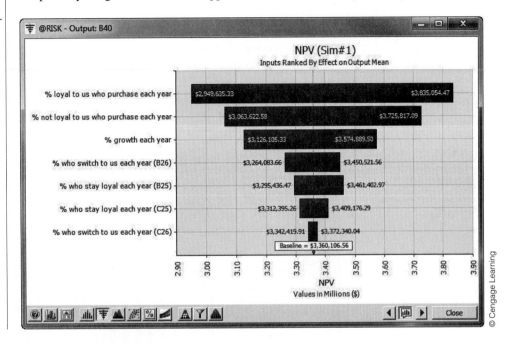

© Cengage Learning

16-4b Marketing and Sales Models

We conclude this marketing section with a model of marketing and selling condos. The main issue is the timing of sales, and we demonstrate how a deterministic model of this timing can provide very misleading results.

EXAMPLE | **16.9 MARKETING AND SELLING CONDOS**

Blackstone Development Company has just finished building 120 high-end condos, each priced at $300,000. Blackstone has hired another company, Pletcher Marketing, to market and sell these condos. Pletcher will incur all of the marketing and maintenance costs, assumed to be $800 per unsold condo per month, and it will receive a 10% commission ($30,000) from Blackstone at the time of each condo sale. Because Blackstone wants these condos to be sold in a timely manner, it has offered Pletcher a $200,000 bonus at the end of the first year if at least half of the condos have been sold, and an extra $500,000 bonus at the end of the second year if all of the condos have been sold. Pletcher estimates that it can sell five condos per month on average, so that it should be able to collect the bonuses. However, Pletcher also realizes that there is uncertainty about the number of sales per month. How should this uncertainty be modeled, and will the resulting simulation model give different qualitative results than a deterministic model where exactly five condos are sold per month?

Objective To develop a simulation model that allows us to see how the uncertain timing affects the monetary outcomes for Pletcher, and to compare this simulation model to a deterministic model with no uncertainty about the timing of sales.

Where Do the Numbers Come From?

The inputs are straightforward from Blackstone's agreement with Pletcher. The only difficulty is determining an appropriate probability model for the timing of sales, which we discuss next.

Solution

To make a fair comparison between a deterministic model with five sales per month and a simulation model with uncertainty in the timing of sales, we need a discrete distribution for monthly sales that has mean 5. One attractive possibility is to use the Poisson distribution discussed briefly in Chapter 5. It is discrete, and it has only one parameter, the mean. The Poisson distribution has one theoretical drawback in that it allows *all* nonnegative integers to occur, but this has no practical effect. As shown in Figure 16.34, the Poisson distribution with mean 5 has virtually no probability of values larger than, say, 15.

Figure 16.34

Poisson Distribution with Mean 5

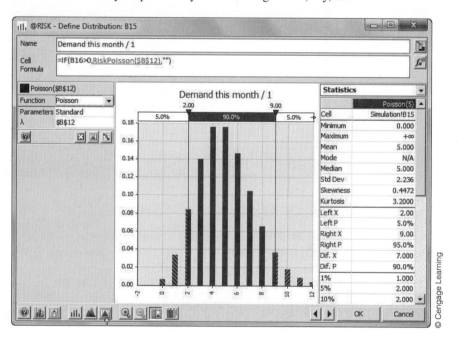

© Cengage Learning

Developing the Simulation Model

Selling Condos Model

The deterministic model is very straightforward and is not shown here. By selling a *sure* five condos per month, Pletcher sells all condos by the end of year 2, receives both bonuses, and realizes an NPV (including bonuses) of $2,824,333. However, this is not very realistic. The steps for creating a more realistic simulation model follow. (See Figure 16.35, with several hidden columns, and the file **Selling Condos.xlsx**.) Note that because of the uncertain timing of sales, we cannot say when all 120 condos will be sold. It could be before 24 months or well after 24 months. Therefore, we model it through 40 months. By experimenting, we found that all 120 condos will almost surely be sold in 40 months.

1. **Inputs.** Enter the inputs in the blue ranges.
2. **Random demands.** Generate the random demands for condos (the number of people who would like to buy) by entering the formula

Figure 16.35 Condo Selling Simulation Model

	A	B	C	D	E	F	AK	AL	AM	AN	AO
1	**Marketing and selling condos**										
2											
3	Number to sell	120									
4	Monthly marketing, maintenance cost	$800									
5	Commission per condo sale	$30,000									
6	Bonus if at least half sold in year 1	$200,000									
7	Extra bonus if all sold in 2 years	$500,000									
8	Discount rate (monthly)	0.8%									
9											
10	**Simulation model**										
11	Distribution of demand for condos each month (Poisson distributed)										
12	Mean demand per month	5									
13											
14	Month	1	2	3	4	5	36	37	38	39	40
15	Demand this month	6	2	7	3	7					
16	Number remaining to be sold	120	114	112	105	102	0	0	0	0	0
17	Number sold this month	6	2	7	3	7					
18	Maintenance cost	$91,200	$89,600	$84,000	$81,600	$76,000					
19	Revenue from sales	$180,000	$60,000	$210,000	$90,000	$210,000					
20	Bonus at end of year 1										
21	Bonus at end of year 2										
22	Net revenue	$88,800	($29,600)	$126,000	$8,400	$134,000					
23											
24	Months to sell out	23									
25	Total bonus	$500,000									
26	NPV	$2,203,928									

=IF(B16>0,RISKPOISSON($B$12),"")

in cell B15 and copying across to month 40. The IF function checks whether there are still any condos available in that month. If there aren't, a blank is recorded. Similar logic appears in many of the other formulas.

3. **Number remaining and sold.** In cell B16, enter a link to cell B3. In cell B17, find the number sold as the minimum of supply and demand with the formula

=IF(B16>0,MIN(B16,B15),"")

In cell C16, find the number remaining to be sold with the formula

=IF(B16>0,B16-B17,0)

Then copy the formulas in cells C16 and B17 across. Note that a 0, not a blank, is recorded in row 16 after all condos have been sold. This makes all the other IF functions work correctly.

4. **Monetary values.** Enter the formulas

=IF(B16>0,$B$4*(B16-B17),"")

=IF(B16>0,$B$5*B17,"")

and

=IF(B16>0,SUM(B19:B21)-B18,"")

in cells B18, B19, and B22, and copy these across. For the bonuses, enter the formulas

=IF(SUM(B17:M17)>=B3/2,B6,0)

and

=IF(SUM(B17:Y17)=B3,B7,0)

in cells M20 and Y21. These capture the all-or-nothing nature of the bonuses.

5. **Outputs.** Three interesting outputs are the number of months required to sell out, the total bonus earned, and the NPV of the cash flows, including bonuses. Calculate these in cells B24–B26 with the formulas

=COUNTIF(B16:AO16,">0")

=M20+Y21

and

=NPV($B$8,B22:AO22)

Then designate them as @RISK output cells.

Running the Simulation

Set @RISK to run 1000 iterations for a single simulation. Then run the simulation in the usual way.

Discussion of the Simulation Results

Recall that the deterministic model sells out in 24 months, receives both bonuses, and achieves an NPV of about $2.82 million. As you might guess, the simulation model doesn't do this well. The main problem is that there is a fairly good chance that one or both bonuses will not be received. Distributions of the three outputs appear in Figures 16.36 through 16.38. Figure 16.36 shows that although 24 months is the *most likely* number of months to sell out, there was at least one scenario where it took only 19 months and another where it took 32 months. Figure 16.37 shows the four possibilities for bonuses: receive neither, receive one or the other, or receive both. Unfortunately for Pletcher, the first three

Figure 16.36

Distribution of Months to Sell Out

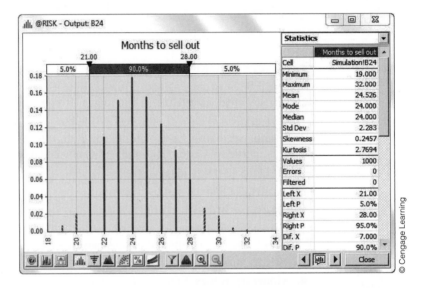

Figure 16.37

Distribution of Total Bonus Received

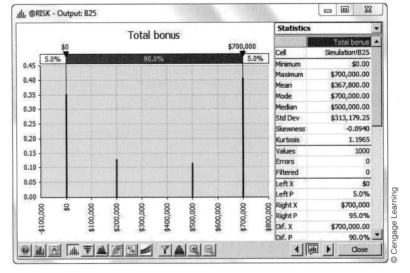

Figure 16.38

Distribution of NPV

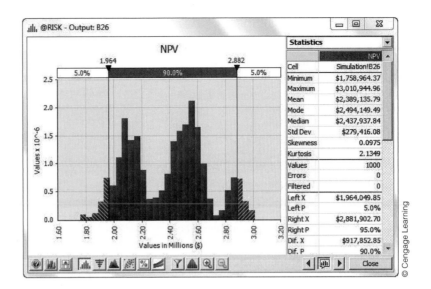

possibilities are fairly likely; the probability of receiving both bonuses is only about 0.41. Finally, the shape of the NPV distribution (Figure 16.38), with three separate peaks, is influenced heavily by the bonuses or lack of them. On average, the NPV is only about $2.39 million, *much* less than estimated by the deterministic model. This is still one more example—a dramatic one—of the flaw of averages. ∎

PROBLEMS

Level A

21. Suppose that Coke and Pepsi are fighting for the cola market. Each week each person in the market buys one case of Coke or Pepsi. If the person's last purchase was Coke, there is a 0.90 probability that this person's next purchase will be Coke; otherwise, it will be Pepsi. (You can assume that there are only two brands in the market.) Similarly, if the person's last purchase was Pepsi, there is a 0.80 probability that this person's next purchase will be Pepsi; otherwise, it will be Coke. Currently half of all people purchase Coke, and the other half purchase Pepsi. Simulate one year (52 weeks) of sales in the cola market and estimate each company's average weekly market share and each company's ending market share in week 52. Do this by assuming that the total market size is fixed at 100,000 customers. (*Hint*: Use the RISKBINOMIAL function. However, if your model requires more RISKBINOMIAL functions than the number allowed in the academic version of @RISK, remember that you can instead use the CRITBINOM function to generate binomially distributed random numbers. This takes the form **=CRITBINOM**(*ntrials*,*psuccess*,**RAND**()).)

22. Seas Beginning sells clothing by mail order. An important question is when to strike a customer from

the company's mailing list. At present, the company strikes a customer from its mailing list if a customer fails to order from six consecutive catalogs. The company wants to know whether striking a customer from its list after a customer fails to order from four consecutive catalogs results in a higher profit per customer. The following data are available:

- If a customer placed an order the last time she received a catalog, then there is a 20% chance she will order from the next catalog.

- If a customer last placed an order one catalog ago, there is a 16% chance she will order from the next catalog she receives.

- If a customer last placed an order two catalogs ago, there is a 12% chance she will order from the next catalog she receives.

- If a customer last placed an order three catalogs ago, there is an 8% chance she will order from the next catalog she receives.

- If a customer last placed an order four catalogs ago, there is a 4% chance she will order from the next catalog she receives.

- If a customer last placed an order five catalogs ago, there is a 2% chance she will order from the next catalog she receives.

It costs $2 to send a catalog, and the average profit per order is $30. Assume a customer has just placed an order. To maximize expected profit per customer, would Seas Beginning make more money canceling such a customer after six nonorders or four nonorders?

23. *Based on Babich (1992).* Suppose that each week each of 300 families buys a gallon of orange juice from company A, B, or C. Let p_A denote the probability that a gallon produced by company A is of unsatisfactory quality, and define p_B and p_C similarly for companies B and C. If the last gallon of juice purchased by a family is satisfactory, the next week they will purchase a gallon of juice from the same company. If the last gallon of juice purchased by a family is not satisfactory, the family will purchase a gallon from a competitor. Consider a week in which A families have purchased juice A, B families have purchased juice B, and C families have purchased juice C. Assume that families that switch brands during a period are allocated to the remaining brands in a manner that is proportional to the current market shares of the other brands. For example, if a customer switches from brand A, there is probability $B/(B + C)$ that he will switch to brand B and probability $C/(B + C)$ that he will switch to brand C. Suppose that the market is currently divided equally: 10,000 families for each of the three brands.

  a. After a year, what will the market share for each firm be? Assume $p_A = 0.10$, $p_B = 0.15$, and $p_C = 0.20$. (*Hint*: You will need to use the RISKBINOMIAL function to see how many people switch from A and then use the RISKBINOMIAL function again to see how many switch from A to B and from A to C. However, if your model requires more RISKBINOMIAL functions than the number allowed in the academic version of @RISK, remember that you can instead use the CRITBINOM function to generate binomially distributed random numbers. This takes the form =**CRITBINOM**(*ntrials*,*psuccess*,**RAND**()).)

  b. Suppose a 1% increase in market share is worth $10,000 per week to company A. Company A believes that for a cost of $1 million per year it can cut the percentage of unsatisfactory juice cartons in half. Is this worthwhile? (Use the same values of p_A, p_B, and p_C as in part **a.**)

Level B

24. The customer loyalty model in Example 16.7 assumes that once a customer leaves (becomes disloyal), that customer never becomes loyal again. Assume instead that there are two probabilities that drive the model, the retention rate and the *rejoin* rate, with values 0.75 and 0.15, respectively. The simulation should follow a customer who starts as a loyal customer in year 1. From then on, at the end of any year when the customer was loyal, this customer remains loyal for the next year with probability equal to the retention rate. But at the end of any year the customer is disloyal, this customer becomes loyal the next year with probability equal to the rejoin rate. During the customer's nth loyal year with the company, the company's mean profit from this customer is the nth value in the mean profit list in column B. Keep track of the same two outputs as in the example, and also keep track of the number of times the customer rejoins.

25. We are all aware of the fierce competition by mobile phone service companies to get our business. For example, AT&T is always trying to attract Verizon's customers, and vice versa. Some even give away prizes to entice us to sign up for a guaranteed length of time. This example is based on one such offer. We assume that a mobile provider named Syncit is willing to give a customer a free laptop computer, at a cost of $300 to Syncit, if the customer signs up for a guaranteed two years of service. During that time, the cost of service to the customer is a constant $60 per month, or $720 annually. After two years, we assume the cost of service increases by 2% annually. We assume that in any year after the guaranteed two years, the probability is 0.7 that the customer will stay with Syncit. This probability is the retention rate. We also assume that if a customer has switched to another mobile service, there is always a probability of 0.1 that the customer will (without any free laptop offer) willingly rejoin Syncit. The company wants to see whether this offer makes financial sense in terms of NPV, using a 10% discount rate. It also wants to see how the NPV varies with the retention rate. Simulate a 15-year time horizon, both with and without the free offer, to estimate the difference. (For the situation without the free offer, assume the customer has probability 0.5 of signing up with Syncit during year 1.)

26. Suppose that GLC earns a $2000 profit each time a person buys a car. We want to determine how the expected profit earned from a customer depends on the quality of GLC's cars. We assume a typical customer will purchase 10 cars during her lifetime. She will purchase a car now (year 1) and then purchase a car every five years—during year 6, year 11, and so on. For simplicity, we assume that Hundo is GLC's only competitor. We also assume that if the consumer is satisfied with the car she purchases, she will buy her next car from the same company, but if she is not satisfied, she will buy her next car from the other company. Hundo produces cars that satisfy 80% of its customers. Currently, GLC produces cars that also satisfy 80% of its customers. Consider a customer whose first car is a GLC car. If profits are discounted at 10% annually, use simulation to estimate the value of this customer to GLC. Also estimate the value of a customer to GLC if it can raise its customer satisfaction rating to 85%, to 90%, or to 95%. You can interpret the satisfaction value as the probability that a customer will not switch companies.

27. Mutron Company is thinking of marketing a new drug used to make pigs healthier. At the beginning of the current year, there are 1,000,000 pigs that could use the product. Each pig will use Mutron's drug or a competitor's drug once a year. The number of pigs is forecast to grow by an average of 5% per year. However, this growth rate is not a sure thing. Mutron assumes that each year's growth rate is an independent draw from a normal distribution, with probability 0.95 that the growth rate will be between 3% and 7%. Assuming it enters the market, Mutron is not sure what its share of the market will be during year 1, so it models this with a triangular distribution. Its worst-case share is 20%, its most likely share is 40%, and its best-case share is 70%. In the absence of any *new* competitors entering this market (in addition to itself), Mutron believes its market share will remain the same in succeeding years. However, there are three potential entrants (in addition to Mutron). At the beginning of each year, each entrant that has not already entered the market has a 40% chance of entering the market. The year after a competitor enters, Mutron's market share will drop by 20% for each *new* competitor who entered. For example, if two competitors enter the market in year 1, Mutron's market share in year 2 will be reduced by 40% from what it would have been with no entrants. Note that if all three entrants have entered, there will be no more entrants. Each unit of the drug sells for $2.20 and incurs a variable cost of $0.40. Profits are discounted by 10% annually.

   a. Assuming that Mutron enters the market, use simulation to find its NPV for the next 10 years from the drug.

   b. Again assuming that Mutron enters the market, it can be 95% certain that its *actual* NPV from the drug is between what two values?

16-5 SIMULATING GAMES OF CHANCE

We realize that this is a book about business applications. However, it is instructive (and fun) to see how simulation can be used to analyze games of chance, including sports contests. Indeed, many analysts refer to Monte Carlo simulation, and you can guess where that name comes from—the gambling casinos of Monte Carlo.

16-5a Simulating the Game of Craps

Most games of chance are great candidates for simulation because they are, by their very nature, driven by randomness. In this section, we examine one such game that is extremely popular in the gambling casinos: the game of craps. In its most basic form, craps is played as follows. A player rolls two dice and observes the sum of the two sides turned up. If this sum is 7 or 11, the player wins immediately. If the sum is 2, 3, or 12, the player loses immediately. Otherwise, if this sum is any other number (4, 5, 6, 8, 9, or 10), that number becomes the player's *point*. Then the dice are thrown repeatedly until the sum is the player's point or 7. In case the player's point occurs before a 7, the player wins. But if a 7 occurs before the point, the player loses. Example 16.10 uses simulation to determine the properties of this game.

EXAMPLE | 16.10 ESTIMATING THE PROBABILITY OF WINNING AT CRAPS

Joe Gamble loves to play craps at the casinos. He suspects that his chances of winning are less than fifty-fifty, but he wants to find the probability that he wins a single game of craps.

Objective To use simulation to find the probability of winning a single game of craps.

Where Do the Numbers Come From?

There are no input numbers here, only the rules of the game.

Solution

The simulation is of a single game. By running this simulation for many iterations, you can find the probability that Joe wins a single game of craps. If his intuition is correct (and surely it must be, or the casino could not stay in business), this probability is less than 0.5.

Developing the Simulation Model

The simulation model is for a single game. (See Figure 16.39 and the file **Craps.xlsx.**) There is a subtle problem here: The number of tosses of the dice necessary to determine the outcome of a single game is unknown. Theoretically, the game could continue forever, with the player waiting for his point or a 7. However, it is extremely unlikely that more than, say, 40 tosses are necessary in a single game. (This can be shown by a probability argument not presented here.) Therefore, you can simulate 40 tosses and use only those that are necessary to determine the outcome of a single game. The steps required are as follows.

Figure 16.39   Simulation of Craps Game

	A	B	C	D	E	F	G	H	I	J
1	Craps Simulation									
2										
3	Simulated tosses									
4	Toss	Die 1	Die 2	Sum	Win on this toss?	Lose on this toss?	Continue?		Summary results from simulation	
5	1	4	5	9	0	0	Yes		Win? (1 if yes, 0 if no)	1
6	2	5	5	10	0	0	Yes		Number of tosses	3
7	3	5	4	9	1	0	No			
8	4	2	1	3					Pr(winning)	1.000
9	5	1	1	2					Expected number of tosses	3.000
10	6	6	3	9						
11	7	6	3	9						
12	8	1	4	5						
13	9	5	1	6						
14	10	1	5	6						
41	37	6	3	9						
42	38	4	5	9						
43	39	3	2	5						
44	40	1	2	3						

---

1. **Simulate tosses.** Simulate the results of 40 tosses in the range B5:D44 by entering the formula

   =RANDBETWEEN(1,6)

   in cells B5 and C5 and the formula

   =SUM(B5:C5)

   in cell D5. Then copy these to the range B6:D44. (Recall that the RANDBETWEEN function was new in Excel 2007. It generates a random integer between the two specified values such that all values are equally likely, so it is perfect for tossing a die. You could also use @RISK's RISKINTUNIFORM function, which works exactly like RANDBETWEEN.)

   @RISK Function: RISKINTUNIFORM
   *The @RISK function RISKINTUNIFORM in the form **=RISKINTUNIFORM(N1,N2)** works exactly like Excel's RANDBETWEEN function.*

2. **First toss outcome.** Determine the outcome of the first toss with the formulas

   =IF(OR(D5=7,D5=11),1,0)

=IF(OR(D5=2,D5=3,D5=12),1,0)

and

=IF(AND(E5=0,F5=0),"Yes","No")

in cells E5, F5, and G5. Note that the OR condition checks whether Joe wins right away (in which case a 1 is recorded in cell E5). Similarly, the OR condition in cell F5 checks whether he loses right away. In cell G5, the AND condition checks whether both cells E5 and F5 are 0, in which case the game continues. Otherwise, the game is over.

3. **Outcomes of other tosses.** Assuming the game continues beyond the first toss, Joe's point is the value in cell D5. Then he is waiting for a toss to have the value in cell D5 or 7, whichever occurs first. To implement this logic, enter the formulas

=IF(OR(G5="No",G5=""),"",IF(D6=$D$5,1,0))

=IF(OR(G5="No",G5=""),"",IF(D6=7,1,0))

and

=IF(OR(G5="No",G5=""),"",IF(AND(E6=0,F6=0),"Yes","No"))

in cells E6, F6, and G6, and copy these to the range E7:G44. The OR condition in each formula checks whether the game just ended on the previous toss or has been over for some time, in which case blanks are entered. Otherwise, the first two formulas check whether Joe wins or loses on this toss. If both of these return 0, the third formula returns Yes (and the game continues). Otherwise, it returns No (and the game has just ended).

4. **Game outcomes.** Keep track of two aspects of the game in @RISK output cells: whether Joe wins or loses and how many tosses are required. To find these, enter the formulas

=SUM(E5:E44)

and

=COUNT(E5:E44)

in cells J5 and J6, and designate each of these as an @RISK output cell. Note that both functions, SUM and COUNT, ignore blank cells.

Recall that the mean (or average) of a sequence of 0s and 1s is the fraction of 1s in the sequence. This can typically be interpreted as a probability.

5. **Simulation summary.** Although you can get summary measures in the various @RISK results windows after you run the simulation, it is useful to see some key summary measures right on the model sheet. To obtain these, enter the formula

=RISKMEAN(J5)

in cell J8 and copy it to cell J9. As the labels indicate, the RISKMEAN in cell J8, being an average of 0s and 1s, is just the fraction of iterations where Joe wins. The average in cell J9 is the average number of tosses until the game's outcome is determined.

Running the Simulation

Set the number of iterations to 10,000 (partly for variety and partly to obtain a very accurate answer) and the number of simulations to 1. Then run the simulation as usual.

Discussion of the Simulation Results

Perhaps surprisingly, the probability of winning in craps is 0.493, only slightly less than 0.5.

After running @RISK, the summary results in cells J8 and J9 of Figure 16.39 (among others) are available. Our main interest is in the average in cell J8. It represents the best estimate of the probability of winning, 0.487. (It can be shown with a probability argument that the exact probability of winning in craps is 0.493.) You can also see that the average number of tosses needed to determine the outcome of a game was about 3.3. (The maximum number of tosses ever needed on these 10,000 iterations was 25.) ∎

16-5b Simulating the NCAA Basketball Tournament

Each year the suspense reaches new levels as "March Madness" approaches, the time of the NCAA Basketball Tournament. Which of the 68 teams in the tournament will reach the "Sweet Sixteen," which will go on to the prestigious "Final Four," and which team will be crowned champion? The excitement at Indiana University is particularly high, given the strong basketball tradition here, so it has become a yearly tradition at IU (at least for the authors) to simulate the NCAA Tournament right after the brackets have been announced. We share that simulation in the following example.

EXAMPLE	16.11 March Madness

A t the time this example was written, the most recent NCAA Basketball Tournament was the 2013 tournament, won by the University of Louisville. Of course, on the Sunday evening when the 68-team field was announced, we did not know which team would win. All we knew were the pairings (which teams would play which other teams) and the team ratings, based on Jeff Sagarin's nationally syndicated rating system. We now show how to simulate the tournament and keep a tally of the winners.

Objective To simulate the NCAA basketball tournament and keep a tally on the number of times each team wins the tournament.

Where Do the Numbers Come From?

As soon as you learn the pairings for the *next* NCAA tournament, you can perform a Web search for "Sagarin ratings" to find the latest ratings.

Solution

We model the point spread as normally distributed, with mean equal to the difference between the Sagarin ratings and standard deviation 10.

We need to make one probabilistic assumption. From that point, it is a matter of "playing out" the games and doing the required bookkeeping. To understand this probabilistic assumption, suppose team A plays team B and Sagarin's ratings for these teams are, say, 85 and 78. Then Sagarin predicts that the actual point differential in the game (team A's score minus team B's score) will be the difference between the ratings, or 7.[4] We take this one step further. We assume that the *actual* point differential is normally distributed with mean equal to Sagarin's prediction, 7, and standard deviation 10. (Why 10? This is an estimate based on an extensive analysis of historical data. However, the spreadsheet is set up so that you can change the standard deviation to a different value if you prefer.) Then if the actual point differential is positive, team A wins. If it is negative, team B wins.

Developing the Simulation Model

March Madness Model

We provide only an outline of the simulation model. You can see the full details in the file **March Madness 2013.xlsx**. (This file includes the data for the 2013 tournament, but you can easily modify it for future tournaments.) The entire simulation is on a single Model sheet. Columns A through C list team indexes, team names, and Sagarin ratings. If two teams are paired in the first round, they are placed next to one another in the list. Also, all teams in a given region are listed together. (The regions are color-coded.) Columns E through K contain the simulation. (Extra calculations on upsets appear in columns L and M, but these are not an essential part of the simulation.) The first-round results are at the top, the second-round results are below these, and so on. Winners from one round are automatically carried over to the next round with appropriate formulas. Selected portions of the Model sheet appear in

---

[4]In general, there is also a home-court advantage, but we assume all games in the tournament are on "neutral" courts, so that there is no advantage to either team.

Figure 16.40

Teams and Sagarin Ratings

	A	B	C
3	**Final Sagarin ratings of teams**		
4	Index	Team	Sagarin rating
5	1	Louisville	95.01
6	2	NC A&T	67.99
7	3	Liberty	66.73
8	4	Colorado State	84.21
9	5	Missouri	87.26
10	6	Oklahoma State	86.80
11	7	Oregon	82.91
12	8	Saint Louis	87.74
13	9	New Mexico State	79.12
14	10	Memphis	85.67
15	11	Middle Tennessee	81.94
16	12	St. Mary's	84.58
17	13	Michigan State	89.80
18	14	Valparaiso	80.37
19	15	Creighton	86.59
20	16	Cincinnati	84.52
21	17	Duke	90.79
22	18	Albany	72.71
23	19	Gonzaga	91.20
24	20	Southern U	69.69
25	21	Pittsburgh	89.08
26	22	Wichita State	83.37
27	23	Wisconsin	88.80
28	24	Ole Miss	85.03
29	25	Kansas State	86.61
30	26	Boise State	81.50
31	27	La Salle	81.60
32	28	Arizona	86.20
33	29	Belmont	82.44
34	30	New Mexico	86.90

© Cengage Learning

Figures 16.40 and 16.41. (Of course, Florida did *not* win the tournament; Figure 16.41 just shows one possible scenario.) We now describe the essential features of the model.

1. **Teams and ratings.** The first step is to enter the teams and their ratings, as shown in Figure 16.40. Most of the teams shown here (the top 18) were in the Midwest region in the 2013 tournament. Louisville played the winner of the preliminary round between NC A&T and Liberty in the first round, Colorado State played Missouri, and so on.

2. **Simulate rounds.** Jumping ahead to the fourth-round simulation in Figure 16.41, the winners from the previous round 3 are captured, and then the games in round 4 are simulated. The key formulas are in columns H and I. For example, the formulas in cells H137 and I137 are

=VLOOKUP(F137,LTable,3)−VLOOKUP(F138,LTable,3)

and

=RiskNormal(H137,$I$1)

Figure 16.41   NCAA Basketball Simulation Model (Last Three Rounds Only)

	E	F	G	H	I	J	K
135	**Results of Round 4**						
136	Game	Indexes	Teams	Predicted	Simulated	Index of winner	Winner
137	1	8	Saint Louis	−2.06	0.78	8	Saint Louis
138		13	Michigan State				
139	1	25	Kansas State	1.96	−8.06	33	Iowa State
140		33	Iowa State				
141	1	42	Michigan	−3.25	−6.84	46	Florida
142		46	Florida				
143	1	52	Indiana	4.16	5.08	52	Indiana
144		67	Miami (Fla)				Number of upsets
145							P(no upsets)
146	**Semifinals**						
147	Game	Indexes	Teams	Predicted	Simulated	Index of winner	Winner
148	1	8	Saint Louis	3.09	13.70	8	Saint Louis
149		33	Iowa State				
150	2	46	Florida	−0.19	6.55	46	Florida
151		52	Indiana				Number of upsets
152							P(no upsets)
153	**Finals**						
154	Game	Indexes	Teams	Predicted	Simulated	Index of winner	Winner
155	1	8	Saint Louis	−4.55	−6.76	46	Florida
156		46	Florida				
157							
158	**Winner**	46	Florida				

© Cengage Learning

The first of these looks up the ratings of the two teams involved and subtracts to get the predicted point spread. The second formula simulates a point spread with the predicted point spread as its mean and the value in cell I1,10, as its standard deviation. The rest of the formulas do the appropriate bookkeeping. You can view the details in the file.

3. **Outputs.** By counting the indexes of winners in column I, it is possible to find the number of wins for each team, whether it made it to the final 16, the final 8, the final 4, the semi-finals, and whether it won the tournament. These are all designated as @RISK outputs—six outputs for each team. (You can check how the names such as "Wins-Louisville" inside the RiskOutput functions are created from the row and column headings.) RiskMean functions are then used in adjacent columns to calculate the means of the outputs. For example, each mean in the Final 4 column is the percentage of iterations where the team made it to the Final 4. As usual, these means are relevant only *after* running the simulation.

The Simulation Data report in @RISK lists the outputs from each iteration of the simulation, which allows us to tally the winners.

Some of the results appear in Figure 16.42. These are based on 1000 iterations. Conditional formatting has been used in the Means columns to highlight the most successful teams, based on the cutoff values in row 2. As you can see, for example, the top-rated team in the Midwest region, Louisville, won the tournament in 215 of the 1000 iterations and reached the Final Four 470 times. In contrast, the lowly rated NC A&T (and a few others) did not make the Final Four in any of the 1000 iterations. ∎

Figure 16.42   Selected Results of 1000 Iterations

	O	P	Q	R	S	T	U	V	W	X	Y	Z	AA
1	Results section							Cutoffs for conditional format coloring					
2								2.5	50%	40%	30%	20%	10%
3		Tallies						Means					
4	Team	Wins	Sweet 16	Final 8	Final 4	Semis	Winner	Wins	Sweet 16	Final 8	Final 4	Semis	Winner
5	Louisville	6	1	1	1	1	1	3.48	81.0%	65.2%	47.0%	33.8%	21.5%
6	NC A&T	1	0	0	0	0	0	0.55	0.0%	0.0%	0.0%	0.0%	0.0%
7	Liberty	0	0	0	0	0	0	0.45	0.0%	0.0%	0.0%	0.0%	0.0%
8	Colorado State	0	0	0	0	0	0	0.46	5.4%	1.7%	0.9%	0.2%	0.1%
9	Missouri	1	0	0	0	0	0	0.87	13.6%	6.7%	3.0%	0.8%	0.4%
10	Oklahoma State	1	0	0	0	0	0	1.18	36.1%	9.8%	3.9%	1.9%	0.7%
11	Oregon	0	0	0	0	0	0	0.50	12.4%	2.2%	0.7%	0.3%	0.0%
12	Saint Louis	2	1	0	0	0	0	1.52	46.9%	14.0%	5.7%	3.3%	1.3%

© Cengage Learning

PROBLEMS

Level A

28. The game of Chuck-a-Luck is played as follows: You pick a number between 1 and 6 and toss three dice. If your number does not appear, you lose $1. If your number appears *x* times, you win $*x*. On the average, use simulation to find the average amount of money you will win or lose on each play of the game.

29. A *martingale* betting strategy works as follows. You begin with a certain amount of money and repeatedly play a game in which you have a 40% chance of winning any bet. In the first game, you bet $1. From then on, every time you win a bet, you bet $1 the next time. Each time you lose, you double your previous bet. Currently you have $63. Assuming you have unlimited credit, so that you can bet more money than you have, use simulation to estimate the profit or loss you will have after playing the game 50 times.

30. You have $5 and your opponent has $10. You flip a fair coin and if heads comes up, your opponent pays you $1. If tails comes up, you pay your opponent $1. The game is finished when one player has all the money or after 100 tosses, whichever comes first. Use simulation to estimate the probability that you end up with all the money and the probability that neither of you goes broke in 100 tosses.

Level B

31. Assume a very good NBA team has a 70% chance of winning in each game it plays. During an 82-game season what is the average length of the team's longest winning streak? What is the probability that the team has a winning streak of at least 16 games? Use simulation to answer these questions, where each iteration of the simulation generates the outcomes of all 82 games.

32. You are going to play the Wheel of Misfortune Game against the house. The wheel has 10 equally likely numbers: 5, 10, 15, 20, 25, 30, 35, 40, 45, and 50. The goal is to get a total as close as possible to 50 points without exceeding 50. You go first and spin the wheel. Based on your first spin, you can decide whether you want to spin again. (You can spin no more than twice.) After you are done, it is the house's turn. If your total is more than 50, the house doesn't need a turn; it wins automatically. Otherwise, the house spins the wheel. After its first spin, it can spin the wheel again if it wants. (The house can also spin no more than twice.) Then the winner is determined, where a tie goes to you. Use simulation to estimate your probability of winning the game if you and the house both use best strategies. What are the best strategies?

33. Consider the following card game. The player and dealer each receive a card from a 52-card deck. At the end of the game the player with the highest card wins; a tie goes to the dealer. (You can assume that Aces count 1, Jacks 11, Queens 12, and Kings 13.) After the player receives his card, he keeps the card if it is 7 or higher. If the player does not keep the card, the player and dealer swap cards. Then the dealer keeps his current card (which might be the player's original card) if it is 9 or higher. If the dealer does not keep his card, he draws another card. Use simulation with at least 1000 iterations to estimate the probability that the player wins. (*Hint*: See the file **Sampling Without Replacement.xlsx** to see a clever way of simulating cards from a deck so that the same card is never dealt more than once.)

34. *Based on Morrison and Wheat (1984).* When his team is behind late in the game, a hockey coach usually waits until there is one minute left before pulling the goalie out of the game. Using simulation, it is possible to show that coaches should pull their goalies much sooner. Suppose that if both teams are at full strength, each team scores an average of 0.05 goal per minute. Also, suppose that if you pull your goalie you score an average of 0.08 goal per minute and your opponent scores an average of 0.12 goal per minute. Suppose you are one goal behind with five minutes left in the game. Consider the following two strategies:

- Pull your goalie if you are behind at any point in the last five minutes of the game; put him back in if you tie the score.
- Pull your goalie if you are behind at any point in the last minute of the game; put him back in if you tie the score.

Which strategy maximizes your probability of winning or tying the game? Simulate the game using 10-second increments of time. Use the RISKBINOMIAL function to determine whether a team scores a goal in a given 10-second segment. This is reasonable because the probability of scoring two or more goals in a 10-second period is near zero.

35. You are playing Andy Roddick in tennis, and you have a 42% chance of winning each point. (You are *good*!)
   a. Use simulation to estimate the probability you will win a particular game. Note that the first player to score at least four points and have at least two more points than his or her opponent wins the game.
   b. Use simulation to determine your probability of winning a set. Assume that the first player to win six games wins the set if he or she is at least two games ahead; otherwise, the first player to win seven games wins the set. (We substitute a single game for the usual tiebreaker.)
   c. Use simulation to determine your probability of winning a match. Assume that the first player to win three sets wins the match.

16-6 AN AUTOMATED TEMPLATE FOR @RISK MODELS

As explained in the third edition of Albright's *VBA for Modelers* book, the macro language for Excel, VBA, can also be used to automate @RISK. We took advantage of this to create an automated template that you can use for any of your simulations. The template appears in Figure 16.43. (See the file **Simulation Template.xlsm**.) The text boxes provide the motivation and instructions. There are two basic ideas. First, you often have particular inputs you would like to vary in a sensitivity analysis. Once you specify these in the Inputs section, the program will run a separate simulation for each *combination* of the input values. In the example shown, it would run $1 \times 2 \times 3 = 6$ simulations. Second, you typically have outputs that you want to summarize in certain ways. The Outputs section lets you

Figure 16.43 Simulation Template

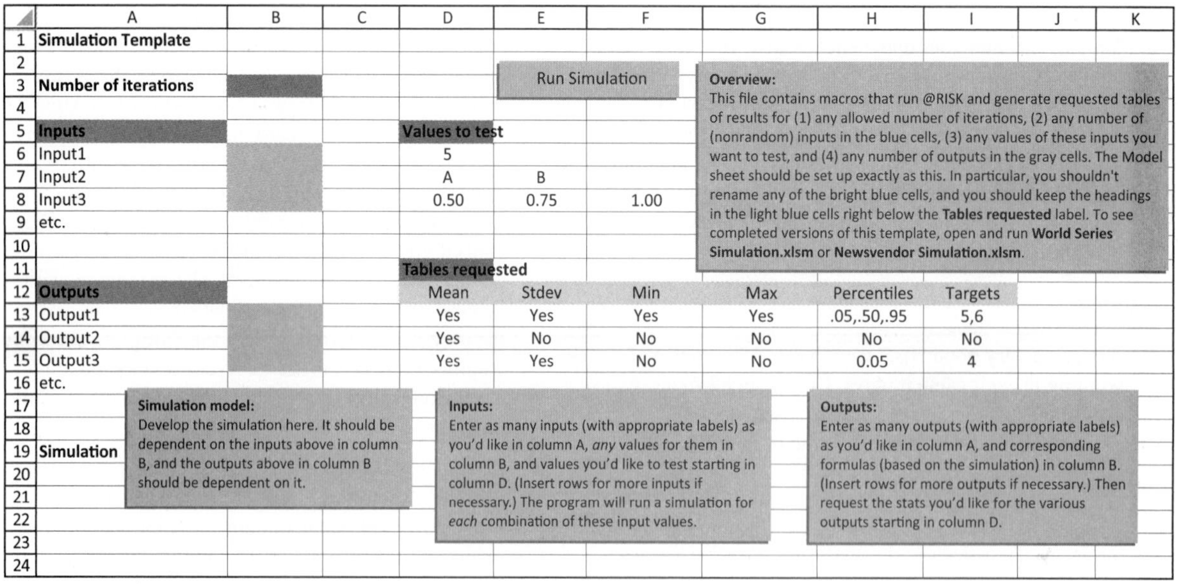

Using the Automated @RISK Template

specify the summary measures you want for each of your outputs. The program then lists the results on separate worksheets.

This template is not a magic bullet. It is still up to you to develop the logic of the simulation. However, you no longer have to worry about RISKSIMTABLE functions or statistical functions such as RISKMEAN. The program takes care of these automatically, using your entries in the Inputs and Outputs sections. To see how the template can be used, we have included two simulations based on it. They are included in the files **World Series Simulation.xlsm** and **Newsvendor Simulation.xlsm**. (Again, remember that you must enable the macros when you open any of these .xlsm files.)

16-7 CONCLUSION

We claimed in the previous chapter that spreadsheet simulation, especially together with an add-in like @RISK, is a very powerful tool. After seeing the examples in this chapter, you should now appreciate how powerful and flexible simulation is. Unlike Solver optimization models, where you often make simplifying assumptions to achieve linearity, say, you can allow virtually anything in simulation models. All you need to do is relate output cells to input cells with appropriate formulas, where any of the input cells can contain probability distributions to reflect uncertainty. The results of the simulation then show the distribution of any particular output. It is no wonder that companies such as GM, Eli Lilly, and many others are increasingly relying on simulation models to analyze their corporate operations.

Summary of Key Terms

Term	Explanation	Excel	Page
Gamma distribution	Right-skewed distribution of nonnegative values useful for many quantities such as the lifetime of an appliance		886
RISKGAMMA function	Implements the gamma distribution in @RISK	=RISKGAMMA *(alpha,beta)*	888
Value at risk at the 5% level (VaR 5%)	Fifth percentile of distribution of some output, usually a monetary output; indicates nearly the worst possible outcome		899
Churn	When customers stop buying a product or service and switch to a competitor's offering		913
RANDBETWEEN function	Generates a random integer between two limits, where each is equally likely	=RANDBETWEEN (1,6), for example	928

PROBLEMS

Conceptual Questions

C.1. We have separated the examples in this chapter into operations, finance, marketing, and sports categories. List at least one other problem in each of these categories that could be attacked with simulation. For each, identify the random inputs, possible probability distributions for them, and any outputs of interest.

C.2. Suppose you are an HR (human resources) manager at a big university, and you sense that the university is becoming too top-heavy with full professors. That is, there do not seem to be as many younger

professors at the assistant and associate levels as there ought to be. How could you study this problem with a simulation model, using current and/or proposed promotions, hiring, firing, and retirement policies?

C.3. You are an avid basketball fan, and you would like to build a simulation model of an entire game so that you could compare two different strategies, such as man-to-man versus zone defense. Is this possible? What might make this simulation model difficult to build?

C.4. Suppose you are a financial analyst and your company runs many simulation models to estimate the profitability of its projects. If you had to choose just two measures of the distribution of any important output such as net profit to report, which two would you choose? Why? What information would be missing if you reported only these two measures? How could they be misleading?

C.5. Software development is an inherently risky and uncertain process. For example, there are many examples of software that couldn't be "finished" by the scheduled release date—bugs still remained and features weren't ready. (Many people believe this was the case with Office 2007.) How might you simulate the development of a software product? What random inputs would be required? Which outputs would be of interest? Which measures of the probability distributions of these outputs would be most important?

C.6. Health care is continually in the news. Can (or should) simulation be used to help solve, or at least study, some of the difficult problems associated with health care? Provide at least two examples where simulation might be useful.

Level A

36. You now have $3000. You will toss a fair coin four times. Before each toss you can bet any amount of your money (including none) on the outcome of the toss. If heads comes up, you win the amount you bet. If tails comes up, you lose the amount you bet. Your goal is to reach $6000. It turns out that you can maximize your chance of reaching $6000 by betting either the money you have on hand or $6000 minus the money you have on hand, whichever is smaller. Use simulation to estimate the probability that you will reach your goal with this betting strategy.

37. You now have $10,000, all of which is invested in a sports team. Each year there is a 60% chance that the value of the team will increase by 60% and a 40% chance that the value of the team will decrease by 60%. Estimate the mean and median value of your investment after 50 years. Explain the large difference between the estimated mean and median.

38. Suppose you have invested 25% of your portfolio in four different stocks. The mean and standard deviation of the annual return on each stock are shown in the file **P16_38.xlsx**. The correlations between the annual returns on the four stocks are also shown in this file.
 a. What is the probability that your portfolio's annual return will exceed 20%?
 b. What is the probability that your portfolio will lose money during the year?

39. A ticket from Indianapolis to Orlando on Deleast Airlines sells for $150. The plane can hold 100 people. It costs Deleast $8000 to fly an empty plane. Each

person on the plane incurs variable costs of $30 (for food and fuel). If the flight is overbooked, anyone who cannot get a seat receives $300 in compensation. On average, 95% of all people who have a reservation show up for the flight. To maximize expected profit, how many reservations for the flight should Deleast book? (*Hint*: The function RISKBINOMIAL can be used to simulate the number who show up. It takes two arguments: the number of reservations booked and the probability that any ticketed person shows up.)

40. *Based on Marcus (1990).* The Balboa mutual fund has beaten the Standard and Poor's 500 during 11 of the last 13 years. People use this as an argument that you can beat the market. Here is another way to look at it that shows that Balboa's beating the market 11 out of 13 times is not unusual. Consider 50 mutual funds, each of which has a 50% chance of beating the market during a given year. Use simulation to estimate the probability that over a 13-year period the best of the 50 mutual funds will beat the market for at least 11 out of 13 years. This probability turns out to exceed 40%, which means that the best mutual fund beating the market 11 out of 13 years is not an unusual occurrence after all.

41. You have been asked to simulate the cash inflows to a toy company for the next year. Monthly sales are independent random variables. Mean sales for the months January through March and October through December are $80,000, and mean sales for the months April through September are $120,000. The standard deviation of each month's sales is 20% of the month's mean sales. Model the method used to collect monthly sales as follows:
 ▪ During each month a certain fraction of new sales will be collected. All new sales not collected become one month overdue.
 ▪ During each month a certain fraction of one-month overdue sales is collected. The remainder becomes two months overdue.
 ▪ During each month a certain fraction of two-month overdue sales is collected. The remainder is written off as bad debt.

You are given the information in the file **P16_41.xlsx** from past months. Using this information, build a simulation model that generates the total cash inflow for each month. Develop a simple forecasting model and build the error of your forecasting model into the simulation. Assuming that there are $120,000 of one-month-old sales outstanding and $140,000 of two-month-old sales outstanding during January, you are 95% sure that total cash inflow for the year will be between what two values?

42. Consider a device that requires two batteries to function. If either of these batteries dies, the device will not work. Currently there are two new batteries in the device, and there are three extra new batteries. Each battery, once it is placed in the device, lasts a random amount of time that is triangularly distributed with parameters 15, 18, and 25 (all expressed in hours). When any of the batteries in the device dies, it is immediately replaced by an extra if an extra is still available. Use @RISK to simulate the time the device can last with the batteries currently available.

43. Consider a drill press containing three drill bits. The current policy (called *individual replacement*) is to replace a drill bit when it fails. The firm is considering changing to a *block replacement* policy in which all three drill bits are replaced whenever a single drill bit fails. Each time the drill press is shut down, the cost is $100. A drill bit costs $50, and the variable cost of replacing a drill bit is $10. Assume that the time to replace a drill bit is negligible. Also, assume that the time until failure for a drill bit follows an exponential distribution with a mean of 100 hours. This can be modeled in @RISK with the formula **=RISKEXPON(100)**. Determine which replacement policy (block or individual replacement) should be implemented.

44. Appliances Unlimited (AU) sells refrigerators. Any refrigerator that fails before it is three years old is replaced for free. Of all refrigerators, 3% fail during their first year of operation; 5% of all one-year-old refrigerators fail during their second year of operation; and 7% of all two-year-old refrigerators fail during their third year of operation.
   a. Use simulation to estimate the fraction of all refrigerators that will have to be replaced.
   b. It costs $500 to replace a refrigerator, and AU sells 10,000 refrigerators per year. If the warranty period were reduced to two years, how much per year in replacement costs would be saved?

45. The annual demand for Prizdol, a prescription drug manufactured and marketed by the NuFeel Company, is normally distributed with mean 50,000 and standard deviation 12,000. Assume that demand during each of the next 10 years is an independent random number from this distribution. NuFeel needs to determine how large a Prizdol plant to build to maximize its expected profit over the next 10 years. If the company builds a plant that can produce x units of Prizdol per year, it will cost $16 for each of these x units. NuFeel will produce only the amount demanded each year, and each unit of Prizdol produced will sell for $3.70. Each unit of Prizdol produced incurs a variable production cost of $0.20. It costs $0.40 per year to operate a unit of capacity.
   a. Among the capacity levels of 30,000, 35,000, 40,000, 45,000, 50,000, 55,000, and 60,000 units per year, which level maximizes expected profit? Use simulation to answer this question.
   b. Using the capacity from your answer to part **a**, NuFeel can be 95% certain that *actual* profit for the 10-year period will be between what two values?

46. A company is trying to determine the proper capacity level for its new electric car. A unit of capacity provides the potential to produce one car per year. It costs $10,000 to build a unit of capacity and the cost is charged equally over the next five years. It also costs $400 per year to maintain a unit of capacity (whether or not it is used). Each car sells for $14,000 and incurs a variable production cost of $10,000. The annual demand for the electric car during each of the next five years is believed to be normally distributed with mean 50,000 and standard deviation 10,000. The demands during different years are assumed to be independent. Profits are discounted at a 10% annual interest rate. The company is working with a five-year planning horizon. Capacity levels of 30,000, 40,000, 50,000, 60,000, and 70,000 are under consideration. You can assume that the company never produces more than demand, so there is never any inventory to carry over from year to year.
   a. Assuming that the company is risk neutral, use simulation to find the optimal capacity level.
   b. Using the answer to part **a**, there is a 5% chance that the *actual* discounted profit will exceed what value, and there is a 5% chance that the *actual* discounted profit will be less than what value?
   c. If the company is risk averse, how might the optimal capacity level change?

47. The DC Cisco office is trying to predict the revenue it will generate next week. Ten deals may close next week. The probability of each deal closing and data on the possible size of each deal (in millions of dollars) are listed in the file **P16_47.xlsx**. Use simulation to estimate total revenue. Based on the simulation, the company can be 95% certain that its total revenue will be between what two numbers?

Level B

48. A common decision is whether a company should buy equipment and produce a product in house or outsource production to another company. If sales volume is high enough, then by producing in house, the savings on unit costs will cover the fixed cost of the equipment. Suppose a company must make such a decision for a four-year time horizon, given the following data. Use simulation to estimate the probability that producing in house is better than outsourcing.
   ■ If the company outsources production, it will have to purchase the product from the manufacturer for $18 per unit. This unit cost will remain constant for the next four years.

- The company will sell the product for $40 per unit. This price will remain constant for the next four years.
- If the company produces the product in house, it must buy a $400,000 machine that is depreciated on a straight-line basis over four years, and its cost of production will be $7 per unit. This unit cost will remain constant for the next four years.
- The demand in year 1 has a worst case of 10,000 units, a most likely case of 14,000 units, and a best case of 16,000 units.
- The average annual growth in demand for years 2–4 has a worst case of 10%, a most likely case of 20%, and a best case of 26%. Whatever this annual growth is, it will be the same in each of the years.
- The tax rate is 40%.
- Cash flows are discounted at 12% per year.

49. Consider an oil company that bids for the rights to drill in offshore areas. The value of the right to drill in a given offshore area is highly uncertain, as are the bids of the competitors. This problem demonstrates the "winner's curse." The winner's curse states that the optimal bidding strategy entails bidding a substantial amount below the company's assumed value of the product for which it is bidding. The idea is that if the company does not bid under its assumed value, its uncertainty about the actual value of the product will often lead it to win bids for products on which it loses money (after paying its high bid). Suppose Royal Conch Oil (RCO) is trying to determine a profit-maximizing bid for the right to drill on an offshore oil site. The actual value of the right to drill is unknown, but it is equally likely to be any value between $10 million and $110 million. Seven competitors will bid against RCO. Each bidder's (including RCO's) estimate of the value of the drilling rights is equally likely to be any number between 50% and 150% of the actual value. Based on past history, RCO believes that each competitor is equally likely to bid between 40% and 60% of its value estimate. Given this information, what fraction (within 0.05) of RCO's estimated value should it bid to maximize its expected profit? (*Hint*: You can use the RISKUNIFORM function to model the actual value of the field and the competitors' bids.)

50. Suppose you begin year 1 with $5000. At the beginning of each year, you put half of your money under a mattress and invest the other half in Whitewater stock. During each year, there is a 50% chance that the Whitewater stock will double, and there is a 50% chance that you will lose half of your investment. To illustrate, if the stock doubles during the first year, you will have $3750 under the mattress and $3750 invested in Whitewater during year 2. You want to estimate your annual return over a 30-year period. If you end with F dollars, your annual return

is $(F/5000)^{1/30} - 1$. For example, if you end with $100,000, your annual return is $20^{1/30} - 1 = 0.105$, or 10.5%. Run 1000 replications of an appropriate simulation. Based on the results, you can be 95% certain that your annual return will be between which two values?

51. Mary Higgins is a freelance writer with enough spare time on her hands to play the stock market fairly seriously. Each morning she observes the change in stock price of a particular stock and decides whether to buy or sell, and if so, how many shares to buy or sell. Assume that on day 1, she has $100,000 cash to invest and that she spends part of this to buy her first 500 shares of the stock at the current price of $50 per share. From that point on, she follows a fairly simple "buy low, sell high" strategy. Specifically, if the price has increased three days in a row, she sells 25% of her shares of the stock. If the price has increased two days in a row (but not three), she sells 10% of her shares. In the other direction, if the price has decreased three days in a row, she buys up to 25% more shares, whereas if the price has decreased only two days in a row, she buys up to 10% more shares. The reason for the "up to" proviso is that she cannot buy more than she has cash to pay for. Assume a fairly simple model of stock price changes, as described in the file **P16_51.xlsx**. Each day the price can change by as much as $2 in either direction, and the probabilities depend on the previous price change: decrease, increase, or no change. Build a simulation model of this strategy for a period of 75 trading days. (You can assume that the stock price on each of the previous two days was $49.) Choose interesting @RISK output cells, and then run @RISK for at least 1000 iterations and report your findings.

52. You are considering a 10-year investment project. At present, the expected cash flow each year is $10,000. Suppose, however, that each year's cash flow is normally distributed with mean equal to *last* year's actual cash flow and standard deviation $1000. For example, suppose that the actual cash flow in year 1 is $12,000. Then year 2 cash flow is normal with mean $12,000 and standard deviation $1000. Also, at the end of year 1, your best guess is that each later year's expected cash flow will be $12,000.
   a. Estimate the mean and standard deviation of the NPV of this project. Assume that cash flows are discounted at a rate of 10% per year.
   b. Now assume that the project has an abandonment option. At the end of each year you can abandon the project for the value given in the file **P16_52 .xlsx**. For example, suppose that year 1 cash flow is $4000. Then at the end of year 1, you expect cash flow for each remaining year to be $4000. This has an NPV of less than $62,000, so you should abandon the project and collect $62,000 at

the end of year 1. Estimate the mean and standard deviation of the project with the abandonment option. How much would you pay for the abandonment option? (*Hint*: You can abandon a project at most once. So in year 5, for example, you abandon only if the sum of future expected NPVs is less than the year 5 abandonment value *and* the project has not yet been abandoned. Also, once you abandon the project, the actual cash flows for future years are zero. So in this case the future cash flows after abandonment should be zero in your model.)

53. Play Things is developing a new Hannah Montana doll. The company has made the following assumptions:

- The doll will sell for a random number of years from 1 to 10. Each of these 10 possibilities is equally likely.
- At the beginning of year 1, the potential market for the doll is one million. The potential market grows by an average of 5% per year. The company is 95% sure that the growth in the potential market during any year will be between 3% and 7%. It uses a normal distribution to model this.
- The company believes its share of the potential market during year 1 will be at worst 20%, most likely 40%, and at best 50%. It uses a triangular distribution to model this.
- The variable cost of producing a doll during year 1 has a triangular distribution with parameters $8, $10, and $12.
- The current selling price is $20.
- Each year, the variable cost of producing the doll will increase by an amount that is triangularly distributed with parameters 4.5%, 5%, and 6.5%. You can assume that once this change is generated, it will be the same for each year. You can also assume that the company will change its selling price by the same percentage each year.
- The fixed cost of developing the doll (which is incurred right away, at time 0) has a triangular distribution with parameters $4, $6, and $12 million.
- Right now there is one competitor in the market. During each year that begins with four or fewer competitors, there is a 20% chance that a new competitor will enter the market.
- Year t sales (for $t > 1$) are determined as follows. Suppose that at the end of year $t - 1$, n competitors are present (including Play Things). Then during year t, a fraction $0.9 - 0.1n$ of the company's loyal customers (last year's purchasers) will buy a doll from Play Things this year, and a fraction $0.2 - 0.04n$ of customers currently in the market who did not purchase a doll last year will purchase a doll from Play Things this year. Adding these two provides the *mean* sales for this year. Then the *actual* sales this year is normally distributed with

this mean and standard deviation equal to 7.5% of the mean.
- **a.** Use @RISK to estimate the expected NPV of this project.
- **b.** Use the percentiles in @RISK's output to find an interval such that you are 95% certain that the company's *actual* NPV will be within this interval.

54. An automobile manufacturer is considering whether to introduce a new model called the Racer. The profitability of the Racer depends on the following factors:

- The fixed cost of developing the Racer is triangularly distributed with parameters $3, $4, and $5, all in billions.
- Year 1 sales are normally distributed with mean 200,000 and standard deviation 50,000. Year 2 sales are normally distributed with mean equal to actual year 1 sales and standard deviation 50,000. Year 3 sales are normally distributed with mean equal to actual year 2 sales and standard deviation 50,000.
- The selling price in year 1 is $25,000. The year 2 selling price will be 1.05[year 1 price + $50 (% diff1)] where % diff1 is the number of percentage points by which actual year 1 sales differ from expected year 1 sales. The 1.05 factor accounts for inflation. For example, if the year 1 sales figure is 180,000, which is 10 percentage points below the expected year 1 sales, then the year 2 price will be 1.05[25,000 + 50(−10)] = $25,725. Similarly, the year 3 price will be 1.05[year 2 price + $50(% diff2)] where % diff2 is the percentage by which actual year 2 sales differ from expected year 2 sales.
- The variable cost in year 1 is triangularly distributed with parameters $10,000, $12,000, and $15,000, and it is assumed to increase by 5% each year.

Your goal is to estimate the NPV of the new car during its first three years. Assume that the company is able to produce exactly as many cars as it can sell. Also, assume that cash flows are discounted at 10%. Simulate 1000 trials to estimate the mean and standard deviation of the NPV for the first three years of sales. Also, determine an interval such that you are 95% certain that the NPV of the Racer during its first three years of operation will be within this interval.

55. It costs a pharmaceutical company $40,000 to produce a 1000-pound batch of a drug. The average yield from a batch is unknown but the best case is 90% yield (that is, 900 pounds of good drug will be produced), the most likely case is 85% yield, and the worst case is 70% yield. The annual demand for the drug is unknown, with the best case being 22,000 pounds, the most likely case 18,000 pounds, and the worst case 12,000 pounds. The drug sells for $60 per pound and leftover amounts of the drug can be sold for $8 per pound. To maximize annual expected profit, how many batches of the drug should the company produce? You can assume that it will produce the batches only once, *before* demand for the drug is known.

56. A truck manufacturer produces the Off Road truck. The company wants to gain information about the discounted profits earned during the next three years. During a given year, the total number of trucks sold in the United States is $500,000 + 50,000G - 40,000I$, where G is the number of percentage points increase in gross domestic product during the year and I is the number of percentage points increase in the consumer price index during the year. During the next three years, Value Line has made the predictions listed in the file **P16_56.xlsx**. In the past, 95% of Value Line's G predictions have been accurate within 6%, and 95% of Value Line's I predictions have been accurate within 5%. You can assume that the actual G and I values are normally distributed each year.

At the beginning of each year, a number of competitors might enter the trucking business. The probability distribution of the number of competitors that will enter the trucking business is also given in the same file. Before competitors join the industry at the beginning of year 1, there are two competitors. During a year that begins with n competitors (after competitors have entered the business, but before any have left, and not counting Off Road), Off Road will have a market share given by $0.5(0.9)^n$. At the end of each year, there is a 20% chance that any competitor will leave the industry. The selling price of the truck and the production cost per truck are also given in the file. Simulate 1000 replications of the company's profit for the next three years. Estimate the mean and standard deviation of the discounted three-year profits, using a discount rate of 10% and Excel's NPV function. Do the same if the probability that any competitor leaves the industry during any year increases to 50%.

57. Suppose you buy an electronic device that you operate continuously. The device costs you $300 and carries a one-year warranty. The warranty states that if the device fails during its first year of use, you get a new device for no cost, and this new device carries exactly the same warranty. However, if it fails after the first year of use, the warranty is of no value. You plan to use this device for the next six years. Therefore, any time the device fails outside its warranty period, you will pay $300 for another device of the same kind. (We assume the price does not increase during the six-year period.) The time until failure for a device is gamma distributed with parameters $\alpha = 2$ and $\beta = 0.5$. (This implies a mean of one year.) Use @RISK to simulate the six-year period. Include as outputs (1) your total cost, (2) the number of failures during the warranty

period, and (3) the number of devices you own during the six-year period.

58. Rework the previous problem for a case in which the one-year warranty requires you to pay for the new device even if failure occurs during the warranty period. Specifically, if the device fails at time t, measured relative to the time it went into use, you must pay $300t$ for a new device. For example, if the device goes into use at the beginning of April and fails nine months later, at the beginning of January, you must pay $225. The reasoning is that you got 9/12 of the warranty period for use, so you should pay that fraction of the total cost for the next device. As before, however, if the device fails outside the warranty period, you must pay the full $300 cost for a new device.

59. *Based on Hoppensteadt and Peskin (1992).* The following model (the Reed–Frost model) is often used to model the spread of an infectious disease. Suppose that at the beginning of period 1, the population consists of five diseased people (called infectives) and 95 healthy people (called susceptibles). During any period there is a 0.05 probability that a given infective person will encounter a particular susceptible. If an infective encounters a susceptible, there is a 0.5 probability that the susceptible will contract the disease. An infective lives for an average of 10 periods with the disease. To model this, assume that there is a 0.10 probability that an infective dies during any given period. Use @RISK to model the evolution of the population over 100 periods. Use your results to answer the following questions. [*Hint:* During any period there is probability $0.05(0.50) = 0.025$ that an infective will infect a particular susceptible. Therefore, the probability that a particular susceptible is not infected during a period is $(1 - 0.025)^n$, where n is the number of infectives present at the end of the previous period.]

    a. What is the probability that the population will die out?
    b. What is the probability that the disease will die out?
    c. On the average, what percentage of the population is infected by the end of period 100?
    d. Suppose that people use infection "protection" during encounters. The use of protection reduces the probability that a susceptible will contract the disease during a single encounter with an infective from 0.50 to 0.10. Now answer parts **a** through **c** under the assumption that everyone uses protection.

60. Chemcon has taken over the production of Nasacure from a rival drug company. Chemcon must build a plant to produce Nasacure by the beginning of 2010. Once the plant is built, the plant's capacity cannot be changed. Each unit sold brings in $10 in

revenue. The fixed cost (in dollars) of producing a plant that can produce x units per year of the drug is $5,000,000 + 10x$. This cost is assumed to be incurred at the end of 2010. In fact, you can assume that all cost and sales cash flows are incurred at the ends of the respective years. If a plant of capacity x is built, the variable cost of producing a unit of Nasacure is $6 - 0.1(x - 1,000,000)/100,000$. For example, a plant capacity of 1,100,000 units has a variable cost of $5.90. Each year a plant operating cost of $1 per unit of capacity is also incurred. Based on a forecasting sales model from the previous 10 years, Chemcon forecasts that demand in year t, D_t, is related to the demand in the previous year, D_{t-1}, by the equation $D_t = 67,430 + 0.985D_{t-1} + e_t$, where e_t is normally distributed with mean 0 and standard deviation 29,320. The demand in 2009 was 1,011,000 units. If demand for a year exceeds production capacity, all demand in excess of plant capacity is lost. If demand is less than capacity, the extra capacity is simply not used. Chemcon wants to determine a capacity level that maximizes expected discounted profits (using a discount rate of 10%) for the time period 2010 through 2019. Use simulation to help it do so.

61. Tinkan Company produces one-pound cans for the Canadian salmon industry. Each year the salmon spawn during a 24-hour period and must be canned immediately. Tinkan has the following agreement with the salmon industry. The company can deliver as many cans as it chooses. Then the salmon are caught. For each can by which Tinkan falls short of the salmon industry's needs, the company pays the industry a $2 penalty. Cans cost Tinkan $1 to produce and are sold by Tinkan for $2 per can. If any cans are left over, they are returned to Tinkan and the company reimburses the industry $2 for each extra can. These extra cans are put in storage for next year. Each year a can is held in storage, a carrying cost equal to 20% of the can's production cost is incurred. It is well known that the number of salmon harvested during a year is strongly related to the number of salmon harvested the previous year. In fact, using past data, Tinkan estimates that the harvest size in year t, H_t (measured in the number of cans required), is related to the harvest size in the previous year, H_{t-1}, by the equation $H_t = H_{t-1}e_t$, where e_t is normally distributed with mean 1.02 and standard deviation 0.10.

Tinkan plans to use the following production strategy. For some value of x, it produces enough cans at the beginning of year t to bring its inventory up to $x + \hat{H}_t$, where $\hat{H}_t$ is the predicted harvest size in year t. Then it delivers these cans to the salmon industry. For example, if it uses $x = 100,000$, the predicted harvest size is 500,000 cans, and 80,000 cans are already in inventory, then Tinkan produces and delivers 520,000 cans. Given that the harvest size for the previous year

was 550,000 cans, use simulation to help Tinkan develop a production strategy that maximizes its expected profit over the next 20 years. Assume that the company begins year 1 with an initial inventory of 300,000 cans.

62. You are unemployed, 21 years old, and searching for a job. Until you accept a job offer, the following situation occurs. At the beginning of each year, you receive a job offer. The annual salary associated with the job offer is equally likely to be any number between $20,000 and $100,000. You must immediately choose whether to accept the job offer. If you accept an offer with salary x, you receive $x per year while you work (assume you retire at age 70), including the current year. Assume that cash flows are discounted so that a cash flow received one year from now has a present value of 0.9. You decide to accept the first job offer that exceeds w dollars.

  a. Use simulation to determine the value of w (within $10,000) that maximizes the expected NPV of earnings you will receive the rest of your working life.

  b. Repeat part **a**, but now assume that you get a 3% raise in salary every year after the first year you accept the job.

63. A popular restaurant in Indianapolis does a brisk business, filling virtually all of its seats from 6 P.M. until 9 P.M. Tuesday through Sunday. Its current annual revenue is $2.34 million. However, it does not currently accept credit cards, and it is thinking of doing so. If it does, the bank will charge 4% on all receipts during the first year. (To keep it simple, you can ignore taxes and tips and focus only on the receipts from food and liquor.) Depending on receipts in year 1, the bank might then reduce its fee in succeeding years, as indicated in the file **P16_63.xlsx**. (This would be a one-time reduction, at the end of year 1 only.) This file also contains parameters of the two uncertain quantities, credit card usage (percentage of customers who will pay with credit cards) and increased spending (percentage increase in spending by credit card users, presumably on liquor but maybe also on more expensive food). The restaurant wants to simulate a five-year horizon. Its base case is not to accept credit cards at all, in which case it expects to earn $2.34 million in revenue each year. It wants to use simulation to explore other options, where it will accept credit cards in year 1 and then continue them in years 2–5 if the bank fee is less than or equal to some cutoff value. For example, one possibility is to accept credit cards in year 1 and then discontinue them only if the bank fee is less than or equal to 3%. You should explore the cutoffs 2% to 4% in increments of 0.5%. Which policy provides with the largest mean *increase* in revenue over the five-year horizon, relative to never using credit cards?

64. The Ryder Cup is a three-day golf tournament played every other year with 12 of the best U.S. golfers against 12 of the best European golfers. They play 16 team matches (each match has two U.S. golfers against two European golfers) on Friday and Saturday, and they play 12 singles matches (each match has a single U.S. golfer against a European golfer) on Sunday. Each match is either won or tied. A win yields 1 point for the winning team and 0 points for the losing team. A tie yields 0.5 point for each team. A team needs 14.5 points to win the Cup. If each team gets 14 points, the tournament is a tie, but the preceding winner gets to keep the Cup. In 1999, the U.S. was behind 10 points to 6 after the team matches. To win the Cup, the U.S. needed at least 8.5 points on Sunday, a very unlikely outcome, but they pulled off the miracle and won. Use simulation to estimate the probability of the U.S. scoring at least 8.5 points in the 12 singles matches, assuming all golfers in the tournament are essentially equal. Proceed as follows.

a. Use simulation to estimate the probability, call it h (for half), that a given match ends in a tie. To do this, you can assume that any of the 18 holes is tied with probability 0.475 and won with probability 0.525. (These are the historical fractions of holes that have been tied and won in singles matches in the past few Ryder Cups.) Note that each match is "match play," so the only thing that counts on each hole is whether a golfer has fewer strokes than the other golfer—winning a hole by one stroke is equivalent to winning the hole by two or more strokes in match play. The player winning the most holes wins the match, unless they tie.

b. Run another simulation, using the estimated probability h as an input, to estimate the probability that the U.S. will score at least 8.5 points in the 12 singles matches.

CASE   16.1 COLLEGE FUND INVESTMENT

Your next-door neighbor, Scott Jansen, has a 12-year-old daughter, and he intends to pay the tuition for her first year of college six years from now. The tuition for the first year will be $17,500. Scott has gone through his budget and finds that he can invest $200 per month for the next six years. Scott has opened accounts at two mutual funds. The first fund follows an investment strategy designed to match the return of the S&P 500. The second fund invests in short-term Treasury bills. Both funds have very low fees.

Scott has decided to follow a strategy in which he contributes a fixed fraction of the $200 to each fund. An adviser from the first fund suggested that in each month he should invest 80% of the $200 in the S&P 500 fund and the other 20% in the T-bill fund. The adviser explained that the S&P 500 has averaged much larger returns than the T-bill fund. Even though stock returns are risky investments in the short run, the risk should be fairly minimal over the longer six-year period. An adviser from the second fund recommended just the opposite: invest 20% in the S&P 500 fund and 80% in T-bills, because treasury bills are backed by the United States government. If you follow this allocation, he said, your average return will be lower, but at least you will have enough to reach your $17,500 target in six years.

Not knowing which adviser to believe, Scott has come to you for help.

Questions

1. The file **C16_01.xlsx** contains 261 monthly returns of the S&P 500 and Treasury bills from January 1970 through September 1991. (If you can find more recent data on the Web, feel free to use it.) Suppose that in each of the next 72 months (six years), it is equally likely that any of the historical returns will occur. Develop a spreadsheet model to simulate the two suggested investment strategies over the six-year period. Plot the value of each strategy over time for a single iteration of the simulation. What is the total value of each strategy after six years? Do either of the strategies reach the target?

2. Simulate 1000 iterations of the two strategies over the six-year period. Create a histogram of the final fund values. Based on your simulation results, which of the two strategies would you recommend? Why?

3. Suppose that Scott needs to have $19,500 to pay for the first year's tuition. Based on the same simulation results, which of the two strategies would you recommend now? Why?

4. What other real-world factors might be important to consider in designing the simulation and making a recommendation?

CASE 16.2 BOND INVESTMENT STRATEGY

An investor is considering the purchase of zero-coupon U.S. Treasury bonds. A 30-year zero-coupon bond yielding 8% can be purchased today for $9.94. At the end of 30 years, the owner of the bond will receive $100. The yield of the bond is related to its price by the following equation:

$$P = \frac{100}{(1 + y)^t}$$

Here, P is the price of the bond, y is the yield of the bond, and t is the maturity of the bond measured in years. Evaluating this equation for $t = 30$ and $y = 0.08$ gives $P = 9.94$.

The investor is planning to purchase a bond today and sell it one year from now. The investor is interested in evaluating the *return* on the investment in the bond. Suppose, for example, that the yield of the bond one year from now is 8.5%. Then the price of the bond one year later will be $9.39 [=100/(1 + 0.085)^{29}]$. The time remaining to maturity is $t = 29$ because one year has passed. The return for the year is −5.54% [= (9.39 − 9.94)/9.94].

In addition to the 30-year-maturity zero-coupon bond, the investor is considering the purchase of zero-coupon bonds with maturities of 2, 5, 10, or 20 years. All of the bonds are currently yielding 8.0%. (Bond investors describe this as a *flat yield curve*.) The investor cannot predict the future yields of the bonds with certainty. However, the investor believes that the yield of each bond one year from now can be modeled by a normal distribution with mean 8% and standard deviation 1%.

Questions

1. Suppose that the yields of the five zero-coupon bonds are all 8.5% one year from today. What are the returns of each bond over the period?

2. Using a simulation with 1000 iterations, estimate the expected return of each bond over the year. Estimate the standard deviations of the returns.

3. Comment on the following statement: "The expected yield of the 30-year bond one year from today is 8%. At that yield, its price would be $10.73. The return for the year would be 8% [= (10.73 − 9.94)/9.94]. Therefore, the average return for the bond should be 8% as well. A simulation isn't really necessary. Any difference between 8% and the answer in Question 2 must be due to simulation error."

PART

6

Advanced Data Analysis

CHAPTER 17
Data Mining

CHAPTER

17

Data Mining

Veni/Jeremy Edwards/iStockphoto.com

LIVEHOODS IN PITTSBURGH

One characteristic of many problems that are analyzed with data mining methods is that the problem is simple to conceptualize, but the methods used to analyze it are quite complex and the corresponding data sets are extremely large. This is exactly the case with a study of "livehoods" by Cranshaw et al., a team of researchers at Carnegie Mellon University in Pittsburgh, Pennsylvania. Their goal was to use data mining to study the social/spatial structure of a large city, based on the social media its residents generate. Their results are discussed in the article by Cranshaw et al. (2012), and they can be viewed interactively at livehoods.org.

The researchers' hypothesis is that the character of an urban area is defined not just by the types of places found there, but also by the people who make the area part of their daily routines. To explore this hypothesis, they collected data from over 18 million foursquare check-ins. Location-based social networks such as foursquare have created new ways of interacting online, based on the physical location of their users. In these systems, users can "check in" to a location by selecting it from a list of named nearby venues. Their check-ins are then broadcast to other users of the system.

The researchers then developed a model that groups nearby venues into areas, based on patterns in the set of people who check in to them. By examining patterns in these check-ins, they were able to learn about the different areas that comprise the city. Specifically, they were able to study the social dynamics, structure, and character of cities on a large scale. They did this with a powerful data mining technique called clustering. Their model takes into account both the *spatial* proximity between venues, as given by their geographic coordinates, as well as the *social* proximity which they derive from the distribution of people who check in to them. The underlying hypothesis of their model is that the "character" of an urban area is defined

947

not just by the types of places found there, but also by the people that choose to make that area part of their daily lives. They call these clusters *livehoods*, reflecting the dynamic nature of activity patterns in the lives of city inhabitants.

The resulting clusters are *not* necessarily the same as the traditional neighborhoods, as the researchers explain in several specific examples. For instances, one example involves the traditional and very different adjacent neighborhoods of Shadyside (wealthy) and East Liberty (poor). A recent development project in East Liberty, including the opening of a Whole Foods store, has made a significant transformation in behavior patterns across the two neighborhoods, and this is reflected in the "spilling over" behavior captured in the livehood clusters.

Again, the goal of such a study and even the results are quite intuitive. However, a quick look at the Clustering Model section of the researchers' paper reveals that very technical algorithms were used to analyze a massive amount of data. This is typical of data mining studies. ■

17-1 INTRODUCTION

The types of data analysis discussed throughout this book are crucial to the success of most companies in today's data-driven business world. However, the sheer volume of available data often defies traditional methods of data analysis. Therefore, new methods—and accompanying software—have recently been developed under the name of data mining. **Data mining** attempts to discover patterns, trends, and relationships among data, especially nonobvious and unexpected patterns. For example, an analysis might discover that people who purchase skim milk also tend to purchase whole wheat bread, or that cars built on Mondays before 10 a.m. on production line #5 using parts from supplier ABC have significantly more defects than average. This new knowledge can then be used for more effective management of a business.

The place to start is with a data warehouse. Typically, a **data warehouse** is a huge database that is designed specifically to study patterns in data. A data warehouse is not the same as the databases companies use for their day-to-day operations. A data warehouse should (1) combine data from multiple sources to discover as many relationships as possible, (2) contain accurate and consistent data, (3) be structured to enable quick and accurate responses to a variety of queries, and (4) allow follow-up responses to specific relevant questions. In short, a data warehouse represents a relatively new type of database, one that is specifically structured to enable data mining. Another term you might hear is data mart. A **data mart** is essentially a scaled-down data warehouse, or part of an overall data warehouse, that is structured specifically for one part of an organization, such as sales. Virtually all large organizations, and many smaller ones, have developed data warehouses or data marts in the past decade to enable them to better understand their business—their customers, their suppliers, and their processes.

Once a data warehouse is in place, analysts can begin to mine the data with a collection of methodologies and accompanying software. Some of the primary methodologies are classification analysis, prediction, cluster analysis, market basket analysis, and forecasting. Each of these is a large topic in itself, but some brief explanations follow.

■ *Classification analysis* attempts to find variables that are related to a categorical (often binary) variable. For example, credit card customers can be categorized as those who pay their balances in a reasonable amount of time and those who don't. Classification analysis would attempt to find explanatory variables that help predict which of these two categories a customer is in. Some variables, such as salary, are natural candidates for explanatory variables, but an analysis might uncover others that are less obvious.

- *Prediction* is similar to classification analysis, except that it tries to find variables that help explain a continuous variable, such as credit card balance, rather than a categorical variable. Regression, the topic of Chapters 10 and 11, is one of the most popular prediction tools, but there are others not covered in this book.

- *Cluster analysis* tries to group observations into clusters so that observations within a cluster are alike, and observations in different clusters are not alike. For example, one cluster for an automobile dealer's customers might be middle-aged men who are not married, earn over $150,000, and favor high-priced sports cars. Once natural clusters are found, a company can then tailor its marketing to the individual clusters.

- *Market basket analysis* tries to find products that customers purchase together in the same "market basket." In a supermarket setting, this knowledge can help a manager position or price various products in the store. In banking and other settings, it can help managers to cross-sell (sell a product to a customer already purchasing a related product) or up-sell (sell a more expensive product than a customer originally intended to purchase).

- *Forecasting* is used to predict values of a time series variable by extrapolating patterns seen in historical data into the future. (This topic is covered in some detail in Chapter 12.) This is clearly an important problem in all areas of business, including the forecasting of future demand for products, forecasting future stock prices and commodity prices, and many others.

Only a few years ago, data mining was considered a topic only for the experts. In fact, most people had never heard of data mining. Also, the required software was expensive and difficult to learn. Fortunately, this is changing. Many people in organizations, not just the quantitative experts, have access to large amounts of data, and they have to make sense of it right away, not a year from now. Therefore, they must have some understanding of techniques used in data mining, and they must have software to implement these techniques.

Data mining is a huge topic. A thorough discussion, which would fill a large book or two, would cover the role of data mining in real business problems, data warehousing, the many data mining techniques that now exist, and the software packages that have been developed to implement these techniques. There is not nearly enough room to cover all of this here, so the goal of this chapter is much more modest. We begin with a discussion of powerful tools for exploring and visualizing data. Not everyone considers these tools to be data mining tools—they are often considered preliminary steps to "real" data mining—but they are too important not to discuss here. Next, we discuss classification, one of the most important types of problems tackled by data mining. Finally, the chapter concludes with a brief discussion of clustering.

It is not really possible, or at least not as interesting, to discuss data mining without using software for illustration. There is no attempt here to cover any data mining software package in detail. Instead, we highlight a few different packages for illustration. In some cases, you already have the software. For example, the NeuralTools add-in in the Palisade DecisionTools® Suite, available with this book, can be used to estimate neural nets for classification. In other cases, we illustrate popular software that can be downloaded for free from the Web. However, you should be aware that there are numerous other software packages that perform various data mining procedures, and many of them are quite expensive. You might end up using one of these in your job, and you will then have to learn how it works.

17-2 DATA EXPLORATION AND VISUALIZATION

Data mining is a relatively new field—or at least a new term—and not everyone agrees with its definition. To many people, data mining is a collection of advanced algorithms that can be used to find useful information and patterns in large data sets. Data mining does indeed include a number of advanced algorithms, but we believe its definition should be broadened to include relatively simple methods for exploring and visualizing data. This section discusses some of the possibilities. They are basically extensions of methods discussed in Chapters 2 and 3, and the key ideas—tables, pivot tables, and charts—are not new. However, advances in software now enable you to analyze large data sets quickly and easily.

17-2a Online Analytical Processing (OLAP)

We introduced pivot tables in Chapter 3 as an amazingly easy and powerful way to break data down by category in Excel®. However, the pivot table methodology is not limited to Excel or even to Microsoft. This methodology is usually called **online analytical processing**, or **OLAP**. This name was initially used to distinguish this type of data analysis from online *transactional* processing, or OLTP. The latter has been used for years by companies to answer specific day-to-day questions: Why was there a shipment delay in this customer's order? Why doesn't the invoice amount for this customer's order match the customer's payment? Is this customer's complaint about a defective product justified? In fact, database systems have been developed to answer such "one-off" questions quickly. In contrast, OLAP is used to answer broader questions: Are sales of a particular product decreasing over time? Is a particular product selling equally well in different stores? Do customers who pay with our credit card tend to spend more?

When analysts began to realize that the typical OLTP databases are not well equipped to answer these broader types of questions, OLAP was born. This led to much research into the most appropriate database structure for answering OLAP questions. The consensus was that the best structure is a **star schema**. In a star schema, there is at least one **Facts** table of data that has many rows and only a few columns. For example, in a supermarket database, a Facts table might have a row for each line item purchased, including the number of items of the product purchased, the total amount paid for the product, and possibly the discount. Each row of the Facts table would also list "lookup information" (or foreign keys, in database terminology) about the purchase: the date, the store, the product, the customer, any promotion in effect, and possibly others. Finally, the database would include a **dimension** table for each of these. For example, there would be a Products table. Each row of this table would contain multiple pieces of information about a particular product. Then if a customer purchases product 15, say, information about product 15 could be looked up in the Products table.

One particular star schema, for the Foodmart Access database created by Microsoft for illustration, appears in Figure 17.1. (This database is available in the **Foodmart.mdb** file if you want to view it in Access.) The Facts table in the middle contains only two "facts" about each line item purchased: Revenue and UnitsSold. (There are over 250,000 rows in the Facts table, but even this is extremely small in comparison to many corporate facts tables.) The other columns in the Facts table are foreign keys that let you look up information about the product, the date, the store, and the customer in the respective dimensions tables. You can see why the term "star schema" is used. The dimension tables surround the central Facts table like stars. (If you are new to relational databases, you can read a brief introduction to this topic in Section 18-4 of the accompanying online Chapter 18.)

Most data warehouses are built according to these basic ideas. By structuring corporate databases in this way, facts can easily be broken down by dimensions, and—you guessed it—the methodology for doing this is pivot tables. However, these pivot tables are not just the "standard" Excel pivot tables. You might think of them as pivot tables on steroids. The OLAP methodology and corresponding pivot tables have the following features that distinguish them from standard Excel pivot tables.

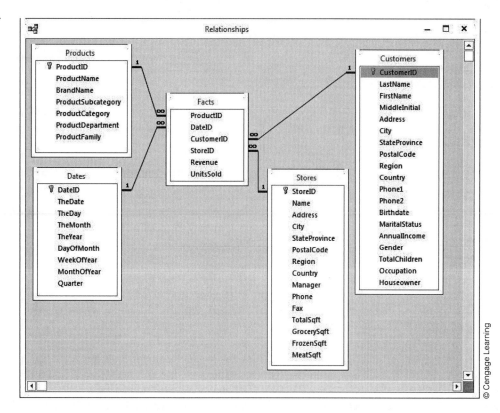

Figure 17.1

Star Schema for Foodmart Database

- The OLAP methodology does not belong to Microsoft or any other software company. It has been developed by many computer scientists, and it has been implemented in a variety of software packages. Of course, Microsoft is included in this group. Its OLAP tools are located in the Analysis Services section of its SQL Server database software.

- In OLAP pivot tables, you aren't allowed to drag any field to any area of the pivot table, as you can in Excel. Only facts are allowed in the Values area, and only dimensions are allowed in the Rows, Columns, and Filters areas. But this is not much of a limitation. The whole purpose of these pivot tables is to break down facts, such as Revenue, by dimensions such as Date and Product.

- Some dimensions have natural hierarchies. For example, the Products dimension in Figure 17.1 has the natural hierarchy ProductFamily, ProductDepartment, ProductCategory, and ProductSubcategory. Similarly, the Stores and Customers dimensions have geographical hierarchies, and the Date dimension always has hierarchies such as Year, Quarter, Month, and Day. OLAP software lets you specify such hierarchies. Then when you create a pivot table, you can drag a hierarchy to an area and "drill down" through it. For example, looking at Revenue totals, you can start at the ProductFamily level (Drink, Food, or Non-Consumable). Then you can drill down to the ProductDepartment level for any of these, such as Beverages, Dairy, and Alcoholic for the Drink family. Then you can drill down further to the ProductCategory level and so on. Figure 17.2 shows what a resulting pivot table might look like. (You will see how to create this pivot table in the next bullet.)

- OLAP databases are typically huge, so it can take a while to get the results for a particular pivot table. For this reason, the data are often "preprocessed" in such a way

Figure 17.2

Drilling Down a
Hierarchy in the
Foodmart Database

◢	A	B
1	**Row Labels** ▼	**Revenue**
2	⊟ **Drink**	**$142,578.37**
3	⊞ **Alcoholic Beverages**	**$41,137.07**
4	⊟ **Beverages**	**$80,152.27**
5	⊞ Carbonated Beverages	$17,754.68
6	⊞ Drinks	$17,028.38
7	⊟ Hot Beverages	$26,227.46
8	⊞ Chocolate	$4,085.95
9	⊞ Coffee	$22,141.51
10	⊞ Pure Juice Beverages	$19,141.75
11	⊞ **Dairy**	**$21,289.03**
12	⊞ **Food**	**$1,187,171.39**
13	⊞ **Non-Consumable**	**$314,635.84**
14	**Grand Total**	**$1,644,385.60**

© Cengage Learning

that the results for any desired breakdown are already available and can be obtained immediately. Specifically, the data are preprocessed into files that are referred to as **OLAP cubes**. (The analogy is to a Rubik's cube, where each little sub-cube contains the result of a particular breakdown.) In Excel 2003, Microsoft let you build your own OLAP cubes, but this feature was removed in subsequent versions of Excel. Now you need Analysis Services in SQL Server (or some other company's software) to build cubes. Nevertheless, it is still possible to use an "offline" cube that someone has created as a source for a pivot table in Excel. This is illustrated in Example 17.1. Also, the PowerPivot tool included in Excel 2013 and discussed later in the chapter can be used to implement much of the OLAP cube functionality.

EXAMPLE | **17.1 EXPLORING AN OFFLINE CUBE FOR FOODMART**

The Foodmart database illustrated in Figure 17.1 is structured as a star schema. By using the Analysis Services tools in SQL Server (which do *not* accompany this book), the cube file **Foodmart.cub** was created. It not only allows you to break down the facts by dimensions, but it includes several hierarchies for drilling down through dimensions. How can this be done in Excel?

Objective To learn how an offline cube file can be used as the source for an Excel pivot table.

Solution

Keep in mind that throughout this example the **Foodmart.cub** file is a special kind of file that had to be created in SQL Server and is not directly viewable. However, you can build a pivot table from it very easily, as illustrated in the following steps.

1. Starting with a blank workbook in Excel, click PivotTable from the Insert ribbon.
2. In the Create PivotTable dialog box shown in Figure 17.3, choose the **Use an external data source** option, and click the **Choose Connection** button.

Figure 17.3
Create PivotTable Dialog Box

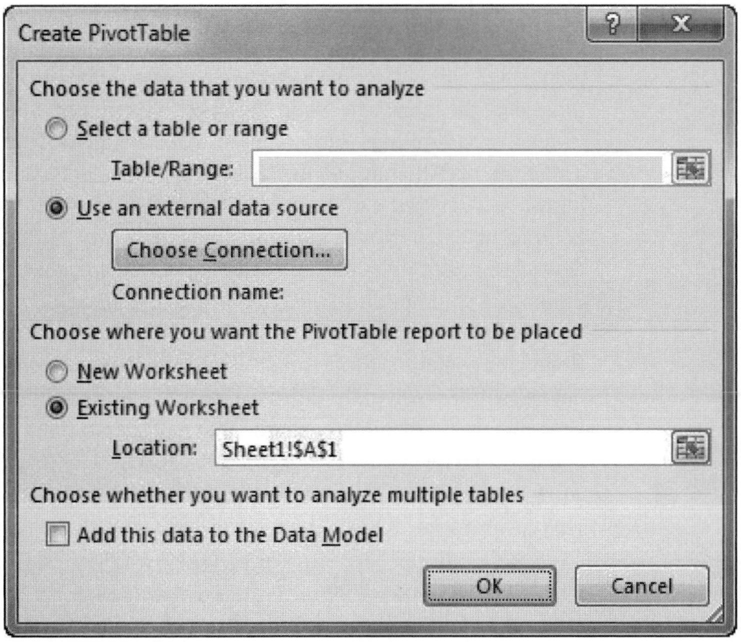

© Cengage Learning

3. In the resulting Existing Connections dialog box (not shown here), click the **Browse for More** button and search for the **Foodmart.cub** file. (If you do this again, you won't have to browse for the cube file. It will be in the list of existing connections, and you can simply select it.)
4. Click Open to return to the Create PivotTable dialog box.
5. Click OK to see a blank pivot table.

As shown in Figure 17.4, the pivot table field list is not the same as for a standard pivot table. First, the Σ sign above the top three items reminds you that these are the only items that can be placed in the Values area of the pivot table. You can get a count of records or a

Figure 17.4
PivotTable Field List for OLAP Cube

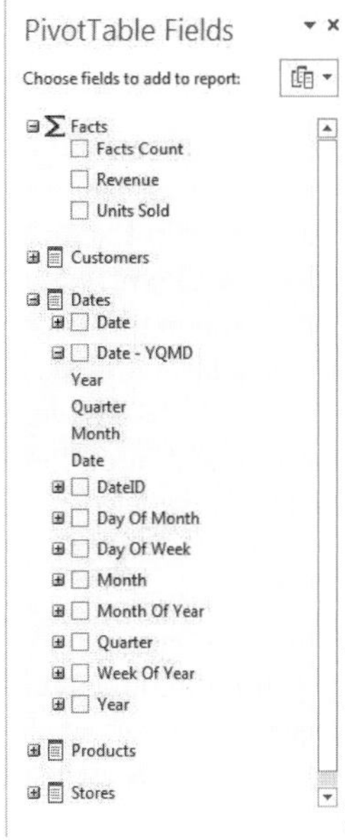

© Cengage Learning

sum of Revenue or UnitsSold. (Actually, you are limited to the Sum operator with OLAP pivot tables. There is a way to get averages, but it requires extra steps in the cube development stage and is not discussed here.) Second, the dimensions you can break down by are limited to those chosen when the cube was first built. You can expand the various items to see the possibilities. For example, you see the YQMD hierarchy for Dates in the figure. There are also hierarchies for Customers, Products, and Stores, and there are individual items, such as Week of Year for Dates. Any of these hierarchies or individual items can be dragged to the Rows, Columns, or Filters areas of the pivot table. Of course, the cube developer has to think carefully about the questions users might want to answer. If a given dimension isn't built into the cube in the first place, it can't be used in a pivot table later on.

One possible pivot table is shown in Figure 17.5. Each value is a sum of revenues. The Rows area contains a Store dimension hierarchy, where Mexico and Canada have been filtered out and a drill-down to the cities in Oregon is shown. Similarly, the Columns area contains the Date dimension hierarchy, where 1997 has been filtered out, and a drill-down to the months in the second quarter of 1998 is shown. Clearly, a lot of useful information can be found with a few mouse clicks. This has made OLAP a very popular technology in the business world. ∎

Figure 17.5 One Possible Foodmart Pivot Table

	A	B	C	D	E	F	G	H	I	J
1	Revenue	Column Labels ⊤								
2		⊟1998							1998 Total	Grand Total
3		⊞Q1	⊟Q2			Q2 Total	⊞Q3	⊞Q4		
4	Row Labels ⊤		⊞April	⊞June	⊞May					
5	⊟USA	$148,402.64	$48,655.54	$48,891.11	$47,947.75	$145,494.40	$145,158.20	$111,753.18	$550,808.42	$550,808.42
6	⊞CA	$42,396.97	$12,130.69	$12,502.35	$12,395.37	$37,028.41	$41,034.28	$34,053.83	$154,513.49	$154,513.49
7	⊟OR	$35,145.11	$11,432.20	$10,157.87	$11,249.15	$32,839.22	$35,509.13	$25,105.04	$128,598.50	$128,598.50
8	⊞Portland	$15,224.56	$4,728.27	$4,477.37	$3,765.01	$12,970.65	$14,635.95	$10,802.10	$53,633.26	$53,633.26
9	⊞Salem	$19,920.55	$6,703.93	$5,680.50	$7,484.14	$19,868.57	$20,873.18	$14,302.94	$74,965.24	$74,965.24
10	⊞WA	$70,860.56	$25,092.65	$26,230.89	$24,303.23	$75,626.77	$68,614.79	$52,594.31	$267,696.43	$267,696.43
11	Grand Total	$148,402.64	$48,655.54	$48,891.11	$47,947.75	$145,494.40	$145,158.20	$111,753.18	$550,808.42	$550,808.42

© Cengage Learning

17-2b PowerPivot and Power View in Excel 2013

The general approach to data analysis embodied in pivot tables is one of the most powerful ways to explore data sets. You learned about basic Excel pivot tables in Chapter 3, and you learned about the more general OLAP technology in the previous subsection. This subsection describes new Microsoft tools of the pivot table variety, **PowerPivot** and **Power View**, that were introduced in Excel 2013.

Actually, PowerPivot was available as a free add-in for Excel 2010, but two things have changed in the version that is described here. First, you no longer need to download a separate PowerPivot add-in. In Excel 2013, you can simply add it in by checking it in the add-ins list. Second, the details of PowerPivot have changed. Therefore, if you find a tutorial for the older PowerPivot add-in on the Web and try to follow it for Excel 2013, you will see that the new version doesn't work in the same way as before. So be aware that the instructions in this section are relevant only for PowerPivot for Excel 2013 and *not* for the older version. (If you don't have Excel 2013 yet and you want to try PowerPivot for Excel 2010, you can search the Web for "PowerPivot 2010 Excel." There is plenty of information out there.)

Before getting into the details of PowerPivot and Power View, it is worth asking why these add-ins are necessary at all. After all, Excel already has pivot tables and pivot charts; it has had them for years. So why are extra tools of the pivot table variety necessary? The short answer is that these newer tools are considerably more flexible and powerful than the basic pivot table/pivot chart combinations discussed in Chapter 3. (A good discussion of their features appears in a Microsoft Web page at http://office.microsoft.com/en-us/excel-help/ whats-new-in-powerpivot-in-excel-2013-HA102893837.aspx. If this link doesn't work, search for "What's new in PowerPivot in Excel 2013.") Among other things, the PowerPivot add-in allows you to do the following:

- Import millions of rows from multiple data sources
- Create relationships between data from different sources, and between multiple tables in a pivot table
- Create implicit calculated fields (previously called measures)—calculations created automatically when you add a numeric field to the Values area of the Field List
- Manage data connections

Interestingly, Microsoft refers to building a **data model** in Excel in its discussion of PowerPivot. This is a somewhat new Microsoft term, and they have provided the following definition.

> **Data Model:** A collection of tables and their relationships that reflects the real-world relationships between business functions and processes—for example, how Products relates to Inventory and Sales.

If you have worked with relational databases, this definition is nothing new. It is essentially the definition of a relational database, a concept that has existed for decades. The difference is that the data model is now contained entirely in Excel, not in Access or some other relational database package.

The Power View add-in for Excel 2013 is used to create various types of reports, including insightful data visualizations. You can read more about Power View at http:// office.microsoft.com/en-us/excel-help/whats-new-in-power-view-in-excel-2013-and-in-sharepoint-2013-HA102901475.aspx. (If this link doesn't work, search for "What's new in Power View in Excel 2013.") As this page states, Power View in Excel 2013 provides an interactive data exploration, visualization, and presentation experience, where you can pull your data together in tables, matrices, maps, and a variety of charts in an interactive view. You will see how it works shortly.

To get started, you must load the following add-ins. From Excel 2013, select Options from the File menu, and select Add-Ins. From the Manage dropdown list at the bottom, select COM Add-ins, and click Go. This takes you to the add-ins list shown in Figure 17.6, where you can check the PowerPivot and Power View items. (If the Developer tab is visible, you can get to this list directly from the Developer ribbon.) Note that your list will probably differ from the one shown here, depending on the add-ins you have installed. In fact, the unchecked PowerPivot for Excel item in this list is the older add-in for Excel 2010, so it probably won't be in your list.

The rest of this subsection leads you through a tutorial on PowerPivot and Power View. It is based on the tutorial presented at http://office.microsoft.com/en-us/excel-help/tutorial-pivottable-data-analysis-using-a-data-model-in-excel-2013-HA102922619.aspx?CTT=3, and it uses a scaled-down version of the data set used in that tutorial. The Facts table in their tutorial contains over 2 million records, which challenges some computers. The Facts table in our data set contains only about 33,000 records, and a number of unnecessary tables and fields have been deleted to save space. Nevertheless, our version is definitely large enough to be interesting. If you are interested, you can download the complete data set from the above site, but the files for our tutorial are included in the example files for this chapter.

Figure 17.6 Add-Ins List with PowerPivot and Power View

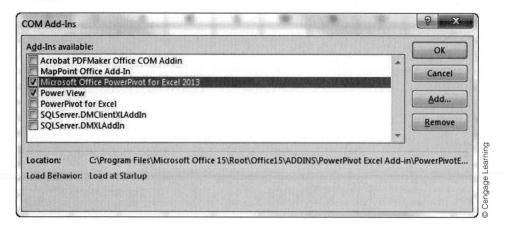

The data set is stored in four separate, currently unrelated, files. There are two Access files, **ContosoSales.accdb** and **ProductCategories.accdb**, and there are two Excel files, **Geography.xlsx** and **Stores.xlsx**. The ContosoSales database has four related tables, DimDate, DimProduct, DimProductSubcategory, and FactSales. Each fact is a sale of some product on some date. The four tables are related through primary and foreign keys as indicated in Figure 17.7. There would normally be a fifth table, DimProductCategory, to the right, joined by ProductCategoryKey fields, with information on the product categories. For illustration, however, this data has been stored separately in the ProductCategories database, which contains a single table, DimProductCategory.

Figure 17.7 Relationships Diagram for ContosoSales Database

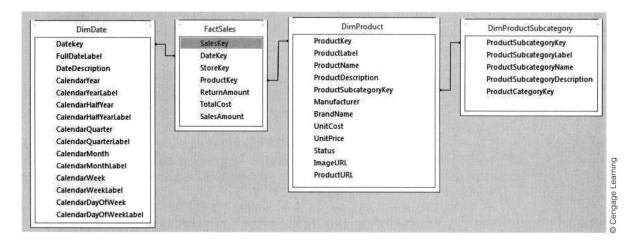

Similarly, each of the two Excel files contains a single table of data that will eventually be related to the ContosoSales data. The Stores file contains data about the stores where the products are sold, which will be related through StoreKey fields. The Geography file has information about the locations of the stores, which will eventually be related to the Stores data through GeographyKey fields. This geography data will permit us to view the sales data on a map.

As stated, these four data sources are currently unrelated. However, they contain the primary and foreign key fields that enable us to relate them with PowerPivot.

Here is an overview of the entire process.

1. Enter the data from the four sources into four worksheets of a single Excel workbook.
2. Use PowerPivot to create relationships between the sources.
3. Modify the data model to enable useful pivot tables.
4. Use Power View to create a map report of sales.

Step 1: Enter the Data into Excel

1. Open a new workbook, open four blank worksheets, Sheet1 through Sheet4, and save the file as **PowerPivot Tutorial.xlsx**.
2. Select cell A1 of Sheet1. From the Data ribbon, select **From Access** in the Get External Data group and browse for the ContosoSales.accdb file. In Excel 2013, you can now select multiple tables. Select all four tables and click OK. Then click OK to import the data into a PivotTable report. You can populate the pivot table in the usual way. As an example, drag SalesAmount from FactSales to the Values area, ProductSubcategoryName from DimProductSubcategory to the Rows area, and CalendarYear from DimDate to the Columns area.
3. You now have the beginnings of a data model. To see it, click **Manage** from the PowerPivot ribbon. This opens the PowerPivot window, where you see a spreadsheet-like view with four tabs at the bottom for the four related database tables. To see that they are indeed related, click **Diagram View** on the PowerPivot Home ribbon. To get back to the previous view, click **Data View** from this ribbon. The PowerPivot window is essentially a "backstage" view for manipulating the data model. You can go back and forth between the PowerPivot and Excel windows as you like. You can also close the PowerPivot window at any time, and you can always get back to it by clicking Manage from the PowerPivot ribbon in Excel.
4. Go back to the Excel window and select cell A1 of Sheet2. From the Data ribbon, select **From Access** again, browse for the ProductCategory.accdb file, and import its single table, DimProductCategory, as a Table into Excel.
5. Open the **Geography.xlsx** file in a separate workbook. Copy its contents and paste them into Sheet3 of the tutorial workbook, starting in cell A1. Designate the data in Sheet3 as an Excel table, and name the table Geography. Then you can close the **Geography.xlsx** file.
6. Repeat the previous step for the Stores data, creating a table named Stores in Sheet4 of the tutorial workbook.

Step 2: Use PowerPivot to Create Relationships between the Sources

1. Select the pivot table in Sheet1. In the PivotTable Fields pane, click ALL. (This is a new PowerPivot option.) You should see all sources, including the currently unrelated Geography, Stores, and Table_ProductCategories.accdb sources. Expand the latter and drag its ProductCategoryName field to the Rows area, *above* ProductSubcategory. You will see a message that "Relationships between tables may be needed." Click the CREATE button to its right to bring up the Create Relationship dialog box. Fill it out as shown in Figure 17.8 and click OK. You want to link the ProductCategoryKey primary key in the ProductCategory table to the foreign key of the same name in the ProductSubcategory table. Then if you revisit Diagram View in the PowerPivot window, you will see that the new relationship exists.

Figure 17.8   Create Relationships Dialog Box for Product Categories

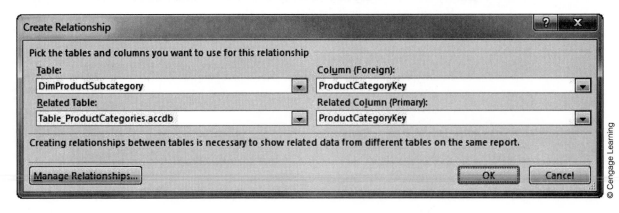

2. Again select the pivot table in Sheet1 and click ALL in the PivotTable Fields pane. Expand Stores and drag StoreName to the Filters area. Another relationship is needed, so click CREATE again, fill out the resulting dialog box as shown in Figure 17.9, and click OK. Now the foreign key is in the FactSales table, and the primary key is in the Stores table. You can filter on various stores in the pivot table to see that everything is working correctly.

Figure 17.9   Create Relationships Dialog Box for Stores

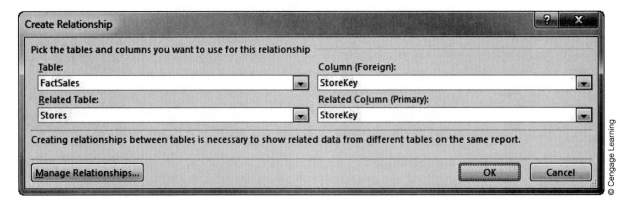

3. As an alternative method of creating a relationship, select cell A1 of Sheet3 (the Geography sheet) and click **Add to Data Model** from the PowerPivot ribbon in Excel. This opens the PowerPivot window with a new Geography tab at the bottom. Click Diagram View to see this new table, and drag it closer to the Stores table. Then drag GeographyKey in Stores (the foreign key) to GeographyKey in Geography (the primary key) to create the relationship. You should see a link between the two tables.

Now all of the data sources are related. You can see this in the Diagram View of the PowerPivot window. You can also see (and manage) the list of relationships by clicking **Relationships** in the Data ribbon of Excel.

Step 3: Modify the Data Model
Now that you have a data model, you can fine-tune it in the PowerPivot window to meet your reporting needs. A few of the many possibilities are described here.

1. Activate the PowerPivot window. (Click Manage from the PowerPivot ribbon in Excel if this window isn't already open.)

2. Right-click the Table_ProductCategories.accdb tab and select **Rename**. Rename it as ProductCategories. This name will be referenced later on, so a friendlier name is convenient.

3. If there are fields in any of the tables that will never be used in a pivot table report, you can hide them to reduce clutter. As an example, select the ProductDescription column in the DimProduct table, right-click, and select **Hide from Client Tools**. This column is then grayed out and is no longer in the pivot table field list.

4. You can create calculated fields (new columns) in the data model. To do this, you type Excel-like formulas in the "formula bar" of the PowerPivot window, but these formulas are actually in the Data Analysis Expressions (DAX) language. As one possibility, select the FactSales tab and click **Add** from the Columns group of the Design ribbon. Then type

   =[SalesAmount] - [Total Cost] - [ReturnAmount]

   in the formula bar and press Enter. Right-click the new column, select **Rename Column**, and name it Profit. This becomes a new field that can be included in a pivot table.

5. In the same way, create two new calculated fields in the DimProduct table. These two calculated fields will be used later on to build a product hierarchy. The formula for the first, which should be renamed ProductCategory, is

   =RELATED(ProductCategories[ProductCategoryName])

   The RELATED function in DAX creates a column of values from a field in a related table. (Note how the table name, ProductCategories, is the name you created earlier.) The formula for the second calculated field, which should be renamed ProductSubcategory, is

   =RELATED(DimProductSubcategory[ProductSubcategoryName])

6. You can also create hierarchies for drilling down in your pivot tables. The first one will be for dates: year, quarter, month, and day. To create this, switch to Diagram View. In the DimDate table, click the Maximize button at the upper right so that you can see all of the fields. Hold the Ctrl key and select CalendarYear, CalendarQuarter, and CalendarMonth. Then right-click and select **Create Hierarchy**. Rename this hierarchy Dates. Then right-click the FullDateLabel field and select **Add to Hierarchy**. This field (which contains individual days) will automatically be added to the bottom of the Dates hierarchy. You can now click the upper right Restore button to return the table to its original size.

7. In a similar way, create a hierarchy called Product Categories in the DimProduct table. It should contain the fields ProductCategory, ProductSubcategory, and ProductName. (Remember that you created two of these fields as calculated fields earlier, exactly for this purpose.)

8. Now switch back to Excel (and save your work!). You can see the effect of the hierarchies in the pivot table. Specifically, drag the current fields from the Rows and Columns areas and replace them with the Dates and Product Categories hierarchies. You now have the ability to drill down through dates or products. One possible pivot table, with data for the Contoso Lancashire Store only, appears in Figure 17.10.

Figure 17.10   Pivot Table with Hierarchies

	A	B	C	D	E
1	StoreName	Contoso Lancashire Store .T			
2					
3	**Sum of SalesAmount**	Column Labels ▼			
4	**Row Labels** ▼	⊞ 2007	⊞ 2008	⊞ 2009	**Grand Total**
5	⊞ **Audio**	2999.252		779.922	3779.174
6	⊞ **Cameras and camcorders**	15481.04	9935.2	22582.6	47998.84
7	⊞ **Cell phones**	10933.296	5260.8	2384	18578.096
8	⊞ **Computers**	57302.19	13870.4107	24347.057	95519.6577
9	⊞ **Music, Movies and Audio Books**	5067.788	4041.9621	3464.3	12574.0501
10	⊟ **TV and Video**	8975.784	6699.7	16228.1	31903.584
11	⊞Car Video			5895	5895
12	⊞Home Theater System	5592		9143.1	14735.1
13	⊟Televisions	3383.784	6699.7		10083.484
14	Adventure Works 20" Analog CRT TV E45 Brown		2000		2000
15	Adventure Works 26" 720p LCD HDTV M140 Black	3383.784			3383.784
16	Adventure Works 26" 720p LCD HDTV M140 Silver		4699.7		4699.7
17	⊞ VCD & DVD			1190	1190
18	**Grand Total**	100759.35	39808.0728	69785.979	210353.4018

© Cengage Learning

Step 4: Use Power View to Create a Map of Sales

The built-in Power View add-in enables you to create a variety of reports that are based on your data model. It will be used here to create a map of sales at the company's stores.

1. Make sure the Excel window is active. In fact, you can close the PowerPivot window for now.

2. Select Power View from the Insert ribbon. (If this item is not active, you need to check Power View in the list of COM add-ins. Also, if this is the first time you are using Power View on this machine, you might be prompted to install the Microsoft Silverlight first.) This creates a new sheet called Power View1 with a list of available Power View fields in the right pane.

3. Check the Profit field in the FactSales list and the RegionCountryName field in the Geography list. Then click **Map** in the Power View ribbon to see a world map with a bubble for each country that reflects the size of its profit. (The maps in Power View are derived from Bing Maps. In fact, you need an Internet connection to access these maps.) If you hover the cursor over any bubble, you can see the summarized data for that country. You can also add a title to the map, as shown in Figure 17.11.

4. This map is just the start of what you can do. Several possibilities follow, and you can experiment with others. First, drag the ProductCategory field from DimProduct to the VERTICAL MULTIPLES area in the Power View Fields pane. This creates a separate map for each of the six product categories.

5. Next, drag the CalendarYear field from DimDate to the COLOR area of the Power View Fields pane. This creates a pie chart for each bubble broken down by year.

6. Next, drag CalendarQuarterLabel from DimDate to the Filters pane just to the right of the maps. This allows you to filter by quarter.

7. Finally, click MAP in the Filters pane. This allows you to filter on other fields, such as ProductCategory. For example, Figure 17.12 shows maps for two of the six product categories.

Figure 17.11

Map of Profit by Country

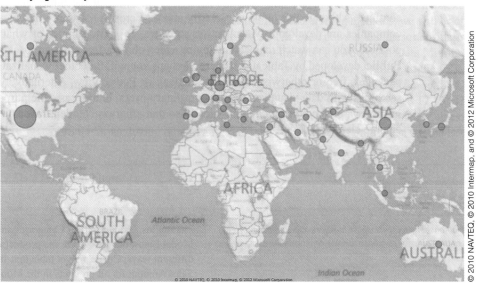

Profit by RegionCountryName

Figure 17.12 Map for Two Product Categories

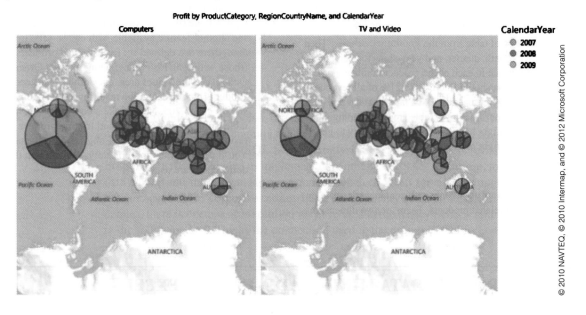

Profit by ProductCategory, RegionCountryName, and CalendarYear

In summary, it will probably take users a while to become comfortable with the new PowerPivot and Power View tools in Excel 2013, but for data analysts, these tools are extremely valuable.

management overhead, and it provides many step-by-step instruction documents that lead you through the process. It even provides several large databases containing real (if somewhat old) data, such as Sam's Club transaction data. If you are an instructor and are planning to teach a significant amount of data mining in your course, this consortium is well worth your consideration.

To create a connection to an SSAS server, you click the Connection button (on either ribbon), click New in the resulting dialog box, and then enter the connection information as illustrated in Figure 17.15. Of course, this information will depend on the SSAS server you have access to.

Figure 17.15
SSAS Server Connection Information

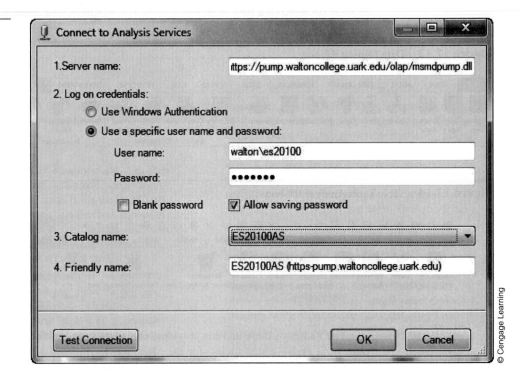

Once you have a connection, you can start exploring the tools with data sets that reside in Excel. That's correct—although the number crunching is performed on the SSAS server, the data and results are in Excel.

Microsoft Table Tools Add-In

To save space, these tools are not covered in detail here, but videos and tutorials are available from the Help dropdown list on either of the ribbons. To see a quick glimpse of what is possible, two of the tools on the Table Tools Analysis ribbon are demonstrated with the same lasagna triers data set that was used to illustrate pivot tables in Chapter 3. You can see this demonstration in the accompanying video, Microsoft Table Tools Add-In.

17-4 CLASSIFICATION METHODS

The previous section introduced one of the most important problems studied in data mining, the classification problem. This is basically the same problem attacked by regression analysis—using explanatory variables to predict a dependent variable—but now the

Figure 17.11

Map of Profit by Country

Profit by RegionCountryName

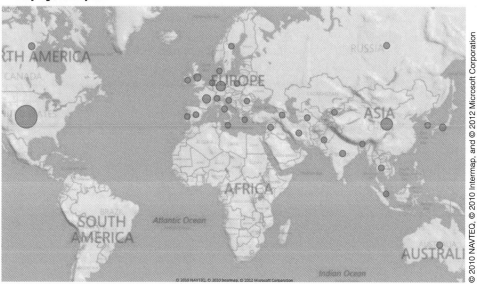

Figure 17.12   Map for Two Product Categories

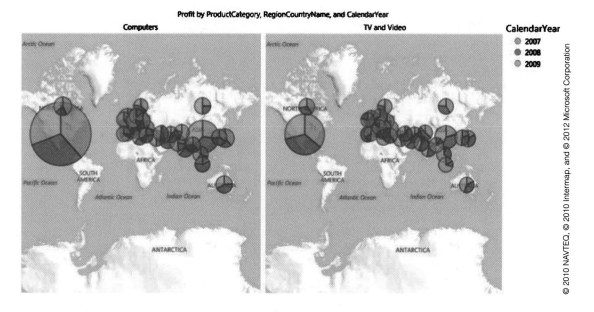

In summary, it will probably take users a while to become comfortable with the new PowerPivot and Power View tools in Excel 2013, but for data analysts, these tools are extremely valuable.

17-2c Visualization Software

Using Tableau Public

As the Power View tool from the previous subsection illustrates, you can gain a lot of insight by using charts to view your data in imaginative ways. This trend toward powerful charting software for data visualization is the wave of the future and will certainly continue. Although this book is primarily about Microsoft software—Excel—many other companies are developing visualization software. To get a glimpse of what is currently possible, you can watch the accompanying video about a free software package, **Tableau Public**, developed by Tableau Software. Perhaps you will find other visualization software packages, free or otherwise, that rival Tableau or Power View. Alternatively, you might see blogs with data visualizations from ordinary users. In any case, the purpose of charting software is to portray data graphically so that otherwise hidden trends or patterns can emerge clearly.

PROBLEMS

Note: Student solutions for problems whose numbers appear within a colored box are available for purchase at www.cengagebrain.com.

Level A

1. Create a pivot table from the **Foodmart.cub** file. Then for each product family and each product department, find the percentage of line items (from the Fact Count measure) of Canada, Mexico, and the three regions of the USA. For example, you should find that 48.27% of all line items in the Alcoholic Beverages department were sold in the Northwest region of the USA.

2. Create a pivot table from the **Foodmart.cub** file. Then for each month, quarter, and year, show the percentage of revenue in each of the product families. For example, you should find that 72.21% of all revenue in March 1997 was in the Food family. Make sure the months in your final pivot table are in chronological order. You might have to drag them manually to get them in the right order.

Level B

3. The file **Adventure Works.cub** contains sales data on biking and related products. There are two dimension

hierarchies, Product Model Categories and Product Model Lines, that categorize the products in slightly different ways. Create a pivot table that shows Internet Sales Amount for all products in the Mountain line in the Rows area, broken down by all product model categories in the Columns area. Then do whatever is necessary to find the percentage of all Internet Sales Amount in the Mountain line due to Tires and Tubes Accessories.

4. Continuing the previous problem, when you create a pivot table from the Adventure Works cube, you see another feature available with cubes: sets. In this case, there is a defined set for long lead products (those with long lead times). Drag Internet Order Quantity to the Values area, check the Long Lead Products box, and sum the resulting values. You should get 15,205. Next, make a copy of this pivot table (to the right or below) and try to reproduce the results *without* checking the Long Lead Products box. You'll need to filter appropriately. Why do you think defined sets are useful?

17-3 MICROSOFT DATA MINING ADD-INS FOR EXCEL

The methods discussed so far in this chapter, all of which basically revolve around pivot tables, are extremely useful for data exploration, but they are not always included in discussions of "data mining." To many analysts, data mining refers only to the algorithms discussed in the remainder of this chapter. These include, among others, algorithms for classification and for clustering. (There are many other types of data mining algorithms not discussed in this book.) Many powerful software packages have been developed by software companies such as SAS, IBM SPSS, Oracle, Microsoft, and others to implement these data mining algorithms. Unfortunately, this software not only takes time to master, but it is also quite expensive. The only data mining algorithms discussed here that are included in the software that accompanies the book are logistic regression and neural nets, two classification methods that are part of the Palisade suite, and they are discussed in the next section.

To provide you with illustrations of other data mining methods, we will briefly discuss **Microsoft data mining add-ins for Excel**. The good news is that these add-ins are free and easy to use. You can find them by searching the Web for Microsoft Data Mining Add-ins.

Once you download these add-ins, you can load them by going to the COM Add-Ins list in Excel and checking SQLServer.DMClientXLAddIn and SQLServer.DMXLAddIn. The first of these provides the Data Mining ribbon shown in Figure 17.13. The second provides the Table Tools Analyze ribbon shown in Figure 17.14. This provides a number of tools for analyzing data in an Excel table. It is available only when a table is selected.

Figure 17.13 Data Mining Ribbon

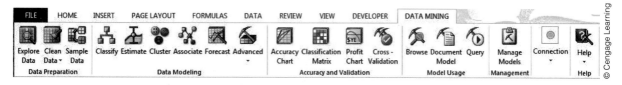

Figure 17.14 Table Tools Analyze Ribbon

The names of these add-ins provide a clue to their downside. These add-ins are really only front ends—client tools—for the Microsoft engine that actually performs the data mining algorithms. This engine is called Analysis Services and is part of Microsoft's **SQL Server** database package. (**SQL Server Analysis Services** is often abbreviated as **SSAS**.) In short, Microsoft decided to implement data mining in SSAS. Therefore, to use its Excel data mining add-ins, you must have a connection to an SSAS server. This might be possible in your academic or corporate setting, but it can definitely be a hurdle. Fortunately for academics, there is one possible solution we have used at the Kelley School, and it is described in the following box. This is the connection used in the examples that follow.

For several years, we have taken advantage of the Microsoft Enterprise Consortium (MEC) set up at the Walton College at the University of Arkansas. As explained at http://enterprise.waltoncollege.uark.edu/mec.asp, this consortium provides instructors and individual students with SQL Server accounts so that you can interact with the SQL Server Management Studio and SSAS tools. You can either connect to their server remotely and use their tools hands-on, or you can connect to their "pump" server to use the data mining add-ins discussed in this section. The MEC provides all of the database

---

management overhead, and it provides many step-by-step instruction documents that lead you through the process. It even provides several large databases containing real (if somewhat old) data, such as Sam's Club transaction data. If you are an instructor and are planning to teach a significant amount of data mining in your course, this consortium is well worth your consideration.

To create a connection to an SSAS server, you click the Connection button (on either ribbon), click New in the resulting dialog box, and then enter the connection information as illustrated in Figure 17.15. Of course, this information will depend on the SSAS server you have access to.

Figure 17.15
SSAS Server Connection Information

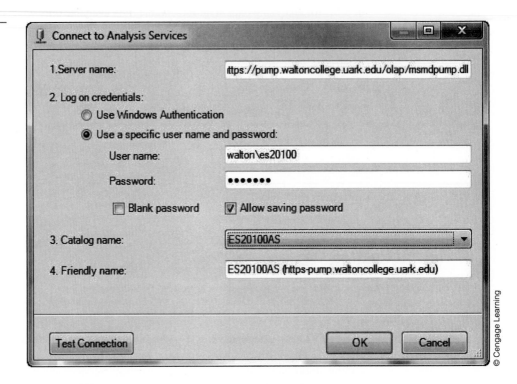

Connect to Analysis Services

1. Server name: `ttps://pump.waltoncollege.uark.edu/olap/msmdpump.dll`

2. Log on credentials:
   ○ Use Windows Authentication
   ● Use a specific user name and password:
      User name: `walton\es20100`
      Password: ●●●●●●●
      ☐ Blank password   ☑ Allow saving password

3. Catalog name: `ES20100AS`

4. Friendly name: `ES20100AS (https-pump.waltoncollege.uark.edu)`

Test Connection   OK   Cancel

Once you have a connection, you can start exploring the tools with data sets that reside in Excel. That's correct—although the number crunching is performed on the SSAS server, the data and results are in Excel.

Microsoft Table Tools Add-In

To save space, these tools are not covered in detail here, but videos and tutorials are available from the Help dropdown list on either of the ribbons. To see a quick glimpse of what is possible, two of the tools on the Table Tools Analysis ribbon are demonstrated with the same lasagna triers data set that was used to illustrate pivot tables in Chapter 3. You can see this demonstration in the accompanying video, Microsoft Table Tools Add-In.

17-4 CLASSIFICATION METHODS

The previous section introduced one of the most important problems studied in data mining, the classification problem. This is basically the same problem attacked by regression analysis—using explanatory variables to predict a dependent variable—but now the dependent variable is categorical. It usually has two categories, such as Yes and No, but it can have more than two categories, such as Republican, Democrat, and Independent. This problem has been analyzed with very different types of algorithms, some regression-like and others very different from regression, and this section discusses three of the most popular **classification methods**. But each of the methods has the same objective: to use data from the explanatory variables to classify each record (person, company, or whatever) into one of the known categories.

Before proceeding, it is important to discuss the role of **data partitioning** in classification and in data mining in general. Data mining is usually used to explore very large data sets, with many thousands or even millions of records. Therefore, it is very possible, and also very useful, to partition the data set into two or even three distinct subsets before the algorithms are applied. Each subset has a specified percentage of all records, and these subsets are typically chosen randomly. The first subset, usually with about 70% to 80% of the records, is called the **training** set. The second subset, called the **testing** set, usually contains the rest of the data. Each of these sets should have *known* values of the dependent variable. Then the algorithm is trained with the data in the training set. This results in a model that can be used for classification. The next step is to test this model on the testing set. It is very possible that the model will work quite well on the training set because this is, after all, the data set that was used to create the model. The real question is whether the model is flexible enough to make accurate classifications in the testing set.

Most data mining software packages have utilities for partitioning the data. (In the following subsections, you will see that the logistic regression procedure in StatTools does not yet have partitioning utilities, but the Palisade NeuralTools add-in for neural networks does have them, and the Microsoft data mining add-in for classification trees also has them.) The various software packages might use slightly different terms for the subsets, but the overall purpose is always the same, as just described. They might also let you specify a third subset, often called a **prediction** set, where the values of the dependent variable are unknown. Then you can use the model to classify these unknown values. Of course, you won't know whether the classifications are accurate until you learn the actual values of the dependent variable in the prediction set.

17-4a Logistic Regression

Logistic regression is a popular method for classifying individuals, given the values of a set of explanatory variables. It estimates the *probability* that an individual is in a particular category. As its name implies, logistic regression is somewhat similar to the usual regression analysis, but its approach is quite different. It uses a *nonlinear* function of the explanatory variables for classification.

Logistic regression is essentially regression with a dummy (0–1) dependent variable. For the *two*-category problem (the only version of logistic regression discussed here), the dummy variable indicates whether an observation is in category 0 or category 1. One approach to the classification problem, an approach that is sometimes actually used, is to run the usual multiple regression on the data, using the dummy variable as the dependent variable. However, this approach has two serious drawbacks. First, it violates the regression assumption that the error terms should be normally distributed. Second, the predicted values of the dependent variable can be between 0 and 1, less than 0, or greater than 1. If you want a predicted value to estimate a *probability*, then values less than 0 or greater than 1 make no sense.

Therefore, logistic regression takes a slightly different approach. Let X_1 through X_k be the potential explanatory variables, and create the linear function $b_0 + b_1X_1 + \cdots + b_kX_k$.

Unfortunately, there is no guarantee that this linear function will be between 0 and 1, and hence that it will qualify as a probability. But the nonlinear function

$$1/\left(1 + e^{-(b_0 + b_1 X_1 + \cdots + b_k X_k)}\right)$$

is *always* between 0 and 1. In fact, the function $f(x) = 1/(1 + e^{-x})$ is an "S-shaped logistic" curve, as shown in Figure 17.16. For large negative values of x, the function approaches 0, and for large positive values of x, it approaches 1.

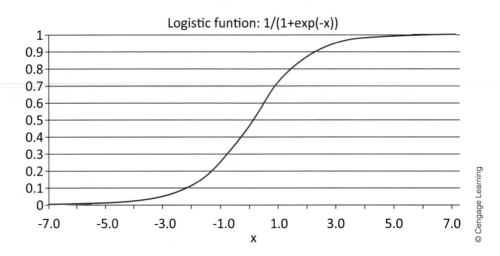

The logistic regression model uses this function to estimate the probability that any observation is in category 1. Specifically, if p is the probability of being in category 1, the model

$$p = 1/\left(1 + e^{-(b_0 + b_1 X_1 + \cdots + b_k X_k)}\right)$$

is estimated. This equation can be manipulated algebraically to obtain an equivalent form:

$$\ln\left(\frac{p}{1 - p}\right) = b_0 + b_1 X_1 + \cdots + b_k X_k$$

This equation says that the natural logarithm of $p/(1 - p)$ is a *linear* function of the explanatory variables. The ratio $p/(1 - p)$ is called the **odds ratio**.

The odds ratio is a term frequently used in everyday language. Suppose, for example, that the probability p of a company going bankrupt is 0.25. Then the odds that the company will go bankrupt are $p/(1 - p) = 0.25/0.75 = 1/3$, or "1 to 3." Odds ratios are probably most common in sports. If you read that the odds against Indiana winning the NCAA basketball championship are 4 to 1, this means that the probability of Indiana winning the championship is 1/5. Or if you read that the odds against Purdue winning the championship are 99 to 1, then the probability that Purdue will win is only 1/100.

The logarithm of the odds ratio, the quantity on the left side of the above equation, is called the **logit** (or **log odds**). Therefore, the logistic regression model states that the logit is a linear function of the explanatory variables. Although this is probably a bit mysterious and there is no easy way to justify it intuitively, logistic regression has produced useful results in many applications.

Although the numerical algorithm used to estimate the regression coefficients is complex, the important goal for our purposes is to interpret the regression coefficients correctly. First, if a coefficient b is positive, then if its X increases, the log odds increases, so the probability of being in category 1 increases. The opposite is true for a negative b. So just by looking at the *signs* of the coefficients, you can see which Xs are positively correlated with being in category 1 (the positive bs) and which are positively correlated with being in group 0 (the negative bs).

You can also look at the magnitudes of the bs to try to see which of the Xs are "most important" in explaining category membership. Unfortunately, you run into the same problem as in regular regression. Some Xs are typically of completely different magnitudes than others, which makes comparisons of the bs difficult. For example, if one X is income, with values in the thousands, and another X is number of children, with values like 0, 1, and 2, the coefficient of income will probably be *much* smaller than the coefficient of children, even though these two variables might be equally important in explaining category membership.

In any case, it is useful to take the antilogarithm of both sides of the equation for log odds to obtain

$$\frac{p}{1-p} = e^{b_0 + b_1 X_1 + \cdots + b_k X_k}$$

Now suppose that X_1, say, increases by an amount Δ and the other Xs do not change. What happens to the odds ratio $p/(1-p)$? Using the law of exponents, it can be shown that the odds ratio changes by a *factor* of $e^{b_1 \Delta}$. In particular, if $\Delta = 1$, this factor is e^{b_1}. This latter value is usually reported in software packages that implement logistic regression.

As an example, suppose that category 1 represents people who have had a heart attack and category 0 represents people who have not. You run a logistic regression with several explanatory variables, one of which is Cholesterol (the person's cholesterol level), and its estimated coefficient turns out to be $b = 0.083$. Then for every unit increase in cholesterol level, the odds of having a heart attack increase by a factor of $e^{0.083} = 1.087$. Because 1 unit of cholesterol is so small, you might prefer to think in terms of 10-unit increases. Then the appropriate factor is $e^{0.083(10)} = 2.293$. In words, if a person's cholesterol level increases by 10 points, you estimate that his or her odds of having a heart attack increase by a factor of 2.293.

However, this does *not* mean that the *probability* of having a heart attack increases by a factor of 2.293. To see this, suppose that the probability of the person having a heart attack, before the cholesterol increase, was $p_0 = 0.25$. Then the person's odds of having a heart attack were $p_0/(1 - p_0) = 0.25/0.75 = 1/3$. After a 10-unit increase in cholesterol, the odds increase to $2.293(1/3) = 0.764$. Now, if p_1 is the new probability of a heart attack, $p_1/(1 - p_1) = 0.764$. This can be solved for p_1 to get $p_1 = 0.764/(1 + 0.764) = 0.433$. [In general, if r is the odds ratio, so that $r = p/(1 - p)$, this can be solved algebraically to get $p = r/(1 + r)$.] If this person experiences another 10-unit increase in cholesterol level, the odds ratio again increases by a factor of 2.293, to $2.293(0.764) = 1.752$, and the new probability of a heart attack occurring is $p_2 = 1.752/(1 + 1.752) = 0.637$. Admittedly, it is not as easy to interpret the regression coefficients as in regular regression, but it *is* possible.

In many situations, especially in data mining, the primary objective of logistic regression is to "score" members, given their Xs. The score for any member is the estimated value of p, found by plugging into the logistic regression equation to get the logit and then solving algebraically to get p. (This is typically done automatically by the software package.) Those members who score highest are the most likely to be in category 1; those who score lowest are most likely to be in category 0. For example, if category 1 represents the responders to some direct mail campaign, a company might mail brochures to the top 10% of all scorers.

These scores can also be used to classify members. Here, a cutoff probability is required. All members who score below the cutoff are classified as 0s, and the rest are classified as 1s. This cutoff value is often 0.5, but any value can be used. For example, it is sometimes chosen to minimize the expected misclassification costs, where the "cost" of misclassifying a 0 as a 1 might be different from misclassifying a 1 as a 0.

Fortunately, StatTools has a logistic regression procedure, as illustrated in Example 17.2.

EXAMPLE | **17.2 CLASSIFYING LASAGNA TRIERS**

The **Lasagna Triers Logistic Regression.xlsx** file contains the same data set from Chapter 3 on 856 people who have either tried or not tried a company's new frozen lasagna product. The categorical dependent variable, Have Tried, and several of the potential explanatory variables contain text, as shown in Figure 17.17. Some logistic regression software packages allow such text variables and implicitly create dummies for them, but StatTools requires all numeric variables. Therefore, the StatTools Dummy utility was used to create dummy variables for all text variables. Using the numeric variables, including dummies, how well is logistic regression able to classify the triers and nontriers?

Figure 17.17 Lasagna Data Set with Text Variables

	A	B	C	D	E	F	G	H	I	J	K	L	M
1	Person	Age	Weight	Income	Pay type	Car Value	CC Debt	Gender	Live Alone	Dwell Type	Mall Trips	Nbhd	Have Tried
2	1	48	175	65500	Hourly	2190	3510	Male	No	Home	7	East	No
3	2	33	202	29100	Hourly	2110	740	Female	No	Condo	4	East	Yes
4	3	51	188	32200	Salaried	5140	910	Male	No	Condo	1	East	No
5	4	56	244	19000	Hourly	700	1620	Female	No	Home	3	West	No
6	5	28	218	81400	Salaried	26620	600	Male	No	Apt	3	West	Yes
7	6	51	173	73000	Salaried	24520	950	Female	No	Condo	2	East	No
8	7	44	182	66400	Salaried	10130	3500	Female	Yes	Condo	6	West	Yes
9	8	29	189	46200	Salaried	10250	2860	Male	No	Condo	5	West	Yes

© Cengage Learning

Objective To use the StatTools Logistic Regression procedure to classify users as triers or nontriers, and to interpret the resulting output.

Solution

A StatTools data set already exists. It was used to create the dummy variables. To run the logistic regression, you select Logistic Regression from the StatTools Regression and Classification dropdown list. Then you fill out the usual StatTools dialog box as shown in Figure 17.18. At the top, you see two options: "with no Count Variable" or "with Count Variable." The former is appropriate here. (The latter is used only when there is a count of the 1s for each joint category, such as males who live alone.) The dependent variable is the dummy variable Have Tried Yes, and the explanatory variables are the original numeric variables (Age, Weight, Income, Car Value, CC Debt, and Mall Trips) and the dummy variables (Pay Type Salaried, Gender Male, Live Alone Yes, Dwell Type Condo, and Dwell Type Home). As in regular regression, one dummy variable for each categorical variable should be omitted.

The logistic regression output is much like regular regression output. There is a summary section and a list of coefficients, shown in Figure 17.19. The summary section is analogous to the ANOVA table in a regression output. The Improvement value indicates how much better the logistic regression classification is than a classification with no explanatory variables at all. The corresponding *p*-value indicates that this improvement is definitely statistically significant, exactly like a small *p*-value in an ANOVA table.

The coefficient section is also analogous to regular regression output. The Wald value is like the *t*-value, and each corresponding *p*-value indicates whether that variable could be excluded from the equation. In this case, Income, Car Value, CC Debt, Gender Male, and the two Dwell Type dummies could possibly be excluded. (You can check that if these variables are indeed excluded and the logistic regression is run again, very little changes.) The signs of the remaining coefficients indicate whether the probability of being

Figure 17.18

StatTools Logistic Regression Dialog Box

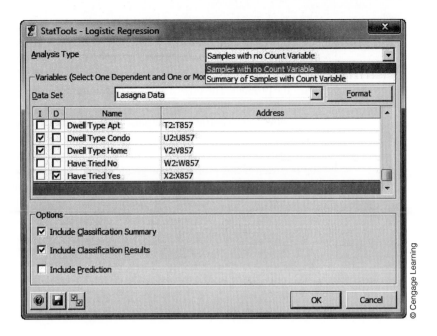

© Cengage Learning

Figure 17.19 **Summary and Coefficients in Logistic Regression Output**

	A	B	C	D	E	F	G	H
8	*Logistic Regression for Have Tried Yes*							
9	*Summary Measures*							
10	Null Deviance	1165.605						
11	Model Deviance	687.943						
12	Improvement	477.662						
13	p-value	< 0.0001						
14								
15		Coefficient	Standard Error	Wald Value	p-value	Lower Limit	Upper Limit	Exp(Coef)
16	*Regresseion Coefficients*							
17	Constant	−2.540588	0.909698	−2.792781	0.0052	−4.323596	−0.757579	0.078820
18	Age	−0.069689	0.010808	−6.447602	< 0.0001	−0.090873	−0.048504	0.932684
19	Weight	0.007033	0.003850	1.827036	0.0677	−0.000512	0.014579	1.007058
20	Income	0.000005	0.000004	1.260222	0.2076	−0.000003	0.000012	1.000005
21	Car Value	−0.000027	0.000020	−1.307318	0.1911	−0.000067	0.000013	0.999973
22	Cc Debt	0.000078	0.000091	0.852025	0.3942	−0.000101	0.000257	1.000078
23	Mall Trips	0.687006	0.059764	11.495247	< 0.0001	0.569868	0.804144	1.987754
24	Pay Type Salaried	1.332747	0.220913	6.032913	< 0.0001	0.899758	1.765736	3.791445
25	Gender Male	0.255542	0.191544	1.334117	0.1822	−0.119884	0.630969	1.291162
26	Live Alone Yes	1.322630	0.283886	4.659013	< 0.0001	0.766213	1.879047	3.753280
27	Dwell Type Condo	−0.080928	0.275087	−0.294191	0.7686	−0.620099	0.458243	0.922260
28	Dwell Type Home	0.176722	0.248864	0.710115	0.4776	−0.311051	0.664495	1.193299

© Cengage Learning

a trier increases or decreases when these variables increase. For example, this probability decreases as Age increases (a minus sign), and it increases as Weight increases (a plus sign). Again, however, you have to use caution when interpreting the magnitudes of the coefficients. For example, the coefficient of Weight is small because Weight has values in the hundreds, and the coefficient of Live Alone Yes is much larger because this variable is either 0 or 1.

The Exp(Coef) column is more interpretable. It contains the e^b values discussed earlier. For example, if Live Alone Yes increases from 0 to 1—that is, a person who doesn't live alone is compared to a person who does live alone—the odds of being a trier increase by a factor of about 3.75. In other words, the people who live alone are much more likely to try the product. The other values in this column can be interpreted in a similar way, and you should be on the lookout for values well above or below 1.

Below the coefficient output, you see the classification summary shown in Figure 17.20. To create these results, the explanatory values in each row are plugged into the logistic regression equation, which results in an estimate of the probability that the person is a trier. If this probability is greater than 0.5, the person is classified as a trier; if it is less than 0.5, the person is classified as a nontrier. The results show the number of correct and incorrect classifications. For example, 422 of the 495 triers, or 85.25%, are classified correctly as triers. The bottom summary indicates that 82.01% of all classifications are correct. However, how good is this really? It turns out that 57.83% of all observations are triers, so a naïve classification rule that classifies everyone as a trier would get 57.83% correct. The last number, 57.34%, represents the improvement of logistic regression over this naïve rule. Specifically, logistic regression is 57.34% of the way from the naïve 57.83% to a perfect 100%.

Figure 17.20

Classification Summary

	A	B	C	D
30		1	0	Percent
31	Classification Matrix			Correct
32	1	422	73	85.25%
33	0	81	280	77.56%
34				
35			Percent	
36	Summary Classification			
37	Correct	82.01%		
38	Base	57.83%		
39	Improvement	57.34%		

© Cengage Learning

The last part of the logistic regression output, a small part of which is shown in Figure 17.21, lists all of the original data and the scores discussed earlier. For example, the first person's score is 75.28%. This is the probability estimated from the logistic regression equation that this person is a trier. Because it is greater than 0.5, this person is classified as a trier. However, this is one of the relatively few misclassifications. The first person is actually a nontrier. In the same way, explanatory values for *new* people, those whose trier status is unknown, could be fed into the logistic regression equation to score them. Then

Figure 17.21

Scores for the First Few People

	M	N	O
41		Analysis	Original
42	Probability	Class	Class
43	75.28%	1	0
44	35.15%	0	1
45	7.65%	0	0
46	9.18%	0	0
47	60.22%	1	1

© Cengage Learning

perhaps some incentives could be sent to the top scorers to increase their chances of trying the product. The point is that logistic regression is then being used as a tool to identify the people most likely to be the triers. ■

Before leaving this subsection, you have probably noticed that StatTools includes another classification procedure called **discriminant analysis**. This is a classical technique developed many decades ago that is still in use. It is somewhat similar to logistic regression and has the same basic goals. However, it is not as prominent in data mining discussions as logistic regression. Therefore, due to space limitations, discriminant analysis is not discussed here.

17-4b Neural Networks

The **neural network** (or simply, **neural net**) methodology is an attempt to model the complex behavior of the human brain. It sends inputs (the values of explanatory variables) through a complex nonlinear network to produce one or more outputs (the values of the dependent variable). Methods for doing this have been studied by researchers in artificial intelligence and other fields for decades, and there are now many software packages that implement versions of neural net algorithms. Some people seem to believe that data mining is synonymous with neural nets. Although this is definitely not true—data mining employs many algorithms that bear no resemblance to neural nets—the neural net methodology is certainly one of the most popular methodologies in data mining. It can be used to predict a categorical dependent variable, as in this section on classification, and it can also be used to predict a numeric dependent variable, as in multiple regression.

The biggest advantage of neural nets is that they often provide more accurate predictions than any other methodology, especially when relationships are highly nonlinear. They also have a downside. Unlike methodologies like multiple regression and logistic regression, neural nets do not provide easily interpretable equations where you can see the contributions of the individual explanatory variables. For this reason, they are often called a "black box" methodology. If you want good predictions, neural nets often provide an attractive method, but you shouldn't expect to understand exactly how the predictions are made.

A brief explanation of how neural nets work helps to clarify this black box behavior. Each neural net has an associated network diagram, something like the one shown in Figure 17.22. This figure assumes two inputs and one output. The network also includes a "hidden layer" in the middle with two hidden nodes. Scaled values of the inputs enter the network at the left, they are weighted by the W values and summed, and these sums are sent to the hidden nodes. At the hidden nodes, the sums are "squished" by an S-shaped logistic-type function. These squished values are then weighted and summed, and the sum is sent to the output node, where it is squished again and rescaled. Although the details of this process are best left to researchers, small illustrative examples are available in the file **Neural Net Explanation.xlsm**. (The file is an .xlsm file because the logistic function

Figure 17.22

Neural Net with Two Inputs and Two Hidden Nodes

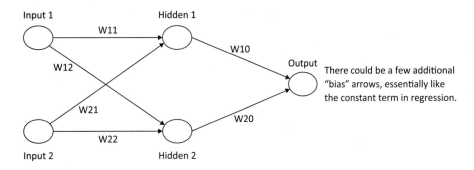

© Cengage Learning

is implemented with a macro, so make sure you enable macros.) There is one sheet for a one-input neural net and another for a two-input neural net. You can see how everything works by studying the cell formulas. However, the main insight provided by this file is that you can see how different sets of weights lead to very different nonlinear behaviors.

A neural net can have any number of hidden layers and hidden nodes, and the choices for these are far from obvious. Many software packages make these choices for you, based on rules of thumb discovered by researchers. Once the structure of the network is chosen, the neural net is "trained" by sending many sets of inputs—even the *same* inputs multiple times—through the network and comparing the outputs from the net with the known output values. Based on many such comparisons, the weights are repeatedly adjusted. This process continues until the weights stop changing in any significant way or some other stopping criterion is reached. Depending on the size of the data set, this iterative process can take some time.

As research continues, the algorithms implemented with neural net software continue to change. The ideas remain basically the same, but the way these ideas are implemented, and even the results, can vary from one implementation to another.

StatTools does not implement neural nets, but another add-in in the Palisade suite, **NeuralTools**, does. It is used for classification in the following continuation of the lasagna triers example.

| EXAMPLE | **17.2 CLASSIFYING LASAGNA TRIERS (CONTINUED)** |

Logistic regression provided reasonably accurate classifications for the lasagna triers data set. Can a neural net, as implemented in Palisade's NeuralTools add-in, provide comparable results?

Objective   To learn how the NeuralTools add-in works, and to compare its results to those from logistic regression.

Solution

The data for this version of the example are in the file **Lasagna Triers NeuralTools.xlsx**. There are two differences from the file used for logistic regression. First, no dummy variables are necessary. The NeuralTools add-in is capable of dealing directly with text variables. Second, there is a Prediction Data sheet with a second data set of size 250 to be used for prediction. Its values of the dependent Have Tried variable are unknown.

You launch NeuralTools just like StatTools, @RISK, or any of the other Palisade add-ins. This produces a NeuralTools tab and ribbon, as shown in Figure 17.23. As you can see, NeuralTools uses a Data Set Manager, just like StatTools. The only difference is that when you specify the data set, you must indicate the role of each variable in the neural net. The possible roles are Independent Numeric, Independent Categorical, Dependent Numeric, Dependent Categorical, Tag, and Unused. Except for Tag, which isn't used here, these have the obvious meanings. So the first step is to create two data sets, one for each sheet, with Have Tried as Dependent Categorical, Person as Unused, and the other variables as Independent Numeric or Independent Categorical as appropriate. (NeuralTools usually guesses the roles correctly.) We call these data sets Lasagna Data and Prediction Data, respectively.

To train the data in the Lasagna Data set, you activate the Data sheet and click Train on the NeuralTools ribbon to get a Training dialog box with three tabs. The Train tab shown in Figure 17.24 provides three basic options. The first option allows you to partition the data set into training and testing subsets. The default shown here is to set aside a random 20%

Figure 17.23

NeuralTools Ribbon

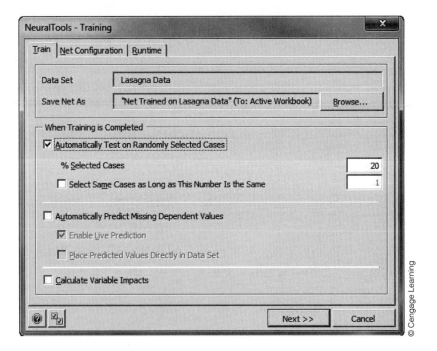

Figure 17.24

Train Tab of Training Dialog Box

of cases for testing. The second option is for predicting cases with missing values of the dependent variable. There are no such cases in the Data sheet. Prediction will be performed later on the Prediction Data set. The third option is to calculate variable impacts. This is useful when you have a large number of potential explanatory variables. It lets you screen out the ones that seem to be least useful. You can check this option if you like. However, its output doesn't tell you, at least not directly, how the different explanatory variables affect the dependent variable.

The Net Configuration tab shown in Figure 17.25 lets you select one of three options for the training algorithm. The PN/GRN (probabilistic neural net) algorithm is relatively new. It is fairly quick and it usually gives good results, so it is a good option to try, as is done here.[1] The MLF option (multi-layer feedforward) algorithm is more traditional, but it is considerably slower. The Best Net Search tries both PN/GRN and various versions of MLF to see which is best, but it is quite slow. (The finished version of the file has results from MLF, and they are very similar to those from PN/GRN.)

The Runtime tab (not shown here) specifies stopping conditions for the algorithm. You can accept the defaults, and you can always stop the training prematurely if it doesn't seem to be making any improvement.

Once you click Next on any of the tabs, you will see a summary (not shown here) of the model setup. Then you can click its Train button to start the algorithm. You will see a

---

[1]The abbreviation PN/GRN is a bit confusing. For classification problems, the algorithm is called probabilistic neural net (PNN). However, if the dependent variable is continuous, the same basic algorithm is called generalized regression neural net, which explains the GRN abbreviation.

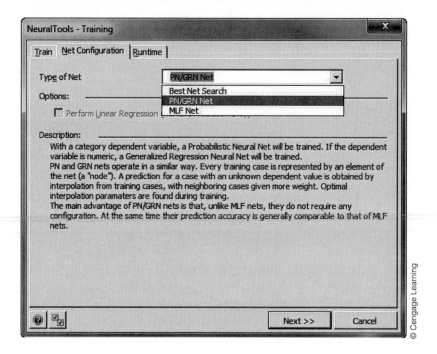

Figure 17.25

Net Configuration Tab of Training Dialog Box

NeuralTools - Training

Train | Net Configuration | Runtime

Type of Net: PN/GRN Net
- Best Net Search
- PN/GRN Net
- MLF Net

Options:

☐ Perform Linear Regression

Description:

With a category dependent variable, a Probabilistic Neural Net will be trained. If the dependent variable is numeric, a Generalized Regression Neural Net will be trained.

PN and GRN nets operate in a similar way. Every training case is represented by an element of the net (a "node"). A prediction for a case with an unknown dependent value is obtained by interpolation from training cases, with neighboring cases given more weight. Optimal interpolation paramaters are found during training.

The main advantage of PN/GRN nets is that, unlike MLF nets, they do not require any configuration. At the same time their prediction accuracy is generally comparable to that of MLF nets.

Next >>   Cancel

© Cengage Learning

progress monitor, and eventually you will see results on a new sheet, the most important of which are shown in Figure 17.26. (As in other Palisade add-ins, the results are stored by default in a new workbook. You can change this behavior from the Application Settings dialog box, available from the Utilities dropdown list.)

Figure 17.26

Selected Training Results

	B	C	D	E
33	**Classification Matrix**			
34	(for training cases)			
35			No	Yes	Bad(%)
36	No		250	41	14.0893%
37	Yes		43	351	10.9137%
38					
39	**Classification Matrix**			
40	(for testing cases)			
41			No	Yes	Bad(%)
42	No		56	14	20.0000%
43	Yes		15	86	14.8515%

© Cengage Learning

The top part shows classification results for the 80%, or 685, cases used for training. About 14% of the No values were classified incorrectly, and close to 11% of the Yes values were classified incorrectly. The bottom part shows similar results for the 20%, or 171, cases used for testing. The incorrect percentages, 20% and about 15%, are not as good as for the training set, but they are not that much worse. Also, these results are slightly better than those from logistic regression, where about 18% of the classifications were incorrect. (Remember, however, that the data set wasn't partitioned into training and testing subsets for logistic regression.)

Now that the model has been trained, it can be used to predict the unknown values of the dependent variable in the Prediction Data set. To do so, you activate the Prediction

Data sheet, click Predict on the NeuralTools ribbon, and then fill out the resulting dialog box as shown in Figure 17.27. If there are multiple trained nets, you can browse for the one you want to use in the Net to Use box. The Enable Live Prediction option provides real-time predictions: If values of the explanatory variables change for any cases in the prediction set, the predictions will update automatically.

Figure 17.27
Prediction Dialog Box

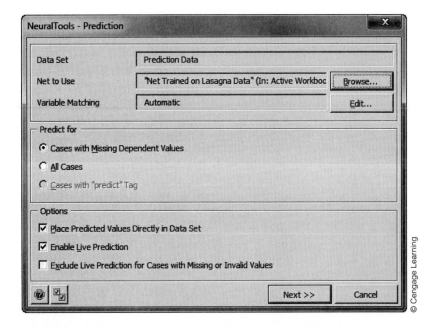

When the Enable Live Prediction option is checked and you click Next, you will see another Options for Live Prediction Cells dialog box (not shown here), where you can accept the defaults and click OK to see the Prediction setup. Then you click its Predict button to create the predictions. At this point, NeuralTools runs each of the cases in the Prediction Data sheet through the trained net and displays the results next to the prediction data. A few of these are shown in Figure 17.28. However, be careful about interpreting the Prediction% column. Unlike the StatTools logistic regression output, each percentage shown here is the probability that the prediction is *correct*, not the probability that the person is a trier. For example, the first person is classified as a nontrier, and there is 89.53% confidence that this classification is correct. Equivalently, the probability is only 10.47% that this person is a trier.

Figure 17.28
Prediction Results

	M	N	O	P	Q
1			Prediction Report: "Net Trained on Lasagna Data"		
2	Have tried		Tag Used	Prediction	Prediction%
3	No		predict	No	89.53%
4	Yes		predict	Yes	81.04%
5	Yes		predict	Yes	72.06%
6	No		predict	No	57.67%
7	Yes		predict	Yes	90.28%
8	Yes		predict	Yes	99.64%
9	No		predict	No	52.81%
10	No		predict	No	79.08%
11	Yes		predict	Yes	98.50%

As indicated earlier, these results are live. For example, if you change the Live Alone and Mall Trips data for the first person to Yes and 8, you will see that the prediction changes to Yes, with 86.62% confidence. This feature lets you experiment with explanatory data values to see their effect on the predictions. This doesn't explain exactly how the neural net "black box" is working, but it helps. ∎

17-4c Classification Trees

Decision Trees with Microsoft Data Mining Add-In

The two classification methods discussed so far, logistic regression and neural networks, use complex nonlinear functions to capture the relationship between explanatory variables and a categorical dependent variables. The method discussed in this subsection, **classification trees** (sometimes called **decision trees**, not to be confused with the very different decision trees in Chapter 6), is also capable of discovering nonlinear relationships, but it is much more intuitive. This method, which has many variations, has existed for decades, and it has been implemented in a variety of software packages. Unfortunately, it is not available in any of the software that accompanies this book, but it is available in the free Microsoft Data Mining Add-Ins discussed earlier. The essential features of the method are explained here, and the accompanying video, Decision Trees with Microsoft Data Mining Add-In, illustrates the method.

Referring to the lasagna data again, imagine that you have all 856 observations in a single box. If you choose one case randomly, there is considerable uncertainty about the Have Tried status of this person because the box is divided about 57% Yes to 43% No. The basic idea of classification trees is to split the box into two or more boxes so that each box is more "pure" than the original box, meaning that each box is more nearly Yes than No, or vice versa. There are many possible splits. For example, one possible split is on Mall Trips: those with fewer than 4 and those with 4 or more. You can check (with a pivot table, say) that the first box is divided 25.8% Yes to 74.2% No and the second box is divided 76.4% Yes to 23.6% No. Each of these boxes (or subsets, if you prefer) is purer than the original box, so this is a promising split.

Each of these boxes can now be split on another variable (or even the same variable) to make them even purer, and this splitting can continue. Eventually, the boxes are either sufficiently pure or they contain very few cases, in which case further splitting is not useful. This sounds simple enough, but the trick is to find the best splits and a good criterion for stopping. The details are implemented in different ways in different software packages.

The attractive aspect of this method is that the final result is a set of simple rules for classification. As an example, the final tree might look like the one in Figure 17.29. (You will see this tree in the accompanying video.) Each box has a bar that shows the purity of the corresponding box, where blue corresponds to Yes values and red corresponds to No values. (These colors show up in the software.) The first split, actually a three-way split, is on Mall Values: fewer than 4, 4 or 5, and at least 6. Each of these is then split in a different way. For example, when Mall Trips is fewer than 4, the split is on Nbhd West versus Nbhd not West. The splits you see here are the only ones made. They achieve sufficient purity, so the algorithm stops splitting after these.

Predictions are then made by majority rule. As an example, suppose a person has made 3 mall trips and lives in the East. This person belongs in the second box down on the right, which has a large majority of No values. Therefore, this person is classified as a No. In contrast, a person with 10 mall trips belongs in one of the two bottom boxes on the right. This person is classified as a Yes because *both* of these boxes have a large majority of Yes values. In fact, the last split on Age is not really necessary.

This classification tree leads directly to the following rules.

Figure 17.29

Possible
Classification Tree

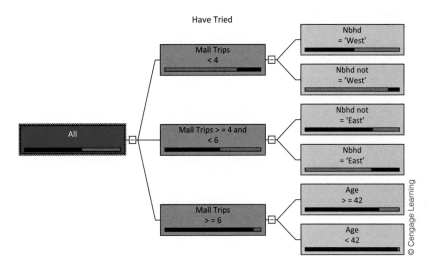

- If the person makes fewer than 4 mall trips:
  - If the person lives in the West, classify as a trier.
  - If the person doesn't live in the West, classify as a nontrier.
- If the person makes 4 or 5 mall trips:
  - If the person doesn't live in the East, classify as a trier.
  - If the person lives in the East, classify as a nontrier.
- If the person makes at least 6 mall trips, classify as a trier.

The ability of classification trees to provide such simple rules, plus fairly accurate classifications, has made this a very popular classification technique.

17-4d Classification and Lift

One concept that often accompanies discussions of classification is **lift**. Imagine that you have a large population where 5% of the people, if they received one of your sales brochures, would actually purchase something from you. You have enough money to mail 10,000 sales brochures, and you naturally want to mail these to the people most likely to respond by making a purchase. If you randomly choose 10,000 people, you can expect to reach 500 purchasers (5% of 10,000) by luck alone. But if you use one of the classification techniques discussed here to *score* the people on their probability of purchasing, and you then mail brochures to the top 10,000 scorers, you ought to reach more—hopefully many more—than 500 purchasers. Lift is defined (loosely) as the increase in the number of purchasers you reach over the random mailing. (There is a very precise definition of lift, but the intuitive meaning given here will suffice.) Presumably, better classification methods will have higher lift.

Many software packages illustrate lift with a **lift chart**. The accompanying Decision Trees with Microsoft Data Mining Add-In video illustrates how you can obtain a lift chart (which it calls an accuracy chart) for the lasagna data. This chart is shown in Figure 17.30. You can think of the horizontal axis as the percentage of the population you mail to, and the vertical axis as the percentage of the triers you reach. In this data set, the 5% from the previous paragraph is replaced by about 57%, the percentage of triers total. The bottom line in the chart corresponds to the random mailing. If you mail to a random x% of the customers, you will reach about x% of the triers just by luck. At the other extreme, the top line is the

Figure 17.30

Lift (Accuracy)
Chart for Lasagna
Data

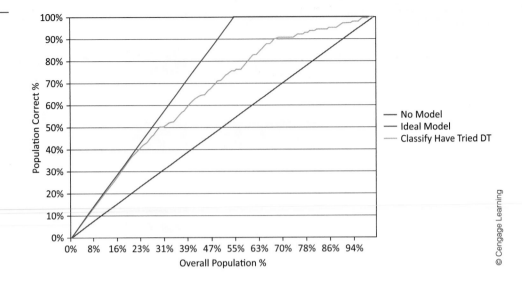

perfect choice—it is when you have the perfect foresight to mail *only* to the triers, at least until there are no triers left (the flat part past 57%). The curve in between is from the classification tree. As an example, if you mail to the top 31% of scorers, you will reach about 50% of the triers, not just 31% as in the random mailing. (From 31%, read up and to the left to get the 50%.) This is a reasonably good lift. Obviously, you want the middle curve to be as close as possible to the upper (perfect) line.

17-4e Classification with Rare Events

Classification methods are often used on data sets with rare events. As an example, suppose a company has data on millions of customers and is trying to classify them as either defaulting on credit card payments (Yes) or not (No). There is probably a very small percentage of Yes values in the data, maybe even less than 1%. In this case, unless special techniques are used, it is very likely that any classification algorithm in any software package will classify *everyone* as No. The algorithm can then claim that over 99% of its classifications are correct. Of course, this sounds good, but the predictions are worthless.

However, all is not lost. Most packages, including NeuralTools, accompany predictions of new observations with probabilities that the predictions are correct. So even if all of these probabilities are above 50%, you can still sort on the probability column to see the predictions that are least likely to be correct. Then if you are forced to choose some observations who, say, will default on credit card payments, you can choose the ones with the lowest probabilities of being classified as No.

PROBLEMS

Level A

5. The file **P17_05.xlsx** contains data on 100 consumers who drink beer. Some of them prefer light beer, and others prefer regular beer. A major beer producer believes that the following variables might be useful in discriminating between these two groups: gender, marital status, annual income level, and age. Use logistic regression to classify the consumers on the basis of these explanatory variables. How successful is it? Which variables appear to be most important in the classification?

6. Admissions directors of graduate business programs constantly review the criteria they use to make admission decisions. Suppose that the director of a particular top-20 MBA program is trying to understand how she and her staff discriminate between those who are admitted to their program and those who are rejected. To do this, she collects data on each of the following variables for 100 randomly selected individuals who applied in the past academic year: whether the applicant graduated in the top 10% of his or her undergraduate class, whether the admissions office interviewed the applicant in person or over the telephone, the applicant's overall GMAT score (where the highest possible score is 800), and the applicant's undergraduate grade-point average (standardized on a four-point scale). These data are provided in the file **P17_06.xlsx**. How useful is logistic regression in discriminating between those who are admitted to this MBA program and those who are not on the basis of these variables?

7. A company that sells through a catalog and online through the Web has collected data on 10,000 potential customers. The data are in the file **P17_07.xlsx**. They include RFM (recency, frequency, and monetary) variables, which are popular in marketing research, as well as yes/no data on whether the person has received various advertising, and yes/no data on whether the person has made a catalog purchase or an online purchase in the latest time period.
   a. Use pivot tables to explore how or whether the Catalog Purchase variable in column I is influenced by the variables in columns B–H.
   b. Repeat part **a** for the Online Purchase variable in column J.

8. Continuing the previous problem, the same data have been split into two sets in the file **P17_08.xlsx**. The first 9500 observations are in the Training Data sheet, and the last 500 observations are in the Prediction Data sheet. In this latter sheet, the values in the Catalog Purchase and Online Purchase columns have been deleted. The purpose of this problem is to use NeuralTools to train a neural net with the data on the first sheet and then use this neural net to predict values on the second sheet. Proceed as follows.
   a. Designate a NeuralTools data set for each sheet. The Customer and Catalog Purchase columns should be marked Unused, and the Online Purchase column should be marked Category Dependent. (The Catalog Purchase column is ignored in this problem.)
   b. Use the NeuralTools Train option to train a neural net on the first data set, using the PNN algorithm. You can accept the option to set aside 20% of the 9500 observations for testing. Then interpret the outputs. In particular, can you tell how the neural net making its predictions?
   c. Use the NeuralTools Predict option to predict Online Purchase for the observations in the

Prediction Data sheet. What can you say about the resulting predictions? If you were forced to choose some people as most likely to make an online purchase, which people would you choose?

9. The file **P17_09.xlsx** contains data on 74 companies that have either gone bankrupt or haven't. The data set also contains data on five frequently quoted accounting ratios.
   a. Create a pivot table that shows the average of each ratio, broken down by the Yes/No values in column G. Comment on which ratios seem to have an effect on whether a company goes bankrupt.
   b. Use logistic regression to classify companies as bankrupt or not, using all five of the accounting ratios. Does this do a good job of classifying? Are any of the ratios insignificant?
   c. Experiment with logistic regressions that use only two of the accounting ratios. Which pair classifies about as well as in part **b**, but with both ratios significant? Could the high p-values in part **b** be due to multicollinearity?

10. Using the same data as in the previous problem, use NeuralTools, with the PNN algorithm, to perform the classification. Even though there are only 74 companies, you can still use 20% of them for testing. Then at the end of the run, respond Yes to the sensitivity analysis. This lets you see how sensitive the percentage of bad predictions in the test data is to size or composition of the test data set. Comment on the results.

Level B

11. The file **P17_11.xlsx** contains customer data on acceptance of products with various attributes. This is explained more fully in the file. There are three potential Yes/No dependent variables, Accept1, Accept2, and Accept3. To keep the outputs straight, it is a good idea to store the results from the following three parts in separate files.
   a. Use NeuralTools to classify the Accept1 dependent variable, ignoring Accept2 and Accept3. Try the PNN algorithm and then the MLF algorithm. Comparing their outputs, do they classify equally well? (Keep in mind that MLF takes a *lot* more computing time, but you can stop it prematurely if it doesn't seem to be making progress.)
   b. Repeat part **a**, using Accept2 as the dependent variable and ignoring Accept1 and Accept3. You can skip the MLF algorithm for this part. However, respond Yes to run a sensitivity analysis at the end of the run. This lets you see how sensitive the percentage of bad predictions in the test data is to size or composition of the test data set. Comment on the results.

c. Repeat part **b**, using Accept3 as the dependent variable and ignoring Accept1 and Accept2.

12. The file **P17_12.xlsx** contains data on 178 wines. They are categorized into three types, labeled A, B, and C. The rest of the variables are numeric properties of the wines. Use NeuralTools to classify these wines. Use the PNN algorithm, and check the Variable Impact Analysis option in the Train dialog box. This ranks the variables on their impact, which provides some information on which variables might not be needed for the neural net. Then run the algorithm a second time, using only the top five variables in terms of their impact percentages. (In the Data Set Manager, mark the others Unused.) Comment on the results. Is the prediction accuracy much different without the deleted variables?

13. Continuing the previous problem, the file **P17_13. xlsx** contains the same wine data. Using the Microsoft Data Mining add-in, a decision tree classification was performed (with 0% of the cases held out for testing). You can see the resulting tree in the Decision_Tree sheet. Write out the corresponding decision rules implied by this tree. Then use a nested IF formula to make the classifications in column O of the Data sheet, and find the percentage of incorrect classifications. Would you say the decision tree is very accurate?

14. Neural nets (and NeuralTools) can also be used when the dependent variable is continuous, not categorical. In this case, the method is an alternative to multiple regression. The file **P17_14.xlsx** contains fairly old Boston housing data that appears frequently in data mining discussions. The original purpose was to use regression to see how the median value of a house (MEDVAL) depends on air quality, as measured by the variable NOX, after controlling for a number of other variables. The results of this regression appear in the Original Analysis sheet. As you can see on this sheet, the resulting RMSE (root mean squared error) is about 4 (in thousands of dollars). See if you can get better results with NeuralTools. Unlike the regression analysis, you don't need to create any nonlinear transformations—NeuralTools does this internally. Use the GRN algorithm, make sure the Perform Linear Regression option in the Net Configuration tab is *unchecked*, and don't use any test cases. That is, use all of the cases for training. Discuss your results.

15. Continuing problem 8, there is another method that has been suggested when the dependent variable has only a small percentage of one category, in this case Y (yes). This is *oversampling*. To do this, you train the neural net on a subset that is more equally divided between Y and N values. This allows the net to "learn" better about the Y cases because it sees a much higher percentage of them. NeuralTools lets you do this fairly easily by creating a Tag variable, as explained in the file **P17_15.xlsx**. Then when you define the data set, you mark this variable as Tag. In general, each Tag value can be Train, Test, or Predict, depending on how you want that case to be treated.

   a. Run the PNN algorithm on the data in this file, using Online Purchase as the dependent variable, ignoring the Catalog Purchase variable, and using the given Tag variable. You will see in the Train dialog box how the Tag variable is recognized.

   b. In the resulting output, you should see that the percentage of bad predictions for the training data is *larger* than the percentage of bad predictions for the testing data. However, using the classification matrices in the output, argue why this is actually misleading—that is, why the predictions are really *better* in the training data.

   c. Are there any Y predictions for the prediction data (the last 500 rows)? What percentage?

17-5 CLUSTERING

In data mining terminology, the classification methods in the previous section are called **supervised** data mining techniques. This term indicates that there is a dependent variable the method is trying to predict. In contrast, the clustering methods discussed briefly in this section are called **unsupervised** data mining techniques. Unsupervised methods have no dependent variable. Instead, they search for patterns and structure among all of the variables. *Clustering* is probably the most common unsupervised method, and it is the only one discussed here. However, another popular unsupervised method you might encounter is **market basket analysis** (also called **association analysis**), where patterns of customer purchases are examined to see which items customers tend to purchase together, in the same "market basket." This analysis can be the basis for product shelving arrangements, for example.

Clustering, known in marketing circles as **segmentation**, tries to group entities (customers, companies, cities, or whatever) into similar clusters, based on the values of their variables. This method bears some relationship to classification, but the fundamental difference is that in clustering, there are no fixed groups like the triers and nontriers in classification. Instead, the purpose of clustering is to *discover* the number of groups and their characteristics, based entirely on the data.

Clustering methods have existed for decades, and a wide variety of clustering methods have been developed and implemented in software packages. The key to all of these is the development of a dissimilarity measure. Specifically, to compare two rows in a data set, you need a numeric measure of how dissimilar they are. Many such measures are used. For example, if two customers have the same gender, they might get a dissimilarity score of 0, whereas two customers of different genders might get a dissimilarity score of 1. Or if the incomes of two customers are compared, they might get a dissimilarity score equal to the squared difference between their incomes. The dissimilarity scores for different variables are then combined in some way, such as normalizing and then summing, to get a single dissimilarity score for the two rows as a whole.

Once a dissimilarity measure is developed, a clustering algorithm attempts to find clusters of rows so that rows within a cluster are similar and rows in different clusters are dissimilar. Again, there are many ways to do this, and many variations appear in different software packages. For example, the package might let you specify the number of clusters ahead of time, or it might discover this number automatically.

In any case, once an algorithm has discovered, say, five clusters, your job is to understand (and possibly name) these clusters. You do this by exploring the distributions of variables in different clusters. For example, you might find that one cluster is composed mostly of older women who live alone and have modest incomes, whereas another cluster is composed mostly of wealthy married men.

As with classification trees in the previous section, there is unfortunately no software accompanying this book that implements clustering. Again, however, it is possible to do so with the free Microsoft Data Mining Add-Ins discussed earlier. You can view how this works in the accompanying video Microsoft Table Tools Add-In that was mentioned earlier in the chapter. (In its data mining add-ins, Microsoft implements clustering in both the Table Tools Analyze ribbon and the Data Mining ribbon, and it even implements these in slightly different ways. The video illustrates only the former.)

PROBLEMS

Level A

16. The file **P17_16.xlsx** contains various data on 325 metropolitan cities in the UnitedStates. Cell comments in row 1 explain some of the variables. The Microsoft Data Mining add-in was used to cluster these cities, with the results shown in the file. There are four clusters, cluster membership is listed in column V of the Data sheet, and the composition of clusters is in the Categories Report sheet. Study this report carefully, and then write a short report about the clusters. Does the clustering make sense? Can you provide descriptive, meaningful names for the clusters?

17. Continuing problem 12, the file **P17_17.xlsx** contains the same wine data. Instead of trying to use a classification algorithm to classify wines into the three

known types (A, B, and C), it is interesting to see if a clustering algorithm can *discover* these known categories. The file contains the results of two runs of the Microsoft Data Mining Detect Categories algorithm. Of course, neither uses the Type variable in column A. The first run didn't specify the number of categories, and the add-in found 7, with category membership in column O of the Data sheet. The second run specified the number of categories as 3, with category membership in column P of the Data sheet. Analyze the results closely. Do either (or both) of the runs seem to discover the known A, B, and C types?

Level B

18. This problem lets you see how dissimilarity, the key to clustering, might be calculated and then used for prediction. The file **P17_18.xlsx** contains data for

10 people. The value of Amount Spent for person 10 is unknown, and the ultimate purpose is to use the data for the first 9 people to predict Amount Spent for person 10. To do so, a common "nearest neighbor" approach is used. You find the three most similar people to person 10 and then use the average of their Amount Spent values as a prediction for person 10. (In the data mining literature, this approach is called k-means, with $k = 3$.) Proceed as follows.

a. For each of the five attributes, Gender to Marital Status, fill in the corresponding yellow boxes as indicated. Each box shows how dissimilar each person is to each other person, based on a single attribute only. The box for Gender has been filled in to get you started.

b. These yellow values can be combined in at least three ways, as indicated by the cell comments above the orange boxes. Fill in these orange boxes.

c. Find the dissimilarity between each person and person 10 in three ways in the blue box at the top, following the cell comment in cell I2.

d. Use Excel's RANK function in the green box to rank the dissimilarities in the blue box.

e. Find three predictions of Amount Spent for person 10, each an average of Amount Spent for the three most similar people to person 10. There will be *three* predictions because each set of rankings in the green box can lead to a different set of three nearest neighbors.

17-6 CONCLUSION

Data mining is a huge topic, and its importance is only starting to be appreciated in business and other areas. This is not because data analysis has not played an important role for many years, but it is because large data sets are now more common than ever before, and it is also because better algorithms, better software, and better technology in general are now available to mine large data sets. The discussion in this chapter provides only a glimpse into the variety of problems data mining can attack and the types of methods it can employ. Indeed, an increasing number of books on data mining, some highly technical and others much less technical, are being written[2]. Finally, it is important to realize that data mining is only part, although a very important part, of "business analytics." For example, business analytics often uses the insights from data mining to optimize a system. The optimization aspect is not usually included in the realm of data mining, but data mining as a first step often enables an intelligent optimization.

Summary of Key Terms

Term	Explanation	Excel	Page
Data mining	Variety of methods used to discover patterns in data sets, usually large data sets		948
Data warehouse	Specially constructed database that can be used for data mining		948
Data mart	Scaled-down data warehouse for a particular business function or department		948
Online analytical processing (OLAP)	Methodology for developing fast, flexible pivot table reports		950
Star schema	Database where a Facts table is surrounded by Dimensions tables		950
OLAP cube	Special type of file where aggregates are preprocessed to produce quick pivot table analyses		950

[2]To appreciate how big this topic is becoming, you might want to read two recent books: *In the Plex*, by Levy and Ganser, Simon & Schuster, 2011; and *Big Data*, by Mayer-Schonberger and Cukier, Eamon Dolan/Houghton Mifflin Harcourt, 2013. The former, mostly about the many ways data mining is used at Google, is mind-blowing.

Term	Explanation	Excel	Page
PowerPivot	New built-in add-in for Excel 2013 that enables analysis of large unrelated tables, all within Excel	PowerPivot tab and window, requires add-in to be loaded	954
Power View	New feature in Excel 2013 for creating a variety of reports	Insert tab, requires add-in to be loaded	954
Data model	New terminology in Excel 2013, essentially a relational database structure created in Excel with PowerPivot	PowerPivot window	955
Tableau Public	Non-Microsoft product for creating interesting data visualizations; Public version is free		962
SQL Server	Microsoft's server-based database package		963
SQL Server Analysis Services (SSAS)	Part of SQL Server that performs data mining operations		963
Microsoft Data Mining Add-ins for Excel	Free add-ins that provide a front end to the data mining algorithms in SSAS	Data Mining tab and Table Tools Analyze tab	963
Classification methods	Methods for predicting a dependent categorical variable from given explanatory variables		965
Data partitioning	Dividing large data set into training and testing subsets so that algorithms trained on one set can be tested on the other	Available in NeuralTools, not in StatTools	965
Logistic regression	Classification method where the logit is estimated as a linear function of the explanatory variables	StatTools Regression & Classification group	965
Odds ratio	Ratio of p to $1-p$, where p is the probability of a given category		966
Logit	Logarithm of the odds ratio		966
Neural network (or neural net)	Complex nonlinear method for classification or prediction, attempts to mimic the human brain		971
NeuralTools	Add-in in the Palisade DecisionTools suite, used for implementing neural nets	NeuralTools tab	972
Classification Trees (or Decision Trees)	Classification method that splits sets of cases so that subsets become purer in terms of composition of categories	Microsoft Data Mining Add-ins for Excel	976
Lift	Data mining term, the ability to determine the most likely responders to a mail campaign, for example		977
Supervised versus unsupervised data mining methods	Supervised methods try to predict a dependent variable; unsupervised methods don't have a dependent variable		980
Clustering (or segmentation)	Unsupervised method, tries to attach cases to categories (clusters), with high similarity within categories and high dissimilarity across categories	Microsoft Data Mining Add-ins for Excel	980
Market basket analysis (or association analysis)	Where patterns of customer purchases are examined to see which items customers tend to purchase together, in the same "market basket."		980

PROBLEMS

Conceptual Questions

C.1. Explain what a star schema is all about. How does it help to provide useful information in pivot tables?

C.2. Suppose a hospital wants to create a database with the star schema structure. What dimensions and facts might it store?

C.3. How does the OLAP methodology allow you to "drill down" in a pivot table?

C.4. What is the advantage of creating an OLAP cube file, especially for extremely large databases?

C.5. Explain briefly what a Data Model in Excel 2013 represents. Also, explain briefly what you can now do in Excel with the new PowerPivot tool that you couldn't do in previous versions of Excel.

C.6. What does it mean that Microsoft's free Data Mining Add-Ins for Excel represents a "front end" to a "back end" SQL Server Analysis Services (SSAS) server?

C.7. What is the main purpose of logistic regression, and how does it differ from the type of regression, discussed in Chapters 10 and 11?

C.8. Suppose that a term in a logistic regression equation is 0.687*MallTrips, as in Figure 17.19. Explain, exactly what this means.

C.9. Suppose you are trying to classify a variable where 96% of its observations equal 0 and only 4% equal 1. You run a logistic regression, and the classification table shows that 97% of the classifications are correct. Why might this large percentage still not be cause for celebration?

C.10. What are the strengths and drawbacks of neural nets versus classification trees?

C.11. Clustering algorithms always start with a dissimilarity measure. Why it is not always obvious how to develop such a measure?

Level A

19. The lasagna data discussed in the chapter is repeated in the file **17_19.xlsx**. Instead of trying to classify a dependent variable, Have Tried, this file shows the result of clustering. Specifically, the Microsoft Data Mining Detect Categories algorithm was used, arbitrarily specifying the number of categories as 3. Also, the Have Tried variable was treated just like all of the other variables. Using the results in the Categories_Report sheet, what can you say about the composition of the categories the algorithm found? How might you "name" these categories?

20. (*Requires PowerPivot*) The file **P17_20.xlsx** contains salaries of all Major League Baseball players in 2011 in one sheet and geographical information about the teams in another sheet. Use PowerPivot and Power View to create a map with bubbles indicating the size of total salary, either by city or by state. The directions for doing this are a bit different from the example in the text because this data set resides in Excel.

a. Select any cell in the Salary data and click Add to Data Model on the PowerPivot ribbon. (Make sure you check that your table has headers.) This does two things. It designates the data set as an Excel table, and it adds this table to the PowerPivot window.

b. From the Excel window, select any cell in the Geography data, and again click Add to Data Model on the PowerPivot ribbon. Now you should have two tabs in the PowerPivot window.

c. Although it is not absolutely necessary, it is useful to rename the Excel tables as Salaries and Teams, respectively, and to do the same to the tabs in the PowerPivot window.

d. In the PowerPivot window, click Diagram View on the Home ribbon. Then drag from Team in the Salaries table to Team in the Teams table to create a relationship.

e. Go back to Excel, activate the Geography sheet, and click Power View from the Insert ribbon. In the Power View Fields pane on the right, click ALL to see a list of all fields in both tables. In the Salaries table, check Salary, and in the Teams table, check either State or City. Uncheck any other fields that might be checked. Then click Map from the ribbon. You will probably have to move the fields around to get the desired map. The Salary field should be in the Size box, and the City (or State) field should be in the Locations box.

f. To fine tune the map, click MAP in the Filters pane to expand it. Then drag Team to this area. This lets you filter out teams, such as either of the New York or Los Angeles teams. Next, drag Pitcher to the Color box to see a pie chart for each bubble.

Level B

21. The file **P17_21.xlsx** contains Gender, Age, Education, and Success (Yes/No) data of 1000 people. The purpose is to see how a classification tree method can use the first three variables to classify Success. You start with 564 Yes values and 436 No values. This is quite diverse (close to 50–50), and as explained in the file, it has a diversity index of 0.9836, the highest being 1. The question you are asked to explore is which splits you should make to reduce this diversity index—that is, to make the subsets purer. Directions are given in the file. (Note that the method suggested is only one variation of splitting and measuring diversity in classification trees. When the Microsoft Data Mining add-in is used on this data set, it finds an extremely simple rule: Classify as Yes if Education is UG or G, and classify as No if Education is HS. This is slightly different from what your method will find.)

REFERENCES

Afshartous, D. "Sample Size Determination for Binomial Proportion Confidence Intervals: An Alternative Perspective Motivated by a Legal Case." *The American Statistician* 62, no. 1 (2008): 27–31.

Appleton, D., J. French, and M. Vanderpump. "Ignoring a Covariate: An Example of Simpson's Paradox." *The American Statistician* 50 (1996): 340–341.

———. "Research on Forecasting: A Quarter-Century Review, 1960–1984." *Interfaces* 16, no. 1 (1986): 89–103.

Babich, P. "Customer Satisfaction: How Good Is Good Enough?" *Quality Progress* 25 (1992): 65–68.

Balson, W., J. Welsh, and D. Wilson. "Using Decision Analysis and Risk Analysis to Manage Utility Environmental Risk." *Interfaces* 22, no. 6 (1992): 126–139.

Barnett, A. "Genes, Race, IQ, and *The Bell Curve.*" *ORMS Today* 22, no. 1 (1994): 18–24.

Bean, J., C. Noon, and G. Salton. "Asset Divestiture at Homart Development Company." *Interfaces* 17, no. 1 (1987): 48–65.

———, C. Noon, S. Ryan, and G. Salton. "Selecting Tenants in a Shopping Mall.". *Interfaces* 18, no. 2 (1988): 1–10.

Berger, P., and R. Maurer. *Experimental Design.* Belmont, CA: Duxbury, 2002.

Blyth, C. "On Simpson's Paradox and the Sure-Thing Principle." *Journal of the American Statistical Association* 67 (1972): 364–366.

Brinkley, P., D. Stepto, J. Haag, K. Liou, K. Wang, and W. Carr. "Nortel Redefines Factory Information Technology: An OR-Driven Approach." *Interfaces* 28, no. 1 (1998): 37–52.

Brown, G., J. Keegan, B. Vigus, and K. Wood. "The Kellogg Company Optimizes Production, Inventory, and Distribution." *Interfaces* 31, no. 6 (2001): 1–15.

Cawley, J., and P. Sommers, "Voting Irregularities in the 1995 Referendum on Quebec Sovereignty." *Chance* 9, no. 4 (Fall 1996): 29–30.

Cranshaw, J., R. Schwartz, J. I. Hong, and N. Sadeh. "The Livehoods Project: Utilizing Social Media to Understand the Dynamics of a City." The 6th International AAAI Conference on Weblogs and Social Media. Dublin, Ireland, June 2012.

Deming, E., *Out of the Crisis.* Cambridge, MA: MIT Center for Advanced Engineering Study, 1986.

DeVor, R., T. Chang, and J. Sutherland. *Statistial Quality Design and Control.* New York: Macmillan, 1992.

Duffy, T., M. Hatzakis, W. Hsu, R. Labe, B. Liao, X. Luo, J. Oh, A. Setya, and L. Yang. "Merrill Lynch Improves Liquidity Risk Management for Revolving Credit Lines." *Interfaces* 35, no. 5 (2005): 353–369.

Feinstein, C. "Deciding Whether to Test Student Athletes for Drug Use." *Interfaces* 20, no. 3 (1990): 80–87.

Hoppensteadt, F., and C. Peskin. *Mathematics in Medicine and the Life Sciences.* New York: Springer-Verlag, 1992.

Howard, R. "Decision Analysis: Practice and Promise." *Management Science* 34, no. 6 (1988): 679–695.

Keefer, D., and S. Bodily. "Three-Point Approximations for Continuous Random Variables." *Management Science* 29, no. 5 (1983): 595–609.

Kelly, J. "A New Interpretation of Information Rate." *Bell System Technical Journal* 35 (1956): 917–926.

Kimes, S., and J. Fitzsimmons. "Selecting Profitable Hotel Sites at La Quinta Motor Inns." *Interfaces* 20, no. 2 (1990): 12–20.

Kirkwood, C. "An Overview of Methods for Applied Decision Analysis." *Interfaces* 22, no. 6 (1992): 28–39.

Kutner, M. H., C. J. Nachtsheim, J. Neter, and W. Li. *Applied Linear Statistical Models.* 5th ed. New York: McGraw-Hill/Irwin, 2005.

Levy, P., and S. Lemeshow. *Sampling of Populations: Methods and Applications.* 3rd ed. New York: Wiley, 1999.

Lindsey, George. "Statistical Data Useful for the Operation of a Baseball Team." *Operations Research* 7, no. 2 (1959): 197–207.

Love, R., and J. Hoey. "Management Science Improves Fast Food Operations." *Interfaces* 20, no. 2 (1990): 21–29.

Marcus, A. "The Magellan Fund and Market Efficiency." *Journal of Portfolio Management* (Fall 1990): 85–88.

McDaniel, S., and L. Kinney. "Ambush Marketing Revisited: An Experimental Study of Perceived Sponsorship Effects on Brand Awareness, Attitude Toward the Brand, and Purchase Intention." *Journal of Promotion Management* 3 (1996): 141–167.

Metters, R., C. Queenan, M. Ferguson, L. Harrison, J. Higbie, S. Ward, B. Barfield, T. Farley, H. A. Kuyumcu, and A. Duggasani. "The Killer Application of Revenue Management: Harrah's Cherokee Casino & Hotel." *Interfaces* 38, no. 3 (2008): 161–175.

Miser, H., "Avoiding the Corrupting Lie of a Poorly Stated Problem." *Interfaces* 23, no. 6 (1993): 114–119.

Morrison, D., and R. Wheat. "Pulling the Goalie Revisited." *Interfaces* 16, no. 6 (1984): 28–34.

Pankratz, A. *Forecasting with Dynamic Regression Models.* New York: Wiley, 1991.

Press, S.J. "Sample-Audit Tax Assessment for Businesses: What's Fair?" *Journal of Business & Economic Statistics* 13, no. 3 (1995): 357–359.

Reichheld, F. *The Loyalty Effect.* Boston, MA: Harvard Business School Press, 1996.

Roselka, Rita. "The New Mantra: MVT." *Forbes* (March 11, 1996): 114–118.

Schmidt, S., and R. Launsby. *Understanding Industrial Designed Experiments.* 4th ed. Colorado Springs: Air Academy Press, 1994.

Schnarrs, S., and J. Bavuso. "Extrapolation Models on Very Short-Term Forecasts." *Journal of Business Research* 14 (1986): 27–36.

Simonoff, J., and I. Sparrow. "Predicting Movie Grosses: Winners and Losers, Blockbusters and Sleepers." *Chance* 13, no. 3 (2000): 15–24.

Sonderman, D., and P. Abrahamson. "Radiotherapy Design Using Mathematical Programming." *Operations Research* 33, no. 4 (1985): 705–725.

Stonebraker, J. "How Bayer Makes Decisions to Develop New Drugs." *Interfaces* 32, no. 6 (2002): 77–90.

Tyagi, R., P. Kalish, K. Akbay, and G. Munshaw. "GE Plastics Optimizes the Two-Echelon Global Fulfillment Network at Its High Performance Polymers Division." *Interfaces* 34, no. 5 (2004): 359–366.

van den Briel, M., R. Villalobos, and G. Hogg. "America West Airlines Develops Efficient Boarding Strategies." *Interfaces* 35, no. 3 (2005): 191–201.

Volkema, R. "Managing the Process of Formulating the Problem." *Interfaces* 25, no. 3 (1995): 81–87.

Westbrooke, I. "Simpson's Paradox: An Example in a New Zealand Survey of Jury Composition." *Chance* 11, no. 2 (1998): 40–42.

Winston, W. L. *Operations Research: Applications and Algorithms.* 4th ed. Belmont, CA: Duxbury Press, 2003.